Handbook of
THE BIOLOGY OF AGING

THE HANDBOOKS OF AGING

Consisting of Three Volumes:

Critical comprehensive reviews of
research knowledge, theories,
concepts, and issues

Editor-in-Chief: **James E. Birren**

Handbook of the Biology of Aging

Edited by Caleb E. Finch and Leonard Hayflick

Handbook of the Psychology of Aging

Edited by James E. Birren and K. Warner Schaie

Handbook of Aging and the Social Sciences

Edited by Robert H. Binstock and Ethel Shanas

Handbook of
THE BIOLOGY OF AGING

Editors
Caleb E. Finch
Leonard Hayflick

With the assistance of Associate Editors
Harold Brody
Isadore Rossman
F. Marott Sinex

 VAN NOSTRAND REINHOLD COMPANY
NEW YORK   CINCINNATI   ATLANTA   DALLAS   SAN FRANCISCO
LONDON   TORONTO   MELBOURNE

Van Nostrand Reinhold Company Regional Offices:
New York Cincinnati Atlanta Dallas San Francisco

Van Nostrand Reinhold Company International Offices:
London Toronto Melbourne

Manufactured in the United States of America

Published by Van Nostrand Reinhold Company
450 West 33rd Street, New York, N.Y. 10001

Published simultaneously in Canada by Van Nostrand Reinhold Ltd.

15 14 13 12 11 10 9 8 7 6 5 4 3 2 1

Library of Congress Cataloging in Publication Data

Main entry under title:

Handbook of the biology of aging.

  (The Handbooks of aging)
  Includes index.
  1. Aging. 2. Cells—Aging. I. Finch, Caleb
Ellicott. II. Hayflick, Leonard. III. Series.
QP86.H35   599.03'72   76-52755
ISBN 0-442-20796-4

CONTRIBUTORS

Richard C. Adelman, Ph.D.
Associate Professor of Biochemistry, Fels Research Institute, Temple University School of Medicine, Philadelphia, Pennsylvania

Reubin Andres, M.D.
Chief, Clinical Physiology Branch, Gerontology Research Center, National Institute on Aging, Baltimore City Hospitals, Baltimore, Maryland

Endre A. Balazs, M.D.
Malcolm P. Aldridch Professor of Opthamology; Director of Research; Department of Opthalmology, College of Physicians and Surgeons, Columbia University, New York, New York

Charles H. Barrows, Jr., Sc.D.
Gerontology Research Center, National Institute on Aging, National Institutes of Health, PHS, U.S. Department of Health, Education and Welfare, Bethesda: Baltimore City Hospitals, Baltimore, Maryland

Renato L. Baserga, M.D.
Department of Pathology and Fels Research Institute, Temple University School of Medicine, Philadelphia, Pennsylvania

Kowit Bhanthumnavin, B.Sc. (Med), MB.BS. (Sydney), F.R.A.C.P.
Department of Medicine, Baltimore City Hospitals; The Johns Hopkins School of Medicine, Baltimore, Maryland

Harold Brody, Ph.D., M.D.
Professor and Chairman, Department of Anatomical Sciences, School of Medicine; Multidisciplinary Center for the Study of Aging, State University of New York, Buffalo, New York

N. O. Calloway, M.D. Ph.D.
Attending Internist, Madison General Hospital, Madison, Wisconsin; Lecturer, University of Wisconsin, Madison, Wisconsin

Jeffrey A. Chesky, Ph.D.
Department of Physiology and Biophysics, University of Miami School of Medicine, Miami, Florida

Charles W. Daniel, Ph.D.
Professor of Biology, Board of Studies in Biology; Fellow of Cowell College, University of California, Santa Cruz, California

Paula L. Dollevoet, Ph.D.
Anatomy Department, University of Nebraska Medical School, Omaha, Nebraska; post-doctoral fellow, Developmental Biology, University of Chicago, Chicago, Illinois

Caleb E. Finch, Ph.D.
Chief, Laboratory of Neurobiology, Andrus Gerontology Center; Associate Professor of Biological Sciences, University of Southern California, Los Angeles, California

Ralph Goldman, M.D.
Chief, Intermediate Care Section, Veterans Administration Wadsworth Hospital Center; Professor of Medicine/Geriatrics in Residence, University of California, Los Angeles, California

Ernest Gutmann, M.D., Ph.D.
Institute of Physiology, Czechoslovak Academy of Sciences, Prague, Czechoslovakia

Leonard Hayflick, Ph.D.
Professor, Department of Medicine Microbiology, Stanford University School of Medicine, Stanford, California

Robert A. Klocke, M.D.
Associate Professor of Medicine, Department of Medicine, State University of New York at Buffalo, Buffalo, New York

Robert R. Kohn, Ph.D., M.D.
Professor of Pathology, Institute of Pathology, School of Medicine, Case Western Reserve University, Cleveland, Ohio

Takashi Makinodan, Ph.D.
Geriatric Research Education and Clinical Center, Veterans Administration, Wadsworth Hospital Center; Professor of Medicine, University of California, Los Angeles, Los Angeles, California

Norman Orentreich, M.D.
Clinical Associate Professor of Dermatology, New York University School of Medicine; Director, Orentreich Foundation for the Advancement of Science, Inc., New York, New York

Jan Pontén, M.D.
The Wallenberg Laboratory, University of Uppsala, Uppsala, Sweden

Ronald L. Rizer, M. A.
Research Associate in Biochemistry and Dermatology, Orentreich Foundation for the Advancement of Science, Inc., New York, New York

Lois M. Roeder, Sc.D.
Department of Pediatrics, University of Maryland School of Medicine, Baltimore, Maryland

Morris Rockstein, Ph.D.
Professor, Department of Physiology and Biophysics, University of Miami School of Medicine; Associate Director, Institute for the Study of Aging, University of Miami, Miami, Florida

Isadore Rossman, Ph.D., M.D.
Medical Director, Home Care and Extended Services Department, Montefiore Hospital and Medical Center, Bronx, New York

George A. Sacher
Division of Biological and Medical Research, Argonne National Laboratory, Argonne, Illinois

D. Rao Sanadi, Ph.D.
Director, Cell Physiology Department, Boston Biomedical Research Institute, Boston, Massachusetts; Associate Professor, Department of Biochemistry, Harvard Medical School, Boston, Massachusetts

Marvin M. Schuster, M.D.
Director, Gastrointestinal Division, Baltimore City Hospitals; Professor of Medicine, The Johns Hopkins University School of Medicine, Baltimore, Maryland

Victor J. Selmanowitz, M.D.
Clinical Associate and Professor of Dermatology, New York Medical College, Metropolitan Hospital Center; Coordinator of Research, Orentreich Foundation for the Advancement of Science, Inc., New York, New York

Nathan W. Shock, Ph.D.
Chief, Gerontology Research Center, National Institute on Aging, National Institutes of Health, Bethesda, Maryland; Baltimore City Hospitals, Baltimore, Maryland

F. Marott Sinex, Ph.D.
Professor and Chairman, Department of Biochemistry, Boston University School of Medicine; Co-Director, Boston University Gerontology Center, Boston, Massachusetts

Marvin L. Sussman, Ph.D.
Department of Physiology and Biophysics, University of Miami School of Medicine, Miami, Florida

George B. Talbert, M.A., Ph.D.
Department of Anatomy, Downstate Medical Center, State University of New York, Brooklyn, New York

Jordan D. Tobin, M.D.
Clinical Physiology Branch, Gerontology Research Center, National Institute on Aging, Baltimore City Hospitals, Baltimore, Maryland

Edgar A. Tonna, Ph.D.
F.R.M.S.; Professor of Histology; Director, Institute for Dental Research and Laboratory for Cellular Research in Aging, New York University Dental Center, New York, New York

Arthur C. Upton, M.D.
Professor of Pathology, Health Sciences Center, State University of New York at Stony Brook, Stony Brook, New York

N. Vijayashankar, M.D., M.S.
Assistant Professor, Department of Anatomical Sciences, School of Medicine, State University of New York, Buffalo, New York

FOREWORD

This volume is one of three handbooks of aging: the *Handbook of the Biology of Aging*; the *Handbook of the Psychology of Aging*; and the *Handbook of Aging and the Social Sciences*. Because of the increase in literature about the many facets of aging, there has been an increasing need to collate and interpret existing information and to make it readily available in systematic form, providing groundwork for the more efficient pursuit of research. The phenomena and issues of aging cut across many scientific disciplines and professions, and a review of research necessarily involves many experts. A decision was made, therefore, to develop a multidisciplinary project, the purpose of which was to organize, evaluate, and interpret research data, concepts, theories, and issues on the biological, psychological, and social aspects of aging.

It is expected that investigators will use these books as the basic systematic reference works on aging, resulting in the stimulation and planning of needed research. Professional personnel, policy-makers, practitioners, and others interested in research, education, and services to the aged will undoubtedly find the volumes useful. The new handbooks will also provide a compendium of information for students entering and pursuing the field of gerontology and will, we hope, also stimulate the organization of new courses of instruction on aging.

The Editorial Committees generated the final outline of each volume, suggested contributors, and discussed sources of information and other matters pertinent to the development of the work. Committee recommendations were reviewed by the Advisory Board and the Editor-in-Chief.

Project Advisory Board

Vern L. Bengtson
Robert H. Binstock
James E. Birren
Sheila M. Chown
Caleb E. Finch
Leonard Hayflick
K. Warner Schaie
Ethel Shanas
Nathan W. Shock
F. Marott Sinex

James E. Birren, *Editor-in-Chief*

Editorial Committees

Handbook of the Biology of Aging

Harold Brody
Caleb E. Finch (Co-Editor)
Leonard Hayflick (Co-Editor)
Isadore Rossman
F. Marott Sinex

Handbook of the Psychology of Aging

James E. Birren (Co-Editor)
Jack Botwinick
Sheila M. Chown
Carl Eisdorfer
K. Warner Schaie (Co-Editor)

Handbook of Aging and the Social Sciences

Vern L. Bengtson
Robert H. Binstock (Co-Editor)

George L. Maddox
Ethel Shanas (Co-Editor)
Dorothy Wedderburn

There are many individuals who contributed to the successful completion of this publication project: Phoebe S. Liebig, Project Coordinator; Julie L. Moore, Research Bibliographer; Project Assistants Barbara H. Johnson, Aelred R. Rosser, Rochelle Smalewitz, and Robert D. Nall; Editorial Assistant V. Jayne Renner; Copy Editors Robert D. Nall and Judy Aklonis (social sciences), James Gollub (psychology), and Peggy Wilson and Carolyn Croissant (biology); Julie L. Moore, Indexing; and Library Assistance, Emily H. Miller and Jean E. Mueller. It is impossible to give the details of their many and varied contributions to the total effort, but they reflect the best traditions of respect for scholarship.

The preparation of the handbooks has been a nonprofit venture; no royalties are paid to any individual or institution. The intent was to give the books a wide circulation on an international level and to reduce publication costs.

The project was supported by a grant from the Administration on Aging under the title "Integration of Information on Aging: Handbook Project," Grant Number 93-P-75181/9, to the University of Southern California, with James E. Birren as the principal investigator. The Editor and his associates wish to thank Dr. Marvin Taves, who encouraged the development of the project as a staff member of the Adminstration on Aging, and also the agency itself, which perceived the value of such work and provided the grant for its support.

JAMES E. BIRREN

PREFACE

The purpose of the *Handbook of the Biology of Aging* is to review the status of the basic biological knowledge in gerontology. This book was designed for those readers, such as graduate students and professionals in other areas of science, who require a serious but fairly broad discussion of specific biological aspects of aging.

The organization of this volume is based on a hierarchical framework, which starts at the molecular level and proceeds to the cellular, physiological, and finally the organismic level. The overall emphasis is on humans and other mammalian species and the varieties of aging changes which they manifest. The relevance of animal models to studies of human aging is a recurrent theme.

The past decade of research in the biology of aging has witnessed a truly enormous increase in the publication of both data and speculation about the nature of aging processes. The scientific literature of gerontology is unusually scattered and is found, for example, in journals of botany, molecular biology, and human clinical medicine. A complete analysis of the biology of aging would require that several authorities present their views in the area of each chapter. Thus, the Editors are painfully aware that some currently controversial topics are only partly elaborated. By necessity, the present volume is a selection from the total literature and represents choices of content and opinion. Although the contributors were instructed to be as comprehensive as possible, each author, of course, retained the scholar's prerogative of critical judgment. Review articles were cited, where possible, to provide wider access to the literature in each area.

Each author was given outlines of the other chapters in the volume and was instructed to write his contribution with a general cognizance of the entire *Handbook*. The Editors wished to encourage communication among the authors in the hopes of minimizing redundancy and increasing general awareness of the interrelationships between chapters. Nonetheless, a great deal of correlation among areas represented in the chapters remains unstated.

Although future research in gerontology will certainly radically alter our views of the nature of biological aging and its relation to the quality of life in the later years, the Editors hope that the scholarship represented in these articles will provide a useful entry into the very diverse areas of this rapidly expanding field.

The Editorial Committee for this volume was: Harold Brody, Caleb E. Finch, Leonard Hayflick, Isadore Rossman, and F. Marott Sinex. We are particularly grateful to the outside reviewers, Joseph Meites and Vincent Cristofalo, and to the Editorial Assistants, Aelred R. Rosser, V. Jayne Renner, and Peggy Wilson, who provided many helpful comments.

CALEB E. FINCH
LEONARD HAYFLICK

CONTENTS

PART THREE

Cellular Level

PART FOUR

Tissue and Organ Level

PART FIVE

Whole Animal Level

PART 1 INTRODUCTORY MATERIAL

1
COMPARATIVE BIOLOGY AND EVOLUTION OF AGING

Morris Rockstein
and
Jeffrey A. Chesky
and
Marvin L. Sussman
University of Miami School of Medicine

THE COMPARATIVE BIOLOGY OF AGING

Although gerontology is the science concerned with the study and understanding of the aging process *per se*, it is common to see the terms *aging* and *senescence* equated with longevity or duration of life. In this connection, species-specific longevity is probably expressed most directly as the mean or average life span, since such a value can be obtained by averaging the age at death of all members of a species or strain, preferably by sex, of a closed (and hopefully sizeable) population of animals. However, in a human population or in one of wild animals, the average life span values are difficult to compute, because there is no way to monitor the births and deaths, since death rates change at different ages with advancing generations. This is strikingly exhibited in the case of humans in America, where the reduction in mortality of infants and young children has increased the mean life span by as much as 20 years from the turn of the century to the present time, without appreciably affecting the known maximum life span (110–115 years) for the whole population. Similarly, in the wild,

the reported mean life span for animals, usually determined by some type of tagging procedure, can be increased simply by the disappearance of a predator. Accordingly, mean life spans determined from captivity data for relatively small numbers of individuals per species are much higher than must actually occur in nature. Maximum longevity data define the survival potential of members of a particular population as the upper limit in terms of time.

More meaningful, perhaps, is the rate of dying or the life expectancy at any one unit of time within the lifetime of any one member of a given population. Based on data obtained from fixed populations maintained under controlled conditions, life expectancy can be expressed either graphically or in tabular form.

The mortality or survival curve, shown in Figure 1 (Rockstein and Lieberman, 1959), is a pictorial representation of the rate of survival from which one can see the rate of dying at any point in the existence of a group of animals born on the same day, i.e., a "cohort." The survival curve also depicts the median and maximum longevity values for the sample tested. In Figure 1 the greatest rate of mortality

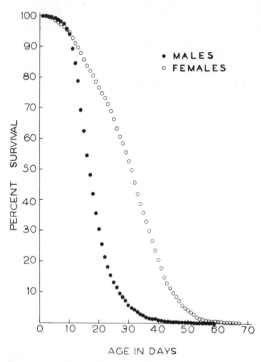

Figure 1. Survival curves for male and female houseflies. (From Rockstein and Lieberman, 1959.)

occurs between the 10th and 20th day of existence for adult male house flies of a highly inbred strain. At the same time, one can see that the rate of dying slows from the 30th through the 60th day for the male sex. Similarly, one can see that the L_{50}, or median death rate, occurs at approximately 17 days of age, which also happens to be very close to the mean life span value for the male of this relatively homogeneous strain.

The life table, on the other hand, represents a more detailed and mathematically more sophisticated way of expressing the rate of dying. It can be employed, as it is by actuaries of life insurance companies, to predict the future life expectancy at any given age in the existence of a particular cohort.

The life table is considered to be the most accurate description of a given population's vital statistics in all dimensions. It is prepared for a given population, all of whose members are starting life on the same day, month, or year. It employs age intervals equal to x, depending on the duration of life in days,

months, or years. The number of individuals dying between ages x and $x + 1$ is represented as d_x; the number of individuals from the cohort membership surviving to age x is called 1_x; the numbers dying between ages x and $x + 1$ per 1000 individuals living at age x is designated as 1000_{qx}; finally, the life expectancy, which is equal to the average number of years lived after age x per person surviving to age x, is designated as e_x. One can see from Table 1 that, for individuals from the total membership of the cohort at age zero, the life expectancy, e_x, is the same as the mean length of life for the entire cohort. In the case of male house flies, this is equal to 16.88 days. If one were to calculate the mean life span by the usual method, one would also obtain the value of 16.88.

It is extremely difficult to prepare a life table for many species, particularly man, because all members of the cohort must be born within the same age interval and, even more importantly, must be reared and maintained under identical, fixed conditions of physical environment, diet, and biological interactions. It is also assumed that the cohort population remains fixed with no migration into or out of the area occurring. For human populations, this is most unlikely, particularly with ever-improving means of transportation. Accordingly, the distribution of mortality is obviously best studied with highly inbred laboratory animals, born the same day or within the same time period, reared under identical conditions, and fixed geographically so that their periodic mortality can be followed exactly.

Aging is variously defined by workers in the field of biological gerontology. Shock (1961, 1962), Weiss (1966), and the authors of this chapter consider aging as the sum total of changes during an individual's life span, which are common to all members of his species or strain. Such a broad definition would normally include divisions of the life span of any organism into three trimesters: embryonic development, maturation, and senescence. However, for this *Handbook*, aging will be considered as "any time-dependent change which occurs *after* maturity of size, form, or function is reached and which is distinct from daily, seasonal, and other biological rhythms." This presumably in-

TABLE 1. A LIFE TABLE FOR 4,627 MALE HOUSE FLIES, *MUSCA DOMESTICA* L. (NAIDM STRAIN).

x	d_x	l_x	$1000 q_x$	e_x	x	d_x	l_x	$1000q_x$	e_x
0–1	1.5	1000.0	1.5	16.88	30–31	8.4	49.1	171.1	5.11
1–2	2.8	998.5	2.8	15.90	31–32	5.6	40.6	137.9	5.07
2–3	3.7	995.7	3.7	14.94	32–33	6.7	35.0	191.4	4.80
3–4	2.8	992.0	2.8	14.00	33–34	4.3	28.3	151.9	4.82
4–5	2.6	989.2	2.6	13.04	34–35	5.0	24.0	208.3	4.59
5–6	5.6	986.6	5.7	12.07	35–36	3.0	19.0	157.9	4.66
6–7	8.6	981.0	8.8	11.14	36–37	2.6	16.0	162.5	4.44
7–8	14.0	972.3	14.4	10.23	37–38	1.5	13.4	111.9	4.21
8–9	19.5	958.3	20.3	9.37	38–39	2.4	11.9	201.7	3.67
9–10	48.0	938.8	51.1	8.56	39–40	2.6	9.5	273.7	3.47
10–11	46.5	890.9	52.2	7.99	40–41	2.8	6.9	405.8	3.59
11–12	57.5	844.4	68.1	7.40	41–42	1.1	4.1	268.3	4.71
12–13	94.9	786.9	120.6	6.91	42–43	0.6	3.0	200.0	5.23
13–14	69.8	692.0	100.9	6.79	43–44	0.2	2.4	83.3	5.42
14–15	77.8	622.2	125.0	6.49	44–45	0.2	2.2	90.9	4.86
15–16	64.2	544.4	117.9	6.35	45–46	0.4	1.9	210.5	4.53
16–17	62.0	480.2	129.1	6.13	46–47	0.4	1.5	266.7	4.60
17–18	61.8	418.2	147.8	5.96	47–48	0.0	1.1	0.0	5.09
18–19	52.7	356.4	147.9	5.91	48–49	0.0	1.1	0.0	4.09
19–20	49.9	303.7	164.3	5.85	49–50	0.4	1.1	363.6	3.09
20–21	41.7	253.7	164.4	5.90	50–51	0.2	0.6	333.3	4.17
21–22	31.8	212.0	150.0	5.97	51–52	0.0	0.4	0.0	5.00
22–23	28.1	180.2	155.9	5.93	52–53	0.0	0.4	0.0	4.00
23–24	22.9	152.2	150.5	5.93	53–54	0.2	0.4	500.0	3.00
24–25	16.6	129.2	128.5	5.90	54–55	0.0	0.2	0.0	4.50
25–26	14.0	112.6	124.3	5.69	55–56	0.0	0.2	0.0	3.50
26–27	14.9	98.6	151.1	5.43	56–57	0.0	0.2	0.0	2.50
27–28	18.8	83.6	165.1	5.32	57–58	0.0	0.2	0.0	1.50
28–29	12.3	69.8	176.2	5.27	58–59	0.2	0.2	1000.0	0.50
29–30	8.4	57.5	146.1	5.29					

SOURCE: Rockstein and Lieberman, 1959.

cludes all of the postmaturational changes in an individual, including senescence! Senescence *per se* connotes to all scientists those manifestations in structure and function of a declining or deteriorating nature which take place during the period of life when the mortality rate of a population is accelerated.

Since unrecorded time, man has not only been aware of his own existence, but has been cognizant that, as part of his biological heritage, he must eventually grow old and die. Unfortunately, the so-called longitudinal study, which follows the course of aging in the individual throughout his life span, is self-defeating in view of the time limitations imposed upon the experimentalist, of limited life span himself. At the same time, the periodic study of the age-related changes in individual organs or cells is obviously impossible when dealing with humans. Accordingly, longitudinal studies on humans should be supplemented with comparative studies on the aging process in other animals of genetically pure, if not long-inbred, strains, with constancy of as many conditions (physical and biological) as possible.

Although objections are frequently raised as to the comparability of data obtained for such animals as highly inbred strains of house flies, mice, rats, rabbits, and dogs, there are certain characteristics of aging common to many different animals. These include characteristic senescent changes in the skin and the hair and in the general posture and physical demeanor of the individual, a definite decrease in speed and vigor of muscular contraction and locomotor function, and finally, a general and decreasing ability to react effectively to stresses of the environment. Therefore, comparative studies involving lower animals serve not only to define the facts of aging but also to pinpoint the mechanisms underlying the aging process.

Invertebrates, such as insects, represent ideal models for the study of aging. They have high reproductive potential, are available in highly inbred strains, are capable of a control of life span by temperature, and possess a short life span relative to that of humans. In addition, most structural and functional features of these complex cold-blooded animals are analogous to those of mammals, including man, even to the extent of virtually identical cellular biochemical processes. Similarly, the microscopic round-worm, the nematode, has been used in aging studies because it can be maintained axenically. As many as 2×10^5 nematodes can be cultured in a milliliter of medium (Gershon, 1970; Zuckerman, 1974). With the exception of the gonads and possibly the intestinal epithelium, their tissues have a constant cell number. Nematodes lack the capacity to regenerate body parts, presumably because they are made up of postmitotic cells, an important factor in the study of aging. Their organ systems exist in the differentiated state, and some tissues resemble those of higher animals (e.g., the intestinal biciliary layer of *Caenorhabditis briggsae* is similar to that of the rat). Most organ systems contain limited numbers of cells (e.g., the intestinal epithelium of *Turbatrix aceti* has 64 cells, and the nervous system of *C. elegans* contains fewer than 300 cells). It is estimated that the entire nematode, *C. briggsae*, contains fewer than 1,000 cells. Genetic mutants of nematodes are readily inducible, and nematodes are apparently free of viral pathogens. Most important to the gerontologist, the nematode is short-lived (e.g., *C. briggsae* matures in approximately 5 days, ceases reproduction in 12–14 days, and dies at 25–28 days). Despite their low phylogenetic position, nematodes possess most of the criteria for being good models for aging research (see Zuckerman, 1974).

COMPARATIVE LONGEVITY IN VERTEBRATES AND INVERTEBRATES

The maximum life span in mammals ranges from as low as approximately 1 year in the insectivore *Sorex fumeus*, the smoky shrew (Hamilton, 1940), to approximately 3 years in a number of small rodents, to as high as 70 years in the elephant, and to at least 114–115 years in man [see the *Handbook of Biological Data* (Spector, 1956), further revised and condensed in the two editions of the *Biology Data Book* (Altman and Dittmer, 1964, 1972)]. In the invertebrates, the 17-year Cicada and one species of parasitic nematode have recorded actual longevity values of 17 years; in the case of one of the tapeworms (living in man) a life span of 35 years has been reported (Spector, 1956). The *Handbook of Biological Data* (Spector, 1956) also cites maximum longevity values of as long as 11 years for some species of beetles. In contrast, numerous species of invertebrates have maximum adult life spans of as low as 3 weeks, as in the case of the vestigial mutant of *Drosophila melanogaster* (Clark and Rockstein, 1964), and as short as 24 hours in the common mayfly (Howard, 1939). For the aquatic invertebrates, two species of Crustacea, including the European lobster, have been reported as having maximum life spans of at least 30 years (Spector, 1956). Unfortunately, the second edition of the *Biology Data Book* (Altman and Dittmer, 1972) cites maximum longevities from dated sources and of only a limited selection of animals. For the investigator seeking known longevity data for more species of vertebrates and invertebrates, now excluded in the 1972 *Biology Data Book*, both the 1956 *Handbook of Biological Data* (Spector, 1956) and Table VI in Comfort's classical text (1964) should be consulted.

In selecting a laboratory animal for the study of aging, the two most important criteria are: (1) similarity in the animal's manifestations of aging to those of man, and (2) a sufficiently short life span to permit a sufficient number of replicate studies within the lifetime of the investigator.

FACTORS CONTRIBUTING TO THE LONGEVITY OF ANIMALS

Unfortunately, most of the experiments done on the contributory role of environmental factors appear to have been made with invertebrates. (See Chapter 24 of this *Handbook* for further details on life span modification by environmental factors.)

Thus, when studying the comparative biology of aging, one must be aware of a number of factors which may affect survival and, therefore, life expectancy. For example, animals that are domesticated or those that have been reared under laboratory conditions have longevities considerably different than their wild counterparts (Comfort, 1956). Such data are well known to wildlife management experts who compare life spans of tagged animals released in the field versus the same species maintained in captivity. The recent study by Andersen and Rosenblatt (1965) points to the role of accidents in affecting the 50 percent survival values for beagles maintained in a simulated "natural" (field) environment in contrast to those kept in a protected environment. Therefore, one must be aware of the likelihood that environmental influences in natural conditions may result in the failure to realize the potential longevity of the species.

As is further emphasized below (see Parental Age), the potential maximum longevity of a species is certainly influenced by genetic factors. Indeed, longevity may be correlated with a number of intrinsic, genetic attributes. For example, the female of any one species generally lives longer than the male (Hamilton, 1948; Rockstein, 1958). There are exceptions to this rule among mammals, however [e.g., the stallion has a greater life span than the mare (Comfort, 1959), and the male Syrian hamster outlives the female (Kirkman and Yau, 1972)].

There also appears to be some correlation between different species for body size and potential longevity (Bourlière, 1957, 1960; Sacher, 1959). However, there are some exceptions to this generalization, e.g., domestic dogs are larger than cats, but have a shorter life expectancy (Bourlière, 1960). Similarly, man, one of the longest-lived species of mammals, is considerably smaller than a number of shorter-lived domesticated animals, such as the cow and the horse (Spector, 1956; Bourlière, 1960).

Diet

McCay, Maynard, Sperling, and Barnes (1939) and Ross (1959, 1961) have shown that nu-

trition is indeed an important factor in modifying the life span of male rats, either directly or through modifying the incidence of disease contributing to early death. (See Chapter 23 of this *Handbook* for a detailed discussion of this subject.)

In the classical study by McCay, Crowell, and Maynard (1935), it was shown that restricted diets fed to newly-weaned rats increased the maximum life span in the males (but not the females) to approximately twice the age of those allowed to feed *ad libitum*. This was confirmed in a later study by Berg and Simms (1960, 1961). Bourlière (1960) has been critical of this study as being inapplicable to all mammals because the lifelong growth of some rodents is atypical of most mammals. Comfort, in a similar comparative study (1963), found that dietary restrictions also increased the life span of the common guppy, *Lebistes*.

In a more recent study on female hooded rats reared on different nutritional diets, Miller and Payne (1968) found that rats fed a diet which supported maximal growth for 120 days had a greater longevity than those maintained on a restricted diet which would just maintain body weight. However, their rats never had the stunted appearance of the McCay diet-deficient animals, in contrast to those on an *ad libitum* diet. Everitt and Webb (1957), on the other hand, found the greatest positive coefficient of correlation between life duration and the age of maximal weight in the male albino Wistar rat.

In insects, a number of nutritional studies have been made in the common house fly (Rockstein, 1959) and in several species of cockroaches (Haydak, 1953); see Clark and Rockstein, 1964; and Rockstein and Miquel, 1973, for reviews of such studies in insects. Clark and Rockstein (1964) have pointed out that the role of diet is highly complicated by such factors as activity [especially in the case of the worker honey bee (Maurizio, 1959)] and the interrelationship of diet and egg-laying in affecting longevity in the house fly (Berberian, Rockstein, and Gray, 1971; Rockstein, Gray and Berberian, 1971; Gray and Berberian, 1971). There appear to be many interacting factors contributing to life span in relation to diet and dietary restriction and, at this time, it is unlikely that a restricted diet can be considered as the most important deterrent to early death or, conversely, uniquely important in prolongation of life.

Temperature

The studies from comparative gerontology on the role of temperature and longevity of invertebrates has led to the proposal that lowering the body temperature of mammals, including man, will extend the life span. Such comparative studies have little, if any, significance insofar as aging in mammals is concerned, because invertebrates such as insects are poikilothermal, and their metabolic rates are influenced by environmental temperatures. In the case of some cold-blooded vertebrates, some species of lizards and certain amphibians living in warm climates have shorter life spans than the same species in more northern, cooler latitudes (Bourlière, 1958, 1960). Liu and Walford (1966, 1970) found that three species of South American annual fishes, maintained at 15–16°C and 20–22°C, grew faster, were larger, and lived longer at the lower temperature ranges. On the other hand, mammals, capable of maintaining their internal body temperature and a fairly constant rate of metabolism, show little, if any, relationship between the temperature of their environment and their longevity. Indeed, mammals capable of surviving severe winters by going into hibernation generally have considerably shorter life spans than other mammals. Among the cold-blooded vertebrates, some tropical forms like the alligator and other aquatic forms living at higher temperatures have the greatest life spans, contradicting the suggestion that low-temperature exposure results in greater longevity.

Several studies on the longevities of rats reared at different temperatures (Kibler and Johnson, 1961, 1966; Kibler, Silsby, and Johnson, 1963; Heroux and Campbell, 1960) have shown that mean life expectancies are lower in rats reared in colder environments, primarily due to a greater incidence of lesions at an earlier age in the cold, stressful environment. (See discussion below concerning survival and ability to adapt to stressful stimuli.) Conversely, the ability of male rats to maintain constant internal body temperature at higher

temperatures actually resulted in an increase in the life expectancy of male rats. Thus, comparative studies involving animals of differing abilities to meet environmental stress, such as poikilothermous versus homeothermous animals, are of academic rather than practical comparative interest.

Parental Age

Classical studies of Lansing (1947, 1954) on the rotifers, a microscopic, complex multicellular aquatic animal, have shown that offspring produced parthenogenetically from young rotifers have a longer life span than those born of old rotifers. The factor for increasing longevity appears to be cumulative, in that selecting such offspring from young mothers over successive generations produced increasingly greater longevities, while those from senile, maternal lines had progressively decreasing life spans. Such trends can be reversed by back-selecting, i.e., shorter-lived animals orginally derived from older maternal parents could be transformed into longer-lived lines by back-selecting thereafter from young parents. In the house fly, Rockstein (1959) and Rockstein and Miquel (1973) could not demonstrate a "Lansing" factor in the NAIDM strain of house fly over several successive generations using eggs laid by young versus old females. After selection of three generations of eggs from older mothers, *longer-lived* males were actually produced, suggesting the presence of a sex-limited genetic factor transmitted only to the males from genetically longer-lived and presumably more viable mothers. Similarly, in the smaller species of fly, *Drosophila subobscura*, Wattiaux (1968a, 1968b) produced longer-lived as well as more fecund offspring from the oldest adults, in contrast to the earlier study by Comfort (1953), which reported the "absence of a Lansing factor" in the same species.

In mammals, such studies have been scarce. Strong and Johnson (1964) could find no consistent evidence for the presence of a "Lansing factor" operating with regard to female parental age and offspring longevity in C57/st mice. Comfort (1958) noted that although there was no effect of parental age upon longevity, longer-lived parents in thoroughbred mares had longer-lived progeny, in keeping with the findings in insects and mice cited above. Such data, although conflicting (see Clark and Rockstein, 1964), suggest support for the concept of the inheritance of longevity, just as the age at death of one's grandparents, parents, and siblings is a prime factor in anticipating the life expectancy of humans by insurance companies (Rockstein, 1958). In this connection, the maternal age at death in humans appears to have a stronger influence on the offspring's age at death than paternal age at death, which may suggest extrachromosomal inheritance (Abbott, Murphy, Bolling, and Abbey, 1974).

Longevity and Reproduction

Finally, in vertebrates, particularly mammals, attempts have been made to relate reproductive period as well as period of gestation to longevity. Among the primates, man, with the female menopause and long postmenopausal period of about 25 years, possesses the longest life span. Talbert (1968) has stressed that the menopausal period (when present) of subhuman female primates represents a very small portion of their life spans, unlike the human female.

Hammond and Marshall (1952), in a table adapted from Asdell (1946), show a positive correlation between life span and length of gestation and age at puberty for a number of species of mammals. Similar data (without being related to life span) have been recorded by Altman and Dittmer (1972) in the *Biology Data Book*, including age at sexual maturity, length of estrus cycle, and gestation period. Table 2 (a compilation of data from both of these sources) shows that man's long life span appears to be related in part to a delay in

TABLE 2. SPECIFIC LONGEVITY, GROWTH, AND REPRODUCTIVE VALUES FOR VARIOUS MAMMALIAN SPECIES.

Scientific Name	Common Name	Life span Mean (mo.)	Life span Maximum (mo.)	Length of gestation (mo.)	Age at puberty (mo.)	Length of growth period (mo.)	Estrus cycle (da.)
PRIMATES							
Homo sapiens	Man	849	1380	9	144	240	28
Gorilla gorilla	Gorilla	–	472	9	–	–	39
Pan troglodytes	Chimpanzee	210	534	8	120	–	36
Saimiri sciureus	Squirrel monkey	–	252	5	36	–	12
Macaca mulatta	Rhesus monkey	–	348	5.5	36	–	28
ARTIODACTYLA							
Bos taurus	Domestic cattle	276	360	9	6	47	19
Sus scrofa	Swine	192	324	4	4	8	21
Ovis aries	Sheep	144	240	5	7	15	17
Capra hircus	Goat	108	216	5	7	15	21
PERISSODACTYLA							
Equus caballus	Horse	300	744	11	12	49	24
PROBOSCIDEA							
Elephus maximus	Indian elephant	480	840	21	156	–	–
CARNIVORA							
Felis catus	Cat	180	336	2	15	–	22
Canis familiaris	Domestic dog	180	408	2	7	–	9
Ursus arctos	Brown bear	–	442	7	72	–	–
CETACEA							
Balaenoptera physalus	Whale	–	960	12	–	–	–
RODENTIA							
Sciurus carolinensis	Gray squirrel	108	180	1.5	12	–	–
Mus musculus	Mouse	18	42	0.7	1.5	6.3	4
Rattus rattus	House rat	30	56	0.7	2	6.6	4.5
Oryctolagus cuniculus	European rabbit	66	156	1	12	–	–
Cavia porcellus	Guinea pig	24	90	2	2	11	18
Mesocricetus auratus	Golden hamster	24	48	0.5	2	6	4.5

puberty and a longer growth period, as it does in the Indian elephant, the horse, and domestic cattle. However, there are an equal number of cases in which short-lived animals, like the gray squirrel and the European rabbit, show late maturity and much longer growth periods than other species of comparable mean and maximum longevities.

The relationship of longevity to reproductive maturity, length of reproductive period, and, in the case of mammals like man, the onset of menopause is difficult to evaluate. However, the occurrence of death in several species of Pacific salmon following spawning is one well-documented example of the relationship between sexual maturation and longevity (Robertson, 1957). The regularity with which several species of Pacific salmon (genus *Oncorhynchus*) die after their first reproduction suggests a causal relationship between spawning and subsequent death. This occurs whether the normal life cycle of a particular species is 2, 3, or 4 years and is a fairly rare phenomenon in vertebrates—only a few other species, such as some eels, lampreys, and small annual fishes, die after a single reproduction (Robertson, 1957). Robertson's classical study (1961) showed that in the Kokanee salmon, *Oncorhynchus nerka kennerlyi*, prevention of spawning by castration prolonged the life span by several years and inhibited the morphological degenerative changes that normally occur during spawning. When the longer-lived, castrated salmon died, they exhibited evidence of testicular regeneration and histological degenerative changes similar to those found in spawning salmon (Robertson and Wexler, 1962). Accordingly, they suggested that the deteriorative alterations accompanying spawning may represent an acceleration of the aging process for these species. In his earlier report, Robertson (1961) also suggested that the maturation of gonadal tissue (and not the act of spawning *per se*) is the cause of death in these species, probably through an indirect influence on the adrenal corticoid secretion (i.e., hyperadrenocorticism). This suggestion was further supported by Robertson, Hane, Wexler, and Rinfret (1963), by experimentally inducing hyperadrenocorticism in trout (*Salmo gairdnerii*), which then exhibited histological

changes similar to those seen in spawning salmon.

At the same time, it should be pointed out that castrated mice have a longer *maximal* life span [although the 50 percent mortality is the same as noncastrates (Mühlbock, 1959)], whereas castrated male cats have a higher mean age at death than noncastrates (Hamilton, Hamilton, and Mestler, 1969). Orchiectomy in cats and in man appears to result in a longer mean duration of life, lower incidence of deaths from infections, a higher incidence of death from cancer, and no change in frequency of death from cardiovascular disease. Spaying female cats also increases their life expectancy but not to as great an extent as in normally shorter-lived male cats (Hamilton, Hamilton, and Mestler, 1969).

MANIFESTATIONS OF AGING

Morphological Aspects of Aging

Part of our knowledge of morphological changes with age comes from careful as well as casual observations of domesticated animals and of wild animals in captivity. Different methods of age estimation have been employed, based on a number of morphological criteria; these include the scales in fish (Lux, 1973), the plumage in birds (Greenberg, Etter, and Anderson, 1972), the baleen in whales (Jonsgard, 1969), and the degree of ossification of the bony skeleton in many mammals, including man and bison (Duffield, 1973). In some animals, such as mice and rabbits, there is a slight increase in the *rate* of nail growth with advancing age (Lavelle, 1968). Hair growth is known to diminish as some animals grow old, especially for primates and CBA mice (Whiteley and Horton, 1962; Finch, 1973). Baldness occurs as a genetic trait in some primates, like the South American red uacaris (*Cacajao rubicundus*), which shows a progression of baldness with age similar to that of man (Uno, Adachi, and Montagna, 1969). Although most mammals show little or no change in hair pigmentation with age, a few domesticated species like the dog, the sheep, and the horse show graying with advancing age. As suggested by Kirby (1974), for animals in the wild, death may occur before the expression of this genetic characteristic. Thus, in attempting to estimate the age of an individual, there may be one or more morphological criteria used to ascertain the animal's age with some degree of accuracy. Dorney and Holzer (1957), for example, employed six criteria for determining the age of the ruffed grouse (*Bonasa umbellus*) involving diameters and lengths of various feathers and the contour and degree of shedding of the primary feathers.

Dentition. In the same fashion, the condition of the teeth may yield a fair degree of accuracy in defining the age of some species of animals. Robins and Rowlatt (1971) reported a high incidence of abnormal incisor teeth (i.e., broken

incisors or discolored or grooved enamel) in C57BL/Icrf mice in the 22- to 23-month-old group as opposed to 14- to 15-month (middle-aged) individuals. Such abnormalities were accompanied by a large increase in the mortality rate at this age. However, Finch, in a personal communication, stated that "damaged teeth in old C57BL/6J mice are atypical in our experience." Finch (1971) quotes Breeden (1967) as stating that old kangaroos in the wild lose their incisor teeth and often die from starvation.

The degree of tooth wear has also been used to estimate the ages of animals captured in the wild. Severinghaus (1949) has shown (Figure 2) that the height of the lingual crest of the molars of the white-tailed deer (*Odocoileus virgin-*

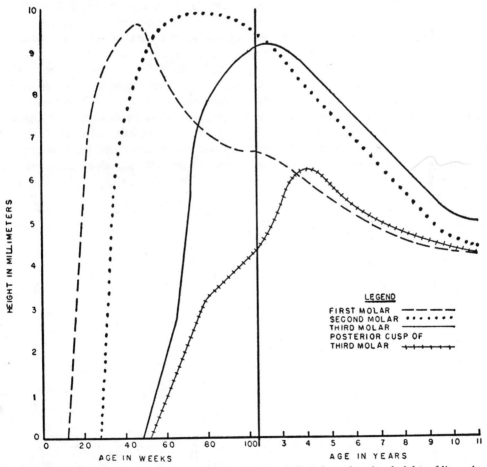

Figure 2. Development and decline of molars of white-tailed deer showing height of lingual crest above the gum at various ages. (From Severinghaus, C. W. 1949. *The Journal of Wildlife Management*, Vol. 13: 195–216. Fig. 3 [p. 205]. The Wildlife Society.)

ianus) declined steadily for each of the three molars, i.e., beginning at 25 weeks for the first molar, at 70 weeks for the second molar, and at 2 years and 3 years for the third molar and its posterior cusp. Accordingly, Severinghaus (1949) suggested that the wearing of the teeth to the gum might be a limiting factor to life expectancy of this species in the wild. Similarly, the age of the African elephant (*Loxodonta africana*) has been estimated accurately up to 30 years of age by relating the pattern of molar progression to a fixed point in the lower jaw (Sikes, 1967).

Another technique for estimating ages of wild animals is counting the "annual layers" in the cementum of the teeth. Scheffer (1950) noted that the age of the Alaskan fur seal (*Callorhinus ursinus*) corresponds to the number of concentric ridges around the roots of the teeth in an examination of skulls from this species of seal at different ages. Laws (1952) has pointed out that in the elephant seal (*Mirounga leonina*) such rings are laid down annually, so that the age of these animals in the wild can be estimated from their tooth cementum. Similarly, growth layers may be used as an index of age in the sperm whale, *Physeter catodon*, L., although in older animals the amount of wear and distortion may prevent accurate readings

(Gaskin and Cawthorn, 1973). Indeed, this particular criterion for determining the ages of wild animals has been applied in several recent studies, including the deer *Odocoileus hemionus* (Thomas and Bandy, 1973); the bobcat *Lynx rufus* (Crowe, 1972); the red fox *Vulpes fulva* (Manson, Stone, and Parks, 1973); the antelope *Antilocapra americana* (McKutchen, 1969); and the grizzly bear *Ursus arctos* (Craighead, Craighead, and McKutchen, 1970).

The Eye Lens. One of the most consistent and perhaps universal manifestations of aging in mammals is the series of changes which takes place in the composition of the lens of the eye with advancing age. The lens is morphologically rather simple, lacking blood vessels, and, because of its comparatively simple chemical composition, has proved to be a useful criterion for estimating the ages of animals, particularly those captured in the wild.

Dische, Borenfreund, and Zelmenis (1956) reported a direct correlation between eye-lens weight and age in Sprague-Dawley rats up to approximately 60 weeks of age (see Figure 3). Similarly, for animals collected from wild populations, eye-lens weight has been employed as one of the best methods for determining age

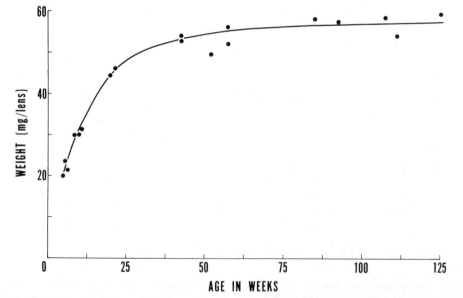

Figure 3. Eye lens weight as a function of age in the Sprague-Dawley rat. (Adapted from data of Dische *et al.*, 1956.)

up to maturity, as in the case of the spotted skunk (*Spilogale putorius*) by Mead (1967); in the gray squirrel (*Sciurus carolinensis*) by Fisher and Perry (1970); and in the black-tailed jack rabbit (*Lepus californicus*) by Connolly, Dudzinski, and Longhurst (1969).

Dische, Borenfreund, and Zelmenis (1956) also included the measurement of total protein content of the lens and found that while this increases during the entire life span of the animal, after maturity there is primarily an increase in the insoluble protein fraction of the lens. Dapson and Irland (1972) evaluated the criterion of protein content of the lens in relation to age in the field mouse (*Peromyscus polionotus*) and found that the insoluble

protein fraction of the eye lens continues to increase with age through the entire life span (approximately 2 years). Since rearing these animals under a variety of conditions (with resulting differences in body weights and sizes) had no appreciable effect upon the insoluble protein fraction of the eye lens, the authors concluded that this was superior to all other measurements for estimating age in small mammals (see Figure 4).

Not all studies have confirmed these findings. Labisky, Mann, and Lord (1969) found that the weight of the eye lens in pheasants could not be related to age. Henny and Ludke (1974) found that there was no consistent age-related pattern of distribution for either the insoluble or

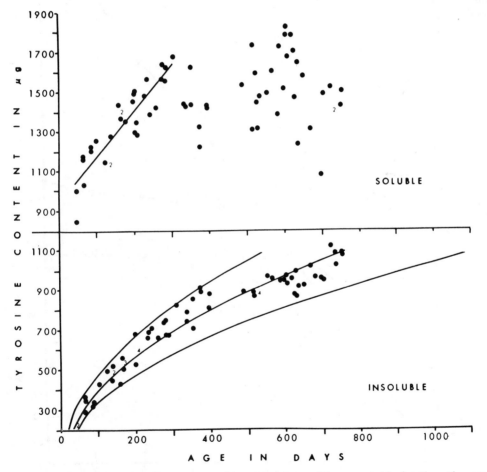

Figure 4. Changes in the tyrosine content of lenses with age. Upper: soluble fraction; the regression line includes animals from 45 to 308 days of age. Lower: insoluble fraction; 95 percent confidence limits for individual predictions are shown. Numbers in the body of the graphs were used in place of dots wherever several data points coincided. (From Dapson and Irland, 1972. By permission of American Society of Mammalogists.)

soluble protein fractions in the eye lens of the mallard. Pirie (1968) has suggested that changes in the lens proteins may be related to decreasing transparency with age as well as failure of the elastic nature of the lens in the development of presbyopia of middle-aged humans. Since birds are much more dependent upon sight and rapid accommodation of the eye in seeking food, mating, and escaping danger, the persistence of the elastic nature of the lens in the avian eye with advancing age may indeed be a manifestation of selective adaptation in birds.

Aging in Body Weight. Lansing's classical studies on aging rotifers (1947, 1954) were the first to experimentally support the earlier suggestion of Minot (1908) and the later observations in fish by Bidder (1925) that postmaturational aging begins with the cessation of growth. Among other papers supporting this viewpoint, those by Kohn (1965) and Goss (1974) are particularly emphatic in stressing the use of growth cessation as the onset of postmaturational aging or senescence. However, Comfort (1964), in discussing the so-called indeterminant growth of fishes, justifiably minimizes Bidder's (1925)

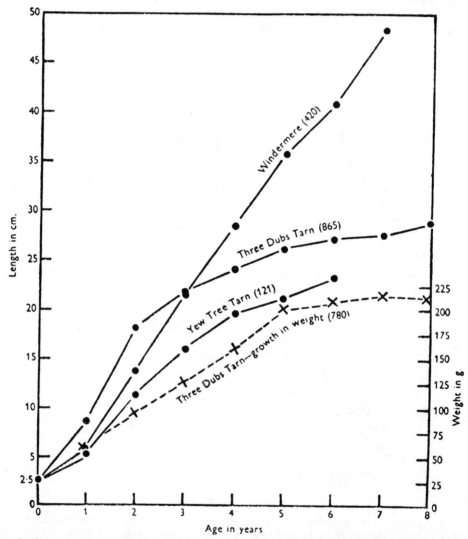

Figure 5. General pattern of growth in length of trout from three waters in the English Lake District; growth in weight also given for Three Dubs Tarn (numbers of fish given in parentheses). (From Frost and Smyly, 1952.)

original theory. Indeed, Figure 5, by Frost and Smyly (1952), shows that the same species of trout may show either limited or indefinite growth, depending on the environment in which the animal is being maintained. Furthermore, the fact that death occurs in some fish after spawning (discussed under Longevity and Reproduction, above) indicates the multifaceted nature of the aging process and the danger of oversimplification in attempting to pinpoint which factor or factors contribute to the onset of aging and to the process of aging itself.

Nevertheless, it is generally true that mammals increase in weight until they reach maturity. In some species, like man, it is unfortunately true that weight gain continues well beyond that point in life as well, even with the onset of postmaturational aging in a number of different parts of the body. As shown in Figure 6, by Rosenstein and Berman (1973), body weight of male cats increases with age from birth with a very definite leveling off sometime beyond the first year, although there is a wide range of weight values in older animals. A similar curve for female cats was obtained with a lower maximum weight being attained and at an earlier age than in the case of the male cats. Exceptions to this general case of weight increase with advanced age have been found. Robertson and Ray (1919) noted that senescent white mice weighed less than the younger

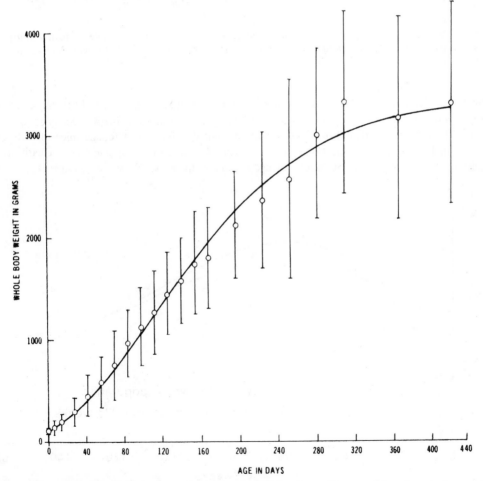

Figure 6. Changes in whole body weight as a function of age for normal male cats (mean ± 1 S.D.). (From Rosenstein, L., and Berman, E. 1973. Postnatal body weight changes of domestic cats maintained in an outdoor colony. *American Journal of Veterinary Research*, Vol. 34, p. 576.)

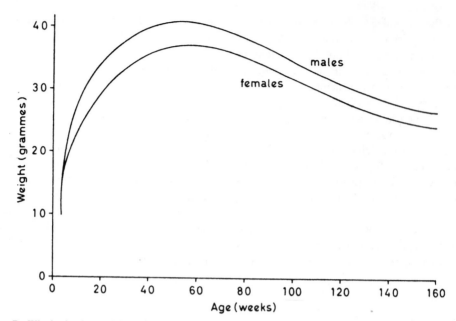

Figure 7. Whole body weight of male and female mice as a function of age. (From Lindop, P. 1961. Growth rate, lifespan, and causes of death in SAS/4 mice. *Gerontologia*, Vol. 5, p. 196 [Fig. 1]. S. Karger AG, Basel.)

individuals. Lindop (1961) studied weight changes with age in SAS/4 white mice (see Figure 7) and found that both males and females had a normal maturational rise in weight up to approximately 50 weeks of age, with a gradual decline in weight through old age (3 years). Lindop's further analysis of the weight distribution of female mice of different ages (see Figure 8) showed very clearly that female mice which survive longer than 123

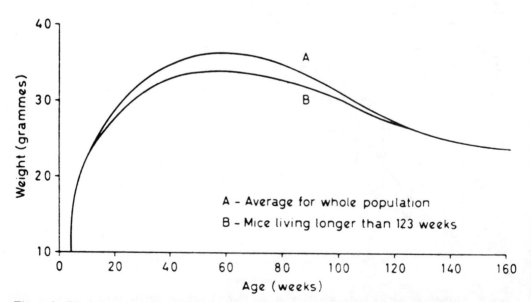

Figure 8. Whole body weight of female mice as a function of age. (From Lindop, P. 1961. Growth rate, lifespan, and causes of death in SAS/4 mice. *Gerontologia*, Vol. 5, p. 208 [Fig. 8]. S. Karger AG, Basel.)

weeks (curve B of Figure 8) had body weights 5 percent lower than the population as a whole throughout their lives. In males, the longer-lived animals showed only a 2 percent lower body weight than all other males. All individuals, then, show an age-related distribution of weight which is of the same general pattern, i.e., there is an onset of weight loss beginning sometime after the first year of life.

Everitt (1957a) studied the body weight changes in noninbred Wistar rats, which he separated into four population subgroups based on their mean longevity: "very short-lived," "short-lived," "long-lived," and "very long-lived." For each of these subgroups, he found a 30 percent loss in body weight during the last 200 days of life. A different result was found by Lesser, Deutsch, and Markofsky (1973) in a combined cross-sectional and longitudinal study in two different Sprague-Dawley rat colonies. They claim that they were able to identify two different subgroups as shorter-lived versus longer-lived animals, with the longer-lived subgroup having a body composition considerably different from that of the rest of the population at all adult ages. For example, at 350–550 days of age, the longer-lived subgroup (i.e., those still apparently healthy at up to 900 days of age) had a significantly lower body weight and lower fat-free mass (although the proportion of lean to fat tissue was similar to that of the rest of the population). Even during old age these longer-lived, leaner animals maintained their body weight with no appreciable loss, while the animals of the shorter-lived, heavier subgroup lost weight during later life. Although a cross-sectional study might show that the older animals of any colony would be the lighter animals, this is really the result of a selection of the more vigorous, longer-lived, and yet leaner animals. Lesser, Deutsch, and Markofsky (1973) concluded that ". . . the widely-held concept of senescent loss of lean tissue in animals needs to be reevaluated."

Finally, one cannot ignore the question of whether senile weight loss is a true manifestation of aging rather than "aging" and death being a consequence of disease, as has been stressed by investigators such as Berg and Simms (1962) and Everitt and Cavanagh (1963).

Hrachovec and Rockstein (1962) and Rockstein and Brandt (1962) reported consistently longer periods of weight stability in the longer-lived, disease-free CFN strain of white rats, in contrast to the much shorter comparable period of weight stability for aging (shorter-lived) Sprague-Dawley animals. In this respect, Finch, Foster, and Mirsky (1969) reported that in their colony of C57BL/6J mice there was no general loss of body weight before death in their healthy individuals (up to 30 months of age).

Numerous studies have been made to relate changes in specific organ weights to age. (Specific data on this subject will be presented in later chapters.) However, one cannot touch upon this subject without considering skeletal muscle, which makes up a considerable portion of the soft tissue weight of man. Indeed, such muscle shows an age-related loss in mass, primarily due to the fact that muscle is a post-mitotic tissue, incapable of replacing its component fibers destroyed by environmental stresses. Barrows, Roeder, and Falzone (1962) reported an age-dependent decrease in the ratio of the weight of the gastrocnemius muscle to total body weight, pointing out that the rate of loss of muscle tissue with advancing age was proportionately higher than that of the total body weight. They suggested that loss in weight of the gastrocnemius muscle was a more sensitive index of aging than loss of weight in other tissues or that of the total body, confirming the earlier findings of Yiengst, Barrows, and Shock (1959) of a decreasing skeletal mass/body weight in aging McCollum rats. In this connection, Tauchi, Yoshioka, and Kobayashi (1971) reported that the senile decrease in weight of skeletal muscle in both Wistar and Donryu rats was due both to a decrease in the *number* of fibers in the case of red skeletal muscle fibers and to a decrease in the *volume* of fibers in the case of the white skeletal muscle fibers.

Aging in the Nervous System. Since aging of the nervous system will be covered extensively in subsequent chapters, reference is now made to general principles of the aging of the nervous system as discussed in the recent publication by Rockstein and Sussman (1973). In general, as a postmitotic tissue, the nervous system characteristically shows a decline in cell number with advancing age in the white rat (Andrew, 1952; Bondareff and Pysh, 1968; Bondareff, 1973), the insect (Rockstein and Miquel, 1973), and man (Brody, 1973). In mice, Andrew (1939) reported progressive brain cell loss with age accompanied by neuronophagia in the white mouse. In BALB/C mice, Wright and Spink (1959) found that the number of large nerve cells of the spinal cord, expressed as a percentage of the cell number in 6-week-old animals, showed a significant decline from 50-week-old to 110-week-old mice, as shown in Figure 9.

Age changes in specific parts of the nervous system, both in structure and function, are beyond the scope of this chapter. It should be noted that with decline in cell number and intracellular degeneration as well as with advancing age, concomitant dysfunction may occur at the cellular level and at the total organismic level, in terms of response to environmental influences and behavior in general. For a detailed review of various aspects of aging in the nervous system, see Ford (1973).

Aging of the Blood. It is a common observation that a so-called normal blood picture in man may change in relation to nutrition, time of day, stresses upon the individual, etc. Despite this, norms have been established in different species of animals, including man, for red and white blood cell counts and for the hematocrit of the blood. It is also important to know how "normal" blood values may vary with age, since laboratory blood tests are routinely employed to aid in the diagnosis of disease.

Studies concerning the blood picture have been conflicting. Dougherty and Rosenblatt (1965) reported that aging beagles show a decrease in the red blood cell count with age. Ewing and Tauber (1964) had previously reported a decrease in the red blood cell count and hemoglobin concentration in C57BL/6 Jax mice, the hemoglobin decreasing from 16.5 grams per 100 ml at 4 months of age to 13.6 grams per 100 ml at 24 months of age. Reports have also been made of a decrease in the hemoglobin content of blood in C57BL mice from 6 to 18 months of age (Talbot, Abel, and Davison, 1965) and of a decrease in hematocrit

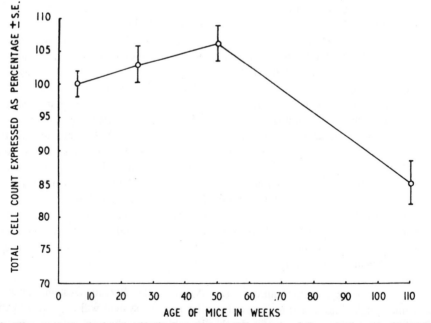

Figure 9. The percentage changes in the large nerve cell counts of the spinal cord of BALB/C mice with age. (From Wright, E., and Spink, J. 1959. A study of the loss of nerve cells in the central nervous system in relation to age. *Gerontologia*, Vol. 3, p. 289 [Fig. 6]. S. Karger AG, Basel.)

during senescence for the same strain of mouse (Finch and Foster, 1973). A slight decrease in the hematocrit had also been found previously by Grunt, Berry, and Knisely (1958) from blood samples of old Osborne-Mendel rats. At the other extreme, Everitt and Webb (1958) found an increase in both the hemoglobin concentration and red blood cell count in the aging Wistar rat during the last 200–300 days of life.

No age-dependent changes in the hemoglobin content from the blood of dairy cattle aged 3 months to 11 years were found by Brooks and Hughes (1932), while Ring, Kurabatov, Hernandez, and Dunn (1964) reported that the hematocrit remains fairly constant in the aging Fischer rat, although the very oldest survivors did have somewhat lowered values.

White blood cells have been reported to decrease with age in cattle (Riegle and Nellor, 1966) and to increase with age in the C57BL/6J mouse (Finch and Foster, 1973). White blood cell count has also been reported to remain unchanged with advancing age in the Wistar rat free of lung disease (Everitt and Webb, 1958) and in the C57BL mouse (Talbot, Abel, and Davison, 1965). Nevertheless, in the same study, Talbot, Abel, and Davison (1965) did report a change in the differential white blood cell distribution, such that the percentage of neutrophiles rose at 12 months and dropped at 18 months, whereas lymphocytes showed the opposite trend. In such animals as camels, goats, and water buffalo, Sharma, Malik, and Sapra (1973) reported that the neutrophile counts increased while lymphocyte counts decreased with advancing age. However, in a similar study on white blood cell distribution in sheep, goats, rats, and cattle, Riegle and Nellor (1966) found no consistent pattern of age-related changes in differential white blood cell counts or in gamma globulin content from species to species.

Therefore, it appears that there are no consistent age-dependent changes in many hematological values. On the other hand, it is not unlikely, since there is a greater incidence of certain diseases during senescence, that some of the conflicting age-related hematological values reported by a number of workers may, as suggested by Finch and Foster (1973), repre-sent pathologies, just as abnormal blood values occurring at any other time of life may represent the diseased state.

Aging Pigments. Obvious manifestations of aging include wrinkling of the skin, slowness of movement, and inability of the eye to accommodate for near vision. Another more cryptic manifestation of aging is the widespread accumulation of pigmented granules within the cytoplasm of cells of many organs, particularly skeletal and cardiac muscle and neurons. Such pigments are classed as "lipofuscin," the most common term applied thereto, although the structure and composition of pigments may vary from species to species and from tissue to tissue (see Figure 10). The genesis of these pigments is still quite hypothetical, and the correlation between such pigment accumulation and the effect on function of the organ or tissue involved is still to be clearly demonstrated. Nevertheless, there is a fairly consistent accumulation of pigment with age in such tissues in a considerable number of cases studied. This is exemplified in Figure 10 by Munnell and Getty (1968), which shows a linear accumulation of pigment at the rate of 0.36 percent pigment volume per unit of myocardial volume per year in the dog. Munnel and Getty stressed the importance of this accumulation in dog myocardial tissue in view of the fact that such pigment accumulation is 5 1/2 times as fast in the dog (with one-fifth of man's life span) as it is in man, as reported by Strehler, Mark, Mildvan, and Gee (1959).

An extensive review by Szabo (1935) gives descriptions of age-related morphological changes in many invertebrates from protozoa to insects, including the accumulation of age pigments as one indication of aging in these lower forms. In Rotatoria, the appearance of a brown substance in the hind portions of *Proales decipiens* occurs late in the animal's life according to Noyes (as cited by Szabo, 1935), with an increase in the quantity of this material until the entire body of the animal is colored. In Nemertini, Sekera (cited by Szabo, 1935) described the appearance of black spots on the body of *Prostoma clepsinoides* as an indication of the onset of senescence. In the

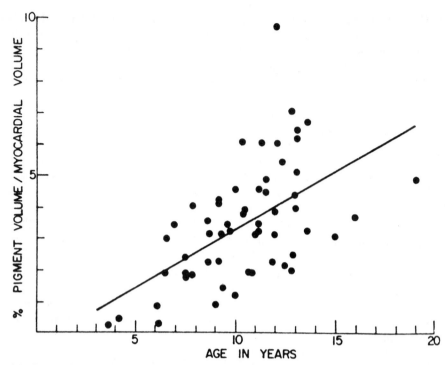

Figure 10. Percentage of pigment volume per myocardial volume *vs.* age in years for dogs older than 3.5 years. (Reproduced with the permission of the *Journal of Gerontology*, Munnell and Getty, 1968.)

polychaete worm (*Hydroides pectina*), Harms (as cited by Szabo, 1935) noted gray and black patches on the formerly yellowish hind parts of the intestine of this animal. Szabo (1935) described the accumulation of age pigment in ganglia and nerve cells of many different species of molluscs, as well.

In insects, a yellowish-green pigment accumulates with advancing age in the Malpighian tubules and in the oenocytes (epidermally derived cells involved in intermediary metabolism and molting). Miquel (1971) reported the accumulation with age of an "age pigment" in the oenocytes of *Drosophila melanogaster*, which appears to be similar to mammalian lipofuscin in color and size. However, in insects, such pigments are either uncommon or absent in muscle and central nervous tissue, where they are normally found to accumulate in aging mammals. Sondhi (1967) noted that the sternal pigment is not present in very young *D. melanogaster* adults, but is always present in senescent flies. In any one individual, the rate of accumulation of pigment was observed to

be related to the life span, so that flies with lowered longevity induced by elevated environmental temperature showed an increased rate of pigment formation. Furthermore, in inbred females, the life span of which was extended by injection of hemolymph from hybrid donors, the appearance of this sternal pigment was delayed. Sondhi concluded that the accumulation of pigment is a true age-dependent phenomenon, the rate of which is genetically determined.

Physiological Aspects of Aging

Aging of Motor Function. Since the cells of the nervous system, the skeletal muscle, and the heart in postembryonic humans are nondividing and therefore not self-replacing, the functional capacity of these tissues or organs characteristically exhibits *true* postmaturational aging or senescence. This attribute is, of course, completely unlike that of all other organs or tissues of the body with cells capable of self-replacement. Accordingly, it is not surprising that major research studies have been undertaken in animals which have the characteristics of a unique model for the study of senescence, such as the *adult form* of insects possessing complete metamorphosis (see Clark and Rockstein, 1964). All structures of the adult forms of such insects, except for the reproductive organs (and the midgut in some cases) are postmitotic. Consequently, cells become nonfunctional and die due to normal attrition or environmental assaults. However, the postulates for complete evaluation of the aging process in any system would include a correlation of gross functional changes with structural and physiological-biochemical changes of a deteriorating nature with age. In this vein, the study of motor function in insects with relatively short life spans, using large numbers of highly inbred individuals of the same sex, has been pioneered by Rockstein and coworkers (see Clark and Rockstein, 1964; Rockstein and Miquel, 1973).

Rockstein and Bhatnagar (1966) first studied gross functional changes in aging male and female house flies of a long-established NAIDM strain by actually measuring wing-beat frequency and duration of flight, beginning with the first day postemergence through the 22nd day, in the case of the female, and the 9th day in the case of the male. These workers found that 1-day-old females flew an average of 500 minutes on the first day, falling to 110 minutes by the 22nd day. In the case of the male flies, an even more striking failure was seen with a flight duration of 420 minutes for 1-day-old, to one of 63 minutes for 9-day-old flies. Rockstein and coworkers have investigated many details of the biochemical-physiological aspects of aging in the male house fly in relation to the gross functional changes and structural deterioration (i.e., wing abrasion and ultimate loss of wings in the case of males) accompanying the deterioration of flight ability. They found a well-integrated pattern of interrelated biochemical changes before, during, and after the failure of flight ability. Table 3 (modified from Rockstein, 1972) shows the changes in various parameters, including enzyme activity for the major enzyme systems concerned with the various aspects of energy metabolism of flight muscle contraction in the NAIDM strain

TABLE 3. TIME SEQUENCE OF AGING OF FLIGHT ABILITY IN THE MALE HOUSE FLY, *MUSCA DOMESTICA* L. [a]

Biological Parameter	Maximum
Acid phosphatase	emergence[b]
Trehalose content	4 hours
Brain cholinesterase	1 day
Duration of flight	1 day
Arginine phosphokinase	2 days
Actomyosin adenosine triphosphatase	2 days
Wing-beat frequency	4–9 days
Thiamine content	4 days
Alpha-glycerophosphate dehydrogenase	4 days
Arginine phosphate	5 days
Alkaline phosphatase	5 days
Onset of wing loss	6 days
Magnesium activated adenosine triphosphatase	6 days
Adenosine triphosphate	8 days
Number of mitochondria	8–12 days
Cytochrome *c* oxidase	11 days

[a]Mean life span—16.88 days
 Maximum life span—58 days
[b]minimum at 5 days

SOURCE: Rockstein, M. 1972. The role of molecular genetic mechanisms in the aging process. *In*, M. Rockstein and G. T. Baker III (eds.), *Molecular Genetic Mechanisms in Development and Aging*, p. 7. New York: Academic Press.

of the common house fly. The corresponding changes in some of the important substrates are also shown. Most recently, Rockstein and Chesky (1973) found that the male house fly flight muscle shows a change in quantity and in specific activity of the natural actomyosin ATPase. After reaching a peak with maturation of flight ability during the first 24 hours, both parameters show a steady, rapid decline, virtually coincidental with the previously observed decline in flight ability as measured by duration of flight in the earlier study by Rockstein and Bhatnagar (1966). In this connection, preliminary studies (Chesky and Rockstein, submitted for publication) show a similar age-related decline in this primary energy-producing enzyme in cardiac muscle in the aging male Fischer white rat. It is interesting that Rowley and Graham (1968), in a study relating histological observations to flight performance in the virgin female mosquito (*Aedes aegypti*), were able to relate changing flight performance directly to the degree of utilization of glycogen, rather than to the glycogen content per animal with advancing age. This suggests the need for further study of (declining) changes in enzyme activity of biochemical systems concerned with the utilization of carbohydrate stores.

In a recently completed electron microscopic study, it was found (Rockstein, Chesky, Philpott, Takahashi, Johnson, and Miquel, 1975) by exhaustive examination of sections of the flight muscle of young and old male NAIDM strain house flies that the following occurs:

1. There is a loss in the glycogen content of the flight muscle of aging male house flies.
2. There is an apparent increase in the size of the flight muscle giant mitochondria with age, even into old age, confirming earlier studies (Rockstein and Bhatnagar, 1965).
3. There is no significant mitochondrial or myofibrillar degeneration, in contrast to the report by Sohal and Allison (1971) of "marked dissolution of myofibrils" in their strain of house fly.

Studies by Tribe and Ashhurst (1972), Webb and Tribe (1974), Sacktor and Shimada (1972), and Bulos, Shukla, and Sacktor (1972) on the house fly and on two species of blow flies agree with the above-mentioned observations of Rockstein *et al.* (1975), particularly with respect to age changes in glycogen content and the relative intactness of myofibrils of the flight muscle, even in very old male flies.

Flight muscle, having basic structural and biochemical features (see Clark and Rockstein, 1964; Chefurka, 1965) analogous to muscles of higher vertebrates including man, is a convenient system for aging studies. Indeed, the above-mentioned workers have laid the groundwork for similar studies in vertebrates on the aging of skeletal and cardiac muscle, both of which have essentially the same structural components as the flight muscle of these short-lived animals.

Reproductive Senescence. Postmaturational aging or senescence is marked by a gradual or even a climactic decline in reproductive activity

and fertility. In man, this is the female menopause. Declining mammalian fertility is discussed in greater detail in Chapter 13 of this *Handbook*. Here it should be mentioned that many female mammals produce a decreased number of offspring per unit time with advancing maternal age. This is partly a consequence of a greater interval between litters and a decreased size of litters (usually after the second litter) with advancing age, in such species as pigs (Perry, 1954), beagles (Andersen, 1965), mice (Russell, 1954; Roman and Strong, 1960), rats (Ingram, Mandl, and Zuckerman, 1958; Chesky and Rockstein, 1975), and the golden hamster (Soderwall, Kent, Turbyfill, and Britenbaker, 1960). Such decreased litter size may be the result of increased embryonic mortality as shown in mice by Finn (1962, 1963). There may also be an increase in the length of the gestation period with advancing maternal age, as occurs in the golden hamster (Soderwall *et al.,* 1960) and sheep (Terrill and Hazel, 1947).

Male fertility also decreases with age and plays some role in determining the reproductive potential of any given species as a function of age. For example, reciprocal mating studies of young versus old animals of either sex have demonstrated a decrease in fertility with advancing age in the male rat (Soderwall and Britenbaker, 1955). Sperm production declines in the rabbit after 24 months of age (Ewing, Johnson, Desjardins, and Clegg, 1972). Larsson reported (1958) that there is a decrease in the number of ejaculations and copulations per hour, as well as in the number of intromissions preceding ejaculation in old male rats, suggesting that such changes in sexual activity may be the basis for the overall decline in fertility in the aging male rat. Drori and Folman (1969) found that the mean life span of 28 male rats mated at least once a week was 734 days as opposed to 578 days for unmated littermates. They suggested that since mated rats produce more testosterone than unmated ones (Herz, Folman, and Drori, 1969), such increases in testosterone result in more exercise and, consequently, in increased longevity in mated male rats.

Similar declines in reproductive output occur

in lower classes of vertebrates. Oliver (1972) reported a decrease in the fertility, with age, of the Chinese male goose; Brody, Henderson, and Kempster (1923) reported a loss in the egg production of domestic fowl of about 12 percent per year; Daniels (1968) reported a rapid decrease in egg production in Japanese quail following the first year to zero egg production by the end of the second. Older female snakes lay fewer eggs than young ones (Bourlière, 1957). Likewise, Comfort (1961) reported that older guppies produced fewer live fish per brood than younger ones, and Gerking (1959) reported a similar, decreasing reproductive capacity in live-bearing fish of the family Poeciliidae.

In the planarian flatworm, *Dugesia lugubris,* Balázs and Burg (1962a) found that cocoon production was low during the first through fifth month of postembryonic development, reaching a maximum by the tenth to eleventh month, and decreasing gradually thereafter. Futhermore, fertility of this animal also decreases with age (Balázs and Burg, 1962b), so that during the eleventh of twelfth postembryonic month, 50 percent to 90 pecent of the cocoons were barren. In addition, there appeared to be a relationship between the ages of the parents at the time of the cocoon production and the number of offspring produced, i.e., the number of offspring from aged parents (20 months old) was at least 566 percent less than that from middle-aged (10-month-old) parents.

In general, the few comparative studies involving invertebrates have indicated that there is an inverse relationship between egg production and life span, in the cases of female *Drosophila subobscura* (Maynard Smith, 1959) and in the cockroach *Periplaneta americana* (Griffiths and Tauber, 1942). In *Ephestia kühniella,* Norris (1933) showed that virgin females live longer and produce fewer eggs than mated ones. Finally, in the studies on the honey bee, *Apis mellifica,* Maurizio (1954) showed that worker bees in a queenless or broodless summer colony resembled in longevity the worker bees from overwintering hives. However, the studies of Berberian, Rockstein, and Gray (1971) clearly show the influence of diet as well as egg laying in determining adult longevity, since *staggered* egg laying increased the longevity of adult female flies in contrast to those provided with a medium for *continuous* egg laying.

Metabolism. This area of interest has been popular since the early part of the twentieth century, with the observation of a decline in metabolism with advancing age in man as well as in lower animals.

Early studies by Child (1915) used susceptibility to toxins (cyanide, ethyl alcohol, chloroform) to determine the age of invertebrates. He reported that younger animals of some species of coelenterates and crustaceans (presumably because of their higher metabolic rates) were more susceptible than adults. Parthenogenetically reproducing *Hydra fusca* were more susceptible in budding parts than in other regions of the body. If low toxin concentrations were used, however, young animals could adjust more completely and lived longer than adults. Child's observations were derived primarily from experiments with the flatworms, *Planaria dorotocephala, P. maculata,* and *P. velata.* In *P. maculata,* which reproduces sexually, he also demonstrated that the rate of metabolism decreases as the animal ages, with a slower decrease in advanced age than just after hatching.

Total body metabolism has been more readily studied by using Warburg respirometers to measure oxygen uptake per unit time under highly controlled (water bath) temperature conditions. Indeed, the metabolism of a small animal like the mouse can be measured in the larger Warburg vessels; smaller, complex invertebrates like flies or honey bees (see Allen, 1959; Stussi, 1972) can be studied in the Warburg microrespirometer flasks under controlled conditions of temperature, oxygen levels, carbon dioxide, etc. In brief, earlier, more general studies involving total body metabolic rate changes with age have given way to measurements of metabolic changes with age both in organs and tissues, as well as at the cellular and subcellular levels, including specific enzyme systems. (The comparative biology of aging at the cellular and subcellular levels, insofar as metabolism is concerned, will be discussed in subsequent chapters.)

Changes in metabolic rate with advancing age can be determined in a number of ways (i.e., by measuring the rate of oxygen consumption, carbon dioxide production, or heat production). Shock and Yiengst (1955) showed that there is a reduction in basal heat production and carbon dioxide elimination in both men and women with advancing age, based upon body surface area. Yet, studies on lower animals have yielded conflicting results. Benedict and MacLeod (1929) found that old female rats (26 months) produced 50 percent more heat per square meter of body surface per 24 hours than young (2-month-old) females (see Figure 11). Ring, Dupuch, and Emeric (1964) reported that the whole body oxygen consumption of Fischer rats increases during aging. These results are in contrast to those of Davis (1937), who measured oxygen consumption in dozing and sleeping rats

throughout life and found that there was a precipitous drop in relation to age, being very rapid in the first 4 to 5 months and more gradual thereafter throughout the remainder of the 30-month life span of the animals. The average oxygen consumption for man, based upon surface area, appears to be quite parallel to that of rats. Denckla (1974) (see Figure 12) has shown that the minimal oxygen consumption in resting Zivic-Miller rats declines by 77 percent from 3 weeks to 2 years of age. Denckla suggests that the decline in minimal oxygen consumption with advancing age is partly related to pituitary function because (1) response curves indicate that young rats are three times more responsive to injected thyroxine than old rats; (2) bovine pituitary extracts can decrease the responsiveness of immature rats to thyroxine; (3) hypophysectomy in young rats arrests the normal age-associated decrease in responsiveness to thyroxine; and (4) hypophysectomy in adults restores some of the responsiveness to thyroxine.

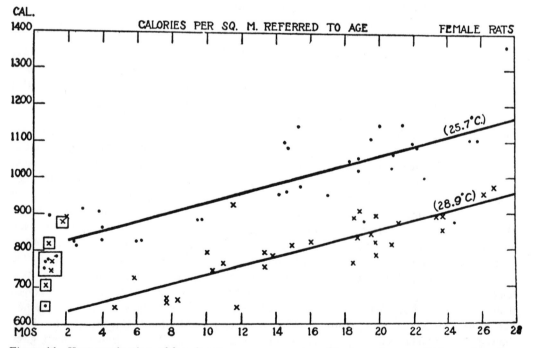

Figure 11. Heat production of female rats per square meter of body surface per 24 hr., referred to age. The data represented by dots were obtained at an average temperature of 25.7°C and those represented by crosses at an average temperature of 28.9°C. The dots and crosses enclosed in squares represent mixed groups of male and female rats. The two curves deal with rats over 2 months old. (From Benedict and MacLeod, 1929.)

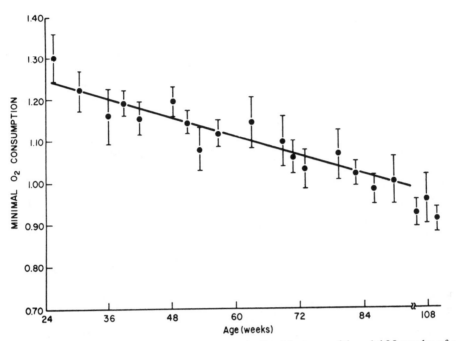

Figure 12. Decline in MOC (minimal oxygen consumption) between 24 and 108 weeks of age in the female rat. MOC values are given for 8–20 female rats per point. Standard deviations are indicated by vertical bars. All rats were fed a low iodine diet. (From Denckla, W. D. 1974. Role of the pituitary and thyroid glands in the decline of minimal O_2 consumption with age. *J. Clin. Invest.*, **53**, 572–581 [Fig. 2].)

Stress. In general, the aged organism shows a decrease in a number of physiological functions concomitant with age-related changes in corresponding organs and their cells. On the other hand, different organ systems and their organs do not age at the same rate and to the same extent; such changes vary from individual to individual within one strain or species and, more dramatically, between members of different strains or species. A number of studies involving changes in blood pressure and cardiac function have produced conflicting data. In the Wistar rat, for example, completely contradictory results have been reported by Medoff and Bongiovanni (1945) and by Rothbaum, Shaw, Angell, and Shock (1973). In the case of the white leghorn chicken, Sturkie, Weiss, and Ringer (1953) have reported increases in blood pressure with age similar to that of humans. Similarly, Rothbaum et al. (1973) noted an 18 percent decline in stroke index in the aging rat heart from 1 to 2 years of age, which is almost identical to the decline in the stroke index of men from 30 years to 70 years of age reported

by Brandfonbrener, Landowne, and Shock (1955). A decrease in heart rate with age in the Wistar and the Sprague-Dawley rat has been reported by Everitt (1957b) and Berg (1955), whereas Rothbaum et al. (1973) reported a higher heart rate despite a decline in cardiac output in older Wistar rats.

Finch (1971) made a rather sweeping, but nevertheless significant comment on the variability in manifestations of aging for different species: " . . . when aging is considered from a comparative viewpoint, it is clear that there is no aging process common to all higher organisms." Nevertheless, the present authors believe that in addition to the universality of aging in motor function and structural and physiological states of the nervous system, there is indeed a decreased ability to adapt to the environment with advancing age which leads to an increase in the rate of mortality in any population of animals. As later chapters of this *Handbook* will show, man shows a decrease in ability to react to stress, particulary to such physiological stresses as (1) the rate of return to equilibrium value by the blood upon displacement of blood pH by the administration of acid or alkali, (2) the decrease in response to administration of glucose intravenously, i.e., the glucose tolerance test, and (3) a return to normal of pulse rate displaced, by standard exercise tests. In Wistar rats a similar decline in response to environmental stress is seen with advancing age. Flückiger and Verzár (1955) found that the body temperature of rats drops markedly when subjected to 350 mm atmospheric pressure; while body temperature returns to normal in animals less than 7 months of age, rats 17–20 months old are unable to restore normal body temperature upon exposure to such atmospheric pressures.

Finch, Foster, and Mirsky (1969) found that 30-month-old C57BL/6J mice, after fasting for 20 hours, showed a steady drop in colon temperature over a period of 3 hours of exposure to lowered ambient temperature (9–10°C), in contrast to that of similarly fasted 10-month-old mice, as shown in Figure 13.

As in the case of humans, senescent lower animals respond differently to the stress of exercise than younger animals. Bloor and Leon (1970) showed that a continuous swimming program produced cardiac hypertrophy in young Walter Reed rats, while 12-month-old rats actually showed a loss of myocardial mass.

One would expect that age-dependent changes in physiological capacity would be reflected in intracellular changes, particularly in enzyme systems concerned with effecting such physiological function. Adelman (1971) suggests that age-dependent modifications in the ability to synthesize certain enzymes in response to environmental alterations may be a general biochemical expression of aging. The studies of Barrows, Roeder and Falzone (1962) in the white rat and of Rockstein and colleagues in the house fly (Rockstein, 1972) have shown such to be the case, particularly as regards the locomotor function of flight and of movement in vertebrates and invertebrates. More recent studies have clearly pointed to an underlying age-related decrease in protein synthesis, even of synthesis of specific enzymes concerned with the energy metabolism of locomotor function (Rockstein and Baker,

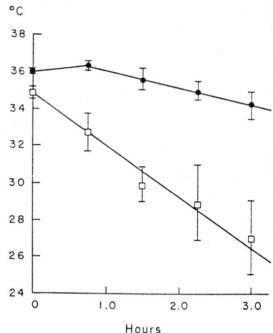

Figure 13. The effect of age on colon temperature during cold stress (9–10°C) (average values). Solid circles indicate 10-month-old mice; open squares, 30-month-old mice; I ± SEM, 7 mice per age group. (Finch et al., 1969. Reproduced from the *Journal of General Physiology*, Vol. 54, pp. 690–712 by copyright permission of the Rockefeller University Press.)

1974; Mecklenburg, personal communication). Thus, in an age of molecular biology, the molecular genetic approach to a declining functional capacity in any organ system appears to be the ultimate approach to the clarification of the nature of the aging process.

THE EVOLUTION OF AGING AND LONGEVITY

This condensed overview of the known distribution of various manifestations of aging in animals should offer these three major conclusions concerning the aging process:

1. It is clear that aging of a number of body functions, organ systems, and their cells appears to be more or less universally distributed among multicellular animals.
2. Not all organs or organ systems age in the same way or at the same rate or extent in

any individual of a given species or strain of animals.

3. The same organs or organ systems do not necessarily age in the same way nor at the same rate or extent in different species.

It is for these reasons that Rockstein (1974) suggested the difficulty in accepting a single theory of aging (also see Wilson, 1974). However, it is patently clear from the longevity data cited earlier in this chapter that for each species, and even for known genotypes in a given species, there exists a specific maximum life span. Intrinsic in the meaning of "aging" is a definite time course and direction for the individual changes in various parts of an organism, the sum total of which results in the failure of the individual to withstand the stress of his environment, ultimately leading to his death. Specific life span is really the reflection of the sum total of deleterious changes accumulated during the lifetime of species representatives, which we describe collectively as "aging" or "senescence."

The concept that species-specific life spans have evolved as an adaptation for maximum survival of each species living in its particular ecosystem has been the subject of both critical analysis by scientists working in the field of gerontology and philosophical conjecture by others from peripheral to unrelated areas of science (Comfort, 1956; Medawar, 1957; Williams, 1957; Strehler, 1960; Clark and Rockstein, 1964; Kohn, 1965; Hamilton, 1966). Certainly, the existence of programmed aging of certain functions, particularly those involving postmitotic tissues like nerve and muscle, together with the existence of a known maximum specific life span for different animals, suggests that, good or bad, such aging has indeed evolved. However, whether or not such an evolved biological attribute is necessarily beneficial is the real heart of the question of aging as an evolved adaptation.

The case of the Pacific salmon cited earlier (Robertson, 1961) is a relatively isolated instance of support for the concept that aging and death follow the end of the reproductive period of a particular species, especially in the case of those producing large numbers of offspring per parent. Many species of fish (trout, sturgeon,

herring, and sardines) survive (if uncaught by sports and commercial fishermen) many years beyond their initial and subsequent egg layings. Among reptiles, the production of large numbers of offspring may reciprocally be matched by fairly long life spans, as in the case of the sea turtle (Spector, 1956). In primates, like man, the menopause (a rare phenomenon among mammals) hardly coincides with the time of death of the female. Indeed, the comparatively long life of the human male and female, as well as of the Asiatic elephant, with their small number of offspring, argues against the case for the adaptive evolution of aging as a desirable phenomenon of species survival value.

The relationship between aging, death, and reproductive period varies in different species. The female parents (queens) of the social insects (honey bees, ants, and termites) produce large numbers of offspring (as many as 3,000 per day in the case of the honey bee), yet possess comparatively long life spans—6 years or better—whereas the mayfly is highly prolific but short-lived (Howard, 1939).

Williams (1957) has suggested that if evolution favors selection for a gene which confers a "survival" advantage during a period of maximum reproduction, the species will in turn evolve an increased longevity. This view leads to the conclusion that there should be no extended period of life after the time of reproduction and parental care. However, in the case of long-lived mammals like man, the postreproductive life span of a human female exceeds that of the reproductive period, on the average by more than 20 years and maximally by 50 years—well beyond the age of parental responsibility. Williams (1957) describes this as an "artifact of civilization." His suggestion agrees with the fact that the onset of senescence usually occurs some time before the termination of reproduction, as in the case of man himself.

Since there is little evidence available for determining what processes play a significant role in determining differences in species-specific maximum life span, one might speculate that the varied processes of evolution, which have been demonstrated for other areas of biology, may also be at work in selecting for or against long life. Indeed, if the propensity to live long in one species is an evolved process, it must necessarily be the result of a *balance* between positive selective pressures which favor long life and negative factors which cause a decline in reproductive function in later age. The survival value of any individual in evolutionary terms is signified by his ability to produce the greatest number of surviving offspring. Accordingly, selection pressures would favor maximum survival in the young, reproductively functioning individuals, rather than in the old, nonreproductive members. The gene which acts to produce a maximum number of offspring early in the life span of the parent and which is linked to the gene which produces weakness later in life (i.e., during the postreproductive period) would, in all probability, be favored (see Williams, 1960, for further discussion on this subject). Any selection pressures for long life would therefore have to be linked either to some earlier beneficial effect or to some benefit which the older, nonreproductive individual confers upon the reproducing members of the population. In human society this would involve the contributions of the more mature members of the populations, such as productivity, inventiveness, leadership, and communication of the accumulated cultural and behavioral values which have a survival value for the species.

Such contributions of older, postreproductive individuals give the younger, reproducing members greater capability for survival and expansion of successive generation populations.

SUMMARY

In this chapter the authors have attempted to point out the universal nature of the aging process for all complex animals, from the lowest, but nevertheless complex, invertebrate animals through the highest vertebrate orders, including man. The increasing number of reports concerned with various aspects of aging in different tissues in different animal species has made it necessary to be both selective and critical in discussing the comparative biology of aging. The one underlying theme of this chapter has been that, although aging is a universal biological phenomenon, its various morphological and physiological manifestations make impossible the acceptance of a single process or theory which adequately describes aging.

As time progresses, cumulative biological changes that occur in all species ultimately result in a decreased ability of the individual to function in its environment. To what extent true senescence is complicated by one or more pathological conditions is a moot question. Whatever the answer, the net result is a greater increase in mortality in a population with advancing age. Although these time-related deteriorative changes may be in part biologically inherited, they may likewise be modified by environmental conditions. Although the specific maximum longevity appears to be universally genetically determined, the percentage of an individual's potential life span that is ultimately realized depends upon the physical and biological factors in its environment. Very few individuals of any species actually attain their potential maximum longevity, so that, especially in the case of wild species, senescence may not be the major cause of death. To determine the comparative influences of heredity and environment on the individual's or species' life span, studies in gerontology must be made under carefully controlled conditions. To this end, invertebrates with short life spans, but with tissues and systems analogous to those of higher vertebrates, including man, should not be overlooked as models for aging studies. It must be obvious, considering the limited life span of the human investigator himself, and, therefore, the relatively short period of time available for any kind of in-depth research in any phase of gerontology, that research findings obtained from extensive study of aging in inbred animals with short life spans which are available in large numbers will make possible the formulation of a basic hypothesis concerning the complex process of aging.

ACKNOWLEDGMENT

The authors acknowledge with appreciation and thanks the role of Mrs. Estella Cooney in the preparation of the manuscript of this contribution.

REFERENCES

Abbott, M., Murphy, E., Bolling, D., and Abbey, H. 1974. The familial component in longevity—A study of offspring of nonagenarians. II. Preliminary analysis of the completed study. *Johns Hopkins Med. J.*, **134**, 1-16.

Adelman, R. 1971. Age-dependent effects in enzyme induction–A biochemical expression of aging. *Exp. Geront.*, **6**, 75-87.

Allen, M. D. 1959. Respiration rates of worker honeybees of different ages and at different temperatures. *J. Exp. Biol.*, **36**, 92-101.

Altman, P., and Dittmer, D. (eds.) 1964. *Biology Data Book*, pp. 57-58. Washington, D.C.: Federation of American Societies for Experimental Biology.

Altman, P., and Dittmer, D. (eds.) 1972. *Biology Data Book*, 2nd ed., pp. 233-235. Bethesda, Maryland: Federation of American Societies for Experimental Biology.

Andersen, A. C. 1965. Reproductive ability of female beagles in relation to advancing age. *Exp. Geront.*, **1**, 189-192.

Andersen, A. C., and Rosenblatt, L. S. 1965. Survival of beagles under natural and laboratory conditions. *Exp. Geront.*, **1**, 193-199.

Andrew, W. 1939. Neuronophagia in the brain of the mouse as a result of inanition and in the normal aging process. *J. Comp. Neurol.*, **70**, 413-430.

Andrew, W. 1952. *Cellular Changes With Age*. Springfield, Illinois: Charles C. Thomas.

Asdell, S. 1946. *Patterns of Mammalian Reproduction*. Ithaca, New York: Comstock.

Balázs, A., and Burg, M. 1962a. Quantitative data to the changes of propagation according to age. I. Cocoon production of *Dugesia lugubris*. *Acta Biol. Acad. Sci. Hung.*, **12**, 287-296.

Balázs, A., and Burg, M. 1962b. Quantitative data to the changes of propagation according to age. II. Fertility and number of embryos in *Dugesia lugubris*. *Acta Biol. Acad. Sci. Hung.*, **12**, 297-304.

Barrows, C., Roeder, L., and Falzone, J. 1962. Effect of age on the activities of enzymes and the concentrations of nucleic acids in the tissues of female wild rats. *J. Geront.*, **17**, 144-147.

Benedict, F. G., and MacLeod, G. 1929. The heat production of the albino rat. II. Influence of temperature, age, and sex; comparison with the basal metabolism of man. *J. Nutr.*, **1**, 367-398.

Berberian, P. A., Rockstein, M., and Gray, F. H. 1971. The effect of egg laying on the longevity of the adult female house fly, *Musca domestica*, L. *J. Geront.*, **26**, 485-489.

Berg, B. 1955. The electrocardiogram in aging rats. *J. Geront.*, **10**, 420-423.

Berg, B., and Simms, H. 1960. Nutrition and longevity in the rat. II. Longevity and onset of disease with different levels of food intake. *J. Nutr.*, **71**, 255-263.

Berg, B., and Simms, H. 1961. Nutrition and longevity in the rat. III. Food restriction beyond 800 days. *J. Nutr.*, **74**, 23-32.

Berg, B., and Simms, H. 1962. Disease, rather than aging, as the cause of weight loss and muscle lesions in the rat. *J. Geront.*, **17**, 452.

Bidder, G. P. 1925. The mortality of plaice. *Nature*, **115**, 495-496.

Bloor, C., and Leon, A. 1970. Interaction of age and exercise on the heart and blood supply. *Lab. Invest.*, **22**, 160-164.

Bondareff, W. 1973. Age changes in the neuronal microenvironment. *In*, M. Rockstein and M. L. Sussman (eds.), *Development and Aging in the Nervous System*, pp. 1-17. New York: Academic Press.

Bondareff, W., and Pysh, J. J. 1968. Distribution of the extracellular space during postnatal maturation of rat cerebral cortex. *Anat. Record*, **160**, 773-780.

Bourlière, F. 1957. The comparative biology of ageing: A physiological approach. *In*, G. E. W. Wolstenholme and C. M. O'Connor (eds.), *Methodology of the Study of Ageing*, CIBA Foundation Colloquia on Ageing, Vol. 3, pp. 20-38. Boston: Little, Brown.

Bourlière, F. 1958. The comparative biology of aging. *J. Geront., Suppl. 1*, **13**, 16-24.

Bourlière, F. 1960. Species differences in potential longevity of vertebrates and their physiological implications. *In*, B. Strehler (ed.), *The Biology of Aging*, pp. 128-131. Washington, D.C.: American Institute of Biological Sciences.

Brandfonbrener, M., Landowne, M., and Shock, N. 1955. Changes in cardiac output with age. *Circulation*, **12**, 557-566.

Breeden, S. 1967. *The Life of the Kangaroo*, p. 25. New York: Taplinger.

Brody, H. 1973. Aging of the vertebrate brain. *In*, M. Rockstein and M. L. Sussman (eds.), *Development and Aging in the Nervous System*, pp. 121-133. New York: Academic Press.

Brody, S., Henderson, E., and Kempster, H. 1923. The rate of senescence of the domestic fowl as measured by the decline in egg production with age. *J. Gen. Physiol.*, **6**, 41-45.

Brooks, H., and Hughes, J. 1932. The hemoglobin of the blood of dairy cattle. *J. Nutr.*, **5**, 35-38.

Bulos, B., Shukla, S., and Sacktor, B. 1972. Bioenergetic properties of mitochondria from flight muscle of aging blowflies. *Arch. Biochem. Biophys.*, **149**, 461-469.

Chefurka, W. 1965. Intermediary metabolism of nitrogenous and lipid compounds in insects. *In*, M. Rockstein (ed.), *The Physiology of Insecta*, Vol. II, pp. 669-768. New York: Academic Press.

Chesky, J., and Rockstein, M. 1975. Survival data for a colony of male Fischer rats. *Gerontologist*, **15**, 29.

Chesky, J. A., and Rockstein, M. 1976. Reduced myocardial actomyosin adenosinetriphosphatase activity in the aging male Fischer rat. Submitted for publication.

Child, C. M. 1915. *Senescence and Rejuvenescence*. Chicago: University of Chicago Press.

Clark, A. M., and Rockstein, M. 1964. Aging in insects. *In*, M. Rockstein (ed.), *The Physiology of Insecta*, Vol. I, pp. 227-281. New York: Academic Press.

Comfort, A. 1953. Absence of a Lansing effect in *Drosophila subobscura*. *Nature*, **172**, 83-84.

Comfort, A. 1956. *The Biology of Senescence*, pp. 37-42, 190-191. New York: Rinehart.

Comfort, A. 1958. The longevity and mortality of thoroughbred mares. *J. Geront.*, **13**, 342-350.

Comfort, A. 1959. The longevity and mortality of thoroughbred stallions. *J. Geront.*, **14**, 9-10.

Comfort, A. 1961. Age and reproduction in female *Lebistes. Gerontologia*, **5**, 146-149.

Comfort, A. 1963. Effect of delayed and resumed growth on the longevity of a fish (*Lebistes reticulatus*, Peters) in captivity. *Gerontologia*, **8**, 150-155.

Comfort, A. 1964. *Ageing: The Biology of Senescence*. San Francisco: Holt, Rinehart & Winston.

Connolly, G., Dudzinski, M., and Longhurst, W. 1969. The eye lens as an indicator of age in the black-tailed jack rabbit. *J. Wildlife Management*, **33**, 159-163.

Craighead, J., Craighead, C., and McKutchen, H. 1970. Age determination of grizzly bears from fourth premolar tooth sections. *J. Wildlife Management*, **34**, 353-363.

Crowe, D. 1972. The presence of annuli in bobcat tooth cementum layers. *J. Wildlife Management*, **36**, 1330-1332.

Daniels, G. L. 1968. Ovulation and longevity in the Japanese quail (*Coturnix coturnix japonica*) under constant illumination. *Poultry Sci.*, **47**, 1875-1878.

Dapson, R., and Irland, J. 1972. An accurate method of determining age in small mammals. *J. Mammalogy*, **53**, 100-106.

Davis, J. 1937. The effect of advancing age on the oxygen consumption of rats. *Am. J. Physiol.*, **119**, 28-33.

Denckla, W. D. 1974. Role of the pituitary and thyroid glands in the decline of minimal O_2 consumption with age. *J. Clin. Invest.*, **53**, 572-581.

Dische, Z., Borenfreund, E., and Zelmenis, G. 1956. Changes in lens proteins of rats during aging. *Arch. Ophth.*, **55**, 471-483.

Dorney, R., and Holzer, S. 1957. Spring aging methods for ruffed grouse cocks. *J. Wildlife Management*, **21**, 268-274.

Dougherty, J., and Rosenblatt, L. 1965. Changes in the hemogram of the beagle with age. *J. Geront.*, **20**, 131-138.

Drori, D., and Folman, Y. 1969. The effect of mating on the longevity of male rats. *Exp. Geront.*, **4**, 263-266.

Duffield, L. 1973. Aging and sexing the post-cranial skeleton of bison. *Plains Anthropologist*, **18**, 132-139.

Everitt, A. 1957a. The senescent loss of body weight in male rats. *J. Geront.*, **12**, 382-387.

Everitt, A. 1957b. Systolic blood pressure and heart rate in relation to lung disease and life duration in male rats. *J. Geront.*, **12**, 379-381.

Everitt, A., and Cavanagh, L. M. 1963. The effect of lung disease and the process of dying on the body weight and blood picture of the ageing male rat. *Gerontologia*, **8**, 132-139.

Everitt, A., and Webb, C. 1957. The relation between body weight changes and life duration in male rats. *J. Geront.*, **12**, 128-135.

Everitt, A., and Webb, C. 1958. The blood picture of the aging male rat. *J. Geront.*, **13**, 255-260.

Ewing, L., Johnson, B., Desjardins, C., and Clegg, R. 1972. Effect of age upon spermatogenic and steroidgenic elements of rabbit testes. *Proc. Soc. Exp. Biol. Med.*, **140**, 907-910.

Ewing, K., and Tauber, O. 1964. Hematological changes in aging male C57BL/6 Jax mice. *J. Geront.*, **19**, 165-167.

Finch, C. 1971. Comparative biology of senescence: Some evolutionary and developmental questions. *In, Animal Models for Biomedical Research*, VI, pp. 47-67. Washington, D.C.: National Academy of Science.

Finch, C. 1973. Retardation of hair regrowth, a phenomenon of senescence in C57BL/6J male mice. *J. Geront.*, **28**, 13-17.

Finch, C., and Foster, J. 1973. Hematologic and serum electrolyte values of the C57BL/6J male mouse in maturity and senescence. *Lab. Animal Sci.*, **23**, 339-349.

Finch, C., Foster, J., and Mirsky, A. 1969. Ageing and the regulation of cell activities during exposure to cold. *J. Gen. Physiol.*, **54**, 690-712.

Finn, C. 1962. Embryonic death in aged mice. *Nature*, **194**, 499-500.

Finn, C. 1963. Reproductive capacity and litter size in mice: Effect of age and environment. *J. Reprod. Fertility*, **6**, 205-214.

Fisher, E., and Perry, A. 1970. Estimating ages of gray squirrels by lens-weights. *J. Wildlife Management*, **34**, 825-828.

Flückiger, E., and Verzár, F. 1955. Lack of adaptation to low oxygen pressure in aged animals. *J. Geront.*, **10**, 306-311.

Ford, D. H. (ed.) 1973. *Neurobiological Aspects of Maturation and Aging. Progress in Brain Research*. Vol. 40. Amsterdam: Elsevier Scientific Publishing.

Frost, W. E., and Smyly, W. J. P. 1952. The brown trout of a moorland fishpond. *J. Animal Ecol.*, **21**, 62-86.

Gaskin, D., and Cawthorn, M. 1973. Sperm whales (*Physeter catodon* L.) in the Cook Strait Region of New Zealand: Some data on age, growth and mortality. *Norw. J. Zool.* **21**, 45-50.

Gerking, S. 1959. Physiological changes accompanying ageing in fishes. *In*, G. E. W. Wolstenholme and M. O'Connor (eds.), *The Lifespan of Animals*, CIBA Foundation Colloquia on Ageing, Vol. 5, pp. 181-207. Boston: Little, Brown.

Gershon, D. 1970. Studies on aging in nematodes. I. The nematode as a model organism for aging research. *Exp. Geront.*, **5**, 7-12.

Goss, R. J. 1974. Aging versus growth. *Perspectives Biol. Med.*, **17**, 485-494.

Gray, F. H., and Berberian, P. A. 1971. The effect of limited milk feeding on the longevity of the house fly, *Musca domestica* L. *Exp. Geront.*, **6**, 205-210.

Greenberg, R. E., Etter, S. I., and Anderson, W. L. 1972. Evaluation of proximal primary feather criteria for aging wild pheasants. *J. Wildlife Management*, **36**, 700-705.

Griffiths, J. T., and Tauber, D. E. 1942. Fecundity, longevity and parthenogenesis of the American roach (*Periplaneta americana* L.). *Physiol. Zool.*, **15**, 196.

Grunt, F., Berry, R., and Knisely, W. 1958. Effects of castration and/or hormonal therapy upon the hematocrit in aged male rats. *J. Geront.*, **13**, 359-361.

Hamilton, J. B. 1948. The role of testicular secretions as indicated by the effects of castration in man and by studies of pathological conditions and the short lifespan associated with maleness. *Proc. Laurentian Horm. Conf.*, **3**, 257-269.

Hamilton, J. B., Hamilton, R., and Mestler, G. 1969. Duration of life and causes of death in domestic cats: Influence of sex, gonadectomy, and inbreeding. *J. Geront.*, **24**, 427-437.

Hamilton, W. D. 1966. The moulding of senescence by natural selection. *J. Theoret. Biol.*, **12**, 12-45.

Hamilton, W. J. 1940. The biology of the smoky shrew (*Sorex fumeus fumeus* Miller). *Zoologica, N. Y.*, **23**, 473.

Hammond, J., and Marshall, F. 1952. The life cycle. *In*, A. Parkes (ed.), *Marshall's Physiology of Reproduction*, II, pp. 793-846. New York: Longmans, Green.

Haydak, M. H. 1953. Influence of the protein level of the diet on the longevity of cockroaches. *Ann. Entomol. Soc. Amer.*, **46**, 547-560.

Henny, C., and Ludke, J. 1974. An attempt to age mallards using eye lens proteins. *J. Wildlife Management*, **38**, 138-141.

Heroux, O., and Campbell, J. 1960. A study of the pathology and life span of 6°C- and 30°C-acclimated rats. *Lab. Invest.*, **9**, 305-315.

Herz, Z., Folman, Y., and Drori, D. 1969. The testosterone content of the testes of mated and unmated rats. *J. Endocrinol.*, **44**, 127-128.

Howard, L. O. 1939. Ageing of insects. *In*, E. V. Cowdry (ed.), *Problems of Ageing*, pp. 53-70, London: Bailliere, Tindall and Cox.

Hrachovec, J. P., and Rockstein, M. 1962. Biochemical criteria for senescence in mammalian structures. I. Age changes of the cholesterol to phospholipid ratio in the rat liver and skeletal muscle. *Gerontologia*, **6**, 237-248.

Ingram, D., Mandl, A., and Zuckerman, S. 1958. The influence of age on litter-size. *J. Endocrinol.*, **17**, 280-285.

Jonsgard, A. 1969. Age determination of marine mammals. *In*, H. Andersen (ed.), *The Biology of Marine Mammals*, pp. 1-30. New York: Academic Press.

Kibler, H., and Johnson, H. 1961. Metabolic rate and aging in rats during exposure to cold. *J. Geront.*, **16**, 13-16.

Kibler, H., and Johnson, H. 1966. Temperature and longevity in male rats. *J. Geront.*, **21**, 52-56.

Kibler, H., Silsby, H., and Johnson, H. 1963. Metabolic trends and life span of rats at 9°C and 28°C. *J. Geront.*, **18**, 235-240.

Kirby, G. C. 1974. Greying with age: A coat-color variant in wild Australian populations of mice. *J. Heredity*, **65**, 126-128.

Kirkman, H., and Yau, P. 1972. Longevity of male and female, intact and gonadectomized, untreated and hormone-treated, neoplastic and non-neoplastic Syrian hamsters. *Am. J. Anat.*, **135**, 205-220.

Kohn, R. R. 1965. Aging as a consequence of growth cessation. *In, Reproduction: Molecular, Subcellular, and Cellular*, pp. 291-324. New York: Academic Press.

Labisky, R., Mann, S., and Lord, R. 1969. Weights and growth characteristics of pheasant lenses. *J. Wildlife Management*, **33**, 270-275.

Lansing, A. I. 1947. A transmissible, cumulative and reversible factor in aging. *J. Geront.*, **2**, 228-239.

Lansing, A. I. 1954. A nongenic factor in the longevity of rotifers. *Ann. N. Y. Acad. Sci.*, **57**, 455-464.

Larsson, K. 1958. Sexual activity in senile male rats. *J. Geront.*, **13**, 136-139.

Lavelle, C. 1968. The effect of age on the rate of nail growth. *J. Geront.*, **23**, 557-559.

Laws, R. 1952. A new method for age determination of mammals. *Nature*, **169**, 972-973.

Lesser, G., Deutsch, S., and Markofsky, J. 1973. Aging in the rat: Longitudinal and cross-sectional studies of body composition. *Am. J. Physiol.*, **225**, 1472-1478.

Lindop, P. 1961. Growth rate, life span, and causes of death in SAS/4 mice. *Gerontologia*, **5**, 193-208.

Liu, R., and Walford, R. 1966. Increased growth and life span with lowered ambient temperature in the annual fish, *Cynolebias adloffi*. *Nature*, **212**, 1277-1278.

Liu, R., and Walford, R. 1970. Observations on the life spans of several species of annual fish, and of the world's smallest fishes. *Exp. Geront.*, **5**, 241-246.

Lux, F. E. 1973. Age and growth of the winter flounder, *Pseudopleuronectes americanus*, on Georges Bank. *Fishery Bull.*, **71**, 505-512.

McCay, C., Crowell, M., and Maynard, L. 1935. The effect of retarded growth upon the length of life span and upon the ultimate body size. *J. Nutr.*, **10**, 63-79.

McCay, C., Maynard, L., Sperling, G., and Barnes, L. 1939. Retarded growth, life span, ultimate body size and age changes in the albino rat after feeding diets restricted in calories. *J. Nutr.*, **18**, 1-13.

McKutchen, H. 1969. Age determination of pronghorns by incisor cementum. *J. Wildlife Management*, **33**, 172-175.

Maurizio, A. 1954. Pollenernährung und lebensvorgange bei der honigbiene (*Apis mellifica* L.). *Landwird. Jahrb. Schweiz.*, **68**, 115-182.

Maurizio, A. 1959. Factors influencing the life span of bees. *In*, G. E. W. Wolstenholme and M. O'Connor (eds.), *The Lifespan of Animals*, CIBA Foundation

Colloquia on Ageing, Vol. 5, pp. 231-246. Boston: Little, Brown.

Maynard Smith, J. 1959. The rate of aging in *Drosophila subobscura*. *In*, G. E. W. Wolstenholme and M. O'Connor (eds.), *The Lifespan of Animals*, CIBA Foundation Colloquia on Ageing, Vol. 5, pp. 269-281. Boston: Little, Brown.

Mead, R. 1967. Age determination in the spotted skunk. *J. Mammalogy*, **48**, 606-616.

Mecklenburg, H. C. Personal communication.

Medawar, P. B. 1957. *The Uniqueness of the Individual*. New York: Basic Books.

Medoff, H., and Bongiovanni, A. 1945. Age, sex, and species variations on blood pressure in normal rats. *Am. J. Physiol.*, **143**, 297-299.

Miller, D., and Payne, P. 1968. Longevity and protein intake. *Exp. Geront.*, **3**, 231-234.

Minot, C. S. 1908. *The Problem of Age, Growth, and Death*. New York: G. P. Putnam's Sons.

Miquel, J. 1971. Aging of male *Drosophila melanogaster*. Histological, histochemical and ultrastructural observation. *Advan. Geront. Res.*, **3**, 39-71.

Monson, R., Stone, W., and Parks, E. 1973. Aging red foxes (*Vulpes fulva*) by counting the annular cementum rings of their teeth. *New York Fish and Game Journal*, **20**, 54-61.

Mühlbock, O. 1959. Factors influencing life span of inbred mice. *Gerontologia*, **3**, 177-183.

Munnell, J., and Getty, R. 1968. Rate of accumulation of cardiac lipofuscin in the aging canine. *J. Geront.*, **23**, 154-158.

Norris, M. J. 1933. Contributions towards the study of insect fertility. III. Experiments on the factors influencing fertility of *Ephestia kühniella* Z. (Leipdoptera, Phycitidae). *Proc. Zool. Soc. London*, **103**, 903-934.

Oliver, M. 1972. Effect of age on productivity of Chinese geese. *Agroanimalia*, **4**, 47-52.

Perry, J. 1954. Fecundity and embryonic mortality in pigs. *J. Embryol. Exptl. Morphol.*, **2**, 308-322.

Pirie, A. 1968. Cataract protein color and solubility. *Invest. Ophthalmol.*, **7**, 634-650.

Riegle, G., and Nellor, J. 1966. Changes in blood cellular and protein components during aging. *J. Geront.*, **21**, 435-438.

Ring, G., Dupuch, G., and Emeric, D. 1964. Aging and the whole body metabolism. *J. Geront.*, **19**, 215-219.

Ring, G., Kurabatov, T., Hernandez, G., and Dunn, R. 1964. Changes in erythrocytes related to the age of rats. *J. Geront.*, **19**, 352-356.

Robertson, O. H. 1957. Survival of precociously mature king salmon male parr (*Oncorhynchus tshawytscha* Juv.) after spawning. *Calif. Fish Game*, **43**, 119-130.

Robertson, O. H. 1961. Prolongation of the life span of kokanee salmon (*Oncorhynchus nerka kennerlyi*) by castration before beginning of gonad development. *Proc. Nat. Acad. Sci.*, **47**, 609-621.

Robertson, O. H., Hane, S., Wexler, B. C., and Rinfret, A. P. 1963. The effect of hydrocortisone on immature rainbow trout (*Salmo gairdnerii*). *Gen. Comp. Endocrinol.*, **3**, 422-436.

Robertson, O. H., and Wexler, B. C. 1962. Histological changes in the organs and tissues of senile, castrated kokanee salmon (*Oncorhynchus nerka kennerlyi*). *Gen. Comp. Endocrinol.*, **2**, 458-472.

Robertson, T., and Ray, L. 1919. Experimental studies on growth. *J. Biol. Chem.*, **37**, 377-391.

Robins, M., and Rowlatt, C. 1971. Dental abnormalities in aged mice. *Gerontologia*, **17**, 261-272.

Rockstein, M. 1958. Heredity and longevity in the animal kingdom. *J. Geront.*, **13**, 7-12.

Rockstein, M. 1959. The biology of ageing in insects. *In*, G. E. W. Wolstenholme and M. O'Connor (eds.), *The Lifespan of Animals*, CIBA Foundation Colloquia on Ageing, Vol. 5, pp. 247-268. Boston: Little, Brown.

Rockstein, M. 1972. The role of molecular genetic mechanisms in the aging process. *In*, M. Rockstein and G. T. Baker III (eds.), *Molecular Genetic Mechanisms in Development and Aging*, pp. 1-10. New York: Academic Press.

Rockstein, M. 1974. Preface. *In*, M. Rockstein, M. L. Sussman, and J. Chesky (eds.), *Theoretical Aspects of Aging*, p. ix. New York: Academic Press.

Rockstein, M., and Baker, G. 1974. Effects of X-irradiation of pupae on aging of the thoracic flight muscle of the adult male house fly, *Musca domestica* L. *Mech. Age. Dev.*, **3**, 271-278.

Rockstein, M., and Bhatnagar, P. L. 1965. Age changes in size and number of the giant mitochondria in the flight muscle of the common house fly (*Musca domestica* L.). *J. Insect Physiol.*, **11**, 481-489.

Rockstein, M., and Bhatnagar, P. L. 1966. Duration and frequency of wing beat in the aging house fly, *Musca domestica* L. *Biol. Bull.*, **131**, 479-486.

Rockstein, M., and Brandt, K. 1962. Muscle enzyme activity and changes in weight in ageing white rats. *Nature*, **196**, 142-143.

Rockstein, M., and Chesky, J. 1973. Age-related changes in natural actomyosin of the male house fly, *Musca domestica* L. *J. Geront.*, **28**, 455-459.

Rockstein, M., Chesky, J., Philpott, D., Takahashi, A., Johnson, J., Jr., and Miquel, J. 1975. An electron microscopic investigation of age-dependent changes in the flight muscle of *Musca domestica* L. *Gerontologia*, **21**, 216-222.

Rockstein, M., Gray, F. H., and Berberian, P. A. 1971. Time-correlated neurosecretory changes in the house fly, *Musca domestica* L. *Exp. Geront.*, **6**, 211-217.

Rockstein, M., and Lieberman, H. M. 1959. A life table for the common house fly, *Musca domestica*. *Gerontologia*, **3**, 23-36.

Rockstein, M., and Miquel, J. 1973. Aging in insects. *In*, M. Rockstein (ed.), *The Physiology of Insecta*, Vol. I, pp. 371-471. New York: Academic Press.

Rockstein, M., and Sussman, M. L. (eds.) 1973. *Devel-*

opment and Aging in the Nervous System. New York: Academic Press.

Roman, L., and Strong, L. 1960. Maternal age, polydactylism, and litter size in mice. J. Geront., 15, 242-245.

Rosenstein, L., and Berman, E. 1973. Postnatal body weight changes of domestic cats maintained in an outdoor colony. Am. J. Vet. Res., 34, 575-577.

Ross, M. 1959. Protein, calories, and life expectancy. Federation Proc., 18, 1190-1207.

Ross, M. 1961. Length of life and nutrition in the rat. J. Nutr., 75, 197-210.

Rothbaum, D., Shaw, D., Angell, C., and Shock, N. 1973. Cardiac performance in the unanesthetized senescent male rat. J. Geront., 28, 287-292.

Rowley, W. A., and Graham, C. L. 1968. The effect of age on the flight performance of female Aedes aegypti mosquitoes. J. Insect Physiol., 14, 719-728.

Russell, E. 1954. Search for new cases of parental and seasonal influences upon variation within inbred strains. Ann. N. Y. Acad. Sci., 57, 597-605.

Sacher, G. A. 1959. Relation of lifespan to brain weight and body weight in mammals. In, G. E. W. Wolstenholme and M. O'Connor (eds.), The Lifespan of Animals, CIBA Foundation Colloquia on Ageing, Vol. 5, pp. 115-141. Boston: Little, Brown.

Sacktor, B., and Shimada, Y. 1972. Degenerative changes in the mitochondria of flight muscle from aging blowflies. J. Cell Biol., 52, 465-477.

Scheffer, V. 1950. Growth layers on teeth of pinnipedia as an indicator of age. Science, 112, 309-311.

Severinghaus, C. 1949. Tooth development and wear as criteria of age in white-tailed deer. J. Wildlife Management, 13, 195-216.

Sharma, D., Malik, P., and Sapra, K. 1973. Age-wise and species-wise haematological studies in farm animals. Indian J. Anim. Sci., 43, 289-295.

Shock, N. W. 1961. Physiological aspects of aging in man. Ann. Rev. Physiol., 23, 97-122.

Shock, N. W. 1962. The physiology of aging. Sci. Am., 206 (1), 100-111.

Shock, N. W., and Yiengst, M. 1955. Age changes in basal respiratory measurement and metabolism in males. J. Geront., 10, 31-40.

Sikes, S. 1967. The African elephant, Loxodonta africana: A field method for estimation of age. J. Zoology, London, 154, 235-248.

Soderwall, A., and Britenbaker, A. 1955. Reproductive capacities of different-age hamsters (Cricetus auratus, Waterhouse). J. Geront., 10, 469-470.

Soderwall, A., Kent, H., Turbyfill, C., and Britenbaker, A. 1960. Variation in gestation length and litter size of the golden hamster, Mesocricetus auratus. J. Geront., 15, 246-248.

Sohal, R. S., and Allison, V. F. 1971. Age-related changes in the fine structure of the flight muscle in the house fly. Exp. Geront., 6, 167-172.

Sondhi, K. C. 1967. Studies in ageing—V. The physio-logical effects of stress in Drosophila. Exp. Geront., 2, 233-239.

Spector, W. S. (ed.) 1956. Handbook of Biological Data, pp. 182-184. Ohio: Wright Air Development Center, U. S. Air Force.

Strehler, B. L., Mark, D., Mildvan, A., and Gee, M. 1959. Rate and magnitude of age pigment accumulation in the human myocardium. J. Geront., 14, 430-439.

Strong, L., and Johnson, F. 1964. Longevity of mice influenced by maternal age. Exp. Geront., 1, 21-30.

Sturkie, P., Weiss, M., and Ringer, R. 1953. Effects of age on blood pressure in the chicken. Am. J. Physiol., 174, 405-407.

Stussi, T. 1972. The honey bee, a heterothermic animal. Arch. Sci. Physiol., 26, 131-159.

Szabo, I. 1935. Senescence and death in invertebrate animals. Riv. Biol., 19, 377-435.

Talbert, G. 1968. Effect of maternal age on reproductive capacity. Am. J. Obstet. Gynecol., 102, 451-457.

Talbot, R., Abel, M., and Davison, F. 1965. Age changes in blood parameters of C57BL mice. Lab. Animal Care, 15, 393-396.

Tauchi, H., Yoshioka, T., and Kobayashi, H. 1971. Age change of skeletal muscles of rats. Gerontologia, 17, 219-227.

Terrill, C., and Hazel, L. 1947. Length of gestation in range sheep. Am. J. Vet. Res., 8, 66-72.

Thomas, D., and Bandy, P. 1973. Age determination of wild black-tailed deer from dental annulations. J. Wildlife Management, 37, 232-235.

Tribe, M. A., and Ashhurst, D. E. 1972. Biochemical and structural variation in the flight muscle mitochondria of aging blowflies, Calliphora erythrocephala. J. Cell Sci., 10, 443-469.

Uno, H., Adachi, K., and Montagna, W. 1969. Baldness of the red uacari (Cacajao rubicundus): Histological properties and enzyme activities of hair follicles. J. Geront., 24, 23-27.

Wattiaux, J. M. 1968a. Parental age effects in Drosophila pseudobscura. Exp. Geront., 3, 55-61.

Wattiaux, J. M. 1968b. Cumulative parental age effects in Drosophila subobscura. Evolution, 22, 406-421.

Webb, S., and Tribe, M. A. 1974. Are there major degenerative changes in the flight muscle of aging Diptera? Exp. Geront., 9, 43-49.

Weiss, P. 1966. Aging: A corollary of development. In, N. W. Shock (ed.), Perspectives in Experimental Gerontology, pp. 311-322. Springfield, Illinois: Charles C Thomas.

Whiteley, H., and Horton, D. 1962. The effect of age on the hair regrowth cycle in the CBA mouse. J. Geront., 17, 272-275.

Williams, G. C. 1957. Pleiotropy, natural selection, and the evolution of senescence. Evolution, 11, 398-411.

Williams, G. C. 1960. Pleiotropy, natural selection, and the evolution of senescence. *In,* B. L. Strehler (ed.), *The Biology of Aging*, pp. 332–337. Washington, D.C.: American Institute of Biological Sciences.

Wilson, D. L. 1974. The programmed theory of aging. *In*, M. Rockstein, M. L. Sussman, and J. Chesky (eds.), *Theoretical Aspects of Aging*, pp. 11-21. New York: Academic Press.

Wright, E., and Spink, J. 1959. A study of the loss of nerve cells in the central nervous system in relation to age. *Gerontologia*, **3**, 277-287.

Yiengst, M., Barrows, C., and Shock, N. 1959. Age changes in the chemical composition of muscle and liver in the rat. *J. Geront.*, **14**, 400-404.

Zuckerman, B. M. 1974. The effects of procaine on aging and development of a nematode. *In*, M. Rockstein, M. L. Sussman, and J. Chesky (eds.), *Theoretical Aspects of Aging*, pp. 177-186. New York: Academic Press.

PART 2 MOLECULAR LEVEL

2

THE MOLECULAR GENETICS OF AGING

F. Marott Sinex

Boston University School of Medicine

This chapter will discuss the possibility that aging results when inappropriate information is provided for normal cell function from the cell nucleus. This approach is consistent with the views of Burnet (1974) who states that aging is too important a matter to be left to the vague general events of cellular metabolism and must be closely related to some form of mutagenesis.

The fundamental genetic information presumably found in all cells is coded in DNA. When DNA is replicated, histone and other regulatory molecules are arranged on newly synthesized DNA in such a way as to insure that daughter cells reproduce the parent cell or are suitably modified for the next stage of differentiation. A description of how this might occur is given by Tsanev and Sendov (1971).

The expression of genetic information by an aging cell might become altered in at least four ways.

1. Through changes in the base pairs or coding of the DNA, the result of:
    (a) coding errors in replication
    (b) point mutation
    (c) chromosome aberrations
2. Through increasing levels of error in:
    (a) RNA synthesis
    (b) charging of transfer RNA
    (c) protein synthesis
3. Through deteriorative alterations in the arrangement of fundamental control elements in chromatin such as histone and nonhistone protein and RNA.
4. Through expression of a normal program of differentiation which includes aging as the final step.

We will now discuss these possibilities.

MUTATION AND ERROR

DNA replication is a very accurate procedure. The level of error per base pair must be less than 1×10^{-8}, probably around 1×10^{-9} (Watson, 1965). The accumulation of replicative error would be dependent on generational number, the more doublings in a particular cell's descent, the more error.

Lewis and Holliday (1970) have presented evidence for this type of error in the aging of the tips of hyphae in fungi. Replicative error is often assumed to be present in tissue culture and may well occur in the body where somatic cells are the products of many doublings. Note however, that this type of error would not be introduced after the cessation of cell division.

Point mutations, on the other hand, may result from other chemical changes which occur with the passage of time in resting cells. An example of a point mutation of the type which might occur in aging would be the conversion of a cytosine to uracil which codes for adenine rather than guanine during DNA synthesis. Estimates of the rate of spontaneous conversion of cytosine to uracil in the body have been made by Lindahl and Nyberg (1974).

The rate of accumulation of aging injury to DNA within a cell would be a function of the rate at which aging injury was being produced and the rate that it was being removed. The rate of repair is therefore as important as the rate of injury. One may consider two models for the kinetics of repair. One is to assume that aging hits, when they occur, are either immediately repaired or never repaired. The other is a more dynamic model. It assumes that at any one time a cell carries a burden of potentially repairable but at that moment unrepaired aging mutations. With time, such mutations may increase if the repair system itself becomes less efficient.

These two approaches are not mutually exclusive, and their relative importance in impairing normal functions may vary with age. In our later discussions these two approaches will be referred to as the more static and more dynamic models.

Somatic mutations of DNA would also be eliminated if the cells produced could not compete with normal cells. Mutant cells are propagated and increase if they are competitive and divide more rapidly. A tissue such as the brain is particularly vulnerable to aging injury because damaged neurons are not replaced. Age-injured cells may not be lost.

If a point mutation is not corrected within the first generation, it cannot be corrected, since the required information is no longer available in the complementary strand, and there is no longer a stress in the double helix. Similarly, after chronic low-level radiation, many cells with double strand breaks and chromosomal aberrations are eliminated (Curtis, 1966).

In malignancy, and perhaps in aging, cells with altered but not necessarily impaired function may dominate a population. The genetics of our bodies thus resembles the genetics of populations, with a potential for diversity of individual clones. There may be more cells in an individual than there are individuals in the world. Inappropriate cell function, a thrombus, a cancer, a scarred liver is more often an obvious cause of death than cell loss.

CHROMOSOMAL ABERRATIONS

Chromosomal aberrations are a form of mutation in which both strands of DNA are broken, lost, or inappropriately rejoined. The may be observed directly in dividing cells. Chromosomal aberrations in postmitotic cells such as brain cells cannot be visualized cytologically in a resting nucleus. Curtis and Miller (1971) attempted to surmount this problem in liver by treating mice with carbon disulfide or carbon tetrachloride. This produces such severe liver injury that many cells die. During liver regeneration and thus renewed mitoses, it is then possible to count the percentage of anaphases which show chromosome bridges and chromosomal fragments. Under the conditions of his experiments, the percentage of cells showing chromosomal aberration increased steadily with age.

In such experiments, radiation is much more effective in producing visible chromosomal aberrations than in shortening life, and the ratios of this discrepency are large, sometimes 6- to 20-fold depending on the type of radiation. Cells with chromosomal aberrations produced by acute irradiation in the young animal are slowly eliminated; Curtis (1963) found that doses of irradiation which produce chromosomal abnormalities to the extent observed in old mice fail to shorten life. This is evidence for point mutations or single strand breaks being responsible for life shortening in aging (rather than double strand breaks), unless the common mechanism is cell death.

In humans, the effect of aging on chromosomal aberrations can be scored by stimulating lymphocytes to divide. Chromosome aberrations in the lymphocytes of the elderly have been studied by many researchers (Jacobs, Brunton, and Brown, 1963; Goodman, Feckheimer, Miller, Miller, and Zartman, 1969; Bettner, Jarvik, and Blem, 1971; Jarvik, Yen, and Moralishvili, 1974). In such studies, lymphocytes were stimulated to divide by phytohemagglutinin. In elderly subjects, and particularly in females, the number of cells showing hypoploidy increased. Jarvik and her coworkers correlated observations of altered karyotype with senescent impairment. Senescent individuals had more hypoploidy, in other words, more cells with less than the normal 2N number of chromosomes. For example, of the cells of aged women, 11.3 percent had 45 chromosomes compared to 6.5 percent in the cells of young women.

Bochkov and Kuleshov (1972) found that leukocytes of older persons, when challenged by two alkylating agents which produce mutations, showed more cells with chromosomal aberrations and more chromosomal aberrations per cell.

The dramatic increase in the trisomy responsible for Down's syndrome with maternal age is a special case of particular concern to older mothers (Stern, 1973; Cavalli-Sforza and Bodmer, 1971). Down's syndrome involves a translocation of a piece of chromosome 21 to chromosome 15. The frequency markedly increases with maternal age. (Penrose and Smith, 1966).

Another type of chromosomal rearrangement is somatic recombination. Somatic recombination may be equal or unequal, and may involve sister or homologous chromosomes. The most common form is exchange between newly synthesized and parental strands of DNA prior to separation at mitosis. Recombination between even equal sister chromatids is subject to errors of deletion and insertion so that the products of sister chromatid exchanges may carry a number of mutations. Sister chromatid exchanges can be followed through labeling with bromodeoxyuridine and staining with fluorescent dye. The fluorescence is quenched in the regions containing bromodeoxyuridine. Sister chromatid exchange occurs more frequently than strand breakage. Exchange between homologous chromosomes is much less frequent in mitotic cells but is another potential source of mutation.

There is one well-studied example of unequal crossing over. This occurs in *Drosophila* and is known as the bob mutation, in which *Drosoph-*

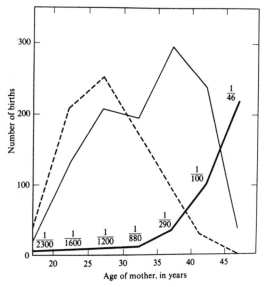

Figure 1. Incidence of Down's syndrome at birth as a function of mother's age. The dashed line plots all births, in thousands. The lighter solid line plots the number of babies born with Down's syndrome. The darker solid line shows the incidence of Down's syndrome relative to maternal age. (From Penrose and Smith, 1966.)

ila have short or "bobbed" bristles. Flies with this mutation have 40 rather than 140 genes coding for ribosomal RNA as in the case of the wild fly. When the unequal crossing over occurs, cells are also produced with 250 ribosomal genes. The frequency of the bob event is quite high, of the order of several percent, and it is remarkable that the wild type number is stabilized in the germ line. Recombination in the germ line of *Drosophila* occurs during the somatic development of germinal cells and not at the time of meiosis.

MUTATION IN THE GERM LINE

Mutation in the germ line is of exceptional importance because it determines the mutational burden of the species. The usual figure given for mutational error per cell division per base pair in the genome is 1×10^{-8}, a figure developed from rates of evolution of protein sequences and from known rates of mutation in microorganisms. Human geneticists estimate that for the human germ line, the spontaneous mutation rate is as low as 1×10^{-5} to 1×10^{-6} per generation per gene. The germ line appears to accumulate between 0.1 and 0.5 detectable mutations per generation (Stern, 1973; Cavalli-Sforza and Bodmer, 1971). An entirely consistent treatment is difficult because only half of the genome of 1.5×10^9 base pairs is single copy message, and only a portion of this may code for structural genes. In any event, the rate of mutation in the germ line is low.

The germ line probably has an exceptionally efficient repair system for altered DNA. Furthermore, selection for fitness is undoubtedly very strong in the germ line. Otherwise gametes would be excellent cells for comparison of the relative importance of miscoding during replication versus point mutation as a consequence of time, sperm presumably being the product of many more doublings than ova.

What we find is that there is, in certain instances, a relation between metabolic disease and maternal age. The principal example is the chromosomal translocation of Down's syndrome, neither a coding error nor a point mutation.

There are two excellent examples of age-correlated incidence in sex-linked dominants in males—chondrodystrophy, involving development of cartilage and bone, and acrocephalo-syndacty, or Apert's syndrome (Mørch, 1941; Blank, 1960). Unlike Down's syndrome, chondrodystrophy and acrocephalosyndacty are rare diseases with average mutation rates in gametes of 1×10^{-5} and 3×10^{-5}, respectively (Vogel, 1965).

THE RATE OF SOMATIC MUTATION

When considering mutation rates in somatic cells, we must consider not only replicative error, but also mutation rate as a function of time. If the comparison is made on the basis of time, the mutation rate in the germ line is an exceptionally small number compared with the mutation rate in tissue culture which seems to be about 4×10^{-6} per gene per generation of 2 or 3 days (Albertini and DeMars, 1973; Harris, 1973). This comparison is made in Table 2. On the other hand, the similarity is

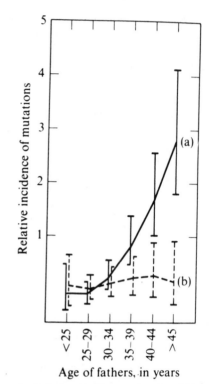

Age of fathers, in years

Figure 2. Relative incidence of dominant mutations among individuals grouped according to their fathers' ages (at birth of offspring) in (a) chondrodystrophy (from a study of 175 cases done by Mørch, Greve, and Stevenson and reported by Vogel, 1963), and in (b) neurofibromatosis, tuberous sclerosis, and osteogenesis imperfect (from a study of 108 cases done by Borberg and Seedorff and reported by Vogel, 1963). Ninety-five percent confidence limits are indicated in the figure by the vertical bars. Relative incidences are based on the Danish age distribution of fathers in 1930 (see Mørch, 1941). These data illustrate a striking effect of father's age on the rate of occurrence of the dominant mutation for chondrodystrophy. The other data are given for comparison (From Vogel, 1963.)

much closer if the comparisons are made in terms of elapsed generations, even though it is not possible to say how many cell generations are required to produce an ova or a sperm.

It is a very important matter in gerontology to know what this rate of somatic mutation is in postmitotic cells where replicative error is eliminated and time and temperature are the predominate variables. Since errors in DNA can arise in at least two ways, through miscoding in

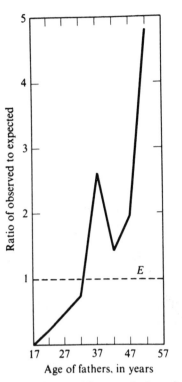

Figure 3. Relative incidence of Apert's syndrome (acrocephalosyndactyly) among individuals grouped according to their fathers' ages. This graph is based on a study of 37 cases; data on patients and normal controls are quoted from Blank, 1960. The dashed line, marked E, indicates the value that would be expected if there were no age dependence. This is another striking example of a dependence of mutation rate on father's age. (From Vogel, 1963.)

replication, or through point mutation in resting cells, it is unfortunate that we have so little information as to whether time or generational number is the critical variable.

The cells of the body go through many generations; and it is difficult to give an average number, although we can try and estimate this from cell size and body mass. Cells vary in mass from 10^{-5} gram for very large cells to $10^{-6} - 10^{-8}$ gram for more typical cells. An average cell mass of 2.6×10^{-6} and a cellular mass of 40 kg would require approximately 34 doublings. In classical genetics, the number of genes is estimated to be between 1×10^4 and 5×10^4 (Stern, 1973). Recent molecular insights into chromosome structure have made gene count difficult to interpret (Britten and David-

son, 1969), since structural genes may comprise only a small fraction of the genome. Such numbers are based on estimates of gene density in the chromosomes of organisms (such as *Drosophila*) rather than numbers of base pairs.

If the number of cell generations were critical, then 4.5×10^{-6} mutations per generation multiplied by 2×10^4 genes and 34 generations would equal approximately three mutations per cell in a lifetime. The effect of such mutations would depend on the importance of the genes in which they were found.

Similar estimates, based not on number of generations but rather on hours in culture or in the body, would give much higher values for accumulated mutations, e.g., hundreds. This is because there is such a large differential between life span and generation time in culture, 25,000 versus 2-3 days. Somatic mutation is tenable as an explanation for aging if one is willing to accept mutation rates based on tissue culture data.

If the number of generations were critical, then large animals might be expected to age faster than small animals, since they have more cells. This difference however might not be as great as it seems. Given identical body composition, an 80 kg dog is four times as big as a 20 kg dog, but represents only 2×2 or 2 more cell doublings of a clonal expansion.

Small mammals in fluctuating environments have exploited rapid reproduction and evolutionary adaption for survival advantage in contrast to a longer-lived, large animals who dominate their environment and reproduce more slowly. In very short-lived species, such as most insects and plants, the life span may not permit the accumulation of somatic mutation. Time-dependent mutation might be more important in long-lived species than short.

The concept that a particular rate of mutation in a population might have a survival advantage for bacteria or the cells of the body is controversial (Cox and Gibson, 1974; Burnet, 1974; and Lewis and Holliday, 1970, argue in favor; Leigh, 1973, against).

Burnet's (1974) recent book deserves critical attention. His argument is as follows: Aging is the result of intrinsic mutation associated with the reproduction of cells. The rate is determined by the characteristics of organ-specific DNA polymerase. This ultimately leads to impaired function and death of cells. This is most critical in the cell system responsible for immunity because suppression of autoimmunity is lost. The death of postmitotic cells, such as neurons, is the result of loss of immune recognition as self and their destruction by a misguided immune defense.

This is contrary to classical views of aging advanced by Cowdry (1952) and his successors that aging occurred primarily in postmitotic cells. This was the reason that aging was so prominent in the brain, kidney, and heart and not in the crypt cells of the small intestine and bone marrow.

Note that if the number of dividing cells in a tissue culture decreases through repetitive propagation, then it is the properties of the dividing population which are changing, not the resting population.

It is unfortunate that no one has yet compared accurately the mutation rate of the dividing population in cultures with the mutation rate of the resting population. It is difficult to recover nondividing cells and return them to the cycle, although Hayflick's (1965) experience with WI 38 fibroblasts would argue for replicative error.

Atwood and Pepper's (1961) study of the incidence of non-A or B red cells (i.e., reversion to O type cells) in AB subjects indicated that most mutations of stem cells occurred early in life, and only a minor fraction of reversions occurred as a function of age. This result suggests that replicative error may be restricted to erythropoiesis in early life and counterindicates the significance of mutational changes during aging.

In summary, there are two models concerning somatic mutation as a cause of aging, (1) somatic mutation as the result of intrinsic mutagenesis at the time of division, advanced by Burnet, Holliday, and Orgel, and (2) a time-dependent mutagenesis in resting cells advanced by Curtis and ourselves (Sinex, 1974). The validity of these two models is an important question in gerontology, and ultimately it should be possible to test them experimentally.

ARE AGING MUTATIONS DOMINANT OR RECESSIVE?

We will now review evidence that the majority of aging hits occurring in somatic cells are expressed as weak dominants. If such mutations occurred in the germ line, many would be considered recessives although their importance in somatic cell occurrence lies not in the probability that a homozygote would be created but in their number and their relatively limited expression as heterozygotes.

For true recessives the odds against double hits are long, both for occurrence twice in one cell, or for matching a recessive previously present, since there are at least 10,000 genes.

This touches on two important questions—first, the relation between gene dose and enzyme products, and second, the ability of the product of single locus, such as a regulator gene, to repress structural genes for enzymes on both alleles.

The partial loss of a gene will produce more impairment if its enzyme product is in limited supply. If it is in vast excess, there will be no effect. If the turning on or turning off of a gene on both alleles is interlocked, an accident to a control gene will have a larger effect than if they are independent.

Studies on *Drosophila* by Maynard Smith (Lamb and Maynard Smith, 1964) show that seemingly recessive mutant alleles induced by radiation reduce the fitness of heterozygote individuals as measured by premature death from all causes on an average of 2.5 percent. Since heterozygote alleles are much more common than homozygote alleles, the over-all impairment of cells made heterozygotes by aging hits may be more important than the injury in those few cells made homozygotes. In our opinion, the assumption made by Szilard (1959) that, in order to be expressed, aging hits must be paired with previously existing mutation on the other allele is not valid.

The classical observation that doubling or halving the sets of chromosomes present in cells has little effect on aging is evidence for the dominant character of aging mutations.

Harris (1971) was one of the first to study

the expression of mutation in diploid, tetraploid, and octaploid Chinese hamster cells. He studied resistance to 8-azaguanine and to heating in suspension to 43–44° as expressions of mutation. He observed that tetraploid cells expressed roughly twice the number of mutations as diploid cells, while octaploid showed about one-half as many. The more chromosomes there are, the more probable a hit will be, and tetraploid cells should have twice as many hits as diploid cells. If they are dominant, twice as many should be expressed. On the other hand, there may be limitations on how many alleles a dominant gene can override. The fifteen other alleles in an octaploid cell may be too many to permit expression.

Harris' data are strong evidence against aging hits being recessives. Once a single chromatid has been hit, the probability of a similar hit on the same gene in a sister chromatid is quite small, of the order of less than 1 in 10,000. In a tetraploid cell for hits to occur in a third sister chromatid, the probability is 1×10^{-8} and for a fourth, 1×10^{-12}. Harris favors an epigenetic control over dominance as an explanation (Harris, 1973) for his experiments. We will discuss epigenetic effects in a later section.

Metzger-Freed (1972) worked with a frog embryo cell line, ICR-2A. This was the first haploid vertebrate cell line to be established. If spontaneous mutations were recessive, then one would expect the mutation rate to be more than 10^4 times as great in haploid as in diploid cells since a chromatid would only have to be hit once rather than twice. The loss of thymidine kinase activity was used to follow mutation. If thymidine kinase disappears, the cells can no longer take up the BrdU. Cells which contain BrdU may be destroyed by exposure to ultraviolet light, whereas mutated cells survive. The results were rather surprising. The frequency of mutations in haploid cells was 5 percent that in diploid cells, not half and certainly not 10^4 times as great. This fits a dominant model of aging hits better than a recessive model. If the hits were completely dominant, there should be twice as many mutations in diploid cells as in haploid cells, not 20 times. The two cell lines

were about equally resistant to mutagens and ionizing radiation. Intact haploid amphibians, however, become edematous and age. In the wasp, *Habrabracon inglandis*, Clark and Rubin (1961) showed that diploid female pupae are 2 to 3 times as resistant to ionizing radiation as haploid male pupae, the larva, 1.3 times as resistant using longevity as an end point.

In this section we have pointed out that the effects of varying ploidy on aging and radiation injury are reasonably consistent and suggest that both aging and radiation hits behave predominately as dominant mutations.

CHEMICAL CHANGES IN DNA

We will consider first the chemical changes which may occur in DNA as the result of reaction with active radicals, and then more conventional chemistry.

One of the more probable sources of an endogenous mutagen is superoxide $\cdot O_2^-$. This substance is produced by the reduction of oxygen through the addition of a single electron. Oxygen is reduced in this manner by a number of oxygenase systems (among which the classical example is xanthine oxidase [Gregory and Fridovich, 1973; McCord and Salin, 1975]) but not ordinarily in the course of mitochondrial respiration.

Other enzymes which may produce an excess of superoxide are glutathione reductase, aldehyde oxidase, dehydro-orotic dehydrogenase, and diamine oxidase. The production of superoxide is characteristic of ferridoxine iron-sulfer enzymes or copper enzymes, coupled to FAD (Fridovich, 1974b). The electron paramagnetic resonance signal of superoxide is produced during the reoxidation of reduced flavins and ferridoxins. Tryptophan dioxygenase is an example of an enzyme which utilizes superoxide, either as superoxide or as its cytochrome P_{450} complex. The active form of the cytochrome P_{450} complex of the endoplasmic reticulum is a superoxide-iron-porphyrin product. This reacts with a number of specific enzymes responsible for metabolism of many drugs including barbiturates and steroids.

The concept of superoxide can be understood if one considers oxygen as an electron acceptor. Oxygen has two unpaired electrons, and in the ground state these have similar spins. For two electrons to be added; the spins of one electron must be inverted, either in both separate orbitals or in the same orbital. Such an oxygen molecule is no longer in the ground state and is called singlet oxygen. It is very chemically active even though it still contains the same number of electrons. Unless oxygen is so activated, it will tend to accept electrons one at a time rather than in pairs. Singlet oxygen is produced by macrophages (Foote, 1974), probably by reduction of superoxide. To review the products formed by the addition of electrons to oxygen:

$$O_2 + e \longrightarrow \cdot O_2^-$$
$$O_2 + 2e + 2H^+ \longrightarrow H_2O_2$$
$$O_2 + 3e + 3H^+ \longrightarrow H_2O + \cdot OH$$
$$O_2 + 4e + 4H^+ \longrightarrow 2H_2O$$

Superoxide is formed by the addition of one electron to oxygen. The addition of two electrons gives peroxide. The addition of three gives water and hydroxy-free radical, and four, two molecules of water.

Superoxide dismutase rearranges two molecules of superoxide to one of oxygen and one of peroxide. Catalase rearranges two molecules of peroxide to one of oxygen and one of water.

The real danger inherent in the production of both superoxide and peroxide in cells is the reaction between these two reduction products to form hydroxyl ion, hydroxy radical, and oxygen.

$$\cdot O_2^- + H_2O_2 \longrightarrow OH^- + \cdot OH + O_2$$

This reaction is called the Haber-Weis reaction.

The hydroxyl-free radical has the property of adding to the 5-6 double bond of thymidine, (Lagercrantz, 1973) and destroying the biological activity of the DNA, a serious problem for cells. Superoxide is active in deaminations (Anbar and Pecht, 1969). Peroxide and oxygen are particularly effective in maintaining autoxidations initiated by active radicals. Tissue contains an enzyme, glutathione peroxide reductase, which reduces organic hydroperoxides and is coupled to NADPH.

Peroxide is also less reactive than $\cdot OH$. In the presence of ferrous ion or cuprous ion, hydrogen peroxide also forms hydroxyl radical.

$$2Fe^{2+} = HOOH \longrightarrow Fe^{3+} + \cdot OH + :OH^-$$

Not enough attention has been paid in the gerontological literature to the distinction between free radical scavengers and antioxidants. Scavengers use up radicals, particularly hydroxyl radical. Hydroxyl radical initiates but does not maintain autoxidation of lipid. This is a property of peroxide or oxygen itself. Antioxidants such as BHT (which were fed to mice by Harman [1968], Comfort, Yokotsky-Gore, and Pathmanathan [1971], and others, and which extended the mean life span of mice) and vitamin E are primarily inhibitors of autoxidation. Radical scavengers have not been as thoroughly explored. It may bring pleasure to some to know that one compound with promise as a radical scavenger is ethyl alcohol.

One should make it clear that a role for hydroxyl radical and superoxide in aging is of great theoretical interest, but is far from proven. Because of the presence of superoxide dismutase in tissue, the concentration of superoxide in tissue has never been measured.

The observation that antioxidants may extend the life span of rodents is indirect evidence that superoxide, hydrogen peroxide, and oxygen may be significant in aging. The longevity extension is most effective in middle life so that the extension is primarily of average life expectancy. It would be interesting to know if a scavenger effective against $\cdot OH$ plus an antioxidant would give more protection than either alone.

The production of the most potent radical of all, $\cdot OH$, is a function of the concentration of superoxide and hydrogen peroxide. Oshino, Chance, Seis, and Bucher (1973) estimate that the concentration of peroxide in rat liver ranges from $10^{-7} - 10^{-9}$ M or lower. Both superoxide and peroxide are produced in tissue by oxygenases and oxidases, utilized in tissue by oxygenases and peroxidases, and dismutated by dismutase or catalase.

In plants, carotenoids are thought to protect

the cell from O_2 radicals generated in the chloroplasts. It is possible that a combination of oxidizable lipid and chain-terminating anti-oxidants could serve a similar function in mammalian cells. Lipotuscin, the oxidized proteolipid which accumulates with age in mammalian tissue, may at times serve a useful purpose. $\cdot OH$ is very short-lived and is primarily a hazard to DNA, whereas superoxide and peroxide are much more stable, diffuse considerable distances, and are present in considerably higher concentrations. Almost nothing is known about the effect of oxygen tension on the presumed concentration of $\cdot OH$ and superoxide.

Injury by ionizing radiation and injury from aging differ to some extent biologically. Acute radiation results in the death of the more rapidly dividing cell populations. The assignment of injury from chronic low level radiation and from aging hits between dividing and non-dividing cells is more difficult. The classical article on the differences and similarities between radiation injury and aging is that of Upton (1957). (See Chapter 21 in this Handbook.) Radiation injury does produce life shortening. Animals injured by chronic low level irradiation look older and are susceptible to some of the same diseases as old animals. Qualitatively at least, chromosomal aberrations are elevated in both.

The survivors of acute doses of radiation which kill one-half of the animals have shorter life expectancy for the rest of their lives. The life-shortening potential is greatest if the radiation is given to young animals. The effects of cell death and of loss of stem cells or their function may become more pronounced in older animals as the supply of such cells is depleted.

For a discussion of -SH compounds as free radical scavengers successfully used to protect cells against ionizing radiation, see the paper of Bacq (1974).

Radicals such as $\cdot OH$ and $\cdot HO_2$ are very reactive. To scrub them with an administered protective agent, significant concentrations must be maintained, since they are capable of reacting with so many other cell constituents such as DNA or protein. This makes chronic protection difficult, since as is in the case with ethanol, there are other pharmacological actions.

As the earth has evolved an oxygen-rich atmosphere, aerobic organisms have had to evolve defenses against oxygen-derived radicals. In the human body there are some very considerable variations in oxygen tension. The oxygen tension in alveoli in the lung is at least 90 mm of Hg. In other tissue it is much lower, in the brain 11 mm (Bicher, Bruley, Reneau, and Knirely, 1973), in rabbit arteries 27-22 mm (Niinikoski, Heughan, and Hunt, 1973a), and in the vena cava 20-11 mm (Niinikoski, Heughan, and Hunt 1973b). Crapo and Tierny (1974) have shown that superoxide dismutase is partially inducible by elevated oxygen tensions in rat lung.

Ionizing radiation is known to produce three products, hydrated electrons, hydrogen radical, and hydroxyl radical. One of these, the hydroxyl radical, may also be produced in aging. It follows that there might be radiation-like components of biological injury associated with aging, but not involving electron ejection as with radiation. Conceptually, the quantitative comparison of aging dose and radiation dose is at least theoretically possible even though very difficult. Rapidly metabolizing cells may produce more radicals, but they also operate at a lower oxygen tension. Is the inverse correlation between metabolic rate of an animal and longevity mediated through $\cdot HO$?

Cadet and Teoule (1974) and Teoule and Cadet (1974) find that the principal product of the reaction of $\cdot OH$ with thymine appears to be trans-6-hydroperoxy-5-hydroxy 5,6-dihydrothymine. The reaction of $\cdot OH$ with DNA in vitro has been shown by Gregory and Cohen (1975) not to produce schism of the phosphate diester backbone. See also Teoule and Cadet (1974) and Ducolomb, Cadet, and Teoule (1974).

The product of the reaction of $\cdot OH$ with DNA is thus available for study of the properties of repair endonuclease; however, the endonuclease required may be different than that for thymidine dimers.

We are now going to discuss a very different kind of chemistry, ordinary hydrolysis.

With single stranded DNA or RNA, estimates can be made of the rate of spontaneous hydrolysis in neutral solution by extrapolating the rates of hydrolysis at elevated temperatures to 37°C (Eigner, Boedtker, and Michaels, 1961). Single stranded RNA, such as transfer RNA, folds back on itself to produce double stranded RNA for stability. Double stranded DNA is at least ten times as stable as single stranded DNA, and it is difficult to obtain evidence for spontaneous hydrolysis below its melting temperature. Its hydrolysis is not as susceptible to catalyses by metal ions as is single stranded. However, experiments with formaldehyde, a reagent which reacts with aliphatic and ring NH groups including those involved in Watson-Crick base pairing, would suggest that there is a small fraction of the DNA which is single stranded even *in vitro*, namely, 1×10^{-9} (Von Hippel and McGhee, 1972). *In vivo* this fraction may be considerably larger.

Spontaneous hydrolysis would result in strand gaps between a 5'-phosphodiester group and a 3'-hydroxyl, a situation very favorable for repair by the usual system of DNA polymerases and ligase. Even if the split were the wrong way, that is, so as to give a 3'-phosphate or a 5'-hydroxyl, the unwanted 3'-phosphate still can be removed, breaks enlarged, and the required 5'-phosphate added. The repair of spontaneous hydrolysis may account for much of the repair observed. Such repair would require no special repair endonuclease, merely polymerase and ligase.

Depurination and oxidation of the deoxyribofuranose rings result in the release of a purine from its bond to deoxyribose, followed by spontaneous hydrolysis of the phosphate ester backbone. Depurination proceeds rapidly at a low pH. It is difficult to estimate how much depurination might be anticipated *in vitro* at neutral pH over a period of years. The data of Lindahl and Nyberg (1972) suggest 1×10^{-11} per purine per second at 37°C. Because of the spontaneous esterolysis which follows depurination, this would appear to be a repairable change (Verly, Paquette, and Thibodeau, 1973).

REPAIR

Repair in simplest form requires endonucleases to recognize injury and excise it, a DNA polymerase to fill the gap, and a ligase to rejoin the ends. There are several repair endonucleases in a cell (Churchill, Urbanczyk, and Studzinski, 1973; Straus, 1974). By analogy with bacteria there may be at least four. Two chromotograph closely together and are responsible for the repair of distortions in one strand of DNA produced between two bases, or large alkyl adducts. These are the enzymes responsible for the repair of the thymidine dimers produced by untraviolet light. The chain is cleaved on the 5' side of the dimer; an exonuclease is still required to remove the dimer.

Another enzyme is required to remove the simple O_2 adducts of pyrimidine monomers. If ·OH was particularly significant in aging, this enzyme would be the more important for repair. In bacteria it splits the wrong way to give a 3'-phosphate and a 5'-hydroxyl which must be cleaned up by a proper exonuclease and resynthesized.

The final endonuclease excises apurinic sites the right way. It thus catalyzes a reaction which would otherwise occur spontaneously but much more slowly. This may be the enzyme which also removes mismatches.

In all repair systems, the strand which is injured is first identified by the repair system, excised, and then corrected using information on the complementary strand to guide the repair. Therefore, double stranded breaks cannot be repaired.

The type of repair we have been discussing is excision repair. Repair can also occur at the time of DNA replication. Under these circumstances a long segment of the strand complementary to the flawed area is read and the new segment is inserted. Cell division in a growing animal thus increases the opportunities for repair or removal of a segment of DNA which could not otherwise be read.

Surprisingly enough, repair does not always decrease the level of error as measured by mutation. A repair during which coding errors are made is known as an error prone repair. Many types of injury must be excised before the strand can again be duplicated, so that even error prone repair serves a purpose. While both postreplicative repair and excision repair can show error proneness, the phenomenon is often more prominent in postreplicative repair. The sequences of new DNA introduced in postreplicative repair are larger than in excision repair. Thus cells dividing under conditions injurious to DNA such as in ultraviolet light may acquire a mutational burden from postreplicative repair in excess of the injury being introduced.

In our more static model, the mutations which contribute to the aging process are viewed as fairly stable. A study of the repair of mutation induced by nitrous acid would seem relevant to what might be happening in aging. Adenine, which bonds to thymine, loses an amino group and becomes hypoxanthine, which at the next division will code for cytosine. The result is that an AT pair becomes a GC pair. Guanine, which bonds to cytosine, loses an amino group and changes to xanthine, which at the next division will code for cytosine; consequently the error is not propagated. Cytosine, which bonds to guanine, becomes thymine, which at the next division will code for adenine; consequently a GC pair is replaced by AT. Thymine is unaffected by nitrous acid. Prior to any division, the code of translated RNA will be similarly altered, uracil replacing thymine. Such mutations would be propagated and are thus particularly threatening.

We now must consider what happens to mutations producing a single miscoded base prior to the next cell division. If aging was due to intrinsic mutagenesis during replication, this would be the predominant type of error. However, such errors could also be produced through deamination of cytosine to uracil with the passage of time (Lindahl and Nyberg, 1974) or through the replacement of amino groups by oxygen as occurs with nitrous acid. Such changes produce simple mismatch. First generation revertants would be almost impossible to detect since the detection of the original mutation depends on the propagation of the mutant and, if corrected, would disappear. Correction of mismatch of SV 40 virus in monkey kidney cells has been demonstrated (Lai and Nathans, 1975). In this system it is not known exactly how many base pairs were mismatched. Furthermore, in a mismatch situation in eukaryotic chromatin, it is hard to see how the chances of revertance could be better than 50-50 since the wrong strand would have an equal probability of being selected.

Attempts to use chemical mutagens to induce a model of aging have been disappointing. Nothing as effective as ionizing radiation has been found. Mutagens are often toxic, and animals may suffer appreciable injury on both acute and chronic dosage. The experiments may merely reflect technical difficulties in experimentally simulating aging with some very toxic compounds. Perhaps the monofunctional and bifunctional alkylating agents, which have been used in attempts to show a gerontomimetic effect, alkylate and distort the double helix so much that they are too efficiently excised. The effects of cigarette smoking on human life tables resemble those of chronological age. This might be fortuitous, or there might be mechanistic implications.

REPAIR AND LIFE SPAN

There is a definite correlation between the capability for the repair of ultraviolet-induced thymidine dimers as measured by thymidine incorporation and life span. Hart and Setlow (1974) grew primary fibroblast cultures out of the dermis of several species. The cultures were irradiated with 1.0 j/m^2 of ultraviolet. Hydroxyurea (2M) was added to inhibit DNA synthesis, and tritium-labeled thymidine was added to detect unscheduled DNA synthesis. Most active in repair were human, elephant, and cow fibroblasts. They were nearly 5 times as active as the fibroblasts of rats, mice, or shrews. The repair system of hamsters was intermediate between the other groups, although the life span of the hamster more resembles that of a rat than a man.

Repair capability and life span are not proportional. Man for example, lives 25 times as long as a rat, not 5 times. Patients with xeroderma pigmentosum do not age prematurely. These results do suggest, however, that long-lived species may have more active repair systems and that their excision systems might also be more sophisticated in detecting a broader spectrum of injury. One must also consider whether or not the efficiency of the repair system changes with age.

Goldstein (1971) has studied DNA repair with autoradiography, following ultraviolet irradiation of skin fibroblasts from normal and

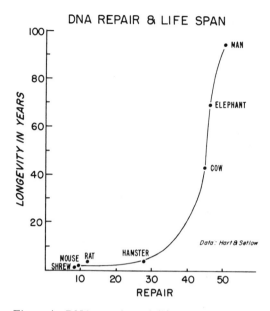

Figure 4. DNA repair and life span. The data reported from Hart and Setlow (1974) has been plotted to show the relationship between longevity and the incorporation of isotopic nucleotide into the DNA of fibroblasts under standardized conditions during repair following untraviolet radiation.

xeroderma pigmentosum individuals. Although there is no change in DNA repair in young cells and in late passage cells, repair decreases at very late passage. He concludes that the DNA repair mechanism is not altered in aging cells *in vitro*. One must note, however, that although radiation and aging damage may appear similar, the repair processes, particularly the initial steps, may be quite different. Purposefully damaging DNA with ultraviolet may not reflect what actually occurs in senescence, nor is the late passage fibroblast necessarily the perfect model of mammalian aging.

Longevity is not correlated with the size of the genome (Cutler, 1973), but with the size of the animals, particularly the size of the brains, and is correlated inversely with metabolic rate (see Sacher, 1968). Many species of invertebrates and plants are both short-lived and radiation-resistant. This presents a paradox. Such short-live species often show a clearly defined sequence of hormonal events leading to aging, e.g., plants (Woolhouse, 1967), or Pacific

salmon (see Chapter 1). Somatic mutation is probably not involved in the aging of such species. The problem in resolution of this paradox is in proving that longer-lived species are also not hormonally programmed.

The speculations concerning the three types of somatic mutation in DNA are given in Table 1. Spontaneous hydrolysis is relatively unimportant in aging if breaks are repaired immediately, but would contribute to the pool of inactivated genes if breaks remained open and repair was delayed. Approximately two-thirds of the breaks resulting from ionizing radiation are repairable, depending on the nature of the radiation. The injuries of aging may be repaired with difficulty and accumulate even though produced quite slowly. By definition, the energy associated with the primary events in injury from ionizing irradiation exceeds 34 eV or about 800 kcal/mole, while the energy of hydrolysis of the polynucleotide backbone is about 4 kcal/mole. The energy of aging hits may be presumed to be in the range of 4–10

TABLE 1.

Type of Mutation	Repairability	Significance in Aging
Spontaneous hydrolysis	high	limited (static model) high (dynamic model)
Radiation type	intermediate	some
Aging type	low	high

kcal/mole. In a dynamic model in which repair rather than injury is limiting, spontaneous hydrolysis becomes a much more important type of injury because it may contribute the largest number of unrepaired breaks open at any one instant in time. Table 1 summarizes these concepts in a qualitative manner. Unfortunately, quantitative data are unavailable.

If repair systems were important in human aging, could we make such systems work better and thus extend human life? Unfortunately, we know more about what inhibits repair than about what stimulates it.

There is one additional type of repair system used in bacteria, but not yet demonstrated in mammalian tissue, and that is restriction endonuclease. In bacteria, certain base sequences, often about six base pairs long, can be recognized as foreign and are digested along with much of the molecule. Such a device is capable of recognizing point mutations or recombinations which do not involve linked molecules but only miscoded sequences. The evolution of such restriction endonucleases in a long-lived vertebrate would favor longevity.

An attempt to demonstrate increased DNA strand breaks as a correlate of age was that of Price, Modak, and Makinodan (1971). They prepared sections of brain, liver, and heart from young and senescent mice, fixed them in ethanol, and embedded them in paraffin at 52°C. Sections were then treated with calf thymus DNA polymerase and tritiated deoxyadenosine triphosphate. Following autoradiography, nuclear grain counts for the tritium were made. Grain counts over neuron and astrocyte nuclei in the brain, over Kupfer cell nuclei in the liver, and over the nuclei of cardiac and skeletal muscle cells were increased with age. Microglia and hepatocyte nuclei showed low incorporation and no age effect. Lymphatic tissues showed such extremely high activity that age differences could not be observed due to the high background. They concluded that at the time of fixation, older tissue had more open gaps in the DNA capable of incorporating thymidine.

While extremely interesting, these experiments are relatively crude. One would like to directly measure strand breaks in postmitotic cells where karyotyping is not possible. Assuming that the nucleus of a human cell has 30×10^{11} daltons of DNA and 46 chromosomes, the average chromosome has a molecular weight of around 6.5×10^{10} daltons. Such molecular weights are usually outside the range of sedimentation constants ordinarily resolvable, by ultracentrifugation in sucrose gradients. When DNA is released into an alkaline sucrose gradient, it forms units of 5×10^8 daltons rather than the expected 6×10^{10}. The characterization of these units was performed by Lett, Klucis, and Sun (1970), who believe that they represent fundamental units of chromosomal organization. As the DNA is released in the alkaline sucrose it denatures and becomes single stranded. Initially, the DNA is found in a relatively buoyant fraction which Elkind and Liu (1972) believe is either associated with attached nuclear membrane or represents a buoyant double stranded DNA complex. The released units, while smaller than chromosomes, are still quite large. In an ordinary gradient run, there would be considerable entanglement unless extremely dilute solutions are used. Unfortunately, these solutions must be so dilute that the DNA can only be detected if first labeled with tritium or carbon-14 in culture or in a young growing animal. A method for determining DNA, based on the phosphorescence of silver-DNA complexes, may have sufficient sensitivity to permit direct analysis of DNA from older animals (Sheridan, O'Donnell, and Pautler, 1973). In Lett's studies, a special rotor developed by Anderson at Oak Ridge

National Laboratory permitted enough DNA to be collected for optical measurements (Klucis and Lett, 1970). In experiments designed to detect any differences in repair of DNA injury induced by X-rays in young and old beagles (Wheeler and Lett, 1972), no differences were found. The complexities of the protocol would require that before definitive conclusions could be reached, experiments should be done with age as the major dependent variable. For one thing, the time course for the release of DNA from the membrane material must be studied as a possible variable in the behavior of the tissue.

Perhaps as relevant to aging injury as measurement of single strand or double strand breaks are estimates of somatic mutation based on mutation rates in tissue culture. Of course conditions in tissue culture are not the same as in tissue, and the mutation rate and stability of the differentiated state may be greater or less. One problem in extrapolating mutation rates in tissue culture to adult tissue concerns the use of mutation rate per cell division in culture or the mutation rate per unit time.

To make such calculations we must make certain assumptions. For example we might assume that there are 20,000 genes, that a human lifetime is 75 years, that doubling occurs, on the average, every 40 hours in culture, and that an average cell is the product of 30 doublings. The mutation rate for cells in culture is about 4×10^{-6} per gene division, as found for example by Albertini and deMars (1973). If one assumes 30 generations in a lifetime and 20,000 genes, then $4 \times 10^{-6} \times 30 \times 2 \times 10^4$ would predict 2.4 mutations per cell per lifetime. This rate of mutation is greater than for the germ line where, as we have discussed, the mutation rate is between 0.1 and 0.5 mutations per generation. If, on the other hand, one believed that mutations accumulated because of chemical events occurring with the passage of time one would calculate differently. The number of hours in 75 years 6.6×10^5, divided by the 40 hours in an average generation time in tissue culture, times the mutation rate of 4×10^{-6} per generation times 2×10^4 genes would give 1.3×10^3 mutations per cell per lifetime, quite a large number of mutations and certainly enough to affect organ function. Because of this discrepancy, 2.4 mutations per cell per lifetime as opposed to 1.3×10^3, it would seem important to estimate mutations directly in primary cultures from older tissues or directly in the tissue itself by some histologic technique. Only by the direct comparison of older tissue with cellularly homogenious younger tissue can hard and fast conclusions be reached. Even here it would be important to use more than one marker for mutation, and to carefully study reversion rates for evidence of altered differentiation rather than mutation of DNA.

To produce a mutation in 10 percent of the cells in every structural gene would require $2 \times 10^4 \times 0.1$ or 2×10^3 mutations per cell. This number exceeds our estimate of replicative error, but not necessarily of time dependent error. Mutations are more serious than errors in charging or messenger or protein synthesis since they affect all of the molecules produced by a particular gene rather than being distributed among all cells.

Under ideal circumstances it might be possible to estimate mutation rate from the rate of repair. However data such as Painter and Young (1972) and Regan, Setlow and Ley (1971) do not permit such an estimate. Furthermore there is a logical inconsistency in using the rate of repair as a quantitative measure of aging hits, since almost by definition, in a static model, aging hits are not repairable.

We may conclude that the rate of somatic mutation in culture is sufficient to account for the changes observed in aging tissue, based on replication error alone, and even more easily account for the loss of function in older tissue based on time dependent mutation. A rate of mutation approaching that of time dependent mutation in culture could produce detectable modification of tissue enzymes in older animals.

The fact that somatic mutation could account for the changes observed in older animals does not prove that such mutations are responsible for aging. It is at least equally possible that aging results from altered states of differentiation the effects of which are somewhat similar to a mutation. In either case the cells produced, if they continue to divide, are subject to natural selection, a more fit cell in terms of its own survival and reproduction would not necessarily be more supportive of the welfare of the organism as a whole.

AGING, MUTATION AND REPAIR

The gerontologist observing the activity of an enzyme is in a difficult position as he has little information about the actual cellular genetics. He usually has no way of knowing whether the phenomenon he is observing applies equally to all cells, or to some cells, or whether within a single cell it applies in an all or none manner.

Suppose one observes that in an aging cell population the activity of a certain enzyme has been decreased. This could be due to:

1. miscoding of DNA in some cells
2. point mutation of DNA in some cells
3. generally increased error in translation in all cells
4. generally increased error in protein synthesis in all cells
5. error in phenotypic expression in some cells
6. expression of an actual genetic program of aging

It would seem likely that a cell would tolerate general errors in translation and protein synthesis better than specific mutations which might entirely suppress out the functions of specific key enzymes. Specific dominant mutations, while lethal to specific cells, might not be readily detectable by general observation of overall enzyme function in tissues.

The number of breaks present in a cell at any one time is really not measurable by repair *in vivo*, since the amount of repair is dependent on both the number of lesions made available for repair during the time of the experiment as well as the activity of repair enzymes. However, in isolated DNA, the number of breaks is relatively fixed in time, and if natural substrate is used, repair activity can be used to quantitate the number of breaks.

The increased variation in cellular size seen among cells in aging tissue could be taken as evidence for mutation of different genes in each cell rather than a general phenomenon in all cells. This variation in size is most conspicuous in nerve tissue and liver, as is discussed in Andrew's book (1971).

PROGRAMMED AGING

If we restrict ourselves to the nucleus, there are two principal alternatives in considering somatic mutation in DNA as a cause of aging. The first is to consider aging as a result of a well-ordered genetic program operating without appreciable error, and the second is to view aging as arising through defects in the control of the genetic program.

First, let us consider embryogenesis as a possible model of aging. Somatic mutation of DNA would not necessarily be involved in a number of situations associated with cell death in embryos. Here cell death often seems to be part of a definite biological program. For example, Saunders (1966) found that after 4 days of development in the formation of the wing of a chick embryo a necrotic zone appears at the posterior junction of the wing bud and body wall. Similar changes occur between the toes and fingers of human, rat, and mouse embryos. In the case of the wing bud of the chick embryo, cell death occurs at stage 24. Cells can be rescued if they are removed prior to stage 17 and grafted to another site. Thus, a program is started at stage 17 that leads to death at stage 24, although this program is reversible up to stage 22. The wing bud is an example of programmed cell death in development.

As an example of a program leading to death of an adult organism, consider the slime mold. Wright (1966) has shown that when a slime mold differentiates, the stalk cells are unable to digest nutrient and therefore have only a limited capacity for survival. A May fly, born without mouth parts resembles the slime mold, as does a plant in which the setting of seed triggers hormonally signaled events leading to cell death. While the product of the final insect metamorphoses, the adult, is the life form which appears to age, it is not certain that a human is programmed for aging. It is possible that in later life, our program is inadequate to deal with aging injury, due to deficits in biochemical repair tools.

It is not clear whether aging cells are formed as the product of the previous cell division or whether cells cease to divide because they age.

Age may not necessarily lead to cell death. In the mature animal, many cells appear to be locked into G_1 by some poorly understood physiological mechanism and to be progressing through mitosis very slowly, similar to cells given very low doses of radiation (see Chapter 5).

ALTERED PHENOTYPE AS A CAUSE OF AGING

It is often difficult to distinguish a mutation which results in altered DNA from a relatively irreversible change in the expression of phenotype. Some of the inconsistencies which beset a somatic mutation theory of aging based on the genotype would be resolved if aging were seen as merely an inappropriate change in the differentiated state. The fundamental changes would occur not within the genetic message of the DNA but within the associated RNA and protein.

For example Shin (1974) studied two mouse cell mutants A_9 and RAG. They are both resistant to 8-azaguanine and therefore seem to lack the enzyme, hypoxanthine-guanine phosphoribosyl transferase. It was found that A_9 actually had enzyme, but it was extremely heat-labile, whereas in the case of RAG, the enzyme seemed to be entirely lacking. Shin concluded that RAG was a regulatory mutation and A_9 a structural mutation.

A study of reversion of 8-azaguanine insensitive mutants detected reversion rates of as high as 10^{-2} (Van Zeeland, Van Diggelen, and Simons, 1972). It is unlikely that such a high reversion rate could be attributable to a back mutation, and these data are suggestive of some sort of alteration in the stability of the phenotype. Harris (1973) concurs and reviews a number of instances where the fluctuations in vari-

ants arising in tissue cultures exceed 2.4×10^{-4} mutants/cell/generation in thymidine transport, and 1.1×10^{-3}/cell/generation in conversion of heavy immunoglobulin producers to light chain producers. He cites the failure of the mutation rate of 8-azaguanine resistance or heat resistance to decrease as the number of chromosomes sets increases as evidence of an epigenetic change rather than mutation of DNA.

Is there such a thing as an aged phenotype? In order to evaluate the possibility that aging arises from altered control capabilities and not from altered DNA, it will be necessary to discuss the organization of chromatin. Chromatin contains, in addition to its DNA and RNA, several types of protein including histones and nonhistone proteins. The placement of these determines the phenotype. At the time of cell division, this placement must be duplicated, and in the resting cell the placement must be maintained. Early amphibian embryos, however, can receive transplanted nuclei from the differentiated tissue of tadpoles which then direct normal early embryonic function. Thus, in an amphibian egg the process is entirely reversible.

CHROMATIN COMPOSITION

The key structural features about which the chromatin of mammalian cells probably is organized are the histones. There are five major types of histone. By weight, the concentration of histone is approximately the same as DNA. The concentration of nonhistone protein varies, being greater in cells which are more active metabolically. The total amount of histone per cell remains fairly constant during development and aging. (For a recent reference see Carter and Chae, 1975.)

The question of whether there are small variations in histone patterns in young and older tissue has proven difficult to answer. Some of the differences which have been observed in apparent histone content could be artifactual or secondary to significant changes in the association and nonhistone protein within the chromatin complex. Older tissue does not always homogenize as readily as younger tissue, and more debris is likely to be trapped in the nuclear pellet. During these earlier stages of isolation, proteolysis is likely to occur, and depending on the condition and the inhibitors which are used, either H_1 or arginine-rich histone may be destroyed. The initial amount of proteolytic activity in the nucleus and the amount of proteolytic enzyme in lysosomal vesicles may vary with age and may give false impressions of histone variabiiity. An increase in histone protease in older cells may reflect an increased need for restructuring chromatin protein as well as, or together with, the repair of DNA. In addition, as Chalkley has shown, severe illness may affect the integrity of histones (Panyim, Bilek, and Chalkley, 1971). Quantitative variation in the histones of older animals is therefore not established. The more recent literature, such as the Carter and Chae (1975) paper, would suggest that there is no gross variation in the patterns of histones with age.

While the amount of histone remains fairly constant, the amount of nonhistone protein does vary with age, e.g., in rodent liver (Zhelabov and Berdyshev, 1972). The amount of nonhistone protein usually decreases between birth and maturation as growth and total metabolic activity decreases. In many tissues there is a further decrease in amount of nonhistone protein during senescence although there are exceptions (Kurtz and Sinex, 1967).

The majoriity of the proteins contributing to the electrophoretic pattern observed for nonhistone protein are probably not specific repressors or inducers but proteins of more general function. Specific repressors and inducers may be present in a relatively low concentration and not ordinarily visible in an electrophoretic pattern.

CHROMATIN ORGANIZATION

Of the major classes of histone, Kornberg and Thomas (1974) have pointed out that H_4, H_{2a}, H_{2b} and H_3 are present in approximately equal molecular quantities. There is about half as much H_1. There is a suggestion in x-ray patterns of a repeating unit about 100Å along the double helix. Experiments with nuclease suggest that there is a basic repeat in the histone pattern every 180 base pairs. Depending on the conditions of dissociation, $(H_4, H_3, H_{2a}, H_{2b})$ tetramer occurs every 180 base pairs. It is not clear what determines the spacing of protein in a differentiated cell and how the information concerning this spacing and the nature of the differentiated state is passed on to the daughter cell. It seems doubtful, because of the diversity of cell types, that the information would be totally reconstituted *de novo* from specific repressor substances as would seem to be the case for bacteria. What is the process which insures that the daughter cells remain true to the phenotype or change in a specific manner at the time of the cell division, and can this ordering alter with age?

When a solution of chromatin is warmed, the base pairs of DNA separate just as they do with purified DNA. The separation, however, occurs at a higher temperature because the presence of the protein tends to stabilize the DNA. Kurtz, Russell and Sinex (1974) programmed a computer to plot the differential of change in melting temperatures per degree. This gives a series of peaks. Older animals showed less open DNA than mature animals as indicated by a smaller hyperchromic shift at the temperature of 50–64°C. This is the temperature at which DNA melts when it is not associated with any protein or with protein such as F1 which dissociates fairly easily. The older animals have more hyperchromicity associated with some of the higher melting fractions, 54 percent vs. 42 percent in the 78–92°C range. It is interesting to note that the positions of the peaks do not seem to change, merely the amount of hyperchromicity observed in relation to particular peaks, thus indicating true phase transitions.

Another way to study the state of chromatin is to study its ability to serve as a template for RNA polymerase (templatability). O'Meara and Herrmann (1972) extracted the chromatin from 3-, 14-, and 21-month-old mice with different concentrations of salt. They then incubated the partially associated chromatin with *Escherichia coli* RNA polymerase and the appropriate nucleotides. Templatability increased as the protein was dissociated by the salt. At low concentrations, old chromatin showed more templatability than the chromatin from young

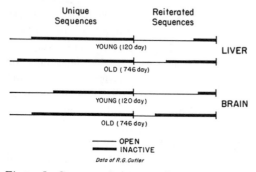

Figure 5. Open and repressed sequences of DNA. This data plotted from a paper by Richard Cutler (1974) shows the fraction of RNA hybridizable to DNA in young and old rat liver and brain in neat and reiterated sequences.

animals, but a higher salt concentration was necessary to dissociate the protein. These studies suggest that F1 may be more readily removed from the chromatin of older animals, leaving a residue of other histones and nonhistone protein which is more tightly bound.

Preliminary studies suggest changes in transcription during aging. Cutler (1974) isolated RNA with DNA and studied both the rapidly reannealing fractions of high redundancy and the slower annealing single copy messenger in young and old C57BL/6J female mice. In the liver, the percentage of DNA hybridizing with both single copy messenger and reiterated RNA decreased with age. In the brain, the fractions hybridizing increased during development and then decreased. The biphasic nature of the brain curve is probably due to the changes in the cellular composition of the brain during development. A fairly loose interpretation of such experiments might be that changes occur in the distribution and aggregation of protein in chromatin with age. The effect *in vivo* is to make chromatin a less favorable substrate for DNA and RNA synthesis.

The reader interested in pursuing the chromatin study further should see the papers of Tsanev and Sendov (1971) and Weintraub and Van Lente (1974).

STABILITY OF ASPARAGINE AMIDE

Just as with DNA, the most likely chemical event to occur in chromatin with the passage of time is spontaneous hydrolysis, and specifically the hydrolysis of primary amides.

Because turnover is limited, the proteins of chromatin would seem to be particularly susceptible to aging injury. Many of these proteins persist for the lifetime of the organism, turning over, if at all, with quite extended lifetimes (Sadgofsal and Bonner, 1969).

In any event some amide loss is not only possible, but probable. Thermodynamic arguments in support of this are given by Sinex (1960), Robinson, McKerrow, and Cary (1970), and Robinson (1974). Moreover, proteins incubated at 37°C for long periods of time would seem susceptible to hydrolysis of their amide nitrogen, particularly the primary amide of asparagine. The amount of amidation may be a factor in determining the turnover of a protein (Robinson, 1974).

Flatmark and Sletten (1968) have demonstrated that the multiple forms of cytochrome c, CyII, and CyIV are formed by deamidation of CyI. Palmer and Papaconstantinou (1969) believe that subunit II_B of crystallin, the eye lens protein, is formed from the subunit of crystallin II_a by deamidation. It is possible that such deamidation occurs in nuclear protein. As a practical matter the study of nuclear proteins in this regard becomes a study of histones, since nonhistone protein is not as well characterized.

MUST AGING REPAIR RECAPITULATE ONTOGENY?

If one compares embryogenesis with aging there are some interesting problems. Embryogenesis occurs in a series of very discrete steps in a particular order. What happens if there is an aging injury and part of this pathway must be retraced?

Let us speculate on a series of steps in differentiation. In this model the switches must be thrown in the proper order. Gene C can only be activated if gene B is activated. After C is activated, B may become inactive. When F is activated the cell becomes postmitotic. What happens if there is aging injury to the protein activating gene C, for example. If it is altered and must be replaced, can such repair be initiated directly or is it necessary for the cell to dedifferentiate to the point where B is first activated, as in the following:

Hypothetical Repair of a Differentiated State

A	b	c	d	e	f	initial state, only A active
A	B	c	d	e	f	B activated
A	B	C	d	e	f	B activates C, which activates D, E, and F
A	b	C	D	E	F	normal maturity, B becomes inactive
A	b	₵	D	E	F	aging hit on C
A	b	ₓ	d	e	f	dedifferentiation back to initial state
A	B	ₓ	d	e	f	B reactivated in repetition of first step
A	B	C	d	e	f	C activated
A	b	C	D	E	F	repair complete, B once again inactivated

Do resting postmitotic cells actually have a reservoir of histone for repair? If chromatin lost protein with age and was unable to replace it in resting cells not undergoing cell division, this would result in an altered phenotype.

RESIDUAL PROTEIN OF DNA

Salser and Baylis (1972) studied the residual amino acids remaining on DNA after extensive purification. They found that the differences in the residual amino acid between different organs and between the two sexes did not show a consistent effect of age.

In certain instances protein may serve as a cross-linking agent. While a particular protein might normally react specifically with both strands at a particular site on the double helix, there may be situations involving reiterated sequences where a single strand of DNA might fold back on itself forming a hairpin loop stabilized by protein.

Herrmann, Dowling, and Russel (1975) attribute their observations concerning hairpin loops in older DNA to the presence of protein. Herrmann prepared his DNA from mouse brain and liver. It was sonicated, denatured, and eluted from hydroxyapatite columns. The DNA was purified by the Marmer procedure which utilizes chloroform and isoamyl alcohol. The amount of spontaneously reassociating DNA in these fractions was measured. Fractions of DNA were prepared which reassociated with a cot number of 10^{-5} or more. In young liver, this consists of 0.7 percent of the total DNA, in the liver of 27-month-old animals, 1.7 percent. In the brain of 2 month animals, the fraction was 2.1 percent and for 27-month-old animals, 4.4 percent. These fractions from older animals showed hairpin loops under an electron microscope. These were not seen in significant numbers in young and mature animals. Herrmann interpreted the hairpin as representing a single stranded loop (which has partially melted out) from a double stranded sequence. The double stranded portion was considered cross-linked either through protein or with itself.

SATELLITE AND REDUNDANT DNA

While eukaryotes are more complex than bacteria and therefore should contain the larger number of structural enzymes, they have considerably more DNA than would seem to be required for this purpose. A human has 750 to 1,000 times as much DNA in its genome as a bacterium. Two or three times might be attributable to humans requiring more structural genes; however, this still leaves a great excess of DNA to cover. Some eukaryotes have even more DNA than humans. The lung fish, *Protopterns*, and the amphibian *Amphiuma* have more than ten times as much DNA as humans. The major portion of this extra DNA contains repetitive or redundant sequences. Redundant fractions can be isolated or identified because when double stranded DNA is melted, to separate the strands, and then cooled to 60°C, the reassociation of the redundant fractions is favored. If it is desirable to separate single copy and reiterated sequences, the materials are chromatographed on a hydroxyapatite column. Double stranded DNA binds to hydroxyapatite, whereas single stranded DNA passes through. If the temperature of the column is raised, successive fractions of DNA can be eluted. If it is desirable to elute double stranded DNA this can be done by elevating the salt concentration. In mammals 10 percent of the DNA reassociates very rapidly, 20 or 30 percent in the intermediate range, and 60-70 percent quite slowly. The latter contains sequences transcribed as single copy messenger.

Reiterated sequences may have a number of functions; one is in control. A number of isolated sequences of genome may be controlled by combination with the same RNA or protein. This concept was advanced by Britten and Davidson (1969). The reappearance of the same sequences throughout the genome may result from the groupings of control function of promoter genes with the same sequences.

Cutler (1973), Medvedev (1972), and others have suggested that redundancy serves to protect mammals from the loss of vital genetic information during their life span. Cutler, considering both the number of genes coding for ribosomal RNA as well as the relative metabolic rate, believes that human ribosomes are required to participate in fewer cycles of protein synthesis than mouse ribosomes, and that this is a factor in the more rapid aging of mice.

A corollary of the central dogma is the constancy of chromosomal DNA. There are isolated exceptions of this corollary throughout the phyla. Strehler (1972) has reported experiments not yet confirmed, in which the amount of brain DNA hybridizing with ribosomal RNA appears to decrease. There are some problems in such experiments with respect to assuring the sampling of all of the DNA. Strehler believes that DNA is eliminated through the formation and loss of loops. A loop would be most likely to form when there was an inversion in a tandem sequence. Another possibility is that some abnormal sequences are covered by tightly bound protein.

MESSENGER RNA

As we have stated, single stranded DNA is considerably less stable than double stranded DNA. Single stranded RNA is less stable than single stranded DNA because of the possibility for formation of cyclic phosphate esters. *In vivo*, however, there is considerable variation in the stability of RNAs. Transfer RNA, for example, actually has a double stranded structure because of internal looping. This may even be true of certain messenger RNAs. If one considers the

code for glycine, proline-hydroxyproline, and alanine, the three most common amino acids in collagen, GGX, CCX, and GCX, it is easy to see how collagen messenger might be looped back on itself. The rate of spontaneous hydrolysis is affected by the concentration of divalent cation and trace metals. Cations such as Mg^{2+} stabilize internal loops at physiological concentrations, while others such as Cr^{2+} or Zn^{2+} promote hydrolysis. RNA is also stabilized through association with protein.

Under ordinary circumstances, the half life of messenger RNA would not be considered a factor in aging because it turns over quite rapidly. In active bacteria, its half life may be of the order of minutes. On the other hand there is evidence of the considerably longer half life of messenger RNA in adult organs, e.g., 1 hour–2 weeks in rat liver. Under these circumstances the RNA is presumably stabilized by protein or internal looping. The most familiar example of the persistence of RNA is in the reticulocytes where hemoglobin synthesis occurs for a period of days after the excision of the nucleus. In the lens of the eye, it appears that messenger RNA persists for quite some time. The synthesis of crystallin in the cells of the lens occurs after the destruction of the cell nucleus. So it would at least appear possible to package messenger. If messenger can be packaged, it would seem possible that the packages would be depleted with time. The stability of messenger may be favored by the attachment of the polyadenylate oligopolymer to its terminal end.

TRANSFER RNA

The genetic code is redundant. There are 64 combinations of 4 base pairs taken 3 at a time and only 20 amino acids. Therefore, each amino acid may be coded in more than one way and by more than one transfer RNA. Transfer RNAs for a particular amino acid may change during the development as the codes utilized by the available messenger RNA shift. This being the case, we must consider the possibility that the transfer RNAs of older tissue may differ from those of younger tissue. Strehler, Hirsch, Gusseck, Johnson, and Bick (1971) suggested that if a transfer RNA coded for its own synthetase, the mature animal might become locked into a particular system of transfer RNA and transfer RNA charging and be unable to adapt to a situation in which it might be required to read more diverse messages rapidly. Changes in transfer RNA seem to occur in early development, for example, in pea cotyledons. Whether or not they occur in aging is speculative, but this is an interesting concept.

Transfer RNAs contain pseudouridine and a number of unusual purines and pyrimidines. Some of these are methylated derivatives. The specificity of the synthetases which charge transfer RNA with the appropriate amino acids serves to protect the cell from errors arising from defective transfer.

END PRODUCT ANALYSIS

End product analysis permits an estimate of the total error in all the events leading up to and including protein synthesis. By the end product analysis we mean attempts to measure the amount of error accumulating from all causes in the sequences of a particular structural protein or enzyme. Such error can arise from:

1. coding error
2. point mutation
3. charging error
4. error in protein synthesis

Coding error and error due to point mutation would tend to be propagated in the descendants of individual cells. Charging error and errors in protein synthesis would be randomized over all the proteins of all cells. In a population of mixed descent these would not be distinguishable.

With respect to a mutation or error the result may be:

1. silent
2. highly deleterious
3. in between or leaky

In practice, Michaelis-Menten kinetics, heat stability, (Holliday and Tarrant, 1972), and antigenic titer as a function of enzymatic activity are studied. In most experiments, Mi-chaelis-Menten kinetics seem unaffected, in the sense that K_m does not change. In other words, that enzyme which binds substrate binds it just as well. When exceptions occur, there is often the question of more than one form of the enzyme being present and its synthesis being directed by more than one set of genes. The relative concentration of the subunits might vary with age. Gandhi and Kanungo (1974) have done a careful study of the apparent K_m of malic dehydrogenase in the liver and brain of young and old rats and the effect of ATP and glucose-1-phosphate on the enzyme. Their results illustrate the complexity of the situation when more than one form of an enzyme is present. Malic dehydrogenase exists in both a cytoplasmic and a mitochondrial form. The K_m (for oxalacetate) values of the cytoplasmic are higher, i.e., there appears to be a lower affinity for substrate in older animals. However, the authors point out that this could be due to contamination with the mitochondrial form.

Orgel (1973) points out that aging cell populations are a mixture of dividing, stationary, and impaired cells. A homogenate samples all cells, including those in which proteolysis may have been initiated. The homogenization distributes proteolytic enzymes which may have been activated in a few cells across enzyme substrate from all cells.

Measurement of the heat stability of an enzyme or its activity is only presumptive evidence of altered structure at the time of synthesis. Within a cell, enzymes are often synthesized in a precursor form, assembled into a variety of dimeric and tetrameric forms, often containing isoenzymes, stabilized by substrates and coenzymes, and then ultimately degraded. All of these processes may affect heat stability. The measurement of heat stability is a simple test which can be made on an enzyme in crude homogenates. However, it is also one of the least reliable.

The estimation of the inactive enzyme present in aging tissues by immunological methods was pioneered by the Gershons. Most of their work (Gershon and Gershon, 1973; Zeelon, Gershon, and Gershon, 1972) has been done on fructose-1,6-diphosphate aldolase in aging mice, and nematodes. In the technique utilized by the Gershon group, total enzyme protein is estimated by immunoprecipitation and compared with enzymatic activity. In the older organism, some enzymes appear to be present in an active and an inactive form, e.g., aldolase in mouse liver and isocitrate lyase in nematodes. These studies on nematode isocitrate lyase were done by Reiss and Rothstein (1974) who believe that old enzyme is altered either by a sequence change or by postsynthetic modification. It would be important to know if inactive enzyme molecules are only found with particular enzymes. Negative findings are significant in this regard. Holliday and Tarrant (1972) mention such negative findings but have not published details. However, immunoprecipitation studies showed no change in mouse liver lactic dehydrogenase (Oliveira and Pfuderer, 1973). Clearly not all enzymes accumulate an inactive component during aging. It would also be interesting to know if the enzymatically inactive but immunologically reactive molecules found by the Gershons are synthetically older or younger than the active species.

It is not at all certain that random variation in the coding of structural genes in somatic cells can be detected by sequential analysis because of the large number of possible variations. Isolation of mutated protein is difficult (Loftfield and Vanderjagt, 1972). In such work an attempt is made to label a protein with an amino acid which it does not normally contain. One must then purify the enzyme without losing the variant. Alternatively, one may attempt to concentrate variants by heat precipitation. Sequencing of fingerprinting must then be done with a sensitivity which will detect significant label above background.

The expectations of success are not high. If aging is the result of point mutation and the impaired function or death of a cell is due to loss of a few key enzymes, then in a mixed population of cells, little will be observed. The number of enzymes and the number of amino acids per enzyme make it unlikely that anything would ever be seen without cloning, since each cell would be unique.

It would be difficult to detect an amino acid substitution at a particular position in the sequence. Supposing that in an enzyme of 300 amino acids, 10 percent of the molecules are substituted. Assume that on the basis of the genetic code, 6 substitutions are probable, including the one being sought. Then working with a particular amino acid, the odds against finding a particular substitution at a particular site in the sequence are 1 in 10 X 1 in 300 X 1 in 6, or 1 in 18,000. This level of error might be detectable technically. However, such levels of error have never been found.

The very cells that one would most want to clone, e.g., the descendants of a single old cell with mutated enzymes, are the most difficult to clone because they may not divide. It would seem important, however, to compare the properties of clones descended from old cells with those of mixed populations. Would clones from individual cells have a few but differently altered enzymes, or would the descendants of all cells show mixed and random error? The former is consistent with mutational error, the latter with transcriptional or protein synthetic error.

Holland et al. (1973) infected young and late passage WI-38 fibroblasts with polio, Herpes simplex, and vesicular stomatitis viruses. They found that mature infectious virus was produced more rapidly in the older cultures and that there was no evidence of impaired synthesis of viral coat protein in older viruses.

It is not clear how random mutations or error would distribute in terms of function. In classical genetics we tend to deal with all-or-none situations, and leaky mutations are rare. They may reflect a convenience for geneticists as much as a true distributive phenomenon. Enzyme inactivation kinetics might seem to show two compartments, one sensitive and the other less so. It is possible that random amino acid substitutions would also tend to give such a distribution, with either stable or unstable molecules predominating.

SUMMARY

Many molecular hazards threaten the integrity of genes and their control. To these, evolution has evolved a number of protective devices.

Aging may well be the result of coding error or point mutation in DNA. Assuming this is the case, it is important to know if aging is the result of intrinsic mutagenesis, dependent on generational number, or a result of mutation in postmitotic cells, dependent on the passage of time. In either case, differences in the apparent rates of aging in different tissues must be explained.

The greatest hazard to DNA would be a hydroxyl radical if this were produced from superoxide and peroxide. Superoxide is removed from tissue by superoxide dismutase, and peroxide by catalase. Endonucleases excise the major types of injury. Aging injury accumulates because it is relatively subtle.

Changes in aging tissue may reflect altered control rather than altered DNA. Spontaneous hydrolysis of amide nitrogen in protein is possible with the passage of time. The repair of altered states of differentiation may be as significant as the repair of DNA.

REFERENCES

Abrahamson, S., Bender, M. A., Conger, A. D., and Wolf, S. 1973. Uniformity of radiation-induced mutation rates among different species. *Nature*, **245**, 460.

Albertini, R. J., and DeMars, R. 1973. Detection and quantification of x-ray-induced mutation in cultured diploid human fibroblasts. *Mutation Res.*, **18**, 199–224.

Anbar, M., and Pecht, I. 1969. Oxidative deamination of ethylene-diamine by OH radicals. *J. Physiol. Chem.*, **71**, 1246–1249.

Andrew, W. 1971. *The Anatomy of Aging in Man and Animals*. New York: Grune & Stratton.

Atwood, K. C., and Pepper, F. J. 1961. Erythrocyte automosaicism in some persons of known genotype. *Science*, **134**, 2110–2101.

Bacq, Z. M. (ed.) 1974. *Sulfur Containing Radioprotective Agents* (International Encyclopedia of Pharmacology and Therapeutics Series: Sec. 74). Elmsford, New York: Pergamon Press.

Bettner, L. G., Jarvik, L. F., and Blem, J. E. 1971. Stroop color-word test, non-psychotic organic brain syndrome and chromosome loss in aged twins. *J. Geront.*, **26**, 45–69.

Bicher, H. I., Bruley, D. F., Reneau, D. D., and Knirely, M. H. 1973. Autoregulation of oxygen supply to microareas of brain tissue under hypoxic and hyperbaric conditions. *Bibl. Anat.*, **11**, 526–531.

Blank, C. E. 1960. Aperts syndrome (a type of acrocephalosyndectyly), Observations on a British series of 39 cases. *Ann. Hum. Genet.*, **24**, 151–164.

Bochkov, M. P., and Kuleshov, N. P. 1972. Age sensi-

tivity of human chromosomes to alkylating agents. *Mutation Res.*, **14**, 345–353.

Britten, R. J., and Davidson, E. H. 1969. Gene regulation for higher cells: A theory. *Science*, **165**, 349–357.

Brookhaven Symposia in Biology. 1968. No. 20 U.S. Depart. Comm. Springfield, Virginia.

Burnet, Sir Macfarlane. 1974. *Intrinsic Mutagenesis: A Genetic Approach to Aging*. New York: John Wiley.

Cadet, J., and Teoule, R. 1974. Radiation chemistry of nucleic acids–characterization of thymine hydroxyhydroperoxide. *Biochem. Biophys. Res. Commun.*, **59**, 1047–1055.

Carter, D. B., and Chae, C. 1975. Composition of liver histones in aging rat and mouse. *J. Geront.*, **30**, 28–32.

Casarett, G. W. Similarities and contrasts between radiation and time pathology. *In*, B. L. Strehler (ed.), *Advances in Gerontological Research*, Vol. 1. New York: Academic Press.

Cavalli-Sforza, L., and Bodmer, W. F. 1971. *The Genetics of Human Populations*. San Francisco: W. H. Freeman.

Churchill, J. R., Urbanczyk, J., and Studzinski, G. P. 1973. Multiple deoxyribonuclease activities in nucleus of HeLa cells. *Biochim. Biophys. Res. Comm.*, **53**, 1009–1016.

Clark, A. M., and Rubin, M. A. 1961. The modification by x irradiation of the life span of haploids and diploids of the wasp *Habrabracon S. P.. Radiation Res.*, **15**, 244.

Comfort, A., Yokotsky-Gore, I., and Pathmanathan, K. 1971. Effect of ethoxyquin on the longevity of C_3H mice. *Nature*, **229**, 232.

Cowdry, E. V. 1952. *Problems of Aging. Biological and Medical Aspects*. 3rd ed. Baltimore: Williams & Wilkins.

Cox, E. C., and Gibson, T. G. 1974. Selection for high mutation rates in chemostats. *Genetics*, **77**, 169–184.

Crapo, J. V., and Tierny, D. F. 1974. Superoxide dismutase and pulmonary oxygen toxicity. *Am. J. Physiol.*, **226**, 1401–1407.

Curtis, H. J. 1963. Biological mechanisms underlying the aging process. *Science*, **141**, 686–694.

Curtis, H. J. 1966. *Biological Mechanisms of Aging*. Springfield, Illinois: Charles C. Thomas.

Cutler, R. (1975). Transcription of unique and reiterated DNA sequences in mouse liver and brain tissues as a function of age. *Exp. Gerontol.* **10**, 37–59.

Cutler, R. 1973. Redundancy of information content in the genome of mammalian species as a protective mechanism determining aging rate. *Mech. Age. Dev.*, **2**, 381–408.

Cutler, R. Transcription of unique and reiterated DNA sequences in mouse liver and brain tissues as a function of age. *J. Gerontol.*, **10**, 37–59.

Deshmukh, K. 1974. Synthesis of tissue nonspecific collagen by bovine articular cartilage as a result of aging *in vitro*. *Proc. Soc. Exp. Biol. Med.*, **147**, 726.

Ducolomb, R., Cadet, J., and Teoule, R. 1974. Gamma irradiation of uridine and uridylic acid in aerated aqueous solutions: 1 Identification of the major product. *Z. Naturforsh.*, **29C**, 643-646.

Eickhorn, G. L., Tarien, E., and Butzow, J. J. 1971. Specific cleavage effects in the depolymerization of ribonucleic acids by zinc (II) ions. *Biochemistry*, **10**, 2014-2018.

Eigner, J., Boedtker, J., and Michaels, G. 1961. The thermal degradation of nucleic acid. *Biochim. Biophys. Acta*, **51**, 165-168.

Elkind, M. M., and Liu, C. 1972. Repair of a DNA complex from x-irradiated Chinese hamster cells. *Intern. J. Radiation Biol.*, **22**, 75-90.

Flatmark, T., and Sletten, K. 1968. Multiple forms of cytochrome c in the rat precursor-product relationship between the main components Cy II and Cy III *in vivo*. *J. Biol. Chem.*, **243**, 1623-1629.

Foote, S. 1974. See *Chem. Eng. News* 25 (Aug.19).

Fridovich, I. 1974a. Oxygen boon and bane. *Am. Scientist*, **63**, 54-59.

Fridovich, I. 1974b. Superoxide dismutases. *Advan. Enzymol.* **41**, 35-97.

Gandhi, B., and Kanungo, M. S. 1974. Modulation of malate dehydrogenase of young and old rats by various effectors. *Exp. Geront.*, **9**, 199.

Gershon, J., and Gershon, D. 1973. Altered enzyme molecules in senescent organisms, mouse muscle aldolase. *Mech. Age. Dev.*, **2**, 33-41.

Goldstein, S. 1971. The role of DNA repair in aging of cultured fibroblasts from xeroderma pigmentosum and normals. *Proc. Soc. Exp. Biol. Med.*, **137**, 730-734.

Goodman, R. M., Feckheimer, N. S., Miller, F., Miller, R., and Zartman, D. 1969. Chromosome alterations in three groups of human females. *Am. J. Med. Sci.*, **258**, 26-34.

Gregory, E. M., and Cohen, B. N. 1975. Effects of oxygen radicals on DNA *in vitro*. *Federation Proc.*, **34**, 229.

Gregory, E. M., and Fridovich, I. 1973. Oxygen toxicity and the superoxide dismutase. *J. Bacteriol.*, **114**, 1193-1197.

Harman, D. 1968. Free radical theory of aging. Effect of free radical reaction inhibitors on the mortality rate of male LAF, mice. *J. Geront.*, **23**, 476.

Harris, M. 1971. Mutation rates at different ploidy levels. *J. Cellular Physiol.*, **78**, 177-184.

Harris, M. 1973. Anomolous patterns of mutation in cultured mammalian cells. *Genetics*, **73**, Supp., 181-185.

Hart, R. W., and Setlow, R. B. 1974. Correlation between deoxyribonucleic acid excision repair and lifespan in a number of mammalian species. *Proc. Nat. Acad. Sci.*, **71**, 2169-2173.

Hayflick, L. 1965. The limited *in vitro* lifetime of human diploid cell strains. *Exp. Cell. Res.*, **37**, 614.

Herrmann, R., Bick, M. D., Dowling, L. E., and Russel, A. (1975). *Mech. Age. Dev.*, **4**, 181-89.

Holliday, R., and Tarrant, G. M. 1972. Altered enzymes in aging human fibroblasts. *Nature*, **238**, 26-30.

Holland, J. J., Kohne, D., and Doyle, M. V. 1973. Analysis of virus replication in aging human fibroblast cultures. *Nature*, **245**, 316-319.

Jacobs, P. A., Brunton, M., and Brown, C. W. 1963. Change of human chromosome count distributions with age: Evidence of a sex difference. *Nature*, **197**, 1080-1081.

Jarvik, L. F., Yen, F., and Moralishvili, E. 1974. Chromosome examinations in aging institutionalized women. *J. Geront.*, **29**, 269-276.

Johnson, R., and Strehler, B. L. 1972. Loss of genes coding for ribosomal RNA in aging brain cells. *Nature*, **240**, 412-414.

Kinkade, J. M., and Cole, R. D. 1966. The resolution of four lysine-rich histones derived from calf thymus. *J. Biol. Chem.*, **241**, 5790-5797.

Klucis, E. S., and Lett, J. T. 1970. Zonal centrifugation of mammalian DNA. *Anal. Biochem.*, **35**, 480-488.

Kornberg, R. D. 1974. Chromatin structure: A repeating unit of histones and DNA. *Science*, **184**, 865-868.

Kornberg, R. D., and Thomas, J. O. 1974. Chromatin structure: Oligomers of histones. *Science*, **184**, 865-868.

Kurtz, D. I., and Sinex, F. M. 1967. Age related differences in the association of brain DNA and nuclear protein. *Biochim. Biophys. Acta*, **145**, 840-842.

Kurtz, D. I., Russell, A. P., and Sinex, F. M. 1974. Multiple peaks in the derivative melting curve of chromatin from animals of varying age. *Mech. Age. Dev.*, **3**, 37-49.

Lagercrantz, C. 1973. Trapping of radicals formed in the photochemical reaction between hydrogen peroxide and some pyrimidine bases, nucleosides, nucleotides and yeast nucleic acid. *J. Am. Chem. Soc.*, **95**, 220-225.

Lai, C. J., and Nathans, D. 1975. Cell mediated correction of mismatched bases in heteroduplex molecules of Simian Virus 40 DNA. *Federation Proc.* (abst.), 1663.

Lamb, M. J., and Maynard Smith, J. 1964. Radiation and aging in insects. *Exp. Geront.*, **1**, 11-20.

Leigh, E. F., Jr. 1973. The evolution of mutation rates. *Genetics*, **73**, Supp. 1-18.

Lett, J. T., Klucis, E. S., and Sun, C. 1970. On the size of the DNA in the mammalian chromosome. Structural subunits. *Biophys. J.*, **10**, 277-292.

Lewis, C. M., and Holliday, R. 1970. Mistranslation and aging in *Neurospora*. *Nature*, **228**, 877-880.

Lindahl, T., and Nyberg, B. 1972. Rate of depurination of native deoxyribonucleic acid. *Biochemistry*, **11**, 3610-3618.

Lindahl, T., and Nyberg, B. 1974. Heat-induced deamination of cytosine residues in deoxyribonucleic acid. *Biochemistry*, **13**, 3405-3410.

Loftfield, R. B., and Vanderjagt, D. 1972. The frequency of errors in protein biosynthesis. *Biochem. J.*, **128**, 1353-1356.

McCord, J. M., and Salin, M. L. 1975. Free radicals and inflammation: studies on superoxidemediated NBT reduction by leukocytes. *In*, G. J. Brewer (ed.), *Erythrocyte Structure and Function*. Vol. 1. New York: Liss.

Macieria-Coelho, A. 1973. Aging and cell division *Matrix. Biol.*, **1**, 46-77.

Medvedev, Z. 1972. Possible role of repeated nucleotide sequences in DNA in the evolution of life spans of differentiated cells. *Nature*, **237**, 453-454.

Meldefort, C. F., and Mehler, A. H. 1972. Deamidation *in vivo* of an asparagine residue of rabbit muscle aldolase. *Proc. Nat. Acad. Sci.*, **69**, 1816-1819.

Metzger-Freed, L. 1972. Effect of ploidy and mutagens on bromodeoxyuridine resistance in haploid and diploid frog cells. *Nature New Biol.*, **235**, 245-246.

Mørch, E. T. 1941. *Chondrodystrophic Dwarfs in Denmark*, Opera ex Domo Biologiae Hereditariae Humanae Universitatis Hafniensis, Vol. 3. Copenhagen: Munksguard.

Niinikoski, J., Heughan, C., and Hunt, T. K. 1973a. Oxygen tensions in the aortic wall of normal rabbits. *Atherosclerosis*, **17**, 353-359.

Niinikoski, J., Heughan, C., and Hunt, T. K. 1973b. Transmural oxygen tensions in the wall of the inferior vena cava. *Acta Chir. Scand.*, **139**, 34-36.

Oliveira, R. J., and Pfuderer, P. 1973. Test for missynthesis of lactate dehydrogenase in aging mice by use of a monospecific antibody. *Exp. Geront.*, **8**, 193-198.

O'Meara, A. R., and Herrmann, R. L. 1972. A modified mouse liver chromatin preparation displaying age-related differences in salt dissociation and template ability. *Biochim. Biophys. Acta*, **269**, 419-427.

Orgel, L. E. 1973. Aging of clones of mammalian cells. *Nature*, **243**, 441-445.

Oshino, N., Chance, B., Seis, H., and Bucher, T. 1973. The role of H_2O_2 generation in perfused rat liver and the reaction of catalase compound with hydrogen doners. *Arch. Biochem. Biophys.*, **154**, 117.

Painter, R. B., and Young, B. R. 1972. Repair replication in mammalian cells after x irradiation. *Mutation Res.*, **14**, 225-235.

Palmer, W. G., and Papaconstantinou, J. 1969. Aging of γ-crystalins during development of the lens. Proc. Nat. Acad. Sci., **64**, 404-410.

Panyim, S., Bilek, D., and Chalkley, R. 1971. An electrophoretic comparison of vertebrate histones. *J. Biol. Chem.*, **246**, 4206-4215.

Pelc, S. R. 1965. Renewal of DNA in non-dividing cells and aging. *Exp. Geront.*, **1**, 215-221.

Penrose, L. S., and Smith, G. F. 1966. *Downs Anomaly*. Boston: Little, Brown.

Price, G. B., Modak, S. P., and Makinodan, T. 1971. Age-associated changes in the DNA of mouse tissues. *Science*, **171**, 917-920.

Regan, J. D., Setlow, R. B., and Ley, R. D. 1971. Normal and defective repair of damaged DNA in human cells. A sensitive assay utilizing the photolysis of bromodeoxyuridine. *Proc. Nat. Acad. Sci.*, **68**, 708.

Reiss, U., and Rothstein, M. 1974. Isocitrate lyase from the free-living nematode *Turbatrix aceti:* Purification and properties. *Biochemistry*, **13**, 1796-1800.

Robinson, A. B. 1974. Evaluation and the distribution of glutaminyl and asparaginyl residues in proteins. *Proc. Nat. Acad. Sci.*, **71**, 885-888.

Robinson, A. B., McKerrow, J. H., and Cary, P. 1970. Controlled deamidation of peptides and proteins. An experimental hazard and a possible biological dimer. *Proc. Nat. Acad. Sci.*, **66**, 753-757.

Sacher, G. A. 1968. Molecular versus systemic theories on the genesis of aging. *Exp. Geront.*, **3**, 265-271.

Sadgofsal, A., and Bonner, J. 1969. The relationship between histone and DNA synthesis in HeLa cells. *Biochim. Biophys. Acta*, **186**, 349-357.

Salser, J. S., and Baylis, M. E. 1972. Alterations in deoxyribonucleic acid bound amino acids with age and sex. *J. Geront.*, **27**, 1-9.

Saunders, J. W., Jr., 1966. Death in embryonic systems. *Science*, **154**, 604-612.

Sheridan, R. E., O'Donnell, C. M., and Pautler, E. L. 1973. The determination of submicrogram quantities of DNA by phosphorescence analysis. *Anal. Biochem.*, **52**, 657.

Shin, S. 1974. Nature of mutations conferring resistance to 8-azaguanine in mouse cell lines. *J. Cell Sci.*, **14**, 235-251.

Sinex, F. M. 1960. Aging and the lability of irreplaceable molecules. II Amide Groups of collagen. *J. Geront.*, **15**, 15-18.

Sinex, F. M. 1974. The mutation theory of aging. In, Morris Rockstein (ed.), *Theoretical Aspects of Aging*. New York: Academic Press.

Stern, C. 1973. *Principles of Human Genetics*. 3rd ed. San Francisco: W. H. Freeman.

Straus, B. S. 1974. Repair of DNA in mammalian cells. *Life Sci.*, **15**, 1685.

Strehler, B., and Johnson, R. 1972. A 30 percent decrease in DNA dosage during aging of dog brain. *Federation Proc.*, **31**, A910.

Strehler, B., Hirsch, G., Gusseck, D., Johnson, R., and Bick, M. 1971. Codon restriction theory of aging and development. *J. Theoret. Biol.* **33**, 429-474.

Szilard, L. 1959. On the nature of the aging process. *Proc. Nat. Acad. Sci.*, **45**, 30-45.

Teoule, R., and Cadet, J. 1974. Influence of the pH in the ·OH radical attached on the pyrimidic ring. *Z. Naturforsh.*, **29c**, 645-646.

Tsanev, R., and Sendov, B. L. 1971. Possible molecular mechanisms for cell differentiation in multicellular organisms. *J. Theoret. Biol.*, **30**, 337-393.

Upton, A. C. 1957. Ionizing radiation and the aging process, A review. *J. Geront.*, **12**, 306-313.

Vanyushin, B. F., Nemirovsky, L. E., Kilminko, V. V., Vasilev, V. K., and Beloyersky, A. N. 1973. The 5-methylcytosine in DNA of rats, tissue and age specificity and the change induced by hydrocortisone and other agents. *Gerontologia*, **19**, 138.

Van Zeeland, A. A., Van Diggelen, M. C. E., and Simons, J. W. I. M. 1972. The role of metabolic cooperation in selection of hypoxanthine-guanine-phosphoribosyl-transferase (HGPRT) deficient mutants from diploid mammalian cell strains. *Mutation Res.*, **14**, 355–363.

Verly, W. G., and Paquette, Y. 1973. An endonuclease for depurinated DNA in rat liver. *Can. J. Biochem.*, **51**, 1003.

Verly, W. G., Paquette, Y., and Thibodeau, L. 1973. Nuclease for DNA apurinic sites may be involved in the maintenance of DNA in normal cells. *Nature New Biol.*, **244**, 67–69.

Vogel, F. 1963. Mutations in man. *In,* S. J. Gierts (ed.), *Genetics Today, Proc. XI. Int. Cong. Genetics,* The Hague, Oxford: Pergamon Press.

Von Hippel, P. H., and McGhee, J. D. 1972. DNA protein interaction. *Ann. Rev. Biochem.*, **41**, 231–300.

Watson, J. D. 1965. *The Molecular Biology of the Gene.* 1st ed. New York: W. A. Benjamin.

Weintraub, H. 1972. A possible role for histone in the synthesis of DNA. *Nature*, **240**, 449–453.

Weintraub, H., and Van Lente, F. 1974. Dissection of chromosome structure with trypsin and nucleases. *Proc. Nat. Acad. Sci.*, **71**, 4249–4253.

Wheeler, K. T., and Lett, J. T. 1972. Formation and rejoining of DNA strand breaks in irradiated neurons, *in vivo. Radiation Res.*, **52**, 59-67.

Woolhouse, H. W. (ed.) 1967. *Symposia of the Society for Experimental Biology: Aspects of the Biology of Ageing,* Vol. XXI, New York: Academic Press.

Wright, B. 1966. Multiple causes and controls in differentation. *Science*, **153**, 830–837.

Zeelon, P., Gershon, J., and Gershon, D. 1972. Inactive enzyme molecules in aging organisms. Nematode-fructose-1, 6-diphosphate aldolase. *Biochemistry*, **12**, 1743-1750.

Zhelabov, S. M., and Berdyshev, G. D. 1972. Composition, template activity and thermostability of the liver chromatin in rats of various ages. *Exp. Geront.*, **7**, 313-320.

3
MACROMOLECULAR METABOLISM DURING AGING

Richard C. Adelman[*]
Temple University School of Medicine

INTRODUCTION

Alterations in the regulation of macromolecular metabolism during aging now are well recognized in the areas of DNA, RNA, and protein. These apparent biochemical manifestations of senescence were detected as alterations in physical properties of macromolecules, such as electrophoretic and chromatographic mobility, susceptibility to heat denaturation, structural resiliency, and binding to other molecules; in intrinsic biological properties of macromolecules, such as enzymatic activity; in the magnitude and time course of stimulated rates of macromolecular synthesis and/or degradation; etc. Unfortunately, the overwhelming majority of these studies have not progressed beyond the stage of phenomenology followed, in many instances, by premature theorization. For example, it is not unfair to suggest that at one time or another each of the types of alterations mentioned immediately above probably were attributed, based on no conclusive experimental evidence, to either deficiencies in gene expression or the accumulation of free radicals. This purposely provocative remark is in no way intended to demean the potential

*Established Investigator of the American Heart Association. Support by the following research grants from the NIH also is gratefully acknowledged: AG-00431, AG-00368, CA-12227 and RR-05417.

importance of specific research interests to the eventual comprehension of underlying mechanisms of biological aging. Its intent, along with the following pages of this article, is to encourage a long overdue mechanistic approach in the research laboratory.

By far the most prolific topic within the framework of macromolecular metabolism and aging is the regulation of enzyme activity. Therefore, the phenomenology of this topic will be reviewed in depth followed by discussion of potential mechanisms. Finally, selected examples of previously reported, age-dependent modifications in the general metabolic schemes of protein, RNA, and DNA will be presented in capsular form.

REGULATION OF ENZYME ACTIVITY

Levels of Enzyme Activity

More than 1,000 publications describe the measurement of more than 100 different enzyme activities as a function of lifespan in various tissues from many different species, as reviewed elsewhere (Freeman, 1974). Numerous reviewers cited in the historical section of that dissertation attempted to identify trends of changing enzyme activity based on tissue location, metabolic function, etc. Perhaps the best documentation of the overwhelming difficulties of drawing general conclusions from such studies was presented recently by Finch (1972). Clearly, direct comparison of the various reports is hampered by species and strain variations, ages of the animals and the conditions of their environmental maintenance, innate characteristics of the enzymes themselves during seasonal and diurnal variations, and in many cases, the methodology employed. In any event, from an overall perspective, these reviews suggest generally that aging has no catastrophic effects on steady-state levels of enzymes.

Aberrant Behavior of Enzyme Molecules

The most convincing evidence supporting the accumulation of aberrantly behaving enzyme molecules during aging is the report in which a mono-specific antibody prepared against homogeneous mouse liver aldolase precipitates approximately half as much aldolase activity from liver extracts of 31-month-old mice as from 3-month-old mice (Gershon and Gershon, 1973). However, another report of similar quality suggests that the phenomenon probably cannot be regarded as universal in its occurrence. Oliveira and Pfuderer (1973) reported that a mono-specific antibody prepared against commercially supplied lactate dehydrogenase from pig muscle inactivates the same amount of lactate dehydrogenase activity in liver extracts from male and female mice aged approximately 2, 20, and 45 months. One hypothetical explanation for these differences, which apparently has avoided consideration, is that only antibodies prepared against enzyme isolated from the particular species and/or strain of animals to be monitored are capable of recognizing an extremely subtle age-dependent modification of protein structure. Indeed, in passing, consideration also might be given to the possibility that the structural modification results in enhanced antigenicity and/or impaired catalytic function. Furthermore, there is no logical reason to exclude the possibility that, for at least certain enzymes, age-dependent differences may be detectable only in regulatory behavior involving interactions between effectors and geographical sites other than those portions of the enzyme that are respon-

sible for characteristic values of K_m and V_{max}. Other types of examples of the age-dependent accumulation of aberrantly behaving protein molecules include: altered heat lability of glutathione reductase activity obtained *post mortem* from human lenses; changes in electrophoretic behavior of hexokinase isoenzymes, and in physical properties of glucose 6-phosphate dehydrogenase from aging human erythrocytes; etc., as reviewed by Freeman (1974). Similar conclusions in support of the accumulation of altered protein molecules also were obtained using serially cultured normal human fibroblasts as a cellular model of senescence (Freeman, 1974).

Protein Missynthesis

The mechanisms by which altered proteins may accumulate during aging include changes in amino acid sequence and/or in posttranslational reactions. A theoretical basis for the accumulation of missynthesized protein during aging was proposed by Orgel (1963). He predicted that random protein missynthesis, initially a low frequency event, could result in a gradual accumulation of protein errors with age. Errors in various enzymes of the protein-synthesizing apparatus would be self-propagating and could eventually lead to an error catastrophe that would be lethal to the cell. He has since corrected his original contention regarding the inevitability of the error catastrophe (Orgel, 1970). However, his "elementary protein error theory" (Orgel, 1973) remains one of the more fashionable notions proposed to account for biological aging. More recently, the concept itself was taken to task by Hoffman (1974) who points out the likelihood that translation may be at least one order of magnitude more accurate than would be necessary for stability. Furthermore, the fidelity of viral replication and subsequent translation of viral genetic information, such as specific replicase (Holland, Kohne and Doyle, 1973) and electrophoretically distinguishable viral proteins (Tomkins, Stanbridge, and Hayflick, 1974), following infection of early and late passage human fibroblasts are not in accord with generalized translational error during cellular senescence *in vitro*. Consequences of similar tissue-specific viral infection *in vivo*, of hosts of different ages, are not yet known. On the other hand, some type of structural modification is evident in a specific polypeptide generated by cyanogen bromide cleavage of liver aldolase from aging rabbits (Anderson, 1974). This type of approach, although not yet sufficiently conclusive to define the nature of the structural modification, is to be applauded. The fact still remains that sequence analysis of a homogeneous polypeptide is prerequisite to the conclusive demonstration of the absence or presence of protein missynthesis. Whether or not it will be possible to distinguish between synthetic error and genetic variance remains to be seen.

Posttranslational Reactions

The recognized abundant occurrence of an extremely diverse spectrum of posttranslational reactions provides potential explanations, that are *at the very least* as plausible as the concept of protein missynthesis, for the age-dependent accumulation of altered enzymes. It is far beyond the scope of this article to attempt to review the nature of posttranslational reactions. Therefore, only select examples will be chosen for brief discussion in order to demonstrate the fantastic potentiality for relevance to gerontological research; a potentiality which, thus far, has been all but totally ignored.

Selective Proteolysis. Limited proteolytic degradations are responsible for the induction of biological activity in such diverse reactions as the formation of proteolytic enzymes and polypeptide hormones from their inactive precursors, the clotting of blood and milk, perhaps albumin and collagen formation, etc. A particularly illustrative example of potential relevance to gerontology is the conversion of proinsulin to insulin. This enzyme-catalyzed extraction of a specific amino acid sequence by multiple proteolysis of the single polypeptide chain of proinsulin generates the characteristic insulin structure of two polypeptide chains that are connected by disulfide bonds (Steiner, Hallund, Rubenstein, Cho, and Bayliss, 1968). More to the point, whereas insulin and pro-

insulin are similar antigenically, proinsulin is far less effective as a hormone (Rubenstein and Steiner, 1971). Therefore, any physiological situation which results in the impaired conversion of proinsulin to insulin and the subsequent secretion of abnormally large amounts of proinsulin into the circulation would bring about the following: (1) modified reactivity of insulin-sensitive physiological systems; (2) very little difference, if any, in the *apparent* amount of circulating insulin as determined by the routinely employed radioimmunoassay; and (3) isolated insulin preparations which exhibit a decreased ratio of hormonal to immunological reactivity (reminiscent of the results of Gershon and Gershon (1973), as described above).

Two recent articles should dramatize the potential importance of this concept even further. The first report (Krieger, 1974) concerns a human patient afflicted with rapidly progressive Cushing's syndrome associated with clinical and laboratory evidence of hypothyroidism and hypoadrenalism. Immunoassayable plasma ACTH and TSH levels were elevated, but there was adequate end organ responsiveness to exogenous ACTH and TSH. Plasma ACTH levels exhibited normal circadian variation and responded markedly to insulin-induced hypoglycemia, with no associated change in plasma cortisol levels. Plasma TSH levels increased following TRH administration, with no change in serum T_3 levels. Bioassay demonstrated markedly diminished levels of ACTH and absent TSH, indicating that the target organ deficiencies were secondary to lack of stimulation by biologically active hormone. Trypsinization of the patient's plasma resulted in levels of bioassayable ACTH that were equivalent to those obtained by immunoassay, suggesting conversion of biologically inactive, "big" ACTH (Yalow and Berson, 1971) to "little" ACTH. The second report (Singh, Seavey, Rice, Lindsey, and Lewis, 1974) demonstrates that human growth hormone, isolated from pituitary extracts, exists in several forms which represent the degradation products of specific proteases. Whereas the various forms are indistinguishable from intact growth hormone by radioimmunoassay, the most biologically active form is not the intact hormone.

General Proteolysis. Total cellular regulation of enzyme levels includes not only their synthesis, but also their subsequent removal when no longer required, either as a result of altered physiological status or as a part of a developmental sequence (Schimke, Ganschow, Doyle, and Arias, 1968). Vital to the comprehension of protein turnover is thorough evaluation of the protein-degrading system which may consist of lysosomes, neutral proteases, or specific inactivating enzymes, as well as the nature of the protein substrate as discussed both above and below. Clearly, a defect at any stage in the inactivation and/or degrading machinery conceivably could result in the accumulation of degradative intermediates of enzymes which retain all, part, or none of the physical and/or biological properties characteristic of the native state. For example, trypsin digestion of insulin splits lysylalanine and arginylglycine bonds in the B chain, generating free alanine, a heptapeptide, and a desoctapeptide-insulin which is devoid of hormonal activity although still antigenically active (Humbel, Bosshard, and Zahn, 1972). Appropriate characterization of homogeneous preparations of enzymes or other proteins isolated from animals of different ages has not yet been accomplished.

Modification Reactions Involving Specific Amino Acid Sidechains. The catalytic activity of many enzymes is susceptible to physiological modulation exerted *in vivo* by both enzyme-catalyzed and nonenzymatic covalent modification of the active functional groups of specific amino acid residues. Recognized modification reactions include phosphorylation, methylation, deamidation, acylation, hydroxylation, adenylation, glycosylation, sulfation, peroxidation, cross-linking reactions, etc. Each of these types of reactions is capable of modifying specific sites on a broad spectrum of proteins localized within virtually any cell population of any tissue. For example, sites of methylation, mechanisms of methyl group transfer, and implications of the structural and functional modifications of target proteins were reviewed by Paik and Kim (1971, 1975).

A given modification reaction can virtually abolish the activity of an enzyme molecule,

thereby switching off entire metabolic pathways. For example, epinephrine-induced degradation of glycogen to glucose 1-phosphate in mammalian skeletal muscle is catalyzed in part by the enzyme, phosphorylase (Krebs and Fischer, 1962). The muscle enzyme is a tetramer, composed of four identical subunits. Each of these subunits contains one serine residue which must be esterified to orthophosphate in order to demonstrate full enzyme activity. When the phosphate of the phosphoserines is hydrolyzed under the influence of the specific enzyme, phosphorylase phosphatase, phosphorylase disaggregates into dimers which are inactive, although activity is partially recovered in the presence of cAMP. The physiological mechanism for activation of phosphorylase involves phosphorylation of the four serine residues by four molecules of ATP in the presence of the specific enzyme, phosphorylase kinase.

Nonenzymatic, sequence-controlled modification reactions, such as the deamidation of glutaminyl and asparaginyl residues, were proposed to serve as a general molecular timer of protein turnover and organismic development and aging (Robinson, McKerrow, and Cary, 1970; McKerrow and Robinson, 1974). This suggestion is particularly intriguing in view of the earlier observations that an age-dependent heterogeneity in rabbit muscle aldolase resulted specifically from deamidation of the asparaginyl residue that is the fourth residue from the carboxyl end of the protein (Koida, Lai, and Horecker, 1969; Lai, Chen, and Horecker, 1970).

It seems appropriate at this point to reemphasize that nearly all types of posttranslational reactions have been almost totally ignored by gerontological research.

Enzyme Adaptation

The ability to initiate adaptive increases in the activity of a large number of enzymes is impaired during aging when examined in a variety of tissues from several different species in response to a broad spectrum of environmental stimuli, as reviewed previously (Adelman, 1970a, 1971, 1972, 1973, 1975a, 1975b, and

1976; Adelman, Freeman, and Cohen, 1972). These age-dependent modifications of enzyme adaptation were expressed as changes in the time course and/or magnitude of response, as illustrated generally in Figure 1, and are susceptible to variation related to differences in sex, strain, species, and conditions of environmental maintenance. Indeed, it still is not generally recognized that reproducibility of

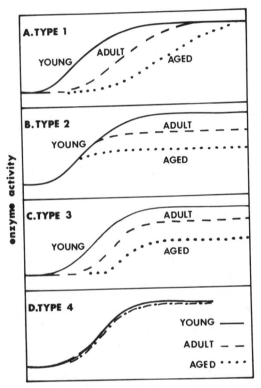

time following administration of stimulus

Figure 1. Patterns of age-dependent enzyme adaptation. The four major categories of effects of aging on the time course and magnitude of a hypothetical adaptive change in enzyme activity are illustrated generally. For the sake of convenience identical basal levels of enzyme activity are presented at the three indicated ages, changes in magnitude are presented as increases, and temporal modifications are presented as delays. Specific examples of each category may be found as follows: Type 1 (Adelman, 1970b); Type 2 (Rahman and Peraino, 1973); Type 3 (Roth *et al.*, 1974b); and Type 4 (Adelman and Freeman, 1972). (From Adelman, R. C. 1975. Disruptions in enzyme regulation during aging. *In*, D. V. Parke (ed.), *Enzyme Induction*, pp. 303-311. London: Plenum Press.)

this type of biochemical data, as well as of life span and pathology studies, is absolutely dependent upon the choice, source, and maintenance of the experimental animal model. At least until pending publications on this subject are completed, interested investigators should address their inquiries to Dr. Donald Gibson, National Institue on Aging, Landow Building, Bethesda, Maryland 20014.

The most thoroughly studied group of those enzyme adaptations which are impaired during aging are those whose initiation times, i.e., adaptive latent periods, are progressively delayed as male Sprague-Dawley CD rats age from 2 to 24 months. These rats were maintained throughout their lifetime at the Charles River Breeding Laboratories under as nearly constant environmental and genetic conditions as possible and are virtually free of detectable pathology up to nearly 2 years of age. The liver enzyme adaptations include the increases in activity of glucokinase and tyrosine aminotransferase following administration, respectively, of glucose and ACTH (Adelman, 1970a, 1970b, 1971). We observed a similarly impaired adaptive increase in microsomal NADPH: cytochrome c reductase activity following phenobarbitol treatment in male Sprague-Dawley rats (obtained from A.R. Schmidt). In each case, more time is required to adapt to the same degree as the rats increase in age. Indeed, for the adaptations of glucokinase and NADPH: cytochrome c reductase, the duration of the adaptive latent periods increases progressively and is directly proportional to chronological age between 2 and at least 24 months (Adelman, 1970a).

The immediate essential question in approaching the mechanism of these age-dependent modifications in liver enzyme regulation entails determination of whether or not the changes are intrinsic to liver. This was investigated in three different manners. (1) Adaptive responsiveness of hepatic glucokinase activity to administration of glucose *in vivo* was compared in fully regenerated livers following partial hepatectomy and in surgically untreated rats of corresponding ages (Adelman, 1970c). Between 2 and 24 months of age, such replacement of a substantial portion of the liver cell population had no effect on either the time course or the magnitude of the glucokinase adaptation. Unfortunately, there is no obvious way of distinguishing between two alternative interpretations of these results. On the one hand, age-dependent changes in liver enzyme adaptation may be the consequence of genetic alterations which are copied during the cell proliferation that accompanies the regenerative process. On the other hand, impaired liver enzyme adaptation may reflect alterations in the availability or effectiveness of crucial extrahepatic factors, e.g., neural or hormonal regulatory mechanism, etc. (2) Adaptive responsiveness of hepatic glucokinase activity to administration of glucose *in vivo* also was examined in parabiotic partnerships of 2-month to 24-month-old rats (Adelman, 1972). Both the time course and the magnitude of the glucokinase adaptation were identical in parabiosed and untreated rats of corresponding ages. These results are consistent with the absence of any age-dependent influence of humoral factors on liver enzyme adaptation, unless the rate of turnover of any such crucial factors in rats of different ages differs significantly from the rate of parabiotic exchange. (3) The third method of attempting to localize the age-dependent lesion of liver enzyme adaptation entailed the following: (a) elucidation of at least certain hormones whose presence is crucial to the adaptive regulation of liver enzyme activity *in vivo*; and (b) assessment of the ability of liver in rats of different ages to increase enzyme activity in response to injection of these hormones. For example, increases both in glucokinase activity following administration of glucose and also in tyrosine aminotransferase activity following administration of ACTH require the presence of at least insulin and corticosterone (Adelman and Freeman, 1972), each of which interact with liver directly. Adaptive increases both in glucokinase activity following injection of insulin and also in tyrosine aminotransferase activity following injection of glucocorticoids, insulin, or glucogan are identical in time course and magnitude of response during aging (Finch, Foster, and Mirsky, 1969; Adelman and Freeman, 1972). Furthermore, the binding affinity and number of binding

sites with respect to glucocorticoids and their hepatic cytoplasmic binding proteins and to insulin and its receptors on the hepatic plasma membrane apparently do not change after 12 months of age (Freeman, Karoly, and Adelman, 1973; Roth, 1974). Thus, it was tempting to conclude that the capability of liver to increase enzyme activity in response to direct hormonal stimulation does not deteriorate during aging; in which case impairments in the availability and/or effectiveness of crucial intermediary hormones must assume an added potential importance.

However, such a conclusion also is not without its difficulties. As indicated orginally by Finch (1969) for mouse liver tyrosine aminotransferase, and more recently by this laboratory (Britton, Britton, Rotenberg, Freeman, and Adelman, 1974) for glucokinase and tyrosine aminotransferase in rat liver, the *minimal* amount of corticosterone or insulin required by injection in order to initiate adaptive increases in the activities of hepatic glucokinase and tyrosine aminotransferase still generates blood hormone levels that are much greater than could be considered physiological. What everyone thus far has failed to appreciate is the possibility that extremely high concentrations of hormones may overwhelm the hormone receptor systems, the hepatocellular protein-synthesizing machinery, etc. Therefore, certain age-dependent changes in hepatic responsiveness may be detectable only in the face of more physiological amounts of hormone, such as those generated *in vivo* in response to administration of ACTH or glucose.

It should be evident that one fundamental, unresolved issue in this *and all other* areas of *in vivo* gerontological research relates to the localization of the origin of any observed lesion of aging, irrespective of the tissue in which the original experimental observation was noted. Moreover, assuming that such a tissue of major responsibility can be determined, a number of yet unapproached difficulties still remain. For example, suppose that the age-dependent modifications in liver enzyme adaptation are, indeed, intrinsic to liver. What is the cellular capacity of the individual hepatocyte to increase enzyme activity in response to direct hormonal stimulation? How many of those cells which comprise the entire liver actually respond in rats of different ages? Do subpopulations of hepatocytes emerge as rats age beyond maturity?

Finally, in concluding this section of the present article, it seems appropriate to emphasize the potential significance of this type of experimental approach to the eventual comprehension of underlying mechanisms of biological aging. Living systems depend on adaptive regulation, deterioration of which would lead eventually to death. Incidence of most diseases increases with increasing age. This suggests that progressive impairment of adaptive response is associated with many illnesses and decrements in performance which are common to advanced age. One biochemical expression of this impairment is the age-dependent inability to initiate certain enzyme inductions following administration of the appropriate stimulus. Such a biochemical parameter of aging may provide a unique opportunity to determine a sequence of events responsible for at least certain phenomena of aging.

GENERAL METABOLISM OF DNA, RNA, AND PROTEIN (SELECTED EXAMPLES)

This area of gerontological research is terribly difficult to evaluate and to present in a rational manner. The difficulties described above relevant to investigations of steady-state enzyme levels during aging of intact organisms also are applicable here. That is to say, there is little constancy from laboratory to laboratory regarding either species, strain, sex, and environmental maintenance of the experimental animal model, or the methodology employed, or the results obtained. Therefore, in order to illustrate a few of those areas which seem to radiate the most promise, and at the same time to avoid repetition of material covered elsewhere in this book in chapters by Baserga and Sinex, I have selected for discussion only those examples indicated below. Those readers who consequently gain the impression that unmentioned subject matter desperately awaits proper

experimental exploitation are correct for all intents and purposes.

Metabolism of Collagen

With increasing animal age, collagen fiber stability becomes increasingly more pronounced when subjected to physiochemical tests, e.g., thermal denaturation and swelling and solubilization with various solvents (as reviewed by Fujii and Tanzer, 1974). These altered properties during collagen maturation may be related to the total number and chemical nature of the covalent intermolecular cross-links of collagen (Bailey, Robins, and Balian, 1974). Over a wide range of ages, apparently no new compounds are formed other than hexosyllysine derivatives, at least with regard to reducible components. Variations with age in the proportion of reducible cross-links parallel the rate of growth (Robins, Shimokamaki, and Bailey, 1973). Thus, the initial rapid rise in their amounts during the deposition of new collagen is followed by a gradual decrease. At maturity, the reducible cross-links are virtually absent. In order to account for increasing insolubility in the face of retained tensile strength, it was proposed that reducible cross-links represent intermediates which are converted into a nonreducible, more stable form during the maturation process. Therefore, it is no longer necessary to propose a continuous increase in the number of cross-links during aging, a notion for which no conclusive evidence exists. Of course, the nature of the stable cross-links present in the insoluble mature tissue remains to be completely elucidated.

Methylation of tRNA

Catalytic activity of glycine methyltransferase increases significantly in the organs of rodents during postnatal development and aging (Mays, Borek, and Finch, 1973). It was suggested that such a finding may indicate restricted activity of tRNA methyltransferases in aging animals, possibly accompanied by deficiencies in the modification of tRNA populations. Indeed, several earlier reports also indicate both qualitative and quantitative changes in isoaccepting species of various tRNAs (as reviewed by Hoffman and McCoy, 1974). Clearly, implications with respect to the functioning of tRNA both in protein synthesis and in transcriptional control are far-reaching.

On the other hand, it also was reported that no alterations occur in the total population of tRNAs in aging mouse liver and mosquitoes (Hoffman and McCoy, 1974). The conclusion of this report was that tRNA-modifying enzymes may have no significant role in biological aging. As a consequence, an intriguing discussion ensued between Borek (1974) and Hoffman (1974) concerning, among other things, the relative potential importance of analyzing gross versus specific populations of modified tRNAs. Borek maintains that a deficiency in one modified nucleoside in one regulatory tRNA can have profound physiological effects; thus, analysis of those tRNAs with altered chromatographic profiles are most important, and not the mass of total tRNAs in a crude preparation. Hoffman concurs with the documented physiological significance of single nucleosides in individual tRNA molecules but, in contrast, contends that an observed deficiency due to altered activity of a tRNA-modifying enzyme should be reflected in all those tRNAs which are substrates for that enzyme. Thus, he continues, analysis of nucleoside composition of total tRNA would indicate a significant deficit in one compartment.

Potential Role of Hormones in Age-Dependent Regulation of Nucleic Acid Metabolism

The impaired ability to stimulate DNA synthesis, mitosis, and cell proliferation during aging is well recognized in a broad variety of experimental systems, including mouse antibody-forming cells *in vivo* (Makinodan, Perkins, and Chen, 1971), mouse mammary gland epithelial cells following serial transplantation (Daniel, 1972), human fibroblasts *in vitro* (Cristofalo, 1972), and rodent salivary glands *in vivo* (Adelman, Stein, Roth, and Englander, 1972). In the latter case, the time required to initiate DNA synthesis increases progressively from 18 to 54 hours as Sprague-Dawley male rats age from 2 to 24 months, and proliferative

capacity appears to be abolished. Age-dependent biochemical markers which precede chronologically the initiation of DNA synthesis include delays in adaptive increases in the activities of thymidine kinase and deoxythymidylate synthetase, and in the appearance of crucial RNA species (Roth, Karoly, Britton, and Adelman, 1974b). The initial age-dependent modification apparently is related to either the synthesis or extranuclear transport of the crucial RNA species, or to an early biochemical action of the mitogen, isoproterenol (Roth and Adelman, 1973), distinct from its membrane-receptor binding. The significance of age-dependent changes in chromatin template activity and in binding of nuclear proteins to DNA is uncertain (Stein, Wang, and Adelman, 1973).

Administration of physiological amounts of glucocorticoid hormones both delays the onset and reduces the magnitude of stimulated DNA synthesis in salivary gland of 2-month-old rats, and also abolishes proliferative capacity in a manner remarkably similar to the effects produced by aging (Roth, Karoly, Adelman, and Adelman, 1974a; Roth and Adelman, 1974). Inhibitory action of the glucocorticoids also is related to the delayed appearance of RNA species required for DNA synthesis. That DNA synthesis may be regulated *in vivo* in this system by endogenous glucocorticoids is suggested by the following: (1) acceleration and increased magnitude of stimulated DNA synthesis in adrenalectomized rats; (2) specific binding of ^{3}H-glucocorticoids to macromolecules derived from cytoplasmic extracts of salivary gland; and (3) reduced uptake of ^{3}H-glucocorticoids following injection of mitogen. Whether age-dependent impairments in RNA and DNA synthesis and cell proliferation *in vivo* actually are attributable to changes in the action and/or availability of glucocorticoid and other hormones remains to be determined.

CONCLUDING REMARKS

An elderly rat, having escaped from even the best of animal facilities, upon madly dashing across the nearby busy thoroughfare, is far less likely to avoid oncoming traffic than its younger counterpart. From the time of emergence of sufficient technological ingenuity required for the need for such a thoroughfare, it probably was appreciated by some that survival of the aged escapee depended upon at least the following: extent of decline in the rat's muscular strength, cardiovascular and respiratory efficiency, sensory perception, etc.; suicidal tendencies of the rat; agility and/or homicidal tendencies of the nearest vehicle operators; and weather conditions. Today, in far more sophisticated times, we also know that the trauma of such a situation will not be expressed as well in the aged rodent when recorded as the cascade of neuroendocrine events which culminate, at least in part, in an enhanced rate of *de novo* synthesis of specific hepatic gene products.

In which specific cell population(s) of which particular tissue(s) is localized the origin of any phenomenon that characterizes an aging organism?

What are the effects of aging on the functional capability of the crucial cell population(s)?

What is the biochemical basis of the modification?

At what age in the life span is the modification first expressed?

What is the nature and origin of molecular events responsible for its emergence?

In what ways does expression of such events relate to the potential vigor and maximal life span of the individual, its species, and other species?

Can these events be tampered with?

At what cost?

REFERENCES

Adelman, R. C. 1970a. Reappraisal of biological aging. *Nature*, 228, 1095-1096.

Adelman, R. C. 1970b. An age-dependent modification of enzyme regulation. *J. Biol. Chem.*, 245, 1032-1035.

Adelman, R. C. 1970c. The independence of cell division and age-dependent modification of enzyme induction. *Biochem. Biophys. Res. Commun.*, 38, 1149-1153.

Adelman, R. C. 1971. Age-dependent effects in enzyme induction—a biochemical expression of aging. *Exp. Geront.*, 6, 75-87.

Adelman, R. C. 1972. Age-dependent control of enzyme adaptation. *Advan. Geront. Res.*, 4, 1-23.

Adelman, R. C. 1973. Hormonal regulation of macromolecular synthesis during aging. *In, Mecanismes du vieillissement moleculaire et cellulare*, pp. 141-152. Paris: Les Colloques de L'Institut National de la Sante et de la Recherche Medicale, Vol. 27.

Adelman, R. C. 1975a. Disruptions in enzyme regulation during aging. *In*, D. V. Parke (ed.), *Enzyme Induction*, pp. 303-311. London: Plenum Press.

Adelman, R. C. 1975b. Impaired hormonal regulation of enzyme activity during aging. *Federation Proc.*, 34, 179-182.

Adelman, R. C. 1976. Age-dependent hormonal regulation of mammalian gene expression. *In*, A. V. Everitt and J. A. Burgess (eds.), *Hypothalamus, Pituitary and Aging*. Springfield, Illinois: Charles C. Thomas, pp. 668-675.

Adelman, R. C., and Freeman, C. 1972. Age-dependent regulation of glucokinase and tyrosine aminotransferase activities of rat liver *in vivo* by adrenal, pancreatic and pituitary hormones. *Endocrinology*, 90, 1551-1560.

Adelman, R. C., Freeman, C., and Cohen, B. S. 1972. Enzyme adaptation as a biochemical probe of development and aging. *Advan. Enz. Reg.*, 10, 365-382.

Adelman, R. C., Stein, G., Roth, G. S., and Englander, D. 1972. Age-dependent regulation of mammalian DNA synthesis and cell proliferation *in vivo*. *Mech. Age. Dev.* 1, 49-59.

Anderson, P. J. 1974. Aging effects on the liver aldolase of rabbits. *Biochem. J.*, 140, 341-343.

Bailey, A. J., Robins, S. P., and Balian, G. 1974. Biological significance of the intermolecular cross-links of collagen. *Nature*, 251, 105-109.

Borek, E. 1974. tRNA and ageing. *Nature,* 251, 260.

Britton, G., Britton, V., Rotenberg, S., Freeman, C., and Adelman, R. C. 1974. Unpublished data.

Cristofalo, V. J. 1972. Animal cell cultures as a model system for the study of aging. *Adv. Geront. Res.*, 4, 45-79.

Daniel, C. W. 1972. Aging of cells during serial propagation *in vivo*. *Adv. Geront. Res.*, 4, 167-199.

Finch, C. E. 1969. Cellular activities during ageing in mammals. Ph.D. dissertation, pp. 141-144.

Finch, C. E. 1972. Enzyme activities, gene function and ageing in mammals. *Exp. Geront.*, 7, 53-67.

Finch, C. E., Foster, J. R., and Mirsky, A. E. 1969. Aging and the regulation of cell activities during exposure to cold. *J. Gen. Physiol.*, 54, 690-712.

Freeman, C. 1974. The effect of age on insulin-liver interaction. Ph.D. dissertation, pp. 2-9.

Freeman, C., Karoly, K., and Adelman, R. C. 1973. Impairments in availability of insulin to liver *in vivo* and in binding of insulin to purified hepatic plasma membrane during aging. *Biochem. Biophys. Res. Commun.*, 54, 1573-1580.

Fujii, K., and Tanzer, M. L. 1974. Age-related changes in the reducible crosslinks of human tendon collagen. *FEBS Letters*, 43, 300-302.

Gershon, H., and Gershon, D. 1973. Inactive enzyme molecules in aging mice: Liver aldolase. *Proc. Nat. Acad. Sci.,* **70,** 909–913.

Hoffman, G. W. 1974. On the origin of the genetic code and the stability of the translation apparatus. *J. Mol. Biol.,* **86,** 349–362.

Hoffman, J. L. 1974. tRNA and ageing. *Nature,* **251,** 260.

Hoffman, J. L., and McCoy, M. T. 1974. Stability of the nucleoside composition of tRNA during biological ageing of mice and mosquitoes. *Nature,* **249,** 558–559.

Holland, J. J., Kohne, D., and Doyle, M. V. 1973. Analysis of viral replication in ageing human fibroblasts. *Nature,* **245,** 316–318.

Humbel, R. E., Bosshard, H. R., and Zahn, H. 1972. Chemistry of insulin. *In,* D. F. Steiner and N. Freinkel (eds.), *Endocrine Pancreas,* pp. 111–132. Baltimore: Waverly Press.

Koida, M., Lai, C. Y., and Horecker, B. L. 1969. Subunit structure of rabbit muscle aldolase: Extent of homology of the α and β subunits and age-dependent changes in their ratio. *Arch. Biochem. Biophys.,* **134,** 623–631.

Krebs, E. G., and Fischer, E. H. 1962. Molecular properties and transformations of glycogen phosphorylase in animal tissues. *Advan. Enzymol.,* **24,** 263–290.

Krieger, D. T. 1974. Glandular end organ deficiency associated with secretion of biologically inactive pituitary peptides. *J. Clin. Endocrinol. Metab.,* **38,** 964–975.

Lai, C. Y., Chen, C., and Horecker, B. L. 1970. Primary structure of two COOH-terminal hexapeptides from rabbit muscle aldolase: A difference in the structure of the α and β subunits. *Biochem. Biophys. Res. Commun.,* **40,** 461–468.

McKerrow, J. H., and Robinson, A. B. 1974. Primary sequence dependence of the deamidation of rabbit muscle aldolase. *Science,* **183,** 85.

Makinodan, T., Perkins. E. H., and Chen, M. G. 1971. Immunological activity of the aged. *Advan. Geront. Res.,* **3,** 171–198.

Mays, L. L., Borek, E., and Finch, C. E. 1973. Glycine N-methyl-transferase is a regulatory enzyme which increases in ageing animals. *Nature,* **243,** 411–413.

Oliveira, R. J., and Pfuderer, P. 1973. Test for missynthesis of lactate dehydrogenase in aging mice by use of a monospecific antibody. *Exp. Geront.,* **8,** 193–198.

Orgel, L. E. 1963. The maintenance of the accuracy of protein synthesis and its relevance to aging. *Proc. Nat. Acad. Sci.,* **49,** 517–521.

Orgel, L. E. 1970. The maintenance of the accuracy of protein synthesis and its relevance to ageing: A correction. *Proc. Nat. Acad. Sci.,* **67,** 1476.

Orgel, L. E. 1973. Ageing of clones of mammalian cells. *Nature,* **244,** 441–445.

Paik, W. K., and Kim, S. 1971. Protein methylation. *Science,* **174,** 114–119.

Paik, W. K., and Kim, S. 1975. Protein methylation: Chemistry, enzymology and biological significance. *Advan. Enzymol.,* **42,** 227–286.

Rahman, Y. E., and Peraino, C. 1973. Effects of age on patterns of enzyme adaptation in male and female rats. *Exp. Geront.,* **8,** 93–100.

Robins, S. P., Shimokomaki, M., and Bailey, A. J. 1973. Chemistry of the collagen cross-links. *Biochem. J.,* **131,** 771–780.

Robinson, A. B., McKerrow, J. H., and Cary, P. 1970. Controlled deamidation of peptides and proteins: An experimental hazard and a possible biological timer. *Proc. Nat. Acad. Sci.,* **66,** 753–757.

Roth, G. S. 1974. Age-related changes in specific glucocorticoid binding by steroid-responsive tissues of the rat. *Endocrinology,* **94,** 82–90.

Roth, G. S., and Adelman, R. C. 1973. Possible changes in tissue sensitivity in the age-dependent stimulation of DNA synthesis *in vivo. J. Geront.,* **28,** 298–301.

Roth, G. S., and Adelman, R. C. 1974. Age-dependent regulation of mammalian DNA synthesis and cell division *in vivo* by glucocorticoids. *Exp. Geront.,* **9,** 27–31.

Roth, G. S., Karoly, K., Adelman, A., and Adelman, R. C. 1974a. Regulation of isoproterenol-stimulated DNA synthesis in rat salivary gland *in vivo* by adrenal glucocorticoids. *Exp. Geront.,* **9,** 13–26.

Roth, G. S., Karoly, K., Britton, V. J., and Adelman, R. C. 1974b. Age-dependent regulation of isoproterenol-stimulated DNA synthesis in rat salivary gland *in vivo. Exp. Geront.,* **9,** 1–11.

Rubenstein, A. H., and Steiner, D. F. 1971. Proinsulin. *Ann. Rev. Med.,* **23,** 1–18.

Schimke, R. T., Ganschow, R., Doyle, D., and Arias, I. M. 1968. Regulation of protein turnover in mammalian tissues. *Federation Proc.,* **27,** 1223–1230.

Singh, R. N. P., Seavey, B. K., Rice, V. P., Lindsey, T. T., and Lewis, V. J. 1974. Modified forms of human growth hormone with increased biological activities. *Endocrinology,* **94,** 883–891.

Stein, G. S., Wang, P. L., and Adelman, R. C. 1973. Age-dependent changes in the structure and function of mammalian chromatin. *Exp. Geront.,* **8,** 123–133.

Steiner, D. F., Hallund, O., Rubenstein, A. H., Cho, S., and Bayliss, C. 1968. Isolation and properties of proinsulin, intermediate forms, and other minor components from crystalline bovine insulin. *Diabetes,* **17,** 725–736.

Tomkins, G. A., Stanbridge, E. J., and Hayflick, L. 1974. Viral probes of aging in the human diploid cell strain WI-38. *Proc. Soc. Exp. Biol. Med.,* **146,** 385–390.

Yalow, R. S., and Berson, S. A. 1971. Size heterogeneity of immunoreactive human ACTH in plasma and extracts of pituitary glands and ACTH-producing thymoma. *Biochem. Biophys. Res. Commun.,* **49,** 439–445.

4
METABOLIC CHANGES AND THEIR SIGNIFICANCE IN AGING*

D. Rao Sanadi
Boston Biomedical Research Institute

CONTROL OF METABOLIC REACTIONS

General Aspects

The major pathways of intermediary metabolism in different organisms were essentially elucidated over a decade ago. From these studies it has become evident that the utilization of food material for the production of energy and for the build-up of tissues proceeds by essentially the same route in all organisms. Since then the interest has branched in two directions. One is the detailed study of the molecular mechanism of the enzymes catalyzing these reactions, using the methods of organic and physical chemistry (e.g., chemical kinetics, X-ray crystallography). Since the principles of these methods have been known for many decades and modern technology has speeded the analysis of the data, progress in understanding the mechanisms has been significant and fairly rapid. The second direction is the evaluation of the relative importance of the related metabolic pathways and how they are regulated in maintaining homeostasis in the living organism. We are barely beginning to recognize the variety of the control mechanisms that seem to operate in the regulation of each individual metabolic reaction and of overall metabolism, and the interplay of these several

*Some of the research reported in this article was supported by NIH grant PO1 HD 05970.

competing and interlocking pathways. Superimposed is the exquisite regulation by hormones on specific enzyme reactions and on complex phenomena such as transport across biological membranes. As more insight is gained into these regulatory processes, they should have a strong impact on research on complex biological phenomena such as cell differentiation, growth, and senescence, and may eventually yield information on the critical parameters governing them.

In this article, I shall attempt to outline the principles of metabolic regulation and mention a few relevant metabolic alterations occurring in senescent organisms. No attempt will be made to be comprehensive since much of the research has involved random assays of enzymes, which have been recently reviewed at length (Wilson, 1973; Finch, 1972).

The regulatory mechanisms can be divided broadly into two groups. One involves alteration of the concentration of *active* enzyme, and the other affects the *operation* (or activity) of the existing enzyme (kinetic factors). Some overlap between these mechanisms occurs in the regulatory enzymes which control overall metabolic processes.

Enzyme Concentration

Changes in the intracellular concentration of enzymes can be brought about in a variety of ways. Enzymes, and most other cell constituents, are known to be in a state of dynamic turnover, with continuous breakdown and resynthesis of the molecules as follows:

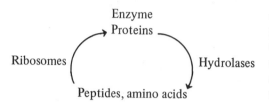

The steady-state concentration of the enzyme is determined by the balance between the two processes, both of which can be independently altered. The rate of enzyme synthesis can be altered by inducers and repressors (particularly in bacteria) which act at the level of the gene or mRNA (see reviews by Greengard, 1969; Schimke and Doyle, 1970). Although such gene involvement has been established in bacteria, little direct evidence is available in mammalian systems. Presumably, the action of some hormones involves similar mechanisms. Specific examples in mammalian systems are the induction of tyrosine transaminase (Kenney, 1962), glutamate-alanine transaminase (Segal and Kim, 1963), and serine dehydratase (Jost, Khairallah, and Pitot, 1968). Enhanced rates of enzyme synthesis (Greengard, 1969) accompany differentiation in mammals (e.g., in the fetus); however, it is difficult to be certain that enhancement is not due to the action of the hormones, which undergo concomitant changes. In fact, Wright (1973) claims that increased protein synthesis attributable directly to differentiation has not been unequivocally demonstrated, in spite of numerous claims.

Another mechanism, unrelated to protein synthesis, is the conversion of inactive proenzymes to active enzymes, as in the classical examples of trypsinogen. The activation of masked enzymes may also be an important control mechanism during differentiation (Daggs and Halcro-Wardlaw, 1933; Epel, Waver, Muchmore and Schimke, 1969; Mayer and Shain, 1968; Tatibana and Cohen, 1965).

Reliable evidence that enzyme concentration in the cell may increase as a result of retarded degradation without any apparent change in the rate of synthesis is now available. The increase

in tryptophan oxygenase in response to tryptophan administration, for example, is a consequence of the stabilization of the enzyme by the substrate (Schimke and Doyle, 1970). The increase in UDPG pyrophosphorylase in *D. discoideum* during differentiation is most probably due to decreased degradation of the enzymes (Wright, 1973). Similar stabilization could occur from binding of cofactors or allosteric modifiers (see later). The tissue-specific patterns of lactate dehydrogenase may not be determined solely by differential activation of the genes controlling the production of the subunits, but may arise from tissue differences in the rate of subunit synthesis and degradation (Fritz, Vesell, White, and Pruitt, 1969).

So it is clear that the synthesis of enzyme molecules and their degradation could be regulated by the changing concentration of the substrates and cofactors produced during metabolism. The profound changes in enzymes initiated by starvation (Swick, Rexroth, and Stange, 1968) may be mediated by the declining availability of specific metabolites. This type of regulation may be of considerable significance in differentiation and senescence, although direct examples of their involvement are lacking.

Kinetic Factors

One of the important considerations that is often neglected is the environment of the enzymes within the cell. For *in vitro* assay, the conditions (pH, temperature, -SH/-S-S-, redox state, enzyme concentration, ions) are generally optimized and are likely to be considerably different from those in the native milieu. Srere (1967) has pointed out that most enzymes in the cell are in high concentration (roughly 10^{-5} M) in contrast to the assay concentration (10^{-7} to 10^{-10} M depending upon their turnover number). Their kinetic behavior at high concentrations can be quite different, and rapid kinetic measurements in the micro- or millisecond range with high concentrations of enzyme would simulate more closely their operation *in vivo*. Also, many enzymes are on solid or semisolid surfaces which affect their kinetics. Association with other enzymes in a multienzyme system (e.g., glycolysis, oxidative phosphorylation, fatty acid oxidation and synthesis) would aid their efficiency since the intermediates can be passed directly from one enzyme to another rather than by diffusion through the medium. Some enzymes are integral, functional parts of membrane, as in the mitochondrial respiratory system, and their kinetic properties (K_m, V_{max}) change on dissociation from the membrane (Sanadi, Huang, and Pharo, 1971). Compartmentalization within membranous organelles and the consequent differences in the environment of different enzymes is another uncertainty in

ectomy did not produce a change in the formation of $^{14}CO_2$ from ^{14}C-tryptophan in both intact and perfused livers. However, large changes in $^{14}CO_2$ production occurred without changes in enzyme concentration when the amino acids in the perfusing medium were increased, which emphasizes the major role of substrate concentration in the regulatory process.

Many multienzyme systems have built-in regulatory steps which are controlled by the first enzyme (regulatory enzyme) in the series by a feedback mechanism as illustrated in the following sequence:

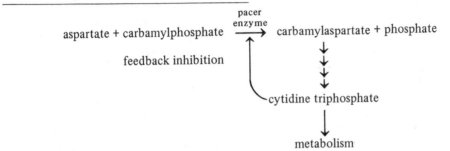

relating *in vitro* enzymes assays to intracellular function.

Metabolic reactions generally occur in a sequence of small changes, with the end result of gross transformations (e.g., breakdown of hexoses, C_6 compounds, to two C_3 fragments). Some of the enzymes acting in the sequence may be far in excess of that needed to maintain the overall rate, and large changes in these enzymes may not affect metabolism. A well-analyzed example is the formation of arginine from ornithine in *Neurospora* (Kacser, 1963), which proceeds in several steps:

ornithine $\longrightarrow$ citrulline

$\longrightarrow$ arginosuccinate $\longrightarrow$ arginine

From a simplified kinetic treatment of the multienzyme reaction, Kacser predicted that the accumulation of arginine should be independent of the last enzyme arginosuccinase. With the use of mutants having striking differences (as much as ten-fold) in arginosuccinase. activity, the prediction was fully confirmed. In another example, Kim and Miller (1968) found that changing the concentration of tryptophan oxygenase and tyrosine transaminase several-fold by hydrocortisone treatment following adrenal-

Cytidine triphosphate (CTP) inhibits its own formation by inactivating the pace-setting first step. When the metabolic demand for CTP is low, its steady-state concentration is high, inhibiting the carbamylaspartate synthetase. When CTP concentration is low due to increased metabolism, the inhibition is relieved and the production of CTP is accelerated. The highly specific inhibitory metabolite is called the effector (negative effector in the inhibitory instances) or modulator. The homotropic regulatory enzymes are modulated by the substrate itself, possibly by binding to a noncatalytic secondary site. The effect is generally a stimulation as in the oxidation of tryptophan or tyrosine mentioned above. The heterotropic regulatory enzymes also have a binding site for the effector which is different from the substrate binding site. These enzymes show a sigmoid substrate-saturation curve, distinct from the hyperbolic Michaelis-Menton curve, indicating that binding of one molecule aids the binding of the second, and thus enhances activity. Small changes in substrate concentration can thus cause profound acceleration of the reaction.

The modulation of activity is believed to be

brought about by a conformational change in the three-dimensional structure of the enzyme upon binding to the effector. Although it is not an enzyme, hemoglobin and its interaction with oxygen offers an excellent example. Its saturation by oxygen shows a sigmoid relationship at low oxygen levels as in the sigmoid substrate saturation curves of homotropic regulatory enzymes. Hemoglobin has four peptides with four hemes, each capable of binding one oxygen molecule. The binding of one oxygen molecule by a hemoprotein appears to cause a conformation change in it as well as in the neighboring hemoprotein, which improves the oxygen binding capacity of the latter subunit. Recent X-ray diffraction data appear to support this explanation.

It is thus clear that one of the important factors regulating intracellular metabolic activity is the concentration of intermediates (which are substrates for the succeeding enzyme in a sequence) and their flux. The excellent monograph by Wright (1973) illustrates and documents the often crucial role of specific metabolites in determining the flux through competing pathways and the formation of desired products. Some examples have been already mentioned.

In addition to the interactions between regulatory enzymes and their modulators, the regulation by modulation of energy flow is another important cellular mechanism.

Interlinking all of the metabolic reactions, both catabolic and biosynthetic, is the flow of energy. Lipman (1941) represented the cata-

bolic reactions as an energy-transducing device which generated ATP for subsequent utilization in the biosynthetic systems (Figure 1). Atkinson (1973) has recently reiterated the stoichiometric nature of the ATP-coupling coefficient, i.e., the number of moles of ATP formed or utilized per mole of starting material consumed or product synthesized. The synthesis of a compound is metabolically more expensive than the energy derived from its breakdown. For example, the synthesis of palmityl-S-CoA from 8 moles of acetyl-S-CoA uses up 49 ATP mole equivalents (7 ATP + 14 NADPH), or 63 mole equivalents (if NADPH is produced by transhydrogenation from NADH), but the breakdown of palmityl-S-CoA to 8 acetyl-S-CoA regenerates only 35 ATP equivalents (7 NADH and 7 $FADH_2$). Different sets of reactions are used for the synthesis and the breakdown, a principle which appears to be universal in nature. The biosynthetic processes are thermodynamically favorable *in vivo* only because of the coupling of catabolic and anabolic processes, with an overall loss of energy.

ENZYME CHANGES WITH AGE

The literature on enzyme activity changes in aging animals is quite extensive. A variety of enzymes (from simple hydrolases to complex Na^+-K^+ activated ATPase), in a profuse number of tissues (from liver to ventral prostate) in different animals (from nematodes to wild rats), have been assayed. Finch (1972) and Wilson

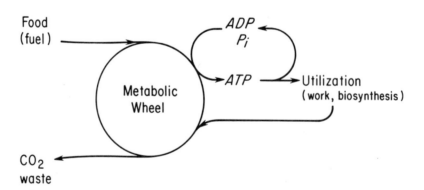

Figure 1. Lipman's concept of the metabolic wheel. This illustrates the links between oxidative metabolism and aspects of cellular function such as muscle contraction, transport of nutrients across cell membranes, etc.

(1973) have reviewed the data with detailed listings of individual enzymes and the reported age-related changes. In a summary table, Finch indicates that 21 liver enzymes have been analyzed with 47 measurements. Of these, 80 percent showed little or no change (0 to 25 percent), 13 percent showed a large increase (25 percent) and 7 percent a large decrease (25 percent). Wilson (1973) provides an even more extensive listing of enzymes that have been examined. Some of the significant age-related changes are shown in Table 1.

Age-related changes in the activities of membrane-bound enzymes also have been reported. (Grinna and Barber, 1972). The kidney microsomal NADH cytochrome c reductase, NADPH cytochrome c reductase, and glucose-6-phosphatase activites of aged (24-month) rats were substanially lower than the activities of the younger (6-month) animals. The K_m of the glucose-6-phosphatase from the kidneys of old rats was increased approximately three-fold, but there was no change with the liver enzyme. The V_{max} of the enzyme in both tissues was decreased. The K_m changes are indicative of alteration at the enzyme active site and have so far not been reported with other enzymes tested.

Wilson (1973) points out that most of the tissues analyzed consist of a heterogeneous cell population in which the changes in enzyme activity may not be similar or of the same magnitude in all cells. A combination of histochemical assays, which unfortunately cannot be quantitated satisfactorily, together with assays of homogenates may be more indicative of the real situation.

The value of the measurements is also limited

TABLE 1. AGE-RELATED CHANGES IN ENZYME ACTIVITIES.

Enzyme	Animal	Tissue	Compared ages	% Change (average)	Change per unit of	References
1. Cathepsin	Rat	Liver	13 vs. 27 mo	+27	DNA	Beauchene, Roeder, and Barrows, 1967
	Rat	Kidney	12 vs. 24 mo	+50	DNA	Barrows, Roeder, and Glewine, 1962 Barrows and Roeder, 1961
2. Glucokinase	Rat	Liver	2 vs. 24 mo	+20	Wt.	Adelman, 1970
3. Glucose-6-phosphatase	Rat	Liver	6 vs. 24 mo	−31	Microsomal protein	Grinna and Barber, 1972
	Rat	Kidney	6 vs. 24 mo	−42	Microsomal protein	Grinna and Barber, 1972
	Mouse	Kidney	6 vs. 23 mo	−20	DNA	Zorzoli and Li, 1967
4. α-Glycerophosphate dehydrogenase	Rat	Liver	6 vs. 24 mo	−30	Mitochondrial protein	Bulos, Sacktor, Grossman, and Altman, 1971
5. Cytochrome oxidase	Rat	Heart	5 vs. 27 mo	−30	Protein	Abu-Erreish, Wohlrab, and Sanadi, 1974
6. Fructose-1,6-diphosphate aldolase	Nematode		10 vs. 40 days	−54	Protein	Zeelon, Gershon, and Gershon, 1973
	Mouse	Liver	3 vs. 31 mo	−50	Protein	Gershon and Gershon, 1973
7. Isocitrate lyase	Nematode		5 vs. 40 days	−71	Protein	Gershon and Gershon, 1970
8. α-amylase	Nematode		5 vs. 35 days	−60	Protein	Erlanger and Gershon, 1970
9. Acetylcholine esterase	Nematode		5 vs. 35 days	−26	Protein	Erlanger and Gershon, 1970

by the differences in the basic reference parameters. For example, the data have been expressed in terms of protein, nitrogen, dry or wet weight, DNA, and cell number, although cell counting techniques are somewhat unreliable. The constancy of some of these parameters during aging has not been established. As a result, comparison between the determinations in the different laboratories is difficult.

Perhaps because of the above uncertainties, or because different strains of animals have been used or their chronological ages have not been related to the mean life span of the animal colony, there are significant differences in the results. For example, alkaline phosphatase was reported to increase 30 percent with age (Zorzoli, 1955), remain unchanged (Barrows, Roeder, and Falzone, 1962), and decrease about 30–40 percent (Ross, 1969).

Mainwaring (1968) has found striking differences in the enzyme activities of the ventral prostate in C57 black and tan mice. Fructose diphoshate (FDP) aldolase increased by 300 percent, lactate dehydrogenase by 220 percent and alkaline phosphatase decreased by 50 percent. These large differences in a tissue that is under the control of hormones are not surprising and may be attributable, at least in part, to development and/or dedifferentiation.

It is unfortunate that in spite of some interesting leads provided by these data, no attempts have been made to examine whether the enzyme alterations affect the *in vivo* metabolism of the tissue in any way. Unless this relationship can be established, the enzyme changes are of little value in providing insight into the metabolic changes in the whole organism.

Recently Gershon and Gershon (1970, 1973) have related the decline in specific activity of isocitrate lyase and FDP aldolase to the accumulation of inactive enzyme molecules, which are still capable of reacting with the antibody to the enzyme. It is not clear whether the inactive enzyme arises from errors in synthesis or post-transcriptional alterations. Also, the metabolic consequence, if any, of the decline in specific activity has not been established.

In a recent study, Erlanger and Gershon (1970) found that the activity of acetylcholine esterase, α-amylase, and malate dehydrogenase decreased considerably with age in the nematode, *T. aceti* (mean life span of 25 days) (Table 1). The malate dehydrogenase activity was separated into its isozymes by polyacrylamide gel electrophoresis. Of the three isozymes found in the young worms (0- and 5-day), the slowest migrating isozyme was decreased in the 15-day worms and disappeared completely in the 25- and 35-day worms. The acid phosphatase activity rose between 0 and 5 days, remained nearly constant on days 15 and 25, and rose again by day 35. Separation of the phosphatase into its four isozymes by gel electrophoresis showed no direct correlation between phosphatase activity and isozyme distribution. The disappearance of the slow band of malate dehydrogenase was attributed to either inactivation of the gene responsible for its formation or missynthesis resulting in inactive protein. Post-transcriptional changes in the isozyme leading to inactivation is yet another possibility for consideration.

LIPID METABOLISM

Despite the apparent importance of lipid metabolism in aging organisms, there have been few studies, and these largely limited to comparative compositional analyses, of lipids in the tissues. Analyses for cholesterol have been of interest in view of the implications in cardiovascular disease. In an extensive study involving a random group of 3,000 visitors to the 1968 San Francisco Health Fair, Werner, Tolls, Hultin, and Mellecker (1970) observed that the cholesterol level of serum increased gradually after the age of 20 (Table 2). Other studies (Das and Bhattacharya, 1961; Kipshidze, 1967) have yielded similar data showing an increase in serum cholesterol with age. Smith (1965) found that all lipids increased with age (from 10 to 70 years) in the aortic initma. Cholesterol esters increased four times faster than other lipids (Figure 2).

Studies with rats have revealed a strain dependence in cholesterol increase with age. Carlson, Froberg, and Nye (1968) have analyzed the lipid content of plasma, liver, heart, and white

TABLE 2. SERUM CHOLESTEROL LEVELS IN MAN.

Age (yrs)	Cholesterol male	mg/100 ml female
0–12	194	197
13–19	197	198
20–29	227	224
30–39	242	230
40–49	246	215
50–59	254	272
60–69	259	265
70–79	258	275

Data from Werner *et al.*, 1970; after Kritchevsky, 1972.

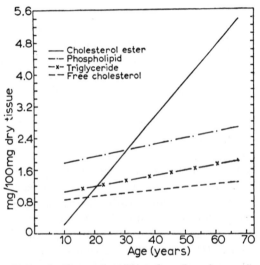

Figure 2. Regression lines for the change in concentration of major lipids with age in normal intima. (Reproduced with permission from Smith, 1965.)

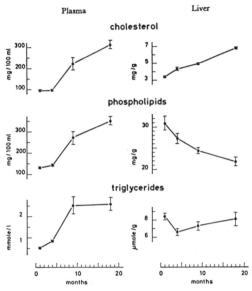

Figure 3. Lipid levels of plasma and liver of rats of different ages. (From Carlson, L. A., Froberg, S. O., and Nye, E. R. 1968. Effect of age on blood and tissue lipid levels in the male rat. *Gerontologia*, **14**, 65. By permission of S. Karger AG, Basel.)

The lipid content of heart and liver reached a peak at weaning age in Sprague-Dawley rats and decreased during growth and maturation (Grollman and Costello, 1972). Lipid content of aorta and epididymal fat pad also reached a maximum at 6 months. Exercise reduced the lipid content significantly in the aorta and epididymal pad, but had no effect on the lipids of heart and liver. In the BN and Lewis inbred strains, the serum cholesterol levels fell at 90 days (Kritchevsky and Tepper, 1964), in contrast to the above-stated results with Sprague-Dawley rats.

The serum cholesterol level reflects a balance between absorption from the diet, degradation, and biosynthesis. All parameters have to be determined in order to evaluate the significance of the serum level. Using isotope incorporation methods, Bloch, Borek, and Rittenberg (1946) observed a striking decrease in rate of cholesterol synthesis in growing rats. The rate decreased roughly 90 percent from 120–130-gram rats to 230-gram rats, which may reflect the high cholesterol requirement for membrane formation. The incorporation of acetate-2-^{14}C into cholesterol decreased appreciably (50

and red skeletal muscle in male Sprague-Dawley rats from ages 1 to 18 months. The cholesterol and phospholipids in plasma remained unchanged from 1 to 4 months, then increased continuously (Figure 3). The triglycerides increased sharply from 4 to 9 months and were constant thereafter. In the liver, the cholesterol increased steadily from 1 to 18 months, and the phospholipids declined. No significant change was observed in the liver triglycerides. There was no consistent age-related trend in the lipid content of heart.

percent) in liver slices of old rats (25+ months) compared with adult animals (4-5 months) (Perry and Bowen, 1957). The output of cholesterol in the bile, which may be derived largely from biosynthesis, also decreased by 50 percent between 6 and 44 weeks of life (Rosenman and Shibata, 1952). The incorporation of ^{14}C-acetate into cholestrol and the excretion of ^{14}C from labeled cholesterol have been compared in rats of ages 2, 5, and 8 months (Yamamoto and Yamamura, 1971). There was 50-60 percent decline in the 5-month rats and 60-70 percent decline in the 8-month rats compared to the 2-month controls. These changes appeared significant in the growth phase of the animals.

Benjamin, Gelhorn, Wagner, and Kundel (1961) and Moore (1968) have carried out an extensive study of several parameters related to lipid metabolism in aging rats. The percentage of lipids increased and that of nitrogen decreased in growing animals (up to 215 days) in all adipose samples that were measured. After 215 days and up to 687 days, there was no further change in the testicular, renal, inguinal, and interscapular adipose tissue, but mesenteric adipose showed continued changes. The incorporation of ^{14}C-acetate into the epididymal fat pad of young (100-130 gram) rats was about sevenfold higher than that of old (250-430 gram) rats, a change which may reflect maturation. Between the ages of 215 days and 647 days, the decline in the rate of acetate incorporation into epididymal and mesenteric depot fat was roughly 50 percent. It should be noted that these isotope incorporation measurements could reflect changes in pool sizes or breakdown and reutilization as well as new synthesis. The *in vitro* incorporation of labeled palmitate into triglycerides showed a large decrease with age (Table 3), with or without added glucose. Addition of epinephrine in the presence of glucose enhanced the incorporation to the same extent in young and old rats.

Benjamin *et al.* (1961) also found that glucose-1-^{14}C and glucose-6-^{14}C were oxidized more rapidly in adipose tissue from young rats. Also, glucose-1-^{14}C was oxidized relatively more rapidly than glucose-6-^{14}C in young adipose tissue compared to old adipose tissue

TABLE 3. INCORPORATION OF PALMITATE INTO THE TRIGLYCERIDE FRACTION OF RAT EPIDIDYMAL FAT TISSUE.

| | μmoles/2hr/g | | |
	+ glucose	− glucose	+ glucose + epinephrine
Young (90–130 g, 38–50 days)	15.1	1.8	3.7
Old (250–430 g, 100–300 days)	5.2	0.83	1.9

From Benjamin *et al.*, 1961.

(Table 4). The latter finding indicates a decrease in the proportion of glucose metabolized by the pentose phosphate pathway.

Since depot lipids serve as a major source of oxidative substrates, their breakdown in aging is of considerable interest. Rat aorta slices can hydrolyze serum triglycerides to free fatty acids, although at a very slow rate. There was a slow, gradual increase in the lipolytic activity of rat aorta from 2 to 24 months of age (Zemplenyi and Grafnetter, 1959). Similar results were obtained in the lipolysis of fat emulsions when aortas from rats of ages 3-4 months and 15-18 months were compared (Dury, 1961). Interestingly, heparin administration 15 min. before killing the animals, produced an increase in the lipolytic activity in young rats but not in the old. Similarly, heparin-induced lipolysis was more active in the serum of adult (20-39 years) compared to old (63-92 years) individuals ($p < 0.01$) (Nikkila and Niemi, 1957). A decreased lipolytic response

TABLE 4. $^{14}CO_2$ PRODUCTION FROM CARBONS 1 AND 6 OF SPECIFICALLY LABELLED GLUCOSE BY RAT ADIPOSE TISSUES.

| | μmoles/3 hr/g tissue | | |
	C_1	C_6	C_1/C_6
Young (90–125 g)	5.90 ± 1.43	1.03 ± 0.29	5.7
Old (300–400 g)	1.26 ± 0.17	0.37 ± 0.04	3.4

From Benjamin *et al.*, 1961.

to adrenalin has been reported in old persons (Stuchlikova, Hruskova, Hruza, Jelinkova, Novak, and Soukupova, 1966). *In vitro* exposure of adipose tissue to adrenalin yielded less free fatty acids from old rats compared to young rats (Benjamin et al., 1961; Jelinkova-Tenorova and Hruza, 1963; Altschuler, Lieberson, and Spitzer, 1962).

It is also known that after the age of 60 days, cell number of the rat adipose tissue remains constant, and further increase in the size of tissue occurs by increase in cell size (Hirsch and Han, 1969). In view of this, Greenwood, Johnson, and Hirsch (1970) have studied the conversion of glucose-1-^{14}C to $^{14}CO_2$ in isolated adipose cells from epididymal fat pads of C57B mice. There was no discernible difference in mice of 3–4 months and 12 months when the rates were calculated on the basis of number of cells used in the incubation.

A number of studies on the changing pattern of lipid composition of nervous tissue, particularly brain, during early development have been carried out. Similar studies on the postmaturation and senescent phase of life have been quite limited. Rouser and Yamamoto (1968) have recently carried out a detailed study of the lipid compositon or normal human brain. The age range of the samples was 6 months (fetal) to 98 years. The authors point out that semilogarithmic plots of values for different lipid classes gave a series of straight lines indicating periods of curvilinear regression in a precise pattern. A typical plot of total phospholipid as a percentage of total lipid (excluding gangliosides) is shown in Figure 4. Although one of the segments had only two points, a steady decline up to about age 33 years and then an increase is apparent. The inflection points, i.e., ages at which the slope of regression line changes, may reflect differences in regional development of the brain or changes in physiological control factors such as blood flow or hormone effects. The annual change in ten lipid parameters have been calculated from the regression lines. They reveal gradual, orderly, and continuous changes in the lipid with increasing age.

The above findings suggest that the size of the adipose tissue depots, size of its cells, their composition, metabolism, and response to

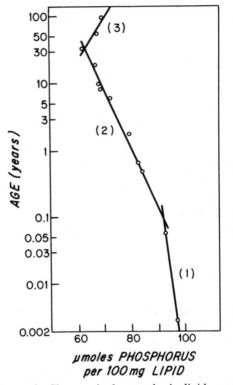

Figure 4. Changes in human brain lipid composition with age. (From Rouser, G., and Yamamoto, Y., *Lipids,* 3: 284(1968), American Oil Chemists' Society.)

hormone change with age. Studies on the mechanisms responsible for these changes should be interesting and merit pursuit.

Modification of the membrane lipids of cells with aging has been recently examined by Grinna and Barber (1972). The phospholipid content of the kidney and liver microsomal fractions derived from old rats (24 months) was considerably reduced (42 and 21 percent respectively) compared to the microsomes from young (6-month) rats. No change in phospholipid content was observed in heart microsomes or in the mitochondria from these three tissues. Changes in membrane lipids could produce pleiotropic alterations in several membrane enzymes and their functions, and merit further examination.

ENERGY METABOLISM

The breakdown of glucose to pyruvate in mammalian cells occurs primarily by way of glycolysis, and the C_3 compounds generated by this or the less prominent pentose phosphate pathway are further oxidized in the mitochondria via the tricarboxylic acid cycle and the respiratory chain to CO_2 and H_2O. Of the several multienzyme cycles operating in this overall conversion of carbon compounds to CO_2, the mitochondrial system has lately received considerable attention in aging research. The pentose phosphate pathway has hardly been screened, and studies on the glycolytic cycle have been relatively rare.

Anaerobic glycolysis in tissue slices and homogenates is measured by CO_2 production resulting from acidification of the suspending bicarbonate buffer due to production of lactic acid, or by direct measurement of lactate formation. Some of the data summarized in Table 5 show a decrease in the glycolytic activity of tissue slices. Reiner (1947), on the other hand, could find no significant difference in CO_2 production in the liver or brain homogenates of rats varying in age from 2 to 24 months. The homogenates were fortified with coenzymes, etc., which may have masked any difference if it existed. Frolkis and Bogatskaya (1967) report that anaerobic glycolysis increases and respiration decreases in the heart muscle "slurry" from aging rats. Angelova-Gateva (1969) has measured anaerobic glycolysis in "sections" of rat skeletal and heart muscle and found no significant alteration between ages 6-8 months and 24-25 months.

Mitochondria are a typical example of a self-contained organelle with all the necessary machinery to convert several compounds (pyruvate, glutamate, fatty acids, etc.) into CO_2 and H_2O and capture much of the oxidative energy in the form of ATP. The substrates, ADP and phosphate, are transported into the mitochondria by an energy-requiring process, and ATP and CO_2 are transported out. Of the several dozen enzymes concerned with the process, many (including dehydrogenases of the tricarboxylic acid cycle) are located within the matrix (i.e., space confined by the inner membrane). A large number (including the electron carriers and ATP synthetase) are arranged precisely in the inner membrane and perform both a catalytic and a structural role in maintaining the integrity of the membrane. This structural organization appears to serve the purpose of juxtapositioning the catalytic units and thereby increases the efficiency of the energy conservation process. The substrates and coenzymes do not diffuse away from the site of their action, but provide the experimenter with additional difficulties in knowing the concentration of the intermediates for simulating *in vivo* conditions.

It has not been possible to establish the rate-limiting steps in the overall process, although indications are that early steps, such as entry of substrate or a specific dehydrogenation, might be important. It is generally known that the turnover numbers (or catalytic efficiency) of the cytochromes, measured with purified preparations, are far in excess of that necessary to account for the overall rate of oxygen uptake (Wainio, 1970). Assay of individual

TABLE 5. EFFECT OF AGE ON ANAEROBIC GLYCOLYSIS.

Tissue	Age	Activity	References
Rat liver slices	12 mo	$2.0\mu l\ CO_2$/mg dry wt $\times$ hr	Hawkins, 1927
	22 mo	$0.8\mu l\ CO_2$/mg dry wt $\times$ hr	
Rat liver slices	5-6 mo	$0.86 \pm 0.07\mu l\ CO_2$/mg wet wt $\times$ hr	Ross and Ely, 1954
	21 mo	$0.57 \pm 0.07\mu l\ CO_2$/mg wet wt $\times$ hr	
Bovine articular cartilage slices	1-7 yr	$0.44 \pm 0.089\mu l\ CO_2$/mg wet wt $\times$ hr	Rosenthal, Bowie, and Wagoner, 1941
	8-11 yr	$0.26 \pm 0.059\mu l\ CO_2$/mg wet wt $\times$ hr	
Rat liver slices	10-12 mo	$59 \pm 3.0\mu l\ CO_2$/100 mg wet wt $\times$ hr	Barrows, Yiengst, and Shock, 1958
	24-27 mo	$69 \pm 4.3\mu l\ CO_2$/100 mg wet wt $\times$ hr	

enzymes (e.g., succinate dehydrogenase, cytochrome *c* oxidase) would only provide a measure of their concentration in mitochondria, but could have little bearing on the question of whether the concentration change is affecting overall oxidation and ATP formation.

It has been established that oxidation and ATP formation are tightly coupled processes and that inhibiting or accelerating one process would similarly affect the other. The rate of oxidation (i.e., oxygen uptake) is determined by the phosphate potential, i.e., (ATP/ADP · P_i) ratio (see Sanadi and Wholrab, in press). When the ATP level declines as a result of its utilization by the cell, the phosphate potential decreases and the respiratory rate is increased. When mitochondria are respiring at a high phosphate potential, which occurs when essentially all of the available ADP has been converted to ATP, they are said to be in state 4 respiration (Lehninger, 1965). Maximal respiration (or state 3) occurs when excess ADP is present. The liver under basal conditions is believed to respire at a rate roughly midway between states 3 and 4, and respiration in normal heart is probably closer to state 3. State 3 may be achieved intracellulary only under conditions of extreme stress and associated high respiratory activity.

An age-related decrease in respiratory activity has been observed in slices from heart (Wollenberger and Jehl, 1952; Pearce, 1936), liver (Pearce, 1936; Ross and Ely, 1954), kidney (Pearce, 1936; Barrows, Yiengst, and Shock, 1958), articular cartilage (Rosenthal, Bowie, and Wagoner, 1941), and homogenates of kidney (Rafsky, Newman, and Horonick, 1952) and liver (Reiner, 1947). Other reports failed to find changes in homogenates and slices of liver (Rafsky, Newman, and Horonick, 1952; Barrows, Yiengst, and Shock, 1958). In a recent study, Frolkis, Verzhikovskaya and Valueva (1973) found that the Q_{O_2} (respiratory quotient) of the myocardium of 8- to 10-month rats was 3.78, and that of 28- to 30-month rats was 2.25. In another series of experiments, Frolkis and Bogatskaya (1967) report a 50 percent decrease in the Q_{O_2} in 28- to 32-month rats compared to 10- to 12-month rats. In most of

these experiments, only endogenous substrate oxidation was measured, which may represent respiration near state 4 levels. It is likely that if state 3 could be approached, the changes might be much greater, and perhaps there would be greater agreement between the different laboratories.

Ermini and Verzar (1968) found that the recovery of creatine phosphate (which is generated from ATP produced during oxidative phosphorylation) in resting rat skeletal muscle was slower in old rats, which also is consistent with decreased *in vivo* respiratory capacity.

Much of the recent work has been carried out with isolated mitochondria which, as it will become evident, has its advantages and disadvantages. Weinbach and Garbus (1959) noted a decline in the oxidative rate with β-hydroxybutyrate (β-OH butyrate), but not with other substrates, in the liver mitochondria from old (24-month) compared to young (3- to 4-month) rats, as well as more rapid decline in the activity of the stored mitochondria from older rats. This has been taken as an indication of poorer stability of the mitochondrial structure in the old animal. The poor stability characteristics have been noted also by Arcos, Stacey, Mathison, and Argus (1967). Gold, Gee, and Strehler (1968) repeated the studies with myocardial mitochondria and could find no age-related difference in the rate of β-OH butyrate oxidation or in ADP/O. The comparison was between adult (12- to 14-month) and old (24- to 27-month) rats. Chen, Warshaw, and Sanadi (1972) compared the oxidative activity of the myocardial and skeletal muscle mitochondria from rats of different ages and found that the state 3 rate declined with some substrates, but not with others, in the same preparations. Some typical data are summarized in Figure 5 and Table 6. It should be noted that in no case were the state 4 rate and ADP/O affected in the old rats. In view of the disagreements in the literature, three sets of experiments were carried out by Chen, Warshaw, and Sanadi (1972) with 6 or 7 animals in a group, using glutamate-malate as one of the substrates. In each experiment a difference between the adult and senescent animals was observed with $p < 0.001$ in all cases.

HEART MUSCLE MITOCHONDRIA

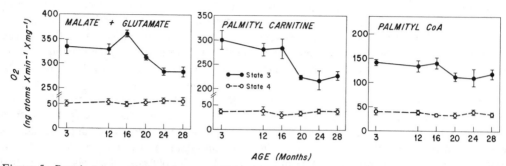

AGE (Months)

Figure 5. Respiratory activity of myocardial mitochondria from aging rats. (From Chen, J. C., Warshaw, J. B., and Sanadi, D. R. 1972. *Journal of Cellular Physiology*, **80**, 141–148.)

In a recent report, Inamdar, Person, Kohnen, Duncan, and Mackler (1974) have studied the activities of heart and skeletal muscle mitochondria from aging hamsters. Unfortunately, they fail to provide lifespan data on these animals, which are seldom used in aging research. They find (a) a progressive decrease in the yield of mitochondria with age; (b) no change in the state 3 oxidation or ADP/O rates of pyruvate-malate, succinate, or glutamate-malate (although the latter does show a change in liver according to their data); and (c) increased fragility indicated by a faster decline in state 3 oxidation rates (compared to mitochondria from the young) during prolonged storage of isolated mitochondria. The increased fragility is in agreement with other findings (Weinbach and Garbus, 1959; Arcos *et al.*, 1967; Abu-Erreish, Wohlrab, and Sanadi unpublished). Chen, Warshaw, and Sanadi (1972) had noted that the state 3 respiration fell off sharply at about 20 months of age in rats. The data of Inamdar *et al.* (1974) go only up to 20 months in hamsters, and not knowing the life span, they could have missed the decline.

Abu-Erreish, Wohlrab, and Sanadi (unpublished) have also examined the *in vitro* stability of myocardial mitochondria from young and old rats. The state 3 rate did show a slightly

TABLE 6. DECLINE IN THE RESPIRATORY RATE OF MYOCARDIAL MITOCHONDRIA FROM SENESCENT RATS.

Substrate	Age (mos)	State 3	State 4	ADP/O
		ng atoms 0 $\times$ min^{-1} $\times$ mg^{-1}		
Glutamate +	9	346 ± 9.4[a]	63.1 ± 3.7	2.88 ± 0.12
malate	24	284 ± 9.9	61.7 ± 3.1	2.89 ± 0.07
Glutamate +	8	252 ± 9.8	69.0 ± 8.5	2.71 ± 0.11
pyruvate	24	180 ± 13	67.7 ± 6.5	2.82 ± 0.07
β-OH butyrate	8	177 ± 3.5[a]	60.2 ± 8.1	2.63 ± 0.11
	24	136 ± 11	57.3 ± 10.0	2.66 ± 0.12
Pyruvate +	8	252 ± 15	72.9 ± 7.5	2.80 ± 0.09
malate	24	237 ± 13	74.5 ± 3.2	2.79 ± 0.10
α-Ketoglutarate	8	142 ± 14	63.7 ± 9.5	2.66 ± 0.09
	24	141 ± 12	66.0 ± 11	2.66 ± 0.07
Succinate	9	458 ± 25	163 ± 7.4	1.52 ± 0.03
	24	436 ± 6.3	170 ± 8.0	1.49 ± 0.07

[a]$p < 0.005$.

After Chen, Warshaw, and Sanadi, 1972.

greater tendency to decline in the mitochondria from old rats, but the difference was not statistically significant.

Insects and nematodes are becoming increasingly popular as models for research on aging in view of their shorter life span and the ease of maintenance and growth. In spite of several differences from mammals, such as absence of the vascular and skeletal system, and change in life span with temperature, there is sound rationale in the choice of these models. The basic parameters in aging, particularly at the genetic and cellular levels, are likely to be quite similar in all species, although specialized properties arising from the differences may also impinge and modulate the more basic mechanisms. This viewpoint is supported by the present finding that the functional changes associated with aging in the mitochondria from rat heart and blowfly flight muscle are similar.

The decline in state 3 oxidation rate with advancing age has been observed also with the flight muscle mitochondria from the blowfly, *Phormia regina* (Bulos, Shukla, and Sacktor, 1972) (Table 7); there was no significant change in state 4 respiration or ADP/O as in the myocardial mitochondria. In these experiments the mitochondria were isolated and maintained in the presence of bovine serum albumin (BSA) to improve ultrastructural and enzymatic stability. If BSA was left out of the medium, there was a 50 percent decline in the state 3 rate in both age groups, but the difference between the mature and senescent flies was still noted. Also, state 4 and ADP/O were unaffected by the omission of BSA.

Tribe and Ashhurst (1972) have observed no significant age-related change in the oxidation of α-glycerophosphate or pyruvate in the flight muscle mitochondria of the blowfly, *Calliphora erythrocephala*. However, they report a high pre–state 3 rate (i. e., with substrate but no added ADP) indicative of loose coupling. The ADP/O was substantially decreased with α-glycerophosphate but not significantly with pyruvate, which is surprising since the oxidation of the former involves the two phosphorylation sites which participate in the three site phosphorylation with pyruvate. Oxidation rates with NADH alone were higher with mitochondria from old than from young. The authors conclude that uncoupling of mitochondrial oxidative phosphorylation increases with age. They also point out an alternative explanation, viz., that the mitochondria in the flight muscle of old flies may be more susceptible to damage during isolation. The higher NADH oxidation and pre–state 3 rates seen in mitochondria from senescent flies may in fact be taken as evidence for damage.

There seems to be general agreement from *in vitro* storage experiments regarding the lower stability of mitochondria isolated from older animals. This is also supported by electron microscopic observations on the greater proportion of degenerating mitochondria in the heart muscle of older rats. The data with tissue slices and homogenates also indicate a decline in respiratory capacity with age. The discrepancies in the respiratory measurements on isolated mitochondria may therefore merely reflect the strong possiblity that under certain isolation conditions, the damaged mitochondria might be discarded and an unrepresentative popula-

TABLE 7. DECLINE WITH AGE IN STATE 3 RESPIRATORY RATE OF THE FLIGHT MUSCLE MITOCHONDRIA OF *Phormia regina*.

Substrate	Age	State 3	State 4	ADP/O
		ng atoms 0/min × mg mito		
Pyruvate +	Mature	0.77 ± 0.05	0.069 ± 0.007	2.15 ± 0.08
Proline	Senescent	0.52 ± 0.05	0.076 ± 0.005	2.33 ± 0.12
Glycerol-1-	Mature	1.35 ± 0.09	0.55 ± 0.04	0.94 ± 0.04
phosphate	Senescent	0.92 ± 0.09	0.43 ± 0.04	0.79 ± 0.06

After Bulos, Shukla, and Sacktor, 1972.

tion might be inadvertently assayed. This would not be surprising since the yield of mitochondria during isolation is hardly quantitative; from heart it is at best 10–20 percent (see addendum).

Chen, Warshaw, and Sanadi (1972) present several possible explanations for the molecular lesion that could account for their observations on the differential effect of substrates on the state 3 rates in myocardial mitochondria:

a. Since the oxidations of succinate, which feeds electrons at the second phosphorylation site, and of malate-pyruvate or α-ketoglutarate, which feeds electrons at site 1, are unaffected with age, the entire respiratory chain from NADH to O_2 should be unimpaired. So also the phosphorylation reactions seem to be unaffected since ADP/O is constant, as seen with mammalian as well as flight muscle mitochondria. On the other hand, the oxidation rates of some other substrates which produce NADH in the mitochondria (i.e., malate-glutamate, pyruvate-glutamate, β-OH butyrate) are distinctly lower. A reasonable explanation for the differences could be that the production of NADH from certain substrates is decreased while that from other substrates is unaffected.

b. The reduced NADH production from some substrates, but not from others, could be due to differential changes in the activitiy of certain dehydrogenases. For example, the data could be accounted for if there is a decrease in the β-OH butyrate dehydrogenases but no decrease in succinate dehydrogenase. Also, these reactions will have to be the rate-limiting steps in the entire sequence of oxidation by oxygen, for which there is no direct evidence.

c. If the different dehydrogenases have independent pools of NAD (for which there is no experimental support), and some pools should decrease preferentially, the differences in rates could be explained.

d. The most likely explanation, however, is that the transport of some substrates into mitochondria is affected in aging, but not that of others. The transport, a complex process involving utilization of respiratory energy, (Klingenberg, 1970) could be altered by changing the translocase or the substrate-binding protein molecules. This area of mitochondrial

research is currently very active and has promise of interesting developments. The net result of the change in transport activity would be a decrease in substrate concentration or flux.

It is interesting to note that among the substrates that have been tested with myocardial mitochondria, those involved exclusively in the tricarboxylic acid cycle, i.e., succinate, pyruvate-malate, and α-ketoglutarate are the ones whose oxidation is unimpaired. On the other hand, those substrates that interface the tricarboxylic acid cycle with protein or lipid oxidation, i.e., malate-glutamate, pyruvate-glutamate, β-OH butyrate, and palmityl carnitine, are oxidized at reduced rates. If the correlation is not just a coincidence, the data would indicate that the older animals have a reduced capacity to utilize proteins and fats for energy production.

It is interesting that the utilization of ATP following brief (10 sec) periods of anoxia in brain produces a slower decline in ATP levels in the old rat (29 month) compared to the young (4 month). The difference was most pronounced in the striatum (48 percent) but less in other regions of the brain (Ferrendelli, Sedgwick, and Suntzeff, 1971).

I have commented earlier that it is important to relate changes in enzyme activity to a physiological alteration. Cross-sectional studies on BMR (basal metabolic rate) indicate a decline of roughly 3 percent per decade in man (Shock and Yiengst, 1955) from maturity to age 89. A more recent study (Keys, Taylor, and Grande, 1973) has taken into account the changes in fat content with age and estimates the regression to be between 1 and 2 percent per decade. It is possible that the differences in metabolic rates may conceivably increase if the comparison is made under actively working conditions (approaching mitochondrial state 3) rather than the basal conditions (near state 4).

Oxidative metabolism in aging animals was assessed somewhat differently by Sanadi, Barrows, and Crowder (1966). They measured the rate of $^{14}CO_2$ appearance in the expired air after administration of related compounds to rats. The oxidation rates of DL-glutamate-3, 4-^{14}C, DL-alanine-3-^{14}C, succinate-2-^{14}C, D-glucose-1-^{14}C, propionate-2-^{14}C, octanoate-1-^{14}C, and acetate-1-^{14}C were unaltered, but acetate-2-^{14}C was oxidized more rapidly in senescent than in adult rats. The increased rate of acetate-2-^{14}C oxidation was taken as an indication of a decreased rate of incorporation of label into biosynthetic (anabolic) reactions (e.g., lipid synthesis), resulting in increased oxidation in old animals. The fact that the increased rate is seen only with acetate-2-^{14}C and not with acetate-1-^{14}C or the other compounds was attributed to the unique disposition of C_2 in the Krebs cycle. Its dwell time in the cycle is considerably larger than that of C_1 due to the recycling of the isotope, which may amplify the difference in the young and old animals and bring it within the range of detection by the method.

As mentioned earlier, if these measurements could only be carried out under actively working conditions where the animals are stressed to approach mitochondrial state 3 respiration, the differences could well be larger. The flight muscle system also offers uncertainties in the interpretation of the data. It is known that the flight muscles of insects are asynchronous and, once contraction is initiated by nerve impulses, an oscillatory contraction-relaxation cycle is set up which is independent of the neural impulses. The wing beat frequency is said to be set (Tregear, 1967). The duration of flight is then the only available convenient measure of flight performance. Using this criterion, it has been established that senescent insects have a decreased capacity for flight (Williams, Barnes, and Sawyer, 1943; Tribe, 1966). However, it is important to note that in the above measurements, flight may cease when the substrates (e.g., glycogen or lipid) are exhausted, and the decreased performance of old flies may be indicative of decreased food reserves rather than of decreased oxidative metabolism. Consistent with this, Tribe and Ashhurst (1972) have observed that the glycogen granules appear far less frequently in thin sections of old blowfly flight muscle. Similar findings have been reported with *D. melanogaster* (Takahashi, Philpot, and Miguel, 1970).

Ultrastructure of Mitochondria in Aging

A number of reports have presented evidence that ultrastructural changes occur in mitochondria during aging. Tauchi and Sato (1968) observed that the mitochondria in human hepatic cells decrease in number and increase in size. The mitochondria from retinal receptor cells of 1-year-old rats, but not of younger ones, were associated with glycogen deposits (Ishikawa and Pei, 1965). In aging *D. melanogaster*, Takahashi, Philpot, and Miguel (1970) found areas of severe mitochondrial and myofibrillar degeneration and reduction of glycogen. Travis and Travis (1972) also noted that some of the myocardial mitochondria from old rats appeared to be in a degenerative state while the young rats showed no such damage.

Two interesting and probably consistent ultrastructural abnormalities appear in the mitochondria of older flies. They are the appearance of giant forms of mitochondria and abnormal membranous inclusions. In 1963, Smith observed that the flight muscle mitochondria of *Calliphora erythrocephala* occasionally contained lamellar bodies (myelin-like whorls) with dense granules in the middle. He proposed that they were degenerating organelles. Sohol (1970), Sohol and Allison (1971), and Rockstein and Bhatnagar (1965) established that the heart mitochondria of *Drosophila repleta* and the flight muscle of the housefly accumulated glycogen within structures similar to those seen by Smith and became much larger with age. These abnormal lamellar stuctures are frequently seen in thin sections of the flight muscle mitochondria of old *Phormia regina* (Bulos, Shukla, and Sacktor, 1972; Sacktor and Shimada, 1972). However, compared to the 30 percent frequency noted by Sacktor and Shimada (1972) in the isolated mitochondrial pellet, J. Hall (unpublished observations) found them much less frequently (in approximately 2 percent of the mitochondrial profiles) with a different strain of blowfly, *Sarcophaga bulata* (Figure 6). The difference was not due to differences in the environment of the two laboratories, since mitochondria from *Phormia regina* (pupae kindly supplied by Dr. B. Sacktor and raised in this laboratory) showed myelin-like whorls with a frequency similar to that reported by Sacktor and Shimada. Since the probability of a section missing a whorl which is confined to a small portion of mitochondria is quite high, the above estimates merely give

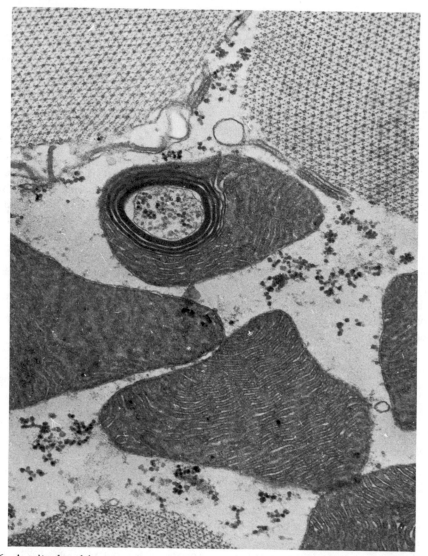

Figure 6. A mitochondrion seen in a thin section of flight muscle from a blowfly, *Sarcophaga bullata*, of age 60 days. The electron micrograph was taken by Dr. J. D. Hall in this laboratory.

the lower limit of the frequency. Tribe and Ashhurst (1972) have quantitated the enlargement of mitochondria with age and report a diameter increase from 1.66 μm at age 2 days to 2.64 μm at 95 days.

It is of interest that abnormal membrane whorls of pathological origin have been seen in the cytoplasm of nervous tissue (Moore and Strasberg, 1970). These have been attributed to abnormal lipid composition. Thus, studies on lipid metabolism in relation to membrane composition may be interesting in the context of aging.

A third mitochondrial abnormality associated with senescence is the change in the composition of mitochondria. Abu-Erreish, Wohlrab, and Sanadi (1974) found that the total cytochrome oxidase activity and content (determined by spectral measurement) in myocardial mitochondria declined with age (Table 8), but the turnover number of the enzyme was unaltered. There was a parallel decline in cytochrome b and cytochrome c-c_1 content. There is considerable evidence that the cytochromes are in constant ratios in the mitochondria, and the parallel decline in all cytochromes

TABLE 8. CYTOCHROME CHANGES IN MYOCARDIAL MITOCHONDRIA DURING AGING.

Age (mos)	5	15	26
Number	6	4	6
		μg atoms O_2/min $\times$ mg	
Cytochrome oxidase	$14.5^a \pm 0.36$	13.0 ± 0.36	$10.6^a \pm 1.03$
		nmoles/mg protein	
Cytochrome aa3	0.468 ± 0.056	0.432 ± 0.040	0.363 ± 0.050
Cytochrome C-C$_1$	0.750 ± 0.040	0.740 ± 0.060	0.560 ± 0.050
Cytochrome b	0.447 ± 0.033	0.466 ± 0.047	0.263 ± 0.075

[a]$p < 0.005$
After Abu-Erreish, Wohlrab, and Sanadi, 1974.

with age is thus consistent with the concept of elimination of entire respiratory assemblies. It should be noted that this decrease in cytochromes is probably not responsible for the decline in state 3 oxidative rate since the decline is selective with some substrates and is not seen with succinate, pyruvate-malate, etc. However, it may be a marker of other changes in composition occurring in mitochondria, which could be responsible for the respiratory decrease.

Abu-Erreish, Wohlrab, and Sanadi (1974) also found that the cytochrome oxidase activity of the homogenate of rat myocardium and brain declined parallel to the activity of isolated mitochondria. There was no change in liver and kidney homogenates (Table 9). From a comparison of the specific activity of the homogenate and the mitochondria, it was concluded that the mitochondrial content of the myocardium does not change with age. In order to detect these changes it was necessary to assay the oxidase activity in the presence of optimal deoxycholate to expose fully the

controlled activity. It is of interest that the tissues which show a decrease in total cytochrome oxidase (i.e., homogenate activity) have mitochondria with relatively long half lives (heart–17.8 days, brain–24.4 days) compared to tissues with no significant change in oxidase (liver–9.3 days, kidney–8.7 days) (Menzies and Gold, 1971).

Fletcher and Sanadi (1961) established that liver mitochondria are constantly broken down and resynthesized in the cell with a relatively short half life. They observed that the half lives for mitochondrial insoluble protein, soluble protein, lipid, and cytochrome were identical. These results have been confirmed by Beattie, Basford, and Koritz (1967) and Menzies and Gold (1971). However, the turnover rates of soluble and insoluble proteins in kidney mitochondria were different (Beattie, Basford, and Koritz, 1966). Thus, it has been amply confirmed that the inner membrane components and mitochondrial DNA have the same half life, although some of the soluble proteins turn over at different rates (see Menzies and Gold, 1971).

TABLE 9. CYTOCHROME OXIDASE ACTIVITY OF RAT TISSUE HOMOGENATES.

Av. Age (mos)	N	μg atoms O_2/min $\times$ g heart		μg atoms O_2/min $\times$ mg mito	
		Heart	Kidney	Heart	Kidney
7	6	639 ± 65^a	269 ± 4	$3.26 \pm .25$	$1.67 \pm .05$
14	7	771 ± 31		$2.87 \pm .18$	
29	6	457 ± 26^a	241 ± 5	$1.57 \pm .05$	$1.57 \pm .05$

[a]$p < 0.005$.
After Abu-Erreish, Wohlrab, and Sanadi, 1974.

The present picture is that two processes occur. One is the turnover of the entire mitochondrion by processes including digestion in an autophagic vacuole (Essner and Novikoff, 1960). The second process is a selective turnover of certain components with widely differing half lives. For example, the δ-aminolevulinate synthetase has a half life of a few hours (Swick, Rexroth, and Stange, 1968) compared to several days for the inner membrane components. It seems likely that the components with shorter half lives are inducible enzymes (e.g., orthnithine aminotransferase, Swick, Rexroth, and Stange, 1968) concerned with a regulatory role. These may merit close examination in relation to aging.

Sanadi and Fletcher (1961) also found that the turnover rates of liver mitochondria from young and old rats were identical. In a more extensive study, Menzies and Gold (1971) compared the half lives of mitochondria (inner membrane) from several tissues of adult (12-month) and old (24-month) rats and also found no statistically significant difference.

The experiments of Comolli, Ferioli, and Azzola (1972) using the double isotope labeling technique also showed little or no change in mitochondrial turnover rate with age.

The weight of evidence based on biochemical studies with tissue slices, homogenates, and isolated mitochondria clearly points to a functional decline in the mitochondria in aged animals. The abnormality could result from (a) defective synthesis of the mitochondrial protein or lipids, (b) increased breakdown of precursor proteins, (c) defective membrane assembly process, or (d) damage subsequent to formation of normal mitochondria. In view of the central role of ATP in the metabolic processes, small changes in its steady-state level could subtly affect a variety of metabolic reactions, such as those seen in senescence, and could lead to a slow decline in the vitality of the organism.

LIPID PEROXIDATION AND VITAMIN E

Free Radicals and Their Detection

Free radicals are molecules containing an unpaired electron (e.g., $OH^{\bullet}$), which makes them highly reactive, and as a consequence,

shorter lived. They are produced by irradiation (e.g., UV radiation), heat (temperatures over $450°C$), or oxidation-reduction reactions. Typical examples of well-known reactions are:

homolysis of peroxides:

$$R{-}O{:}O{-}R_2 \longrightarrow R_1{-}O^{\bullet} + R_2{-}O^{\bullet}$$

homolysis of hydrogen peroxide:

$$H{-}O{:}O{-}H \longrightarrow 2OH^{\bullet}$$

homolysis by redox coupling:

$$metal^+ + R_1{-}O{:}O{-}R_2 \longrightarrow$$
$$Metal^{2+} + R_1{-}O^{\bullet} + R_2O^{-}$$

production by hydrogen addition or abstraction, as in semiquinone formation:

$$Flavin \xrightarrow{H^+ + e} Flavin\ H^{\bullet} \xrightarrow{H^+ + e} Flavin\ H_2$$

The free radicals can and often do initiate chain reactions involving the production of other free radicals as in the decomposition of H_2O_2:

$$Fe^{2+} + H_2O_2 \longrightarrow Fe^{3+} + OH^- + OH^{\bullet}$$

$$Fe^{3+} + H_2O_2 \longrightarrow Fe^{2+} + HO_2{}^{\bullet} + H^+$$

$$Fe^{2+} + OH^{\bullet} \longrightarrow Fe^{3+} + OH^-$$

$$Fe^{2+} + HO_2{}^{\bullet} \longrightarrow Fe^{3+} + HO_2{}^-$$

$$Fe^{3+} + HO_2{}^- \longrightarrow Fe^{2+} + H^+ + O_2{}^-$$

$$OH^{\bullet} + H_2O_2 \longrightarrow HO_2{}^{\bullet} + H_2O$$

$$O^{\bullet}{}_2{}^- + H_2O_2 \longrightarrow O_2 + OH^- + OH^{\bullet}$$

Lipid peroxidation (Figure 7) is an example of a free radical chain reaction of biological relevance. It leads to the formation of end products with reduced efficiency or perhaps even deleterious effects.

Several methods of free radical detection have been devised, although none is entirely suitable for quantitation in biological material. The ability of free radicals to initiate chain reactions is a sensitive tool. The addition of free radicals to a stabilized solution of sulfite produces readily measurable, rapid oxygen uptake (Fridovich and Handler, 1961). Another elegant and highly sensitive procedure suitable for the detection of superoxide anion radicals ($O_2{}^{\bullet}$) involves their dismutation, as shown

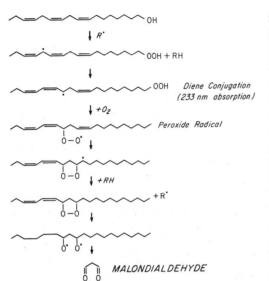

Figure 7. Scheme for the peroxidation of unsaturated fatty acids leading to malondialdehyde formation. (After Dahle, Hill, and Holman, 1962.)

below, by copper proteins such as haemocuprein and erythrocuprein (McCord and Fridovich, 1969):

$$O_2{}^{\cdot-} + O_2{}^{\cdot-} + 2H^+ \longrightarrow O_2 + H_2O_2$$

Similar dismutase activity has been found in many tissues. The superoxide dismutase strongly inhibits sulfite oxidation, but not in the absence of EDTA. The inhibition is an example of a free radical quenching reaction. Other examples of free radical scavengers of biological importance include oxygen, quinones, antioxidants such as ascorbic acid, purine bases, and -SH compounds. Some of these have been used as antioxidants to stabilize less readily oxidizable compounds. They appear to be in sufficiently high concentrations in the tissue to offer some protection from free radical damage.

Spectrophotometric methods of determining free radicals are available for chemical reactions but are unsuitable for biological systems.

Lipid peroxidation has been considered by several workers to be a particularly likely event in tissue injury, and a number of methods have been devised to detect and estimate the reaction (see the excellent monograph by Slater, 1972). Measurement of oxygen consumption during peroxidation of lipids containing unsaturated fatty acids is a convenient kinetic assay for tissue extracts or fractions (Hochstein and Ernster, 1963), although care has to be taken that other oxidations do not occur simultaneously. The reaction is accompanied by production of malondialdehyde and related products, which provide the basis for another method for the determination of peroxidation. Malondialdehyde can be measured by its color reaction with thiobarbituric acid (TBA) (Bernheim, Bernheim, and Wilbur, 1948). Although a number of aldehydes will react with TBA to yeild similarly colored products which can be distinguished by their absorption maxima, Sidwell, Salwin, and Mitchell (1955) found that the TBA index was proportional to the concentration of lipid peroxide and the carboxyl content during oxidation of fats in food materials. Under well-defined conditions, the relationship between TBA index and lipid peroxidation seems to hold, but extrapolation to other conditions requires close scrutiny.

Other more sensitive assays for lipid peroxidation in tissue extracts involve measurement of diene conjugation by the absorbance increase at 233 nm. Lipid peroxidation is accompanied by rearrangement of double bonds leading to diene conjugation. Fletcher, Dillard, and Tappel (1973) have devised a sensitive method for the assay of peroxidation products. They first studied the interaction between malondialdehyde and amino acids (Dillard and Tappel, 1973) and, based on the properties of the product, developed a fluorescence assay.

An effective and direct method for detecting free radicals is by electron spin resonance (ESR) spectrum (see Wertz and Bolton, 1972; Pryor, 1966). Free radicals with short lifetimes can be stabilized by freezing and holding them at low temperatures (e.g., liquid N_2). A further increase in sensitivity can be obtained by coupling the spectrometer to a computer that will average the data from several repeated scans in order to cancel the noise. Quantitation by this method, however, is difficult.

Free Radicals in Tissues and Their Potentially Deleterious Effects

A number of metabolic reactions are known to produce free radicals as obligatory intermediates. Among these, the flavin semiquinone in the mitochondrial respiratory chain (Rieske, Zangg, and Hansen, 1964; Commoner and Hollocher, 1960) and radicals associated with the microsomal drug metabolizing system (Hashimoto, Yamamo, and Mason, 1962) appear the strongest by ESR measurements. These signals can be seen best in frozen samples of whole tissue, e.g., rat liver at -180°C (Slater, 1972). Speculations that these free radicals could initiate damaging chain reactions may be warranted, but probably only under abnormal conditions. Under ordinary conditions, they are designed to proceed on their normal pathway, particularly in membranous systems.

In vitro experiments have established conclusively that *in vitro* peroxidation of membrane lipids is accompanied by extensive damage to the structure of membrane with attendant functional decline. Hunter, Gebicki, Hoffsten, Weinstein, and Scott (1963) found that lipid peroxidation in the isolated mitochondrial system induced by Fe^{2+}- catalyzed ascorbate oxidation resulted in swelling of mitochondria and uncoupling of phosphorylation. Desai and Tappel (1963) showed that lysosomal enzymes were released when lipid peroxidation was promoted in a suspension of the purified organelles. In a third example, lipid peroxidation of the erythrocyte membrane produced lysis, particularly in the erythrocytes from vitamin E-deficient animals (Mengel and Kann, 1966). Many more such experiments have been carried out with similar results (see Slater, 1972).

Lipid peroxidation can also damage biological molecules such as cytochrome c (Desai and Tappel, 1963), ATP (Roubal and Tappel, 1967), and α-tocopherol (vitamin E) (O'Brien and Titmus, 1967; O'Brien and Little, 1969).

Free Radicals, Peroxidation of Lipids, and Aging

The occurrence of the fluorescent inclusions generally referred to as lipofuscin or age pigment in cells, particularly in the brain, was reported first by Stübel (1911). Strehler (1962) has extensively reviewed the early work on this interesting phenomenon. The pigment particles have been isolated (Björkerud, 1963; Strehler

et al., 1959) and partially characterized. They contain protein, carbohydrate, and the pigment which can be partially extracted by organic solvents (Strehler, 1959). They have phosphatase and esterase activity (Gedigk and Bontke, 1956). This association together with the evidence for their presence in lysosomes (Essner and Novikoff, 1960) suggests that they may arise from incomplete digestion of membranes in autophagic vacuoles (lysosomes). The degraded membrane could be from any intracellular organelle, and the process could represent normal turnover or some pathological response. Several workers have proposed that the fluorescent chromophore may arise from the polymerization of oxidized unsaturated lipids (Hartcroft, 1951; Casselman, 1951; Tappel, 1955).

Strehler, *et al.* (1959) found that the lipofuscin granules accumulate linearly with age in the human myocardium. The accumulation increased at the rate of 0.3 percent/decade (or about 0.6 percent of the intracellular volume/decade) and by the age of 90, 6 to 7 pecent of the intracellular volume was taken up by the pigment. There is also evidence that the pigment can result from stress, such as that following injection of cortisone, hypoxia, or acetanilide feeding (Sulkin and Srivanij, 1960). In nervous tissue, it can arise from several pathological conditions. Ceroid is a more general term for such degenerate products. Of all the tissues, brain probably has the highest concentration and most consistent distribution of ceroid (Siakotos, Watanabe, Saito, and Fleischer, 1970; Siakotos, Watanabe, Pennington, and Whitfield, 1973). On the basis of Strehler's attempts at quantitation of the lipofuscin by fluorescence microscopy, there is much reference in the literature to its association with the aging phenomenon. The fact that (1) some old persons have little pigment while some younger individuals are deeply pigmented; and (2) ceroid has been associated with pathology, particularly in the nervous tissue, raise some doubts with regard to lipofuscin accumulation as an obligatory process in aging.

The hypothesis that free radicals generated in excessive amounts from cellular reactions or from environmental factors such as ozone, radiation, or drug administration may damage cellular membranes and other components merits further consideration. In a logical extension of this hypothesis, Harman (1960) and Tappel (1968) have argued that such damage could accelerate aging and bring about death of the organism before its natural life span is attained. In a test of this hypothesis, Harman (1961) reported that inclusion of antioxidants in the diet increased the mean life span of experimental animals by 15–30 percent without changing the maximum life span. The animals receiving the antioxidants were lower in weight, which raises the possibility of dietary restriction in the experimental animals which by itself can prolong the mean life span. Another effect of feeding antioxidants was a reduction in tumor production (Harman, 1968). Comfort, Youhotsky-Gore, and Pathmanathan (1971) have reproduced the extension of mean life span in C3H mice, which were reported to be resistant to the antioxidant effect (Harman, 1961). Several alternatives to the free radical hypothesis of aging have been considered by Comfort et al. (1971) to explain the data. In these experiments the antioxidant was mixed with the diet which could help maintain its nutritive value in a better state than in the absence of the antioxidant. Epstein and Gershon (1972) have also reported that including α-tocopherol or tocopherol-quinone in the medium of the nematode, Caenorhabditis briggsae, increased the mean life span from 35 ± 2 days to 46 ± 2 days, and the normal life span from 56 ± 3 days to 69 ± 4 days. The authors also state that the accumulation of lipofuscin, as seen by electron microscopy, was delayed in the animals receiving the tocopherol. Since the quinone was just as effective as the quinol, and since butylated hydroxytoluene (BHT) (also an antioxidant) was ineffective in prolonging the mean life span, the authors point out that the tocopherol must act intracellularly. On the other hand, Harman (1961) has claimed that BHT was quite effective in rats and mice. It is not known whether tocopherol is an essential nutrient for the nematode. Should it be a requirement, supplementation of an inadequate medium with tocopherol could extend the mean life span. Against this possibility, Epstein and Gershon (1972) found that the duration of the reproductive period and the number of offspring per animal were not altered by the inclusion of tocopherol in the medium.

Consistent with the "free radical hypothesis" of aging, Harman (1960) has also reported that the serum mercaptan (-SH) levels in men and women decline significantly, i.e., from 550 μM at age 20–40 to the range of 400 μM at age 80. Analyses were not carried out for a corresponding increase in -S-S- compounds, which could have strengthened the arguments for peroxidation.

A number of examples have been given to illustrate the in vitro structural and molecular changes induced by free radicals. The evidence that free radicals actually do produce these changes in tissues, however, is purely circumstantial. Even granting this, the more questionable assumption is that the products are deleterious in the slow process of aging. One of the characteristics of the living organism is its ability to eliminate unwanted material or to neutralize its effect by encapsulation in a membrane and then to repair any damage. An example of a repairable damage is reduction of -S-S- compounds back to -SH by active enzyme systems. If the production of free radicals exceeds normal rates, e.g., in carbon tetrachloride poisoning (Slater, 1972) or UV irradiation, the normal steady-state concentration of free radicals can be exceeded beyond levels that can be dealt with by the quenching process and repair systems. The result could be serious tissue injury. But does this kind of damage happen under physiological conditions in senescence which is a slow change? Unfortunately, there is little data to answer this question satisfactorily, and further research is needed.

ADDENDUM

The occurrence of enlarged, foamy mitochondria in the liver cells of aging mice has been quantitated by Wilson and Franks (1975). Extensive loss of these abnormal forms did occur during isolation of the mitochondrial pellet. Representative sampling of the mitochondria in the tissues is thus a serious problem. In fact, improving the isolation methods to obtain better and better mitochondria may lead to even larger errors in the sampling and may be self-defeating.

Contrary to the data of Abu-Erreish, Wohlrab, and Sanadi (1974) shown in Tables 8 and 9, Wilson, Hill, and Franks (1975) observed no change in the cytochrome oxidase activity of the isolated mitochondria. However, their assays were not done under conditions that expressed maximal activity of the oxidase.

REFERENCES

Abu-Erreish, G. M., Wohlrab, H., and Sanadi, D. R. 1974. *In vitro* and *in vivo* changes of mitochondria from hearts of senescent rats. *Federation Proc.*, 33, 1518.

Adelman, R. C. 1970. An age-dependent modification of enzyme regulation. *J. Biol. Chem.*, 245, 1032–1035.

Altschuler, H., Lieberson, M., and Spitzer, J. J. 1962. Effect of body weight on free fatty acid release by eclipse tissue *in vitro*. *Experientia*, 18, 91–92.

Angelova-Gateva, P. 1969. Tissue respiration and glycolysis in quadriceps femoris and heart of rats of different ages during hypodynamia. *Exp. Geront.*, 4, 177–187.

Arcos, J. C., Stacey, R. E., Mathison, J. B., and Argus, M. F. 1967. Kinetic parameters of mitochondrial swelling. Effect of animal age. Tissue distribution of the mitochondrial "contractile protein." *Exp. Cell Res.*, 48, 448–460.

Atkinson, D. E. 1973. Adenine nucleotides as universal stoichiometric coupling agents. *In*, G. Weber (ed.), *Advances in Enzyme Regulation*, Vol. 9, pp. 207–219. New York: Pergamon Press.

Barrows, C. H., and Roeder, L. M. 1961. Effect of age on protein synthesis in rats. *J. Geront.*, 16, 321–326.

Barrows, C. H., Roeder, L. M., and Falzone, J. A. 1962. Effect of age on the activities of enzymes and the concentrations of nucleic acids in the tissues of female wild rats. *J. Geront.*, 17, 144–147.

Barrows, C. H., Roeder, L. M., and Glewine, D. A. 1962. Effect of age on the renal compensatory hypertrophy following unilateral nephrectomy on the rat. *J. Geront.*, 17, 148–153.

Barrows, C. H., Yiengst, M. J., and Shock, N. W. 1958. Senescence and the metabolism of various tissues of rats. *J. Geront.*, 13, 351–355.

Beauchene, R. W., Roeder, L. M., and Barrows, C. H. 1967. The effect of age and ethinine feeding on the RNA and protein synthesis of rats. *J. Geront.*, 22, 318–324.

Beattie, D. S., Basford, R. E., and Koritz, S. B. 1966. Studies on the biosynthesis of mitochondrial protein components. *Biochemistry*, 5, 926–930.

Beattie, D. S., Basford, R. E., and Koritz, S. B. 1967.

The turnover of the protein components of mitochondria from rat liver, kidney and brain. *J. Biol. Chem.*, 242, 4584.

Benjamin, W., Gelhorn, A., Wagner, M., and Kundel, H. 1961. Effect of aging on lipid composition and metabolism in the adipose tissue of the rat. *Am. J. Physiol.*, 201, 540–546.

Bernheim, F., Bernheim, M. L. C., and Wilbur, K. M. 1948. The reaction between thiobarbituric acid and the oxidation of certain lipids. *J. Biol. Chem.*, 174, 257–264.

Björkerud, S. 1963. The isolation of lipofuschin granules from bovine cardiac muscle, with observations on the properties of the isolated granules on the light and electron microscopic levels. *J. Ultrastruct. Res. Supp. 5*, 5–49.

Bloch, K., Borek, E., and Rittenberg, D. 1946. Synthesis of cholesterol in surviving liver. *J. Biol. Chem.*, 162, 441–449.

Bulos, B., Sacktor, B., Grossman, I. W., and Altman, N. 1971. Thyroid control of mitochondrial α-glycerolphosphate dehydrogenase in rat liver as a function of age. *J. Geront.*, 26, 13–19.

Bulos, B., Shukla, S., and Sacktor, B. 1972. Bioenergetic properties of mitochondria from flight muscle of aging blowflies. *Arch. Biochem. Biophys.*, 149, 461–469.

Carlson, L. A., Froberg, S. O., and Nye, E. R. 1968. Effect of age on the blood and tissue lipid levels in the male rat. *Gerentologia*, 14, 65–79.

Casselman, W. G. B. 1951. The *in vitro* preparation and histochemical properties of substances resembling ceroid. *J. Exp. Med.*, 94, 549–562.

Chen, J. C., Warshaw, J. B., and Sanadi, D. R. 1972. Regulation of mitochondrial respiration in senescence. *J. Cellular Physiol.*, 80, 141–148.

Comfort, A., Youhotsky-Gore, I., and Pathmanathan, K. 1971. Effect of ethoxyquin on the longevity of C3H mice. *Nature*, 229, 254–255.

Commoner, B., and Hollocher, J. C. 1960. Free radicals in heart muscle mitochondrial particles: General characteristics and localization in the electron transfer system. *Proc. Nat. Acad. Sci*, 46, 405–416.

Comolli, R., Ferioli, M. E., and Azzola, S. 1972. Protein turnover of the lysosomal and mitochondrial fractions of rat liver during aging. *Exp. Geront.*, 7, 369–376.

Daggs, R. G., and Halcro-Wardlaw, H. S. 1933. Conversion of fat to carbohydrate in the germinating castor bean. *J. Gen. Physiol.*, 17, 303–309.

Dahle, L. K., Hill, E. G., and Holman, R. T. 1962. The thiobarbituric acid reaction and the autoxidations of polyunsaturated fatty acid methyl esters. *Arch. Biochem. Biophys.*, 98, 253–261.

Das, B. C., and Bhattacharya, S. K. 1961. Variation in lipoprotein level with age, weight and cholesterol ester. *Gerontologia*, 5, 25–34.

Desai, I. D., and Tappel, A. L. 1963. Will anti-oxidant nutrients slow aging processes? *J. Lipid Res.*, 4, 204.

Dillard, C. J., and Tappel, A. L. 1973. Fluorescent

products from reaction of peroxidizing polyunsaturated fatty acids with phosphatidyl ethanolamine and phenylalanine. *Lipids*, **8**, 183-189.

Dury, A. 1961. Lipolytic activity of aorta of young and old rats and influence of heparin *in vivo*. *J. Geront.*, **16**, 114-117.

Epel, D., Weaver, A. M., Muchmore, A. V., and R. T. Schimke. 1969. β-1,3-gluconase of sea urchin eggs: Release from particles at fertilization. *Science*, **163**, 294-296.

Epstein, J., and Gershon, D. 1972. Studies on aging in nematodes. IV. The effect of antioxidants on cellular damage and lifespan. *Mech. Age. Dev.*, **1**, 257-264.

Erlanger, M., and Gershon, D. 1970. Studies on aging in nematodes. II. Studies of the activities of several enzymes as a function of age. *Exp. Geront.*, **5**, 13-19.

Ermini, M., and Verzar, F. 1968. Decreased restitution of creatine phosphate in white and red skeletal muscle during aging. *Experientia*, **24**, 902-904.

Essner, E., and Novikoff, A. 1960. Human hepatocellular pigments and lysosomes. *J. Ultrastruct. Res.*, **3**, 374-379.

Ferrendelli, J. A., Sedgwick, W. G., and Suntzeff, V. 1971. Regional energy metabolism and lipofuscin accumulation in mouse brain during aging. *J. Neuropathol.*, **30**, 638-649.

Finch, C. 1972. Enzyme activities, gene function and aging in mammals. *Exp. Geront.*, **7**, 53-68.

Fletcher, B. L., Dillard, C. J., and Tappel, A. L. 1973. Measurement of fluorescent lipid peroxidation products in biological systems and tissues. *Arch. Biochem. Biophys.*, **52**, 1-9.

Fletcher, M., and Sanadi, D. R. 1961. Turnover of rat liver mitochondria. *Biochim. Biophys. Acta*, **51**, 356-360.

Fridovich, I., and Handler, P. 1961. Detection of free radicals generated during enzymic oxidations by initiation of sulfite oxidation. *J. Biol. Chem.*, **236**, 1836-1840.

Fritz, P. J., Vesell, E. S., White, E. L., and Pruitt, K. M. 1969. The role of synthesis and degradation in determining tissue concentration of lactic dehydrogenase -5. *Proc. Nat. Acad. Sci.*, **62**, 558-565.

Frolkis, V. V., and Bogatskaya, L. N. 1967. The energy metabolism of myocardium and its regulation in animals of various age. *Exp. Geront.*, **3**, 199-210.

Frolkis, V. V., Verzhikovskaya, N. V., and Valueva, G. V. 1973. The thyroid and age. *Exp. Geront.*, **8**, 285-296.

Gedigk, P., and Bontke, E. 1956. Uber den Nachweis von hydrolytischen Enzymen in dipopigmenten. *Z. Zellforsch.*, **44**, 495-518.

Gershon, H., and Gershon, D. 1970. Detection of inactive enzyme molecules in aging organisms. *Nature*, **227**, 1214-1217.

Gershon, H., and Gershon, D. 1973. Inactive enzyme molecules in aging mice: Liver aldolase. *Proc. Nat. Acad. Sci.*, **70**, 909-913.

Gold, P. H., Gee, M. V., and Strehler, B. L. 1968. Ef-

fect of age on oxidative phosphorylation in the rat. *J. Geront.*, **23**, 509-512.

Greengard, P. 1969. Enzymic differentiation in mammalian liver. *Science*, **163**, 891-895.

Greenwood, M. R. C., Johnson, P. R., and Hirsch, J. 1970. Relationship of age and cellularity to metabolic activity in C57B mice. *Proc. Soc. Exp. Biol. Med.*, **133**, 944-947.

Grinna, L. S., and Barber, A. A. 1972. Age-related changes in membrane lipid content and enzyme activities. *Biochim. Biophys. Acta*, **288**, 347-353.

Grollman, S., and Costello, L. 1972. Effect of age and exercise on lipid content of various tissues of the male albino rat. *J. Appl. Physiol.*, **32**, 761-765.

Harman, D. 1960. The free radical theory of aging: The effect of age on serum mercaptan levels. *J. Geront.*, **15**, 38-40.

Harman, D. 1961. Prolongation of the normal lifespan and inhibition of spontaneous cancer by antioxidants. *J. Geront.*, **16**, 247-254.

Harman, D. 1968. Free radical theory of aging. *J. Geront.*, **23**, 476-482.

Hartcroft, W. S. 1951. *In vitro* and *in vivo* production of ceroid-like substance from erythrocytes and certain lipids. *Science*, **113**, 673-674.

Hashimoto, Y., Yamamo, T., and Mason, H. S. 1962. An electron spin resonance study of microsomal electron transport. *J. Biol. Chem.*, **237**, PC3843-PC3844.

Hawkins, J. 1927. The metabolism of liver tissue from rats of different ages. *J. Gen. Physiol.*, **11**, 645-647.

Hirsch, J., and Han, J. 1969. Cellularity of rat adipose tissue: Effect of growth, starvation and obesity. *J. Lipid. Res.*, **10**, 77-82.

Hochstein, P., and Ernster, L. 1963. ADP-activated lipid peroxidation coupled to the TPNH oxidase system of microsomes. *Biochem. Biophys. Res. Comm.*, **12**, 388-394.

Hunter, F. E., Gebicki, J. M., Hoffsten, P. E., Weinstein, J., and Scott, A. 1963. Swelling and lysis of rat liver mitochondria induced by ferrous ions. *J. Biol. Chem.*, **238**, 828-835.

Inamdar, A. R., Person, R., Kohnen, P., Duncan, H., and Mackler, B. 1974. Effect of age on oxidative phosphorylation in tissues of hamsters. *J. Geront.*, **29**, 638-642.

Ishikawa, T., and Pei, Y. F. 1965. Intramitochondrial glycogen particles in rat retinal receptor cells. *J. Cell Biol.*, **25**, 402-407.

Jelinkova-Tenorova, M., and Hruza, Z. 1963. The effect of epinephrine on fat metabolism in old rats. *Gerontologia*, **7**, 168-180.

Jost, J. O., Khairallah, E. A., and Pitot, H. C. 1968. Studies on the induction and repression of enzymes in rat liver. *J. Biol. Chem.*, **243**, 3057-3066.

Kacser, H. 1963. Kinetic structure of organisms. *In*, R. J. C. Harris (ed.), *Biological Organization at the Cellular and Supercellular Level*, pp. 25-41. New York: Academic Press.

Kenney, F. T. 1962. Induction of tyrosine-α-ketoglutarate transaminase in rat liver. *J. Biol. Chem.*, **237**, 3495-3498.

Keys, A., Taylor, H. L., and Grande, F. 1973. Basal metabolism and age of adult man. *Metabolism*, **22**, 579-587.

Kim, J. H., and Miller, L. L. 1968. The functional significance of changes in activity of enzymes after inclusion in intact rats and in isolated, perfused rat liver. *J. Biol. Chem.*, **244**, 1410-1416.

Kipshidze, N. N. 1967. Quantitative changes in lipid, protein, and carbohydrate metabolism in relation to age. Thule International Symposium on Cancer and Aging, pp. 49-57.

Klingenberg, M. 1970. Metabolite transport in mitochondria: An example for intracellular membrane function. *Essays in Biochem.*, **6**, 119-159.

Kritchevsky, D. 1972. Lipid metabolism and aging. *Mech. Age. Dev.*, **1**, 275-284.

Kritchevsky, D., and Tepper, S. A. 1964. Serum cholesterol levels of inbred rats. *Am. J. Physiol.*, **207**, 631-633.

Lehninger, A. L. 1965. *The Mitochondrion*. New York: W. A. Benjamin.

Lipman, F. 1941. Metabolic generation and utilization of phosphate bond energy. *Advan. Enzymol.*, **1**, 99-162.

McCord, J. M., and Fridovich, I. 1969. Superoxide dismutase: An enzymatic function for erythrocuprein (hemocuprein). *J. Biol. Chem.*, **244**, 6049-6055.

Mainwaring, W. I. P. 1968. The effect of testosterone on the age-associated changes in the ventral prostate gland of the mouse. *Gerontologia*, **14**, 133-141.

Mayer, A. M., and Shain, Y. 1968. Zymogen granules in enzyme liberation and activation in pea seeds. *Science*, **162**, 1283-1284.

Mengel, C. E., and Kann, H. E. 1966. Effects of *in vivo* hyperoxia on erythrocytes. III. *In vivo* peroxidation of erythrocyte lipid. *J. Clin. Invest.*, **45**, 1150-1158.

Menzies, R. A., and Gold, P. H. 1971. The turnover of mitochondria in a variety of tissues of young adult and aged rats. *J. Biol. Chem.*, **246**, 2425-2429.

Moore, C. L., and Strasberg, P. M. 1970. Cytochromes and oxidative phosphorylation. *In*, A. Lajtha (ed.), *Handbook of Neurochemistry*, Vol. 3, pp. 53-85. New York: Plenum Press.

Moore, R. O. 1968. Effect of age of rats on the response of adipose tissue to insulin and the multiple forms of hexokinase. *J. Geront.*, **23**, 45-49.

Nikkila, E. A., and Niemi, T. 1957. Effect of age on the lipemia cleaning activity of serum after administration of heparin to human subjects. *J. Geront.*, **12**, 44-47.

O'Brien, P. J., and Little, C. 1969. Intracellular mechanisms for the decomposition of lipid peroxide by subcellular fractions. *Can. J. Biochem.*, **47**, 493-499.

O'Brien, P. J., and Titmus, G. 1967. The effects of a lipid peroxide on vitamin E. *Biochem. J.*, **103**, 33P-34P.

Pearce, J. M. 1936. Age and tissue respiration. *Am. J. Physiol.*, **114**, 255-260.

Perry, W. F., and Bowen, H. F. 1957. The utilization of acetate by liver and adipose tissue of growth hormone treated rats of different ages. *Can. J. Biochem. Physiol.*, **35**, 759-766.

Pryor, W. A. 1966. *Free Radicals*. New York: McGraw-Hill.

Rafsky, H. A., Newman, B., and Horonick, A. 1952. Age differences in respiration of guinea pig tissues. *J. Geront.*, **7**, 38-40.

Reiner, J. M. 1947. The effect of age on the carbohydrate metabolism of tissue homogenates. *J. Geront.*, **2**, 315-320.

Rieske, J. S., Hansen, R. E., and Zaugg, W. S. 1964. Studies on the electron transfer system. LVIII. Properties of a new oxidation-reduction component of the respiratory chain as studied by electron paramagnetic resonance spectroscopy. *J. Biol. Chem.*, **239**, 3017-3022.

Rockstein, M., and Bhatnagar, P. L. 1965. Age changes in size and number of the giant mitochondria in the flight muscle of the common housefly (*Musca domestica L.*). *J. Insect Physiol.*, **11**, 481-491.

Rosenman, R. H., and Shibata, E. 1952. Effect of age upon hepatic synthesis of cholesterol in the rat. *Proc. Soc. Exp. Biol. Med.*, **81**, 296-298.

Rosenthal, O., Bowie, M. A., and Wagoner, G. 1941. Studies in the metabolism of articular cartilage. I. Respiration and glycolysis of cartilage in relation to age. *J. Comp. Cell. Physiol.*, **17**, 221-223.

Ross, M. H. 1969. Aging, nutrition and hepatic enzyme activity patterns in the rat. *J. Nutr.*, **96**, 563-601.

Ross, M. H., and Ely, J. O. 1954. Age-related changes in respiration of sliced liver of the rat. *J. Franklin Inst.*, **258**, 63-66.

Roubal, W. T., and Tappel, A. L. 1967. Damage to ATP by peroxidizing lipids. *Biochim. Biophys. Acta*, **136**, 402-403.

Rouser, G., and Yamamoto, Y. 1968. Curvilinear regression course of human brain lipid changes with age. *Lipids*, **3**, 284-287.

Sacktor, B., and Shimada, Y. 1972. Degenerative changes in the mitochondria of flight muscle from aging blowflies. *J. Cell Biol.*, **52**, 465-477.

Sanadi, D. R., Barrows, C. H., and Crowder, S. E. 1966. Oxidation of ^{14}C-labeled compounds in rats of different ages. *J. Geront.*, **21**, 244-247.

Sanadi, D. R., and Fletcher, M. 1961. Turnover of liver mitochondrial components in adult and senescent rats. *J. Geront.*, **16**, 255-257.

Sanadi, D. R., Huang, P-k.C., and Pharo, R. L. 1971. NADH-ubiquinone reductase. *In*, T. E. King and M. Klingenberg (eds.), *Electron and Coupled Energy Transfer in Biological Systems*, Vol. 1, pp. 159-175. New York: Marcel Dekker.

Schimke, R. T., and Doyle, D. 1970. Control of enzyme levels in animal tissues. *Ann. Rev. Biochem.*, **39**, 929-976.

Segal, H. L., and Kim Y. S. 1963. Glycocorticoid stimulation of the biosynthesis of glutamic-alanine transaminase. *Proc. Nat. Acad. Sci.*, **50**, 912–918.

Shock, N. W., and Yiengst, M. J. 1955. Age changes in basal respiratory measurements and metabolism in males. *J. Geront.*, **10**, 31–40.

Siakotos, A. N., Watanabe, I., Pennington, K., and Whitfield, M. 1973. Procedure for mass isolation of pure lipofuscins from normal human heart and liver. *Biochem. Med.*, **7**, 25–38.

Siakotos, A. N., Watanabe, I., Saito, A., and Fleischer, S. 1970. Procedures for the isolation of two distinct lipopigments from human brain: Lipofuschin and ceroid. *Biochem. Med.*, **4**, 361–375.

Sidwell, C. G., Salwin, H., and Mitchell, J. H. 1955. Measurement of oxidation in dried milk products with thiobarbituric acid. *J. Am. Oil Chemists' Soc.*, **32**, 13–16.

Slater, T. F. 1972. *Free Radical Mechanisms in Tissue Injury*. London: Pion.

Smith, D. S. 1963. The structure of flight muscle sarcosomes in the blowfly *Calliphora erythrocephala*. *J. Cell Biol.*, **19**, 115–138.

Smith, E. B. 1965. The influence of atherosclerosis on the chemistry of the aortic intima. *J. Atherosclerosis Res.*, **5**, 224–240.

Sohol, R. S. 1970. Mitochondrial changes in the heart of *Drosophila replita*, Wallaston, with age. *Exp. Geront.*, **5**, 213–216.

Sohol, R. S., and Allison, V. F. 1971. Age-related changes in the fine structure of the flight muscle in the house fly. *Exp. Geront.*, **6**, 167–172.

Srere, P. A. 1967. Enzyme concentrations in tissues. *Science*, **158**, 936, 937.

Strehler, B. L. 1962. *Time, Cells and Aging*. New York: Academic Press.

Strehler, B. L., Mark, D. D., Mildvan, A. S., and Gee, M. V. 1959. Rate and magnitude of age pigment accumulation in the human myocardium. *J. Geront.*, **14**, 430–439.

Stübel, H. 1911. Die Fluoreszenz tienscher Gewebe Licht. Pfluger's *Arch. ges. Physiol.*, **142**, 1–14.

Stuchlikova, E., Hruskova, J., Hruza, Z., Jelinkova, M., Novak, P., and Soukupova, K. 1966. Effect of adrenalin on lipolysis in glycogenolysis in relation to age and stress. *Exp. Geront.*, **2**, 15–21.

Sulkin, N. M., and Srivanij, P. 1960. The experimental production of senile pigments in the nerve cells of young rats. *J. Geront.*, **15**, 2–9.

Swick, R., Rexroth, A. K., and Stange, J. L. 1968. The metabolism of mitochondrial proteins. III. The dynamic state of rat liver mitochondria. *J. Biol. Chem.*, **243**, 3581–3587.

Takahashi, A., Philpot, D. E., and Miguel, J. 1970. Electron microscopic studies on aging *D. melanogaster*. III. Flight muscle. *J. Geront.*, **25**, 222–228.

Tappel, A. L. 1955. Studies of the mechanism of vitamin E action. III. *In vitro* copolymerization of oxidized fat and protein. *Arch. Biochem. Biophys.*, **54**, 266–280.

Tappel, A. L. 1968. Will antioxidant nutrients slow aging processes? *Geriatrics*, **23**, 97.

Tatibana, M., and Cohen, P. P. 1965. Formation and conversion of macromolecular precursor(s) in the biosynthesis of carbonyl phosphate synthetase. *Proc. Nat. Acad. Sci.*, **53**, 104–111.

Tauchi, H., and Sato, T. 1968. Age changes in size and number of mitochondria of human hepatic cells. *J. Geront.*, **23**, 454–461.

Travis, D. F., and Travis, A. 1972. Ultrastructural changes in the left ventricular rat myocardial cells with age. *J. Ultrastruct. Res.*, **39**, 124–148.

Tregear, R. J. 1967. The oscillation of insect flight muscle. *In*, D. R. Sanadi (ed.), *Current Topics in Bioenergetics*, Vol. 2, pp. 269–284. New York: Academic Press.

Tribe, M. A. 1966. Some physiological studies in relation to age in the blowfly, *Calliphora erythrocephala*. *J. Insect Physiol.*, **12**, 1577–1593.

Tribe, M. A., and Ashhurst, D. E. 1972. Biochemical and structural variations in the flight muscle mitochondria of aging blowflies, *Calliphora erythrocephala*. *J. Cell Sci.*, **10**, 443–469.

Wainio, W. W. 1970. *The Mammalian Mitochondrial Respiratory Chain*. New York: Academic Press.

Weinbach, E. C., and Garbus, J. 1959. Oxidative phosphorylation in mitochondria from aged rats. *J. Biol. Chem.*, **234**, 412–417.

Werner, M., Tolls, R. E., Hultin, J. V., and Mellecker, J. 1970. Influence of sex and age on the normal range of eleven serum constituents. *Z. Klin. Chem. Biochem.*, **8**, 105–115; quote by Kritchevsky, 1972.

Wertz, J. E., and Bolton, J. R. 1972. *Electron Spin Resonance. Elementary Theory and Practical Applications*. New York: McGraw-Hill.

Williams, C. M., Barnes, L. A., and Sawyer, W. H. 1943. The utilization of glycogen by flies during flight and some aspects of the physiological aging of *Drosophila*. *Biol. Bull.*, **84**, 263–272.

Wilson, P. 1973. Enzyme changes in aging mammals. *Gerontologia*, **19**, 79–125.

Wilson, P. D., and Franks, L. M. 1975. The effect of age on mitochondrial ultrastructure. *Gerontologia*, **21**, 81–94.

Wilson, P. D., Hill, B. T., and Franks, L. M. 1975. The effect of age on mitochondrial enzymes and respiration. *Gerontologia*, **21**, 95–101.

Wollenberger, A., and Jehl, J. 1952. Influence of age on rate of respiration of sliced cardiac muscle. *Am. J. Physiol.*, **170**, 126–130.

Wright, B. W. 1973. *Critical Variables in Differentiation*. Englewood Cliffs, New Jersey: Prentice-Hall.

Yamamoto, M., and Yamamura, Y. 1971. Changes of cholesterol metabolism in the aging rat. *Atherosclerosis*, **13**, 365–374.

Zeelon, P., Gershon, H., and Gershon, D. 1973. Inactive enzyme molecules in aging organisms. Nematode fructose-1,6-diphosphate aldolase. *Biochemistry*, **12**, 1743–1750.

Zemplenyi, T., and Grafnetter, D. 1959. The lipolytic activity of the aorta: Its relation to aging and to atherosclerosis. *Gerontologia*, **3**, 55–64.

Zorzoli, A. 1955. Effect of age on phosphatase activity in the liver of the mouse. *J. Geront.*, **10**, 156–164.

Zorzoli, A., and Li, J. B. 1967. Gluconeogenesis in mouse kidney cortex. Effect of age and fasting on glucose production and enzyme activities. *J. Geront.*, **22**, 151–157.

PART 3 CELLULAR LEVEL

5
CELL DIVISION AND THE CELL CYCLE

Renato L. Baserga

Temple University School of Medicine

INTRODUCTION

This chapter deals with cell division and the cell cycle *in vivo*, i.e., in experimental animals and man. There are two fundamental reasons why a knowledge of the cell cycle is of interest to the student of the aging process, namely: (1) the *in vitro* aging of human diploid fibroblasts is characterized by a failure of cell proliferation; and (2) aging causes changes in the kinetics of the cell cycle. Since the *in vitro* aging process, pioneered by Hayflick and coworkers, is considered elsewhere in this volume (see Chapter 7), this chapter will be limited to a study of the effect that aging has on the cell cycle of mammalian cells *in vivo*. Both the kinetics and the basic biochemical events that control the flow of cells through the cell cycle will be considered.

Methodology for Studying the Cell Cycle

The concept of the cell cycle was first developed in 1951 by Howard and Pelc studying cell division in root tips of *Vicia faba*. Howard and Pelc, using autoradiography and ^{32}P to label the DNA of root tip cells, found that mitosis was always preceded by incorporation of ^{32}P into DNA. Furthermore, they found that a discrete interval existed between cessation of ^{32}P incorporation into DNA and cell division. On the ba-

sis of their studies, which were by necessity rather approximate, Howard and Pelc developed the concept of the cell cycle as a sequence of cyclic events occurring between one mitosis and the subsequent mitosis of one or both daughter cells. The study of the cell cycle gained considerable impetus with the development of a radioactive compound which was rightfully considered as a specific precursor of DNA, i.e., thymidine [^{3}H]. Thymidine is a deoxynucleoside which is incorporated exclusively into DNA. Since thymidine and its degradation products are soluble in ordinary fixatives in which DNA is insoluble, any radioactivity found in fixed tissues or cells after exposure to radioactive thymidine is due to newly synthesized DNA. In addition, thymidine, when injected into experimental animals is either promptly incorporated into DNA or catabolized to nonutilizable products. The time during which injected thymidine is available for incorporation into DNA is, in most cases, between 30 min. and 1 hr, so that for all practical purposes an *in vivo* exposure to thymidine results in pulse labeling of newly synthesized DNA (detailed references on the biochemistry of radioactive thymidine are given in a review by Baserga and Wiebel, 1969).

The use of thymidine [^{3}H] has greatly simplified the study of the cell cycle, not only because of its specificity and its short availability time, but also because of the high resolution that can be obtained with the tritium label. The classical approach for study of the cell cycle is the one originally described in 1959 by Quastler and Sherman and is based on the time of appearance of labeled mitoses after a pulse exposure to thymidine [³H]. However, before describing the method of Quastler and Sherman we will spend a few words on the technique of high resolution autoradiography.

Autoradiography. The cell cycle is, so to speak, a creature of autoradiography and although new and different methodologies have been developed in the past few years, autoradiography is still the best method available for a comprehensive study of the kinetics of the cell cycle in experimental animals.

Since little has been added to autoradiographic techniques in the past few years, the reader is referred for details to the monographs by Rogers (1967), Feinendegen (1967), Epifanova and Terskikh (1969a), and Baserga and Malamud (1969); or to the review articles by Prescott (1964a) and Baserga (1967).

Determination of the Cell Cycle and its Phases. Let us suppose a synchronous population of cells which, at least for the moment, we shall imagine as being composed exclusively of cells capable of division. The Ehrlich ascites tumor of mice in the first two or three days of intraperitoneal growth is a good example of such a population. When Ehrlich ascites tumor cells are exposed to thymidine [³H], cells that are synthesizing DNA at the time of exposure take up thymidine and become labeled. The availability time of thymidine in Ehrlich ascites tumors is only 10 min. (much shorter than the usual availability time for other cells of experimental animals). Thus cells that are not syn-

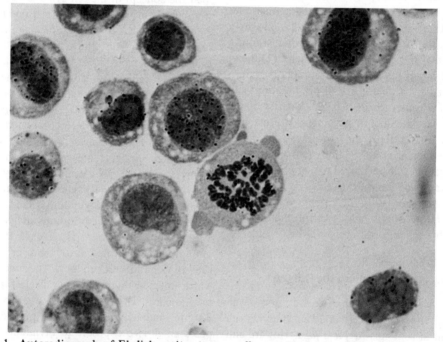

Figure 1. Autoradiograph of Ehrlich ascites tumor cells growing in the peritoneal cavity of mice and labeled with [³H]-thymidine. The animals were injected with [³H]-thymidine 6 hr before a sample was taken for autoradiography. Cells that were synthesizing DNA at the time [³H]-thymidine was injected can be recognized by the presence of black dots over the nuclei. These black dots represent the image produced in the nuclear emulsion by the β-particles emitted by the disintegrating [³H] atoms. The tumor cell in the middle is in mitosis. Notice that the radioactivity is confined to the chromosomal masses. The autoradiograph was done with Kodak NTB emulsion, and the cells were stained with hematoxilin. Magnification: 620 X.

thesizing DNA at the time of exposure ± 10 min. are not labeled. An autoradiograph of a smear of such cells taken within 30 min. after injection of thymidine [³H] discloses three types of cells: cells in mitosis (all unlabeled), unlabeled cells in interphase (cells not synthesizing DNA), and labeled cells in interphase (cells synthesizing DNA). The information obtained thus far is that DNA is synthesized during interphase and not during mitosis, since all cells in mitosis are unlabeled.

We can now follow the fate of cells that were in DNA synthesis at the time of exposure by taking tissue samples at various intervals after exposure to thymidine [³H]. For a few hours after exposure to thymidine [³H], all mitoses are unlabeled. Since mitosis lasts between 30 min. and 1 hr, one must conclude that cells do not synthesize DNA for a defined period before mitosis. After a few hours, the percentage of labeled mitoses (see Figure 1) begins to increase rapidly. The interval between the administration of thymidine [³H] and the time at which 50 percent of the mitoses are labeled gives the median duration of the premitotic phase, the G_2 phase, during which no DNA is synthesized. As more and more cells that were in DNA syn-

thesis at the time of exposure enter mitosis, the percentage of labeled mitoses increases until 100 percent of mitoses are labeled (Figure 2). Then the percentage of labeled mitoses begins to decrease. The interval between the 50 percent points on the ascending and descending limbs of the curve representing percentage of labeled mitoses, gives the median duration of the phase during which DNA is synthesized, the S phase (Howard and Pelc, 1951, Quastler and Sherman, 1959). The length of the entire cell cycle can be estimated on the basis of the time elapsing between two successive peaks of labeled mitoses (Fry, Lesher, and Kohn, 1961; see also review by Baserga and Wiebel, 1969). Because cells desynchronize very rapidly, the second peak of labeled mitoses may be dampened and it is therefore customary to take the time elapsing between equal points of the first two ascending limbs of the curve of percentage of labeled mitoses as the length of the entire cell cycle. For instance, in Figure 2, the interval between the 50 percent labeling points of the first and second ascending limbs is 22 hr (from 4 to 26 hr after the injection of thymidine [³H]), and the length of the entire cell is thus estimated at 22 hr. From Figure 2, one can also

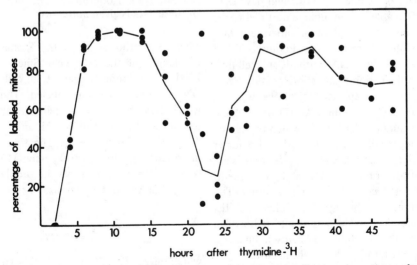

Figure 2. Percentage of labeled mitoses in Ehrlich ascites tumor cells at various times after a single injection of [³H]-thymidine. The radioactive compound was injected into the peritoneal cavity of mice at zero time. Appropriate samples were taken at the intervals indicated on the abscissa and autoradiographed, as described in Figure 1. The percentage of labeled mitoses was determined on a minimum of 50 mitoses/slide. The interpretation of the labeled mitoses curve is given in the text. Each point represents one animal.

calculate the duration of G_2 (4 hr) and of the S phase (16 hr), as decribed above. Since mitosis usually lasts less than 1 hr (Fry, Lesher, and Kohn, 1962a), another phase must be postulated to complete the cell cycle. The existence of this phase is also indicated by the decrease in percentage of labeled mitoses occurring after the first peak which suggests a period preceding DNA synthesis during which no DNA is synthesized. The duration of this period, the G_1 phase, can be calculated by subtracting the duration of G_2 plus S plus mitosis (1 hr in the case of Figure 2) from the entire length of the cell cycle. We can now give a definition of the cell cycle and its four phases. The cell cycle is the interval between mid-point of mitosis in the parent cell and mid-point of the subsequent mitosis in one or both daughter cells.

Another method that has been extensively used to determine the various parameters of the cell cycle employs repeated injections of thymidine [³H] into experimental animals. With this method one can not only determine the length of the cell cycle and its four component phases, but also the growth fraction, i.e., that fraction of cells in a given cell population that participates in the cell cycle. As mentioned above, not all cells participate in the proliferating cycle, and while some of them have definitely left the cell cycle and are destined to die without any further division, others are in a kind of limbo where they remain quiescent but capable of entering DNA synthesis and cell division again if an appropriate stimulus is received. The method of repeated injections was described originally by Fujita (1967) and is essentially a continuous labeling in which thymidine [³H] is repeatedly injected at intervals shorter than the length of the S phase. The animals are sacrificed at various intervals and the percentage of labeled cells determined as usual. The same continuous labeling can be achieved in tissue cultures by simply adding the radioactive isotope to the medium (see below). Figure 3 shows this pattern for HeLa cells in culture.

Thirty min. after exposure to thymidine [³H], about 33 percent of the cells were labeled, which can be expressed by the equation:

$$33 = 100 \times T_s/T_c \tag{1}$$

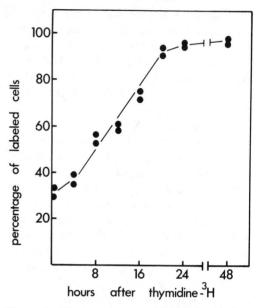

Figure 3. The percentage of labeled cells in a culture of HeLa cells continuously exposed to [³H]-thymidine. Monolayer cultures of HeLa cells were grown under standard conditions and [³H]-thymidine was added to the culture medium at time zero. Individual samples were harvested at the time indicated on the abscissa, and autoradiographs of the cultured cells were made, as described in Figure 1. Each point represents one set of tissue culture. The percentage of labeled cells was determined on a minimum of 1,000/point. The interpretation of these data is given in the text.

where T_s is the length of the S phase and T_c the length of the cell cycle. Since thymidine [³H] is continuously present, all cells entering DNA synthesis become labeled. The time at which 100 percent of the cells are labeled corresponds to the sum of G_2, M, and G_1, that is, $T_{G2} + T_M + T_{G1} = T_c - T_s$. The time of maximum labeling (close to 100 percent) in Figure 3 is 20 hr. We can now solve the problem with a set of simultaneous equations:

$$33\ T_c = 100\ T_s \tag{2}$$

$$T_c = 20 + T_s \tag{3}$$

which gives $T_c = 30$ hr and $T_s = 10$ hr. The growth fraction is near 1.0, i.e., by observation, nearly all cells are proliferating.

The limits of these methodologies, their degree of accuracy, and shortcomings have been discussed at length in a number of monographs and reviews. The reader is again referred to these works, in particular the book by Lamerton and Fry (1962) and the review articles by Tubiana (1968) and Baserga and Wiebel (1969). The reader interested in a more sophisticated mathematical treatment of the percentage of labeled mitoses curve can find nourishment to his heart's content in two articles by Barrett (1966) and by Mendelsohn and Takahashi (1971).

Determination of the Cell Cycle in Tissue Culture. The methods for determining the length of the cell cycle in cells in culture are essentially the same as those described for experimental animals. The second method described, i.e., the one of continuous exposure to thymidine [³H] is especially effective in tissue cultures where, in most cases, the growth fraction is 1.0 or near 1.0. The method for determining percentage of labeled mitoses needs a variation in tissue cultures because thymidine is not catabolized in tissue cultures as efficiently as it is in experimental animals. In fact, since most of thymidine catabolism is carried out in the liver, if thymidine is added to a tissue culture it will label cells continuously. This is an ideal situation if one wishes to carry out method 2 for the determination of the cell cycle, but it is obviously not feasible if one wishes to carry out method 1, i.e., the percentage of labeled mitoses curve. In such a case, an artificial pulse-labeling has to be carried out by labeling the

cells with thymidine [³H] for a period of only 30 min. followed by a replacement of the radioactive medium with nonradioactive medium. This introduces a few complications. Apart of course from the shock caused by the changing of medium (which can be avoided if the procedures are carried out gently), there remains the fact that the addition of fresh medium to a culture may stimulate its rate of growth and shorten the cell cycle so that the figures obtained would actually reflect a special circumstance, that is, the cell cycle of cells that are being stimulated to proliferate. Apart from these considerations, however, the methodologies are substantially the same and are as reliable as those carried out in experimental animals.

Table 1 gives the length of the cell in a few tissues of adult experimental animals and in selected cell cultures. Variations due to age will be considered in a later section.

Determination of the Length of the Various Phases of the Cell Cycle. *S phase.* Apart from the methods described above, the S phase of mammalian cells can also be determined by a double labeling technique. This method was originally introduced by Pilgrim and Maurer (1962) and developed by Wimber and Quastler (1963), who described the theoretical aspects of the method and applied it to the study of *Tradescantia* root tips. Briefly, to determine the duration of the S phase by a double labeling procedure, a population of cells is labeled with

TABLE 1. CELL CYCLE TIMES IN REPRESENTATIVE MAMMALIAN CELL PUPULATIONS[a].

Cell Type	T_C	T_{G_1}	T_S	T_{G_2}	T_M	Reference
Mouse embryo ependymal cells	111.0	3.5	5.5	1.0	1.0	Atlas and Bond, 1965
Mouse esophageal epithelium	41.0	–[b]	8.5	–	–	Blenkinsopp, 1969
Mouse mammary gland alveolar epithelium	71.0	38	21.7	–	–	Bresciani, 1965
Man, colon, epithelial cells	25.0	–	14.0	1.0	–	Lipkin, Bell, and Sherlock 1963
Man, bronchial epithelium	220.0	–	11.3	–	–	Fabrikant, 1970
Man, colon carcinoma	–	–	20.0	–	–	Clarkson, Ota, Ohkita, and O'Connor, 1965
Man, bronchial carcinoma	196–260	–	23.0	–	–	Fabrikant, 1970
Human diploid cells in culture	24.5	12.0	7.5	4.0	–	Defendi and Manson, 1963
L mouse cells	23.2	6.2	12.2	4.8	–	Cleaver, 1965
HeLa S₃ cells	21.0	8.0	9.5	3.0	–	Terasima and Tolmach, 1963

[a] T_C, T_{G_1}, T_S, T_{G_2} and T_M: respective duration (in hours) of cell cycle, G_1, S, G_2 and mitosis.
[b] –, not determined.

two thymidines, for example, thymidine [³H] and thymidine [¹⁴C], given separately at a measured interval. Some cells are labeled only by the first isotope, others only by the second, and still others by both. The ratio of cells labeled only by the first isotope to all the other labeled cells is equal to the ratio of the interval between the two isotopes to the total length of the S phase. This relationship in the simplest case and assuming that each time element of the generation cycle is represented by the same number of cells can be expressed by the equation $R1/R2 = I/S$; where $R1$ is the fraction of cells that have left or entered the S phase during the interval between the two radioisotopes, $R2$ is the fraction of cells labeled by a single injection of radioactive thymidine, T is the interval between the two isotopes, and S the length of DNA synthesis phase (Baserga and Lisco, 1963). All double labeling techniques require the identification of the fraction of cells labeled by the first isotope, and the accuracy of each technique depends essentially (if one neglects the counting error) on the accuracy with which the labeled cells can be identified. The pitfalls of the various methods used for the determination of the S phase by a double labeling technique have been discussed in detail by Baserga and Lisco (1963). The method when properly applied is reliable and can give a good idea of the length of the S phase. Its extrapolation to the measurement of other phases, however, is far from being reliable and reproducible and should not be used.

The methods for the determination of the length of G_2 and G_1 have been described above. Mitosis can actually be determined accurately only by time-lapse cinematography. Using this method, Sisken and Morasca (1965) found that T_M in cultured human amnion cells was 0.5 hr.

Cycling and Noncycling Cells. It is now generally accepted that mammalian cells can be divided into three large classes, namely: (1) continuously dividing cells, that go from one mitosis to the next one; (2) nondividing cells, that differentiate and die without dividing again; and (3) G_0 cells, that do not divide but can be

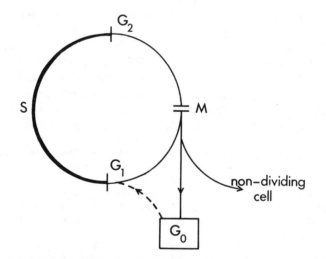

Figure 4. The cell cycle of mammalian cells. M represents mitosis in its classic four phases from prophase to telophase. After mitosis the cells can be divided into three general classes. One class of cells continues throughout the cell cycle, through G_1, S (period of DNA replication), and G_2, to the next mitosis. A second class of cells leaves the cell cycle and becomes nondividing cells destined to die without any further division. A third class of cells goes into a G_0 state in which the cell populations are resting, do not synthesize DNA, or divide. However, they can be stimulated to do so if an appropriate stimulus is applied. Cells of the lining epithelium of the crypts of the small intestine are representative of the first class of cells. Keratinizing epithelial cells of the skin are representative of the second class of cells, while hepatocytes, kidney cells, and many other cells of the adult animal are representative of the third class, G_0 cells.

stimulated to do so by an appropriate stimulus (Baserga, 1968). This situation is illustrated in the diagram of Figure 4.

BIOCHEMISTRY OF THE CELL CYCLE

Continuously Dividing Cells

We shall consider here, separately, the biochemical events that occur in the various phases of continuously dividing cells and those that occur in the prereplicative phase of G_0 cells stimulated to proliferate by an appropriate stimulus. There are very good reasons for keeping separate these two types of cells, i.e., continuously dividing cells and G_0 cells stimulated to proliferate. A discussion of why G_0 cells can be rightfully considered distinct from cells with a long G_1 will be included later. In the meantime we shall analyze separately the various phases of the cell cycle before considering the biochemical events occurring in the prereplicative phase of stimulated G_0 cells. Most of the information given in the following sections is contained in the reviews by Baserga, 1968; Mueller, 1969; Stein and Baserga, 1972; and a recent book by Baserga, 1971, to which the reader is referred also for the appropriate references. Only more recent or special references are singled out for further information.

G_1 **Phase.** The first biochemical event in G_1 that could be related to the onset of DNA synthesis was the finding by Baserga, Estensen, and Petersen (1965) and Baserga, Estensen, Petersen, and Layde (1965) that in the G_1 of Ehrlich ascites tumor cells, there was a step sensitive to small doses of actinomycin D. If this step (presumably RNA synthesis) was inhibited, the onset of DNA synthesis was prevented. A similar actinomycin D-sensitive step was identified by Baserga, Estensen, and Petersen (1966) in the G_1 phase of epithelial cells lining the crypts of the mouse jejunum. Several reports since have shown that in mammalian cells, synthesis of RNA occurs during the G_1 period and is a prerequisite for DNA synthesis. A more specific step was described by Borun, Scharf, and Robbins (1967) who found that 1 hr before the onset of DNA synthesis, a messenger RNA for histone synthesis was made in synchronized HeLa cells. The messenger RNA for histones appeared on cytoplasmic ribosomes 1 hr before the onset of DNA synthesis, and since inhibition of histone synthesis promptly leads to inhibition of DNA synthesis, the lack of the appropriate messenger RNA also led to failure in DNA synthesis initiation.

Protein synthesis was also found to be necessary for the orderly flow of G_1 cells into the S phase. The first demonstration goes back to the findings of Terasima and Yasukawa (1966) in synchronized L cells where they found that 2-hr periods of exposure to either puromycin or cycloheximide produced a 2-hr delay in the onset of DNA synthesis.

Other distinguishing features of the G_1 period include: (1) two enzymes are missing from G_1 cells that are present in cells in S phase, thymidine kinase and deoxycytidylate deaminase; (2) in human lymphoid cell lines the synthesis of immunoglobulins begins in late G_1 and continues throughout S phase up to mitosis; (3) polyribosomes that disaggregate during mitosis are re-formed immediately after mitosis using preexisting messenger RNA; (4) in mouse leukemic lymphoblasts at the end of the G_1 period and extending into the very early part of the S phase, there is a marked decrease in potassium content of the cell, accompanied by an increase in cellular sodium content; (5) the inducibility by steroids of the enzyme tyrosine aminotransferase is absent in hepatoma cells in the early phase of the G_1 period. These results, although fragmentary, seem to indicate that during the G_1 period there is a series of orderly metabolic events, some of which involve gene expression, which are directly related to the onset of DNA synthesis. Reviews of the events occurring in the G_1 period can be found in the references given above.

S **Phase.** Throughout the S phase, the activities of enzymes associated with DNA synthesis remain high. Among the enzyme activities increased during the S phase are: DNA polymerase, thymidine kinase, thymidylate kinase, thymidylate synthetase, and deoxycytidylate deaminase (see review by Stein and Baserga, 1972). In addition, ribonucleotide reductase activity increases considerably during the S phase and remains elevated in G_2. RNA synthesis continues during the S phase. Although Prescott (1964b) has demonstrated in the protozoan *Euplotes* that DNA cannot replicate and transcribe RNA simultaneously, this does not appear to be the situation in mammalian cells where DNA synthesis is markedly asynchronous in individual chromosomes, as well as in various segments of each chromosome. Thus, although RNA synthesis may not occur in the actual segment of DNA that is being replicated, the asynchrony of DNA replication in individual chromosomes and in various chromosomes within the same nucleus, over a period of 6 to 8 hr, averages out in such a manner that the small decrease in the rate of synthesis of RNA goes undetected.

Protein synthesis also continues at an elevated rate during S phase, and the synthesis of nonhistone chromosomal proteins which was evident during G_1 continues during the S phase. The synthesis of histones has been shown to be tightly coupled to DNA synthesis both in stimulated G_0 cells and in continuously dividing cells, and what has been provisionally designated as histone messenger RNA is present during the S phase (Borun, Scharf, and Robbins, 1967).

G_2 Phase. During the G_2 phase of the cell cycle, RNA and protein synthesis continue. However, their rates of synthesis decrease as the cell approaches mitosis. Kishimoto and Lieberman (1964) were the first to demonstrate that puromycin (5 μg/ml), when administered during G_2, effectively prevents the flow of cultured cells from G_2 to mitosis. Low doses of actinomycin D (0.33 μg/ml) were ineffective in producing a G_2 block. However, subsequent studies with higher doses of actinomycin D (2 μg/ml) have clearly established that the synthesis of RNA during the G_2 phase of the cell cycle is essential for entry of cells into mitosis (see review by Tobey, Petersen, and Anderson, 1971).

The synthesis of nonhistone chromosomal proteins continues during the G_2 phase. Furthermore, polyacrylamide gel electrophoretic profiles of nonhistone chromosomal proteins suggest that there are qualitative differences in nonhistone chromosomal proteins synthesized in G_2.

Mitosis. In addition to the condensation and segregation of chromosomes, a number of biochemical events also occur during the mitotic phase of the cell cycle. In 1960, Taylor demonstrated that mammalian cells synthesized RNA in all phases of the cell cycle, except during mitosis when there is cessation of RNA synthesis. These findings, indicating an interruption of gene expression, have been confirmed by several other investigators (see review by Prescott, 1964b). A decreased rate of total cellular protein synthesis has also been observed during mitosis (Baserga, 1962; Prescott and Bender, 1962). However, Stein and Baserga (1970) have found that nonhistone chromosomal proteins are synthesized during mitosis almost at the same rate as during S phase. Johnson and Holland (1965) have reported that the *in vitro* template activity of mitotic chromatin is severalfold less than that observed in interphase chromatin, and their findings have been confirmed by Farber, Stein, and Baserga (1972). Finally, Fox, Shepherd, and Burger (1971) have shown that mitotic cells are agglutinated by wheat agglutinins, whereas interphase cells are not, indicating changes in the structure of the cell surface.

Prereplicative Phase of Stimulated G_0 Cells

Table 2 gives a few selected *in vitro* and *in vivo* models of stimulated DNA synthesis and cell division, that is, situations in which quiescent cells can be stimulated to proliferate by the application of an appropriate stimulus. These models vary considerably, especially in terms of the extent of cell proliferation and the interval between the application of the stimulus and the onset of DNA synthesis or mitosis. However, the biochemical events occurring between the application of the stimulus and the onset of DNA synthesis (S, G_2, and mitosis are the same as in continuously dividing cells) are essentially similar in the various situations listed in Table 2.

For convenience, the events that occur in the prereplicative phase of stimulated G_0 cells will be divided into late events and early events. Late events are those that occur after the peak of ribosomal RNA synthesis, early events are those that precede it. The division is obviously arbitrary but it is necessary for an orderly un-

TABLE 2. STIMULATION OF CELL PROLIFERATION IN QUIESCENT CELLS.

Target Tissue	Stimulus	Reference
	In vivo	
Rat liver	partial hepatectomy	Grisham, 1962
Rat uterus	estrogens	Hamilton, 1968
Rat salivary gland	isoproterenol	Barka, 1965
Mouse mammary gland	estrogens	Bresciani, 1965
	In vitro	
Stationary cell cultures	nutritional changes	Todaro, Lazar, and Green, 1965
		Wiebel and Baserga, 1969
	DNA oncogenic viruses	Dulbecco, Hartwell, and Vogt, 1965
	RNA oncogenic viruses	Macieira-Coelho and Ponten, 1967
	trypsin	Burger, 1970
Lymphocytes	phytohemagglutinin	Cooper, 1971
Rabbit kidney cells	explantation	Lieberman, Abrams, and Ove, 1963
Chinese hamster cells	isoleucine	Ley and Tobey, 1970

derstanding of the sequence of events that lead from the application of the stimulus to the onset of DNA synthesis.

Late Events of the Prereplicative Phase. These include the appearance and/or increased activity of enzymes associated with DNA synthesis (see above). The templates for these enzymes are usually synthesized a few hours before the appearance of the enzymes themselves (Pegoraro and Baserga, 1970). An increase in ribosomal RNA synthesis has been described in a number of situations in which quiescent cells are stimulated to proliferate (Lieberman, Abrams, and Ove, 1963; Fujioka, Koga, and Lieberman, 1963; Hamilton, 1968; Cooper, 1971; Ellem and Mironescu, 1972; Zardi and Baserga, 1974) and is usually associated with an increased protein synthesis.

Early Biochemical Events of the Prereplicative Phase. A number of biochemical events have been described in the early prereplicative phase of G_0 cells stimulated to proliferate. These include an early increase in RNA synthesis, first demonstrated in 1963 by Lieberman and coworkers in primary explants of rabbit kidney cortex cells (Lieberman, Abrams, and Ove, 1963). These investigators also showed that low doses of actinomycin D which did not affect DNA synthesis *per se*, or the rate of RNA syn-

thesis in nonproliferating kidney cells, were capable of inhibiting the increase in RNA synthesis that occurred during the prereplicative phase, as well as the subsequent onset of DNA synthesis. This increased RNA synthesis and sensitivity to actinomycin D was quickly confirmed by Lieberman's group in the regenerating liver following partial hepatectomy (Fujioka, Koga, and Lieberman, 1963) and subsequently in several other situations in which quiescent cells are stimulated to proliferate. These include phytohemagglutinin-stimulated lymphocytes, the isoproterenol-stimulated salivary gland of rats and mice, the folic acid-stimulated kidney, and the estrogen-stimulated uterus (see reviews mentioned above). Additional evidence for increased transcriptional activity in the early prereplicative phase of the cell cycle includes: (1) an increased chromatin template activity for *in vitro* RNA synthesis which has been observed in a number of situations in which quiescent cells are stimulated to proliferate (see Table 3); (2) an increased binding of actinomycin D and acridine orange (Rigler and Killander, 1969; Ringertz and Bolund, 1969; Darzynkiewicz, Bolund, and Ringertz, 1969; Zetterberg and Auer, 1970); (3) an increased synthesis of RNA in nuclear monolayers of confluent cells stimulated to proliferate (Mauck and Green, 1973; Bombik and Baserga, 1974); (4) an increased number of chromatin binding sites for *E. coli*

RNA polymerase (Hill and Baserga, 1974; Bombik and Baserga, 1974); and (5) the synthesis of new species of RNA which has been reported by Church and McCarthy (1967) in the regenerating mouse liver following partial hepatectomy.

An increased protein synthesis has been observed during the prereplicative phase of the cell cycle in most situations in which quiescent cells are stimulated to proliferate. These include: serum-stimulated, contact-inhibited cells; the regenerating liver following partial hepatectomy; the folic acid-stimulated kidney; the estrogen-stimulated uterus; and the isoproterenol-stimulated salivary gland of mice. Some of the proteins synthesized during the prereplicative phase have been characterized. They include phosphoproteins, glycoproteins, nonhistone chromosomal proteins, and probably a number of enzymes associated with the synthesis of RNA. Chemical modifications of pre-existing proteins have also been reported during the prereplicative phase. They include the phosphorylation of histones as well as non-histone chromosomal proteins (see review by Stein, Spelsberg, and Kleinsmith, 1974), the acetylation of histones (Allfrey, 1969), and methylation (Paik and Kim, 1971). The meaning of histone acetylation in terms of stimulation of cell proliferation, however, is still obscure. Finally, a number of changes in membrane transport function have been reported in continuously dividing cells and in G_0 cells stimulated to proliferate (see reviews by Burger, 1972 and Pardee, 1971).

EFFECT OF AGING ON THE CELL CYCLE TIMES AND THE GROWTH FRACTION

Cell Cycle Changes in Old Animals

In a pioneer series of experiments Lesher, Fry, and Kohn (1961a) showed that the length of the cell cycle of duodenal epithelial cells increased in aging CAF_1 mice. For instance, in young (93 day old) and middle-aged (372 day old) mice, the length of the cell cycle was 11.5 hr, but in old mice (940 day old), T_C increased to more than 15 hr. This increase in the length of the cell cycle caused a corresponding increase in transit time, that is, in the time required for a crypt cell in DNA synthesis to reach the extrusion zone at the tips of the villi. Thus in mice of the three ages mentioned above, the overall transit times were respectively 41, 48, and 53 hr (Lesher, Fry, and Kohn, 1961b). The increase in T_C and in transit time was not limited to duodenal epithelial cells but could also be demonstrated in crypt cells of the jejunum and of the ileum (Fry, Lesher, and Kohn, 1962b).

TABLE 3. TEMPLATE ACTIVITY OF CHROMATIN IN QUIESCENT TISSUES STIMULATED TO PROLIFERATE.

Tissue	Stimulus	Effect[a]	References
rat uterus (ovariect.)	estradiol-17	↑ (120)	Barker and Warren, 1966; Teng and Hamilton, 1968
rat prostate (castrated)	testosterone	↑ (240)	Couch and Anderson, 1973
oviduct immature chickens	estradiol	↑ (120)	Cox, Haines, and Carey, 1973
rat liver	partial hepatectomy	↓ (120)	Thaler and Villee, 1967
rat liver	partial hepatectomy	↑ (360)	Thaler and Villee, 1967
fibroblasts in culture	serum	↑ (60)	Farber, Rovera, and Baserga, 1971
mouse salivary gland	isoproterenol	↑ (60)	Novi and Baserga, 1972a, 1972b
lens culinaris roots	indole-3-acetic acid	↑ (90)	Teissere, Penon, and Ricard, 1973

[a] ↑ increase; ↓ decrease. The number in parenthesis is the earliest time (in min), in which a change was detected.

A typical study of the effects of age on the duration of the cell cycle and its phases was also carried out in BDF_1 mice, and the results are summarized in Table 4 (Lesher, 1966). It can be seen from Table 4 that T_C increases from 10.1 hr in 55-day-old mice to 15.7 hr in 1050-day-old animals. The increase, though, is not a gradual one but takes the shape of two rather abrupt increases between 55 and 100 days and between 675 and 825 days. T_{G_2} and T_M are essentially unaffected by age, but T_{G_1} and T_S do increase with age.

A careful inspection of Figure 1 (curve of percentage of labeled mitoses) in the original paper by Lesher, Fry, and Kohn (1961a) indicates that in old mice there is not only an increase in the length of the cell cycle, but that the second half of the first cycle is broadened and the second cycle smeared out, while in young and middle-aged animals, the first cell cycle is followed by a clearly indicated second cycle. This would suggest that the crypt cell population in old animals has become more heterogeneous with age (Fry, Tyler, and Lesher, 1966), a phenomenon that could be, at least in part, related to the well-known failure to proliferate noted in normal diploid cells aging in culture (described in detail elsewhere in this volume). Finally, at least in BDF_1 mice, the proliferative population is decreased from about 126 cells/crypt in 100-day-old mice to 89 cells/crypt in 825-day-old animals (Lesher, 1966). It seems, therefore, that the following conclusions can be drawn from the pioneer work of Lesher and his collaborators on the effect of age on the cell cycle of the lining epithe-

lium of the small intestine of mice. (1) There is an increase in the length of the cell cycle in T_{G_1} and in T_S with age. (2) The growth fraction in the crypts of the small intestine is decreased in old animals. (3) Transit time is increased, and (4) the proliferative population in old animals shows considerably more heterogeneity than the proliferative population in younger mice.

It is interesting to note that mitosis *per se* is not appreciably affected by increasing age. However, changes in the chromosomal apparatus must occur with age since the incidence of chromosomal aberrations in lymphocytes of elderly individuals (75 to 92 years of age) is 5 times higher than in lymphocytes of individuals with an average age of 35 years (Lisco, Lisco, Adelstein, and Banks, 1973).

Th work of Lesher and collaborators has been repeated by a number of investigators on other tissues, other strains of mice, and other animals, but the results have not added much to the conclusions reached in this early work. Thus Thrasher (1967) found an increase in the length of the cell cycle in the lining epithelium of the colon of mice of from 15 hr in infant mice to 21 hr in senescent mice. It should be noted that Thrasher used male Swiss albino mice, that the infants were 10 days old, and that the senescent mice were between 579 and 638 days of age, somewhat younger than the mice used as "old mice" by Lesher and co-workers. Mitotic incidence and mean generation time of alveolar cells in mouse lungs were studied by Simnet and Hepplestone (1966). The results were substantially the same as those described above, i.e., there was generally an increase in the mean generation time of alveolar wall cells with increasing age. For instance, the mean generation time of alveolar wall cells of types A and B increased from 94 days in C57 black male mice of 3 months of age to 314 days in 24-month-old mice. The increase was much less spectacular in other mouse strains, and indeed, in one strain the females did not show any increase in mean generation time with age.

In the ear epithelium of the mouse, the mitotic index has been reported to fall from 30.1 at 9 days of age 2.4–5.6 in mice 30–33 months of age (Whiteley and Horton, 1963). Since, as discussed before, the duration of mitosis is not affected by increasing age, these data indicate

TABLE 4. CELL CYCLE TIMES OF THE LINING EPITHELIUM OF THE CRYPTS OF THE SMALL INTESTINE OF BCF$_1$ MICE OF DIFFERENT AGES.

Age in days	T_C	T_{G_1}	T_S	T_{G_2}	T_M
55	10.1	1.8	6.9	0.6	0.8
100	13.2	4.8	6.7	0.9	0.8
300	14.1	4.3	8.1	0.8	0.9
675	14.2	4.5	8.2	0.7	0.8
825	15.2	5.4	8.2	0.8	0.8
1050	15.7	5.4	8.9	0.7	0.7

All times in hours. Symbols (T_C, etc.) as in Table 1. Adapted from Lesher, 1966.

that in the ear epithelium of the mouse there is a true decrease in proliferating activity with age. In human skin, however, Thuringer and Katzberg (1959) obtained opposite results. The mitotic index rose from birth to about the fifth decade. For instance, in the group from 0–20 years of age, the mitotic index was 0.245; in the group 21–40 years of age, it was 0.268. It increased to 0.497 in the group 41–60 years of age and then remained steady at 0.489 in the group 61–80 years of age. There is no explanation yet for the discrepancy between the effect of age on mitotic indices in human epidermis and mouse epidermis except for the profound consideration that mice are different from men.

Cell Cycle Changes in Development

Another group of studies has dealt with changes occurring in the cell cycle during development. These do not properly belong in a study of aging since they are usually a comparison of cell cycle times of tissues in embryos, or newborn animals, versus cell cycle times in adult animals. Typical of this is the paper by Graham and Morgan (1966) on changes in the cell cycle during early amphibian development. The most interesting part about this report is that during cleavage there is no G_1 phase and the G_2 phase is either very short or absent. In late blastula there is a substantial G_2 phase and the G_1 phase becomes apparent. Similarly, age-related changes have been reported in the proliferative activity of the renal corpuscle and the nephron tubule region in mice (Litvak and Baserga, 1964). The length of the cell cycle in embryonic tissue and the changes occurring in the cell cycle and its various phases during development have been summarized and discussed in detail by Malamud (1971).

EFFECT OF AGING ON BIOCHEMICAL EVENTS OCCURRING IN THE CELL CYCLE

Effect of Chronological Time on the Length of G_0

Available Data. It has been known since the classical studies of Bucher and coworkers that age affects liver regeneration after partial hepatectomy. Thus rapidly growing young rats re-

store tissue mass and cell population number more rapidly than adults, while the older animals lag in new cell production. When the incorporation of thymidine [^{14}C] into DNA is used as an index of growth, the peak of incorporation in weanlings is obtained at 22 hr after partial hepatectomy, in young adults at 25 hr, and in 1-year-old rats at 32 hr (Bucher, 1963). In addition, there is in weanlings a second peak at 35 hr which is absent in other animals. The results of Bucher and coworkers have therefore established that in older animals there is a progressive lengthening of the prereplicative phase of the cell cycle, that is, of the time required for a G_0 cell to enter DNA synthesis, although the original mass of the liver is eventually restored even in the older animals.

Similar findings were reported by Adelman, Stein, Roth, and Englander (1972) in the isoproterenol-stimulated salivary gland of rats. In a 2-month-old rat, a single injection of isoproterenol caused a stimulation of DNA synthesis which began at about 18 hr after stimulation, reaching a peak at about 28 hr. A similar treatment of 12-month-old rats produced a wave of DNA synthesis which began to increase very slowly at 24 hr after the injection of isoproterenol and reached a peak only between 36 and 38 hr after stimulation. The increased length of the prereplicative phase was also accompanied by a decrease in the fraction of cells responding to isoproterenol with DNA synthesis. Thus in 2-month-old rats about 17 percent of the submandibular gland cells responded to a single injection of isoproterenol with DNA synthesis. In 12-month-old rats the percentage of cells thus responding was decreased to about 10 percent. A decrease with age in the fraction of cells capable of responding to a proliferating stimulus has also been reported by Oh and Conard (1972a). These authors studied lymphocyte transformation in blood cultures treated with phytohemagglutinin in a Marshallese population. They found that the fraction of lymphocytes transformed by phytohemagglutinin decreased from 50 percent in young individuals (15–29 years of age) to about 40 percent in old individuals (50–79 years of age).

A lengthening of the prereplicative phase has also been found in WI-38 human diploid fibroblasts kept quiescent for increasing lengths of time. For instance, when confluent monolayers of WI-38 are stimulated by a change of medium containing 10 percent serum at 5 days after plating, at a time, that is, when they have just become quiescent, the prereplicative phase is relatively short, 8 hr. If the same monolayers are stimulated 9 days after plating, the prereplicative phase is considerably longer, 14 hr. In fact, the cells apparently go into a deeper G_0, and the prereplicative phase becomes very long, up to 22 hr, when the cells are stimulated 17 or 18 days after plating (Augenlicht and Baserga, 1974).

It therefore seems from these data that the length of the prereplicative phase in quiescent cells stimulated to proliferate by an appropriate stimulus is lengthened in old animals, or in cells left quiescent for increasing periods of time (which is the same thing). The increased length of the prereplicative phase is not due to the type of cell but it seems truly to be due to the length of time the cell has been quiescent, that is, age in adult animals or a longer time in a nonstimulated condition in tissue culture. A similar situation has also been described in human lymphocytes stimulated and subsequently re-stimulated with phytohemagglutinin (Younkin, 1972).

If aging in the adult animal or prolonged quiescence in tissue culture causes an increase in the length of the prereplicative phase and a decrease in the fraction of cells capable of responding to a proliferative stimulus, a legitimate question that we may now ask is whether some of the biochemical events that are known to occur in quiescent cells stimulated to proliferate may be altered by aging. In particular, we would be interested in two phenomena that, as mentioned above, seem to play a major role in the transition of G_0 cells to the proliferative cycle: the increase in synthesis of nuclear proteins and the template activity of chromatin.

Effect of Aging on Certain Biochemical Events Occurring in Quiescent Cells Stimulated to Proliferate

We omit here a consideration of the effect of aging on DNA synthesis which has already been discussed above. Since chromatin and nuclear proteins play a major role in the control of cell proliferation (see above), we will especially consider, in this section, those changes that have been described with aging in DNA, nuclear proteins, and chromatin of animals and cells in culture. However, some of the events occurring in the late prereplicative phase will also be examined.

Chemical Composition of Nuclei. In 1971 Price, Modak, and Makinodan reported an increased accumulation of DNA strand breaks with aging in brain, liver, and heart from young and senescent mice. Studying the cerebellar neurons of beagle dogs, Wheeler and Lett (1974) found that there is no age-associated decrease in the ability of the cells to rejoin single-strand breaks induced by radiation, but that there may be an age-associated decline in the size of the DNA-containing species which can be extracted from unirradiated cells. Perhaps more important, in view of the well-known role of ribosomal RNA in cell growth, is the finding by Johnson and Strehler (1972) of a loss of genes coding for ribosomal RNA in brain cells of aging dogs. In an investigation carried out on human epidermis, Tschahargane, Haag, and Goerttler (1971) reported that in male individuals over 65 years of age, there is a reduction in nuclear volume and in average nucleic acid content in abdominal epidermal cells of approximately 35 percent. Reports on protein and RNA content of nuclei in relation to age have been recently summarized by von Hahn (1970). The results are not always consistent. The protein/DNA ratio definitely decreases in nuclei of liver and kidney of rats from 4 to 33 months of age, but an opposite trend was noticed in mouse brain and in beef thymus. The same inconsistency appears in the very few data on RNA/DNA ratios in isolated nuclei. Mainwaring (1968) found a decrease in total nuclear protein/DNA ratio, and especially in acidic protein/DNA ratio in purified nuclei of liver, lung, and prostate of aged mice in comparison to younger animals. A careful study was carried out by O'Meara and Herrmann (1972) on chromatin prepared from purified nuclei isolated from livers of mice of different ages. The protein/DNA ratio in chromatin decreased from 1.8 in young mice to 1.7 in old mice, and while the percentage of histones slightly increased, the percentage of non-histones decreased from 46 to 37 percent. In addition, the facility with which proteins are removed from chromatin at high ionic strength diminishes with increasing age. These latter studies, therefore, seem to indicate in general a decrease in the amount of nonhistone nuclear proteins with increasing age. Because of the importance of nonhistone chromosomal proteins in the control of cell proliferation (see above), it is possible that part of the delay in the onset of DNA synthesis that occurs in cells from senescent animals may be due to a partial loss of nonhistone chromosomal proteins from the nucleus. This will be discussed further.

Histone acetylation has also been proposed as a regulatory step in cell proliferation, and a number of studies have been reported showing differences in histone acetylation in aged cells. Thus, Ryan and Cristofalo (1972) found an age-associated decrease in the rate of histone acetylation in WI-38 cells. Decreased acetylation of nuclei with increasing age is also found in lymphocytes stimulated with phytohemagglutinin (Oh and Conard, 1972a). Histone acetylation in rat liver declines to minimal levels by the time the animals have reached 6 months of age. After partial hepatectomy, acetylation of liver histones is also higher in young growing rats than in older animals (Oh and Conard, 1972b). These differences in histone acetylation may play a role in determining the template activity of chromatin.

Effect of Aging on Chromatin Template Activity: Devi, Lindsay, Raina, and Sarkar (1966) and Mainwaring (1968) have reported a marked diminution of RNA synthesis in purified nuclei from tissues of aged mice. In the experiments of Mainwaring (1968), the decrease in chromatin template activity was minimal in livers of 30-month old mice when compared to 6-month-old mice, in agreement with the results of Samis and Wulff (1969). However, in the same groups of animals, chromatin template activity was decreased in the lung and markedly decreased in the prostate of older animals where the priming ability of chromatin was 50 percent of the value for younger animals. It

should be noted at this point that Stein, Wang, and Adelman, (1973) while not finding any decrease in chromatin template activity in the liver of aged rats, found a marked increase in chromatin template activity in submandibular glands of older rats. An increase in template activity in a tissue of an aged animal, as the one reported by Stein, Wang, and Adelman (1973) is unique and is at variance with other reports in the literature. Related to chromatin template activity is the ability of chromatin to bind reporter molecules like actinomycin D (see above). Lymphocytes from young rats bind actinomycin D at a higher rate than do cells from older animals (Darzynkiewicz and Anderson, 1971). This decreased transcriptional activity is also confirmed by the reduced rate of RNA synthesis and of transfer of RNA from the nucleus to the cytoplasm observed in aging fibroblasts (see review by Macieira-Coelho, 1973).

Finally, both Dingman and Sporn (1964), as well as Pyhtila and Sherman (1968) found an age-related reduction in the RNA content of chromatin.

Physico-chemical Characteristics of Chromatin: The findings here have also been summarized by Von Hahn (1970), who has tabulated the reports on thermal denaturation of nucleoproteins and DNA in relation to age. There are no differences in the melting point of protein-free DNA in beef thymus (age: 8 weeks to 10 years) or in pooled viscera of mice (age: 3 to 24 months). The T_m of nucleoproteins from thymus increased from 69.5 in 8-month-old calves to 76.3 in 10-year-old cows. However, the T_m of nucleoprotein from brain was reported to be the same in 1-month-old and 30-month-old mice (Kurtz and Sinex, 1968).

We have examined the structure of chromatins from early passages, middle passages, and late passages of WI-38 human diploid fibroblasts by circular dichroism. Circular dichroism is a useful technique for investigating changes in the asymmetry of a macromolecule (in this case DNA) containing chromophores (i.e., nucleotide bases).

Table 5 shows that chromatin from late passage WI-38 has a decreased maximum positive

TABLE 5. CHANGES IN CIRCULAR DICHROISM SPECTRA AND ETHIDIUM BROMIDE BINDING IN AGING WI-38 CELLS.

Passage Number	θ_{308}	θ_{279}
21	7500	2750
53	5500	1600
21 after salt extraction	3400	1700
53 after salt extraction	3300	1700

Circular dichroism was measured in a Jasco spectropolarimeter and is expressed in degree cm^2/dmol of DNA nucleotide (θ) at 279 nm. Ethidium bromide binding was also measured by spectropolarimetry and is expressed in degree cm^2/dmol of ethidium bromide (θ) at 308 nm.

The last two rows give the value of both chromatins after extraction with 0.25 M NaCl.

ellipticity and a red shift in the 250–300 nm region of circular dichroism spectra when compared to the chromatin of middle passage WI-38. The chromatins of early and middle passage WI-38 were indistinguishable by circular dichroism (Maizel, Nicolini, and Baserga, 1975). The chromatin from aged WI-38 cells also has a decreased capacity for binding the intercalating dye, ethidium bromide. In fact, the results of Table 5 clearly show that in aged diploid fibroblasts, there are functional and structural changes in chromatin that mimic those of quiescent cells (Lin, Nicolini, and Baserga, 1974). Furthermore, the differences between the chromatins of middle and late passage WI-38 cells are abolished when both chromatins are extracted with 0.25 M NaCl, a procedure that removes only 10-12 percent of nonhistone chromosomal proteins and no histones.

In conclusion, some changes have been reported in chromatin and chromosomal proteins in old animals and aging cells, but the findings are far from being consistent. Yet, this is a worthy area of investigation because of the well-established role of chromatin and chromosomal proteins in the control of cell proliferation in mammalian cells.

Other Events in the Prereplicative Phase: We have mentioned above that age causes a length-ening of the prereplicative phase in the iso-proterenol-stimulated salivary gland of rats. There is also a delay in the induction of two enzymes that are associated with DNA synthesis, thymidine kinase and deoxythymidylate synthetase (Roth, Karoly, Britton, and Adelman, 1974). In contrast, stimulated incorporation of uridine [^{3}H] into RNA is initiated several hours earlier in 12-month than in 2-month-old rats (Roth, Karoly, Britton, and Adelman, 1974). It should be noted at this point that the impaired ability to initiate DNA synthesis and cell division in submandibular glands of aging rats may be the consequence of an increased susceptibility to regulation by endogenous glucocorticoids (Roth, Karoly, Adelman, and Adelman, 1974b; Roth and Adelman, 1974).

LENGTHENING OF G_0 AS AN EXPRESSION OF SENESCENCE

Comparison of G_0 and G_1 Cells

The concept of G_0 cells was introduced in 1963 by Lajtha to designate quiescent cells that do not synthesize DNA or divide, but that can be stimulated to do so by the application of an appropriate stimulus. A typical example of G_0 cells, according to this definition, would be hepatocytes, cells of the renal tabules, salivary gland cells, and other similar cells of the adult animal which do not synthesize DNA or undergo mitosis in physiological conditions but can be induced to do so by appropriate stimuli. The concept of G_0 cells has been opposed for a number of years by several investigators who felt that the term G_0 simply reflected an artificial division and that G_0 cells are simply cells with a very long G_1, which can be shortened under certain specific condition. More recently, however, evidence has accumulated that G_0 cells can be distinguished on a functional basis from cells with a long G_1, and the current general consensus is that G_0 cells do exist as separate entities (Epifanova and Terskikh, 1969b; Sander and Pardee, 1972; Rovera and Baserga, 1973; Smets, 1973; Baserga, Costlow, and Rovera, 1973). G_0 cells can be distinguished from G_1 cells on the basis of several parameters which include: (a) time differences in the length of the prereplicative phase, (b) ability to respond with an increase in cell proliferation to nutritional changes, (c) differences in constituent proteins, (d) time differences in changes occurring in membrane functions, and (e) differences in the levels of chromatin template activity.

Time Differences in the Prereplicative Phase. The best demonstration that G_0 cells are not simply cells with a very long G_1 is shown by the fact that, in many instances, putative G_0 cells can actually shorten the prereplicative phase under appropriate conditions. For instance, in the isoproterenol-stimulated salivary glands of mice, the length of the prereplicative phase is 20 hr, if a single injection of isoproterenol is given. However, if a second injection of isoproterenol is given 48 hr after the first, at which time the salivary gland cells are again totally quiescent, the prereplicative phase is shortened to 14 hr (Novi and Baserga, 1972b). A similar situation has been described in human lymphocytes stimulated and subsequently restimulated with phytohemagglutinin (Younkin, 1972). Even better is the system described by Choie and Richter (1973). The length of the prereplicative phase in tubular epithelial cells of rat kidneys, stimulated to proliferate by a single injection of lead, is 20 hr. A second injection, 48 hr after the first, causes a second wave of DNA synthesis within 6 hr. The situation can also be reproduced *in vitro*. For instance, Sander and Pardee (1972) studied Chinese hamster ovary cells in culture synchronized in two different ways. When cells were synchronized by the isoleucine deficiency technique, the interval between the application of the stimulus, in this case isoleucine, and the onset of DNA synthesis was 2.5 hr longer than the interval between completion of mitosis and the onset of DNA synthesis. Similar differences in the length of the prereplicative phase have been described in WI-38 human diploid fibroblasts kept confluent for various lengths of time (see above in the first subsection under "Effect of Aging on Biochemical Events Occurring in the Cell Cycle").

Ability to Respond With an Increase in Cell Proliferation to Nutritional Changes. This is especially true when a comparison is made between transformed and untransformed cells. Often transformed cells will stop in G_1, whereas untransformed cells are capable of entering G_0. While the transition from G_0 to S requires serum, transformed cells in G_1 can often be stimulated to resume the cell cycle traverse by addition of medium or even amino acids (Baserga, Costlow, and Revera, 1973).

Differences in Protein Complement. Differences in the nonhistone chromosomal proteins of G_0 and G_1 cells have been reported by Becker and Stanners (1972) and by Tsuboi and Baserga (1972). In addition, in human fibroblasts quiescent for 3 or more weeks, there is a 30 percent loss in the amount of total cellular proteins (Dell'Orco, Mertens, and Kruse, 1973).

Changes in Membrane Transport Function. These have been discussed in detail by Costlow and Baserga (1973) and by Baserga, Costlow, and Rovera (1973). In general, cells in G_1 show a prompt increase in membrane transport function immediately after mitosis, whereas cells in G_0 show an increase in membrane transport function 2 to 3 hr after the application of the stimulus.

Differences in the Levels of Chromatin Template Activity. It was mentioned above that a characteristic of putative G_0 cells is to respond with an increase in template activity to a proliferation stimulus. This increase, about 50 to 70 percent above control values, seems to be characteristic of all kinds of G_0 cells from the estrogen-stimulated uterus to the isoproterenol-stimulated salivary gland. On the other hand, continuously dividing cells behave in a different way (Rovera and Baserga, 1973). As already mentioned, quiescent, confluent monolayers of WI-38 human diploid fibroblasts show an increase in chromatin template activity within 1 hr after they are stimulated by a change of medium (Farber, Rovera, and Baserga, 1971). However, density-inhibited SV40 transformed WI-38 human fibroblasts, 2RA cells, arrested in

G_1 do not show an increase in chromatin template activity when stimulated to proliferate by an appropriate nutritional change (Costlow and Baserga, 1973). Similarly, 3T6 cells do not show any change in chromatin template activity when stimulated to proliferate after reaching the stationary phase (Rovera and Baserga, 1973). A prediction of this model is that chromatin template activity (a) should not increase in WI-38 cells stimulated on the fifth day after plating when they are still in G_1 (see above), (b) should increase in WI-38 stimulated between the seventh and ninth day after plating when they have entered G_0, and (c) should also increase, but with a delay, in cells stimulated on the eighteenth day after plating that have a prolonged prereplicative phase. This prediction was borne out precisely as stated above by the experiments of Augenlicht and Baserga (1974). Similar results were obtained by Smets (1973) with 3T3 cells left quiescent for different lengths of time.

Lengthening of G_0 in Aging Cells

The results obtained with the regenerating liver after partial hepatectomy, and with the isoproterenol-stimulated salivary gland in intact animals, as well as those obtained with WI-38 cells left quiescent for an increasing length of time (see the first subsection under "Effect of Aging on Biochemical Events Occurring in the Cell Cycle"), do suggest that the lengthening of the prereplicative phase may be a characteristic of senescence in mammalian cells. In the case of the tissues of the adult animal this is easy to understand. The results clearly state that the length of the prereplicative phase increases with increasing age. More uncertain is the significance of the results obtained in WI-38 cells. In these cells, senescence is usually considered to be failure to proliferate after a certain number of generations, as described in detail elsewhere in this *Handbook*. It is difficult, at this moment, to relate this increase in the length of the prereplicative phase in WI-38 cells left quiescent for an increasing length of time to their failure to reproduce after several generations. It is possible, however, that the failure to reproduce may be due to an abnormal increase

of the prereplicative phase that goes beyond physiological boundaries and causes unbalanced growth and eventually not only failure to proliferate, but the actual death of the cells. If this were true, then the study of chromatin and nonhistone chromosomal proteins that play such an important role in the control of cell proliferation in G_0 cells stimulated to proliferate could throw considerable light on our understanding of the aging mechanisms *in vivo* and *in vitro*.

CONCLUSIONS

In the past 20 years, considerable evidence has accumulated on the various biochemical parameters that control the flow of cells from one mitosis to the other. It seems to be increasingly apparent that DNA synthesis, that is, the replication of the genetic material, precedes and determines mitosis so that in many respects a study of the factors that control cell division in mammalian cells is a study of the factors that control DNA replication. In turn, DNA replication is controlled by a number of other factors which are arranged in an orderly fashion throughout the cell cycle. The earliest events that determine the transition of resting cells into the proliferative cycle include changes in membrane function, changes in gene activation, and the synthesis of certain nonhistone chromosomal proteins.

Aging causes, in general, an increase in the length of the cell cycle and in the length of the prereplicative phase in stimulated G_0 cells. It also causes changes in the template activity of chromatin and in the synthesis and storage of nonhistone chromosomal proteins. The tentative conclusions are that aging cells are cells that go into deeper states of G_0 from which it becomes increasingly difficult to rescue them. This, in turn, could be due to changes in chromatin and its components in aging cells.

REFERENCES

Adelman, R. C., Stein, G., Roth, G. S., and Englander, D. 1972. Age dependent regulation of mammalian DNA synthesis and cell proliferation *in vivo*. *Mech. Age. Dev.*, **1**, 49–59.

Allfrey, V. G. 1969. The role of chromosomal proteins in gene activation. *In*, R. Baserga (ed.), *Biochem. of Cell Division*, pp. 179–205. Springfield, Illinois: Charles C. Thomas.

Atlas, M., and Bond, P. 1965. The cell generation cycle of the 11-day mouse embryo. *J. Cell Biol.*, **26**, 19–24.

Augenlicht, L. H., and Baserga, R. 1974. Changes in the G_0 state of WI-38 fibroblasts at different times after confluence. *Exp. Cell Res.*, **89**, 255–262.

Barka, T. 1965. Stimulation of DNA synthesis by isoproterenol in the salivary glands. *Exp. Cell Res.*, **39**, 355–364.

Barker, K. L., and Warren, J. C. 1966. Template capacity of uterine chromatin controlled by estradiol. *Proc. Nat. Acad. Sci.*, **56**, 1298–1302.

Barrett, J. C. 1966. A mathematical model of the mitotic cycle and its application to the interpretation of percentage labeled mitosis data. *J. Nat. Cancer Inst.*, **37**, 443–450.

Baserga, R. 1962. A radio autographic study of the uptake of ^{14}C leucine by tumor cells in deoxyribonucleic acid synthesis. *Biochim. Biophys. Acta.*, **61**, 445–450.

Baserga, R. 1967. Autoradiographic methods. *In*, Harris Busch (ed.), *Methods in Cancer Research*, Vol. 1, pp. 45–116. New York: Academic Press.

Baserga, R. 1968. Biochemistry of the cell cycle. A review. *Cell Tissue Kinetics*, **1**, 167–191.

Baserga, R. 1971. *The Cell Cycle and Cancer*. New York: Marcel Dekker.

Baserga, R., Costlow, M., and Rovera, G. 1973. Changes in membrane function and chromatin template activity in diploid and transformed cells in culture. *Federation Proc.*, **32**, 2115–2118.

Baserga, R., Estensen, R. D., and Petersen, R. O. 1965. Inhibition of DNA synthesis in Ehrlich ascites cells by actinomycin D. 2. The presynthetic block in the cell cycle. *Proc. Nat. Acad. Sci.*, **54**, 1141–1148.

Baserga, R., Estensen, R. D., and Petersen, R. O. 1966. Delay inhibition of DNA synthesis in mouse jejunum by low doses of actinomycin D. *J. Cellular Physiol.*, **68**, 177–184.

Baserga, R., Estensen, R. D., Petersen, R. O., and Layde, J. P. 1965. Inhibition of DNA synthesis in Ehrlich ascites cells by actinomycin D. 1. Delayed inhibition by low doses. *Proc. Nat. Acad. Sci.*, **54**, 745–751.

Baserga, R., and Lisco, E. 1963. Duration of DNA synthesis in Ehrlich ascites cells as estimated by double-labeling with C^{14} and H^3 thymidine and autoradiography. *J. Nat. Cancer Inst.*, **31**, 1559–1571.

Baserga, R., and Malamud, D. 1969. *Autoradiography*. New York: Harper & Row.

Baserga, R., and Wiebel, F. 1969. The cell cycle of mammalian cells *Intern. Rev Exp. Path.*, **7**, 1–30.

Becker, H., and Stanners, C. P. 1972. Control of macromolecular synthesis in proliferating and resting Syrian hamster cells in monolayer culture. III. Electrophoretic patterns of newly synthesized proteins in synchronized proliferating cells, and resting cells. *J. Cellular Physiol.*, **80**, 51–61.

Blenkinsopp, W. K. 1969. Comparison of multiple injections with continuous infusion of tritiated thymidine and estimation of the cell cycle time. *J. Cell Sci.*, **5**, 575–582.

Bombik, B. M., and Baserga, R. 1974. Increased RNA synthesis in nuclear monolayers of WI-38 cells stimulated to proliferate. *Proc. Nat. Acad. Sci.*, **71**, 2038–2042.

Borun, T. W., Scharf, M. D., and Robbins, E. 1967. Rapidly labeled polyribosome associated RNA having the properties of histone messengers. *Proc. Nat. Acad. Sci.*, **58**, 1977–1967.

Bresciani, F. 1965. A comparison of the cell generative cycle in normal, hyperplastic and neoplastic mammary gland of the C^3H mouse, *In*, *Cellular Radiation Biology*, pp. 547–557, Symposium on Fundamental Cancer Research, University of Texas, M.D. Anderson Hospital and Tumor Inst. Baltimore: Williams & Wilkins.

Bucher, N. L. R. 1963. Regeneration of mammalian liver. *Intern. Rev. Cytol.*, **15**, 245–300.

Burger, M. M. 1970. Proteolytic enzymes initiating cell division and escape from contact inhibition and growth. *Nature*, **227**, 170–171.

Burger, M. M. 1972. Surface changes detected from lectins and implications for growth regulation in normal and transformed cells. *Biomembranes*, **2**, 247–270.

Choie, D. D., and Richter, G. W. 1973. Stimulation of DNA synthesis in rat kidney by repeated administration of lead. *Proc. Soc. Exp. Biol. Med.*, **142**, 446–449.

Church, R. B., and McCarthy, B. J. 1967. Ribonucleic acid synthesis in regenerating and embryonic rat liver. 1) The synthesis of new species of RNA during regeneration of mouse liver after partial hepatectomy. *J. Mol. Biol.*, **23**, 459–475.

Clarkson, B., Ota, K., Ohkita, T., and O'Connor, A. 1965. Kinetics of proliferation of cancer cells in neoplastic effusions of man. *Cancer*, **18**, 1189–1213.

Cleaver, J. E. 1965. The relationship between the duration of the S phase and the fraction of cells which incorporate ^3H thymidine during exponential growth. *Exp. Cell Res.*, **39**, 297–300.

Cooper, H. L. 1971. Biochemical alterations accompanying initiation of growth in resting cells. *In*, R. Baserga (ed.), *The Cell Cycle and Cancer*, pp. 197–226. New York: Marcel Dekker.

Costlow, M., and Baserga, R. 1973. Changes in membrane transport function in G_0 and G_1 cells. *J. Cellular Physiol.*, **82**, 411–420.

Couch, R. M., and Anderson, K. M. 1973. Rat ventral prostate chromatin. Effect of androgens on the chemical composition, physical properties and template activity. *Biochemistry*, **12**, 3114–3121.

Cox, R. F., Haines, M. E., and Carey, N. H. 1973. Modification of the template capacity of chick-oviduct chromatin from RNA polymerase by estradiol. *Eur. J. Biochem.*, 32, 513-524.

Darzynkiewicz, Z., and Anderson, J. 1971. Effect of prednisolone on thymus lymphocytes. *Exp. Cell Res.*, 67, 39-48.

Darzynkiewicz, Z., Bolund, L., and Ringertz, N. R. 1969. Nuclear protein changes and initiation of RNA synthesis in PHA stimulated lymphocytes. *Exp. Cell Res.*, 56, 418-424.

Defendi, V., and Manson, L. A. 1963. Analysis of the life-cycle in mammalian cells. *Nature*, 198, 359-361.

Dell'Orco, R. T., Mertens, J. G., and Kruse, P. F. Jr. 1973. Doubling potential calendar time and senescence of human diploid cells in culture. *Exp. Cell Res.*, 77, 356-360.

Devi, A., Lindsay, P., Raina, P. L., and Sarkar, N. K. 1966. Effect of age on some aspects of the synthesis of ribonucleic acid. *Nature*, 212, 474-475.

Dingman, V. W., and Sporn, M. D. 1964. Studies on chromatin. 1) Isolation and characterization of nuclei complexes of deoxyribonucleic acid and protein from embryonic and adult tissues of the chicken. *J. Biol. Chem.*, 2, 3483-3492.

Dulbecco, R., Hartwell, L. H., and Vogt, M. 1965. Induction of cellular DNA synthesis by polyoma virus. *Proc. Nat. Acad. Sci.*, 53, 403-410.

Ellem, K. A. O., and Mironescu, S. 1972. The mechanism of regulation of fibroblastic cell replication. 1) Properties of the system. *J. Cellular Physiol.*, 79, 389-406.

Epifanova, O. I., and Terskikh, V. V. 1969a. Radio autographic techniques in the study of cell cycles. Moscow: Mauka.

Epifanova, O. I., and Terskikh, V. V. 1969b. On the resting periods in cell life cycle. *Cell Tissue Kinetics*, 2, 75-93.

Fabrikant, J. I. 1970. The kinetics of cellular proliferation in human tissues. Determination of duration of DNA synthesis using double labeling autoradiography. *Brit. J. Cancer*, 24, 122-127.

Farber, J., Rovera, G., and Baserga, R. 1971. Template activity of chromatin during stimulation of cellular proliferation in human diploid fibroblasts. *Biochem. J.*, 122, 189-195.

Farber, J., Stein, G., and Baserga, R. 1972. The regulation of RNA synthesis during mitosis. *Biochem. Biophys. Res. Comm.*, 47, 790-797.

Feinendegen, L. E. 1967. *Tritium Labeled Molecules In Biology and Medicine*. New York: Academic Press.

Fox, T. O., Shepherd, J. R., and Burger, M. M. 1971 Cyclic membrane changes in animal cells. Transformed cells permanently display a surface architecture detected in normal cells only during mitosis. *Proc. Nat. Acad. Sci.*, 68, 244-247.

Fry, R. J. M., Lesher, S., and Kohn, H. I. 1961. Estimation of time of generation of living cells. *Nature*, 191, 290-291.

Fry, R. J. M., Lesher, S., and Kohn, H. I. 1962a. A method for determining mitotic time. *Exp. Cell Res.*, 25, 469-471.

Fry, R. J. M., Lesher, S., and Kohn, H. I. 1962b. Influence of age on the transit time of cells of the mouse intestinal epithelium. III. Ilium. *Lab. Invest.*, 11, 289-293.

Fry, R. J. M., Tyler, S. A., and Lesher, S. 1966. Relationships between age and variability. *In*, P. J. Lindopp and G. A. Sacher (eds.), *Radiation and Aging*, pp. 43-55. London: Taylor and Francis.

Fujioka, M., Koga, M., and Lieberman, I. 1963. Metabolism of ribonucleic acid after partial hepatectomy. *J. Biol. Chem.*, 238, 3401-3406.

Fujita, S. 1967. Quantitative analysis of cell proliferation and differentiation in the cortex of the postnatal mouse cerebellum. *J. Cell Biol.*, 32, 277-288.

Graham, C. S., and Morgan, R. W. 1966. Changes in the cell cycle during early amphibian development. *Develop. Biol.*, 14, 439-460.

Grisham, J. W. 1962. A morphologic study of deoxyribonucleic acid synthesis and cell proliferation in regenerating rat liver. Autoradiography with thymidine ^{3}H. *Cancer Res.*, 22, 842-849.

Hamilton, T. H. 1968. Control by estrogen of genetic transcription and translation. *Science*, 161, 649-661.

Hill, B. T., and Baserga, R. 1974. Changes in the number of binding sites for ribonucleic acid polymerase in chromatin of WI-38 fibroblasts stimulated to proliferate. *Biochem. J.*, 141, 27-34.

Howard, A., and Pelc, S. R. 1951. Nuclear incorporation of ^{32}P as demonstrated by autoradiographs. *Exp. Cell Res.*, 2, 178-187.

Johnson, R., and Strehler, E. L. 1972. Loss of genes coding for ribosomal RNA in aging brain cells. *Nature*, 240, 412-414.

Johnson, T. C., and Holland, J. J. 1965. Ribonucleic acid and protein synthesis in mitotic HeLa cells. *J. Cell Biol.*, 27, 565-574.

Kishimoto, S., and Lieberman, I. 1964. Synthesis of RNA protein required for the mitosis of mammalian cells. *Exp. Cell Res.*, 36, 92-101.

Kurtz, D. I., and Sinex, F. M. 1968. Aged related differences in the association of brain DNA and nuclear proteins. *Biochim. Biophys. Acta*, 145, 840-842.

Lajtha, L. G. 1963. On the concept of the cell cycle. *J. Cellular Comp. Physiol.*, 62, Suppl. 1, 143-145.

Lamerton, L. F., and Fry, R. J. M. 1962. *Cell Proliferation*. Oxford: Blackwell Scientific Publications.

Lesher, S. 1966. Chronic irradiation and aging in mice and rats. *In*, P. J. Lindopp and G. A. Sacher (eds.), *Radiation and Aging*, pp. 183-206. London: Taylor and Francis.

Lesher, S., Fry, R. J. M., and Kohn, H. I. 1961a. Influence of age on the transit time of cells of the mouse intestinal epithelium. I. Duodenum. *Lab. Invest.*, 10, 291-300.

Lesher, S., Fry, R. J. M., and Kohn, H. I. 1961b.

Age and the generation time of the mouse duodenal epithelial cells. *Exp. Cell Res.*, 24, 334-343.

Ley, K. D., and Tobey, R. A. 1970. Regulation of initiation of DNA synthesis in Chinese hamster cells. 2) Induction of DNA synthesis and cell division by isoleucine and glutamine in G_1 arrested cells in suspension culture. *J. Cell Biol.*, 47, 453-459.

Lieberman, I., Abrams, R., and Ove, P. 1963. Changes in the metabolism of ribonucleic acid preceding the synthesis of deoxyribonucleic acid in mammalian cells cultured from the animal. *J. Biol. Chem.*, 38, 21-49.

Lin, J-G., Nicolini, C., and Baserga, R. 1974. A comparative study of some properties of chromatin from normal diploid and SV-40 transformed human fibroblasts. *Biochemistry*, 13, 4127-4133.

Lipkin, M., Bell, D., and Sherlock, P. 1963. Cell proliferation kinetics in the gastrointestinal tract of man. 1: Cell renewal in colon and rectum. *J. Clin. Invest.*, 42, 767-776.

Lisco, H., Lisco, E., Adelstein, S. A., and Banks, H. H. 1973. Cytogenetic studies on blood lymphocytes of 4 patients with fracture of the femur, injected with tritiated thymidine. *Intern. J. Radiation Biol.*, 24, 45-47.

Litvak, R. M., and Baserga, R. 1964. An autoradiographic study of the uptake of ^{3}H thymidine by kidney cells of mice at different ages. *Exp. Cell Res.*, 33, 540-552.

Macieira-Coelho, A. 1973. Aging and cell division. *Front. Matrix Biol.*, 1, 46-77.

Macieira-Coelho, A., and Ponten, J. 1967. Induction of the division cycle in resting stage human fibroblasts after RSV infection. *Biochem. Biophys. Res. Comm.*, 29, 316-321.

Mainwaring, W. I. P. 1968. Changes in the ribonucleic acid metabolism of aging mouse tissues, with particular reference to the prostate gland. *Biochem. J.*, 110, 78-86.

Maizel, A., Nicolini, C., and Baserga, R. 1975. Structural alterations of chromatin in phase-III WI38 human diploid fibroblasts. *Exp. Cell Res.*, 96, 351-359.

Malamud, D. 1971. Differentiation and the cell cycle. *In*, R. Baserga (ed.), *The Cell Cycle and Cancer*, pp. 132-141. New York: Marcel Dekker.

Mauck, J. C., and Green, H. 1973. Regulation of RNA synthesis in fibroblasts during transition from resting to growing state. *Proc. Nat. Acad. Sci.*, 70, 2819-2822.

Mendelsohn, M. L., and Takahashi, M. 1971. A critical evaluation of the fraction of labeled mitosis method as applied to the analysis of tumor and other cell cycles. *In*, R. Baserga (ed.), *The Cell Cycle and Cancer*, pp. 58-95. New York: Marcel Dekker.

Mueller, G. C. 1969. Biochemical events in the animal cell cycle. *Federation Proc.*, 28, 1780-1789.

Novi, A. M., and Baserga, R. 1972a. Changes in chromatin template activity and the relationship to DNA synthesis in mouse parotid glands stimulated by isoproterenol. *J. Cell Biol.*, 55, 554-562.

Novi, A. M., and Baserga, R. 1972b. Correlation between synthesis of ribosomal RNA and stimulation of DNA synthesis in mouse salivary glands. *Lab. Invest.*, 26, 540-547.

Oh, Y. H., and Conard, R. A. 1972a. Effect of aging on thymidine incorporation in nuclei of lymphocytes stimulated with phytohemagglutinin. *Life Sci.*, 11, 677-684.

Oh, Y. H. and Conard, R. A. 1972b. Effect of aging on histone acetylation of the normal and regenerating rat liver. *Life Sci.*, 11, 1207-1214.

O'Meara, A. R., and Herrmann, R. L. 1972. A modified mouse liver chromatin preparation displaying age-related differences in salt dissociation and template ability. *Biochem. Biophys. Acta*, 269, 419-427.

Paik, W. K., and Kim, S. 1971. Protein methylation. *Science*, 174, 114-119.

Pardee, A. B. 1971. The surface membrane as a regulator of active cell division. *In Vitro*, 7, 95-104.

Pegoraro, L., and Baserga, R. 1970. Time of appearance of deoxythymidylate kinase and deoxythymidylate synthetase and of their templates in isoproterenol-stimulated deoxyribonucleic acid synthesis. *Lab. Invest.*, 22, 266-271.

Pilgrim, Ch., and Maurer, W. 1962. Autoradiographische der DNS-Verdopplungszeit vershidener Zellarten von Maus und Ratte bei Doppelmarkierung mit ^{3}H und ^{14}C-Thymidin. *Naturwissenschaften*, 23, 1-4.

Prescott, D. M. 1964a. Autoradiography with liquid emulsion. *In*, D. M. Prescott (ed.), *Methods in Cell Physiology*, pp. 365-370. New York: Academic Press.

Prescott, D. M. 1964b. Cellular sites of RNA synthesis. *In*, J. N. Davidson and W. E. Cohn (eds.), *Progress in Nucleic Acid Research and Molecular Biology*, pp. 33-57. New York: Academic Press.

Prescott, D. M., and Bender, M. A. 1962. Synthesis of RNA and protein during mitosis in mammalian tissue culture cells. *Exp. Cell Res.*, 26, 260-268.

Price, G. B., Modak, S. P., and Makinodan, T. 1971. Age associated changes in the DNA of mouse tissue. *Science*, 171, 917-920.

Pyhtila, M. J., and Sherman, F. G. 1968. Age-associated studies on thermal stability and template effectiveness of DNA and nuclear protein from bovine thymus. *Biochem. Biophys. Res. Comm.*, 31, 340-344.

Quastler, H., and Sherman, F. G. 1959. Cell population kinetics in the intestinal epithelium of the mouse. *Exp. Cell Res.*, 17, 420-438.

Rigler, A., and Killander, D. 1969. Activation of deoxyribonuclear protein in human leukocytes stimulated by phytohemagglutinin. *Exp. Cell Res.*, 54, 171-180.

Ringertz, N. R., and Bolund, L. 1969. Activation of hen erythrocyte deoxyribonuclear protein. *Exp. Cell Res.*, 55, 205-214.

Rogers, A. W. 1967. *Techniques of Autoradiography*, p. 335. Amsterdam: Elsevier.

Roth, G. S., and Adelman, R. C. 1974. Age-dependent regulation of mammalian DNA synthesis and cell division *in vivo* by glucocorticoids. *Exp. Geront.*, 9, 27–31.

Roth, G. S., Karoly, K., Adelman, A., and Adelman, R. C. 1974. Regulation of isoproterenol stimulated DNA synthesis in rat salivary gland *in vivo* by adrenal glucocorticoids. *Exp. Geront.*, 9, 13–26.

Roth, G. S., Karoly, K., Britton, V. G., and Adelman, R. C. 1974. Age dependent regulation of isoproterenol stimulated DNA synthesis in rat salivary gland *in vivo*. *Exp. Geront.*, 9, 1–11.

Rovera, G., and Baserga, R. 1973. Effect of nutritional changes on chromatin template activity and non-histone chromosomal protein synthesis in WI-38 and 3T6 cells. *Exp. Cell Res.*, 78, 118–126.

Ryan, J., and Cristofalo, V. J. 1972. Histone acetylation during aging of human cell in culture. *Biochem. Biophys. Res. Comm.*, 48, 735–742.

Samis, H. V., and Wulff, V. J. 1969. The template activity of rat liver chromatin. *Exp. Geront.*, 4, 111–117.

Sander, G., and Pardee, A. B. 1972. Transport changes in synchronously growing CHO and L cells. *J. Cellular Physiol.*, 80, 267–272.

Simnet, J. D., and Hepplestone, A. G. 1966. Cell renewal in the mouse lung. *Lab Invest.*, 15, 1793–1801.

Sisken, J. E., and Morasca, L. 1965. Intrapopulation kinetics of the mitotic cycle. *J. Cell Biol.*, 25, 179–189.

Smets, L. A. 1973. Activation of nuclear chromatin and their release from contact inhibition of 3T3 cells. *Exp. Cell Res.*, 79, 239–243.

Stein, G., and Baserga, R. 1970. Continued synthesis of non-histone chromosomal proteins during mitosis. *Biochem. Biophys. Res. Comm.*, 41, 715–722.

Stein, G., and Baserga, R. 1972. Nuclear proteins and the cell cycle. *Advan. Cancer Res.*, 15, 287–330.

Stein, G. S., Spelsberg, T. C., and Kleinsmith, L. J. 1974. Non-histone chromosomal proteins and gene regulation. *Science*, 183, 817–824.

Stein, G. S., Wang, P. L., and Adelman, R. C. 1973. Age dependent changes in the structure and function of mammalian chromatin. 1) Variations in chromatin template activity. *Exp. Geront.*, 8, 123–133.

Taylor, J. H. 1960. Nucleic acid synthesis in relation to the cell division cycle. *Ann. N. Y. Acad. Sci.*, 90, 409–421.

Teissere, M., Penon, T., and Ricard, J. 1973. Hormonal control of chromatin availability and of the activity of purified RNA polymerases in higher plants. *FEBS Letters*, 30, 65–70.

Teng, C. S., and Hamilton, T. H. 1968. The role of chromatin in estrogen action in the uterus. 1) The control of template capacity and chemical composition and the binding of H^3 estradiol 17β. *Proc. Nat. Acad. Sci.*, 60, 1410–1417.

Terasima, T., and Tolmach, L. J. 1963. Growth and nucleic acid synthesis in synchronously divided populations of HeLa cells. *Exp. Cell Res.*, 30, 344–362.

Terasima, T., and Yasukawa, M. 1966. Synthesis of G_1 protein preceding DNA synthesis in cultured mammalian cells. *Exp. Cell Res.*, 44, 669–672.

Thaler, M. M., and Villee, C. A. 1967. Template activities in normal regenerating and developing rat liver chromatin. *Proc. Nat. Acad. Sci.*, 58, 2055–2062.

Thrasher, J. D. 1967. Age and the cell cycle of the mouse colonic epithelium. *Anat. Record*, 157, 621–626.

Thuringer, J. M., and Katzberg, A. A. 1959. The effect of age on mitosis in human epidermis. *J. Invest. Dermatol.*, 33, 35–39.

Tobey, R. A., Petersen, D. F., and Anderson, E. C. 1971. Biochemistry of G_2 and mitosis. *In*, R. Baserga (ed.), *The Cell Cycle and Cancer*, pp. 309–353. New York: Marcel Dekker.

Todaro, P. J., Lazar, G. K., and Green, H. 1965. The initiation of cell division in a contact-inhibited mammalian cell line. *J. Cellular Comp. Physiol.*, 66, 325–334.

Tschahargane, C., Haag, D., and Goerttler, K. 1971. Über den Altersformwandel der Zellkerne in der menschlichen Epidermis. *Z. Zellforsch.*, 119, 434–450.

Tsuboi, A., and Baserga, R. 1972. Synthesis of nuclear acidic proteins in density inhibited fibroblasts stimulated to proliferate. *J. Cellular Physiol.*, 80, 107–118.

Tubiana, M. 1968. La cinetique des populations de cellules. *Ann. Biol. Clin.*, 26, 793–823.

von Hahn, H. P. 1970. Structural and functional changes in nuclear protein during the aging of the cell. *Gerontologia*, 16, 116–128.

Wheeler, K. T., and Lett, J. T. 1974. On the possibility that DNA repair is related to age in non-dividing cells. *Proc. Nat. Acad. Sci.*, 71, 1862–1865.

Whiteley, H. J., and Horton, D. L. 1963. The effect of age on the mitotic activity of the ear epithelium in the CBA mouse. *J. Geront.*, 18, 335–339.

Wiebel, F., and Baserga, R. 1969. Early alterations in amino acid pools and protein synthesis of diploid fibroblasts stimulated to synthesize DNA by addition of serum. *J. Cellular Physiol.*, 74, 191–202.

Wimber, B. E., and Quastler, H. 1963. A ^{14}C and ^3H thymidine double labeling technique in the study of cell proliferation in *Tradescantia* root tip. *Exp. Cell Res.*, 30, 8–22.

Younkin, L. H. 1972. *In vitro* response of lymphocytes to phytohemagglutinin as studied with antiserum to PHA. *Exp. Cell Res.*, 75, 1–10.

Zardi, L., and Baserga, R. 1974. Ribosomal RNA synthesis in WI-38 cells stimulated to proliferate. *Exp. Molec. Path.*, 20, 69–77.

Zetterberg, A., and Auer, G. 1970. Proliferative activity and cytochemical properties of nuclear chromatin related to local cell density of epithelial cells. *Exp. Cell Res.*, 62, 262–270.

6
CELL LONGEVITY:
In Vivo

Charles W. Daniel
University of California

INTRODUCTION

The purpose of this chapter is to review evidence relating to the question of whether the potential life span of certain component cells from complex metazoan organisms is infinite or finite.

Since the general acceptance of the cell theory, generations of biologists have been intrigued by this question (e.g., Weissman, 1891). This was particularly the case following the early years of this century, when the first cell culturists discovered that tissues removed from a variety of vertebrate species could be studied *in vitro*. During the course of these experiments, it quickly became evident that tissue cells could adhere to an artificial substrate, move about, and, perhaps most remarkably, proliferate with vigor for long periods of time. It thus became evident that cells from even very advanced, complex, and highly evolved organisms had the potential for independent or semiindependent existence (Harrison, 1907; Carrel, 1912; Sanford, Earle and Likely, 1948).

The demonstration of this remarkable biological capacity had a considerable impact upon thinking in the biological sciences, for it raised questions regarding the nature of those homeostatic restraints which, in the organism, restrict cell movement and curb the explosive potential

for cell division so clearly demonstrated in culture—problems which remain at the heart of much contemporary research. With regard to aging, the question became, given the limited and predictable life span of birds and mammals, to what extent can their inevitable senescence and death be attributed to a possible limitation upon the life span of their component cells?

The direct approach to this question is the inspection of dead or senescent animals with the aim of determining whether cell death, or possibly the inability of cells to divide, is causally related to mortality. The general finding is that most cells and tissues of recently deceased animals are alive and in satisfactory condition at the time of natural death (Kohn, 1965). Local areas of cell degeneration or death are in most cases related to cardiovascular or other disease processes, and intrinsic cellular aging mechanisms are not clearly revealed. Indeed, rather than discovering that death is related to the large-scale degeneration of tissue cells, the more common finding is that unrestrained proliferation of cells has given rise to a wide spectrum of neoplastic pathologies.

It is important to establish at the beginning that in approaching the question of cellular mortality, there are biological precedents for cell lines with both limited and unlimited life spans. The germ cell line, in which there is periodic rearrangement of the genome through sexual exchanges, is by necessity and definition potentially immortal. There are also many examples of somatic cells, as well as microorganisms, which appear to have an unlimited potential for cell division. Whereas certain protozoa display the phenomenon of clonal aging, in which the proliferating population progressively loses mitotic capability (e.g., Smith-Sonneborn and Klass, 1974), many others, such as the amoeba, appear capable of limitless division in the complete absence of known sexual activity. It is characteristic of bacteria in general that asexual division can continue indefinitely.

Perhaps the most striking example in metazoans of the lack of senescent changes during serial propagation is found in the perennial plants, where vegetative propagation may be carried on indefinitely either *in vitro* or *in vivo*. The distribution of senescence among various animal phyla has been reviewed by Strehler (1962) and Comfort (1964) and is described in Chapter 7 of this volume.

CELL CULTURE

The problem of cellular aging, the characteristics and parameters of aging processes, and the mechanisms which underlie them have been most intensely studied by the technique of continuous cell culture (see Chapter 7 for discussion of this subject).

It has been reported several times, particularly in the older literature (Carrel, 1912; Ebeling, 1913), that certain lines of vertebrate cells grow indefinitely when provided with a suitable cultural environment. It now appears likely that this conclusion, which had considerable influence upon biological thinking, was obtained from experiments in which improper technique permitted the reintroduction of young cells into older cultures (Hayflick, 1965a).

The more contemporary view is that whereas transformed cells may often be propagated as continuous cell lines, those cells which are phenotypically and karyotypically normal display a limited *in vitro* life span. This conclusion is based upon evidence such as that presented by Swim and Parker (1957), who reported that human fibroblasts obtained from various tissues proliferated for an extended period but finally died out. This work was greatly extended by Hayflick and Moorhead (1961), who grew cells derived from human fetal tissues and found that they could not be propagated indefinitely; in most cases the cultures could be carried for approximately 50 population doublings before entering a Phase III period in which cell death exceeded cell replacement and the cultures were lost. Hayflick (1965a, 1965b) therefore formulated the concept that the limited life span of normal cells in culture was related to aging and could provide a useful model system in which the declining vitality of cells is considered as an expression of senescence at the cellular level.

It now appears that a finite *in vitro* life span is a general, and perhaps universal, characteristic of primary cell strains obtained from mammalian and avian sources. The techniques of cell culture, which make *in vitro* aging studies possible, provide a number of powerful experimental advantages. Perhaps most importantly, the investigator is provided with a means for manipulating the physical and chemical environment of the cells. The cells are visible, and progressive changes may be monitored with ease. Large numbers of cells may be obtained for biochemical studies. Finally, and of great significance, is the fact that human cells may be employed, which is presently impossible with *in vivo* serial transplantation methods.

The methodology of cell culture also introduces substantial difficulties in interpretation. The cellular environment is necessarily artificial, or in the forcefully stated assessment of Moore and McLimans (1968), "Present cell culture systems are very imperfect. Indeed, it is a tribute to the biological flexibility of isolated mammalian cells that they can survive in the adverse physical and chemical environments provided by cell culture methods." It may of course also be argued that although the cell culture milieu may not be optimal, it is demonstrably adequate. Furthermore, by removing cells from their normal homeostatic and morphogenetic restraints, they are freed to demonstrate their biological potential in a manner not otherwise possible.

Whatever one's position is with respect to this argument, it would be generally agreed that a central concern in gerontological studies is to what extent the aging changes observed *in vitro* reflect a fundamental property intrinsic to the cell. It is difficult to design experiments which eliminate the possibility that during long term culture, cellular changes gradually accumulate that are directly related to some aspect of the cultural situation—composition of the medium, attachment to unfamiliar substrates, lack of normal cell associations, or some combination of these. For this reason many workers experimenting *in vitro* attempt, where possible, to relate their findings to analogous results obtained *in vivo*. The degree of confidence one can have in such analogies requires careful assessment. In addition to substantial differences in technique, there is the serious difficulty that long term cell culture studies generally use cells of fibroblastic morphology, because epithelial cells appearing in young cultures are generally overgrown by the more vigorously growing fibroblasts. This is not the case *in vivo*, where the most rapidly proliferating cells are of either epithelial or hemopoeitic type. It has not yet been possible to serially passage fibroblasts in animals, a limitation which must be taken into serious consideration when relating cell culture findings to animal systems.

IN VIVO AGING STUDIES: EXPERIMENTAL DESIGN

The most desirable experimental protocol, in terms of providing a meaningful *in vivo* corollary continuous cell culture, is the serial transfer of cells or tissues between animals in such a manner that optimal conditions are provided for them to display their full potential for survival, proliferation, and function. In practice, it has been difficult to devise experimental conditions which meet these requirements, and the number of serial transplant systems available for use in aging research is presently limited to a few. Below are some of the considerations that enter into the design of such experiments.

Identification of Transplants

The most desirable manner in which to conduct serial transplantation experiments is to return the transplants to their normal position in a new host, thus providing the cells under study with their normal cell and tissue associations. This can be easily accomplished in the case of neoplastic cells, which overgrow surrounding tissues and may be easily identified. Normal transplants, however, are easily confused with host material, and this difficulty imposes a severe restriction upon the design of transplantation experiments. In order to minimize this difficulty, cells have been placed in unusual sites such as the anterior chamber of the eye (Grobstein, 1950), or into unrelated organs such as the brain (Sigel, 1958). These methods may provide for positive identification, but it is not known to what extent the unfamiliar environment may restrict cell proliferation and other activities.

Another type of experiment involves the ablation of host tissue, eliminating potential sources of ambiguity. In some cases such a procedure may have little effect upon the host, and the technique is acceptable. In others, the removal of host tissues may have serious secondary effects upon the host, and questions as to the interpretation of results are raised. The use of genetic markers to provide for cell identification suggests elegant experimental possibilities and has been used successfully by Harrison (1972, 1973) in studies on transplanted erythrocyte precursor cells. Still another means of providing identification was used by Williamson and Askonas (1972), who followed cell lines during serial transplantation by their manufacture of specific antibody.

Growth of Transplants

In order to test the proliferative potential of transplanted cells, sufficient free space for growth must be made available. Whereas neoplastic transplanted cells will characteristically ignore growth restraints imposed by the host, normal transplants are subject to such restraints. Transplanted cells must compete with host cells of similar type, and surgical procedures or chemical or physical means must be used to minimize this competitive restriction upon cell division.

Histocompatibility Factors

The use of highly inbred animals is desirable because it eliminates the need for immunosuppressive measures which often have generalized systemic effects. Syngeneic animals are available in only a handful of species, thus limiting the variety of possible experimental programs. Indeed, serial transplantation experiments which are relevant to aging research have been carried out mainly in the laboratory mouse.

If it is necessary to perform transplants across histocompatibility barriers, it is worthwhile to note that some tissues, such as skin, are readily rejected even in the face of weak histocompatibility antigens, whereas others, such as mammary epithelium, will grow normally even in the presence of a moderate lymphocytic response (Moretti and Blair, 1966). Because these experiments tend to be very long term, and genetic drift is a possible complication, isogenicity should be regularly monitored. A satisfactory method involves the use of reciprocal second-set skin grafts between randomly selected animals within a particular strain (Daniel, De Ome, Young, Blair, and Faulkin, 1968).

Function of Transplants

In some cases, such as the production of hair by skin transplants, functional activity is apparent and may be easily monitored during serial passage. In other cases, function is the criteria for successful transplantation, as in the production of hemoglobin by erythrocytes derived from transplanted stem cells. In still other cases, the transplants may be capable of a differentiated function which is demonstrated only by special procedures, as in the case of milk production by transplanted mammary gland in pregnant or lactating hosts.

Quantification

It is necessary to have some objective measure of what is being studied; this is perhaps most important with respect to cell proliferative capacity. The growth span of cells in culture is generally described in terms of population doublings. Similar indexes of cell division *in vivo* are clearly desirable, but at present the population dynamics of most transplanted cells and tissues are not sufficiently understood to permit meaningful estimates.

IN SITU OBSERVATIONS ON CELL PROLIFERATION

Tissues composed of continuously renewing epithelia have not, in general, been studied in cell culture. The proliferative potential of these cells with respect to age is critical for the maintenance of stable steady-state kinetics in rapidly proliferating tissues such as the skin and the lining of the gut.

Studies of possible age-related changes in proliferation or in characteristics of the cell cycle conducted in nontransplanted tissues offer difficulties in interpretation. These arise because it is not easily possible to distinguish between events which are intrinsically timed by the component cells and those which are related to extracellular influences. The latter, because of the deteriorating environment of the aging animal, may be responsible for the observed results.

In spite of this reservation, information regarding the activities of proliferating cell populations *in situ* has been obtained which is of potential importance to experimental gerontology; of particular interest are studies conducted on the proliferating epithelia of the gut (Lesher, Fry, and Kohn, 1961; Thrasher and Greulich, 1965a, 1965b). Dividing cryptal cells of the duodenum offer a system in which terminally differentiated cells at the luminal interface are progressively lost through attrition and are replaced by cells derived by mitosis from those located near the central region of the crypt. The dividing cryptal cell is currently considered to be a stem or progenitor cell, which serves to provide a continuous supply of differentiated postmitotic cells at a rate which exactly balances the rate of cell loss. Because the dividing and differentiating populations can be located geographically with some precision, the duodenal crypts provide an excellent physiological and morphological system in which to study the causal relationships existing between the positioning of cells in relation to proliferative activity (Figure 1).

Thrasher and Greulich (1965a) studied proliferation in the progenitor cell population in young (10 days), young adult (30–70 days), adult (380–399 days), and senescent (579–638 days) Swiss mice; longevity data for these animals was not given. Using the method of

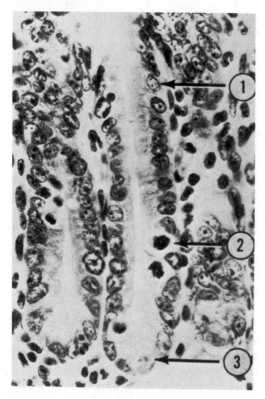

Figure 1. A longitudinally sectioned crypt of Lieberkühn, demonstrating the cryptovillal junction (1), the central region of mitotic activity (2), and the cryptal base with Paneth cells (3). (From Thrasher and Greulich, 1965a.)

Quastler and Sherman (1959), mice were administered a single injection of ^{3}H-thymidine and sacrificed at intervals thereafter. Samples of duodenum were prepared for autoradiography, and microscopic counts were made in order to determine the percent labeled metaphase figures at various times after injection, the percentage of labeled cells, and the mitotic index. Curves describing the rate of appearance of labeled metaphase figures were obtained (Figure 2) and showed two waves of labeled mitoses, with the midpoint of the first wave falling at about 5.2 hr for all age groups. The midpoint of the second wave occurred after an interval of time which gradually increased with advancing age. From these data the mean duration of the S phase was calculated by measuring the interval between the 50 percent labeling point on the ascending and the descending limbs of the first peak, and the G_2 + prophase period was measured from the time at which labeled metaphase figures first appeared and when they attained 100 percent labeling. The results are summarized in Table 1.

The DNA synthetic index declined progressively and substantially with age. The mitotic index was similar among the first three age groups, but the senescent animals differed significantly ($p < 0.01$). Both the duration of the S phase and that of the G_2 + prophase were constant, which is typical of other cell types.

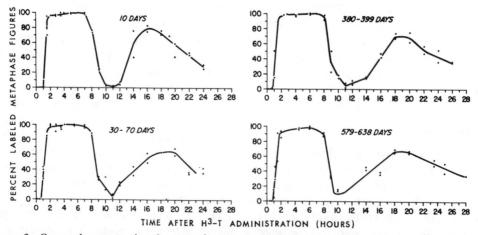

Figure 2. Curves demonstrating the rate of appearance of labeled metaphase figures in the four age groups of mice plotted as a function of the time between ^{3}H-T administration and sacrifice. Each symbol represents at least one animal, and in some cases two or more. (From Thrasher and Greulich, 1965a.)

TABLE 1. MEAN DURATIONS OF THE PROGENITOR CYCLE, ITS PHASES, AND THE DNA SYNTHETIC AND MITOTIC INDICES.[a]

Age (days)	DNA synthetic index (%)	Mitotic index (%)	T** (hours)	T* (hours)	S-phase (hours)	G₂ + prophase (minimum-maximum) (hours)
Infant	48.0	5.52	15	12	7.2	0.75–2.0
Young adult	40.7	5.90	18	13	7.4	0.75–2.0
Adult	34.7	5.78	22	14	7.5	0.75–2.0
Senescent	30.4	4.93	24	18	7.4	0.75–2.0

[a]From Thrasher and Greulich, 1965b.
 T**, S-phase duration/DNA synthetic index.
 T*, Calculated from the peak to peak analysis of Metaphase Curves.

The mean transit time was estimated by two methods (T* and T**), which give somewhat disparate absolute values. It is evident, however, that there is a consistent trend towards increased transit times with age. Given the relative constancy of other phases of the cell cycle, it was concluded that the age-related extension of the interdivision periods was the result of increased duration of the G_1 phase. Similar results were obtained in studies of aging colonic progenitor cells (Thrasher, 1967).

In a closely related study, Thrasher and Greulich (1965b) measured the mean percentage of labeled cells for each cell position in the crypt for each age group (Figure 3). Comparisons of the curves reveal that for each position in the young adult, adult, and senescent mice, the frequency of labeling fell slightly with

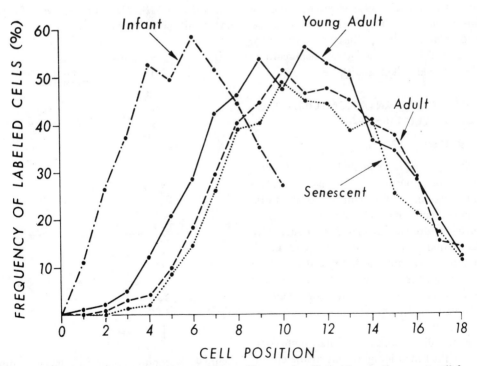

Figure 3. The percentage of labeled progenitor cells at each cell position in the crypt wall for each age group of mice demonstrating the consistent decrease in labeling with age. (From Thrasher and Greulich, 1965b.)

increasing age. The most dramatic differences were found in the infant group, suggesting that substantial developmental changes occur in the location of the progenitor cell population.

In discussing these results, the authors conclude that although the observed changes in the net DNA-synthetic index with age could be caused by a change in the progenitor pool size, the fact that labeled cells could be found to extend from the crypto-villar junction to the cryptal base in all adult age groups suggests that the most likely explanation is lengthening of the cell cycle duration, by extension of the G_1 period, with advancing age.

A few additional studies of changes in proliferative activity with age have been reported. Whiteley and Horton (1963) made mitotic counts on the ear epidermis of the mouse and found that the number of mitotic figures per unit area declined from 30.1 at 9 days to one-half that value at 3 months. Senescent animals (33–36 months) displayed a reduction to only 2-6 mitotic figures per cm. Age-related changes in the proliferative capacity of regenerating rat liver (Norris, Blanchard, and Polovny, 1942; Bucher and Glinos, 1959) and regenerating hair (Whiteley and Horton, 1962) have been reported as having changes in compensatory hypertrophy following unilateral nephrectomy (McCreight and Sulkin, 1959).

SERIAL TRANSPLANTATION: LIMITED OR UNLIMITED LIFE SPAN?

Imaginal Discs

The life cycle of holometabolous insects, such as *Drosophila,* consists of two dramatically different phases of development. Following fertilization and embryogenesis, the larva undergoes a period of growth associated with successive molts. Within the larva are groups of undifferentiated cells known as imaginal discs, which have the responsibility of giving rise to adult structures during the dramatic developmental events associated with pupation (see review by Nöthiger, 1972).

Imaginal discs appear in later embryonic stages as thickened invaginations of the epidermis; it is not known to what extent mesodermal

cells may contribute. They arise in definite numbers and sites throughout the embryo and grow by a process of cell division until they acquire a shape which is characteristic of each type of disc. Each disc has a highly specific destiny and, depending upon type, may develop into a remarkable variety of complex structures such as the compound eye, mechanoreceptors and chemoreceptors, hairs and bristles, legs, wings, genital apparatus, and many others. Indeed the adult, or imago, is a mosaic of structures arranged in a manner that is predetermined by the location and nature of imaginal discs. Each disc is fully committed to a specific differentiative pathway and is said to be developmentally *determined.*

In view of the interest in *Drosophila* genetics, and the enormous literature which surrounds it, it is not surprising that the biology of the imaginal disc has become an active field of investigation in the discipline of developmental genetics. Methods have been devised which permit the discs to be manipulated, dissociated and reaggregated, transplanted and cloned. Transplantation, originally introduced by Ephrussi and Beadle (1936), was further developed (Figure 4) by Hadorn (1963).

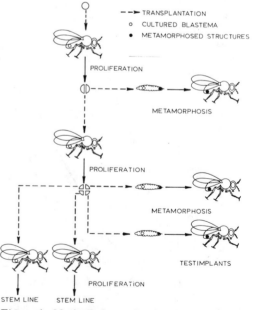

Figure 4. Method for culturing imaginal discs *in vivo.* (From Gehring, 1972.)

Imaginal discs may be transplanted into the body cavity of larva, after which they maintain an undifferentiated state until pupation. At this time, the transplants differentiate into their previously determined structures, which may be readily identified and characterized. Following differentiation, no further proliferation or development occurs. Alternatively, discs may be implanted into the abdomen of adult flies, where the host's hemolymph provides a culture medium which allows proliferation without differentiation. The culture period is restricted to the life span of the host, and the discs may be subsequently transplanted at 2- to 4-week intervals. At each transplant the imaginal disc tissue, which has undergone considerable proliferation, is cut into several fragments. These may then be implanted into subsequent adult hosts where proliferation continues (stem line). Alternatively, the differentiative potential, or state of determination, may be tested by implanting fragments in larva and studying the adult structures appearing following pupation (Figure 4). By all criteria, this transplantation technique is technically excellent; the implants may be positively identified, and ample opportunity is available for growth and specialization.

The general finding (Hadorn, 1967, 1969) is that imaginal disc cells cultured *in vivo* maintain their capacity for continuous proliferation for very long periods, extending in some cases over many years. They maintain the normal karyotype (Gehring, 1966; Remensberger, 1968), and only rarely are abnormalities observed. Certainly there is no correlation between unlimited proliferative capacity and chromosomal abnormalities, for long-term transplant lines are characteristically normal with regard to karyotype.

Transplants also maintain their ability to differentiate into normal adult structures for extended periods. An interesting change in differentiative potential occurs after a period of time. Cells, which might for example have been originally or "autotrophically" determined for anal plates, undergo a change and instead differentiate into "allotypic" structures such as head parts, legs, or wings. This phenomena, termed *transdetermination*, is illustrated in Figure 5. In

Figure 5a and b, two transplant lines which originated from primary transplants of anal plate discs are depicted and have been serially propagated for 3 years, 9 months (Hadorn, 1967). The sequence of determination and differentiation in the lines may be followed, and it is apparent that even in early generations, transdetermination from anal plate to head parts, legs, palpus, and wings occurred. With subsequent transplantation, the frequency of transplants in the various categories of determination changed, and at generation 90, the majority were determined to produce thorax. From the distribution and association of auto- and allotypic structures along the time axis, it was concluded that transdetermination follows a sequence (Figure 5f). Certain transdeterminational events are reversible, others only rarely so, and some not at all; thorax does not undergo further changes and remains stable indefinitely. The amount of transdetermination observed is directly related to proliferation (Figure 6).

These very convincing experiments were undertaken in connection with developmental studies, and relevance to aging has not been extensively discussed. Although it is admittedly difficult to make comparisons between vertebrate and insect cells, and although vertebrates do not have tissues which are formally comparable to imaginal discs, it is nevertheless important to note that this system provides numerous examples of immortal transplant lines within which the cells are phenotypically and karyotypically normal.

It is also significant that certain rules govern these transplantations, and that the phenomenon of transdetermination restricts the type of imaginal disc which may be carried beyond a certain point. Anal plate, for example, cannot be transplanted indefinitely, for it inevitably undergoes transdetermination. The significance of this is unclear, but it may be speculated that limitless division potential in these tissues may be associated with certain patterns of gene activation, and that during continuous propagation, selective pressures favor those cells with certain activation patterns associated with both the state of determination and proliferative capability.

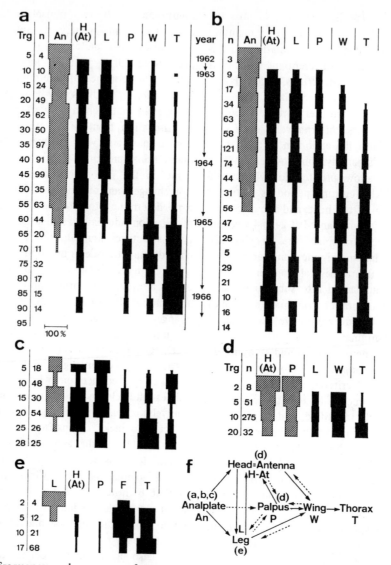

Figure 5. Frequency and sequence of auto and allotypic differentiations in test implants derived from various culture lines which were started with imaginal discs of *Drosophila melanogaster*. Trg, transfer generations (the results of several Trg are assembled as a group); n, number of test implants in each group of Trg; An, anal plates; H (At), head structures (mainly antennal); L, leg parts; P, palpus; W, wing; T, thorax. The blocks indicate the percentage of implants which differentiated into one or the other autotypic (hatched) or allotypic structures (black). Scale of 100 percent is given in a; a and b: male genital lines; c: female genital lines; d: antennal discs lines; e: leg lines; f: scheme of transdetermination; the starting points of the different lines are indicated in brackets. (From Hadorn, 1967.)

Skin

Krohn (1962, 1966) has performed a series of very long-term experiments in which small explants of skin, taken from the body, ear, or tail, were maintained by serial transplantation within inbred strains of mice. By grafting parental strain skin into F_1 hybrids, hair color could be used as a means of identification. It was found that transplants survived for extended periods and could be successively grafted for several generations (Table 2). Although the grafts sur-

TABLE 2. THE BEHAVIOR OF SERIAL SKIN TRANSPLANTS.[a]

Month/year of birth of original donor	Grafts to host I	Good grafts	To host II	Good grafts	To host III	Good grafts	Total age (years/ months)
2/59	14	13	11	3	3	2	6-8/12
11-12/59	30	30	25	16	13	5	6
7/60	10	10	10	6	1[b]	1	5-4/12
10/60	13	11	10	9	8[b]	6	5
12/60	30	25	23	18	11[b]	7	4-10/12
2/61	26	24	20	20	2[b]	2	4-9/12
	123	113	99	72	38[b]	23	

[a]From Krohn, 1966.
[b]More still to be transferred at time of writing.

vived transplantation for periods substantially exceeding the life span of the laboratory mouse, it was found that with successive transfers the grafts became smaller, more shrunken, and because of failure of hair growth, identification became progressively more uncertain. The data in Table 2 represents the last published report of this work, but recently, Krohn indicated that several of these transplant lines have been continued. From a total of 305 primary transplants, 32 could still be identified at 7 years, 7 transplants survived for more than 8 years, and one

survived serial passage for 10.25 years (Krohn, 1972)*. These are impressive life spans, clearly indicating that transplanted skin can survive and function for a period far beyond what is normally required. A large amount of cell proliferation must have been involved in these studies, for both skin maintenance and hair production depend upon cell replication.

It is uncertain whether the ultimate demise of the transplant was due to an exhaustion of proliferative potential. It is equally likely that the gradual increase of extensive scar tissue, as well as other traumatic events associated with repeated transplantation, were the cause. In grafting a complex organ such as the skin, considerable time is required for revascularization and reinnervation, and accumulative damage may result. This may possibly explain why with short transplant intervals of only 42 or 48 days, only four transfer generations could be obtained.

Another difficulty in interpreting the results of skin transfer experiments arises because of the possibility that the graft may be invaded by host material such as nerves, blood vessels, or even tissue cells. It is debated as to what extent this actually occurs in grafting situations (Converse, Filler, and Ballantyne, 1965; Halber and Billingham, 1964), but any such infiltration makes assessment of the total age of the graft uncertain. The presence of identifiable hair after many years and several transfers is unequivocal, however, and provides evidence for remarkable longevity of at least certain components of mouse skin.

*Personal communication.

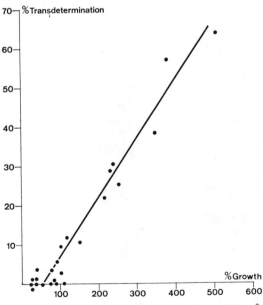

Figure 6. Correlation between amount of growth and rate of transdetermination in blastemas of leg and wing disc. (From Hadorn, 1967.)

Krohn did not attempt to estimate, or even speculate upon, the number of cell divisions that may have been experienced by the basal cells during more than a decade of serial propagation. If one assumes a conservative pattern of cell proliferation in which each stem cell divides every 48 hours, then it appears likely that hundreds, perhaps even thousands, of cell divisions occurred during passage. This estimate, if correct, far exceeds that attributed to human fibroblasts in culture (Hayflick, 1965a).

Hemopoietic Cells

Erythropoiesis. The hemopoietic system consists of a proliferating cell population, the stem or progenitor cells, which must give rise to both additional stem cells and to prodigious numbers of terminally differentiated descendants. Because of the dependence of life upon the proliferative capacity of erythropoietic cells, it has long been a subject of interest to gerontologists. An important initial observation is that although individual circulating cells have well defined life spans and undergo characteristic degenerative changes, an association between aging and cell turnover, cell production, and cell function is difficult to establish (Das, 1969). It also appears that the ability of the hemopoietic system to tolerate certain types of environmental stress, requiring increased proliferative capacity, is little affected by age. The ability of both young and old rats to respond to experimentally induced hypoxia by increased erythrocyte production is, for example, reasonably similar (Garcia, 1957). The ability of old rodents to recover from severe bleeding is somewhat impaired, however (Grant and LeGrande, 1964; Harrison, 1975b).

The ultimate capacity of this system can therefore be tested only by transplantation into hosts whose own hemopoietic cells have been eradicated; this may be accomplished by massive, whole-body irradiation (usually 800–1,000 rads). Host mice so prepared die unless transplanted with hemopoietic cells with sufficient proliferative capacity to repopulate the spleen and bone marrow. Recipient mice which have been saved by hemopoietic transplants may then serve as donors for another transplant

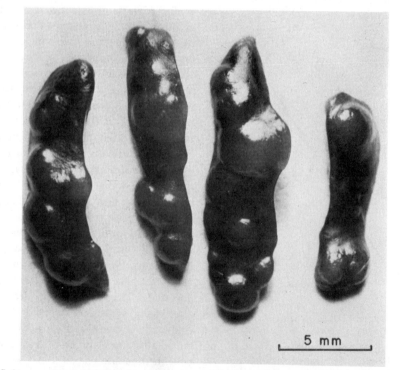

Figure 7. Spleens of irradiated mice 10 days after injection of 6×10^4 nucleated cells. The nodules on which the assay is based are readily seen. (From Till and McCulloch, 1961.)

generation. It has been shown by a number of investigators that as this procedure is repeated, the protection afforded by the transplanted cells decreases (Barnes, Ford, and Loutit, 1959; Barnes, Loutit, and Micklem, 1962; Koller and Doak, 1963). Radiation death usually results from failure of the hemopoietic system, and these results suggest that serial passage reduces the ability of grafts to supply the recipient with mature, functionally competent cells, perhaps as a result of limitations in proliferative potential of stem cells.

It has been possible to repeat these results using methods that provide for excellent quantitation. Till and McCulloch (1961) described a method for studying the proliferative potential of stem cells, which has subsequently been well characterized (McCulloch and Till, 1964). The method makes use of the observation that an intravenous injection of viable cells derived from bone marrow, fetal liver, or in some cases, spleen, will give rise to colonies of hemopoietic cells in the spleens of irradiated recipients. Within 9–14 days after injection, the colonies grow to macroscopic dimensions and are readily recognized and enumerated (Figure 7). The results are expressed in terms of colony forming units (CFU) and, because there is evidence that each colony is derived from a single progenitor cell (Becker, McCulloch, and Till, 1963), each CFU is approximately equivalent to one stem cell. It must be considered, of course, that only a fraction of the injected cells take up residence in the spleen.

Because spleens containing growing cell colonies may be used as both a source for further transplantation and for conducting additional assays, serial passage is possible. In Figure 8, a typical experimental design employed by Siminovitch, Till, and McCulloch (1964) is pictured. The results of two such experiments performed by these workers are summarized in Table 3. It is apparent that the colony-forming ability and the protective ability of these transplants declined markedly and progressively during serial passage. Comparable results have been reported by Lajtha and Schofield (1971).

In slightly different experiments, Cudkowicz, Upton, and Shearer (1964) studied the effect of serial transplantation on the rate of DNA synthesis in the spleens of irradiated, inoculated mice. Five days after transplantation, the recipient mice were injected with ^{131}I-labeled 5-iodo-2'-deoxyuridine, a thymidine analogue, and the incorporated radioactivity was used as an index of cell proliferation. The results (Table 4) also indicate a progressive decline in the rate of cell multiplication.

It is possible that these results are influenced by the necessity for lethal doses of irradiation. It is likely that such effects, if they exist, are particularly serious in later transplant generations where the number of CFUs is reduced, host protection by the grafted cells is lessened, and it is apparent that the transplants are surrounded by a moribund environment.

This difficulty was avoided in an elegant series of transplantation experiments conducted by Harrison (1972, 1973), who used genetically anemic mice as recipients. Anemic hosts, carrying two dominant mutant alleles at the W (dominant spotting) locus, comprise 25 percent of the offspring produced from WB/Re-W/+ × C57BL/6J-W^v/+ parents, hereafter called W/W^v

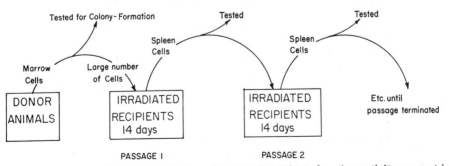

Figure 8. Diagram illustrating the method used to test for colony-forming activity present in marrow cells subjected to serial transplantation in the spleens of irradiated hosts. (From Siminovitch, Till, and McCulloch, 1964.)

TABLE 3. DECLINE IN COLONY-FORMING ABILITY OF HEMOPOIETIC CELLS DUE TO SERIAL TRANSPLANTATION.[a]

Exp.	Passage number	Transplanted[b] cell source	Transplanted cell number	No. of CFU in transplant	Duration of passage	Cells recov. per spleen	CFU per 10^5 cells	CFU per spleen	Survival
1	1	Marrow	10^7	appr. 1500	14 days	3.5×10^7	5.3	1.9×10^3	9/12
	2	Passage 1 spleen	5×10^6	260	14 days	8.7×10^7	2.6	2.3×10^3	21/22
	3	Passage 2 spleen	3×10^6	78	14 days	7.8×10^7	0.49	3.8×10^2	13/31
	4	Passage 3 spleen	10^7	49	14 days	$-^c$	−	−	2/31
2	1	Marrow	10^6	appr. 150	14 days	9.0×10^7	3.5	3.2×10^3	28/34
	2	Passage 1 spleen	10^7	350	14 days	7.6×10^7	>1	$>7.6 \times 10^2$	27/31
	3	Passage 2 spleen	10^7	>100	14 days	1.3×10^8	1.2	1.6×10^3	19/24
	4	Passage 3 spleen	10^7	120	14 days	7.3×10^7	0.41	3.0×10^2	16/32
	5	Passage 4 spleen	1.3×10^7	53	14 days	1.6×10^7	appr. 0.035	appr. 6	6/31

[a] After Siminovitch, Till, and McCulloch, 1964.
[b] Transplanted at 14-day intervals.
[c] Indicates that no measurement was made.

TABLE 4. EFFECT OF SERIAL TRANSPLANTATION ON THE ABILITY OF MARROW CELLS TO PROMOTE ^{131}IUdR UPTAKE IN THE SPLEEN OF IRRADIATED MICE.[a]

Transplant generation	INTERVAL (DAYS)		^{131}IUdR UPTAKE (%)[b]
	Since original passage	Since last passage	Weighted average and 95% confidence intervals
Controls			
(100–120 days old)			0.98 (0.90–1.06)
(200–250 days old)			0.81 (0.75–0.88)
First	30	30	0.50 (0.45–0.55)
	150	150	0.55 (0.48–0.62)
Second	65	30	0.25 (0.21–0.29)
	150	115	0.30 (0.03–0.36)
Third	100	30	0.43 (0.38–0.48)
	150	80	0.38 (0.34–0.42)
Fourth	150	45	0.08 (0.03–0.13)
(with lymph node cells)	150	45	0.10 (0.08–0.12)

[a] After Cudkowicz, Upton, and Shearer, 1964.
[b] The uptake values for spleens of marrow injected mice are given as percentage of the total ^{131}IUdR radioactivity administered, above percentage retention in spleens of uninjected radiation control animals.

recipients. They are easily identified by coat color and are characterized by severe macrocytic anemia. Donor cells were obtained from C57BL/6J (B6) mice which are histocompatible with the hosts and whose hemoglobin may be distinguished electrophoretically from that of the W/W^v mouse. In the course of these studies (Harrison, 1973), marrow cell transplants from both young and old donors were carried in W/W^v hosts. After as long as 36 months and four serial transplants, marrow cell lines from both old and younger donors continued to produce erythrocytes normally, and in one case a cell line produced erythrocytes in an apparently normal fashion for 73 months. Normal production was demonstrated by curing of anemia, their normal rate of recovery after severe bleeding, and normal response of cured recipients to erythropoietin. Hemoglobin patterns indicated that at least 90 percent of the circulating erythrocytes were of the donor type.

These results clearly demonstrate the ability of hemopoietic cells to function normally for periods far in excess of what could be required during a single life cycle. Nevertheless, the data do not indicate an unlimited proliferative potential for hemopoietic stem cells. When colony forming units were studied, they were found to decline slowly with successive transplants, and the decline was more pronounced in the fourth transplant generation in lines derived from older than from younger donors (Table 5).

All transplantation studies so far conducted suggest a finite proliferative capacity for erythropoietic stem cells. At present it is not possible to determine the total number of cell generations of which a stem cell population is capable. It has been postulated that in the normal animal the turnover of stem cells is slow, due to the fact that a majority of such cells may not be in a state of proliferation at all, but are in a resting, or G_0 state. At the presentation of some stimuli, the nature of which remains to be identified, a stem cell may resume proliferation, giving rise to both committed cells and additional progenitors (Lajtha, 1963; Lajtha, Oliver, and Gurney, 1962; Lajtha and Schofield, 1971). Evidence supporting this was obtained

TABLE 5. EFFECT OF MARROW CELL AGE ON ABILITY TO CURE W/W^v ANEMIC MICE.[a]

Transplant	Original donor	Cell age months[b]	No. CFU (SE)[c]	% CURED (n) AFTER MONTHS	
				1–3	6–9
I	Old	29–39	10.6(0.7)	94(33)	63(27)
	Young	1–13	10.7(0.9)	81(36)	69(29)
I[b]	Old	30–34	10.4(0.6)	87(45)	86(37)
	Young	4–12	11.6(0.9)	100(48)	93(44)
II	Old	37–50	6.3(1.2)	96(47)	75(45)
	Young	14–27	8.7(0.9)	91(42)	73(41)
II[b]	Old	43–47	7.7(0.7)	97(29)	–
	Young	18–23	9.1(0.9)	100(29)	–
III	Old	43–64	5.6(0.6)	72(102)	54(76)
	Young	21–41	7.4(0.7)	80(86)	59(44)
IV	Old	63–70	3.7(0.3)	64(36)	53(30)
	Young	38–43	7.2(0.9)[c]	87(23)[c]	80(10)
Untreated W/W^v		3–6	<0.01	–	–

[a] After Harrison, 1973.
[b] C57BL/6J donors; others were WCB6F$_1$ donors.
[c] After the fourth transplant, the younger control marrow cell lines did not decline in either ability to cure W/W^v recipients or in CFU numbers, while these factors continued to decline in the marrow cell lines from old donors. This may have occurred because only two carriers donated half of the younger marrow. Their marrow contained twice as many CFUs as that of the best of the 11 carriers of old cells. When additional younger cell carriers have been transplanted for the fourth time, they may approach the pattern followed for the first three transplants.

by Becker, McCulloch, Siminovitch, and Till (1965), using the ^{3}H-thymidine suicide method, in which DNA-synthetic cells incorporate lethal amounts of radioactivity.

If many or most of the progenitor cells are mitotically inactive, or divide very slowly, with the responsibility for the production of differentiated descendants falling upon cells one or more generations removed from the progenitor population, it is possible that extremely large numbers of potential cell doublings are not required.

Antibody-producing Cells. Williamson and Askonas (1972) have used another marker, the production of specific antibody, to study clonal senescence *in vivo*. Primary spleen cell donors were immunized with bovine gamma globulin which had been conjugated with DNP (Askonas, Williamson, and Wright, 1970). Antibody produced was highly specific and could be identified by isoelectric focusing techniques. Using the isoelectric spectrum as a phenotypic marker, the authors were able to follow a single clone of anti-DNP forming cells through successive transfers in syngeneic mice.

Serial transfer of these cells showed that they (clone E9) had a finite life span. The loss of E9 production was not a precipitous event; a relatively constant production continued during the first four transfers, after which maximum production declined progressively (Figure 9). Although this result could be due to diminished productivity by antibody-producing cells, Williamson and Askonas (1972) present evidence that production is reasonably constant, and the level of E9 is proportional to the number of secreting cells. It is concluded that limitations in ultimate proliferative capacity provide the most direct explanation for the observed results.

Based upon a model for cell division and differentiation patterns in antibody forming clones (Figure 10), it is postulated that the decline in antibody production is due to a progressive failure to regenerate memory cells. Based upon a number of assumptions regarding the probable number of cell divisions involved at various levels in this clonal hierarchy, it was calculated that from the first differentiation from an

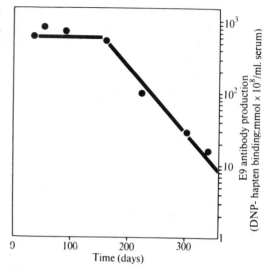

Figure 9. Maximum production of E9 antibody in each transplant generation plotted as a function of the age of the clone. Each point represents the time at which the highest producer in each generation was killed for transplantation of clone E9. (From Williamson and Askonas, 1972.)

original precursor cell, in which the descendants became committed to the production of antibody-forming populations, the overall proliferative potential is not more than 90 cell doublings. If true, or even if nearly true, this figure is remarkably consistent with the estimated cell doubling potential of diploid human fibroblasts *in vitro* (Martin, Sprague, and Epstein, 1970). What the significance of this correlation might be, even if verified, is for discussion. Were it possible to accurately enumerate the mitotic events of various mammalian cells, it would not be unexpected to find that the proliferative potential of cells of murine origin, a species with a life span of two or three years, would differ significantly from that of human cells, which must continue in many cases for nearly a century.

Calculations of the estimated doubling potential of a cell, whether in the animal or in culture, must be interpreted with great caution, for they rest upon a variety of important assumptions and estimates. This is particularly troublesome in the case of hemopoietic tissues where, unlike the gut or the skin, the progenitor cells

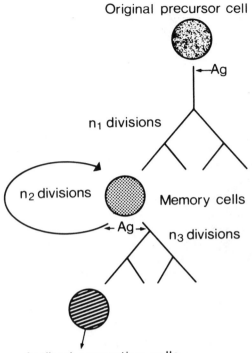

Original precursor cell

n_1 divisions

n_2 divisions

Memory cells

Ag

n_3 divisions

Antibody secreting cells

Figure 10. Model of the development of an antibody-forming cell clone. The clonal precursor cell carries receptors recognizing antigen. Antigen-dependent divisions: n_1, generation of memory cells from precursor cell; n_2, regeneration of memory cells on further antigenic stimulation; n_3, division and differentiation leading to terminal antibody secreting cells. (From Williamson and Askonas, 1972).

cannot be identified visually, and experimentation with them is done at a certain level of abstraction. Information needed to accurately assess division potential includes data on the length of the cell cycle, as well as information on how it may change during aging. An understanding of the pattern of proliferation kinetics is also necessary. That is, whether replication proceeds by a clonal pattern, a tangential pattern, or something between the two. It is also necessary to take into account the phenomenon of cell death, which may be an important factor not only as a result of terminal differentiation, but also later in clonal expansions. Rates and patterns of cell death may, of course, change with cell age.

Mammary Epithelium

Mouse mammary epithelium, which at first may appear an unlikely tissue to employ in the study of cellular aging, has provided a useful model system for the investigation of cell behavior during long term serial transplantation. This is largely because certain growth characteristics of the gland, and the existence of uniquely suitable transplantation techniques, make possible a number of interesting experimental designs.

The method is based upon the technique of mammary transplantation devised by De Ome, Faulkin, Bern, and Blair, (1959) in connection with experiments involving mammary tumors and preneoplastic tissues. The grafted tissue is placed in its natural environment, white fat, and by means of a simple surgical technique, the competing host gland is removed; ample opportunity is provided for growth, differentiation, and function. The hosts are little disturbed by the gland-clearing operation, and their growth, reproductivity, and longevity are normal.

The gland-clearing operation is depicted in Figure 11. The procedure is based upon the observation that in prepubertal female mice the glandular epithelial component of the organ is rudimentary and consists only of the nipple and a network of very short ductal elements. The fatty stromal tissue, termed the fat pad, is well developed at this time however, and by surgically removing the epithelial component, it becomes available for transplantation. It has been demonstrated by Soemarwoto and Bern (1958) that this surgery does not interfere with circulation to the remaining portions of the fat pad.

Transplants consist of 0.5-mm pieces of mammary gland removed either from a primary source or from previously transplanted fat pads; in some cases trypan blue is administered to the donor in order to make glandular elements more easily visible. Transplants are placed in a small incision in the fat pad, and hosts are maintained under standard conditions. Primary transplants placed in young or adult hosts fill the fat pad within 8–12 weeks and are normal in appearance. They are entirely capable of completing the mammary cycle of lobuloalveolar devel-

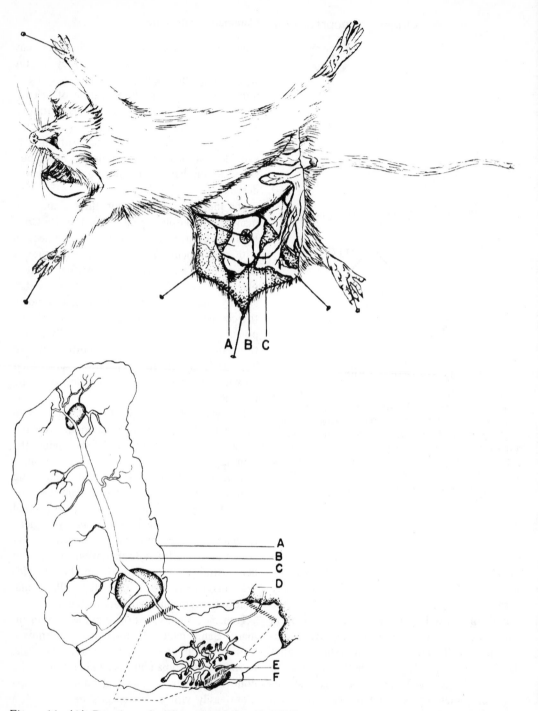

Figure 11. (A) Drawing of a 3-week-old female C3H mouse prepared for the removal of the mammary gland elements from the right No. 4 (inguinal) fat pad. A, nipple area; B, right No. 4 fat pad; C, right No. 5 fat pad. (B) Drawing of a right No. 4 fat pad from a 3-week-old female mouse. The blood vessels, fat pad, and nipple area were cauterized along the slant lines. The fat pad and the surrounding connective tissue bounded by the dashed line (---) were removed with fine scissors. A, boundary of No. 4 fat pad; B, large vein; C, inguinal lymph node; D, portion of No. 5 fat pad; E, branching ducts of the No. 4 mammary gland; F, nipple area. (After De Ome *et al.*, 1959.)

opment, secretion, and involution, if hosts are bred.

The serial transplantation of mammary tissue was first reported by Hoshino and Gardner (1967). The longest life span obtained was 3 years and 9.5 months (transplant generation 7), and it was concluded that mammary parenchyma can survive indefinitely if conditions are favorable. It is important to note that very long transplant intervals were used, and one host was 812 days old at necropsy.

Somewhat different results were reported by Daniel *et al.* (1968). In a large-scale series of experiments, mammary tissue was passaged in young mice using constant intervals of either 2 or 3 months, a period that provides opportunity for the gland to grow continuously (Figure 12). Growth rate, rather than simple survival was measured by estimating the amount of available fat occupied by the glandular outgrowths. This provided the *mean percent fat pad filled*, a figure which may be related to either transplant generation or time.

Serial transplantation of this normal, nontransformed mammary tissue invariably led to a decline in proliferative capacity (Daniel *et al.*, 1968; Daniel, 1973). After a number of serial transfers, the tissue became progressively unable to fill the available fat (Figure 13), and eventually the lines were lost due to difficulty in identification and in transplantation of the minute, slowly proliferating outgrowths.

Data from eight typical experiments is summarized in Figure 14. The decline in growth takes place at the rate of approximately 15 percent each passage and is linear. This reduced proliferation inevitably occurs in response to serial passage even though all conditions for growth are optimal, and careful selection is exercised for the most vigorously proliferating outgrowths. It is independent of mouse strain and is not related to the presence of Mammary Tumor Virus (Daniel *et al.*, 1968). The loss of proliferative potential is interpreted as an expression of aging at the cell and tissue level, when aging is considered solely in terms of proliferation, rather than survival (Daniel, 1972).

ROLE OF CELL DIVISION IN CELLULAR AGING

A central problem in these studies is whether the limited life span of somatic cells is attributable to a finite and specified number of cell doublings, or alternatively, whether the passage of metabolic time can account for senescence independent of mitotic activity. Limitations

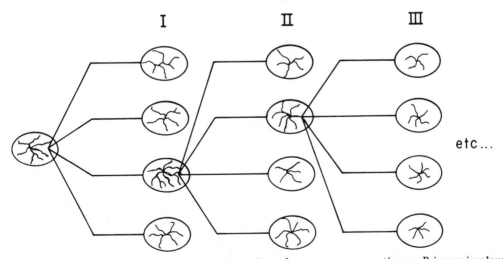

Figure 12. Diagram illustrating serial transplantation of mouse mammary tissues. Primary implants are removed from a single donor gland and transplanted into 10–14 gland-free fat pads, which represent generation 1. Subsequent transplants are always taken from the most vigorously growing outgrowth of the preceding generation. Growth rate is expressed as mean percent fat pad filled at each generation. (From Daniel *et al.,* 1975.)

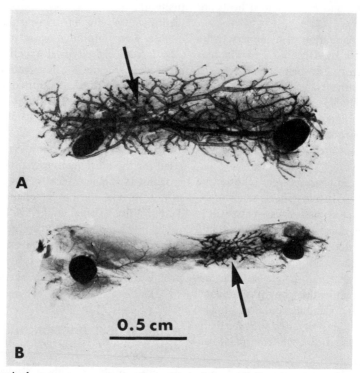

Figure 13. Typical mammary outgrowths arising from serially transplanted mammary tissues, using a transplant interval of 3 mo. Arrows indicate the origin of growth. A, generation I outgrowth which has grown rapidly to fill the available fat; B, generation IV outgrowth which has been propagated for 16 mo and fills about 25 percent of the fat pad. Hematoxylin staining. (From Daniel and Young, 1971.)

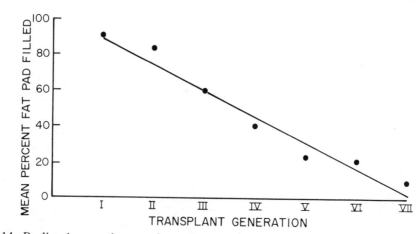

Figure 14. Decline in growth rate of mammary tissue during serial propagation. This plot summarized results of eight transplant lines, and each point represents 80-100 transplants. The regression is approximately linear, and the slope indicates a 15 percent loss of growth potential at each passage. Line fitted by method of least squares. (From Daniel *et al.,* 1975.)

upon division potential are strongly indicated in studies of hemopoietic and antibody forming cell transplants and may well be a factor in the aging of serially grafted skin. In no case, however, has it been possible to manipulate the experimental situation in such a manner as to cleanly distinguish between maintenance and proliferation.

Recently, *in vivo* evidence regarding the relationship of division to cellular aging was obtained using the mammary transplant system. The design of these experiments was dictated by certain morphogenetic features displayed by mammary ducts proliferating in nonpregnant hosts. The mammary gland, which originates in the fetus as a derivative of the developing epidermis, grows by a process of ductal elongation in which mitotic activity is mainly con-

fined to the growing tips, or *end buds* (Bresciani, 1968). This developmental pattern is clearly seen in autoradiographs made from whole-mount preparations, in which structural details may be related to DNA synthetic activity. A representative autoradiograph is pictured in Figure 15, alongside the same gland visualized with hematoxylin staining. It is seen that incorporation is mainly found in the end buds. In addition, it is the large end buds which are most densely labeled and which are clearly the most rapidly growing. The nipple and the terminal ducts on which the end buds have regressed are only slightly labeled.

The gland in Figure 15 has not been transplanted, and retains its full growth potential. Nevertheless, some ducts have ceased growth due to the fact that they have reached the limits

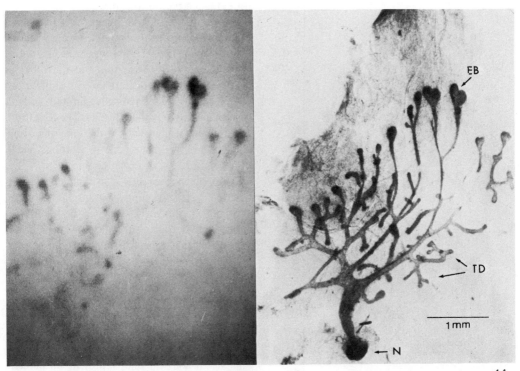

Figure 15. Whole gland autoradiograph. Thirty minutes after a single injection of 25 $\mu C^{14}C$ thymidine, the mammary fat pad was removed, fixed, extracted in acetone, and dried. After gentle compression to a final thickness of 100μ, the gland was sandwiched between emulsion coated slides. After exposure the glands were removed. The slides were then developed, fixed, and cemented together with Permount in original alignment. Left, whole gland autoradiograph of rapidly growing mouse mammary gland. Right, same gland stained with hematoxylin. A point by point comparison reveals that the large end buds (EB) are most intensely labeled. Ducts, terminal ducts (TD), and the nipple (N) display reduced incorporation. (From Daniel, 1975.)

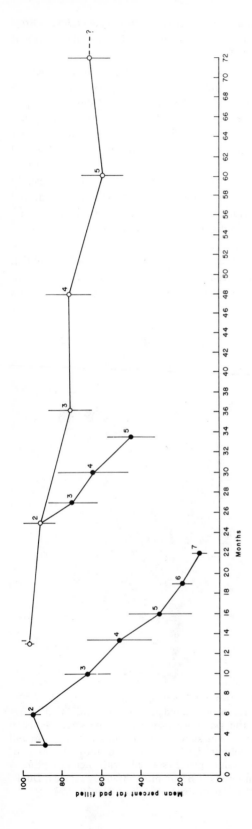

of available fat. This represents a process of growth regulation operating at the tissue level and is the result of normal, but poorly understood, morphogenetic processes (Faulkin and De Ome, 1960). Termination of growth results in the regression of end buds and a simultaneous reduction in cell proliferation (see also Figure 13).

Experiments intended to clarify the relative contributions of metabolic time and cell proliferation were designed, taking into account the fact that a primary mammary transplant requires 2-3 months to fill the fat pad, after which the ducts remain mitotically inactive until subsequent transplantation. By transplanting at short intervals, therefore, the tissue is allowed to proliferate continuously, whereas by extending the transplant interval, the gland may remain mitotically static but metabolically active for extended periods of time.

The results of such an experiment are seen in Figure 16. Two transplant lines were initiated from a single donor; one was transplanted at short intervals of 3 months and the other at yearly intervals. The short interval subline displayed the characteristically limited growth span of slightly less than 2 years. The long interval subline is still growing at the time of writing, at the end of 6 transplant generations and 6 years, although at a decreasing rate.

This extension of life span could not be attributed to the trauma of transplantation. In another experiment, Daniel and Young (1971) initiated two transplant lines, one which was propagated by transplants taken from the pe-

Figure 16. Serial transplantation studies of mouse mammary gland. Circles denote transplant generations and indicate the mean percent of fat pads filled with mammary outgrowths, calculated on the basis of successful transplants. Thirty-two fat pads were transplanted at each generation. Vertical lines represent 95 percent confidence intervals. Two transplant lines were initiated from a single donor at time 0 and transplanted at intervals of 12 months (○——○) or 3 months (●——●). At 24 months a second short-interval line was split from the 12-month series. The experiment is in progress. (From Daniel and Young, 1971; Daniel, 1973; Daniel, 1975.)

riphery of outgrowths and which had experienced maximum proliferation, and another line in which transplants were always removed from the center of the donor outgrowths, where the history of cell division was less. Results of this experiment (Figure 17) indicate that the peripheral subline, which had experienced the largest number of cell divisions, displayed the most rapid decline in growth.

It is concluded that in the case of mammary cells, aging *in vivo* during serial passage is a result of exhaustion of proliferative potential. There is no indication that the life span of these cells, maintained under physiological but static conditions, is necessarily limited, although conclusive evidence in this regard will perhaps not

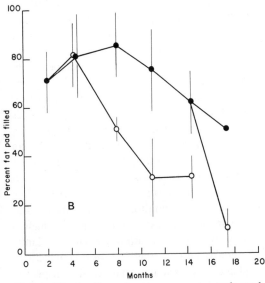

Figure 17. At time 0 mice were transplanted with gland from a single 12-week donor. At the first transplant generation (3 months) a fat pad was selected, and transplants were removed either from its center (●——●) or from peripheral areas (○——○). In subsequent generations, transplants continued to be taken either from the center or periphery, using the most rapidly growing outgrowths as donors. At 14 months the center-propagated line was split into a second peripheral-propagated group. The experiment was terminated at 18 months. The last closed circle is uncertain, and its confidence interval is omitted; due to technical difficulties, only four successful transplants were obtained. (From Daniel and Young, 1971.)

be available for years. In any case, the cells can be maintained for periods far in excess of the murine life span, and during this period they remain in excellent condition as judged by electron microscopy (Daniel, 1972) and by functional competence. Even very old mammary cells which have lost their capacity to proliferate will produce abundant milk in lactating hosts (Daniel, unpublished).

THE INFLUENCE OF DONOR AGE

Skin

With the intention again of distinguishing between intrinsic and extrinsic factors related to aging, Krohn (1962), in a series of "heterochronic" transplantations, studied the behavior of skin when grafted from old donors to young hosts. Old and young A strain skin (680 and 74 days old) and CBA skin (765 and 71 days old) were simultaneously grafted to young CBA × A mice and to either A or CBA mice according to donor strain (Table 6). Old A strain skin deteriorated on either host between 100 and 227 days following transplantation, while young A skin remained in satisfactory condition more than 300 days later. With CBA skin, however, most of the pairs of grafts were equally vigorous, though in some cases there were indications that a turning point had been reached in the behavior of old skin at about 400 days. No explanation for the strain-related difference in behavior following transplantation is available.

In a related experiment, Horton (1967) performed skin grafts into 3-4 month-old hosts from donors aged 30-32 months (strain not specified). Grafts survived in good condition longer than 2 years following transplantation, for a maximum tissue age of 4 years, 8 months. The hair had been plucked from both the grafted areas and from the hosts. Although in old mice the hair regrowth cycle following plucking may be delayed for as long as 4 weeks (see also Finch, 1973), in the transplants the hair regrowth quickly fell into synchrony with that of the host, indicating the presence of systemic factors effecting hair growth that may become deficient or irregular in old age.

TABLE 6. BEHAVIOR OF OLD AND YOUNG SKIN GRAFTS TRANSPLANTED SIMULTANEOUSLY.[a]

Strain combination	No. of mice	SURVIVAL TIME (DAYS) OF	
		Old grafts[b]	Young grafts[b]
A-A	5	5 × 100–200	5 × 325+
A-CBA × A	6	4 × 100–200	5 × 325+
		1 × 300	
		1 (tailskin) × 325+	
CBA–CBA	6	1 × ?200	6 × 325+
		5 × 325+	
CBA-CBA × A	7	7 × 325+	7 × 325+

[a] After Krohn, 1962.
[b] Age of donors: A strain old: 680 days; young: 74 days; CBA strain old: 765 days; young: 71 days.

Hemopoietic Cells

As previously indicated (Table 5), Harrison (1973) has demonstrated that there is little difference in the behavior of serially transplanted marrow derived initially from old and young donors. In both old and younger cell lines, the CFU declined slightly with each passage.

In addition to his studies on erythropoiesis, Harrison and Doubleday (1975) have studied the function of immunological stem cells derived from old and young donors. Donor mice immunized with sheep red blood cells (SRBC) served as donors for marrow or spleen cells, which were grafted into young, lethally irradiated recipients. Immunological function was tested by the Jerne plaque assay at periods following transplantation. The results (Figure 18) suggested that irradiated recipients populated by marrow cell lines from old donors had an immune response almost as effective as recipients populated by cell lines from younger controls. The old marrow lines had functioned normally for a total of 39 to 43 months by 10 months after grafting and still gave immune responses in the normal range; at this time the hosts were 13 months old. These findings contrast with, for instance, those of Wigzell and Stjernswärd (1966) and Makinodan, Perkins, and Chen (1971), who established that immunological competence declines with age. The tentative conclusion reached by Harrison (1975a) is that aging is not intrinsically timed within the immunologically significant stem cells. Rather, the observed changes probably result from the deterioration in the internal environment of the aging mouse which prevents normal differentiation and development of functional cells. These postulated environmental defects may be short-range interactions involving the microenvironment of the cells, or could be long-range, involving nutritional or hormonal deficiencies.

The findings of Harrison appear to be at odds with those of Williamson and Askonas, (1972), but differences in experimental design make comparison difficult. Harrison's transplants were allowed to remain in the host for extended periods, during which antibody forming capacity was monitored. Williamson and Askonas, in contrast, found "aging" changes after only a few short-interval serial transplants. The contradiction is perhaps most convincingly explained by assuming that serial transplantation at short intervals forces stem cells to proliferate far more frequently than would be demanded of them under physiological conditions.

Mammary Epithelium

The mammary transplant system has been used to investigate the interrelationship between host and tissue age (Young, Medina, De Ome, and Daniel, 1971). The growth potential of tissue from old and young mice was investigated by transplanting from 26-month and 3-week Balb/c donors into gland-free fat pads of 3-week hosts. Old and young tissue was transplanted simultaneously on contralateral sides of each recipient, and this pattern was continued in subsequent transplant generations. The

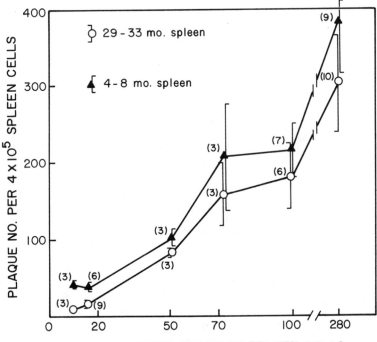

Figure 18. Immune responses of irradiated recipients populated with marrow cells from: O—29 to 33-month-old donors. ▲—3 to 6-month-old donors. Each point is the mean for recipients in that category, with brackets enclosing one standard error, and with the number of recipients in parentheses. At 3 and 6 months, recipients were stimulated by 2×10^9 SRBC ip; at 10 months by 1×10^9 SRBC iv. (From Harrison and Doubleday, 1975.)

results (Figure 19) indicate that it was possible to propagate both the young and old tissue for five generations before both lines were lost because of reduced proliferative capacity. There was no difference in growth potential between tissues derived from young or old donors. This result is predictable, for in the case of mammary transplant the cells from old virgin donors had experienced no more cell divisions than cells taken from young animals, due to growth restrictions imposed by the fat pad.

In the reverse experiment, old and young tissue was transplanted contralaterally into 26-month-old hosts whose fat pads had been cleared of host gland at 3 weeks of age. Neither young nor old transplants grew vigorously in old hosts (Table 7). This result is not unexpected in view of the fact that mammary

TABLE 7. GROWTH OF MAMMARY TRANSPLANTS OF VARIOUS AGES IN OLD HOSTS.[a]

Experiment	Host Age	Age of initial transplant	MEAN % FAT PAD FILLED (95% C.I.) TRANSPLANT GENERATION	
			I	II
A	25–26 months	3 weeks	37(±10)	
	25–26 months	25–26 months	28(±11)	
B	25 months	3 weeks	31(±16)	35(±48)
	25 months	25 months	29(±21)	31(±39)
Control	3 weeks	3 weeks	77(±19)	
	3 weeks	26 months	58(±19)	

[a]After Young *et al.*, 1971.

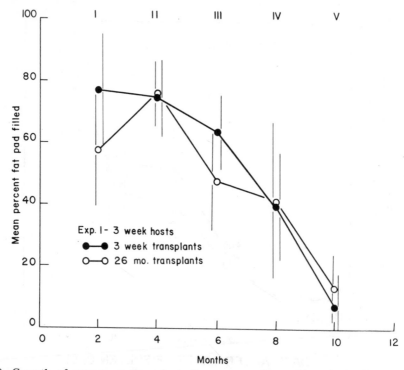

Figure 19. Growth of mammary transplants from young (3 week) and old (26 month) donors during serial passage in young hosts. Each point represents a transplant generation, and vertical lines indicate 95 percent confidence intervals. ●——●, 3-week transplants; ○——○, 26 month transplants. (From Young *et al.*, 1971.)

growth is an endocrine-dependent process and elongation of ducts in virgin females requires stimulation by mammogenic hormones released during regular estrous cycling (Nandi, 1958). Slow growth of gland carried in old hosts could therefore be due to irregular or infrequent estrus. This interpretation is supported by a study of vaginal smears taken from a sample of host mice; all had very irregular cycles ranging from 6 to 10 days or were in constant diestrus.

In summary, the existing *in vivo* evidence regarding the influence of host age on the viability of individual tissues, whether skin, hemopoietic, or mammary, does not provide evidence that the viability of cells obtained from older, but not senescent, animals is significantly less than that of younger cells.

This finding is not necessarily at variance with the previously reported conclusion that a finite proliferative potential is indicated for most tissues and cells so far studied. Rather, it suggests that this potential is so significantly in excess of what is required during a single life-

time that only a fraction of the potential for cell replication has been used up by the time heterochronic transplants are performed.

TISSUE INTERACTIONS AND AGING

Mammary Epithelium

Age-related changes in the physical characteristics of connective tissues have received considerable attention in recent years (Sinex, 1964; Sobel, 1967). It has been suggested that these changes could alter the microenvironment of cells, perhaps by interfering with exchange processes, and thereby contribute to cellular senescence. Direct evidence is difficult to obtain.

In the case of serial transplantation of mammary epithelium, it is possible to make a definite statement regarding the effect of connective tissue on the senescence of associated epithelium. This can be done because of certain growth characteristics of mammary ducts. After transplantation, the elongating ducts invade the fat by means of intense cell proliferation at the end bud. The end bud, which is a multilayered epithelial structure, lacks a structured connective tissue sheath, and except for a very thin basal lamina, the proliferating epithelium is in direct contact with fat and mesenchymal cells (Daniel, 1972). An inductive interaction exists between the advancing mammary epithelium and surrounding cells, with the result that host mesenchyme ahead of the end bud begins to proliferate and, in the region of the subtending duct, the mesenchyme later differentiates into fibrocytes. These fibrocytes then form a well-developed sheath of collagenous connective tissue which is characteristic of the mature duct. These relationships are especially well visualized with the aid of the scanning electron microscope (Figure 20).

From this it is apparent that during serial passage of mammary epithelium, the connective tissue portion of the organ is contributed by the host; even late-passage epithelium which has lost its ability to proliferate is surrounded by young connective tissue. It can be concluded that in this case, aging of connective tissue components is not implicated in cellular aging processes.

Hemopoietic Cells

Although it is difficult to directly visualize the cell interactions involved in erythropoiesis, Harrison (1975b) has devised experiments in

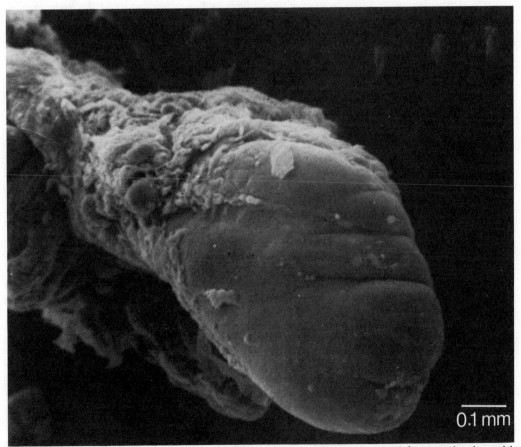

Figure 20. Young mammary end bud dissected from fat pad and prepared for examination with the scanning electron microscope. Note that the anterior surface of the end bud has separated easily from surrounding tissues, while the subtending duct is surrounded by adherent fibrous and cellular material. The smooth surface of the leading edge is the thin basal lamina overlying end bud epithelium. (From Daniel, 1975.)

which it is possible to draw inferences regarding environmental influences upon stem cell proliferation. Female C57BL/6J mice were bled severely, and their ability to recover was measured by hematocrit and by hemoglobin concentration. Old mice consistently recovered more slowly than younger controls and resembled rats in this respect (Grant and LeGrande, 1964). In an attempt to improve the response of old mice, large numbers of young marrow cells were injected. Although these injections were effective in genetically anemi W/W^v controls, they failed to influence erythrocyte production in old animals. Assuming that the injected cells were able to populate the host, which was not demonstrated, it could be concluded that the cause of the decline in old age was not intrinsically timed within the marrow stem cells, but resulted from an alteration in the mouse's internal environment where the stem cells multiply and differentiate.

TRANSPLANTATION-INDUCED ALTERATIONS IN CELL REGULATION

Imaginal Discs

In addition to transdetermination, which leads in an all-or-none fashion from one normal differentiative pathway to another, Hadorn (1969) has reported occasional examples of anomalous behavior in certain serially transplanted imaginal disc cells lines. One type of alteration, termed "anormotypic", resulted in true breeding lines whose test pieces differentiated into aberrant structures. It is not known whether the explanation for this phenomenon lies in alteration of regulatory processes controlling patterns of gene activation, or whether somatic mutations might be responsible. The latter explanation is favored by Hadorn on the basis that each type of anormotypic line originated only once, and reversion to normal type has never been found to occur. The unusual developmental patterns are maintained in stable fashion during serial propagation in adult flies.

A second type of abnormality, termed "atelotypic," gave rise to cell lines that grew very rapidly but failed to differentiate. The method of identifying the state of determination involved implanting test pieces into larva

and examining them following pupation. The implants are required, during the course of this process, to respond to a complex spectrum of hormones, appearing and waning in a sequential fashion, by specific patterns of differential gene activation. It is apparent that these atelotypic lines have lost the competence to respond to the hormones of pupation. Again, the mechanisms involved are unclear. Mutations or chromosomal abnormalities are a possibility, but although Remensberger (1968) found occasional karyotypic abnormalities in these lines, it was clear that atelotypic behavior could be established and propagated in cells whose karyotypes remained normal. The possibility of viral involvement was raised, for virus-like particles have been observed in the atelotypic lines. Similar particles have been observed in normal lines and in other tissues of the body (Filshie, Grace, Poulson, and Rehacek, 1967).

Mammary Epithelium

In the case of insect imaginal disks serially passaged *in vivo*, alterations in hormonal responsiveness are only rarely observed. In the case of serially propagated mouse mammary tissue, alterations in the ability of aging cells to respond to endocrine stimuli always occurs, and it is likely that these changes are responsible for the ultimate loss of proliferative capacity.

Mammary tissue propagated in young, nonpregnant females is exposed during its growth span to the regularly cycling hormones of the host, which provides adequate stimulation for ductal elongation. After a period of continuous proliferation, the capacity for growth declines and the line is eventually lost. Two alternative explanations are immediately presented. First, the cells could be accumulating damage which is expressed as the inability to divide, due perhaps to failure to commence DNA synthesis, inability to replicate chromosomes, or even the loss of the capacity to divide resulting from age-related changes in the mitotic apparatus. Alternatively, the cells might retain the capacity for further division but are unable to express that capacity because they have exhausted their ability to respond to the appropriate stimulatory endocrine signals.

Using the mammary system, it is possible to distinguish between these alternatives. Mammary gland has two distinct growth phases. Ductal elongation is characteristic of nonpregnant animals, and lobuloalveolar development, in which massive cell proliferation occurs along the ducts, is a response to the hormones of pregnancy. In order to determine if a continuous hormonal regime might be responsible for proliferative failure, mammary tissue was serially passaged in nonpregnant hosts until the growth rate was markedly reduced. Host mice were placed with males one month following the final transplantation, and the mammary outgrowths were removed and examined following pregnancy. Among more than 80 outgrowths examined from pregnant or lactating animals, all displayed excellent lobuloalveolar development, which could only result from vigorous cell proliferation (Figure 21). These small, densely cellular outgrowths produced milk in an apparently normal fashion during lactation. In the reverse experiment, tissue was serially propagated in mice in which a pseudopregnant endocrine status was continuously maintained during the course of transplantation by means of pituitary isografts (Loeb and Kirtz, 1939). Thus stimulation was provided for both ductal elongation and lobuloalveolar development. As a result, both responses declined in magnitude with serial passage, suggesting that mammary cells lose the ability to respond to any hormonal milieu which is continuously present over a long period of proliferation (Table 8). The secretory capacity of these cells

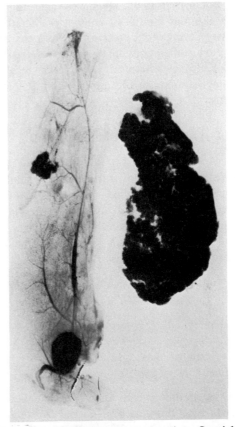

Figure 21. Whole-mount preparation. On right is an old outgrowth that was carried in virgin hosts for 5 transplant generations, after which the generation 6 host was bred (arrow). Only slight ductal growth has occurred (note absence of end buds), but the extensive lobuloalveolar development is identical to that seen in sample of host gland at left. LN, lymph node. Hematoxylin stain. (From Daniel and Young, 1971.)

TABLE 8. EFFECTS OF HORMONAL STIMULATION ON SERIALLY PASSAGED MAMMARY GLAND.[a]

Type of stimulation	Mammogenic effect	Response to serial passage
Virgin, continuous	Ductal proliferation	Decline in ductal proliferation
Pituitaries, continuous	Ductal and alveolar proliferation	Decline in both ductal and alveolar proliferations
Virgin, continuous, followed by one breeding in late passage	Ductal elongation; alveolar proliferation during pregnancy	Decline in ductal proliferation; alveolar proliferation normal during pregnancy

[a] From Daniel, Young, Medina, and DeOme, 1971.

was not investigated. Mammary aging therefore occurs as a result of unusual proliferative activity during serial passage, which is characterized by alterations in those normal regulatory pathways where, in young cells, regular cell replication occurs in response to hormonal signals.

CELLULAR TRANSFORMATION AND *IN VIVO* AGING

A striking relationship exists between cellular growth span and neoplasia. Hayflick (1965a, 1965b) has formulated this relationship into a general scheme in which three fundamental cellular characteristics, unlimited growth, heteroploidy, and neoplasia, are linked:

been performed, and the superficial location of these transplanted tissues would make it difficult to overlook tumors should they appear.

Drosophila Imaginal Discs. Serially transplanted imaginal discs give rise to a spectrum of abnormalities which display characteristics of "benign neoplasms" (Gateff and Schneiderman, 1969). Wild type discs give rise to such neoplasms infrequently, but enough have been discovered to recognize them as a distinct category—the atelotypic tissues described in the preceding section of this review. These are characterized by failure to differentiate, very rapid growth, and unstructured histological appearance. Their rapid proliferation soon leads them to fill the

Heteroploid Cell Lines = Transplantable Tumors		Diploid Cell Strains = Normal Somatic Tissue	
(*in vitro*)	(*in vivo*)	(*in vitro*)	(*in vivo*)
1. Heteroploid		1. Diploid	
2. Cancer cells		2. Normal cells	
(histological criteria)		(histological criteria)	
3. Indefinite growth		3. Finite growth	

Although this generalization may be liable to certain exceptions, such as normal *Drosophila* imaginal disk tissue which may be transplanted indefinitely (Hadorn, 1969), it is generally believed that in vertebrates, cellular transformation is coincident with both the onset of certain neoplastic characteristics and the acquisition of unlimited proliferative potential. This correlation, which holds both *in vitro* and *in vivo,* suggests the possibility that common or shared mechanisms may be involved in these seemingly different processes and is clearly of both theoretical and practical significance to the study of cellular aging.

Transformation Arising During Serial Passage

Many types of cancer are characteristic of advancing age, and it is natural to inquire whether the incidence of spontaneous tumors is more frequent in cells and tissues maintained for extended periods by serial transplantation. In the case of both skin and mammary transplants, no increase in tumor incidence has been observed (Krohn, 1962; Daniel, unpublished), even though large numbers of transplants have

abdominal space when transplanted into adult flies, resulting in a characteristic bloated appearance (Figure 22), which ultimately leads to death of the host.

Abnormalities of this type appear with high frequency and, in fact, are characteristic of transplanted imaginal discs homozygous for recessive mutation 1(2)gl[4] (Gateff and Schneiderman, 1969), hereafter referred to as "mutant larva." This mutation leads to a variety of developmental defects. The mutant larva are incapable of normal metamorphosis and cannot give rise to adult flies.

Comparisons of various *Drosophila* neoplasms are given in Table 9. None of these tumors qualify as malignant neoplasms in that their growth habit is that of a compact tissue, and there is no evidence of invasive behavior. True malignancies are rare in *Drosophila;* perhaps the best example was obtained from the brain of a mutant larva and was classified as an invasive neuroblastoma. Although this tumor is maintained by serial transplantation, it is not considered to be a result of such transplantation (Gateff and Schneiderman, 1969).

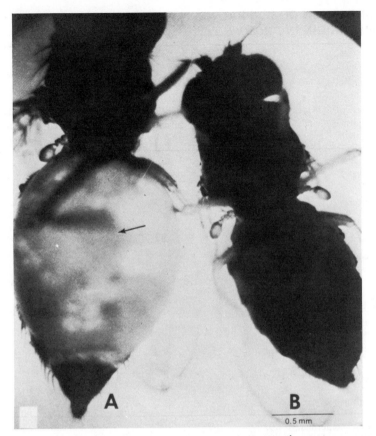

Figure 22. Female adult host bearing benign neoplasm of $1(2)gl^4$ imaginal disc. Fly A shows "bloating" syndrome. Fly B is an uninjected control. Arrow indicates location of neoplasm. Fat body and ovaries are almost completely destroyed, and abdomen appears translucent and swollen, when the host bears a benign neoplasm. (From Gateff and Schneiderman, 1969.)

Hemopoietic Cells. In the course of serial transplantation studies of cells obtained from mouse fetal liver, Till, McCulloch, and Siminovitch (1964) found that although most of their cell lines could be passaged for only a few transplant generations before proliferative capacity was lost, two variant cell lines were able to survive transplantation for extended periods (Table 10). Some of the properties of these variant strains resemble those of lymphoma cell lines. In addition to unlimited proliferative capacity, these cells showed no clear evidence of differentiation within splenic colonies and were able to form colonies in the livers of irradiated hosts. They differ from lymphomas in that when injected into unirradiated, syngeneic mice they could not form spleen colonies, and malignant diseases did not result. The proper-

ties of these variant cells are such that they have an advantage over normal cells in the irradiated, but not in the unirradiated host. The characteristics are somewhat similar to preneoplastic mammary nodule cells (see following).

Transplantation Following Preneoplastic Transformation

It is well established that the genesis of mammary cancer in certain strains of mice is at least a two-step process, with benign nodules as an obligatory intermediate (De Ome *et al.*, 1959). The occurrence of these nodules is usually associated with infection with the mouse Mammary Tumor Virus (MTV), but they may also be induced in MTV-free mice by treatment with

TABLE 9. COMPARISON OF SEVERAL NEOPLASMS AND NEOPLASM-LIKE GROWTHS OF DIFFERENT ORIGIN IN *DROSOPHILA*.[a]

Type of tissue[b]	Cause of abnormal growth	Rate of growth	Mode of growth	Growth after repeated transplantation in adults	Differentiation capacities of cells	Lethality to host	"Bloated" syndrome	Response to hormones	Type of neoplasm
Autotypic		+	Folded cell layers	+	+	0	0	+	Nonneoplastic
Allotypic	Culture	++	Folded cell layers	+	+	+	+	+	Incipient benign neoplasm
Atelotypic	Culture and mutation	+++	Compact	+	0	+	+	+	Benign neoplasm
Mutant disc *in situ*	Mutation	+++	Compact	+	0	+	+	+	Benign neoplasm
Mutant disc in culture	Mutation and culture	+++	Compact	+	0	+	+	+	Benign neoplasm
Mutant brain *in situ*	Mutation	+++	Invasive	+	0	+	+	0	Invasive neoplasm
Mutant brain in culture	Mutation and culture	+++	Invasive	+	0	+	+	0	Invasive neoplasm

[a] After Gateff and Schneiderman, 1969.
[b] Imaginal disc cell lines which grow at a modest rate and differentiate according to their initial state of determination or prospective significance are called *autotypic* (e.g., an eye-antennal disc yields cell lines which differentiate into eye-antennal structures). Imaginal disc cell lines which grow rapidly and undergo a change in determination so that they differentiate into foreign structures are called *allotypic* (e.g., an eye-antennal disc cell line which differentiates into genitalia, wings, etc., in addition to eyes and antenna). Imaginal disc cell lines which grow rapidly and fail to differentiate are called *atelotypic*.

TABLE 10. SUMMARY OF EXPERIMENTS INVOLVING SERIAL TRANSPLANTATION OF CELLS DERIVED FROM FETAL LIVER.[a]

Experiment	Number of passages[b]	Evidence for variant cell type
D35	24	Histology, transplantation
K1	4	None
K2	3	None
K5a	3	None
K5b	3	Histology
K5c	15	Histology, transplantation
K7	5	Histology
K15	5	None

[a] From Till, McCulloch, and Siminovitch, 1964.
[b] Serial transplantation was performed at 7- to 14-day intervals with irradiated (900 rads) hosts.

carcinogenic hydrocarbons (Faulkin, 1966). Nodules may be distinguished because they retain an alveolar morphology in nonpregnant females. That is, nodules have altered hormonal requirements for maintenance of alveolar cells (Nandi, 1961), such that they are maintained under circumstances in which all normal alveoli are regressed, and in which normal mammary tissue exists as a simple network of ducts.

Nodules remain as small, discrete alveolar structures because their growth is completely inhibited by contiguous normal ductal tissue (Faulkin and De Ome, 1960). If transplanted into gland-free fat pads and removed from the growth-inhibiting effects of normal gland, nodules proliferate and retain their characteristic alveolar morphology (Figure 23). Their

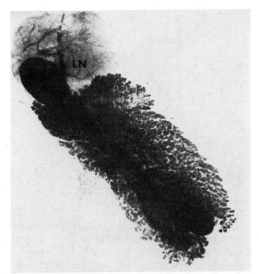

Figure 23. Whole-mount preparation showing preneoplastic outgrowth taken from a virgin host; note extensive lobuloalveolar development. This outgrowth is from transplant generation 31 and has been serially propagated for 7.5 years. The hyperplastic tissue has filled 70 percent of the available fat. LN, lymph node. Hematoxylin stain. (From Daniel *et al.* 1968.)

growth is limited by the boundaries of the fat pads, as is normal gland, and growth stops when the available fat is occupied.

The ability to serially transplant preneoplastic mammary tissue makes it possible to study the cellular life span of these cells. In a long-term study conducted by De Ome and his colleagues at the Cancer Research Genetics Laboratory in Berkeley, outgrowths from two C3H nodules were serially passaged (Figure 24). Both preneoplastic lines grew for longer than 8 years and 30 transplant generations, and both lines were proliferating vigorously when the experiment was terminated. It was concluded that these results indicated an indefinite life span *in vivo*. Control transplants of normal (C3H, MTV-infected) gland could be carried for no more than 6 generations and 15 months (Daniel *et al.*, 1968).

Recently, it has been demonstrated that the acquisition of unlimited division potential is associated with the preneoplastic characteristics of these transformed tissues, regardless of the nature of the transforming agency. Nodules originating spontaneously, as a result of prolonged hormonal stimulation, or from the administration of carcinogenic hydrocarbons grow indefinitely, without known exceptions (Daniel, Aidells, Medina, and Faulkin, 1975).

Using strain GR mice, Aidells and Daniel (1974) reported the establishment of unusual mammary transplant lines which were not

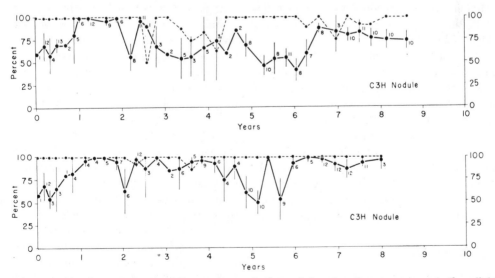

Figure 24. Serial transplantation of two preneoplastic nodules. ●——●, mean percent of available fat occupied by transplants; ●----●, percent successful transplants. Each point denotes a transplant generation, and small numbers beside points refer to the number of successful transplants in each generation. Vertical lines indicate 95 percent confidence intervals. (From Daniel *et al.*, 1968.)

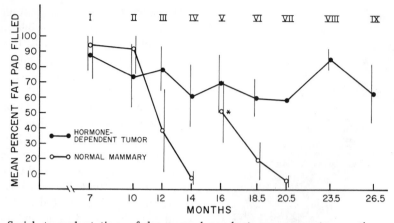

Figure 25. Serial transplantation of hormone-dependent mammary tumor tissue and normal mammary tissue in virgin hosts. Growth rate and mean percent of available fat pad filled by the transplants were calculated from successful transplants only. *Each point* denotes a transplant generation. *Vertical lines* indicate 95 percent confidence intervals and are omitted from points that represent the mean of fewer than 3 outgrowths. *=Start of new normal mammary line. From Aidells and Daniel, 1974.)

alveolar as are nodules, but which displayed a relatively normal ductal appearance during serial transplantation. Their preneoplastic nature became evident only during pregnancy, when they give rise to hormone-dependent tumors. This ductal outgrowth was growing vigorously after nine transplant generations, when the line was accidentally lost. It is not known whether this tissue will proliferate indefinitely, but a very substantial prolongation of the normal growth span is clearly indicated (Figure 25).

These studies indicated that in vertebrate cells an unlimited, or greatly extended, growth span is associated with transformation from a normal to an intermediate, preneoplastic cell type. The release from cellular aging is therefore an early event on the pathway to neoplasia and is not directly associated with malignancy. Indeed, the tumorogenic potential of many of the preneoplastic mammary tissues examined is extremely low, and carcinomas appear only very occasionally during years of serial passage.

CONCLUSIONS

Several *in vivo* serial transplantation techniques have been devised by a number of investigators which are designed to measure the proliferative capacity and the ultimate life span of somatic cells and tissues. Although some transplantation methods offer difficulties in interpretation, the large number of experiments which have been conducted, and the variety of cell types used, lead to the following conclusions.

1. Murine cells of several types—hemopoietic, skin, and mammary—may display an impressive longevity during the course of serial passage in syngeneic hosts. In several cases the transplants were found to display functional adequacy for time periods well beyond the life span of the laboratory mouse. In no case, however, has the unlimited proliferative potential of normal, nontransformed cells been reported.

Imaginal disc cells of *Drosophila* provide an exception, for the undifferentiated tissues may be propagated in adult hosts without apparent limit, and they may retain both a normal karyotype and the capacity to differentiate into normal adult structures, if provided with the opportunity to do so. During transplantation imaginal discs frequently display alterations in their state of determination, and in wild type discs abnormal growth and unusual differentiative patterns are occasionally observed.

2. It is indicated, particularly in transplantation studies of mammary and hemopoietic cells, that the observed decline in rate of proliferation is the result of cell replication *per se,* and the passage of chronological or metabolic time appears to be of secondary importance.

3. A clear influence of donor age upon the

ability of cells to withstand serial transplantation has proved difficult to demonstrate with these techniques, and it is apparent that cells from aged animals may retain much of their potential for growth and function.

4. Mechanisms involved in cell aging *in vivo* are currently being investigated. Possible influences of aging connective tissue upon mammary aging was studied, and it was found that the two were unrelated. Instead it was concluded that mammary aging, and perhaps aging of other cell types, is associated with alterations in cellular regulatory mechanisms which occur progressively during the course of repeated transplantations. These regulatory pathways, which in young cells provide a means for them to respond to mitogenic hormones, eventually become unable to stimulate the cells to further divisions. The stimulation of previously unused regulatory mechanisms, accomplished by changing the hormonal environment of the aged cells, can enable even very old cells to resume division and to develop along a new differentiative pathway.

5. Rescue from cellular senescence is accomplished by "transformation." *In vitro* transformation is generally associated with the acquisition of one or more of the properties of transplantable tumors. *In vivo* transformation is also related to life span—many tumors have been serially passaged in animals for periods of many years. In the case of mammary tissue and perhaps certain others, escape from cell mortality is associated with an intermediate alteration, transformation into a precancerous but nonmalignant cell type.

The acquisition of unlimited division potential is therefore associated with early, rather than later changes leading to malignancy.

REFERENCES

Aidells, B. D., and Daniel, C. W. 1974. Hormone-dependent mammary tumors in strain GR/A mice. I. Alternation between ductal and tumorous phases of growth during serial transplantation. *J. Nat. Cancer Inst.* 52(6), 1855–1863.

Askonas, B. A., Williamson, A. R., and Wright, B. E. G. 1970. Selection of a single antibody-forming cell clone and its propagation in syngeneic mice. *Proc. Nat. Acad. Sci.*, 67(3), 1398–1403.

Barnes, D. W. H., Ford, C. E., and Loutit, J. F. 1959. Greffes en série de moelle osseuse homologue chez des souris irradices. *Le Sang*, 30, 762–765.

Barnes, D. W. H., Loutit, J. F., and Micklem, H. S. 1962. "Secondary disease" of radiation chimeras: A syndrome due to lymphoid aplasia. *Ann. N. Y. Acad. Sci.*, 99, 374–385.

Becker, A. J., McCulloch, E. A., Siminovitch, L., and Till, J. E. 1965. The effect of differing demands for blood cell production on DNA synthesis by hemopoietic colony forming cells of mice. *Blood J. Hematol.*, 26(3), 296–308.

Becker, A. J., McCulloch, E. A., and Till, J. E. 1963. Cytological demonstration of the clonal nature of spleen colonies derived from transplanted mouse marrow cells. *Nature*, 197, 452–454.

Bresciani, F. 1968. Topography of DNA synthesis in the mammary gland of C3H mouse and its control by ovarian hormones: An autoradiographic study. *Cell Tissue Kinetics*, 1, 51–63.

Bucher, N. L. R., and Glinos, A. D. 1959. The effect of age on regeneration of rat liver. *Cancer Res.*, 10, 324–332.

Carrel, A. 1912. On the permanent life of tissues outside of the organism. *J. Exp. Med.*, 15, 516–528.

Comfort, A. 1964. *Ageing: The Biology of Senescence*, New York: Holt, Rinehart & Winston.

Converse, J. J., Filler, M., and Ballantyne, D. L. 1965. Vascularization of split-thickness skin autographs in the rat. *Transplantation*, 3(1), 22–27.

Cudkowicz, G., Upton, A. C., and Shearer, G. M. 1964. Lymphocyte content and proliferative capacity of serially transplanted mouse bone marrow. *Nature*, 201, 165–167.

Daniel, C. W. 1972. Aging of cells during serial propagation *in vivo*. *Adv. Geront. Res.*, 4, 167–199.

Daniel, C. W. 1973. Finite growth span of mouse mammary gland serially propagated *in vivo*. *Experientia*, 29, 1422–1424.

Daniel, C. W. 1975. Regulation of cell division in aging mouse epithelium. *In*, V. Cristofalo (ed.), *Proceedings of the Philadelphia Symposium on Aging 1975*, in press.

Daniel, C. W., Aidells, B. D., Medina, D., and Faulkin, L. J., Jr. 1975. Unlimited division potential of precancerous mouse mammary cells after spontaneous or carcinogen-induced transformation. *Proc. F. A. S. E. B.*, 34, 64–67.

Daniel, C.W., De Ome, K. B., Young, J. T., Blair, P. B., and Faulkin, L. J. 1968. The *in vivo* life span of normal and preneoplastic mouse mammary glands: A serial transplantation study. *Proc. Nat. Acad. Sci.*, 61, 52–60.

Daniel, C. W., and Young, L. J. T. 1971. Life span of mouse mammary epithelium during serial propagation *in vivo:* Influence of cell division on an aging process. *Exp. Cell Res.*, 65, 27–32.

Daniel, C. W., Young, L. J. T., Medina, D., and DeOme, K. B. 1971. The influence of mammogenic hormones on serially transplanted mouse mammary gland. *Exp. Gerontol.* 6, 95–101.

Das, B. C. 1969. An examination of variability of blood chemistry, hematology, and proteins in relation to age. *Gerontologia,* **15,** 275–287.

De Ome, K. B., Faulkin, L. J., Bern, H. A., and Blair, P. B. 1959. Development of mammary tumors from hyperplastic alveolar nodules transplanted into gland-free mammary fat pads of female C3H mice. *Cancer Res.,* **19,** 515–520.

Ebeling, A. H. 1913. The permanent life of connective tissue outside of the organism. *J. Exp. Med.,* **17,** 273–285.

Ephrussi, B., and Beadle, G. W. 1936. A technique of transplantation for *Drosophila. Am. Naturalist,* **70,** 218–225.

Faulkin, L. J., Jr. 1966. Hyperplastic lesions of mouse mammary glands after treatment with 3-methylcholanthrene. *J. Nat. Cancer Inst.,* **36,** 289–298.

Faulkin, L. J., Jr., and De Ome, K. B. 1960. Regulation of growth and spacing of gland elements in the mammary fat pad of the C3H mouse. *J. Nat. Cancer Inst.,* **24**(4), 953–970.

Filshie, B. K., Grace, T. D. C., Poulson, D. G., and Rehacek, J. 1967. Virus like particles in insect cells of three types. *J. Invertebr. Path.,* **9,** 271–273.

Finch, C. E. 1973. Retardation of hair regrowth, a phenomenon of senescence in C57B1/6J male mice. *J. Geront.,* **28**(1), 13–17.

Garcia, J. F. 1957. Erythropoietic response to hypoxia as a function of age in the normal male rat. *Am. J. Physiol.,* **190,** 25–30.

Gateff, E., and Schneiderman, H. A. 1969. Neoplasms in mutant and cultured wild-type tissues of *Drosophila. In,* C. J. Dawe and J. C. Harshbarger (eds.), *National Cancer Institute Monograph 31–Neoplasms and Related Disorders of Invertebrates and Lower Vertebrate Animals,* pp. 365–397. Bethesda, Maryland: National Cancer Institute.

Gehring, W. 1966. Übertragung und Änderung der Determinationsqualitäten in Antennenscheiben-Kulturen von *Drosophila melanogaster. J. Embryol. Exp. Morphol.,* **15,** 77–111.

Gehring, W. 1972. The stability of the determined state in cultures of imaginal disks in drosophila. *In,* H. Urspring and R. Nothiger (eds.), *Results and Problems in Cell Differentiation: The Biology of the Imaginal Disks,* pp. 35–38. New York: Springer-Verlag.

Grant, W. C., and LeGrande, M. C. 1964. The influence of age on erythropoiesis in the rat. *J. Geront.,* **19,** 505–509.

Grobstein, C. 1950. Production of intra-ocular hemorrhage by mouse trophoblast. *J. Exp. Zool.,* **114,** 359–373.

Hadorn, E. 1963. Differenzierungsleistungen wiederholt fragmentierter Teilstücke männlicher Genitalscheiben von *Drosophila melanogaster* nach Kultur *in vivo. Develop. Biol.,* **7,** 617–629.

Hadorn, E. 1967. Dynamics of determination. *In,* M. Locke (ed.), *Major Problems in Developmental Biology,* 25th Symposium of the Society for Developmental Biology. New York: Academic Press.

Hadorn, E. 1969. Proliferation and dynamics of cell heredity in blastema cultures of *Drosophila. In,* C. J. Dawe and J. C. Harshbarger (eds.), *National Cancer Institute Monograph 31–Neoplasms and Related Disorders of Invertebrate and Lower Vertebrate Animals,* pp. 351–364. Bethesda, Maryland: National Cancer Institute.

Halber, J. A., and Billingham, R. E. 1964. *In,* W. R. Montagna and R. E. Billingham (eds.), *Advances in the Biology of Skin,* Vol. 5, p. 165. London: Pergamon Press.

Harrison, D. E. 1972. Normal function of transplanted mouse erythrocyte precursors for 21 months beyond donor life spans. *Nature New Biol.,* **237,** 220–221.

Harrison, D. E. 1973. Normal production of erythrocytes by mouse marrow continuous for 73 months. *Proc. Nat. Acad. Sci.,* **70**(11), 3184–3188.

Harrison, D. E. 1975a. Normal function of transplanted marrow cell lines from aged mice. *J. Geront.,* **30** (3), 279–285.

Harrison, D. E. 1975b. Defective erythropoietic responses of aged mice not improved by young marrow. *J. Geront.,* **30** (3), 286–288.

Harrison, D. E., and Doubleday, J. W. 1975. Normal function of immunological stem cells from aged mice. *J. Immunol.,* **114** (4), 1314–1322.

Harrison, R. G. 1907. Observations on the living developing nerve fiber. *Proc. Soc. Exp. Biol. Med.,* **4,** 140–143.

Hayflick, L. 1965a. The limited *in vitro* lifetime of human diploid cell strains. *Exp. Cell Res.,* **37,** 614–636.

Hayflick, L. 1965b. Cell culture and the aging phenomenon. *In,* P. L. Krohn (ed.), *Topics in the Biology of Aging,* pp. 83–100. New York: John Wiley.

Hayflick, L., and Moorhead, P. S. 1961. The serial cultivation of human diploid cell strains. *Exp. Cell Res.,* **25,** 585–621.

Horton, D. L. 1967. The effect of age on hair growth in the CBA mouse: Observations on transplanted skin. *J. Geront.,* **22,** 43–45.

Hoshino, K., and Gardner, W. U. 1967. Transplantability and life span of mammary gland during serial transplantation in mice. *Nature,* **213,** 193–194.

Kohn, R. R. 1965. Aging as a consequence of growth cessation. *In,* M. Locke (ed.), *Reproduction: Molecular, Subcellular, and Cellular,* pp. 291–324. New York: Academic Press.

Koller, P. C., and Doak, S. M. A. 1963. Serial Transplantation of haematopoietic tissue in irradiated hosts. *In,* R. J. C. Harris (ed.), *Cellular Basis and Aetiology of Late Somatic Effects of Ionizing Radiation,* pp. 59–64. New York: Academic Press.

Krohn, P. L. 1962. Review lectures on senescence: II. Heterochronic transplantation in the study of aging. *Proc. Roy. Soc. (London) Ser. B,* **157,** 128–147.

Krohn, P. L. 1966. Transplantation and aging. *In,* P. L. Krohn (ed.), *Topics of the Biology of Aging,* pp. 125–138. New York: John Wiley.

Lajtha, L. G. 1963. "On the concept of the cell cycle" in Differential Sensitivity of the Cell Cycle (round-table discussion). *J. Cellular Comp. Physiol.*, **62** (Suppl. 1), 143-145.

Lajtha, L. G., Oliver, R., and Gurney, C. W. 1962. Kinetic model of a bone-marrow stem-cell population. *British J. Haematol.*, 8(4), 442-460.

Lajtha, L. G., and Schofield, R. 1971. Regulation of stem cell renewal and differentiation: Possible significance in aging. *In*, B. L. Strehler (ed.), *Advances in Gerontological Research, Vol. 3*, pp. 131-146. New York: Academic Press.

Lesher, S., Fry, R. J. M., and Kohn, H. I. 1961. Age and the generation time of the mouse duodenal epithelial cell. *Exp. Cell Res.*, 24, 334-343.

Loeb, J., and Kirtz, M. M. 1939. The effects of transplants of anterior lobes of the hypophysis on the growth of the mammary gland and on the development of mammary gland carcinoma in various strains of mice. *Am. J. Cancer*, **36**, 56-82.

McCreight, C. E., and Sulkin, N. M. 1959. Cellular proliferation in the kidneys of young and senile rats following unilateral nephrectomy. *J. Geront.*, 14, 440-443.

McCulloch, E. A., and Till, J. E. 1964. Proliferation of hemopoietic colony-forming cells transplanted into irradiated mice. *Radiation Res.*, 22, 383-397.

Makinodan, T., Perkins, E. H., and Chen, M. G. 1971. Immunologic activity of the aged. *In*, B. L. Strehler (ed.), *Advances in Gerontological Research Vol. 3*, pp. 171-198. New York: Academic Press.

Martin, G. M., Sprague, C. A., and Epstein, E. J. 1970. Replicative life-span of cultivated human cells: Effects of donor's age, tissue, and genotype. *Lab. Invest.*, 23(1), 86-92.

Moore, G. E., and McLimans, W. F. 1968. The life span of the cultured normal cell: Concepts derived from studies of human lymphoblasts. *J. Theoret. Biol.*, 20, 217-226.

Moretti, R. L., and Blair, P. B. 1966. The male histocompatibility antigen in mouse mammary tissue: I. Growth of the male mammary gland in female mice. *Transplantation*, 4, 596-604.

Nandi, S. 1958. Endocrine control of mammary gland development and function in the C3H/He Crgl mouse. *J. Nat. Cancer Inst.*, 21, 1039-1055.

Nandi, S. 1961. Effect of hormones on maintenance of hyperplastic alveolar nodules in mammary glands of various strains of mice. *J. Nat. Cancer Inst.*, 27, 187-201.

Norris, J. L., Blanchard, J., and Polovny, C. 1942. Regeneration of rat liver in different ages. *Arch. Pathol.*, 34, 208-217.

Nöthiger, R. 1972. The larval development of imaginal disks. *In*, H. Ursprung and R. Nöthiger (eds.), *Results and Problems in Cell Differentiation: The Biology of Imaginal Disks*, pp. 1-34. New York: Springer-Verlag.

Quastler, H., and Sherman, F. G. 1959. Cell population kinetics in the intestinal epithelium of the mouse. *Exp. Cell Res.*, 17, 420-438.

Remensberger, P. 1968. Cytologische und histologische Untersuchungen an Zellstämmen von *Drosophila melanogaster* nach Dauerkultur *in vivo*. *Chromosoma (Berl.)*, 23, 386-417.

Sanford, K. K., Earle, W. R., and Likely, G. D. 1948. The growth *in vitro* of single isolated tissue cells. *J. Nat. Cancer Inst.*, 9, 229-246.

Sigel, M. 1958. Tubule formation in rat brains by monkey kidney cells previously grown *in vitro*. *Nature*, **182**, 1034-1035.

Siminovitch, L., Till, J. E., and McCulloch, E. A. 1964. Decline in colony-forming ability of marrow cells subjected to serial transplantation into irradiated mice. *J. Cellular Comp. Physiol.*, **64**, 23-32.

Sinex, F. M. 1964. Cross-linkage and aging. *Advan. Geront. Res.*, **1**, 165-180.

Smith-Sonneborn, J., and Klass, M. 1974. Changes in the DNA synthetic pattern of paramecium with increased clonal age and interfission time. *J. Cell Biol.*, **61**, 591-598.

Sobel, H. 1967. Aging of ground substances in connective tissue. *In*, B. L. Strehler (ed.), *Advances in Gerontological Research*, pp. 205-283. New York: Academic Press.

Soemarwoto, I. N., and Bern, H. A. 1958. The effect of hormones on the vascular pattern of the mouse mammary gland. *Am. J. Anat.*, 103, 403-435.

Strehler, B. L. 1962. *Time, Cells and Aging.* New York: Academic Press.

Swim, H. E., and Parker, R. F. 1957. Culture characteristics of human fibroblasts propagated serially. *Am. J. Hyg.*, 66, 235-243.

Thrasher, J. D. 1967. Age and the cell cycle of the mouse colonic epithelium. *Anat. Record*, 157(4), 621-626.

Thrasher, J. D., and Greulich, R. C. 1965a. The duodenal progenitor population: I. Age related increase in the duration of the cryptal progenitor cycle. *J. Exp. Zool.*, 159(1), 39-46.

Thrasher, J. D., and Greulich, R. C. 1965b. The duodenal progenitor population. II. Age related changes in size and distribution. *J. Exp. Zool.*, 159(3), 385-396.

Till, J. E., and McCulloch, E. A. 1961. A direct measurement of the radiation sensitivity of normal mouse bone marrow cells. *Radiation Res.*, 14, 213-222.

Till, J. E., McCulloch, E. A., and Siminovitch, L., 1964. Isolation of variant cell lines during serial transplantation of hematopoietic cells derived from fetal liver. *J. Nat. Cancer Inst.*, 33, 707-720.

Weissman, A. 1891. *Essays upon Heredity and Kindred Biological Problems.* London and New York: Oxford University Press (Clarendon).

Whiteley, H. J., and Horton, D. L. 1962. The effect of age on the hair regrowth cycle in CBA mouse. *J. Geront.*, 17, 272-275.

Whiteley, H. J., and Horton, D. L. 1963. The effect of age on the mitotic activity of the ear epidermis in the CBA mouse. *J. Geront.*, 18, 335-339.

Wigzell, H., and Stjernswärd, J. 1966. Age-dependent

rise and fall of immunological reactivity in the CBA mouse. *J. Nat. Cancer Inst.,* **37,** 513–517.

Williamson, A. R., and Askonas, B. A. 1972. Senescence of an antibody-forming cell clone. *Nature,* **238,** 337–339.

Young, L. J. T., Medina, D., De Ome, K. B., and Daniel, C. W. 1971. The influence of host and tissue age on life span and growth rate of serially transplanted mouse mammary gland. *Exp. Geront.,* **6,** 49–56.

7
THE CELLULAR BASIS
FOR BIOLOGICAL AGING

Leonard Hayflick*
Stanford University School of Medicine

INTRODUCTION

The development of techniques by which vertebrate cells can be cultured in ordinary laboratory glassware (*in vitro*) has had a profound impact in almost all areas of biological inquiry.
Although these methodologies had their genesis
at the turn of this century, they reached full
fruition only within the past 25 years. The
initial effect of the ability to culture vertebrate
cells was felt in the discipline of virology, where
its marriage with cell culture techniques ultimately resulted in a remarkable understanding
of these organisms and the perfection of vaccines against almost all of the important acute
viral diseases of man. In subsequent years, the
disciplines of developmental biology, genetics,
and immunology have been the benefactors.

More recently, however, the impact of cell
culture techniques on gerontology have been
manifest, and the expectation is that we are
now at the threshold of realizing the importance
that cell culture techniques will play in our understanding of the aging process.

Historical Developments

The early work in cell culture that has a bearing
on gerontological thought are those studies

*Supported, in part, by Research Grant AG 00428
from the National Institute on Aging, National Institutes of Health, Bethesda, Maryland

done in the 1920s and whose principal findings
can be summarized as follows:

1. An inverse relationship was found between
the "growth rate" of embryonic chicken fibroblasts cultivated in plasma clots and the age of
the chicken supplying the plasma (Carrel and
Ebeling, 1921). Although this claim is generally
accepted, confirmation has not been reported.

2. The latent period, which is the lapse of
time preceding the first appearance of migrating
cells from cultured tissue fragments (explants),
was found to increase with the age of the donor
(Suzuki, 1925; Cohn and Murray, 1925). This
phenomenon has been amply confirmed in subsequent years and will be more fully discussed
later.

3. It was claimed that cultured fibroblasts
from chicken embryo heart tissue could be kept
in a state of continuous proliferation for at
least 34 years (Ebeling, 1913; Parker, 1961).

Of the aforementioned claims, the last had
the most profound impact on early thought regarding biological aging. If it were true that an
animal's normal cells, released from the usual
in vivo cell control mechanisms, were found to
be capable of long or indefinite function or proliferation *in vitro*, then an important insight
into biological aging could be deduced. That is,
if normal cells, so released, revealed no decrement in division potential or function *in vitro*,

it could be concluded that biological aging was not a function of intrinsic failures within individual cells themselves. One would be forced to the conclusion that biological aging results from decrements occurring at hierarchies of organization greater than that of the indivdual cell, that is, at the tissue or organ level.

It is because of the profound consequences that this observation had on gerontological thought that confirmation of this claim came to be of the utmost importance. Failure to confirm this observation and its impact on the biology of aging will be described in subsequent sections. For detailed reviews of specific areas discussed only generally below, the following reviews should be consulted (Goldstein, 1971; Cristofalo, 1972; Daniel, 1972; Hay, 1967; Krohn, 1966a; Holečková and Cristofalo, 1970; Cristofalo, Howard, and Kritchevsky, 1970; Hayflick, 1966, 1972).

The Finite Lifetime of Cultured Normal Human Cells

In 1961 Moorhead and I, working with cultured normal human fibroblasts, found that these cells underwent a finite number of population doublings and then died (Hayflick and Moorhead, 1961). Although earlier studies had revealed similar results (Swim and Parker, 1957), the cells used were not characterized as normal which is a central requirement for assessing this phenomenon.

The importance of considering only normal cells cannot be overemphasized since, as we pointed out (Hayflick and Moorhead, 1961), cells capable of indefinite proliferation in vitro are abnormal in one or more properties. Prior to our observation, it was fully appreciated that there existed several hundred cultured mammalian cell populations endowed with the singular property of immortality. That is, they are capable of continuous serial propagation in vitro. These cells are abnormal in one or more of their properties, often have the characteristics of cancer cells, and will be referred to here as cell lines. Normal cell populations which have a finite capacity to replicate in vitro will be referred to here as cell strains. Since biological aging results from functional decrements occur-

ring in normal cells in vivo, it follows that the behavior of cultured normal cell strains in vitro must be considered. There are several reports of cell populations claimed to be normal, yet on closer inspection are found to lack unequivocal proof of euploidy and nonmalignancy. These reports are analyzed elsewhere in this chapter.

In Vitro Cell Culture Techniques

How then are normal vertebrate cells cultured in vitro, and what is their fate? Of the several ways in which this can be done, the most common method is the following: the tissue from which cells are to be grown is exposed to an enzyme preparation called trypsin, which, in reality, consists of many enzymes since the material used is an aqueous extract of hog pancreas. The outcome of the tryptic digestion is to release individual cells from the tissue matrix. The cells are then separated from the trypsin by centrifugation and seeded into glass or plastic culture vessels containing an appropriate growth medium. In a few hours, after incubation at 37°C, the cells attach to the glass surface and within a day or so begin to divide. Depending upon the number of cells introduced into the culture vessel, the surface will be fully covered with daughter cells in a few days or a few weeks. When this state is reached (confluency), cell division diminishes considerably. In order to obtain more cells, one can remove the spent growth medium, introduce trypsin to obtain a suspension of single cells, and, finally, introduce the cell suspension into several daughter culture vessels. This provides a greater total surface area which is a prerequisite for further cell replication. If two daughter culture vessels of the same surface area are derived from the initial starting culture (primary culture), this is referred to as a 1:2 subcultivation ratio, and the numbers of cells ultimately produced are twice the number initially seeded. Other ratios can be used, but the principle is the same. For example, a 1:4 ratio would result in two population doublings per subcultivation. The 1:2 subcultivations can be made each 3 to 4 days so that the numbers of culture vessels will be increased by powers of two at each subculture. It is apparent, therefore, that in 5 weeks, for example,

2^{10} (1,024) cultures can be produced with a 1:2 split ratio performed each 3 or 4 days. The usual normal cell type that is capable of dividing for long periods of time *in vitro* is the fibroblast. This cell is the major structural element found in almost all tissues and organs.

Modern Developments

Fifteen years ago we showed that normal human embryonic fibroblasts when cultured *in vitro* undergo a finite number of population doublings and then die. We showed that fibroblasts derived from normal human embryonic tissue undergo approximately 50 population doublings *in vitro* before losing proliferative power. We called the decline period of proliferative capacity the Phase III phenomenon and interpreted the results as a manifestation of senescence at the cellular level (Hayflick and Moorhead, 1961) (Figure 1). Furthermore, we showed that the phenomenon was not a consequence of any medium deficiency or technique artifact but that it was an intrinsic cell phenomenon. This observation has now been confirmed in scores of laboratories.

The beginning of Phase III cannot be determined with precision. Some studies discussed later under the title "The Phase III Phenomenon" have shown that some of the events that become obvious during Phase III may actually have their origins much earlier. From a practical standpoint, the beginning of Phase III is generally realized when a culture does not reach confluency at the time it would ordinarily be expected to do so. This longer time interval becomes lengthened as subsequent subcultivations are made until confluency no longer occurs.

Eleven years ago the author reported that fibroblast populations isolated from human adult tissue undergo only about 20 population doublings *in vitro* and suggested that the finite lifetime of normal human and animal cell replication is a programmed intracellular event under genetic control (Hayflick, 1965). The author further suggested that the limits on cell prolifertion *in vitro* are dictated by donor age (Hayflick, 1965).

Prior to our studies, it was well known that several animal cell populations could be propagated, apparently indefinitely, *in vitro*. However, we pointed out that all such populations are composed of abnormal cells, often displaying the properties of cancer cells (Hayflick and Moorhead, 1961).

The notion that isolated animal cells in culture are capable of unlimited proliferation has profoundly influenced thinking on many fundamental biological questions, not the least of which are theories of senescence. It was once thought that animal cells placed in culture will go on to multiply indefinitely. This is not always the case and seems to depend for its frequency on the animal species from which the cells were obtained. For example, mouse cells very frequently acquire the ability to proliferate indefinitely, but they are always abnormal. It is only the unusual situation that results in the ability of a human cell growing *in vitro* to acquire the property of unlimited capability for division. Furthermore, such cells are inevitably abnormal in one or more properties and frequently resemble cancer cells.

It was Alexis Carrel who, in the 1920s, reported that animal cells released from *in vivo* control mechanisms by *in vitro* cultivation will apparently perpetuate themselves indefinitely. This so-called immortality of cultured cells was based on his series of experiments purporting to show that fibroblasts derived from the heart of a chick embryo could be kept in an active state of division for an indeterminate period of time (Ebeling, 1913; Parker, 1961). Since, even with more modern and sophisticated cell culture techniques, actively dividing chick cells cannot be cultured much beyond 1 year, there is serious doubt that this common interpretation of Carrel's experiment is valid.

An alternative explanation is that the method of preparation of chick embryo extract, used as a source of nutrients for his cultures and prepared daily under conditions easily permitting cell survival, contributed new, viable embryonic cells to the chick heart strain at each feeding. Although it cannot be proven, we believe that the low-speed centrifugation used in Carrel's laboratory allowed for the presence of viable chick cells in the supernatant fluid of the chick embryo extract used to feed his alleged "immortal" chick heart cells. Further support for this contention is that islands of chick fibroblasts were often seen to be growing in the plasma clot some millimeters distant from the "immortal" chick heart cells. Finally, waves of mitotic activity were reported to be coincidental with the periodic addition of chick embryo extract, although this could result simply from the presence of fresh nutrients and not from the addition of new cells (Ebeling, 1913). No one has succeeded in confirming Carrel's studies, despite the fact that the chick embryo has been the most popular source of cells for making tissue cultures.

It is now known that normal cells derived from almost all vertebrate and many insect tissues can be cultivated *in vitro* for varying periods of time. Such cell populations divide for a finite number of generations and, after cessation of mitotic activity, the culture finally undergoes total degeneration. These events may span a period of days, weeks, or months but usually end within 1 or 2 years. We call such cell populations "cell strains" (Hayflick and Moorhead, 1961). However, Gey and Gey (1936), using human tissue, and Earle (1943), using murine tissue, unequivocally demonstrated the existence of cells capable of dividing for an indeterminate period of time. Since then, at least 500 cell populations with the extraordinary capacity to multiply indefinitely *in vitro* have been spontaneously derived from different kinds of vertebrate and insect tissue (Hayflick and Moorhead, 1962). These cell populations previously designated by us as "cell lines" are often morphologically, and always cytogenetically, distinguishable from cell strain populations (Hayflick and Moorhead, 1961). The biological characteristics of cell lines led us to the conclusion that regardless of the tissue of origin, whether normal or cancerous, cell lines are abnormal in one or more properties. This distinction between "cell lines" and cell strains" is not universally accepted, and caution must be exercised when interpreting these differences between cell populations as reported in the literature.

The spontaneous occurrence of a cell line is a rare event in the cultivation of many animal cell strains (Figure 1). The major exception to this generalization is the behavior of mouse cells,

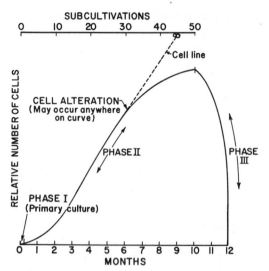

Figure 1. Diagrammatic representation of the history of cell strains and the phenomenon of cell alteration. Phase I, the primary culture, terminates with the formation of the first confluent sheet. Phase II is characterized by luxuriant growth necessitating many subcultivations. Cells in this phase are termed "cell strains." An alteration may occur at any time, giving rise to a "cell line" whose potential life is infinite. Conversely, cell strains characteristically enter Phase III and are lost after a finite period of time.

which when cultured *in vitro* have the unique property of almost always spontaneously transforming from a cell strain to a cell line with the concomitant acquisition of the ability to multiply indefinitely (Rothfels, Kupelwieser, and Parker, 1963; Todaro and Green, 1963). Since, after Carrel's studies, much of the early work in tissue culture was done with murine cells, it was "logical" to extrapolate the observations made with chick and murine cells and to conclude that all animal cells cultivated *in vitro* would, under the proper conditions, divide indefinitely. This generalization, without one critical qualification, is fallacious; normal somatic cells of these two species behave oppositely when cultivated *in vitro*. Chick cells never become cell lines, and mouse cells frequently do. The essential qualification to the generalization is that the only cells capable of unlimited division *in vitro* are those which acquire abnormal properties. On the other hand, the *in vitro* behavior of normal somatic cells, which is pivotal to the development of many theories of vertebrate aging, reveals that normal cells do have a finite lifetime. The importance of a correct interpretation of this phenomenon cannot be overemphasized since the apparent indefinite multiplication of isolated normal vertebrate cells in culture, as purportedly demonstrated by Carrel, has often been cited as evidence for the thesis that senescence in higher animals is a phenomenon resulting from the effects of events at the supracellular level (Bidder, 1925; Comfort, 1964a; Cowdry, 1952; Pearl, 1922; Maynard-Smith, 1962; Medawar, 1940).

It follows, therefore, that if normal animal cells do indeed have only a limited capacity for division in cell culture, then manifestations of aging might very well have an intracellular basis. Consequently, arguments marshalled against cellular theories of aging that are based on the myth of "immortal" cell cultures must be reevaluated since those cells that do proliferate indefinitely *in vitro* are abnormal and often behave like cancer cells. Contrariwise, normal cells *in vitro* do have a finite life span, as do the animals from which such cells have been taken (Figure 1). There is no confirmed evidence that normal cells can be maintained in a state of active proliferation in cell culture longer than the specific age of the species from which the cells were obtained. It is our contention that *in vivo* vertebrate senescence phenomena at the level of the cell also occur *in vitro* when the proper systems are compared. In earlier work with human embryonic diploid cell strains derived from lung tissue, we observed that after a period of active multiplication (generally less than 1 year), these cells demonstrated an increased doubling time (normally 24 hours), gradual cessation of mitotic activity, accumulation of cellular debris, and, ultimately, total degeneration of the culture (Hayflick and Moorhead, 1961). This phenomenon, called Phase III, is now a common observation by cell culturists when growing normal cells from many types of tissue. We view this event as an innate characteristic of all normal cells grown *in vitro*.

Since diploid cell strains have a limited doubling potential *in vitro*, studies on any single strain would be severely curtailed were it not possible to preserve these cells at subzero temperatures for indefinite periods of time. This maneuver allows for the construction of a number of interesting experiments. The reconstitution of frozen human fetal diploid cell strains has revealed that regardless of the doubling level reached by the population at the time it is preserved, the *total* number of doublings that can be expected is about 50 when those made before and after preservation are combined (Hayflick and Moorhead, 1961; Hayflick, 1965). Storage of human diploid cell strains merely arrests the cells at a particular population doubling level but does not influence the total number of expected doublings.

As of this date we have reconstituted a total of 130 ampules of our human diploid cell strain WI-38 which was placed in liquid nitrogen storage 14 years ago. Since 1962, one ampule has been reconstituted approximately each month, and all have yielded cell populations that have undergone 50 ± 10 cumulative population doublings. This represents the longest period of time that viable normal cells have been arrested at subzero temperatures (Hayflick, 1972).

THE INVERSE RELATIONSHIP BETWEEN DONOR AGE AND CULTURE LONGEVITY

In 1965 we reported that all 13 of the human embryo lung fibroblast populations that were studied reached senescence (Phase III) after undergoing between 35 and 63 population doublings. The average number of doublings was 48. We also showed that from 14 to 29 population doublings occurred (an average of 20) in the human adult fibroblast populations studied. The age of the adult donors varied from 26 to 87, and we were unable to find a precise correlation between the age of the adult donors and the number of cell population doublings found (Hayflick, 1965). These data are summarized in Table 1.

We concluded that although no precise correlation could be shown between adult donor age and cell doublings, it was clearly evident that human fibroblast cultures derived from embryo donors as a group underwent significantly more population doublings (40–60) than those derived from adults as a group (10–30). If a precise relationship did exist between the age

TABLE 1. A COMPARISON OF THE PASSAGE LEVELS AT WHICH PHASE III OCCURRED IN HUMAN DIPLOID CELL STRAINS OF ADULT AND FETAL ORIGIN.[a]

	FETAL LUNG		ADULT LUNG	
Strain	Passage level at which Phase III occurred (population doublings)	Strain	Passage level at which Phase III occurred (population doublings)	Age of Donor
WI-1	51	WI-1000	29	87
WI-3	35	WI-1001	18	80
WI-11	57	WI-1002	21	69
WI-16	44	WI-1003	24	67
WI-18	53	WI-1004	22	61
WI-19	50	WI-1005	16	58
WI-23	55	WI-1006	14	58
WI-24	39	WI-1007	20	26
WI-25	41			
WI-26	50			
WI-27	41			
WI-38	48			
WI-44	63			
	Average 48		20	
	Range 35–63		14–29	

[a]All strains cultivated at a 1:2 split ratio. Fetal strains derived from donors of 3–4 months' gestation obtained by surgical abortion. Adult and fetal strains derived from both male and female tissue.

of each adult donor and the number of population doublings undergone by his cultured cells, then we felt that our inability to observe this might be attributed to the lack of precision by which population doublings were then measured *in vitro*. Indeed, as substantiated by our experience with WI-38, which was derived from the lung of a single female human embryo, the number of population doublings undergone by cells from 130 consecutive reconstituted ampules varied between 38 and 65 (Hayflick and Pleibel, in preparation).

Subsequent to these studies, a report appeared which not only confirmed these findings but extended them significantly and showed that, with appropriate statistical analysis of the data, a decrement of 0.20 population doublings per year of donor life occurs in the cultured normal fibroblasts of humans (Martin, Sprague, and Epstein, 1970). These workers cultured the fibroblasts derived from biopsies taken from the mesial aspect of the mid-upperarm of 100 subjects ranging from fetal to 90 years of age. From the first to the ninth decade, the regression coefficient was found to be -0.20 population

doublings per year with a standard deviation of 0.05 and a correlation coefficient of -0.50. The regression coefficient was significantly different from 0 ($p < 0.01$), yet the interpretation of these analyses has been subject to some criticism. An additional notable confirmation of our earlier studies was found by Martin, Sprague, and Epstein (1970), who reported that the numbers of population doublings of skin fibroblasts derived from a group of 12 fetal donors averaged 44 and ranged between 33 and 56. Our earlier studies (Table 1) with lung fibroblasts from 13 different fetal donors averaged 48 and ranged between 35 and 63 population doublings (Hayflick, 1965).

Although our observation has been confirmed in hundreds of laboratories where 40-60 population doublings represents the range of the finite lifetime of cultured human fetal diploid fibroblast strains *in vitro,* this is the first report of a study employing a large enough series of separate fetal donors to make a suitable independent comparison. Further studies (Martin, Sprague, and Epstein, 1970), show that skin fibroblasts produced the greatest number of cell doublings *in vitro,* bone marrow spicules least, with skeletal muscle yielding intermediate results. Similar studies reported earlier by us showed that lung and skin fibroblasts yielded more population doublings than those derived from kidney, muscle, heart, thymus, or thyroid (Hayflick and Moorhead, 1961). These differences remain unexplained. LeGuilly, Simon, Lenoir, and Bourel (1973), studying human liver cells, obtained results similar to these. Thus, it is now generally believed that there is an inverse relationship between the age of a human donor and the *in vitro* proliferative capacity of at least two cell types—fibroblasts derived from skin and lung and cells derived from liver.

PROGERIA AND WERNER'S SYNDROME

Progeria (Hutchinson-Guilford syndrome) is a human condition leading to a severe deceleration of growth, characterized by generalized atherosclerosis involving all major vessels, including the aorta and coronary arteries even in patients as young as 9 years of age (Reichel, Garcia-Bunuel, and Dilallo, 1971). Progeria is a very rare disease and is thought by many to represent a model for precocious aging in which individuals, at the end of the first decade of life, manifest the physical signs of aging typical of their normal counterparts in the seventh decade of life. Werner's syndrome is like progeria in many ways, although its salient manifestations occur in later years. At least 10 percent of these patients develop neoplasms during their average life span of 47 years (Martin, Sprague, and Epstein, 1970). The clinical symptoms are early graying and loss of hair, short stature, juvenile cataracts, proneness to diabetes, atherosclerosis and calcification of the blood vessels, osteoporosis, and a high incidence of malignancy (Epstein, Martin, Schultz, and Motulsky, 1966; Reichel, Garcia-Bunuel, and Dilallo, 1971). Although doubts exist that progeria and Werner's syndrome are genuine examples of accelerated aging, any syndrome that mimics aging as much as these do merits attention in the present context.

Of interest here is the question, if Werner's syndrome and progeria are examples of accelerated aging, then when does senescence of cultured fibroblasts taken from these patients occur? The first such study reported that the replication of skin fibroblasts obtained from a 9-year-old boy with progeria was severely restricted (Goldstein, 1969, 1971). On two separate trials, these cells were found to undergo only two population doublings when cultured *in vitro.* Age-matched control cultures grown under identical conditions confirmed our earlier experiences (Hayflick, 1965) that fibroblasts from young adults were capable of 20–30 population doublings (Goldstein, 1969). Additional data on this question have been forthcoming from another laboratory, and all of the data bearing on this question are summarized in Table 2. Decreased mitotic activity, DNA synthesis, and cloning efficiency of cultured progeria cells have also been reported by other workers (Danes, 1971; Nienhaus, de Jong, and ten Kate, 1971; Singal and Goldstein (1973) have shown that although HL-A specificities can be found on the circulating lymphocytes of progeria patients, they cannot be detected on cultured fibroblasts from the same patients. This is contrary to what is found with normal individuals where HL-A specificities are detectable on both lymphocytes and cultured fibroblasts (Goldstein and Singal, 1972; Brautbar, Payne, and Hayflick, 1972).

A marked reduction in population doubling potential is characteristic of fibroblasts grown from patients with Werner's syndrome, as can be deduced from the data in Table 2. The number of population doublings for the skin fibroblast cultures from the two older patients with Werner's syndrome were found to be more than two standard deviations below the mean of the distribution for control cultures for the fifth decade. The number of population doublings was more than three standard deviations below the mean of the distribution of control cultures for the fourth decade in the case of the 37-year-old patient. The culture from the patient with progeria (Martin, Sprague and Epstein, 1970) is less readily differentiated from the control cultures; yet it ranks 23rd in life span out of 26 cultures in that particular age group. Fibroblast cultures derived from a testes biopsy of the patient with Werner's syndrome and carcinoma of the prostate (patient 2) had a much reduced

TABLE 2. POPULATION DOUBLINGS OF FIBROBLASTS DERIVED FROM PATIENTS WITH PROGERIA AND WERNER'S SYNDROMES.

Syndrome	Age in years	No. of population doublings *in vitro*	Reference
Progeria	9	2[a]	Goldstein, Littlefield, and Soeldner, 1969
Werner's Patient 1	48	2	Martin, Sprague, and Epstein, 1970
Werner's Patient 1	49	5	Martin, Sprague, and Epstein, 1970
Werner's Patient 2	48	8	Martin, Sprague, and Epstein, 1970
Werner's Patient 3	37	10	Martin, Sprague, and Epstein, 1970
Werner's Patient 4	43	4.5	Martin, Sprague, and Epstein, 1970
Progeria	5	30	Martin, Sprague, and Epstein, 1970

[a]Same result with two separate skin biopsies.

life span in comparison with control testes cultures derived from other patients with carcinoma of the prostate (Martin, Sprague, and Epstein, 1970).

Although there is still some question as to the relevance of these two syndromes to aging, it is still of interest that the fibroblast populations derived from such individuals and cultivated *in vitro* undergo significantly fewer doublings than their age-matched controls. Of additional interest is the finding that several patients with diabetes mellitus whose fibroblasts were cultured *in vitro* also displayed a significantly lower potential for division (Goldstein, Littlefield, and Soeldner, 1969; Martin, Sprague, and Epstein, 1970).

However, equivocal results have been obtained with cultured fibroblasts from patients with Down's syndrome. Where one group finds no reduction in doubling potential (Fialkow, Martin, and Sprague, 1973), another does (Schneider and Epstein, 1972).

THE FINITE LIFETIME OF CULTURED NORMAL CHICK CELLS

As previously described, the early work on chick fibroblasts reported by Carrel (Carrel and Ebeling, 1921; Ebeling, 1913; Parker, 1961)

claimed to prove that these cells could be cultured indefinitely, but this has not been confirmed. The most reasonable explanation for his finding is the virtual certainty that at each feeding of these cells, viable new chick fibroblasts were introduced into the so-called immortal culture at each feeding from the nutrient media which was prepared from a fresh extract of chick embryos (Hayflick, 1970). Similar studies on cultured chick fibroblasts in more recent years have revealed that these cells also have a finite capacity to replicate and undergo from 15 to 35 population doublings *in vitro* for periods up to 4 months (Hay and Strehler, 1967; Pontén, 1970; Lima and Macieira-Coelho, 1972) (Table 1).One possible exception to this generalization is the finding (Gey, Svotelis, Foard, and Bang, 1974) that chick embryo muscle explants have been reported to survive successive transplants *in vitro* up to 44 months on a collagen substrate but not on glass surfaces. However, because of the difficulty in determining numbers of population doublings in explant cultures, it is probable that these longevous cultures represent a considerable amount of cell maintenance time and not necessarily an unusually large number of population doublings. Maintenance of slowly dividing cell populations can cover much longer periods of time than serially cultured cell monolayers where rapid cell division constantly occurs. As pointed out by these investigators, "These results in themselves do not then contradict the idea that there is a limit to the number of cell divisions which cells may undergo" (Gey et al., 1974). It remains to be seen whether these longevous chick explant cultures will eventually reach Phase III.

More recently it has been reported that by the addition of HEPES buffer (N-2-hydroxy-ethylpiperazine-N'-2-ethanesulfonic acid) to the culture media, in lieu of the commonly used sodium bicarbonate buffer, substantial increases in population doubling potentials of normal chick fibroblasts can be obtained (Massie, Baird, and Samis, 1974). Ten cultures yielded population doublings ranging from 24 to 52 with an average of 40. This is significantly greater than the range of 15–35 found by other investigators (Table 3). However, these authors (Massie, Baird, and Samis, 1974) obtain only 2 population doublings for chick cell populations grown in the commonly used medium containing sodium bicarbonate which is considerably less than that found by four other groups of investigators (Table 3). Since the cultures grown in medium containing sodium bicarbonate are used as controls and do not compare with results obtained in four other laboratories, it is difficult to interpret the HEPES culture data until control values are found to be compatible with results found in other laboratories.

TABLE 3. THE PHASE III PHENOMENON AS EXPRESSED IN WHITE LEGHORN CHICK EMBRYO FIBROBLASTS.

Number of different embryo cultures studied	Range of population doublings observed	Reference
6	15–25	Hay and Strehler (1967)
16	20–27	Pontén (1970)
8	30–35	Lima and Macieira-Coelho (1972)
2	16–20[a]	Harris (1957)
	Average 23.5	

[a]Chicken strain not given. Doublings not given but calculated from subcultivation ratios and inoculation density of 1×10^6 per T-60 flask.

In recent years there has been a significant amount of work done on the Phase III phenomenon in cultured chick cells, where the findings are in general agreement with data obtained using cultured normal human fibroblasts (Lima and Macieira-Coelho, 1972; Harris, 1957; Pontén, 1970; Azencott and Courtois, 1974; Brock and Hay, 1971; and Lima, Malaise, and Macieira-Coelho, 1972).

THE FINITE LIFETIME OF CULTURED NORMAL FIBROBLASTS FROM OTHER VERTEBRATES

Mouse

Normal mouse embryo fibroblasts have been shown to undergo between 14 and 28 population doublings in vitro (Todaro and Green, 1963; Rothfels, Kupelweiser, and Parker, 1963). Since mouse cells have a very great likelihood of spontaneously transforming to abnormal cell populations, it is important to be aware of assessing the doubling potential of mouse fibroblasts concomitant with the certainty that they are indeed normal cells as determined karyologically and by inoculation into properly inbred host animals.

Other Species

In studies on six cell strains derived from embryonic heart tissue of the marsupial Potorus tridactylis, a limit of 30 population doublings was found (Simons, 1970). Transformation did not occur, and no data are given on the life span of Potorus tridactylis, although the closely related Echidna is reported to live for nearly 40 years (Duetz, 1942). Embryonic bovine lung cells have been found to undergo between 40 and 60 population doublings for the three strains studied, at which time major chromosomal anomalies occurred (Lithner and Pontén, 1966), but transformation did not. The maximum life span for bovines is reported to be 30 years (Flower, 1931).

Although embryonic tissue was unobtainable, studies have been made on cultured normal diploid skin fibroblasts from two young and two mature Galapagos tortoises (Testudo elephantopus) (Goldstein, 1974). Cells from the two younger animals (4–6 years) achieved the highest number of population doublings (112 and 130). Cell populations from the two mature animals (25–100 years) doubled 90 and 102 times *in vitro*. The mean maximum life span of *Testudo elephantopus* is thought to be about 175 years (Comfort, 1964b).

FUNCTIONAL AND BIOCHEMICAL DECREMENTS THAT OCCUR IN CULTURED NORMAL HUMAN CELLS

The likelihood that animals age because one or more important cell populations lose their proliferative capacity is unlikely. It is more probable that, as we have shown, normal cells have a finite capacity for replication and that this finite limit is rarely, if ever, reached by cells *in vivo* but is, of course, demonstrable *in vitro*. We would therefore suggest that the functional losses that occur in cells prior to the cessation of division capacity produce physiological decrements in animals much before their normal cells have reached their maximum proliferative capacity. Indeed, we are now becoming more aware of many functional changes taking place in normal human cells grown *in vitro* and expressed well before they lose their capacity to replicate (Houck, Sharma, and Hayflick, 1971; Cristofalo, Howard, and Kritchevsky, 1970; Holečková and Cristofalo, 1970). It is more likely that those subtler changes which herald the approach of loss of division capacity play the central role in the expression of aging and result in death of the individual animal well before his cells fail to divide. As we have pointed out before (Hayflick, 1970), the *in vitro* endpoint measured by us as loss of capacity for division is simply a convenient and reproducible system but may have little to do with the actual cause of *in vivo* aging.

However, the measurement of loss of potential for cell division is, after all, one of many cell functions that could be studied. If the manifestations of age changes are due to loss of cell function, other than loss of cell division, as we believe is more likely, then *in vitro* systems are all the more important as model systems. We must not lose sight of the fact that cell division is one of a number of functional losses occurring as normal cells proliferate *in vitro*. In recent years a lengthening list of functional changes is being attributed to human diploid cell strains as they age *in vitro*, and it is more likely that these functional decrements, which are manifest well before loss of capacity for division, result in the most important age changes *in vivo* (Table 4).

The biochemistry of the normal human diploid cell strain WI-38 before and during senescence has been the subject of a review covering the years up to 1972 (Cristofalo, 1972). These findings plus those reported until 1974 are summarized in Table 4. The salient findings are that glucose utilization and lactate production can be correlated with the rate of cell proliferation. In the absence of added glucose, growth can be supported by mannose, galactose, and fructose. Mannose is converted to lactic acid at almost the same rate as glucose, whereas galactose and fructose are converted at a slower rate.

Lipid content is about 20 percent of the cell dry weight for both normal and S.V.$_{40}$ transformed WI-38. Of this, about 70 percent is phospholipid and primarily in the form of lecithin. Most of the neutral lipid is cholesterol and free fatty acids, of which the latter are predominantly palmitic, stearic, and oleic. Other than the relatively large amount of free fatty acids, the lipid distribution is comparable to that found in other human tissues generally.

The glycogen and protein contents of rapidly dividing WI-38 at early population doubling levels is respectively 7.7 μg/10^6 cells (1.26 percent) and 227 μg/10^6 cells (32.2 percent). The DNA content is 7.83 μg/10^6 cells, and RNA content is 20.4 μg/10^6 cells.

A higher level of acid phosphatase activity was found in human diploid cell strains derived from adult lung than in cultures derived from fetal lung at equivalent population doubling levels. This may be resolved on the basis that the cells from older donors and at an equivalent doubling level of a culture from a younger donor has actually fewer doublings remaining. The alkaline phosphatase activity of WI-38 is low but much higher than its S.V.$_{40}$ transformed counterpart.

Cristofalo finds that respiration, glycolysis, and lactic dehydrogenase activity do not

TABLE 4. METABOLIC AND CELL PARAMETERS THAT INCREASE, DECREASE, OR DO NOT CHANGE AS NORMAL HUMAN FIBROBLASTS AGE *IN VITRO*.

PARAMETERS THAT INCREASE

Parameter	Reference
Glycogen content	Cristofalo, Howard, and Kritchevsky (1970)
Lipid content	Kritchevsky and Howard (1966); Hay and Strehler (1967)
Lipid synthesis	Chang (1962); Yuan and Chang (1969); Rothblat and Boyd (1971)
Protein content	Cristofalo, Howard and Kritchevsky (1970); Wang *et al.* (1970) (also reported not to change)
RNA content	Cristofalo and Kritchevsky (1969)
RNA turnover	Michl and Svobodá (1967)
Lysosomes and lysosomal enzymes	Cristofalo, Parris, and Kritchevsky (1967); Robbins, Levine, and Eagle (1970); Wang *et al.* (1970); Brandes *et al.* (in press); Milisauskas and Rose (1973)
Heterogeneity in length of division cycle	Macieira-Coelho, Pontén, and Philipson (1966a)
Heat lability of G6PD and 6 phosphogluconate dehydrogenase	Holliday (1972); Holliday and Tarrant (1972)
Proportion of RNA and histone in chromatin	Srivastava (1973)
Activity of "chromatin-associated enzymes" (RNAase, DNAase, protease, nucleoside triphosphatase, DPN pyrophosphorylase)	Srivastava (1973)
5' MNase activity	Turk and Milo (1974)
Esterase activity	Turk and Milo (1974)
Acid phosphatase band 3	Turk and Milo (1974)
Acid phosphatase	Cristofalo and Kabakjian (1975)
β-glucuronidase activity	Turk and Milo (1974); Cristofalo and Kabakjian (1975)
Membrane-associated ATPase activity	Turk and Milo (1974)
Cell size and volume	Simons (1967); Simons and van den Broek (1970); Cristofalo and Kritchevsky (1969)
Number and size of lysosomes	Lipetz and Cristofalo (1972); Robbins, Levine, and Eagle (1970); Brunk *et al.* (1973)
Glucose utilization	Goldstein and Trieman (1974)
Prolongation of doubling time	Hayflick and Moorhead (1961); Hayakawa (1969); Macieira-Coelho, Pontén, and Philipson (1966a)
Number of residual bodies	Brunk *et al.* (1973)
Cytoplasmic microfibrils, constricted and "empty"	Lipetz and Cristofalo (1972)
Endoplasmic reticulum	Lipetz and Cristofalo (1972)
Cyclic AMP level/mg protein	Goldstein and Haslam (1973)
Protein component P8	Stein (1975)
Particulate intracellular fluorescence	Deamer and Gonzales (1974)
Tolerance to sublethal radiation damage	Cox and Masson (1974)

PARAMETERS THAT DECREASE

Glycolytic enzymes	Wang *et al.* (1970) (also reported not to change)
Pentose phosphate shunt	Cristofalo (1970); Cristofalo, Opalek, and Baker (in prep.)
Mucopolysaccharide synthesis	Kurtz and Stidworthy (1969)
Transaminases	Wang *et al.* (1970) (also reported not to change)
Collagen synthesis	Macek, Hurych, and Chvapil (1967); Houck, Sharma, and Hayflick, (1971)
DNA content	Hay and Strehler (1967)
DNA synthesis	Choe and Rose (1974)
Nucleic acid synthesis	Macieira-Coelho, Pontén, and Philipson (1966a, 1966b)

TABLE 4. (Continued)

PARAMETERS THAT DECREASE (continued)

Parameter	Reference
Collagen synthesis and collagenolytic activity	Houck, Sharma, and Hayflick (1971)
Lactic dehydrogenase isoenzyme pattern	Childs and Legator (1965)
Ribosomal RNA content	Levine *et al.* (1967) (may have been due to mycoplasma contamination)
Incorporation of tritiated thymidine	Cristofalo and Sharf (1973)
RNA-synthesizing activity of chromatin	Srivastava (1973); Ryan and Cristofalo (in press)
Alkaline phosphatase	Turk and Milo (1974)
Specific activity of lactic dehydrogenase	Lewis and Tarrant (1972)
Rate of RNA synthesis	Macieira-Coelho, Pontén, and Philipson (1966a)
Synchronous division, constancy of interdivision time and motility	Absher, Absher, and Barnes (1974)
Rate of histone acetylation	Ryan and Cristofalo (1972)
Numbers of cells in proliferating pool	Cristofalo and Sharf (1973); Merz and Ross (1969); Smith and Hayflick (1974)
Cell saturation density	Macieira-Coelho (1970)
Population doubling potential as a function of donor age	Hayflick (1965); Martin, Sprague, and Epstein (1970); Martin, Ogburn, and Sprague (1975); LeGuilly *et al.* (1973)
Proportion of mitochondria with completely transverse cristae	Lipetz and Cristofalo (1972)
HL-A specificities (cloned cells)	Goldstein and Singal (1972)
Adherence to polymerizing fibrin and influence on fibrin retraction	Niewiarowski and Goldstein (1973)
Cyclic AMP level (molar values)	Goldstein and Haslam (1973)
Chromatin template activity	Ryan and Cristofalo (1975); Stein and Burtner (1975)
Rate of DNA chain elongation	Petes *et al.* (1974)
Rate of DNA strand rejoining and repair rate	Epstein, Williams, and Little (1974); Mattern and Cerutti (1975)

PARAMETERS THAT DO NOT CHANGE

Parameter	Reference
Glycolysis	Cristofalo and Kritchevsky (1966); Cristofalo, Opalek, and Baker (in prep.)
Permeability to glucose	Hay and Strehler (1967)
Respiration	Cristofalo and Kritchevsky (1966)
Respiratory enzymes	Hakimi and Pious (1968); Wang *et al.* (1970)
Permeability to amino acids	Hay and Strehler (1967)
Glutamic dehydrogenase	Wang *et al.* (1970)
Nucleohistone content	Ryan and Quinn (1971)
Alkaline phosphatase	Cristofalo, Parris, and Kritchevsky (1967); Wang *et al.* (1970)
Soluble RNAase, soluble DNAase, soluble seryl T-RNA synthetase, soluble and chromatin-associated DNA polymerase	Srivastava (1973)
Mean temperature of denaturation of DNA and chromatin	Comings and Vance (1971)
Numbers of mitochondria	Lipetz and Cristofalo (1972)
HL-A specificities (mass cultures)	Brautbar, Payne, and Hayflick (1972); Brautbar *et al.*, (1973)
Virus susceptibility	Hayflick and Moorhead (1961); Pitha, Adams, and Pitha (1974)
Poliovirus and herpesvirus titer, mutation rate and protein chemistry	Holland, Koline, and Doyle (1973); Tomkins, Stanbridge, and Hayflick (1974)
Cell viability at subzero temperatures	Hayflick (1965)
Diploidy (only changes in Phase III)	Saksela and Moorhead (1963)

TABLE 4. (Continued)

PARAMETERS THAT DO NOT CHANGE (continued)

Parameter	Reference
Histone/DNA ratio	Ryan and Cristofalo (1972)
Irreversible adsorption/uptake of foreign macromolecules	Press and Pitha (1974)
Prematurely condensed chromosomes	Yanishevsky and Carrano (1975)
Cyclic AMP concentration	Haslam and Goldstein (1974)
Superoxide dismutase activity	Yamanaka and Deamer (1974)
Rate of DNA strand rejoining and ability to perform repair replication	Clarkson and Painter (1974)

change as normal diploid cells approach Phase III and concludes that cell senescence does not result from a loss of ability to utilize available energy sources (Cristofalo, Howard, and Kritchevsky, 1970). Alkaline phosphatase activity and DNA and total protein values also remain unchanged. Conversely, there is an increased content of lipid and mean phospholipid components. Glycogen, soluble protein, RNA, and acid phosphatase activity also increase as cells approach Phase III.

It is very likely that additional information will become available on the functional decrements of cultured normal human cells that appear as they approach Phase III. It will be important to determine whether these findings can be correlated with similar *in vivo* physiological decrements of aging. If so, the *in vitro* system will be of even greater importance than it now is in the study of human aging.

POSSIBLE CORRELATION BETWEEN POPULATION DOUBLING POTENTIAL OF CULTURED NORMAL FIBROBLASTS AND MEAN MAXIMUM SPECIES LIFE SPAN

Although the data are fragmentary, it is interesting to explore the possibility that the population doubling potential of normal fibroblasts from the embryonic tissue of a variety of animal species might be correlated with the mean maximum life span for those species. The available data are shown in Table 5. Despite the likelihood that some of this data need confirmation and more exhaustive studies should be done, the notion that the population doubling potential of cultured normal embryonic

fibroblasts might be proportional to the mean maximum life span of the species is intriguing. If this correlation is ultimately found, a significant finding will have been made. Among other important insights would be the possibility of determining the mean maximum life span for any animal species simply by assessing the numbers of population doublings possible in their cultured normal embryonic cells. This would result in (1) more precise figures for the longevity of particular animal species, (2) the determination of species life spans without observing animals for many years, and (3) predicting life spans for hybrid animal species and for species whose records for longevity are scant or nonexistent.

Additionally it would be valuable to determine the longevity of cultured normal fibroblasts from a variety of animal species cultured at intervals throughout their life span. Of equal importance would be the acquisition of similar data obtained from longitudinal as well as from the cross-sectional studies done until now. That is, several animal species should be studied by obtaining tissue biopsies from a single tissue throughout the life span of the same animal. It is not impossible to undertake such studies on man as well. Longitudinal studies of this type might reveal a greater reliability upon population doubling measurements than is now possible.

THE FINITE LIFETIME OF NORMAL CELLS *IN VIVO*

If the concept of the finite lifetime or senescence of cells grown *in vitro* is related to aging

TABLE 5. THE FINITE LIFETIME OF CULTURED NORMAL EMBRYONIC HUMAN AND ANIMAL FIBROBLASTS.

Species	Range of population doublings for cultured normal embryo fibroblasts	Mean maximum life span in years	Reference
Galapagos tortoise	90–125	175 (?)	Goldstein (1974)
Man	40–60	110	Hayflick and Moorhead (1961)
Mink[a]	30–34	10	Porter (1961)[b]
Chicken	15–35	30 (?)	Hay and Strehler (1967); Harris (1957); Lima and Macieira-Coelho (1972); Pontén (1970)
Mouse	14–28	3.5	Rothfels, Kupelwieser, and Parker (1963); Todaro and Green (1963)

[a] Data from 20 embryos.
[b] Personal communication.

in the whole animal, then it is important to know whether normal cells, given the opportunity, can proliferate indefinitely *in vivo*. If all of the multitude of animal cell types were continually renewed, without loss of function or capacity for self-renewal, we would expect that the organs composed of such cells would function normally indefinitely and that their host would live forever. Unhappily, however, renewal cell populations do not occur in most tissues, and when they do, a proliferative finitude is often manifest. Although this important question has been discussed previously (Hayflick, 1966, 1970), much new information has become available in recent years. This subject is extensively treated in Chapter 6 of this *Handbook*, entitled "Cell Longevity *in vivo*."

It is apparent that most animal species have a specific life span and then die. The normal somatic cells composing their tissues obviously die as well. The important question then is: is it possible to circumvent the death of normal animal cells that results from the death of the "host" by transferring marked cells to younger animals *ad seriatum*? If such experiments could be conducted, we would have an *in vivo* counterpart of the *in vitro* experiments and would predict that normal cells transplanted serially

to proper inbred hosts would, like their *in vitro* counterparts, senesce. Such experiments would largely rule out those objections to *in vitro* findings that are based on the artificiality of *in vitro* cell cultures. The question could be answered by serial orthotopic transplantation of normal somatic tissue to new, young, inbred hosts each time the recipient approaches old age. Under these conditions, do transplanted normal cells of age-chimeras proliferate indefinitely?

Data from four different laboratories in which mammary tissue (Daniel, de Ome, Young, Blair, and Faulkin, 1968), skin (Krohn, 1962), and hematopoietic cells (Ford, Micklem, and Gray, 1959; Cudkowicz, Upton, Shearer, and Hughes, 1964; and Siminovitch, Till, and McCulloch, 1964) were employed indicate that normal cells serially transplanted to inbred hosts do not survive indefinitely. Furthermore, the trauma of transplantation does not appear to influence the results (Krohn, 1962). Finally, in heterochronic transplants, survival time is related to the age of the grafted tissue (Krohn, 1962). It is well known that under similar conditions of tissue transplantation, cancer cell populations can be serially passed indefinitely (Stewart, Snell, Dunham, and Schylen, 1959;

Till, McCulloch, and Siminovitch, 1964; and Daniel, Aidells, Medina, and Faulkin, 1975). The implications of this may be that acquisition of potential for unlimited cell division or escape from senescent changes by mammalian cells *in vitro* or *in vivo* can only be achieved by cells which have acquired some or all properties of cancer cells. Paradoxically, this leads to the conclusion that in order for mammalian somatic cells to become biologically "immortal," they first must be induced to the neoplastic state either *in vivo* or *in vitro,* whereupon they can then be subcultivated or transplanted indefinitely.

More recently a series of experiments have been reported (Daniel and Young, 1971; Daniel et al., 1968; and Daniel, 1973) which clearly show that the birth rate of mouse mammary epithelium declines during *in vivo* serial transplantation. Mouse mammary epithelium was propagated in isogenic female hosts by periodic transplantation of tissue samples into the mammary fat pads from which the host gland was surgically removed. These workers repeatedly observed that, unlike cancerous and precancerous mammary tissue, normal mammary epithelium displays a characteristic decline in proliferative capacity with repeated transplantations (Daniel et al., 1968). Cancerous tissue, having an unlimited capacity for replication *in vivo*, is, as we pointed out previously (Hayflick, 1966; Hayflick and Moorhead, 1961), the counterpart of transformed cells *in vitro* in which cell immortality is also observed. It has also been found that when transplants that are allowed to proliferate continuously are compared to transplants in which growth is restricted, the decline in cell proliferation is related to numbers of cell doublings undergone rather than to the passage of metabolic time (Daniel and Young, 1971). This represents the first *in vivo* confirmation of our *in vitro* data and of conclusions reached by us some 15 years ago (Hayflick and Moorhead, 1961; Hayflick, 1965). At that time we suggested that somatic cells have an intrinsic, predetermined capacity for division under the most favorable environmental conditions. Others, however, (Hay and Strehler, 1967; McHale, Mouton, and McHale, 1971) have invoked the passage of "metabolic time" as the determinant of *in vitro* senescence.

That metabolic time is not the governing factor but that population doublings are has been recently demonstrated (Dell'Orco, Mertens, and Kruse, 1974). The *in vivo* finding that population doublings dictate cell senescence and not "metabolic time" (Daniel and Young, 1971) is especially significant as it results from studies on cells grown entirely *in situ* and thus circumvents arguments leveled at similar data obtained from the alleged "artificial" conditions of *in vitro* cell culture. These investigators conclude that "the ability of grafts from old donors to proliferate rapidly in young hosts suggests that the life span of mammary glands is influenced primarily by the number of cell divisions rather than by the passage of chronological or metabolic time" (Young, Medina, de Ome, and Daniel, 1971).

In the past few years, the study of single antibody-forming cell clones *in vivo* has shown that these cells are also capable of only a finite ability to replicate after serial transfer *in vivo* (Williamson and Askonas, 1972; Williamson, 1972). Harrison (1972, 1973), however, reports that when marrow cell transplants from young and old normal donors are made to a genetically anemic recipient mouse strain, the anemia is cured. He further reports that such transplants to anemic mice can be made over a period of 73 months (Harrison, 1973). Subsequent to this publication, these transplants expired, exhibiting once again the finitude of normal cell proliferation *in vivo* (Harrison, 1975). The fact that this normal hematopoietic cell population has replicated far beyond the normal life span of the mouse is in keeping with our speculation that aging is not necessarily due to the loss of cell division capacity but probably due to other functional decrements that are known to occur prior to the loss of ability to replicate. The loss of capacity to divide is presumably an extreme limit, capable of demonstration *in vitro* and by serial transplantation *in vivo*.

In connection with findings that bear upon proliferative capacity of cells *in vivo* as a function of age, several other intriguing reports bear mentioning here. The most informative of such studies are those bearing upon the major cell renewal systems: the hematopoietic cells of the bone marrow, the epidermis, the lymphatic cells of the thymus, the spleen and lymph nodes, the sperm cells in the seminiferous tubules of the testes, and the epithelial cells lining the gastrointestinal tract and in the crypts of the epithelial lining of the small intestine. It has been found, for example, in the latter system in the mouse, that cell generation time increases with age (Lesher, Fry, and Kohn, 1961a, 1961b; Thrasher and Greulich, 1965). The increase in generation time is not a linear increase from early youth to extreme old age (Lesher and Sacher, 1968). Generation time increases up to approximately 1 year of age and levels off during the 2nd year, and between 675 and 825 days, generation time increases again. Furthermore, the intestinal crypt of a 3-month-old mouse contains a population of about 132 dividing cells, while the proliferative compartment of a 27-month-old animal contains only 92 cells. These data support the finding of Thrasher and Greulich (1965), who also found in older animals a decrease in the number of crypt cells that are capable of dividing and synthesizing DNA. Lesher and Sacher (1968) conclude that "because of the increase in generation time and the decrease in the proliferating cell population, production of new cells in old animals is approximately 50% less than the production in 100 day old BCF_1 mice."

Post and Hoffman (1964) find in rats that, following birth, there is an exponential decrease in the rate of body and liver growth as well as in the number of cells engaged in DNA synthesis and mitosis. Furthermore, the size of the replicating pool decreases, and there is lengthening of the replication time and of its component parts, DNA synthesis, G_2, mitosis, and G_1.

Their data reveal that as the rat reaches maturity (6 months), there is a marked decline in the percentage of hepatic cells and hepatocytes engaged in DNA synthesis and mitosis, after which a low level of each is maintained.

Thus we can see a wide variety of examples of *in vivo* constraints on the proliferative capacity of replicating cell cohorts. It is likely that different proliferating cell systems may display variations on this general theme. Based on our *in vitro* data, the fibroblast may represent the upper limit of proliferative potential, although one should not exclude a higher limit being placed on such cell renewal systems as hema-

topoietic cells or skin epithelium, neither of which have been shown to proliferate *in vitro* for long periods of time and still retain normal characteristics and functional capacities.

Is it possible that a limit on cell proliferation or function in some strategic organ could orchestrate the entire phenomenon of senescence? Burnet (1970a, 1970b) has speculated that if this is so, the most likely organ is the thymus and its dependent tissues. Burnet reasons that aging is largely mediated by autoimmune processes that are influenced by progressive weakening of the function of immunological surveillance. He further argues that weakening of immunological surveillance may be related to weakness of the thymus-dependent immune system. He concludes that the thymus and its dependent tissue are subject to a proliferative limit similar to the Phase III phenomenon or senescence *in vitro* described by us for human cells. Whether the role played by the thymus and its dependent tissues as the pacemaker in senescence is important or not still remains to be established. However, the immunological theory of aging, being based on the occurrence of somatic mutations (Walford, 1969), is of doubtful importance in view of the fact that the somatic mutation theory of aging is itself in disrepute (Comfort, 1964a; Strehler, 1962).

ARE KARYOLOGICALLY NORMAL CELLS KNOWN THAT DO NOT DISPLAY SENESCENCE *IN VITRO*?

Since our first report on the finite lifetime of karyologically normal human cells, several authors have purportedly found normal human cell populations that did not senesce *in vitro*.

The first of these reports (Moore and Sandberg, 1964), like those that followed, was later shown to be erroneous (Moorhead, 1965). In recent years reports on the unlimited *in vitro* proliferation of human hematopoietic cells with a normal karyotype have appeared again (Moore and McLimans, 1968), but these reports are unacceptable for a variety of reasons.

The authors of this report claim that hematopoietic cell lines derived from normal human donors and having a normal karyotype exist because "the spectrum of karyotypes, although slightly wider than occurs in temporary cultures of leucocytes stimulated by phytohaemagglutinin, clustered around the mode of 46 (85% or greater of the cells)" and because "these lines qualify as 'normal diploid cells' as defined by a subcommittee of the American Tissue Culture Association (Proposed Usage of Animal Tissue Culture Terms 1967)." Even though the claim for karyological normalcy has been made for these cells by these authors, inadequate data have been provided on karyology and karyotype analyses for hematopoietic cell lines kept in continuous culture for more than 1 year and that meet acceptable criteria for determining whether a given human cell population is karyologically normal (Cell Culture Committee 1970, 1971; Moorhead, Nichols, Perkins, and Hayflick, 1974). The Proposed Usage of Animal Tissue Culture Terms 1967 (Federoff, 1967) was intended as a statement of generalizations and did not lay down strict criteria for establishing karyological normalcy for human cells such as currently exist (Cell Culture Committee 1970, 1971; Moorhead et al., 1974). Since the statement quoted above admits to a "slightly wider spectrum of karyotypes" for the hematopoietic cell lines studied when compared to phytohaemagglutinin stimulated leucocyte cultures, the statement that the hematopoietic cell lines studied are karyologically normal is internally inconsistent. This is especially so since the phytohaemagglutinin stimulated leucocytes are the very cells upon which the normal human karyotype is based, and to admit a "slightly wider spectrum" for hematopoietic cell lines is to admit that they are indeed not karyologically normal.

Of the several publications purporting to describe karyologically normal hematopoietic cell lines, none has given adequate data. Other hematopoietic cell lines have indeed been shown, after continued cultivation, to be karyologically abnormal (Hayflick, 1970). Until such time as at least one hematopoietic cell line (1) has been derived from a normal donor, (2) has been documented to have undergone at least 70 population doublings in vitro, and (3) has been found to conform to the definition of karyological normalcy as defined by experts in

this area (Cell Culture Committee, 1970, 1971; Moorhead et al., 1974), then it cannot be claimed that hematopoietic cell lines exist that are karyologically normal. These workers (Moore and McLimans, 1968) also claim for hematopoietic cell lines (without supporting data) that "the number of aberrant karyotypes around the mode of 46 has remained less than 15% in cell lines for normal individuals." Any human being found to have 15 percent of his cells with "aberrant karyotypes" could hardly be called normal. Nor could such cells be considered normal as stipulated by karyologists in the minimum requirements established for diploidy in normal human cells (Cell Culture Committee, 1970, 1971).

As admitted by these workers (Huang and Moore, 1969) and even after their earlier publication (Moore and McLimans, 1968), "chromosome data for cell lines derived from the peripheral blood of normal persons, however, is scant," and "the cytogenetic stability of these haematopoietic cell lines as a function of time in vitro has not received much attention." They go on to describe karyological data on "14 long-term human haematopoietic cell lines derived from peripheral blood of 11 normal persons. . . ." Of the fourteen "normal lines," they described four as changing to pseudodiploidy, one as "rather complex" (half pseudodiploid, high incidence of aneuploidy), two with an extra chromosome and a large dicentric marker, and four with "no deviation from the normal male karyotype." However, what they do not point out and what is extraordinarily important is that the latter four cell lines were in culture for only 3 to 4 months, which is 1 year less than any of the other ten cell lines that they find undergoing karyological changes. This bears precisely on the point that we have made in describing the lifetime of normal human cells, i. e., these later four cultures have not been cultivated long enough to have transformed or altered karyologically. Thus, we concur with the original statement made by these authors that "the cytogenetic stability of these haematopoietic cell lines as a function of time in vitro has not received much attention." Until these four cell lines are found to undergo several hundred population doublings and retain diploidy, no conclusions can be reached beyond those stated by us previously (Hayflick 1965, 1966, 1970). In a more recent report from these same laboratories on 14 hematopoietic cell lines derived from eight different patients with infectious mononucleosis (Huang, Minowada, Smith, and Osunkoya, 1970), all are claimed to be diploid, yet no data are given nor is the number of population doublings stated. Significantly, no culture is older than 1 year. As we indicated some 15 years ago, cell populations grown *in vitro* are expected to have the karyotype of the tissue of origin until either a transformation or senescence occurs (Hayflick and Moorhead, 1961). Insufficient data are supplied in the aforementioned reports to determine that when transformation has not occurred sufficient population doublings have.

There are also several reports in the literature claiming the existence of karyologically normal animal cell populations, only two examples of which will be given here. The mysterious diploid rat cell population (Truitt, 1970), often discussed but never referenced, has never been authenticated. Despite the verbal report by Puck (Krohn, 1966b) of a diploid rabbit cell population that had undergone "500 replications without visible chromosomal change," this was later retracted when the written version was published (Puck, Waldren, and Tjio, 1966).

In summary then, there are no confirmed studies that show karyological normalcy by current standards for any animal or human cell population that has been in continuous cultivation for a minimum of about 150 population doublings. Krooth, Shaw, and Campbell (1964) report a rat cell population subcultured for 15 months where 85 percent of the cells are diploid and with no chromosomal abnormalities. Although this appears to be a unique finding, it does not conform to our original definition of a normal diploid cell strain in which the cell population should maintain the karyotype of the cells composing the tissue of origin. It would be expected that the tissue of origin would show diploidy at a level nearer to 95 percent. Furthermore, diploidy is not the only criterion for normalcy, and cells thought to be karyologically normal also must be inoculated into immunosuppressed hosts in order to deter-

mine whether malignant properties have been acquired. Krooth describes several other alleged diploid cell strains with properties of continuous growth, each of which can be criticized on the grounds stated above. In general, however, most claims of having developed diploid cell populations capable of indefinite growth suffer from the criticism that karyological analysis is frequently done very early in the history of the culture and then years or even months later when it is concluded that the cell population is probably immortal, the claim is made that the cells are diploid, based on the earlier karyological analysis.

In most of these cases, the assumption is found to be spurious since a spontaneous transformation is often found to have occurred after the karyological analysis was made. What is not appreciated is that, if derived from normal tissue, all cultures at early population doubling levels will undoubtedly be found to be diploid. It is essential that karyological analysis be done after many months or years of continuous propagation *in vitro* since spontaneous transformations in which karyological changes do occur usually account for these longevous cultures. It cannot be assumed that a finding of diploidy at a population doubling level of, say, 10 will be found to exist also at a level of 100. Of equal importance is that normal human diploid fibroblasts do eventually show chromosome aberrations as they enter Phase III, yet spontaneous transformations to permanent cell lines have not been reported.

LATENT PERIOD VERSUS DONOR AGE

In 1927, Suzuki, and independently, Cohn and Murray (1925) showed that the period of time elapsing between explantation of embryo chick tissue in culture and cell migration from the explant increased with embryo age. This observation was later confirmed by many others (Oda and Kamon, 1927; Olivo and Slavich, 1930; Hoffman, Goldschmidt, and Doljanski, 1937; Goldschmidt, Hoffman, and Doljanski, 1937; Doljanski, Goldschmidt, and Hoffman, 1937). Similar studies have been undertaken in more recent years (Soukupová and Holečková, 1964; Soukupová, Holečková, and Cinnerova, 1965; Michl, Soukupová, and Holečková, 1968; Soukupová, Hněvkovsky, Chvapil, and Hruza, 1968) and have shown again that the time necessary for the first cells to emigrate from tissue explants grown *in vitro* (the latent period) correlates inversely with the age of the donor. Most significantly, they report that the latent period increases even after the cessation of active growth in the rat. Similar observations are reported for chicken cells. These workers conclude that explanted tissue behaves like a mosaic of active and inactive cells in which the percentage of slowly migrating cells increases with increasing donor age. These findings are also the result of more sophisticated measurements confirming those made many years earlier by others (Ebeling, 1921; Hoffman, Goldschmidt, and Doljanski, 1937; Mayer, 1939; Medawar, 1940). In studies on chick heart explants, the rate of cell migration was found to be a function of donor age, but the mitotic index did not vary (Chaytor, 1962; Lefford, 1964).

Recently, similar studies on latent periods versus donor age have been reported for human tissue (Waters and Walford, 1970; Soukupová and Hněvkovský, 1972). In one study (Waters and Walford, 1970), measurements were made of the latent periods for outgrowth of epithelial cells and fibroblasts from explants of human skin obtained by punch biopsy from 20 adult forearms and neonatal foreskins. Donor age ranged from newborn to 80 years old. It was found that the latent period of fibroblasts increased linearly with age and was subject to individual variabilities which tended to increase with donor age. For all three categories of migrating fibroblast responses selected (1-6 cells, 7-25 cells, and > 25 cells), there was found a significant difference between neonates and adults, between persons under and over 30 years of age, and between persons under 32 and over 43 years of age. The neonatal epithelial latent periods, however, were significantly greater than explants from adults. No significant difference was found in the time for epithelial cell outgrowth to occur from adult explants under and over 30 years of age or from adult explants under 32 and over 43 years of age. In the extensive study of Soukupová and Hněvkovský, the

latent period of cultured human embryonic heart, liver, and kidney explants was found to be inversely proportional to the age of the embryo (Soukupová and Hněvkovský, 1972). These results in which an increased latent period for human tissue explants is found are compatible with our studies and with those of others (Martin, Sprague, and Epstein, 1970), who find a decrease in population doubling potential for cultured human cells as a function of donor age.

PROTOZOA AND CULTURED CELLS COMPARED

The concept that normal dividing cells never have an opportunity to age because they periodically yield new daughter cells before age changes take place bears consideration in light of the finite lifetime of normal cultured vertebrate cells. What is in question here is whether the product of a cell division is always a pair of daughter cells, each having the same age status. This notion makes the very important assumption that dividing cells yield daughters that are "separate but equal." There is little, if any, evidence that bears on this important point in cultured mammalian cells and no factual data opposing the possibility that one daughter cell may receive one or more old organelles and the other only new organelles. It is also possible to argue that information-containing molecules with different error levels are unequally distributed. Thus, to assume that each daughter mammalian cell is equivalent in age status may be spurious. Cell culture may lead to an examination of this question.

Since populations of vertebrate cells in culture have an independent existence and can be manipulated like microorganisms, it may be useful to compare certain aspects of the behavior of both. Studies with protozoa do not unequivocally demonstrate the "immortality" of unicellular organisms or that the outcome of a protozoan cell division is a pair of rejuvenated infant cells, instead of a mother and daughter cell of different seniorities.

For example, it has been shown (Danielli and Muggleton, 1959; Muggleton and Danielli, 1968) that amebae will multiply indefinitely if kept on a food supply permitting logarithmic vegetative multiplication, but, if kept on a limited food supply and then transferred to the optimum diet, they have a variable life span. This span of from 30 days to 30 weeks is dependent on the conditions of exposure to the deficient diet. Since it is likely that amebae in the natural state do not always have an optimum food supply, their usual fate is probably one in which senescence occurs. A number of other investigators have also concluded that many clones of protozoa do not propagate asexually indefinitely. Such observations have been made with *Uroleptus* (Calkins, 1919), *Paramecium* (Sonneborn, 1938; Smith-Sonneborn, Klass, and Cotton, 1974; Sonneborn, 1954), and with an *Ascomycete* (Rizet, 1953). Other clones of protozoa apparently do reproduce asexually and indefinitely. The extensive studies of Jennings (1945) bear directly on this question and on clonal rejuvenation by conjugation. It was found that the viability of the progeny *Paramecium bursaria* produced by conjugation varies greatly, even when the conjugants are young, and that a high proportion of exconjugants normally die. The rate appears to be highest in those clones that are most closely related. Fifty-three percent of exconjugants die before undergoing five cell divisions, and 30 percent die without dividing at all. Conjugation produced nonviable clones, clones of limited survival, and some vigorous clones apparently capable of unlimited asexual reproduction. It is suggested that it is from these latter clones that laboratory cultures are normally obtained. Jennings concludes that death is not a consequence of multicellularity and that it occurs on a vast scale in the protozoa "from causes which are intrinsic to the organism." He claims that "most if not all clones ultimately die if they do not undergo some form of sexual reproduction . . . Rejuvenation through sexual reproduction is a fact . . . yet conjugation produces, in addition to rejuvenated clones, vast numbers of weak, pathological or abnormal clones whose predestined fate is early death." He adds that some very vigorous clones may be produced "that may continue vegetatively for an indefinite period, without decline or death." Reference should be made to Comfort (1964a) and Strehler (1962) for an exhaustive discussion of this subject.

It is interesting that a similar kind of clonal variation occurs with the human diploid cell strains. Some isolated single embryonic cells give rise to progeny capable of about 50 doublings (Hayflick, 1965), and others yield colonies composed of varying numbers of cells or no clones at all (Merz and Ross, 1969; Smith and Hayflick, 1974). However, the uncloned or wild embryonic cell population always undergoes about 50 doublings. Of equal importance in this context is the intriguing possibility that cultures of bacteria in which exchange of genetic information between organisms is prevented might also reveal a senescence phenomenon. In order to test this hypothesis, daughter microorganisms would have to be kept isolated from other members of the culture as they replicate serially. The technical problems that would be encountered in constructing such an experiment are probably sufficient reason why this experiment has not yet been reported. Perhaps of interest in this connection are reports of the exchange of genetic material by mammalian somatic cells *in vitro* (Barski, Sorieul, and Cornefert, 1960; Ephrussi, Scaletta, Stenchever, and Yoshida, 1964). Is it possible that immortal cell populations can only occur after the exchange of genetic information which somehow recycles the genetic clock?

CAN CELL DEATH BE NORMAL?

The death of cells and the destruction of tissues and organs are indeed a normal part of morphogenic or developmental sequences in animals. It is the common method of eliminating organs and tissues that are useful only in the larval or embryonic stages of many animals, e.g., the pronephros and mesonephros of higher vertebrates, the tail and gills of tadpoles, larval insect organs, and in many cases, the thymus. The degeneration of cells is an important part of development, and it is a widespread occurrence in mammalian cells (Saunders, 1966). During the development of vertebrate limbs, cell death and cell resorption model not only digits but also thigh and upper arm contours (Whitten, 1969). In the limbs of vertebrates, the death clocks function on schedule even when heterochronic tissue grafts are made (Saunders and Fallon, 1966). The following remarks by Saunders (1966) attest to the universality and normality of cell death *in vivo:*

> One confronts less than comfortably the notion that cellular death has a place in embryonic development; for why should the embryo, progressing towards an ever more improbable state, squander in death those resources of energy and information which it has laboriously won from a less ordered environment? Nevertheless, abundant death, often cataclysmic in its onslaught, is a part of early development in many animals: it is the usual method of eliminating organs and tissues that are useful only during embryonic or larval life or that are but phylogenetic vestiges (phylogenetic death). For example, the pronephros and mesonephros of the higher vertebrates, the anuran tail and gills, and larval organs of holometabalous insects; it plays a role in the differentiation of organs and tissues, as exemplified by the histogenesis and remodelling of cartilage and bone (histogenetic death); and it accompanies the formation of folds and the confluence of anlagen (morphogenetic death). It occurs frequently in the early blastoderm of the chick embryo, more or less at random, and dead cells are scattered throughout the tissues of the older embryo. Indeed, degeneration of cells and tissues is a very prominent part of development, and it is unfortunate that little has been done to analyze its significance in the processes with which it is associated, its embryonic control, the biochemical events in the onset and realization of necrosis, and the development of the products of degeneration.

Thus cell death is an intrinsic part of development. To the casual observer the contemplation that normal human embryo cells grown *in vitro* will die after dividing vigorously for 50 population doublings is difficult to accept. Yet, the same logic that makes acceptable aging and death in whole animals as being universal and inevitable should apply when the same phenomenon is seen to occur in cells derived from these animals after they are grown *in vitro*.

THE PHASE III PHENOMENON

From the time the observation was made that cultured normal human fibroblasts had a limited doubling potential and the suggestion made that this phenomenon might be an expression of aging at the cellular level (Hayflick and Moorhead, 1961), a considerable body of knowledge on this event has been accumulated. Although the finite replicative capacity of these cells was at first met with considerable skepticism, the occurrence of the Phase III phenomenon itself is now generally accepted. What is still controversial, however, is the bearing that this phenomenon may or may not have on biological aging.

The most significant argument for an association of the phenomenon with aging are those data showing an inverse relationship between donor age and population doubling potential in a variety of human cell types (Hayflick and Moorhead, 1961; Martin, Sprague, and Epstein, 1970; Martin, Ogburn, and Sprague, in press; Le Guilly *et al.*, 1973). Nevertheless, proof that the phenomenon is directly related to aging is unlikely to be forthcoming because (1) agreement as to what biological phenomena are or are not age-associated is debatable, (2) experiments showing age association to the exclusion of other biological phenomena are very difficult to design, and (3) there is resistance to extrapolating from *in vitro* events to those occurring *in vivo*. Despite these reservations, the Phase III phenomenon, regardless of its real meaning, is of sufficient interest generally to warrant consideration as to its cause.

In the past 15 years, a significant number of investigations relating to his phenomenon have been reported. Table 4, although undoubtedly incomplete, tabulates some of these studies in which a number of variables have been found to increase, decrease, or remain unchanged as normal human cells approach or enter Phase III. Because of the great number of studies reported, it is not possible to discuss all of them here (for a detailed discussion of much of the data in this area, see Macieira-Coelho, 1973); only a brief discussion will be given of general research trends and theoretical considerations as to the cause of Phase III. This is necessitated because the cause of the event is still not understood.

Although some discrepancies in interpretation exist, ability to perform DNA repair replication diminishes with increased population doublings (Epstein, Williams, and Little, 1974; Mattern and Cerutti, 1975). Hart and Setlow (1974) have extended this observation by showing that unscheduled DNA synthesis was approximately proportional to the logarithm of life span in seven animal species including man. The suggestion is made that effective repair mechanisms might be important in determining life span of whole animals and of cells *in vitro*.

Since the proposal was made that accumulation of errors in the protein synthesizing machinery of cells could result in age changes, a substantial amount of experimental evidence has been accumulated that bears on this as an explanation for the Phase III phenomenon. Orgel (1973) has reviewed this area and especially those studies done by Holliday and his colleagues that seem to support the hypothesis (Holliday and Tarrant, 1972). Nevertheless, substantial data have been obtained which do not support the notion that the loss of cell doubling capacity *in vitro* is due to an accumulation of errors in enzymes or other proteins (Ryan, Duda, and Cristofalo, 1974; Holland, Koline, and Doyle, 1973; Pitha, Adams, and Pitha, 1974; Tomkins, Stanbridge, and Hayflick, 1974; Wright and Hayflick, 1975a, 1975b).

One of the first decrements shown to occur as cell populations approach and enter Phase III are the numbers of cells in the proliferating pool (Merz and Ross, 1969; Cristofalo and Sharf, 1973; Smith and Hayflick, 1974). More recently, using phase-contrast time-lapse cinemicrophotography, Absher, Absher, and Barnes (1974) showed that constancy of interdivision time decreased and asynchronous division events occurred in cells at later population doubling levels. It was concluded that noncycling cells are present in increased amounts during *in vitro* cell senescence; nevertheless, a cogent argument in opposition to this view has recently been made (Macieira-Coelho, 1974). A mathematical model describing the variation in length of mitotic cycle as cells approach Phase III has also been put forward (Good and Smith, 1974).

Several reports have appeared in which additives to the usual cell culture medium have resulted in an increase in population doubling potential. The first of these reports (Todaro and Green, 1964) claimed that the addition of serum albumin resulted in a 20 percent increase in population doubling potential. However,

there has been no confirmation of this result. Despite several attempts, there has also been failure to confirm the claim that the addition of vitamin E can significantly prolong the population doubling potential of cultured normal human cells (Packer and Smith, 1974). There is, nevertheless, ample evidence to support the finding that cortisone and hydrocortisone can extend *in vitro* life span by about 20 percent (Macieira-Coelho, 1966; Cristofalo, 1970). The earlier these substances are administered, the greater is the effect, and when hydrocortisone is removed from cells which have grown beyond the life span of controls, cell death occurs within two subcultivations. The mechanism by which these compounds produce this effect is unknown, and future research in this area could provide useful new insights into the Phase III phenomenon.

One approach to understanding the finite lifetime of cultured normal cells that shows considerable promise is the utilization of cell hybridization techniques. Although fusions between pairs of "aged" fibroblasts and pairs of "young" and "senescent" fibroblasts failed to produce viable hybrids (Littlefield, 1973), interspecies hybrids between Galapagos tortoise fibroblasts and those from hamsters showed some ability to replicate (Goldstein and Lin, 1972). "Senescent" human fibroblasts fused to HeLa or to SV_{40} transformed human fibroblasts showed a reinitiation of DNA synthesis in "senescent" nuclei in a high proportion of these heterodikaryons (Norwood, Pendergrass, and Martin, 1975).

Of greater interest, however, is the perfection of techniques by which fusions can be made between whole cells and enucleated cells (Prescott, Myerson and Wallace, 1972, Wright and Hayflick, 1972, 1975a). Our initial results using these techniques have been interpreted to mean that cytoplasmic factors do not appear to control *in vitro* cellular senescence (Wright and Hayflick, 1975b, 1975c). These experiments are not entirely conclusive, and it is our expectation that recently devised techniques by which viable nuclei can be inserted into anucleate cytoplasts will lead to an unequivocal determination of the role of the nucleus or the cytoplasm in cellular aging (Muggleton-Harris and Hayflick, in press).

If it is correct to assume that the cessation of division capacity or function in cultured normal cells is an expression of aging at the cellular level, then the final explanation of this phenomenon may be as complex as is the explanation for age changes in whole animals.

REFERENCES

Absher, P. M., Absher, R. G., and Barnes, W. D. 1974. Genealogy of clones of diploid fibroblasts. *Exp. Cell Res.*, 88, 95-104.

Azencott, R., and Courtois, Y. 1974. Age-related differences in intercellular adhesion for chick fibroblasts cultured *in vitro. Exp. Cell Res.*, 86, 69-74.

Barski, G. Sorieul, S., and Cornefert, F. 1960. Production dans des cultures *in vitro* de deux souches cellulaires en association, de cellules de caractere "hybride." *C. R. Acad. Sci. (Paris)*, 251, 1825.

Bidder, G. P. 1925. The mortality of plaice. *Nature*, 115, 495-496.

Brandes, D., Murphy, D. G., Montes de Oca, H., and Anton, E. (in press).

Brautbar, C., Payne, R., and Hayflick, L. 1972. Fate of HL-A antigens in aging cultured human diploid cell strains. *Exp. Cell Res.*, 75, 31-38.

Brautbar, C., Pellegrino, M. A., Ferrone, S., Reisfeld, R. A., Payne, R., and Hayflick, L. 1973. Fate of HL-A antigens in aging cultured human diploid cell strains. II. Quantitative absorption studies. *Exp. Cell Res.*, 78, 367-375.

Brock, M. A., and Hay, R. J. 1971. Comparative ultrastructure of chick fibroblasts *in vitro* at early and late stages during their growth span. *J. Ultrastruct. Res.*, 36, 291-311.

Brunk, U., Ericsson, J. L. E., Pontén, J., and Westermark, B. 1973. Residual bodies and "aging" in cultured human glia cells. *Exp. Cell Res.*, 79, 1-14.

Burnet, F. M. 1970a. *Immunological Surveillance*, pp. 224-257. New York: Pergamon Press.

Burnett, F. M. 1970b. An immunological approach to aging. *Lancet*, 2, 358-360.

Calkins, G. N. 1919. *Uroleptus mobilis* Eng. II. Renewal of vitality through conjugation. *J. Exp. Zool.*, 29, 121.

Carrel, A., and Ebeling, A. H. 1921. Age and multiplication of fibroblasts. *J. Exp. Med.*, 34, 599-623.

Cell Culture Committee, Permanent Section on Microbiological Standardization. 1970. Minutes of the Sixth Meeting. Available from F. T. Perkins, Medical Research Council, Hampstead Laboratories, London, England.

Cell Culture Committee, Permanent Section on Microbiological Standardization. 1971. Minutes of the Seventh Meeting. Available from F. T. Perkins, Medical Research Council, Hampstead Laboratories, London, England.

Chang, R. S. 1962. Metabolic alterations with senescence of human cells. Some observations *in vitro*. *Arch. Internal Med.*, 110, 563-568.

Chaytor, D. E. B. 1962. Mitotic index *in vitro* of embryonic heart fibroblasts of different donor ages. *Exp. Cell Res.*, 28, 212-213.

Childs, V. A., and Legator, M. S. 1965. Lactic dehydrogenase isozymes in diploid and heteroploid cells. *Life Sci.*, 4, 1643-1650.

Choe, B.-K., and Rose, N. R., 1974. Synthesis of DNA binding protein in WI-38 cells stimulated to synthesize DNA by medium replacement. *Exp. Cell Res.*, 83, 261-270.

Clarkson, J. M., and Painter, R. B. 1974. Repair of X-ray damage in aging WI-38 cells. *Mutation Res.*, 23, 107-112.

Cohn, A. E., and Murray, H. A. 1925. Physiological Ontogeny. A. Chicken Embryos. IV. The negative acceleration of growth with age as demonstrated by tissue cultures. *J. Exp. Med.*, 42, 275-290.

Comfort, A. 1964a. *Ageing: The Biology of Senescence.* New York: Holt, Rinehart & Winston.

Comfort, A. 1964b. *The Process of Ageing.* New York: Signet Science Library, The New American Library.

Comings, D. E., and Vance, C. K. 1971. Thermal denaturation of DNA and chromatin of early and late passage human fibroblasts. *Gerontologia*, 17, 116-121.

Cowdry, E. V. 1952. *In*, A. I. Lansing (ed.), *Problems of Aging*. Baltimore: Williams & Wilkins.

Cox, R., and Masson, W. K. 1974. Changes in radiosensitivity during the *in vitro* growth of diploid human fibroblasts. *Intern. J. Radiation Biol.*, 26, 193-196.

Cristofalo, V. J. 1970. Metabolic aspects of aging in diploid human cells. *In*, E. Holečková and V. J. Cristofalo (eds.), *Aging in Cell and Tissue Culture*, pp. 83-119. New York: Plenum Press.

Cristofalo, V. J. 1972. Animal cell cultures as a model system for the study of aging. *In*, B. Strehler (ed.), *Advances in Gerontological Research*, Vol. 4, pp. 45-80, New York: Academic Press.

Cristofalo, V. J., Howard, B. V., and Kritchevsky, D. 1970. The biochemistry of human cells in culture. *In*, V. Gallo and L. Santamarra (eds.), *Organic, Biological and Medicinal Chemistry*, Vol. 2, pp. 95-150. Amsterdam: N. Holland.

Cristofalo, V. J., and Kabakjian, J. 1975. Lysosomal enzymes and aging *in vitro*: Subcellular enzyme distribution and effect of hydrocortisone on cell lifespan. *Mech. Age. Dev.*, 4, 19-28.

Cristofalo, V. J., and Kritchevsky, D. 1966. Respiration and glycolysis in the human diploid cell strain WI-38, *J. Cellular Comp. Physiol.*, 67, 125-132.

Cristofalo, V. J., and Kritchevsky, D. 1969. Cell size and nucleic acid content in the diploid human cell line WI-38 during aging. *Med. Exp.*, 19, 313-320.

Cristofalo, V. J., Opalek, A. A., and Baker, B. L. (in prep.)

Cristofalo, V. J., Parris, N., and Kritchevsky, D. 1967. Enzyme activity during the growth and aging of human cells *in vitro*. *J. Cellular Physiol.*, 69, 263-271.

Cristofalo, V. J., and Sharf, B. B. 1973. Cellular senescence and DNA synthesis. *Exp. Cell Res.*, **76**, 419-427.

Cudkowicz, G., Upton, A. C., Shearer, G. M., and Hughes, W. L. 1964. Lymphocyte content and proliferative capacity of serially transplanted mouse bone marrow. *Nature*, **201**, 165-167.

Danes, B. S. 1971. Progeria: A cell culture study on aging. *J. Clin. Invest.*, **50**, 2000-2003.

Daniel, C. W., 1972. Aging of cells during serial propagation *in vivo*. *In*, B. Strehler (ed.), *Advances in Gerontological Research*, Vol. 4, pp. 167-200. New York: Academic Press.

Daniel, C. W., 1973. Finite growth span of mouse mammary gland serially propagated *in vivo*. *Experientia (Basel)*, **29** (11), 1422-1424.

Daniel, C. W., Aidells, B. D., Medina, D., and Faulkin, L. J., Jr. 1975. Unlimited division potential of precancerous mouse mammary cells after spontaneous or carcinogen-induced transformation. *Federation Proc.*, **34**, 64-67.

Daniel, C. W., de Ome, K. B., Young, J. T., Blair, P. B., and Faulkin, L. J., Jr. 1968. The *in vivo* life span of normal and preneoplastic mouse mammary glands: A serial transplantation study. *Proc. Nat. Acad. Sci.*, **61**, 53-60.

Daniel, C. W., and Young, L. J. T. 1971. Influence of cell division on an aging process. *Exp. Cell Res.*, **65**, 27-32.

Danielli, J. F., and Muggleton, A. 1959. Some alternative states of amoeba, with special reference to life-span. *Gerontologia (Basel)*, **3**, 76.

Deamer, D. W., and Gonzales, J. 1974. Autofluorescent structures in cultured WI-38 cells. *Arch. Biochem. Biophys.*, **165**, 421-426.

Dell'Orco, R. T., Mertens, J. G., and Kruse, P. F., Jr., 1974. Doubling potential, calendar time, and donor age of human diploid cells in culture. *Exp. Cell Res.*, **84**, 363-366.

Doljanski, L., Goldschmidt, J., and Hoffman, R. 1937. Etude comparative sur la durée de la période de latence pour la croissance de différents tissus et organes d'une poule adulte *in vitro*. *C. R. Soc. Biol.*, *Paris*, **126**, 744-745.

Duetz, G. H. 1942. Revised tables of maximum exhibition periods for animals in the Philadelphia collection. *Lab. Rep. Zool. Soc. Philadelphia*, **70**, 23.

Earle, W. R. 1943. Production of malignacy *in vitro*. IV. The mouse fibroblast cultures and changes seen in the living cells. *J. Nat. Cancer Inst.*, **4**, 165-212.

Ebeling, A. H. 1913. The permanent life of connective tissue outside of the organism. *J. Exp. Med.*, **17**, 273-285.

Ebeling, A. 1921. Measurement of the growth of tissues *in vitro*. *J. Exp. Med.*, **34**, 231-243.

Ephrussi, B., Scaletta, L. J., Stenchever, M. A., and Yoshida, M. C. 1964. Hybridization of somatic cells *in vitro*. *In*, R. J. C. Harris (ed.), *Cytogenetics of Cells in Culture*, pp. 13-25. New York: Academic Press.

Epstein, C. J., Martin, G. M., Schultz, A. L., and Motulsky, A. G. 1966. Werner's syndrome: A review of its symptomatology, natural history, pathologic features, genetics and relationship to the natural aging process. *Medicine (Baltimore)*, **45**, 177-221.

Epstein, J., Williams, J. R., and Little, J. B. 1974. Rate of DNA repair in progeric and normal human fibroblasts. *Biochem. Biophys. Res. Commun.*, **59**, 850-857.

Federoff, S. 1967. Proposed usage of animal tissue culture terms. *J. Nat. Cancer Inst.*, **38**, 607-611.

Fialkow, P. J., Martin, G. M., and Sprague, C. A. 1973. Replicative life-span of cultured skin fibroblasts from young mothers of subjects with Down's syndrome: Failure to detect accelerated ageing. *Am. J. Human Genet.*, **25**, 317-322.

Flower, S. S. 1931. Contributions to our knowledge of the duration of life in vertebrate animals, I. Fishes. *Proc. Zool. Soc. London*, **4**, 145.

Ford, C. E., Micklem, H. S., and Gray, S. M. 1959. Evidence of selective proliferation of reticular cellclones in heavily irradiated mice. *Brit. J. Radiol.*, **32**, 280.

Gey, G. O., and Gey, M. K. 1936. The maintenance of human normal cells and tumor cells in continuous culture. I. Preliminary report: Cultivation of mesoblastic tumors and normal tissue and notes on methods of cultivation. *Am. J. Cancer*, **27**, 45-76.

Gey, G. O., Svotelis, M., Foard, M., and Bang, F. B. 1974. Long-term growth of chicken fibroblasts on a collagen substrate. *Exp. Cell Res.*, **84**, 63-71.

Goldschmidt, J. 1969. Lifespan of cultured cells in progeria. *Lancet*, **1**, 424.

Goldschmidt, J., Hoffman, R., and Doljanski, L. 1937. Etude comparative sur la durée de la période de latence pour la croissance des tissus embryonnaires et adultes explantés *in vitro*. *C. R. Soc. Biol.*, Paris, **126**, 389-392.

Goldstein, S. 1969. Lifespan of cultured cells in progeria. *Lancet*, **1**, 424.

Goldstein, S. 1971. The biology of aging. *New Engl. J. Med.*, **285**, 1120-1129.

Goldstein, S. 1974. Aging *in vitro*. Growth of cultured cells from the Galapagos tortoise. *Exp. Cell Res.*, **83**, 297-302.

Goldstein, S., and Haslam, R. J. 1973. Cyclic AMP levels in young and senescent fibroblasts: Effects of epinephrine and prostaglandin E_1. *J. Clin. Invest.*, **52**, 35a.

Goldstein, S., and Lin, C. C. 1972. Somatic cell hybrids between cultured fibroblasts from the Galapagos tortoise and the golden hamster. *Exp. Cell Res.*, **73**, 266-269.

Goldstein, S., Littlefield, J. W., and Soeldner, J. S. 1969. Diabetes mellitus and aging: Diminished plating efficiency of cultured human fibroblasts. *Proc. Nat. Acad. Sci.*, **64**, 155-160.

Goldstein, S., and Singal, D. P. 1972. Loss of reactivity of HL-A antigens in clonal populations of cultured human fibroblasts during aging *in vitro*. *Exp. Cell Res.*, **75**, 278.

Goldstein, S., and Trieman, G. 1974. Glucose consumption by early and late passage human fibroblasts during growth and stationary phase. *Experientia*, **31**(2), 177-180.

Good, P. I., and Smith, J. R. 1974. Age distribution of human diploid fibroblasts. *Biophys. J.*, **14**, 811-822.

Hakami, N., and Pious, D. A. 1968. Mitochondrial enzyme activity in "senescent" and virus-transformed human fibroblasts. *Exp. Cell Res.*, **53**, 135-138.

Harris, M. 1957. Quantitative growth studies with chick myoblasts in glass substrate cultures. *Growth*, **21**, 149-166.

Harrison, D. E. 1972. Normal function of transplanted mouse erythrocyte precursors for 21 months beyond donor life spans. *Nature New Biol.*, **237**, 220-222.

Harrison, D. E. 1973. Normal production of erythrocytes by mouse marrow continuous for 73 months. *Proc. Nat. Acad. Sci.*, **70**(11), 3184-3188.

Harrison, D. E. 1975. Normal function of transplanted marrow cell lines from aged mice. *J. Geront.*, **30**, 279–285.

Hart, R. W., and Setlow, R. B. 1974. Correlation between DNA excision repair and life-span in a number of mammalian species. *Proc. Nat. Acad. Sci.*, **71**, 2169-2173.

Haslam, R. J., and Goldstein, S. 1974. Adenosine $3^1 : 5^1$-cyclic monophosphate in young and senescent human fibroblasts during growth and stationary phase *in vitro*. *Biochem. J.*, **144**, 253-263.

Hay, R. J. 1967. Cell and tissue culture in aging research. *In*, B. Strehler (ed.), *Advances in Gerontological Research*, **2**, pp. 121-158. New York: Academic Press.

Hay, R. J., and Strehler, B. L. 1967. The limited growth span of cell strains isolated from the chick embryo. *Exp. Geront.*, **2**, 123-135.

Hayakawa, M. 1969. Progressive changes of the growth characteristics of human diploid cells in serial cultivation *in vitro*. *Tohoku J. Exp. Med.*, **98**, 171-179.

Hayflick, L. 1965. The limited *in vitro* lifetime of human diploid cell strains. *Exp. Cell Res.*, **37**, 614-636.

Hayflick, L. 1966. Senescence and cultured cells. *In*, N. Shock (ed.), *Perspectives in Experimental Gerontology*, pp. 195-211. Springfield, Illinois: Charles C. Thomas.

Hayflick, L. 1970. Aging under glass. *Exp. Geront.*, **5**, 291-303.

Hayflick, L. 1972. Cell senescence and cell differentiation *in vitro*. *In*, H. Bredt and J. W. Rohen (eds.), *Aging and Development, Academy of Science and Literature*, Vol. 4, pp. 1-15. Stuttgart/New York: F. K. Schattauer Verlag.

Hayflick, L. (in preparation).

Hayflick, L., and Moorhead, P. S. 1961. The serial cultivation of human diploid cell strains. *Exp. Cell Res.*, **25**, 585-621.

Hayflick, L., and Moorhead, P. S. 1962. Cell lines from non-neoplastic tissue. *In*, P. L. Altman and D. S. Dittmer (eds.), *Growth*, pp. 156-160. Washington, D.C.: Federation of American Societies for Experimental Biology, Biological Handbook Series.

Hayflick, L., and Pleibel, N. (in preparation).

Hoffman, R. S., Goldschmidt, J., and Doljanski, L. 1937. Comparative studies on the growth capacity of tissues from embryonic and adult chickens. *Growth*, **1**, 228-233.

Holečková, E., and Cristofalo, V. J. (eds.) 1970. *Aging in Cell and Tissue Culture*. New York: Plenum Press.

Holland, J. J., Koline, D., and Doyle, M. V. 1973. Analysis of virus replication in ageing human fibroblasts. *Nature*, **245**, 316-318.

Holliday, R. 1972. Ageing of human fibroblasts in culture: Studies on enzymes and mutation. *Humangenetik*, **16**, 83-86.

Holliday, R., and Tarrant, G. M. 1972. Altered enzymes in ageing human fibroblasts. *Nature*, **238**, 26-30.

Houck, J. C., Sharma, V. K., and Hayflick, L. 1971. Functional failures of cultured human diploid fibroblasts after continued population doublings. *Proc. Soc. Exp. Biol. Med.*, **137**, 331-333.

Huang, C. C., Minowada, J., Smith, R. T., and Osunkoya, B. O. 1970. Reevaluation of relationship between C chromosome marker and Epstein-Barr virus: Chromosome and immunoflorescence analyses of 16 human hematopoietic cell lines. *J. Nat. Cancer Inst.*, **45**, 815-829.

Huang, C. C., and Moore, G. E. 1969. Chromosomes of 14 hematopoietic cell lines derived from peripheral blood of persons with and without chromosome anomalies. *J. Nat. Cancer Inst.*, **43**, 1119-1128.

Jennings, H. S. 1945. *Paramecium bursaria*: Life history. V. Some relations of external conditions, past or present, to ageing and to mortality of exconjugants, with summary of conclusions on age and death. *J. Exp. Zool.*, **99**, 15.

Kritchevsky, D., and Howard, B. V. 1966. The lipids of human diploid cell strain WI-38. *Ann. Med. Exp. Biol. Fenniae* (Helsinki), **44**, 343–347.

Krohn, P. L. 1962. Review lectures on senescence. II. Heterochronic transplantation in the study of ageing. *Proc. Roy. Soc.* (London) *Ser. B.*, **157**, 128-147.

Krohn, P. L. (ed.). 1966a. *Topics in the Biology of Aging*. New York: Interscience Publishers, John Wiley.

Krohn, P. L. 1966b. Symposium on Aging, Meeting Report. *Science*, **152**, 391-393.

Krooth, R. S., Shaw, M. W., and Campbell, B. K. 1964. A persistent strain of diploid fibroblasts. *J. Nat. Cancer Inst.*, **32**, 1031-1044.

Kurtz, M. J., and Stidworthy, G. H., 1969. Enzymatic sulfation of mucopolysaccharides as a function of age in cultured rat gut fibroblasts. *Proc. 8th Intern. Congr. Geront.*, *Washington, D.C.*, **II**, 49.

Lefford, F. 1964. The effect of donor age on the emigration of cells from chick embryo explants *in vitro*. *Exp. Cell Res.*, **35**, 557-571.

LeGuilly, Y., Simon, M., Lenoir, P., and Bourel, M. 1973. Long-term culture of human adult liver cells: Morphological changes related to *in vitro* senescence and effect of donor's age on growth potential. *Geron-tologia*, **19**, 303-313.

Lesher, S., Fry, R. J. M., and Kohn, H. I. 1961a. Age and the generation time of the mouse duodenal epithelial cell. *Exp. Cell Res.*, **24**, 334-343.

Lesher, S., Fry, R. J. M., and Kohn, H. I. 1961b. Aging and the generation cycle of intestinal epithelial cells in the mouse. *Gerontologia (Basel)*, **5**, 176-181.

Lesher, S., and Sacher, G. A. 1968. Effects of age on cell proliferation in mouse duodenal crypts. *Exp. Geront.*, **3**, 211-217.

Levine, E. M., Burleigh, I. G., Boone, C. W., and Eagle, H. 1967. An altered pattern of RNA synthesis in serially propagated human diploid cells. *Proc. Nat. Acad. Sci.*, **57**, 431-438.

Lewis, C. M., and Tarrant, G. M. 1972. Error theory and ageing in human diploid fibroblasts. *Nature*, **239**, 316-318.

Lima, L., and Macieira-Coelho, A. 1972. Parameters of aging in chicken embryo fibroblasts cultivated *in vitro. Exp. Cell Res.*, **70**, 279-284.

Lima, L., Malaise, E., and Macieira-Coelho, A., 1972. Effect of low dose rate irradiation on the division potential of chick embryonic fibroblasts. *Exp. Cell Res.*, **73**, 345-350.

Lipetz, J., and Cristofalo, V. J. 1972. Ultrastructural changes accompanying the aging of human diploid cells in culture. *J. Ultrastruct. Res.*, **39**, 43-56.

Lithner, F., and Pontén, J. 1966. Bovine fibroblasts in long-term tissue culture: Chromosome studies. *Intern. J. Cancer*, **1**, 579-588.

Littlefield, J. W. 1973. Attempted hybridizations with senescent human fibroblasts. *J. Cellular Physiol.*, **82**, 129-132.

Macek, M., Hurych, J., and Chvapil, M. 1967. The collagen protein formation in tissue cultures of human diploid strains. *Cytologia* (Tokyo), **32**, 426-443.

McHale, J. S., Mouton, M. L., and McHale, J. T. 1971. Limited culture lifespan of human diploid cells as a function of metabolic time instead of division potential. *Exp. Geront.*, **6**, 89-93.

Macieira-Coelho, A. 1966. Action of cortisone on human fibroblasts *in vitro. Experientia*, **22**, 390-391.

Macieira-Coelho, A. 1970. The decreased growth potential *in vitro* of human fibroblasts of adult origin. *In*, E. Holečková and V. J. Cristofalo (eds.), *Aging in Cell and Tissue Culture*, pp. 121-132. New York: Plenum Press.

Macieira-Coelho, A. 1973. Aging and cell division. *Front. Matrix Biol.*, **1**, 46-77.

Macieira-Coelho, A. 1974. Are non-dividing cells present in ageing cell cultures? *Nature*, **248**, 421-422.

Macieira-Coelho, A., Pontén, J., and Philipson, L. 1966a. The division cycle and RNA-synthesis in diploid human cells at different passage levels *in vitro. Exp. Cell Res.*, **42**, 673-684.

Macieira-Coelho, A., Pontén, J., and Philipson, L. 1966b. Inhibition of the division cycle in confluent cultures of human fibroblasts *in vitro. Exp. Cell Res.*, **43**, 20-29.

Martin, G. M., Ogburn, C. E., and Sprague, C. E. Senescence and vascular disease. *In, Philadelphia Symposium on Aging.* New York: Plenum Press, in press.

Martin, G. M., Sprague, C. A., and Epstein, C. J. 1970. Replicative life-span of cultivated human cells. Effect of donor's age, tissue, and genotype. *Lab. Invest.*, **23**, 86-92.

Massie, H. R., Baird, M. B., and Samis, H. V. 1974. Prolonged cultivation of primary chick cultures using organic buffers. *In Vitro*, **9**, 441-444.

Mattern, M. R., and Cerutti, P. A. 1975. Age dependent excision repair of damaged thymidine from gamma-irradiated DNA by isolated nuclei from fibroblasts. *Nature*, **254**, 450-452.

Mayer, E. 1939. Tissue cell colonies *in vitro. Tabul. Biol. ('s-Grav.)*, **19**, 265-275.

Maynard-Smith, J. 1962. Review lectures on senescence. I. The causes of ageing. *Proc. Roy. Soc.* (London) *Ser. B*, **157**, 115-127.

Medawar, P. B. 1940. The growth, growth energy and ageing of the chicken's heart. *Proc. Roy. Soc.* (London) *Ser. B*, **129**, 332-355.

Merz, G. S., and Ross, J. D. 1969. Viability of human diploid cells as a function of *in vitro* age. *J. Cellular Physiol.*, **74**, 219.

Michl, J., Soukupová, M., and Holečková, E. 1968. Ageing of cells in cell and tissue culture. *Exp. Geront.*, **3**, 129-134.

Michl, J., and Svobodá, J. 1967. RNA turnover and the growth potential of human cells in culture. *Exp. Cell Res.*, **47**, 616-619.

Milisauskas, V., and Rose, N. R. 1973. Immunochemical quantitation of enzymes in human diploid cell line WI-38. *Exp. Cell Res.*, **81**, 279-284.

Moore, G. E., and McLimans, W. F. 1968. The life span of the cultured normal cell: Concepts derived from studies of human lymphoblasts. *J. Theoret. Biol.*, **20**, 217-226.

Moore, G. E., and Sandberg, A. A. 1964. Studies of a human tumor cell line with a diploid karyotype. *Cancer*, **17**, 170-175.

Moorhead, P. S. 1965. Human tumor cell line with a quasi-diploid karyotype (RPMI 2650). *Exp. Cell Res.*, **39**, 190-196.

Moorhead, P. S., Nichols, W. W., Perkins, F. T., and Hayflick, L. 1974. Standards of karyology for human diploid cells. *J. Biol. Stand.*, **2**, 95-101.

Muggleton, A., and Danielli, J. F. 1968. Inheritance of the "life-spanning" phenomenon in *amoeba proteus. Exp. Cell Res.*, **49**, 116-120.

Muggleton-Harris, A. L., and Hayflick, L. Cellular aging studied by the reconstruction of replicating cells from nuclei and cytoplasms isolated from normal human diploid cells. *Exp. Cell Res.*, (in press).

Nienhaus, A. J., de Jong, B., and ten Kate, L. P. 1971. Fibroblast culture in Werner's syndrome. *Hum. Genet.*, **13**, 244-246.

Niewiarowski, S., and Goldstein, S. 1973. Interaction of cultured human fibroblasts with fibrin: Modification by drugs and aging *in vitro*. *J. Lab. Clin. Med.*, **82**, 605-610.

Norwood, T. H., Pendergrass, W. R., and Martin, G. M. 1975. Reinitiation of DNA synthesis in senescent human fibroblasts upon fusion with cells of unlimited growth potential. *J. Cell Biol.*, **64**, 551-556.

Oda, S., and Kamon, H. 1927. *Folia Pharmacol. Japon.*, **6i**, 166.

Olivo, O., and Slavich, E. 1930. *Wilhelm Roux' Arch. Entwicklungsmech. Organ.*, **121**, 408.

Orgel, L. E. 1963. The maintenance of the accuracy of protein synthesis and its relevance to ageing. *Proc. Nat. Acad Sci.*, **49**, 517-521.

Orgel, L. E. 1973. Aging of clones of mammalian cells. *Nature*, **243**, 441-445.

Packer, L., and Smith, J. R. 1974. Extension of the lifespan of cultured normal human diploid cells by vitamin E. *J. Cell Biol.*, **63** (2), A255.

Parker, R. C. 1961. *Methods of Tissue Culture*. New York: Harper & Row.

Pearl, R. 1922. *The Biology of Death*. Philadelphia: J. B. Lippincott.

Petes, T. D., Farber, R. A., Tarrant, G. M., and Holliday, R. 1974. Altered rate of DNA replication in ageing human fibroblast cultures. *Nature*, **251**, 434-436.

Pitha, J., Adams, R., and Pitha, P. M. 1974. Viral probe into the events of cellular (*in vitro*) aging. *J. Cellular Physiol.*, **83**, 211-218.

Pontén, J. 1970. The growth capacity of normal and Rous-virus-transformed chicken fibroblasts *in vitro*. *Intern. J. Cancer*, **6**, 323-332.

Post, J., and Hoffman, J. 1964. Changes in the replication times and patterns of the liver cell during the life of the rat. *Exp. Cell Res.*, **36**, 111-123.

Prescott, D., Myerson, O., and Wallace, J. 1972. Enucleation of mammalian cells with cytochalasin B. *Exp. Cell Res.*, **71**, 480-485.

Press, G. D., and Pitha, J. 1974. Aging changes in uptake of polysaccharides by human diploid cells in culture. *Mech. Age. Dev.*, **3**, 323-328.

Puck, T., Waldren, C. A., and Tjio, J. H. 1966. Some data bearing on the long-term growth of mammalian cells *in vitro*. *In*, P. Krohn (ed.), *Topics in the Biology of Aging*, p. 101. New York: Interscience Publishers, John Wiley.

Reichel, W., Garcia-Bunuel, R., and Dilallo, J. 1971. Progeria and Werner's syndrome as models for the study of normal human aging. *J. Am. Geriat. Soc.*, **19**, 369-375.

Rizet, G. 1953. Sur l'impossibilité d'obtenir la multiplication végétative ininterrompue et illimitée de l'ascomycète, *Podospora anserina*. *C. R. Acad. Sci.* (*Paris*), **237**, 838.

Robbins, E., Levine, E. M., and Eagle, H. 1970. Morphologic changes accompanying senescence of cultured human diploid cells. *J. Exp. Med.*, **131**, 1211-1222.

Rothblat, G., and Boyd, R. 1971. Unpublished data.

Rothfels, K. H., Kupelwieser, E. B., and Parker, R. C. 1963. Effects of x-irradiated feeder layers on mitotic activity and development of aneuploidy in mouse-embryo cells *in vitro*. *Can. Cancer Conf.*, **5**, 191-223.

Ryan, J. M., and Cristofalo, V. J. 1972. Histone acetylation during aging of human cells in culture. *Biochem. Biophys. Res. Commun.*, **48**, 735-742.

Ryan, J. M., and Cristofalo, V. J. 1975. Chromatin template activity during aging in WI-38 cells. *Exp. Cell Res.*, **90**, 456-458.

Ryan, J. M., and Cristofalo, V. J. (in press).

Ryan, J. M., Duda, G., and Cristofalo, V. J. 1974. Error accumulation and aging in human diploid cells. *J. Geront.*, **29**, 616-621.

Ryan, J. M., and Quinn, L. Y. 1971. Nucleohistone content during aging in tissue-culture. *In Vitro*, **6**, 269-273.

Ryan, J. M., and Quinn, L. Y. *In Vitro*. (in press).

Saksela, E., and Moorhead, P. S. 1963. Aneuploidy in the degenerative phase of serial cultivation of human cell strains. *Proc. Nat. Acad. Sci.*, **50**, 390-395.

Saunders, J. W., Jr. 1966. Death in embryonic systems. *Science*, **154**, 604-612.

Saunders, J. W., Jr., and Fallon, J. F. 1966. Cell death in morphogenesis. *In*, M. Locke (ed.), *Major Problems in Developmental Biology*, pp. 289-314. New York: Academic Press.

Schneider, E. L., and Epstein, C. J. 1972. Replication rate and lifespan of cultured fibroblasts in Down's syndrome. *Proc. Soc. Exp. Biol. Med.*, **141**, 1092-1094.

Siminovitch, L., Till, J. E., and McCulloch, E. A. 1964. Decline in colony-forming ability of marrow cells subjected to serial transplantation into irradiated mice. *J. Cellular Comp. Physiol.*, **64**, 23-31.

Simons, J. W. I. M. 1967. The use of frequency distributions of cell diameters to characterize cell populations in tissue culture. *Exp. Cell Res.*, **45**, 336-350.

Simons, J. W. I. M. 1970. A theoretical and experimental approach to the relationship between cell variability and aging *in vitro*. *In*, E. Holečková and V. J. Cristofalo (eds.), *Aging in Cell and Tissue Culture*, pp. 25-39. New York: Plenum Press.

Simons, J. W. I. M., and van den Broek, C. 1970. Comparison of ageing *in vitro* and ageing *in vivo* by means of cell size analysis using a Coulter counter. *Gerontologia*, **16**, 340-351.

Singal, D. P., and Goldstein, S. 1973. Absence of detectable HL-A antigens on cultured fibroblasts in progeria. *J. Clin. Invest.*, **52**, 2259-2263.

Smith, J. R., and Hayflick, L. 1974. Variation in the life-span of clones derived from human diploid cell strains. *J. Cell Biol.*, **62**, 48-53.

Smith-Sonneborn, J., Klass, M., and Cotton, D. 1974. Parental age and life span versus progeny life span in *paramecium*, *J. Cell Sci.*, **14**, 691-699.

Sonneborn, T. M. 1938. The delayed occurrence and total omission of endomixis in selected lines of *Paramecium aurelia*. *Biol. Bull.*, **74**, 76.

Sonneborn, T. M. 1954. The relation of autogamy to senescence and rejuvenescence in *paramecium aurelia. J. Protozool.*, **1**, 38-53.

Soukupová, M., and Hněvkovský, P. 1972. The influence of donor age on the behaviour of human embryonic tissue *in vitro. Physiol. Bohemoslov.*, **21**, 485-488.

Soukupová, M., Hněvkosvký, P. Chvapil, M., and Hruza, S. 1968. Effect of collagenase on the behaviour of cells from young and old donors in culture. *Exp. Geront.*, **3**, 135-139.

Soukupová, M., and Holěcková, E. 1964. The latent period of explanted organs of newborn, adult and senile rats. *Exp. Cell Res.*, **33**, 361-367.

Soukupová, M., Holěcková, E., and Cinnerova, O. 1965. Behaviour of explanted kidney cells from young, adult and old rats. *Gerontologia*, **11**, 141-152.

Srivastava, B. I. S. 1973. Changes in enzymic activity during cultivation of human cells *in vitro. Exp. Cell Res.*, **80**, 305-312.

Stein, G. H. 1975. DNA-binding proteins in young and senescent normal human fibroblasts. *Exp. Cell Res.*, **90**, 237-248.

Stein, G. S., and Burtner, D. L. 1975. Gene activation in human diploid cells. *Biochem. Biophys. Acta*, **390**, 56-68.

Stewart, H. L., Snell, K. C., Dunham, L. J., and Schylen, S. M. 1959. *Transplantable and Transmissible Tumors of Animals.* Washington, D.C.: Armed Forces Institute of Pathology.

Strehler, B. L. 1962. *Time, Cells, and Aging.* New York: Academic Press.

Suzuki, Y. 1925. *Mitt. allg. Path. (Sendai)*, **2**, 191.

Swim, H. E., and Parker, R. F. 1957. Culture characteristics of human fibroblasts propagated serially. *Am. J. Hyg.*, **66**, 235-243.

Thrasher, J. D., and Greulich, R. C. 1965. The duodenal progenitor population. I. Age related increase in the duration of the cryptal progenitor cycle. *J. Exp. Zool.*, **159**, 39-46.

Till, J. E., McCulloch, E. A., and Siminovitch, L. 1964. Isolation of variant cell lines during serial transplantation of hematopoietic cells derived from fetal liver. *J. Nat. Cancer Inst.*, **33**, (4), 707-720.

Todaro, G. J., and Green, H. 1963. Quantitative studies of the growth of mouse embryo cells in culture and their development into established lines. *J. Cell Biol.*, **17**, 229-313.

Todaro, G. J., and Green, H. 1964. Serum albumin supplemented medium for long-term cultivation of mammalian fibroblast strains. *Proc. Soc. Exp. Biol. Med.*, **116**, 688-692.

Tomkins, G. A., Stanbridge, E. J., and Hayflick, L. 1974. Viral probes of aging in the human diploid cell strain WI-38. *Proc. Soc. Exp. Biol. Med.*, **146**, 385-390.

Truitt, A. 1970. Book Review: Aging in Cell and Tissue Culture. *Growth*, **34**, 456-457.

Turk, B., and Milo, G. E. 1974. An *in vitro* study of senescent events of human embryonic lung (WI-38) cells. *Arch. Biochem. Biophys.*, **161**, 46-53.

Walford, R. L. 1969. *The Immunologic Theory of Aging*, p. 169. Baltimore: Williams & Wilkins.

Wang, K. M., Rose, N. R., Bartholomew, E. A., Balzer, M., Berde, K., and Foldvary, M. 1970. Changes of enzymatic activities in human diploid cell line WI-38 at various passages. *Exp. Cell Res.*, **61**, 357-364.

Waters, H., and Walford, R. L. 1970. Latent period for outgrowth of human skin explants as a function of age. *J. Geront.*, **25**, 381-383.

Whitten, J. M. 1969. Cell death during early morphogenesis: Parallels between insect limb and vertebrate limb development. *Science*, **163**, 1456-1457.

Williamson, A. R. 1972. Extent and control of antibody diversity. *Biochem. J.*, **130**, 325-333.

Williamson, A. R., and Askonas, B. A. 1972. Senescence of an antibody-forming cell clone. *Nature*, **238**, 337-339.

Wright, W. E., and Hayflick, L. 1972. Formation of anucleate and multinucleate cells in normal and SV$_{40}$ transformed WI-38 by cytochalasin B. *Exp. Cell Res.*, **74**, 187-194.

Wright, W. E., and Hayflick, L. 1975a. Use of biochemical lesions for selection of human cells with hybrid cytoplasms. *Proc. Nat. Acad. Sci.*, **72**, 1812-1816.

Wright, W. E., and Hayflick, L. 1975b. Contributions of cytoplasmic factors to *in vitro* cellular senescence. *Federation Proc.*, **34**, 76-79.

Wright, W. E., and Hayflick, L. 1975c. Nuclear control of cellular aging demonstrated by hybridization of anucleate and whole cultured normal human fibroblasts. *Exp. Cell Res.*, **96**, 113-121.

Yamanaka, N., and Deamer, D. 1974. Superoxide dismutase activity in WI-38 cell cultures: Effects of age, trypsinization and SV-40 transformation. *Physiol. Chem. Physics*, **6**, 95-106.

Yanishevsky, R., and Carrano, A. V. 1975. Prematurely condensed chromosomes of dividing and nondividing cells in aging human cell cultures. *Exp. Cell Res.*, **90**, 169-174.

Young, L. J. T., Medina, D., de Ome, K. B., and Daniel, C. W. 1971. The influence of host and tissue age on the life span and growth rate of serially transplanted mouse mammary gland. *Exp. Geront.*, **6**, 49-56.

Yuan, G. C., and Chang, R. S. 1969. Effect of hydrocortisone on age-dependent changes in lipid metabolism of primary human amnion cells *in vitro. Proc. Soc. Exp. Biol. Med.*, **130**, 934-936.

4 TISSUE AND ORGAN LEVEL

8
ANATOMIC AND BODY COMPOSITION CHANGES WITH AGING

Isadore Rossman

Montefiore Hospital and Medical Center

INTRODUCTION: SECULAR TRENDS, DIFFERENTIAL SURVIVORSHIP

Much of the literature on human anatomical changes with aging has produced data and conclusions which are to be accepted with some reservations. This derives from the fact that most investigators have been necessarily limited to studies in which a number of age groups are examined at one point in time (cross-sectional analysis) rather than following a cohort for many years (longitudinal analysis). Investigators have generally been aware of the interpretive hazards related to cross-sectional analysis. These are perhaps nowhere more evident than in the reports detailing such readily made basic measurements as height and weight. There seems to be general agreement that if one examines a large number of individuals representing the different decades past maturity, the older ones will be shorter than more youthful ones. Indeed, no adequate series has failed to show this. The presumed loss of height is seen whether the populations are studied on a national basis, such as in Canada (Pett and Ogilvie, 1956), the U.S. (Stoudt, Damon, McFarland, and Roberts, 1965), or France (Marquer and Chamla, 1961), or whether the groups of varying age are assembled on the basis of isolated

criteria such as being veterans (Damon, Seltzer, Stoudt, and Bell, 1972), pilots (Luft, 1973), factory workers (Albrink and Meigs, 1971), or longshoremen (Behnke, 1963). Decreases in stature of 1–3 in. and even more, especially in women, are reported as apparently occurring over the lifetime.

Interpretation of the data is obscured by the well-established fact that there has been an increase in height of the average person in various parts of the world in recent times. The tendency towards progressive increase in height during the twentieth century and even earlier is well known to anthropologists as a secular trend, presumably ascribable to improved environmental conditions, such as nutrition. Apparent shrinkage in height between younger and older persons in a cross-sectional study may partially, even largely, reflect differences which were present at maturity.

The height of American army recruits increased by 0.7 in. between the First and Second World Wars, and a further 0.5 in. between the Second World War and 1958, for a total gain over the 40-year period of 1.2 in. (Karpinos, 1961). Similar increases in height have been demonstrated for French army recruits (ref. in Marquer and Chamla, 1961) and for successive generations of incoming Harvard freshmen (Bowles, 1932; Damon, 1968). The most rapidly occurring intergenerational gap is the 2.1 in. reported by Damon (1965b) for Italian-Americans. Damon (1965a), who did not doubt that people shrink in old age, pointed out nonetheless that the secular increase in height derived from some of the available data could alone explain the 2.4 in. difference between Spanish American War veterans in their 80's and young Americans in their 20's. The possibility of a secular effect on other body proportions is also to be kept in mind, even for such contradictory trends as narrowing of the biacromial diameter coupled with increase in the bicristal (pelvic) diameter with aging. The secular trend toward increased height (and weight) necessarily has repercussions on other kinds of data. Reported decrements in the size of various organs with aging (Rössle and Roulet, 1932; Calloway, Foley, and Lagerbloom, 1965) are to be regarded in the light of the probability that larger human beings have larger internal organs. Relative body size at maturity may well account for the findings of Sato, Miwa, and Tauchi (1970), who reported the mean liver weight of Caucasians at age 50 to be 1814 grams versus 1194 grams for Japanese subjects of similar age.

A further potential difficulty is the factor of differential survivorship. Thus, if it is true that obesity tends to shorten life, a selective survivorship of thin persons would exaggerate the apparent weight loss in late life demonstrable in cross-sectional analysis (cf. Hooton and Dupertuis, 1951). The possibility that other factors may be operative in differential survivorship has hardly been explored. Damon (1965a) raised a similar question regarding height, and one wonders whether being a "pyknic" or "mesomorph" might not also affect survivorship, perhaps through some correlated pathogenic mechanism such as coronary artery disease or hypertension (cf. Damon, 1965c).

Despite the difficulties presented by secular trends and selective survivorship, it would seem that many of the conclusions derived from cross-sectional studies are in fact valid. Important direct validation has come from the small amount of data furnished by the few longitudinal studies described below.

CHANGES IN STATURE

Galton's 1884 data were reevaluated by Ruger and Stoessiger in 1927 and revealed a 1.42-in. shrinkage between the middle years and age 80. In the U.S. Health Examination Survey (Stoudt et al., 1965), average height of males decreased from a maximum of 69.1 in. in the 25-35 group to 65.9 in. in the 75-79 group. Women experienced a similar decline in successive age groups past maturity; the average of 63.8 in. at 18-24 dropped to 61.1 in. at 75-79. Loss in sitting height was the major component in loss of stature, contributing about 1.4 in. to the changes in the males and 2.1 in. in the females. Popliteal height in males, the chief component of which is the tibia, was an inch less at 75-79 than at 25-34, and one-half inch less in the corresponding females. The popliteal height differences presumably reflected the secular trend towards increased height (cf. Hertzog, Garn, and Hempy, 1969).

Perhaps the largest of all such studies is the survey reported by Pett and Ogilvie (1956), in which 23,000 Canadians were weighed and measured between March and October 1953. The maximum average height in males was recorded as 68.3 in. (173.5 cm) in the 25-29 age group; this fell to 65.4 in. (166.4 cm) in the 65 and over group. In females, the maximum average height was 62.8 in. (159.5 cm) in the 20-24 group and dropped progressively to 61.3 in. (155.7 cm) in the 55-64 group and to 60.6 in. (153.9 cm) in the 65 and over group. There was thus almost a 3-in. difference between the young males and the older males and a 2.2-in. difference between the females. Declines in height of the same magnitude (10 cm) were reported in Frenchmen by Marquer and Chamla (1961) and Parot (1961). In the Boston longitudinal study (Damon et al., 1972), initial measurements of the 2,200 healthy male veterans showed them be to somewhat taller, heavier, and more muscular than men in the general population. In cross-sectional terms, decrement in stature with aging is evident with approximately 1-cm drops or more for each decade past 30. Thus, the third decade average mean height of 177.9 ± 5.9 cm fell to 173.7 ± 6.4 cm at 50-59, and 171.9 ± 8.4 cm in the 70+ group. The group of Hutterites reported by Howells (1970) has added value because of the homogeneity of this group. Hutterite males age 20-34 had mean heights of about 171.5 cm; the 50-59 group were some 3 cm shorter; the 65-74 group, 5 cm shorter. The younger women had a maximum height of 158.-159. cm which decreased to around 154. cm in the 55-64 group.

In comparing the different age groups, a factor to be reckoned with is posture. Some older individuals habitually carry themselves with slight flexion at the knees and hips. Stoudt et al. (1965) measured the difference between "normal sitting height" and "erect sitting height"—essentially the change produced by extension of the spine. They found that the difference, "slump," averaged about 1.5 in. in men. The maximum slump, 1.6-1.7 in. in the 18-54 age group, decreased to 1.2 in. at 75-79. This was taken to reflect increased spinal rigidity. On the average, slump was 4.2 percent of the erect sitting height. The increase in height in some Welshmen to age 40 was thought by Miall, Ashcroft, Lovell, and Moore (1967) to be due possibly to more erect posture. In Hutterite females, postural habits seemed to contribute prominently to the shrinkage of height (Howells, 1970).

The comparative aspects of decreased stature in different population groups has been reviewed by Marquer and Chamla (1961). They summarized their overview in Table 1, and the bibliographic references are given in their paper. As can be seen, there is some increase in stature reported in age group 20-40 by some of the investigators, but usually of a minor degree. Decline in stature thereafter is noted in all of the studies over the last 100 years for every racial group, the sole exception being in one group of Yugoslavs (Table 1).

Variability in Decrement in Stature

Longitudinal studies have indicated more variability in onset and extent of the decline in stature. Büchi (1950) found an increase in height to occur into the fourth decade in males. The decrease began at about the age of 47 and amounted to 2.9 cm in the past-70 group. Contrary to most reports, an increase in sitting height was found in males to about the age of

55, and in females to the age of 45, in part compensating for a continuing decrease in lower extremity length found in both sexes from 20 on. Damon (1965a) reported that only 27 of 187 Columbia College men showed any degree of height loss between mean ages 18-19 and 56, and that the net difference for the whole group was a *gain* of 1.62 ± s.e. 0.13 cm. Damon noted that ". . . cross-sectional studies would lead one to expect an appreciable decrement by age 56." In the study of Gsell (1967), some individuals still grew 1 cm after their 25th year; after age 30, body length generally tended to decrease, with an average loss over the first 10 years of 6 mm. By the fifth decade, the decrement was 14 mm, and during the sixth decade, 17 mm. Thus the Gsell study differs from the Büchi study as to age of onset of statural decline, though both dealt with Swiss subjects. A similar difference between two related groups was demonstrable in the longitudinal study of Miall et al. (1967). They compared a group from a mining community, the Rhondda Fach, with another Welsh group in the Glamorgan Vale. There was a slight decline in height of the women in both communities from age 25 to 45 (0.3 to 0.7 cm). By age 45, though Rhondda men would be 0.4 cm shorter, Vale men would be 0.6 cm taller, and their decline in height became apparent only after 55. By age 70, Vale men would be 1.7 cm, Rhondda men 3.6 cm, Vale women 3.5 cm, and Rhondda women 4.3 cm shorter than they had been at age 25 (Figure 1). The increase in height in the 30's and beyond reported in some of these studies may be due, as Büchi (1950) thought, to swelling of the intervertebral discs, or more likely, to an enlargement of individual vertebrae as reported by Israel (1973a). In this connection one notes that Allbrook (1956) demonstrated a 5 mm increment in the total height of lumbar vertebrae in the 25 to 45 age period in male East African skeletons.

The relative constancy of long bone measures has been used to reconstruct height at maturity. Trotter and Gleser (1951) showed that though adult stature decreased with aging, femur length remained fairly constant. In a later study (Merz, Trotter, and Peterson, 1956), mean femur length was 46.2 cm at 18-29 and 46.0 cm at 80-87 for white males; in white females, it

TABLE 1. AGE-RELATED CHANGES IN STATURE REPORTED FOR VARIOUS RACES AND GROUPS. (REFERENCES IN MARQUER AND CHAMLA 1961)

Populations	Age-related change pattern (20, 30, 40, 50, 60, 70, 80, 90 yr)	Increase in %	Decrease in %
Whites			
Icelanders (Hannesson, 1935)	= = = = = = = – – – – – –	0	3.5
Irish (Hooton and Dupertuis, 1951)	+ + + = = – – – – – – – – –	0.3	4.3
Alsatians (Pfitzner, 1899)	+ + + + + – – – – – – – – – –	0.3	3.1
French (Bertillon)	+ + + – – – – – – – – →	0.7	2.4
(Parot, 1959)	= = = = = – – – – – – – –	0	5.9
(Marquer and Chamla, 1961)	– – – – – – – – – – – – –	0	5.8
Belgians (Quételet, 1871)	+ + + = = = = – – – – – – –	0.9	4.5
Swiss (Büchi, 1950)	+ + + + = = = – – – – →	1	1
(Hulse, 1957)	← – – – – →	0	1.3
(Kaufmann, Hägler and Lang, 1958)	– – = = – – – – – – – →	0.6	5.2
Germans (Mühlmann, 1927)	+ + + = = = = – – – – – – –	0.9	4.5
Yugoslavs (Skerlj, 1957)	– – – – – + +	2.3	2.7
Hungarians (Bartucz, 1917)	+ + + – – – – – – – – – –	0.7	3
Poles (Kopernicki, 1885)	+ + + – – – – – – –	1.5	0.7
Russians (Jarcho, 1935)	= = = = = – – →	0	1.3
Jews, Russian (Weissenberg, 1895)	+ + + – – – – – – – – –	0.6	1.3
Armenians (Jarcho, 1935)	– – – – – – →	0	0.7
Albanians (Coon, 1950)	+ + + + + – – – – – →	0.4	1.8
Sicilians (Boas, 1935)	– – – – – – – – –	0	0.6
Cypriots (Buxton, 1920)	+ + + + + = = – –	0.5	2.2
Canadians (Pett and Ogilvie, 1956)	– – – – – – – →	0	3.6
Whites, USA (Lee and Lasker, 1958)	– – – – – – – – →	0	3.9
(Hrdlicka, 1925)	+ + + + + – – – →	0.5	0.5
Yellow			
Kirghiz (Jarcho, 1935)	+ + + + + – – →	0.3	0.1
Uzbeks (Jarcho, 1935)	+ + + + + – – →	0.6	0.7
Eskimo (Sutherland, 1856)	+ + + – – →	0.6	
Iroquois (Gould, 1869)	+ + + + + →	1.4	
Indians, Pueblo (Hrdlicka, 1935)	= = = = = = = – – →	0	0.3
Indians, Mexican (Lasker, 1953)	+ + + + + – – – →	0.6	2.6
(Goldstein, 1943)	– – – – – – – →	0	2.4
Chinese (Drooglever, 1952)	+ + + – – – –	1.2	2.6
Japanese (Takahashi and Atsumi, 1955)	– – – – – – – – –	0	7.5
Javanese (Drooglever, 1952)	= = = = = =	0	0
Blacks			
Blacks, USA (Herskovits, 1927)	– – – – – – – – – – – –	0	1.5
(Gould, 1869)	+ + + = = – – →	2.1	0.1
Mixed			
Hawaiians (Sullivan and Wissler, 1927)	+ + + – – – – – – – – – →	1.3	6.2

Keys: + increase
  – decrease
  = no change
  → insufficient further data

From Marquer and Chamla, 1961.

was 42.9 cm in the youngest, 42.5 cm in the oldest groups (Table 2). Hertzog, Garn, and Hempy (1969) used tibia length as a measure for partitioning the effects of secular trends and aging on adult stature. They derived formulas for predicting height at maturity from measures of tibial length, and age-related shrinkage could be ascertained by subtraction. The methodol-

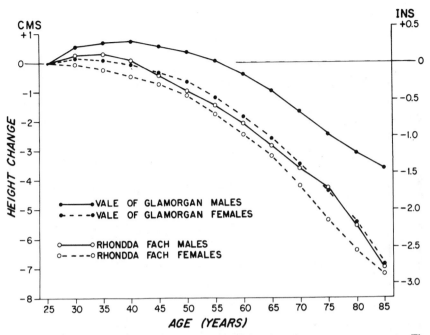

Figure 1. Decrements in height for two groups in Wales, based on remeasurements. The decline appears somewhat earlier and is more marked in the Rhondda Fach (mining area) group, presumably reflecting poorer environmental circumstances. (From Miall *et al.*, 1967.)

ogy was validated for a group of women who had had measurements some decades apart. Both actual and calculated results indicated a decrease of around 1 cm 20-25 years after the initial measurement at age 30, and around 3 cm 30-35 years later. It seems apparent that decline in height may not be as marked or occur as early as older transverse analyses had indicated. Both types of studies agree generally that it will be encountered past 50 and that the rate of decline increases thereafter. The lifetime loss in height in the female is on the order of 4.9 cm, in the male 2.9 cm, with roughly half the decline due to decrease in sitting height.

In addition to individual variability and the sex-related factor, black racial origin may be important with respect to rate of loss in height. Trotter, Broman, and Peterson (1960) found bone density in blacks higher than in whites, and Moldawer, Zimmerman, and Collins (1965) found much less osteoporosis and thus fewer fractures of the lumbar spine and femur in older blacks as compared to whites. In this connection, one notes that an insignificant age-related decrement in the stature of male black

subjects was recorded in the ^{40}K study of Meneely, Heyssel, Ball, Weiland, Lorimer, Constantinides, and Meneely (1963).

CHANGES IN BODY FAT

The body constituent that undergoes major fluctuation past maturity is fat, given circumstances of relatively unhampered access to food. Past maturity, fat can be measured simply by weighing; but at similar weights different individuals vary considerably in fat content, so that density and skin-fold measurements are more accurate (Keys and Brožek, 1953).

Weight

The well-known increase in weight in the middle years followed by a decrease in old age was clear in the U.S. Health Examination Survey (Stoudt *et al.*, 1965). In males the maximum average weight of 172 lb was achieved between 34 and 54 years, followed by decline to 166 lb at 55-64, 160 lb at 65-74, and 140 lb at 75-79. The changes in women were rather different:

TABLE 2. FEMORAL MEASUREMENTS AS RELATED TO AGE, STATURE, RACE, AND SKELETAL WEIGHT.[a]

Cases	Interval	AGE (years)		STATURE (cm)		FEMUR LENGTH (cm)		AREA SHAFT (cm²)		AREA COMPACT (cm²)		% COMPACT (X_5/X_4)		FEMUR WEIGHT (gm)		SKELETON WEIGHT (gm)	
no.		Mean	S.D.	Mean	S.D.	Mean	S.D.	Mean	S.D.	Mean	S.D.	Mean	S.D.	Mean	S.D.	Mean	S.D.
								White male									
4	18–29	21.5	4.4	172.0	12.3	46.2	3.1	60.4	12.4	26.8	7.1	44.2	6.3	364	100	4445	999
8	30–39	35.1	3.4	173.1	10.5	46.2	4.4	68.0	9.1	29.2	2.9	43.5	6.4	388	68	4245	624
9	40–49	44.9	3.0	173.0	7.0	46.2	2.0	70.9	5.6	32.1	4.5	45.6	8.1	435	70	4860	710
9	50–59	55.8	4.0	171.7	4.7	46.1	2.6	68.9	5.5	30.1	3.9	43.6	2.7	395	51	4369	569
9	60–69	66.2	2.3	172.1	4.9	46.3	1.7	71.0	5.1	31.3	4.1	44.0	3.8	415	70	4432	701
8	70–79	73.6	3.3	168.1	2.8	46.3	1.5	69.8	3.1	30.2	3.5	43.3	4.7	410	34	4575	349
8	80–87	82.9	2.5	168.9	7.5	46.0	2.4	69.3	7.5	27.0	3.0	39.1	3.9	358	46	3955	457
55	18–87	56.7	18.8	171.3	7.0	46.2	2.5	69.0	6.9	29.8	4.2	43.3	5.4	398	64	4417	646
								Negro male									
8	18–29	24.1	4.3	174.9	7.0	48.6	3.2	70.2	9.4	29.7	3.3	42.5	2.6	448	71	4915	715
8	30–39	34.2	2.9	178.5	4.4	49.9	2.0	76.2	4.9	33.8	4.7	44.3	4.2	512	65	5621	675
9	40–49	45.7	2.8	170.6	8.4	47.6	4.0	70.2	10.8	31.3	3.6	44.9	3.6	439	94	4882	1009
8	50–59	56.2	2.3	171.4	5.7	48.0	2.1	73.1	7.3	34.2	5.1	46.7	4.1	451	81	4976	890
8	60–69	62.8	3.5	167.9	10.2	48.7	2.1	74.6	8.8	35.8	4.2	47.7	5.5	477	76	4988	480
8	70–79	73.6	3.5	172.8	10.4	48.7	3.5	76.0	11.5	31.5	3.0	42.3	7.4	477	126	5340	946
5	80–91	86.4	4.2	167.8	6.4	46.8	1.8	72.3	4.2	31.0	3.1	43.0	4.0	390	50	4611	832
54	18–91	52.8	19.6	172.2	8.2	48.4	2.8	73.2	8.6	32.5	4.2	44.6	4.9	460	86	5069	822
								White female									
7	17–39	30.0	6.2	163.3	5.0	42.9	2.8	54.5	4.2	22.0	3.0	40.5	5.6	265	38	3197	543
4	40–49	46.5	1.7	161.2	7.8	42.8	2.8	58.9	10.3	20.8	7.1	34.7	6.6	264	105	3002	844
7	50–59	55.0	2.1	164.6	5.8	44.4	1.0	61.5	5.4	24.4	3.8	39.9	5.9	290	58	3320	507
8	60–69	65.0	2.9	158.1	7.4	42.2	2.4	56.4	3.0	18.7	4.0	33.2	7.5	231	31	2984	400
8	70–79	73.0	2.7	161.4	7.8	43.6	2.3	61.3	6.9	17.3	7.0	28.0	11.0	255	67	3022	709
5	80–89	86.4	3.4	153.6	8.3	42.5	2.2	61.9	6.0	11.2	3.7	18.0	4.9	192	51	2182	400
39	17–89	59.4	18.3	160.6	7.4	43.1	2.3	58.9	6.3	19.3	6.1	32.8	10.2	251	62	2989	630
								Negro female									
12	16–29	22.2	3.9	161.6	8.4	43.5	1.9	55.2	5.0	22.8	2.5	41.4	4.8	316	46	3736	487
7	30–39	35.7	3.5	162.1	8.1	44.8	2.9	59.9	6.8	24.8	3.9	41.3	3.0	333	83	4030	790
8	40–49	44.5	2.6	164.4	6.9	46.0	2.3	62.9	6.4	26.4	5.4	42.0	7.8	346	61	3920	646
8	50–59	54.8	3.3	160.0	3.5	43.6	1.4	58.4	3.4	25.6	4.7	43.6	5.9	291	50	3388	443
6	60–69	63.8	2.2	158.8	3.5	43.1	1.5	60.9	5.5	23.4	3.4	38.5	5.3	325	74	3827	656
9	70–79	73.0	3.1	160.0	5.6	44.7	1.9	60.9	3.8	20.8	6.0	33.9	9.1	297	68	3373	634
5	80–91	83.8	4.5	158.4	7.5	44.9	3.2	63.7	6.7	22.8	1.7	36.1	4.4	289	51	3286	612
55	16–91	50.2	20.7	161.0	6.5	44.3	2.2	59.7	5.7	23.7	4.4	39.8	6.7	314	61	3659	628

[a]To be noted: Unchanged length of femur despite decrease in stature, the expansion of shaft, and for white females the marked decline in area of compact with associated decrease in femoral and skeleton weight.
SOURCE: Merz, Trotter, and Peterson, 1956.

the average weight at 25-34 of 136 lb rose progressively to a maximum of 152 lb at 55-65, then dropped to 146 lb at 65-74, and 138 lb at 75-79. Thus in women, weight continued to climb for two decades longer than in men, and the decline in old age was proportionately less. Indeed the 50th percentile for women age 25-34 was 130 lb and for women 75-79, 137 lb. The comparable figures for males were 168 lb at 25-34 and 146 lb at 75-79.

In the Canadian survey of 23,000 individuals (Pett and Ogilvie, 1956), similar weight changes were also seen. In the 10,000 Irish males reported by Hooton and Dupertuis (1951), weight reached a maximum of 164.4 lb at 55-59, fell to 156.6 lb at 70-74, and down to 152.0 lb at 80-94. In the Boston veterans' study (Damon et al., 1972), the mean weight of the veterans in age group 20-29 through 40-49 was 80.1-.2 kg, and this fell by approximately 1.0 kg for each decade thereafter (Figure 5). Parot (1966), who was interested in the question of differential survivorship in relation to height and weight, found for males

of the same heights, that mean value of weight increased to age 50, then decreased. In females, weight increments were relatively higher, reached a maximum later, and decreased after age 70. But where energy expenditures are higher and especially when food supply is restricted, fat gain and weight increase in the middle years do not occur. Bourlière and Parot (1962) in comparing Parisians with a primitive North African Caucasian group, the Kabyles, found the latter showed little change in weight throughout maturity (Figure 2).

Skin Folds

Changes in the skin folds, a measure of the fatty depots, would also be expected to more or less parallel age fluctuations in weight, and in general, skin folds thicken progressively past the third decade. However, in some circumstances, subcutaneous fat may show little of the expected thickening, as in the Kabyles (Figures 2, 3). The same is true of the Cape Verdian Islanders described by Albrink and

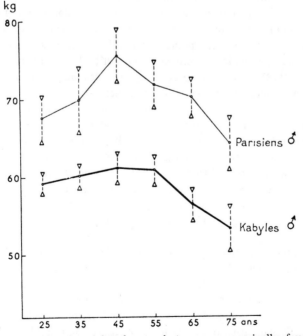

Figure 2. Contrasting age-related weight changes between economically favored Parisians and a North African Caucasian group leading a primitive life (Kabyles). There is but a minimal weight gain in the latter throughout maturity, followed by a decline in old age. (From Bourlière and Parot, 1962.)

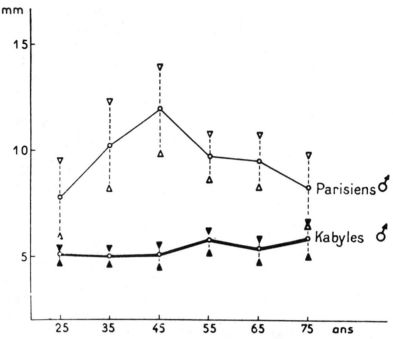

Figure 3. Comparative iliac skinfold changes in the same two groups of men. There is relatively little change throughout the lifetime in the Kabyles.

Meigs (1971), who also show little weight gain or increase in skin-fold thickness with aging and, of more than peripheral interest, have a striking freedom from coronary artery disease. Also in special groups, such as the poorly nourished, indigent male population described by Lee and Lasker (1958), there was no evidence of an age-related increase in skin-fold thickness.

In the typical economic circumstances of Western society, skin-fold measurements increase with aging, falling off only in the seventh or eighth decades but with marked differences between males and females. This was shown for the single skin-fold measurements of the triceps recorded in the Canadian survey of Pett and Ogilvie (1956).

In the Health Examination Survey (Stoudt, Damon, McFarland, and Roberts, 1970), weight and skin folds for U.S. adults were found to be consistently greater than those of Canadian adults. The average right arm skin fold in men did not fluctuate greatly with age but did reach a high of 1.4 cm between 25 and 44 and declined to 1.1 cm at 75-79. In women, the lowest value, 1.8 cm, was found in the youngest age range. It increased stepwise to a high of 2.5 cm at 55-64 and fell to 2.0 cm at 75-79. The infrascapular skin fold in the male also showed little change with age. It averaged 1.3 cm at 18-24, rose to a high of 1.6 cm at 35-65, then fell to 1.3 cm at the oldest ages. In women, infrascapular skin fold showed a mean thickness of 1.8 cm in the youngest group, increased to 2.2 cm at 55-64, and declined to 1.7 cm at 75-79.

Perhaps of more importance are changes in different areas of the body. Ryckewaert, Parot, Tamisier, and Bourlière (1967) emphasized the value of measurements of the subcutaneous skin fold of the back of the hand. This measurement decreased rapidly after 45 in the female, though weight continues to rise; the decrement occurs later in the male (Figure 4). Garn and Young (1956) showed that fat from the upper tibial area started to disappear at around age 45, and Damon et al. (1972) were impressed by the discrepant alterations in triceps and subscapular skin folds with aging. The subscapular skin fold increased slightly from the 20's to the 40's, then remained constant to the 60's, and fell in the 70's to its initial value.

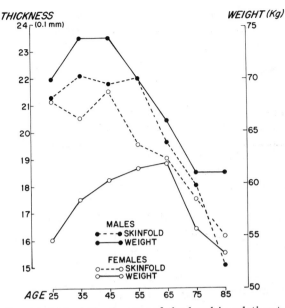

Figure 4. Changes in the skinfold of the dorsum of the hand in relation to age, weight, and sex. The skinfold shrinks earlier in women than in men and has its onset in the middle years despite weight gain. (From Ryckewaert *et al.,* 1967.)

The triceps skin fold remained constant from the 20's to the 50's and then fell; it therefore followed weight more closely than did the subscapular fold (Figure 5). These findings indicate that the subcutaneous fat loss with aging tends to be centripetal: fat is lost earlier and to a greater degree from the extremities and is maintained more consistently and longer on the trunk (cf. Figure 6).

Further evidence that bodily areas undergo variable changes in subcutaneous fat was noted by Parot (1961). He found that in males the maximum thickness of skin folds was attained at around age 45 at the humeral, scapular, iliac, mammillary, and chin areas. However, a continuing thickening occurred in the paraumbilical region up to age 75. Furthermore, in some areas such as the humeral and the iliac, a decline began almost immediately after the maximum had been attained, whereas in other regions there was plateauing for one or more decades. Decrease in thickness of skin folds in the paraumbilical and neck regions did not occur until after 75 years of age (Figure 6). Subcutaneous fat in the female followed a different pattern (Figure 6). The maximum thickness of skin folds occurred by age 45 in

the humeral, iliac, and paraumbilical areas, but increased thickening continued until age 75 in the scapular, mammillary, neck, and chin regions. Most of the skin folds in women tended to remain stationary until around age 65.

In sum, the female could be characterized as showing a greater deposition of fat and a longer maintenance of the thickness of fatty depots. Of the various skin-fold measurements, the humeral (triceps), paraumbilical, and dorsal skin fold of the hand have been singled out by Bourlière (1970) as best correlated with aging.

OTHER ANTHROPOMETRIC CHANGES

A small group of alleged centenarians from the TransCaucasus were described by Basilevich (1958) as having small stature, decreased length of the trunk, relatively long arms with long reach, a rather voluminous thorax, and a decreased circumference of the neck, legs, and thighs. He noted that their faces, noses, and ears were relatively large. Despite skepticism regarding their ages (Medvedev, 1974), many of the observed changes have been corroborated in more extensive anthropometric surveys.

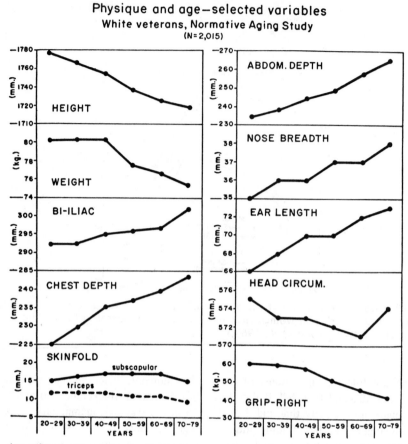

Figure 5. Age-related changes in the Boston veterans group. See text for discussion (From Damon *et al.*, 1972.)

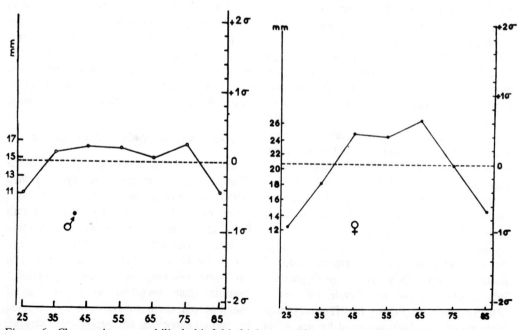

Figure 6. Changes in paraumbilical skinfold thickness with age by sex. The fold is thicker in the female, and its maximum is reached later in life. (From Parot, 1961.)

Similar statural, cranial, and facial changes were noted in Hawaiians by Wissler (1927) and by Hooton and Dupertuis (1951) in a study of 10,000 Irish males with good representation from all of the age groups into the 90's. Other relevant studies are the Health Examination Survey (HES) of Stoudt *et al.* (1970) of 7,710 American individuals, the study of Marquer and Chamla (1961) of 2,089 French males, and the one by Damon *et al.* (1972) of 2,200 American male veterans. Parot's study (1961) included 241 men and 125 women, all clinically healthy, aged 20-90. The study of Howells (1970) contains detailed anthropometric measurements on more than 800 male and female Hutterites, selected as a group of unusual homogeneity. A discussion of the major areas of change follows.

Biacromial Diameter

In Irish males, this declined from a peak average of 38.96 cm at 35-39, to 37.85 cm in the 70-80 group, and to 37.52 cm in the ninth decade. In American males, the average value of 15.8 in. between 18 and 34 was followed by a steady decline to 14.7 in. at 75-79. In women, changes were smaller: the maximum of 14.1 in. at age 35-44 declined to 13.6 in. at 74-79. Similar shrinkages of the biacromial diameter were observed by Marquer and Chamla (1961) and by Parot (1961). Shoulder width includes the deltoid muscles which, like many other muscles, undergo shrinkage with aging. This further accentuates the narrowing in the biacromial diameter.

Chest Changes

Unfortunately, none of the surveys recorded the examinees' extent of smoking which may contribute to "aging changes." However, it seems clear that the chest undergoes an increase in size with aging. Among the Irish males, the chest *diameter* kept rising to a peak, 29.76 cm average at 50-54, with slight diminution in the decades thereafter—to 29.25 cm in the 75-79 group. However, this was followed by a "terminal rise" to 30.15 cm in the oldest group. Chest *depth* also showed a rise throughout the

decades, proceeding from a mean of 22.74 cm at 25-29 to 24.54 cm at 50-54 and 24.66 cm at age 70-74; it remained close to this figure in the older groups. The thoracic index (chest depth times 100 over chest breadth) increased with comparative regularity from the earliest age group through 70-74 with a minimal and obviously not significant drop-off afterwards.

In the U.S. HES, only chest circumference was measured, and results were somewhat different: In males the lowest value of 37.8 in. for chest girth was found in the youngest age group, 18-24 years; the highest was 39.8 in. at 45-54. By 75-79, chest girth had dropped to 37.9 in. American females followed a similar course with chest girth of 32.9 in. at 18-24, followed by a consistent increase to a maximum of 36.2 in. at 55-64. There was then a decline to 34.8 in. in the oldest age group. Marquer and Chamla (1961) found the *width* of the thorax was somewhat less variable in the course of life. It grew until age 25, maintained itself quite stably to 59, and then slowly decreased. *Depth* of the thorax, to the contrary, grew in continuous fashion from 20-24 to 60-64 and then stabilized; it was 3 cm greater in the group aged 75 than in those 20 years of age. In the group studied by Parot (1961), the transverse thoracic diameter in males fell from 27.0 cm at age 25 to 25.5 cm at age 85. This might reflect a secular trend; in the same group the anteroposterior diameter increased from 19.5 cm to 22.4 cm. In the females, transverse diameter fell from 24.4 cm at 25 to 20.7 cm at 85, but again the anteroposterior diameter increased from 17.3 cm to 20.8 cm. It seems clear that an increased anteroposterior diameter of the chest is characteristic of aging and overrides secular trends present in transverse analysis.

Pelvic Changes

In contrast to the narrowing reported for the shoulders, most studies rather uniformly report a *widening* of the pelvis as judged by the bicristal diameter. This diameter was not measured in either the Irish study or the U.S. HES survey. In the French group of Marquer and Chamla (1961), the pelvis seemingly grew progressively from age 20-24 to age 60-64 and

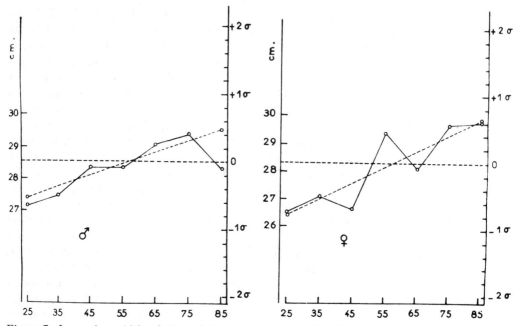

Figure 7. Increasing width of the pelvis in both sexes with aging has been reported by various investigators. (Figure from Parot, 1961.)

then stabilized until the end of life. Parot (1961) reported the bicristal measurement as showing a rise throughout the age span: 27.15 cm in males age 25, peaking to 29.40 cm in males age 75, and averaging 28.33 cm at 85. In women, this diameter rose from 26.52 cm at age 25 to a peak of 29.83 cm in the 85-year-old females (Figure 7). Among the Hutterites, only the measurements of males were available to Howells (1970); they too showed a continued rise throughout life. Though there were too few males available in the age group past 65 to be significant, the widest measurements of all, 32.68 cm average, were recorded in the 75–79 group. A 3.5 percent increase in the bi-iliac diameter in their group of male white veterans was recorded by Damon et al. (1972) (Figure 5).

Damon and others (Howells, 1970; Marquer and Chamla, 1961) have commented on this increment since this is a skeletal dimension not expected to increase with age. An increase in the width of the pelvis with aging is also to be noted in the Midwestern women studied by Ohlson, Biester, Brewer, Hawthorne, and Hutchinson (1956). Similarly, Ries (1967) noted a shrinking biacromial and widening

bitrochanteric diameter to be characteristic of both sexes with aging. This, along with increased fat deposition in the lower abdomen and buttocks, led him to characterize the process as a cranial-caudal redistribution. Damon et al. (1972) refer to a verbal suggestion made by F. S. Hulse, that the change in pelvic diameter might be an unrecognized secular trend, worthy of investigation. However, they were unable to prove this hypothesis in a study of Solomon Islanders.

Extremities

A slight diminution in the length of the extremities is generally ascribed to secular changes in stature rather than to aging. The decreased stature produced by aging would therefore primarily be due to loss of trunk height. Thus, in the white veterans studied by Damon et al. (1972), the sitting height declined by 16 mm from the fifth to the eighth decades, while buttock-knee length declined by 6 mm and knee height by 2 mm. Similarly in the French group of Marquer and Chamla (1961), the length of the lower extremity decreased considerably less than that of the sitting height; the decrease was irregular but also started at age 20–24. In the group studied by Parot (1961), the length of the lower extremities was calculated as the difference between stature and sitting height. In men of 25, it was 81.7 cm with a falloff to 79.8 cm at age 85. In the women, it was 76.65 cm at age 25, falling off to 72.69 cm at age 86. Over the decades this group showed a decline of more than 5 cm in the height of the trunk in the males, and a decline of more than 8 cm in the females, emphasizing that loss in height was due primarily to shrinkage in the trunk. In Büchi's longitudinal study (1950), in which sitting height was found to increase well into the middle years, decrease in the length of the lower extremities was noted even in the youngest group, the rate being maximal in the third decade in the males and in the fourth decade in females. The decline between 20 and 29 was 1.12 percent for males and 0.48 percent for females, and steady declines were recorded thereafter. Büchi ascribed the continuing age-related declines to an ongoing process of shrinkage in the cartilages and flattening of bones in the foot, ascribed to the burden of weight bearing.

Span has been of special interest because of its proportionality to height at maturity. This proportionality was known to the first century Roman, Vitruvius, and was figured in the celebrated drawing of Leonardo da Vinci which related height and span to the geometry of the square and the circle. It has been argued that since span is a measure mostly determined by the length of the arms, it should remain fairly constant, giving a reliable index to height at maturity. Thus Dequeker, Baeyens, and Claessens (1969) noted in a group of women that length exceeded span by 1 cm in the fourth and fifth decades. From the sixth decade on, span exceeded length and was progressively more marked in the older subjects. By the ninth decade, mean span was 8 cm greater than mean body length. Similarly, in elderly hospital subjects, Brown and Wigzell (1964) found mean length/span ratio to be 97.34 at 65–74, 96.70 at 75–84, and 95.15 at 85–94. However, in the Irish males studied by Hooton and Dupertuis (1951), span relative to stature showed relatively minor and insignificant changes, even for the decades where loss in height was occurring. Hooton thought that span, too, was diminishing with age. Büchi (1950) found diminution in span to begin at around 40 and past 65, it amounted to about 2.41 cm in the males and 3.30 cm in the females (Figure 8). In his group, absolute span measures decreased to a greater extent than did height. The differing ratios found by different observers for older age groups may well be due to variability in osteoporosis and loss of trunk height, but clearly span is not a fixed or even relatively fixed body measurement.

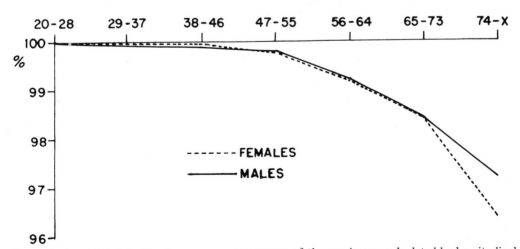

Figure 8. Age-related decline in span as a percentage of the maximum, calculated by longitudinal analysis. The decline is slow in the third to fifth decades, then accelerates. (From Büchi, 1950.)

Facial Changes

Both the ears and the nose become longer with aging, and the nose becomes significantly broader. In the Irish males, age 20-24, mean nose height was 55.22 mm, increased steadily to 57.90 mm at age 65-69, and remained close to this in the older groups. The nose breadth similarly increased from 35.45 mm in the 20-24 group to a maximum of 37.76 mm in the 80-94 group. In the Normative Aging Study (NAS) (Damon et al., 1972), although the circumference, length, and breadth of the head and the length and breadth of the face showed no significant differences over the decades, nose length increased from a mean of 57 mm in the third decade to 59 mm in the 70-plus group. Nose breadth similarly expanded from 35 mm to 38 mm (Figure 5). In the centenarians reported by Basilevich (1958), average nose length was 6.2 cm, width 2.3 cm.

Ears: Hooton and Dupertuis (1951) recorded a progressive thickening of the ear lobe. In the Boston veteran's group, ear length progressed from 66 mm in the youngest group to 73 mm in the oldest, ear breadth from 36 to 39 mm (Figure 5). In the Basilevich centenarian group, 28 percent had an ear length of 8-8.5 cm. In a quarter of the cases, ear length was approximately 5.0-5.5 percent of total body length.

A summary of some of the findings from the NAS aging study is shown in Figure 5. Hooton attempted to distinguish between intrinsic aging changes and changes that might have been brought about by selective survivorship. Table 3 summarized some of his interpretations.

Cranial Changes

The skull exhibits clear evidence of continued change throughout the lifetime, with growth and suture closure extending into old age. These are of further interest in that they cannot be related to weight-bearing or stress, once cited as factors affecting bones elsewhere. Todd and Lyons (1924) found that endocranial suture closure occurred in bursts of activity throughout the life span. There was an initial peak in the third decade, followed by a period of little activity, then by episodes of renewed activity,

TABLE 3. CHANGES IN MEASUREMENTS AND INDICES PROBABLY DUE TO AGING.

Weight: increase to 50; decline from 60.
Stature: increase through 30-34; decline from 40.
Span: increase through 30-34; decline from 40.
Thoracic Index: increase through 70-74.
Biacromial Diameter: increase through 35-39; decline from 55.
Relative Shoulder Breadth: increase through 45-49.
Chest Breadth: increase through 50-54.
Chest Depth: increase through 50-54.
Sitting Height: increase through 35-39; decline thereafter.
Relative Sitting Height: slow decline after 49.
Head Circumference: increase through 35-39; slow decline after 54.
Head Length: increase through 50-54.
Head Breadth: increase to 40 and slight decline thereafter.
Cephalic Index: decline from 35.
Cephalo-facial Index: rise through 75-79.
Total Face Height: increase through 30-34; decline thereafter.
Facial Index: increase through 25-29; decline thereafter.
Upper Face Height: increase through 30-34.
Upper Facial Index: increase through 30-34; decline from 55.
Nose Height: increase through 55-59.
Nose Breadth: increase throughout age groups.

Source: Hooton and Dupertuis, 1951.

with terminations or peaks as late as the seventh, eighth, or ninth decades.

Thus the sphenofrontal suture is three-fourths united by age 30 and remains practically stationary until the final burst of activity in the early 60's. In contrast, the mastooccipital suture only begins to close at about 30 and shows little further change until the 50's, when a second wave of activity occurs. The third and final episode of suture closure takes place at about age 80. Similarly, the parietomastoid suture does not attain complete closure until age 80 or more.

Other growth phenomena also occur relatively late in life. Todd (1924) found a definite tendency of cranial vault thickening to age 60. Ingalls (1931) examined the weight changes in different components of 100 complete skeletons. He found that the cranium increased gradually in weight to about age 35 and then much more rapidly over the next decade. In the following decade, there was a slight loss of weight which was again regained by the late decades. He also noted that the gradual late increase in skull weight occurred despite the loss of numerous teeth and adjacent alveolar bone.

In the study of Boston veterans (Damon et al., 1972), no changes in head dimensions were noted. In Irish males (Hooton and Dupertuis, 1951), head circumference continued to increase to a first mode of 575 mm at 35-39 years. There was then a slight decline, and a second mode of 575 mm was reached at 50-54. Thereafter, there was a small decline attributed to hair loss and shrinkage in the temporal muscles. In his longitudinal study, Büchi (1950) found head circumference to increase continuously in both sexes into his oldest group. The over-65's exhibited a 2.15-2.16 percent increment over those aged 20. There was a similar increase in both breadth and length of the head, the increase in length between the youngest and the oldest groups attaining a mean of 5 mm. In a longitudinal study in which skull sizes were compared after the lapse of 13 to 25 years, Israel (1968) clearly demonstrated an enlargement both of the size of the skull and its thickness. In a more detailed study, Israel (1973b) again presented longitudinal data and x-rays showing a continued growth of the craniofacial complex from early adulthood to later life. All skull diameters increased in thickness, as did endocranial dimensions. There was a disproportionately greater increase in the size of the sella turcica and frontal sinuses (Israel, 1970).

Postmaturational Bone Growth

The existence of continued bone growth past maturity has been demonstrated in many other sites. Using the same roentgenographic material, Israel (1973a) also demonstrated by both longitudinal and cross-sectional methods that an age-associated enlargement of the third cervical vertebra occurred in women through adulthood and into later years. The mean change in height was the increment from 12.06 mm to 12.73 mm over a mean age span of 19.55 years. In two cases, the mean difference in height reached 1.5 mm and in one case, 1.6 mm.

In the data presented by Merz, Trotter, and Peterson (1956) (Table 2), one can discern a significant age-related widening of the femur with age, both in males and females, in spite of the marked decrease in femur weight in older white females characteristic of osteoporosis. This was clear in the femoral radiographs of 2,030 aging women studied by Smith and Walker (1964). They found the femoral diameter at approximately midshaft to progressively increase in each age group from a mean of 31.32 mm at 45-49 to 34.74 mm at 75-90. The increment at the subtrochanteric region was less than half that at midfemur, 1.75 mm, and was only 0.94 mm at the femoral neck. In rib, Epker, Kelin, and Frost (1965) found the mean total cross-sectional area to increase quite consistently with age past maturity, going from 53.07 mm at 20-29 to 59.99 mm at 60-69. This occurred with a concurrent decrease of 23 percent in the amount of cortical bone, and they concluded that the aging change consisted of a negative bone balance at the cortical-endosteal surface which was in excess of a positive balance at the periosteal surface.

The fact that tetracycline is deposited in areas of new bone formation, where it is detectable by fluorescence, enabled Epker and Frost (1966) to demonstrate periosteal appositional bone growth in ribs of individuals of all ages, including one-third of those in their seventh decade. In a study of changes in the second metacarpal in 2,799 subjects using roentgenograms, Garn, Rohmann, Wagner, and Ascoli (1967) demonstrated a gain in width in all populations studied which was continuous over eight decades. This gain was on the order of 4 percent, with increased bone apposition demonstrable in the femur, metacarpal, rib, and cranium at all decades past maturity. Hrdlička's (1936) conclusion comes to mind: "Growth . . . proceeds slowly in some features to the fourth decade, in others to the fifth, and in a few even later. Elements included are stature, various head and face diameters, the chest, hands and feet, especially the mouth, nose and ears".

In Ingalls' (1931) all-male series, cranial weight was highest at 41-49 and remained heavier in the 60-78 group than in the 31-40 group. This diverged from the weight of the ribs, which fell considerably from the fourth decade onwards. In contrast, weight of cervical vertebrae peaked at 41–49, thoracic at 50–59, lumbar at 31–40. Weights of the skeletons as a whole showed no notable reductions except in the 60–78 group.

The study of Merz, Trotter, and Peterson (1956) covers both sexes and both whites and blacks. These authors derived equations for estimating skeletal weight in the living from femoral roentgenograms. For whites of both sexes, only the single variable of area of compact bone was needed. Some of their results are incorporated in Table 2. Skeletal weight declined in the oldest members of the different groups, was more marked in whites than in blacks, and was especially marked in elderly, white females. Also to be noted is that into the eighth decade, skeletal weights in the males of both races did not notably decrease.

Other Skeletal Changes

The skeleton undergoes other complex alterations, often difficult to classify. Though some are regarded as pathologic, e.g., hypertrophic osteoarthrosis, some appear to be inevitable consequences of use. Simultaneously, there may occur a loss of protein matrix and mineral, variously called "senile," "postmenopausal," and even "physiologic" osteoporosis, some degree of which may be an aging phenomenon in the sense of a tissue atrophy universally encountered in old age.

The scapula as described by Graves (1922) and Cobb (1952) illustrates one form of dynamic alteration. It exhibits a variety of changes, including hypertrophic and atrophic, and alterations due to changes in vascular patterns and musculotendinous indentations. By age 50, the number of blood vessels and their size tend to diminish. In old age, formerly regular vascular patterns are in disarray. Graves defined two further processes, one an ossification, the other an atrophy. Ossification involved the cartilage of the glenoid cavity, where it started in one segment of the oval and progressed from the ventral and inferior margins to the dorsal and superior margins.

Atrophic spots, initially minute and discrete, later become merging areas of bone atrophy. Rare under age 45, these become greater in number and size past that age. A further distortion of scapular anatomy is a progressive folding or wrinkling of the formerly relatively smooth surface, mostly of the dorsal aspect. It is first noted to some degree in the early 30's when it often appears as a single, elevated buckle running transverse to the long scapular axis. In old age, besides distortion of formerly regular vascular patterns, musculotendinous attachments become irregular, and areas of atrophy are so common that the bone appears to be spotty or moth-eaten.

Use Changes in Joints

The knee joint is a complicated joint (involving the distal femur, tibial plateau, and patella) and is a good example of the early onset and inevitability of aging. Keefer, Parker, Myers, and Irwin (1934) described the first anatomic changes in the knee as beginning in the fourth decade in both sexes and progressing with age.

Aging in the knee joint is the subject of a monograph by Bennett, Waine, and Bauer (1942). Joints from five individuals between 10 and 19 had macroscopic abnormalities of some articular surface. By the third decade, the patellas in 5 of 7 joints showed linear irregularities with thin strips or shreds of superficial cartilage partially detached. Similar but less marked changes were found on the patellar surface of the femurs, but there were only slight degenerative changes in the femoral and tibial condyles. By the fourth decade, the degree of damage markedly increased, and further progression occurred in the succeeding decades. It is interesting that roentgenograms were often negative when joint changes were marked. In the eighth decade, peripheral lipping became marked. The oldest joint, that of a 90-year-old male, showed flattening and eburnation of tibial and femoral condyles, decalcification of semilunar cartilages, and bony hypertrophy of the periarticular margins of the tibia, fibula, and patella. Despite individual variability, there was no doubt of an age-related progression of changes in the joint (Figure 9).

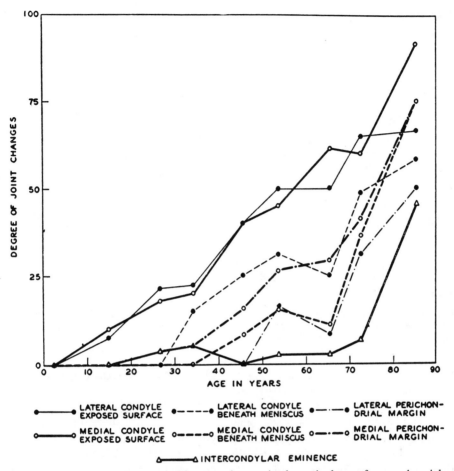

Figure 9. Average degenerative and proliferative changes in the articular surfaces and perichondrial margins of the tibia at each age decade. Changes are apparent in the second decade. A marked increment occurs after the sixth decade. (Figure from Bennett, Wayne, and Bauer, 1942.)

Proliferative Joint Changes

Proliferative bone changes about joints may occur in response to infection, unusual stress, or degeneration in the cartilage. Genetic factors play a role, as in the hypertrophic osteoarthrosis that occurs in the distal finger joints (Heberden's nodes) and more proximal joints (Bouchard's nodes). According to Stecher (1965), Heberden's nodes in women have an 0.4 percent in the 30's and rise to 30 percent in the ninth decade. About 3 percent of males are affected. He thought this condition was due to a single autosomal gene, dominant in women, recessive in males, independent of, and unrelated to other types of osteoarthritis.

The vertebral column exhibits osteoarthritic changes with aging to such a predictable degree as to give it some value as a criterion for age (Nathan, 1962; Howells, 1965). As is indicated in Figure 10, changes are more marked in the more mobile portions of the spine, the cervical and lumbar, and less marked in the intervening thoracic section. Willis (1924) examined the lumbar spine in 625 spinal columns and found hypertrophic proliferative changes related both to aging and to "types" of columns which he divided into slender, average, and heavy. In general, the changes were more severe and appeared earlier in the heavy than in the slender columns.

Friedenberg, Edeiken, Spencer, and Tolentino (1959) and Friedenberg and Miller (1963) in radiologic studies found that 25 percent of

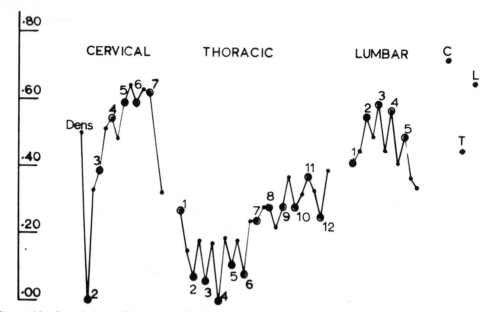

Figure 10. Correlation of vertebral lipping with age. Circled points identify the upper border of a vertebral body. At the right are shown the correlations with age of the mean values for each region. (From Howells, 1965.)

asymptomatic individuals had degenerative changes in their cervical spines by the fifth decade and 75 percent by the seventh decade. DePalma and Rothman (1970) also found degeneration of cervical discs closely associated with aging. The majority of spines after the fourth decade showed implication of one or more discs, and after the fifth decade there was a sharp rise in the severity of degenerative processes. The C5–C6 level was most frequently involved, followed by C6–7.

A high statistical correlation was noted between disc degeneration and posterior osteophyte formation, with anterior osteophyte formation not as closely related. The localization of change is explained by radiological studies (Penning, 1964) which demonstrated clearly that the most mobile joints in the cervical spine are at the C5 and C6 levels.

Howells (1965) concluded that ". . . with the greater experience of movement and stress in the neck and lumbar region, the 'age' effect supervenes, overlying individual proneness to osteophytosis, and induces increased arthritic development in these regions with advancing age." Thus in select skeletal areas, age and use, with degenerative and proliferative changes, are inseparably bound together.

BODY COMPOSITION CHANGES

The various morphological and anthropometric changes discussed above suggest that body composition must undergo major changes with aging. Increasing skin folds, decreasing muscle mass, and alterations in skeletal weight all suggest that water, fat, and mineral changes are to be anticipated. Changes in the viscera are also involved. It has long been known that the organs of healthy older people are smaller (Rössle and Roulet 1932; Calloway, Foley, and Lagerbloom, 1965). Table 4 from Calloway, Foley, and Lagerbloom (1965) illustrates the decrement. Calloway points out the many difficulties involved in the interpretation of this data, such as secular trends, selective survivorship, and various causes of mortality. Unequivocal proof of organ shrinkage in old age does not exist for man since longitudinal analysis feasible by noninvasive methods has not been done. Indeed for some organs of clinical interest, the prostate, lungs, and heart, enlargement is common. Shrinkage of the ovaries and uterus postmenopausally may be considered as special instances of hormone withdrawal regression. But in a number of organs, shrinkage seems evident: in the brain this is indicated by the

TABLE 4. WEIGHT OF ORGANS BY AGE GROUPS AT AUTOPSY.[a]
Organ Size and Age of Subject—Absolute Weights (Average) and Percentages of Body Weights (BW); Vascular Widths

	AGE 20's		AGE 30's		AGE 40's		AGE 50's		AGE 60's		AGE 70's		AGE 80's		AGE 90's	
	AVG.	% BW	AVG.	% BW	AVG.	% BW	AVG.	% BW	AVG.	% BW	AVG.	% BW	AVG.	% BW	AVG.	% BW
Age (yrs)	25.4		35.2		45.2		56.0		64.5		73.3		83.8		92.0	
Adrenal R & L (gm)	24.8	0.03	15.3	0.02	15.4	0.02	25.1	0.04	16.7	0.02	19.6	0.03	14.6	0.02		
Aorta, abd. (width, mm)	30.5		33.5		38.3		42.2		42.4		52.0		48.8		48.0	
Aorta, thor. (width, mm)	37.0		46.5		51.0		52.1		53.8		61.3		65.8		55.0	
Brain (gm)	1325	1.8	1399	1.8	1233	1.8	1350	2.1	1300	1.9	1270	2.0	1198	1.8		
Heart (gm)	345	0.46	466	0.59	429	0.62	425	0.65	444	0.64	463	0.72	369	0.56	390	0.64
Kidney, L (gm)	177	0.24	200	0.26	186	0.27	180	0.28	177	0.26	149	0.23	145	0.22	110	0.18
Kidney, R (gm)	163	0.22	181	0.23	174	0.25	166	0.25	173	0.25	146	0.23	138	0.21	105	0.17
Liver (gm)	1855	2.5	1929	2.5	1662	2.4	1625	2.5	1569	2.3	1398	2.2	1273	1.9	1000	1.6
Lung, L (gm)	513	0.68	601	0.77	572	0.83	605	0.93	575	0.83	539	0.83	612	0.93	690	1.1
Lung, R (gm)	525	0.7	780	0.99	634	0.92	692	1.1	706	0.0	640	0.99	722	1.1	690	1.1
Pancreas (gm)	96.8	0.13	113	0.14	108	0.16	116	0.18	112	0.16	105	0.16	103	0.16	110	0.18
Pituitary (gm)[b]	0.6	0.8	0.5	0.64	0.77	1.1	0.734	1.1	0.72	1.0	0.69	1.1	0.7	1.1		
Prostate (gm)	22.3	0.03	46.3	0.06	28.0	0.04	26.2	0.04	40.6	0.06	52.9	0.08	50.4	0.08		
Spleen (gm)	199	0.27	214	0.27	157	0.23	164	0.25	184	0.27	138	0.21	120	0.18	95	0.16
Testes (L & R) (gm)			35.7	0.05	32.3	0.05	40.8	0.06	42.1	0.06	45.3	0.07	32.9	0.05		
Thyroid (gm)			25.5	0.03	23.2	0.03	53	0.08	32.6	0.05	26.2	0.04	29.5	0.05		
Ventricle wall, L (mm)	16		16.9		17		18.2		18.5		17.9		18.8		17	
Ventricle wall, R (mm)	3.6		3.7		3.7		4.6		4.9		4.6		3.8		3	
Height (ins.)	69.1		70.1		67.9		67.5		67.3		66.1		66.2		64.5	
Weight (lbs.)	165		173		152		144		153		143		145		135	

[a]Note declines in absolute weights of brain, kidney, liver, spleen (cf. Figure 14). See text for discussion.
[b]Percentage of body weight, $\times 10^{-3}$.
SOURCE: Calloway, Foley, and Lagerbloom, 1965.

frequent increase in the size of the ventricles, and in the kidney a longitudinal decline in function to some extent mirroring the anatomical shrinkage is well documented (cf. Chapter 16 in this volume). The clearest evidence comes from animal studies and bears out the existence of a "senile atrophy" for both musculature and internal organs (Tauchi, 1961; Tauchi, Tsuboi, and Okutomi, 1971).

Body Water

Since most of the body water is intracellular, determinations of the total body water (TBW) gives some insights into the possibility of tissue shrinkage. This was done for all the age groups from infancy to old age by Edelman, Haley, Schloerb, Sheldon, Friis-Hansen, Stoll, and Moore (1952). TBW was measured by an injection of deuterium oxide, with which a distribution equilibrium occurs in approximately 2 hours. Their results are summarized in Table 5 for normal males and Table 6 for normal females. It is apparent that there is a drop with aging in the TBW calculated as the percent of body weight—from 61.1 percent in younger men to 54.3 percent in the older

group. The decline is attributable to a rise in body fat, but also, as noted below, reflects a decline in the lean body mass. In females in the third decade, TBW represented 51.2 percent of body weight and decreased to 46.2 percent in old age. Of interest is the lower percentage of TBW of the female at all ages past puberty, indicative of a constantly higher fat content than the male. Fryer (1962) found the percentage of TBW in men age 60 to over 80 to be 50–54 percent of body weight, which is in agreement with the results of Edelman et al. (1952). Since adipose tissue, which contributes most to fluctuations in body weight in normal adults, is low in water (only 14 percent) (Keys and Brožek, 1953), TBW is a good index to the lean or fat-free body mass. Thus, it has been shown by Rathbun and Pace (1945) that the percent fat of the body could be calculated by the formula

$$\% \text{ Fat} = 100 - \frac{\% \text{ H}_2\text{O}}{0.732}$$

It appears that the decline in the ratio of TBW to body weight in aging mirrors a rise in the relative proportion of fat to lean body mass.

TABLE 5. SUMMARY OF TOTAL BODY WATER DATA AS A FUNCTION OF AGE IN NORMAL MALES.

No. subjects	Age, range in years	Weight kgms.	Surface sq.m.	Total body water, liters		TBW per body wt. percent body wt.		TBW per surf. area, liters/sq.m.	
				Mean	Range	Mean	Range	Mean	Range
9	10.5–15.6	46.8	1.42	27.9	19.0–44.3	59.0	51.8–63.2	19.2	15.7–24.1
34	17–34	72.6	1.89	44.1	39.9–54.0	61.1	53.3–70.3	23.3	21.2–26.1
10	35–52	79.4	1.97	43.8	35.4–52.0	55.4	44.7–64.1	22.2	20.0–24.6
6	57–86	70.7	1.88	38.1	34.9–40.5	54.3	47.8–62.8	20.8	19.7–22.5

From Edelman *et al.*, 1952.

TABLE 6. SUMMARY OF TOTAL BODY WATER DATA AS A FUNCTION OF AGE IN NORMAL FEMALES.

No. subjects	Age, range in years	Weight kgms.	Surface sq.m.	Total body water, liters		TBW per body wt. percent body wt.		TBW per surf. area, liters/sq.m.	
				Mean	Range	Mean	Range	Mean	Range
6	12–15	44.6	1.42	25.0	20.1–29.7	56.2	49.8–59.5	17.6	16.0–19.4
18	20–31	57.9	1.64	29.4	22.0–36.0	51.2	45.6–59.9	18.0	15.3–20.0
6	36–54	58.8	1.59	28.3	25.8–33.0	48.2	40.5–54.3	17.7	16.2–19.5
5	60–82	61.5	1.61	28.4	25.1–32.5	46.2	42.0–53.4	17.1	16.1–18.2

From Edelman *et al.*, 1952.

Specific Gravity Changes

Alterations in fat content might be expected to change specific gravity (sp. gr.) determinations of the body throughout the life span. This would follow from the fact that the only body tissue lighter than water is fat. Direct determinations by Pace and Rathbun (1945) revealed for the guinea pig that its fat had a sp. gr. of 0.912 and that the sp. gr. of the whole fat-free guinea pig was 1.0934. From this they derived an equation for percentage of fat, F = 5.135/sp. gr. – 4.694. Using the values of 1.10 as the density of the fat-free human body (found by Behnke, Feen, and Welham, 1942) 0.918 as the sp. gr. of human fat, Pace and Rathbun derived the formula %F = 100 (5.548/sp. gr. – 5.044) for the prediction of the percentage of fat in the human body from a sp. gr. determination. The formula was slightly modified by Keys and Brožek (1953) and Brožek, Grande, Anderson, and Keys (1963) and yields slightly lower percentage figures for body fat. The body volume is calculated by the Archimedean principle of underwater weighing, with a correction for residual air. It is well recognized that this correction increases with aging (Brožek and Keys, 1953; Fryer, 1962; cf. Brožek 1968).

With the fat gain that characteristically occurs in the mature years, a decline in sp. gr. is observed. Thus, in the study of men by Brožek (1952), five age groups were represented: 20.3, 25.2, 46.0, 50.0, and 54.6. Their sp. gr. steadily declined, and the corresponding fat percentages calculated by the method of Rathbun and Pace were respectively 9.9, 14.4, 22.2, 24.0, and 25.2. Of the various skin-fold measurements taken, all of which increased, those from the chest showed the closest parallel to rising fat content. In a corresponding study on women done by Brožek, Chen, Carlson, and Bronczyk (1953), 62 women in three groups with mean ages of 24.2, 39.1, and 56.0 were studied. The sp. gr. showed a marked linear decrement with age, with values of 1.0459, 1.0336, and 1.0218 corresponding to 26.1, 32.4, and 38.8 percent of body fat by the Rathbun and Pace formula.

Sixty older subjects were studied by Fryer

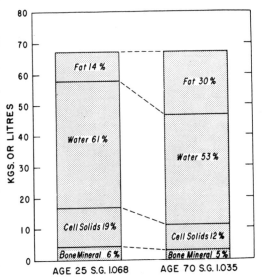

Figure 11. A comparison of major body components and their changes with aging for "reference males" ages 25 and 70. (From Fryer, 1962.)

(1962), who concluded that the mean sp. gr. for men underwent a linear decline from the region of 1.080 at age 20, to 1.033 at around 70. The decrement was roughly 0.01 sp. gr. unit per decade past maturity. At around the eighth decade, the sp. gr. tended to plateau, either because the age-related change in sp. gr. had ended or because of differential survivorship. Fryer noted that the decline in sp. gr. could not be due to rising fat content alone and that there was a discrepancy in the use of the formula of Brožek relating skin-fold measurements to sp. gr. in his older group. He thought this might be explainable by the fact that subcutaneous fat decreased with age and therefore lowered skin-fold measurements, while "internally" situated fat might rise. In conjunction with data for body water, he constructed a diagram (Figure 11) for a hypothetical reference man, aged 70, to be contrasted to the reference man, aged 25, constructed by Brožek (1954).

Multiple Isotope Studies

Study of body composition by injection of isotopes reached a high level in the hands of Moore and his collaborators. Their wide-ranging findings, both in health and disease, are discussed in detail in *The Body Cell Mass and its Supporting Environment* (Moore, Olesen,

McMurrey, Parker, Ball, and Boyden, 1963). In addition to the age-related changes of body water noted above in the work of Edelman et al., (1952), Moore and coworkers, demonstrated an age-related decline in exchangeable potassium using the injectable isotope ^{42}K. Moore promulgated the concept of ^{42}K as a measure of *body cell mass*. This was initially defined as the skeletal muscle and visceral parenchyma cells, to distinguish it from the following two concepts: *fat-free body*, which contains such supportive elements as bone, tendon, collagen, etc.; and the *lean body mass*, regarded as the adipose-tissue-free body still with its structural cellular lipid, and some supportive elements. The body cell mass was defined by Moore as using oxygen, burning calories, emitting creatinine, (or to use his phrase "the engine of the body," in contrast to supporting structures such as bone, which were defined as "the chassis"). Despite their lack of clear definition histologically, functionally, or biochemically, all three concepts (i.e., body cell mass, fat-free body, and lean body mass) are still current.

Moore and coworkers showed that the total exchangeable potassium (Ke) as a function of body weight declines with advancing age. In normal males age 31-60, Ke was 45.1 meq/kg, in males age 61-90, Ke was 37.3 meq/kg (Moore et al., 1963). In the female, reflecting a lower muscle to fat proportion, the figures were lower: age 31-60, 34.2 meq/kg, age 61-90, 29.7 meq/kg (Moore et al., 1963). With declines in body water and exchangeable potassium both age-related, Moore concluded that the body cell mass diminished with aging.

Macgillivray, Buchanan, and Billewicz (1960) gave ^{24}Na and ^{42}K to 52 females aged 16 to 76 and found the K/kg weight ratio to decrease from 44.0 at 25-29 to 33.5 in those over 60. There was a rising Na/K ratio with age as indicated:

Age	Na/K
30–34	0.953
35–39	1.026
40–44	1.077
45–49	1.103
50–59	1.169
60 and over	1.208

TABLE 7. PERCENT DIFFERENCES IN WEIGHT ANALYSES BETWEEN 70-YEAR-OLD AND 30 TO 40-YEAR-OLD HUMAN TISSUES.

Constituent	Kidney	Liver	Spleen	Psoas muscle	Heart	Average of tissues
H_2O	+ 2.6	+ 1.7	+ 2.8	+ 0.8	− 1.4	+ 2. XH
Cl[a]	+ (2)	+(18)	+(12)	+(56)	+(25)	+(23)
Total Base	+ 3.	+ 12.	+ 4.	+ 6.	+ 7.	+ 7.
Na	+ 5.	+ 15.	+ 21.	+ 62.	+ 0.3	+ 20.
Ca	+60.	+ 4.	+ 14.	+ 33.	+ 31.	+ 38.
K	−19.	+ 6.	− 13.	− 7.	− 9.	− 12. XL
Mg	− 9.	+ 17.	− 10.	− 11.	− 2.5	− 8. XL
P	−13.	− 0.1	− 8.	− 12.	− 2.	− 9. XL
N	− 9.	+ 8.5	− 13.	− 3.	− 4.	− 7. XL
Ash	−11.	+ 1.	− 8.	− 1.	0.	− 5. XL

[a]The chloride values are less accurate than the other values in this table.
XH signifies that the average for the tissues does not include the heart.
XL signifies that the average for the tissues does not include the liver.
SOURCE: Simms and Stolman, 1937.

This demonstrates, as Moore has shown, a rise in the ratio of extracellular to intracellular components. These isotope studies are thus in agreement with the chemical analyses of Simms and Stolman (1937), who found rises in sodium and declines in potassium in muscle and viscera of older individuals (Table 7).

Measurement of ^{40}K

An important advance over "exchangeable potassium" by the isotope dilution principle was the development of a technology for the direct measurement of ^{40}K and thus total body potassium. ^{40}K is a gamma emitter which represents 0.0118 percent of all potassium, which can function as a naturally occurring tracer. The various methods have yielded somewhat differing results, and some studies indicate that the ^{42}K dilution method measured only about 92 percent of the body's total potassium (Miller and Remenchik, 1963; Remenchik, Miller, and Kessler, 1968). Methodologies for measuring the body's metabolic mass are reviewed by Parot (1969).

The study of Meneely et al. (1963) deals with 915 normal subjects, representing a sample of the population of Nashville, Tennessee. Past maturity, a rise in total body weight (TBW) due to fat with a decline in lean body weight (LBW) was evident; the fall in LBW was more marked in the males (Figure 12). To be noted was the consistently higher K concentrations in both male and female blacks as compared to white subjects, presumably indicative of a greater musculature. Oberhausen and Onstead (1965) performed 10,000 measurements of ^{40}K and demonstrated that total K decreased with age, starting at about age 25–30 in males. The K decrement proceeded in almost linear fashion thereafter. By using the figures of Edelman et al. (1952) for body water, Oberhausen and Onstead calculated that the K/water ratio declined in constant fashion into the sixth decade. They suggested that this might be due to loss of a constant mixture of muscle and other parenchyma. Thereafter the ratio altered, perhaps indicating that tissue richer in K (presumably muscle) was diminishing. Their interpretation was based on the consideration that muscle had the highest K concentration of any body tissue, 153 meq per liter of intracellular water according to Talso, Spafford, and Blaw (1953), as opposed to estimates that there were 50 meq K per liter total water in other parts of the lean body mass. Corroborating Anderson and Langham (1959) in females K remained constant until about 50, pointing up a sex-related distinction in the fate of the lean body mass.

Reviewing his data on 2,160 individuals,

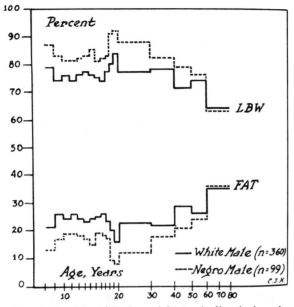

Figure 12. Illustrates the relationship of body weight to decline in lean body weight with age, in white and black males. Lean body weight in the elderly of both groups declines quite apart from fluctuations in body weight due to fat. (From Meneely *et al.*, 1963.)

Anderson (1963) proposed that, "from ages 35 to 70, the development can be interpreted either as replacement of muscle by muscle-free lean with constant adipose fraction or as the replacement of a constant mixture of these three components by connective tissue."

Burmeister and Bingert (1967) studied alterations in the cell mass of 3,292 subjects aged 8 to 90 using K^{40}. They too found the cell mass to diminish in males past 30. The lifetime shrinkage in the cell mass appeared to be on the order of 25 percent in males and 15 percent in females. This was accompanied by a rising proportion of fat, calculated in males to increase from 10 kg at age 20 to 19 kg at 45, and over 20 kg in those past 60. In 20-year-old women, fat was calculated at 18 kg, rising to 30 kg at 70.

Pierson, Lin, and Phillips (1974) studied 3,083 normal subjects of all ages. Males showed an increase of K to a peak of 53.8 meq/kg at age 20. This decreased thereafter at an average rate of 0.25 meq/kg per year. In females, K/weight decreased continuously from puberty onwards because of added fat. The rate of decrease in K in adult females was slower than in the males, averaging 0.23 meq/kg per year.

In females, total K was constant from age 20 to 45 and then declined, in agreement with Oberhausen and Onstead (1965) and Lorimer *et al.* (1965). Using anthropometry to calculate fat content, Pierson, Lin, and Phillips (1974) found the K content in the fat-free body to decrease from age 20 to 90; initial mean levels of 72 meq/kg decreased to 50 meq/kg in males, and declines of from 60 to 47 meq/kg were found in females (Figure 13). As they noted, this finding is in conflict with the concept of an unvarying potassium concentration in the lean body.

These large-scale studies of potassium decline with aging involved cross-sectional analysis, but a few studies show that the age-related decrease in K is measurable in the same subject after an interval. Forbes and Reina (1970) showed that three of four male subjects remeasured after a lapse of some years had sustained a decrease in calculated LBM, though one of them had gained a considerable amount of weight. Another subject, studied over a 29-year period by densitometric and total body water measures, showed a decline of around 5 kg in LBM. Another showed a slight decline between ages 36 to 41, followed by a rise, apparently associ-

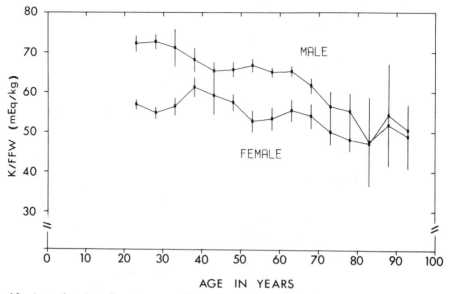

Figure 13. Age-related decline in proportion of potassium to fat-free weight in both sexes. (From Pierson *et al.*, 1974.)

ated with increased physical activity. In 13 other subjects in whom two measurements were available after a span of 4 to 9 ½ years, there was an average decline of 2.78 kg. Forbes and Reina concluded that "the rapid increase in lean body mass which occurs through childhood and adolescence eventually gives way to a decline which characterizes the adult years, a decline which gradually speeds up as the years go by."

Despite problems posed by different methods, all investigators are in agreement that the body's total K decreases with age and more markedly and earlier in males. Potassium can probably be increased temporarily by muscle cell hypertrophy during exercise (Misner, Boileau, Massey, and Mayhew, 1974), but any such increment is to be regarded as a short-term, upward fluctuation in a longitudinal process which over the longer term reduces body K by around 25 percent in the male. If this be a parameter for an aging process, the early onset of K decrement in males is one of the first objective criteria.

K and Densitometric Discrepancies. Forbes, Gallup, and Hursh (1961) proposed a formula for relating body potassium to lean body mass based on cadaver analysis,

$$LBM = \frac{meqK \text{ in body}}{68.1}$$

Counting with ^{40}K would therefore appear to be a simple noninvasive method for estimating a decline in LBM with the years. However, this presumes that the LBM has a constant proportion of K throughout senescence, a concept criticized by Pierson, Lin, and Phillips (1974), who found that the K/fat-free body ratio declines with age. A number of calculations led Pierson to conclude that fat increments produce an increase in K partly because adipose tissue is not fat alone, but chiefly because of a fat mandated increase in muscle tissue. They calculated for males that a potassium level of 15 meq/kg fat at age 21–25, 10 meq/kg fat at 26–30, and 5 meq/kg from 31–50 reduced the variance introduced by weight. Pierson postulated a two-compartment model for body K, the larger being a function of the body cell mass and independent of appended fat and a second which was a direct function of the fat mass. The second component consisted of the K found in adipose tissue (5–8 meq/kg) and a larger K mass contained in a skeletal muscle increment made necessary to maintain mobility with rising weight due to fat. But it is of interest that the postulated K of the second component due to fat is not needed to account for the findings past 50. By pooling the data developed by Pierson with that of the Brookhaven National Laboratory, Ellis, Shukla, Cohn, and Pierson (1974) have developed a series of equations for predicting total body K for different age groups with good accuracy.

Discrepancy in the results found by densitometry and ^{40}K counting are increasingly apparent past the middle years. This was found by Myhre and Kessler (1966), who evaluated the two methods in 100 subjects aged 15–87. The results agreed in most age ranges; in the older group, however, calculations derived from formulas based on ^{40}K counting gave consistently higher values for body fat in 82 of the cases. In the oldest subjects, the discrepancy was the most marked:

				% BODY FAT	
				---	---
Age	Ht (cm)	Wt (kg)	D_B	Hydrostatic Weighing	K-40
87	165.1	55.69	1.034	27.90	49.86
80	168.3	56.72	1.050	20.86	40.99

These subjects were described as very lean, which made the calculated high fat content (derived from low ^{40}K) seem inapplicable even on the assumption that an increasing proportion of body fat becomes "internalized" in old age. The alternate explanation is that the K concentration in the lean body has diminished (Pierson, Lin, and Phillips, 1974).

Until about age 70, no significant decline in skeletal weight of males seems to occur, at least not to an extent which would modify the calculations of body fat by densitometry (Ingalls 1931; Merz, Trotter, and Peterson 1956). If the densitometry can be accepted as reliable, the fat percentage calculated by K^{40} counting and standard formulas must be in error. The discrepancies could be finally resolved by cadaver analysis, which has never been performed on very old subjects. Pending such an analysis, the contention of Pierson that the K content of the lean body mass decreases with age seems valid in resolving the discrepancy. The changing ratio of K to fat-free body could be explained by a variable age-related decrement in the K richer tissue (such as muscle) as suggested also by Oberhausen and Onstead (1965) and by Myrhe and Kessler (1966). In fact, body components such as muscle, viscera, fat, and skin folds, and supportive connective tissue elements all change in a variable manner throughout maturity and into old age. Hence calculations based on measurements and formulas derived from younger groups are in need of modification.

ANATOMIC REGRESSION RELATED TO DIMINISHING K CONTENT

The decline in total body potassium that characterizes aging is so great as to warrant the belief that it might be identifiable at the gross level in the viscera and musculature. The organs of older people are smaller, and data on this have been funished by Rössle and Roulet (1932). Some of these are diagrammed in Figure 14. Similar decrements are reported by Calloway, Foley, and Lagerbloom (1965). Racial differences in apparent regression in the liver have been noted by Sato, Miwa, and Tauchi (1970), who found liver weights to decrease more markedly in old Japanese than in old Caucasian subjects. In the kidney declines in weight were age-related but again were more marked in the Japanese (Tauchi, Tsuboi, and Okutomi, 1971). For some organs, changes in weight may not adequately reveal the extent of regression since the fat and connective tissue content may rise as parenchymatous cells decrease. This can be demonstrated histologically (discussion in Andrew, 1971) and is also implied in analyses which revealed a declining potassium content in the organs of older individuals. This is clear in the report of Simms and Stolman (1937) (Table 7), which was done before the advent of potent potassium-excreting diuretics. Thus the study of Wilkinson, Issler, Hesp, and Raftery (1975) showed a 4 percent decline in total body K during a 1-year course of thiazide therapy for hypertension. In the Simms and Stolman study, the relative decline in intracellular components in all tissues except liver is clear, and the decrement in K is in agreement with the isotope studies.

Since the largest store of potassium is in skeletal muscle, declines in this system are of

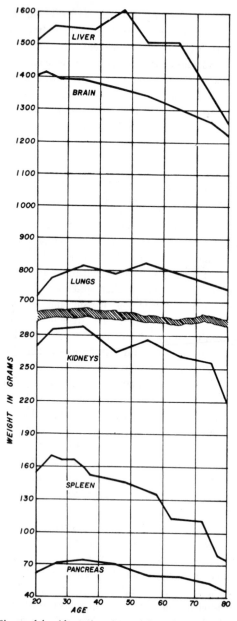

Figure 14. Alteration in weight of body organs with aging. (Redrawn from Rössle and Roulet (1932) in I. Rossman, *Clinical Geriatrics,* J. B. Lippincott, 1971.)

major importance. Rössle and Roulet (1932) recorded sharp declines in muscle weight, especially past age 50. It is clear that muscle is partially replaced by fat and connective tissue with aging (Andrew, Shock, Barrows, and Yiengst, 1959). The unique study of Frantzell and Ingelmark (1951) demonstrated a rising fat content in human muscle by chemical,

histologic, and roentgenographic methods. They found fat appearing for the first time in smaller perimysial spaces by the fourth decade. There was a gross replacement of muscle by adipose tissue after age 40 in the gastrocnemius, though not in the biceps brachii. In the gastrocnemius, fat content rose linearly with age, so that about one-third of the dry muscle tissue was fat by age 70-80. Though some muscle shrinkage in old age is attributed to disuse, this could hardly be the explanation for the same changes in the muscles of the eye (Wohlfart, 1938) or the larynx (Bach, Lederer, and Dinolt, 1941).

In the aged male (24-27 mo) rat, Yiengst, Barrows, and Shock (1959) found the total muscle mass to be 18.45 grams as against 28.05 grams in young (12-14 mo) rats. In the female for the same age groups, the differences were not statistically significant (13.90 *vs.* 14.56 grams). The sex differences here are reminiscent of the sex differences reported for ^{40}K counting. Tauchi, Tsuboi, and Okutomi (1971) found in the rat a roughly 50 percent decline in the weight of the tibialis anterior muscle between 12 and 24 mo, with a parallel decline in red muscle fibers, plus a shrinkage in diameter of white muscle fibers. Atrophic changes were also seen in the psoas muscle. The totality of the above findings suggests that decline in the musculature is a prominent contributor to the decline in ^{40}K and that the sex differences in rate of ^{40}K loss may be attributable to the muscle component. Additional K loss would also occur because of dwindling cell populations elsewhere in the body, including such connective tissue components as dermis (Andrew, Behnke, and Sato, 1964).

OTHER MORPHOLOGIC CHANGES

The catalogue of overt changes that occur with aging is very long. Many are discussed elsewhere in this volume or in standard textbooks in medical specialty areas. A few that can be noted are discussed in the following sections.

Skin Changes

Wrinkling of the skin is inevitable with aging and is markedly increased by exposure to sunlight (Kligman, 1969). Facial wrinkling is recognizable in the second decade in most individuals and tends to be progressive thereafter (Johnson and Hadley, 1964). Wrinkling is use related, and habitual facial expressions such as frowning and smiling accentuate it. Facial wrinkling occurs at an angle to the direction of the pull of the muscle on the skin (Kraissl and Conway, 1949). This leads to curved lines of the skin of the forehead, the "purse-string" wrinkles around the mouth, and the sheaf of linear wrinkles at the lateral aspects of the orbits. Deepening of the nasolabial groove and grooves extending down from the lateral corners of the mouth towards the chin are common in old age. In the neck, both circumferential and longitudinal wrinkling are ascribed to the action of the platysma muscle.

But some wrinkling is clearly not use related, as in the case of the immobile lobe of the ear. The ear lobe often appears puffy or enlarged by the sixth decade and develops variable wrinkling. A prominent wrinkle or groove running more or less at an angle from the horizontal has received special attention because of an alleged relation to coronary artery disease (Lichtstein, Chadda, Naik, and Gupta, 1974). In the very old, one often observes fine wrinkling of the face unrelated to the distribution of the major facial muscles. The wrinkling has an irregular or criss-cross distribution, resembling that of crumpled paper, and is presumably due to atrophy of fat and other dermal components.

Hair loss with aging results from a number of factors and is obviously different in the sexes. Early patterned development of baldness is genetic and androgen related (see Chapter 20 in this volume). In the middle and later years, a slower and progressive loss of scalp hair is often found in both the sexes. Axillary hair appears at puberty in both sexes, tends to diminish past the middle years, and in older women often disappears. Racial factors, which are important to hair distribution, color, and density, are also pointed up by the fact that in Japanese women 10 or more years postmenopausal, axillary hair has virtually disappeared (Hamilton, 1958). Body hairs, including pubic hair, become less numerous with aging; the very old have comparatively little body hair (Melick and Taft, 1959).

Graying of the hair is so well known a marker for the aging process that it was employed by Burch, Murray, and Jackson (1971) to support a theory of aging. Damon *et al.* (1972), in a study of 51 body measurements for aging criteria, found graying of scalp hair to be the most reliable indicator ($r = 0.64$). It is still subject to great variability both in time of onset and distribution (Fitzpatrick, Szabo, and Mitchell, 1965), but to the extent that it can be identified as a visible failure of a single enzyme system (tyrosinase), it is an indicator of clinical and biologic interest. Loss of melanophore activity in the skin, with depigmentation, is more difficult to grade clinically but clearly progresses with age in whites (Fitzpatrick, Szabo, and Mitchell, 1965).

Arcus Senilis

This is a lipid infiltrate into the limbus of the cornea of the eye, which progresses in a variable manner. The initial commalike and parenthesislike deposits expand into annular form, and a dense white border to the limbus results. According to Duke-Elder and Leigh (1965), it is virtually universal after 80. It is, however, found in some blacks in their 20's (Macaraeg, Lasagna, and Snyder, 1968). It remains to be determined whether the arcus in young blacks and older whites carries the same significance. Once thought to be related to coronary artery disease or ECG abnormalities, the relationship is doubtful, though the arcus may be more marked earlier in life in some subjects with hyperlipidemia.

Elongation and Tortuosity of Arteries

A palpable and often visible elongation of the brachial and radial arteries is found in some old subjects. Recently, attention has been directed to a similar change in the labial artery (Howell and Freeman, 1973). Elongation of the aorta is frequently observed in chest roentgenograms, especially in hypertensive individuals. Tortuosity, coiling, and kinking of the carotid arteries and the innominate have been brought to the fore with the development of angiocardiography. Thus Bauer, Sheehan and Meyer (1961) who performed arteriograms of both carotid and vertebral arteries in 71 patients with symptoms of possible cerebrovascular origin, found one or more of the arteries to be tortuous, kinked, or rotated in 30 percent of the cases. There was a frequent but by no means invariable relation to hypertension. However, Metz, Murray-Leslie, Bannister, Bull, and Marshall (1961) found some kinking in 16 percent of their cerebral angiograms and in every decade from the first through the eighth. They considered that much of the abnormalities might be on a developmental basis, with clinical onset decades later due to atherosclerosis. Weibel and Fields (1965) reviewed the carotid angiograms of 1,438 consecutive patients admitted for such study. They too concluded that tortuosity and coiling of the internal carotid artery was a congenital developmental condition, which could worsen with aging of the artery. However, kinking specifically was regarded as an acquired condition, occurring later in life and "always associated with a persistent tortuous coiled, and dilated segment of the artery." Factors such as hypertension and atherosclerosis, important in tortuosity and elongation of the aorta, have not been quantitated for such peripheral arteries as the brachial and radial, but the changes seem to be age-related and not developmental.

Osteoarthritis

Often referred to as a wear-and-tear disorder, the universal evidence of osteoarthritis in the vertebral column has been noted above, as have been the anatomic changes with aging that occur in such joints as the glenoid cavity, the knee, and the fingers. In the hip, the radiologic report by Danielsson (1966) was based on barium enema studies and thus escaped focussing on a clinic population with joint complaints. A rise in major osteoarthritic change in the hip with age was clear: from an 0.2 percent incidence in the fifth decade, it rose to around 10 percent in 84 year olds, with minor degrees of change obviously not reported.

Other anatomic changes which are time related include osteoporosis, sometimes subdivided into physiologic, i.e., age-related, and pathologic, due to such factors as calcium lack or inadequate vitamin D intake. The same

seems true of atherosclerosis, at least in some species, such as the human, in having some aspect of universality but with a variable component dependent on such factors as diet, hypertension, and metabolic disorders.

AGING AND PATHOLOGY

It appears clear that to disentangle universal "true" aging changes as distinct from pathology is difficult and by certain definitions, impossible. The lens illustrates both universal and common aging changes (discussion in Weale, 1963). Because of continued multiplication of its epithelial cells, it thickens and becomes heavier with age. This is universal, progressive, and in a basic sense, predictable and thus would appear to be a true aging change. Cataract formation, in contrast, is far more variable. It appears earlier and is more severe in systemic disease such as diabetes and thyroid-parathyroid disorders, but it seems not to be universally present in the elderly. There is a widespread belief, however, that given enough time, it would be universal. That cataract is an aging change in the lens protein with some specific relation to the life span is emphasized by its frequent occurrence in animals, for example, in dogs past 10 years of age (Bloom, 1959). An age-related, species specific pathology of a different sort is the development of bronchiectasis and pneumonitis in aging rats (Saxton, 1950).

A number of quite distinct and sometimes contradictory processes go on simultaneously in aging, among which the following can be considered.

Growth and Hyperplastic Changes

Apart from the benign growth changes in organs (such as the prostate) which are to be regarded as adenoma formation, or seborrheic hyperkeratotic growths in the skin (which are pathologic and not universal), there are some growth changes which commence early in life and regularly continue into old age. Among them are the thickening of the cranial vault and cranial suture closures which continue into the 80's. Other examples include thickening of the lens, enlargement of the nose and ear, perhaps an increment in lung volume, and increase in many bony diameters such as widths of the femur, ribs, metacarpals, and pelvis.

Use-Related Changes

These are the seemingly inevitable changes that occur with use and motion and thus become evident as the cartilaginous and "arthritic" changes of the vertebral spine or knee joint and in some skin wrinkling.

"Passage of Time" Events

In contrast to the above, these would be processes which leave their marks with the passage of time. They are to be distinguished from universally progressive growth changes or changes quantitatively related to active use. Some may be "passive" in the sense of an imbibition or deposition; such may be the case with the arcus senilis. The palmar and finger varicosities recently described by Clark, Melcher, and Hall-Smith (1974) may also fall into this category. Others are pathologic and implicitly preventable, such as various forms of arteriosclerotic (Mönckeberg and atherosclerotic) changes.

Regression, "Physiological Atrophy"

A constant aspect of aging is a widespread shrinkage of many tissues and organs (Tauchi, 1961). The histological evidence of this is reviewed by Andrew (1971). As noted in this chapter, it is encountered in the skin and subcutaneous tissue including fat deposits, in most muscles, in many but not all parts of the central nervous system (Brody, 1955; Monagle and Brody, 1974; Chapter 10 in this volume), in bone, and despite the reservations discussed above, in many viscera. The shrinkage in cell size which occurs with disuse in a tissue such as skeletal muscle is reversible, but there is no evidence that the senile atrophy observed in muscle is due to disuse or is reversible. A persuasive line of evidence is the progressive shrinkage in the lean body mass first in males, then in females evidenced by ^{40}K counting. The decline in lean body mass pieced together with both gross and microscopic studies indi-

cates that in many (though not all) body sites, progressive dwindling in the number of cells is the cardinal feature of age-related regression; in some cells (e.g., muscle), shrinkage in size is also noteworthy. Anatomically, this decline appears to be the most distinctive and universal of the multiple changes that occur with aging. Its slowing or reversal would serve as an objective parameter of successful therapeutic intervention.

REFERENCES

Albrink, M. J., and Meigs, J. W. 1971. Serum lipids, skin-fold thickness, body bulk and body weight of native Cape Verdeans, New England Cape Verdeans and United States factory workers. *Am. J. Clin. Nutr.*, **24**, 344–352.

Allbrook, D. B. 1956. Change in lumbar vertebral body height with age. *Am. J. Phys. Anthropol.*, **14**, 35–39.

Anderson, E. C. 1963. Three-component body composition analysis based on potassium and water determinations. *Ann. N.Y. Acad. Sci.*, **110**, 189–212.

Anderson, E. C., and Langham, W. H. 1959. Average potassium concentration of the human body as a function of age. *Science*, **130**, 713–714.

Andrew, W. 1971. *The Anatomy of Aging in Man and Animals.* New York: Grune & Stratton.

Andrew, W., Behnke, R. H., and Sato, T. 1964. Changes with advancing age in the cell population of human dermis. *Gerontologia*, **10**, 1–19.

Andrew, W., Shock, N. W., Barrows, C. H., and Yiengst, M. J. 1959. Correlation of age changes in histological and chemical characteristics in some tissues of the rat. *J. Geront.*, **14**, 405–414.

Bach, A. C., Lederer, F. L., and Dinolt, R. 1941. Senile changes in the laryngeal musculature. *Arch. Otolaryngol.*, **34**, 47–56.

Basilevich, I. 1958. The medical aspects of natural old age. An introduction to clinical gerontology. Munich. pp. 317. Also privately printed, Rhode Island State Hospital. Howard, R.I. 1959.

Bauer, R., Sheehan, S., and Meyer, J. M. 1961. Arteriographic study of cerebrovascular disease. *Arch. Neurol.*, **4**, 119–131.

Behnke, A. R. 1963. Anthropometric evaluation of body composition throughout life. *Ann. N.Y. Acad. Sci.*, **110**, 450–463.

Behnke, A. R., Feen, B. G. and Welham, W. C. 1942. The specific gravity of healthy men. *J. Am. Med. Assoc.*, **118**, 495–499.

Bennett, G. A., Waine, H., and Bauer, W. 1942. *Changes in the Knee Joint at Various Ages. With Particular Reference to the Nature and Development of Degenerative Joint Disease.* New York: The Commonwealth Fund.

Bloom, F. 1959. Geriatrics. *In, Canine Medicine,* Ch. XXV, 751–783. Santa Barbara, California: American Veterinary Publications.

Bourlière, F. 1970. The assessment of biological age in man. *Public Health Papers,* No. 37. Geneva: World Health Organization.

Bourlière, F., and Parot, S. 1962. Le vieillissement de deux populations blanches vivant dans des conditions écologiques très différentes, étude comparative. *Rev. France. Etudes Clin. Bio., 7,* 629–635.

Bowles, G. T. 1932. *New Types of Old Americans at Harvard and at Eastern Women's Colleges.* Cambridge, Massachussetts: Harvard University Press.

Brody, H. 1955. Organization of the cerebral cortex, III. A study of aging in the human cerebral cortex. *J. Comp. Neurol., 102,* 511–556.

Brown, O. T., and Wigzell, F. W. 1964. The significance of span as a clinical measurement. In W. F. Anderson and B. Isaacs (eds.) *Current Achievements in Geriatrics,* pp. 246–251. London: Cassell.

Brožek, J. 1952. Changes of body composition in man during maturity and their nutritional implications. *Federation Proc., 11,* 784–793.

Brožek, J. 1954. *Measurement of Body Compartments in Nutritional Research.* Washington, D.C.: Department of the Army, Office Quartermaster General.

Brožek, J. 1968. Interaction of human and animal research on body composition. *In, Body Composition in Animals and Man,* Publication 1598. pp. 3–15. Washington, D. C.: National Academy of Sciences.

Brožek, J., Chen, K. P., Carlson, W., and Bronczyk, R. 1953. Age and sex differences in man's fat content during maturity. *Federation Proc., 12,* 21–22.

Brožek, J., Grande, F., Anderson, J. T., and Keys, A. 1963. Densitometric analysis of body composition: Revision of some quantitative assumptions. *Ann. N.Y. Acad. Sci., 110,* 113–140.

Brožek, J., and Keys, A. 1953. Relative body weight, age and fatness. *Geriatrics, 8,* 70–75.

Büchi, E. C. 1950. Änderung der Körperform beim erwachsenen Menschen, eine Untersuchung nach der Individual-Methode. *Anthrop. Forsch.,* Heft 1. Anthrop. Gesel., Wien.

Burch, P. R. J., Murray, J. J., and Jackson, D. 1971. The age prevalence of arcus senilis, greying of hair, and baldness. Etiological considerations. *J. Geront., 26,* 364–372.

Burmeister, W., and Bingert, A. 1967. Die quantitativen Veränderungen der menschlichen Zellmasse zwischen dem 8 und 90 Lebensjahr. *Klin. Wshr., 45,* 409–416.

Calloway, N. O., Foley, C. F., and Lagerbloom, P. 1965. Uncertainities in geriatric data, II. Organ size. *J. Am. Geriat. Soc., 13,* 20–29.

Clark, A. N. G., Melcher, D. H., and Hall-Smith, P. 1974. Palmar and finger varicosities in the aged. *Brit. J. Dermatol. 91,* 305–314.

Cobb, W. M. 1952. Skeleton. *In,* A. I. Lansing (ed.),

Cowdry's Problems of Ageing, pp. 791–856. Baltimore: Williams & Wilkins.

Damon, A. 1965a. Discrepancies between findings of longitudinal and cross-sectional studies in adult life. Physique and Physiology. *Hum. Develop., 8,* 16–22.

Damon, A. 1965b. Stature increase among Italian-Americans: Environmental, genetic, or both? *Am. J. Phys. Anthropol., 23,* 401–408.

Damon, A. 1965c. Delineation of the body build variables associated with cardiovascular disease. *Ann. N.Y. Acad. Sci., 126,* 711–727.

Damon, A. 1968. Secular trend in height and weight within old American families at Harvard 1870–1965. I. Within twelve four-generation families. *Am. J. Phys. Anthropol., 29,* 45–50.

Damon, A. 1972 Predicting age from body measurements and observations *Aging and Human Development 3,* 169–173.

Damon, A., Seltzer, C. C., Stoudt, H. W., and Bell, B. 1972. Age and physique in healthy white veterans at Boston. *Aging and Human Development., 3,* 202–208.

Danielsson, L. 1966. Incidence of osteoarthritis of the hip (coxarthrosis). *Clin. Ortho., 45,* 67–72.

DePalma, A. F., and Rothman, R. H. 1970. *The Intervertebral Disc.* Philadelphia: W. B. Saunders.

Dequeker, J. V., Baeyens, J. P., and Claessens, J. 1969. The significance of stature as a clinical measurement of aging. *J. Am. Geriat. Soc., 17,* 169–179.

Duke-Elder, S., and Leigh, A. G. 1965. *System of Ophthalmology. Vol VIII. Diseases of the Outer Eye, Part 2.* St. Louis: C. V. Mosby.

Edelman, I. S., Haley, H. B., Schloerb, P. R., Sheldon, D. B., Friis-Hansen, B. J., Stoll, G., and Moore, F. D. 1952. Further observations on total body water, I. Normal values throughout the life span. *Surg. Gynecol. Obstet., 95,* 1–12.

Ellis, K. J., Shukla, K. K., Cohn, S. H., and Pierson, R. N. Jr. 1974. A predictor for total body potassium in man based on height, weight, sex, and age: Applications in metabolic disorders. *J. Lab. Clin. Med., 83,* 716–727.

Epker, B. N., and Frost, H. M. 1966. Periosteal appositional bone growth from age two to age seventy in man. A tetracycline evaluation. *Anat. Record, 154,* 573–578.

Epker, B. N., Kelin, M., and Frost, H. M. 1965. Magnitude and location of cortical bone loss in human rib with aging. *Clin. Ortho., 41,* 198–202.

Fitzpatrick, T. B., Szabo, G., and Mitchell, R. E. 1965. Age changes in the human melanocyte system. *In,* W. Montagna (ed.), *Advances in Biology of Skin. Aging.* Vol. VI. New York: Pergamon Press.

Forbes, G. B., Gallup, J., and Hursh, J. B. 1961. Estimation of total body fat from potassium-40 content. *Science, 133,* 101–102.

Forbes, G. B., and Reina, J. C. 1970. Adult lean body mass declines with age: Some longitudinal observations. *Metabolism, 19,* 653-663.

Frantzell, A., and Ingelmark, B. E. 1951. Occurrence and distribution of fat in human muscles at various age levels. *Acta. Soc. Med. Upsalien,* **56,** 59–87.

Friedenberg, Z. B., Edeiken, J., Spencer, H. M., and Tolentino, S. C. 1959. Degenerative changes in the cervical spine. Anat. Study. *J. Bone Joint Surg.,* **41A,** 61–70.

Friedenberg, Z. B., and Miller, W. T. 1963. Degenerative disc disease of the cervical spine. *J. Bone Joint Surg.,* **45A,** 1171–1178.

Fryer, J. H. 1962. Studies of body composition in men aged 60 and over. *In,* N. W. Shock (ed.), *Biological Aspects of Aging,* pp. 59–78. New York: Columbia University Press.

Garn, S. M., Rohmann, C. G., Wagner, B., and Ascoli, W. 1967. Continuing bone growth throughout life: A general phenomenon. *Am. J. Phys. Anthropol.,* **26,** 313–318.

Garn, S. M., and Young, R. W. 1956. Concurrent fat loss and fat gain. *Am. J. Phys. Anthropol.,* **14,** 497–504.

Graves, W. W. 1922. Observations on age changes in the scapula. *Am. J. Phys. Anthropol.,* **5,** 21–33.

Gsell, O. R. 1967. Longitudinal gerontological research over ten years (Basel Studies, 1955–1965). *Gerontol. Clin.,* **9,** 67–80.

Hamilton, J. B. 1958. Age, sex, and genetic factors in the regulation of hair growth in man: A comparison of Caucasian and Japanese populations. *In,* W. Montagna and R. A. Ellis (eds.), *Hair Growth,* pp. 399–433. New York: Academic Press.

Hertzog, K. P., Garn, S. M., and Hempy, H. O. III. 1969. Partitioning the effects of secular trend and aging on adult stature. *Am. J. Phys. Anthropol.,* **31,** 111–115.

Hooton, E. A., and Dupertuis, C. W. 1951. Age changes and selective survival in Irish males. *Studies in Physical Anthropology* (American Association of Physical Anthropologists and Wenner-Gren Foundation), **2,** 1–130.

Howell, J. B., and Freeman, R. G. 1973. Prominent inferior labial artery. *Arch. Dermatol.,* **107,** 386–387.

Howells, W. W. 1965. Age and individuality in vertebral lipping: Notes on Stewart's data. *Homenaje a Juan Comas,* **2,** 169–178. Mexico.

Howells, W. W. 1970. Hutterite age differences in body measurements. *Peabody Museum Papers,* **57,** 1–123.

Hrdlička, A. 1963. Growth during adult life. *Proc. Am. Phil. Soc.,* **76,** 847–897.

Ingalls, N. W. 1931. Observations on bone weights. *Am. J. Anat.,* **48,** 45–98.

Israel, H. 1968. Continuing growth in the human cranial skeleton. *Arch. Oral Biol.,* **13,** 133–137.

Israel, H. 1970. Continuing growth in sella turcica with age. *Am. J. Roentgenol. Radium Therapy Nucl. Med.,* **108,** 516–527.

Israel, H. 1973a. Progressive enlargement of the vertebral body as part of the process of human skeletal ageing. *Age and Ageing,* **2,** 71–79.

Israel, H. 1973b. Age factor and the pattern of change in craniofacial structures. *Am. J. Phys. Anthropol.,* **39,** 11–128.

Johnson, J. B., and Hadley, R. C. 1964. The aging face. *In,* J. M. Converse (ed.), *Reconstructive Plastic Surgery,* Vol. 3 (*Head and Neck*), Chap. 33, pp. 1306–1342. Philadelphia: W. B. Sauders.

Karpinos, B. D. 1961. Current height and weight of youth of military age. *Human Biol.,* **33,** 335-354.

Keefer, C. S., Parker, F., Myers, W. K., and Irwin, R. L. 1934. Relationship between anatomic changes in knee joint with advancing age and degenerative arthritis. *Arch. Internal Med.,* **53,** 325–344.

Keys, A., and Brožek, J. 1953. Body fat in adult man. *Phys. Rev.,* **33,** 245–325.

Kligman, A. M. 1969. Early destructive effect of sunlight on human skin. *J. Am. Med. Assoc.,* **210,** 2377–2380.

Kraissl, C. J., and Conway, H. 1949. Excision of small tumors of the skin of the face with special reference to the wrinkle lines. *Surgery,* **25,** 592–600.

Lee, M. M. C., and Lasker, G. W. 1958. The thickness of subcutaneous fat in elderly men. *Am. J. Phys. Anthropol.,* **16,** 125–134.

Lichtstein, E., Chadda, K. D., Naik, P., and Gupta, P. K. 1974. Diagonal ear-lobe crease: Prevalence and implications as a coronary risk factor. *New Engl. J. Med.,* **290,** 615–616.

Lorimer, A. R., Sinclair-Smith, B. C., Constantinides, C., Weiland, R. L., Ball, W. T., and Heyssel, R. M. 1965. Clinical applications of whole body potassium determination. *In, Radioactivity in Man,* pp. 248–262. Springfield, Illinois: Charles C. Thomas.

Luft, U. C. 1973. Pulmonary function, body composition and physical fitness of 415 airline pilots in relation to age. *Phys. Fitness, V.* Seliger (Ed.). Prague.

Macaraeg, P. V. J. Jr., Lasagna, L., and Snyder, B. 1968. Arcus not so senilis. *Ann. Internal Med.,* **68,** 345–354.

Macgillivray, I., Buchanan, T. J., and Billewicz, W. Z. 1960. Values for total exchangable sodium and potassium in normal females based on weight, height and age. *Clin. Sci.,* **19,** 17–25.

Marquer, P., and Chamla, M. C. 1961. L'evolution des caractéres morphológiques en fonction del l'âge chez 2089 français de 20 à 91 ans. *Bull. Mém. Soc. Anthropol., Paris,* **XI** (2) 1–78.

Medvedev, Z. A. 1974. Caucasus and Altay longevity: A biological or social problem. *Gerontologist,* **14,** 381–387.

Melick, R., and Taft, H. P. 1959. Observations on body hair in old people. *J. Clin. Endocrinol.,* **19,** 1597–1607.

Meneely, G. R., Heyssel, R. M., Ball, C. O. T., Weiland, R. L., Lorimer, A. R., Constantinides, C., and Meneely, E. V. 1963. Analysis of factors affecting body composition determined from potassium content in 915 normal subjects. *Ann. N.Y. Acad. Sci.,* **110**, 271–281.

Merz, A. L., Trotter, M., and Peterson, R. R. 1956. Estimation of skeleton weight in the living. *Am. J. Phys. Anthropol.,* **14**, 589–609.

Metz, H., Murray-Leslie, R. M., Bannister, R. G., Bull, J. W. D., and Marshall, J. 1961. Kinking of the internal carotid artery in relation to cerebrovascular disease. *Lancet.* **1**, 424–426.

Miall, W. E., Ashcroft, M. T., Lovell, H. G., and Moore, F. 1967. A longitudinal study of the decline of adult height with age in two Welsh communities. *Human Biol.,* **39**, 445–454.

Miller, C. E., and Remenchik, A. P. 1963. Problems involved in accurately measuring the K content of the human body. *Ann. N.Y. Acad. Sci.,* **110**, 175–188.

Misner, J. E., Boileau, A., Massey, B. H., and Mayhew, J. L. 1974. Alterations in the body composition of adult men during selected physical training programs. *J. Am. Geriat. Soc.,* **22**, 33–38.

Moldawer, M., Zimmerman, S. J., and Collins, L. C. 1965. Incidence of osteoporosis in elderly whites and elderly negroes. *J. Am. Med. Assoc.,* **194**, 859–862.

Monagle, R. D., and Brody, H. 1974. The effect of age upon the main nucleus of the inferior olive in the human. *J. Comp. Neurol.,* **155**, 61–66.

Moore, F., Olesen, K. H., McMurrey, J. D., Parker, H. V., Ball, M. R., and Boyden, C. M. 1963. *The Body Cell Mass and its Supporting Environment.* Philadelphia: W. B. Saunders.

Myhre, L. B., and Kessler, W. 1966. Body density and potassium 40 measurements of body composition as related to age. *J. Appl. Physiol.,* **21**, 1251–1255.

Nathan, H. 1962. Osteophytes of the vertebral column. *J. Bone Joint Surg.,* **44**, 243–268.

Oberhausen, E., and Onstead, C. O. 1965. Relationship of potassium content of man with age and sex. *In, Radioactivity in Man.* pp. 179–185. Springfield, Illinois: Charles C. Thomas.

Ohlson, M. A., Biester, A., Brewer, W. D., Hawthorne, B. E., and Hutchinson, M. B. 1956. Anthropometry and nutritional status of adult women. *In,* J. Brožek (ed.), *Body Measurements and Human Nutrition.* pp. 79–92. Detroit: Wayne University Press.

Pace, N., and Rathbun, E. N. 1945. Studies on body composition, III. The body water and chemically combined nitrogen content in relation to fat content. *J. Biol. Chem.,* **158**, 685–691.

Parot, S. 1961. Recherches sur la biométrie du vieillissement humain. *Bull. Mém. Soc. Anthropol., Paris,* **XI** (2), 299–341.

Parot, S. 1966. Les variations de poids liées à l'âge. Etude transversale à taille constante. *Biométrie Humaine,* **1**, 79–91.

Parot, S. 1969. Les méthodes de mesure de la masse métabolique active et de la masse grasse. Principes et étude critique. *In,* F. Bourliére, *Progrès en Gérontologie,* pp. 57–131. Paris: Flammarion.

Penning, L. 1964. Nonpathologic and pathologic relationships between the lower cervical vertebrae. *Am. J. Roentgenol., Radium Therapy Nucl. Med.* **91**, 1036–1050.

Pett, L. B., and Ogilvie, G. F. 1956. The Canadian weight-height survey. *In* J. Brožek (ed.), *Body Measurements and Human Nutrition.* pp. 67–78. Detroit: Wayne University Press. Also in *Human Biol.,* **28**, 177–188.

Pierson, R. N. Jr., Lin, D. H. Y., and Phillips, R. A. 1974. Total body potassium in health: Effects of age, sex, height and fat. *Am. J. Physiol.,* **226**, 206–212.

Rathbun, E. N., and Pace, N. 1945. Studies on body composition, I. Determination of body fat by means of the body specific gravity. *J. Biol. Chem.,* **158**, 667–676.

Remenchik, A. P., Miller, C. E., and Kessler, W. V. 1968. Estimates of body composition derived from potassium measurements. *In, Body Composition in Animals and Man.* pp. 231–253. Washington, D.C.: National Academy of Sciences.

Ries, W. 1967. Zum Alterswandel de Körpergestalt. *Zeitsch. f. Alternsf.,* **20**, 335–346.

Rössle, R., and Roulet, F. 1932. Zahl und Mass in Pathologie. Berlin: J. Springer.

Ruger, H. A., and Stoessiger, B. 1927. Growth curves of certain characters in man (males). *Ann. Eugenics,* **2**, 75–110.

Ryckewaert, A., Parot, S., Tamisier, S., and Bourlière, F. 1967. Variations, selon l'âge et le sexe, de l'epaisseur du pli cutané mesuré au dos de la main. *Rev. Franc. Etudes Clin. Biol.,* **12**, 803–806.

Sato, T., Miwa, T., and Tauchi, H. 1970. Age changes in the human liver of the different races. *Gerontologia,* **16**, 368–380.

Saxton, J. A., Jr. 1950. Pathology of senescent animals. *In, Conference on Problems of Aging.* pp. 136–142. New York: Josiah Macy Jr. Foundation.

Simms, H. S., and Stolman, A. 1937. Changes in human tissue electrolytes in senescence. *Science,* **86**, 269–270.

Smith, R. W., Jr., and Walker, R. R. 1964. Femoral expansion in aging women: Implications for osteoporosis and fractures. *Science,* **145**, 156–157.

Stecher, R. M. 1965. Heredity of osteoarthritis. *Arch. Phys. Med. Rehabil.,* **46**, 178–186.

Steinkamp, R. C., Cohen, N. L., Siri, W. E., Sargent, T. W., and Walsh, H. E. 1965. Measures of body fat and related factors in normal adults. *J. Chronic Diseases,* **18**, 1279–1288.

Stoudt, H. W., Damon, A., McFarland, R. A., and Roberts, J. 1965. Weight, height and selected body measurements of adults. United States, 1960–62. Public Health Service, Publication No. 1000, Series 11, No. 8. Washington. D.C.: Government Printing Office.

Stoudt, H. W., Damon, A., McFarland, R. A., and Roberts, J. 1970. Skinfolds, body girths, biacromial breadth and selected anthropometric indices of adults. United States, 1960–62. U.S. Public Health Service, Publication No. 1000, Series 11, No. 35. Washington, D.C.: Government Printing Office.

Talso, P. J., Spafford, N., and Blaw, M. 1953. The metabolism of water and electrolytes in congestive heart failure, I. The electrolyte and water content of normal human skeletal muscle. *J. Lab. Clin. Med.,* **41,** 281–286.

Tauchi, H. 1961. On the fundamental morphology of the senile changes. *Nagoya J. Med. Sci.,* **24,** 97–132.

Tauchi, H., Tsuboi K., and Okutomi, J. 1971. Age changes in the human kidney of the different races. *Gerontologia,* **17,** 87–97.

Tauchi, H., Yoshioka, R., and Kobayashi, H. 1971. Age changes of skeletal muscles of rats. *Gerontologia,* **17,** 219–227.

Todd, T. W. 1924. Thickness of the male white cranium. *Anat. Record,* **27,** 245–256.

Todd, T. W., and Lyons, D. W., Jr. 1924. Endocranial suture closure. Its progress and age relationship. Part I. Adult males of white stock. *Am. J. Phys. Anthropol.,* **7,** 325–384.

Trotter, M., Broman, G. E., and Peterson, R. R. 1960. Density of bones of white and negro skeletons. *J. Bone Joint Surg.,* **42A,** 50–58.

Trotter, M., and Gleser, G. C. 1951. Trends in stature of American whites and negroes born between 1840 and 1924. *Am. J. Phys. Anthropol.,* **9,** 427–440.

Weale, R. A. 1963. *The Aging Eye.* New York: Harper & Row.

Weibel, J., and Fields, W. S. 1965. Tortuosity, coiling and kinking of the internal carotid artery, I. Etiology and radiographic anatomy. *Neurol.,* **15,** (11), 7–18.

Wilkinson, P. R., Issler, H., Hesp, R., and Raftery, E. B. 1975. Total body and serum potassium during prolonged thiazide therapy for essential hypertension. *Lancet,* **i,** 759–762.

Willis, T. A. 1924. The age factor in hypertrophic arthritis. *J. Bone Joint Surg.,* **6,** 316–325.

Wissler, C. 1927. Age changes in anthropological characters in childhood and adult life. *Proc. Am. Phil. Soc.,* **66,** 431–438.

Wohlfart, G. 1938. Zur Kenntnis der Altersveränderungen der Augenmuskeln. *Zeitsch. f. mikr-anat. Forsch,* **44,** 33–44.

Yiengst, M. J., Barrows, C. H., Jr., and Shock, N. W. 1959. Age changes in the chemical composition of muscle and liver in the rat. *J. Geront.,* **14,** 400–404.

9
INTERCELLULAR MATRIX OF CONNECTIVE TISSUE

Endre A. Balazs

Matrix Biology Laboratory
Department of Ophthalmology
College of Physicians and Surgeons
Columbia University

In this chapter, age-related changes of the intercellular matrix of connective tissue will be reviewed. Only the most important aspects of these changes will be discussed. A complete description of all the work published in this field could very well fill an entire volume. The aim of this review is to bring to the attention of the reader the most important problems related to the structural and functional changes of the matrix during life. These changes occur from birth to death, and therefore, aging is considered in the broadest sense.

The structure and function of the matrix and its macromolecular components are not discussed. The reader is referred to major books on this subject (Balazs, 1970; Ramachandran, 1967–1969; Pigman and Horton, 1970). For review of the aging of cartilage and bone, the reader is referred to other chapters of this treatise (see Chapter 19 in this volume).

THE MATRIX

According to the old and still often quoted concept, the intercellular substance is made up of the collagen-elastin framework and a space-filling ground substance, both permeated by a dilute blood plasma. This definition is highly inaccurate. The macromolecules in the intercellular space form a highly ordered framework in which all elements are interacting with each other in a very specific way. As a matter of fact, the interaction among the framework elements is the central problem in the aging of the matrix. This interaction between collagen, elastin, glycoprotein, proteoglycans, and hyaluronic acid molecules varies according to the nature and function of the cells which produce and maintain these molecules. Therefore, the structure of the matrix is highly specific. This specificity is not only related to the tissue but also, in a topographic sense, to every part of the tissue. This topographic specificity makes it very difficult to describe age-related changes because all sampling for analysis results in an averaging process which often eliminates the possibility for discrimination of changes representative of a small cell population.

The interaction between the macromolecular components of the matrix is so extensive that with two exceptions—the synovial fluid and, in a few species, the vitreous—all matrices are solids rather than fluids. The overall rheological nature of all tissues depends on the intra and intermolecular interactions of these macromolecules. That is, the matrix is responsible for the solid structure of the body of multicellular organisms, and without the matrix the specific compartmentalization of cells with different functions would be impossible and the body in effect would be a random distribution of cells packaged in an epithelial bag.

This highly specific interaction of all the macromolecules of the matrix creates a tremendous problem in accurately defining its nature and describing its topography. This is the reason that today we are only scratching the surface of the knowledge of the fine structure and function of the matrix. The structural variation in the matrix is further complicated by the fact that the movement of the body results in a constant deformation of the soft tissue matrices (not in bone and only partially in cartilage). These deformations, mostly elastic, are determined by the very nature of the matrix. The deformation also causes dislocations of the fluid (water) in the intermolecular space of the matrix and movement of those large and small molecules which are more or less freely diffusible in between the interacting macromolecular components of the matrix. The two important structural elements of the matrix are the immobile macromolecular network, which is deformable, and the mobile fluid in which molecules of various size are dissolved and can move by flow or diffusion between the network elements.

The two components of the matrix—the interacting macromolecular network and the fluid with solutes permeating it—are enclosed in a basal laminar (basement membrane) bag which always forms the boundaries of a connective tissue compartment. This wall or bag has two fundamental roles. First, the solid network of the matrix is attached and anchored to this wall, and second, the movement of the fluid and large molecular solutes are restrained by this bag. Consequently, during the deformation of the matrix, the fluid and the dissolved molecules are more or less restrained within a given compartment. With this mechanism the integrity of a compartment is maintained under the mixing and deforming forces of mechanical stress to which the soft connective tissues are constantly exposed.

From the point of the aging process, the most important questions are: first, how the interaction between the network elements of the matrix are changing; second, what consequence these changes have on the deformations and dislocations of the various elements of the matrix; and third, how these changes of the matrix influence the metabolism of the connective tissue cells that are embedded in it, as well as the epithelial, neural, and muscle cells that are outside of it. Unfortunately, most of the answers to these questions are only hypotheses or speculations at this time.

THE MACROMOLECULES

Collagen

The most studied age changes in the matrix are related to the collagen fibers. It is a generally accepted view that with increasing age these fibers become more and more stable to external influences. In most connective tissue matrices, there is a progressive decrease with aging in the amount of collagen extractable with salt solutions or acetic acid. Similarly, with aging, the tissue becomes less responsive to mechanical stress, losing some if its flexibility (Hall, 1967). On the molecular level these age-related, mostly developmental, changes are usually explained by formation of new intermolecular bonds, often referred to as cross-links. The high structural stability of the extracellular matrix of the connective tissues is largely dependent on the stability of the fiber-forming collagen molecules. For this stability, a unique configuration of the aggregated molecules and their reinforcement with covalent cross-links are responsibile. These cross-links are especially important in conferring high tensile strength and resistance to solubilization upon these fibrils.

The most important intermolecular bond is initiated by a reaction of the enzyme lysyloxidase. This enzyme, catalyzed by copper ions, causes the oxidative deamination of specific lysine or hydroxylysine residues located in the nonhelical region, at N- and C-terminals, of the molecule. The aldehydes produced can condense with various reactive groups, first of all the ϵ-amino groups of hydroxylysine. These groups are situated in the helical region of neighboring molecules, and therefore, a network of intermolecular bonds can form. This aldimine-type bond is extremely labile, and its direct investigation is impossible. Therefore, a technique was developed whereby a mild reduction of the collagen fibrils with borohydride stabilizes these cross-links and makes the isolation of the linked amino acids possible. The borohydride reduced matrix of skin, tendon, bone, and cartilage became the source of several compounds which today are generally believed to represent reduced intermolecular cross-links. These compounds are hydroxylysinonorleucine, hydroxylysinohydroxynorleucine, histidinohydroxymerodesmosine, bysinonorleucine, aldol-histidine, hydroxymerodesmosine, hexosyl-lysine, and hexasyl-hydroxylysine. The evidence for the existence of these compounds *in vivo* and the physiological significance of the cross-links they represent was recently reviewed with penetrating criticism (Bailey, Robins, and Balian, 1974). According to these authors, the identification of these compounds from borohydride treated collagen or peptides does not constitute proof that their nonreduced forms act as intermolecular bonds *in vivo* since the initial condensation reaction could have been promoted by the alkaline reducing conditions. Some of these compounds, such as hexosyllysine and hexosyl-hydroxylysine, which are present in increasing quantity in aging tissue, are derived from the condensation of lysine and hydroxylysine with glucose and mannose. This clearly indicates that they are not involved in the cross-linking of two collagen molecules but rather in the linking of collagen to glycoproteins. This indicates another type of intermolecular cross-link which is age-dependent and results in binding between collagen fibrils and the glycoprotein molecules that envelop these fibrils. From all these compounds only hydroxylysinonorleucine and dihydroxylysinonorleucine were prepared from collagen in significant amounts. The amount of these peptides in a tissue seems to depend on the hydroxylation of the lysine residues in the N- and C-terminal nonhelical regions of the molecules. In skin, these residues are not hydroxylated (Kang, Piez, and Gross, 1969), whereas in bone and cartilage the hydroxylation is virtually completed (Miller, Lane, and Piez, 1969).

In tendon the lysine is about 50 percent hydroxylated. The presence of intermolecular cross-links represented by the hydroxylysinonorleucine and dihydroxylysinonorleucine parallels the tensile strength of the tissue. In the absence of lysine derived aldehydes, the collagen fibers have very little tensile strength, and they are soluble in neutral salt solutions. Such is the case in experimentally produced collagen diseases (lathyrism and copper deficiency) (Traub and Piez, 1971). In rat tail tendon, the presence of dehydro-hydroxylysinonorleucine results in high tensile strength, but the fibers are soluble in dilute acetic acid. In bone, cartilage, skin, and granulation tissues, the presence of hydroxylysino-5-keto-norleucine may be responsible for the high tensile strength and the insolubility of the fibers in salt and acid solutions. One must emphasize, however, that the solubility of the collagen fibrils can be greatly influenced by other important interactions between the collagen fibrils and other matrix elements, such as glycoproteins and proteoglycans. The rheological properties (rigidity, fluidity) of the collagen fibril matrix can also be influenced by proteoglycans or glycosaminoglycans of the matrix, especially in "soft tissues." This is well demonstrated in the case of the vitreous, where hyaluronic acid distributed between the random network of collagen fibrils exerts a "stabilizing" effect which increases the rigidity of the gel.

During the aging process, no new compounds other than hexosyl-lysine derivatives are formed in the matrix. During early development, when large amounts of new fibrils are formed in the matrix, a rapid rise of reducible cross-links was observed (Robins, Shimokomaki, and Bailey, 1973). This phase is followed by rapid decrease of the reducible cross-link content of the fibrils; thus, at maturity these cross-links are virtually absent from the matrix. During this period the fibrils become increasingly resistant to solvents, but they retain their tensile strength. It was proposed that reducible cross-links formed during early development represent an intermediate stage, and they are converted, during the maturation process, into nonreducible, more stable cross-links. That this process may occur *in vivo* is supported by some studies on intermediate cross-links in bone and dentine (Mechanic, Gallop, and Tanzer, 1971;

Deshmukh and Nimni, 1972). Other investigations indicate, however, that reduction of the intermolecular bonds *in vivo* does not occur (Robins, Shimokomaki, and Bailey, 1973). Consequently, the nature of stable crosslinks in the mature tissue remains undefined. It is most likely that these bonds develop in some way from the borohydride reducible cross-links. Bailey, Robins, and Balian (1974) suggested that a spontaneous extracellular (nonenzymatic) reaction within the fiber converts the reducible intermediates to the stable cross-links of the mature tissue.

The fluorescent properties of collagen were described in early research, and the hypothesis has been suggested that the fluorescent material is involved in cross-linking of the peptide chains (LaBella, Vivian, and Thornhill, 1966). Two types of ultra violet fluorescence have been reported. The first, a shortwave fluorescence (272/315 nm), is due to tyrosine residues, and the second, at longer wavelengths (345/440 nm), is related to a cross-link between the peptide chains of the collagen molecule (La Bella and Thornhill, 1965; Fujimori, 1966). After ultraviolet irradiation, the long wavelength fluorescence increases, especially in collagen of old age animals (LaBella and Thornhill, 1965). A compound with identical fluorescent properties could be formed in collagen by the action of ultraviolet light and tyrosinase. A greater amount of this long wavelength fluorescing compound was found in collagen prepared from various tissues (skin, tendon, cornea) of various species (rat, dog, cat, and human) of older ages than of younger (Deyl, Praus, Šulcová, and Goldman, 1969). These authors suggest that this compound "could be possibly of a cross-linking nature," however, there are other alternatives.

When purified collagen (acid soluble) isolated from mouse skin is exposed to oxygen at 37° C for several weeks, it becomes insoluble in acid and its digestibility by a bacterial collagenase decreases (Puleo and Sobel, 1972). This oxygen modified collagen contains a peptide which exhibits the long wavelength fluorescence and contains most of the tyrosine of the collagen. These authors speculated that such an oxygen modified collagen may be found *in vivo* under some pathological conditions related to aging.

With increasing age, collagen from various animal and human tissues becomes more and more resistant to the attack of various proteolytic enzymes (Everitt, Gal, and Steele, 1970). For example, during development the collagen from human diaphragm tendon becomes progressively resistant to digestion by bacterial collagenase (Hamlin and Kohn, 1971). This increase in the amount of insoluble collagen in tendon progresses so predictably with age that the determination of bacterial collagenase resistant collagen in human tendon can be successfully used in age determination (Hamlin and Kohn, 1972).

Food intake in rats can influence certain qualities of the tail tendon fibers. When the food intake was limited to approximately half that of the ad libitum consumption of rats (from 28 to 330 days of age), the solubility of the tendon fibers in urea increased—that is, the time needed to break the tail tendon under constant stress when suspended in 7 M urea decreased. Since the breaking time under these conditions increases progressively throughout life, it was concluded that high food intake accelerates the aging of collagen in tail tendon (Everitt, 1971; Chvapil and Hruza, 1959; Giles and Everitt, 1967). There could be several explanations for this observation. It was reported that food restriction causes decrease in the neutral salt soluble collagen in skin (Gross, 1958; Whitehead and Coward, 1969) and bone (Smith and Armstrong, 1961). Since the tendon weight is lower in chronically underfed rats, impaired collagen synthesis may explain the faster breaking time.

Elastin

The elastic elements of the matrix are the so-called elastic fibers, which are not fibers at all but contain the macromolecular complex, elastin. Electron microscopic observation of the elastic fibers clearly demonstrates that they contain two morphologically distinct components (Fahrenbach, Sandberg, and Cleary, 1966; Greenlee and Ross, 1967). One is amorphous or slightly structured, and the other consists of microfibrils of 110–120 nm in diameter. The fibrils are dispersed within and also surround the interstices of the amorphous component. The microfibrils have an affinity for cationic stains, such as lead or uranyl acetate, while the amorphous component stains well with anionic metal stains, such as phosphotungstic acid. During embryogenesis, only the microfibrils can be identified. With increasing age, the amorphous component appears, and at maturity the "elastic fiber" consists largely of the amorphous component with a relatively small microfibrillar envelope. The solubilities of the microfibrils and the amorphous component are quite different. From fetal tissue, the entire "elastic fiber" complex (microfibrils and amorphous component) can be removed with 5 M guanidine at pH 7, but the complex remains insoluble. The microfibrils can be separated from this complex by dissolving them in dilute sodium hydroxide or with reducing thiols in 5 M guanidine solution (Ross and Bornstein, 1969). The microfibrillar fraction contains glycoprotein, and it is free of hydroxyproline, hydroxylysine, and desmosine, three of the typical amino acids of the amorphous components. The "elastic fiber" of the mature tissue frequently contains an excess of polar amino acids which makes the complex less soluble.

Like collagen, elastin also exhibits fluorescence in the visible region of the spectrum. This fluorescence has been assigned in the past both to fatty acid impurity (Loomeijer, 1961) and to the amino acid component, desmosine (Milch, 1965). Other studies demonstrated that the chromophore and the fluorophore are not related to desmosines (Partridge, Eldsen, and Thomas, 1963) and that a fluorescent fatty acid can be present as a contaminant. After optimal elastase and pronase treatment, 35 percent of the elastin molecule remains as a macromolecule and contains both the chromophore and fluorophore groups. It was speculated that these groups may be involved in a covalent cross-linking (Thornhill, 1972). The yellow color and the fluorescence of elastin increase with the aging process, in contrast to the desmosine content, which is constant from maturity to old age (LaBella and Lindsay, 1963; LaBella, Vivian, and Thornhill, 1966). It was suggested that the fluorescence is due to a cross-linking agent and that elastin "became tanned with age." Quinones and homogentisic acid have been suggested as the tanning agent

(Stoner and Blivaiss, 1967; Morrison, Steele, and Danner, 1969).

The maturation of the elastic fiber occurs in the matrix—that is, fibers which have been synthetized during embryonic or early postnatal life undergo chemical modification later in life. The main change seems to be the reduction of the aldimines which results in formation of cross-links. The major cross-links formed are dehydrolysinonorleucine, dehydromerodesmosine and dehydropyridines. As many as 38 out of 47 lysine residues per 1,000 amino acid residues of elastin are modified during maturation. The nature and mechanism of this reduction of aldimines is not known. Since the reaction occurs extracellularly, the usual reducing coenzyme systems may not be involved but rather some oxydation-reduction carrier systems play a major role (for review see Gallop, Paz, Pereyera, and Blumenfeld, 1974).

Basal Lamina

Basal lamina or basement membranes constitute a chemically and structurally distinct extracellular matrix. These structures separate connective tissue compartments from epithelial, neural, or muscle cells, and therefore, form the boundary of the connective tissue matrix. One can also visualize the basal lamina as a "bag" in which the matrix of the connective tissue is enclosed. The basal lamina on the "outside," that is, towards the retina, is always directly attached to the cell membrane of the neural, epithelial, or muscle cells which are also responsible for the synthesis of the structures of this matrix. On the "inside" the basal lamina is usually attached to the collagen fibrils and is seldom in direct contact with cells of connective tissue.

The biological function of basal lamina is not well understood, but three major functions have been assigned to it.

First, it may serve as a barrier for migration of cells. This does not mean, however, that cells cannot pass through this lamina, but they must have the proper apparatus to break it down. There is some evidence that lymphocytes and mononuclear phagocytes (monocytes, histocytes, hyalocytes) can pass through the basal lamina in normal conditions. In inflammation, all types of leukocytes can pass through this lamina.

Second, it serves as a barrier for the passage of certain macromolecules. Horseradish peroxidase, with a molecular weight of 40,000 daltons does traverse the lamina (Graham and Karnovsky, 1966), but the somewhat larger ferritin molecule does not (Farguhar, 1960).

Third, as an elastic bag of connective tissue, it serves a mechanical function by supporting and containing the structure of this compartment.

Immunochemical studies have shown that three major antigenic determinants are present in the basal lamina. One is represented by its major component, a collagen-type protein; the other two, by low and high molecular weight glycoproteins which contain hexosamine.

The backbone of the basal lamina is a collagen-type protein which contains unusually high amounts of hydroxylysine, hydroxyproline, and carbohydrates (10–12 percent glucose and galactose) when compared to fibrous collagen. The three identical polypeptide chains assume a triple helical conformation in the molecule, which is then organized into a subunit very different from that found in fibrous collagen. The two glycoproteins play important roles in the organization of collagen subunits into the laminar structure. (For review see Kefalides, 1973).

The only data available on the aging of basal lamina are related to its thickness. It has been stated by several authors that with increasing age, the basal lamina becomes thicker, in some cases doubling its original width. This increase in thickness was observed in the basal lamina of the skin capillaries of very old rats (Gersh and Catchpole, 1949). Age-related increase in the thickness of the basal laminae was observed in glomeruli (Caulfield, 1964), and in ciliary processes (Yamashita and Becker, 1961).

Proteoglycans and Hyaluronic Acid

The proteoglycan and hyaluronic acid content of connective tissue have been the subjects of many investigations in which the objective was

correlation of these values with the aging process. The highlights of these studies are discussed in the second part of this review. Very few data are available, however, on the molecular parameters and conformation of these macromolecules as related to the aging of the tissues from which they are obtained.

Changes in the rheological properties of the synovial fluid as related to its hyaluronic acid content have been studied in detail (Balazs, 1968b, 1969). Since synovial fluid contains a substantial amount of protein, the relationship between hyaluronic acid and these rheological changes cannot be arbitrarily assumed as causal.

THE TISSUES

The Vitreous

The vitreous in young adult mammals has two major characteristics: it has very few cells, and its intercellular matrix, a transparent colorless gel, contains only one glycosaminoglycan—hyaluronic acid. To the best of our knowledge, this is true for all young adult mammals except owl monkeys (*Aotus trivirgatus*) and bushbabies (*Galago crassicaudatus*), in which the vitreous space is filled with an elastoviscous fluid. The gel character of the vitreous originates from a network of collagen filaments. These filaments are thin (10–20 nm in diameter) and are randomly distributed in a loose network. The gel is transparent for visible light because the filaments are thin and the distance between them is great as compared to the wavelength of the light. The serum protein content of the vitreous is low (<1 mg/ml), so it appears colorless. The fluid vitreous of the owl monkey and bushbaby do not contain collagen (Balazs, 1968a).

Human Vitreous. Data are not available on the hyaluronic acid content of the embryonic vitreous. Vitreous samples from two stillborns (weights 1050 and 1250 grams) and three infants (1 day, 3 months, and 18 months) were analyzed. Hexuronic acid and glucosamine analyses revealed variations between 0.013–0.022 mg/ml and 0.020–0.060 mg/ml, respectively. The glycosaminoglycans were not identified. The range of hexuronic acid and glucosamine concentrations in the vitreous of adults (22 to 46 years old) was higher (0.065–0.075 mg/ml and 0.044–0.057 mg/ml respectively). In the adult human vitreous, it was found that at least 95 percent of these two carbohydrate moieties originate from high polymer hyaluronic acid. Therefore, we conclude that there is less hyaluronic acid in the vitreous of infants than in young adults. Other investigations support these conclusions (Schweer, 1962; Berman and Michaelson, 1964). They found the hexosamine concentration in the vitreous of 0 to 19-year-old human subjects to be significantly lower than that of young adults. The interpretation of these findings is not straightforward because hexosamine is present not only in glycosaminoglycans, such as hyaluronic acid, but also in glycoproteins. The vitreous is known to contain glycoproteins (Balazs and Sundblad, 1960). In some species (bovine), the embryonic blood glycoprotein-fetuin content of the vitreous is extremely high (Balazs, Laurent, and Laurent, 1959). Nevertheless, the low hexosamine concentration in the vitreous of young subjects further supports the statement that in the growing vitreous, the hyaluronic acid content is lower than in full-grown subjects.

With aging, the picture becomes more complex. More than 30 vitreous samples obtained from the eyes of subjects between the ages of 65 and 95 were analyzed (Balazs, 1960, 1965). It was found that 1.9–4.0 ml of the vitreous can be aspirated easily from the enucleated eyeball (within 24 hours postmortem) through a 22-gauge needle. The rest of the vitreous (0.9–2.2 ml) cannot be aspirated but can be collected as a gel after the eyeball is opened. The appearance of liquid vitreous is not a postmortem phenomenon. It is known from slit lamp examination of the living eye (Busacca, Goldmann, and Schiff-Wertheimer 1957) and from examination of eyes after surgical enucleation, that a progressive liquefaction of the vitreous begins at age 40–45. Liquid vitreous formation during aging is a unique phenomenon in human eyes and, interestingly, it coincides with the onset of aging of the lens.

Analyses of the liquid and gel vitreous revealed that liquid vitreous contains only a small amount of collagen fibrils or soluble collagen, while gel vitreous largely is made up of collagen fibrils (Balazs, 1968a). The hydroxyproline content of 14 liquid vitreous samples obtained from subjects 71 to 95 years old varied between 0.003–0.011 mg/ml, while gel vitreous from the same subjects varied between 0.033–0.359 mg/ml. However, no significant difference was found between the hyaluronic acid concentration in the liquid and in the gel vitreous from these same subjects (liquid vitreous, 0.172 ± 0.045 mg/ml; gel vitreous, 0.144 ± 0.036 mg/ml); nor was there any significant difference in the limiting viscosity numbers of hyaluronic acid in the liquid and in the gel vitreous. The values obtained varied between 7,800 and 3,300 cc/gram. The low limiting viscosity values could be the result of postmortem degradation of hyaluronic acid, either in the eyeball or immediately after exposure to atmospheric oxygen. Under similar conditions, oxidative degradation of hyaluronic acid in bovine vitreous has been observed (Balazs, 1960).

With aging of the human eye, another interesting variation occurs in the hyaluronic acid concentration of the vitreous. Preliminary studies, carried out on 32 eyes from subjects 65–95 years old, clearly show that with regard to hyaluronic acid concentration, two groups can be established—those with low (0.059–0.176 mg/ml) and those with high (0.190–0.500 mg/ml) hyaluronic acid concentration (Balazs, 1968a). When both eyes were available for analysis, the hyaluronic acid concentration was similar in both vitreous samples. The hyaluronic acid concentration in young adults (22 to 60 years old) was the same as that in the low concentration group of old adults. Thus, it seems that during aging, in approximately 30 percent of the population, hyaluronic acid metabolism is altered in the vitreous in such a way that its concentration increases. Since this increase is observable in both eyes of the individual, the possibility of a pathological condition existing in one eye is excluded. These subjects did not have any eye diseases, except mild diffraction problems and presbyopia. In most cases, the cause of death was of cardiovascular origin. It is unlikely, therefore, that some local or general pathological condition is responsible for the change in hyaluronic acid concentration. At this stage it is, of course, impossible to determine whether an increase in the synthesis of hyaluronic acid or a slowing of the passage of hyaluronic acid into the posterior chamber causes this concentration increase. Whatever the explanation may be, it is important to remember that only one-third of the relatively small number of subjects analyzed showed this change.

Hexosamine determinations of the vitreous of adult subjects of various ages showed no (Schweer, 1962) or only slight (Berman and Michaelson, 1964) increase with aging. In our studies on mature human eyes, we found that when the vitreous was free of contamination from blood or cells of adjacent tissues, the hexuronic acid and glucosamine concentrations were very closely equimolar, indicating that most of the hexosamine originates from hyaluronic acid. Hexosamine, however, is present in serum and tissue glycoproteins and, therefore, is not a reliable measure of the hyaluronic acid content of the vitreous.

Bovine Vitreous. The hyaluronic acid content of the vitreous in the 4- to 9-month-old bovine embryo is very low compared to that in the adult (Balazs, Laurent, and Laurent, 1959). In the homogenized vitreous of these embryos, the concentration of hyaluronic acid is approximately 0.050 mg/ml, while in 3-year-old adults it is ten times higher. It is not known at what time the concentration reaches adult levels, but the increase starts during the third month after birth. The vitreous volume increases steadily during embryonic development, but even in the newborn calf it is only approximately one-half that of the full-grown animal. Thus the total hyaluronic acid content of the vitreous increases slowly during embryonic development and very rapidly during postnatal development (Figure 1).

A concentration gradient of hyaluronic acid is maintained throughout the entire development period. That is, the concentration of hyaluronic acid is highest in the cortical gel

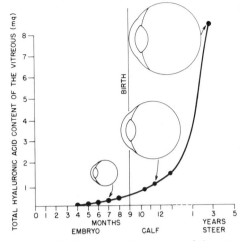

Figure 1. Hyaluronic acid content of the growing bovine vitreous. The sketch indicates the growth of the eyeball and the volume increase of the vitreous.

where hyalocytes—the hyaluronic acid-producing cells—are present and is lowest behind the lens in the central and anterior parts of the gel adjacent to the posterior chamber. The molecular weight of hyaluronic acid calculated from the limiting viscosity number does not change during development of the vitreous (Balazs, Laurent, and Laurent, 1959).

During aging, the hyaluronic acid concentration decreases significantly in bovine vitreous. Table 1 shows four representative samples of many analyses. In the entire vitreous, the concentration of hyaluronic acid is lower in the old (12 years) than in the young (1.5 years) mature cow. The concentration gradient is apparent in the vitreous of young and old animals. In the same cows the hyaluronic acid concentration of the carpal and hock joints also was studied (Table 1). No age-related difference could be found in the fluids of the same animal. One may conclude that the decrease in hyaluronic acid concentration in the vitreous is an aging phenomenon of the eye *per se*, a consequence of some changes in local metabolic control rather than the manifestation of a general change in the metabolism of hyaluronic acid in the body.

Avian Vitreous. The vitreous of the chick embryo is a solid collagen gel until the tenth

TABLE 1. HYALURONIC ACID CONCENTRATION AND LIMITING VISCOSITY NUMBER ([η] , cc/g) IN THE VITREOUS AND SYNOVIAL FLUIDS OF YOUNG AND OLD COWS.

| Animal no. | Age (yrs) | VITREOUS GEL[a] | | | SYNOVIAL FLUID[a] | | | |
| | | | | | CARPAL JOINT | | HOCK JOINT | |
		Cortical (mg/ml)	Central (mg/ml)	Anterior (mg/ml)	(mg/ml)	[η] (cc/g)	(mg/ml)	[η] (cc/g)
1	1.5[b]	0.739	0.602	0.195[c]	0.749	8,700	0.550	5,300
2	1.5	0.668	0.588		0.995	10,200	0.410	7,600
3	12[b]	0.332	0.242	0.155[c]	0.979	8,400	0.491	6,200
4	12	0.250	0.148		0.936	10,300	0.575	9,000

[a]The samples from the pair of eyes and the two joint fluids of the same animals were pooled.
[b]The four cows were of the same breed (Jersey) and were maintained under identical feeding and living conditions for 2 months.
[c]The four anterior samples from the pair of eyes of both animals were pooled.

day. After that, a liquid pocket develops, separating the gel into a larger anterior part and a thin cortical layer lining the retina and the pecten. This lining gel layer contains the hyalocytes, while the anterior gel is cell-free. The gel vitreous reaches its maximum volume around the 30th day after hatching, but the volume of the liquid vitreous continues to increase until the developing chick is 90 to 100 days old. Hyaluronic acid was identified in both the gel and liquid vitreous of full-grown birds; its concentration is, however, much lower than in most mammals. In the full-grown chicken, the hyaluronic acid concentration in both liquid and gel vitreous is in the range of 0.015–0.02 mg/ml. After the gel vitreous has reached its full volume, around the 30th day, the hyaluronic acid concentration remains constant throughout adult life (animals up to 4 years of age were studied) (Balazs, Toth, Jutheden, and Collins, 1965).

The hyaluronic acid or glycosaminoglycan content of the chick embryo vitreous is, however, undergoing rapid changes. Since only the hexuronic acid and hexosamine determinations were carried out on the pronase digested and dialyzed vitreous samples from embryos and young birds, we can only speculate about the hyaluronic acid or glycosaminoglycan content. The hexuronic acid concentrations of both the liquid and gel vitreous are three to four times greater in the 18 to 20-day-old embryo than in the adult. This high hexuronic acid concentration drops rapidly to nearly adult levels

during the first week after hatching. The maximum point of the concentration of hexuronic acid in the gel vitreous is reached when the volume of the gel has reached a maximum and temporary halt at the 18th day of embryonic life. This stage coincides with the full development of the cortical gel and its hyalocyte content (Balazs et al., 1965).

Owl Monkey Vitreous. The ages of the bushbaby (*Galago crassicaudatus*) and owl monkey (*Aotus trivirgatus*) can be related to the weights of the animals. In both species, the vitreous space is filled with a gel in the very small animal (Dartnall, Arden, Ikeda, Luck, Rosenberg, Pedler, and Tansley, 1965). As the weight of the animal increases, the vitreous becomes mostly liquid, and in full-grown animals it remains only a few hundred microns thick, cortical collagen gel adjacent to the retina, ciliary body, and lens. The hyaluronic acid concentration of this cortical gel is highest in the posterior part. In the owl monkey, the concentration varies between 0.5–1.0 mg/ml (Balazs, Laurent, Laurent, DeRoche and Bunney, 1959). The hyaluronic acid in the liquid vitreous is unevenly distributed, forming a concentration gradient decreasing from the cortical gel toward the posterior chamber (Österlin and Balazs, 1968). For this and other reasons, we suggested that the hyaluronic acid produced by the hyalocytes of the cortical gel diffuses toward the posterior chamber from which it is washed by the aqueous humor into the anterior chamber and from there to Schlemm's canal (Balazs, Freeman, Klöti, Meyer-Schwickerath, Regnault, and Sweeney, 1972).

When the entire vitreous of an owl monkey—liquid and gel—is collected by careful dissection of the surrounding tissues from the frozen vitreous, the average concentration and the total hyaluronic acid content can be determined (Österlin and Balazs, 1968). The vitreous of small (90–300 grams) animals contained 0.172 ± 0.025 mg/ml hyaluronic acid (average of 13 eyes). On the other hand, the vitreous of 500–1100 gram-animals contained 0.446 ± 0.019 mg/ml hyaluronic acid (average of 31 eyes). Animals varying in weight from 500–1100 grams did not show any significant difference in the concentration of hyaluronic acid. Thus, it was concluded that during the postnatal maturation of this species, hyaluronic acid synthesis in the hyalocytes is stimulated and that during the growth of the eyeball, as the vitreous volume increases, hyaluronic acid accumulates in this matrix. Therefore, the concentration of hyaluronic acid in the vitreous is significantly higher in the mature adult than in the young growing animal.

Species Differences. In two-thirds of the human vitreous samples investigated, the concentration of hyaluronic acid was unchanged during aging; in the other one-third, it was higher. The hyaluronic acid concentration in the cow vitreous, on the other hand, decreases during aging. Furthermore, in the bovine vitreous, aging is not accompanied by liquefaction of the gel. We suggest that these differences in the aging of the vitreous in these two species are somehow related to the aging process of the adjacent lens and its suspension elements, the zonular fibers. We further suggest that the vitreous is closely coupled with the lens, as its mechanical (shock absorber) and metabolic (molecular filter) buffer.

One can also draw an important conclusion from the comparison of the hyaluronic acid content of the developing bovine and avian vitreous. In the bovine vitreous, hyaluronic acid accumulates after birth, while in the chicken vitreous, the concentration of the hexuronic acid and hexosamine-containing glycosamin-glycans decreases following the last days of embryonic development. Thus, from the point of view of hyaluronic acid content, just as in the liquid-gel state of the vitreous, there seems to be a fundamental difference between species.

The Synovial Fluid

Human Synovial Fluid. The concentration of hyaluronic acid in the synovial fluid of subjects 18 to 29 years old was found to be generally higher than that of older subjects (Balazs, Rydell, Seppälä, Duff, Merrill, and Gibbs, in preparation). This does not mean that every synovial fluid sample of a subject under 29 years of age has a higher concentration of hyaluronic acid than that of older subjects. However, a statistically significant difference was found between the 18 to 29-year-old group and the 27 to 39-year-old group. In the former, the concentration of hyaluronic acid was found to be 2.17 ± 0.3 mg/ml, and in the latter, 2.45 ± 0.04 mg/ml. In an even older group (52–78 years), the concentration was only slightly lower (2.37 ± 0.17 mg/ml). Figure 2 summarizes all data found in the literature, including data obtained in several studies carried out in the author's laboratory (Balazs et al., in preparation; Hamerman and Schuster, 1958; Castor, Prince, and Hazelton, 1966; Balazs, Watson, Duff, and Roseman, 1967; Balazs, 1968b, 1969). There is an apparent tendency for a major decrease in the concentration of hyaluronic acid to occur between the ages of 22 and 27. The extent of changes in the normal joint after the age of 30 is minimal except in this case of osteoarthritis. Figure 2 also shows that in osteoarthritis, the concentration of hyaluronic acid is significantly lower than in symptom-free knee joints of subjects in the same age group.

Bovine Synovial Fluid. It was found that in the course of postnatal development (1 month to 2 years), the volume of synovial fluid and the total amount of hyaluronic acid per joint increased in two specific joints—the carpal (intercarpal and carpometacarpal) and the hock (tibiotarsal and proximal intertarsal) (Seppälä and Balazs, 1969). The concentration

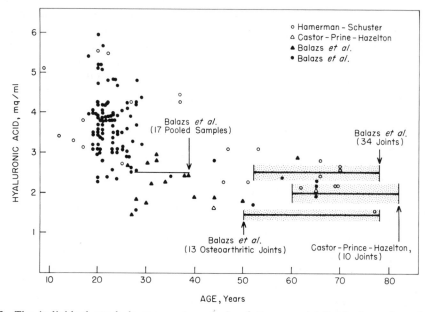

Figure 2. The individual symbols represent analysis of the synovial fluid of one knee joint of a subject with no history of any joint disorder. The only exceptions are the 13 cases represented by the dotted area labeled "osteoarthritic joints." These subjects had longstanding osteoarthritis in one or both knee joints.

The three dotted areas cover the standard error of the mean of 10–34 individual determinations over the age range of subjects. The horizontal solid line represents the hyaluronic acid concentration of a sample in which 17 synovial fluids of the same number of subjects 28–39 years old were pooled.

All analyses reported in this figure were carried out in three laboratories using different analytical methods to determine the hyaluronic acid concentration in synovial fluids. For details see Hamerman and Schuster, 1958; Castor, Prince, and Hazelton, 1966; Balazs, et al., unpublished publication; and Balazs et al., 1967.

of hyaluronic acid in these two joints is significantly different but remains essentially unchanged during the development of the joint (calf carpal 0.90 ± 0.08 mg/ml; cow carpal 0.80 ± 0.05 mg/ml; calf hock 0.47 ± 0.05 mg/ml; cow hock 0.33 ± 0.03 mg/ml). The molecular size (limiting viscosity number) of the hyaluronic acid did not show significant change during development in either of these two joints.

During maturation, the viscoelastic qualities of the fluids obtained from these two joints do not change significantly (Balazs, 1968b, 1969; Seppälä, Gibbs, Balazs, and Merrill, in preparation), but the viscoelastic properties of fluids from these two joints are very different. The fluids from the carpal joints have higher limiting viscosity number (Table 1) and absolute dynamic rigidity, and both the dynamic elas-

tic and viscous moduli are much greater in the carpal than in the joint. The hock joint fluid has a rigidity which is one-sixth that of fluid from the carpal joints. In general, the fluid from the carpal joints has far better lubricating and protective properties than that from the hock joint. This may be related to the fact that the carpal joints in these species support more body weight than do the hock joints.

No significant difference was found in the concentration or molecular size of hyaluronic acid of the fluids obtained from the carpal and hock joints of young (1 to 3 years) and old (10 to 15 years) cows. (Four representative samples are presented in Table 1). Nor could significant differences in the viscoelastic properties of the fluids obtained from normal joints of animals in these two age groups be detected.

A few fluids obtained from hock joints with obvious macroscopic evidence of osteoarthritis were analyzed. The average concentration of hyaluronic acid was considerably lower (0.24 ± 0.05 mg/ml) than in the normal fluids (0.33 ± 0.03 mg/ml), but the limiting viscosity number was unchanged (osteoarthritic 7500 cc/gram; normal 7300 cc/gram). All viscoelastic parameters had considerably lower values in the osteoarthritic than in the normal joints.

Difference During Aging. These results suggest a great difference between the aging process in the bovine and in the human joint. The normal aging of the bovine joint is not accompanied by the same kind of rheological changes in the fluid which occur in the human joint. Osteoarthritis, however, produces the same type of changes in the fluids of both species. Since most cases of osteoarthritis are related to various degrees of trauma or to some chronic functional disorder (misalignment) of the joints, it may be possible that the rheological changes in the human fluids that have been associated with the so-called normal aging process are, in fact, a result of chronic traumatic conditions of the joint. In other words, the human knee joint is "misused" during life, and this chronic, subclinical traumatic condition results in changes that we mistakenly associate in a causal sense with aging. The finding that the fluids from young persons with recognizable osteoarthritis and from the "normal" joints of old persons exhibit the same rheological properties seems to support this hypothesis (Balazs et al., in preparation).

Molecular Size of Hyaluronic Acid. Synovial fluid is much more viscous than a solution of serum proteins of the same concentration (15–25 mg/ml). The viscosity of the synovial fluid is, therefore, due entirely to the hyaluronic acid content, and after degrading the hyaluronic acid with specific enzyme (leech hyaluronidase), the viscosity of the fluid is the same as that of diluted serum. It has been previously shown that one can measure the limiting viscosity number of hyaluronic acid (Balazs and Sundblad, 1959) in the natural protein milieu of synovial fluid. The removal

of all proteins from synovial fluid by electrodeposition does not change the limiting viscosity number of the hyaluronic acid (Balazs et al., 1967). In other words, if there is an interaction between the proteins of synovial fluid and hyaluronic acid, this interaction cannot be detected by measuring the limiting viscosity number of hyaluronic acid in the natural ionic milieu of the fluid or in 0.15 N NaCl.

The limiting viscosity number of the hyaluronic acid measured in the protein milieu of the synovial fluid, after it has been dialyzed against 0.15 N NaCl and all cells and other particles have been removed by centrifugation at 50,000 × g for 2 hr, is not age-dependent (see Table 2).

On the molecular level, the frequency dependence of the dynamic moduli was explained (Gibbs, Merrill, Smith, and Balazs, 1968) by the configurational adjustments of the polymer chain under strain. At any given frequency, the interaction between the chains and between the chain and the solvent determines the relaxation mechanism of the molecular network. It was suggested (Gibbs et al., 1968) that a strongly hydrogen bonded network is responsible for the unusually high elastic behavior. This interaction between the chain elements, rather than increases in molecular weight or concentration, is responsible for the

TABLE 2. LIMITING VISCOSITY NUMBER OF HYALURONIC ACID IN THE SYNOVIAL FLUID OF HUMAN KNEE JOINTS OF SUBJECTS OF VARIOUS AGES.

Age group (yrs)	No. of samples analyzed	Vol. of sample aspirated from one knee	$[\eta]$ (cc/g)
18–20	36	0.4 ± 0.04[a]	5200 ± 100[a]
	9	1.3 ± 0.1	5500 ± 250
21–23	24	0.3 ± 0.1	5300 ± 100
	6	1.2 ± 0.2	5500 ± 200
24–29	20	0.5 ± 0.05	5000 ± 150
	11	1.5 ± 0.1	5400 ± 200
27–39	18	0.6 ± 0.1	5800 ± 300
35	1	2.5	6400
52–78	26	0.7 ± 0.1	5200 ± 400
52	1	2.0	4200
58	1	2.0	5800

[a]Mean and standard error of the mean.
Data taken from Balazs et al., in preparation.

greater elasticity of the fluids obtained from the young. It was further suggested that a conformational change in the molecular network caused by an overall change in the electrostatic potential of the molecule is responsible for the viscoelastic transformation with aging. There are many factors in the ionic and protein milieu of the synovial fluid that can cause such changes in the hyaluronic acid chain network, but without experimental data it would be fruitless to speculate about them. However, it is important to emphasize that the elasticity of hyaluronic acid networks in biological ionic milieu could increase if the electrostatic potential generated by the carboxyl groups is reduced by the shielding effect of bulky mono or multivalent counterions or by another molecule which changes the effective dielectric constant in the immediate environment of the charged groups. It is known that hyaluronic acid in concentrations over 0.2 percent forms a highly elastic putty in salt solution (0.01–0.2 N NaCl) when the hydrogen ion concentration is adjusted to pH 2.5 (Balazs, 1966). At lower or higher hydrogen ion concentrations, the putty is less elastic. At pH 2.5 in the presence of guanidine hydrochloride, the putty loses its elastic nature. It was suggested that decreasing the electrostatic repulsion between the hyaluronic acid chains in solution of high hydrogen ion concentration, would cause a chain-chain interaction via hydrogen bonds to occur. The conformational change, which makes the chain segments "stiffer," is responsible for the greater elasticity.

The change in concentration of hyaluronic acid and its rheological properties in aspirated synovial fluid of the knee joint from subjects of various age groups could also be explained by the difference in the properties of the fluid in the joint space and in the connected bursae. It is possible that with aging the anatomical communication between the joint space and the bursae is changed and, consequently, the samples collected represent different compartments. This possibility seems to be unlikely, however, because the properties of the fluid within a given age group do not seem to depend on the volume of fluid collected. Some knee joints, without any objective or subjective

signs of abnormality, yield 1.0–2.5 ml of fluid, two to five times more than the average. There was no difference in the hyaluronic acid concentration and its rheological properties between the samples with large and small volume. The possible effect of the physical activity of the knee joint on the chemical and rheological qualities of the fluid was also tested (Balazs *et al.*, in preparation). The hyaluronic acid and protein concentrations and the rheological properties of the fluid did not show significant difference when collected from a knee joint after resting or after five minutes' exercise of bending and stretching with or without bearing full body weight.

It was concluded, therefore, that the differences in the concentration of hyaluronic acid reflect a change in the metabolism (anabolic or catabolic) of hyaluronic acid with aging. There is, however, another possibility that is related to the hyaluronic acid "lining" on the surface of the joint. It was pointed out that this hyaluronic acid layer ("protective cushion") changes with age (Balazs, Bloom and Swann, 1966). Recently, it was found that pure hyaluronic acid injected into rabbit joints coats the surfaces of the articular cartilage. Therefore, it is possible that with aging, an increasing amount of hyaluronic acid is deposited on the cartilage and synovial surfaces, and hence, the concentration in the fluid decreases. This would also explain why the thickness of the "protective cushion" on the articular cartilage increases with aging.

The Surface of Bovine Articular Cartilage

Hyaluronic acid forms a "surface cushion" on the articular cartilage (Balazs and Gibbs, 1970; Balazs, Bloom, and Swan, 1966). This layer is a few microns thick on the surface of the cartilage in load-bearing joints and has a fine structure that is different from the underlying network of collagen filaments. This surface cushion resists extensive washing but can be removed readily by incubation with testis or leech hyaluronidase. Chemical analyses revealed that the surface cushion contains hyaluronic acid, which presumably originates from the synovial fluid. It also contains proteins

TABLE 3. DYNAMIC RHEOLOGICAL PROPERTIES OF SYNOVIAL FLUID ASPIRATED FROM THE HUMAN KNEE JOINTS OF SUBJECTS OF VARIOUS AGES.

Age (yrs)	NO. OF SAMPLES ANALYZED		G' and G'' at crossover (dyne cm^{-2})	ω at crossover (cycle sec^{-1})	G' at 2.5 cycle sec^{-1} (dyne cm^{-2})	G'' at 2.5 cycle sec^{-1} (dyne cm^{-2})
	Pooled	Individual				
18–29	$4(12)^a$	4	259 ± 36^b	0.13 ± 0.02^b	1170 ± 130^b	450 ± 82^b
27–39	$2(17)^a$	1	59 ± 6	0.21 ± 0.004	226 ± 7	72 ± 8
52–78	$5(26)^a$		61 ± 7	0.41 ± 0.12	189 ± 33	101 ± 12

[a] Figures in parentheses are the number of individual fluids pooled.
[b] Mean and standard error of the mean.
All rheological measurements were carried out in an oscillating Couette type rheometer (21) at a temperature range of 4–37°C. The data presented in this table are "reduced" to 37°C.
Data taken from Balazs et al., in preparation.

which are responsible for the structures visible in electron micrographs. Its staining characteristics, with cationic dyes, strongly suggest that most of the negative sites of hyaluronic acid are blocked or are associated with a counterion which is not replaced by the dye ions.

This surface cushion is absent in embryos and newborn animals (rat and calf). It develops rapidly after the joint starts to bear weight, and it is present in 2-week-old calves. With aging, the surface cushion becomes thicker and undergoes easily recognizable morphologic changes. The biological function of this surface cushion is not well understood. One may assume that it forms a seal on the surface of the cartilage, preventing diffusion of the proteoglycans of the cartilage into the synovial fluid. It can serve as a protective layer that prevents deterioration of the loops of collagen filaments which form the outer layer of the articular cartilage matrix. This cushion can serve as a shock absorber for the first layer of cartilage cells which are located only 10-20 μm below it. Furthermore, it can prevent cells (such as fibroblasts from the neighboring connective tissue and mononuclear phagocytes, granulocytes, and lymphocytes from the synovial fluid) from adhering to and proliferating on the articular surface. We were able to show that fibroblasts, leukocytes, and peritoneal exudate cells do not adhere to or move on the surface of jellies made from pure, high polymer (molecular weight: $1-5 \times 10^6$) hyaluronic acid of high concentration (>1 percent. Thus, it is conceivable that the surface cushion represents a connective tissue matrix

surface that maintains the cell-free status of normal articular cartilage surfaces. This surface cushion was demonstrated by scanning electron microscopy (Walker, Unsworth, Dowson, Sikorski and Wright, 1970), and it was suggested that it represents the "squeeze film" which is generated during loading of the joints and provides the mechanism for "boundary lubrication" (Walker et al., 1970). Further extensive studies on the structure and biological function of this surface cushion are needed before its significance is well understood. However, it seems clear at this point that the surface cushion plays some role in the protection of the articular cartilage and that it changes as the joint ages.

Skin

The water content of the skin decreases during development. For example, in pig skin from the 90-day-old fetus to adult, a 25 percent decrease in water content was observed. The concentration of ions (Na^+, K^+ Cl^-, Ca^{2+}, Mg^{2+}) in the tissue water is, however, unchanged. The collagen content per wet tissue weight increases nearly 20 times. Thus, the most dramatic quantitative change in the skin connective tissue matrix is the increase of collagen content during maturation (Table 4).

Another important change in the collagen component of the matrix occurring during maturation is the change in the solubility. For example, from the skin of a 5-week-old rat, 37 percent of the total collagen can be extracted

**TABLE 4. SOME ANALYTICAL VALUES OF THE
DEVELOPING PIG SKIN.**

Water per kg tissue		90-DAY-OLD FETUSES	NEWBORN	4 to 6-WEEK-OLD	ADULT
		902	836	778	685
Na^+		106.4	131.6	111.5	119.1
K^+	m Egn	43.8	47.2	53.8	38.2
Cl^-	per kg	89.8	95.7	99.6	110.9
Ca^{2+}	water	12.5	10.9	10.8	13.4
Mg^{2+}		8.0	7.9	10.0	6.4
Collagen N g per kg tissue		4.0	1.5	39.7	70.6

Data from Widdowson and Dickerson, 1960.

with neutral salt solutions and citrate buffer. From the skins of a 10-week-old rat, this amount decreases to 12 percent and in a 40-week-old rat, to 5 percent (Hall, 1967).

The change in the physical properties of human skin during aging was well demonstrated by measuring the tension developed in isometric thermal contraction. This tension increases with maturation, reaching a high value at puberty, after which a slight decrease occurs; and later with aging, it again slowly increases (Hall, 1967).

Another interesting age difference found in rat skin is related to the catabolism of collagen. The catabolism of collagen appears to be the result of two mechanisms: one, a cortisol mediated induction of collagenolytic activity and second, a lysosomal protease activity, both of which are released from the cells into the intercellular matrix. The net result of both collagenolytic activities is a limited and localized degradation of the collagen fibrils. The aged rat skin apparently does not have the inductive mechanism for activation of the collagenolytic activity in response to cortisol treatment (Hall, 1967). This means that the skin of the old rat contains more collagen than that of the young rat and at the same time it has less capacity to catabolize this collagen than has the young rat.

The turnover rate of glycosaminoglycans hyaluronic acid and dermatan sulfate) in rabbit skin is faster in young (4-week-old) than in mature (12-month-old) animals (Davidson and

Small, 1963). It is not known whether the decreasing metabolic rate is a result of change in the synthetic or the breakdown process. The biological half time of chondroitin sulfate is 2–3 days in newborn, 7–9 days in adult, and 12–14 days in old rat skin (Hauss and Junge-Hülsing, 1963). The relative amount of glycosaminoglycans in the skin also varies with age. Hyaluronic acid comprises almost 80 percent of the total skin glucosaminolycans in the embryo but only 30 percent in the adult. On the other hand, chondroitin sulfate represents about 10 percent of the glycosaminoglycans in the embryonic skin but 66 percent of the adult (Loewi and Meyer, 1958). The increase of the dermatan sulfate to hyaluronic acid ratio with aging was also observed, and it was pointed out that parallel with this the water content of the skin also decreases (Meyer, 1958). Others found that in rat skin, the hyaluronic acid of chondroitin sulfate content decreases from newborn to maturation, at which level it remains constant for the rest of life (Schiller and Dorfman, 1960).

Heart Valves

The incorporation of $[^{35}S]$ sulfate into the sulfated glycosaminoglycans, expressed as radioactivity per mg dry tissue or per mg of sulfated glycosaminoglycans (dermatan sulfate and chondroitin-6-sulfate), was found to be higher in the metral, aortic, and pulmonary valves of young (1-to-8-day-old) calves than in full-grown

(1-to-1.5-year-old) cows. There was, however, no difference between the values obtained from full-grown (1-to-5-year-old) and old (8-to-10-year-old) cows. The sulfated glycosaminoglycan content of the aortic and pulmonary valves (expressed as GAG per dry tissue weight) of the young (1-to-8 day-old) cattle was 57 percent, and 35 percent lower, respectively, than that of old (8-to-10-year-old) cattle. These findings indicate that the composition and metabolism of the sulfated GAG in the connective tissue matrix changes with aging (Boström, Moretti, and Whitehouse, 1963).

The aminotransferase activity was also lower in the cow than in young calf aortic valves, indicating a possible decrease of turnover rate of the sulfated glycosaminoglycans (Jacobson and Boström, 1964).

The collagen content of the heart valves increases with age, while the cell content, measured by DNA analysis, decreases (Trnavsky, Kopecky, Tranavská, and Cehecauer, 1965).

Granuloma

Granulation in the subcutanous connective tissue of rats can be caused by injection of carrageenin or by implantation of cellulose sponges. Several authors have shown that the age of the animal in which the granulation of tissue is induced does not affect the collagen content of this newly formed tissue (Németh-Csóka, 1970; Heikkinen, Aalto, Viherssaari, and Kulonen, 1971). This is an interesting observation since the DNA and RNA-ribose content of the granulomas of young (1-month-old) animals was higher than that of old (1.5-year-old) animals, indicating a higher cell content in the young animal's granuloma. Probably because of this higher cell content some metabolic rates, such as the incorporation of proline into collagen, the oxygen consumption, and protein synthesis were considerably higher in the younger animals (Heikkinen et al., 1971). On the other hand, the granulomas of 4-to-5-week-old growing rats contained considerably more (61-90 percent) hyaluronic acid than those of adult rats (10-67 percent). During the development of granulomas (20-day period), the hyaluronic acid content was found to be the highest at the initial stage, gradually decreasing to the 20th day. The other sulfated glycosaminoglycans gradually increased with time in the granuloma to a value at the 20th day of 39 percent in the very young and 90 percent in the adult animals (Németh-Csóka, 1970). The biological significance of this difference in the glycosaminoglycan content of granulomas of animals with various ages is not known.

CONCLUSION

The major macromolecular components of the matrix are collagen (fibrils and soluble collagen), elastin, glycoproteins, proteoglycans, hyaluronic acid, and the proteins forming basal laminae. Among these macromolecules only collagen and elastin were studied in detail from the point of view of age-related changes. Both of these macromolecules form water insoluble fibrils or filaments which are organized in fibers and sheaths. The rheological properties and the solubility of these structures change during development and aging. These changes are explained in the literature as development of "cross-links". The "cross-links" represent a great variety of intermolecular bonds between two chemically identical molecules and various types of interactions between chemically different molecules; they are mainly accrued during development. While much research is in progress in this area, the nature of the mechanism of the formation of cross-links in collagen and elastin is yet unsolved.

Changes in the rheological and chemical properties of hyaluronic acid in the synovial fluid and vitreous during development and aging are controlled by factors that are specific for the species. Such oversimplified notions that hyaluronic acid is in general the major component of the growing and developing matrix or that it is associated with the formation of a specific type of collagen filaments cannot be verified experimentally. The mechanism of this process and its relationship with structural changes in the articular cartilage and synovial tissue were not yet explored. Practically nothing is known about the chemical and physicochemical changes of proteoglycans during maturation and aging.

A considerable amount of data is available in the literature about the morphological, physical, and chemical changes in the matrix of tendon, vitreous, synovial fluid, cartilage, skin, and heart valves during development and aging. This information clearly indicates that the matrix undergoes a continuous change during life, providing a most consistent chronological marker of the body. The fundamental question, however, is yet unanswered. Are age-related changes in the matrix caused solely by cells which are responsible for its synthesis, or does there exist an extracellular apparatus built into some structural elements of the matrix which is partially or fully responsible for these changes? In the first case the matrix only reflects cellular changes, while in the second it represents an important determinant of development, maturation, and aging.

REFERENCES

Bailey, A. J., Robins, S. P., and Balian, G. 1974. Biological significance of the intermolecular cross-links of collagen. *Nature,* 251, 105–109.

Balazs, E. A. 1960. Physiology of the vitreous body. *In,* C. L. Schepns (ed.), *Importance of the Vitreous Body in Retina Surgery with Special Emphasis on Reoperations* (Proceedings of the II Conference of the Retina Foundation, Ipswich, May 30–31, 1958), pp. 29–48. St. Louis: C. V. Mosby.

Balazs, E. A. 1965. Amino sugar-containing macromolecules in the tissues of the eye and the ear. *In,* E. A. Balazs and R. W. Jeanloz (eds.), *The Amino Sugars: The Chemistry and Biology of Compounds Containing Amino Sugars. II-A. Distribution and Biological Role,* pp. 401–460. New York: Academic Press.

Balazs, E. A. 1966. Sediment volume and visocelastic behavior of hyaluronic acid solutions. *Federation Proc.,* 25, 1817–1822.

Balazs, E. A. 1968a. Die mikrostruktur und chemie des glaskörpers. *In,* W. Jaeger (ed.), *Bericht über die 68. Zusammenkunft der Deutschen Ophthalmologischen Gesellschaft in Heidelberg 1967,* pp. 536–572 Munich: J. F. Bergmann Verlag.

Balazs, E. A. 1968b. Viscoelastic properties of hyaluronic acid and biological lubrication (Symposium: Prognosis for Arthritis: Rheumatology Research Today and Prospects for Tomorrow, Ann Arbor, Michigan, 1967). *Univ. Mich. Med. Ctr. J. Suppl.,* Special Arthritis Issue, 255–259.

Balazs, E. A. 1969. Some aspects of the aging and radiation sensitivity of the intercellular matrix with special regard to hyaluronic acid in synovial fluid and vitreous. *In,* A. Engel and T. Larsson (eds.), *Thule International Symposium: Aging of Connective Skeletal Tissue,* pp. 107–122. Stockholm: Nordiska Bokhandelns Förlag.

Balazs, E. A. (ed.) 1970. *The Chemistry and Molecular Biology of the Intercellular Matrix.* London: Academic Press.

Balazs, E. A., Bloom, G. D., and Swann, D. A. 1966. Fine structure and glycosaminoglycan content of the surface layer of articular cartilage. *Federation Proc.* 25, 1813–1816.

Balazs, E. A., Freeman, M. I., Klöti, R., Meyer-Schwickerath, G., Regnault, F., and Sweeney, D. B. 1972. Hyaluronic acid and the replacement of vitreous and aqueous humor. *In,* E. B. Streiff (ed.). *Modern Problems in Ophthalmology* (Secondary Detachment of the Retina, Lausanne, 1970), Vol. X, pp. 3–21. Basel: S. Karger.

Balazs, E. A., and Gibbs, D. A. 1970. The rheological properties and biological function of hyaluronic acid. *In,* E. A. Balazs (ed.), *The Chemistry and Molecular Biology of the Intercellular Matrix,* pp. 1241–1254. London and New York: Academic Press.

Balazs, E. A., Laurent, T. C., and Laurent, U. B. G. 1959. Studies on the structure of the vitreous body. VI. Biochemical changes during development. *J. Biol. Chem.,* 234, 422–430.

Balazs, E. A., Laurent, T. C., Laurent, U. B. G., DeRoche, M. H., and Bunney, D. M. 1959. Studies on the structure of the vitreous body. VIII. Comparative biochemistry. *Arch. Biochem. Biophys.,* 81, 464–479.

Balazs, E. A., Rydell, N. W., Seppälä, P. O., Duff, I. R., Merrill, E. W., and Gibbs, D. A. Hyaluronic acid in synovial fluid. II. Macromolecular composition and rheological properties of synovial fluid from humans of different ages (in preparation).

Balazs, E. A., and Sundblad, L. 1959. Viscosity of hyaluronic acid solutions containing proteins. *Acta Soc. Med. Upsalien.,* 64, 137–146.

Balazs, E. A., and Sundblad, L. 1960. Studies on the structure of the vitreous body. V. Soluble protein content. *J. Biol. Chem.,* 235, 1973–1978.

Balazs, E. A., Toth, L. Z. J., Jutheden, G. M., and Collins, B. A. 1965. Cytological and biochemical studies on the developing chicken vitreous. *Exp. Eye Res.,* 4, 237–248.

Balazs, E. A., Watson, D., Duff, I. F., and Roseman, S. 1967. Hyaluronic acid in synovial fluid. I. Molecular parameters of hyaluronic acid in normal and arthritic human fluids. *Arthritis Rhuemat.,* 10, 357–375.

Berman, E. R., and Michaelson, I C. 1964. The chemical composition of the human vitreous body as related to age and myopia. *Exp. Eye Res.,* 3, 9–15.

Boström, H., Moretti, A., and Whitehouse, M. 1963. I.

On the biosynthesis of mucopolysaccharides in bovine heart valves. *Biochim. Biophys. Acta,* 74, 213-221.

Busacca, A., Goldmann, H., and Schiff-Wertheimer, S. 1957. *Biomicroscopie du Corps Vitre et du Fond de l'Oeil.* Paris: Masson Cie.

Castor, C. W., Prince, R. K., and Hazelton, M. J. 1966. Hyaluronic acid in human synovial effusions; a sensitive indicator of altered connective tissue cell function during inflammation. *Arthritis Rheumat.,* 9, 783-794.

Caulfield, J. B. 1964. Medical progress application of the electron microscope to renal diseases. *New Engl. J. Med.,* 270, 183-194.

Chvapvil, M., and Hruza, Z. 1959. The influence of aging and undernutrition on chemical contractility and relaxation of collagen fibres in rats. *Gerontologia,* 3, 241.

Dartnall, H. J. A., Arden, G. B., Ikeda, H., Luck, C. P., Rosenberg, M. E., Pedler, C. M. H., and Tansley, K. 1965. Anatomical, electrophysiological and pigmentary aspects of vision in the bush baby: An interpretative study. *Vision Res.,* 5, 399-424.

Davidson, E. A., and Small, W. 1963. Metabolism *in vivo* of connective tissue mucopolysaccharides. II. Chondroitin sulfate B and hyaluronic acid of skin. *Biochim. Biophys. Acta,* 69, 453-458.

Deshmukh, K., and Nimni, M. E. 1972. Identification of stable intermolecular crosslinks present in reconstituted native collagen fibers. *Biochem. Biophys. Res. Commun.,* 46, 175-182.

Deyl, Z., Praus, R., Sulcová, H. and Goldman, J. N. 1969. Fluorescence of collagen-properties of tryosine residues and another fluorescent element in calf skin collagen. *FEBS Letters,* 5, 187-191. (November).

Everitt, A. V. 1971. Food intake, growth and the ageing of collagen in rat tail tendon. *Gerontologia,* 17, 98-104.

Everitt, A. V., Gal, A., and Steele, M. G. 1970. Age changes in the solubility of tail tendon collagen throughout the life span of the rat. *Gerontologia,* 16, 30-40.

Fahrenbach, W. H., Sandberg, L. G., and Cleary, E. G. 1966. Ultrastructural studies on early elastogenesis. *Anat. Record,* 155, 563-568.

Farguhar, M. G. 1960. An electron microscopic study of glomerular permeability. *Anat. Record.,* 136, 191.

Fujimori, E. 1966. Ultraviolet light irradiated collagen macromolecules. *Biochemistry,* 5, 1034-1040.

Gallop, P. M., Paz, M. A., Pereyera, B., and Blumenfeld, O. O. 1974. The maturation of connective tissue proteins. *Israel J. Chem.,* 12, 305-317.

Gersh, I., and Catchpole, H. R. 1949. The organization of ground substance and basement membrane and its significance in tissue injury, disease and growth. *Am. J. Anat.,* 85, 457-522.

Gibbs, D. A., Merrill, E. W., Smith, K. A., and Balazs,

E. A. 1968. The rheology of hyaluronic acid. *Biopoly.,* 6, 777-791.

Giles, J. S., and Everitt, A. V. 1967. The role of the thyroid and food intake in the ageing of collagen fibres. I. In the young rat. *Gerontologia,* 13, 65.

Graham, R. C., Jr., and Karnovsky, M. J. 1966. Glomerular permeability ultrastructural cytochemical studies using peroxidases as protein traces. *J. Exp. Med.,* 124, 1123-1133.

Greenlee, T. K., Jr., and Ross, R. 1967. The development of the rat flexor digital tendon, a fine structure study. *J. Ultrastruct. Res.,* 18, 354-376.

Gross, J. 1958. Studies on the formation of collagen. II. The influence of growth rate on neutral salt extracts of guinea pig dermis. *J. Exp. Med.,* 107, 265.

Hall, D. A. 1967. The ageing of connective tissue. *In, Aspects of the Biology of Ageing* (Symposia No. 21 of the Society for Experimental Biology), pp. 101-126. New York: Academic Press.

Hamerman, D., and Schuster, H. 1958. Synovial fluid hyaluronate in rheumatoid arthritis. *Arthritis Rheumat.,* 1, 523-531.

Hamlin, C. R., and Kohn, R. R. 1971. Evidence for progressive, age-related structural changes in post-mature human collagen. *Biochim. Biophys. Acta,* 236, 458-467.

Hamlin, C. R., and Kohn, R. R. 1972. Determination of human chronological age by study of a collagen sample. *Exp. Geront.,* 7, 377-379.

Hauss, W. H., and Junge-Hülsing, G. 1963. Modifications du métabolisme de l'acide chondroitine-sulfurique observées dans différentes conditions. *Exposes Ann. Biochem. Med.,* 24, 239-251.

Heikkinen, E., Aalto, M., Vihersaari, T., and Kulonen, E. 1971. Age factor in the formation and metabolism of experimental granulation tissue. *J. Geront.,* 26 (3), 294-298.

Jacobson, B., and Boström, H. 1964. II. The effect of aging and anti-inflammatory drugs on the synthesis of glucosamine 6-phosphate and phosophoadensine phosphosulfate by bovine heart valves. *Biochim. Biophys. Acta,* 83, 152-164.

Kang, A. H., Piez, K. A., and Gross, J. 1969. Characterization of the cyanogen bromide peptides from the $\alpha 1$ chain of chick skin collagen. *Biochemistry,* 8, 1506-1514.

Kefalides, K. N. 1973. Structure and biosynthesis of basement membranes. *In,* D. A. Hall and D. S. Jacson (eds.), *International Review of Connective Tissue Research,* Vol. 6, pp. 63-104. New York: Academic Press.

LaBella, F. S., and Lindsay, W. G. 1963. The structure of human aortic elastin as influenced by age. *J. Geront.,* 18, 111-118.

LaBella, F. S., and Thornhill, D. P. 1965. Effects of ultraviolet irradiation on human and bovine collagen and elastin: Relationship of tyrosine to native fluorescence. *In, Studies of Rheumatoid Diseases*

(Proceedings of the Third Canadian Conference for Research in Rheumatic Disease), pp. 246-254.

LaBella, F. S., Vivian, S., and Thornhill, D. P. 1966. Amino acid composition of human aortic elastin as influenced by age. *J. Geront.*, **21**, 550-555.

Loewi, G., and Meyer, K. 1958. The acid mucopolysaccharides of embryonic skin. *Biochim. Biophys. Acta*, **27**, 453-456.

Loomeijer, F. J. 1961. The lipid compound of elastin. *J. Atherosclerosis Res.*, **1**, 62-66.

Mechanic, G. L., Gallop, P. M., and Tanzer, M. L. 1971. The nature of crosslinking in collagens from mineralized tissues. *Biochem. Biophys. Res. Commun.*, **45**, 644-653.

Meyer, K. 1958. *In*, G. F. Springer (ed.), *Conference on Polysaccharides in Biology*, Vol. 4, pp. 11-56. New York: Macy Foundation.

Milch, R. A. 1965. Matrix properties of the aging arterial wall. *In, Monographs in the Surgical Sciences*, Vol. 2, pp. 261-341. Baltimore: Williams & Wilkins.

Miller, E. J., Lane, J. M., and Piez, K. A. 1969. Isolation and characterization of the peptides derived from the α1 chain of chick bone collagen after cyanogen bromide cleavage. *Biochemistry*, **8**, 30-39.

Morrison, M., Steele, W., and Danner, D. J. 1969. The reaction of benzoquinone with amines and proteins. *Arch. Biochem. Biophys.*, **134**, 515-523.

Németh-Csóka, M. 1970. Importance of sulphated acid mucopolysaccharides for fibrillogenesis in carrageenin granulomata of rats at different ages. *Exp. Geront.*, **5**, 67-75.

Österlin, S., and Balazs, E. A. 1968. Macromolecular composition and fine structure of the vitreous in the owl monkey. *Exp. Eye Res.*, **7**, 534-545.

Partridge, S. M., Elsden, D. F., and Thomas, J. 1963. Constitution of the cross-linkages in elastin. *Nature*, **197**, 1297-1298.

Pigman, W., and Horton, D. (eds.) 1970. *The Carbohydrates*, Vol. IIB. New York and London: Academic Press.

Puleo, L. E., and Sobel, H. H. 1972. Oxygen-modified collagen and its possible pathological significance. *Aerospace Med.*, **43**, 429-431.

Ramachandran, G. N. (ed.) 1967-1969. *Treatise on Collagen*, Vol. 1, 2, 3. New York and London: Academic Press.

Robins, S. P., Shimokomaki, M., and Bailey, A. J. 1973. The chemistry of the collagen cross-links. Age-related changes in the reducible components

of intact bovine collagen fibres. *Biochem. J.*, **131**, 771-780.

Ross, R., and Bornstein, P. 1969. The elastic fiber. I. The separation and partial characterization of its macromolecular components. *J. Cell Biol.*, **40**, 366-381.

Schiller, S., and Dorfman, A. 1960. Effect of age on the heparin content of rat skin. *Nature*, **185**, 111-112.

Schweer, G. 1962. Glaskörper und hyaluronsäure-hyaluronidase-system. *Samml. Zwangl. Abh. Augenheilk.*, **25**, 1-74.

Seppälä, P., and Balazs, E. A. 1969. Hyaluronic acid in synovial fluid. III. Effect of maturation and aging on the chemical properties of bovine synovial fluid. *J. Geront.*, **24**, 309-314.

Seppälä, P., Gibbs, D. A., Balazs, E. A., and Merrill, E. W. Hyaluronic acid in synovial fluid. V. The rheological properties of bovine synovial fluid in animals of different ages (in preparation).

Smith, Q. T., and Armstrong, W. D. 1961. Collagen metabolism of rats in various hormonal and dietary conditions. *Am. J. Physiol.*, **200**, 1330.

Stoner, R., and Blivaiss, B. B. 1967. Reaction of quinone of homogentisic acid with biological amines. *Arthritis Rheumat.*, **10**, 53-60.

Thornhill, D. P. 1972. Elastin: Locus and characteristics of chromophore and fluorophore. *Conn. Tis. Res.*, **1**, 21-30.

Traub, W., and Piez, K. A. 1971. The chemistry and structure of collagen. *Advan. Protein Chem.*, **25**, 243-352.

Trnavský, K., Kopecký, Š., Trnavská, Z., and Cehecauer, L. 1965. Influence of age on biochemical composition of the mitral valve connective tissue. *Gerontologia*, **2** (3/4), 169-178.

Walker, P. S., Unsworth, A., Dowson, D., Sikorski, J., and Wright, V. 1970. Mode of aggregation of hyaluronic acid protein complex on the surface of articular cartilage. *Ann. Rheumatic Diseases*, **29**, 591-602.

Whitehead, R. G., and Coward, D. G. 1969. Collagen and hydroxyproline metabolism in malnourished children and rats. *In, Bibl. Nutr. Diet.*, Vol. 13, p. 74. Basel: S. Karger.

Widdowson, E. M., and Dickerson, J. W. T. 1960. Effect of growth and function of the chemical composition of soft tissues. *Biochem. J.* **77**, 30-43.

Yamashita, T., and Becker, B. 1961. The basement membrane in the human diabetic eye. *Diabetes*, **10**, 167-174.

10
ANATOMICAL CHANGES IN THE NERVOUS SYSTEM

Harold Brody
and
N. Vijayashankar
State University of New York at Buffalo

INTRODUCTION

The past decade has witnessed a veritable revolution in the orientation of scientific thought regarding the study of the nervous system. The emphasis upon these studies ought to be of interest for researchers at both theoretical and applied levels, but it should be recognized that the increased attention being given to neurophysiological and behavioral studies with increasing age depends upon the understanding of morphological changes occurring in the nervous system.

A basic difficulty in the study of changes in the aging nervous system is the scarcity of suitable material for examination. In this regard, Tomlinson (1972) has emphasized that the selection of "normal" brains is made difficult by a lack of information regarding the behavior and intellectual capacity of the individual before death. It is obvious that in keeping with the increased attention being given the aging nervous system, longitudinal studies must be developed which will provide information about individuals during their lifetimes as well as their brain material for anatomical and biochemical studies. This integrated approach would provide the proper baseline currently unavailable in studies of the human central nervous system.

In the absence of such criteria, use must be made of studies which have restricted the "control" subjects to individuals who had not been under neurologic or psychiatric care and had not demonstrated nervous system involvement before death (Brody, 1955; Hirano and Zimmerman, 1962).

In this section of the chapter, emphasis will be placed upon the morphological changes in the nervous system of man and animals, as these may be considered to be essential in the interpretation of changes in function. The gross features of the aging nervous system will be examined first including the question of brain weight and volume as well as changes in meninges, convolutional size, and ventricular system. The consideration of the microscopic structure of the aging central nervous system will include a review of studies of neuronal cell number as well as an examination of the neuron and its organelles with respect to aging.

Studies of the nervous system as related to aging may provide a basis for a better understanding of biological and clinical aspects of development. The statement of Medawar (1971),

"I do want to emphasize that the purpose of research on aging is to enlarge our understanding of biological processes in a way that will ultimately be of value to human beings," emphasizes the value of gerontological research in providing answers not only to the aging process but also to the living process as well.

NEUROANATOMY AND NEUROPATHOLOGY

Gross Appearance and Changes

Brain Weight. An early study of brain weight is that of Boyd (1860) who showed that the human brain in his series increased in weight in the male from 493 grams at 3 months of age to a peak value of 1,374 grams between 14 and 20 years. By 80 years, the brain had lost approximately 90 grams or 6.6 percent by weight. Relatively similar findings were reported in the female. In 1878, Broca reported the weight of the brain to be at its maximum between 25 and 35 years of age. In an extensive report, the biometrician, Pearl (1922) in a study of 3,134 adult brains (2,100 male and 1,034 female) observed a linear regression in brain weight during the period from 20 to 80 years which amounted to a 7 percent decrease by the latter age.

This decrease in brain weight was confirmed by Appel and Appel (1942a), whose study of 2,752 specimens indicated a mean weight of 1,300 grams in the male. Earlier, Scammon and Dunn (1922) had examined 2,956 male and female brains between birth and 20 years and concluded that a smooth curve could be drawn which after a sharp rise during the first 2 years, gradually flattens out during the next 18 years. Appel and Appel in a later study (1942b) found that brain weight decreased at a uniform rate, by 96 years amounting to 11 percent of the mean weight in a series of 2,080 brains. But, as these latter authors and Bailey and von Bonin (1951) point out, it is highly improbable that any standardization exists in the technique of weighing brain material.

In the study of forensic material conducted by Pakkenberg and Voigt (1964) upon 1,090 Danish specimens, the mean weight found for adult males was 1,440 grams and for adult females 1,282 grams. At least in the statistically significant male group, the weight loss found from the age of 25 to 70 years was about 100 grams, very similar to the 90-gram loss Boyd had determined 104 years earlier.

Attention must be directed to the fact that rarely are descriptions included in the literature of the exact caudal and rostral extent of the brain removed for weight determination, whether the meninges and blood vessels are included in the weight, and information as to the body weight of the individual before death.

It is an accepted fact among neuroanatomists and neuropathologists that with few exceptions, there is a direct correlation between body weight and brain weight. Younger people of today are larger and heavier than younger people of earlier generations, and one would expect that at this point in time the average larger 20-year-old should possess a heavier brain (and larger body size) than the average 75-year-old. Were these two individuals autopsied for the same study, the variation in body size could be a factor in a brain weight differential and provide an erroneous conclusion that brain weight decreases with increasing age. In C57B1/6J male mice that have attained a maximum, stable value of skeletal size and body weight, Finch (1973) did not observe changes in wet brain weight between 10–12-month-old and 28–30-month-old animals.

Gross Brain Structure

Cortical Size. Differentiation must be made between the effect of age upon convolutional size in the "control" where only a moderate degree of atrophy is noted and the severe atrophy seen in Alzeimer's disease and some cases of senile dementia.

Ventricular Size. Cammermeyer (1959) had demonstrated an increase in ventricular size with age in dogs. However, Last and Tompsett (1953) found no evidence of increased size of the ventricles with age in a series of human specimens, but only three specimens were from individuals over 65 years of age.

In 60 percent of Tomlinson's series (1972), the ventricles of aged specimens were similar in size to those of young adults. Also based on these cases, it was Tomlinson's impression that unless there has been a dementing process, there is a lack of widespread softening in the brains of aging persons.

The detailed studies of Tomlinson, Blessed, and Roth (1968, 1970) indicate a need for further studies to determine whether the changes usually described in brain weight and ventricular size with increasing age are truly age-dependent.

Microscopic Anatomy

General Considerations—Autopsy Time, Fixation, and Tissue Preparation. A good deal of confusion regarding the microscopic study of the nervous system has been introduced by studies reported in the literature in which improper use of autopsied material had been employed. Neural tissue is very sensitive to procedural treatment, and it is imperative that the investigators introduce as little artifact as possible. Earlier, we alluded to the problem of selection of material for aging studies in the human. Care must be exercised that the specimens used are not from individuals with a previous history of neurologic disease or symptomatology. The risk of misinterpretation of data may result if this initial criterion is not applied. The specific brain or spinal cord specimen must be removed at autopsy as rapidly as possible after death and quickly fixed. For any study, the investigator must determine a maximal time for specimen use. A practical difficulty exists which may make rapid procurement of a specimen difficult. In our own studies, specimens are removed and fixed by injection of physiological saline followed by 10 percent formalin saline solution through the internal carotid and vertebral arteries within 4 hours after death.

The need for rapid removal and fixation is further emphasized in the preparation of tissue for ultrastructural studies which to a large extent have not been carried out in the human because of rapid artifactual changes which occur in subcellular elements. Since the need for these studies is required for an understanding of morphology and function in the central nervous system and since the animal model is not comparable to that of the human

in relation to aging (Dayan, 1971), it may be necessary to conduct studies which will illustrate the electron microscopic structure of the human nervous system at specific intervals after death. Thus, the presence of artifactual change occurring with time may be interpreted and separated from that which may occur as a concomitant of aging.

The method of preparation of nerve tissue for examination with the light microscope is variable, depending upon the specific structure to be examined. Various embedding media and stains will be discussed later as each area is examined.

Nerve Cell Number—Quantitative Techniques. Are the changes which occur in early development and maturation of the nervous system specific to the nerve cell body or its processes, and does there exist a relationship as aging occurs between numerical changes in these structures and function? A number of techniques have been developed for the estimation of cell number in the nervous system. These have been reviewed by Konigsmark (1970) and are cited briefly below.

Photographic Method. In one of the earliest techniques used, a section of tissue is photographed and cells counted from the print. The disadvantage of this method is that the cells may be observed and counted in only one plane, and distinguishing between small neurons and glial cells is difficult.

Projection Method. The histological preparation is projected onto a screen and cells counted within predetermined areas.

Microphotometric Method. This involves passage of light through the section onto a photocell of a microphotometer. The current in the photocell may then be recorded as a curve indicating optical density related to cortical depth. The density may then be converted into cell numbers by use of a mathematical formula.

Homogenate Method. Suspensions of cells are produced by homogenation of fresh brain tissue and are examined under the microscope. These cells can provide estimates of cell number per known weight of tissue, but, again, small neurons may not be distinguishable from glial cells. This is particularly critical when examining the brain of the newborn. Johnson and Erner (1972) developed a rapid method for determining the absolute number of neurons in mouse brain. Brains fixed in formalin for several months were placed in a test tube and homogenized in water with a glass rod. After two periods of sonication, a drop of the suspension was stained with thionine and cell counts determined in a hemocytometer. This method has been found to have some value in estimating total neuronal population in small brains since the neurons and glia are distinguishable.

Direct Microscopic Method. This is the most common although laborious method for counting nerve cells as well as other cells of the central nervous system. However, this remains the most dependable of all counting techniques at the present time. After the tissue is embedded in paraffin or celloidin, thin sections are stained and examined under the light microscope, usually with the aid of a micrometer disc which separates the field into smaller squares. The risk of counting a cell more than once is minimized by the use of this equipment. All cells in a specific cellular group may be counted or cells in a percentage of the sections may be counted in serial fashion through the length of the group and the sum of these counts multiplied to give a total. This technique is particularly useful in examining brain stem nuclei or other discrete cellular groups (Van Buskirk, 1945; Tomasch and Malpass, 1958; Tomasch and Ebnessajjade, 1961; Blinkov and Ponomarev, 1965; Moatamed, 1966; Konigsmark and Murphy, 1972; Monagle and Brody, 1974). In less discrete areas of the nervous system (cerebral cortex), the number of cells per unit area may be obtained by counting cells throughout the full thickness of the cortex, e.g., to compare cortical areas (Rowland and Mettler, 1949; Brody, 1955), or the number of cells per unit volume may be used to calculate the total population of the structure by volume.

Automated Methods. In addition to the flying spot scanner (Causley and Young, 1955; Mansberg and Segarra, 1962), the recently developed analyzer (Quantimet) transmits an image of a section on a slide through a light microscope or from a photograph through a camera to a television screen and permits particles to be counted based upon size, shape, and intensity of staining (Manodesley-Thomas and Healey, 1970; Fisher, 1971; Prensky, 1971). The disadvantages of this technique at this time are that thin sections $(1-2\mu)$ must be cut to facilitate counting without cell overlap, and staining techniques must be used which differentiate cell components from each other so that one of these structures may be used as the critical unit for counting. Because of the problems related to the use of automated counting techniques, it appears that the direct microscopic method provides the greatest reproducibility and dependability and is the preferred method for cell counting. However, the speed (8,000 fields/4 hr) and relative simplicity of the apparatus are such that its increased use in quantitative biology should be a high priority of investigators in this field.

RESULTS OF CELL COUNTS AND RELATION TO AGING

Cerebral Cortex

There have been relatively few studies performed on the numbers of nerve cells in the human central nervous system, and the relationship of cell number and aging is only now receiving increased attention. Among these studies of cerebral cortical aging, Brody (1955) reported a decrease in cell number with aging, occurring in varying degrees in specific cortical areas. As substantiated by Hanley (1974) in his review of neuronal fallout in the aging brain, this decrease in cell number was significant in the superior temporal gyrus, precentral gyrus, and area striata and was not significant in the postcentral gyrus or inferior temporal gyrus. A later study (Brody, 1970) reported a decrease in cell number in the superior frontal gyrus comparable to that demonstrated in the superior temporal gyrus, approximately 45 percent by the ninth decade. While within age groups there were differences in cell number, in general there was a clustering by decades and a decrease with increasing age. The decrease in neuronal cell number occurred in all layers but was most marked in layers 2 and 4, the external and internal granule layers in which the Golgi type II short axoned cells are characteristic of the associational cells of the human cerebral cortex. Of particular interest in this regard is the recent work of Scheibel and Scheibel (1975), in which studies of the Golgi of the cerebral cortex of the aging human demonstrated a progressive loss of horizontal dendrites of pyramidal cells of layer 3. As these dendrites normally contact the granule cells of layers 2 and 4, it would appear that the relationship between cortical granule cells and pyramidal cells undergoes quantitative and morphological changes with age. While additional evidence is lacking at this time, it may be hypothesized that changes in one of these cell groups may have influenced changes in the other and that functional disorganization could be expected as a result.

Colon (1972) found a substantial, random loss of neurons in cortex of the frontal pole, area striata, cingulate gyrus, and precentral gyrus by the ninth decade. While he does not supply information as to percentage of cell decrease for each area, Colon reports a total mean cell loss of 44 percent for all areas.

A study of the effect of aging upon nerve cells in layer 3 of the cerebral cortex in a group of subjects with a mean age of 77 years (Shefer, 1973) indicated an average decrease of 20 percent in the absolute number of nerve cells in all regions of cortex examined, particularly marked in the frontal polar region (28 percent), middle temporal gyrus (23 percent), and subiculum (29 percent). Other cortical areas which showed a lesser degree of cell loss were the posterior frontal lobe region, area striata, temporal polar region, and supramarginal gyrus. Most recently, Tomlinson (1976) has repeated the work of Brody (1955, 1970, 1973) using an automatic counting device (Quantimet) and has verified the progressive loss of neurons in cerebral cortex. These quantitative studies of the cerebral cortex indicate a general decrease in cell number in cortex with some variation as to the degree of involvement in different cortical areas.

A concept which has achieved a modicum of popularity was developed by Burns (1958) based on the studies of Leboucq (1929) and Brody (1955). Combining Brody's findings of neuronal decrease between the third and ninth decades and the conclusion of Leboucq that there is a 10 percent decrease in surface area of the brain during these time periods, Burns suggested that "during every day of our adult life more than 100,000 neurones die." While changes described in the brain appear to occur throughout the life span, it is not possible to conclude from this that daily attrition occurs. In fact, as was demonstrated by Brody (1970) in a study of the superior frontal gyrus, the decrease in cell number is greater for this area of cortex during the fifth decade than during the remainder of the life span. It should be obvious, then, that a daily estimation is neither useful nor justifiable.

Cerebellar Cortex

The early studies performed on cerebellar cortex by Hodge (1894), Archambault (1918), Ellis (1919, 1920), and Harms (1927) in the human and by Inukai (1928) in the rat indicated a decrease with age in the number of Purkinje cells. This conclusion was not supported by Delorenzi (1931) or Wilcox (1956) in the guinea pig. However more recently, Hall, Miller, and Corsellis (1975) have examined cerebellar hemispheres from 90 human subjects ranging in age from 1 to 105 years. They report that although there is a wide variation in Purkinje cell number among subjects, there is a tendency for these cells to decrease in number during adult life. This reduction in both males and females amounted to a 25 percent decrease over a 100-year age span but was not appreciable until the sixth decade of life.

Whole Brain Studies

Johnson and Erner (1972) homogenzied the whole brain of Swiss albino mice between 1 month and 29 months of age and examined the cell suspension. They found that by 29 months of age, the neuronal population had declined to about one-third of its original number. Of interest is that by 24 months of age these mice demonstrated only a 5 percent decline in total cell number. Extending the study to older animals showed that a much greater cell decrease occurred very late in life.

Brain Stem

In contrast to the cellular decrease in cerebral and cerebellar cortex noted by some investigators, there is general agreement that cell loss with age does not occur in some brain stem nuclei such as the facial nerve nucleus (Van Buskirk, 1945), the ventral cochlear nucleus (Konigsmark and Murphy, 1970, 1972), the inferior olive (Moatamed, 1966; Monagle and Brody, 1974), and the nuclei of the trochlear and abducens nerves (Vijayashankar and Brody, 1971, 1973). The first change in cell number noted within a brain stem structure occurs in the locus coeruleus, where a significant decrease occurs after the seventh decade (Brody and Vijayashankar, 1975). These findings suggest that within the central nervous system of the human, there are differential rates of cell loss. Clearly, further examination of the central nervous system is essential if an understanding of the relationships among cell number, morphology, and aging is to be obtained. That these studies are best performed on human material is evident from the reviews by Dayan (1971), Buetow (1971), and Hanley (1974).

Nerve Fiber Changes

A considerable difference of opinion exists in the interpretation of changes in nerve fibers with age. Although Dunn (1912) in the ventral root of the rat, Birren and Wall (1956) in the sciatic nerve of the aging rat, Moyer and Kaliszewski (1958) in the C8 and T1 spinal roots of the cat, and Hoffman and Schnitzlein (1961) in human vagus nerve have reported no change with increasing age in the number of fibers, a large number of reports indicate a positive correlation between increasing age and decreasing fiber number. These include: Greenman (1917) in rat peroneal nerve, Duncan (1930) in rat sciatic nerve, Duncan (1934) in

rat ventral root, Cottrell (1940) in human median, femoral, sciatic, and peroneal nerves, and Bruesh and Arey (1942) in human optic nerve. Corbin and Gardner (1937) and Gardner (1940) in human spinal roots and Bergström (1973) in human vestibular nerve found an approximate 35 percent decrease in fiber number in these structures. Bergström also reported a decrease in the proportion of heavily myelinated nerves in the vestibular nerve.

Slowing of motor nerve conduction in association with increased age was first described by Wagman and Leese (1952). However, when measured directly in the sciatic nerve, conduction time has not been shown to change with age (Birren and Wall, 1956). Depression or loss of the ankle reflex is a common finding in the elderly (Critchley, 1931; Howell, 1949), as is impaired appreciation of vibration sense in the feet (Pearson, 1928). The anatomical location of the lesions responsible for these changes has been suggested (Lascelles and Thomas, 1966) to be in the peripheral nerve, manifested as segmental demyelination and remyelination resulting in irregularities of the internodal length. It is explained that this results in a loss of tendon reflexes and vibration sensitivity since both depend upon the ability of the nerve to conduct a synchronous volley of impulses. Kemble (1967) studied the nerve fiber conduction velocities in median nerve between the wrist and the elbow and found that motor conduction time decreased with age to a greater extent in men than women, while sensory conduction time increased with age more in men than women. He suggested that the more pronounced electrophysiological alterations of median nerve conduction with aging in normal males (as compared to normal females) were due to differences in minor degrees of segmental demyelination of peripheral nerve fibers.

GENERAL CYTOLOGY OF AGING NERVOUS SYSTEM

Golgi Complex

Almost every known cytoplasmic organelle has been shown to exhibit subtle changes in structure in the process of aging of neurons. The two alterations in the Golgi complex observed in senescent mice are fragmentation of this reticulated structure and loss of its characteristic perinuclear distribution (Andrew, 1939). Age-associated fragmentation of Golgi apparatus has been described in mouse cortical neurons (Gatenby, 1953) and rabbit spinal ganglion cells (Gatenby and Moussa, 1950). It has been suggested that the genesis of lipofuscin pigment is associated with the resultant Golgi fragments (Gatenby and Moussa, 1950; Bondareff, 1957). In autonomic ganglion cells of dogs over the age of 12 years, Sulkin and Kuntz (1952) observed that the Golgi apparatus loses its characteristic, loosely woven appearance and instead appears in the form of discrete granules. Similar findings were noted in young scorbutic guinea pigs, in young rats on vitamin E-deficient diet, in rats subjected to prolonged administration of acetanilid, and in young rats subjected to chronic hypoxia (Sulkin and Srivanij, 1960).

Sosa and deZorilla (1966), in their study of the age-related morphological variations of the Golgi apparatus in spinal ganglion cells of rabbits, classified them into six stages: (1) complete network; (2) network islets; (3) network fragmented into racemose and curly gangliosomes; (4) network fragmented into bacillary and granular forms; (5) network fragmented into granular gangliosomes; and (6) dissolved network or stage of Golgiolysis. They concluded that the Golgi apparatus fragments increasingly with age and finally occupies a perinuclear position in contrast to the juxtanuclear position in young animals. However, Hasan and Glees (1973) did not detect significant alterations in the Golgi zones of aged animals.

There is little agreement concerning the morphological changes of the Golgi complex and their significance in aging. The Golgi complex is only a part of an extensive membrane system extending throughout the cell (Palade and Porter, 1955).

Mitochondria

Abnormal swelling, vacuolation, and disruption of the cristae have been described in rat spinal ganglia in electromicrographic studies (Hess, 1955). However, Bondareff (1964) cautions against interpreting such findings as age-associated in view of the extreme vulnerability of mitochondria to prefixation insult. Andrew (1956a) reported predominance of the filamentous type of mitochondria in neurons of younger mice and of short rods and granules with a few vesicles in the neurons of older mice. Measurement of mitochondrial concentrations in pyramidal tract fibers of mouse brain revealed that the number of mitochondria in a given area of cytoplasm may decrease with age (Samorajski, Friede, and Ordy, 1971). Little variation exists in the chemical components of the mitochondria from different sources, species, and ages (Samorajski, Friede, and Ordy, 1971). Following injection of labeled precursor, the specific activity of mitochondrial DNA and lipids per unit weight of protein in brains is found to decrease with age (Huemer, Bickert, Lee, and Reeves, 1971).

Endoplasmic Reticulum

Age-associated changes in the endoplasmic reticulum are strongly suggested by the decrease in the amount of Nissl substance in older animals and humans. According to Palay and Palade (1955), Nissl bodies are granular, RNA-containing concentrations of endoplasmic reticulum. They suggested that the more tightly packed, agranular reticulum, particularly in the region of the nucleus, is the Golgi apparatus. Whether or not changes in the Golgi apparatus or endoplasmic reticulum are a result of the changes in the environment of the cell or a result of some other underlying intracellular change is not known (Strehler, 1962). Since endoplasmic reticulum is involved in synthetic activities, its decrease will result in depression of cellular function or conversely may be the result of decreased demand in older cells (Strehler, 1962). Hasan and Glees (1973), in their study of ultrastructural age changes in hippocampal neurons and glia, reported that the well-organized patterns of the rough surfaced endoplasmic reticulum seen in the neurons of younger animals were singularly lacking in older ones.

Nissl Substance

Nissl substance represents aggregates of RNA-rich endoplasmic reticulum in neuronal peri-karyon. Nissl substance, as assayed by basophilic dyes during histochemical procedures is reported to increase (Vogt and Vogt, 1946), decrease (Kuhlenbeck, 1954; Andrew, 1937; Ellis, 1920; Cammermeyer, 1963; Hasan and Glees, 1973), or remain unchanged (Bondareff, 1957; Wilcox, 1959) with age. A summary of RNA content in brain regions (neurons plus glia and other cells) is given in Table 1 of Chapter 11. In general, most regions do not show change with age in healthy rodents.

Bondareff (1962) investigated the dynamics of Nissl substance in aging rats using exhaustive swimming as an experimental stress. He showed a difference in the ability of young and old animals to recover from exhaustive swimming; the Nissl pattern characteristic of the normal unexercised animal was reestablished within hours in the young, but remained "chromatoly-tic" in the older animals. It is unknown if the deficit reflects intrinsic neuronal aging or other factors such as blood flow. Strehler (1962) considers that age-dependent changes in the endoplasmic reticulum are strongly suggested by the decrease in the amount of Nissl substance in the neurons of older animals and humans. Cammermeyer (1963) reported a progressive reduction in cytoplasmic basophilia and Feulgen reactive chromatin with aging, while Hasan and Glees (1973) considered an absence of well organized patterns of rough-surfaced endoplasmic reticulum in older animals as indicative of a reduction in the Nissl substance.

Nucleus and Nucleolus

Varying descriptions are found in the literature of the morphological changes of the nucleus with respect to aging. A decrease in the nuclear chromatin and loss of nucleolus (Hodge, 1894) and a progressive pallor of both nuclei (Hempel and Namba, 1958) and nucleoli (Andrew, 1956b) have been reported. More frequently, an increasing darkening of the nucleoplasm and accumulation of Feulgen-reactive chromatin material are described (Klatzo, 1954; Schiffler, 1954; Andrew, 1956b; Solcher, 1956; Beheim-Schwarzbach, 1957; Sanides, 1957).

An extreme degree of swelling, with transformation of the entire nucleus into a large vacuole has been ascribed to aging (Sayk, 1960). No noticeable alteration of the nuclear and nucleolar structure was reported by Bondareff (1959) and Wilcox (1959). Again, effects of preparational artifacts must not be underestimated (Bondareff, 1959). However, Cammermeyer (1963), using a two-step perfusion procedure followed by a delay of autopsy for at least 4 hours, has compared the brains of young and old rabbits and of young and old chinchillas. He concluded that the brain stem and cerebellar cortical neurons exhibit a reduction in content of cytoplasmic basophil material as evidenced by disappearance of the smallest granules and by a diminution in amount of Feulgen-reactive chromatin in the cerebellar granule cell nuclei. He also stated that these changes progress with age, indicative of a continuous alteration of intracellular nucleic acid synthesis. Andrew (1964) considers that invagination of the nuclear envelope is a common phenomenon in old cells and may be used as a criterion of aging. Hasan and Glees (1973), although repeatedly observing infolding of the nuclear membrane in electron micrographs of aged animals, tend to disagree with the concept that all reported changes in the nucleus and nucleolus may be attributed to aging alone. Age changes of a purely qualitative nature such as changes in shape and spatial displacement of the nucleus or nucleolus are prone to interpretive errors and may be extremely difficult to evaluate. Nevertheless, evidence seems to indicate that decreased cytoplasmic basophila, diminution of Feulgen-reactive chromatin, and infolding of the nuclear membrane are some features observed in aging nerve cells.

Lipofuscin

Definition. A consistently noted change in cell composition during aging is the increase of substances variously known as aging pigment, age pigment, lipofuscin, or "wear and tear" pigment. These brown, autofluorescent, intracellular pigment particles have long been recognized to be increased during aging in a variety of vertebrate cells both dividing and nondividing: myocardial cells, spleen cells, liver cells, adrenals, seminal vesicles, corpus luteum, prostate, interstitial cells of testes, and nerve cells. That the accumulation of lipofuscin in nonreplaceable, fixed postmitotic cells is an age-correlated process is well established (Jayne, 1950; Strehler, Mark, Mildvan, and Gee, 1959; Brody, 1960; Dayan, 1971; Brizzee, Ordy, and Kaack, 1974; Miquel, Tappel, Dillard, Herman, and Bensch, 1974). Indeed it is claimed that pigment formation and accumulation are the most constant findings in morphological studies of aging. Because of its apparent universal occurrence in phylogeny (Timiras, 1972) and its progressive and irreversible accumulation in postmitotic cells, this process has been proposed as a "basic law" of cellular aging (Strehler and Barrows, 1970).

Properties. No single histochemical method will identify this pigment, indicating its heterogeneous chemical composition. Various histochemical tests reveal that lipofuscin contains lipid, carbohydrate, and protein (Bjorkerud, 1964; Hendley, Mildvan, Reporter, and Strehler, 1963). Lipofuscin has an affinity for lipid stains such as Sudan Black B. It stains with carbolfuchsin, as well as with ferric ferricyanide, methyl green, PAS, and Nile Blue (Wolf and Pappenheimer, 1945; Lillie, 1950, 1956a, 1956b; Dixon and Herbertson, 1950). A histochemical study of the pigment of Nandy (1971) indicated the presence of possibly two types of lipofuscin pigment. The type predominant in the younger animals was more easily stained with Sudan Black B and PAS, had a greenish yellow autofluorescence, and was generally scattered in the neuronal cytoplasm. On the other hand, the type frequently encountered in older animals was easily stained by Nile Blue and ferric ferricyanide methods, was deposited in clumps, and had a golden yellow autofluorescence. Braak (1971) also noted a difference in the staining character of lipofuscin in the inferior olivary nucleus and dentate nucleus of the cerebellum. The former is PAS-positive and gives a strong reaction with aldehyde fuchsin while the pigment of the latter

does not react or reacts very faintly with this technique.

The presence of lipoprotein has been demonstrated in lipofuscin by both histochemical and biochemical methods (Siebert, Heidenreich, Böhmig, and Lang, 1955; Gedigk and Fischer, 1959), and the procedure for the isolation of lipopigments has been reviewed by Siakatos and Koppang (1973).

The absorption spectrum of lipofuscin has been studied both in brain sections by microspectrophotometry and on isolated lipofuscin particles and appears to consist of a gradually increasing absorption at shorter wavelengths. No clear peaks in the visible portion of the spectrum are discernible in the purified preparations (Strehler, 1962), although two peaks in the ultraviolet range were reported by Hydén and Lindström (1950). With either visible or near ultraviolet light, they emit a bright yellow green to orange fluorescence extending from about 5,000Å to 6,200Å–6,300Å.

Age pigments are poorly defined except for their histologic characteristics, and they are insoluble in polar and nonpolar solvents. Analytical biochemical studies have not yet shown if all pigments exhibiting these properties are identical or even closely related regardless of the tissue, species, or age of the subject. Some authors consider lipofuscin and age pigment as synonymous and insist on a clear-cut differentiation from ceroid. The latter term was introduced by Lillie, Ashbwin, Sebrell, Daft, and Lowry (1942) to designate a lipopigment in the liver of rats with dietary cirrhosis. It is now commonly applied to lipopigments induced by various manipulations (Zeman, 1971). Porta and Hartroft (1969) conclude that the available "evidence even now seems fairly clear that age-pigment and ceroid could be regarded as essentially synonymous with only their historical connotations retained." Nishioka, Takahata, and Iizuka (1968) in their comparative histochemical studies on ceroid pigment appearing in the brain and liver of experimental vitamin E–deficient rats and in hogs with yellow fat disease (naturally occurring vitamin E deficiency) and lipofuscin in the brain and liver of people over 70 years of age, found it impossible to draw a sharp distinction between the two. They support the view that ceroid and lipofuscin represent different degrees in the autoxidative polymerization of unsaturated fatty acids.

A number of amino acids have been demonstrated in age pigment employing highly specific, histochemical reactions (Gedigk and Fischer, 1959; Pearse, 1960). These include arginine, tryptophan, histidine, lysine, cysteine, and cystine.

Among the enzymes reported to be associated with lipofuscin are acid phosphatase, esterase, β-glucuronidase, alkaline phosphatase, ATPase, and succinyl dehydrogenase (Gedigk and Bontke, 1956; Essner and Novikoff, 1960; Gedigk and Fischer, 1959). Some of these enzymes are thought to be equivalent to the so-called lysosomal enzymes (de Duve, Pressman, Gianetto, Wattiaux, and Appelman, 1955).

Ultrastructure of Lipofuscin. Hess (1955) reported that the pigment was noted to form aggregations towards the periphery and more frequently was located around the entire border of the cell. It exhibited very marked electron density approaching that of lipoidal or nucleolar material and varied in shape from spheroidal to highly irregular bodies. It was also noted that the granules formed a lacework of dense material surrounding a number of lucent vesicles. Bondareff (1957), however, in his studies of spinal ganglia in senescent rats, indicated that such vesicles, which may be of large size, were always clearly delineated by an intact "single" membrane. Often the pigment would appear as dense, relatively isolated particles about 0.5μ in diameter, not demonstrating a noticeable association with any intracellular organelles. The pigment was also observed as a round dense body containing dense granules or small vesicles of a diameter similar to that of the granules.

Recent electron microscopic studies of lipofuscin have revealed considerable variability in the fine architecture of the individual granules. Certain investigators (Gonatas, Gambetti, Tucker, Evangelista, and Baird, 1969) consider only lobulated granules with a dense granular matrix and large lucent vacuoles surrounded by a single membrane to represent lipofuscin. Samorajski, Ordy, and Keefe (1965) found this type frequently but not exclusively in the ventral horn cells of aged mice. Goldfischer and Bernstein (1969) also refer to dense pigment granules without lucent vacuoles observed in the newborn human liver as "lipofuscin (aging) pigment." It is interesting to note that these granules bear a strong resemblance to those found in the hearts of aged humans by Malkoff and Strehler (1963) and Zeman (1971). There is a striking similarity in the electron micrographs of human lipofuscin in situ and isolated lipofuscins. There is no gross disruption of the particulate structure as a result of the isolation procedure (Strehler, 1964).

More recent electron microscopic studies have revealed electron-dense, osmiophilic particles bound by a single membrane with polymorphic internal structures ranging from fine particles in early stages to aggregates of coarse laminated bodies composed of dense bands or dense granular material (Samorajski, Keefe, and Ordy, 1964; Samorajski, Ordy, and Keefe, 1965; Samorajski, Ordy, and Rady-Reimer, 1968; Brizzee, Cancilla, Sherwood, and Timiras, 1969; Porta and Hartroft, 1969; Brizzee and Johnson, 1970). Miyigashi, Takashata, and Iizuka (1971) proposed an ultrastructural classification of neuronal lipofuscin as Type I, granular; Type II, homogeneous; Type III, lamellated; Type IV, compound (various combinations of I, II, and III).

Origin of Lipofuscin. The origin of lipofuscin has been attributed to many of the cytoplasmic organelles including mitochondria, endoplasmic reticulum, Golgi apparatus, and lysosomes. For an extensive review on the genesis of lipofuscin, the reader is referred to Toth (1968) and Porta and Hartroft (1969). Reference will be made here only to the literature on the subject since these publications. Hasan and Glees (1973) in their study of the deafferented, lateral geniculate nucleus, observed a close topographical association of mitochondria and lipofuscin granules, implying a mitochondrial origin of the latter, supporting the findings of Miquel (1971) and Spoerri and Glees (1973). Barden (1970) observed in the aging rhesus monkey that in neurons containing lipofuscin, Golgi apparatus retreated from the accumulating pigment and was diminished in amount in direct relation to the quantity of the pigment; "while neuromelanin accumulates in the presence of an intact Golgi apparatus, this being the converse of the process following lipofuscin formation in the nerve cell in which a functional depression in the Golgi apparatus related to aging appears to occur." These results suggest that fully formed neuromelanin and lipofuscin granules are residual bodies derived from small lysosomes present in the neurons of immature and aging monkeys.

Pallis, Duckett, and Pearse (1967) in their study of a case of diffuse lipofuscinosis of the central nervous system observed the lipofuscin granules to be the sites of acid phosphatase activity, providing further evidence of a lysosomal origin. Brünk and Ericsson (1972) in their study of the neurons in rat cerebral cortex and pontine ganglia observed apparent transitional forms between autophagic vacuoles and lipofuscinlike bodies showing acid phosphatase activity and thus supporting a lysosomal origin. The weight of evidence thus far seems to favor a lysosomal origin for lipofuscin (Figure 1).

Location (Intracellular Distribution). Studies on the intracellular distribution of the pigment showed different patterns during aging. Höpker (1951) noted a variable distribution pattern relative to certain cell types and aging. Whiteford and Getty (1966) grouped the intracellular distribution of the pigment in various areas of the brain of dogs and pigs into four categories:

a. diffuse type with small particles evenly scattered throughout the cytoplasm;
b. perinuclear clusters, usually concentrated in a crescent-shaped configuration;
c. polar or axonal concentration when the pigment was collected at or near the axon hillock;
d. bipolar type with aggregations in relation to both axon hillock and the principal dendrite.

Brody (1960) and Monagle, Brody, and Vijayashankar (in preparation) based on their studies of human cerebral cortex and inferior olive, divided the cells into four groups according to the amount and distribution pattern of lipofuscin:

a. Group I with no pigment;
b. Group II in which pigment granules are scattered throughout the cytoplasm;
c. Group III in which the pigment is clumped and concentrated in one pole;
d. Group IV in which the pigment occupies almost the entire cytoplasm, pushing the nucleus to an eccentric position.

The depth distribution of lipofuscin in the cerebral cortex of rats was studied by Brizzee and Johnson (1970), who analyzed the absolute and proportional accumulation with age at various depths. They observed that the proportional increase of neuron somata occupied by the autofluorescent pigment granules from young adulthood to old age was greater in lamina III than in other laminae. These authors also suggested a lysosomal origin for lipofuscin.

Significance. The biological implications of this pigment continue to be debated because it is not known whether the pigment accumulation is a fundamental part of the aging process *per se* or whether it is the result of various types of insult and injury to the animal. Lipofuscin is widely distributed throughout the nervous system, although differences in the localization as well as differences related to species have been noted. Whiteford and Getty (1966) demonstrated that the pigment was not present in significant amounts prior to the age of 2 years in the pig and 2½ years in the dog. They also noted that the pigment appeared at approximately the same time in the same nuclei of the same species.

Based on the observation that the pigment was absent in the continually active cochlear nucleus of guinea pigs, Wilcox (1956) presented the hypothesis that the deposition of the pigment may be indirectly related to the functional activity of the nerve cells. However, Whiteford and Getty (1966) observed a heavy pigmentation of the cochlear nucleus in senescent dogs.

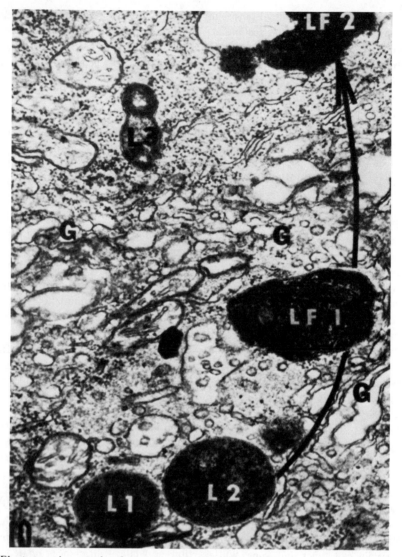

Figure 1. Electron micrograph of anterior horn cell from spinal cord of a 15-month-old mouse. Possible transformation of lipofuscin pigment from lysosome (L1) to a more complex lipofuscin pigment configuration (LF2) is indicated by a large arrow. Note early membrane formation in dense body (L2) and presence of small vacuole and numerous membranes in pigment body (LF1). Pigment body (LF2) displays a large, peripherally placed vacuole. The Golgi apparatus (G) and a sysosome with laminated bands (L3) are indicated. O_sO_4 fixation, Maraglas embedding, lead tartrate strain. 22,000 X. (Reproduced with the permission of the authors and the Journal of Gerontology. Samorajski, Keefe, and Ordy, 1964).

In this regard Reichel, Hollander, Clark, and Strehler (1968) considered any speculation on the relationship between activity level and pigment accumulation to be premature until a complete quantitative survey of the distribution of age pigment throughout the nervous system is accomplished.

More recent studies conducted on the effects of prolonged acetanilid feeding, chronic vitamin E deficiency, and chronic hypoxia in very young rats indicated that these environmental factors resulted in a marked deposition of ceroid in nerve cells at an age in which the pigment does not normally occur (Sulkin, 1958). In addition, prolonged treatment of unilaterally nephrectomized rats with ACTH resulted in the deposition of the pigment in various parts of the nervous system in amounts greater than those normally found in senescent rats raised under the usual laboratory conditions (Sulkin, 1958; Sulkin and Srivanij, 1960). However, as pointed out by Strehler (1962), such observations cannot rule out an intrinsic role of pigments in the aging process since any factor that accelerates their accumulation might well operate by a different pathway than the normally occurring one.

Porta and Hartroft (1969) raised the questions as to "whether the pigment should be regarded as an ornament of the autopsy and a laboratory curiosity or do they have greater significance in terms of health and disease, whether their accumulation in the old hastens the onset of clinical evidence of senility or even death and whether suppression of their formation has a beneficial effect." They concluded that these fundamental questions still remain unanswered, although more recent studies have attempted to answer some of these questions. Tappel (1968, 1970) observed that the critical initiating reaction in the formation of lipofuscin is polyunsaturated lipid peroxidation and that if the aging processes are to be slowed, attention should be given to naturally occurring biological antioxidants, in particular vitamin E. Because the biochemistry of vitamin E deficiency and aging processes runs parallel, Tappel points out that research should continue to explore more fully the optimum intake of vitamin E which inhibits lipid peroxidation and the possible use of multiple synthetic antioxidants.

The early appearance and experimental modification of lipofuscin by drugs, hormones, antioxidants, and immunoregulation have suggested that the pigment may represent an innocuous by-product of cellular metabolism (Kormendy and Bender, 1971; Nandy, 1968). There is evidence that the mere presence of the pigment in residual bodies does not materially impair the formation of the affected cell, unless the accumulation reaches enormous proportions (Zeman, 1971). On the other hand, if the rate of pigment production is higher than the rate of regenerative molecular synthesis, nerve cells undergo specific pathological changes. First, a stunting of the dendritic apparatus occurs, then the perikaryon becomes rounded, the cytoplasm rarified, and the cells die and eventually disappear (Zeman, 1971). However, studies on the rate of *in vivo* high energy phosphate utilization as a measure of metabolic rate in young and senescent mice (Ferrendelli, Sedgwick, and Suntzeff, 1971) indicate that the lipofuscin accumulation *per se* does not result in a decrease in brain metabolic rate and that the effect of advanced age on brain energy metabolism is a regionally selective process.

It has been established that under experimental circumstances in rodents and monkey, the drug Centrophenoxine can reduce the lipofuscin present in nerve cells without affecting the lipofuscin in other tissues (Bourne, 1973; Nandy and Bourne, 1966; Nandy, 1968). Although the above mentioned studies do not answer the questions regarding the functional significance of lipofuscin accumulation unequivocally, they do reflect some recent advances. An unexplored area of research would be single unit electrical and microchemical studies which may provide direct experimental evidence concerning the functional consequences at the cellular level.

Kormendy and Bender (1971) have summarized the most significant attempts made in recent years to decelerate physiological aging by chemical intervention, including tissue culture studies, antioxidants, lipofuscin and cross-link inhibitors, immunoregulators, hormones, and learning enhancing agents. They have pointed out that the future course of research should be to determine whether prolongation of either mean or maximum life span brings about a true deceleration of the overall aging process or only of certain biological functions.

There are indications that the reduction of reserve capacity of the brain is due to a loss of functional cells occurring throughout the entire adult life span (Hollander, 1970). The question is still not resolved as to whether this reduction is due to a decrease of functional cells or to a decreased function per cell, for example, as a result of lipofuscin accumulation. While Mann and Yates (1974) have proposed that cell death may be a result of accumulation of lipofuscin pigment, this is probably not the case. At least within the cells of the inferior olive where the largest amount of intracellular lipofuscin occurs Monagle, Brody, and Vijayashankar, (in preparation), Moatamed (1966), and Monagle and Brody (1974) have reported no loss of cells with increasing age. At this time we do not know what effect lipofuscin has on cells; we know only that it accumulates with age.

Neuroglia

Neuroglial changes in the senescent human brain were studied by Ravens and Calvo (1965). The astrocytes showing gliofibril degeneration are mostly confined to the cerebral cortex and subcortex, especially in the frontal lobe, middle portion of the superior temporal gyrus, hippocampus, and occipital lobes, but they also are distributed throughout the subependymal area and in the cortex and subcortex of the cerebellum. This type of degeneration is seen in astrocytes with the following characteristics or combination of characteristics: (1) an increase in volume; (2) a slight disintegration of the cytoplasmic extensions; and (3) astrocytes more or less intact. The degenerated gliofibrils of the cortex exhibit a number of varying forms being "filamentous," "tangled," "fragmented," "serpentine," "spiral," "signet ring," and "conglomerate." These features progressively increase in frequency and degree with further aging. The alterations suggest a progressive aging phenomenon manifested initially in the degeneration of the sucker-feet with eventual production of intracellular hypoxic metabolic changes and subsequent gliofibrillary degeneration. Neuroglial alterations in aged rats have also been reported by Hasan and Glees (1973). They have observed binucleate oligodendrocytes with increasing age but observed no significant alterations in astrocytes. They also reported the occurrence of numerous vacuoles in microglia but did not consider this to be an age-related phenomenon.

Synapses

Changes in the acetylcholinesterase activity, norepinephrine content, and serotonin concentration in brain homogenates of mice have been associated with increasing age (Samorajski,

Rolsten, and Ordy, 1971). Electric shock stress for 15 days altered the norepinephrine and acetylcholinesterase concentrations to a variable degree depending upon the age of the animal. But the exact relationship between these findings and the ultrastructure of the synapses has not been established. Very few studies have been reported on the morphological changes of the synapse with aging. Hasan and Glees (1973) in their study of age changes in the hippocampus noted that axosomatic contacts were a prominent feature of the younger animals while these decreased in older animals, and characteristic membrane thickenings and accumulation of synaptic vesicles were seldom observed in aged rats.

There are no quantitative data about the effects of aging on the number of synapses.

Extracellular Space in Aging

The extracellular space of the brain is composed primarily of submicroscopic channels between cellular elements. It is believed to be the site of physiologically important reactions involving metabolites and ions, upon which neuronal metabolism depends. The extracellular space of the brain appears to contain certain anionic substances that may be glycoproteins or mucopolysaccharides. In this regard, it resembles the ground substance of connective tissue. It has been reported that the ground substance of the connective tissue condenses, becomes less hydrated, and is replaced by collagen as animals age (Gersh and Catchpole, 1960). Bondareff and Narotzky (1972), in estimating the volume of the tissue occupied by the extracellular space stereometrically in rats of various ages, found that it decreases from 20.8 percent in the 3-month-old rat to 9.6 percent in senescent animals 26 months of age. They concluded that this decrease in extracellular space reflects an age-associated change in the microenvironment of nerve cells, indicating that the transport of catecholamines through brain tissue is reduced greatly in senescent animals and suggesting a generalized decrease in transport of materials through the extracellular space (Bondareff, 1973). However, Finch, Jonec, Hody, Walker, Smith, Alper, and Dougher (1975) reported no reduction in the extracellular space with increasing age. The possible contribution of the age-related changes in the extracellular space to decreased uptake was determined to be negligible by wash-out studies of tyrosine and by the uptake of inulin. A significant age-related increase of inulin uptake *in vitro* was observed under ionic conditions which minimize tissue swelling (Finch *et al.*, 1975).

Neuroaxonal Dystrophy

This lesion which consists of spheroidal or ovoid swellings on the terminal parts of the axis cylinders has been described as a concomitant of aging in various animals. Several extensive surveys have been undertaken in man in order to discover the distribution of this type of change within the brain and to correlate its occurrence with advancing age (Sung, 1964; Brannon, McCormick, and Lampert, 1967; Fujisawa, 1967; and Sroka, Bornstein, Strulovici, and Sandbank, 1969). Although many areas may be affected, the greatest number of lesions have been found in the gracile nucleus. None has been reported in individuals less than 10 years old, and they become increasingly common in later life, so that by 60 years of age the majority of specimens are affected. A direct correlation was found between the frequency of neuroaxonal dystrophy and increasing age in 82 out of 459 consecutive autopsies (Sroka *et al.*, 1969). Fujisawa (1967), employing routine histochemical techniques, demonstrated intense focal swellings, mainly of preterminal axons. These lesions were rarely seen in younger specimens and were frequent and severe in the aged. Of 541 consecutive autopsies, Brannon, McCormick, and Lampert (1967) found neuroaxonal dystrophy in all patients over 20 with few exceptions, but could not establish a clear relationship between the severity of involvement, age of the patient, chronic alcoholism, or any underlying disease process.

Noncentral Nervous System Structures

Receptor Organs of the Skin. Age changes in the receptor organs of human skin were studied in 200 individuals ranging in age from birth to 93 years using silver impregnation, histochemical staining, electron microscopy, and wax plate reconstruction (Cauna, 1965). It was found that:

a. Some Pacinian corpuscles increased in size, others were remodelled or formed anew on the axons of obsolete corpuscles;
b. Merkel's corpuscles were reduced in number and restricted to certain sites in relation to the epidermis during late fetal stages and shortly after birth;
c. Meissner's corpuscles were progressively reduced in number. They increased in length continuously from birth to old age. As a result, they became coiled and lobulated to varying degrees. Nerve endings within the Meissner's corpuscles underwent changes from neurofibrillary networks to coarse winding terminals and later to fine irregular filaments;
d. The free nerve endings underwent the least changes. Cauna concluded that these changes may represent a morphological adaptation to functional requirements and that they do not signify senescence of either neural or associated nonnervous tissue of these organs.

Motor Nerve Endings. Age changes in human motor nerve endings in distal muscles were studied by Harriman, Taverner, and Wolf (1970). They reported spherical axonic swelling of the longest axons of the motor nerves and elaborate and multiple motor end plates with elevation of terminal innervation ratio to be expressions of aging in motor end plates. Swash and Fox (1972) studied the effect of age on the morphology and innervation of the muscle spindles in 22 subjects from birth to 81 years and reported that the mean capsular thickness increased linearly with age with a slight decrease in the mean number of intrafusal fibers in the oldest subject. They also found some changes in the spindles consistent with denervation and changes in the fine structure of the muscle spindle innervation consisting of spherical axonal swellings and expanded abnormal motor end plates. The reader is referred to a review article on the neuromuscular system by Gutmann and Hanzliková (1972).

CONCLUSIONS

This review of changes in the nervous system with increasing age emphasizes a need for continued anatomical studies at gross, microscopic, and ultrastructural levels. Disagreement exists today on changes which for many years have been accepted as true concomitants of aging including gross changes in brain weight, narrowing of gyri, meningeal thickening, and ventricular enlargement. Quantitative measurements of neuronal numbers and glial-neuronal ratios, as well as the use of several morphological techniques to relate cell number to possible structural changes in nerve cells are necessary. The ultrastructural study of the aging brain, including the blood-brain barrier, membrane systems of the central nervous system, as well as the morphology of neurons and glia has not been accomplished. If there is truth in the statement that we are as old as our nervous system, then it behooves us to make this system a major target area for future gerontological research.

REFERENCES

Andrew, W. 1937. The Purkinje cell in man from birth to senility. *Z. Zellforsch.*, **27**, 534–554.

Andrew, W. 1939. The Golgi apparatus in the nerve cells of the mouse from youth to senility. *Am. J. Anat.*, **64**, 351–376.

Andrew, W. 1956a. The neurologic and psychiatric aspects of the disorders of aging. *In*, J. E. Moore, H. H. Merritt, and R. J. Masselink (eds.), *Structural Alterations with Aging in the Nervous System*, Vol. 35, pp. 129–170. Baltimore: Williams and Wilkins.

Andrew, W. 1956b. Structural alterations with aging in the nervous system. *J. Chronic Diseases.*, **3**, 575–596.

Andrew, W. 1964. Changes in the nucleus with advancing age of the organism. *In*, B. L. Strehler (ed.), *Advances in Gerontological Research*, pp. 87–108. New York: Academic Press.

Appel, F. W., and Appel, E. M. 1942a. Intracranial variation in the weight of the human brain. *Human Biol.*, **14**, 48–68.

Appel, F. W., and Appel, E. M. 1942b. Intracranial variation in the weight of human brain. *Human Biol.*, **14**, 235–250.

Archambault, La S. 1918. Parenchymatous atrophy of the cerebellum. *J. Nervous Mental Disease*, **48**, 273.

Bailey, P., and von Bonin, G. 1951. *The Isocortex of Man*, pp. 13–20. Urbana, Illinois: University of Illinois Press.

Barden, H. 1970. Relationship of Golgi thiamine-pyrophosphatase and lysosomal acid phosphatase to neuromelanin and lipofuscin in cerebral neurons of the aging rhesus monkey. *J. Neuropath.*, **29**, 225–240.

Beheim-Schwarzbach, D. 1957. Weitere Beobachtungen an Nervenzellkernen. *J. Hirnforsch*, **3**, 105–142.

Bergström, B. 1973. Morphology of the vestibular nerve. II. The number of myelinated vestibular nerve fibers in man at various ages. *Acta Otolaryng.* (Stockh), **76**, 173–179.

Birren, J. E., and Wall, P. D. 1956. Age changes in the conduction velocity, refractory period, number of fibers, connective tissue space and blood vessels in the sciatic nerve of rats. *J. Comp. Neurol.*, **104**, 1–16.

Bjorkerud, S. 1964. Studies of lipofuscin granules of human cardiac muscle. II. Chemical analysis of isolated granules. *Exp. Molec. Path.*, **3**, 377–389.

Blinkov, S. M., and Ponomarev, V. S. 1965. Quantitative determinations of neurons and glial cells in the nuclei of facial and vestibular nerves in man, monkey and dog. *J. Comp. Neurol.*, **125**, 295–302.

Bondareff, W. 1957. Genesis of intracellular pigment in the spinal ganglia of senile rats. An electron microscope study. *J. Geront.*, **12**, 364–369.

Bondareff, W. 1959. Morphology of the aging nervous system. *In*, J. E. Birren (ed.), *Handbook of Aging and the Individual*, pp. 136–173. Chicago: University of Chicago Press.

Bondareff, W. 1962. Distribution of Nissl substance in the neurons of rat spinal ganglia as a function of age and fatigue. *In*, N. W. Shock (ed.), *Biological Aspects of Aging*, pp. 147–154. New York: Columbia University Press.

Bondareff, W. 1964. Histophysiology of the aging nervous system. *In*, B. L. Strehler (ed.), *Advances in Gerontological Research*, pp. 1–22. New York: Academic Press.

Bondareff, W. 1973. Age changes in the neuronal environment, *In*, M. Rockstein and M. Sussman (eds.), *Development and Aging in the Nervous System*, pp. 1–18. New York: Academic Press.

Bondareff, W., and Narotzky, R. 1972. Age changes in the neuronal microenvironment. *Science*, **176**, 1135–1136.

Bourne, G. H. 1973. Lipofuscin. *In*, D. H. Ford (ed.), *Neurobiological Aspects of Maturation and Aging. Progress in Brain Research*, pp. 187–202. New York: Elsevier Scientific Publishing.

Boyd, R. 1860. The average weights of human body and brain. Philosophical Transactions. *In*, Schafer and Thane (eds.), Reference in *Quain's Anatomy*, p. 219. London: Longmans and Green, 1895.

Braak, H. 1971. Über das Neurolipofuscin in der unteren olive und dem Nucleus dentatus cerebelle in Gehirn des Menschen. *Z. Zellforsch.*, **121**, 573–592.

Brannon, W., McCormick, W., and Lampert, P. 1967.

Axonal dystrophy in gracile nucleus of man. *Acta Neuropathol.*, **9**, 1-6.

Brizzee, K. R., Cancilla, P. A., Sherwood, N., and Timiras, P. S. 1969. The amount and distribution of pigments in neurons and glia of the cerebral cortex. *J. Geront.*, **24**, 127-135.

Brizzee, K. R., and Johnson, F. A. 1970. Depth distribution of lipofuscin pigment in cerebral cortex of albino rat. *Acta Neuropathol.*, **16**, 205-219.

Brizzee, K. R., Ordy, J. M., and Kaack, B. 1974. Early appearance and regional differences in intraneuronal and extraneuronal lipofuscin accumulation with age in the non-human primate (*Macaca mulatta*). *J. Geront.*, **29**, (4), 366-381.

Broca, P. 1878. Anatomie comparée des circonvolutions cérébrales le grand lobe limbique et la Scissure limbique dans la série des Mammifères. *Rev. Anthrop.*, **1**, 384-498.

Brody, H. 1955. Organization of cerebral cortex. III. A study of aging in the human cerebral cortex. *J. Comp. Neurol.*, **102**, 511-556.

Brody, H. 1960. The deposition of aging pigment in the human cerebral cortex. *J. Geront.*, **15**, 258-261.

Brody, H. 1970. Structural changes in the aging nervous system. *In*, H. T. Blumenthal (ed.), *Interdisciplinary Topics in Gerontology*, Vol. 7, pp. 9-21. New York: Karger, Basel/München.

Brody, H. 1973. Aging of the vertebrate brain. *In*, M. Rockstein and M. Sussman (eds.), *Development and Aging in the Nervous System*, pp. 121-133. New York: Academic Press.

Brody, H., and Vijayashankar, N. 1975. Neuronal loss in the human brainstem and its relation to sleep in the elderly. Tenth International Congress of Gerontology, Congress Abstracts. Vol. II, p. 9.

Bruesh, S. R., and Arey, L. B. 1942. The number of myelinated and unmyelinated fibers in the optic nerve of vertebrates. *J. Comp. Neurol.*, **77**, 631-665.

Brünk, U., and Ericsson, J. L. E. 1972. Electron microscopical studies on the rat brain neurons. Localization of acid phosphatase and mode of formation of lipofuscin bodies. *J. Ultrastruct. Res.*, **38**, 1-15.

Buetow, D. E. 1971. Cellular content and cellular proliferation changes in the tissues and organs of the aging mammal. *In*, I. L. Cameron and J. D. Thrasher (eds.), *Cellular and Molecular Renewal in the Mammalian Body*, pp. 87-106. New York: Academic Press.

Burns, B. D. 1958. *The Mammalian Cerebral Cortex*. London: Edward Arnold.

Cammermeyer, J. 1959. Third round-table discussion. *In*, J. E. Birren, H. A. Imus, and W. F. Windle (eds.), *The Process of Aging in the Nervous System*, pp. 131-134. Springfield, Illinois: Charles C. Thomas.

Cammermeyer, J. 1963. Cytological manifestations of aging in rabbit and chinchilla brains. *J. Geront.*, **18**, 41-54.

Cauna, N. 1965. The effects of aging on the receptor organs of human dermis. *In*, W. Montagna (ed.), *Advances in Biology of Skin*. Oxford: Pergamon Press.

Causley, D., and Young, J. Z. 1955. Counting and sizing of particles with flying-spot microscope. *Nature* (London), **176**, 453-454.

Colon, E. J. 1972. The elderly brain. A quantitative analysis of cerebral cortex in two cases. *Psychiat. Neurol. Neurochir* (Amst.), **75**, 261-270.

Corbin, K. B., and Gardner, E. D. 1937. Decrease in number of myelinated fibers in human spinal roots with age. *Anat. Record*, **68**, 63-74.

Cottrell, L. 1940. Histologic variations with age in apparently normal peripheral nerve trunks. *Arch. Neurol. Psychiat.*, **43**, 1138-1150.

Critchley, M. 1931. The neurology of old age. II. Clinical manifestations in old age. *Lancet*, **I**, 1221-1230.

Dayan, A. D. 1971. Comparative neuropathology of aging. Studies on the brains of 47 species of vertebrates. *Brain*, **94**, 31-42.

de Duve, C., Pressman, B. C., Gianetto, R., Wattiaux, R., and Appelman, F. 1955. Intracellular distribution patterns of enzymes in rat liver tissue. *Biochem. J.*, **60**, 604-617.

Delorenzi, E. 1931. Constanza numerica delle cellule del Purkinje in individui di varia eta. *Bull. Soc. Ital. Biol. Sper.*, **6**, 80-82.

Dixon, K. C., and Herbertson, B. M. 1950. Cytoplasmic constituent of brain. *J. Physiol.* (London), **111**, 244-247.

Duncan, D. 1930. The incidence of secondary (Wallerian) degeneration in normal mammals compared to that in certain experimental and diseased conditions. *J. Comp. Neurol.*, **51**, 197-228.

Duncan, D. 1934. A determination of the number of nerve fibers in the eighth thoracic and the largest lumbar and ventral roots of albino rat. *J. Comp. Neurol.*, **59**, 47-60.

Dunn, E. H. 1912. The influence of age, sex, weight and the relationship upon the number of medullated fibers in the ventral root of II cervical nerve of albino rat. *J. Comp. Neurol.*, **22**, 131-157.

Ellis, R. S. 1919. A preliminary quantitative study of Purkinje cells in normal, subnormal and senescent human cerebella. *J. Comp. Neurol.*, **30**, 229-252.

Ellis, R. S. 1920. Norms for some structural changes in the human cerebellum from birth to old age. *J. Comp. Neurol.*, **32**, 1-33.

Essner, E., and Novikoff, A. B. 1960. Human hepatocellular pigments and lysosomes. *J. Ultrastruct. Res.*, **3**, 374-391.

Ferrendelli, J. A., Sedgwick, W. G., and Suntzeff, V. 1971. Regional energy metabolism and lipofuscin accumulation in the mouse brain during aging. *J. Neuropathol. Exp. Neurol.*, **30**, 638-649.

Finch, C. E., 1973. Catecholamine metabolism on the brains of aging male mice. *Brain Res.*, **52**, 261-276.

Finch, C. E., Jonec, V., Hody, G., Walker, J. P., Smith, M., Alper, A., and Dougher, G. J. 1975. Aging and passage of L-tyrosine, L-dopa and inulin into mouse brain slices *in vitro*. *J. Geront.*, **30**, (1), 33-40.

Fisher, C. 1971. The new Quantimet-720. *Microscope*, **19**, 1-20.

Fujisawa, K. 1967. A unique type of axonal alteration (so-called axonal dystrophy) as seen in Goll's nucleus in 277 cases of controls. *Acta Neuropathol.*, 8, 255–275.

Gardner, E. D. 1940. Decrease in human neurones with age. *Anat. Record*, 77, 529–536.

Gatenby, J. B. 1953. The Golgi apparatus of the living sympathetic ganglion cells of the mouse, photographed by phase contrast microscopy. *J. Roy. Microscop. Soc.*, 73, 61–68.

Gatenby, J. B., and Moussa, T. A. 1950. The sympathetic ganglion cell, with Sudan Black and Zernika microscope. *J. Roy. Microscop. Soc.*, 70, 342–364.

Gedigk, P., and Bontke, E. 1956. Über den Nachweis von hydrolytiachen Enzymen in Lipopigmenten. *Z. Zellforsch.*, 44, 495–518.

Gedigk, P., and Fischer, R. 1959. Über die Entstehung von Lipopigmenten in Muskelfascern. Untersuchungen beim experimentallen Vitamin E Mangel der Ratte und an Organen des Menschen. *Virchows Arch. Pathol. Anat.*, 332, 431–468.

Gersh, I., and Catchpole, H. R. 1960. The nature of the ground substance of connective tissue. *Perspectives Biol. Med.*, 3, 282–319.

Goldfischer, S., and Bernstein, J. 1969. Lipofuscin (aging) pigment granules of the newborn human liver. *J. Cell Biol.*, 42, 253–261.

Gonatas, N. K., Gambetti, P., Tucker, S. H., Evangelista, I., and Baird, H. W. 1969. Cytoplasmic inclusions in juvenile amaurotic idiocy. *J. Pediat.*, 75, 796–805.

Greenman, M. J. 1917. The number, size and axis sheath relation of the large myelinated fibers in the peroneal nerve of inbred Albino rat under normal conditions, in disease and after stimulation. *J. Comp. Neurol.*, 27, 403–420.

Gutman, E., and Hanzlikova, V. 1972. Basic mechanisms of aging in the neuromuscular system. *Mech. Age. Dev.*, 1, 327–349.

Hall, T. C., Miller, A. K. H., and Corsellis, J. A. N. 1975. Variations in the human Purkinje cell population according to age and sex. *Neuropathol. Appl. Neurobiol.*, 1, 267–292.

Hanley, T. 1974. "Neuronal Fall-out" in aging brain: A critical review of the quantitative data. *Age and Ageing*, 3, 133–151.

Harms, J. W. 1927. Alterscheinungen im Hirn von Affen und Menschen. *Zool. Anz.*, 74, 249–256.

Harriman, D. G., Taverner, D., and Wolf, A. L. 1970. Ekborn's Syndrome and burning parasthesia. A biopsy study by vital staining and electron microscopy of the intramuscular innervation with a note on age changes in motor nerve endings in distal muscles. *Brain*, 93, 393–406.

Hasan, M., and Glees, P. 1973. Ultrastructural age changes in hippocampal neurons, synapses and neuroglia. *Exp. Geront.*, 8, 75–83.

Hempel, K.-J., and Namba, M. 1958. Die involution des Supranucleus medialis dorsalis. Sowie der lamella medialis und der lamella interna thalami. *J. Hirnforsch.*, 4, 43–77.

Hendley, D. D., Mildvan, A. S., Reporter, M. C., and Strehler, B. L. 1963. The properties of isolated human cardiac age pigment. II. Chemical and enzymatic properties. *J. Geront.*, 18, 250–259.

Hess, A. 1955. The fine structure of young and old spinal ganglia. *Anat. Record*, 123, 399–424.

Hirano, A., and Zimmerman, H. M. 1962. Alzheimer's neurofibrillary changes. *Arch. Neurol.* (Chic.), 7, 227–242.

Hodge, C. F. 1894. Changes in ganglion cells from birth to senile death. Observations on man and honey bee. *J. Physiol.*, 17, 129–134.

Hoffman, H. H., and Schnitzlein, H. N. 1961. The number of nerve fibers in the vagus nerve of man. *Anat. Record*, 139, 429–435.

Hollander, C. F. 1970. Model systems in experimental gerontology. *Ned. T. Geront.*, 1, 144–148.

Höpker, W. 1951. Das Altern des Nucleus Dentatus. *Z. Alternsforsch.*, 5, 256–277.

Howell, T. H. 1949. Senile deterioration of the central nervous system. *Brit. Med. J.*, 1, 56–58.

Huemer, R. P., Bickert, C., Lee, K. D., and Reeves, A. E. 1971. Mitochondrial studies in senescent mice. I. Turnover of brain mitochondrial lipids. *Exp. Geront.*, 6, 259–265.

Hydén, H., and Lindström, B. 1950. Microspectrographic studies on the yellow pigment in nerve cells. *Discussions Faraday Soc.*, 9, 436–441.

Inukai, T. 1928. On the loss of Purkinje cells with advancing age from cerebellar cortex of Albino rat. *J. Comp. Neurol.*, 45, 1–31.

Jayne, E. P. 1950. Cytochemical studies of age pigments in the human heart. *J. Geront.*, 5, 319–325.

Johnson, H. A., and Erner, S. 1972. Neuron survival in the aging mouse. *Exp. Geront.*, 7, 111–117.

Kemble, F. 1967. Conduction in the normal adult median nerve. The different effect of aging in men and women. *Electromyography*, 7, 275–289.

Klatzo, I. 1954. Über das Verhalten des Nukleolarapparates in den Menschlichen Pallidunzellen. *J. Hirnforsch.*, 1, 47–60.

Konigsmark, B. W. 1970. Methods for the counting of neurons. *In*, S. O. E. Ebbessen, and W. J. H. Nauta (eds.), *Contemporary Research Methods in Neuroanatomy*, pp. 313–340. Berlin/Heidelberg: Springer-Verlag.

Konigsmark, B. W., and Murphy, E. A. 1970. Neuronal populations in the human brain. *Nature*, 299, 1335.

Konigsmark, B. W., and Murphy, E. A. 1972. Volume of ventral cochlear nucleus in man: Its relationship to neuronal population and age. *J. Neuropathol. Exp. Neurol.*, 31, 304–316.

Kormendy, C. G., and Bender, A. D. 1971. Chemical interference with aging. *Gerontologia*, 77, 52–64.

Kuhlenbeck, H. 1954. Some histologic age changes in the rat's brain and their relationship to comparable changes in the human brain. *Confinia Neurol.*, 14, 329–342.

Lascelles, R. G., and Thomas, P. K. 1966. Changes due to age in the internodal length on the sural nerve in man. *J. Neurol. Neurosurg. Psychiat.*, 29, 40–44.

Last, R. J., and Tompsett, D. H. 1953. Casts of cerebral ventricles. *Brit. J. Surg.*, **40**, 525-543.

Leboucq, G. 1929. Le rapport entre lipoids et la surface de l'hemisphere cérébrale chez l'homme et les singes. *Men. Acad. Roy. Belg.*, **10**, 55.

Lillie, R. D. 1950. Further exploration of the HIO$_4$ Schiff reaction with remarks on its significance. *Anat. Record*, **108**, 239-253.

Lillie, R. D. 1956a. A Nile blue staining technique for the differentiation of melanin and lipofuscins. *Stain Technol.*, **31**, 151-152.

Lillie, R. D. 1956b. The mechanism of Nile blue staining of lipofuscins. *J. Histochem. Cytochem.*, **4**, 377-381.

Lillie, R. D., Ashbwin, L. L., Sebrell, W. H. J., Daft, F. S., and Lowry, J. V. 1942. Histogenesis and repair of hepatic cirrhosis in rats produced on low protein diets and preventable with choline. *Public Health Rept.*, *U.S.*, **57**, 502-508.

Malkoff, D. B., and Strehler, B. L. 1963. The ultrastructure of isolated and *in situ* human cardiac age pigment. *J. Cell Biol.*, **16**, 611-616.

Mann, D. N. A., and Yates, P. O. 1974. Lipoprotein pigments—their relationship to ageing in the human nervous system. I. The lipofuscin content of nerve cells. *Brain*, **97**, 481-488.

Manodesley-Thomas, L. E., and Healey, P. 1970. Automating quantitative histopathology. *Laboratory Management* **8**, 22-24. (January).

Mansberg, H. H., and Segarra, J. M. 1962. Counting of neurons by flying-spot microscope. *Ann. N.Y. Acad. Sci.*, **99**, 309-322.

Medawar, P. B. 1971. Aging, The Listener. *8*, 7. Ageing as a Human Concern. Quoted by Beerling, R. F. *In*, H. M. VanPraag, and A. F. Kalverboer (eds.), *Ageing of the Central Nervous System*. Haarlem: De Erven F. Bohn N.V.

Miquel, J. 1971. Aging of male *Drosophila melanogaster*: Histological, histochemical and ultrastructural observations. *Advan. Geront. Res.*, **3**, 39-71.

Miquel, J., Tappel, A. L., Dillard, C. J., Herman, M. M., and Bensch, K. G. 1974. Fluorescent products and lysosomal components in ageing *Drosophila melanogaster*. *J. Geront.*, **29**, (6), 622-637.

Miyigashi, T., Takashata, M., and Iizuka, R. 1971. Electronmicroscopic studies on the lipopigments in the cerebral cortex nerve cells of senile and Vitamin E-deficient rats. *Acta Neuropathol.* (Berl), **9**, 7-17.

Moatamed, F. 1966. Cell frequencies in human inferior olivary complex. *J. Comp. Neurol.*, **128**, 109-116.

Monagle, R. D., and Brody, H. 1974. The effects of age upon the main nucleus of the inferior olive in the human. *J. Comp. Neurol.*, **155**, 61-66.

Monagle, R. D., Brody, H., and Vijayashankar, N. The distribution of lipofuscin in cells of the human inferior olive (in preparation).

Moyer, E. K., and Kaliszewski, B. F. 1958. The number of nerve fibers in motor spinal nerve roots of young, mature and aged cats. *Anat. Record*, **131**, 681-698.

Nandy, K. 1968. Further studies on the effects of centrophenoxine on the lipofuscin pigment in the neurons of senile guinea pigs. *J. Geront.*, **23**, 82-92.

Nandy, K. 1971. Properties of neuronal lipofuscin pigment in mice. *Acta Neuropathol.* (Berl), **19**, 25-32.

Nandy, K., and Bourne, G. H. 1966. Effect of centrophenoxine on the lipofuscin pigments in the neurons of senile guinea pigs. *Nature* (London), **210**, 313-314.

Nishioka, N., Takahata, N., and Iizuka, R. 1968. Histochemical studies on the lipopigments in the nerve cells. A comparison with lipofuscin and ceroid pigment. *Acta Neuropathol.* (Berl), **11**, 174-181.

Pakkenberg, H., and Voigt, J. 1964. Brain weight of the Danes. *Acta Anat.*, **56**, 297-307.

Palade, C., and Porter, K. R. 1955. Studies on the endoplasmic reticulum. *J. Biophys. Biochem. Cytol.*, **1**, 59-68.

Palay, S. L., and Palade, G. E. 1955. The fine structure of neurons. *J. Biophys. Biochem. Cytol.*, **1**, 69-88.

Pallis, C. A., Duckett, S., and Pearse, A. G. E. 1967. Diffuse lipofuscinosis of the central nervous system. *Neurol.*, **17**, 381-394.

Pearl, R. 1922. *The Biology of Death*. Philadelphia: J. B. Lippincott.

Pearse, A. G. E. 1960. *Histochemistry, Theoretical and Applied*. London: J. A. Churchill.

Pearson, G. H. J. 1928. Effect of age on vibratory sensibility. *Arch. Neurol. Psychiat.* (Chic), **20**, 482-496.

Porta, E. A., and Hartroft, W. S. 1969. Lipid pigments in relation to aging and dietary factors (lipofuscin). *In*, M. Wolman (ed.), *Pigments in Pathology*, pp. 191-233. New York: Academic Press.

Prensky, W. 1971. Automated image analysis in autoradiography. *Exp. Cell Res.*, **68**, 388-394.

Ravens, J. R., and Calvo, W. 1965. Neuroglial changes in the senile brain. *In*, Proceedings of the Fifth International Congress of Neuropathology, pp. 506-513. New York: Excerpta Medica Fdn, International Congr. Ser. No. 100.

Reichel, W., Hollander, J., Clark, J. H., and Strehler, B. L. 1968. Lipofuscin pigment accumulation as a function of age and distribution in rodent brain. *J. Geront.*, **23**, 71-78.

Rowland, L., and Mettler, F. 1949. Number of cells in frontal cortex of psychotic patients. Studies of cortex removed at operation. *J. Comp. Neurol.*, **90**, 281-319.

Samorajski, T., Friede, R. L., and Ordy, J. M. 1971. Age difference in the ultrastructure of axons in the pyramidal tract of mouse. *J. Geront.*, **26**, 542-551.

Samorajski, T., Keefe, J. R., and Ordy, J. M. 1964. Intracellular localization of lipofuscin age pigment in the nervous system of aged mice. *J. Geront.*, **19**, 261-276.

Samorajski, T., Ordy, J. M., and Keefe, J. R. 1965. The fine structure of lipofuscin age pigment in the nervous system of aged mice. *J. Cell Biol.*, **26**, 779-795.

Samorajski, T., Ordy, J. M., and Rady-Reimer, P.

1968. Lipofuscin pigment accumulation in the nervous system of aging mice. *Anat. Record*, **160**, 555–574.

Samorajski, T., Rolsten, C., and Ordy, J. M. 1971. Changes in behavior, brain and neuroendocrine chemistry with age and stress in C57 BL/10 male mice. *J. Geront.*, **26**, 168–175.

Sanides, F. 1957. Untersuchungen über die histologische struktur des Mandelkernigebietes. *J. Hirnforsch.*, **3**, 56–77.

Sayk, J. 1960. Über die Kernhomogenisierung in Nervenzellen der menschlichen Hirnrinde bei verschiedenen Erkrankungen. *Arch. Psychiat. Nervenkr.*, **200**, 197–202.

Scammon, R. E., and Dunn, H. L. 1922–23. Empirical formulae for postnatal growth of human brain and its major subdivisions. *Proc. Soc. Exp. Biol. Med.*, **19**, 114–117.

Scheibel, M. D., and Scheibel, A. B. 1975. *In*, H. Brody, D. Harmon, and J. M. Ordy (eds.), *Clinical, Morphological and Neurochemical Aspects of the Aging Nervous System*. New York: Raven Press.

Schiffler, D. 1954. Sur l'action réparatrice du noyau des cellules nerveuses. *J. Hirnforsch.*, **1**:326–336.

Shefer, V. F. 1973. Absolute number of neurons and thickness of cerebral cortex during aging, senile and vascular dementia and Pick's and Alzheimer's Disease. *Neurosci. Beh. Physiol.*, **6**, 319–324.

Siakatos, A. N., and Koppang, N. 1973. Procedures for the isolation of lipopigments from brain, heart and liver, and their properties: A review. *Mech. Age and Ageing*, **2**, 177–200.

Siebert, G., Heidenreich, O., Böhmig, R., and Lang, K. 1955. Isolierung und chemische Untersuchung von Lipofuscin. *Naturasenschaften*, **42**, 156.

Solcher, H. 1956. Die Involutionsveränderungen des Corpus subthalamicus und des Niger reticulatus. *J. Hirnforsch.*, **2**, 148–155.

Sosa, J. M., and deZorilla, N. B. 1966. Morphological variations of the Golgi apparatus in spinal ganglion nerve cells, related to aging. *Acta Anat.*, **64**, 475–497.

Spoerri, P. E., and Glees, P. 1973. Neuronal aging in cultures, an electronmicroscopic study. *Exp. Geront.*, **8**, 259–263.

Sroka, C. H., Bornstein, B., Strulovici, N., and Sandbank, U. 1969. Neuroaxonal dystrophy: Its relation to age and central nervous system lesions. *Israel J. Med. Sci.*, **5**, 373–377.

Strehler, B. L. 1962. *Time, Cells and Aging*. New York: Academic Press.

Strehler, B. L. 1964. On the histochemistry and ultrastructure of age pigment. *In*, B. L. Strehler (ed.), *Advances in Gerontological Research*, pp. 343–384. New York: Academic Press.

Strehler, B. L., and Barrows, C. H. 1970. Senescence. Cell biological aspects of aging. *In*, O. A. Schjeide and J. deVallis (eds.), *Cell Differentiation*. New York: Van Nostrand Reinhold.

Strehler, B. L., Mark, D. D., Mildvan, A. S., and Gee, M. S. 1959. Rate and magnitude of age pigment accumulation in the human myocardium. *J. Geront.*, **14**, 430–439.

Sulkin, N. M. 1958. The occurrence and duration of senile pigments experimentally induced in the nerve cells of young rats. *Anat. Record*, **130**, 377–378.

Sulkin, N. M., and Kuntz, A. 1952. Histochemical alterations in autonomic ganglion cells associated with aging. *J. Geront.*, **7**, 533–543.

Sulkin, N. M., and Srivanij, P. 1960. The experimental production of senile pigments in the nerve cells of young rats. *J. Geront.*, **15**, 2–9.

Sung, J. H. 1964. Neuroaxonal dystrophy in mucoviscidosis. *J. Neuropathol. Exp. Neurol.*, **23**, 567–583.

Swash, M., and Fox, K. P. 1972. The effect of age on human skeletal muscle. Studies of the morphology and innervation of muscle spindles. *J. Neurol. Sci.*, **16**, 417–432.

Tappel, A. L. 1968. Will antioxidant nutrients slow aging process? *Geriatrics*, **23**, 97–105 (October).

Tappel, A. L. 1970. Biological antioxidant protection against lipid peroxidation damage. *Am. J. Clin. Nutr.*, **23**, 1137–1139.

Timiras, P. S. 1972. Degenerative changes in cells. *In*, P. S. Timiras, *Developmental Physiology and Aging*, pp. 429–449. New York: Macmillan.

Tomasch, J., and Ebnessajjade, D. 1961. The human nucleus ambiguus. *Anat. Record*, **141**, 247–252.

Tomasch, J., and Malpass, A. J. 1958. The human motor trigeminal nucleus. A quantitative study. *Anat. Record*, **130**, 91–103.

Tomlinson, B. E. 1972. Morphological brain changes in non-demented old people. *In*, H. M. VanPraag and A. F. Kalverbove (eds.), *Ageing of the Central Nervous System, Biological and Psychological Aspects*, pp. 38–57. Haarlem: DeErven F. Bohn N. V.

Tomlinson, B. E. 1976. Some quantitative cerebral findings in normal and demented old people. *In*, R. D. Terry and S. Gershon (eds.), *Neurobiology of Aging*. New York: Raven Press.

Tomlinson, B. E., Blessed, G., and Roth, M. 1968. Observations on the brains of non-demented people. *J. Neurol. Sci.*, **7**, 331–356.

Tomlinson, B. E., Blessed, G., and Roth, M. 1970. Observations on the brains of demented old people. *J. Neurol. Sci.*, **11**, 205–242.

Toth, S. E. 1968. The origin of lipofuscin age pigments. *Exp. Geront.*, **3**, 19–30.

Van Buskirk, C. 1945. The seventh nerve complex. *J. Comp. Neurol.*, **82**, 303–333.

Vijayashankar, N., and Brody, H. 1971. Neuronal population of human abducens nucleus. *Anat. Record*, **169**, (2), 447.

Vijayashankar, N., and Brody, H. 1973. The neuronal population of the nuclei of the trochlear nerve and the locus coeruleus in the human. *Anat. Record*, **172**, (2), 421–422.

Vogt, C., and Vogt, O. 1946. Ageing of nerve cells. *Nature*, **158**, 304.

Wagman, I., and Leese, H. 1952. Conduction velocity of ulnar nerves in human subjects of different ages and sizes. *J. Neurophysiol.*, **15**, 235–244.

Whiteford, R., and Getty, R. 1966. Distribution of lipofuscin in canine and porcine brain as related to aging. *J. Geront.*, **21**, 31–44.

Wilcox, H. H. 1956. A quantitative study of Purkinje cells in guinea pigs. *J. Geront.*, **11**, 442.

Wilcox, H. H. 1959. Structural changes in the nervous system related to the process of aging. *In*, J. E. Birren, H. A. Imus, and W. F. Windle, (eds.), *The Process of Aging in the Nervous System*, pp. 16–23. Springfield, Illinois: Charles C. Thomas.

Wolf, A., and Pappenheimer, A. M. 1945. Occurrence and distribution of acid fast pigment in the central nervous system. *J. Neuropathol. Exp. Neurol.*, **4**, 402–406.

Zeman, W. 1971. The neuronal ceroid lipofuscinosis-Batten-Vogt Syndrome. A model for human aging? *In*, B. L. Strehler (ed.), *Advances in Gerontological Research*, Vol. 3, pp. 147–169. New York: Academic Press.

11
NEUROENDOCRINE AND AUTONOMIC ASPECTS OF AGING

Caleb Ellicott Finch
University of Southern California

INTRODUCTION

The past 150 years of physiological research have established the commanding role of the central nervous system (CNS) in regulating the functions of the body at the behavioral, organ, cellular, and molecular levels. How aging affects the central nervous system is therefore a question of great importance. Because of evidence for the roles of extracellular factors such as hormones and neural influences as regulators of changes in cellular activities during aging (see Chapters 1 and 3), and because of evidence for changes in endocrine regulation [gonad (Chapter 13), adrenal, and thyroid (Chapter 14)], attention is drawn to the seats of endocrine and autonomic control in the brain.

Little is now known about cellular functions of the central nervous system during aging in mammals. This review therefore will indicate important areas of ignorance. The available evidence, slight as it is, shows us that aging does not randomly alter cell functions in the central nervous system, and that significant changes do occur in neural metabolism which may be related to changing functions elsewhere in the body.

THE PROBLEM OF AGING AND DISEASE IN THE CENTRAL NERVOUS SYSTEM

A major technical problem of investigating the CNS of mammals during aging is distinguishing between normal aging processes and those which are *pathogeric* (Finch, 1972a) or secondary to age-related diseases. For example, cerebral vascular disease is a tremendously widespread phenomenon in aging human populations, e.g., nearly 90 percent of all men and women over the age of 75 in the United States show atherosclerotic changes in the cerebral blood vessels (Flora, Baker, Loewenson, and Klassen, 1968). Although these changes vary in degree, there is no question of their widespread incidence, which causes much difficulty in distinguishing normal changes in neural function from those which are consequences of cerebral vascular diseases. For example, the performance of men on intelligence tests does not decrease appreciably during the ages of 60 to 70 unless there has been evidence of high blood pressure (Wilkie and Eisdorfer, 1971). Such pathogeric changes must be distinguished from the normal (*eugeric*) phenomena of aging (Finch, 1972a). Examples of eugeric phenomena are female reproductive senescence (menopause in humans; see Chapter 13), accumulation of aging pigment (lipofuscins, Chapter 10), and reduced immune function (Chapter 15). These changes occur in all mammalian populations and are not the result of rare genetic determinants, bizarre life-style, or exposure to unusual diseases or diets. The data reviewed in this article will exclude pathogeric changes to the extent possible at present. Unfortunately, few researchers provide adequate statements of husbandry protocols and necropsy procedures for animals or adequate clinical profiles for humans. Most populations studied therefore are heterogeneous with respect to one or more pathological conditions. Perhaps in the next 10 years this difficult problem in experimental gerontology will be more frankly dealt with, even if never completely conquered.

OVERVIEW OF CELLULAR FUNCTIONS IN THE CENTRAL NERVOUS SYSTEM DURING AGING

A brief survey of cell functions in the brain will be presented here, prior to discussions of the neuroendocrine and autonomic aspects of aging.

Neural-Vascular Relationships

Cell functions in the brain are acutely dependent on blood supply. The literature on cerebral blood flow and aging indicates that basal rates of flow may not be significantly altered in healthy humans (Oldendorf and Kitano, 1965) and rodents (Haining, Turner, and Pantall, 1970). Major blood flow alterations with age may be more disease-related than age-related (Chapter 12). However, studies on cerebral blood flow do not inform us about microcirculation in the brain during aging.

The transport of substances from the blood into the brain tissue has not been fully investigated. A study from the author's laboratory indicates that uptake of L-tyrosine and L-DOPA from slices of hypothalamus, brain stem, and neostriatum of C57BL/6J male mice is not age-related between 10–30 mo. at concentra-

tions >0.1 μg/ml (Finch, Jonec, Hody, Walker, Morton-Smith, Alper, and Dougher, 1975). Further *in vitro* studies are needed, as well as studies of the blood-brain barrier, about which nothing is known with respect to postmaturational aging.

DNA, RNA, Proteins

The seat of cellular control mechanisms in the brain is the cell nucleus. Genetic information residing in nuclear DNA is transcribed into RNA and is then translated to direct the synthesis of specific proteins. It is a matter of profound interest to know if gene expression changes during aging.

As a whole, the brain does not appear to show significant age-related changes in total DNA (Table 1). In brief, there is little evidence for general loss of brain cells in rodents during the average life span; the loss of neurons which may occur in humans does not occur in all brain regions (Chapter 10). The nucleic acid and protein content of the whole brain or of most brain regions does not change markedly with age. The amount of DNA per neuron is also probably not greatly altered. In one study, direct measurements of the quantity of DNA of Purkinje neurons of the cerebellum through the age of 52 years showed no change (Lapham, 1968). According to the studies of Johnson, Chrisp, and Strehler (1972), there is a loss of ribosomal RNA genes in the brain and myocardium of aging dogs. No loss was detected in the liver and brain of aging mice and men (Gaubatz, Prashad, and Cutler, 1976).

Postmaturational age-related changes in the RNA contents of various brain regions and in individual neurons are summarized in Table 1. There is some evidence of selectivity of change in the rodent brain regions, e.g., the neostriatum (chiefly putamen), which was the only brain region in a population of healthy old mice to show RNA loss (Chaconas and Finch, 1973). In all of the existing data, no regions or neurons show an increase in relative RNA or protein content during aging. The trend is generally towards a reduced level, although it is clear that most brain regions are not affected. These gross measurements of

TABLE 1. THE EFFECT OF AGE ON NUCLEIC ACID AND PROTEIN CONTENT OF NEURAL TISSUE.

	DNA	RNA	Pro-tein	RNA/DNA	Protein/DNA	Species	Age	Sex	Ref.
A. *Whole Brain*									
	0	0	0	0	0	mouse (C57BL/6J)	4 *vs.* 28 mo	M	a
	0	0	−20%	0	0	mouse (C57BL/6J)	4 *vs.* 28 mo	F	a
B. *Brain Regions*									
1. brain stem	0			0	0	mouse (C57BL/6J)	12 *vs.* 30 mo	M	b, e
brain stem	0	0	0	0	0	rat (Wistar)	4 *vs.* 28 mo	F	a
2. cerebellum	0	0	−10%			rat (Wistar)	4 *vs.* 28 mo	F	a
cerebellum	0			0	0	mouse (C57BL/6J)	12 *vs.* 30 mo	M	b, e
3. cerebral cortex	0	0	0	0	0	rat (Wistar)	4 *vs.* 28 mo	F	a
4. hippocampus				0	0	mouse (C57BL/6J)	12 *vs.* 30 mo	M	b
5. hypothalamus and preoptic region				0	0	mouse (C57BL/6J)	12 *vs.* 30 mo	M	b
6. septum				0	0	mouse (C57BL/6J)	12 *vs.* 30 mo	M	b
7. neostriatum				−15%	−20%	mouse (C57BL/6J)	12 *vs.* 30 mo	M	b
C. *Studies of Individual Cells (microspectro-photometry)*									
1. cerebellum (Purkinje cells)		−30%				rat (albino)	8–31 mo		c
2. hypothalamus—supraoptic neurons		0				rat (albino)	2–32 mo		f
3. spinal neurons		−20%				human	>60 yr		d
		−10%–0				rat (albino)	3–32 mo		f

[a] Hollander and Barrows, 1968.
[b] Chaconas and Finch, 1973.
[c] Wulff and Freshman, 1961.
[d] Hydén, 1960.
[e] Finch, 1973.
[f] Wulff, Piekielniak, and Wayner, 1963.

RNA contents do not distinguish changes among the different types of RNA (heterogeneous nuclear RNA, messenger RNA, ribosomal RNA, etc.). Because ribosomal RNA is the major (>80 percent) RNA species in the brain, as in other tissues, it may be surmised that aging does not involve diminution of this species. The turnover of ribosomal RNA and transfer RNA is not affected by aging in the whole rat brain (Menzies, Mishra, and Gold, 1972). It would also be of great interest to know about the messenger RNA populations of individual neurons.

The effect of age on genomic transcription is of particular interest because three to five times more of the nonrepeated DNA (unique or single copy DNA) is transcribed in the brain (Brown and Church, 1971; Hahn and Laird, 1971; Grouse, Omenn, and McCarthy, 1973) than in other tissues (e.g., liver or kidney). This large amount of transcription, reported to include up to 40 percent of the unique DNA sequences of the rat brain (Bantle and Hahn, 1976), may reflect the summation of transcription from the numerous differentiated cell types in the brain. Cutler (1975) concludes that the total number of unique DNA sequences transcribed decreases progressively in the C57BL/6J mouse brain during aging and that some genes may be selectively repressed during aging in the brain (Cutler, 1972, 1975).

The effect of aging on protein synthesis in the brain has not been investigated thoroughly. The incorporation of leucine into total proteins of some brain regions (measured as total specific activity without evaluation of $tRNA_{leu}$ pools) does not change with age in C57BL/6J male mice (Finch, 1973; Gordon and Finch, 1974). However, patterns of leucine incorporation into electrophoretically separated proteins of the hypothalamus, preoptic, hippocampus, caudate, cerebellum, and septum indicates that the apparent rate of synthesis of other proteins is decreased in each region (Gordon and Finch, 1974). Regionally selective changes in the content of the brain-specific proteins S100 and 14-3-2 are also reported for C57BL/6J mice during aging (Cicero, Ferendelli, Suntzeff, and Moore, 1972).

Membranes, Electrical Activities, and Aging

The brain contains diverse membranes with highly specialized functions. Although the data are far from complete at the present time, substantial changes occur after maturity in the composition and architecture of neural membranes. In both rodents and humans, myelin deposition around some neurons continues long after puberty, e.g., in rats (Davison, 1969) and mice (Samorajski, Friede, and Ordy, 1971). The increased thickness of the myelin layers around the pyramidal tracts of C57BL/10J mice observed by transmission electron microscopy (Samorajski, Friede, and Ordy, 1971) parallels the chemical findings of increased myelin (Sun and Samorajski, 1972).

Rouser and colleagues (Rouser and Yamamoto, 1969; Rouser, Kritchevsky, Yamamoto, and Baxter, 1972) have observed substantial changes in the lipid composition of the human brain after maturity. The selectivity of the changes is noteworthy. Some lipid constituents such as cholesterol, cerebral sulfatides, ceramides, triglycerides, and gangliosides decrease whereas cholesterol esters and phosphoinositides increase. The changes occur within so-called *lipid substitution groups,* in such a way that the total content of each group remains constant: cerebrosides and sphingomyelin replace phosphatidyl choline, sulphatides replace phosphatidyl ethanolamine, and acidic phospholipids replace each other (Rouser et al., 1972). There are no comparable studies

on animal models; the functional consequences of these changes are entirely obscure. The changes are much smaller than those which occur in some degenerative diseases which severely affect mental function, e.g., the ganglioside diseases, such as Gaucher's, Tay-Sach's, and Nieman-Pick's diseases; no changes in lipid composition were detected in brains afflicted by Alzheimer's disease (Rouser et al., 1972).

Little is known about the effect of age on lipid turnover. The half life of phosphatidyl ethanolamine is slowed in old mice, whereas the half life of other lipids (e.g., cardiolipin and phosphatidyl serine associated with the mitochondrial faction) did not change (Huemer, Bickert, Lee, and Reeves, 1971).

SYNAPTIC FUNCTION AND NEUROTRANSMITTERS

Although many neural phenomena are slowed with age [e.g., reaction time (Birren, 1964), the α-rhythm (Marsh and Thompson, 1976)], axonal conduction velocity may not be significantly slowed with age in rodents (Birren and Wall, 1956; Wayner and Emmers, 1958; Chambers, Dunihue, Smith, Blanchard, Taylor, and Hill, 1966). On the other hand, transmission over multisynaptic pathways appears to be substantially retarded during aging (Wayner and Emmers, 1958; Chambers et al., 1966). The status of the neural synapse during aging is therefore of prime interest. Although there is little direct evidence about the effect of aging on synaptic function, substantial metabolic changes within the synaptic machinery which have direct relevance to endocrine function and some neurological diseases of aging are indicated in mice.

The mechanisms by which axonal depolarization initiates a similar impulse on the dendritic side of the synapse is poorly understood. A chemical mechanism at the synapse is now generally presumed, in which the secretion of substances by the nerve ending causes the depolarization or hypopolarization of the membrane at the other side (reviewed in Cooper, Bloom, and Roth, 1974). The metabolism of substances found in nerve endings undoubtedly has a profound effect on electrical activity in the brain and in peripheral organs. The best established neurotransmitters in vertebrates are acetylcholine (at the neural-skeletal muscle synapse) and norepinephrine (released by sympathetic nerves) (reviewed in Cooper, Bloom, and Roth, 1974). These substances are concentrated in storage particles in the presynaptic terminals of nerve cells. Both acetylcholine and norepinephrine are also found in presynaptic locales of neurons in the brain. Although the exact role of these substances in the brain in neural transmission has not been determined, it is generally presumed to be analagous to their role in peripheral neurons. In addition, dopamine, serotonin, glycine, glutamic acid, histamine, and γ-aminobutyric acid have been localized in particulate brain fractions which may correspond to presynaptic stores (Cooper, Bloom, and Roth, 1974). The catecholamines are thought to participate in the regulation of the hypothalamic oligopeptide hormones, e.g., LH-RH (Kalra and McCann, 1973; Ojeda, Harms, and McCann, 1974) and are thus of considerable interest because of their potential relationship to endocrine changes during aging (Finch, 1973, 1976).

Aging changes in the metabolism of the putative neurotransmitters are just now coming to light. It has been known for 10 years that a major age-related disease, Parkinson's disease, involves large losses of monoamines, particularly dopamine, in the basal ganglia (Hornykiewicz, 1965; Bernheimer, Birkmayer, Hornykiewicz, Jellinger, and Seitelberger, 1973). The effect of age on the various putative neurotransmitters in healthy human subjects is largely unknown, as is the contribution of possible aging changes to the large deficits in monoamines observed in Parkinson's disease. To resolve the effect of "normal" aging on the central catecholamines, the mouse was studied in the author's laboratory.

Disease and mortality in a colony of C57BL/6J male mice (established in 1965) have been extensively characterized. The age-specific mortality rate remains very low until 22-24 mo; it increases rapidly thereafter (Finch, Foster, and Mirsky, 1969). These mice have an average longevity of 28-30 mo and a maximum

longevity of 44 mo (Finch, 1971). Spontaneous pathological lesions of aging (not found before 22 mo of age) are reticulum cell sarcomas involving the liver, spleen, and mesenteric lymph nodes (Finch, Foster, and Mirsky, 1969) and necrotic seminal vesicles (Finch and Girgis, 1974). Mice with these lesions or with weight loss of 15 percent (Finch, Foster, and Mirsky, 1969) are not utilized in our studies. Enlarged, atrophic seminal vesicles (Finch and Girgis, 1974) and lower circulating erythrocyte concentrations (Finch and Foster, 1973) occur in nearly all mice as a consequence of aging and are not considered abnormal. In apparently healthy aged mice, there is no change in plasma levels of corticosterone or corticosterone binding globulin (Latham and Finch, 1976), testosterone (Nelson, Latham, and Finch, 1975), or the pituitary hormones FSH, TSH, GH, or PRL (Finch, Jonec, Wisner, Sinha, DeVellis, and Swerdloff, in preparation). It is relevant for neuroendocrine studies that no tumors of the brain, adrenal, or testes have been detected by gross observation in C57BL/6J male mice between the ages of 8-30 mo. (Finch, 1973). In contrast, pituitary adenomas are frequent in some strains of rats used for aging studies, e.g., Sprague-Dawley females (Durbin, Williams, Jeung, and Arnold, 1966; Simms and Berg, 1957; Ross and Bras, 1971). Animal strains and sexes without major endocrine disturbances are desirable for studying the effect of aging on catecholamine metabolism, since gonadal steroids (Bapna, Neff, and Costa, 1971) and ACTH (Versteeg, 1973) appear to alter brain catecholamine metabolism at any age.

Employing apparently healthy old C57BL/6J male mice, we found that the turnover of catecholamines of the hypothalamus and neostriatum (chiefly putamen) is slowed (Finch, 1973); levels of dopamine are also reduced in the neostriatum, although changes were not found in other brain regions of those mice. This selectivity probably has biological significance, because it implicates specific cell populations which may be sensitive to aging, in particular, the dopaminergic neurons of the substantia nigra which project to the putamen (Andén, Fuxe, Hamberger, and Hökfelt, 1966). The available data are summarized in Table 2. In

TABLE 2. EFFECT OF AGING ON CATECHOLAMINE METABOLISM.

	Change	Species	Age	Sex	Ref.
A. Tyrosine Hydroxylase					
1. neostriatum	-35%	rat (Wistar)	(4–15) vs. (25–28) mo	M	a
2. brain, minus cerebellum and neostriatum	0	rat (Wistar)	(4–15) vs. (25–28) mo	M	a
3. substantia nigra	>-50%	human	15–60 yr		b
4. hypothalamus	0	human	15–60 yr		b
B. Dopa decarboxylase					
1. hypothalamus	0	mouse (C57BL/6J)	12 vs. 28 mo	M	c
2. neostriatum	0	mouse (C57BL/6J)	12 vs. 28 mo	M	c
3. heart	0	rat (albino)	15 vs. 24 mo	both	d
C. Dopamine					
1. levels					
a. whole brain	0	mouse (C57BL/6J)	12 vs. 28 mo	M	c
b. neostriatum	-20%	mouse (C57BL/6J)	12 vs. 28 mo	M	c
c. whole brain, minus neostriatum and cerebellum	0	rat (Wistar)	7 vs. (24–29) mo		a
2. turnover neostriatum	-50%	mouse (C57BL/6J)	12 vs. 28 mo	M	c
D. Dopamine β hydroxylase serum levels	+20%	human	(21–40) vs. (41–60) yr	both	e
E. Norepinephrine					
1. levels					
a. whole brain	0	mouse (C57BL/6J)	12 vs. 28 mo	M	c
b. whole brain	0	mouse (C57BL/10)	9 vs. 28 mo	M	f
c. whole brain, minus neostriatum and cerebellum	0	rat (Wistar)	7 vs. (24–28) mo	M	a
d. cerebellum	0	mouse (C57BL/6J)	12 vs. 28 mo	M	c
e. hypothalamus	0	mouse (C57BL/6J)	12 vs. 28 mo	M	c
f. brain stem	0	mouse (C57BL/6J)	12 vs. 28 mo	M	c
g. hindbrain	-40–50%	human	25 vs. 65+ yr	both	g
2. turnover hypothalamus	-50%	mouse (C57BL/6J)	12 vs. 28 mo	M	c
F. Monoamine Oxidase					
1. heart	0	rat (albino)	8 vs. 24 mo	F	d
2. heart	+300%	rat (albino)	8 vs. 24 mo	M	d
3. plasma	>+35%	human	25–55 vs. >65 yr	both	g, h
4. platelets	>+35%	human	25–35 vs. >65 yr	both	g, h
5. hindbrain	+50%	human	25–55 vs. >65 yr	both	g, h
G. Catechol -0-methyl transferase					
1. heart	0	rat (albino)	8 vs. 24 mo	F	d
2. heart	0	rat (albino)	12 vs. 24 mo	F	d
H. Homovanillic acid cerebrospinal fluid	+50%	human	30 vs. 80 yr	both	i

[a] McGeer, Fibiger, McGeer, and Wickson, 1971.
[b] Côte and Kremzner, 1974.
[c] Finch, 1973.
[d] Gey, Burkard, and Pletscher, 1965.
[e] Freedman, Ohuchi, Goldstein, and Axelrod, 1972.
[f] Samorajski, Friede, and Ordy, 1971.
[g] Robinson, Nies, Davis, Bunney, Davis, Colburn, Bourne, Shaw, and Coppen, 1972.
[h] Robinson, Davis, Nies, Ravaris, and Sylvester, 1971.
[i] Gottfries, Gottfries, Johansson, Olsson, Persson, Roos, and Sjöström, 1971.

TABLE 3. EFFECT OF AGING ON SEROTONIN METABOLISM.

	Change	Species	Age	Sex	Ref.
A. *Serotonin*					
1. whole brain	0	mouse (C57BL/6J)	12 *vs.* 28 mo	M	a
2. whole brain	0	mouse (C57BL/6J)	15 *vs.* 28 mo	M	b
3. hindbrain	0	human	25 *vs.* 65+ yr	both	c
B. *5-hydroxyindole acetic acid*					
1. hindbrain	0	human	25 *vs.* 65 yr	both	c
2. hindbrain	+30%	human	65 *vs.* 70 yr	both	c
3. urine/24 hr	−50%	human	(20–40) *vs.* >80 yr	both	d
4. CSF	+20%	human	30 *vs.* 80 yr	both	e
C. *Hydroxyindole-O-methyl transferase*					
1. pineal	−20%	human	(40–55) *vs.* (55–70) yr	both	f

[a] Finch, 1973
[b] Samorajski, Friede, and Ordy, 1971
[c] Robinson, Davis, Nies, Ravaris, and Sylwester, 1971
[d] Földes, Csotortok, and Beregi, 1965
[e] Gottfries *et al.*, 1971
[f] Wurtman, Axelrod, and Burchas, 1964

TABLE 4. EFFECT OF AGING ON ACETYLCHOLINE METABOLISM.

	Change	Species	Age	Sex	Ref.
A. *Choline Acetylase*					
1. cerebellum, cerebral cortex and hypothalamus	0	rat (Long Evans)	12, 14, 20 mo	M	a
2. spinal cord	−15%	rat (Long Evans)	12, 14, 20 mo	M	a
3. neostriatum	−25%	rat (Wistar)	(7, 15) *vs.* (24, 28) mo	M	b
4. "rest of brain" (minus neostriatum or cerebellum)	0	rat (Wistar)	(7, 15) *vs.* (24, 28) mo	M	b
B. *Acetylcholine Esterase*					
1. whole brain	0	mouse (C57BL/6J)	11, 26 + mo	both	c
2. prosencephalon	0	rat (Wistar)	6, 12, 24 mo	F	c
3. cerebral cortex	0	mouse (C57BL/6J)	4 *vs.* 28 mo	both	c
4. cerebral cortex	0	mouse (C57BL/10)	9 *vs.* 28 mo	M	d
5. cerebral cortex	0	rat (Wistar)	4, 7, 23, 24, 28 mo	M	b
6. cerebral cortex	−20%	rat (Wistar)	7 *vs.* 15 mo	F	e
7. cerebellum	0	rat (Wistar)	7 *vs.* 15 mo	F	e

[a] Vulcana and Timiras, 1969
[b] McGeer *et al.*, 1971
[c] Hollander and Barrows, 1968
[d] Samorajski, Friede, and Ordy, 1971
[e] Moudgil and Kanungo, 1973b

this very preliminary phase of research, aging appears to alter the metabolism of catecholamines more than the metabolism of serotonin (Table 3), acetylcholine (Table 4), or the putative amino acid transmitters (Table 5).

The enzymes which synthesize the neurotransmitters are also known to be important modulators of this metabolism. For example, tyrosine hydrozylase is considered to be the rate limiting enzyme for catecholamine synthesis (Nagatsu, Levitt, and Udenfriend, 1964). Large decreases have been reported in the basal ganglia of humans and rodents, although other regions may be unaffected (Table 2).

TABLE 5. EFFECT OF AGING ON AMINO ACID NEUROTRANSMITTER METABOLISM.

	Change	Species	Age	Sex	Ref.
A. *Glutamic acid*					
1. whole brain	0	mouse (C57BL/6J)	10, 29 mo	M	a
B. *Glutamic acid Decarboxylase*					
1. whole brain	–15%	mouse (C57BL/6J)	(10, 24) *vs.* (33, 37) mo	M	a
2. brain stem	0	rat	2, 12, 26 mo		b
3. cerebellum	0				
4. prosencephalon	0				
5. neostriatum	0	rat (Wistar)	2–29 mo	M	c
6. "whole brain" (minus neo- striatum and cerebellum)	0				
C. *γ-aminobutyric acid (GABA)*					
whole brain	0	rat (Wistar)	10, 18, 29 mo	M	a
D. *GABA-transferase*					
whole brain	+20%	mouse (C57BL/6J)	(10, 24) *vs.* 33 mo	M	a
E. *Aspartic acid*					
	0	mouse (C57BL/6J)	10, 18, 29 mo	M	a
F. *Aspartate Aminotransferase*					
	0	mouse (C57BL/6J)	10, 24, 33 mo	M	a

G. *Succinic Dehydrogenase*
  "whole brain" (minus
  caudate and cerebellum)
	0	rat (Wistar)	4, 24, 29 mo	M	c

H. *Glutamic-Oxalacetic Transaminase* cerebrospinal fluid	+100%	human	(25–35) *vs.* (55–65) yr	both	d
I. *Malate Dehydrogenase* cerebrospinal fluid	0	human	(25–35) *vs.* (55–65) yr	both	d
J. *Lactic Dehydrogenase* cerebrospinal fluid	+100%	human	(25–35) *vs.* (55–65) yr	both	d

[a] Fonda, Acree, and Auerbach, 1973
[b] Epstein and Barrows, 1969
[c] McGeer *et al.*, 1971
[d] Hain and Nutter, 1960

The activity of the complex enzyme "mono-amine oxidase" may increase with age (Table 2F). The few published studies (Table 2F) do not justify overly enthusiastic speculation about the value of monoamine oxidase inhibitors such as procaine as a rejuvenator (Aslań, Vrăbiescu, Domílescu, Câmpeanu, Costiniu, and Stănescu, 1965); much more information is needed.

The preliminary evidence available indicates that the enzymes of catecholamines may be more altered during aging than those of the other putative neurotransmitters (Tables 3–5). It must be cautioned that studies of the entire cell populations of brain regions represent the summations of individual neuronal pathways which may change independently during aging. Differences in neurotransmitter metabolism between neural loci (Fuxe, 1965; Palkovits,

Brownstein, Saavedra, and Axelrod, 1974b) are well established. It is only when the analysis of aging can be brought to the level of functionally distinct pathways and cell groups that an adequate understanding of the effect of aging on the brain will be achieved.

The alteration in monoamine metabolism which may occur in the brain during aging is of considerable interest in view of the increasing incidence of Parkinson's disease during aging (Hoehn, 1976). The altered levels of dopamine in the mouse neostriatum and of other monoamines in the human brain during aging may lower the threshold for the induction of extra-pyramidal symptoms. The incidence of reversible, drug-induced Parkinson's symptoms by phenothiazine tranquilizers approximates the spontaneous age-related incidence (Ayd, 1961). It is thus plausible that disturbances

TABLE 6. EFFECT OF AGING ON MISCELLANEOUS ENZYMES AND METABOLITES.

	Change	Species	Age	Sex	Ref.
A. *ATPase*					
1. prosencephalon	0	rat (Wistar)	11 *vs.* 26 + mo	F	a
2. brain stem	0	rat (Wistar)	11 *vs.* 26 + mo	F	a
3. cerebellum	0	rat (Wistar)	11 *vs.* 26 + mo	F	a
B. *Na-K activated ATPase*					
1. prosencephalon	0	rat (Wistar)	11 *vs.* 26 + mo	F	a
2. brain stem	0	rat (Wistar)	11 *vs.* 26 + mo	F	a
3. cerebellum	0	rat (Wistar)	11 *vs.* 26 + mo	F	a
4. whole brain	0	mouse (C57BL/6J)	4–28 mo	F	a
C. *Adenyl cyclase*					
1. basal					
a. neostriatum	+60%	rat (Sprague-Dawley)	3 *vs.* 24 mo	M	b
b. cerebellum	+60%	rat (Sprague-Dawley)	3 *vs.* 24 mo	M	b
c. cortex	0	rat (Sprague-Dawley)	3 *vs.* 24 mo	M	b
d. hippocampus	0	rat (Sprague-Dawley)	3 *vs.* 24 mo	M	b
2. catecholamine activated					
a. neostriatum	reduced	rat (Sprague-Dawley)	3 *vs.* 24 mo	M	b
D. *Cyclic AMP*	0	rat (Fisher)	6, 12, 24 mo	M	c

[a] Hollander and Barrows, 1968
[b] Walker and Boas-Walker, 1973
[c] Zimmerman and Berg, 1974

in monoamine metabolism during aging may establish preconditions for Parkinson's disease, as well as other age-related diseases which may be a result of disturbed monoamine metabolism. Possibly included among such disorders are tardive dyskinesia (Seide and Muller, 1967) and senile tremor (Doshay, 1961). It is pertinent that tardive dyskinesia, e.g., involuntary writhing movements of the mouth, may be irreversibly induced in older humans by prolonged treatment with phenothiazines (Seide and Muller, 1967). Possibly, a reduced dose threshold for inducing irreversible neurological damage occurs as the result of lowered dopamine or inhibited dopamine uptake (see below) during aging (Finch, 1973; Jonec and Finch, 1975). Another example of altered drug sensitivity which may be related to impaired dopamine reuptake is the greater hyperactivity of old rats in response to amphetamines (Puri, Volicer, Choma, Williams, and Pelikan, 1976), since amphetamines also impair dopamine reuptake by synaptosomes (Horn, Coyle, and Snyder, 1971).

Another aspect of neurotransmitter regulation concerns the ability of some neural membranes to actively transport monoamines. Such transport or reuptake from the synaptic cleft by the presynaptic membrane is considered to be an important means of biologically inactivating released monoamines (Cooper, Bloom, and Roth, 1974). This process may be studied *in vitro,* employing partially purified preparations of synaptosomes or "pinched off nerve endings" (Whittaker, 1966; Bretz, Baglioni, Hauser, and Hodel, 1974). In exploratory studies of synaptosomes from the hypothalamus and neostriatum of C57BL/6J male mice, no effect of age was found on the stability of endogenous dopamine stores, or on the uptake of norepinephrine, serotonin, or L-tyrosine (Jonec and Finch, 1975). However, the uptake of dopamine was reduced by 20–30 percent in mice between the ages of 18 and 28 months. Kinetic analysis indicated an increased K_m for DA uptake, but no change in V_{max} (Jonec and Finch, 1975). This observation could imply a selective effect of aging on dopaminergic cells. If dopamine uptake is also inhibited during aging in humans, this change could account for the greater sensitivity of older humans to phenothiazines (*vide infra*) since phenothiazines appear to inhibit dopamine uptake (Horn, Coyle, and Snyder,

1971). A study of ATPase (Na^+, K^+ dependent) in synaptosomal fractions of C57BL/10J male mice revealed another age change: although the basal levels of the enzyme from synaptosomes of whole brains of mice was unchanged between 3 and 29 months, the inhibitory effect of ethanol increased gradually with age (Sun and Samorajski, 1975). A similar trend was observed in a very limited sample of human frontal cortex grey matter (Sun and Samorajski, 1975). The origins of the increased sensitivity to ethanol are unkown but suggest a change in membrane structure. An increasing amount of cholesterol has been observed in the brains of aging mice by these workers (Sun and Samorajski, 1972). Possibly, as Sun and Samorajski (1975) observe, changes in the sensitivity of neural membranes with age underlie reduced tolerance to alcohol with age in rats (Wiberg, Trenholm, and Caldwell, 1970).

In conclusion, the exploratory studies described above indicate that there may be a number of age-related alterations in subcellular loci which pertain to neurotransmitter metabolism. The consequences of such changes to the use of drugs in the elderly could be profound and, at the very least, require evaluation of dosimetry as a function of age.

NEUROENDOCRINE FUNCTION AND AGING

The regional selectivity of age-related change as manifested in RNA, protein, and monoamine synthesis implies that certain cell groups and functions may be more sensitive to aging. This selectivity may be a key to understanding the alterations of neuroendocrine controls during aging, because the functions of the pituitary are regulated by specific brain regions and groups of cells. The neuroendocrine axes about which the most is known with respect to aging are the ovarian-pituitary-brain relationships.

The onset of irregularities in ovarian cycles during midlife is a widely distributed phenomenon in mammals (Chapter 13). Although a severe and irreversible loss of ovarian oocytes occurs during aging (Chapter 13), transplantation of ovaries from (old) noncycling rats to young rats in two laboratories resulted in reinitiation of estrous cycles (Ascheim, 1964; Peng and Huang, 1972).* Therefore, a diminished store of oocytes of the old rat can not be considered as sufficient cause for the loss of estrous cycles. Other factors are probably involved, since young ovaries transplanted to an old host rat did not regain cycles (Ascheim, 1964; Peng and Huang, 1972). Thus, extraovarian factors (e.g., in the brain or pituitary) may contribute to the loss of ovarian cycles in rats. Certainly there is no failure of gonadotropin production by the pituitary during aging; on the contrary, loss of ovarian cycles during aging is characteristically followed by an increased output of gonadotropins in humans (Tsai and Yen, 1971). Clinical studies indicate an absence of daily variation in postmenopausal gonadotropin output (Tsai and Yen, 1971). Tentatively, then, the age-related defect resides in the brain centers which regulate the cyclic output of gonadotropin releasing factors.

Ovarian cycles in a majority of old rats were reinitiated by the administration of L-DOPA, epinephrine, and iproniazide (Clemens, Amenomori, Jenkins, and Meites, 1969; Quadri, Kledzik, and Meites, 1973; Huang and Meites, 1975). These experiments indicate that the aging defect may be a hypothalamic deficiency in catecholamines, which are strongly implicated in the central mechanism producing cycling discharge of releasing factors: L-DOPA is converted to dopamine and norepinephrine in the brain (Wurtman, Chou, and Rose, 1970; Dowson and Laszlo, 1971); epinephrine is a catecholamine; and iproniazide, a monoamine oxidase inhibitor, increases brain catecholamines (Spector, Prockop, Shore, and Brodie, 1957). Hence these drugs, by increasing hypothalamic catecholamine levels may overcome the deficiency, which has been observed

---

*Evidence from hamsters (Blaha, 1964) implicates ovarian aging as the primary cause of reproductive senescence in this species. In the CBA strain of mouse, young ovaries regain cycles after transplantation to noncycling 12-month-old females (Krohn, 1962). The younger age of the host or strain differences are factors here, since CBA mice show an unusually early loss of fertility by 10 months and, unlike most other mice, lose all oocytes before midlife (Jones and Krohn, 1961).

in male mice (Finch, 1973). A drug-induced deficiency of brain catecholamines will also cause the loss of ovarian cycles in rodents (Kalra and McCann, 1973). Stereotaxic implants of catecholamines are needed to identify the particular regions of the brain which are deficient in catecholamines. *A priori,* the hypothalamus and the preoptic regions are of much interest because of their high content of catecholamines (Palkovits *et al.,* 1974b) and releasing factors (Palkovits, Arimura, Brownstein, Schally, and Saavedra, 1974a) and because of their critical role in regulating gonadotropin cyclicity (Halazs and Gorski, 1967).

• The role of the brain in regulating endocrine changes is highly speculative (Finch, 1976): other hormonal changes which may result from altered monoamines include the increased production of prolactin in female rats (Clemens and Meites, 1971) the reduced secretion of pregnanediol and other adrenal steroids in men (Romanoff, Baxter, Thomas, and Ferrechio, 1969; Romanoff, Thomas, and Baxter, 1970), smaller elevation of corticosterone in fasted aging rats (Britton, Rottenburg, and Adelman, 1975), impaired elevation of LH after castration of aging rats (Shaar, Euker, Riegle, and Meites, 1975) and mice (Finch, Jonec, Wisner, Sinha, DeVellis, and Swerdloff, in preparation), and an absence of LH output after ether stress in aging rats (Riegle and Meites, 1976).

Steroid Receptors of the Brain

The regulation of pituitary hormone output requires that the brain detect levels of steroids and other endocrine gland products. One of the currently considered mechanisms for this control involves the steroid-binding proteins which carry steroid molecules into the nucleus in steroid-sensitive tissues such as the uterine epithelium (Hamilton, 1968). Similar molecules and mechanisms have been described in neurons, e.g., the hippocampal pyramidal cells have corticosterone binding proteins (Gerlach and McEwen, 1972), and the tubero-infundibular neurons of the arcuate nucleus in the hypothalamus have estrogen-binding capacity (Stumpf, 1968). The precise functions of these

molecules is not described, although their distribution in the brain generally corresponds to loci known to influence hypothalamic and pituitary functions (reviewed by McEwen and Pfaff, 1973).

The effect of aging on the potentially crucial steroid receptor proteins has just recently been probed for glucocorticoids. Total cytosol binding capacity for dexamethasone decreased with age in rat "cerebral hemisphere" (Roth, 1974). Isolated neuronal perikarya of old rats showed a 30 percent loss of specific glucocorticoid binding sites (Roth, 1976). In contrast, no age-related change in corticosterone binding capacity of cytosols from cerebral cortex, hippocampus, or hypothalamus was detected in C57BL/6J male mice (Nelson, Holinka, Latham, Allen, and Finch, 1976). Cytosols from whole brain regions contain contributions from many cell types which could obscure age changes in specific cells. Decreased sex steroid receptors may occur in the old rat brain, since there is evidence for decreased uptake of ^{3}H-estradiol in old female rat hypothalamus (Peng and Peng, 1973), decreased sensitivity of single unit electrical activity to estrogen and testosterone in the preoptic region and arcuate nucleus (Babichev, 1973), and decreased induction of acetylcholinesterase by estrogens (Moudgil and Kanungo, 1973a). It may be speculated that changes in steroid receptor levels, by altering steroid sensitive parameters of hypothalamic catecholamine metabolism (Kizer, Palkovits, Zivin, Brownstein, Saavedra, and Kopin, 1974), could influence the feedback sensitivity of the hypothalamic-pituitary axis (Finch, 1976).

AUTONOMIC MECHANISMS AND AGING

There are many indications that functional changes occur in autonomic mechanisms during aging. However, the literature is fragmentary, and the majority of studies are insufficiently controlled for age-related diseases. At present, no change has been analyzed sufficiently to reveal the mechanism involved (see Wollner and Spalding [1973] for a clinically oriented discussion of autonomic changes of aging). This section will illustrate autonomic associated changes with two examples which may be particularly accessible to analysis of the molecular changes in future studies.

Blood Pressure Regulation: The Baroreceptor Reflex

The age-related trend for higher systolic and diastolic pressure is well documented in humans, although a similar phenomenon may not occur in aging rodents (Chapter 12). The role of the autonomic controls in these changes is virtually undefined but is suggested by the hemodynamic response to change in body position, which reveals an interesting age difference in humans. In young subjects, tilting from supine to upright positions causes a sudden increase of urinary norepinephrine content, which results from the vasomotor reflex involving the baroreceptors of the aorta and carotid sinus to prevent loss of blood pressure. This compensation is much reduced in older humans (Strandall, 1964; Johnson, Smith, Spalding, and Wollner, 1965; Hedfors, 1973) and is accompanied by reduced output of urinary norepinephrine (Benetato and Găleşanu, 1966; Hedfors, 1973). Several points in this system may be considered for possible age changes: first, consider the baroreceptors.

The baroreceptors in the aorta and carotid sinus, which contain high concentrations of dopamine (Zapata, Hess, Bliss, and Eyzaguirre, 1969), showed some evidence of impaired sensitivity by variants of the Valsalva manoeuvre (transitory reduction of venous return to the heart) in aging humans (Johnson et al., 1965; Gribbin, Pickering, Sleight, and Peto, 1971); in rabbits and cats (Shchegoleva, 1962); and in rats (Rothbaum, Shaw, Angell, and Shock, 1974).

The pathways from the baroreceptors to the brain stem and thence to the sympathetic chain are uninvestigated with respect to aging. Presumably, some of the urinary norepinephrine detected after tilting comes from the noradrenergic neurons in the vascular beds of the skeletal muscles and heart. Thus the reduced secretion of norephinephrine could result from reduced signals from the baroreceptors as well as from intermediate relays. The possibility

that sympathetic innervation is reduced with age in some organs is shown by the loss of catecholamine terminals in the follicles of the aging mouse thyroid (Melander, Sundler, and Westgren 1975).

The response of blood vessels to adrenergic agents appears to change markedly during maturation and during later aging. Fleisch observed substantial impairment of the relaxation (vasodilation) induced by isoproterenol (an adrenergic receptor mediated function) in the aorta of rats, rabbits and cats. Although the isoproterenol induced relaxation was impaired, complete relaxation was obtained with nitrite (Fleisch, Maling, and Brodie, 1970; Fleisch, 1970); thus, at least some components of the vasodilation mechanism are not impaired. Similar changes occur in the tracheal smooth muscle of rats and guinea pigs (Åberg, Adler, and Ericsson, 1973). These observations have been confirmed and extended: there is also a maturation-related impairment in the relaxatory response to dopamine (Cohen and Berkowitz, 1975) and to cyclic AMP (Cohen and Berkowitz, 1974). However, there was no maturation-related impairment in basal or nucleotide stimulated adenyl cyclase in the aorta (Cohen, 1976). Thus, the impairment may reside in some interaction of cyclic AMP with the aortic smooth muscle cells. A relationship of some of these changes to hypertension is suggested by further impairments of aortic relaxation in spontaneous and renal hypertensive rats (Cohen and Berkowitz, 1976). Another aspect of vascular aging is the decreased contractility of the aorta of old rats in response to norepinephrine (Tuttle, 1966). Decreases in rat aortic contractility in response to norepinephrine in the old rat aorta may also result from increased thickness of the tunica media; hence, a primary change in adrenergic receptors cannot be determined (Tuttle, 1966). Age-related decreases in the response of vascular beds to catecholamines were also observed during maturation (Hrůza and Zweifach, 1967). Thus, the reduced response to tilting may result from lowered sensitivity of the baroreceptors as well as from changes in peripheral receptors. These aging changes of hemodynamic controls may be difficult to analyze because of the generally increasing rigidity and thickness of blood vessels (Chapter 12).

Reports of changed cardiac and hemodynamic response of aging humans and animals to injected catecholamines are numerous but cannot be easily analyzed because of the complexity of the systems, the problem of vascular disease which is present to varying degrees in human and animal populations (Chapters 12 and 21), and because of the frequent error of comparing young, growing animals with senescent animals (thus, it can not be established if the changes observed are due to maturation or aging). Examples of reported changes include increased heart rate in response to atropine in older humans (Frolkis, 1968) and increased electrical thresholds for a variety of autonomic responses (Frolkis, Bezrukov, Bogatskaya, Verkhratsky, Zamostian, Shevtchuk, and Shtchegoleva, 1970).

Thermoregulation

Maintenance of body temperature during exposure to heat or cold is governed by hypothalamic mechanisms (thermostats) which control heat by exchange with the environment, by shivering, by activation of caloric depots, such as in fat cells and in the liver, and by controlling appetite. There are many studies of humans and rodents which demonstrate age-related defects in thermoregulation during exposure to cold (*mice:* Grad and Kral, 1957; Finch, Foster and Mirsky, 1969, *rats:* Rapaport, 1967; and *humans:* Krag and Kountz, 1950; Horvath, Radcliffe, Hutt, and Spurr, 1955) and to heat (*rats:* Rapaport, 1969; and *humans:* Shattuck and Hilferty, 1932; Krag and Kountz, 1952; Hellon and Lind, 1956; Hellon, Lind, and Weiner, 1956). There are obviously so many loci involved in thermoregulation that it is currently impossible to estimate the contribution of specific neural, endocrine, metabolic, and mechanical components to the age changes observed. Indications of changes at many loci are indicated by the following studies.

The Liver. In young fasted mice (4–16 mo), there is a rapid induction of hepatic tyrosine aminotransferase (Finch, Foster, and Mirsky,

1969), an enzyme considered to be involved in gluconeogenesis (Feigelson and Feigelson, 1966). In old mice (>26 mo.) which show marked defects of thermoregulation, exposure to cold results in a delayed induction of tyrosine aminotransferase. The contribution of the delayed induction of tyrosine aminotransferase to the major loss of body temperature observed in fasted old mice during short exposures to cold is probably negligible. Disturbances of neural and endocrine control mechanisms of thermoregulation are clearly indicated, however.

The Adrenal Cortex. The secretion of corticosterone during exposure of mice to cold is not significantly altered by age (Finch, Foster, and Mirsky, 1969).

Lipolysis. Fatty acids, released by adrenergic stimulation of fat cells, are a major source of thermogenesis. Much evidence shows age-related impairments of lipolytic response to stress in rats (Hrůza and Jelínková, 1963; Hrůza and Jelínková, 1964), to insulin in mice (Greenwood, Johnson, and Hirsch, 1970) and rats (Di Girolamo and Rudman, 1968), and to catecholamines in rats (Bunnel and Griffith, 1943; Hrůza and Jelínková, 1965; Jelínková and Hrůza, 1963, 1967; and Nakano, Gin, and Ishii, 1971). The origin of these changes is unknown, but the impaired lipolytic response could be a major cause of defective thermogenesis during exposure to cold. The adipocyte could provide valuable material for analysis of changed hormone-target cell interactions during aging.

CONCLUSIONS

The fragmentary and scattered evidence discussed above indicates the very early stage of development of the neurobiology of aging. The conjectures advanced by Dilman (1971), Everett (1973), and by this author (Finch 1972b, 1973, 1976) that many phenomena of aging may ultimately be traced to neuroendocrine and autonomic loci cannot be seriously evaluated until a great deal more information is available.

ACKNOWLEDGMENTS

This research was supported by grants to Caleb E. Finch from the N. I. H. (HUD-07539 and AG-00446), the N. S. F. (GB-352336) and by assistance from the Orentreich Foundation for the Advancement of Science (N. Y. C.) and the Glenn Foundation for Medical Research (Manhasset, N.Y.).

Contribution XX from the Laboratory of Neurobiology, Andrus Gerontology Center.

REFERENCES

Åberg, G., Adler, G., and Ericsson, E. 1973. The effect of age on β-adrenoceptor activity in tracheal smooth muscle. *Brit. J. Pharmacol., 47*, 181-182.

Andén, N. E., Fuxe, K., Hamberger, B., and Hökfelt, T. 1966. A quantitative study on the nigro-neostriatal dopamine neurone system in the rat. *Acta Physiol. Scand., 67*, 306-312.

Ascheim, P. 1964. Résultats fournis par la greffe hétérochrone des ovaire dans l'étude de la régulation hypothalamo-hypophyso-ovarienne de la ratte sénile. *Gerontologia, 10*, 65-75.

Aslań, A., Vrăbiescu, A., Domílescu, C., Câmpeanu, L., Costiniu, M., and Stănescu, S. 1965. Long-term treatment with procaine (Gerovital H_3) in albino rats. *J. Geront., 20*, 1-8.

Ayd, F. J. 1961. A survey of drug-induced extrapyramidal reactions. *J. Am. Med. Assoc., 175*, 1054-1060.

Babichev, V. N. 1973. Characteristics of hypothalamic neurons controlling the pituitary gonadotropic function in old female and male rats. Translated from *Byul. Eksperim. Biol. i Med., 75*, 3-5.

Bantle, J. A., and Hahn, W. E. 1976. Complexity and characterization of polyadenylated RNA in the mouse brain. *Cell, 8*, 139-150.

Bapna, J., Neff, N. H., and Costa, E. 1971. A method for studying norepinephrine and serotonin metabolism in small regions of rat brains: Effect of ovariectomy on amine metabolism in anterior and posterior hypothalamus. *Endocrinology, 89*, 1345-1349.

Benetato, G., and Găleşanu. 1966. Vanatiile catecolaminelor urinare si sanguine în raport cu vîrto si postura. *St. Cerc. Fiziol., 11*, 121-133.

Bernheimer, H., Birkmayer, W., Hornykiewicz, O., Jellinger, K., and Seitelberger, F. 1973. Brain dopamine and the syndromes of Parkinson and Huntington. Clinical, morphological and neurochemical correlations. *J. Neurol. Sci., 20*, 415-455.

Birren, J. E. 1964. *The Psychology of Aging*, p. 303. Englewood Cliffs, New Jersey: Prentice-Hall.

Birren, J. E., and Wall, P. D. 1956. Age changes in conductive velocity, refractory period, number of fibers, connective tissue space, and blood vessesls in sciatic nerve of rats. *J. Comp. Neurol., 104*, 1-16.

Blaha, G. C. 1964. Effect of age of the donor and recipient on the development of the transferred golden hamster ova. *Anat. Record, 150*, 413-416.

Bretz, U. M., Baglioni, M., Hauser, R., and Hodel, C. 1974. Resolution of three distinct populations of nerve endings from rat brain homogenates by zonal isopycnic centrifugation. *J. Cell Biol., 61*, 466-480.

Britton, G. W., Rotenberg, S., and Adelman, R. C. 1975. Impaired regulation of corticosterone levels during fasting in aging rats. *Biochem. Biophys. Res. Comm., 64*, 184-188.

Brown, I. R., and Church, R. B. 1971. RNA transcription from nonrepetitive DNA in the mouse. *Biochem. Biophys. Res. Comm., 42*, 850-854.

Bunnell, I. L., and Griffith, F. R. 1943. Age and the calorigenic response to subcutaneously administered adrenalin in the rat. *Am. J. Physio., 138*, 669-675.

Chaconas, E., and Finch, C. E. 1973. The effect of aging on RNA/DNA ratios in brain regions of the C57BL/6J male mouse. *J. Neurochem., 21*, 1469-1473.

Chambers, W. F., Dunihue, F. W., Smith, C. J., Blanchard, R. R., Taylor, C. H., and Hill D. B. 1966. Effect of vasopressin and adrenal steroids on cortical responses evoked at mid-brain level in aged rats. *Gerontologia, 12*, 65-73.

Cicero, T. J., Ferendelli, J. A., Suntzeff, V., and Moore, B. W. 1972. Regional changes in CNS levels of the S100 and 14-3-2 proteins during development and aging of the mouse. *J. Neurochem., 19*, 2119-2125.

Clemens, J. A., Amenomori, Y., Jenkins, T., and Meites, J. 1969. Effects of hypothalamic stimulation, hormones, and drugs on ovarian function in old female rats. *Proc. Soc. Exp. Biol. Med., 132*, 561-563.

Clemens, J. A., and Meites, J. 1971. Neuroendocrine status of old constant-estrous rats. *Neuroendocrinology, 7*, 249-256.

Cohen, M. L. 1976. Vascular adenyl cyclase: Role of age and guanine nucleotide activation. *Federation Proc., 35*, 423.

Cohen, M. L., and Berkowitz, B. A. 1974. Age-related changes in vascular responsiveness to cyclic nucleotides and contractile agonists. *Pharmacol. Exp. Therapeut., 191*, 147-155.

Cohen, M. L., and Berkowitz, B. A. 1975. Differences between the effects of dopamine and apomorphine on rat aortic strips. *European Pharmacol., 34*, 49-58.

Cohen, M. L., and Berkowitz, B. A. 1976. Decreased vascular relaxation in hypertension. *Pharmacol. Exp. Therapeut., 196*, 396-406.

Cooper, J. R., Bloom, F. E., and Roth, R. H. 1974. *The Biochemical Basis of Neuropharmacology*. 2nd ed. New York: Oxford University Press.

Côté, L. J., and Kremzner, L. T. 1974. Changes in neurotransmitter systems with increasing age in human brain, *In,* Transactions of the American Society for Neurochemistry, 5th Annual Meeting: New Orleans, Louisiana, p. 83.

Cutler, R. G. 1972. Transcription of reiterated DNA sequence classes throughout the lifespan of the mous. *Advan. Geront. Res.,* 4, 219–321.

Cutler, R. G. 1975. Transcription of unique and reiterated DNA sequences in mouse liver and brain tissues as a function of age. *Exp. Gerontol.,* 10, 37–60.

Davison, A. N. 1969. Biochemistry and the Myelin Sheath. *In, Scientific Basis of Medicine, Annual Reviews,* Chap. XIII, London: Athlone Press.

Di Girolamo, M., and Rudman, D. 1968. Variations in glucose metabolism and sensitivity to insulin of the rat's adipose tissue, in relation to age and body weight. *Endocrinology,* 82, 1133–1141.

Dilman, V. M. 1971. Age associated elevation of hypothalamic threshold to feedback control, and its role in development, aging, and disease. *Lancet,* 1, 1211–1219.

Doshay, L. J. 1961. Senile tremor versus Parkinson's disease. *Postgrad. Med.,* 30, 550–554.

Dowson, J. H., and Laszlo, I. 1971. Quantitative histochemical studies of formaldehyde-induced parenchymal fluorescence following L-DOPA administration. *J. Neurochem.,* 18, 2501.

Durbin, P. W., Williams, M. H., Jeung, N., and Arnold, J. S. 1966. Development of spontaneous mammary tumors over the lifespan of the female Charles River (Sprague-Dawley) rat: The influence of ovariectomy, thyroidectomy, and adrenalectomy-ovariectomy. *Cancer Res.,* 26, 400–411.

Epstein, M. H. and Barrows, C. H., Jr. 1969. The effects of age on the activity of glutamic acid decarboxylase in various regions of the brains of rats *J. Geront.,* 24, 136–139.

Everett, A. V. 1973. The hypothalamic-pituitary control of aging and age-related pathology. *Exp. Geront.,* 8, 265–277.

Feigelson, M., and Feigelson, P. 1966. Relationships between hepatic enzyme induction, glutaminate formation, and purine nucleotide biosynthesis in glucocorticoid action. *J. Biol. Chem.,* 241, 5819.

Finch, C. E. 1971. Comparative biology of senescence: some evolutionary and developmental considerations. *In, Animal Models for Biomedical Research, IV.,* pp. 47–67. Washington, D.C.; National Academy of Sciences.

Finch, C. E. 1972a. Enzyme activities, gene function, and aging in mammals (review). *Exp. Geront.,* 7, 53–67.

Finch, C. E. 1972b. Cellular pacemakers of aging in mammals. *In,* R. Harris and D. Viza (eds.), *Proceedings of the 1st European Conference on Cell Differentiation,* Nice, 1971, pp. 123–126. Copenhagen: Munksgaard.

Finch, C. E. 1973. Catecholamine metabolism in the brains of aging male mice. *Brain Res.,* 52, 261–276.

Finch, C. E. 1976. Physiological changes of aging in mammals. *Quart. Rev. Biol.,* 51, 49–83.

Finch, C. E., and Foster, J. R. 1973. Hematologic and serum electrolyte values of C57BL/6J male mouse in maturity and senescence. *Lab. Animal Sci.,* 23, 339–349.

Finch, C. E., Foster, J. R., and Mirsky, A. E. 1969. Aging and the regulation of cell activities during exposure to cold. *J. Gen. Physiol.,* 54, 690–712.

Finch, C. E., and Girgis, F. 1974. Enlarged seminal vesicles in C57BL/6J male mice. *J. Geront.,* 29, 134–138.

Finch, C. E., Jonec, V., Hody, G., Walker, J. P., Morton-Smith, W., Alper, A., and Dougher, G. J. 1975. Aging and the passage of L-tyrosine and inulin into mouse brain slices *in vitro. J. Geront.,* 30, 33–40.

Finch, C. E., Jonec, V., Wisner, J. R., Jr., Sinha, Y. N., deVellis, J., and Swerdloff, R. S. Hormone production by the pituitary and testes in male C57BL/6J mice during aging. In preparation.

Fleisch, J. H. 1971. Further studies on the effect of aging on β-adrenoreceptor activity of rat aorta. *Brit. J. Pharmacol.,* 42, 311–313.

Fleisch, J. H., Maling, H. M., and Brodie, B. B. 1970. Beta-receptor activity in aorta. Variations with age and species. *Circulation Res.,* 26, 151–162.

Flora, G. C., Baker, A. B., Loewenson, R. B., and Klassen, A. C. 1968. A comparative study of cerebral atherosclerosis in males and females. *Circulation,* 38, 859–869.

Foldes, I., Csotortok, L., and Beregi, E. 1965. Decrease of 5-hydroxyindole acetic acid (5-HIAA) excretion in old age. *Gerontol. Clin.,* 7, 92–95.

Fonda, M. L., Acree, D. W., and Auerback, S. B. 1973. The relationship of γ-aminobutyrate levels and its metabolism to age in brains of mice. *Arch. Biochem. Biophys.,* 159, 622–628.

Freedman, L. S., Ohuchi, T., Goldstein, M., Axelrod, R., Fish, I., and Dancis, J. 1972. Changes in human serum dopamine-β-hydroxylase activity with age. *Nature,* 236, 310–311.

Frolkis, V. V. 1968. The autonomic nervous system in the aging organism. *Triangle,* 8, 322–328.

Frolkis, V. V., Bezrukov, V. V., Bogatskaya, L. N., Verkhratsky, N. S. Zamostian, V. P., Shevtchuk, V. G., and Shtchegoleva, I. V. 1970. Catecholamines in the metabolism and functions regulation in aging. *Gerontologia,* 16, 129–140.

Fuxe, K. 1965. Evidence for the existence of monoamine-containing neurones in the central nervous system. IV. Distribution of monoamine nerve terminals in the central nervous system. *Acta. Physiol. Scand.,* 64, Suppl., 247. pp 37–85.

Gaubatz, J., Prashad, N., and Cutler, R. G. 1976. Ribosomal RNA gene dosage as a function of tissue and age for mouse and human. *Biochim. Biophys. Acta,* 418, 358–375.

Gerlach, J. L., and McEwen, B. S. 1972. Rat brain

binds adrenal steroid hormone: Radioautography of hippocampus with corticosterone. *Science,* **175,** 1133–1136.

Gey, K. F., Burkard, W. P., and Pletscher, A. 1965. Variation of the norepinephrine metabolism of the rat heart with age. *Gerontologia,* **11,** 1–11.

Gordon, S. M., and Finch, C. E. 1974. An electrophoretic study of protein synthesis in brain regions of senescent male mice. *Exp. Geront.,* **9,** 269–273.

Gottfries, C. G., Gottfries, I., Johansson, B., Olsson, R., Persson, T., Roos, B.-E., and Sjöström. 1971. Acid monoamine metabolites in human cerebrospinal fluid and their relations to age and sex. *Neuropharmacol.,* **10,** 665–672.

Grad, B., and Kral, V. A. 1957. The effect of senescence on resistance to stress. *J. Geront.,* **12,** 172–181.

Greenwood, M. R. C., Johnson, P. R., and Hirsch, J. 1970. Relationship of age and cellularity to metabolic activity in C57BL mice. *Proc. Soc. Exp. Biol. Med.,* **133,** 944–947.

Gribbin, B., Pickering, T. G., Sleight, P., and Peto, R. 1971. Effect of age and high blood pressure on baroreflex sensitivity in man. *Circulation Res.,* **29,** 424–431.

Grouse, L., Omenn, G. A., and McCarthy, B. J. 1973. Studies by DNA-RNA hybridization of transcriptional diversity in human brain. *J. Neurochem.,* **20,** 1063–1073.

Hahn, W. E., and Laird, C. D., 1971. Transcription of nonrepeated DNA in mouse brain. *Science,* **173,** 158–161.

Hain, R. F., and Nutter, J. 1960. Cerebrospinal fluid enzymes as a function of age. *Arch. Neurol.,* **2,** 109–115.

Haining, J. L., Turner, M. D., and Pantall, R. M. 1970. Local cerebral blood flow in young and old rats during hypoxic hypercapnia. *Am. J. Physiol.,* **218,** 1020–1024.

Halázs, B., and Gorski, R. A. 1967. Gonadotrophic hormone secretion in female rats after partial or total interruption of neural afferents to the medial basal hypothalamus. *Endocrinology,* **80,** 608–622.

Hamilton, T. H. 1968. Control by estrogen of genetic transcription and translation. *Science,* **161,** 649–661.

Hedfors, E. 1973. Urinary excretion of noradrenaline in response to tiliting in aged. *Acta Physiol. Scand.,* **88,** 528-532.

Hellon, R. F., and Lind. A. R. 1956. Observations on the activity of sweat glands with special reference to the influence of aging. *J. Physiol.,* **133,** 132–144.

Hellon., R. F., Lind, A. R., and Weiner, J. S. 1956. The physiological reactions of men of two age groups to a hot environment. *J. Physiol.,* **133,** 118–131.

Hoehn, M. M. 1976. Age distribution of patients with Parkinsonism. *J. Am. Ger. Soc.* **24,** 79–85.

Hollander, J., and Barrows, C. H. 1968. Enzymatic studies in senescent rodent brain. *J. Geront.,* **23,** 174–179.

Horn, A. S., Coyle, J. T., and Snyder, S. H. 1971. Catecholamine uptake by synaptosomes from rat brain. Structure activity relationships of drugs with differential effects on dopamine and norepinephrine neurones. *Molecular Pharmacol.,* **7,** 66–80.

Hornykiewicz, O. 1966. Metabolism of brain dopamine in human Parkinsonism: Neurochemical and clinical aspects. *In,* E. Costa, L. J. Côté, and M. D. Yahr (eds.), *Proceedings of the 2nd Symposium of the Parkinson's Disease Information and Research Center.* (1965). New York: Raven Press.

Horvath, S. M., Radcliffe, C. E., Hutt, B. K., and Spurr, G. B. 1955. Metabolic responses of old people to a cold environment. *J. Appl. Physiol.,* **8,** 145–148.

Hrůza, Z., and Jelínková, M. 1963. The metabolism of fat and proteins in trauma and adaptation to trauma in rats of different ages. *Gerontologia,* **8,** 36–45.

Hrůza, Z., and Jelínková, M. 1965. Carbohydrate metabolism after epinephrine, glucose and stress in young and old rats. *Exp. Geront.,* **1,** 139–147.

Hrůza, Z., and Zweifach, B. W. 1967. Effect of age on vascular reactivity to catecholamines in rats. *J. Geront.,* **22,** 469–473.

Huang, H. H., and Meites, J. 1975. Reproductive capacity of aging female rats. *Neuroendocrinology,* **17,** 289–295.

Huemer, R. P., Bickert, C., Lee, K. D., and Reeves, A. E. 1971. Mitochondrial studies in senescent mice-1. Turnover of brain mitochondrial lipids. *Exp. Geront.,* **6,** 259–265.

Hydén, H. 1960. The neuron. *In,* J. Brachet and A. E. Mirsky (eds.), *The Cell,* Vol 4, Part 1, Chapter 5, pp. 215–324.

Jelínková-Tenorová, M., and Hrůza, Z. 1963. The effect of epinephrine on fat metabolism in old rats. *Gerontologia,* **7,** 168–180.

Jelínková, M., and Hrůza, Z. 1967. The influence of endocrine factors on the decreased reactivity of adipose tissue to epinephrine in old rats. *Physiol. Bohemoslov.,* **16,** 48–52.

Johnson, R., Chrisp, C., and Strehler, B. 1972. Selective loss of ribosomal genes during the aging of postmitotic tissues. *Mech. Age. Dev.,* **1,** 183–198.

Johnson, R. H., Smith, A. C., Spalding, J. M. K., and Wollner, L. 1965. Effect of posture on blood-pressure in elderly patients. *Lancet,* i, 731–733.

Jonec, V. J., and Finch, C. E. 1975. Senescence and dopamine uptake by subcellular fractions of the C57BL/6J male mouse brain. *Brain Res.,* **91,** 197–215.

Jones, E. C. and Krohn, P. L. 1961. The relationships between age, numbers of oocytes, and fertility in virgin and multiparous mice. *J. Endocrinol.,* **21,** 469–495.

Kalra, S. P. and McCann, S. M. 1973. Effect of drugs modifying catecholamine synthesis on LH release induced by preoptic stimulation in the rat. *Endocrinology*, 93, 356–362.

Kizer, J. S., Palkovits, M., Zivin, J., Brownstein, M., Saavedra, J. M., and Kopin, I. J. 1974. The effect of endocrinological manipulations on tyrosine hydroxylase and dopamine-β-hydroxylase activities in individual hypothalamic nuclei of the adult male rat. *Endocrinology*, 95, 799–812.

Krag, C. L. and Kountz, W. B. 1950. Stability of body function in the aged I. Effect of exposure of the body to cold. *J. Geront.*, 5, 227–235.

Krag, C. L., and Kountz, W. B. 1952. Stability of body function in the aged II. Effect of exposure of the body to heat. *J. Geront.*, 7, 61–70.

Krohn, P. L. 1962. Review lectures on senescence. II. Heterochronic transplantation in the study of aging. *Proc. Roy. Soc. (London) Ser. B*, 157, 128–147.

Lapham, L. W. 1968. Tetraploid DNA content of Purkinje neurons of human cerebellar cortex. *Science*, 159, 310–312.

Latham, K. R. 1974. Aging and glucocorticoid binding proteins in the liver and brain of C57BL/6J mice. Ph.D. dissertation. Los Angeles: University of Southern California.

Latham, K. R., and Finch, C. E. 1976. Hepatic glucocorticoid binders in mature and senescent C57BL/6J male mice. *Endocrinol.*, 98, 1480–1489.

McEwen, B. S., and Pfaff, D. W. 1973. Chemical and physiological approaches to neuroendocrine mechanisms: Attempts at integration. *In*, W. F. Ganong and L. Martini (eds.), *Frontiers in Neuroendocrinology*, Chap. 9., pp 267–335. New York: Oxford University Press.

McGeer, E. G., Fibiger, H. C., McGeer, P. L., and Wickson, V. 1971. Aging and brain enzymes. *Exp. Geront.*, 6, 391–396.

Marsh, G. R., and Thompson, L. W. 1976. Psychophysiology of aging. *In*, J. E. Birren and K. W. Schaie (eds.), *Handbook of the Psychology of Aging*. New York: Van Nostrand Reinhold.

Melander, A., Sundler, F., and Westgren, U. 1975. Sympathetic innervation of the thyroid: Variation with species and with age. *Endocrinology*, 96, 102–106.

Menzies, R. A., Mishra, R. K., and Gold, P. H. 1972. The turnover of ribosomes and soluble RNA in a variety of tissues of young adult and aged rats. *Mech. Age. Dev.*, 1, 117–132.

Moudgil, V. K., and Kanungo, M. S. 1973a. Effect of age of the rat on induction of acetylcholinesterase of the brain by 17β estradiol. *Biochim. Biophys. Acta*, 329, 211–220.

Moudgil, V. K., and Kanungo, M. S. 1973b. Effect of age on the circadian rhythm of acetylcholinesterase of the brain of the rat. *Comp. Gen. Pharmacol.*, 4, 127–130.

Nagatsu, T., Levitt, M., and Udenfriend, S. 1964. Tyrosine hydroxylase. The initial step in norepinephrine biosynthesis. *J. Biol. Chem.*, 239, 2910–2917.

Nakano, J., Gin, A. C., and Ishii, T. 1971. Effect of age on norepinephrine-, ACTH-, theophylline-, and dibutryl cyclic AMP-induced lipolysis in isolated rat fat cells. *J. Geront.*, 26, 8–12.

Nelson, J. F., Holinka, C. F., Latham, K. R., Allen, J. K., and Finch, C. E. 1976. Corticosterone binding in cytosols from brain regions of mature and senescent C57BL/6J male mice. *Brain Res.* In press.

Nelson, J. F., Latham, K. R., and Finch, C. E. 1975. Plasma testosterone levels in C57BL/6J male mice: Effects of age and disease. *Acta Endocrinol.*, 80, 744–752.

Ojeda, S. R., Harms, P. G., and McCann, S. M. 1974. Effect of blockade of dopaminergic receptors of prolactin and LH release: Median eminence and pituitary sites of action. *Endocrinology*, 94, 1650–1657.

Oldendorf, W. H., and Kitano, M. 1965. Isotope study of brain blood turnover in vascular disease. *Arch. Neurol.*, 12, 30–38.

Palkovits, M., Arimura, A., Brownstein, M., Schally, A. V., and Saavedra, J. M. 1974a. Luteinizing hormone-releasing hormone (LH-RH) content of the hypothalamic nuclei in rat. *Endocrinology*, 95, 554–558.

Palkovits, M., Brownstein, M., Saavedra, J., and Axelrod, J. 1974b. Norepinephrine and dopamine content of hypothalamic nuclei of the rat. *Brain Res.*, 77, 137–149.

Peng, M.-T., and Huang, H.-O. 1972. Aging of hypothalamic-pituitary-ovarian function in the rat. *Fertility Sterility*, 23, 535–542.

Peng, M.-T., and Peng, Y. M. 1973. Changes in the uptake of tritiated estradiol in the hypothalamus and adenohypophysis of old female rats. *Fertility Sterility*, 24, 534–539.

Puri, S. K., Volicer, L., Choma, P., Williams, R., and Pelikan, E. W. 1976. Age-related changes of locomotor activity after amphetamine administration. *Federation Proc.*, 35, 785.

Quadri, S. K., Kledzik, G. S., and Meites, J. 1973. Reinitiation of estrous cycles in old constant-estrous rats by central-acting drugs. *Neuroendocrinology*, 11, 248–255.

Rapaport, A. 1967. L'adaptation du comportement du rat jeune, adulte et âgé aux variation de la température ambiante I. Adaptation an froid. *Gerontologia*, 13, 14–19.

Rapaport, A. 1969. L'adaptation du comportement du rat jeune, adulte et âgé aux variation de la température ambiante II. Adaptation à la chaleur. *Gerontologia*, 15, 288–292.

Riegle, G. D., and Meites, J. 1976. Effects of aging on LH and prolactin after LHRH, L-DOPA methyl-DOPA and stress in male rat. *Proc. Soc. Exp. Biol. Med.*, 151, 507–511.

Robinson, D. S., Davis, J. M., Nies, A., Ravaris, C. L., and Sylwester, D. 1971. Relation of sex and aging to monoamine oxidase activity of human brain, plasma, and platelets. *Arch. Gen. Psychiat.*, 24, 536–539.

Robinson, D. S., Nies, A., Davis, J. N., Bunney, W. E., Davis, J. M., Colburn, R. W., Bourne, H. R., Shaw, D. M., and Coppen, A. J. 1972. Aging, monoamines and monoamine-oxidase levels. *Lancet*, **i**, 290–291.

Romanoff, L. P., Baxter, M. N., Thomas, A. W., and Ferrechio, G. B. 1969. Effect of ACTH on the metabolism of pregnenolone-7α-^{3}H and cortisol-4-^{14}C in young and elderly men. *J. Clin. Endocrinol. Metab.*, **29**, 819–830.

Romanoff, L. P., Thomas, A. W., and Baxter, M. N. 1970. Effect of age on pregnanediol excretion by men. *J. Geront.*, **25**, 98–101.

Ross, M. H., and Bras, G. 1971. Lasting effect of early caloric restriction on prevention of neoplasms in the rat. *J. Nat. Cancer Inst.*, **47**, 1095–1113.

Roth, G. S. 1974. Age-related changes in specific glucocorticoid binding by steroid-responsive tissues of rats. *Endocrinology*, **94**, 82–90.

Roth, G. S. 1976. Reduced glucocorticoid binding site concentration in cortical perikarya from senescent rats. *Brain Res.*, **107**, 345–354.

Rothbaum, D. A., Shaw, D. J., Angell, C. S., and Shock, N. W. 1974. Age differences in the baroreceptor response of rats. *J. Geront.*, **29**, 488–492.

Rouser, G., Kritchevsky, G., Yamamoto, A., and Baxter, C. 1972. Lipids in the nervous system of different species as a function of age. Brain, spinal cord, peripheral nerve, purified whole cell preparations, and subcellular particulates: Regulatory mechanisms and membrane structure. *In*, R. Paoletti and D. Kritchevsky (eds.), *Advances in Lipid Research*, pp. 261–360. New York: Academic Press.

Rouser, G., and Yamamoto, A. 1969. Lipids. *In*, A. Lajtha (ed.), *Handbook of Neurochemistry*, Vol. 1, Chap. 8., pp. 121–169. New York: Plenum Press.

Samorajski, T., Friede, R. L., and Ordy, J. M. 1971. Age differences in the ultrastructure of axons—the pyramidal tract of the mouse. *J. Geront.*, **26**, 542–551.

Seide, H., and Müller, H. 1967. Choreiform movements as side effects of phenothiazine medication in geriatric patients. *J. Am. Geriat. Soc.*, **15**, 517–522.

Shaar, C. J., Euker, J. S., Riegle, G. D., and Meites, J. 1975. Effects of castration and gonadal steroids on serum luteinizing hormone and prolactin in old and young rats. *J. Endocrinol.*, **66**, 45–51.

Shattuck, G. C., and Hilferty, M. M. 1932. Sunstroke and allied conditions in the United States. *Am. J. Trop. Med.*, **12**, 233–245.

Shchegoleva, I. V. 1962. Changes in the sensitivity of the carotid sinus receptors during aging. *Bull. Exp. Biol. Med.* (USSR), **54**, 850–852.

Simms, H. S., and Berg, B. N. 1957. Longevity and the onset of lesions in male rats. *J. Geront.*, **12**, 244–252.

Spector, S., Prockop, D., Shore, P. A., and Brodie, B. B. 1957. Effect of iproniazid on brain levels of nonrepinephrine and serotonin. *Science*, **127**, 704.

Strandall, T. 1964. Mechanical systole at rest, during and after exercise in supine and sitting position in young and old men. *Acta Physiol. Scand.*, **61**, 279–298.

Stumpf, W. E. 1968. Estradiol-concentrating neurones: Topography in the hypothalamus by dry mount autoradiography. *Science*, **162**, 1001–1003.

Sun, G. Y., and Samorajski, T. 1972. Age changes in the lipid composition of whole homogenates and isolated myelin fractions of mouse brain. *J. Geront.*, **27**, 10–17.

Sun, A. Y., and Samorajski, T. 1975. The effects of age and alcohol on ($Na^+ + K^+$)-ATPase activity of whole homogenate and synaptosomes prepared from mouse and human brain. *J. Neurochem.*, **24**, 161–164.

Tsai, C. C., and Yen, S. S. C. 1971. Acute effects of intravenous infusion of 17β-estradiol on gonadotrophin release in pre- and post-menopausal women. *J. Clin. Endocrinol. Metab.*, **32**, 766–771.

Tuttle, R. S. 1966. Age-related changes in the sensitivity of rat aortic strips to norepinephrine and associated chemical and structural alterations. *J. Geront.*, **21**, 510–516.

Versteeg, D. H. G. 1973. Effect of two ACTH-analogs on noradrenaline metabolism in rat brains. *Brain Res.*, **49**, 483–485.

Vulcana, T., and Timiras, P. S. 1969. Choline acetyltransferase activity in various brain areas of aging rats. *In*, *Proc. of 8th Int'l Cong. of Gerontol.*, Vol. 2, p. 24. Washington, D.C.: Federation of American Societies for Experimental Biology.

Walker, J. B., and Walker, J. P. 1973. Properties of adenyl cyclase from senescent rat brain. *Brain Res.*, **54**, 391–396.

Wayner, M. J., and Emmers, R. 1958. Spinal synaptic delay in young and aged rats. *Am. J. Physiol.*, **194**, 403–405.

Whittaker, V. J. 1966. Catecholamine storage particles in the central nervous system. *Pharmacol. Rev.*, **18**, 401–412.

Wiberg, G. S., Trenholm, H. L., and Caldwell, B. B. 1970. Increased ethanol toxicity in old rats: Changes in LD50, *in vivo* and *in vitro* metabolism, and liver alcohol dehydrogenase activity. *Toxicol. Appl. Pharm.*, **16**, 718–727.

Wilkie, F., and Eisdorfer, C. 1971. Intelligence and blood pressure in the aged. *Science*, **172**, 959–962.

Wollner, L., and Spalding, J. M. K. 1973. The autonomic nervous system. *In*, J. C. Brocklehearst (ed.), *Textbook of Geriatric Medicine and Gerontology*, Chap. 8e, pp. 235–254. Edinburgh: Churchill Livingston.

Wulff, V. J., and Freshman, M. 1961. Age-related reduction of the RNA content of rat cardiac muscle and cerebellum. *Arch. Biochem. Biophys.*, **95**, 181–182.

Wulff, V. J., Piekielniak, M., and Wayner, M. J., Jr. 1963. The ribonucleic acid content of tissues of rats of different ages. *J. Geront.*, **18**, 322–325.

Wurtman, R. J., Chou, C., and Rose, C. 1970. The fate of C^{14}-dihydroxyphenylalanine (C^{14}-DOPA) in the whole mouse. *J. Pharmacol. Exp. Therap.*, **174,** 351–356.

Wurtman, R. J., Axelrod, J. A., and Barchas, J. D. 1964. Age and enzyme activity in the human pineal. *J. Clin. Endocrinol. Metab.*, **24,** 299–301.

Zapata, P., Hess, A., Bliss, E. L., and Eyzaguirre, C. 1969. Chemical, electron microscopic, and physiological observations on the role of catecholamines in the carotid body. *Brain Res.*, **14,** 473–496.

Zimmerman, I., and Berg, A. 1974. Levels of adenosine 3′, 5′ cyclic monophosphate in the cerebral cortex of aging rats. *Mech. Age. Dev.*, **3,** 33–36.

12
HEART AND CARDIOVASCULAR SYSTEM

Robert R. Kohn

Case Western Reserve University

INTRODUCTION

Aging processes are usually considered to be normal processes in that they occur in all members of the population. Further, they are progressive and physiologically irreversible. Progressive and irreversible processes are generally harmful to the system involved. A consideration of aging should emphasize those processes that are inevitable, occurring in spite of optimal nutrition, environment, activity patterns, and an ideal genetic background. Such inevitable processes may, however, show altered rates of progression, depending on these other factors.

Aging and developmental processes are similar in many ways, and it is often difficult to identify a given process as one or the other. Developmental processes usually slow or stop at maturity, while aging processes accelerate or become more obvious during the postmature period, although they may be evident at earlier periods. Maturity is the point in the life span of mammals at which growth of long bones stops. It is essential in the study of aging processes to determine progressive change after this point. Comparisons between immature animals and old ones can yield misleading data.

Changes involving the cardiovascular system are central to major questions about aging. Aging of the cardiovascular system may under-

lie, in part, the generalized physiological decline and progressive debilitation that characterize the aging syndrome. This is an old idea; Leonardo da Vinci wrote, on the basis of his dissections, that the cause of aging was "veins which by the thickening of their tunics in the old restrict the passage of the blood, and by this lack of nourishment destroy the life of the aged without any fever, the old coming to fail little by little in slow death" (cited by Belt, 1952).

The major causes of death in an aging population are diseases of the cardiovascular system. Some of these diseases may represent aging processes themselves, while others are undoubtedly influenced by, or are dependent on, underlying basic aging processes.

An enormous number of studies have been carried out on age-related diseases of the cardiovascular system. It is beyond the scope of this review to deal in detail with each disease as a disease, in terms of etiology and pathogenesis. Rather, the emphasis will be on aspects of these diseases that appear to represent aging processes and on ways in which aging processes may initiate or accelerate disease. Some diseases show increasing incidences with age but lack the universality of aging processes; they occur only in certain subgroups in a population. They are somewhat peripheral to major questions about aging but are worthy of some consideration because of the obvious role of age-related factors.

Every complex system will be found to change in some way with age. The significance of an observed change at the molecular or cellular level is often not obvious from the observation itself. In the evaluation of information on aging, it is useful to start with the questions—that is, with the most general observations at high levels of biological organization and then attempt to work through cause-and-effect sequences to the tissue and molecular levels where the ultimate answers must lie. Age-related changes in function of the cardiovascular system and diseases characteristic of aging will be considered first. Discussions of changes at the tissue, cell, and chemical levels will follow, in attempts to find explanations for the functional decline and disease.

FUNCTIONAL CHANGES WITH AGE

Heart

Virtually everything that the heart can do has been measured as a function of age. Some functions change markedly, while data on others are equivocal and of uncertain significance.

The effect of age on heart rate has been determined in several studies. A tendency for this to decrease with age was reported in men under resting conditions (Brandfonbrener, Landowne, and Shock, 1955). Contradictory results, showing a decreased heart rate in 15 to 18-year-old males, compared with 60 to 75 year olds, have also been reported (De Vries and Adams, 1972). In the latter study, heart rate was determined in the young and old groups at various workloads up to 100 watts, employing a bicycle ergometer. Heart rate in the young group increased slightly, but consistently more than in the old group, as the workload was increased. The resting heart rate in men 20 to 92 years of age was found to be slightly increased with age, but when tilted from the horizontal position, young individuals showed a greater increase in heart rate than old (Norris, Shock, and Yiengst, 1953). The heart

rate in 22 to 30 and 64 to 73-year-old men without cardiopulmonary disease was studied under conditions of hypoxia and hypercapnia; the increase was significantly greater in the young group (Kronenberg and Drage, 1973). Resting heart rate was found to be greater in 24-month-old rats than in 12-month-old animals. The age difference was abolished by propranolol, a beta adrenergic blocking agent (Rothbaum, Shaw, Angell, and Shock, 1973).

While the effect of age on resting heart rate is equivocal, it appears clear that the heart rate increase in response to stress is less effective with increasing age.

Cardiac output, studied in 67 males 19 to 86 years old, free of disease, was found to drop off in a linear fashion at a rate of around 1 percent per year (Figure 1) (Brandfonbrener, Landowne, and Shock, 1955). Calculations of cardiac index (cardiac output per unit surface area) showed a decrease of 0.79 percent per year. In the same study, stroke volume and stroke index were found to decrease 0.70 percent and 0.49 percent per year respectively. It was estimated that about one-half of the cardiac output decrease with age was related to decreases in body size and heart rate, while the remaining one-half was due to a reduction in blood pumped per heart beat per unit body size. A study of the same population indicated that heart work (stroke volume X mean systolic blood pressure) decreased around 0.5 percent per year (Landowne, Brandfonbrener, and Shock, 1955). Figure 2 shows that heart power, which is heart work per beat per duration of systole, falls around 0.9 percent per year.

An investigation of 500 airline pilots without cardiovascular or pulmonary disease did not reveal any correlation between age and cardiac output or stroke volume (Proper and Wall, 1972). This raises the question about the use of selected populations in aging studies. Cardiovascular disease is a very common finding in an aging population. Depending on one's definition of disease and the thoroughness of physical and laboratory examinations, it might be possible to find some evidence of disease in all aging individuals. With regard to the healthy pilots, who clearly represent a selected pop-

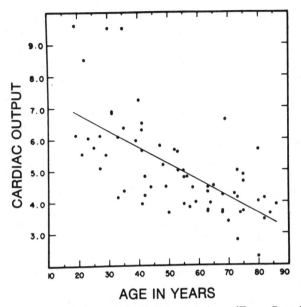

Figure 1. Cardiac output as a function of age in human beings. (From Brandfonbrener, M., Landowne, M., and Shock, N. W. 1955. Changes in cardiac output with age. *Circulation*, **12**, 567–576. By permission of The American Heart Association, Inc.)

ulation, it would be useful to know if their cardiac status proves that the declines shown in Figures 1 and 2 are not inevitable, or whether the individual pilots have shown similar functional declines with age. However, because of the selection methodology, only those at the upper ranges at older ages were available for study. While most data would

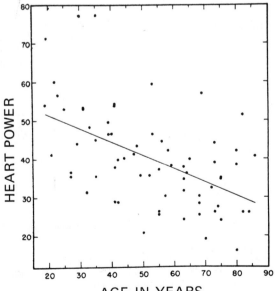

Figure 2. Heart power as a function of age in human males. (From Brandfonbrener, M., Landowne, M., and Shock, N. W. 1955. Changes in cardiac output with age. *Circulation*, **12**, 567–576. By permission of The American Heart Association, Inc.)

favor the latter possibility, only longitudinal studies of individuals can answer these questions.

Several studies of heart function in laboratory animals have provided useful information on changes with age. Cardiac output and stroke volume are significantly reduced in 24-month-old male rats as compared to 12-month-old animals, and the age difference was not abolished by beta adrenergic blockade (Rothbaum, et al., 1973). It was concluded that the decreased function with age was probably not due to decreased perfusion demand but to a decrease in the ability to maintain output per heart beat. Angiotensin II was administered to male rats from which baroreceptor reflexes were removed by vagotomy and stripping of nerve fibers from the carotid sinus and aortic arch. Left ventricular stroke work increase caused by the angiotensin II was 115 percent in 6-month-old rats but only 49 percent by 24 months of age (Lee, Karpeles, and Downing, 1972).

Investigations of performance of the aging heart have been taken to more basic levels by the study of isolated systems in vitro. Rat heart-lung preparations were stressed to produce failure while aortic flow was followed with time (Shreiner, Weisfeldt, and Shock, 1969). Flow fell much faster in 24-month-old males than in 12-month-old animals. The age difference was less in virgin females, while retired female breeders showed less initial flow and an equivocal change with age. This study raised the question of age-related coronary disease in male rats and retired female breeders.

Mechanical properties of left ventricular muscle from 11 to 13 and 26 to 31-month-old male rats were studied in vitro (Weisfeldt, Loeven, and Shock, 1971). Resting tension increased more with increasing length in the old than in the young group (Figure 3). Stress relaxation was more rapid in the young (Figure 4). There was no age difference in maximum isometric tension or in the length at which maximum tension occurred. On the other hand, the time to peak isometric contraction, the

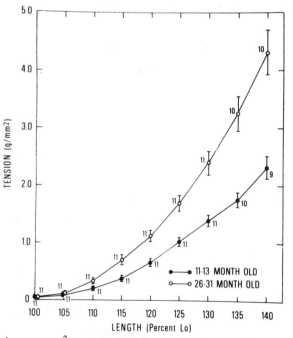

Figure 3. Resting tension per mm² cross-sectional area with increases in muscle length in trabeculae carnae from 11–13 (●) and 26–31 (○) month old rats. (From Weisfeldt, M. L., Loeven, W. A., and Shock, N. W. 1971. Resting and active mechanical properties of trabeculae carnae from aged male rats. *Am. J. Physiol.*, **220**, 1921–1927.)

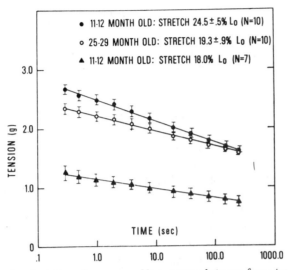

Figure 4. Stress relaxation in trabeculae carnae. Upper two plots are from trabeculae of 11–12 and 25–29-month-old rats stretched to length achieved after 1 hr at 1.75 g tension. Lowest plot is for muscles from 11–12-month old rats stretched to 18% of L_O. (From Weisfeldt, M. L., Loeven, W. A., and Shock, N. W. 1971. Resting and active mechanical properties of trabeculae carnae from aged male rats. *Am. J. Physiol.*, **220**, 1921–1927.)

duration of contraction, and the relaxation time were shorter in the young group. These suggested age changes in a viscous component of heart muscle.

In a study of rat myocardial muscle properties during the growth period (40 to 300 days of age), there was no change in isometric properties, but force and velocity of contraction decreased during growth and maturation (Heller and Whitehorn, 1972).

Hearts increase in size when stressed over long periods to do more work. The stress can result from an increased work load or from a decrease in the work capacity per unit of organ weight. In a human population dying from trauma or acute illness, there is marked variation in heart weight at all ages with no very significant change after maturity (Roessle and Roulet, 1932). When heart weight was expressed as percentage of body weight, there was a clear increase in later decades, particularly in males. This would appear to be due to an age-related decrease in body weight. On the other hand, the exclusion of significant fractions of the aging population from the study because of the presence of disease may have resulted in misleading low values for mean weights of aging hearts.

A study of heart weight in male rats showed increases with age; left ventricular weights were 0.8, 0.9, and 1.1 grams in 6-, 12-, and 24-month-old animals respectively (Lee, Karpeles, and Downing, 1972). Increases in heart weight in rats between 12 and 24 months of age were confirmed for males and retired breeder females, but no age difference was found in virgin females (Shreiner, Weisfeldt, and Shock, 1969). These data suggest the possibility of age-related disease in rats that spares virgin females.

Accumulated data suggest that large subfractions of aging populations have enlarged hearts but that hypertrophy is not inevitable in all individuals and should, therefore, not be considered a basic aging process.

The capacity to undergo cardiac hypertrophy following treatment with thyroxin was studied in 8- and 26-month-old mice (Florini, Saito, and Manowitz, 1973). Early development of hypertrophy was sluggish in the old group, but by 9 days heart size was the same in both groups. Such sluggishness of physiological reactivity, and response of homeostatic mechanisms with age is characteristic of virtually all organ systems. Explanations for this will be sought when aging of cells and tissues is considered.

Arteries

The large arteries change in very characteristic ways with age. These alterations are likely to play an important role in aging of the cardiovascular system and, therefore, in the generalized aging syndrome.

Thoracic aortas from 27 normotensive individuals 22 to 85 years of age were studied by determining relative volume increase at 100 mm Hg pressure (Bader, 1967). As shown in Figure 5, the volume fell off in a linear fashion with age. This indicates a progressive stiffening of the arteries, such that at older ages they had the elastic properties of rigid tubes. It was proposed that the change was due to a declining role of elastin and smooth muscle in determining elastic properties and an increasingly prominent role of collagen, which has very limited extensibility. Data in these studies also showed a marked increase in the elastic modulus of aorta with age, and a linear decrease in tangential wall stress.

It was pointed out in this study that about one-half of the cardiac output is stored in the aorta during systole and ejected during diastole. The aorta has a buffering action in maintaining blood pressure at 100 ± 20 mm Hg during the cardiac cycle. As the aorta stiffens with age, there is some compensation by an increase in

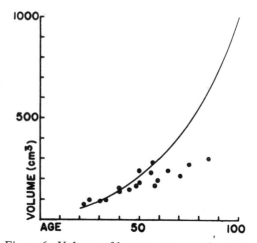

Figure 6. Volume of human aorta as a function of age. (From Bader, H. 1967. Dependence on wall stress in the human thoracic aorta of age and pressure. *Circulation Research,* **20,** 354–361. By permission of The American Heart Association, Inc.)

volume. Aortic volume increases until around 60 years of age (Figure 6), but thereafter, the increasing vessel stiffness in the absence of increasing volume should cause increasing systolic blood pressure and pulse pressure. Further, the decrease in tangential wall stress with age should affect the function of baroreceptors that respond to stress. If these receptors do not adapt to lower wall stresses, or smooth muscle cells do not adapt by exerting more stress on elastic fibers, increased blood pressure would result.

The increasing stiffness of human arteries with age has been confirmed in a number of studies. Iliac arteries show increasing resistance to both longitudinal and circumferential stretch with increasing age (Roach and Burton, 1959). Tension develops much more rapidly in old than mature arteries as they are elongated (Figure 7). The age differences appeared independent of the presence of vascular disease and vessel wall thickness. It was suggested that the slope of the length-tension curve was proportional to the number of collagen fibers being stretched and that the slack was taken up sooner in the old specimens.

In an angiographic study of mechanical properties of the aorta and pulmonary artery, the pressure strain elastic modulus (stiffness index)

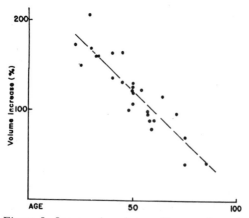

Figure 5. Increase in volume of human thoracic aorta, at a pressure of 100mm Hg, as a function of age. (From Bader, H. 1967. Dependence on wall stress in the human thoracic aorta of age and pressure. *Circulation Research,* **20,** 354–361. By permission of The American Heart Association, Inc.)

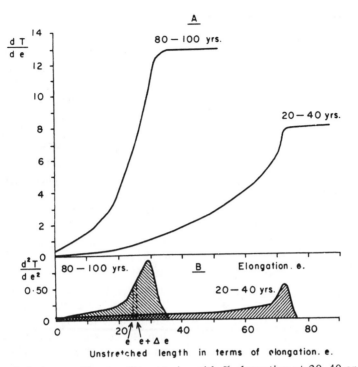

Figure 7. Rise of elastance of human iliac arteries with % elongation at 20–40 and 80–100 years of age. (From Roach and Burton, 1959.)

and pulse wave velocity were observed to increase linearly with age, doubling between 20 and 60 years of age (Gozna, Marble, Shaw, and Holland, 1974). Transcutaneous measurements of elastic properties of arteries in living subjects by an ultrasonic method have shown increasing stiffness with age in femoral and brachial arteries (Mozersky, Sumner, Hokanson and Strandness 1972, 1973). Increasing arterial stiffness with age is also manifested in living subjects by a decreasing amplification of the pressure wave between the proximal aorta and iliac arteries (Figure 8) and by an increased pulse wave velocity (O'Rourke, Blazek, Morreels, and Kravetz, 1968). It was concluded from these observations that the age-related stiffness extended throughout the arterial system, impairing pulsatile flow and increasing the load presented to the left ventricle.

In the case of human arteries, the question arises of the possible role of vascular disease, particularly atherosclerosis, in age-related changes in elastic properties. No correlation between degree of atherosclerosis and loss of vessel compliance was observed in

several of the cited studies. Further, the age-related loss of aortic distensibility is similar in American and Japanese populations, although the incidence and severity of atherosclerosis are much greater in Americans (Nakashima and Tanikawa, 1971).

That arterial stiffening may be characteristic of mammalian aging is suggested by the observation that between 6 and 18 months of age, rat aorta becomes less distensible (Band, Goedhard, and Knoop, 1972).

As noted above and as observed in additional studies, an increasing stiffness of arterial walls would tend to make baroreceptor reflexes sluggish. The heart rate response to hypoxia and hypercapnia in rats is reduced with increasing age (Kronenberg and Drage, 1973). In a study of human beings, baroreceptor sensitivity was studied during the response to phenylephrin (Gribbin, Pickering, Steight, and Peto, 1971). Sensitivity, as pulse interval per mm Hg of blood pressure, decreased with increasing age (Figure 9). It is of interest that a hypertensive population showed greater sensitivity than the normotensives at all ages. Both

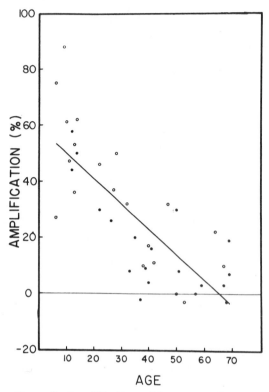

Figure 8. Amplification of human aortic pressure wave as a function of age. (From O'Rourke, M. F., Blazek, J. V., Morreels, C. L., and Kravetz, L. J. 1968. Pressure wave transmission along the human aorta. *Circulation Research*, 23, 567–579. By permission of The American Heart Association, Inc.)

groups showed decreases at about the same rate with increasing age.

It was proposed in a number of the cited studies that the age-related increase in arterial stiffness was related to a decreasing role of elastin and smooth muscle in determining mechanical properties and to a prominent role being taken over by collagen. And, although it appears that the presence of an atheroma does not influence mechanical properties, the question remains of a possible relationship between age changes in mechanical properties and other diseases categorized under the heading of arteriosclerosis. These questions will be dealt with in later sections.

Peripheral Vascular Function

Aging of the cardiovascular system should have the most important consequences at the micro-

vascular level where exchanges between cells and blood occur. Useful data have been acquired by measurements of resistance to blood flow, rate of flow through tissues, and rate of removal of substances in the blood.

Total peripheral resistance, as determined by ratio of mean arterial pressure to cardiac output, increases with age (Landowne, Brandfonbrener, and Shock, 1955). As shown in Figure 10, the average increase is 1.11 percent per year. Increasing peripheral resistance would tend to decrease perfusion rates of organs in the absence of an increase in heart work; the latter has been shown to decrease rather than increase with age (Landowne, Brandfonbrener, and Shock, 1955).

Studies of the role of age in blood flow through organs and the interpretation of observations are complicated by a number of factors. Age effects may become most apparent when the system is stressed by a demand for greater flow and may be masked under resting conditions. Rate of flow may be secondary to tissue demand or amount of tissue present, and these might vary with age. Excluding subjects with disease may remove a large and significant fraction of the aging population from a study, while individuals with disease but without clinical symptoms might be included.

In reviewing a large number of studies of blood flow through human organs (Bender, 1965), it was concluded that total peripheral resistance increased and systemic blood flow decreased with age and that these changes were not related to disease. There were, however, changes in distribution of cardiac output with age. Cerebral, coronary, and skeletal muscle flow changes were minimal "in the absence of arteriosclerosis," while splanchnic, renal, and finger-hand flow decreased significantly. The latter age-related decreases in flow were greater than could be accounted for on the basis of decreased cardiac output, or decreased metabolic rate, or amount of tissue present.

The cerebral circulation has received a great deal of attention. Although age changes are not as marked as in some other organs, decreases in flow rate seem established. For example, cerebral blood flow per 100 grams of tissue drops from 65.3 ml/min. at 18 to 36 years of age to 50.6 ml/min. at 56 to 79 years (Scheinberg,

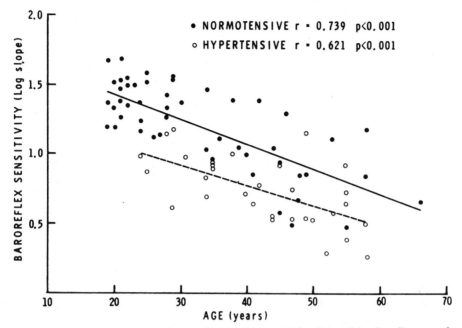

Figure 9. Effect of age on human baroreflex sensitivity. The solid and broken lines are for nor-motensives and hypertensives respectively. (From Gribbin, B., Pickering, T. G., Steight, P., and Peto, R. 1971. Effect of age and high blood pressure on baroreflex sensitivity in man. *Circulation Research*, **29**, 424–431. By permission of The American Heart Association, Inc.)

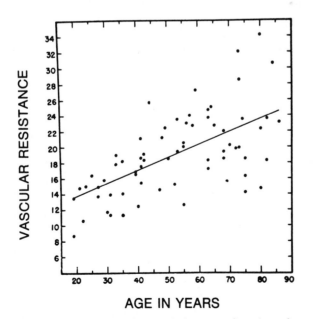

Figure 10. Peripheral vascular resistance in human beings as a function of age. (From Landowne, M., Brandfonbrener, M., and Shock, N. W. 1955. The relation of age to certain measures of performance of the heart and circulation. *Circulation*, **12**, 567–576. By permission of The American Heart Association, Inc.)

Blackburn, Rich, and Saslow, 1953). In a study of 32 subjects without neurological disease, transit time for cerebral blood flow, with wide variation at each age, increased from an average of 9.0 seconds (left hemisphere) and 9.8 seconds (right hemisphere) at 10 to 20 years of age to 13.0 seconds (both hemispheres) in those over 50 years old (Klanova and Heinis, 1972).

Measurements of blood flow in the human tibialis anterior muscle, based on rate of removal of a radioactive tracer injected into the muscle, showed decreases with age both in resting blood flow and in maximum flow in response to ischemia and weighting (Kuchar, Kuba, and Tomsu, 1972). There is marked variability in muscle blood flow at all ages (Amery, Bossaert, and Verstraete, 1969). An exception to decreased flow with age was observed in studies of forearm blood flow, where rate of flow was found to increase with age (Kravec, Eggers, and Kettel, 1972). Increased flow in response to hypoxemia was greater in the young than in old subjects. The basal forearm flow increase with age might be peculiar to this region because of a large flow through the skin, and the arteriovenous anastomoses and dilator mechanisms that characterize this site (Bender, 1965).

Blood flow in laboratory animals as a function of age has been studied by measuring rate of removal of radioactive tracers injected into organs. There is a marked decrease with age in myometrial blood flow in rabbits (Larson and Foote, 1972). Subcutaneous and muscle blood flow in rats and mice was observed to decrease rapidly during growth, but showed little change between 6 and 12 months of age (Robert, Marignac, Holtier, and Bertrand, 1970). It should be noted that removal of an injected tracer will depend on diffusion in tissue and vascular permeability in addition to rate of blood flow.

Effective renal plasma flow under basal conditions in human males without evidence of cardiovascular or renal disease showed a drop of 53 percent between 20 and 90 years of age (Davies and Shock, 1950). The data, shown in Figure 11, provide an extreme example of change in peripheral vascular function with age. The decrease could not be accounted for on the basis of decreased cardiac output. In studying renal blood flow by a xenon washout technique, it was found that the reduction with age was greater than the reduction in kidney mass, suggesting that aging of the vasculature might be a primary cause of reduced perfusion

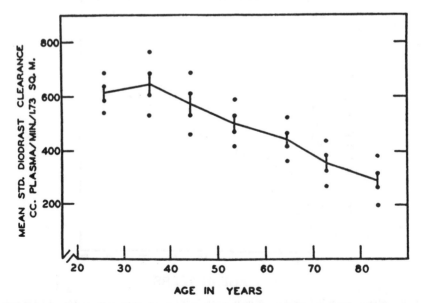

Figure 11. Renal plasma flow (diodrast clearance) in human beings as a function of age. (From Davies, D. F., and Shock, N. W. 1950. Age changes in glomerular filtration rate, effective renal plasma flow, and tubular excretory capacity in adult males. *J. Clin Invest.*, **29**, 496–507.)

(Hollenberg, Adams, Solomon, Rashid, Abrams and Merrill, 1974). Injected antigen is removed from the circulation much more slowly with increasing age in mice (Hanna, Nettesheim, and Snodgrass, 1971). Such a change could be due to either reduced peripheral blood flow or reduced efficiency of the reticuloendothelial system.

Accumulated data on peripheral resistance, blood flow, and clearance of substances strongly support the generality that organ perfusion decreases with age, although there are certainly differences between organs in degree of change. Also, compensatory mechanisms, such as vasodilation or increased vascularization at some sites may come into play with age that could mask basic vascular and tissue alterations that would tend to reduce flow.

Age changes in organ perfusion could be caused by less blood being supplied to capillary beds because of changes in cardiac output or in properties of large vessels. Investigators who have speculated on this have concluded that decreased flow through organs is not due, to any great extent, to decreased cardiac output, while stiffening of major arteries has been frequently documented. Variations in numbers of capillaries per unit volume of tissue or changes in properties of individual small vessels could also affect flow. Changes might also be secondary to such tissue alterations as decreased metabolic demand or loss of compliance. The increasing peripheral resistance with age very likely plays an important role in the decreased blood flow. Causes for this must be sought when basic aging processes at the tissue level are considered.

A progressive decrease in organ perfusion with age is capable of explaining many debilities that characterize aging.

Blood Pressure

Factors changing with age that would be expected to cause increased blood pressure would be increasing stiffness of large arteries and increasing peripheral resistance. Decreasing renal blood flow might also cause high blood pressure by the renin-angiotensin system. Blood pressure would tend to decrease with age because of de-

creased cardiac stroke volume and the increasing volume of the aorta. Blood pressure could also be influenced by many other factors that might change with age, such as obesity, salt intake, stress, aldosterone secretion, and nervous system function. The balance of such factors in individuals and populations determines what happens to blood pressure with increasing age. In terms of aging, the central question is whether blood pressure changes in progressive and irreversible ways in every individual.

Cross-sectional studies of American and European populations generally show increasing systolic pressure with age and a slower rate of increase in diastolic pressure, with the latter leveling off or decreasing in old age, resulting in increased pulse pressure (Bender, 1965). The frequency distribution of blood pressure yields a symmetrical curve in the young population and, as the population ages, the curve is skewed to higher values, as shown in Figure 12 (Harlan, Oberman, Mitchell, and Graybiel, 1973). The mean blood pressure rises with age, but some aging individuals have blood pressures comparable to those in young adults. In a longitudinal study, changes in blood pressure from 25–30 to 50–54 years of age were determined (Harris, 1968). Frequency plots of the changes showed generalized rises in blood pressure with age, but small numbers of individuals showed little or no change over the 25-year period (Figure 13).

A Welsh population also showed an increase in systolic blood pressure with age and equivocal changes in diastolic pressure, as shown in Figure 14 (Miall and Lovell, 1967). This investigation included a longitudinal study of individuals over a period of 10 years. It was found that the rate of increase was related to the original pressure; the greater the initial pressure, the greater was the increase during the period of observation. It was concluded that in individuals, increasing blood pressure was only indirectly related to age.

An investigation of 140 healthy males 20 to 92 years old confirmed an increase in systolic pressure with age, and an increase in diastolic pressure between the ages of 20 to 29 years and 60 to 69 years but with an equivocal difference

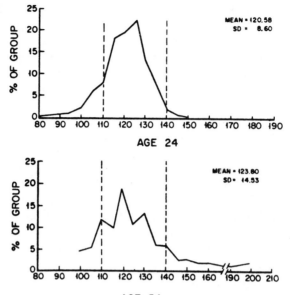

Figure 12. Frequency distribution curves for systolic blood pressures in the same cohort at 24 and 54 years of age. (From Harlan, W. R., Oberman, A., Mitchell, R. E., and Graybiel, A. 1973. A 30-year study of blood pressure in a white male cohort. *In*, G. Onesti, K. E. Kim, and J. H. Moyer (eds.), *Hypertension: Mechanisms and Management, 26th Hahnemann Symposium*. New York and London: Grune & Stratton. By permission.)

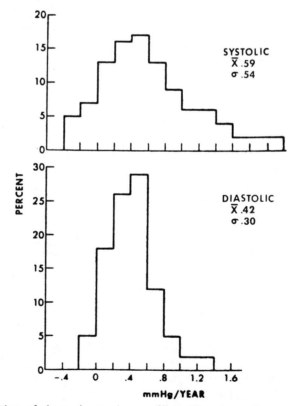

Figure 13. Distribution of slopes (regression coefficients) representing rates of increase in pressure from 25–30 to 50–54 years of age in human beings. (From Harris, 1968.)

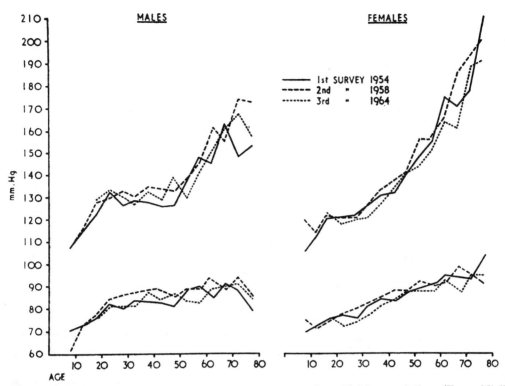

Figure 14. Relationship between age and blood pressure in a Welsh population. (From Miall, W. E., and Lovell, H. G. 1967. Relation between change of blood pressure and age. *British Medical Journal,* 2, 660–664.)

between the latter group and those 80 to 92 years old (Norris, Shock, and Yiengst, 1953). When individuals were tilted 45°, systolic blood pressure fell in the two older groups but remained constant in the youngest group, while diastolic pressure rose in all except the oldest group. Response to tilting was associated with an increased heart rate that was greatest in the youngest group. Exercise caused increased systolic and decreased diastolic pressures without significant age differences. Times required for return of blood pressure to resting levels were proportional to age, however. In a comparison of blood pressure increase at varying work loads in men 15 to 18 and 60 to 75 years old (De Vries and Adams, 1972), it was concluded that vasomotor response to exercise was not affected by age, and that differences with age in blood pressure levels are manifestations of the increased peripheral resistance that is present at rest. These data suggest an age-related sluggishness in cardiovascular reactivity that is apparent during postural change and

recovery from exercise, but not in response to exercise.

Pulmonary artery systolic and diastolic pressure increase with exercise. The influence of increased cardiac output and increased pulmonary capillary pressure in causing the blood pressure rise has been reported to be more marked with increasing age (Tartulier, Bourret, and Deyrieux, 1972).

Changes in blood pressure with age differ in different populations, and blood pressure in individuals is clearly modifiable. A 3-month physical training program for 8 subjects 55 to 78 years of age resulted in a mean drop in systolic blood pressure from 147.5 to 127.5 mm Hg (Barry, Daly, Pruett, Steinmetz, Page, Birkhead, and Rodahl, 1966). Training did not affect diastolic pressure. Four groups of Amish with different religious and cultural characteristics all showed increased systolic pressure with age, with diastolic pressure rising more slowly and leveling off or decreasing after 50 to 60 years of age, which is consistent with studies of other American populations, but the most conservative group showed the least increase in systolic pressure (Jorgenson, Balling, Yoder, and Murphy, 1972). Indian tribes in Surinam show a slight increase with age in systolic pressure in females but an apparent decrease in males. No change in diastolic pressure was observed in either sex (Glanville and Geerdink, 1972). In bushmen of Botswana, it has been reported that there is a slight decrease in both systolic and diastolic pressures with age in men, while in women there is a slight rise in systolic pressure and a slight decrease in diastolic pressure, the latter occurring after the menopause (Truswell, Kennelly, Hansen, and Lee, 1972). In a comparison of Londoners with natives of the Fiji and Gilbert Islands, the same rising blood pressures were observed in all groups until the fifth decade, after which both systolic and diastolic pressures rose in the English but remained constant in the islanders (Maddocks, 1961). No significant change in blood pressure with age was observed in a New Guinea population (Sinnett and Whyte, 1973).

Mean blood pressure in 24-month-old rats has been reported to be lower than that in 12-month-old animals (Rothbaum *et al.,* 1973); the difference (105 *vs.* 114 mm Hg) may be due to decreased cardiac output in the old animals. Another investigation of rats indicated that 31 percent of males and 19 percent of females were hypertensive when over 677 days of age (Berg and Harmison, 1955); renal disease may have played a role in these subgroups of the aging population.

Cross-sectional studies may be misleading, in that individuals whose blood pressure increases markedly with age might be selected out of the population by death or might alter their lifestyle in such a way as to decrease their blood pressure. This could explain in part the tendency of diastolic pressure to level off or decrease in old age in some populations. Data might also be complicated by possible environmental and nutritional changes in a population over a life span. The incidence of hypertension in Papago Indians has been increasing in recent decades; changing dietary habits, particularly increased salt intake, could be responsible (Strotz and Shorr, 1973).

Although increasing blood pressure with age is characteristic of many populations, the evidence is not convincing that this is an aging process, in the sense that it occurs in all individuals and is progressive and irreversible. Rather, it would appear that there are vascular changes that in themselves would tend to raise blood pressure with age, but that some individuals and populations are capable of compensating by bringing other factors into play.

Overview of Age and Cardiovascular Function

Age-related alterations in various components of the cardiovascular system are, of course, manifested in measurements of overall function. Central elasticity of the vascular system, calculated from resistance of the greater circulation times the fractional rate of fall of pressure in diastole, rises 1.58 percent per year, indicating an age change in volume distensibility (Landowne, Brandfonbrener, and Shock 1955). Circulation time increases with age but with marked variablity at each age (Brandfonbrener, Landowne, and Shock, 1955; Willems, Roelandt, Van de Vel, and Joossens, 1971). There is a decline with age in the ability to transport oxygen (Davies, 1972). Thermoregulation, which depends in part on heat conductance by cutaneous blood flow, becomes sluggish with age (Wagner, Robinson, Tzankoff, and Marino, 1972).

Central questions about aging of the cardiovascular system deal with those processes that are intrinsic to that system rather than those caused by changes in other organs. A change in one component of the cardiovascular system will influence properties or reactivity of other components, and it is difficult to distinguish primary from secondary age changes. It is possible, however, to explain most of the changes with age on the basis of a small number of factors that may be primary and intrinsic. These are: (1) a decrease in the ability of the heart to contract, (2) increased stiffness of large arteries, that is partially compensated for by an increased volume of the aorta, and (3) an increase in peripheral resistance. Basic tissue and molecular processes that might underlie such factors will be taken up in a later section.

CARDIOVASCULAR DISEASE AND AGE

Diseases of the cardiovascular system comprise the major causes of death in an aging population. Medical progress and improved sanitation and nutrition have had the most effect on decreasing the mortality rate amongst younger age groups and have had little or no effect on degenerative processes in aging populations. Progress has enabled large numbers of people to live to the age at which they die of these degenerative processes. In terms of vital statistics, it appears that the limits of progress have been reached in modern societies. These populations have shown little increase in life expectancy at birth or in shape of survivor curves in recent years. There is little reason to expect the cure or modification of the debilities and diseases of age until mechanisms of basic aging processes are better understood.

Although ways in which aging processes influence cardiovascular disease are poorly understood, it is possible to categorize various diseases in relationship to the criteria of such processes. Most significant in a discussion of aging would of course be diseases that are aging processes themselves, in being universal, progressive, and irreversible. Age-related changes in the morphology and elastic properties of arterial walls, generally and loosely referred to as "arteriosclerosis," represent the best and perhaps the only example of this kind of cardiovascular disease. A second category consists of those diseases that become prominent in certain populations or subgroups of a population—that is, they lack the universality of an aging process but appear to be dependent on basic underlying aging mechanisms. Examples are atherosclerosis and one or more forms of hypertension. A third category is of a disease whose incidence is clearly age-dependent, such as amyloidosis. In addition, there are diseases that occur in subgroups of a population and have serious consequences late in life simply because they take a long time to develop. These diseases, such as rheumatic valvulitis and the sequelae of syphilis, are only peripherally related to aging and will not be considered in this review. Also, any process requiring the interaction of factors is more likely to occur given more time. Thus, a number of lesions such as valve vegetations, granulomas, and tumors, which turn up in older individuals, do not appear to depend on aging *per se* and will not be considered here. On the basis of currrent knowledge, it may be difficult to decide on the proper category for a given disease or lesion.

The role of cardiovascular disease in deaths of an aging population can be seen in Figure 15, where the log of the age-specific death rate for all causes and for major individual causes is plotted as a function of age. The "all causes" curve is a straight line that is characteristic of an aging population (Gompertz function), indicating that the rate and probability of dying doubles around every 8.5 years after maturity. Curves for specific causes of death that are parallel to or rise faster than the "all causes" curve indicate a very strong age-dependence for the given cause. Thus, arteriosclerotic heart disease, vascular lesions of the central nervous system, hypertension, and renal disease of vascular origin are very age-dependent and together play a major role in characterizing overall mortality data. The curve for all deaths if cancer did not exist (ALL-NEOPL.) is mainly produced by cardiovascular disease and is very close to the curve for all causes. In other words, aging of a human population as manifested in mortality rates can be almost entirely accounted for on the basis of cardiovascular disease.

Another way of looking at mortality data is shown in Figure 16. Deaths due to major causes are plotted for a cohort of females as a function of age. Females live longer than males, and the inevitability of age-related deaths is emphasized in this population. The dominant role of arteriosclerotic heart disease is obvious. It is of interest that this disease, hypertension, pneumonia, and accidents all show the same modal value of 86 to 88 years, suggesting that a small number of basic aging processes may be responsible for these apparently different causes of death and that the human female life span should be considered to be around 87 years.

The accumulated mortality data indicate that if individuals do not die of other specific diseases, they will die from cardiovascular disease, pneumonia, or accidents. Which cause

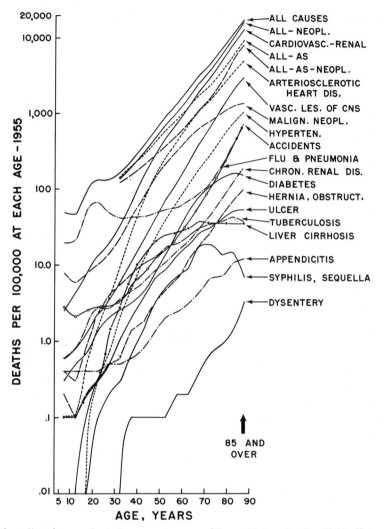

Figure 15. Mortality from selected causes by age. (From Kohn, R. R. 1963. Human aging and disease. *The Journal of Chronic Diseases,* Vol. 16, page 6, fig. 1.)

they will die from cannot be predicted, but the cause would appear to be fortuitous because deaths will occur at around the same age regardless of the terminal disease or injury.

Arteriosclerosis

The term *arteriosclerosis* is in common usage, and most clinicians and basic scientists interested in cardiovascular disease have a general understanding of its connotations. The term is, however, imprecise and difficult to use with reference to modern knowledge of vascular disease and aging of the cardiovascular system.

A standard text (Robbins, 1967) states "arteriosclerosis literally means 'hardening of the arteries,' but more accurately it refers to a group of processes which have in common thickening and loss of elasticity of arterial walls." This is a description of age changes in arteries that will be dealt with at the tissue level in a later section. Definitions then go on, however, to describe the three major kinds of arteriosclerosis: atherosclerosis, medial calcific sclerosis, and arteriolosclerosis. Thus, there is no specific form of arteriosclerosis that fits the original definition of the term. In practice, arteriosclerosis is used interchangeably with

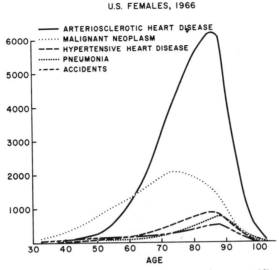

DEATHS IN COHORT OF 100,000 BORN
U.S. FEMALES, 1966

——— ARTERIOSCLEROTIC HEART DISEASE
········· MALIGNANT NEOPLASM
— — — HYPERTENSIVE HEART DISEASE
·········· PNEUMONIA
— - — ACCIDENTS

Figure 16. Deaths in a U.S. female cohort, at the 1966 rate, from specific major diseases. (Plotted from U.S. Vital Statistics, 1966.)

atherosclerosis; when discussing arteriosclerotic heart disease, for example, what is meant is disease due to atherosclerotic lesions.

It would be more useful to restrict the term arteriosclerosis to its original and literal meaning—hardening of the arteries—and to consider the other varieties of vascular changes as separate entities.

Both arteriosclerosis and atherosclerosis are readily apparent in the arteries of virtually all older Americans. There does not appear to be any correlation or cause-and-effect relationship between degree of atherosclerosis and loss of distensibility (Nakashima and Tanikawa, 1971). While loss of distensibility is a general aging phenomenon, occurring in all populations and possibly developing at comparable rates, degree of atherosclerosis in individuals and populations is variable.

Atherosclerosis is dealt with rather thoroughly in medical and pathological texts and is the subject of a continuing production of comprehensive reviews and symposium volumes in which epidemiology, comparative and experimental aspects, etiology and pathogenesis, and the chemical composition and morphology of lesions are described in detail (Geer and Haust, 1972; Likoff, 1972; Porter and Knight, 1973; Brusis and McGandy, 1971; Getty, 1966;

Solomon, 1967; and Vogel, 1973). In this discussion, emphasis will be placed only on those observations and phenomena that appear to bear on the role of aging in atherosclerosis.

Probably all human beings show increasing atherosclerosis with increasing age. There are, however, marked variations in the degree of arterial involvement in individuals at every age, as noted above. The risk factors that have been identified include overnutrition, high serum lipids, hypertension, diabetes mellitus, maleness, a stressful life-style, and recently, prolonged hemodialysis (Lindner, Charra, Sherrard, and Scribner, 1974). A number of racial and geographic differences in risk have also been observed, but these probably depend on special risk factors such as the preceding rather than on genes that cause atherosclerosis. Also, large numbers of atherosclerotic deaths will only occur in populations with decreased death rates due to the elimination of other causes—that is, only in advanced societies. Atherosclerosis also occurs in subhuman primates, horses, swine, dogs, and rabbits (Getty, 1966; Solomon, 1967; Garbarsch, Matthiessen, Helin, and Lorenzen, 1970), but the lesions are absent in untreated laboratory rodents.

The greatest risk factor in the development of atheromas is increasing age. This is clearly

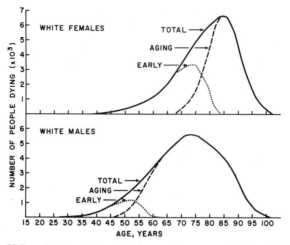

Figure 17. Deaths in U.S. cohorts, at the 1966 rate, from arteriosclerotic heart disease. (Plotted from U.S. Vital Statistics, 1966.)

shown in Figure 17, where deaths in cohorts due to coronary artery atherosclerosis at the 1966 rate are plotted as a function of age. Males are more susceptible at earlier ages (Keys, Aravanis, Blackburn, van Buckem, Buzina, Djordjevic, Fidanza, Karvonen, Menotti, Puddu and Taylor, 1972; Anderson, 1973). The incidence rises with age to a modal value that corresponds roughly with the mode for all deaths in the population; the descending limb corresponds with the dying out of the entire population. The overall curve can be resolved into two curves: one, a symmetrical bell-shaped curve that could represent atherosclerotic deaths primarily due to aging, and a second curve appearing at earlier ages that could represent a subpopulation with special risk factors. It should be noted that deaths due to atherosclerosis are only an indirect indication of the prevalence and degree of this disease in a population. Death occurs when circulation to vital organs is diminished by obliterative atherosclerosis or by thrombi forming on atherosclerotic plaques. Such catastrophes can occur in individuals with small numbers of plaques and not take place in individuals with widespread atherosclerosis. The increasing atherosclerosis with age has been confirmed, however, in clinical and autopsy studies of different populations (Sasaki, Horiuchi, Suzuki, and Inui, 1972; Heath, et al., 1973; Zhdanov, Lifshits, and Vikhert, 1973).

A number of the risk factors for atherosclerosis increase in incidence and/or severity with age. Hypertension is an important predictor of severe atherosclerosis (Keys et al., 1972; Sasaki et al., 1972). As noted in an earlier section, blood pressure increases with age in modern societies. Diabetes in the adult onset form does, of course, show an increasing incidence with age and would be expected to influence vascular disease to a degree proportional to the length of the time the diabetes had been present. Serum cholesterol, another useful predictor of clinically significant atherosclerosis (Keys et al., 1972; Aronow, Uyeyama and Cassidy, 1973), increases in American men until 45 to 54 years and then remains constant and increases in women until at least 65 years of age (Pincherle, 1971). The leveling off in males may be caused in part by the dying off of those with very high values. A New Guinea population did not show increased plasma lipids with age (Sinnett and Whyte, 1973). Although these risk factors are age-dependent in certain populations, they lack the universality of true aging processes as originally defined.

It has been reported that the rise in plasma-free fatty acids in response to epinephrine decreases with age in man (Hrůza, 1967). This was interpreted as an age-related decrease in the ability to catabolize fats that could play a role in atherosclerosis. A diurnal increase in plasma fibrinolytic activity was found to be decreased in a significant percentage of older people and in most older individuals with clinical coronary artery atherosclerosis and hyperlipoproteinemia (Rosing, Redwood, Brakman, Astrup, and Epstein, 1973). It was hypothesized that this represented an age-related decrease in responsiveness of the fibrinolytic system that might permit complications of atherosclerosis to occur.

Arterial lesions begin to develop early in life. In childhood focal thickening of the intima and fatty streaks consisting of accumulation of neutral fat, phospholipids, cholesterol and cholesterol esters in intimal smooth muscle cells are apparent. By maturity in addition to these lesions which have progressed, atherosclerotic plaques are identified. The plaques are raised lesions. They contain collagen, mucopolysaccharides, capillaries, intra and extracellular lipids, and often lymphocytes and macrophages. The lesions involve both intima and media. Elastic fibers are split and fragmented. It has been reported that the amino acid composition of elastin is altered in atherosclerotic plaques and that it has an increased affinity of lipid (Yu, 1971; Kramsch and Hollander, 1973). It is not known whether the intimal thickening and fatty streaks of young individuals evolve into the plaques or are separate entities (Solomon, 1967).

With increasing age, areas of vessel involvement increase, and plaques contain more collagenous connective tissue (often with cholesterol crystals), become less cellular, and involve more of the media with a corresponding loss of smooth muscle cells. Similar changes occur in veins but without lipid accumulation (Solomon, 1967). The arterial lesions become progressively scarlike, eventually consisting largely of mature collagen. In later stages many lesions are complicated by ulceration, formation of surface thrombi, hemorrhages, and the deposition of large amounts of calcium salts.

Perhaps the most important feature of the atherosclerotic plaque, with regard to etiology, is its nonspecificity—both morphologic and chemical. Morphologically, the lesions are characteristic of inflammation, as seen in old granulomas, degenerating cysts, and chronic liver disease. If one were to examine a plaque at high power through a microscope without knowing the tissue was arterial wall, the diagnosis would usually be organizing and chronic inflammation. Similarly, chemical analyses of evolving lesions can in most cases be interpreted as indicating inflammation in which there are cell proliferation, synthesis and turnover of mucopolysaccharides, synthesis of collagen, and accumulation of lipid. Experimentally, virtually any kind of injury to arterial walls causes lesions very similar to the plaque. For example, both decreased oxygen supply and mechanical injury to rabbit vessels caused lesions that were essentially identical to atherosclerosis (Garbarsch et al., 1969; Helin, Lorenzen, Garbarsch, and Matthiessen, 1971). An enormous number of experiments have been carried out in which short-lived animals that normally do not develop atherosclerosis have been treated in various ways to cause vessel injury that results in lesions with some resemblance to atherosclerotic plaques. These studies have been of use in the description of vascular injury and repair and have served to demonstrate the nonspecificity of atherosclerotic lesions, but they are of limited value regarding the etiology of naturally occurring atherosclerosis.

Observations have been made that suggest that the atherosclerotic plaque may represent a focal exaggeration of changes that are occurring diffusely in arteries with increasing age. Intimal thickening and fibrosis of arterial walls occur with age in the pig and dog (Nanda and Getty, 1971). Collagen, mucopolysaccharides, and lipids increase in human arteries with increasing age (Solomon, 1967; Levene and Poole, 1962; Khominskaya 1973), and lipids increase in rhesus monkeys' arteries with age (Portman and Alexander, 1972). The accumulation of lipids may be a generalized aging process in man in that it occurs in many nonvascular tissues, particularly in collagenous connective tissue (Crouse, Grundy, and Ahrens, 1972; Broekhuyse, 1972).

It is possible to view all risk factors in atherosclerosis as causing or contributing to vascular injury. Since aging is a major risk factor, it is appropriate to ask if any basic aging processes, other than those suggested above, occur in vessel walls and could result in injury. This is an old idea; much data and many inferences support the view that diffusion processes in vessel walls are altered with age and that there could be a deficit in metabolites, such as oxygen, that could cause degenerative, inflammatory changes over long periods of time (Kohn, 1963; Chisolm, Gainer, Stoner, and Gainer, 1972). The increase in connective tissue and lipids has been mentioned. Other basic aging processes that could play a role in atherogenesis will be taken up in a later section.

Medial calcification, usually classified as a variant of arteriosclerosis, occurs progressively with age in the media of elastic arteries. This change apparently satisfies the definition of a basic aging process and will be discussed with those processes.

Arteriolosclerosis, also considered a variant of arteriosclerosis, occurs in arterioles and consists of proliferation of intimal cells and thickening of media, with fibrosis, hyalinization, and loss of smooth muscle cells. It has been reported to increase in severity with age in man, dog, and pig (Getty, 1966). Arteriolosclerosis can be viewed as representing the same response to injury, as occurs in atherosclerosis, but taking place in very small vessels where there is simply not enough room and not enough cell types present for the formation of plaques. Such changes in small vessels could be responsible, in part, for the age-related increase in peripheral vascular resistance discussed earlier.

Hypertension

As seen in Figures 15 and 16, deaths from hypertension, at least in developed societies, are clearly age dependent. The rate and probability of dying from hypertension doubles at regular intervals, and the modal age for hypertensive deaths corresponds with the deaths from arteriosclerosis and with what would appear to be the human life span (Figure 16). Thus, hypertensive deaths would appear to be caused by aging processes—or better, agelike processes,

because the underlying processes affect only a segment of the population. The mechanism of death in hypertension is usually either heart failure, kidney failure, or stroke. Numbers of hypertensive deaths are indirect indications of the incidence, severity and duration of hypertension in a population.

It has frequently been pointed out that the diagnosis of hypertension is an arbitrary one depending on where one wants to draw the line between health and disease. Also, frequency plots of blood pressure in a population do not show clearly identifiable subgroups with different mean blood pressures (Harlan et al., 1973; Harris and Forsyth, 1973; Kannel and Dawber, 1973).

In the section on blood pressure, data were presented showing that almost all individuals in modern societies showed increased blood pressure with age. Some individuals do not, however, show this increase, and in some less developed societies there is no or little increase in pressure with age. The rise with age is dependent on pressure at younger ages; those with high initial pressure show the greatest increase; those with low pressure when young show little increase or even a decreasing pressure with increasing age (Harlan et al., 1973; Miall and Lovell, 1967).

A large number of causes of hypertension have been suspected or identified. These include abnormalities in the renin-angiotensin-aldosterone system, stress-neurogenic mechanisms, obesity, altered baroreceptor sensitivity, and excessive salt intake (Harris and Forsyth, 1973; Kannel and Dawber, 1973; Laragh, 1974). In spite of the known mechanisms, no specific cause is identified in up to 90 percent of those diagnosed as having hypertension (Laragh, 1974). Could aging processes be responsible for some or most of these cases? If so, and considering the requirement of universality in the definition of an aging process, why don't all members of all populations develop hypertension with increasing age?

As mentioned earlier, aging processes that should cause increased blood pressure would be increasing stiffness of arteries, decreased baroreceptor sensitivity, increased peripheral resistance, and decreased renal blood flow. If everything else affecting the cardiovascular system were constant with age, blood pressure would inevitably rise in all individuals. Other aging processes would tend, however, to counteract the rise. These are increasing volume of the aorta, which occurs until around 60 years of age, and decreasing cardiac output. There are the regulatory processes affecting blood pressure that are extrinsic to the cardiovascular system and probably do not change very significantly with age—that can cause hypertension, and also probably can decrease blood pressure when acting in the opposite direction. In other words, lack of obesity, decreased salt intake, decreased stress, etc., could compensate for factors that increase blood pressure with age. A reasonable working hypothesis could be that in many "essential" hypertensives, high blood pressure is due to aging processes combined with an inability to compensate by bringing into play those factors that could cause lower pressure.

Hypertension affects other age-related diseases and also influences basic aging changes at the tissue level. Cardiac hypertrophy, atherosclerosis, and arteriolosclerosis are accelerated in hypertension. Rat aorta shows increased collagen and elastin content with increasing age, and these substances accumulate at greater rates in experimental hypertension (Wolinsky 1971, 1972).

Amyloidosis

Amyloid has been of interest to many gerontologists. Although the accumulation of this mysterious substance is associated with a variety of diseases, in a significant fraction of cases the only underlying cause would appear to be aging. Various classification schemes for amyloidosis have been proposed. One form affects primarily the tongue, heart, gastrointestinal tract, skeletal, and smooth muscle and is associated with aging, multiple myeloma, and plasma cell dyscrasias. A second category involves liver, spleen, kidney, and the adrenal gland and is associated with long-standing chronic inflammatory processes such as rheumatoid arthritis. There are also mixtures of

these two as well as localized nodular aggregates (Isobe and Osserman, 1974). Amyloidosis also develops in some mouse strains and in experimental animals in response to a large number of different kinds of treatment (Cohen, 1965).

In histological sections amyloid is a hyaline eosinophilic material that is mostly in extracellular masses, causing atrophy of adjacent cells. In the cardiovascular system, amyloid is deposited between cardiac myofibers, beneath epicardium and endocardium, in valves, and in the walls of arteries, arterioles, and capillaries (Friedberg, 1966; Buerger and Braunstein, 1960). It gives a characteristic green birefringence with the Congo Red stain and is metachromatic when stained with Crystal Violet. Its formation has been observed in reticuloendothelial cells, but it may also be synthesized by other cells of mesodermal origin such as fibroblasts, endothelial, and smooth muscle cells. In the electron microscope, amyloid is seen to consist of beaded fibrils (Cohen, 1965). The original identification of amyloid was by staining properties rather than by chemical composition, and there is currently a great deal of confusion about the latter. Chemical studies of amyloid isolated from patients with plasma cell dyscrasias have led to the conclusion that it is composed of immunoglobulin light chains or antibody fragments (Isobe and Osserman, 1974), while analyses of amyloids from familial Mediterranean fever and rheumatoid arthritis patients have shown no relationship to immunoglobulins (Levin, Franklin, Frangione, and Pras, 1972; Ein, Kimura, Terry, Magnotta, and Glenner, 1972). Thus, a material with characteristic staining properties and ultrastructure appears to have different chemical compositions when associated with different diseases. Furthermore, a protein has been extracted from normal skin and joints with an amino acid composition very similar to at least one form of amyloid, suggesting the latter may be a normal constituent of connective tissue (Timpl, Wolff, and Weiser, 1968).

Studies of amyloidosis of the cardiovascular system with age have been based on histological examinations of tissues. Data have provided information primarily on incidence rather than on rates of accumulation in individuals and populations. In 100 unselected autopsies of males 65 to 95 years old, amyloidosis was diagnosed in 15 percent. In 5 of the 15, cardiac amyloid without known predisposing processes was identified (Cohen, 1965). In another series of 986 autopsies of individuals over 55 years of age, the incidence of cardiac amyloidosis increased with age, occurring in 8 out of 33 persons in the 90 to 99-year-old group (Buerger and Braunstein, 1960). No race or sex differences or predisposing factors were identified. The role of age appeared to be in incidence rather than a progressive accumulation in individuals; the impression was gained that the amount of amyloid reached a plateau in each case.

Additional surveys have shown cardiac amyloid in 21 percent of individuals over 80 years of age, and in 15 percent of males and 10 percent of females over 70 years old. Cerebral vessel amyloidosis was identified in 12 percent of persons over 80 years old (Wright, Calkins, Breen, Stolte, and Schultz, 1969). A very thorough sampling of hearts from 100 persons 60 to 90 years old revealed the presence of amyloid in 70 percent (Katenkamp and Stiller, 1971). A study of individuals without diseases known to be associated with amyloidosis showed a cardiac amyloidosis incidence of 30 percent and aortic amyloidosis of 39 percent in individuals over 60 years of age. A comparison of persons under and over 70 years of age showed a clear increase in incidence with age (Wright et al., 1969).

Thus, significant fractions of aging populations show conspicuous amyloid accumulation in the heart and vessels. Heart failure can result from amyloidosis, and cor pulmonale has been observed in cases of amyloidosis of pulmonary vessels (Friedberg, 1966).

Questions remain about the origin of this substance, its chemical nature, and the causes of its accumulation. It is not clear at this point if deposition of amyloid is an aging process, in that it occurs in all members of a population, or if it is formed only in some subgroups. There is suggestive evidence that some form of amyloid may be a normal component of connective tissue (Timpl, Wolff, and Weiser, 1968). It has been suggested that individuals diagnosed as having amyloidosis simply have excessive amounts of this normally occurring substance (Wright et al., 1969). It is possible that all individuals accumulate amyloid with increasing age but that it is diagnosed only in those who show the very large amounts required for identification by the present histological techniques. As amyloid becomes better characterized chemically, and as more sensitive methods for its analysis become available, answers to these questions may be forthcoming.

BASIC AGING PROCESSES

The fundamental aging processes are those that are intrinsic to tissues, cells, and molecules, that occur in all individuals, and that are progressive and irreversible. These processes must underlie age changes at higher levels of organization, such as decreased heart work, increased arterial stiffness, dilatation, tortuosity, increased peripheral resistance, and the predisposition to atherosclerosis.

The cardiovascular system was not designed to last indefinitely. Whereas many organs are composed of cell populations that are turning over, the cardiovascular system is composed of postmitotic cells that remain present for the life of the animal. Myocardial cells do not have the capacity to divide. Smooth muscle and endothelial cells can divide when blood vessels proliferate or are injured but probably do not divide to any significant extent unless they receive some special stimulus. Such stable cells persisting for long periods of time would be expected to undergo progressive morphological and chemical alterations. Structural connective tissue proteins are prominent components of the heart and blood vessels, particularly arteries. Collagen and elastin at most sites are quite inert metabolically and are subjected to continual stress; these substances would similarly be expected to undergo progressive changes with age.

Heart

Many hearts in an aging population show thickening of the valves and endocardium caused by the deposition of collagenous connective tissue. These changes probably have the same etiology as atherosclerosis and should be viewed as manifestations of age-related disease rather than basic aging processes. Similarly, many old hearts show fibrosis of the myocardium secondary to coronary artery occlusion or insufficiency. Cardiomegaly and myocardial hypertrophy are common in an aging population and can usually be related to anemia, hypertension, coronary insufficiency, or valvular disease. Again, these changes lack the universality of true aging processes.

Studies of the ultrastructure of myocardial cells in aging rats have shown increased numbers of residual bodies and lipid droplets, increased numbers of lysosomes that apparently degrade organelles and glycogen, numerous Golgi structures, dilated vesicles in the intercalated disc region, and numerous surface vesicles (Travis and Travis, 1972; Tomanek and Karlsson, 1973). The number of mitochondria per unit of cell has been reported to increase with age in rats, but the mitochondria are smaller. Oxidative phosphorylation of mitochondria and the response to ADP have not been observed to change with age (Limas, 1971). In terms of synthetic and degradative capacities, it is significant that rate of heart mitochondria turnover does not change with age (Menzies and Gold, 1971).

A very large number of cardiac enzymes have been studied as a function of age. A review of many of these studies leads to the conclusion that there is no pattern of change with age

(Limas, 1971). As is the case with many other organs, heart enzymes either increase, decrease, or stay the same with age (Table 1). As additional examples, malate dehydrogenase shows a slight drop with age in rat heart (Singh, 1973), while β glucuronidase and cathepsin D increase, and acid phosphatase does not change significantly (Comalli, 1971). Lipolytic activity of rat myocardium, as determined by release of free fatty acids and glycerol in response to epinephrine, has been reported to decrease with age (Stuchliková, Jelinková, Faltová and Smrž, 1971).

The amount and state of organelles and enzymes that turn over are very labile, varying with diet, activity, and presence of disease and debility. There is no assurance that changes in ultrastructure and enzyme levels that have been described represent true aging processes in being progressive and irreversible. They could be secondary to the general debilitated state of old animals or to altered dietary or activity patterns. The fact that many key enzymes and organelles show no changes with age suggests that some or all of the changes that have been described are secondary and reversible.

Total nitrogen and protein of heart have not been found to change with age. Myosin and myoglobin either remain constant or increase in concentration. Water and electrolyte changes with age can be interpreted in terms of a relative increase in the extracellular compartment with age (Limas, 1971). Cardiac muscle cells of dogs show no age-related changes in protein/

TABLE 1. CHANGES IN MYOCARDIAL ENZYMES ASSOCIATED WITH AGING.

Enzyme	Type of Change	Reference
Monoamine oxidase	Increase	Prange et al., 1967; Gey et al., 1965
Dopamine-β-oxidase	Decrease	Burkard et al., 1966; Studer et al., 1964
Dopa-decarboxylase	Decrease	Gey, 1965
Catechol-O-methyl-transferase	No change	Sinex, 1966
Dopa/α-ketoglutarate transaminase	No change	Sinex, 1966
Lactic dehydrogenase	Decrease	Kanungo et al., 1965; Shirley and Davis, 1959
Cytochrome oxidase	Decrease	Myer and King, 1968
Succinic oxidase	No change	Shirley and Davis, 1959
Glucose-6-phosphate dehydrogenase	Decrease	Shukla and Kanungo, 1968
Malic dehydrogenase	Increase	Shukla and Kanungo, 1968
β-hydroxyacyl CoA dehydrogenase	No change	Heilbrunn, 1965

From Limas, 1971.

DNA or RNA/DNA ratios or in the amount of DNA transcribed (Shirey and Sobel, 1972).

One of the best characterized age changes in myocardium is the deposition of lipofuscin pigment. This insoluble and inert substance, also referred to as ceroid, lipochrome, and wear-and-tear pigment, accumulates in many organs, particularly neurons and cardiac muscle cells. The origin of lipofuscin is not certain, but it is generally thought to arise from the oxidative polymerization of unsaturated lipids and to exist in combination with components of lysosomes. In the heart it consists of aggregates of granules near the poles of nuclei (Figure 18). Lipofuscin accumulates linearly with age— about 0.36 percent of heart volume per year in the dog (Munnell and Getty, 1968) and 0.0285 percent per year in man (Strehler, Mark, Mild-

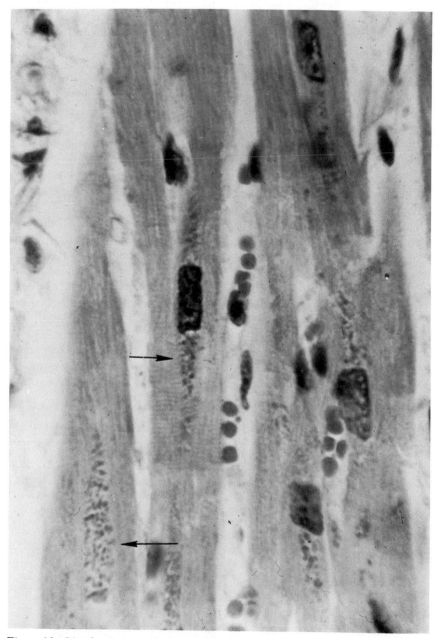

Figure 18. Lipofuscin granules (arrows) in cardiac muscle. Photograph by R. Kohn.

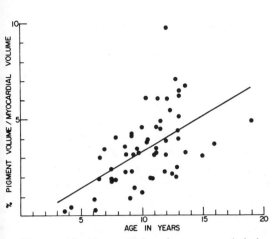

Figure 19. Myocardial volume occupied by lipofuscin pigment as a function of age in dogs. (From Munnell and Getty, 1968.)

van, and Gee, 1959). It is interesting that rate of accumulation in relation to life span is very similar in dog and man. There is marked variability in the amount present at each age (Figure 19). The amount present has not been related to any disease or abnormality in cardiac function.

The amount and state of connective tissue in the heart are of interest because of the role of connective tissue in determining elastic properties of tissue. An increase with age in human heart collagen in subendocardial and subepicardial zones, but not in central myocardium, has been observed (Lenkiewicz, Davies, and Rosen, 1972). A histological study of muscle and collagen fibers in the sinoatrial node of 100 human hearts showed a clear decrease in muscle and increase in collagen with age (Davies and Pomerance, 1972). Muscle, as percentage of heart, decreased from 46 percent in individuals under 50 years of age to 27 percent in those over 75, while collagen fibers increased from 17 percent to 36 percent in the two groups. It appeared that the muscle loss and fibrosis started at around 60 years of age. A study of left ventricular myocardium free of epi and endocardium from 148 individuals without lesions revealed no significant change in collagen concentration with age (Kohn and Rollerson, 1959a).

In male rats left ventricular trabeculae carnae had a hydroxyproline content of 331 mg per 100 grams dry weight in 11 to 12-month-old

animals and 483 mg in 26 to 31-month-old animals (Weisfeldt, Loeven, and Shock, 1971). In another study of male rats, a 28 percent increase in left ventricular hydroxyproline was observed in 22-month-old animals as compared to animals 6 months old (Tomanek, Taunton, and Liskop, 1972). The increase was mainly at sites of valve attachment and in the atrioventricular bundle, with focal increases in the subendocardium.

Available data suggest that the increase with age in connective tissue of heart is, for the most part, localized at certain sites and may not occur diffusely through the myocardium. In a study of mechanical properties of heart muscle described earlier (Weisfeldt, Loeven, and Shock, 1971), it was suggested that alterations with age were associated with changes in a viscous component, perhaps in the compliance of connective tissue. In an investigation of swelling properties of human myocardium (Kohn and Rollerson, 1959a), it was found that there was a drop in ability to swell after the age of around 35 years (Figure 20). This was interpreted as an age-related increase in myocardial stiffness. A subsequent study (Kohn and Roller-

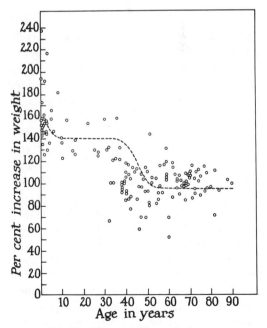

Figure 20. Swelling ability of human myocardium as a function of age. (From Kohn and Rollerson, 1959a.)

son, 1959b) suggested that the change was due to age-altered connective tissue in the heart.

Changes in properties of heart connective tissue may be of greater significance than changes in concentration. This possibility will be considered in a later section.

Arteries

The cliché that a man is as old as his arteries was used before much was known about arterial aging. As more knowledge is acquired, however, this concept continues to gain support. Many changes that satisfy the criteria of aging processes and that probably underlie arteriosclerosis, atherosclerosis, and age-related changes in properties have been described. These include alterations in proportions of the cellular and extracellular compartments, changes in the morphology, chemistry, and properties of cells and fibers, and the accumulation of various substances.

A rather complete picture of overall morphological changes in arteries with age is now available from studies of man, pig, dog, and rat (Solomon, 1967; Nanda and Getty, 1971; Gerrity and Cliff, 1972; Cliff, 1970; Lindner and Johannes, 1973). The intima thickens because of cell proliferation and the formation of connective tissue. Modified smooth muscle cells enter the intima from the media and apparently synthesize connective tissue proteins and polysaccharides. There is progressive fibrosis of the media and increasing numbers of fibroblasts or macrophages. Total cellularity of both intima and media decreases as extracellular material accumulates. Necrosis of smooth muscle cells has been observed in the media of aging rat cerebral arteries (Kojimahara, Sekiya, and Ooneda, 1973).

A large number of enyzme and coenzyme activities of arteries has been measured as a function of age. Many of these studies have been reviewed (Kirk, 1969). As in other organs, no general pattern is discernible. In the case of human aortic intima-media, for example, there is no change with age in hexokinase, glucose-6-phosphate isomerase, or malate dehydrogenase, while fumarase and phenosulfatase decrease, and aldolase increases; lactate dehydrogenase

and β glucuronidase reach a peak in middle age and then decline. The isoenzyme pattern of lactate dehydrogenase has been observed to change with age in rat aorta (Gerlach and Fegeler, 1973). The amount of glucose metabolized to lactate did not change with age in rat aorta from 2 to 12 months of age (Newmark, Malfer, and Wiese, 1972). Release of free fatty acids from rat aorta in response to epinephrine has been reported to decrease with age (Jelinková, Stuchliková, Hrůza, Deyl, and Smrž, 1972). The hydrolytic activity of rat aorta on cholesterol oleate was found to be increased over threefold in 24-month-old as compared to 12-month-old animals (Kritchevsky, Genzano, and Kothari, 1973).

Although some enzyme changes with age may represent very important basic aging processes, the significance of the described changes is difficult to ascertain because cell populations change with age and the altered morphology and accumulation of substances could bring about secondary and potentially reversible changes in cells.

One of the more characteristic changes in aging arteries is the accumulation of lipids. Lipid accumulates progressively in the media of human arteries with age (Khominskaya, 1973; Bertelsen, 1961). In the intima and inner media of rhesus monkey arteries, sphingomyelin and free and esterified cholesterol increase with age (Portman and Alexander, 1972). The lipids are in a microsomal fraction with properties of the plasma membrane. In the aorta of rats over 2 years old there is conspicuous lipid accumulation in endothelial and intimal cells (Gerrity and Cliff, 1972). Sphingomyelin, lecithin, and phosphatidyl ethanolamine increase in concentration in old rat aorta in association with smooth muscle cells that are altered in having increased plasma membrane surfaces and decreased endoplasmic reticulum (Stein, Eisenberg, and Stein, 1969).

Other very characteristic features of aging arteries involve mineralization and elastin changes and their interrelationship. Elastin is a major component of arteries, representing up to 30 percent of the dry weight in man and 47 percent in the rat (Lindner and Johannes, 1973). The thick, discrete, wavy elastic lamellae

Figure 21. Human iliac arteries stained for elastin, X 90. Top, 18 year old showing wavy lamellae. Bottom, 58 year old showing thinning and fragmentation of elastin. (From Blumenthal, H. T., Lansing, A. L., and Gray, S. H. 1950. The interrelation of elastic tissue and calcium in the genesis of arteriosclerosis. *Am. J. Pathol.,* **26**, 989–1009.)

seen in young animals become thin with age and rather uniformly distributed intercellularly through the media (Cliff, 1970). In man, as seen in Figure 21, the fibers become diffusely arranged, thin, and fragmented (Blumenthal, Lansing, and Gray, 1950). There is probably destruction of elastin in that the amount present has been reported to drop by around one-third in advanced age (Lindner and Johannes, 1973). Human arterial elastin has been reported to lose around 30 percent of the cross-links desmosine and isodesmosine and to almost double the amount of bound or insoluble carbohydrate (John and Thomas, 1972). Chemical studies of old elastin are difficult to carry out and interpret because of the extreme insolubility of elastin and the possibility of contamination of preparations by other insoluble materials.

Calcification of the media occurs progressively with age and precedes intimal thickening and lipid deposition, possibly playing a role in the latter (Bertelsen, 1961). The progressive calcification with age can be seen in Figure 22. Rate of mineralization with age varies in different arteries, being greatest in arteries with the most elastin (Figure 23). The mineral appears bound to elastin; the amount of calcium bound to isolated arterial elastin increases with age (Figure 24). It has been suggested that elastin undergoes alterations with age that enable it to bind more calcium (Eisenstein, Ayer, Papajiannis, Hass, and Ellis, 1964), and studies of the calcium binding capacity of isolated human arterial elastin support this possibility (Figure 25). The binding capacity increases until around 50 years of age, then levels off, and is greater in aortic elastin than in elastin from the pulmonary artery.

There are concentration gradients of collagen and elastin through arterial media, and these change over the life span. Elastin decreases and collagen increases from the intima to the adventitia in the human aorta during growth. In old adults the pattern is reversed; medial collagen decreases and elastin increases going from the intimal zone to the adventitia (Feldman and Glagov, 1971).

Collagen comprises 22–28 percent of the dry weight of human and rat aorta (Lindner and Johannes, 1973). It comprises around 20 percent of the normal human aortic intima (Levene and Poole, 1962). The adventitia is almost pure collagen. In the media, collagen is distributed around all smooth muscle cells. Chemical and histochemical studies confirm the histological observations of increasing fibrosis with age and are consistent with what is known about the synthesis of collagen. Collagen synthesis is always associated with the synthesis of mucopolysaccharides. The latter are synthesized in greatest amounts and show the fastest turnover early in relation to collagen synthesis. As collagen accumulates, polysaccharide synthesis slows, and the amount present decreases in mature and aging collagenous tissue.

Human aortic collagen increases continuously over the life span in both intima and media;

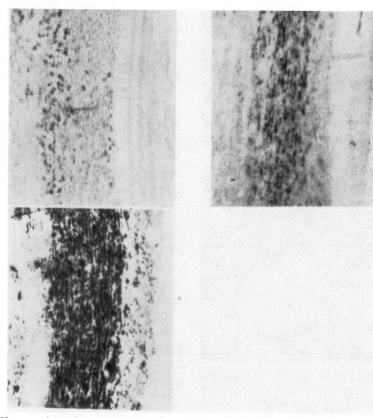

Figure 22. Human thoracic aorta stained for calcium, X 35. Upper left, 30 year old; upper right, 40 year old; lower left, 59 year old. (From Bertelsen, S. V. 1961. Alterations in human aorta and pulmonary artery with age. *Acta Pathol. Microbiol. Scand.*, **51**, 206–228.)

there are some reports of a sharp increase after 60 years of age (Lindner and Johannes, 1973). Intimal collagen in human aorta increases from around 20 percent of dry weight at 21 to 30 years of age to around 26 percent at 81 to 90 years (Levene and Poole, 1962). In rat aortic media, collagen accumulation with age is observed around every smooth muscle cell. This progresses to scarlike tissue that replaces cells (Cliff, 1970).

Data on mucopolysaccharide amounts and rates of synthesis are varied, probably because syntheses of these substances are related to the synthesis of that collagen which forms during growth, the collagen synthesized with aging, and the collagen synthesized as part of atherosclerosis. Sulfated acid mucopolysaccharides accumulate in some arteries from birth to around 40 years of age and then decrease. In other arteries these substances

increase only after 30 years of age (Khominskaya, 1973). Rate of synthesis and turnover of arterial mucopolysaccharides decrease with age. In human aorta, in the absence of frank atherosclerosis, total neutral and acidic mucopolysaccharides decrease during aging. Age-related hybridization between chondroitin sulfate and keratin sulfate, and an increase in the glucosamine/galactosamine ratio have been reported (Lindner and Johannes, 1973).

Diffusion across membranes of arterial components has been studied as a function of age. Increases with age in diffusion coefficients for nitrogen, CO_2, lactate, iodide, and glucose were obtained with membranes of media and of intima plus subintimal tissue (Kirk and Laursen, 1955). These observations may not reflect *in vivo* phenomena because cells in the specimens were dead, and vessel motility which could play an important role in age-

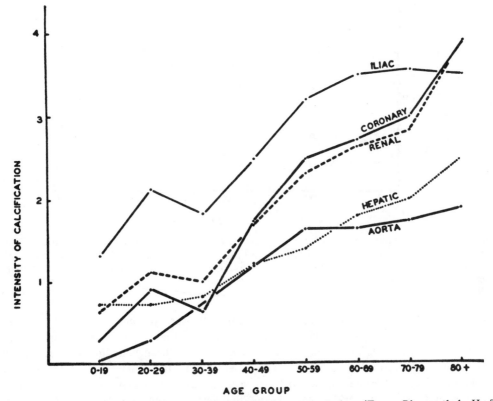

Figure 23. Rates of calcification of several major human arteries. (From Blumenthal, H. T., Lansing, A. L., and Gray, S. H. 1950. The interrelation of elastic tissue and calcium in the genesis of arteriosclerosis. *Am. J. Pathol.*, **26**, 989–1009.)

related differences in diffusion was not part of the study. It is likely, however, that the altered diffusion is a manifestation of basic changes in the vessel walls.

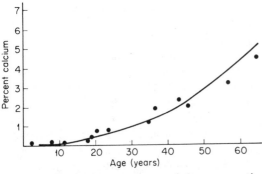

Figure 24. Calcium content of human aortic elastin as a function of age. (From Lansing, A. L. 1959. Elastic tissue in atherosclerosis. *In*, I. H. Page (ed.), *Connective Tissue, Thrombosis, and Atherosclerosis*, p. 167. New York: Academic Press.)

The most striking and consistent age changes in arteries are the redistribution, thinning, and fragmentation of elastin and the accumulation of collagen, calcium salts, and lipid. It is possible that the elastin changes represent responses to severe and prolonged stresses. The age-related increase in calcium-binding of elastin is greater in the case of highly stressed aorta than in pulmonary artery (Eisenstein, *et al.*, 1964). Excessive stress in the form of experimental hypertension causes increases in both arterial collagen and elastin (Wolinsky, 1972). The accumulation of collagen, mineral, and lipid is very similar to what is seen in tissues in low-grade chronic inflammation. This suggests an underlying injury to vessel walls.

The fibrosis and accumulations are also very similar to the changes that characterize atherosclerosis. It is often difficult in evaluating studies to decide if given data are referable to basic aging or atherosclerosis. This similarity

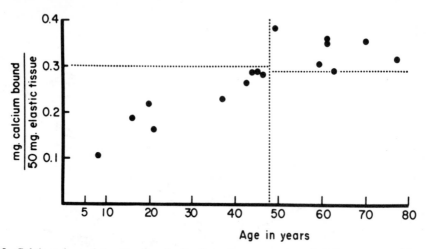

Figure 25. Calcium bound *in vitro* by elastin from human aortas of different ages. (From Eisenstein, R., Ayer, J., Papajiannis, S., Hass, G., and Ellis, H. 1964. Mineral binding by human arterial elastic tissue. *Lab. Invest.*, **13**, 1198–1204. © 1964, U.S.-Canadian Division of the International Academy of Pathology.)

between the two phenomena lends support to the view that accumulation of collagen, calcium, and lipids represents basic aging processes occurring diffusely through arterial walls and that additional factors cause plaques to form at various sites (Bertelsen, 1961). It has been noted that lipid and mucopolysaccharides are not deposited at the same sites at the same rate and to the same degree with age (Khominskaya, 1973), that fibrosis of the media can occur in the absence of atherosclerosis (Feldman and Glagov, 1971), and that mucopolysaccharides decrease at some sites with age, while increasing in atherosclerosis (Lindner and Johannes, 1973). These observations would tend to support the concept that atherosclerosis is not a consequence of aging alone, but that other complicating factors are required.

Veins and Lymphatic Vessels

The veins and lymphatics have not received the same attention from students of aging as have the other components of the cardiovascular system. It is likely that they undergo many of the same kinds of changes as arteries, perhaps to a lesser degree because of the lower stresses to which they are subjected.

Increased tortuosity of veins and phlebosclerosis are commonly observed in older individuals and may represent generalized age changes. The thoracic duct wall in man becomes thicker until the fourth decade. Thickening of the intima and progressive fibrosis of the media occur throughout life. Thickness of the medial smooth muscle zone increases until middle age and then decreases (Borchard, Borchard, and Huth, 1972).

Microvasculature

Some of the same changes described in large arteries would be expected to occur, with modifications, down the arterial tree. A study of the human inner ear showed a gradual involution of small arteries throughout life (Johnsson and Hawkins, 1972). A progressive thickening of arteriole walls was also observed. Thickening of walls of small myocardial arteries with age in man has also been described (Danilova, 1972). The wall thickening was accompanied by narrowing of lumens at some sites and vessel ectasia at others. There appeared to be some compensation for these degenerative changes by the formation of new vessels. A number of deformities of small arteries, such as spiraling and looping, have been reported to occur with age (Hassler, 1969). Small arteries in undiseased human kidney show splitting of elastin fibers with increasing age (Darmady, Offer, and Woodhouse, 1973).

An ultrastructural study of human conjunctival capillaries showed a diminution of endothelial pores and thickening of the basement membrane with increasing age (Brancato, and Pellegrini, 1973). In the human inner ear, a marked loss of capillaries with age was observed (Johnsson and Hawkins, 1972). Capillary basement thickening with age has also been reported in the case of human skeletal muscle (Jordan and Perley, 1972; Kilo, Vogler, and Williamson, 1972) and in the retina of rats and mice (Leuenberger, 1973).

In a study of hearts from rats 4 and 26 to 27 months old, the number of capillaries per mm^2 was observed to decrease from 2,637 to 2,305 with age, and the diffusion distance (one-half the distance between capillaries) decreased from 10.43 to 9.77 microns (Rakušan and Poupa, 1964). In human heart it has been reported that the number of capillaries remains constant with age with a myofiber/capillary ratio of 1:1 (Wearn, 1940). In cases of cardiac hypertrophy, the constant number of capillaries results in a decreased number of capillaries per unit heart mass. Number of capillaries per unit cross-section in human skeletal muscle show little change with age but, because of an age-related increase in number of muscle fibers per unit area, the capillary/fiber ratio decreases with age (Parizkova, Eiselt, Sprynarova, and Wachtlova, 1971).

Collagen and Elastin

Aging of connective tissue is described in detail elsewhere in these volumes. It is worthwhile, however, to draw attention here to the probable role of collagen and elastin in aging of the cardiovascular system. Collagen is a major component of the epi and endocardium and valves and also comprises around 3.5 percent of the dry weight of myocardium (Kohn and Rollerson, 1959a). Collagen surrounds every myofiber; cell contraction occurs within a collagenous matrix. As indicated earlier, collagen and elastin are also major components of blood vessels, and smooth muscle cells must contract within a meshwork of these proteins. Collagen and elastin are highly polymerized and, when mature in tissues, have little turnover under normal circumstances (Walford, Carter, and Schneider, 1964). These fibrous proteins play key roles in limiting deformation, transmitting forces, and determining elastic properties of tissues (Harkness, 1961; Wiederhielm,

1965; Wolinsky and Glacov, 1964; Mullins and Guntheroth, 1965). Polymers in general, such as paint, rubber, plastics, and paper, become stiff and brittle with age.

The changes that have been described in the amounts of collagen and elastin present as a function of age are probably secondary to prolonged severe stress, inflammation, and/or atherosclerosis. The most basic aging processes in these proteins are altered properties rather than concentration changes. It is difficult to study connective tissue proteins in parenchymatous organs such as heart because of the low concentrations in such organs. In arteries, new collagen is synthesized throughout life, and the age of a given sample from this tissue is uncertain. Most of what is known about the aging of collagen has been learned from the study of tissue such as tendon where collagen exists in high concentration and has been present since maturity. Aging of collagen is characterized by progressive insolubility, increased chemical stabilization, and particularly by increased stiffness (Kohn and Rollerson, 1959c; Hamlin and Kohn, 1971). The chemistry of these changes is not known, but the changes are similar to those occurring with age in many polymers and are often assumed to be caused by chemical cross-linking of subunits. To the extent it has been studied, the changes with age appear to take place in collagen throughout the body (Schaub, 1963). Changes in the properties of collagen probably constitute the most definitive basic aging process that has been observed in mammals.

Aging of elastin has not been studied to the same extent as collagen. The thinning and fragmentation of aortic elastin could be caused by wear and tear of structures that do not turn over. Elastin has been described as becoming yellow and brittle with age and as binding calcium salts. It is very likely that this metabolically inert polymer eventually will be found to undergo progressive cross-linking with age.

COMMENT

As noted earlier, the cardiovascular system was not designed for a very long life. In addition to containing fixed postmitotic cells and being rich in connective tissue that loses its elasticity, there is a poor blood supply to the media of arteries, even in young individuals (Kohn, 1963). Smooth muscle cells of arteries are in a precarious state in that metabolites must diffuse over long distances. These structures are then subjected to continuous, severe mechanical stress.

The simplest explanation of major functional debilities of the aging cardiovascular system, in terms of what is known, is based largely on the aging of connective tissue. The heart might function less efficiently as a pump with age because of stiffening of the connective tissue matrix in which the myocardium contracts. Mechanical data on aging heart muscle have suggested this possibility (Weisfeldt, Loeven, and Shock, 1971).

Stiffening of arteries would similarly be caused in part by stiffening of connective tissue components. Changes in elastic properties of arteries have suggested that collagen becomes more restrictive with increasing age (Roach and Burton, 1959). Elastin and smooth muscle cells apparently have decreasing roles in the mechanical properties of aging arteries; the elastic modulus of the vessel approaches that of collagen by 85 years of age in man (Bader, 1967). Even in the absence of such connective tissue aging, it would be anticipated that because of the normally poor diffusion through the media, materials such as lipids and minerals would be trapped, possibly injuring cells and eliciting a low-grade inflammatory reaction. Trapping of extracellular material would be accelerated by the loss of motility caused by increasing stiffness and by the synthesis of additional collagenous connective tissue. It is of interest that lipids accumulate in collagen and adjacent to mucopolysaccharides elsewhere in the body with age (Crouse, Grundy, and Ahrens, 1972; Broekhuyse, 1972; Adams and Bayliss, 1973). Trapping of substances may be a characteristic property of aging collagenous connective tissue. Atherogenesis could represent a complication of these basic processes. With increasing stiffness, arteries would react to continuous stress by dilatation. Signals to baroreceptors would be damped.

Similarly, increased peripheral resistance with age could result from increased stiffness of connective tissue in and around small blood vessels and throughout the parenchyma of organs.

An alternative explanation of cardiovascular aging is based on primary intrinsic aging of cells. Myocardial cells could contract less efficiently. Cells of vessels could undergo degenerative changes, and the accumulation of connective tissue, minerals, and lipids could represent a secondary inflammatory reaction. There is no convincing evidence at present that such primary cellular changes with age exist. These cells have not been studied in detail with age, however, and the possibility of significant intrinsic changes has not been excluded.

SUMMARY

Aging processes in the cardiovascular system are those that occur in all individuals and are progressive and physiologically irreversible. Functionally, these appear to include a decreased heart rate in response to stress, decreased efficiency of the heart as a pump, decreased velocity of contraction and relaxation of isolated heart muscle, and decreased rate of cardiac hypertrophy. Arteries stiffen and dilate and demonstrate decreased baroreceptor sensitivity. Elastin and smooth muscle play diminishing roles in determining elastic properties; the latter are determined progressively by collagen. Peripheral vascular resistance increases, and organ perfusion, in general, decreases. Blood pressure tends to rise, but this is avoided in some individuals and populations.

Atherosclerosis and essential hypertension appear strongly dependent on underlying basic aging processes, but additional complicating factors or an absence of compensating factors are required for their development. The atheroma may represent an inflammatory lesion consisting of a focal exaggeration of processes that occur diffusely in arterial walls with age. Amyloid accumulates in heart and blood vessels with age.

Ultrastructural changes in the myocardium have been observed with age. No pattern of enzyme decrease or defect in protein synthesis has been demonstrated. Lipofuscin increases in myofibers. Collagen increases focally with age in the heart.

In the arterial system, collagen accumulates in the intima and media. Mucopolysaccharide concentration is variable. Smooth muscle cells decrease. There is no generalized decrease in cellular concentration of enzymes. Lipids and minerals increase. Elastin concentration decreases, and elastin fibers appear redistributed, thin, and fragmented and bind increasing amounts of calcium salts. There is an involution with age of small arteries and capillaries, and thickening of basement membranes.

Fibrous connective tissue proteins become stiff with age. The simplest explanation of major age changes in the cardiovascular system is based on the consequent stiffening of heart and blood vessels. Additional degeneration would also be expected because of the original poor design of the system and the continual stress to which it is subjected. An important role for primary intrinsic cell aging has not been excluded.

REFERENCES

Adams, C., and Bayliss, O. 1973. Acid mucosubstances underlying lipid deposits in ageing tendons and atherosclerotic arteries. *Atherosclerosis*, 18, 191–195.

Amery, A., Bossaert, H., and Verstraete, M. 1969. Muscle blood flow in normal and hypertensive subjects. *Am. Heart J.*, 78, 211–216.

Anderson, T. W. 1973. Mortality from ischemic heart disease: Changes in middle-aged men since 1900. *J. Am. Med. Assoc.*, 224, 336–338.

Aronow, W. S., Uyeyama, R. R., and Cassidy, J. 1973. Serum lipids, serum uric acid and glucose tolerance in coronary heart disease. *J. Am. Geriat. Soc.*, 21, 58–62.

Bader, H. 1967. Dependence of wall stress in the human thoracic aorta on age and pressure. *Circulation Res.*, 20, 354–361.

Band, W., Goedhard, W. J. A., and Knoop, A. A. 1972. Effects of aging on dynamic viscoelastic properties of the rat's thoracic aorta. *Pflüg. Arch.*, 331, 357–364.

Barry, A. J., Daly, J. W., Pruett, E. D., Steinmetz, J. R., Page, H. F., Birkhead, N. C., and Rodahl, K. 1966. The effects of physical conditioning in older individuals. I. Work capacity, circulatory-respiratory function, and work electrocardiograms. *J. Geront.*, 21, 182–191.

Belt, E. 1952. Leonardo da Vinci's study of the aging process. *Geriatrics*, 7, 205–210.

Bender, A. D. 1965. The effect of increasing age on the distribution of peripheral blood flow in man. *J. Am. Geriat. Soc.*, 13, 192–198.

Berg, B. N., and Harmison, C. R. 1955. Blood pressure and heart size in aging rats. *J. Geront.*, 10, 416–419.

Bertelsen, S. V. 1961. Alterations in human aorta and pulmonary artery with age. *Acta Pathol. Microbiol. Scand.*, 51, 206–228.

Blumenthal, H. T., Lansing, A. L., and Gray, S. H. 1950. The interrelation of elastic tissue and calcium in the genesis of arteriosclerosis. *Am. J. Pathol.*, 26, 989–1009.

Borchard, F., Borchard, H., and Huth, F. 1972. Beitrag zur lymphvascualeren Sklerose des Ductus thoracicus: Morphometrische Untersuchungen von 99 Faellen. *Beitr. Pathol.*, 146, 145–161.

Brancato, R., and Pellegrini, M. S. F. 1973. Etude ultramicroscopique sur le vieillissement des capillaires de la conjonctive. *Ophthalmologica*, 166, 105–109.

Brandfonbrener, M., Landowne, M., and Shock, N. W. 1955. Changes in cardiac output with age. *Circulation*, 12, 557–566.

Broekhuyse, R. M. 1972. Lipids in tissues of the eye: VII. Changes in concentration and composition of sphingomyelins, cholesterol esters and other lipids in aging sclera. *Biochim. Biophys. Acta*, 280, 637–645.

Brusis, O. A., and McGandy, R. B. 1971. Nutrition and man's heart and blood vessels. *Federation Proc.*, 30, 1417–1420.

Buerger, L., and Braunstein, H. 1960. Senile cardiac amyloidosis. *Am. J. Med.*, 28, 357–367.

Burkard, W. P. *et al.* 1966. Alteration of the catecholamine metabolism of the rat heart in old age. *Proc. 7th Intern. Congr. Geront.*, 1, 237.

Chisolm, G. M., Gainer, J. L., Jr., Stoner, G. E., and Gainer, J. V. 1972. Plasma proteins, oxygen transport and atherosclerosis. *Atherosclerosis*, 15, 327–343.

Cliff, W. J. 1970. The aortic tunica media in aging rats. *Exp. Molec. Path.*, 13, 172–189.

Cohen, A. S. 1965. The constitution and genesis of amyloid. *Intern. Rev. Exp. Path.*, 4, 159–243.

Comalli, R. 1971. Hydrolase activity and intracellular pH in liver, heart, and diaphragm of aging rats. *Exp. Geront.*, 6, 219–225.

Crouse, J. R., Grundy, S. M., and Ahrens, E. H., Jr. 1972. Cholesterol distribution in the bulk tissues of man: Variation with age. *J. Clin. Invest.*, 51, 1292–1296.

Danilova, K. M. 1972. Starcheskaya perestroika intramural 'nykh so sudov serdtsa cheloveka. *Arkh. Patol.*, 34, 21–29.

Darmady, E. M., Offer, J., and Woodhouse, M. A. 1973. The parameters of the ageing kidney. *J. Pathol.*, 109, 195–207.

Davies, C. T. M. 1972. The oxygen-transporting system in relation to age. *Clin. Sci.* (OXF), 42, 1–13.

Davies, D. F., and Shock, N. W. 1950. Age changes in glomerular filtration rate, effective renal plasma flow, and tubular excretory capacity in adult males. *J. Clin. Invest.*, **29**, 496–507.

Davies, M. J., and Pomerance, A. 1972. Quantitative study of ageing changes in the human sinoatrial node and internodal tracts. *Brit. Heart. J.*, **34**, 150–152.

De Vries, H. A., and Adams, G. M. 1972. Comparison of exercise responses in old and young men: I. The cardiac effort total body effort relationship. *J. Geront.*, **27**, 344–348.

Ein, D., Kimura, S., Terry, W. D., Magnotta, J., and Glenner, G. W. 1972. Amino acid sequence of an amyloid fibril protein of unknown origin. *J. Biol. Chem.*, **247**, 5653–5655.

Eisenstein, R., Ayer, J., Papajiannis, S., Hass, G., and Ellis, H. 1964. Mineral binding by human arterial elastic tissue. *Lab. Invest.*, **13**, 1198–1204.

Feldman, S. A., and Glagov, S. 1971. Transmedial collagen and elastin gradients in human aortas: Reversal with age. *Atherosclerosis*, **13**, 385–394.

Florini, J. R., Saito, Y., and Manowitz, E. J. 1973. Effect of age on thyroxine-induced cardiac hypertrophy in mice. *J. Geront.*, **28**, 293–297.

Friedberg, C. K. 1966. *Diseases of the Heart*, pp. 1006–1008. 3rd ed. Philadelphia: W. B. Saunders.

Garbarsch, C., Matthiessen, M. E., Helin, P., and Lorenzen, I. 1969. Arteriosclerosis and hypoxia: I. Gross and microscopic changes in rabbit aorta induced by systemic hypoxia. Histochemical studies. *J. Atherosclerosis Res.*, **9**, 283–294.

Garbarsch, C., Matthiessen, M. E., Helin, P., and Lorenzen, I. 1970. Aortic arteriosclerosis in rabbits of the Danish country strain. *Atherosclerosis*, **12**, 291–300.

Geer, J. C., and Haust, M. D. 1972. Smooth muscle cells in atherosclerosis. *In, Monographs on Atherosclerosis*. New York: S. Karger.

Gerlach, U., and Fegeler, W. 1973. Variations with age in the lactate dehydrogenase isoenzyme pattern in the aorta of rats. *Enzyme* (Basel), **14**, 1–12.

Gerrity, R. G., and Cliff, W. J. 1972. The aortic tunica intima in young and aging rats. *Exp. Molec. Path.*, **16**, 382–402.

Getty, R. 1966. Histomorphological studies in the dog and hog as related to aging. *In*, G. Sacher and P. Lindop (eds.), *Radiation and Ageing*, pp. 245–276. London: Taylor and Francis.

Gey, K. F. 1965. *In, Age With a Future*, p. 181. New York: Academic Press.

Gey, K. F. *et al.* 1965. Variation of the norepinephrine metabolism of the rat heart with age. *Gerontologia*, **11**, 1.

Glanville, E. V., and Geerdink, R. A. 1972. Blood pressure of Amerindians from Surinam. *Am. J. Phys. Anthropol.*, **37**, 251–254.

Gozna, E. R., Marble, A. E., Shaw, A., and Holland, J. G. 1974. Age-related changes in the mechanics of the aorta and pulmonary artery of man. *J. Appl. Physiol.*, **36**, 407–411.

Gribbin, B., Pickering, T. G., Steight, P., and Peto, R. 1971. Effect of age and high blood pressure on baroreflex sensitivity in man. *Circulation Res.*, **29**, 424–431.

Hamlin, C. R., and Kohn, R. R. 1971. Evidence for progressive age-related structural changes in post mature human collagen. *Biochim. Biophys. Acta*, **236**, 458–467.

Hanna, M. G., Jr., Nettesheim, P., and Snodgrass, M. J. 1971. Decreasing immune competence and development of reticulum cell sarcomas in lymphatic tissue of aged mice. *J. Nat. Cancer Inst.*, **46**, 809–824.

Harkness, R. D. 1961. Biological function of collagen. *Biol. Rev. Cambridge Phil. Soc.*, **36**, 399–463.

Harlan, W. R., Oberman, A., Mitchell, R. E., and Graybiel, A. 1973. A 30-year study of blood pressure in a white male cohort. *In*, G. Onesti, K. E. Kim, and J. H. Moyer (eds.), *Hypertension: Mechanisms and Management, 26th Hahnemann Symposium*. New York and London: Grune & Stratton.

Harris, R. E. 1968. Long-term studies of blood pressure recorded annually, with implications for the factors underlying essential hypertension. *Trans. Assoc. Life Ins. Med. Dir.*, **LI**, 30.

Harris, R. E., and Forsyth, R. P. 1973. Personality and emotional stress in essential hypertension in man. *In*, G. Onesti, K. E. Kim, and J. H. Moyer (eds.), *Hypertension: Mechanisms and Management, 26th Hahnemann Symposium*. New York and London: Grune & Stratton.

Hassler, O. 1969. A senile change resulting from excessive spiraling of arteries. *J. Geront.*, **24**, 37–41.

Heath, D., Smith, P., Harris, P., and Winson, M. 1973. The atherosclerotic human carotid sinus. *J. Pathol.*, **110**, 49–58.

Heilbrunn, L. V. 1965. Cellular physiology and aging. *Federation Proc.*, **15**, 948.

Helin, P., Lorenzen, I., Garbarsch, C., and Matthiessen, M. E. 1971. Repair in arterial tissue: Morphological and biochemical changes in rabbit aorta after a single dilation injury. *Circulation Res.*, **29**, 542–554.

Heller, L. J., and Whitehorn, W. V. 1972. Age-associated alterations in myocardial contractile properties. *Am. J. Physiol.*, **222**, 1613–1619.

Hollenberg, N. K., Adams, D. F., Solomon, H. S., Rashid, A., Abrams, H. L., and Merrill, J. P. 1974. Senescence and the renal vasculature in normal man. *Circulation Res.*, **34**, 309–316.

Hrůza, Z. 1967. Changes in lipid metabolism with aging. *In*, H. W. Woolhouse (ed.), *Aspects of the Biology of Ageing*, pp. 375–401. Cambridge: Cambridge University Press.

Isobe, T., and Osserman, E. F. 1974. Patterns of amyloidosis and their association with plasma-cell dyscrasia, monoclonal immunoglobulins and Bence-Jones proteins. *New Engl. J. Med.*, **290**, 473–477.

Jelinková, M., Stuchlíková, E., Hrůza, Z., Deyl, Z., and Smrž, M. 1972. Hormone-sensitive lipolytic activity of the aorta of different age groups of rats. *Exp. Geront.*, **7**, 263–271.

John, R., and Thomas, J. 1972. Chemical composition

of elastins isolated from aortas and pulmonary tissues of humans of different ages. *Biochem. J.*, 127, 261–269.

Johnsson, L., and Hawkins, J. E., Jr. 1972. Vascular changes in the human inner ear associated with aging. *Ann. Otol. Rhinol. Laryngol.*, 81, 364–376.

Jordan, S. W., and Perley, M. J. 1972. Microangiopathy in diabetes mellitus and aging. *Arch. Pathol.*, 93, 261–265.

Jorgenson, R. J., Balling, D. R., Yoder, O. C., and Murphy, E. A. 1972. Blood pressure studies in the Amish. *Johns Hopkins Med. J.*, 131, 329–350.

Kannel, W. B., and Dawber, T. R. 1973. Hypertensive cardiovascular disease: The Framingham study. *In*, G. Onesti, K. E. Kim, and J. H. Moyer (eds.), *Hypertension: Mechanisms and Management, 26th Hahnemann Symposium*. New York and London: Grune & Stratton.

Kanungo, M. S. *et al.* 1965. Effect of age on the isoenzyme of lactic dehydrogenase of the heart and brain of rat. *Biochem. Biophys. Res. Commun.*, 21, 454.

Katenkamp, D., and Stiller, D. 1971. Histotopographische untersuchungen zur senilen herzamyloidose. *Pathol. Eur.*, 6, 109–121.

Keys, A., Aravanis, C., Blackburn, H., van Buchem, F., Buzina, R., Djordjevic, B., Fidanza, F., Karvonen, M., Menotti, A., Puddu, V., and Taylor, H. 1972. Probability of middle-aged men developing coronary heart disease in five years. *Circulation*, 45, 815–828.

Khominskaya, M. B. 1973. Sravnitel 'noe gistokhimicheskoe issledovanie vozrastnykh izmenenii krupnykh arterii cheloveka. *Arkh. Patol.*, 35, 33–38.

Kilo, C., Vogler, N., and Williamson, J. R. 1972. Muscle capillary basement membrane changes related to aging and to diabetes mellitus. *Diabetes*, 21, 881–905.

Kirk, J. E. 1969. *Enzymes of the Arterial Wall*. New York: Academic Press.

Kirk, J. E., and Laursen, T. J. S. 1955. Changes with age in diffusion coefficients of solutes for human tissue membranes. *In*, G. E. W. Wolstenholme and M. P. Cameron (eds.), *Aging- General Aspects*, pp. 69–76. Boston: Little, Brown.

Klanova, J., and Heinis, P. 1972. The mean transit time determined with the gamma camera as a value of the cerebral blood flow. *Radiol. Clin. Biol.*, 41, 193–197.

Kohn, R. R. 1963. Human aging and disease. *J. Chronic Diseases*, 16, 5–21.

Kohn, R. R., and Rollerson, E. R. 1959a. Age changes in swelling properties of human myocardium. *Proc. Soc. Exp. Biol. Med.*, 100, 253–256.

Kohn, R. R., and Rollerson, E. R. 1959b. Studies on the mechanism of the age-related change in swelling ability of human myocardium. *Circulation Res.*, 7, 740–745.

Kohn, R. R., and Rollerson, E. R. 1959c. Studies of the effect of heat and age in decreasing ability of human collagen to swell in acid. *J. Geront.*, 14, 11–15.

Kojimahara, M., Sekiya, K., and Ooneda, G. 1973. Age-induced changes of cerebral arteries in rats: An electron microscope study. *Virchows Arch. Abt. A. Pathol. Anat.*, 361, 11–18.

Kramsch, D. M., and Hollander, W. 1973. Interaction of serum and arterial lipoproteins with elastin of the arterial intima and its role in the lipid accumulation in atherosclerotic plaques. *J. Clin. Invest.*, 52, 236–247.

Kravec, T. F., Eggers, G. W. N., Jr., and Kettel, L. J. 1972. Influence of patient age on forearm and systemic vascular response to hypoxaemia. *Clin. Sci.* (OXF), 42, 555–565.

Kritchevsky, D., Genzano, J., and Kothari, H. 1973. Influence of age on aortic cholesterol esterase in rats. *Mech. Age. Dev.*, 2, 345–347.

Kronenberg, R. S., and Drage, C. W. 1973. Attenuation of the ventilatory and heart rate responses to hypoxia and hypercapnia with aging in normal men. *J. Clin. Invest.*, 52, 1812–1819.

Kuchar, O., Kuba, J., and Tomsu, M. 1972. Messung der Muskeldurchblutung in den unteren Extremitaeten nach der lokalen Xenon[133]-Clearance-Methode: I. Normalwerte und ihre Abhaengigkeit vom Lebensalter. *Radiobiol. Radiother.*, 13, 217–224.

Landowne, M., Brandfonbrener, M., and Shock, N. W. 1955. The relation of age to certain measures of performance of the heart and circulation. *Circulation*, 12, 567–576.

Lansing, A. L. 1959. Elastic tissue in atherosclerosis. *In*, I. H. Page (ed.), *Connective Tissue, Thrombosis, and Atherosclerosis*, p. 167. New York: Academic Press.

Laragh, J. H. 1974. An approach to the classification of hypertensive states. *Hosp. Pract.*, pp. 61–73 (January).

Larson, L. L., and Foote, R. H. 1972. Uterine blood flow in young and aged rabbits. *Proc. Soc. Exp. Biol. Med.*, 141, 67–69.

Lee, J. C., Karpeles, L. M., and Downing, S. E. 1972. Age-related changes of cardiac performance in male rats. *Am. J. Physiol.*, 222, 432–438.

Lenkiewicz, J. E., Davies, M. J., and Rosen, D. 1972. Collagen in human myocardium as a function of age. *Cardiovascular Res.*, 6, 549–555.

Leuenberger, P. M. 1973. Ultrastructure of the ageing retinal vascular system, with special reference to quantitative and qualitative changes of capillary basement membranes. *Gerontologia*, 19, 1–15.

Levene, C. I., and Poole, J. C. F. 1962. The collagen content of the normal and atherosclerotic human aortic intima. *Brit. J. Exp. Pathol.*, 43, 469–471.

Levin, M., Franklin, E. C., Frangione, B., and Pras, M. 1972. The amino acid sequence of a major non-immunoglobulin component of some amyloid fibrils. *J. Clin. Invest.*, 51, 2773–2776.

Likoff, W. (ed.). 1972. *Atherosclerosis and Coronary Heart Disease, 25th Hahnemann Symposium*. New York: Grune & Stratton.

Limas, C. J. 1971. Aging of the myocardium. *Acta. Cardiol.*, 26, 249–259.

Lindner, A., Charra, B., Sherrard, D. S., and Scribner, B. H. 1974. Accelerated atherosclerosis in prolonged maintenance hemodialysis. *New Engl. J. Med.*, **290**, 697–700.

Lindner, J., and Johannes, G. 1973. Contribution on the ageing of arterial connective tissue. *In*, H. G. Vogel (ed.), *Connective Tissue and Aging*, pp. 68–78. Amsterdam: Excerpta Medica.

Maddocks, I. 1961. Possible absence of essential hypertension in two complete Pacific island populations. *Lancet*, **2**, 396–399.

Menzies, R. A., and Gold, P. H. 1971. The turnover of mitochondria in a variety of tissues of young adult and aged rats. *J. Biol. Chem.*, **246**, 2425–2429.

Miall, W. E., and Lovell, H. G. 1967. Relation between change of blood pressure and age. *Brit. Med. J.*, **2**, 660–664.

Mozersky, D. J., Sumner, D. S., Hokanson, D. E., and Strandness, D. E. 1972. Transcutaneous measurement of the elastic properties of the human femoral artery. *Circulation*, **46**, 948–955.

Mozersky, D. J., Sumner, D. S., Hokanson, D. E., and Strandness, D. E. 1973. Transcutaneous measurement of arterial wall properties as a potential method of estimating aging. *J. Am. Geriat. Soc.*, **21**, 18–20.

Mullins, C. L., and Guntheroth, W. G. 1965. A collagen net hypothesis for force transference of smooth muscle. *Nature*, **206**, 592–594.

Munnell, J. F., and Getty, R. 1968. Rate of accumulation of cardiac lipofuscin in the aging canine. *J. Geront.*, **23**, 154–158.

Myer, Y. P., and King, T. E. 1968. Effects of the oxidation state, ligands, detergents and aging on the conformation of cytochrome oxidase. *Biochem. Biophys. Res. Commun.*, **33**, 43.

Nakashima, T., and Tanikawa, J. 1971. A study of human aortic distensibility with relation to atherosclerosis and aging. *Angiology*, **22**, 477–490.

Nanda, B. S., and Getty, R. 1971. Age-related histomorphological changes in the cerebral arteries of domestic pig. *Exp. Geront.*, **6**, 453–460.

Newmark, M. Z., Malfer, C. D., and Wiese, C. D. 1972. Regulation of arterial metabolism. I. The effects of age and hormonal status upon the utilization of glucose *in vitro* by rat aorta. *Biochim. Biophys. Acta*, **261**, 9–20.

Norris, A. H., Shock, N. W., and Yiengst, M. J. 1953. Age-changes in heart rate and blood pressure responses to tilting and standardized exercise. *Circulation*, **8**, 521–526.

O'Rourke, M. F., Blazek, J. V., Morreels, C. L., and Kravetz, L. J. 1968. Pressure wave transmission along the human aorta. *Circulation Res.*, **23**, 567–579.

Parizkova, J., Eiselt, E., Sprynarova, S., and Wachtlova, M. 1971. Body composition, aerobic capacity, and density of muscle capillaries in young and old men. *J. Appl. Physiol.*, **31**, 323–325.

Pincherle, G. 1971. Factors affecting the mean serum cholesterol. *J. Chronic Diseases*, **24**, 289–297.

Porter, R., and Knight, J. (eds.) 1973. *Atherogenesis: Initiating Factors, A Ciba Foundation Symposium*. Amsterdam and New York: Associated Scientific Publishers.

Portman, O. W., and Alexander, M. 1972. Changes in arterial subfractions with aging and atherosclerosis. *Biochim. Biophys. Acta*, **260**, 460–474.

Prange, A. J. *et al.* 1967. Influence of age on monoamine oxidase and catechol-o-methyl transferase in rat tissues. *Life Sci.*, **6**, 581.

Proper, R., and Wall, F. 1972. Left ventricular stroke volume measurements not affected by aging. *Am. Heart J.*, **83**, 843–845.

Rakušan, K., and Poupa, O. 1964. Capillaries and muscle fibers in the heart of old rats. *Gerontologia*, **9**, 107–112.

Roach, M. R., and Burton, A. C. 1959. The effect of age on the elasticity of human iliac arteries. *Can. J. Biochem. Physiol.*, **37**, 557–570.

Robbins, S. L. 1967. *Pathology*, pp. 573–574. 3rd ed. Philadelphia: W. B. Saunders.

Robert, J., Marignac, T., Holtier, D., and Bertrand, A. 1970. Variations du débit capillaire spécifique du muscle et du tissu cellulaire sous-cutané de la souris et du rat en fonction de l'age et du poids. *Compt. Rend. Soc. Biol.*, **164**, 1324–1330.

Roessle, R., and Roulet, F. 1932. *Mass und Zahl in der Pathologie*, pp. 26–36. Berlin: Springer Verlag.

Rosing, D. R., Redwood, D. R., Brakman, P., Astrup, T., and Epstein, S. E. 1973. Impairment of the diurnal fibrinolytic response in man: Effects of aging, type IV hyperlipoproteinemia, and coronary disease. *Circulation Res.*, **32**, 752–758.

Rothbaum, D. A., Shaw, D. J., Angell, C. S., and Shock, N. W. 1973. Cardiac performance in the unanesthetized senescent male rat. *J. Geront.*, **28**, 287–292.

Sasaki, A., Horiuchi, N., Suzuki, T., and Inui, H. 1972. Clinical features of arteriosclerotic heart disease in Japanese diabetics. *J. Jap. Diabetic Soc.*, **15**, 95–103.

Schaub, M. C. 1963. Qualitative and quantitative changes of collagen in parenchymatous organs of the rat during aging. *Gerontologia*, **8**, 114–122.

Scheinberg, P., Blackburn I., Rich, M., and Saslow, M. 1953. Effects of ageing on cerebral circulation and metabolism. *Arch. Neurol. Psychiat.*, **70**, 77–85.

Shirey, T. L., and Sobel, H. 1972. Compositional and transcriptional properties of chromatins isolated from cardiac muscle of young-mature and old dogs. *Exp. Geront.*, **7**, 15–29.

Shirley, R. L., and Davis, G. K. 1959. Effect of dietary proteins, vitamin E and age on the lactic dehydrogenase and succinoxidase of the hearts of rats. *J. Nutr.*, **67**, 635.

Shreiner, D. P., Weisfeldt, M. L., and Shock, N. W. 1969. Effects of age, sex, and breeding status on the rat heart. *Am. J. Physiol.*, **217**, 176–180.

Shukla, S. P., and Kanungo, M. S. 1968. Effect of age on the activity of glucose-6-phosphate dehydrogenase in different tissues of rat. *Exp. Geront.*, **3**, 31.

Sinex, F. M. 1966. Biochemistry of aging. *Perspectives Biol. Med.*, **9**, 208.

Singh, S. N. 1973. Effect of age on the activity and citrate inhibition of malate dehydrogenase of the brain and heart of rats. *Experientia*, **29**, 42–43.

Sinnett, P. F., and Whyte, H. M. 1973. Epidemiological studies in a total highland population, Tukisenta, New Guinea. *J. Chronic Diseases*, **26**, 265–290.

Solomon, R. D. 1967. Biology and pathology of vascular disease. *Advan. Geront. Res.*, **2**, 285–354.

Stein, O., Eisenberg, S., and Stein, Y. 1969. Aging of aortic smooth muscle cells in rats and rabbits. *Lab. Invest.*, **21**, 386–397.

Strehler, B. L., Mark, D., Mildvan, A. S., and Gee, M. V. 1959. Rate and magnitude of age pigment accumulation in the human myocardium. *J. Geront.*, **14**, 430–439.

Strotz, C. R., and Shorr, G. I. 1973. Hypertension in the Papago Indians. *Circulation*, **48**, 1299–1303.

Stuchlíková, E., Jelínková, M., Faltová, E., and Smrž, M. 1971. Age-dependent lipolytic activity of the rat myocardium in relation to its triglyceride content. *Exp. Geront.*, **6**, 297–304.

Studer, A. *et al.* 1964. Histochemical evidence of monoamine oxidase activity in rats of different ages. *Histochemie*, **4**, 43.

Tartulier, M., Bourret, M., and Deyrieux, F. 1972. Les pressions arterielles pulmonaires chez l'homme normal: Effets de l'age et de l'exercice musculaire. *Bull. Physio. -Pathol. Respir.*, **8**, 1295–1321.

Timpl, R., Wolff, I., and Weiser, M. 1968. A new class of structural proteins from connective tissue. *Biochim. Biophys. Acta*, **168**, 168–170.

Tomanek, R. J., and Karlsson, U. L. 1973. Myocardial ultrastructure of young and senescent rats. *J. Ultrastruct. Res.*, **42**, 201–220.

Tomanek, R. J., Taunton, C. A., and Liskop, K. S. 1972. Relationship between age, chronic exercise, and connective tissue of the heart. *J. Geront.*, **27**, 33–38.

Travis, D. F., and Travis, A. 1972. Ultrastructural changes in the left ventricular rat myocardial cells with age. *J. Ultrastruct. Res.*, **39**, 124–148.

Truswell, A. S., Kennelly, B. M., Hansen, J. D. L., and Lee, R. B. 1972. Blood pressures of Kung bushmen in northern Botswana. *Am. Heart J.*, **84**, 5-12.

Vogel, H. G. (ed.) 1973. *Connective tissue and aging.* Amsterdam, *Exerpta Medica.*

Wagner, J. A., Robinson, S., Tzankoff, S. P., and Marino, R. P. 1972. Heat tolerance and acclimatization to work in the heat in relation to age. *J. Appl. Physiol.*, **33**, 616–622.

Walford, R. L., Carter, P. K., and Schneider, R. B. 1964. Stability of aortic elastic tissue with age and pregnancy in the rat. *Arch. Pathol.*, **78**, 43–45.

Wearn, J. T. 1940. Morphological and functional alterations of the coronary circulation. *Harvey Lectures Ser.*, **35**, 243–270.

Weisfeldt, M. L., Loeven, W. A., and Shock, N. W. 1971. Resting and active mechanical properties of trabeculae carnae from aged male rats. *Am. J. Physiol.*, **220**, 1921–1927.

Wiederhielm, C. A. 1965. Distensibility characteristics of small blood vessels. *Federation Proc.*, **24**, 1075–1084.

Willems, J. L., Roelandt, J. R., Van de Vel, H. R., and Joossens, J. V. 1971. The circulation time in the aged. *Am. J. Cardiol.*, **27**, 155–161.

Wolinsky, H. 1971. Effects of hypertension and its reversal on the thoracic aorta of male and female rats: Morphological and chemical studies. *Circulation Res.*, **28**, 622–637.

Wolinsky, H. 1972. Long-term effects of hypertension on the rat aortic wall and their relation to concurrent aging changes: Morphological and chemical studies. *Circulation Res.*, **30**, 301–309.

Wolinksy, H., and Glacov, S. 1964. Structural basis for the static mechanical properties of the aortic media. *Circulation Res.*, **14**, 400–413.

Wright, J. R., Calkins, E., Breen, W. J., Stolte, G., and Schultz, R. T. 1969. Relationship of amyloid to aging. *Medicine*, **48**, 39–60.

Yu, S. Y. 1971. Cross-linking of elastin in human atherosclerotic aortas: I. A preliminary study. *Lab. Invest.*, **25**, 121–125.

Zhdanov, V. S., Lifshits, A. M., and Vikhert, A. M. 1973. Atherosclerosis of the aortic arch. *Kardiologiya*, **13**, 47–52.

13
AGING OF THE REPRODUCTIVE SYSTEM

George B. Talbert
Downstate Medical Center
State University of New York

Aging of the reproductive system in the human has always been of interest to laymen as well as to investigators. The dramatic transformation which occurs in both sexes at puberty primarily involves the reproductive system and for centuries has had religious, sociological, as well as biomedical significance. The alterations which accompany the menopause have also attracted considerable attention, particularly since this event occurs at a relatively early age, when changes in other systems of the body are not as obvious. The aging of the reproductive system of the male who is in good health is generally far more gradual and variable in time. As a result, these modifications, with the exceptions of those in the notorious prostate gland, have attracted far less attention from the biologist or the physician.

The present discussion will be largely confined to the changes which occur as the individual passes from a period of full reproductive function into the period of decline and eventual cessation of reproductive capacity, but some consideration must be given to earlier changes in many instances. Fortunately, many review articles have been written in recent years which the reader can utilize to follow some of the earlier work. Examples of review papers which have dealt with different aspects of reproductive aging are: Lanman (1968a, 1968b), Talbert (1968), Biggers (1969), Adams (1970), Austin (1970), Bishop (1970), Finn (1970), Francis (1970), Labhsetwar (1970), Jones (1970), and Noyes (1970).

FEMALE REPRODUCTIVE SYSTEM

Reproductive Life Span

The relationship between total life span and reproductive life span in female mammals varies considerably from one species to another and even between different strains of the same species. Unfortunately satisfactory data are largely confined to man and a few small laboratory animals. Information on farm animals is limited because they are usually killed relatively early in life for economic reasons, and data on wild animals in their natural habitat are very difficult to obtain.

The initiation of reproductive life in mammalian species is specifically related to the age when eggs are first shed from the ovary. In the human and some other primates, this event is typically related to the first menses, while in other mammalian species, which are spontaneous ovulators, the initial release of ova is temporally associated with the first estrous period.

The early postpubertal period in humans is an age of relative infertility, and when pregnancy does occur, it is more likely to be complicated by anemia and symptons of preecalmpsia such as headache, nausea, and jaundice. This early period is followed by a variable number of years when reproductive capacity is usually optimal. Finally there ensues a span of a few months to a few years when cycles tend to be irregular, and pregnancy again becomes hazardous for both mother and fetus.

The termination of reproductive capacity is quite well defined by the cessation of menstrual periods in the human and probably other primates. In other mammals which have been studied, termination of reproductive life is less predictable, primarily because the ovaries of these animals generally contain ova into old age, whereas the human ovary rarely has any normal appearing ova after the menopause.

Primates. The menarche in the human has tended to occur at an earlier age in more recent times. Although genetic factors may be partly responsible, this change has generally been attributed to better nutrition in the populations which have been studied.

Dreizen, Spirakis, and Stone (1967) compared a group of 30 undernourished with 30 well-nourished girls and found that the girls in the latter group reached the menarche about 2 years earlier, although their skeletal age showed a difference of less than 4 months. Frisch (1972) also compared two such groups of girls and found that the former group reached the menarche nearly 2 years earlier. The important concept derived from this study was that there was no significant difference in body weight between the two groups at the menarche, although the undernourished girls were slightly taller. It is of further interest that the weight at the menarche is about 46 kg in several Caucasian populations, but it is lower in a Japanese population who have a smaller mean body weight. For a review of the older literature the reader is referred to Tanner (1962).

Van Wagenen (1952) found considerable range in both age and body weight at the menarche in her colony of *Macaca mulatta*. The earliest menarche occurred at 17 months and the latest at 31 months with a mean of about 24 months while the body weight varied from 2,800 to 4,110 grams with a mean of 3,428.

Although there is general agreement that the age at the menarche has decreased with time, there are conflicting data as to whether there has been any change in age at the menopause. Frommer (1964) reported that the age at the menopause had increased in Great Britian and Germany over the last 100 years, but McKinlay, Jeffreys, and Thompson (1972) found no evidence of any change in a London population during essentially the same period of time. Many studies indicate that the menopause now occurs at 48 to 51 years of age in a wide variety of populations.

Socioeconomic factors and the widespread use of contraceptive measures make it very difficult to obtain reliable data on the decline in reproductive capacity due to age in women. Tietze (1957) made a study of the Hutterites, who do not use contraceptives, and found that they continued to bear children until a mean age of about 49, which is close to the average age of the menopause. Snaith and Williamson (1947) compiled reports of 15 pregnancies after the menopause had presumably taken place. Although amenorrhea had existed for at least 18 months in the women included in this compilation, this still is not positive evidence that the menopause had been reached.

In summary, it is clear that births after the age of 50 are extremely rare (Figure 1), which coincides very well with the average age at the menopause.

Surprisingly little data are yet available concerning the reproductive life span of other primates. Van Wagenen (1970) reported that the age of menopause in her colony of *Macaca mulatto* appears to be between 25 and 30 years of age, and Guilloud (1968) observed that chimpanzees are still menstruating at up to 44 years of age. Both of these reports indicate that the postmenopausal period in these species may be relatively short compared to the human.

Laboratory Animals. Considerable data have become available in recent years with respect to the decline in reproductive capacity in a variety of small laboratory animals. The availability of

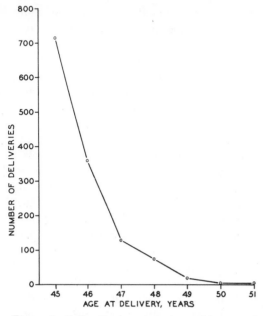

Figure 1. Deliveries in women over 44 years of age in England and Wales in 1957. (This Text-figure is reproduced from an article by Winifred J. A. Francis entitled "Reproduction at menarche and menopause in women," *J. Reprod. Fert.* (1970) Suppl. **12**, 90, by permission of the author and Editor.)

a number of inbred strains and their relatively short life span make them particularly attractive for this type of investigation. Another advantage of these animals for studies of reproductive aging is that they are polytocous (give birth to litters) so that reproductive failure can be quantitated by a decline in litter size.

Asdell, Bogart, and Sperling (1941), Ingram, Mandl, and Zuckerman (1958), and Bloch (1961) studied reproductive decline in aging rats. All of these investigations indicate that reproduction ends in this species at about 15 to 18 months of age with only an occasional reference to individual animals delivering a litter at an older age. Since rats often live for 3 years under laboratory conditions, much of their life is spent in a postreproductive state.

In an investigation of three strains of rats, Ingram, Mandl, and Zuckerman (1958) found that the second litter was the largest, with subsequent litters gradually declining in size through eight litters. A somewhat similar pattern of decline was observed by Asdell, Bogart,

and Sperling (1941); however, the decline in litter size was minimal until about the sixth litter. Up to 12 litters were delivered by rats which were initially bred at 100 days of age, with the last litter born at about 17 months of age.

The pattern of reproductive decline in the mouse is very similar to that observed in the rat. Numerous studies (see Talbert, 1968) show that there are strain differences in litter size and in reproductive life span, but litters are rare after 16 months of age in any inbred strain (Figure 2). Eaton (1953) and Jones and Krohn (1961a) have shown that litter size is larger and fertility maintained longer in some hybrid strains. Kirkham (1920) found that his colony-bred mice did not stop reproducing until they were 18 to 22 months of age.

Soderwall, Kent, Turbyfill, and Britenbaker (1960) and Blaha (1964a) found that hamsters also show a decline in litter size with advancing age and spend a significant portion of their lives in a postreproductive condition. Studies by Rogers and Taylor (1955), Adams (1970), and Arrington, Beaty, and Kelley (1973) on guinea pigs, rabbits, and gerbils indicate that these laboratory animals also live some time after reproduction ceases.

Domestic Animals. The most reliable data on reproductive life span in large domestic animals are found in records of valuable lines of thoroughbred horses in the *General Stud Book.* These records were studied by Hammond and Marshall (1952) who found that up to that time, 31 horses had been bred successfully at 27 to 33 years of age, which is near their normal life span. However, it has also been shown that Morgan mares are most fertile at 7 to 14 years of age, with a marked decline in fertility by 19 years.

Little information is available concerning the decline in reproductive capacity in cattle, and much of these data come from areas of the world where conditions might not be optimal for maintaining these animals in good reproductive condition. Data were tabulated on 2,000 Hariana cattle in India by Kohli and Suri (1957) which showed that the average age at the last calving was 13.5 years, with a maximum of 16

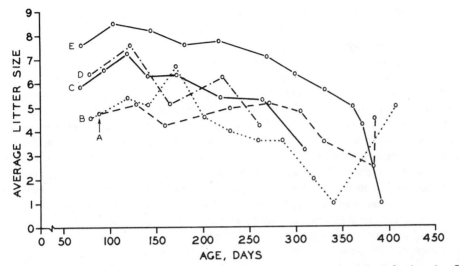

Figure 2. Relationship between maternal age and litter size in several strains of mice. A = Strain A, B = RIII, C = CBA, D = CBA♂ X A♀, E = CBA♀ X A♂. (From Jones, E. C., and Krohn, P. L. 1961. The relationship between age, number of oocytes, and fertility in virgin and multiparous mice. *Journal of Endocrinology*, **21**, 469–495.)

years. Comparable data were reported by Ahmed and Tantawy (1959) on Egyptian cattle and buffalo. Hammond and Marshall (1952) summarized many reports of cows producing calves at 15 to 21 years of age in the United States and Great Britain. Since cattle often live to be over 30 years of age, it appears that successful pregnancies are rare during the last several years of life in this species.

Desai and Winters (1951) and Turner and Dolling (1965) reported that ewes lamb on rare occasions up to 20 years of age, but several studies of different breeds agree reasonably well that reproductive performance declines considerably after 7 years of age.

Little data are available on reproductive decline in small domestic animals, but Anderson (1965) did report that the females in a colony of beagles reached peak breeding capacity by 3 years of age. By 6 years of age, over half the animals failed to conceive after mating, and by 7.5 years the mean litter size was less than one-third of the peak value.

Age Changes in Individual Organs And Tissues

The preceding discussion of the reproductive life span in different species of mammals shows that as a general rule the female loses ability to produce young well before she reaches her normal life span. There is also clear evidence that for a variable period prior to the ultimate cessation of reproduction, the efficiency of the process is declining. This decline is shown by smaller litters in polytocous species; increasing intervals between litters or individual births; increased resorbtions, abortions and stillbirths; increase in some types of malformed offspring and greater risk to the health of the mother during pregnancy and at delivery. (See Francis, 1970 and Talbert, 1968 for references.)

These aging problems can be initiated in the ovary, in one of the accessory reproductive organs, or they may be primarily the result of age changes in the anterior pituitary-hypothalamic complex. As will become evident in the following discussion, the aging process in this system may follow quite different courses in different species which have been studied.

Hypothalamic-Pituitary Complex. During the past 25 years, increasing emphasis has been placed on the relationship between the central nervous system (CNS) and more specifically, the hypothalamus and the anterior lobe of the pituitary gland.

At the present time there is very little evidence of morphological changes in the hypothalamus which have been specifically associated with decline in reproductive function. It is clear, however, from functional and biochemical studies that age changes will almost certainly be demonstrable by histochemical or electron microscopic techniques in the future.

In contrast to the paucity of morphological changes which have been observed in the hypothalamus, the anterior lobe of the pituitary gland does undergo marked histological changes in postmenopausal women. As might be anticipated, the most prominent structural changes occur in the gonadotrophin-secreting basophil cells. Sevringhaus (1944) and Randall (1962) noted vacuolation of these cells in postmenopausal women. Biggart (1935) and Shanklin (1953) observed that there is a small increase in basophils and a decrease in acidophils closely associated with the beginning of the menopause. Similar, but more pronounced, changes were observed in women who had been ovariectomized prior to the menopause. These more striking changes in the basophils of castrated women may have been due to a more sudden reduction in circulating estrogen than that following the menopause, but alternatively, the ovaries of postmenopausal women may continue to secrete enough of these steroids to reduce morphological changes in the pituitary gland.

Histological changes in the anterior pituitary gland of aging rodents appear to be less definitive than those observed in postmenopausal women. Spagnoli and Charipper (1955) did find some increase in the percentage of basophils in the anterior pituitary gland of aging hamsters. Wolfe (1943) failed to find an increased proportion of basophils in aged rats, but he did note an increase in vacuolation of these cells. These smaller changes in rodents are not surprising, since the ovaries of these species do not show as precipitous a decline in function as does the aging human ovary. Such an interpretation is supported by the pronounced changes which follow castration in these species.

Weiss and Lansing (1953) appear to have made the initial study of the fine structure of the pituitary gland in aging laboratory animals.

These investigators observed degenerative changes in the mitochondria in this organ in 12 to 14-month-old Swiss mice. These structures increase two to five times in diameter in all cell types, while the double-membered septa which extend into the middle of the mitochondria were reduced to stumps. Such changes have generally been associated with reduced function. A recent study of Balough, Takaks, Ládanyi, and Árvay (1970) compared the adenohypophysis of 3 and 32-month-old rats. Several age-associated changes were noted in the gonadotrophin-secreting cells. Of particular interest was the presence of nuclear inclusions surrounded by a membrane and containing finely granulated material of low electron density. Cytoplasmic inclusions were also commonly observed in the gonadotrophin-secreting cells but were not confined to them. These complex structures were of variable electron density and were surrounded by a membrane. These investigators speculated that these bodies might be associated with lysosomes.

The endoplasmic reticulum (ER) in the gonadotrophin-secreting cells of old rats contain marked cisternlike spaces which are considered characteristic of the well-known castration cells. Vesicular dilation was also noted in the ER of luteotrophin-secreting cells, and there was some indication of mitochondrial damage in these cells in the 32-month-old rats. In contrast to the observations of Weiss and Lansing (1953) in 12 to 14-month-old mice, the mitochondria in the gonadotrophin cells of old rats usually appeared normal.

It is clear that studies of morphological age changes in the hypothalamus and in the pituitary are still quite fragmentary, and little relationship has been established to functional changes. Information is particularly lacking in the human where the abrupt cessation of ovarian function might be expected to produce more striking alterations than in laboratory animals where ovarian function declines more gradually.

Pituitary Hormones. Pituitary gonadotrophin content has been assayed in laboratory animals at different ages and under a variety of experimental conditions. The early assay methods were relatively crude and failed to differentiate between FSH and LH activity, but even with such a method, Lauson, Golden, and Sevringhaus (1939) were able to detect an increase in pituitary gonadotrophin in old rats.

More recently biological and immunological test methods have been developed which separate FSH from LH activity and are also much more sensitive. Using the HCG augmentation method of Steelman and Pohley (1953) for FSH and the ovarian ascorbic acid depletion method of Parlow (1961) for LH, Labhsetwar (1969) found that the pituitary glands of 9-month-old multiparous rats with irregular cycles had a marked increase in FSH and a less pronounced increase in LH content over that found in young adults. Clemens and Meites (1971) also found an increase in pituitary FSH content in 21-month-old constant estrous rats when compared with 3-month-old rats in the estrous stage of their cycle. However, the LH content was lower and the prolactin level higher in the old rats (Table 1). A lower level of hypophyseal LH was also noted by Matsuyama, Weisz, and Lloyd (1966) in 11 to 12-month-old rats when compared with 4-month-old animals at all stages of their cycle, although the difference was least in rats autopsied during estrus. The reduced content of LH in the pituitary gland of old constant-estrous rats might be due to a continuous negative feedback of estrogen on the hypothalamus, since this inhibitory effect on LHRF release has been shown by Redding, Schally, Arimura, and Matsuo (1972) to reduce LH synthesis.

There is general agreement that there is an increase in total gonadotrophin in the hypophysis of postmenopausal women, but the relative change in FSH and LH is open to question. Bahn, Lorenz, Bennett, and Albert (1953) assayed pituitary glands from 60 to 90-year-old women and found a considerable increase in FSH but no change in LH in comparison with the levels found in premenopausal women. Ryan (1962) reported a tendency for LH content to be higher in postmenopausal women, but the difference was not significant because of wide individual variations. There seems to be little doubt that FSH content is influenced more by the decline in circulating estrogen in postmenopausal women than is LH, but it is premature to conclude that LH content is not affected by age.

Plasma Levels of Gonadotrophins. Plasma levels of gonadotrophins are dependent on the relationship between the rate of secretion by the adenohypophysis and the rate of metabolism and excretion of these hormones. The significant work of Kohler, Ross, and Odell (1968) and Coble, Kohler, Cargille, and Ross (1969) has shown that there is no difference in the metabolic clearance rate of LH and FSH from the plasma of premenopausal and postmenopausal women; consequently plasma levels of these hormones reflect their rate of secretion into the circulation (Table 2). It can also be seen from these data that the rate of secretion (production rate) of FSH increases about 15-fold after the menopause, whereas LH increases about 3-fold. These observations agree with the much greater increase in pituitary FSH

TABLE 1. COMPARISON OF GONADOTROPHIN CONCENTRATION IN THE PITUITARY GLAND OF OLD CONSTANT-ESTROUS RATS AND YOUNG ADULT RATS IN ESTRUS.

Age	No. of rats	FSH[a] conc. (μg/mg)	No. of rats	LH[b] conc. (μg/mg)
Young	30	2.50 (1.75–3.56)[c]	15	8.51 (5.60–12.82)[c]
Old	30	4.95 (3.66–6.76)[c]	15	3.07 (2.04–4.60)[c]

[a] Expressed as μg equivalents of NIH-FSH-S3.
[b] Expressed as μg equivalents of NIH-LH-S1.
[c] Mean and 95% confidence limits.
Data of Clemens and Meites, 1971.

TABLE 2. COMPARISON OF PLASMA CONCENTRATIONS, METABOLIC CLEARANCE RATE, AND PRODUCTION RATE OF GONADOTROPHIC HORMONES IN PRE AND POSTMENOPAUSAL WOMEN.

		FSH				LH		
Age	No.	Plasma conc.	MCR[b]	PR[c]	No.	Plasma conc.	MCR[b]	PR[c]
Yr		mU[a]/ml	ml/min.	mU[a]/min.		mU[a]/ml	ml/min.	mU[a]/min.
21–27	6	10 ± 1.8	14.3 ± 1.1	146 ± 27	5	32.0 ± 9.6	24.4 ± 1.8	784 ± 170
45–56	5	172 ± 24	12.6 ± 1.1	2141 ± 264	4	99.2 ± 23.2	25.6 ± 4.1	2400 ± 410

[a]In terms of 2nd International Reference Preparation of Human Menopausal Gonadotrophin.
[b]Metabolic clearance rate.
[c]Production rate.
Data of Kohler, Ross, and Odell, 1968 and Coble, *et al.*, 1969.

content after the menopause but also suggest that further study may reveal an increase in LH content.

It has been generally accepted that the high level of circulating and urinary gonadotrophins in postmenopausal women is a reflection of the low level of circulating estrogens acting back on the hypothalamus and possibly on the pituitary, but the influence of different levels of estrogens is less well understood. Keller (1970) found that 6 mg per day of estrone or 10 mg per day of estradiol benzoate administered over a 6-day period sharply depressed both LH and FSH excretion without altering the FSH/LH ratio. On the other hand, 0.3 mg per day of estrone, estradiol, or estriol for 6 days produced a considerable increase in the excretion of FSH and a lesser increase in LH. Franchimont, Legros, and Meurice (1972) observed only a negative feedback effect on both LH and FSH with three different estrogens at levels of 20 to 100 μg per day for 12 to 27 days. Low doses of estrogen depressed serum levels of only FSH whereas higher doses depressed both LH and FSH.

As an alternative to the widely accepted role of estrogen exerting a negative feedback effect on FSH and LH secretion Sherman and Korenman (1975) and Sherman, West and Korenman (1976) have recently speculated that the dramatic increase in serum FSH after the menopause and much smaller change at this time in serum LH may be explained by the presence of an ovarian regulatory hormone, an inhibin, which specifically controls FSH but not LH by a negative feedback mechanism. It was sug-

gested that this hormone may be closely associated with the number of maturing follicles which decreases around the menopause. A decrease in the output of this hormone would thus permit an increase in FSH secretion. It is clear, as has been stated by the authors, that this proposal is highly speculative at this time but it does appear to be worthy of further investigation.

Direct measurements of serum gonadotrophins in young and old laboratory animals do not appear to have been carried out, and less satisfactory indirect methods have produced conflicting data.

Labhsetwar (1967) applied the well-established principle of ovarian compensatory hypertrophy which follows unilateral ovariectomy. In this study, less growth took place in the remaining ovary of 9-month-old rats than in younger adults. The smaller ovarian hypertrophy in the older animals was apparently due to a reduced gonadotrophin secretion rather than to a decline in ovarian sensitivity to these hormones since the ovaries of the older rats were shown in a supplementary experiment to respond to exogenous gonadotrophin to the same degree as did those of young adults.

However, Takasugi (1963) placed young and old adult ovariectomized mice in parabiosis with young adult partners and found that the ovaries of the intact partner were stimulated to a greater degree by gonadotrophin from the old rats.

Comparison of these studies is of limited value since different species were involved, and the old mice were up to 15 months of age whereas the older rats were only 9 months of age. Clearly, more work with modern methods is needed to resolve this problem

Reproductive Cycles. Treolar, Boynton, Behn and Brown (1967) have clearly shown that the menstrual cycle in women is more irregular for some time following the menarche and for months and sometimes years preceding the menopause than it is during the period of optimal reproductive capability. Sherman and Korenman (1975) and Sherman, West and Korenman (1976) noted that women approaching the menopause frequently had shorter cycles than they had had earlier in their adult life and that the shorter cycle was due to a reduction in the length of the follicular phase of the cycle. Following the menopause there is little indication of reproductive cycles.

Age changes in reproductive cycles in laboratory rodents follow a far less predictable pattern than has been observed in humans. The underlying reason for this difference is that the ovaries in these rodents continue to secrete sex steriods well after their reproductive capacity has been lost, although major changes in the balance of these hormones almost invariably take place in association with increasing age (Thung, Boot, and Mühlbock, 1956).

The most complete studies of age changes in reproductive cycles were conducted by Thung, Boot, and Mühlbock, (1956) in mice and by Bloch (1961) and Aschheim (1961) in the laboratory rat. Their work showed that following the cessation of reproductive cycles, these animals have periods of constant estrus, repetitive pseudopregnancy, or both which can last for many months. The ovaries of rats in constant estrus contain only a large number of follicles of variable size, while the pseudopregnant rat ovaries contain many large functional corpora lutea. Not all rats demonstrate both of these conditions during their life span but may show only one condition or the other (Aschheim, 1961).

In a subsequent experiment, Aschheim (1964-65) provided evidence that these changes in the estrous cycle of the aging rat are probably the result of alterations in the pituitary-hypothal-amic axis which interferred with cyclic gonadotrophic stimulation. In this study ovaries from old constant-estrous or pseudopregnant rats were transplanted into castrated young rats of the same strain. When the ovarian grafts became established with a good blood supply, they performed in a regular cyclic manner for 3 or 4 months. Conversely, ovaries which were transplanted from immature rats into old rats assumed either a constant-estrous or pseudopregnant condition, which was dependent on the state of the recipient at the time it was ovariectomized. Although proof was lacking, the author suggested that the hypothalamus of aging rats might become less sensitive to the feedback control of estrogen so that the reciprocal relationship between the hypothalamic-pituitary axis and the ovary, which is essential for normal cycling, no longer exists. Some evidence has recently been obtained by Peng and Peng (1973) to support this suggestion. They found in both *in vivo* and *in vitro* experiments that the anterior hypothalamus and the anterior pituitary gland of 2-year-old female rats which were in constant estrus or anestrus at the time they were killed showed less uptake of ^{3}H-estradiol than did those structures in 3 to 5 month-old rats. Aged rats which were in a condition of repetitive pseudopregnancy at the time of autopsy did not show a difference in uptake of the isotope when compared with young adult cycling or pseudopregnant rats.

Further investigation by Aschheim (1965) has shown that constant estrus in aged rats can be interrupted by an injection of LH which induces ovulation. More recently, Clemens, Amenomori, Jenkins, and Meites (1969) demonstrated that ovulation and even cycling could be induced in old constant-estrous rats by injections of epinephrine or progesterone or by electrical stimulation of the preoptic area of the hypothalamus. The ability of epinephrine to produce these effects suggests that there may be a deficiency of this neurotransmitter substance in the hypothalamus of old female rats. Quadri, Kledzik, and Meites (1973) provided further evidence that deficiency of catecholamines may be responsible for age changes in the functioning of the hypothalamus by injecting epinephrine, L-dopa, or ipronaizid into 20 to

23-month-old constant-estrous rats. Each of these treatments usually induced one to six regular estrous cycles, but after termination of the injections, most of the animals either resumed a constant-estrous condition or became anestrous.

Wuttke and Meites (1973) furthermore demonstrated that electrochemical stimulation of the medial preoptic area in 20 to 24-month-old constant-estrous rats results in a significant increase in serum prolactin and LH levels, whereas similar treatment of old pseudopregnant rats results in only a small increase in serum prolactin and no increase in LH. The authors hypothesized that this difference could be due to relatively low estrogen and high progesterone in the blood of the latter group, which might reduce the sensitivity of the preoptic area to electrochemical stimulation.

Attempts have been made to separate the roles of the pituitary gland and the hypothalamus in the loss of reproductive cycles in old rats. Peng and Huang (1972) found that anterior pituitary glands from 2-year-old rats which had ceased to cycle did produce cycling in 10 out of 30 hypophysectomized young adult recipients when these glands were transplanted under the median eminence. These results indicate that the central nervous system of young rats can restore cyclic function in about one-third of the anterior pituitary glands of aged rats, but in the same experiment eight out of nine anterior pituitary glands from young adult rats performed cyclically after transplantation into the same site. As the authors stated, these data suggest that either age changes usually take place in the pituitary gland of aged rats which precludes functioning in a cyclic manner, or alternatively pituitary grafts from old rats are less likely to become well established than are those from young adults.

The Ovary. The ovary in mammals performs two basic functions: (1) It is a center for maturation of the female germ cells, and (2) it is a source of the female sex hormones. These two functions, although closely related to each other, do not necessarily develop or age at the same rate and must therefore be considered somewhat independently.

Influence of Age on Oocyte Population and Quality. There is general agreement that the initial supply of germ cells in both the male and female gonads are the result of migration of the primordial germ cells from the wall of the yolk sac into the dorsal mesentery of the primitive gut and finally laterally and ventrally into the developing genital ridges. For many years there was considerable controversy as to whether all germ cells are derived from this initial invasion of cells or whether there is a subsequent proliferation of cells from the germinal epithelium of the ovary (Thung, 1961).

At the present time there is increasing tendency to accept the evidence presented by Zuckerman (1956) that there is no renewed proliferation, but very few species have been studied, so caution must be used in generalizing on this point. The importance of this issue cannot be overestimated because as Thung (1961) has pointed out, if there is no means of replenishment of ova beyond fetal or early postnatal life, there is little hope of recovery of fertility once the initial stock of ova has been exhausted. Alternatively, if the germinal epithelium of the adult mammal can produce more germ cells, it might be possible to develop means of stimulating it to renewed activity.

The decline in the population of female germ cells in the ovary begins prior to birth in the species which have been studied and continues until these cells are exhausted or the individual dies. The relationship between exhaustion of developing oocytes and normal life span is extremely variable among the few mammalian species and even strains of the same species which have been studied.

Mandl and Shelton (1959) found that there was a steady decline in oocytes in the rat ovary beginning at birth, but a considerable number were still present at the normal age of death. Jones and Krohn (1961a) showed that there are wide strain differences in the rate of exhaustion of germ cells in inbred and hybrid mice and, perhaps even more important, there is great strain variation in the number of oocytes remaining in the ovaries at the age when reproductive capacity terminates. Mice of the CBA strain were found to be far more efficient in utilizing their oocytes than were the other strains which were studied, since the number of these cells had dropped to less than 100 when the last litter was born. In the other strains, there were still over 1,000 developing ova in each pair of ovaries when reproduction ceased.

The human pattern of oocyte decline has been studied by Block (1952, 1953). The data obtained in this study (Table 3) show that the number of these cells in the ovary declines rapidly from birth to 25 to 30 years of age. No decrease could then be detected until after 38, when a rapid decline was again observed.

No data were obtained by Block (1952, 1953) in women over 45 years of age, and no satisfactory counts of ova in the ovaries of older women appear to have been made since that time. Novak (1970) observed an occasional follicle or corpus luteum in a group of 200 women past the age of 50, so a few ova may obviously persist into the sixth decade, but no quantitative data were obtained.

The decline in oocytes in the ovary has also been studied in dogs by Schotterer (1928) and in cows by Erickson (1966). Both investigations indicate that oocytes are still present in dogs which are over 10 years old and in old cows.

The question has often been raised as to the factors which control the rate of depletion of oocytes. It is obvious that the rate of decline is not significantly affected by ovulation since only one ovum is lost by ovulation to 1,000 lost by atresia in the human. Furthermore, Jones and Krohn (1961b) and Shelton (1959) have shown in mice and rats that the rate of

loss in virgin animals which ovulated regularly every 4 to 5 days throughout their reproductive life span was no greater than in repeatedly bred animals which ovulated much less frequently. It seems clear that factors which control the rate of atresia will have the greatest influence on the rate of loss of oocytes.

Ingram (1953) and Jones and Krohn (1961b) found that the rate of loss of oocytes could be considerably reduced by hypophysectomy. It is tempting to conclude from these data that atresia is promoted by one or more of the gonadotrophic hormones, but as Jones and Krohn (1961b) have pointed out, more oocytes are undergoing atresia prior to puberty, when gonadotrophin output is less, than during the reproductive period. Consequently, it is possible that other pituitary hormones directly, or through an effect on other endrocrine glands, may have an influence on this aspect of ovarian aging.

The rate of decline of oocytes has also been slowed in mice by a restriction in caloric intake. Huseby and Ball (1945) found that C3H mice which had reduced food intake beginning at weaning had large numbers of primary follicles and small follicles at 17 to 18 months of age, whereas animals fed ad lib had very few such follicles remaining. Ball, Barnes, and Visscher (1947) also reported that mice kept on a restricted diet until 9 months of age and then fed *ad libitum* produced 13 times as many litters in the next 4 months as did similar mice which had not been restricted. However, it is unlikely that this difference was due completely to an increase in available oocytes, since this strain of mice has been shown by Jones and Krohn (1961a) to have no reduction in Graafian follicles until they are over 1 year of age.

The decrease in quantity of oocytes associated with increasing age cannot be considered apart from possible age changes in the quality of these cells. Krohn (1962) suggested that the relative viability of ova from young and aging rodents might best be judged by transplantation into the uterus of young adults. Blaha (1964b), using this method, recovered fertilized ova from the uteri of young and old hamsters and transferred them into the uteri of young adult hosts which had been made pseudopregnant by mating with vasectomized males. Approxi-

TABLE 3. EFFECT OF AGE OF HUMAN FEMALE ON NUMBER OF OOCYTES IN THE OVARY.

Age (yr)	No. of cases	No. of oocytes
Birth	7	733,000
4 to 10	5	499,200
11 to 17	5	389,300
18 to 24	7	161,800
25 to 31	11	62,500
32 to 38	8	80,200
39 to 45	7	10,900

Data of Block, 1952.

TABLE 4. EFFECT OF AGE OF DONOR ON PERCENTAGE SURVIVAL TO TERM OF OVA TRANSPLANTED INTO THE UTERUS OF YOUNG ADULTS OF THE SAME SPECIES.

Age of donor	Mouse[a]	Hamster[b]	Rabbit[c]	Rabbit[d]
Young adult	48	49.2	45	33.5
Old	54	4.5	26	12.9

[a] Data of Talbert and Krohn, 1966.
[b] Data of Blaha, 1964b.
[c] Data of Maurer and Foote, 1971.
[d] Data of Adams, 1970.

mately half of the ova from young females developed normally, but few ova from the old females survived to term. A similar study was carried out by Talbert and Krohn (1966) on several strains of mice, but no difference in viability was found between the ova obtained from young or old donors. Adams (1970) and Maurer and Foote (1971) conducted somewhat comparable experiments in rabbits and observed some loss of viability with age. The results obtained in these species are compared in Table 4.

These data appear to indicate that there is considerable species difference in ovum viability in aging laboratory animals, but the cause of the age difference has not been established. Parkening and Soderwall (1973) have shown that the preimplantation ovum of the aged hamster develops slower than that of the young adult hamster, which might result in premature exhaustion of the intrinsic food supplies of the blastocyst. This in turn might interfere with normal implantation and early development. However, Talbert and Krohn (1966) also found evidence of delayed preimplantation development in the mouse, but there was no evidence that this resulted in increased failure of implantation and early postimplantation development. Consequently more work is needed to clarify the cause of the loss of viability of ova from aging rodents.

There is conclusive evidence that aneuploidy is much more frequent in ova in women approaching the menopause than in women under 40 years of age. The most highly documented change of this type is trisomy of chromosome 21 which produces Down's Syndrome, but Turpin and Lejeune (1969) have reported that trisomy of other small chromosomes also tend to increase in the offspring of older women. The immediate cause is nondisjunction, which in turn may be due to failure of separation of chromatids at anaphase II or chromosomes at anaphase I of meiosis. Henderson and Edwards (1968) presented evidence that reduction in the number of chiasmata and an increase in terminal chiasmata at the first meiotic division might be followed by unequal segregation of univalents and that this was associated with increasing maternal age in CBA mice. These investigators speculated that gradients in oocyte production may be present during fetal and neonatal life, so that oocytes formed earliest ovulate first and have the highest chiasma frequency. Therefore, a greater proportion of the oocytes have a low chiasma frequency as the oocyte population is reduced with increasing age. Luthardt, Palmer, and Yu (1973) also found a decrease in chiasma and univalent frequency in aging mice and showed that the decrease in univalents was most common in small chromosomes which have fewer chiasmata. Since Goodlin (1965) found no increase in aneuploidy in the offspring of aged mice, these authors suggested that the decrease in implantation associated with increasing age might, in part, be the result of selection against blastocysts with univalents at this stage of development.

Noyes (1970) discussed the possibility that oocytes that spend many years in the ovary may be more exposed to damage by viruses, autoantibodies, or irradiation than are those ovulated early in life. Convincing proof, however, is lacking at the present time.

Although oocytes in the ovary are capable of remaining viable and normal for years during the prolonged prophase of the first meiotic division, their life is reduced to hours in laboratory animals after the second meiotic division begins unless the ovum is fertilized (Austin, 1970). A detailed consideration of this microaging process is beyond the scope of this paper, but it is important to note that there is evidence from studies of laboratory animals that aneuploidy and abnormal development are more common following delayed fertilization.

Salisbury (1965), Lanman (1968b), and Austin (1970) have reviewed this literature together with less satisfactory data from human studies.

Follicular Development. Talbert (1968) and Jones (1970) have summarized data which show that the number of Graafian follicles forming each cycle in laboratory mice, rats, and hamsters decreases in old animals, but this decline does not typically take place until after reproductive capacity has been reduced due to uterine failure or loss of viability of ova.

Block (1952) studied follicular development in different ages of women and found that the number of follicles that reach at least 100μ in diameter decreases from childhood to the preclimacteric period. However, this decline is not as steep as the decline in primary follicles, so that the ratio of growing follicles to primary follicles changes from 1 to 50 at puberty to 1 to 3 in 39–45-year old women. The decline in growing follicles does not result in any significant change in the number of Graafian follicles forming each cycle in women 18 to 38 years old, but from 39 to 45 the decrease is appreciable.

Development of Graafian follicles does not ensure that ovulation will take place, and there is evidence that failure of this process increases with age. One pathological condition which has been shown to increase is development of follicular cysts. This change has been reported in aging rodents by Dickie, Atkinson, and Fekete (1957), Burack and Wolfe (1959), and Adams (1970) and in humans by Hertig (1944) and Riley (1964).

Another abnormality which is more prevalent in aging rodents is luteinization of follicles without ovulation. Thung (1961) found corpora lutea with entrapped ova in 28 percent of 18 to 21-month-old mice but in only 5 percent of 16 to 17-month-old animals. A similar increase was shown in rats by Burack and Wolfe (1959). The development of follicular cysts and entrapped ova may be due to an inappropriate balance of gonadotrophic hormones which is essential for ovulation, but failure of the ovary to respond properly to a normal stimulus is also possible. It is important to emphasize that neither cyst formation nor luteinization without ovulation appears to be a significant factor in causing a decline in reproductive capacity in rodents because uterine failure or loss of viability of ova generally occurs at an earlier age.

Corpora Lutea. Jones (1970) has summarized the evidence that fewer corpora lutea develop per cycle in aging rodents, but this change does not typically occur until reproductive capacity has greatly decreased.

Several different studies have been undertaken in an attempt to determine the functional capability of corpora lutea of old rodents to maintain pregnancy. Harman and Talbert (1970) found a correlation between morphological changes in corpora lutea of pregnancy and a decline in the number of implantation sites per corpus luteum in aging mice. However, there was no evidence that these changes were associated with a decline in circulating estrogen or progesterone. Thorneycroft and Soderwall (1969b) reported that the corpora lutea in pregnant, aged hamsters displayed markedly reduced secondary growth at 12 to 14 days of pregnancy, indicating that there may be a quantitative rather than a qualitative change in luteal tissue in aging hamsters. This observation lends some support to the work of Blaha (1968), who found that ovariectomized aged hamsters which had received ovarian transplants from young adult donors were better able to achieve implantation of transferred morulae than were aged hamsters with intact ovaries. This worker concluded that the greater number of corpora lutea in the grafted ovaries might have been responsible for the increased number of implantation sites in the grafted animals.

In a different approach to the same question, Finn (1963) tied off one uterine tube in aging mice to increase the ratio of corpora lutea to embryos. This experimental procedure failed to increase the reproductive life span of these animals. From these results, it was suggested that deficiency of luteal tissue is not a major factor in causing embryonic loss in aging mice. This concept is supported by the work of Spilman, Larson, Concannon, and Foote (1972), who studied the relationship between the level of progesterone in plasma and corpora lutea and the number of implantation sites in young and aged rabbits. This study indicated that the corpora lutea in aged rabbits were just as functional as those in young adults except when no viable fetuses were present, in which case plasma progesterone was sharply reduced by the 18th day of pregnancy. These investigators concluded that luteal failure in this species was secondary to the death of the fetuses.

Luteal failure in women approaching the menopause appears to be a more common occurrence than in younger women. Using basal body temperature, Collett, Wertenberger, and Fiske (1954) found evidence that corpora lutea in such women may be less stable, resulting in shortened cycles or early interruption of pregnancy. It is tempting to blame this type of luteal failure on LH deficiency, but a decline in the ability of the ovary to respond to this hormone has not been ruled out.

Novak (1970) studied ovaries of 200 women past the age of 50 and found that 46 had corpora lutea which were judged to be less than 6 months old. Twenty-one of the 46 showed evidence of a secretory endometrium, but it was conjectured that such progesterone stimulation may have come from luteinized stromal cells.

Although the aged human ovary is generally fibrotic (Figure 3), there may be hyperplasia of stromal and interstitial cells several years after the menopause. Bigelow (1958) reviewed the evidence that stromal cells are the source of estrogens after the menopause. More recently, Mestwerdt, Brandau, and Müller (1972) observed that stromal tissue cells of early postmenopausal women often possess well-developed smooth endoplasmic reticulum and tubular, vesicular mitochondria, which are believed to be indicative of steroid secretion. This conclusion was supported by the presence of endometrial stimulation. In another study Lajos, Illei, Kecskés, Görcs, Mutschler, and Kóbor (1963) found that ovaries of women with significant levels of urinary estrogen

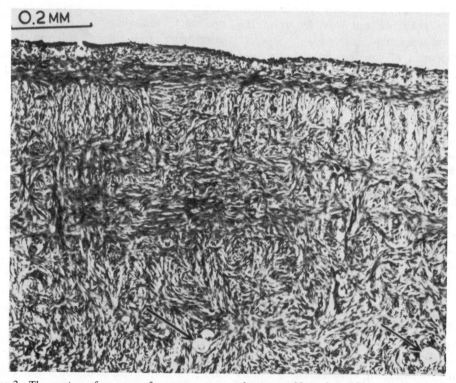

Figure 3. The cortex of an ovary from a menopausal women. Note dense fibrous nature of stroma. Arrows indicate two primordial follicles. (Reproduced [by permission] from Franchi, L. L. 1970. The ovary. *In*, E. E. Philipp, J. Barnes, and M. Newton (eds.), *Scientific Foundation of Obstetrics and Gynecology*, Fig. 26, Section III, Chap. 1. Philadelphia: F. A. Davis.)

showed diffuse or nodular thecal cell hyperplasia, direct assay of which confirmed the presence of estrogen. Following ovariectomy, urinary estrogen could no longer be detected.

Hilus cells, which closely resemble and appear to be embryologically related to the Leydig cells in the testis, also may become hyperplastic after the menopause. Such hyperplasia has been associated by Lenters (1954) with testosterone secretion and consequent masculinization.

Green (1957) and Biggers, Finn, and McLaren (1962a) have described the presence of large cells containing lipochrome pigment, which may be remnants of corpora lutea, in aging mouse ovaries. Thung, Boot, and Mühlbock (1956) stressed the accumulation of ceroid pigment and amyloid deposits in the ovaries of old mice.

Ovarian Sensitivity to Gonadotrophic Hormones. There is no question that the human postmenopausal ovary usually shows little response to gonadotrophic hormones. Paulson, Leach, Sandberg, and Maddock (1955) did find an increase in urinary estrogens in postmenopausal women following administration of gonadotrophin, but more recently Mattingly and Huang (1969) showed that cultured stromal tissue from postmenopausal ovaries produced only very small quantities of estrogens when 4-androstene-3, 17-dione-7H^3 was used as a substrate and no estrogens with pregnanolone-7H^3 as a substrate. With both substrates, considerably more androgenic steroid was produced. The low output of estradiol by postmenopausal ovaries has been associated with the small number of follicles in such organs but direct proof of this hypothesis has not been obtained. (Sherman and Korenman, 1975). These data suggest that any significant levels of plasma or urinary estrogen in postmenopausal women may be the result of conversion of androgens to estrogens at an extragonadal site or from suprarenal secretion. Another interpretation of these data is that estrogen formation from ovarian stromal tissue requires the presence of gonadotrophin which was not added to the culture medium.

There are some data which indicate that the ovaries of aging laboratory animals are also not as responsive as those in young adults. Ortiz

(1955) and Green (1957) found that the ovaries of 12 to 14-month-old hamsters and mice showed a smaller weight increase in response to gonadotrophin than did young adults. In a more recent investigation, Adams (1970) reported that rabbits over 4 years of age show a reduced number of ovulations in response to FSH.

Estrogens and Progestins in the Blood and Urine. Pincus, Romanoff, and Carlo (1954) and Furuhjelm (1966) found that there is a decline in urinary estrogens with increasing age in 40 to 60 and 45 to 75-year-old women respectively (Table 5). Very small amounts of estrogens have also been detected after menopause by gas-liquid chromatography (Kaplan and Hreshchyshen, 1971). By radioimmunoassay, Procope and Adlercreutz (1969) detected no difference in mean values for urinary estrogens among six age groups of postmenopausal women and a group of ovariectomized women, all of whom had an atrophic endometrium and normal liver function. Furthermore, Rader, Flickinger, deVilla, Mikuta and Mikhail (1973) and Judd, Judd, Lucas and Yen (1974) detected little difference in the concentration of estrone and estradiol in the ovarian vein plasma and in peripheral plasma in postmenopausal women. The low level of urinary estrogen which was found in these women must therefore have come from extraovarian sources. In support of this concept, Grodin, Siiteri, and MacDonald (1973) found that estrone is the principal circulating estrogen in postmenopausal women and that the level of this hormone could be accounted for almost exclusively by aromatization of plasma androstenedione. This conversion increases with age (Hemsell, Grodin, Brenner, Siiteri and McDonald, 1974) and the precursor appears to be primarily of adrenal cortical origin (Vermeulen, 1976).

Longcope (1971) studied the metabolic clearance rate (MCR) and the blood production rate (BPR) of estradiol and estrone in young women and in women over 70. They found a 25 percent reduction in the MCR for both hormones in the old group. In spite of the slower clearance in aged women, the plasma concentration of estradiol fell to between 5 and 10

TABLE 5. EFFECT OF AGE ON URINARY ESTROGEN EXCRETION IN WOMEN.

Age	No.	Estradiol[a]	Estrone[a]	Estriol[a]
20–29	25	9.6 ± 1.6	6.1 ± 1.2	16.6 ± 2.8
30–39	21	10.2 ± 2.2	4.8 ± 0.8	19.5 ± 3.4
40–49	17	4.7 ± 0.8	2.8 ± 0.5	11.3 ± 2.8
50–59	17	3.7 ± 0.8	2.2 ± 0.5	4.9 ± 1.1
60–69	18	2.3 ± 0.6	2.3 ± 0.5	2.0 ± 0.6
70–79	47	2.2 ± 0.3	2.2 ± 0.3	3.0 ± 0.4
80+	42	1.9 ± 0.3	1.6 ± 0.3	3.3 ± 0.5

[a]Rat units/24 hours ± Standard Error.
Data of Pincus, Romanoff, and Carlo, 1954.

percent of the level found in young women, whereas the less active steroid, estrone, dropped to only 25 to 30 percent of its former level. These results are not surprising since Baird, Uno, and Melby (1969) observed that the ovary is virtually the sole source of estradiol, whereas estrone is only partially of ovarian origin.

Uterus. The human uterus grows slowly from birth until puberty and then increases rapidly to the nulliparous adult size of about 8 X 4 X 2.5 cm. Lang and Aponte (1967) reported that following the menopause it often atrophies to as little as 1 cm in very old women. In this study the myometrial blood vessels were frequently observed to be thick-walled as a result of obliterative subintimal sclerosis, which was often associated with calcification of the media.

Dilts and Greene (1964) found that the relative amount of myometrial fibrous tissue does not increase with age or parity throughout reproductive life. Woessner (1963) also observed that total collagen and elastin as well as the wet weight of the uterus reach a maximum at around 30 years of age and remain constant until about 50. After this age, the net weight and the fibrous tissue decline by about 50 percent over the next 15 years.

The histological appearance of the postmenopausal human endometrium is subject to wide variation, which is largely dependent on the functional status of the ovary. McBride (1954) carried out a curettage on 1,521 postmenopausal women who had had no irregular bleeding and found that 31.5 percent had simple atrophy and an additional 40.7 percent had

inactive cystic glands (Figure 4). Active hyperplasia was confined almost exclusively to women who were in their first 5 years after the menopause, and only 1 percent showed any evidence of actively secreting glands which would be indicative of progesterone stimulation.

A large number of studies have shown that there is an increase in fibrous connective tissue in the uterus of laboratory animals (see Talbert, 1968 for references). This increase does not appear to be due to greater production of collagen since Kao, Chen Lu, Hitt, and McGavack (1962) found that collagen synthesis from rat uterine slices diminishes with age. The more likely explanation is that there is an increase in cross-linked collagen in aging uteri which resists degradation and turnover. Such a change has been demonstrated in aging rats by Schaub (1964-65). The concept of reduced breakdown of collagen is given further support by the work of Maurer and Foote (1972), who found that collagenase activity is reduced in the uterus of aging rabbits. The increase in the collagen content of aging mice does not appear to be related to the number of fetuses which have been carried since Finn, Fitch, and Harkness (1963) found no difference between barren and repeatedly pregnant horns of 2-year-old mice.

Greene (1941) observed that spontaneous uterine tumors occur with increasing frequency in aging rabbits. Adenomas and adenocarcinomas were found in 42 percent of 2 to 3-year-old does, and this percentage increased to 79 percent in 5 to 6-year-old animals. Adams (1965) has suggested that this high rate of tumorogenesis which has been observed in laboratory rabbits, usually in estrus, may be the result of unopposed estrogen action. It would be interesting to compare tumor development in such animals with repeatedly pregnant or pseudopregnant animals which have high levels of circulating progesterone.

There is still a paucity of information on age changes in the blood supply to the uterus, although a study of uterine blood flow in young and aged rabbits was conducted by Larson and Foote (1972) using the inert gas ([85]Krypton) wash-out technique. No difference was observed in 3, 6, and 30-month-old rabbits, but the blood flow was significantly

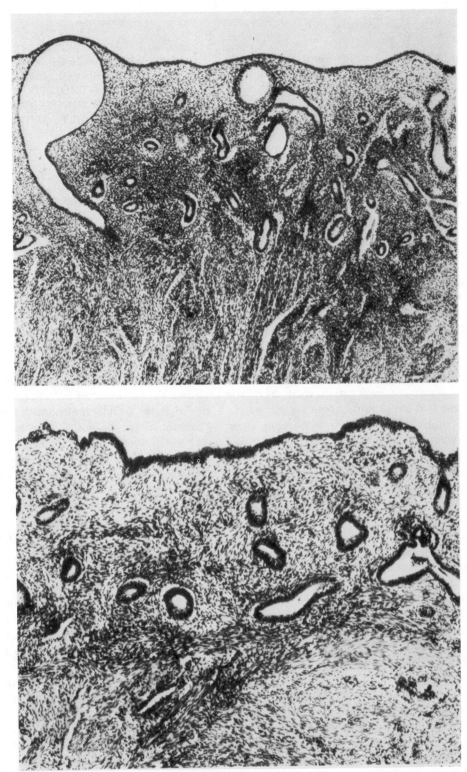

(a)

(b)

Figure 4. Types of postmenopausal endometria. (a) Nonfunctioning endometrium of woman 7 years after the menopause. Note thin epithelium, isolated cystic glands, and fibrous stroma. (b) Distinct glandular proliferation and dense stroma in endometrium of woman 1 year after the menopause. (From Witt, H. J. Structural elements and general function of the endometrium. Light microscope morphology. *In,* H. Schmidt-Matthiesen (ed.), *The Normal Human Endometrium.* Copyright Used with permission of McGraw-Hill Book Company.)

slower in 45-month-old animals. The authors suggested that inadequate blood supply might contribute to reproductive decline by reducing the nutritional and hormonal support of this organ.

Increasing quantities of pigment deposits have been observed in the uterus of aging animals. Biggers, Finn, and McLaren (1962a) found such granules, which gave a strong positive reaction for ferric iron, in all layers of the uterine wall of mice. However, this condition was more prevalent in the uterine horn which had been repeatedly pregnant than in the opposite horn which had been barren throughout reproductive life. Bal and Getty (1973) found increasing quantities of lipofuscin associated with increasing age in the myometrium and in the walls of large endometrial veins of pigs, but the role, if any, that such accumulations play in the functional deterioration of the uterus has not been established.

Although the investigations cited above have shown that recognizable morphological and biochemical changes do occur in the aging uterus of laboratory animals, these changes have not been definitely linked to the decline in the ability of the uterus to support pregnancy. However, there is good evidence that failure of implantation and failure to maintain pregnancy after implantation are more common in the uterus of older animals. This problem has been studied by transplanting fertilized ova from the uterus of young donors into the uterus of young and old adult hosts. Blaha (1964b), Talbert and Krohn (1966), and Maurer and Foote (1971) uniformly found that the uteri of old hamsters, mice, and rabbits are far less able to implant and maintain embryos until term than are uteri of young adults of these species. These data are summarized in Table 6.

The results of all these studies support the concept that, at least in common laboratory animals, there are age changes in the uterus which reduce its ability to support pregnancy. In this respect, it is important to know whether these changes are related to the number of litters which have been borne and/or the size of these litters. Does the uterus age as a result of use? Asdell, Bogart, and Sperling, (1941) approached this problem by delaying breeding in

TABLE 6. PERCENTAGE OF OVA SURVIVING TO TERM FOLLOWING TRANSPLANTATION FROM YOUNG ADULT DONORS TO THE UTERUS OF YOUNG AND OLD ADULTS OF THE SAME SPECIES.

Age of host	Mouse[a]	Hamster[b]	Rabbit[c]	Rabbit[d]
Young adult	48	49.2	50.0	48.1
Old	14	8.3	1.5	37.2

[a] Data of Talbert and Krohn, 1966.
[b] Data of Blaha, 1964b.
[c] Data of Adams, 1970.
[d] Data of Maurer and Foote, 1971.

a group of rats until they were 9 months of age and comparing their reproductive performance with a group bred first at 100 days of age. There was no indication that sparing the uterus for about 6 months resulted in the extension of reproductive life. Finn (1963) provided supporting data when he observed that mice which were kept virgin or pseudopregnant until they were 9 months of age did not perform better than mice which were bred continuously throughout their reproductive life.

Another approach to this problem has been to determine if crowding of the uterus during several pregnancies will result in a more rapid decline in the ability of the uterus to maintain pregnancy. Such a condition can be readily achieved in laboratory animals with a bicornuate uterus by unilateral ovariectomy. This procedure results in nearly doubling the number of eggs ovulated into one uterine cornu, and there is a consequent large number of implantations in one side of the uterus. This technique was used by Jones and Krohn (1960) and Biggers, Finn, and McLaren (1962a) in mice and by Blaha (1964a) in hamsters. All of these studies showed that the number of litters produced was considerably less in the animals where the uterus was crowded than in others where the uterine horns carried a normal load. In none of these studies was there any indication that the reduction in the number of litters was the result of exhaustion of oocytes in the remaining ovary. There is evidence that overcrowding of the uterus can cut short its reproductive capacity, but there is no indication that normal use is a major influence on the length of time that it is able to efficiently support pregnancy. The reason for the overcrowding effect is not known, but a study of the local blood supply in such a uterus, as suggested by Biggers (1969), is worthy of investigation.

Probably the most common stage of pregnancy for reproductive failure in aging laboratory animals is at implantation. This has been well documented in the hamster by Connors, Thorpe, and Soderwall (1972), who found that the mean number of ova in the uterine tube 56 hours after ovulation was 6.6 in young and 4.9 in old hamsters. At 132 hours, however, there were 6.1 implantation sites in the young adult hamsters and only 2.8 in the old aminals. At the implantation stage in mice, the uterine lumen is normally closed so that the blastocysts appear to be pressed against the luminal epithelium. Finn and Martin (1969) studied this closure in ovariectomized young adults and in 19 to 21-month-old mice which had been treated with progesterone and estrogen. In this experiment, all of ten young adults showed good closure, whereas only one out of six old animals showed this response (Figure 5). The authors speculated that this age change might influence implantation.

Another critical aspect of the implantation process which has been shown to change with age is the ability of the uterus to undergo the decidualization reaction. Qualitative and quantitative studies of this reaction have been carried out in aging mice and hamsters. Finn (1966) was the first to show that the uterus of 14 to 16-month-old mice which had produced six litters was less responsive to an artificial decidualizing stimulus (arachis oil injected into the uterine lumen) than was the uterus of 4 to 5-month-old virgin animals. In a later study, Shapiro and Talbert (1974) found that C57BL/6J mice show a decline in the size of the decidual response at 9 months, which corresponds to the age when reproductive capacity begins to decline in this strain. Blaha (1967) also found that the uterus of pseudopregnant 15.5 to 18-month-old multiparous and virgin hamsters was less responsive to intraluminal oil or air than was the uterus of 4 to 7-month-old hamsters.

Hollander and Strong (1950), Sugiyama (1961), Biggers, Finn, and McLaren (1962b), Finn (1962), and Talbert (1971) have shown in mice and Thorneycroft and Soderwall (1969a) in the hamster that there is also an increase in resorbtions primarily around midpregnancy in aging animals, but the reason for vulnerability at this stage has not been established.

In conclusion, it is clear that the potential duration of fertility in women is limited ultimately by the irreversible exhaustion of oocytes in the ovaries. Although some viable oocytes may survive through the menopause, it is well documented that pregnancy is more difficult to achieve and abortions increase in women during the few years preceding the menopause. Such problems are undoubtedly due in part to a decline in the viability and loss of ova but also may be the result of uterine failure. This failure may in turn be due to intrinsic changes in the uterus or to inadequate hormonal or nutritional support. This premenopausal period is therefore more comparable to the period of reproductive decline in laboratory animals, which is characterized universally by failure of the uterus to support pregnancy with a variable contribution in different species from decline in viability of ova.

Vagina. The vagina of postmenopausal women undergoes considerable contraction, so that the organ is shorter and the caliber of the lumen smaller. Lang and Aponte (1967) reported that there is a marked loss of elasticity which may be related to fragmentation of elastic fibers in the tunica propria, although Toth and Gimes (1964) stated that elastic fibers appeared to be unimpaired.

In the absence of a significant level of circulating estrogen the postmenopausal vaginal epithelium becomes thin, pale, and dry. Lang and Aponte (1967) observed that the epithelial cells frequently contain pycnotic nuclei and show increased beta glucuronidase, acid phosphatase, and nonspecific esterase activity. However, the significance of these enzyme changes has not been determined.

During reproductive life as well as during the postreproductive period, considerable attention has been paid to the exfoliation of cells from

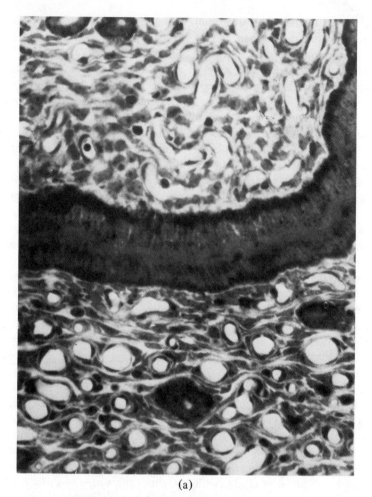

(a)

Figure 5. Uterine luminal closure in mice. (a) Tightly closed uterine lumen typical of young adult at about time of implantation. Tissue fixed by perfusion with gluteraldehyde. (b) Open uterine lumen typical of many aged mice at time of implantation. Gluteraldehyde fixation. (The plate figures are reproduced from an article by C. A. Finn and L. Martin entitled "The cellular response of the uterus of the aged mouse to oestrogen and progesterone," *J. Reprod. Fert.* (1969), **20,** opposite p. 546, by permission of the authors and Editor.)

the vaginal epithelium. The proportion of basal, parabasal, intermediate, and superficial cells which are sloughed from the vaginal epithelium varies during the menstrual cycle. The basal cells predominate during the proliferative portion of the cycle, whereas high levels of estrogen near midcycle result in a preponderance of cornified superficial cells. After ovulation, the cells tend to cluster and become basophilic with large vesicular nuclei.

With increasing years after the menopause Masukawa (1960) noted a decreasing number of superficial cells in the smear. However, McLen-nan and McLennan (1971) found that 9 percent of women over 75 years of age still had vaginal smears which were composed almost exclusively of intermediate cells, and 25 percent had some superficial cells. The presence of these cells is usually interpreted to indicate a higher than normal level of estrogen in the circulation, but Procope (1970) has pointed out that vaginal smears are not always in agreement with plasma estrogen determinations, since changing of inactive to active steroids by the target organ or changes in target organ sensitvity must be considered.

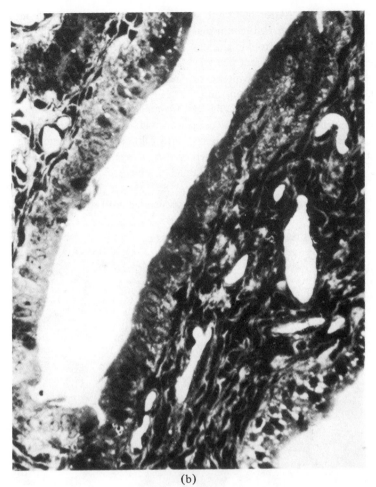

(b)

Figure 5 (*Continued*)

Age changes in the rat vaginal smear have been studied extensively by Mandl (1961) and Aschheim (1961). During the postreproductive period, considerable variation in the smear has been noted which aids in identifying the condition of the ovary. One type of smear consists of a continuous high percentage of cornified epitheliel cells which appear to result from uninterruped estrogen secretion by the ovary and little or no progesterone. Another condition commonly observed in aged rats is repetitive pseudopregnancy during which time corpora lutea are inferred to continually secrete progesterone because of a psuedopregnant-type of vaginal smear (noncornified epithelial cells and leucocytes as well as mucus). Finally, in some very old rats, the vaginal epithelium and the ovary may become atrophic, and often few cells are found in the smear. Thung, Boot, and Mühlbock (1956) studied the vaginal smears of several inbred and hybrid strains of mice and found that in some strains, cyclic activity often continued throughout the lifespan, but these cycles tended to become less regular in very old mice. These investigators also observed that the vagina of old mice was less sensitive to either local or systemic administration of estrogen.

Uterine Tubes. Novak and Everett (1928) made one of the earliest extensive studies of this organ. These authors noted that the ciliated and secretory cells, which are the predominant cells in the epithelium, do not atrophy for several years after the menopause, and there is little evidence of secretion. After 60, there is lessening in the height of the epithelium and gradual loss of cilia, but these atrophic changes do not progress uniformly in different portions of the uterine tube. The earliest evidence of decline in function is found typically in the isthmus region where Shimoyama (1965) noted that the mitochondria of the secretory cells tended to swell and secretory droplets were no longer evident. This observation was confirmed by scanning electron microscopy by Patek, Nilsson, and Johannisson (1972), who noted large areas of flattened epithelium with no cilia

or indication of secretion in the isthmus of women 20 to 30 years after the menopause. At the same time, there was little or no evidence of deciliation in the ampullar or infundibular regions (Figure 6).

Mammary Glands. The human breast during reproductive life consists of glandular, stromal and adipose tissue. Beginning as early as 35 years of age, there is a gradual replacement of glands by fat.

By far the most important clinical problem associated with the aging breast in women is the

(a)

Figure 6. Scanning electron microscopy of uterine tube of pre and postmenopausal women. (a) Ampulla of uterine tube of premenopausal woman. Note numerous ciliated cells and abundant secretory material. (b) Ampulla of uterine tube of woman 14 years after the menopause. Note persistence of cilia and absence of secretory material. (c) Isthmus of uterine tube of woman 27 years after the menopause. Note absence of both cilia and secretory material and flattened hexagonal appearance of cells. (From Patek, E., Nilsson, L., and Johannisson, E. 1972. Scanning electron microscopic study of the human fallopian tube. *Fertility and Sterility*, **23**, 719–733.)

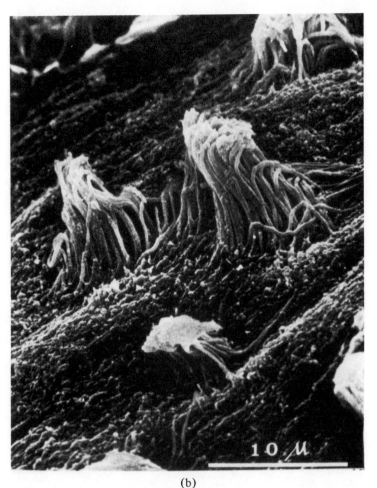

(b)

Figure 6 (*Continued*)

increasing risk of malignancy with the maximum risk occurring after 70 according to Trichopoulos, MacMahon, and Cole (1972). It is beyond the scope of this review to discuss all the clinical studies which provide indirect evidence that some type of breast carcinoma depend on estrogen stimulation. However, benign hyperplastic changes in the breasts of elderly women have recently been associated with breast carcinoma or its subsequent development (Tellem, Shane, and Imbriglia, 1965). The authors considered it likely that these conditions might both be due to continued presence of circulating estrogens from ovarian or adrenal sources. However, blood levels of these hormones were not studied. Clearly more work is needed to support this hypothesis.

Kramer and Rush (1973) found a clear relationship between intraductal hyperplasia and subsequent development of atypical hyperplasia and carcinoma in 70 women over 70 years of age. The authors felt that stimulation at this age was most likely from adrenal estrogens, but other possibilities such as conversion of androgens to estrogens in the plasma were not explored. Furthermore, Korenman and Dukes (1970) made the interesting observation that certain human mammary neoplasms contain a much larger quantity of highly specific estrogen-binding protein than is found in nonneoplastic breast tissue. They suggested that such tumors might be most favorably influenced by ovariectomy or hypophysectomy.

Schneider (1970) compared the risk of breast

(c)

Figure 6 (*Continued*)

cancer in 1,632 women and 460 female dogs. Up to the menopause and the corresponding age in the dog, the risk was similar in both species. After this age the risk increased at a slower rate in the human, yet continued unabated in the dog. At the age of the menopause (48 to 51 years) the risk of breast cancer in women was 149/100,000, and in dogs at a comparable age (8 years), it was 226/100,000. In women the risk increased to only about 200/100,000 in the next 16 years whereas the risk increased to over 1000/100,000 during a comparable relative age span in dogs. Although comparisons of this type between species are difficult to interpret, the authors suggest that this difference might be due to continuing high levels of estrogen secretion in the dog whereas the human level of circulating estrogen is typically much reduced. Indirect support for this suggestion was provided by Trichopoulos, MacMahon and Cole (1972) who gathered data which indicated that ovariectomy in the human before 35 years of age reduced the risk of carcinoma to ⅓ thirty or more years later. Furthermore, women with a natural menopause before 45 had only half the risk of women with a menopause after 55.

The development of mammary gland tumors in rats and mice also appear to be promoted by ovarian hormones. Pullinger (1961) found that late ovariectomy greatly reduced the incidence of mammary carcinoma and adenoma in C_3H mice and that administration of estrone returned the incidence to the noncastrate level.

Durbin, Williams, Jeung, and Arnold, (1966) noted that ovariectomy reduced the incidence of mammary gland tumors from 71 percent to less than 7 percent, and ovariectomy plus adrenalectomy eliminated all tumors in aging Charles River (Sprague-Dawley) rats. In this study the incidence of neoplasms in virgin and uniparous rats were similar. However, Howell and Mandl (1961), using the Birmingham strain of rats, found that multiparous females had markedly fewer tumors and less benign hyperplasia than did virgin animals. This observation supports the concept that unopposed estrogen secretion tends to promote tumor development and that this tendency can be greatly reduced by the frequent presence of progesterone-secreting corpora lutea which are found only during pregnancy, pseudopregnancy, and lacation.

In recent years evidence has accumulated that the incidence of spontaneous mammary adenomas or fibroadenomas, which are common in Sprague-Dawley and other strains of aging rats, can be substantially increased by raising the level of plasma prolactin. This can be brought about by grafting of multiple pituitary glands (Welsch, Jenkins, and Meites, 1970), by placing lesions in the median eminence area in the hypothalamus (Welsch, Nagasawa, and Meites, 1970) or by utilization of central acting drugs such as reserpine which increases prolactin secretion (Quadri and Meites, 1975). Administration of low doses of estrogen has also been shown to stimulate release of prolactin, whereas higher doses of estrogen, although still stimulating the release of prolactin, apparently reduces its tumor-producing effect on the mammary tissue (Meites, 1972). The important role of prolactin in stimulating mammary tumor growth has been further substantiated by Quadri and Meites (1975), who demonstrated that the age of onset of spontaneous mammary tumors could be delayed by drugs such as L-dopa, which inhibits the release of prolactin.

Sex Steriod Therapy After the Menopause

Clinical studies of sex hormone therapy for the treatment of the human female during the climacteric and continuing throughout the postmenopausal period are extremely numerous,

and the conclusions reached are highly divergent. At one extreme are Wilson and Wilson (1972), who favor hormone treatment to the extent that menstrual cycles may be maintained from puberty to very old age. At the other extreme are investigators such as Pundel (1969), who are opposed to the use of sex hormones for the treatment of transitory menopausal symptoms on the basis that such treatment could prevent the natural adaptation of the body to a new condition. It is indisputable that menopause results in drastic loss of estrogens (Kaplan and Hreshchyshen, 1971) and that a great many cell functions are thereby affected. Normal longer-range consequences of estrogen loss include hot flushes (Martin, Burnier, Segre, and Huix, 1971), atrophy of the uterus and vagina (Lin, So-Bosita, Brar, and Roblete, 1973), and loss of the morning surge of growth hormone (Frantz and Rabkin, 1965; also see Chapter 14 in this volume). Many of these changes are reversed by steroid replacement therapy in most women (Martin et al., 1971; Lin et al., 1973). Probably the majority of investigators favor a middle-of-the-road approach, in which estrogen, estrogen-progesterone, or estrogen-androgen regimens are used selectively for alleviation of symptoms of the climacteric, such as hot flushes.

The significant increase in the incidence of arteriosclerosis and acute osteoporosis in postmenopausal women has prompted the use of sex steroids on a long-term basis in an attempt to lessen this problem. However, Novak (1967) examined a group of 85 women who had been ovariectomized at different ages and found no evidence of an increase in either arteriosclerosis or osteoporosis. In addition, there is not clear evidence that administration of estrogens after the menopause will restore the protection against vascular disease that seems to exist in premenopausal women even though the high alpha to beta lipoprotein ratio which exists in the plasma of young women is restored. Saville (1968) found that there is also little convincing evidence that estrogen therapy will be beneficial for the treatment of previously established osteoporosis, even though calcium excretion is reduced. However, Meema (1968) believes that this disease can be delayed if estrogens and androgens are given before the disease becomes manifest.

The possible role of sex hormone therapy in the stimulation of endometrial and breast cancer appears to be undecided at the present time. Cupr, Druckmuller, and Kucera (1969) and Schleyer-Saunders (1971) believe that tumor development is not increased if care is taken in the selection of women for long-term treatment, but Novak (1967) and Staemmler and Willie-Schörcher (1966) are more skeptical.

Estrogen alone or in combination with progesterone or androgen have all produced different degrees of endometrial stimulation and subsequent irregular bleeding in many instances. New synthetic steroids and some non-steroidal substances have been recently tested for the treatment of climacteric and menopausal problems, yet none appears to be completely free of annoying side effects (Lin *et al*, 1973; Kistner, 1973).

MALE REPRODUCTIVE SYSTEM

The decline in reproductive function in the human male is generally a gradual process, often decreasing with the general fitness of the individual. In many cases all parts of the system retain sufficient functional capability so that reproduction is possible into extreme old age. Seymour, Duffy, and Koerner (1935) reported a case of a 94-year-old man who carried out a successful paternity.

There has been less investigation of the effect of age on gonadotrophin secretion in aging males than in females. In general the increase with age in circulating gonadotrophins appears to be smaller and occurs more gradually, which suggests that the negative feedback of gonadal hormones on gonadotrophin secretion is maintained to a considerable degree in older men. Nevertheless Schlach, Parlow, Boon, and Reichlin (1968) and also Nieschlag, Kley, Wiegelmann, Solbach, and Krüskemper (1973) found an increase in plasma LH but not FSH in elderly men. Recently, however, Rubens, Dhont, and Vermeulen (1974) found higher levels of both FSH and LH in men over 65 than in men under 50. In contrast to these changes in men, Finch (1975) could detect no change in LH or prolactin in 8 to 28-month-old C57BL/6J mice.

Testis

The rate and age of decline in function of the human testis are quite varible. In fact Harbitz (1973a) could find no correlation between testis weight and age in a study of 182 men over 40.

In male animals, in contrast to the female, there is a constant replenishment of male germ cells from puberty to old age. The length of time required for the male gamete to develop from a spermatogonium to a spermatozoan in the testis does not appear to be influenced by the age of the individual but is species-specific. This process typically requires several weeks, whereas the completion of oogenesis may require 45 to 50 years. This sex difference may explain why there is little evidence that the age of the father is an important factor in the production of aneuploid babies. Nevertheless, this problem requires considerably more investigation before the male gamete can be exonerated from a role in embryonic deaths or major abnormalities of presently unknown etiology.

Sasano and Ichijo (1969) found that 90 percent of the seminiferous tubules had spermatids in 20 to 39 year-old men. This incidence dropped to about 50 percent during the fifth decade and remained at this level until about 70. After this age, there was a gradual decline to near 10 percent in men over 80. Spermiogenesis also continues into old age; Blum (1936) found spermatozoa in the ejaculate of 68.5 percent of men between 60 and 70, 59.5 percent between 70 and 80, and 48 percent between 80 and 90.

Bishop (1970) observed that there is thickening of the basement membrane and tunica propria of the seminiferous tubules in the aging human testis. This is followed by thinning of the spermatogenic epithelium, decrease in the diameter of the tubules, and eventual obliteration of the tubule lumen (Figure 7). There is also evidence of progressive intertubular fibrosis. Burgi and Hedinger (1959) noted that these aging changes occur frequently in focal areas with completely fibrotic tubules adjacent to normal ones.

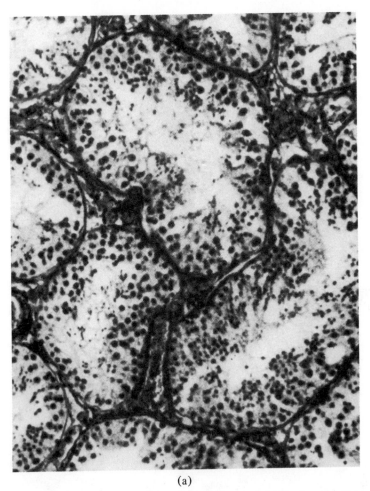

(a)

Figure 7. Variation in functional condition of seminiferous tubules in aged men. (a) Persisting active spermatogenesis in seminiferous tubules of 94-year-old man. (b) Atrophic and sclerosed seminiferous tubles from 91-year-old man. (From Burgi, Von H., and Hedinger, C. 1959. Histologische Hodenveränderugen im hohen Alter. *Schweiz. Med. Wochschr.,* **89**, 1236–1239.)

Sasano and Ichijo (1969) and Suoranta (1971) found that degenerative areas in the testis were associated with fewer capillaries, suggesting that inadequate blood supply might be a factor in this process. Furthermore, Ewing (1967) reported that the blood flow in the rabbit testis declined from 10.7 ml/gram of testis in 6-month-old animals to 4.3 ml/gram in 3-year-old (middle-aged) rabbits. Additional work is clearly necessary, however, to determine if aging changes in the testis are the result or the cause of a reduction in blood supply.

There is conflicting data with respect to age changes in the number of Leydig cells. Harbitz (1973b) observed some decrease in the popula-

tion of these cells in very old men, but Sokal (1964) found no alteration with age in a study of men up to 85 years of age. However, there does appear to be a decline in the ability of these cells to produce testosterone in response to gonadotrophin in aged men. Nieschlag, *et al.* (1973) could find no decline in the production of this androgen following gonadotrophin administration until 60, but after this age a decrease was noted. Longcope (1973) also observed that administration of gonadotrophin to young and old men resulted in higher levels of testosterone and 17β-estradiol in the young group, yet the percentage increase over the pre-injection level was the same in the two age

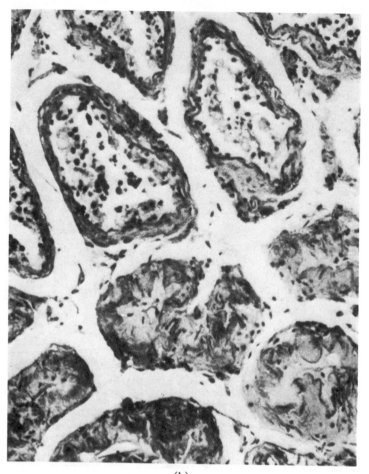

(b)

Figure 7 (*Continued*)

groups. Conversely, Rubens, Dhont, and Vermeulen (1974) found a smaller percentage as well as absolute increase in plasma testosterone following gonadotrophin administration in old men. Less testosterone secretion was also noted following gonadotrophin secretion in 36-month-old rabbits than in young adults (Ewing, Johnson, Desjardins, and Clegg, 1972).

Support of the concept of an age decline in androgen synthesis by Leydig cells was obtained by Piotti, Ghiringhelli, and Magrini (1967). These investigators observed that 3β hydroxysteroid dehydrogenase activity, which is involved in androgen synthesis, decreased in these cells in men over 72. Collins, Bell, and Tsang (1972) also found a decrease in the activity of this enzyme in the Leydig cells of 15-month-old rats.

Much less information is available on aging of the Sertoli cells. Lynch and Scott (1950) did find, however, that the lipid content of these cells remains high into old age, whereas the lipid content of Leydig cells begins to decline by 35 years of age in some cases. The Sertoli cells have been reported to be a source of estrogen, but firm proof is still lacking.

In contrast to the ovum, which has a very limited postovulation life span unless fertilized, the male germ cells undergo a period of physiological maturation of several days to a few weeks as they pass through the epididymis. Only after ejaculation into the female vagina does the life span of these cells become a matter of hours to a few days, which is comparable to the status of ovulated mammalian eggs. For a detailed discussion of this "microaging" process, the reader is referred to articles by Salisbury (1965), Lanman (1968a), and Bishop (1970).

Plasma Testicular Steriods

There is increasing evidence that secretion of testosterone decreases in elderly men. This was shown directly by Hollander and Hollander (1958), who compared testosterone levels in spermatic vein blood of young and old men. Kent and Acone (1965) found no age difference in plasma testosterone; however they did observe a decline in the metabolic clearance rate (MCR) so that the blood production rate (BPR) must have declined with age. Longcope (1973), Pirke and Doerr (1973), and Vermeulen, Rubens, and Verdonck (1972) all found lower levels of plasma testosterone in elderly men. The results of the study of Vermeulen, Rubens, and Verdonck are shown in Table 7.

Vermeulen, Rubens, and Verdonck (1972), as well as Pirke and Doerr (1973), also made the observation that the capacity of testosterone-binding globulin (TeBG) increases with age, which results in a smaller percentage of free testosterone in the plasma of aging men (Table 7). In addition there is evidence from the work of Vermeulen, Verdonck, Van der Straeten, and Orie (1969) that the age increase in the capacity of TeBG is the result and not the cause of decreasing plasma testosterone levels. Recently Nelson, Latham, and Finch (1975) reported that the plasma level of testosterone in healthy

TABLE 7. PLASMA T[a] LEVELS, FREE T FRACTION, AND CAPACITY OF TeBG[b] IN MEN.

Age yr	T ng/100 ml	FREE T %	CAPACITY TeBG 10^{-8} M
20–50	633 ± 25[c]	2.08 ± 0.8[c]	5.2 ± 0.07[c]
50–60	582 ± 62	} 1.68 ± 0.9	6.5 ± 0.8
60–70	462 ± 70		
70–80	373 ± 46	} 1.36 ± 0.9	8.2 ± 0.7
80–90	245 ± 26		

[a]Testosterone.
[b]Testosterone-binding globulin.
[c]Mean ± Standard error.
  Data of Vermeulen, Rubens, and Verdonck, 1972.

8 to 11-month and 29 to 31-month-old male C57BL/6J mice was similar, but diseased mice in both age groups had lower levels. This indicated that care must be taken to determine the general health of either humans or experimental animals before they are included in this type of study.

Less data are available on the effect of age on the plasma level of 17β-estradiol than on testosterone, and the data that are available are difficult to interpret. Nagai and Longcope (1971), Longcope (1973) Pirke and Doerr (1973), and Rubens, Dhont, and Vermeulen (1974) all found 21 to 24 picograms of estradiol per milliliter of plasma in men over 65. In younger men, the results ranged from 43 pg/ml in 21 to 30-year-old men (Longcope, 1973) to 14 pg/ml in men under 50 (Rubens, Dhont, and Vermeulen, 1974). Data is obviously needed on more uniformly aged young men in order to resolve this problem.

Epididymis

It is surprising that so little work has been done on the aging of this organ because of its important role in sperm maturation. Clermont and Flannery (1970) studied mitotic activity in the epithelium of the epididymis of 2½, 4, and 12-month-old rats and noted that the labeling indices of ^{3}H-thymidine injected animals was 2.2 percent in principal cells and 1.4 percent in basal cells. This dropped to 0.18 percent in principal cells and 0.42 percent in basal cells of 12-month-old rats. The label stayed in the epithelium for at least 50 days, indicating that few cells are extruded or lost by degeneration. Mitotic indices also fell off greatly with age in both the principal and the basal cells. Altogether, these data indicate that this organ is growing slowly during adult life with little evidence of cell renewal.

Seminal Vesicle

Nilsson (1962) made a detailed study of morphological age changes in the human seminal vesicle. He found that there is little alteration from childhood to puberty. In adults, the fluid capacity of the gland increases from 1.75 ml in the upper teens to 5 ml in 21 to 60-year-old men and then decreases to a mean of about 2.25 ml in aged men.

In prepubertal boys, the wall of the seminal vesicle is quite thick compared to the lumen. It then decreases with age. The mucosal folds, which are numerous in young men, tend to decrease in number between 30 and 40 and may be absent in the seminal vesicles of aged men. The epithelium decreases in height with age, and the subepithelial connective tissue replaces the muscle layer in the wall. Alveoli are commonly seen as irregularities in the mucosa of young men, yet as early as 40 years of age, they decrease in size beginning in the distal portion of the organ and proceeding toward the duct. Andrew (1971) reported that yellow pigment granules accumulate with increasing age in the columnar cells but not in the basal cells of the epithelium. Goldman (1963) observed that amyloid is frequently seen in the wall of the seminal vesicle of men past middle age.

Very little attention has been paid to aging of the seminal vesicles of laboratory animals, but Finch and Girgis (1974) observed that this organ was greatly enlarged in over 60 percent of C57BL mice which were over 28 months of age. This hypertrophy was due entirely to fluid accumulation, since the empty gland weighed the same as in young adults and DNA determinations indicated that the number of cells in the gland had decreased in the old animals. The cause of the fluid accumulation was not positively determined; however occlusion of the ejaculatory duct was considered to be a reasonable possibility since the atrophic condition of the epithelium in the old animals made increased secretion unlikely.

Kruszel (1967) investigated the fructose and citric acid concentrations in the seminal vesicles of rats from puberty to 80 weeks of age and found that fructose levels did not change, but citric acid, which is believed to be a sensitive indicator of hormonal stimulation of this gland, reached a maximum at 12 to 20 weeks and then decreased gradually.

Prostate Gland

Until puberty the human prostate gland shows little evidence of secretory activity, but from this age until the fifth decade, it has well-developed tubulo-alveolar glands which make an important contribution to the ejaculate. Moore (1952) found that beginning typically after 40 years of age the epithelial cells gradually change from columnar to cuboidal and the stromal tissue shows a loss of muscle and replacement with dense collagen. These changes are rarely uniform throughout the gland, with some lobules showing more atrophic changes than do others. In men past 60, these degenerative changes progress to the point of complete atrophy of acini and loss of secretory activity by the glandular epithelium. With increasing age, these changes become more uniform so that there is less variation among lobules (Figure 8). A unique characteristic of the aging prostate gland is the formation of laminated concretions, called corpora amylacea, in the acini. These bodies, which may be the result of stagnation of secretion, increase in size and number, particularly in men past 65.

Nodular hyperplasia of the prostate gland is very common in Caucasians and American Negroes after the age of 50, but it is less common in Chinese, according to Moore (1952). There is still controversy as to whether the initial change in nodular hyperplasia occurs in the glandular tissue or in the surrounding stroma, although the latter origin seems to be favored by most investigators. Ultimately, hyperplasia of both tissues is most common; however pure adenomas, which consist only of glandular tissue, or leimyomata, which are of fibromuscular origin, have also been observed. These hyperplastic changes generally arise in the wall of the urethra and spread into the medial and lateral lobes. These portions of the gland are homologous to the rudimentary female prostate gland, whereas the posterior lobe, which is usually only indirectly involved in benign hypertrophy, is a discrete male structure. The posterior lobe of the prostate is the largest and is susceptible to both focal and diffuse atrophy. Focal atrophy is confined to a few adjacent ducts and is frequently observed in relatively young men who have had chronic prostatitis and, according to McNeal (1968), it does not appear to be age related. Diffuse atrophy is often less acute but involves many more glands, so that there may be more loss of function. It is common after 45 years of age, and this trend continues into old age. Carcinoma of the prostate arises almost exclusively in the posterior lobe but may, and frequently does, invade the other lobes. This type of malignancy clearly increases with age, yet often goes unrecognized until autopsy. Latent carcinoma has been observed in about 10 percent of glands from 50 to 59-year-old men, in 36 percent of glands of men from 60 to 69, and in 50 percent of glands of men over 80 (Harbitz and Haugen, 1972).

The blood supply to the human prostate gland decreases with age according to Leutert and Jahn (1970). The periurethral arteries are particularly affected so that the gland becomes more dependent on capsular arteries, as was shown in a study by Ivanov (1966).

Jahn, Leutert, and Rotzsch (1971) made biochemical determinations of 40 prostate glands of 17 to 89-year-old men and showed that the total protein content decreases after 60 years of age, but collagen increases absolutely and in relation to total protein. A similar drop in protein content was noted by Mainwaring (1967) in 30-month-old mice when compared with 9 to 24-month-old animals.

There is, as yet, no clear understanding of the cause of hypertrophic changes in the aging prostate gland, yet there is no doubt that at least some types are strongly influenced by sex hormones. Siiteri and Wilson (1970) found that the concentration of dihydrotestosterone was five times as great in hypertrophic prostate glands as in normal glands and was two to three times more concentrated in the periurethral area where nodular hypertrophy starts than in more

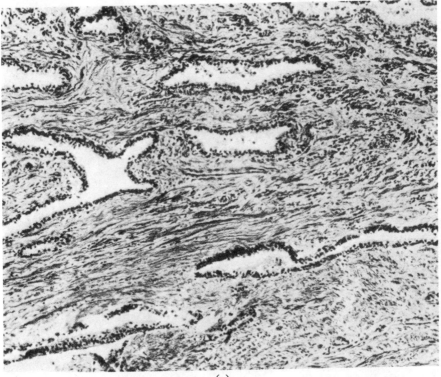

(a)

Figure 8. Aging changes in human prostate gland. (a) Slit-like acini characteristic of prostate after 50 years of age. Note little evidence of secretion and increase in fibrous tissue in stroma. (b) Complete atrophy of a lobule of the prostate with mesenchymal tissue replacing glands. (c) Nodular hyperplasia in lateral lobe of prostate. Note large number of nuclei in nodule and high columnar epithelium in nodule compared to atrophic epithelium in encircling glands. (From Moore, R. A. 1952. Male secondary sexual organs. *In,* A. I. Lansing (ed.), *Cowdry's Problems of Aging,* 3rd ed., pp. 686–707.

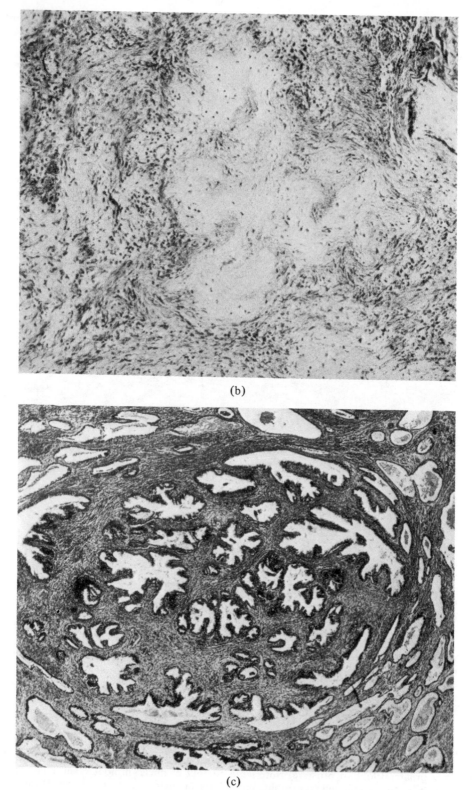

(b)

(c)

Figure 8 (*Continued*)

peripheral portions of the gland. This increased concentration in hypertrophic glands was not due to increased conversion of testosterone to dihydrotestosterone, so the authors suggested that this hormone accumulation may be the result and not the cause of hypertrophy.

Animal experiments have also been utilized to explore the relationship between dihydrotestosterone and prostatic hypertrophy. Gloyna, Siiteri, and Wilson (1970) injected dihydrotestosterone into castrated dogs and showed that the formation and degradation of dihydrotestosterone was similar in immature, mature, and hypertrophic prostate glands. As in the human, this steroid was five times more concentrated in hypertrophic than in mature prostate glands.

Another aspect of the relationship between dihydrotestosterone and the aging prostate gland was explored in the rat by Shain and Axelrod (1973). These investigators found that cytoplasmic extracts of ventral prostate glands obtained from 50 to 90-day-old rats contained high affinity binding sites for 5α dihydrotestosterone, but 80 percent of 10 to 14-month-old rats showed no evidence of such binding sites. However, this animal does not typically display age-related prostatic hypertrophy, so this observation may not have a direct application to the human.

Gasparyan and Portnoy (1970) suggested that hormone-dependent prostatic tumors might be the result of a shift in androgen-estrogen balance, since it is well established that androgens stimulate the epithelium and estrogens the fibromuscular tissue.

Penis

Tyukov (1967) found that the first indications of involuntionary changes occur in the penis of 30 to 40-year-old men. The initial changes consist of fibroelastosis of trabeculae in the corpus spongiosum, followed by progressive sclerosis of both arteries and veins. Similar sclerotic changes follow in the corpora cavernosa, so that the condition becomes generalized in 55 to 60-year-old men. The author suggests that the rate of degenerative changes in the veins may be of particular importance in age-associated impotence.

Sexual Activity in the Male

Sexual activity in the male in relation to age is influenced by morphological, physiological, and, at least in the human, by psychological factors. There is no doubt that sex drive does decline with age. Most bulls tend to be slow in serving behavior after they reach about 5 or 6 years of age, although Bishop (1970) has reported that some may maintain satisfactory drive until 15 years of age or even more.

In the human male, erectal impotence may occur on occasion in relatively young men, but there is no doubt that it becomes increasingly prevalent in older individuals (Kinsey, Pomeroy, and Martin, 1948). General fitness and psychological factors are undoubtedly involved in the maintenance of sexual activity in aging males; however, Goy and Jakway (1962) have presented evidence that inherited factors may also be of importance.

CONCLUSIONS

The mammalian reproductive organs undergo many age changes which are similar to those occurring in other organs and tissues in the body. However, this system is uniquely dependent on a complex interrelationship of hormones secreted by the hypothalamus, anterior pituitary, and gonads for its continuing function. The pattern of change which occurs in these hormones during the period of reproductive decline is still poorly understood, yet it is already obvious that there are major species differences during this period which are particularly evident in the female.

During the past few years, important advances have been made in achieving a better understanding of the role of the hypothalamic-pituitary axis in the control of reproduction, but unfortunately little of this work has been carried out on humans or animals during the period of reproductive decline.

Highly sensitive and discriminating methods are now available for the study of the level of many hormones in the blood, and these techniques have been applied to a limited degree in aged individuals. Far less is known about age changes in the ability of target organs to respond to these hormones, although considerable evidence now exists that prostaglandins and cyclic AMP play an important role in the response of tissues to hormonal stimulation so that extension of such studies to the study of aging of reproductive organs might well prove to be valuable.

It is still not possible to fully evaluate the contribution of genetic and chromosomal abnormalities in gametes to reproductive failure in the human, since many losses occur prior to, or immediately following implantation. However, there is enough evidence from experimental animals, abortions, and births of defective children to indicate that the age of the mother and the "microaging" of the gametes may be of considerable importance.

Only through a more thorough understanding of all aspects of the aging of the male and female reproductive systems will it be possible to not only improve the chances of conception, maintenance, and delivery of a normal child by the older mother, but also to maintain better health in the postreproductive years.

REFERENCES

Adams, C. E. 1965. The influence of maternal environment on preimplantation stages of pregnancy in the rabbit. *In*, G. E. W. Wolstenholme and M. O'Connor (eds.), *Preimplantation Stages of Development*, p. 345. London: L. A. Churchill.

Adams, C. E. 1970. Ageing and reproduction in the female mammal with particular reference to the rabbit. *J. Reprod. Fertility Suppl.*, 12, 1–16.

Ahmed, I. A., and Tantawy, A. O. 1959. Breeding efficiency of Egyptian cows and buffalo. *Empire J. Exp. Agric.*, 27, 17–26.

Anderson, A. C. 1965. Reproductive ability of female beagles in relation to advancing age. *Exper. Geront.*, 1, 189–192.

Andrew, W. G. 1971. *The anatomy of aging in man and animals*, p. 286. New York: Grune & Stratton.

Arrington, L. R., Beaty, T. C. Jr., and Kelley, K. C. 1973. Growth, longevity, and reproductive life of the Mongolian gerbil. *Lab. Animal Sci.*, 23, 262–265.

Aschheim, P. 1961. La pseudogestation á répetition chez les rattes séniles. *C. R. Acad. Sci.*, 253, 1988–1993.

Aschheim, P. 1964–65. Résultats fournis par la greffehétérochrome des ovaires dans è étude de la regulation hypothalamo-hypophyso-ovarienne de la ratte sénile. *Gerontologia*, 10, 65–70.

Aschheim, P. 1965. La réactivation des rattes séniles en oestrus permanent au moyen d'hormones go-

nadotropes de la mise á l'obscurité. *C. R. Acad. Sci.*, 260, 5627–5630.

Asdell, S. A., Bogart, R., and Sperling, G. 1941. The influence of age and rate of breeding upon the ability of the female rat to reproduce and raise young. *Mem. Cornell Univ. Agr. Exp. Sta.*, No. 238.

Austin, C. R. 1970. Ageing and reproduction: Postovulatory deterioration of the egg. *J. Reprod. Fertility, Suppl.*, 12, 39–53.

Bahn, R. C., Lorenz, N., Bennett, W. A., and Albert, A. 1953. Gonadotropins of the pituitary of postmenopausal women. *Endocrinology*, 53, 455–457.

Baird, D. T., Uno, A., and Melby, J. C. 1969. Adrenal secretion of androgens and oestrogens. *J. Endocrinol.*, 45, 135–136.

Bal, H. S., and Getty R. 1973. Changes in the histomorphology of the uterus of the domestic pig (Sus scrofa domesticus) with advancing age. *J. Geront.*, 28, 160–172.

Ball, Z. B. Barnes, R. H., and Visscher, M. 1947. The effects of dietary caloric restriction on maturity and senescence with particular reference to fertility and longevity. *Am. J. Physiol.*, 150, 511–519.

Balough, A., Takaks, I., Ladányi, P., Árvay, A., 1970. Electron microscopic studies of the adenohypophyses of aged rats. *Gerontologia*, 16, 313–324.

Bigelow, B. 1958. Comparison of ovarian and endometrial morphology spanning the menopause. *Obstet. Gynecol.*, 11, 487–513.

Biggart, J. H. 1935. Some observations on the basophilic cells of the human hypophysis. *Edinb. Med. J.*, 42, 113–124.

Biggers, J. D. 1969. Problems concerning the uterine causes of embryonic death with special reference to the effects of ageing of the uterus. *J. Reprod. Fertility Suppl.*, 8, 27–43.

Biggers, J. D., Finn, C. A., and McLaren, A. 1962a. Long-term reproductive performance of female mice. I. Effect of removing one ovary. *J. Reprod. Fertility*, 3, 303–312.

Biggers, J. D., Finn, C. A., and McLaren, A. 1962b. Long-term reproductive performance of female mice. II. Variation of litter size with parity. *J. Reprod. Fertility*, 3, 313–330.

Bishop, M. W. H. 1970. Ageing and reproduction in the male. *J. Reprod. Fertility Suppl.*, 12, 65–87.

Blaha, G. C. 1964a. Reproductive senescence in the female golden hamster. *Anat. Record*, 150, 405–412.

Blaha, G. C. 1964b. Effect of age of the donor and recipient on the development of transferred golden hamster ova. *Anat. Record*, 150, 413–416.

Blaha, G. C. 1967. Effects of age, treatment and method of induction on deciduomata in the golden hamster. *Fertility Sterility*, 18, 477–485.

Blaha, G. C. 1968. The effect of grafted ovaries on the implantation and development of transferred ova in aged and young golden hamsters. *Anat. Record*, 160, 318.

Bloch, S. 1961. Investigations of genital aging of female rats. *Gerontologia*, 5, 55–62.

Block, E. 1952. Quantitative morphological investigations of the follicular system in women. Variations at different ages. *Acta Anat.,* 14, 108–123.

Block, E. 1953. A quantitative morphological investigation of the follicular system in newborn female infants. *Acta Anat.,* 17, 201–206.

Blum, V. 1936. Das Problem des mannlichen Klimacteriums. *Wien. Klin. Wochschr.,* 49, 1133–1139.

Burack, E., and Wolfe, J. M. 1959. The effect of anterior hypophyseal administration on the ovaries of old rats. *Endocrinology,* 64, 676–684.

Burgi, Von H., and Hedinger, C. 1959. Histologische Hodenveränderugen im hohen Alter. *Schweiz. Med. Wochschr.,* 89, 1236–1239.

Clemens, J. A., Amenomori, Y., Jenkins, T., and Meites, J. 1969. Effects of hypothalamic stimulation, hormones and drugs on ovarian function in old female rats. *Proc. Soc. Exp. Biol. Med.,* 132, 561–563.

Clemens, J. A., and Meites, J. 1971. Neuroendocrine status of old constant estrous rats. *Neuroendocrinology,* 7, 249–254.

Clermont, Y., and Flannery, J. 1970. Mitotic activity in the epithelium of the epididymis in young and old adult rats. *Biol. Reprod.,* 3, 283–292.

Coble, Y. D. Jr., Kohler, P. O., Cargille, C. M., and Ross, G. T. 1969. Production rates and metabolic clearance rates of human FSH in pre-menopausal and post-menopausal women. *J. Clin. Invest.,* 48, 359–363.

Collett, M. E., Wertenberger, G. E., and Fiske, V. M. 1954. The effect of age upon the pattern of the menstrual cycle. *Fertility Sterility,* 5, 437–448.

Collins, P. M., Bell, J. B., and Tsang, W. N. 1972. The effect of vasectomy on steroid metabolism by the seminiferous tubules and interstitial tissue of the rat testis—A comparison with the effects of ageing. *J. Endocrinol.,* 55, XVIII–XIX.

Connors, T. J., Thorpe, L. W., and Soderwall, A. L. 1972. Analysis of preimplantation embryonic death in senescent golden hamsters. *Biol. Reprod.,* 6, 131–135.

Cupr, Z., Druckmuller, V., Kucera, F. 1969. Zur Problematik langfristiger Behandlung mit depot Oestrogenen beim klimacterischen Syndrom. *Zentr. Gynaekol.,* 91, 873–880.

Desai, R. N., and Winters, L. M. 1951. An appraisal of factors affecting fertility in sheep. *Indian J. Vet. Sci.,* 21, 177–189.

Dickie, M. M. Atkinson, W. B., and Fekete, E. 1957. The ovary estrous cycle and fecundity of DBA x CE and reciprocal hybrid mice in relation to age and the hyperovarian syndrome. *Anat. Record,* 127, 187–200.

Dilts, P. V., and Greene, R. R. 1964. Effects of increasing parity on the myometrium. *Am. J. Obstet. Gynecol.,* 89, 1049–1059.

Dreizen, S., Spirakis, C. N., and Stone, R. E. 1967. A comparison of skeletal growth and maturation in undernourished and well-nourished girls before and after menarche. *J. Pediat.,* 70, 256–263.

Durbin, P. Williams, M. H., Jeung, N., and Arnold, J. S. 1966. Development of spontaneous mammary tumors over the lifespan of the female Charles River (Sprague-Dawley) rat. Influence of ovariectomy, thyroidectomy, and adrenalectomy-ovariectomy. *Cancer Res.,* 26, 400–411.

Eaton, O. N. 1953. Heterosis in performance in mice. *Genetics,* 38, 609–629.

Erickson, B. H., 1966. Development and senescence of the post-natal bovine ovary. *J. Animal Sci.,* 25, 800–805.

Ewing, L. L. 1967. Effect of aging on testicular metabolism in the rabbit. *Am. J. Physiol.,* 212, 1261–1267.

Ewing, L. L., Johnson, B. H., Desjardins, C., and Clegg, R. F. 1972. Effect of age upon the spermatogenic and steroidogenic elements of rabbit testes. *Proc. Soc. Exp. Biol. Med.,* 140, 907–910.

Finch, C. E. 1975. Personal communication.

Finch, C. E., and Girgis, F. G., 1974. Enlarged seminal vesicles of senescent C57BL/6J mice. *J. Geront.,* 29, 134–138.

Finn, C. A. 1962. Embryonic death in aged mice. *Nature,* 194, 499–500.

Finn, C. A. 1963. Reproductive capacity and litter size in mice: Effect of age and environment. *J. Reprod. Fertility,* 6, 205–214.

Finn, C. A. 1966. Initiation of the decidual cell reaction in the uterus of the aged mouse. *J. Reprod. Fertility,* 11, 423–428.

Finn, C. A. 1970. The ageing uterus and its influence on reproductive capacity. *J. Reprod. Fertility Suppl.,* 12, 31–38.

Finn, C. A., Fitch, S. M., and Harkness, R. D. 1963. Collagen content of barren and previously pregnant uterine horns in old mice. *J. Reprod. Fertility,* 6, 405–408.

Finn, C. A., and Martin, L. 1969. The cellular response of the uterus of the aged mouse to oestrogen and progesterone. *J. Reprod. Fertility,* 20, 545–547.

Franchi, L. L. 1970. The ovary. *In,* E. E. Philipp, J. Barnes, and M. Newton (eds.), *Scientific Foundations of Obstertrics and Gynaecology,* pp. 107–131. Philadelphia: F. A. Davis.

Franchimont, P., Legros, J. J., and Meurice, J. 1972. Effect of several estrogens on serum gonadotropin levels in postmenopausal women. *Horm. Metab. Res.,* 4, 288–292.

Francis, W. J. A. 1970. Reproduction at menarche and menopause in women. *J. Reprod. Fertility Suppl.,* 12, 89–98.

Frantz, A. G. and Rabkin, M. T. 1965. Effects of estrogen and sex difference on secretion of human growth hormone. *J. Clin. Endocrinol.,* 25, 1470–1480.

Frisch, R. E. 1972. Weight at menarche: Similarity for well-nourished and undernorished girls at differing ages, and evidence for historical constancy. *Pediatrics,* 50, 445–450.

Frommer, D. J. 1964. Changing age of the menopause. *Brit. Med. J.* 5405, 349–351.

Furuhjelm, M. 1966. Urinary excretion of hormones during the climacteric. *Acta Obstet. Gynecol. Scand.,* 45, 352–364.

Gasparyan, A. M., and Portnoy, A. S. 1970. Reaction of the prostate to experimental endocrine disorders. *Int. Urol. Nephrol.,* 2/3, 277–285.

Gloyna, R. E., Siiteri, P. K., and Wilson, J. D. 1970. Dihydrotesterone in prostatic hypertrophy II. The formation and content of dihydrotesterone in the hypertrophic canine prostate and the effect of dihydrotesterone on prostatic growth in the dog. *J. Clin. Invest.* 49, 1746–1753.

Goldman, H. 1963. Amyloidosis of seminal vesicles and vas deferens. Primary localized cases. *Arch. Pathol.,* 75, 94–98.

Goodlin, R. 1965. Non-disjunction and maternal age in the mouse. *J. Reprod. Fertility,* 9, 355–356.

Goy, R. W., and Jakway, J. S. 1962. Role of inheritance in determination of sexual behavior patterns. *In,* E. L. Bliss (ed.), *Roots of Behaviour,* pp. 96–112. New York: Harper.

Green, J. A. 1957. Some effects of advancing age on the histology and reactivity of the mouse ovary. *Anat. Record,* 129, 333–348.

Greene, H. S. N. 1941. Uterine adenomata in the rabbit. III. Susceptibility as a function of constitutional factors. *J. Exp. Med,* 73, 273–292.

Grodin, J. M., Siiteri, P. K., and MacDonald, P. C. 1973. Source of estrogen production in postmenopausal women. *J. Clin. Endocrinol.,* 36, 207–214.

Guilloud, N. B. 1968. Personal communication.

Hammond, J., and Marshall, F. H. A. 1952. The life cycle. *In,* A. S. Parkes (ed.), *Marshall's Physiology of Reproduction,* pp 793–846. London: Longmans, Green.

Harbitz, T. B. 1973a. Testis weight and the histology of the prostate in elderly men. Analysis in an autopsy series. *Acta Pathol. Microbiol. Scand.,* 81A, 148–158.

Harbitz, T. B. 1973b. Morphometric studies of the Leydig cells in elderly men with special reference to the histology of the prostate. An analysis in an autopsy series. *Acta Pathol. Microbiol. Scand.,* 81A, 301–314.

Harbitz, T. B., and Haugen, O. A. 1972. Histology of the prostate in elderly men. *Acta Pathol. Microbiol. Scand.,* 80A, 756–768.

Harman, S. M., and Talbert, G. B. 1970. The effect of maternal age on ovulation, corpora lutea of pregnancy and implantation failure in mice. *J. Reprod. Fertility,* 23, 33–39.

Hemsell, D. L., Grodin, M., Brenner, P. F., Siiteri, P. K. and McDonald, P. C. 1974. Plasma precursors of estrogen. II. Correlation of the extent of conversion of plasma androstenedione with age. *J. Clin. Endocrinol.,* 38, 476–479.

Henderson, S. A., and Edwards, R. G. 1968. Chiasma frequency and maternal age in mammals. *Nature,* 218, 22–28.

Hertig, A. T. 1944. The aging ovary–A preliminary note, *J. Clin. Endocrinol.,* 4, 581–582.

Hollander, N., and Hollander, V. P. 1958. The microdetermination of testosterone in human spermatic vein blood. *J. Clin. Endocrinol. Metab.,* 18, 966–971.

Hollander, W. F., and Strong, L. C. 1950. Intra-uterine mortality and placental fusions in the mouse. *J. Exp. Zool.,* 115, 131–150.

Howell, J. S., and Mandl, A. M. 1961. The mammary glands of senile nulliparous and multiparous rats. *J. Endocrinol.,* 22, 241–255.

Huseby, R. A., and Ball, Z. B. 1945. A study of the genesis of histological changes produced by caloric restrictions in portions of the endocrine and reproductive systems of strain A female mice. *Anat. Record,* 92, 135–155.

Ingram, D. L. 1953. The effect of hypophysectomy on the number of oocytes in the adult albino rat. *J. Endocrinol.,* 9, 307–311.

Ingram, D. L., Mandl, A. M., and Zuckerman, S. 1958. The influence of age on litter size. *J. Endocrinol.,* 17, 280–285.

Ivanov, A. I. 1966. Age changes in the blood and lymphatic vessels in the prostate gland in adults. *Arkh. Anat. Gistol. i Embriol.,* 51, 87–94.

Jahn, K., Leutert, G., and Rotzsch, W. 1971. Age dependent morphological and biochemical examinations of the human prostate. *Z. Alternsforsch.,* 23, 323–335.

Jones, E. C. 1970. The ageing ovary and its influence on reproductive capacity. *J. Reprod. Fertility Suppl.,* 12, 17–30.

Jones, E. C., and Krohn, P. L. 1960. Effect of unilateral ovariectomy on reproductive lifespan of mice. *J. Endocrinol.,* 20, 129–134.

Jones, E. C., and Krohn, P. L. 1961a. The relationship between age, number of oocytes and fertility in virgin and multiparous mice. *J. Endocrinol.,* 21, 469–495.

Jones. E. C., and Krohn, P. L. 1961b. Effect of hypophysectomy on age changes in the ovaries of mice. *J. Endocrinol.,* 21, 497–509.

Judd, H. L., Judd, G. E., Lucas, W. E. and Yen, S.S.C. 1974. Endocrine function of the postmenopausal ovary: concentration of androgens and estrogens in ovarian and peripheral vein blood. *J. Clin. Endocrinol.,* 39, 1020–1024.

Kao, K. Y. T., Chen Lu, S. O., Hitt, W., and McGavack, T. H. 1962. Connective tissue VI. Synthesis of collagen by rat uterine slices. *Proc. Soc. Exp. Biol. Med.,* 109, 4–7.

Kaplan, H. G., and Hreshchyshen, M. M. 1971. Gas-liquid chromatographic quantitation of urinary estrogens in nonpregnant women, postmenopausal women and men. *Am J. Obstet. Gynecol.,* 111, 386–390.

Keller, P. J. 1970. Effect of natural sex steroids on the excretion of follicle-stimulating and luteinizing hormone in post-menopausal women. *Acta Endocrinol.,* 64, 479–488.

Kent, J. Z., and Acone, A. B. 1965. Plasma testosterone levels and aging in males. *In,* A. Vermeulen and

D. Exley (eds.), *Androgens in Normal and Pathological Conditions*, pp. 31–35. Amsterdam: Excerpta Medica Foundation, Int. Cong. Series No. 191.

Kinsey, A. C., Pomeroy, W. B., and Martin, C. E. 1948. *Sexual Behavior in the Human Male*. Philadelphia: W. B. Saunders.

Kirkham, W. B. 1920. The life of the white mouse. *Proc. Soc. Exp. Biol. Med., 17,* 196–198.

Kistner, R. W. 1973. The menopause. *Clin. Obstet. Gynecol.* 16 (4), 106–219.

Kohler, P. O., Ross, G. T., and Odell, W. D. 1968. Metabolic clearance and production rates of human luteinizing hormone in pre- and post-menopausal women. *J. Clin. Invest., 47,* 38–47.

Kohli, M. L., and Suri, K. R. 1957. Longevity and reproductivity in Hariana cattle. *Indian J. Vet. Sci., 27,* 105–110.

Korenman, S. G., and Dukes, B. A. 1970. Specific estrogen bonding by the cytoplasm of human breast carcinoma. *J. Clin. Endocrinol., 30,* 639–645.

Kramer, W. M., and Rush, B. F. Jr. 1973. Mammary duct proliferation in the elderly. A histo-pathologic study. *Cancer, 31,* 130–137.

Krohn, P. L. 1962. Review lectures on senescence. II. Heterochronic transplantation in the study of ageing. *Proc. Roy. Soc. Ser. B, 157,* 128–147.

Kruszel, T. 1967. Fructose and citric acid concentrations in the seminal vesicles of rats in relationship to age. *Endokrynol. Polska, 18,* 287–296.

Labhsetwar, A. P. 1967. Age-dependent changes in the pituitary-gonadal relationship. A study of ovarian compensatory hypertrophy. *J. Endocrinol, 39,* 387–393.

Labhsetwar, A. P. 1969. Age-dependent changes in the pituitary-gonadal relationship. II. A study of pituitary FSH and LH content in the female rat. *J. Reprod. Fertility, 20,* 21–28.

Labhsetwar, A. P. 1970. Ageing changes in pituitary-ovarian relationships. *J. Reprod. Fertility Suppl., 12,* 99–117.

Lajos, L. Illei, Gy., Kecskés. L., Görcs, J., Mutschler, F., and Kóbor, J. 1963. Hyperoestrogenism after the menopause *J. Obstet. Gynaecol. Brit. Commonwealth, 70,* 1016–1023.

Lang, W. R. and Aponte, G. E. 1967. Gross and Microscopic anatomy of the aged female reproductive organs. *Clin. Obstet. Gynecol., 10,* 454–465.

Lanman, J. 1968a. Delays during reproduction and their effects on the embryo and the fetus. 1. Aging of sperm. *New. Engl. J. Med., 278,* 993–999.

Lanman, J. 1968b. Delays during reproduction and their effects on the embryo and the fetus. 2. Aging of eggs. *New Engl. J. Med., 278,* 1047–1054.

Larson, L. L., and Foote, R. H. 1972. Uterine blood flow in young and aged rabbits. *Proc. Soc Exp. Biol. Med., 141,* 67–69.

Lauson, T. C., Golden, H. B., and Sevringhaus, E. L. 1939. The gonadotropic content of the hypophysis throughout the life cycle of the normal female rat. *Am. J. Physiol., 125,* 396–404.

Lenters, G. J. V. H. 1954. Ovarian hilus cells. *Ned. Tijdschr. Verlosk. Gynec., 54,* 284–291.

Leutert, G., and Jahn, K. 1970. Über altersabhängige histologische und histochemische Befunde an der Prostata des Menschen. *Acta Histochem., 37,* 136–147.

Lin, T. J., So-Bosita, J. L, Brar, H. K., and Roblete, B. V. 1973. Clinical and cytologic responses of postmenopausal women to estrogen. *Obstet. Gynecol., 41,* 97–107.

Longcope, C. 1971. Metabolic clearance and blood production rates of estrogens in postmenopausal women. *Am. J. Obstet. Gynecol., 111,* 778–781.

Longcope, C. 1973. Effect of HCG on plasma steroid levels in young and old men. *Steroids, 21,* 583–592.

Luthardt, F. W., Palmer, C. G., and Yu, P. L. 1973. Chiasma and univalent frequencies in aging female mice. *Cytogenet. Cell Genet., 12,* 68–79.

Lynch, K. M., and Scott, W. W. 1950. The lipid content of the Leydig cell and Sertoli cell in the human testis as related to age, benign prostatic hypertrophy and prostatic cancer. *J. Urol., 64,* 767–776.

McBride, J. M. 1954. The normal postmenopausal endometrium. *J. Obstet. Gynaec. Brit. Empire, 61,* 691–697.

McKinlay, S., Jeffreys, M., and Thompson, B. 1972. An investigation of the age at menopause. *J. Biosoc. Sci., 4,* 161–173.

McLennan, M. T., and McLennan, C. E. 1971. Estrogenic status of menstruating and menopausal women assessed by cervicovaginal smears. *Obstet. Gynecol., 37,* 325–331.

McNeal, J. E. 1968. Regional morphology of the prostate. *Am. J. Clin. Pathol., 49,* 347–357.

Mainwaring, W. I. P. 1967. The aging process in the mouse ventral prostate gland. A preliminary biochemical survey. *Gerontologia, 13,* 177–189.

Mandl, A. M., 1961. Cyclical changes in vaginal smears of senile nulliparous and multiparous rats. *J. Endocrinol., 22,* 257–268.

Mandl, A. M., and Shelton, M. 1959. A quantitative study of oocytes in young and old nulliparous laboratory rats. *J. Endocrinol., 18,* 444–450.

Martin, P. L., Burnier, A. M., Segre, E. J., and Huix, F. J. 1971. Graded sequential therapy in the menopause: A double-blind study. *Am. J. Obstet. Gynecol., 111,* 178–186.

Masukawa, T. 1960. Vaginal smears in women past 40 years of age with emphasis on their remaining hormonal activity. *Obstet. Gynecol., 16,* 407–413.

Matsuyama, E., Weisz, J., and Lloyd, C. W. 1966. Gonadotrophin content of pituitary glands of testosterone-sterilized rats. *Endocrinology, 79,* 261–267.

Mattingly, R. F., and Huang, W. Y. 1969. Steroidogenesis of the menopausal and postmenopausal ovary. *Am. J. Obstet. Gynecol, 103,* 679–693.

Maurer, R. R., and Foote, R. H. 1971. Maternal ageing and embryonic mortality in the rabbit. I. Repeated superovulation, embryo culture and transfer. *J. Reprod. Fertility, 25,* 329–341.

Maurer, R. R., and Foote, R. H. 1972. Uterine collagenase and collagen in young and ageing rabbits. *J. Reprod. Fertility,* 30, 301–304.

Meema, H. E. 1968. Prevention of postmenopausal osteroporosis by hormone treatment of the menopause. *Can. Med. Assoc. J.,* 99, 248–251.

Meites, J. 1972. Relation of prolactin and estrogen to mammary tumorigenesis in the rat. *J. Nat. Cancer Inst.,* 48, 1217–1224.

Mestwerdt, W., Brandau, H. and Müller, O. 1972. Struktur und Funktion steroidaktiver Zellen in Postmenopauseovar. *Arch. Gynak.,* 212, 268–284.

Moore, R. A. 1952. Male secondary sexual organs. *In,* A. I. Lansing (ed.), *Cowdry's Problems of Ageing,* 3rd ed., pp. 686–707. Baltimore: Williams & Wilkins.

Nagai, N., and Longcope, C. 1971. Estradiol-17β and estrone: Studies on their binding to rabbit uterine cytosol and their concentration in plasma. *Steroids,* 17, 631–647.

Nelson, J. F., Latham, K. R., and Finch, C. E. 1975. Plasma testosterone levels in C57Bl/6J male mice: Effects of age and disease. Acta Endocrinol., in press.

Nieschlag, E., Kley, H. K., Wiegelmann, W., Solbach, H. G., and Krüskemper, H. L. 1973. Lebensalter und endokrine Funktion der testes des erwachsenan Mannes. *Deut. Med. Wochscher.,* 98, 1281–1284.

Nilsson, S. 1962. The human seminal vesicle. A morphogenetic and gross anatomic study with special regard to changes due to age and to prostatic adenoma. I, II, III. *Acta Chir. Scand. Suppl.,* 296, 5–96.

Novak, E., and Everett, H. S. 1928. Cyclical and other variations in the tubal epithelium. *Am. J. Obstet. Gynecol.,* 16, 499–530.

Novak, E. R. 1967. Replacement therapy of the menopause. *Johns Hopkins Med. J.,* 120, 408–415.

Novak, E. R. 1970. Ovulation after fifty. *Obstet. Gynecol.,* 36, 903–910.

Noyes, R. W. 1970. Physiology of ovarian aging. *Ann. N.Y. Acad. Sci.,* 171, 517–525.

Ortiz, E. 1955. The relation of advancing age to reactivity of the reproductive system in the female hamster. *Anat. Record.,* 122, 517–537.

Parkening, T. A., and Soderwall, A. L. 1973. Delayed embryonic development and implantation in senescent golden hamsters. *Biol. Reprod.,* 8, 427–434.

Parlow, A. F. 1961. Bioassay of pituitary luteinizing hormone by depletion of ovarian ascorbic acid. *In,* A. Albert (ed.), *Human Pituitary Gonadotropins,* p. 300. Springfield, Illinois: Charles C. Thomas.

Patek, E., Nilsson, L., and Johannisson, E. 1972. Scanning electron microscopic study of the human fallopian tube. Report 2. Fetal life, reproductive life and postmenopause. *Fertility Sterility,* 23, 719–733.

Paulson, C. A., Leach, R. B., Sandberg, H., and Maddock, W. O. 1955. Function of the postmenopausal ovary, urinary estrogen excretion and the response to administered FSH. *J. Clin. Endocrinol.,* 15, 846.

Peng, M., and Huang, H. 1972. Aging of hypothalamic-pituitary-ovarian function in the rat. *Fertility Sterility,* 23, 535–542.

Peng, M., and Peng, Y. 1973. Changes in the uptake of tritiated estradiol in the hypothalamus and adenohypophysis of old female rats. *Fertility Sterility,* 24, 534–539.

Pincus, G., Romanoff, L. P., and Carlo, J. 1954. The excretion of urinary steroids by men and women of various ages. *J. Geront.,* 9, 113–132.

Piotti, L. E., Ghiringhelli, F., and Magrini, U. 1967. A propos de la fonction testiculaire du vieillard: Observations histochimiques et biologiques. *Revue Fr. Endocr. Clin.,* 8, 479–491.

Pirke, K. M., and Doerr, P. 1973. Age related changes and interrelations between plasma testosterone, oestradiol and testosterone binding globulin in normal adult males. *Acta Endocrinol.,* 74, 792–800.

Procope, B. J. 1970. Urinary excretion of oestrogens and the oestrogenic effect in vaginal smears in postmenopausal women with uterine bleeding. *Acta Obstet. Gynecol. Scand.,* 49, 243–247.

Procope, B. J., and Adlercreutz, H. 1969. Studies on the influence of age on oestrogens in postmenopausal women with atrophic endometrium and normal liver function. *Acta Endocrinol.,* 62, 461–467.

Pullinger, B. D. 1961. The effect of oestrone on the incidence of mammary carcinoma and adenoma in C_3Hf breeders after late ovariectomy. *Brit. J. Cancer,* 15, 127–132.

Pundel, J. P. 1969. La place des oestrogenes dans la prevention et la traitement de la menopause et de ses troubles. *Gynéc. Prat.,* 20, 177–200.

Quadri, S. K., Kledzik, G., and Meites, J. 1973. Reinitiation of estrous cycles in old constant-estrous rats by central-acting drugs. *Neuroendocrinology,* 11, 248–255.

Quadri, S. K., and Meites, J. 1975. Stimulation of development of spontaneous mammary tumors in female rats by reserpine: Inhibition by L-Dopa. *Proc. Soc. Exp. Biol. Med.,* in press.

Rader, M. D., Flickinger, G. L., deVilla, G. O., Mikuta, J. J. and Mikhail, G. 1973. Plasma estrogens in postmenopausal women. *Am. J. Obstet. Gynecol.,* 116, 1069–1073.

Randall, R. V. 1962. The pituitary body and aging. *J. Am. Geriat. Soc.,* 10, 6–9.

Redding, T. W., Schally, A. V., Arimura, A., and Matsuo, H. 1972. Stimulation of release and synthesis of luteinizing hormone (LH) and follicle stimulating hormone (FSH) in tissue cultures of rat pituitaries in response to natural and synthetic LH and FSH releasing hormone. *Endocrinology,* 90, 764–770.

Riley, G. M. 1964. Endocrinology of the climacteric. *Clin. Obstet. Gynecol.,* 7, 432–450.

Rogers, J. B., and Taylor, R. C. 1955. Age changes in the uterus and ovary of the guinea pig. *Anat. Record,* 121, 448.

Rubens, R., Dhont, M., and Vermeulen, A. 1974. Further studies on Leydig cell function in old age. *J. Clin. Endocrinol. Metab.,* 39, 40–45.

Ryan, R. J. 1962. The luteinizing hormone content of human pituitaries. I. Variations with age and sex. *J. Clin. Endocrinol.*, **22**, 300–303.

Salisbury, C. W. 1965. Aging phenomena in gametes: A review. *J. Geront.*, **20**, 281–288.

Sasano, N., and Ichijo. S. 1969. Vascular patterns of the human testis with special reference to its senile changes. *Tohoku J. Exp. Med.*, **99**, 265–272.

Saville, P. D. 1968. Treatment of postmenopausal osteoporosis. *Modern Treatment*, **5**, 571–580.

Schalch, D. D., Parlow, A. F., Boon, R. C., and Reichlin, S., 1968. Measurement of human luteinizing hormone in plasma by radioimmunoassay, *J. Clin. Invest.*, **47**, 665–678.

Schaub, M. C. 1964-65. Changes of collagen in the aging and in the pregnant uterus of white rats. *Gerontologia*, **10**, 137–149.

Schleyer-Saunders, E. 1971. Result of hormone implants in the treatment of the climacteric. *J. Am. Geriat. Soc.*, **19**, 114–121.

Schneider, R. 1970. Comparison of age, sex and incidence rates in human and canine breast cancer. *Cancer*, **26**, 419–426.

Schotterer, A. 1928. Veitrag zur Festellung der Eianzahl in verschiedenen Altersperioden bei der Hündin. *Anat. Anz.*, **65**, 177–192.

Sevringhaus, A. E. 1944. Cytology of the anterior pituitary of the postmenopausal woman. *J. Clin. Endocrinol.* **4**, 583–588.

Seymour, F. I., Duffy, C., and Koerner, A. 1935. A case of authenticated fertility in a man of 94. *J. Am. Med. Assoc.*, **105**, 1423–1424.

Shain, S. A., and Axelrod, L. R. 1973. Reduced high affinity 5-dihydrotestosterone receptor capacity in the ventral prostate of the aging rat. *Steroids*, **21**, 801–812.

Shanklin, W. M. 1953. Age changes in the histology of the human pituitary. *Acta Anat.*, **19**, 290–304.

Shapiro, M., and Talbert, G. B. 1974. The effect of maternal age on decidualization in the mouse. *J. Geront.*, **29**, 145–148.

Shelton, M. 1959. A comparison of the population of oocytes in nulliparous and multiparous senile laboratory rats. *J. Endocrinol.*, **18**, 451–455.

Sherman, B. M. and Korenman, S. G. 1975. Hormonal characteristics of the human menstrual cycle throughout reproductive life. *J. Clin. Invest.*, **55**, 699–706.

Sherman, B. M., West, J. H. and Korenman, S. G. 1976. The menopausal transition: Analysis of LH, FSH, estradiol and progesterone concentrations during menstrual cycles of older women. *J. Clin. Endocrinol.*, **42**, 629–636.

Shimoyama, T. 1965. Electron microscopic studies of the mucous membrane of the human fallopian tube in the embryonal, pregnancy and senile period. *J. Jap. Obstet. Gynecol. Soc.*, (English Edition), **12**, 132.

Siiteri, P. K., and Wilson, J. D. 1970. Dihydrotestosterone in prostate hypertrophy. I. The formation and content of dihydrotestosterone in the hypertrophic prostate of man. *J. Clin. Invest.*, **49**, 1737–1745.

Snaith, L., and Williamson, M. 1947. Pregnancy after the menopause. *J. Obstet. Gynaecol. Brit. Empire.*, **54**, 496–498.

Soderwall, A. L., Kent, H. A., Turbyfill, C. L. and Britenbaker, A. I., 1960. Variation in gestation length and litter size of the golden hamster (Mesocricetus auratus). *J. Geront.*, **15**, 246–248.

Sokal, Z. 1964. Morphology of the human testes in various periods of life. *Folia Morphol.* **23**, 102–111.

Spagnoli, H. H., and Charipper, H. A. 1955. The effects of aging on the histology and cytology of the pituitary gland of the golden hamster (Cricetus auatus) with brief reference to simultaneous changes in the thyroid and testis. *Anat. Record,* **121**, 117–139.

Spilman, C. H., Larson, L. L., Concannon, P. W., and Foote, R. H. 1972. Ovarian function during pregnancy in young and aged rabbits: Temporal relationship between fetal death and corpus luteum regression. *Biol. Reprod.*, **7**, 223–230.

Staemmler, J. J., and Wille-Schörcher, C. 1966. Probleme der Sexual-steroid-therapie bei der alternden Frau. *Geburtsh. Franuenheilk.*, **26**, 357–370.

Steelman, S. L., and Pohley, F. M. 1953. Assay of the follicle stimulating hormone based on the augmentation with human chorionic gonadotrophin. *Endocrinology*, **53**, 604–616.

Sugiyama, T. 1961. Reproductive power of mother mice of different ages. *Acta Schol. Med. Univ. Kioto*, **37**, 172–179.

Suoranta, H. 1971. Changes in the small blood vessels of the adult human testis in relation to age and to some pathological conditions. *Virchow's Arch. Path. Anat.*, **352**, 165–181.

Takasugi, N. 1963. Gonadotropic activity of the anterior hypophysis of old female mice as demonstrated by parabiosis with young partners. *J. Fac. Sci. Tokyo Univ. Sect. 4*, **10**, 193–210.

Talbert, G. B. 1968. Effect of maternal age on reproductive capacity. *Am. J. Obstet. Gynecol.*, **102**, 451–477.

Talbert, G. B. 1971. Effect of maternal age on postimplantation reproductive failure in mice. *J. Reprod. Fertility*, **24**, 449–452.

Talbert, G. B., and Krohn, P. L. 1966. Effect of maternal age on viability of ova and uterine support of pregnancy in mice. *J. Reprod. Fertility,* **11**, 399–406.

Tanner, J. M. 1962. *Growth at Adolescence.* 2nd ed. Oxford: Blackwell Scientific Publications.

Tellem, M., Shane, J. J., and Imbriglia, J. E. 1965. Breast cancer in the postmenopausal years. *Surg. Gynecol. Obstet.*, **120**, 17–24.

Thorneycroft, I. H., and Soderwall, A. L., 1969a. The nature of the litter size loss in senescent hamsters. *Anat. Record*, **165**, 343–348.

Thorneycroft, I. H., and Soderwall, A. L., 1969b.

Ovarian morphological and functional changes in reproductively senescent hamsters. *Anat. Record,* **165,** 349–354.

Thung, P. J. 1961. Ageing changes in the ovary. *In,* J. Bourne (ed.), *Structural Aspects of Ageing,* pp. 109–142. New York: Hafner.

Thung, P. J., Boot, L. M., and Mühlbock, O. 1956. Senile changes in the oestrous cycle and in ovarian structure in some imbred strains of mice. *Acta Endocrinol.,* **23,** 8–32.

Tietze, C. 1957. Reproductive span and rate of reproduction among Hutterite women. *Fertility Sterility.,* **8,** 89–97.

Toth, F., and Gimes, R. 1964. Senile changes in the female endocrine glands and internal sex organs. *Acta Morph. Hung,* **12,** 301–313.

Treolar, A. E., Boynton, R. E., Behn, B. G., and Brown, B. W. 1967. Variation of the human menstral cycle through reproductive life. *Intern. J. Fertility,* **12,** 77–126.

Trichopoulos, D. B., MacMahon, B., and Cole, P., 1972. Menopause and breast cancer risk. *J. Nat. Cancer Inst.,* **48,** 605–613.

Turner, H. N., and Dolling, C. H. S. 1965. Vital statistics for an experimental flock of Merino sheep. II. The influence of age on reproductive performance. *Australian J. Agri. Res.,* **16,** 699–712.

Turpin, R., and Lejeune, J. 1969. *Human Afflictions and Chromosomal Abnormalities,* pp. 57–58. Oxford: Pergamon Press.

Tyukov, A. I. 1967. Age changes in the vessels in the corpora cavernosa of the penis. *Arkh. Patol.,* **29,** 29–34.

Van Wagenen, G. 1952. Age at menarche of the laboratory rhesus monkey. *Anat. Record,* **112,** 436.

Van Wagenen, G. 1970. Menopause in a subhuman primate (Macaca mulatta). *Anat. Record,* **166,** 392.

Vermeulen, A. 1976. The hormonal activity of the postmenopausal ovary. *J. Clin. Endocrinol.,* **42,** 247–253.

Vermeulen, A., Rubens, R., and Verdonck, L. 1972. Testosterone secretion and metabolism in male senescence. *J. Clin. Endocrinol. Metab.,* **34,** 730–735.

Vermeulen, A., Verdonck, L., Van der Straeten, M., and Orie, N. 1969. Capacity of the testosterone-binding globulin in human plasma and influence of specific binding of testosterone on its metabolic clearance rate. *J. Clin. Endocrinol. Metab.,* **29,** 1470–1480.

Weiss, J., and Lansing, A. I. 1953. Age changes in the fine structure of anterior pituitary of the mouse. *Proc. Soc. Exp. Biol. Med.,* **82,** 460–466.

Welsch, C. W., Jenkins, T. W., and Meites, J., 1970. Increased incidence of mammary tumors in the female rat grafted with multiple pituitaries. *Cancer Res.,* **30,** 1024–1029.

Welsch, C. W., Nagasawa, H., and Meites, J. 1970. Increased incidence of spontaneous mammary tumors in female rats with induced hypothalamic lesions. *Cancer Res.,* **30,** 2310–2313.

Wison, R. A., and Wilson, T. A. 1972. The basic philosophy of estrogen maintenance. *J. Am. Geriat. Soc.,* **20,** 521–523.

Witt, H-J., 1963. Structural elements and general function of the endometrium. Light microscope morphology. I. *In.* H. Schmidt-Matthiesen (ed.), *The Normal Human Endometrium,* pp. 24–64. New York: McGraw-Hill.

Woessner, J. F., Jr., 1963. Age related changes of the human uterus and its connective tissue framework. *J. Geront.,* **18,** 220–226.

Wolfe, J. M. 1943. The effects of advancing age on the structure of the anterior hypophysis and ovaries of female rats. *Am. J. Anat.,* **72,** 361–383.

Wuttke, W., and Meites, J. 1973. Effects of electrochemical stimulation of medial preoptic area on prolactin and luteinizing hormone release in old female rats. *Pflüg. Arch.,* **341,** 1–6.

Zuckerman, S. 1956. The regenerative capacity of ovarian tissue. *In,* G. E. W. Wolstenholme and E. C. P. Millar (ed.), *Aging in Transient Tissues,* Vol. 2, Ciba Found. Colloq. Aging, pp. 31–58. Boston: Little, Brown.

14
ENDOCRINE SYSTEMS

Reubin Andres

and

Jordan D. Tobin

National Institute on Aging

INTRODUCTION

Initiation of interest in the gerontologic aspects of endocrinology is generally attributed to Brown-Sequard (1889) who reported the rejuvenating effects in himself of an extract of young dog's testes. The fact that he used an aqueous extract which could not have contained the steroid hormone, testosterone, lends piquancy to the story. Nevertheless this endocrine-gerontology link had an obvious impact on both fields, the effects of which still linger in the wistful and wishful thinking that some simple "replacement therapy" of waning hormonal function will reverse, stop, or decelerate the effects of aging.

The pace of research on endocrine glands in gerontology may be judged by the fact that over half of the references in this chapter were published within the past 5 years and 90 percent in the past 10 years. Among these are several recent summaries which are also indicative of this burgeoning interest. Gregerman and Bierman (1974) contributed an innovative chapter entitled "Aging and Hormones" which appeared for the first time in the 5th edition of the important *Textbook of Endocrinology,* edited by R. H. Williams. This article, as well as those by Gusseck (1972) and Roth (1975b), are much more than mere catalogues; they point out the remarkable complexities involved in interpreting the literature on the endocrines and aging.

This chapter will focus primarily on the pancreatic hormones (insulin and glucagon), the hypothalamic and anterior pituitary hormones (omitting the gonadotropins), the thyroid hormones, and the adrenal glucocorticoids. The little information available on the primary hormones of calcium metabolism (parathyroid hormone and calcitonin), the gonadal steroids, the nervous system hormones (including those of the posterior pituitary), and gastrointestinal hormones is discussed elsewhere in the *Handbook.*

We have, where information is available, summarized age effects on: structure and hormonal content of the individual glands, responses of the glands to stimuli, kinetics of hormonal distribution and metabolism, and sensitivity of the end organs to the hormones; and we have called attention to the important new areas of hormone receptors, "secondary messengers," and adaptive cell responses. Both the information available and the gaps in knowledge are awesome. Discrepancies are common and are, for example, evident in the tabular summaries of the end-organ sensitivity to hormones in the three review articles noted above. Another important but necessary omission from this chapter is that of the special presentation or manifestations of the endocrine diseases in the elderly and special problems in the therapy of these diseases in the aged. In general, the problems of endocrine diagnosis in the elderly have not been discussed with the exception of diabetes. The discussion of diabetes serves to illustrate the difficulties of differentiating a normal age change from a disease state. The decision concerning the setting of age-adjusted normative standards for endocrine function is a corollary of the aging *vs.* disease dilemma.

There is, of necessity, a mingling of data derived from studies on man and on experimental animals. These diverse studies are as essential for endocrinology as for other fields. In general the human studies, which demand an element of "non-invasiveness," has forced the clinical investigator to expend considerable effort on the design of experiments which, although taking place in a relatively intact organism, can still lead to an understanding of the mechanisms underlying age changes. This goal is, unfortunately, not always met.

INSULIN

From the standpoint of gerontologic interests, insulin is undoubtedly the most extensively studied of the hormones. This is probably due to the clinical importance of the strongly age-related disease of insulin deficiency, diabetes mellitus. The advent of immunoassay has also provided a remarkable stimulus to research. Before insulin measurements were feasible, indirect studies of insulin pathophysiology were conducted using the glucose tolerance test.

The effect of aging on deterioration of glucose tolerance was first noted over 50 years ago, and there has been an uninterrupted stream of publications since then (Andres, 1971). An overwhelming consensus on certain aspects of these studies has emerged: (1) The deterioration of "tolerance" (i.e., the ability to dispose of administered glucose efficiently) is progressive throughout the adult span of life. (2) A variety of diagnostic tests for diabetes all show this age effect (oral glucose tolerance, intravenous glucose tolerance, steroid primed oral glucose tolerance, and intravenous tolbu-

tamide tolerance). (3) The deterioration in performance is so large that approximately half of older subjects lie above an arbitrary mean + 2SD cut-off point of data derived from young adults. Here perhaps the consensus ends. Among questions of great theoretical and clinical importance but still in serious dispute are: (1) Should age adjustments of standards of normality be made, or should all subjects be judged by standards derived from young adults? (2) Is the mechanism of the deterioration in performance identical with, similar to, or entirely different from the mechanism underlying the disease, diabetes mellitus? (3) In a quantitative sense, just how common is the deterioration of performance? (Some reports show only a slight change with age, while others report that 100 percent of older subjects are abnormal.) The overriding question can be put simply: (4) Is the change with age physiologic (i.e., "normal") or pathologic (i.e., "disease" associated)?

Underlying the diversity of estimates of the degree of "abnormality" associated with aging are many experimental variables in the performance of the diagnostic tests and in the techniques used to select the young and old subjects (Committee on Statistics, 1969). Among the more important technical variables are: the dose of glucose, blood sampling times, time of day of glucose administration, prohibition or allowance of physical activity during the test, use of venous or capillary blood, measurement of glucose concentration in whole blood, plasma, or serum, and chemical method for glucose analysis. Among the diverse subjects used are: carefully stratified samples of large populations, entire smaller communities, self-recruited volunteer populations, veterans groups, food-handlers, residents of old age homes, or patients in chronic disease hospitals. There are also different procedures for including or excluding subjects with known histories of diabetes (or with positive family histories of diabetes), gross obesity, medication with drugs known to influence test performance, or with known diseases associated with abnormal performance (hyperlipidemia, coronary heart disease, etc.). Even though there is much qualitative information concerning the impact of these technical and personal variables on test performance, it is not possible to present a cogent summary of the many studies performed.

Representative studies of the effect of aging on performance for the oral glucose tolerance test (OGTT), the intravenous glucose tolerance test (IVGTT), and the intravenous tolbutamide response test (TRT) are summarized in Tables 1-3. Aging effects on the cortisone primed oral glucose tolerance test were discussed by Pozefsky, Colker, Langs, and Andres (1965) (Figure 1). The OGTT (Table 1) is performed by administering glucose either in fixed amounts or adjusted for body size. As glucose is absorbed, the blood glucose concentration rises; then as glucose utilization by the body increases, the blood glucose concentration falls. Performance level thus is judged by the level of glucose at fixed times (usually 1 and 2 hr) after glucose ingestion.

The IVGTT (Table 2) is most commonly performed by infusing a pulse of glucose in a 2 to 5-minute period. The dose varies in the several studies and is either a fixed amount or an amount adjusted for body size. The blood glucose concentration increases with the infusion and begins to fall at the end of the infusion. The fall in the logarithm of the glucose concentration with time from about 15 to 60 min. tends to be remarkably linear. Performance can thus be expressed as a decay constant, K, in terms of percent fall per minute.

The TRT (Table 3 and Figure 2) consists of the infusion of either 1 gram of tolbutamide to all subjects or, in one case, (Swerdloff, Pozefsky, Tobin, and Andres, 1967) of 1 gram per 70 kg body weight. Tolbutamide induces the rapid secretion of insulin, and blood glucose concentration consequently falls. Test performance is judged by the percentage fall in

TABLE 1. ORAL GLUCOSE TOLERANCE TEST.
(References for this table are given in Andres and Tobin, 1972)

Study[a]	Glucose dose (g)	Source of blood[d]	AGE (YR) Young	AGE (YR) Old	Mean Blood Gluc.[e] (mg%) 1 HR Young	1 HR Old	2 HR Young	2 HR Old	Age Effect on Glucose Conc. (mg% per decade life) 1 hr	2 hr
1. U.S. Nat. Center Health Stat., 1964	50	V	18-24	75-79	100	166	–	–	12	–
2. Welborn et al., 1969	50	V	21-29	>70	86	135	–	–	10	–
3. Boyns et al., 1969	50	V	<24	>55	89	125	74	78	9	1
4. Nilsson et al., 1967	(50)[b]	C	20-39	60-79	111	154	–	–	11	–
5. Butterfield, 1966	50	C	20-29	70-79	125	194	86	121	14	7
6. Diabetes Survey Working Party, 1963	50	C	<29	>70	122	186	98	119	13	4
7. Hayner et al., 1965	100	V	16-19	70-79	100	177	–	–	13	–
8. Unger, 1957	100	V	18-29	50-59	–	–	99	131	–	11
9. Studer et al., 1969	100	C	25-34	65-74	–	–	98	127	–	7
10. Gerontology Research Center, 1972	(122)[c]	V	20-29	70-79	144	174	113	145	6	6

[a]In studies 3-6 and 8-10, glucose was ingested in the morning after an overnight fast. In studies 1, 2, and 7, subjects presented themselves for testing at various times of the day and at various time intervals after the last meal.

[b]30 g glucose per m^2 surface area—50 g for man of average size.

[c]1.75 g per kg body weight = 122 g per 70 kg man.

[d]V = antecubital venous blood; C = capillary blood.

[e]It should be stressed that these values should *not* be taken as the upper limits of normality. They represent mean values. Note that at 2 hours the *mean* value for the old subjects is equal to or exceeds 120 mg%, a level commonly taken to be the upper limit of normality.

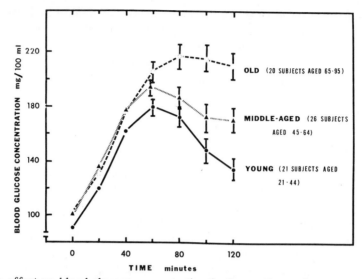

Figure 1. Age effect on blood glucose concentration in the cortisone glucose tolerance test. The test requires administration of cortisone acetate in doses of approximately 0.78 mg per kg body weight, 8.5 and 2 hr prior to the ingestion of 1.75 g glucose per kg body weight. (From Pozefsky, T., Colker, J. L., Langs, H. M., and Andres, R. 1965. The cortisone-glucose tolerance test. *Annals of Internal Medicine,* **63**: 988–1000.)

TABLE 2. INTRAVENOUS GLUCOSE TOLERANCE TEST.
(References for this table are given in Andres and Tobin, 1972)

Study	Glucose dose	AGE OF SUBJECTS[a] Young	AGE OF SUBJECTS[a] Old	MEAN DECAY CONSTANT, K[b] Young	MEAN DECAY CONSTANT, K[b] Old	Age effect on K (percent per decade of life)[c]
1. Schneeberg and Finestone, 1952[d]	0.33 g/kg	16–39 (48)	60–90 (39)	1.88	1.14	0.15
2. Conard, 1955	0.33 g/kg	20–39 (33)	60–88 (27)	1.85	1.09	0.19
3. Silverstone et al., 1957	25 g	23–37 (12)	65–87 (11)	1.68	0.98	0.15
4. Streeten et al., 1964	25 g	21–32 (23)	70–92 (15)	2.35	1.16	0.21
5. Dyck and Moorhouse, 1966[e]	50 g/1.73 m²	18–39 (31)	60–75 (13)	2.61	1.48	0.28
6. Cerasi and Luft, 1967[f]	25 g	20–39 (49)	60–79 (14)	1.76	1.45	0.09
7. Gerontology Research Center, 1972	0.375 g/kg	20–39 (70)	60–79 (111)	1.37	1.01	0.09

[a]The number of subjects in each age group is given in parentheses.
[b]The decay constant is computed from the absolute glucose concentration, not from the increment in glucose over the fasting value. K has the dimensions of percent glucose disappearance per minute.
[c]Computed from the difference between mean K of the young and old groups, divided by the difference between the mean age of these two groups, multiplied by 10.
[d]K values computed from table of mean glucose concentrations at 30 and 60 min.
[e]The higher mean K values in this study are due to the high glucose dose used. The authors consider the limit of normality to be 1.50 with this dose.
[f]The high mean K value in the older subjects in this study is at least partly due to the elimination of subjects with $K < 1.00$; the authors wish to study "normal" old subjects. The mean is thus arbitrarily raised.

TABLE 3. INTRAVENOUS TOLBUTAMIDE RESPONSE TEST.[a]
(References for this table are given in Andres and Tobin, 1972)

	AGE OF SUBJECTS		MEAN GLUCOSE CONC. AT 30 MIN. (% of fasting value)		Prescreening by oral GTT[b]
Study	Younger	Older	Young	Old	
1. Unger and Madison, 1958	–	–	– 51	–	*
2. Vecchio et al., 1965	App 20–58	–	54	–	*
3. Kaplan, 1961	18–59	60+	57	63	*
4. Oberdisse et al., 1962[c]	App 18–45	–	58	–	*
5. Haas, 1964[c]	Young adults	–	60	–	
6. Swerdloff et al., 1967	20–29	50–81	60	75	
7. Pereira et al., 1962	14–48	–	61	–	
8. Marigo et al., 1962	20–59	60+	63	75	
9. Bronzini et al., 1964	–	64–89	–	65	
10. Mazzi et al., 1964	–	65+	–	78	
11. Ortone, 1964[d]	–	64–86	–	84	

[a]Studies selected for this table have met the following criteria: (1) the age of the subject must be given reasonably clearly, (2) the age range of the younger subjects must not have exceeded 59 years, and (3) the number of subjects in an age group must be at least 19. The Unger and Madison study is included despite uncertainty of the age range since it is the original publication which provides the generally accepted standards for judging performance.

[b]In the studies marked by an asterisk, in order to be included for tolbutamide testing, subjects had to first pass a stringently interpreted oral glucose tolerance screening test. Subjects in these studies therefore represent that fraction of the population which performs superiorly on diabetes testing. This probably explains the lower glucose concentrations (i.e., the better tolbutamide performance) in the 4 studies marked with the asterisks as compared to the 7 done on subjects not preselected in this manner.

[c]These data were computed by us from illustrations, not from tabular data and are therefore subject to minor errors in our readings of the illustrations.

[d]One subject with fasting glucose values of 140 and 122 mg% was included by Ortone but excluded in our computations in the table above.

glucose concentration from the preinjection value; 20 and 30-minute values are generally used—the table presents 30-minute values only.

These summaries reveal marked *quantitative* differences in the magnitude of the age effect, although the effect itself is hardly in dispute. From a practical standpoint, a decision must be made concerning adjustment of normative standards for age. (These tables present only mean values; the papers themselves may be consulted to obtain data concerning distributions of values at different ages.) The arguments for and against the use of age adjustment have been presented recently by O'Sullivan (1974) and Andres, (1971). An approach to providing an age adjustment is shown in Figure 3. From data on the OGTT, a nomogram was constructed. An individual's test performance can be derived in comparison to his own age cohort and expressed in terms of a percentile rank (see legend of Figure 3). The decision as to "normality" or "abnormality" of various percentiles is, at this time, arbitrary (Andres, 1971).

There are at least two approaches for the resolution of this question. One is "actuarial" and involves long-term follow-up of large numbers of individuals over the entire adult age span. This approach is identical to studies which established the importance of hypertension and obesity as risk factors for coronary heart disease and requires longitudinal studies.

The other approach is "experimental." It aims to define the mechanism of the deterioration in performance with age and aims to differentiate the aging mechanism from that of the disease state, diabetes. Two basic questions have been posed: (1) Is the pancreatic beta cell response to hyperglycemia decreased with advancing age? (2) Is the sensitivity of tissues to insulin reduced with age?

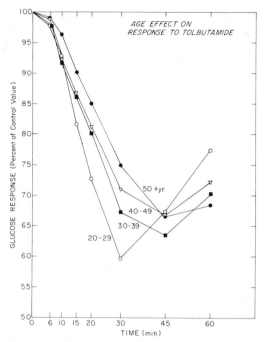

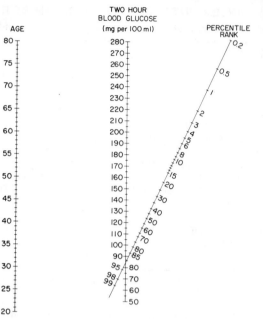

Figure 2. Age effect on blood glucose response to tolbutamide. The number of subjects were: 20-29 years, $n = 26$; 30-39 years, $n = 13$; 40-49 years, $n = 17$; 50-81 years, $n = 85$. The oldest three decades were grouped together since no age change occurred after age 50 in this test. (From Swerdloff, R. S., Pozefsky, T., Tobin, J. D., and Andres, R. 1967. Influence of age on the intravenous tolbutamide response test. *Diabetes,* **15,** 161–170.)

Figure 3. Nomogram for the oral glucose tolerance test. A line extending from the subject's age through the subject's 2-hr blood glucose concentration will intersect the percentile rank line; thus a 51-year-old subject with a 2-hr glucose of 130 mg per 100 ml will have a rank of 50%, an exactly average performance, while a 49-year-old with a glucose value of 190 will rank at 3%, a very poor performance. (From Andres, R.: Aging and diabetes. 1971 *Medical Clinics of North America,* **55**: 835–846.)

Most studies have administered glucose to young adult and old subjects either orally or intravenously. Insulin concentration in serum is then assayed as a measure of the beta cell (pancreatic) response. Interpretation of these results is generally difficult since older subjects have higher glucose responses and it is the level of blood glucose which is the major stimulus for insulin release. Thus, a low insulin response in the older subjects may be clear-cut evidence of a beta cell defect, but an elevated or "normal" response is difficult to interpret. Table 4 summarizes results of studies in man. The lack of consistency in the results is all too evident.

A recently developed technique, the "glucose-clamp" (Andres, Pozefsky, Swerdloff, and Tobin, 1970), avoids the problem of uncontrolled glucose concentrations in studies as noted above. The blood glucose concentration is placed under the investigator's control by rapid analysis of the arterial glucose concentration and by appropriate negative feedback servo-control of a continuous but variable intravenous glucose infusion rate. Steady-state hyperglycemia at four levels (140, 180, 220, and 300 mg/100 ml) for 2 hours results in biphasic serum insulin responses, a rapid peak followed by a fall and a secondary slow rise. Older subjects at the lower three glucose plateaus show miniature insulin curves as compared to younger subjects. Thus, since the pancreas is perfused solely by arterial blood and since the hyperglycemic stimulus to insulin release is identical in all subjects, these studies lead us to conclude that beta cell sensitivity to glucose decreases with age.

Several studies on insulin levels in the rat

TABLE 4. EFFECT OF AGE ON SERUM INSULIN RESPONSE TO GLUCOSE IN MAN.[a]

	Oral glucose	Intravenous glucose
Barbagallo-Sangiorgi et al., 1970		↓ at 2, 5, and 10 min.
Boyns et al., 1969	0(F); ↑(M)[b] at 60 min.	
Björntorp, Berchtold, and Tibblin, 1971	0	
Chlouverakis, Jarrett, and Keen, 1967	↑ at 60 min. ($.05 < p < .10$)	
Crockford, Harbeck, and Williams, 1966		↓ at 6 min.
Dudl and Ensinck, 1972		↓ at 3–5 min.
Hales et al., 1968	↑ at 90 and 120 min.	
Johansen, 1973		0
Nolan et al., 1973	↑ at 60 min.	
Palmer and Ensinck, 1974		0
Reaven and Miller, 1968	0	
Sandberg et al., 1973	↑ at 60–120 min.	
Schreuder, 1972		↑ (total 0–60 min. area)
Sensi et al., 1972	↓ at 30 min.; ↑ at 120 min.	↓ at 3 min.; ↑ at 40 and 60 min.
Streeten et al., 1965[c]		↑ at 20 min.
Welborn et al., 1966	0	
Zhukov, 1965[c]	↓ at ? time	

[a]↑ = increase with age; ↓ = decrease with age; 0 = no significant difference with age.
[b]F = female; M = male.
[c]"Insulin-like activity" by fat pad assay (Streeten) and by rat diaphragm assay (Zhukov); all other studies measured insulin by immunoassay.

(Table 5) are difficult to interpret. Such variables as the strain used, use of anesthesia, number of hours of fasting, and breeding status interact to give these diverse results.

Other insulinotropic stimuli have also begun to be explored. Johansen (1973) reported no significant age differences in serum insulin responses to intravenous tolbutamide administration. Palmer and Ensinck (1974) showed no age differences in plasma insulin responses to intravenous secretin, but Dudl and Ensinck (1972) reported a decreased insulin response to intravenous arginine infusion with increasing age. Arginine infusion also stimulates growth hormone secretion (see below), and interpretation of insulin responses is therefore complex. It is worth pointing out that the hormonal as well as the nonhormonal control of the glucose

TABLE 5. EFFECT OF AGE ON SERUM INSULIN LEVELS IN THE RAT.

Study	Fast (hr)	Anesthesia	Strain	AGE (mo)[a] Younger	Older	Effect of age on insulin level[b]
1. Berdanier, Marshall, and Moser, 1971	16	yes	Wistar	3.3	10	↑
			BHE	3.3	10	0
			BHE-IN	3.3	10	0
2. Freeman, Karoly, and Adelman, 1973[c]	72	yes	Chas. River	12	24	↓
	0	yes	Chas. River	12	24	↓
3. Frolkis et al., 1971	?	?	"albino"	6–8	24–26	↓
4. Gommers and de Gasparo, 1972	16	no	Wistar	12	24	0
5. Lewis and Wexler, 1974	4	no	Sprague-Dawley	6–8	15–18	↑

[a]In general, studies on very young rats are not included in this table. The first study is included to illustrate strain differences obtained in one laboratory.
[b]↑ = increase with age; ↓ = decrease with age; 0 = no significant difference with age.
[c]Portal venous blood in this study; in other studies blood obtained from tail vein, intracardiac puncture, or decapitation.

economy of the body is extremely complex, and the interaction of these factors with aging processes has hardly been examined. Some of these factors were reviewed by Ensinck and Williams (1972); the absence of age studies is conspicuous in their authoritative summary.

An important hormone or group of hormones, the "gastrointestinal insulin-stimulating hormone(s)" have been shown to play an important role in the body's glucose economy. The oral administration of glucose causes much greater insulin release than does intravenous glucose. The mediation of this effect is undoubtedly via one or more hormones released from the small intestine into the bloodstream when glucose is ingested. The quantification of this effect and possible age differences in their release and in their effectiveness as insulin-stimulators are unknown (Tobin, Swerdloff, and Andres, 1966).

The effectiveness of insulin at its target organs has been explored by the "intravenous insulin tolerance test." The nearly instantaneous injection of the dose ordinarily used in human studies (100 mU of insulin per kg body weight) results in a sudden surge of plasma insulin concentration to levels well above 1,000 μU/ml, greatly in excess of levels achievable by normal physiological mechanisms (several hundred μU/ml at most). Studies in man by Kalk, Vinik, Pimstone, and Jackson (1973) and by Martin, Pearson, and Stocks (1968) showed no age effects on insulin sensitivity. However, Frolkis, Bogatskaya, Bogush, and Shevchuk (1971) using a smaller insulin dose in the rabbit (25mU/kg), reported a surprising increase in sensitivity to insulin with age. The fall in blood sugar was 29 ± 2.4 mg per 100 ml in the old rabbits and 14 ± 2.1 mg per 100 ml in adults.

The concentration curves of insulin relative to the concentration curves of glucose during glucose tolerance tests have been examined to assess the effectiveness of the released insulin. Barbagallo-Sangiorgi, Laudicina, Bompiani, and Durante (1970) and Johansen (1973) report discrepant results and conclusions. Both investigators selected superior older subjects whose glucose curves resembled those of young subjects on the intravenous glucose tolerance test. Barbagallo's subjects, however, had lower insulin responses with age (and thus must have been hypersensitive to insulin since their glu-

cose curves fell rapidly), while Johansen's insulin levels were slightly, albeit insignificantly, higher in the older subjects.

An alternative approach to the assessment of insulin sensitivity is also offered by the glucose-clamp technique (Tobin, Sherwin, Liljenquist, Insel, and Andres, 1972). After a priming infusion, insulin was infused continuously at rates of 1 or 2 mU/kg body wt/min; steady-state arterial plasma insulin concentrations of 100 or 200 μU/ml were achieved—well within the physiologic range. Hypoglycemia was prevented by a servo-controlled intravenous glucose infusion. The rate of glucose infused under steady-state conditions is a measure of sensitivity of body tissues to insulin. No differences in sensitivity with age were present in these studies.

The measurement of insulin in plasma is at best an indirect index of the rate at which it is being secreted. In order to interpret plasma levels, the kinetics of insulin distribution and catabolism must be understood. Welsh, Henley, Williams, and Cox (1956) reported no differences in the percent of ^{131}I-insulin remaining in plasma 60 min. after intravenous injection. More recent studies by Orskov and Christensen (1969) have shown that ^{131}I-insluin does not behave kinetically as "native" insulin. They therefore infused 8 units of human insulin intravenously into young and old subjects. The disappearance rates were much more rapid for unlabeled than for labeled insulin, but again no age differences were found.

A further refinement in the analysis of insulin kinetics has recently been reported by Sherwin, Kramer, Tobin, Insel, Liljenquist, Berman, and Andres (1974). A computer simulation technique was used to define the parameters of a three-compartment insulin system. Tobin *et al.* (1972) in a preliminary report, showed that there are no differences with age in any of the pool sizes or exchange constants of the model. Furthermore, neither the metabolic clearance rate for insulin nor the delivery rate of insulin to the systemic circulation under basal conditions was influenced by age.

PROINSULIN

Insulin is synthesized in the beta cell as a single chain molecule (proinsulin) which is then cleaved intracellularly to form the double-chain insulin molecule (Steiner, Kemmler, Clark, Oyer, and Rubenstein, 1972). Proinsulin is also released intact to some extent. In circulating plasma, the proinsulin is detected immunologically by the usual immunoassay procedures for insulin, but its biological potency is only a small fraction of that of insulin. Measurement of serum insulin levels may therefore be deceptive unless the secretion of proinsulin relative to insulin is known. In the only study reported to date, Duckworth and Kitabchi (1972) found no differences in proinsulin levels in man under basal conditions; after an oral glucose challenge, proinsulin levels rose earlier and higher in 40 to 60 year-old subjects than in 21 to 35 year olds. Over the 3 hr period after oral glucose, 8 percent of the total immunoreactive insulin was proinsulin in the younger subjects versus 14 percent in the older subjects. These results imply that less of the secreted insulin in older subjects is biologically effective. Further studies are required as interpretation of beta cell responses to insulinotropic agents and sensitivity of tissues to "insulin" may be misinterpreted if this differential proinsulin response is confirmed.

GLUCAGON

The alpha cell hormone of the pancreas may play a critical role in the pathophysiology of diabetes mellitus (Unger, 1971). The recent availablility of a highly specific immunoassay for glucagon has stimulated intensive investigations of its role in diabetes. It is therefore disappointing that so little has been reported on age and glucagon physiology. There has been one report on age differences in response to exogenously administered glucagon and one abstract on endogenous glucagon responses. Korkushko and Orlov (1972) examined the hyperglycemic effect of glucagon administration in apparently healthy subjects aged 19–25, 60–74, and 75–84 years (10 per group). The increase in blood glucose was delayed in time and reduced in magnitude in the older groups. Dudl and Ensinck (1972) in studies on 44 subjects aged 22 to 81 years reported no differences either in fasting plasma levels of glucagon or in the glucagon response to intravenous arginine stimulation. These results

require confirmation and extension before a role for glucagon in aging physiology can be assigned. The lack of agreement in the studies on insulin, noted in the previous section, emphasizes the need for further evaluations of glucagon metabolism in aging.

THICKENING OF CAPILLARY BASEMENT MEMBRANE—RELATION TO AGING AND TO DIABETES MELLITUS

A characteristic microangiopathy in a variety of tissues has been identified in diabetics. This lesion of the capillary bed can devastate the renal glomerulus and the retina but is also seen in skin, muscle, and indeed in most, if not all, tissues of the body. At issue is the question of the pathogenesis of the glycoprotein which accumulates and thickens the basement membrane of the capillaries. Siperstein, Unger, and Madison (1968) contend that the lesion is due to a primary genetic defect, that it occurs in diabetics at a stage of the disease when no metabolic abnormalities are demonstrable, and that no change in basement membrane thickness (BMT) occurs with age. Kilo, Vogler, and Williamson (1972) on the other hand present evidence that the BMT in diabetes is secondary to a demonstrable derangement in glucose and insulin metabolism; they further show that BMT occurs normally with aging and that careful age control is essential in evaluating the lesion in disease groups. The effects of diabetes and of aging on BMT are confirmed by Jordan and Perley (1972). BMT is an important new marker for diabetes; further studies on the time course of its development and on its interactions with aging and with glucose tolerance test performance could be of great value in clarifying procedures for diagnosing diabetes at different ages.

ANTERIOR PITUITARY

Studies on the weight and morphology of the pituitary gland in a variety of species were summarized by Verzár (1966) and Bourne (1967), and those reviews should be consulted for original references.

Pituitary weight in the male rat declined from 38 mg/kg body weight in the 2- and 3-month-old animals to 27 mg/kg in the 6-, 10-, and 20-

month-animals. Pituitary weight increased commensurate with body size during development in the dog (Das and Magilton, 1971) and in swine (Das, Haensly, and Getty, 1971). In male and female beagles, the relative pituitary weight (gland wt/body wt) did not change during the adult years (1–13.6 years). In swine, the relative weight did not change in males or in females from 1-7 years of age. Only females were studied from 7-10 years; relative gland weight showed a marked increase in this older group and was due to lower body weight as well as greater absolute weight of the gland .

Autopsy studies in adult man show unimpressive effects of age on relative pituitary weight. Calloway, Foley, and Lagerbloom (1965) reported 400 autopsies from a Veterans Administration hospital. There was no change in relative gland weight from age 40 to 80; although the subjects in the 20-39 year age group had lower weights, the statistical significance of these results is unclear, because the number of subjects dying at those ages and the variance in weight was not given. Bakke, Lawrence, Knudtson, Roy, and Needman (1964) reported from 175 autopsies also in a Veterans Administration hospital that there was no significant age effect on pituitary weight or on body weight. As both groups of authors point out, the results in man must be interpreted cautiously since effects of the diverse terminal diseases may play an important role in weight, hormonal content, and histology of the gland.

Microscopic changes in human pituitary glands during adult aging include decreased vascularity, increased connective tissue, and a change in distribution of cell types. Between the ages of 18-50 and 51-78 years, eosinophils (growth hormone and prolactin-producing) decreased and chromophobes increased by about 4 percent. No studies have been reported using modern and more specific techniques for the indentification of specific hormone-producing cells. Verzár (1966) summarizes that the number of mitoses in the 300-day-old rat decreases to less than one-tenth the number in the 96-day-old animal. Mitochondria of basophils become swollen and vesicular, and their membranes become fragmented. The anterior pituitary of aged mice showed irregularity of outline of the nuclear membranes of all cells and increased density of the cortex of the nucleus.

GROWTH HORMONE (GH)

Interpretation of the hormonal content of the human pituitary obtained at autopsy is subject to the difficulties inherent in post mortem studies. With this caution in mind, the content of GH is reported to be relatively constant with age (Gershberg, 1957).

Basal (AM) Levels

The effects of aging are complicated by sex and obesity differences in GH physiology. Thus young men have lower basal GH levels and lower GH responses to stimuli than young women; furthermore, estrogen administration to men causes a female pattern of response (Frantz and Rabkin, 1965; Merimee, Rabinowitz, Riggs, Burgess, Rimoin, and McKusick, 1967). In the aged, differences between men and women in basal GH is in dispute (F > M, Laron, Doron, and Amikam, 1970; F = M, Cartlidge, Black, Hall, and Hall, 1970; F < M, Kalk et al., 1973).

Vidalon, Khurana, Chae, Gegick, Stephan, Nolan, and Danowski (1973) studied the effects of age and obesity on basal GH levels in 1,185 women between the ages of 20 and 59 years. Normal weight women, 40-59 years of age, had lower GH levels that 20-39 year-old subjects. Though estrogen levels were not measured, the authors suggested that the low GH might be associated with the menopause and be secondary to lower estrogen levels.

The young, obese women had lower GH levels than did the young nonobese, which agrees with the known effects of obesity on GH secretion (Rabinowitz, 1970). There were no significant GH differences with age in the obese subjects. In the oldest decade studied, 50-59 years, the GH levels were the same in the obese and nonobese groups, a result of the decline with age in the nonobese group and the constancy of GH levels in the obese group. The authors concluded that in the presence of obesity, estrogen did not exert its usual GH-enhancing effects.

These studies demonstrate the complexity of interpretation of age effects on hormone levels.

Variables which both change with age and influence the hormone under study (for example, obesity and estrogens in the case of growth hormone) may obscure or confound the primary effects of aging.

Sleep Induced Secretion

Bursts of GH secretion have been observed during the early stages of deep (slow wave) sleep in young adults (Takahashi, Kipnis, and Daughaday, 1968; Sassin, Parker, Mace, Gotlin, Johnson, and Rossman, 1969; Carlson, Gillin, Gorden, and Snyder, 1972), and the bursts have been proposed as a "physiologic" test of GH secretion (Mace, Gotlin, Sassin, Parker and Rossman, 1970). There have been only two reports on GH bursts during sleep in older adults, both dealing primarily with middle-aged subjects. Carlson et al., (1972) reported that four of five subjects aged 52–57 years and a single 73 year-old subject failed to show GH bursts during sleep. None of these subjects was obese, and only one was male. It is of interest that among the younger subjects, the largest GH bursts occurred in a 44-year-old postmenopausal woman who was receiving estrogen therapy. Finkelstein, Roffwarg, Boyar, Kream, and Hellman (1972) studied three postmenopausal woman (47–57 years) and two men (62 years). GH secretory levels during sleeping and waking were decreased in all and approached zero in three of the five subjects.

With aging there is a reduction in slow wave sleep (Roffwarg, Muzio, and Dement, 1966); this could be an explanation for the reduction in GH bursts. Carlson et al. (1972), however, could not demonstrate the close association of slow wave sleep and GH peaks, and they do not believe that altered sleep patterns with aging are responsible for the diminished GH bursts.

The interrelated variables of sex, obesity, and aging on the pattern of GH secretion require further study. Almost no very old subjects have been investigated.

The size of the pituitary gland, its hormone content, the basal plasma levels, and even sleep induced secretion do not fully test aging effects on GH secretion; the ability of the gland to secrete hormones in response to appropriate stimuli has been investigated.

Hypoglycemia Induced Secretion

Hypoglycemia, induced by the intravenous (IV) injection of insulin, has been used as such a stimulus. It has been emphasized that a fall of blood sugar to less than 50 percent of basal levels is required to assure a potent enough stress (Greenwood, Landon, and Stamp, 1966). Laron, Doron, and Amikam (1970), reported significantly lower mean GH responses in ten women and nine men over the age of 68 than in young subjects. They concluded that in seven individuals the response was slightly reduced; in four, the response was markedly reduced to levels compatible with GH insufficiency. The obesity of these subjects was not stated. Also, seven of the nineteen did not have glucose fall of 50 percent, including three of the four poorest responders.

Cartlidge et al. (1970), studied eight individuals aged 80–95 years after insulin injection. They found that "the GH production under the stress of insulin-induced hypoglycemia was normal in each instance" when compared to control values from the literature.

Kalk et al. (1973) also found that the mean GH response to insulin hypoglycemia in 30 subjects aged 63–99 years was similar to the mean response of 26 younger controls. They also reported that though the mean *fasting* GH concentration was lower in obese, elderly subjects than in lean elderly, the former group's response to hypoglycemia was not lower. In addition they found that elderly women had lower responses than did men. They concluded, however, that the small numbers in each subgroup make interpretation of these sex and obesity findings difficult.

The level of hypoglycemia required to elicit reliable growth hormone output causes discomfort and possible danger to elderly subjects. For this reason, the amino acid arginine has been used as a stimulus for GH release.

Arginine Induced Secretion

Studies in 44 men aged 22–81 years (Dudl, Ensinck, Palmer and Williams, 1973) showed that neither basal nor GH responses to an arginine infusion were significantly influenced by aging. Using ^{40}K to determine lean body mass, they noted a highly significant increase in adiposity with age and a highly significant inverse correlation between peak GH responses to arginine infusions and obesity. They suggested that the trend toward lower GH response to arginine with age, though not statistically significant in the whole sample, was attributable to the effect of adiposity in some individuals.

Responses to GH Administration

The effect of daily injection of GH for 10 days was studied in three men aged 75–85 years by Root and Oski (1969). Responses in the elderly were similar to young subjects previously studied in that there were an increase in net nitrogen retention, a decrease in BUN, an increase in plasma FFA concentrations, and a decrease in urinary sodium excretion. However, the elderly differed from young subjects in that there was no increase in hydroxyprolinuria in any subject, their red cells were resistant to the GH-induced inhibition of glucose consumption *in vitro*, and only one subject increased in urinary excretion of calcium.

These results should be accepted with caution, because the three subjects studied were hospitalized patients with serious, multiple medical complications. Further studies of metabolic responses to growth hormone on larger numbers of healthy aged men and women are needed.

THYROTROPIN (TSH)

The plasma content of TSH does not change with age. Mayberry, Gharib, Bilstad, and Sizemore (1971), measured plasma TSH levels in 307 subjects aged 4–89 years. Variance was very large over the entire age span. Mean values were highest in children and adolescents; during the adult years no distinct age trends are evident in the data. No age changes were observed in C57BL/6J male mice 9–28 months.*

Snyder and Utiger (1972) studied the secretion of TSH in response to synthetic thyrotropin-

*C. E. Finch, personal communication.

releasing hormone (TRH) in man. The maximal increase in TSH in 12 young (20–39 years) men occurred with a TRH dose of 400 μg intravenously; a higher TRH dose gave no further increase in TSH. The 400 μg dose gave intermediate TSH responses in 12 middle-aged (40–59 years) and the lowest responses in 12 old (69–79 years) men. The age differences are large and highly significant. They point out the necessity of using age-adjusted criteria in judging pituitary responsiveness to TRH. Since a dose:response curve was determined only for the young men, two possible explanations of the age effect cannot be differentiated: (1) a decreased maximal capacity of the pituitary response, and/or (2) a shift in the sensitivity curve of the pituitary to TRH.

The Snyder and Utiger finding of decreased TSH response to TRH administration in men has been confirmed by Azizi, Vagenakis, Portnay, Rapoport, Ingbar, and Braverman (1975). They gave 2 mg TRH intramuscularly to nine young men (20–33 years) and eight older men (50–72 years). In addition, they studied an equal number of women in the two age groups and found no age differences in TSH response. Both young and old women had greater TSH responses than the comparably aged man.

SOMATOSTATIN

This recently described hypothalamic hormone (Brazeau and Guillemin, 1974) acts to inhibit the release of insulin, glucagon, and growth hormone. The quantification of its role in the total scheme of endocrine checks and balances is under intensive investigation. Whether changes in its function occur with age is unknown at this time.

CORTICOTROPIN (ACTH)

The pituitary content of ACTH does not appear to change with age (Verzár, 1966). Jensen and Blichert-Toft (1971) found that there was no significant difference in the 8:00 A.M. serum ACTH concentration between 28 elderly and 25 young subjects. Studies in five of these elderly subjects indicated that the circadian rhythms of both ACTH and cortisol were intact, with highest values in the morning and lowest in the evening.

With the exception of the one study noted above, measurements of ACTH levels in plasma have not been performed as a function of age. The status of endogenous ACTH secretion has been inferred by bioassay, i.e., by assay of adrenal glucocorticoid responses in plasma or urine. Thus, intactness of the adrenal response mechanism must be assumed if the studies noted in this section are to be taken as evidence of anterior pituitary function (see section on glucocorticoids below).

Stress is a known stimulus to the secretion of ACTH. Insulin induced hypoglycemia in man and ether anesthesia in rats have been used as provocative tests of the hypothalamic-pituitary axis. It is assumed that the elderly and the young perceive the stimulus identically, that is, that the stress is the same in both age groups.

Studies on the effect of insulin induced hypoglycemia have yielded conflicting results. Hochstaedt, Schneebaum and Shadel (1961) found that at 30 and 60 min. after insulin administration, the plasma 17-hydroxycorticosteroids (17-OHCS) in 28 elderly subjects (mean age 76 years) were significantly lower than the values in 20 younger volunteers (mean age 23 years). These results were interpreted as a failure of the hypothalamic-pituitary portion of the axis, since plasma levels of 17-OHCS were similar in young and old subjects after an injection of exogenous ACTH. These latter studies indicate that the old adrenal responds adequately to maximal levels of ACTH.

Other investigators (Friedman, Green, and Sharland, 1969; Cartlidge et al., 1970) report that the maximal rise in 17-OHCS after insulin hypoglycemia was not altered in elderly subjects. The reason for the discrepancies in these studies is not clear.

Hess and Riegle (1970) studied the effect in rats of the stress of ether anesthesia on plasma corticosterone in 45 young males (5.6 months), 27 old males (22.0 months), 39 young females (5.2 months), and 133 old females (25.4 months). Females had significantly greater responses than males at both ages. In both sexes there was a small but significantly decreased response with age (old females 20 percent lower, old males 14 percent lower than young controls).

The hypothalamus-anterior pituitary axis also responds to the negative feedback effects of the glucocorticoids (17-OHCS). Thus elevation of 17-OHCS levels inhibits ACTH secretion, and depression of 17-OHCS levels stimulates ACTH release. This aspect of hypothalamus-anterior pituitary function can be tested by administration of metyrapone, which inhibits the synthesis of cortisol in the adrenal cortex by blocking 11-hydroxylase. The sequence of events after metyrapone is therefore a fall in 17-OHCS, then a rise in plasma ACTH, followed by a rise in the sterioid intermediate product, 11-deoxycortisol (Compound S). Direct measurement of ACTH is difficult; therefore assay of the rise in Compound S levels is the measure of the feedback effect. Blichert-Toft, Blichert-Toft, and Jensen (1970) demonstrated that with the intravenous administration of metyrapone (as opposed to the conflicting results from oral administration), there is no significant difference between young and old subjects. They recognize that possible differences with age in clearance of Compound S might mask age differences (Gregerman and Bierman, 1974), but data are not available on the effect of age on the metabolism of Compound S.

The sensitivity of the anterior pituitary (ACTH) to the negative feedback effects of glucocorticoids can also be measured by administration of synthetic steroids which are biologically much more active than cortisol; thus, they exert a suppressive effect on the pituitary while contributing little or nothing to the steroid measurements. In a complex set of experiments, Riegle and Hess (1972) studied the effects of age, sex, synthetic steroid dosage, and duration of administration on plasma corticosterone responses to the stress of ether anesthesia in the rat. With high doses and chronic administration, the corticosterone responses were markedly suppressed in all groups. At lower doses and shorter duration of drug administration, there was less suppression of stress activation of the adrenal cortex in old than in young rats, male and female.

Two studies of pituitary suppression in man

have been reported. Gittler and Friedfeld (1962) administered 9 alpha fluorohydrocortisone to five elderly subjects and measured urinary steroid excretion, and Freidman, Green, and Sharland (1969) administered dexamethasone to 21 elderly subjects and assayed plasma steroid levels. In both studies, normal responsiveness of the pituitary to the suppressive effect of circulating steroids was demonstrated.

The findings of similar basal ACTH levels, a generally adequate response to stress, and an intact negative feedback effect of plasma cortisol levels in elderly subjects indicate that there is no gross deficit in the hypothalamus-pituitary-adrenal axis with age.

ADRENAL CORTEX

The weight of the adrenals in dogs increases proportionately with body weight and age, that is, there is no increase in the *relative* adrenal weight with age (Das, Haensly, and Getty, 1971; Haensly and Getty, 1965). Data from a series of 400 autopsies in man (Calloway, Foley, and Lagerbloom, 1965) showed no consistent changes in either absolute or relative weight over the age of 30. Khelimskii (1964) showed that there was little change in cortical thickness after age 20. Histological changes (reviewed by Bourne, 1967), include accumulation of pigment, proliferation of connective tissue, loss of characteristic lipids, vascular dilatation, hemorrhage, and fragmentation of mitochondria. Dobbie (1969) found an increase in nodular hyperplasia in man which was multifocal and bilateral. He reported a high correlation between distinct nodularity and capsular arteriopathy and suggested that "focal hyperplasia may represent a response to loss of cortical substance—segmental atrophy—due to focal ischemia."

GLUCOCORTICOIDS

Diurnal Plasma Levels

The basal plasma levels of the glucocorticoids (cortisol, corticosterone) do not change with age in cattle (Riegle and Nellor, 1967), goats (Riegle, Przekop, and Nellor, 1968), or rats (Hess and Riegle, 1970, 1972). Numerous stud-

ies in man (Friedman, Green, and Sharland, 1969; Cartlidge et al., 1970; Blichert-Toft, Blichert-Toft, and Jensen, 1970; West, Brown, Simons, Carter, Kumagai, and Englert, 1961; Grad, Kral, Payne, and Berenson, 1967; Gherondache, Romanoff, and Pincus, 1967) indicate that basal plasma levels are not different in young and old subjects. Cortisol levels in man are known to have a diurnal rhythm, with highest values in the morning and lowest in the evening. Friedman, Green, and Sharland (1969) measured 9:00 A.M. and midnight cortisol levels in 23 elderly subjects. The 9:00 A.M. level was higher than the midnight level in all but one subject. The mean A.M. level was similar to that reported for young adults, while the midnight level, though lower than the A.M. level, was higher than reported values in young subjects. Serio, Piolanti, Romano, De Magistris, and Giusti (1970) reported a circadian rhythm of plasma cortisol in 25 subjects over 70 years of age. The timing of the peak appeared later (towards 10:00 A.M.) in the old subjects and did not seem to be influenced by sleep disturbances. Grad, Rosenberg, Liberman, Trachtenberg, and Kral (1971) noted a normal diurnal variation in 18 of 23 elderly control subjects. They also noted that the presence of combinations of heart disease, chronic brain syndrome, or diabetes increased the prevalence of abnormal diurnal patterns (morning values not the highest and/or evening values not the lowest). This study serves to emphasize an important point: The common presence of multiple chronic diseases in the aged and their effects on various endocrine functions introduces serious complexities into efforts to evaluate "pure" biological changes of aging from those secondary to disease states.

Cortisol Kinetics

The plasma level of a hormone is not determined solely by its rate of secretion. It is also influenced by the kinetics of distribution and catabolism. Circulating levels can be misleading if these other factors are altered with age. In the case of cortisol, there is indeed evidence of an alteration with age in the metabolism of the hormone. West et al., (1961) infused cortisol into young and old men and reported that while there was no change in the apparent volume of distribution, there was significant slowing of the disposal rate as measured by its half life. $T_{1/2}$ in elderly subjects (mean age 73) was 40 percent longer than in younger subjects (mean age 33). Serio, Piolanti, Cappelli, De Magistris, Ricci, Anzalone, and Giusti (1969) used a tracer (tritiated cortisol) to study these variables in ten subjects (mean age 73) in order to avoid administration of large doses of the steroid. They too found that the volume of distribution was not different between young and old subjects. Although the half life was 40 percent longer in old subjects, this difference was not significantly different statistically because of the large variances.

Secretion and Urinary Excretion Rates

The combination of a decreased disposal rate and an unchanged plasma level in the aged can only occur if secretion rate is also decreased. This was directly confirmed by Romanoff, Morris, Welch, Rodriguez, and Pincus (1961), who found that the 24-hour secretion rate of cortisol in eight elderly men was 75 percent of that of their young controls.

The activity of the adrenal cortex has also been studied by measuring the urinary excretion of 17-hydroxycorticosteroids (17-OHCS). Though Gittler and Friedfeld (1962) observed normal excretion, others (West et al., 1961; Romanoff et al., 1961; Moncloa, Gómez, and Pretell, 1963; Grad et al., 1967) found a decreased excretion in the elderly.

There is a problem of the "reference base" used in interpreting the excretion rates of hormones. Clearly, when individuals of markedly different body size are compared, some correction for the mass of metabolically active tissue must be made. Thus, two lean young men of different size (say, 50 and 90 kg)—or, more dramatically, a mouse and an elephant—would not be expected to produce and therefore to excrete the same amount hormone. The urinary excretion of creatinine has been used as an index of active cellular mass. If 17-OHCS excretion is expressed per mg creatinine excreted, then indeed the reported age differences disap-

pear (Romanoff et al., 1961; Gherondache, Romanoff, and Pincus, 1967). The rationale for this "correction," however, is not accepted by all investigators (Moncloa, Gómez, and Pretell, 1963; Gregerman and Bierman, 1974).

The reduced rate of metabolism and excretion of the glucocorticoids with age in the face of unchanged plasma levels might be secondary to the known decrease in renal function with age (West et al., 1961). Other suggestions, so far unsupported by evidence, are that hepatic metabolism of the hormone is reduced either due to intrinsic hepatic mechanisms or to reduction in hepatic blood flow with age.

Cortisol Response to ACTH Administration

Though the basal plasma level of cortisol is well maintained in the elderly, the ability of the adrenal cortex to increase its secretion in response to ACTH is not as clear. Studies in cattle (Riegle and Nellor, 1967), goats (Riegle, Przekop, and Nellor, 1968), rats (Hess and Riegle, 1970), and mice (Eleftheriou, 1975) indicate a marked diminution in the response of old animals to exogenous ACTH. In man given porcine ACTH intramuscularly (IM), Friedman, Green, and Sharland (1969), found a larger increase in plasma cortisol in old subjects than in young. When these volunteers were given synthetic ACTH, the response was similar in young and old subjects. West et al., (1961) using intravenous (IV) ACTH infusions and Hochstaedt, Schneebaum, and Shadel (1961) using IM injections of a lower dose of ACTH noted an equal plasma cortisol response in young and old subjects. Gittler and Friedfeld (1962) reported 24-hour urinary excretions of 17-OHCS after IM ACTH that were the same in old subjects as those reported for young subjects, while Moncloa, Gómez, and Pretell (1963) found lower 24-hour excretion in response to ACTH IV infusions in older men than in their young controls. Romanoff, Baxter, Thomas, and Ferrechio (1969) also found a significantly lower excretion in old than in young men after IM ACTH injections. The percent increase, however, was similar in old and young subjects since the baseline values were significantly lower in the elderly. Whether absolute levels or percentage response should be considered as the better indicator of hormone function is a difficult, pervasive, and unresolved problem in endocrinology.

West *et al.,* (1961) pointed out that given the decreased disposal of cortisol noted in the elderly, one would expect a greater plasma level after ACTH in the elderly were the glucocorticoid secretion in the old equal to that in the young. Therefore, an equal plasma response to ACTH indicates less adrenal secretion and therefore a lower sensitivity of the adrenal in older subjects to maximum stimulation with ACTH.

It may be premature to attempt to summarize the effect of aging on the ACTH-glucocorticoid (GC) axis since not all of the facts are "hard." It would appear that (1) basal levels of ACTH and GC are unchanged with age, (2) sensitivity of the pituitary to both positive stimuli and to negative feedback by GC is unchanged; but (3) disposal of the corticoids is reduced with age, and (4) sensitivity of the adrenal to ACTH is reduced. Thus homeostatic levels of GC are maintained by a combination of two age changes (items 3 and 4 above). Teleologically one could agree that if the primary age change were a reduced rate of destruction of GC, and if adaptation at the pituitary level does not occur, then sensitivity of the adrenal to ACTH must be reduced in order to avoid excessively high GC levels. The reverse adaptive mechanism is equally attractive, that is, that the primary age change is a decrease in sensitivity of the adrenal to ACTH; in order to maintain normal GC levels, the rate of its destruction must be appropriately reduced. Further studies, hopefully with measurements of ACTH levels, are needed.

ADRENAL ANDROGENS

Adrenal secretion of androgens has been shown to decrease with age. As reviewed by Gherondache, Romanoff, and Pincus (1967), the urinary excretion of androgens (24-hour 17-ketosteroids) is predominantly made up of androsterone and etiocholanolone—the end products of the metabolism of testosterone, androstenedione, and dehydroepiadrosterone (DHE)—

and epiandrosterone and DHE. DHE excretion decreased by 65 percent, and androsterone plus etiocholanolone decreased by 53 percent; these account for the bulk of the decrease in the 17-KS excretion.

Plasma levels of DHE have been shown to decrease in the elderly (Migeon, Keller, Lawrence, and Shepard, (1957). Yamaji and Ibayashi (1969) measured plasma levels of the sulfated form of DHE and also noted lower levels in the elderly. They found that ACTH administration caused a definite increase in the plasma levels and that there was no difference between young and aged groups in the percent increase. Since older individuals have lower basal levels, their stimulated levels were always lower than those of the young subjects.

As pointed out by Gregerman and Bierman (1974) the biological significance of the adrenal androgens is not known. "In terms of the quantities produced, the adrenal androgens equal or even exceed those of all the other adrenal steroids combined. It would be most remarkable, considering merely the amounts secreted, if they were proved to be devoid of physiologic effects, but until such time as a functional role is demonstrated, we shall remain ignorant of the significance of one of the most striking age-related alterations of hormone secretion."

THYROID

The age-related changes in the physiology of the thyroid have recently been extensively reviewed by Gregerman and Bierman (1974). Despite the accepted microscopic changes of fibrosis, cellular infiltrations, follicular alterations, and nodularity, and controversy over changes in gross size of the gland, from a functional point of view, "the thyroid of even very elderly persons appears to function adequately and maintain its reserve capacity." They point out that "while basal metabolic rate (BMR) and thyroid hormone secretion decrease with age, the two events are not causally related. The decrease of BMR is best explained by an age-related decrease of metabolic mass; oxygen comsumption per unit of metabolic mass does not decrease with age." Denckla

(1974) reported lower "minimal oxygen consumption" in anesthetized female rats with aging. He states that this test is more specific for the determination of thyroid status than the BMR (awake animals) and that the difference between young and old rats is not a function of differences in body composition. The fall was most dramatic (67 percent) from 3 to 32 weeks but was less pronounced (25 percent) between 32 and 100 weeks.

Hormone Levels

The bulk of thyroid hormone does not exist in a free state in the blood but is bound to plasma proteins. The thyroxine-binding globulin (TBG) rises slightly with age while thyroxine-binding prealbumin, a relatively minor carrier, falls. The plasma thyroxine, both protein-bound (measured as either protein-bound iodine or thyroxine, T_4) and the free T_4, shows no change with age (Gregerman and Bierman, 1974). Triiodothyronine (T_3), a quantitatively smaller but more potent form of thyroid hormone, did show a highly significant decrease with age in two studies (Snyder and Utiger, 1972; Rubenstein, Butler, and Werner, 1973) but no decrease in a third study (Azizi et al., 1975). These measurements represent total T_3, and no estimates of free and bound T_3 fractions are available in the aged.

Thyroxine Disposal and Secretion

There is a progressive decrease in the rate of T_4 disposal with increasing age such that there is a loss of about 50 percent over the entire adult age range. Since plasma T_4 levels do not change with age, the secretion rate of the thyroid in the steady state must also decrease. The mechanisms of the decreased disposal rate are not clear. Gregerman and Bierman (1974) suggested that it is linked to an alteration of an adaptive enzyme system of the liver, though the possible effect of a decrease in physical activity (strenuous activity accelerates T_4 disposal) in the elderly has not been adequately examined. They also point out that both the disposal rate and the secretion rate can be markedly accelerated in elderly as well as

young subjects during the course of an acute infectious illness.

Thus, with aging, circulating levels of T_4 are unchanged, and responses of the thyroid to physiologic stimulation (TSH administration) and pathophysiologic stimulation (fever) are unchanged. These facts would indicate that the thyroid gland functions normally in the elderly. The significance of the lower levels of plasma T_3 remains to be determined. If this is indeed the metabolically significant circulating form of the thyroid hormone, then there may be a marked drop in effective hormone at the periphery. This would in turn imply a deficiency of the negative feedback control of TSH release, since plasma TSH is not elevated with age (Gregerman and Bierman, 1974).

Hyperthyroidism and Hypothyroidism in the Elderly

Hyperfunction of the thyroid results in a clinical picture in the aged that in many respects is different from the classic textbook description of this disorder. Davis and Davis (1974) have summarized the "oligosymptomatic" features of the hyperthyroid state; diagnostic errors are common because of the masked or apathetic presentation by the patient. Serious diagnostic problems are also presented by hypofunction of the thyroid in the aged. Zellmann (1968) pointed out the similarity in the symptoms of hypothyroidism to multiple changes which are more or less expected to occur with advancing age (e.g., lack of energy, change in facial appearance, dry skin, mental slowing, etc.).

EFFECT OF AGE ON THE MECHANISMS OF HORMONAL ACTION

The mechanisms underlying the responsiveness of tissues to hormones are currently under intensive investigation. There is accumulating evidence of changes in tissue responsiveness with aging (Gusseck, 1972; Roth and Adelman, 1975; Gregerman and Bierman, 1974). The results are by no means consistent, and a unifying hypothesis to explain not only the diversity of responses to different hormones but also the diversity of reports on individual hormones has not been forthcoming.

Roth (1975A) has recently summarized these new concepts: "The initial step in the action of most hormones appears to be specific binding to target cell receptors. The subcellular location of the receptors and the subsequent biochemical events depend upon the type of hormone and target cell. For example, steroid hormones bind to cytoplasmic receptors and are translocated to the nucleus where they interact with the chromatin. In contrast, catecholamines and certain polypeptide hormones associate with membrane receptors which activate adenyl cyclase and thus act through cyclic AMP . . . . The degree of response is dependent upon the amount of hormone which binds to receptor."

As reviewed elsewhere in the *Handbook,* there are now a number of examples of reduction in hormone binding during senescence, and Roth (1975A) calls attention to three studies which support the hypothesis that the reduction in binding is responsible for changes in biochemical responsiveness to hormones (salivary gland response to isoproterenol, hepatic response to androgen, and splenic leukocyte response to glucocorticoid).

Gregerman and Bierman (1974) summarize evidence that there are age differences in plasma membrane-bound adenyl cyclase levels and cyclase activation by catecholamines. They caution that age-related loss of cyclase responsiveness is selective for specific hormones within a given tissue and varies from one tissue to another, as well as between species.

Not only will it be necessary to catalogue these species-specific, organ-specific, hormone-specific age changes in hormone receptors and in "secondary messengers," but the mechanism by which aging causes these changes will need to be investigated. Thus a shift in the proportion of hormone-specific target cells within an organ with increasing age rather than a loss of receptor density in each cell is conceivable. Changes in the milieu of the receptor with aging might also play a role.

The absence of aging effects on enzyme induction by some hormones was first pointed out by Gregerman (1959). More recently Adelman and his coworkers have summarized their exten-

sive investigations into the effect of aging on the time course and peak responses of the induction of enzymes by rat liver (Adelman, 1972; Adelman, Freeman, and Cohen, 1972; Adelman, 1975). They have emphasized the induction of glucokinase by glucose (via insulin) and of tyrosine aminotransferase by ACTH (via glucocorticoids). These studies are reviewed in detail in Chapter 3.

ADDENDUM: An extensive monograph (Blichert-Toft, M. 1975. Secretion of Corticotrophin and Somatotrophin by the Senescent Adenohypophysis in Man. Acta Endocrinol. [Supp.] 78 (195): 15-154.) has recently been published. It is only possible here to quote the author's Conclusion (p. 136). "The conclusions to be drawn must be:

(1) The functional state of the adenohypophysis was not found to be impaired in old age. (2) The theory according to which an age-related hypofunction of the adenohypophysis might be assumed to contribute to the high risks involved in surgery on elderly patients was not corroborated."

REFERENCES

Adelman, R. C. 1972. Age-dependent control of enzyme adaptation. *Advan. Geront. Res.,* 4, 1–23.

Adelman, R. C. 1975. The roles of insulin and corticosterone in age-dependent liver enzyme adaptation. *Proc. 10th Intern. Congr. Geront.,* 1, 42–43.

Adelman, R. C., Freeman, C., and Cohen, B. S. 1972. Enzyme adaptation as a biochemical probe of development and aging. *Advan. Enz. Reg.,* 10, 365–382.

Andres, R. 1971. Aging and diabetes. *Med. Clin. N. Am.,* 55, 835–846.

Andres, R., Pozefsky, T., Swerdloff, R. S., and Tobin, J. D. 1970. Effect of aging on carbohydrate metabolism. *In,* R. A. Camerini-Davalos and H. S. Cole (eds.), *Early Diabetes,* pp. 349–355. New York: Academic Press.

Andres, R., and Tobin, J. D. 1972. Aging, carbohydrate metabolism, and diabetes. *Proc. 9th Intern. Congr. Geront.,* 1, 276–280.

Azizi, F., Vagenakis, A. G., Portnay, G. F., Rapoport, B., Ingbar, S. H., and Braverman, L. E. 1975. Pituitary-thyroid responsiveness to intramuscular thyrotropin-releasing hormone based on analysis of serum throxine, tri-iodothyronine and thyrotropin concentrations. *New Engl. J. Med.,* **292,** 273–277.

Bakke, J. L., Lawrence, N., Knudtson, K. P., Roy, S., and Needman, G. H. 1964. A correlative study of the content of thyroid stimulating hormone (TSH) and cell morphology of the human adenohypophysis. *Am. J. Clin. Pathol.,* **41,** 576–588.

Barbagallo-Sangiorgi, G., Laudicina, E., Bompiani, G. D., and Durante, F. 1970. The pancreatic beta-cell response to intravenous administration of glucose in elderly subjects. *J. Am. Geriat. Soc.,* **18,** 529–538.

Berdanier, C. D., Marshall, M. W., and Moser, P. 1971. Age change in the level of serum immunoreactive insulin in three strains of rats. *Life Sci.,* **10,** (Pt. 1), 105–109.

Björntorp, P., Berchtold, P., and Tibblin, G. 1971. Insulin secretion in relation to adipose tissue in man. *Diabetes,* **20,** 65–70.

Blichert-Toft, M., Blichert-Toft, B., and Jensen, H. K. 1970. Pituitary-adrenocortical stimulation in the aged as reflected in levels of plasma cortisol and Compound S. *Acta Chir. Scand.,* **136,** 665–670.

Bourne, G. H. 1967. Aging changes in the endocrines. *In,* L. Gitman (ed.), *Endocrines and Aging,* pp. 66–75. Springfield, Illinois: Charles C. Thomas.

Boyns, D. R., Crossley, J. N., Abrams, M. E., Jarrett, R. J., and Keen, H. 1969. Oral glucose tolerance and related factors in a normal population sample. I. Blood sugar, plasma insulin, glyceride and cholesterol measurements and effect of age and sex. *Brit. Med. J.,* **1,** 595–598.

Brazeau, P., and Guillemin, R. 1974. Somatostatin: Newcomer from the hypothalamus. *New Engl. J. Med.,* **290,** 963–964.

Brown-Sequard, C. E. 1889. Des effets produits chez l'homme par des injections souscutanées d'un liquide retiré des testicules frais de cobayes et de chiens. *Compt. rend. Soc. Biol.,* **41,** 415–422.

Calloway, N. O., Foley, C. F., and Lagerbloom, P. 1965. Uncertainties in geriatric data. II. Organ size. *J. Am. Geriat. Soc.,* **13,** 20–28.

Carlson, H. E., Gillin, J. C., Gorden, P., and Snyder, F. 1972. Absence of sleep-related growth hormone peaks in aged normal subjects and in acromegaly. *J. Clin. Endocrinol. Metab.,* **34,** 1102–1105.

Cartlidge, N. E. F., Black, M. M., Hall, M. R. P., and Hall, R. 1970. Pituitary function in the elderly. *Gerontol. Clin.,* **12,** 65–70.

Chlouverakis, C., Jarrett, R. J., and Keen, H. 1967. Glucose tolerance, age, and circulating insulin. *Lancet,* **1,** 806–809.

Committee on Statistics of the American Diabetes Association. 1969. Standardization of the oral glucose tolerance test. *Diabetes,* **18,** 299–307.

Crockford, P. M., Harbeck, R. J., and Williams, R. H. 1966. Influence of age on intravenous glucose tolerance and serum immunoreactive insulin. *Lancet,* **1,** 465–467.

Das, L. N., Haensly, W. E., and Getty, R. 1971. Age changes in the weight of the hypophysis in swine. *Exp. Geront.,* **6,** 63–73.

Das, L. N., and Magilton, J. H. 1971. Age changes in the relationship among endocrine glands of the beagle. *Exp. Geront.,* **6,** 313–324.

Davis, P. J., and Davis, F. B. 1974. Hyperthyroidism in patients over the age of 60 years; clinical features in 85 patients. *Medicine,* **53,** 161–181.

Denckla, W. D. 1974. Role of the pituitary and thyroid glands in the decline of minimal O_2 consumption with age. *J. Clin. Invest.,* **53,** 572–581.

Dobbie, J. W. 1969. Adrenocortical nodular hyperplasia: The ageing adrenal. *J. Pathol.,* **99,** 1–18.

Duckworth, W. C., and Kitabchi, A. E. 1972. Direct measurement of plasma pro-insulin in normal and diabetic subjects. *Am. J. Med.,* **53,** 418–427.

Dudl, R. J., and Ensinck, J. W. 1972. The role of insulin, glucagon, and growth hormone in carbohydrate homeostasis during aging. *Diabetes,* **21,** 357.

Dudl, R. J., Ensinck, J. W., Palmer, H. E., and Williams, R. H. 1973. Effect of age on growth hormone secretion in man. *J. Clin. Endocrinol. Metab.,* **37,** 11–16.

Eleftheriou, B. E. 1975. Changes with age in protein-bound iodine (PBI) and body temperature in the mouse. *J. Geront.,* **30,** 417–421.

Ensinck, J. W., and Williams, R. H. 1972. Hormonal and nonhormonal factors modifying man's response to insulin, *In,* R. O. Greep and E. B. Astwood (eds.), *Handbook of Physiology, Section 7: Endocrinology, Vol I. Endocrine Pancreas,* pp. 655–684. Washington, D.C.: Am. Physiol. Soc.

Finkelstein, J. W., Roffwarg, H. P., Boyer, R. M., Kream, J., and Hellman, L. 1972. Age-related change in the twenty-four-hour spontaneous secretion of growth hormone. *J. Clin. Endocrinol. Metab.,* **35,** 665–670.

Frantz, A. G., and Rabkin, M. T. 1965. Effects of estrogen and sex difference on secretion of human growth hormone. *J. Clin. Endocrinol.,* **25,** 1470–1480.

Freeman, C., Karoly, K., and Adelman, R. C. 1973. Impairments in availability of insulin to liver *in vivo* and in binding of insulin to purified hepatic plasma membrane during aging. *Biochem. Biophys. Res. Commun.,* **54,** 1573–1580.

Friedman, M., Green, M. F., and Sharland, D. E. 1969. Assessment of hypothalamic-pituitary-adrenal function in the geriatric age group. *J. Geront.,* **24,** 292–297.

Frolkis, V. V., Bogatskaya, L. N., Bogush, S. V., and Shevchuk, V. G. 1971. Content and activity of insulin in the blood and the sensitivity of tissues to it during aging. *Geriatrics,* **26** (8), passim.

Gershberg, H. 1957. Growth hormone content and metabolic actions of human pituitary glands. *Endocrinology,* **61,** 160–165.

Gherondache, C. N., Romanoff, L. R., and Pincus, G. 1967. Steroid hormones in aging men. *In,* L. Gitman, (ed.), *Endocrines and Aging,* pp. 76–101. Springfield, Illinois: Charles C. Thomas.

Gittler, R. D., and Friedfeld, L. 1962. Adrenocortical responsiveness in the aged. *J. Am. Geriat. Soc.,* 10, 153–159.

Gommers, A., and de Gasparo, M. 1972. Variation de l'insulinémie en fonction de l'âge chez le rat mâle non traité. *Gerontologia,* 18, 176–184.

Grad, B., Kral, V. A., Payne, R. C., and Berenson, J. 1967. Plasma and urinary corticoids in young and old persons. *J. Geront.,* 22, 66–71.

Grad, B., Rosenberg, G. M., Liberman, H., Trachtengerg, J., and Kral, V. A. 1971. Diurnal variation of the serum cortisol level of geriatric subjects. *J. Geront.,* 26, 351–357.

Greenwood, F. C., Landon, J., and Stamp, T. C. B. 1966. The plasma sugar, free fatty acid, cortisol, and growth hormone response to insulin. I. In control subjects. *J. Clin. Invest.,* 45, 429–436.

Gregerman, R. I. 1959. Adaptive enzyme responses in the senescent rat: Trypotophan peroxidase and tyrosine transaminase. *Am. J. Physiol.,* 197, 63–64.

Gregerman, R. I., and Bierman, E. L. 1974. Aging and hormones. *In,* R. H. Williams (ed.), *Textbook of Endocrinology,* 5th ed., pp. 1059–1070. Philadelphia: W. B. Saunders.

Gusseck, D. J. 1972. Endocrine mechanisms and aging. *Advan. Geront. Res.,* 4, 105–166.

Haensly, W. E., and Getty, R. 1965. Age changes in the weight of the adrenal glands of the dog. *J. Geront.,* 20, 544–547.

Hales, C. N., Greenwood, F. C., Mitchell, F. L., and Strauss, W. T. 1968. Blood-glucose, plasma-insulin, and growth hormone concentrations of individuals with minor abnormalities of glucose tolerance. *Diabetologia,* 4, 73–82.

Hess, G. D., and Riegle, G. D. 1970. Adrenocortical responsiveness to stress and ACTH in aging rats. *J. Geront.,* 25, 354–358.

Hess, G. D., and Riegle, G. D. 1972. Effects of chronic ACTH stimulation on adrenocortical function in young and aged rats. *Am. J. Physiol.,* 222, 1458–1461.

Hochstaedt, B. B., Schneebaum, M., and Shadel, M. 1961. Adrenocortical responsivity in old age. *Gerontol. Clin.,* 3, 239–246.

Jensen, H. K., and Blichert-Toft, M. 1971. Serum corticotrophin, plasma cortisol and urinary excretion of 17-ketogenic steroids in the elderly (age group: 66–94 years). *Acta Endocrinol.,* 66, 25–34.

Johansen, K. 1973. A new principle for the comparison of insulin secretory responses. I. The effect of age on insulin secretion. *Acta Endocrinol.,* 74, 511–523.

Jordan, S. W., and Perley, M. J. 1972. Microangiopathy in diabetes mellitus and aging. *Arch. Pathol.,* 93, 261–265.

Kalk, W. J., Vinik, A. I., Pimstone, B. L., and Jackson, W. P. U. 1973. Growth hormone response to insulin hypoglycemia in the elderly. *J. Geront.,* 28, 431–433.

Khelimskii, A. M. 1964. Age changes in dimensions of adrenal cortex. *Federation Proc.* (Translation Suppl.), 23, T1250–T1252.

Kilo, C., Vogler, N., and Williamson, J. R. 1972. Muscle capillary basement membrane changes related to aging and to diabetes mellitus. *Diabetes,* 21, 881–898.

Korkushko, O. V., and Orlov, P. A. 1972. Age related features of the effect of glucagon on blood sugar level and oxygen consumption in apparently healthy persons. *Probl. Endokr.,* 18/6, 46–49.

Laron, Z., Doron, M., and Amikam, B. 1970. Plasma growth hormone in men and women over 70 years of age. *In, Medicine and Sport, Vol. 4: Physical Activity and Aging,* pp. 126–131. New York: Karger.

Lewis, B. K., and Wexler, B. C. 1974. Serum insulin changes in male rats associated with age and reproductive activity. *J. Geront.,* 29, 139–144.

Mace, J. W., Gotlin, R. W., Sassin, J. F., Parker, D. C., and Rossman, L. G. 1970. Usefulness of post-sleep human growth hormone release as a test of physiologic growth hormone secretion. *J. Clin. Endocrinol.,* 31, 225–226.

Martin, F. I. R., Pearson, M. J., and Stocks, A. E. 1968. Glucose tolerance and insulin sensitivity. *Lancet,* 1, 1285–1286.

Mayberry, W. E., Gharib, H., Bilstad, J. M., and Sizemore, G. W. 1971. Radioimmunoassay for human thyrotrophin. *Ann. Internal Med.,* 74, 471–480.

Merimee, T. J., Rabinowitz, D., Riggs, L., Burgess, J. A., Rimoin, D. L., and McKusick, V. A. 1967. Plasma growth hormone after arginine infusion. *New Engl. J. Med.,* 276, 434–439.

Migeon, C. J., Keller, A. R., Lawrence, B., and Shepard, T. H. 1957. Dehydroepiandrosterone and androsterone levels in human plasma. Effect of age and sex; day-to-day and diurnal variations. *J. Clin. Endocrinol.* 17, 1051–1062.

Moncloa, F., Gómez, R., and Pretell, E. 1963. Responses to corticotrophin and correlation between excretion of creatinine and urinary steroids and between the clearance of creatinine and urinary steroids in ageing. *Steroids,* 1, 437–444.

Nolan, S., Stephan, T., Chae, S., Vidalon, C., Gegick, C., Khurana, R. C., and Danowski, T. S. 1973. Age-related insulin patterns in normal glucose tolerance. *J. Am. Geriat. Soc.,* 21, 106–111.

Orskov, H., and Christensen, N. J. 1969. Plasma disappearance rate of injected human insulin in juvenile diabetic, maturity-onset diabetic and nondiabetic subjects. *Diabetes,* 18, 653–659.

O'Sullivan, J. B. 1974. Age gradient in blood glucose levels. *Diabetes,* 23, 713–715.

Palmer, J. P., and Ensinck, J. W. 1974. Acute insulin response to glucose and secretin in the aged. *In,*

Program of the Gerontological Society 27th Annual Scientific Meeting, p. 46.

Pozefsky, T., Colker, J. L., Langs, H. M., and Andres, R. 1965. The cortisone-glucose tolerance test: Influence of age on performance. *Ann. Internal Med.,* **63**, 988-1000.

Rabinowitz, D. 1970. Some endocrine and metabolic aspects of obesity. *Ann. Rev. Med.,* **21**, 241-258.

Reaven, G., and Miller, R. 1968. Study of the relationship between glucose and insulin responses to an oral glucose load in man. *Diabetes,* **17**, 560-569.

Riegle, G. D., and Hess, G. D. 1972. Chronic and acute dexamethasone suppression of stress activation of the adrenal cortex in young and aged rats. *Neuroendocrinology,* **9**, 175-187.

Riegle, G. D., and Nellor, J. E. 1967. Changes in adrenocortical function during aging in cattle. *J. Geront.,* **22**, 83-87.

Riegle, G. D., Przekop, F., and Nellor, J. E. 1968. Changes in adrenocortical responsiveness to ACTH infusion in aging goats. *J. Geront.,* **23**, 187-190.

Roffwarg, H. P., Muzio, J. N., and Dement, W. C. 1966. Ontogenetic development of the human sleep-dream cycle. *Science,* **152**, 604-619.

Romanoff, L. P., Baxter, M. N., Thomas, A. W., and Ferrechio, G. B. 1969. Effect of ACTH on the metabolism of pregnenolone-7α-^{3}H and cortisol-4-^{14}C in young and elderly men. *J. Clin. Endocrinol.,* **29**, 819-830.

Romanoff, L. P., Morris, C. W., Welch, P., Rodriguez, R. M., and Pincus, G. 1961. The metabolism of cortisol-4-C^{14} in young and elderly men. I. Secretion rate of cortisol and daily excretion of tetrahydrocortisol, allotetrahydrocortisol, tetrahydrocortisone and cortolone (20α and 20β). *J. Clin. Endocrinol.,* **21**, 1413-1425.

Root, A. W., and Oski, F. A. 1969. Effects of human growth hormone in elderly males. *J. Geront.,* **24**, 97-104.

Roth, G. S. 1975A. Altered hormone binding and responsiveness during aging. *Proc. 10th Intern. Cong. Geront.,* **1**, 44-45.

Roth, G. S. 1975B. Changes in hormone binding and responsiveness in target cells and tissues during aging. *In,* V. J. Cristofalo, J. Roberts and R. C. Adelman (eds.), *Explorations in Aging,* pp. 195-208. New York: Plenum Press.

Roth, G. S., and Adelman, R. C. 1975. Age related changes in hormone binding by target cells and tissues: Possible role in altered adaptive responsiveness. *Exp. Geront.,* **10**, 1-11.

Rubenstein, H. A., Butler, V. P., Jr., and Werner, S. C. 1973. Progressive decrease in serum triiodothyronine concentrations with human aging: Radioimmunoassay following extraction of serum. *J. Clin. Endocrinol. Metab.,* **37**, 247-253.

Sandberg, H., Yoshimine, N., Maeda, S., Symons, D., and Zavodnick, J. 1973. Effects of an oral glucose load on serum immunoreactive insulin, free fatty acid, growth hormone and blood sugar levels in young and elderly subjects. *J. Am. Geriat. Soc.,* **21**, 433-439.

Sassin, J. F., Parker, D. C., Mace, J. W., Gotlin, R. W., Johnson, L. C., and Rossman, L. G. 1969. Human growth hormone release: Relation to slow-wave sleep and sleep-waking cycles. *Science,* **165**, 513-515.

Schreuder, H. B. 1972. Influence of age in insulin secretion and lipid mobilization after glucose stimulation. *Israel J. Med. Sci.,* **8**, 832-834.

Sensi, S., Corotenuto, M., Capani, F., Camilli, G., Caradonna, P., and Policicchio, D. 1972. La rispasta insulinemica nel soggetto anziano dopo stimolo glicidico per via orale ed intravenosa. Indagine su piccolo campione. *Giorn. Gerontol.,* **20**, 228-245.

Serio, M., Piolanti, P., Cappelli, G., De Magistris, L., Ricci, F., Anzalone, M., and Giusti, G. 1969. The miscible pool and turnover rate of cortisol in the aged, and variations in relation to time of day. *Exp. Geront.,* **4**, 95-101.

Serio, M., Piolanti, P., Romano, S., De Magistris, L., and Giusti, G. 1970. The circadian rhythm of plasma cortisol in subjects over 70 years of age. *J. Geront.,* **25**, 95-97.

Sherwin, R. S., Kramer, K. J., Tobin, J. D., Insel, P. A., Liljenquist, J. E., Berman, M., and Andres, R. 1974. A model of the kinetics of insulin in man. *J. Clin. Invest.,* **53**, 1481-1492.

Siperstein, M. D., Unger, R. H., and Madison, L. L. 1968. Studies of muscle capillary basement membranes in normal subjects, diabetic, and prediabetic patients. *J. Clin. Invest.,* **47**, 1973-1999.

Snyder, P. J., and Utiger, R. D. 1972. Response to thyrotropin releasing hormone (TRH) in normal man. *J. Clin. Endocrinol.,* **34**, 380-385.

Steiner, D. F., Kemmler, W., Clark, J. L., Oyer, P. E., and Rubenstein, A. H. 1972. The biosynthesis of insulin. *In,* R. O. Greep and E. B. Astwood (eds.), *Handbook of Physiology, Section 7: Endocrinology, Vol I. Endocrine Pancreas,* pp. 175-198. Washington, D.C.: Am. Physiol. Soc.

Streeten, D. H. P., Gerstein, M. M., Marmor, B. M., and Doisy, R. J. 1965. Reduced glucose tolerance in elderly human subjects. *Diabetes,* **14**, 579-583.

Swerdloff, R. S., Pozefsky, T., Tobin, J. D., and Andres, R. 1967. Influence of age on the intravenous tolbutamide response test. *Diabetes,* **15**, 161-170.

Takahashi, Y., Kipnis, D. M., and Daughaday, W. H. 1968. Growth hormone secretion during sleep. *J. Clin. Invest.,* **47**, 2079-2094.

Tobin, J. D., Sherwin, R. S., Liljenquist, J. E., Insel, P. A., and Andres, R. 1972. Insulin sensitivity and kinetics in men. *In,* D. F. Chebotarev, V. V. Frolkis, and A. Ya. Mints (eds.), *Proceedings of the 9th International Congress of Gerontology, Vol. 3, Abstracts,* P. 155. Kiev, U.S.S.R.: The Congress.

Tobin, J., Swerdloff, R., and Andres, R. 1966. GI insulin-stimulating factor in man: Plasma insulin response to oral and IV glucose at controlled arterial glucose concentration. *Clin. Res.,* **14,** 478.

Unger, R. 1971. Glucagon physiology and pathophysiology. *New Engl. J. Med.,* **285,** 443–449.

Verzár, F. 1966. Anterior pituitary function in age. *In,* B. T. Donovan and G. W. Harris (eds.), *The Pituitary Gland,* Vol. 2, pp. 444–459. Berkeley: University of California Press.

Vidalon, C., Khurana, R. C., Chae, S., Gegick, C. G., Stephan, T., Nolan S., and Danowski, T. S. 1973. Age-related changes in growth hormone in nondiabetic women. *J. Am. Geriat. Soc.,* **21,** 253–255.

Welborn, T. A., Rubenstein, A. H., Haslam, R., and Fraser, R. 1966. Normal insulin response to glucose. *Lancet,* **1,** 280–284.

Welsh, G. W., III, Henley, E. D., Williams, R. H., and

Cox, R. W. 1956. Insulin I-131 metabolism in man; Plasma-binding, distribution and degradation. *Am. J. Med.,* **21,** 324–338.

West, C. D., Brown, H., Simons, E. L., Carter, D. B., Kumagai, L. F., and Englert, E., Jr. 1961. Adrenocortical function and cortisol metabolism in old age. *J. Clin. Endocrinol.,* **10,** 1197–1207.

Yamaji, T., and Ibayashi, H. 1969. Plasma dehydroepiandrosterone sulfate in normal and pathological conditions. *J. Clin. Endocrinol.,* **29,** 273–278.

Zellmann, H. E. 1968. Unusual aspects of myxedema. *Geriatrics,* **23** (11), 140–148.

Zhukov, N. A. 1965. Part played by age changes in insular apparatus of pancreas in development of diabetes mellitus in middle and old age. *Federation Proc.* (Translation Suppl.), **24,** T597–T599.

15
IMMUNITY AND AGING

Takashi Makinodan
Gerontology Research Center, NIA

INTRODUCTION

Over the years immunology has made significant contributions to gerontology. Thus, for example, immunologic "breakthroughs" have permitted us to substantially control infectious diseases through vaccination and other means. As a consequence, the survivorship curve commonly used to describe aging has become more rectangular (Kohn, 1971), and we have become more knowledgeable of the "disease of aging" (Walford, 1969). These advances, in turn, have enabled gerontologists to identify which of the multitude of theories of aging (Orgel, 1963; Comfort, 1964; Medvedev, 1964; Curtis, 1966; Krohn, 1966; Strehler, 1967; Burch, 1969) are more probable and therefore should be subjected to experimental scrutiny. These advances also have enabled gerontologists to evaluate which of the various manipulative approaches are most likely to retard and alleviate the severity of diseases of aging.

With these objectives in mind, gerontologists are now systematically investigating many biologic systems. Those who are oriented toward basic science are hopeful that there may be a single underlying mechanism responsible for the various aging conditions and diseases of aging (e.g., either aging results from an accumulation of random "errors" or aging is a genetically programmed event in life following development, growth, and maturation).

Those who are clinically oriented are hopeful that there will be ways to delay the onset, lessen the severity, and possibly prevent the diseases of aging. Of all the systems being examined, the immune system is perhaps the most attractive from both basic and applied points of view. The reasons are as follows:

1. As individuals age, their normal immune functions decline, and associated with the decline is the emergence of diseases that can profoundly affect many tissues.

2. Our understanding of differentiation, ontogenetic, and phylogenetic processes of the immune system at the cellular, molecular, and genetic levels is as comprehensive as, if not more so than, that of most other systems.

3. The complex differentiation process of the immune system is an excellent model for systems in which cells undergo a terminal differentiation process.

4. The immune system is amenable to precise cellular and molecular analyses and therefore offers a great promise for successful manipulation.

5. Delay, reversal, or prevention of the decline in normal immune functions may delay the onset and/or lessen the severity of diseases of aging.

Accordingly, in this chapter I will attempt to describe (a) the immune system, (b) age-related changes in immune functions, (c) diseases associated with reduced normal immune functions,

(d) methods used to analyze immunodeficient states, (e) cellular changes responsible for the decline with age in normal immune functions, and (f) immunoengineering.

THE IMMUNE SYSTEM

The immune system protects the body in a highly specific manner against foreign invasion by viruses, bacteria, fungi, and possibly one's own somatic cells which undergo neoplastic changes by seeking out and destroying them. Obviously, any factor or event that can decrease the normal surveillance or police activity of the immune system will promote growth of invasive antigens (e.g., bacteria and cancer cells) which can, in turn, disrupt various physiological functions of the body. Hence, it should be apparent that the immune system plays a major role not only in the preservation but also in the shortening of life.

The bone marrow, thymus, bursa of Fabricius of birds, spleen, and lymph nodes comprise the major organs of the immune system (Figure 1). The bone marrow, thymus, and bursa of Fabricius are generally referred to as the primary or central organs of the immune system because they become lymphocytic first in embryogenesis and thereafter serve as the source of precursor cells. The spleen and lymph nodes, on the other hand, are referred to as secondary or peripheral organs. It is in these peripheral organs that immunity is initiated.

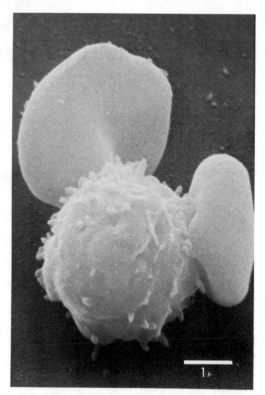

Figure 2A. Scanning electron micrograph. Human B lymphocyte rosette. B cells were separated from T cells on a Ficoll-Hypaque gradient (Kay, 1973), and B cell rosettes were formed by a 5-minute incubation in phosphate buffered saline with washed Type O, Rho positive human red blood cells coated with anti-Rho antibody and complement that was deficient in C'3. Unstimulated human B cells generally have less than 100 microvilli per cell.

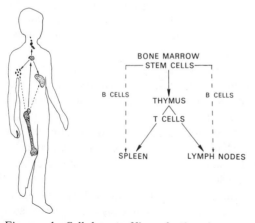

Figure 1. Cellular traffic of the immune system.

The cells found in the secondary lymphoid organs are the lymphocytes, plasma cells, macrophages, and structural cells (reticulum cells, fibroblasts, and endothelial cells). The lymphocytes, which are often referred to as "immunocompetent" cells, look like billiard balls with villi of varying lengths (see Figures 2A and 2B). According to current thinking, there are two distinct types (Moore and Owen, 1967; Claman and Chaperon, 1969). One develops in the bone marrow in mammals and the bursa of Fabricius of birds and is responsible for the humoral antibody response. This type is called the "B" cell. The other develops in the thymus and is responsible for cell-mediated responses (delayed hypersensitivity, rejection

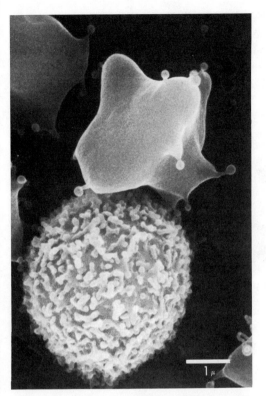

Figure 2B. Human T lymphocyte rosette. The ability of human lymphocytes from nonimmunized individuals to bind sheep red blood cells in the absence of antibody and complement has been shown to be a marker for T cells. This lymphocyte was fixed after a 5-minute centrifugation with sheep red blood cells. Unstimulated T cells generally have more than 300 microvilli per cell.

of foreign cell tissue and organ grafts, immunity against tumor cells, etc.). This type is called the "T" cell. B cells can be distinguished from T cells by their differences in membrane receptors, responsiveness to various stimulants including antigens, mitogens, drugs, and radiation, relative adherence to glass and plastic surfaces, electrophoretic mobility, density, etc. (Ishidate and Metcalf, 1963; Reif and Allen, 1964; Naor and Sulitzneau, 1967; Bianco, Patrick, and Nussenzweig, 1970; Katz, Paul, Goidl, Benacerraf, 1970; Cohen, 1971; Raff, 1971; Basten, Miller, Sprent, and Pye, 1972).

The macrophages are not only the principle scavengers of foreign antigens and effete cells but also the presentors of antigens to the lymphocytes (Mosier, 1967; Roseman, 1969; Shortman and Palmer, 1971). In contrast to the surface membranes of lymphocytes, macrophages possess highly elastic membrane foldings or lamellae which are used to crawl on surfaces and to trap and ingest antigens and effete cells (Figure 2C).

B and T cells respond to specific antigenic stimulation either by generating functional effector cells or by becoming tolerant so that the system will not respond when reexposed to the same antigen. Although the precise mechanisms of these responses are not known, it is clear that B and T cells generally respond to antigenic stimulation in the presence of non-antigen-specific accessory (A) cells which are made up primarily of macrophages (Mosier, 1967; Claman and Chaperon, 1969; Shortman and Palmer, 1971). In an immune response, the antigen triggers B and T cells to proliferate and transform into effector cells. The effector cells derived from antigen-stimulated B cells are primarily plasma cells which synthesize and secrete specific antibodies. Antibodies, together with nonspecific factors (e.g., complement) and cells (e.g., macrophages), provide immunity against many pathogens. The effector cells derived from antigen-stimulated T cells are primarily lymphocytes. Some, which are referred to as killer cells, kill target cells (e.g., tumor cells) without the aid of complement (Brunner, Mauel, Rudolf, and Chapius, 1970). Others synthesize and secrete immunity-promoting factors called lymphokines (Dumonde, Wolstencroft, Panayi, Matthau, Morley, and Howson, 1969; Lawrence and Landy, 1969; Perlman and Holm, 1969; Gorczynski, Miller, and Philips, 1972).

The regulators of differentiation of B and T cells into effector cells are antibodies and T cells. Antibodies can promote or suppress an immune response under various situations by complexing with only the antigen or with the antigen bound to antigen-sensitive precursor T and B cells (Rowley, Fitch, Stuart, Köhler, and Cosenza, 1973). As promoters they increase the stimulatory or immunogenic potency of the antigen and localize the antigen in sites readily available to B and T cells. As suppressors they bind antigens

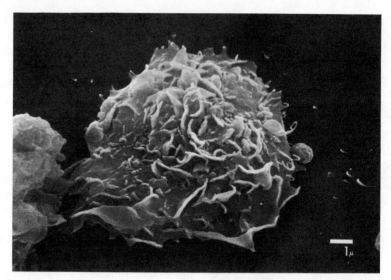

Figure 2C. Scanning electron micrograph of a rat peritoneal macrophage fixed with glutaraldehyde followed by osmium tetroxide after a 60-minute incubation at 37°C. Lamellipodia (ruffles) are a characteristic feature of macrophage surfaces. (Photographs kindly supplied by Marguerite M. B. Kay.)

in such a manner that antigens are less immunogenic and less accessible to B and T cells. In the case where the antigen is a tumor cell, this latter phenomenon has been referred to as immunologic enhancement (Hellstrom and Hellstrom, 1972), for it enhances the growth of tumor cells. More recently it has been shown that antigen-activated T cells can also modulate immune responses, by acting as "helpers" and "suppressors" (Lawrence and Landy, 1969; Baker, Stashak, Amsbaugh, Prescott, and Barth, 1970; Okumura and Tada, 1971; Gershon, Cohen, Hencin, and Liebhaber, 1972; Gorczynski, Miller, and Phillips, 1972). The mechanisms of their actions are not known, but they seem to secrete a fast-acting factor(s). Moreover, it is not known whether one regulator cell can function both as a helper and suppressor, and whether regulatory cells are distinct from effector killer cells involved in cell-mediated immunity. In any event, it is clear that both B and T cells can regulate the differentiation events of both humoral and cell-mediated immune responses. Figure 3 shows schematically the cellular differentiation process of antigen-stimulated B and T cells.

Both lymphocytes and macrophages are descendants of lympho-hematopoietic stem cells (Volkman and Gowans, 1965; Micklem, Ford,

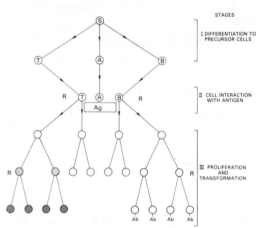

Figure 3. Schematic representation of cellular differentiation process of antigen-stimulated B and T cells. S, stem cells; T, thymic-derived cells; B, bone marrow-derived cells; A accessory cells; Ab, antibody; R, regulators. (From Makinodan, 1973.)

Evans, and Gray, 1966). These stem cells are often referred to as multipotent stem cells because they possess the potential to differentiate into the neutrophil, basophil, eosinophil, megakaryocyte, and erythrocyte series (Wu, Till, Siminovitch, and McCulloch, 1968). Their origin is the yolk sac (Moore and Owen, 1967; Owen, 1972). During embryogenesis they migrate to the liver and from the liver to the bone marrow where they normally reside throughout the life of the individual. At present, we do not know how multipotent stem cells differentiate into unipotent, antigen-sensitive T cells in the thymus although many believe that thymic hormones are somehow involved (White and Goldstein, 1970; Trainin, 1974). Also we do not know how they differentiate into unipotent, antigen-sensitive B cells in the bone marrow.

Phylogenetically the cell-mediated immune response evolved before the humoral immune response (Hildemann and Reddy, 1973). Thus, it has been shown that coelenterates, annelids, and tunicates can be provoked to undergo cell-mediated immune response. However, the ability to respond humorally to antigenic stimulation occurs much later with the vertebrates, and among the vertebrates the birds are the first to possess distinct T and B cells (Good and Gabrielson, 1964).

AGE-RELATED CHANGES IN IMMUNE FUNCTIONS

Indirect Evidence

The first hint that normal immune functions may decline with age came from the findings of classical morphologists who showed rather convincingly that in both laboratory animals and humans the thymic lymphatic mass decreases with age, beginning at the time of sexual maturity (Andrew, 1952). This is due primarily to atrophy of the cortex (Figure 4).

The size of lymph nodes and the spleen of normal individuals remains the same or decreases only slightly with age after adulthood. In long-lived mice, the number of T and B cells in the spleen remains relatively constant at least until 2 years of age (Makinodan and Adler, 1975) when tumors begin to appear in lymphatic and other tissues (Chino, Makinodan, Lever, and Peterson, 1971; Smith, Walford, and Mickey, 1973). Probably more significant than age-related weight changes are the age-related histologic changes of lymphatic tissues; i.e., diminishing numbers of germinal centers, increasing reticulum structures (Chino et al., 1971; Peter, 1973), and increasing numbers of plasma cells and phagocytes (Walford, 1969).

The number of white cells in the blood does not change significantly after sexual maturity (Betke, 1961; Zacharski, Elveback, and Linman, 1971). Information on the number of circulating T cells in humans is still unclear. Some preliminary reports show a progressive

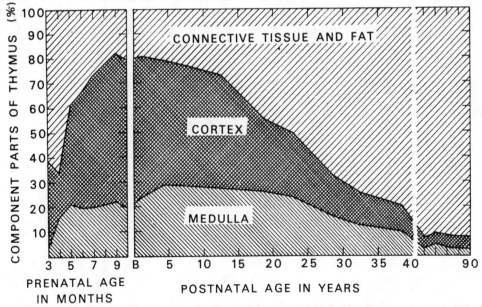

Figure 4. Age-related changes in the components of the thymus of humans (Boyd, 1932). (Reprinted from *Am. J. Diseases Children*, **43**, 1162–1211, Copyright 1932, American Medical Association.)

decline, others show a rise, and still others show no change (Carosella, Monchanko, and Braun, 1974; Proc. of 2nd Intern. Congr. Immunol., 1974). The frequency of aneuploidy (i.e., circulating lymphocytes with abnormal numbers of chromosomes) seems to increase with age (Jacobs, Brunton, and Court-Brown, 1964). The level of circulating immunoglobulins (Ig) tends to increase slightly with age (Walford, 1969), and, in humans, this is due to an increase in the levels of IgG and IgA (Haferkamp, Schlettwein-Gsell, Schwick, and Storiko, 1966; Kalff, 1970; Buckley and Dorsey, 1970; Lyngbye and Kroll, 1971). On the other hand, the level of IgM tends to remain constant or decreases with age. The increase with age in the level of Ig correlates well with the increase in number of Ig-synthesizing plasma cells, suggesting that the net synthetic rate of Ig is increasing slightly with age. This is supported by Quinn, Price, Ellis, and Makinodan (1973) who found that the catabolic rate of Ig increases slightly with age in long-lived mice.

Direct Evidence

Normal B cell immune functions reflective of humoral immunity have been analyzed in terms of circulating levels of natural isoantibodies and heteroantibodies and in terms of antigen-induced antibody response. Circulating levels of natural antibodies have been assessed most systematically in the human, and the results show that they decline with age, starting shortly after the thymus begins to involute (Friedberger, Bock, and Fürstenheim, 1929; Thomsen and Kettel, 1929; Paul and Bunnell, 1932; Furuhata and Eguchi, 1955) and after the level of serum thymosin, alleged to be a thymic hormone, begins to decline (Bach, Dardenne, and Salomon, 1973).

Aging rodents have been used primarily for the study of antibody responses, and the results show that primary, but not secondary, antibody response decreases with age (Makinodan and Peterson, 1962; Goullet and Kaufmann, 1965; Metcalf, Moulds, and Pike, 1966; Wigzell and Stjernswärd, 1966). They also show that the onset of decline in antibody response can also occur as early as the beginning of thymus involution. This would suggest that with many types of primary antibody responses, aging is affecting the regulator T cells and not necessarily the B cells. This suspicion has been verified partially by the subsequent demonstration, as cited earlier in the section entitled "The Immune System," that the antibody response of B cells to complex antigens generally requires the help of T cells (e.g., Claman and Chaperon, 1969). Figure 5 relates B cell immune functions of the human and mouse to their life span. It can be seen that the

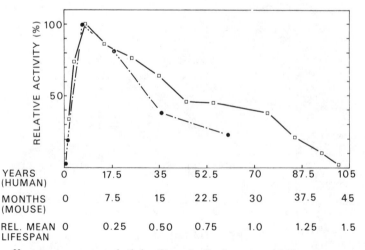

Figure 5. Age effects on serum agglutinin titers in the human and the mouse. □, natural serum anti-A isoagglutinin titers in the human (Thomsen and Kettel, 1929). ●, peak serum agglutinin response titer to sheep red blood cell stimulation by intact long-lived mice (Makinodan and Peterson, 1964). (Reprinted from *Federation Proc.*, **34**, 153–158, 1975.)

patterns of rise and decline in B cell immune functions of the human and mouse are remarkably similar.

There have been exceptions to the "rule"; i.e., reports showing no decline in primary antibody response, especially against bacterial and viral vaccines (Sabin, 1947; Davenport, Hennessy, and Francis, 1953; Kishimoto, Tsuyuguchi, and Yamamura, 1969; Fulk, Fedson, Huber, Fitzpatrick, and Kasel, 1970; Solomonova and Vizev, 1973). Two explanations can be offered: (a) these individuals have been previously exposed to the antigen and therefore are mounting in fact a secondary response, and (b) the response is to antigens which do not require the participation of T cells; i.e., a T-independent antibody response.

Normal T cell immune functions reflective of cell-mediated immunity have been assessed in many ways. The most commonly employed assays are the delayed skin hypersensitivity and graft rejection in intact individuals, the *in vivo* graft-versus-host reaction, and the *in vitro* T cell cytotoxicity, mitogenicity, and lymphokine tests (e.g., World Health Organization, 1973).

Studies with intact humans and animals showed that T cell immune functions generally decline with age, provided the individuals have not been sensitized previously with the antigen (Giannini and Sloan, 1957; Baer and Bowser, 1963; Gross, 1965; Stjernsward, 1966; Davis and Cole, 1968; Waldorf, Willkens, and Decker, 1968; Roberts-Thomson, Whittingham, Youngchaiyud, and Mackay, 1974; Goodman and Makinodan, 1975). Of course, there have been exceptions (e.g., Krohn, 1962). In the case of delayed skin hypersensitivity, it could be argued that the results reflect aging of the skin rather than T cell immune functions. However, the results of the tumor cell rejection tests were comparable. In such tests the tumor cells were injected intraperitoneally, indicating that the aging skin need not be a serious limitation for delayed skin hypersensitivity testing.

The *in vivo* findings also indicate that mouse T cell immune functions decline with age (Krohn, 1962; Stutman, Yunis, and Good, 1968; Teague, Yunis, Rodey, Fish, Stutman, and Good, 1970; Goodman and Makinodan, 1975). However, in general, the magnitude of decline is appreciable only in short-lived auto-

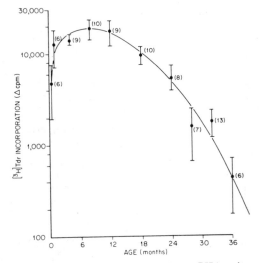

Figure 6. Decline with age in the PHA mitogenic activity of splenic T cells of long-lived mice. (From Hori, Perkins, and Halsall, 1973).

immune disease-susceptible mice, whereas in long-lived mice it is marginal or not apparent.

The *in vitro* findings show that the proliferative capacity of T cells of humans and rodents in response to plant mitogens and allogeneic target cells declines with age (Pisciotta, Westring, Deprey, and Walsh, 1967; Adler, Takiguchi, and Smith, 1971; Heine, 1971; Hallgren, Buckley, Gilbertsen, and Yunis, 1973; Hori, Perkins, and Halsall, 1973; Konen, Smith, and Walford, 1973; Mathies, Lipps, Smith, and Walford, 1973; Roberts-Thomson *et al.*, 1974), and the decline is most striking in mice, regardless of their life span (Figure 6). In contrast, the decline in the cytotoxicity index of T cells of long-lived mice is generally moderate against allogeneic tumor cells (Goodman and Makinodan, 1975) and not apparent against syngeneic tumor cells (Stutman, 1974).

T cells also perform regulatory functions. Both direct and indirect assays have been employed, which are based on the ability of T cells to promote antibody response to "T cell-dependent" antigens (e.g., foreign red blood cells) (Farrar, Loughman, and Nordin, 1974). As discussed earlier in this section, the regulatory function of T cells declines with age, and this has been demonstrated in intact animals and in *in vivo* and *in vitro* assays (Price and Makinodan, 1972a; Heidrick and Makinodan, 1973; Hardin, Chuseo, and Steinberg, 1973).

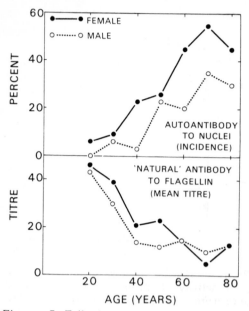

Figure 7. Fall in natural anti-Salmonella flaggellin titer with age and rise in incidence of anti-nuclear factor in humans of both sexes. (From Rowley, Buchanan, and Mackay, 1968).

DISEASE ASSOCIATED WITH AGE-RELATED DECLINE IN NORMAL IMMUNE FUNCTIONS

As normal immune functions decline with age, the incidence of infections, autoimmunity (Figures 7 and 8), and cancer increases (Walford, 1969; Chino et al., 1971; Mackay, 1972; Peterson and Makinodan, 1972; Smith, Walford, and Mickey, 1973), as in the case of

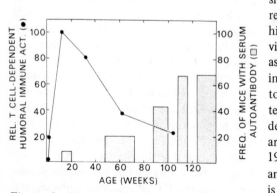

Figure 8. The capacity for T cell-dependent primary antibody response in relation to natural autoantibody formation in long-lived mice. (From Makinodan and Peterson, 1964; Peterson and Makinodan, 1972.)

immunodeficient newborns (Gatti and Good, 1970) and immunosuppressed adults (Penn and Starzl, 1972).

Autoimmunity

According to the surveillance theory (Burnet, 1970a and 1970b), the regulatory mechanism of the immune system normally prevents it from recognizing self components as antigens. However, when there is a breakdown of the regulatory function, production of antibodies which are reactive against self antigens follows. Such antibodies are called autoantibodies. All autoantibodies need not be pathogenic. In fact, it is possible that some may serve a normal physiological role; e.g., to protect the more effete cells from mechanical trauma or to enhance their destruction by the scavenging macrophages. When an autoimmunity is associated with a disease(s), it is classified as an autoimmune disease. Autoimmune diseases have been divided into two groups (Walford, 1969). One group is seen mostly in young women (e.g., lupus erythematosus and scleroderma), and the other is more commonly seen with advancing age (e.g., senile amyloidosis, "maturity-onset" diabetes, certain types of hemolytic anemias, and various forms of periarteritis).

Although serum autoantibody is well documented, its cause(s) and mechanism(s) still remain obscure. One view is that host antigens sequestered in tissues, which are inaccessible to the immune system, are accidentally released into the circulation and then become highly antigenic by binding with, for example, viruses (see Roitt, 1971). Another view is that as the normal immune functions wane, the immune system becomes chronically exposed to microbial agents. As a consequence, the system produces antibodies against unusual determinants of the microbial agents which are cross-reactive against self antigens (Roitt, 1971; Yunis, Fernandes, Teague, Stutman, and Good, 1972). A modification of this view is that host cells harboring viruses can express viral antigens on their surfaces late in life. As a consequence, the immune system can be provoked to make antibodies against these cells, which in turn can lead to autoimmune disease (Hotchin, 1972). Alternatively, the virus-infected cells themselves could be immune cells which upon transformation later in life, recognize other noninfected cells as foreign and the result is autoimmunity (Proffit, Hirsch, and Black, 1973). Still another view is that as regulation of self tolerance breaks down, "forbidden clones" emerge which can attack self tissues (Burnet, 1970b). These, as well as other regulatory theories (Fudenberg, 1971; Phillips and Wegman, 1973), are attractive but can be perplexing. According to these theories, in autoimmunity the regulatory machinery by some unknown mechanism suppresses immune cells reactive against non-self antigens and at the same time promotes immune cells reactive against self antigens to flourish. However, the recent series of studies on the genetics of immunity indicate that this problem on autoimmunity may not be insurmountable. They reveal that the genes responsible for the histocompatibility antigens, the ability to respond to specific antigens, and the susceptibility to certain specific diseases are all closely linked (Amos and Yunis, 1971; Walford, Smith, and Waters, 1971; Benacerraf and McDevitt, 1972). This would further strengthen the view that the fidelity of the immune system is the key to pathogenesis and possible etiology of aging.

Cancer

Suffice it to say that the frequency of cancer in individuals with reduced normal immune functions, regardless of age, sex, and cause, is higher than in individuals with normal immune functions (Defendi and Metcalf, 1964; Dent, Peterson, and Good, 1968; Gatti and Good, 1970; Burnet, 1970b; Penn and Starzl, 1972). However, this inverse relationship between functional immune status and frequency of cancer is most striking among the aged in both humans and animals (e.g., see review by Teller, 1972).

Cause and Effect

It is possible that the relationship between age-related decline in normal immune function and increase in the incidence of infection, auto-immunity, and cancer (immunodeficient diseases) can be a mere coincidence. However, this is very unlikely for two reasons. (1) Among aged humans, mortality is higher among those with reduced normal cell-mediated immune function than those with normal cell-mediated immune function, and death associated with cancer and cardiovascular diseases is higher among those with serum antinuclear autoantibody than those without nuclear antibody (Mackay, 1972; Roberts-Thomson et al., 1974). (2) In individuals where allogeneic tumor has arisen during immunosuppressive therapy, cessation of the therapy has led to its rejection (Penn and Starzl, 1972). Therefore, it is very likely that these two events are causally related; i.e., either the immunodeficient diseases impose on normal immune functions or the fall in normal immune functions predisposes one to immunodeficient diseases.

Several observations favor the former possibility that immunodeficient diseases impose on normal immune functions. (1) Slow virus infection of newborn mice can suppress normal immune function (e.g., Hotchin, 1972). However, it remains to be established whether or not all vertebrates harbor slow viruses responsible for the gradual decline in normal immune functions with age. (2) Infection of mice with leukemogenic virus induces immunosuppression (e.g., see Friedman and Ceglowski, 1971). However, its immunosuppressive effect is rapid and can be marked, whereas the decline in normal immune functions with age in long-lived mice occurs gradually. Moreover, Anderson, Sealetti, and Howarth (1972) have recently found that mice reared in germ-free environment, and therefore under reduced viral load, had a shorter life expectancy, contrary to expectation. (3) In two long-lived strains of mice (C3H and C57BL/6), autoimmune states appear relatively early in life (Linder, Pasternack, and Edgington, 1972), presumably before the onset of decline in normal immune functions. However, Adler, Takiguchi, and Smith (1971) have found in these and other long-lived mice that the onset of decline in certain cellular immune functions occurs very early in life. (4) In short-lived mice, cancer and autoimmunity precede any visible decline in normal immune functions (Metcalf and Moulds, 1967;

Morton and Siegel, 1969; Yunis *et al.*, 1972). It can be argued that this is not unexpected, because these mice are not dying of "true" aging but of life-shortening, virus-induced diseases. Support of this contention comes from the following. One is the demonstration that the life expectancy of a short-lived AKR strain of mice, destined to die of lymphoma originating in the thymus, can be doubled by its early removal (Furth, 1946; Nakakuki, Shisa, and Nishizuka, 1967). The other is the observation that the decline with age in normal immune functions of a short-lived NZB strain of mice, destined to die of autoimmune disease, is associated with a decrease in the number of T cells, whereas the decline with age in normal immune functions of long-lived old mice is not (Makinodan and Adler, 1975).

There are three convincing observations which favor the latter possibility that the decline in normal immune functions predisposes one to increased susceptibility to infection, autoimmunity, and cancer. (1) In humans and long-lived mice, the onset of decline in certain normal immune functions begins shortly after sexual maturity when the thymus begins to involute and atrophy (e.g., Thomsen and Kettel, 1929; Makinodan and Peterson, 1962; Adler, Takiguchi, and Smith, 1971). Obviously, this is long before age-related immunodeficient diseases are manifested. (2) Individuals receiving immunosuppressive therapy are 80 times more vulnerable to cancer than average individuals, and cessation of the immunosuppressive therapy leads to prompt rejection of the tumor (Penn and Starzl, 1972). This is applicable only to allogenic tumors which were transplanted to the patients and which may manifest themselves during immunosuppressive therapy. It is not applicable to those tumors which have arisen from the recipient's own cells and become established as a result of immunosuppression. (3) Death due to cardiovascular diseases and cancer is higher among the aged with antinuclear auto-antibody than among those without (Mackay, 1972). Another consideration is that it is very difficult to imagine how diverse diseases as pneumonia, autoimmunity, and cancer can impose only on certain T cell functions. It is easier to envision how a decline in certain normal immune functions to threshold levels can predispose an individual to any array of diseases.

The above considerations favor the view that the decline with age in certain normal immune functions predisposes one to infection, autoimmunity, and cancer. Thus, until definitive evidence to the contrary emerges, this view has been accepted as a working hypothesis by most experimentalists in this area.

The cause(s) and mechanism(s) of cancer, autoimmunity, and related immunodeficient diseases are still unclear. However, with improved technologies and better understanding of the mechanisms of immune responses, more and more studies are being focused on this problem. Over the past decade, the most popular theory of etiology of autoimmunity and cancer has been the clonal selection theory of Burnet (1970a, 1970b). It states that the breakdown in the T cell surveillance mechanism is responsible for the diseases, and, in general, studies in experimental model animals have been consistent with this theory (e.g., Yunis *et al.*, 1972). However, recent studies on tumor susceptibility of T cell deficient mice (i.e., mice born with only a thymus rudiment) would indicate that T cells involved in cell-mediated immunity are not essential for the surveillance against certain tumor cells (Stutman, 1974; Rygaard and Povlsen, 1974). In this regard, Stjernsward (1966) demonstrated that in normal long-lived mice there is a direct relationship between T cell-dependent humoral immune activity and resistance to syngeneic tumor cells (Figure 9). Moreover it has been found that, although the *in situ* scavenging activity of macrophages against allogeneic tumor cells is reduced in old mice (e.g., see review by Teller, 1972), macrophages *in vitro* are functionally normal if not more active than those of young mice (Aoki and Teller, 1966; Perkins and Makinodan, 1971). These results suggest that one limitation of the old mice in their tumor surveillance function is their inability to produce adequate amounts of lymphokines which promote the scavenging activities of phagocytic cells and/or their ability to overproduce inhibitory factors.

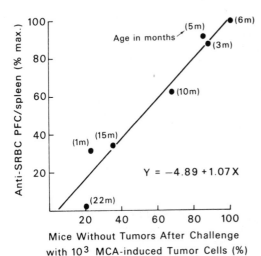

$Y = -4.89 + 1.07X$

Mice Without Tumors After Challenge
with 10^3 MCA-induced Tumor Cells (%)

Figure 9. Relationship between age-related T cell-dependent humoral immunity and resistance to syngeneic tumor cells in CBA mice. (From Stjernsward, 1966.)

METHODS USED TO ANALYZE IMMUNODEFICIENT STATES

In order to understand what changes are responsible for the decline with age in normal immune functions at the cellular and molecular levels, we must first be able to separate immune cells from humoral factors, and the cells and factors into distinct subgroups. Then we must be able to assess their activities in a quantitative manner. Otherwise it would be extremely difficult, if not impossible, to evaluate the nature and relative contribution of changes in the cells and in their environment (nutrient factors, regulatory factors, etc.). Because immunologists have been confronted with cellular and regulatory problems of this nature during the past decade, a great deal of effort has been expended in the area of cell culture and separation techniques.

Thymus, bone marrow, lymph node, and spleen cells are gently dispersed manually and separated according to their differences in density, size, stickiness to glass and plastic surfaces, receptors, net surface charge, and susceptibility to antiserum reagents, antimetabolites, and drugs (Makinodan, Perkins, Shekarchi, and Gengozian, 1960; Rabinowitz, 1964; Mosier, 1967; Raidt, Mishell, and Dutton, 1968; Miller and Phillips, 1969; Roseman, 1969; Kaufman,

1971; Levy and Scott, 1972; Miller, Sprent, Basten, and Warner, 1972; Rutishauser, Millette, and Edelman, 1972; Shortman, Cerottini, and Brunner, 1972; Wekerle, Lonai, and Feldman, 1972; Wigzell, Sundquist, and Yoshida, 1972; Wioland, Sabolovic, and Burg, 1972; Adams, 1973; Julius, Simpson, and Herzenberg, 1973). Their cellular activities are then determined in *in vivo* or *in vitro* cultures. There are advantages and disadvantages to both culture methods. The primary advantage of the *in vivo* method is that the cells are cultured in a natural medium, i.e., the same medium as that utilized by cells *in situ*. In contrast, the *in vitro* culture medium is artificial and chemically undefined, e.g., mouse lymphoid cells grow well in medium containing bovine serum but not mouse serum, and we do not know why. The primary advantage of the *in vitro* method is that the culture condition can be varied and the cells manipulated by the experimenter at any point in time of culture.

In the *in vivo* method, which is often referred to as the cell transfer method, known numbers of dispersed cells are infused together with the antigen into immunologically inert recipients, and their activities subsequently assessed (see Figure 10, path A). Immunologically inert receipients are animals which are genetically compatible with the transfer cells and which have been made unresponsive to the test antigen by pretreating them with either ionizing radiation (Makinodan et al., 1960) or immunosuppressive drugs (Santos and Owens, 1966). In a humoral immune response, only about 10 percent of the infused precursor cells colonize in the spleen of the recipient, but their descendants synthesize practically all the antibodies found in the blood (Bosma, Perkins, and Makinodan, 1968). Thus, the response of the transferred cells can be quantitatively assessed by determining either the amount of antibodies found in the blood or by counting the total number of antibody forming cells found in the recipient's spleen at the height of response. A modification of the cell transfer method is the diffusion chamber method (e.g., Goodman, Chen, and Makinodan, 1972) schematically presented in Figure 11. The primary advantage of the diffusion chamber method is that it is a

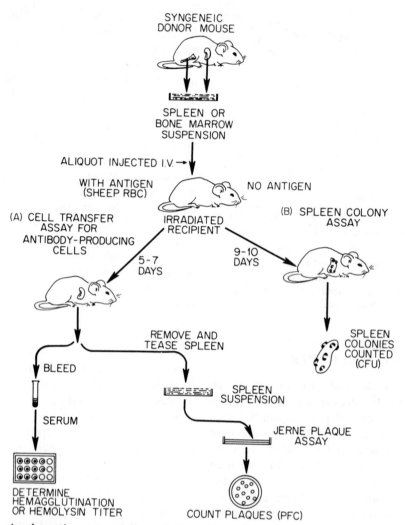

Figure 10. A schematic representation of the cell transfer method for analysis of antibody response and stem cells. (From Makinodan, T., Perkins, E. H., and Chen, M. G. 1971. Immunologic activity of the aged. *Advances in Gerontological Research,* **3,** 171–198.)

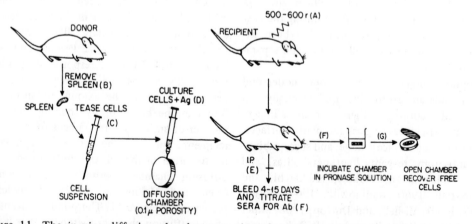

Figure 11. The *in vivo* diffusion chamber procedure for cellular kinetic analysis of immune response. (From Makinodan and Albright, 1967.)

closed system, and this eliminates the problem of cell traffic. Multipotent stem cells which can give rise to T and B cells are generally assessed *in vivo* by the colony-forming unit assay of Till and McCulloch (1961). The number of stem cells colonizing in the spleen is based on the number of nodules appearing 9–10 days after cell infusion (see Figure 10, path B), for it had been demonstrated that each nodule is derived from a single stem cell (Wu *et al.*, 1968).

The Mishell-Dutton (1967) and Marbrook (1967) methods are the two methods employed routinely to assess immune response *in vitro*. The former method utilizes Petri dishes and the latter dialysis membrane or Millipore filter chambers. The advantage of the former method is in the simplicity of the culture apparatus and the latter in the simplicity of the culturing conditions.

Two types of quantitative assays have been used to assess the effects of age on immune cells. One is the limiting dilution assay (Brown, Makinodan, and Albright, 1966; Groves, Lever, and Makinodan, 1970), and the other is the classical dose-response assay. Before discussing the merits of these assays, it would be useful to review cellular differentiation in terms of compartment and triangle models (Figures 12 and 13). The compartment model emphasizes the importance of relative and absolute cell numbers of each stage of competence or differentiation. The triangle model brings in the concept of cell division and its importance in determining the eventual size of a clone of cells. As illustrated in Figures 13B and 13C, a defect in cell division or in differentiation can result in changes in the absolute number of functional cells.

The limiting dilution assay is used to estimate in any given tissue the number of functional immunocompetent units (I.U.) and/or the number of immunocompetent precursor T or B cells making up the I.U. An I.U. is operationally defined as the minimum number of nucleated cells necessary to initiate an immune response. It should be emphasized at this time that in a typical immune response an antigen-specific precursor cell rarely responds to antigenic stimulation in the absence of other cells. Hence, unlike a cancer cell or a bacterium with a high "plating" efficiency, an I.U. is made up of 2 or

COMPARTMENTS

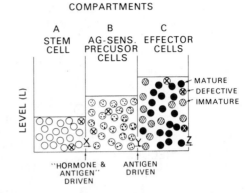

LEVEL OF COMPARTMENT (L) PER UNIT TIME (T)

$$\text{a)} \quad \frac{dL_A}{dT} = f\left[GT, -\frac{dX}{dT} - \frac{dF_A}{dT}\right]$$

$$\text{b)} \quad \frac{dL_B}{dT} = f\left[\frac{dX}{dT} - \frac{dY}{dT} - \frac{dF_B}{dT}, GT(?)\right]$$

$$\text{c)} \quad \frac{dL_C}{dT} = f\left[\frac{dY}{dT} - \frac{dZ}{dT} - \frac{dF_C}{dT}, GT\right]$$

where:
GT, generation time; F, functional impairment ; X, differentiation of A to B cells; Y, differentiation of B to C cells; Z, cell death.

Figure 12. A three-compartment model of cellular differentiation in an immune response (Makinodan and Adler, 1975). Cells of each compartment are identified; those with an "X" denote defective cells. (Reprinted from: *Federation Proc.*, **34**, 153–158, 1975.)

more cells (T-A, T_1-T_2, B-A, T-A-B, etc.), and the number of each cell type can vary from one to many per I.U. Obviously, one of the cell types making up an I.U. is most limiting because it is either few in numbers or there is a factor(s) in the cellular environment that is suppressing it from participation in the union.

A dose-response assay is used to determine (a) the immunologic burst size or the number of effector progenies generated per one antigen-stimulated I.U. or precursor B and T cell (Bosma, Perkins, and Makinodan, 1968, Figure 13), (b) the antigenic acuity or the ability of I.U. or precursor T and B cells to respond to minimal doses of antigen (Price and Makinodan, 1972a), and (c) the ability of precursor T and B cells to proliferate in response to mitogenic stimulation. Immunologic burst size and antigenic acuity are determined on the basis of numbers of effector cells generated, and the mitogenic index on the basis of numbers of cells synthesizing DNA or undergoing mitosis.

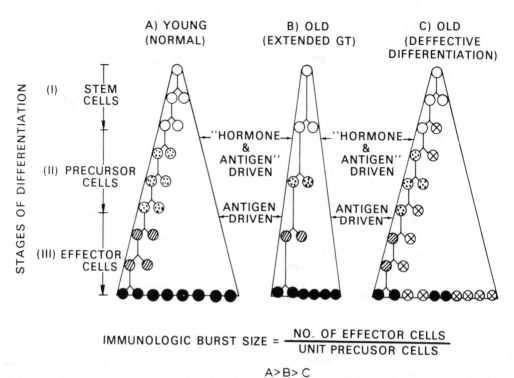

IMMUNOLOGIC BURST SIZE = $\dfrac{\text{NO. OF EFFECTOR CELLS}}{\text{UNIT PRECUSOR CELLS}}$

A > B > C

Figure 13. Triangle models of cellular differentiation in an immune response (Makinodan and Adler, 1975). (Reprinted from: *Federation Proc.*, 34, 153–158, 1975.)

NATURE, CAUSE(S), AND MECHANISMS(S) OF DECLINE WITH AGE IN NORMAL IMMUNE FUNCTIONS

At present we do not know what is responsible for the decline in normal immune functions with age. Obviously we need to find out what is going wrong with the immune system before attempting to find out what is responsible for it. Accordingly, research in this area has been centered about the nature of decline in normal immune functions. Focus has been on the humoral or B cell immune system rather than the cell-mediated or T cell immune system simply because the former system has been more amenable to quantitative evaluation at the cellular level.

Nature of the Decline

In broad terms, the decline with age in normal immune functions must be due to either changes in the environment of cells of the immune system, changes in the cells, or both. This problem was approached by assessing the T cell-dependent humoral activities of spleen cells from young and old mice in young and old recipients rendered immunologically inert beforehand. The activity of spleen cells should vary according to which of the three causes is/are responsible for the decline. Table 1 summarizes the predicted results one would obtain in this experimental model depending on the cause of the loss in activity with age. The experimental results revealed that both factors were involved (Albright and Makinodan, 1966) but that only about 10 percent of the decline can be accounted for by changes in the environment of the cells whereas about 90 percent of the decline was attributable to changes in the old cells (see Table 2) (Price and Makinodan, 1972a, 1972b).

Cellular Environmental Changes. At least two factors appear to be responsible for the changes in the cellular environment. One is noncellular and systemic. This factor(s) was detected by

TABLE 1. A CELL TRANSFER APPROACH TO RESOLVE WHAT ROLE CELLULAR AND ENVIRONMENTAL CHANGES PLAY IN THE DECLINE WITH AGE IN NORMAL IMMUNE ACTIVITY.[a]

Cause of decline in activity	Donors of cell	RECIPIENTS YOUNG OLD	
		Expected response	
Cellular	Young	High	High
	Old	Low	Low
Environmental	Young	High	Low
	Old	High	Low
Both	Young	High	Low
	Old	Low	Low

[a]The immune response of a fixed number of donor spleen cells from young and old mice is assessed in x-rayed syngeneic young and old recipients (Makinodan and Adler, 1975).

TABLE 2. EFFECT OF AGE OF THE RECIPIENT ON THE RELATIVE HUMORAL IMMUNE RESPONSE OF MOUSE SPLEEN CELLS.[a]

	RECIPIENT	
	Young	Old
Donors	%	%
Young	100	50
Old	20	10

[a]From Price and Makinodan, 1972b.

assessing the T cell-dependent humoral immune activity of spleen cells of young mice in immunologically inert young and old recipient mice (Price and Makinodan, 1972b). Fixed numbers of spleen cells were either cultured in the spleen (cell transfer assay) or the peritoneal cavity of recipient (cell-impermeable diffusion chamber assay). A difference in activity was observed between young and old recipients but not between sites of culture. The difference in activity between young and old recipients was twofold for both sites. It is interesting to note that a comparable twofold difference was also observed when the stem cell activity of bone marrow cells was assessed in the spleens of young and old recipient mice (Chen, 1971). We do not know what the factor(s) is. It could be that

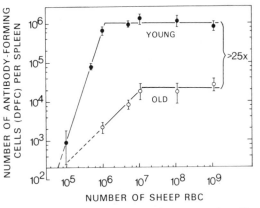

Figure 14. Effect of antigen dose on peak antibody response of young and old mice. Vertical bars indicate 95% confidence limits. (From Price and Makinodan, 1972a.)

there is either too much of a deleterious factor or too little of an essential factor for the cells of the immune system.

Another change appears to be localized in at least the spleen of aging mice (Price and Makinodan, 1972b). It is not known if this change is reflective of noncellular factor(s) and/or accessory cells of the immune system. In any event, it seems to interfere with the ability of splenic antigen-sensitive cells to respond maximally to limiting doses of antigen (Figure 14). This is reflected by the difference in slopes of the regression curves of young and old mice, which incidentally regress to the same starting point. Moreover, ten times more antigen is needed to maximally stimulate old mice than young mice. In contrast, the dose of antigen required to maximally stimulate dispersed spleen cells from young and old mice in vitro is the same.* These findings suggest that changes are taking place in the spleen with age which are preventing limiting amounts of antigen from stimulating the antigen-sensitive T and B cells effectively.

Perhaps the antigens when administered to old mice become coated with a factor(s) which causes them to be trapped in areas of the spleen not easily accessible to antigen-sensitive T and B cells. This may explain why antigens localize poorly in the follicles (Metcalf, Moulds, and Pike, 1966; Legge and Austin, 1968) and why germinal centers are absent in old mice (Makin-

*M. H. Halsall, personal communication.

odan, Perkins, and Chen, 1971). In any event, this phenomenon may have a significant bearing on immune surveillance, because it implies that the ability of individuals to "sense" antigens, especially weak antigens, can decline with age without any appreciable loss of number and activity of antigen-sensitive T and B cells. This could account for the poor surveillance performance of mice to low doses of certain tumor cells (Prehn, 1971).

On the other hand, this may reflect relative changes in the macrophages (Perkins, 1971); i.e., the possibility exists that antigen-destructive macrophages can become more competitive with age against antigen-sensitive T and B cells. In this regard, it should be noted that macrophages in the spleen possess extensive dendritic processes (Nossal, Ada, and Austin, 1964) and therefore should be extremely susceptible to damage when spleen cells are dispersed manually. This can account for the lack of difference between spleen cells of young and old mice in their *in vitro* response to limiting doses of antigen.

Cellular Changes. The three types of cellular changes which could cause a decline in normal immune functions are (a) an absolute decrease in the number of antigen-sensitive T and B cells due to cell death, (b) a relative decrease in their number due to an increase in the number of regulatory "suppressor" cells, and/or (c) a decrease in functional ability of antigen-sensitive T and B cells, either in their division potential, their differentiation potential, or their ability to interact with antigens or other cells.

To resolve this issue, spleens of young and old long-lived mice were assessed for their size, number of cells, and types of cells (Makinodan and Adler, 1975). It was found that the size remains relatively constant and the number of viable T and B cells per unit wet weight remains relatively constant. Preliminary density distribution analysis (Makinodan and Adler, 1975) shows that the frequency of less dense cells increases at the expense of the more dense cells. Figure 15 shows the difference in BSA density profiles between spleen cells of approximately 6-and 24-month-old, long-lived mice.

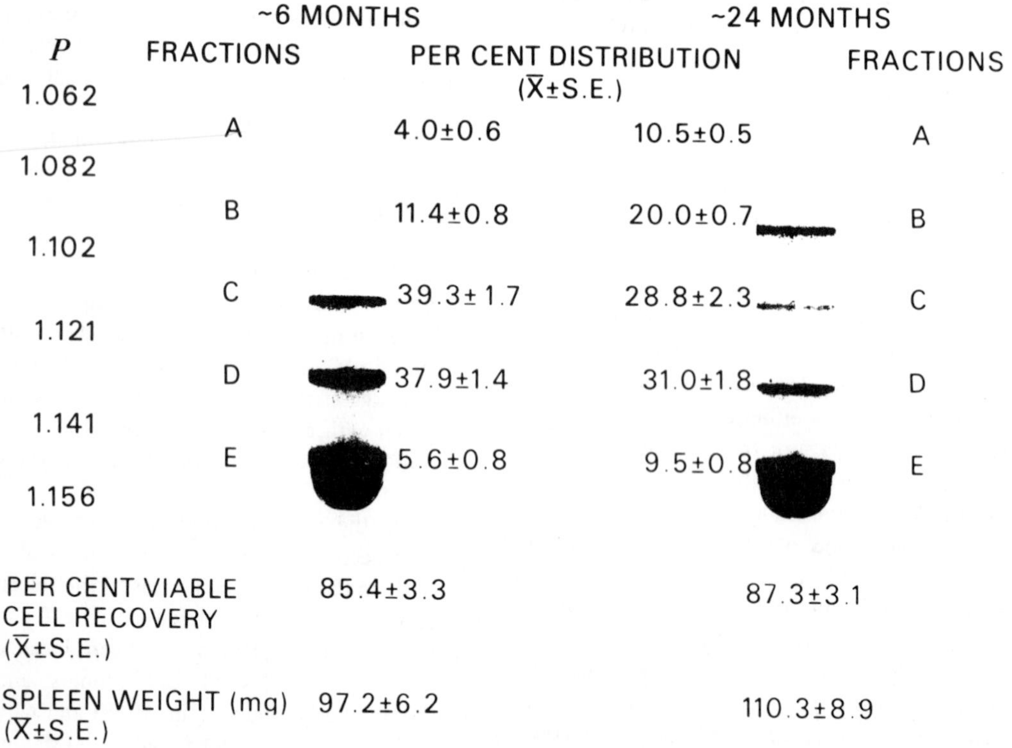

P	FRACTIONS	~6 MONTHS PER CENT DISTRIBUTION ($\bar{X}\pm$S.E.)	~24 MONTHS	FRACTIONS
1.062				
	A	4.0±0.6	10.5±0.5	A
1.082				
	B	11.4±0.8	20.0±0.7	B
1.102				
	C	39.3±1.7	28.8±2.3	C
1.121				
	D	37.9±1.4	31.0±1.8	D
1.141				
	E	5.6±0.8	9.5±0.8	E
1.156				

PER CENT VIABLE CELL RECOVERY ($\bar{X}\pm$S.E.)   85.4±3.3   87.3±3.1

SPLEEN WEIGHT (mg) ($\bar{X}\pm$S.E.)   97.2±6.2   110.3±8.9

Figure 15. Density distribution of spleen cells of young and old long-lived mice (Makinodan and Adler, 1975). (Reprinted from: *Federation Proc.*, **34**, 153–158, 1975.)

Stem Cells. Studies on the effects of age on stem cells have been limited primarily to the mouse. In the bone marrow where the bulk of stem cells reside (about 90 percent), the total number of stem cells remains relatively constant throughout life, i.e., the concentration declines gradually with age after adulthood (Coggle and Proukakis, 1970; Chen, 1971; Davis, Upton, and Satterfield, 1971), but the total cellularity increases proportionately as the concentration declines (Chen, 1971). These studies show that marrow stem cells can self-replicate throughout the natural life span of the mouse without exhausting themselves, unlike passaged stem cells (Siminovitch, Till, and Mc Culloch, 1964; Lajtha and Schofield, 1971).

There is no evidence to indicate that the hematopoietic ability of stem cells declines with age (Harrison, 1973). However, their ability to generate lymphocytes and blood cells at a normal rate may be affected as judged by their impaired ability to generate B cells in thymectomized, x-rayed, young syngeneic recipients (Farrar, Loughman, and Nordin, 1974) and by their ability to recover from fractionated sublethal doses of x-rays and to generate hematopoietic colonies (Chen, 1974). Still to be resolved are issues such as whether the altered functional properties are due to a slowing down with age of their proliferative rate and whether the alterations are permanent or reversible.

Accessory Cells. As defined previously (in "The Immune System" section), the accessory cells, made up primarily of macrophages, participate in both B and T cell immune responses in a nonspecific manner, are relatively radio-resistant, adhere to glass and plastics, do not give rise to functional effector cells, and phagocytize opsonized particles effectively (Mosier, 1967; Roseman, 1969; Shortman and Palmer, 1971). Because they generally confront the antigens before antigen-specific T and B cells do, any defect in them could result in a decreased immune response without any appreciable decline in number or function of T and B cells. Accordingly, in one series of studies, peritoneal accessory cells from young and old mice were assessed for their functional capacities (Perkins, 1971; Perkins and Makinodan,

1971). The results showed that (a) the *in vitro* phagocytic activity of accessory cells of old mice was equal to, if not better than, that of young mice; (b) their hydrolytic activities increased with age; and (c) their ability to initiate antibody response *in vivo* was unaffected by age. In another study, splenic accessory cells of young and old mice were assessed for their ability to cooperate with B and T cells in the initiation of antibody response *in vitro* (Heidrick and Makinodan, 1973). Accessory cells were obtained by allowing them to selectively adhere to plastic dishes. The results, summarized in Table 3, clearly reveal that this functional capacity of accessory cells does not diminish with age and that the deficiency resides in the nonadherent T and B cell fraction.

B Cells. The B cell population in the spleen does not seem to change with age. Thus, for example, the number of B cells in the spleen of disease-free, long-lived, old mice is about the same as that in the spleen of young mice. This is based on the number of cells bearing immunoglobulin receptors, cells susceptible to anti-B cell reagent and, as it will be discussed later, cells responsive to endotoxin (Adler, Takiguchi, and Smith, 1971; Makinodan and Adler, 1975). Of course, subpopulations of B cells may fluctuate, depending upon their susceptibility to various age-associated regulatory forces, including antigenic loads. Support of this view comes from studies showing shifts in the serum concentration of immunoglobulin (see discussion in section entitled "Age-related Changes in Immune Functions") and a slight decline in the number of B cells responsive to bacterial antigen in mice (Price and Makinodan, 1972a).

T Cells. It would appear that the primary age-related effect on the T cell immune system is a defect in the T cell proliferative activity. This conclusion is based on the following data. (1) The total number of lymphocytes in the spleen of long-lived mice carrying the T cell-distinct antigen, theta, remains constant with age (Makinodan and Adler, 1975). (2) The proliferative response of these T cells to plant mitogens, phytohemagglutinin (PHA), and concanavalin A (Con-A), or to the stimulatory effects of allo-

TABLE 3. PRIMARY ANTIBODY RESPONSE OF VARIOUS COMBINATIONS OF ADHERENT AND NONADHERENT SPLENIC CELL POPULATIONS FROM YOUNG AND OLD MICE.[a]

Preparation of interacting spleen cells	RELATIVE ANTIBODY-FORMING RESPONSE (%)	
	Young	Old
Controls		
Unseparated	100	20
Adherent	8	5
Nonadherent	2	1
Adherent + Nonadherent	96	18
Experimental	Young-Old Combinations	
Old Adherent + Young Nonadherent	95	
Young Adherent + Old Nonadherent	20	

[a]The nonadherent splenic cell fraction (95% lymphocytes) from both young and old mice consisted of about 70% of the nucleate cells in the original inoculum and the adherent cell fraction (70% macrophages) about 30%. Therefore a nonadherent cell to adherent cell proportion of 7 to 3 was used in the 4 reconstituted mixtures. From Heidrick and Makinodan, 1973.

geneic cells in the mixed lymphocyte culture, however, decreases markedly with age (Adler, Takiguchi, and Smith, 1971; Konen, Smith, and Walford, 1973; Hori, Perkins and Halsall, 1973) (see Figure 6 which shows that the T cell mitogenic activity can decline with age by more than tenfold). (3) Correlative evidence of a proliferative defect shows a marked decrease in the concentration of cyclic 3',5'-guanosine monophosphate in the lymphoid cells from aged mice (Heidrick, 1973). This compound has been shown to increase when lymphocytes are stimulated by mitogens, and as such, this decrease with age correlates well with the lack of mitogenic response. (4) Another correlative evidence of a proliferative defect shows a decrease in acetylation of histones of PHA-stimulated lymphocytes (Oh and Conrad, 1972).

Perhaps the most intriguing facet of these data is the appreciation of the temporal relationship of aging and a selective decrease in T cell functions occurring very early in life. An experiment which demonstrates the difference in the age effects on the T and B cell systems is one in which the mitogenic effects of PHA, Con-A, and bacterial lipopolysaccharide (LPS) were assayed on spleen cells of long-lived mice

at different ages (Makinodan and Adler, 1975). T cells are considered to be the responsive population to PHA and Con-A and B cells to LPS. Figure 16 shows that at 24 months of age,

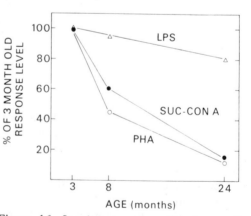

Figure 16. *In vitro* response of spleen cells from different aged, long-lived mice to various mitogenic stimuli. Comparisons of responsiveness are based on the comparative levels of tritiated thymidine incorporation in 72-hr cultures of spleen cells with the labeled thymidine being present for the last 18 hr of culture. PHA, phytohemagglutinin; Suc-Con-A, succinyl-concanavalin A; LPS, bacterial lipopolysaccharide (Makinodan and Adler, 1975). (Reprinted from *Federation Proc.*, **34**, 153–158, 1975.)

when both PHA and Con-A responses are about 10 percent that of the 3 month level, the LPS response is at the 90 percent level.

Studies on age-related changes in T cells involved in the regulation of B cell immune responses have been minimal. This is due in part to our lack of understanding of how these cells function. We know that in general a few will enhance a response and many will suppress it. We do not know whether or not there exist two distinct subpopulations of regulator T cells, suppressor and promotor T cells, or one population of regulator T cells with the potential to promote or suppress a B cell immune response. In any event, Hardin, Chuseo, and Steinberg (1973) showed that in short-lived autoimmune-prone mice, the relative number of T cells participating in a B cell immune response decreases with age. This could account for the emergence of autoantibodies in the older short-lived mice. On the other hand, Price and Makinodan (1972a) showed that in long-lived mice, the relative number increases slightly. Because excessive numbers of regulator T cells tend to interfere with B cells' response to antigenic stimulation, this could account for the slight decline in the number of antibody response precursor cell units, which will be discussed subse-

TABLE 4. EFFECT OF OLD SPLEEN CELLS ON THE MITOGENIC ACTIVITY OF YOUNG SPLEEN CELLS.

Spleen cell (No. $\times 10^{-6}$)	MITOGENS	
	Con A (1 μg/culture)	PHA (5 μg/culture)
	CPM/Culture	
Young (1.5)	5,247	26,326
Old (1.5)	1,082	729
Young + Old (0.75) (0.75)		
a. "Expected"[a]	3,164	13,528
b. Observed	1,314	6,259
c. Observed/ Expected	0.42	0.46

[a] $\dfrac{\text{Young (1.5)} + \text{Old (1.5)}}{2}$.

From Halsall et al., 1973.

quently. To test if these regulator splenic cells of old mice can also affect the proliferative capacity of T cells of young mice, splenic T cells of young mice were assessed for their mitogenic activity in response to PHA and allogeneic target cells, in the presence or absence of splenic cells of old mice (Halsall, Heidrick, Dietchman, and Makinodan, 1973; Gerbase-Delima, Meredith, and Walford, 1975). The preliminary results (Table 4) indicate that indeed splenic cells of old mice can interfere with the mitogenic activity of splenic T cells of young mice.

Finally it should be noted that T cells can also regulate hematopoiesis. This was demonstrated by Goodman and Shinpock (1968) who augmented hematopoiesis of parental stem cells in heavily irradiated F_1 recipients by simultaneously injecting parental T cells.

Immunocompetent Unit of Precursor Cells (I.U.) and Immunological Burst Size (I.B.S.). To investigate what role I.U. plays in the decline with age in B and T cell immune functions, it was assessed by the limiting dilution method (Price and Makinodan, 1972a; Goodman and Makinodan, 1975). The results revealed that it decreases, but its decrease is responsible for only a fraction of the decline in B and T cell immune functions. This would suggest that the differentiation events of antigen-stimulated B and T cells are highly vulnerable to the deleterious effects of the aging process. To test this notion, I.B.S., a quantitative index of differentiation, was determined in the B cell system (Price and Makinodan, 1972a). The results, summarized in Table 5, show a 50-fold difference in the *in situ* antibody response per spleen between young and old mice, but only a fivefold difference in the number of I.U. per spleen. This shows that the I.B.S. has declined by tenfold with age.

Model Animals. Four types of mice have been used extensively as models for old-age associated immune deficiency: thymectomized mice (Teague, Friou, Yunis, and Good, 1972); short-lived, autoimmune-prone mice (Yunis *et al.*, 1972), very short-lived, hypopituitary dwarf mice (Fabris, Pierpaoli, and Sorkin, 1972); and short-lived, athymic "nude" mice

TABLE 5. QUANTITATIVE EVALUATION OF THE DIFFERENTIATION PROCESS OF SPLEEN CELLS OF YOUNG AND OLD BC3F$_1$ MICE IN RESPONSE TO SHEEP RED BLOOD CELL STIMULATION *IN SITU*.

Rel. age of mice (months)	(A) Response (DPFC/spleen)	Ratio of $\frac{young}{old}$	(B) I.U. per spleen	Ratio of $\frac{young}{old}$	(C) I.B.S. per spleen (A/B)	Ratio of $\frac{young}{old}$
	($\times 10^{-6}$)		($\times 10^{-3}$)		($\times 10^{-3}$)	
Young (3–4)	1.0		1.0		1.0	
		50×		5×		10×
Old (30–35)	0.02		0.2		0.1	

Abbreviations: DPFC, direct plaque antibody forming cells; I.U., immunocompetent unit; I.B.S., immunological burst size. Values presented are average; for detail see reference (Price and Makinodan, 1972a, 1972b).

(Panteloris, 1972; Rygaard and Povlsen, 1974; Stutman, 1974). Much has been learned through these studies. Nevertheless, it is still uncertain whether or not these animals are appropriate models for immune deficiency as it occurs in long-lived aging animals and humans. That is, the causes and mechanisms of the decline in normal immune functions and of immunodeficient diseases in these model animals may be different from those occuring in long-lived aged individuals. If so, we may be witnessing phenotypic caricatures of old-age immune deficiency, analogous to the phentotypic features of accelerated aging seen in progeria in humans.

Cause(s) and Mechanism(s) of the Decline

As stated earlier, research efforts in this area have been minimal, for the major emphasis has been centered about the nature of decline in normal immune functions and the associated rise in immunodeficient diseases. Nevertheless, these studies all indicate that involution and atrophy of the thymus is the key to aging of the immune system. It follows then that search for the cause(s) and mechanism(s) of aging of the immune system should be oriented around the thymus.

At this point, it may be fruitful to consider briefly the various possible causes and mechanisms responsible for the involution and atrophy of the thymus. As to the causes, they can be either extrinsic or intrinsic to the thymus. The most likely extrinsic cause is a possible regulatory breakdown in the hypothalamus-pineal-pituitary neuroendocrine axis in relation to the thymus (Pierpaoli and Sorkin, 1967; Bearn, 1968; Fabris, Pierpaoli, and Sorkin, 1972; Everitt, 1973). As to causes intrinsic to the thymus, they can occur at either the DNA level or the non-DNA level (for molecular theories of aging, see, for example, Strehler, 1967).

Three possible mechanisms of involution and atrophy have been and can be proposed. One is through clonal exhaustion (Burnet, 1970a), where thymus cells with a genetically programmed clock mechanism for self destruction die after undergoing a fixed number of divisions. This is similar to the Hayflick phenomenon of human fibroblasts *in vitro* (Hayflick, 1965). Another possible mechanism is that the DNA of thymus cells undergoes alteration either randomly or through viral infection. These DNA-altered or mutated cells can then disrupt the self-tolerance mechanism by destroying normal T cells (Proffit, Hirsch, and Black, 1973). Various types of stable DNA alteration can occur including cross-linking and strand breaks (for review, see, for example, Price and Makinodan, 1973). The third possible mechanism is that stable molecular alteration can occur at the non-DNA level through insidious error accumulating mechanisms, as proposed for those occurring at the DNA Level. At the level of genes, evidence is mounting to indicate that only a few genes may be responsible for the aging process (Walford, 1974). If this were so, the 17th chromosome (IX linkage group) carrying the immune response genes (Ir), the histocompatibility system (H-2), and other immunologically important genes and the chromosome carrying the immune response genes and histocompatibility system (HL-A) in the human might be the probable site of aging genes.

It should be apparent and therefore encouraging that, of the various causes and mechanisms of aging of the immune system proposed here, several of them can be rigorously tested now.

IMMUNOENGINEERING

The exciting possibility exists that the incidence and severity of diseases of aging and the increase in susceptibility of infections among the aged can be reduced through immunoengineering. Immunoengineering is defined here as a method of manipulating the immune system for the purpose of maintaining its normal functions. This optimistic attitude is founded on four lines of evidence derived from clinical, epidemiological, and experimental studies: (a) Age-independent immunodeficient diseases and diseases of aging are both inversely related to immune dysfunction, (b) aging individuals with autoantibodies are more prone to die of vascular diseases and cancer than those without, (c) among very old people, the mortality of those with reduced normal immune functions is higher than those with normal immune functions, and (d) aging can be accelerated in normal individuals by promoting immune dysfunction (Walford, 1969; Fudenberg et al., 1971; Mackay, 1972; Penn and Starzl, 1972; Roberts-Thomson et al., 1974).

Basically two approaches have been taken: (a) selective alteration of the immune system by manipulation of the diet and body temperature, by drug treatment, and by surgery and (b) replenishment or rejuvenation of the immune system by injecting immune cells from histocompatible young donors or by injecting stored autologous immune cells.

Selective Alteration

In an attempt to selectively promote normal immune functions (e.g., antitumor cell immunity) and suppress abnormal immune functions (e.g., production of deleterious autoantibodies), immunologists have subjected young rodents to dietary manipulation (Jose and Good, 1971) following the classical life-extending dietary regime of McCay, Crowell, and Maynard (1935). These studies revealed that with moderate protein restriction, humoral immunity can be depressed while leaving cellular immunity intact. However, with a slightly more severe protein and caloric restriction, maturation of both humoral and cellular immune activities can be delayed or extended (Walford, Liu, Mathies, Gerbase-Delima, and Lipps, 1974). Associated with these changes are the delay in the onset of diseases of aging and extension of the life span (Ross and Bras, 1971). These results indicate that it may be possible to selectively suppress, through dietary restriction, immune functions involved in the production of autoantibodies while leaving immune functions involved in surveillance intact. It may also be possible to keep the immune system "young" for an extended period through dietary restriction. Such an interpretation could account for the life-extending effects of restrictive diet, as first observed by McCay and his colleagues 40 years ago (McCay, Crowell, and Maynard, 1935). It has also been reported that a high fat diet, in contrast to a low fat diet, promotes autoimmunity, decreases cell-mediated immunity, and shortens the life span of mice with propensity for autoimmune disease (Fernandes, Yunis, Smith, and Good, 1972; Fernandes, Yunis, Jose, and Good, 1973). Having established these baseline studies, the pragmatics are now focused on how best to minimize diseases of aging and extend the mature phase of life through dietary manipulation of the immune system.

Another approach that may selectively slow down the decline in normal immune functions and extend the mature phase of life without slowing down the general metabolism is to subject individuals to periodic mild hypothermia (Liu and Walford, 1972). This notion stems from the observation that (a) immune functions are highly temperature dependent (Tait, 1969; Andjus, Rajevski, Rajevski, and Cahurski, 1971; Jaroslow, 1971), (b) among hibernating homeotherms, resistance to infection increases even during mild hypothermia (Fedor, Fisher, and Fisher, 1958; Atwood and Kass, 1964), and (c) the life span of poikilothermic fish can be extended significantly by lowering the water temperature from 20°C to 15°C (Liu and Walford, 1972). Life extension through body temperature lowering may be operating through immunologic mechanisms. This is consistent with the demonstration that in annual fish this action is greatest during the last half of life when autoimmune processes begin to manifest themselves most readily (Liu and Walford, 1972). It remains to be established if intermittent hypothermia can selectively enhance normal immune functions, decrease the incidence and severity of immunodeficient diseases of aging, and extend the mature phase of life among thermostable homeotherms such as man and mouse.

Immunosuppressive chemicals have also been used in an attempt to selectively suppress autoimmune activities and to extend the life span of aging mice (Walford, 1969). Imuran and cyclophosphamide, which have been clinically effective in the treatment of autoimmune diseases and in the extension of foreign graft survival, have had marginal effects in extending life expectancy, possibly because of their toxic nature and their lack of cell specificity. It would seem that a more effective way in selectively suppressing autoimmune activities is to treat animals with specific anit-B cell reagent, for it is nontoxic and inactivates only B cells.

Perhaps another approach is to treat animals with adjuvants (chemicals which nonspecifically promote normal immune activities). Among the adjuvants with potential immune-enhancing activity in the aged are polynucleotides (Jaroslow and Taliaferro, 1956; Johnson, 1973), mercaptoethanol (Fanger, Hart, Wells, and Nisonoff, 1970; Chen and Hirsch, 1972; Click, Benck, and Alter, 1972), vitamin E (Tengerdy, Heinzerling, and Nockels, 1972; Campbell, Cooler, Heinzerling, and Tengerdy, 1974), and polyanions (Diamantstein, Wagner, Beyse, Odenwald, and Schulz, 1971). In fact, preliminary studies by Braun (Braun, Yajima, and Ishizaka, 1970) showed that the T cell-dependent humoral immune response of 1 year-old mice can be greatly enhanced by treating them

with synthetic double stranded polyadenylic acid: polyuridylic acid. More recently, Halsall and Perkins (1974) have reported that mercaptoethanol can enhance the mitogenic activity of T cells of old mice, and we have found that it can rescue in a very dramatic manner the reduced T cell-dependent humoral immune response of spleen cells of old mice (Deitchman and Makinodan, 1975).

Surgery has also been attempted to selectively decrease the deleterious activities of the immune system and to extend the life span of animals. This was first attempted successfully by Furth (1946). He decreased the incidence of thymoma and extended the life expectancy of thymoma-prone, short-lived mice by thymectomizing them during adulthood. A more impressive finding in this area was that of Albright, Makinodan, and Deitchman (1969), for they were able to significantly extend the life expectancy of very long-lived mice (Figure 17) without altering the death rate. They did it by removing the spleen when the mice were about 2 years old, just before they began to manifest immunodeficient diseases. Removal of the spleen at young adulthood or after the diseases had manifested themselves had no beneficial effect. Two explanations can be offered to account for the beneficial effects of extirpation of lymphoid organs at a crucial time in life: (a) The organ at the time of

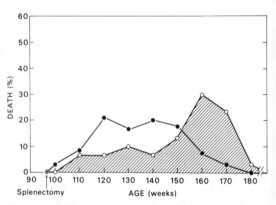

Figure 17. Frequency distribution of death of long-lived mice as affected by splenectomy at 97 weeks of age. ●, control; ○, experimental. (From Albright, Makinodan, and Deitchman, 1969.)

removal is the primary site of self-destroying autoimmune cells, and (b) the organ at the time of removal is the primary site of late viral-induced cancer cells. These two explanations need not be mutually exclusive. In fact, it is very likely that both events are emerging at the same time.

Rejuvenation

Another approach in preventing, delaying the onset of, or decreasing the rate of the decline in normal immune functions and thereby hopefully extending the mature phase of life is to infuse immune cells from healthy young donors into individuals as they begin to age. However, before this approach can be effectively applied to humans, the following considerations must be fulfilled. (1) The immune cells must *not* interact immunologically with the host (i.e., graft-versus-host or host-versus-graft reactions). (2) The cells must be able to persist in the host for an extended period of time. (3) The cells must be able to express their functional potential efficiently in the host. (4) The prospective host must not be subjected to traumatic insult beforehand.

The first consideration presents a logistically formidable problem, because a large complex network of immune cell typing stations must be set up to insure the aged a ready access to immune cells from young histocompatible donors. Alternatively, autologous immune cells can be used, which will eliminate the problem of cell matching. This can be accomplished by having individuals store their immune cells periodically during adolescence and adulthood. Later, as the individuals grow old, they can reclaim their own immune cells. The success of this alternative approach, of course, is dependent upon how well immune cells can be preserved without loss of activity. To this end, we have employed mouse spleen cells as the model immune cells and found that they can be "banked" at −196 C for an extended period without any appreciable loss of activity (Albright, Makinodan, and Mazur, 1963); i.e., no loss of immune cells has been detected since they were banked in 1962—period extending

more than four times the average life span of a long-lived mouse.

Using aging mice as model animals, rejuvenation has been attempted by either implanting thymic tissues, infusing thymic cells, infusing spleen cells, or infusing bone marrow cells from genetically identical young donors. In autoimmune-susceptible, short-lived mice, such treatment was marginally beneficial. Thus, with one strain of mice, the effect was not long lasting, and the treatment did not prevent the production of pathological changes (Yunis *et al.*, 1972). With another strain, the mean life expectancy was extended 1 month longer (Kysela and Steinberg, 1973). In nonautoimmune-susceptible, long-lived mice, immune cell therapy was also marginally beneficial at best (Metcalf, Moulds, and Pike, 1966; Albright and Makinodan, 1966). Two explanations can be offered. One is that the infused immune cells are unable to correct a preexisting immunologic disorder in the aged mice and therefore the disorder must first be diminished by radiation, surgical, or chemical treatment. Another explanation is that a variety of cell types should be employed, i.e., stem cells, T cells, B cells, macrophages, and thymic epithelial cells. Our preliminary findings (Hirokawa and Makinodan, 1975) are consistent with this latter view. We have found that old mice can be immunologically rejuvenated most effectively by simultaneously infusing stem cells into them and implanting thymic tissue of young donors. In this regard, the possibility exists that hormones elaborated by thymic epithelial cells which transform stem cells into T cells (Komuro and Boyse, 1973) may be used in place of thymic tissue implants.

The mouse was also used to look into considerations 1, 2, 3, and 4 stated above. For this study, the effect of cell replenishment on resistance against bacterial infection was assessed (Perkins, Makinodan, and Seibert, 1972). Young donor mice were first immunized with the vaccine, and then their spleen cells were processed and infused into syngeneic test mice at varying intervals before they were challenged with lethal doses of the virulent bacteria. The results revealed that (a) resistance against infection can be markedly enhanced by immune cell therapy, (b) the cells can persist in the recipient for a long time without appreciable loss of activity, (c) the recipients need not be treated beforehand, and (d) the immune cells can be stored effectively at −196 C.

These findings are very preliminary in nature. However, they are most encouraging as they suggest that immunoengineering of aged humans may be feasible, especially through autologous immunologic rejuvenation, and hopefully may offer a rational approach to immune disorders of the aged.

CONCLUDING REMARKS

An attempt has been made here to show that (a) normal immune functions can begin to decline shortly after sexual maturity when the thymus begins to involute, (b) the decline is due to selective changes in certain T cell functions including their inability to proliferate and to promote B cell differentiation, (c) age-related immune dysfunction predisposes one to autoimmunity, immune complex diseases, and cancer, and (d) immunoengineering may offer an effective approach to minimize diseases of aging.

The immune system should continue to serve as an excellent model not only for the etiology of aging at the cellular and molecular levels and for the pathogenesis of aging but also for effective approaches to improve the quality of life. We believe that in future studies these three areas of research should be addressed by investigators in close communication with each other, for only then can fruition of their efforts occur in a minimum of time.

REFERENCES

Adams, P. B. 1973. A physical adherence column method for the preparation of T and B lymphocytes from normal mouse spleen. *Cell. Immunol.*, 8, 356–371.

Adler, W. H., Takiguchi, T., and Smith, R. T. 1971. Effect of age upon primary alloantigen recognition by mouse spleen cells. *J. Immunol.*, 107, 1357–1362.

Albright, J. F., and Makinodan, T. 1966. Growth and senescence of antibody-forming cells. *J. Cellular Physiol.* 67, (Suppl. 1), 185–206.

Albright, J. F., Makinodan, T., and Deitchman, J. W. 1969. Presence of life-shortening factors in spleens of aged mice of long life span and extension of life expectancy by splenectomy. *Exp. Geront.*, 4, 267–276.

Albright, J. F., Makinodan, T., and Mazur, P. 1963. Preservation of antibody-producing cells at low temperature: A method of storage that allows complete recovery of activity. *Proc. Soc. Exp. Biol. Med.*, 114, 489–493.

Amos, D. B., and Yunis, E. J. 1971. A new interpretation of the major histocompatibility gene complexes of man and mouse. *Cell. Immunol.*, 2, 517–520.

Anderson, R. E., Sealetti, J. V., and Howarth, J. W. 1972. Radiation-induced lifeshortening in germfree mice. *Exp. Geront.*, 7, 289–301.

Andjus, R. K., Rajevski, O., Rajevski, V., and Cahurski, A. 1971. Effects of induced hypothermia on the immune response of a hibernator (ground squirrel) and a nonhibernator (rat) to particulate antigen. *Cryobiology*, 8, 306.

Andrew, W. 1952. *Cellular Changes with Age.* Springfield, Illinois: Charles C. Thomas.

Aoki, T., and Teller, M. N. 1966. Aging and cancerigenesis. III. Effect of age on isoantibody formation. *Cancer Res.*, 26, 1648–1652.

Atwood, R. P., and Kass, E. H. 1964. Relationship of body temperature to the lethal action of bacterial endotoxin. *J. Clin. Invest.*, 43, 151–159.

Bach, F. J., Dardenne, M., and Salomon, J. C. 1973. Studies on thymus products. IV. Absence of serum "thymic activity" in adult NZB and (NZB × NZW) F₁ mice. *Clin. Exp. Immunol.*, 14, 247–256.

Baer, H., and Bowser, R. T. 1963. Antibody production and development of contact skin sensitivity in guinea pigs of various ages. *Science*, 140, 1211–1212.

Baker, P. J., Stashak, P. W., Amsbaugh, D. T., Prescott, B., and Barth, R. F. 1970. Evidence for the existence of two functionally distinct types of cells which regulate the antibody response to type III pneumococcal polysaccharide. *J. Immunol.*, 105, 1581–1583.

Basten, A., Miller, J. F. A. P., Sprent, J., and Pye, J. 1972. A receptor for antibody on B lymphocytes. I. Method of detection and functional significance. *J. Exp. Med.*, 135, 610–626.

Bearn, J. G. 1968. The thymus and the pituitary adrenal axis in anencephaly. *Brit. J. Exp. Pathol.*, 49, 136–144.

Benacerraf, B., and McDevitt, H. O. 1972. Histocompatibility-linked immune response genes. *Science*, 175, 273–279.

Betke, K. 1961. Aging changes in blood cells. *In*, G. H. Bourne (ed.), *Structural Aspects of Aging*, pp. 231–245. New York: Hafner.

Bianco, C., Patrick, R., and Nussenzweig, V. 1970. A population of lymphocytes bearing a membrane receptor for antigen-antibody-complement complexes. I. Separation and characterization. *J. Exp. Med.*, **132**, 702–720.

Bosma, M. J., Perkins, E. H., and Makinodan, T. 1968. Further characterization of the lymphoid cell transfer system for the study of antigen-sensitive progenitor cells. *J. Immunol.*, **101**, 963–972.

Boyd, E. 1932. The weight of the thymus gland in health and in disease. *Am. J. Dis. Child.* **43**, 1162–1214.

Braun, W., Yajima, Y., and Ishizaka, M. 1970. Synthetic polynucleotides as restorers of normal antibody-forming capacities in aged mice. *J. Reticuloendothel. Soc.*, **7**, 418–424.

Brown, R. A., Makinodan, T., and Albright, J. F. 1966. Significance of a single hit event in the initiation of antibody response. *Nature*, **210**, 1383–1384.

Brunner, K. T., Mauel, J., Rudolf, H., and Chapius, B. 1970. Studies of allograft immunity in mice. I. Induction, development and *in vitro* assay of cellular immunity. *Immunology*, **18**, 501–515.

Buckley, C. G., III, and Dorsey, F. C. 1970. The effect of aging on human serum immunoglobulin concentrations. *J. Immunol.*, **105**, 964–972.

Burch, P. R. J. 1969. *Growth, Disease and Ageing.* Toronto, Canada: University of Toronto Press.

Burnet, F. M. 1970a. An immunological approach to aging. *Lancet*, **2**, 358–360.

Burnet, F. M. 1970b. *Immunological Surveillance.* Oxford, England: Pergamon Press.

Campbell, P. A., Cooler, H. R., Heinzerling, R. H., and Tengerdy, R. P. 1974. Vitamin E enhances *in vitro* immune response by normal and nonadherent spleen cells. *Proc. Soc. Exp. Biol. Med.,* **146**, 465–469.

Carosella, E. D., Monchanko, K., and Braun, M. 1974. Rosette-forming T cells in human peripheral blood at different ages. *Cell. Immunol.*, **12**, 323–325.

Chen, C., and Hirsch, J. G. 1972. The effects of mercaptoethanol and of peritoneal macrophages on the antibody forming capacity of non-adherent mouse spleen cells *in vitro. J. Exp. Med.*, **136**, 604–617.

Chen, M. G. 1971. Age-related changes in hematopoietic stem cell populations of a long-lived hybrid mouse. *J. Cellular Physiol.*, **78**, 225–232.

Chen, M. G. 1974. Impaired Elkind recovery in hematopoietic colony-forming cells of aged mice. *Proc. Soc. Exp. Biol. Med.*, **145**, 1181–1186.

Chino, F., Makinodan, T., Lever, W. H., and Peterson, W. J. 1971. The immune systems of mice reared in clean and dirty conventional laboratory farms. I. Life expectancy and pathology of mice with long life-spans. *J. Geront.*, **26**, 497–507.

Claman, H. N., and Chaperon, E. A. 1969. Immunologic complementation between thymus and marrow cells. *Transplant. Rev.*, **1**, 92–113.

Click, R. E., Benck, L., and Alter, B. J. 1972. Enhancement of antibody synthesis *in vitro* by mercaptoethanol. *Cell. Immunol.*, **3**, 156–160.

Coggle, J. E., and Proukakis, C. 1970. The effect of age on the bone marrow cellularity of the mouse. *Gerontologia,* **16**, 25–29.

Cohen, J. J. 1971. Hydrocortisone resistance of activated initiator cells in graft-versus-host reactions. *Nature*, **229**, 274–275.

Comfort, A. 1964. *Ageing, the Biology of Senescence.* London: Routledge & Kegan Paul.

Curtis, H. J. 1966. *Biological Mechanisms of Aging.* Springfield, Illinois: Charles C Thomas.

Davenport, F. M., Hennessy, A. V., and Francis, T., Jr. 1953. Epidemiologic and immunologic significance of age distribution of antibody to antigenic variants of influenza virus. *J. Exp. Med.*, **98**, 641–656.

Davis, M. L., Upton, A. C., and Satterfield, L. C. 1971. Growth and senescence of the bone marrow stem cell pool in RFM/Un mice. *Proc. Soc. Exp. Biol. Med.*, **137**, 1452–1458.

Davis, W. J., Jr., and Cole, L. J. 1968. Homograft response in adult-thymectomized mice: Deficiency with aging and after low dose-rate gamma irradiation. *Exp. Geront.*, **3**, 9–17.

Defendi, V., and Metcalf, D. 1964. *The Thymus.* Philadelphia: Wistar Institute Press.

Deitchman, J. W., and Makinodan, T. 1975. Proc. 10th Intern. Congr. Geront., **2**, 25.

Dent, P. B., Peterson, R. D. A., and Good, R. A. 1968. The relationship of immunologic function and oncogenesis. *In*, R. A. Good and D. Bergsma (eds.), *Immunologic Deficiency Diseases in Man*, pp. 443–458. New York: National Foundation Press.

Diamantstein, T., Wagner, B., Beyse, I., Odenwald, M. V., and Schulz, G. 1971. Stimulation of humoral antibody formation by polyanions. I. The effect of polyacrylic acid on the primary immune response in mice immunized with sheep red blood cells. *European J. Immunol.*, **1**, 335–340.

Dumonde, D. C., Wolstencroft, R. A., Panayi, G. S., Matthau, M., Morley, J., and Howson, W. T. 1969. "Lymphokines": Nonantibody mediators of cellular immunity generated by lymphocytes. *Nature*, **224**, 38–42.

Everitt, A. V. 1973. The hypothalamic-pituitary control of ageing and age-related pathology. *Exp. Geront.*, **8**, 265–277.

Fabris, N., Pierpaoli, W., and Sorkin, E. 1972. Lymphocytes, hormones and ageing. *Nature*, **240**, 557–559.

Fanger, M. W., Hart, D. A., Wells, H. J., and Nisonoff, A. 1970. Enhancement by reducing agents of the transformation of human and rabbit peripheral lymphocytes. *J. Immunol.*, **105**, 1043–1045.

Farrar, J. J., Loughman, B. E., and Nordin, A. A. 1974. Lymphopoietic potential of bone marrow cells from aged mice: Comparison of the cellular constituents of bone marrow from young and aged mice. *J. Immunol.*, **112**, 1244–1249.

Fedor, E. J., Fisher, B., and Fisher, E. R. 1958. Observations concerning bacterial defense mechanisms during hypothermia. *Surgery*, **43**, 807–814.

Fernandes, G., Yunis, E. J., Jose, D. G., and Good, R. A. 1973. Dietary influence on antinuclear antibodies and cell-mediated immunity in NZB mice. *Intern. Arch. Allergy*, **44**, 770–782.

Fernandes, G., Yunis, E. J., Smith, J., and Good, R. A. 1972. Dietary influence on breeding behavior, hemolytic anemia, and longevity in NZB mice. *Proc. Soc. Exp. Biol. Med.*, **139**, 1189–1196.

Friedberger, E., Bock, G., and Fürstenheim, A. 1929. Zur normalantikörperkurve des menschen durch die verschiedenen lebensalter und ihre bedeutung für die erklärung der hautteste (Schick, Dick). *Z. Immunitätforsch.*, **64**, 294–319.

Friedman, H., and Ceglowski, W. S. 1971. Immunosuppression by tumor viruses: Effects of leukemia virus infection on the immune response. *Progr. Immunol.*, **1**, 815–829.

Fudenberg, H. H. 1971. Genetically determined immune deficiency as the predisposing cause of "autoimmunity" and lymphoid neoplasia. *Am. J. Med.*, **51**, 295–298.

Fudenberg, H. H., Good, R. A., Goodman, H. C., Hitzig, W., Kunkel, H. G., Roitt, I. M., Rosen, F. S., Rowe, D. S., Seligmann, M., and Soothill, J. R. 1971. Primary immunodeficiencies. *Bull. World Health Organ.*, **45**, 125–142.

Fulk, R. V., Fedson, D. S., Huber, M. A., Fitzpatrick, J. R., and Kasel, J. A. 1970. Antibody responses in serum and nasal secretions according to age of recipient and method of administration of A2/Hong Kong/68 inactivated influenza virus vaccine. *J. Immunol.*, **104**, 8–13.

Furth, J. 1946. Prolongation of life with prevention of leukemia by thymectomy in mice. *J. Geront.*, **1**, 46–52.

Furuhata, T., and Eguchi, M. 1955. The change of the agglutinin titer with age. *Proc. Japan Acad.*, **31**, 555–557.

Gatti, R. A., and Good, R. A. 1970. The immunologic deficiency diseases. *Med. Clin. N. Am.*, **54**, 281–307.

Gerbase-Delima, M., Meredith, P., and Walford, R. L. 1975. Age-related changes, including synergy and suppression, in the mixed lymphocyte reaction in long-lived mice. *Federation Proc.*, **34**, 159–161.

Gershon, R. K., Cohen, P., Hencin, R., and Liebhaber, S. A. 1972. Suppressor T cells. *J. Immunol.*, **108**, 586–590.

Giannini, D., and Sloan, R. S. 1957. A tuberculin survey of 1285 adults with special reference to the elderly. *Lancet*, **1**, 525–527.

Good, R. A., and Gabrielson, A. B. (eds.) 1964. *Thymus in Immunobiology*. New York: Hoeber-Harper.

Goodman, J. W., and Shinpock, S. G. 1968. Influence of thymus cells on erythropoiesis of parental marrow in irradiated hybrid mice. *Proc. Soc. Exp. Biol. Med.*, **129**, 417–422.

Goodman, S. A., Chen, M. G., and Makinodan, T. 1972. An improved primary response from mouse spleen cells cultured *in vivo* in diffusion chambers. *J. Immunol.*, **108**, 1387–1399.

Goodman, S. A., and Makinodan, T. 1975. Effect of age on cell-mediated immunity in long-lived mice. *Clin. Exp. Immunol.*, **19**, 533–542.

Gorczynski, R. M., Miller, R. G., and Phillips, R. A. 1972. Initiation of antibody production to sheep erythrocytes *in vitro*: Replacement of the requirement for T-cells with a cell-free factor isolate from cultures of lymphoid cells. *J. Immunol.*, **108**, 547–551.

Goullet, P., and Kaufmann, H. 1965. Ageing and antibody production in the rats. *Experientia*, **21**, 46–47.

Gross, L. 1965. Immunologic defect in aged population and its relation to cancer. *Cancer*, **18**, 201–204.

Groves, D. L., Lever, W. E., and Makinodan, T. 1970. A model for the interaction of cell types in the generation of hemolytic plaque-forming cells. *J. Immunol.*, **104**, 148–165.

Haferkamp, O., Schlettwein-Gsell, D., Schwick, H. G., and Storiko, K. 1966. Serum protein in an aging population with particular reference to evaluation of immune globulins and antibodies. *Gerontologia*, **12**, 30–38.

Hallgren, H. M., Buckley, E. C., III, Gilbertsen, V. A., and Yunis, E. J. 1973. Lymphocyte phytohemagglutinin responsiveness, immunoglobulins and autoantibodies in aging humans. *J. Immunol.*, **111**, 1101–1107.

Halsall, M. H., Heidrick, M. L., Dietchman, J. W., and Makinodan, T. 1973. Role of suppressor cells in age-related decline in the proliferative capacity of spleen cells. *Gerontologist*, **13**, 46.

Halsall, M. H., and Perkins, E. H. 1974. The restoration of phytohemagglutinin responsiveness of spleen cells from aging mice. *Federation Proc.*, **33**, 736.

Hardin, J. A., Chuseo, T. M., and Steinberg, A. D. 1973. Suppressor cells in the graft-vs-host reaction. *J. Immunol.*, **111**, 650–651.

Harrison, D. E. 1973. Normal production of erythrocytes by mouse marrow continuous for 73 months. *Proc. Nat. Acad. Sci.*, **70**, 3184–3188.

Hayflick, L. 1965. The limited *in vitro* lifetime of human diploid cell strains. *Exp. Cell Res.*, **37**, 614–636.

Heidrick, M. L. 1973. Imbalanced cyclic-AMP and cyclic-GMP levels in concanavalin A-stimulated spleen cells from aged mice. *J. Cell Biol.*, **57**, 139a.

Heidrick, M. L., and Makinodan, T. 1973. Presence of impairment of humoral immunity in nonadherent spleen cells of old mice. *J. Immunol.*, **111**, 1502–1506.

Heine, K. M. 1971. Die Reaktionsfahigkeit der Lymphozyten im Alter. *Folia Haematol.*, **96**, 29–33.

Hellstrom, K. E., and Hellstrom, I. 1972. The role of serum factors ("blocking antibodies") as mediators of immunological non-reactivity to cellular antigens. *In*, R. Porter and J. Knight (eds.), *Ciba Foundation Symposium on Ontogeny of Acquired Immunity*, pp. 133–143. New York: Associated Scientific Publishers.

Hildemann, W. H., and Reddy, A. L. 1973. Phylogeny of immune responsiveness: Marine invertebrates. *Federation Proc.*, **32**, 2188–2194.

Hirokawa, K., and Makinodan, T. 1975. Thymic involution: Effect on T cell differentiation. *J. Immunol.*, **114**, 1659–1664.

Hori, Y., Perkins, E. H., and Halsall, M. K. 1973. Decline in phytohemagglutinin responsiveness of spleen cells from aging mice. *Proc. Soc. Exp. Biol. Med.*, **144**, 48–53.

Hotchin, J. E. 1972. Virus-induced autoimmunity and the aging process. *In*, M. M. Sigel and R. A. Good (eds.), *Tolerance, Autoimmunity and Aging*, pp. 132–157. Springfield, Illinois: Charles C. Thomas.

Ishidate, M., and Metcalf, D. 1963. The pattern of lymphopoiesis in the mouse thymus after cortisone administration or adrenalectomy. *Australian J. Exp. Biol. Med. Sci.*, **41**, 637–649.

Jacobs, P. A., Brunton, M., and Court-Brown, W. M. 1964. Cytogenetic studies in leukocytes on the general population: Subjects of ages 65 years or more. *Ann. Hum. Genet.*, **27**, 353–365.

Jaroslow, B. N. 1971. Hibernation and different stages in the sequence of immune responsiveness. *Cryobiology*, **8**, 306–307.

Jaroslow, B. N., and Taliaferro, W. H. 1956. Restoration of hemolysin-forming capacity of x-irradiated rabbits by tissue and yeast preparations. *J. Infect. Diseases*, **98**, 75–81.

Johnson, A. G. 1973. The adjuvant action of polynucleotides. *J. Reticuloendothel. Soc.*, **14**, 441–448.

Jose, D. G., and Good, R. A. 1971. Absence of enhancing antibody in cell-mediated immunity to tumor heterografts in protein deficient rats. *Nature*, **231**, 323–325.

Julis, M. H., Simpson, E., and Herzenberg, L. A. 1973. A rapid method for the isolation of functional thymus-derived murine lymphocytes. *European J. Immunol.*, **3**, 645–649.

Kalff, M. W. 1970. A population study on serum immunoglobulin levels. *Clin. Chim. Acta*, **28**, 277–289.

Katz, D. H., Paul, W. E., Goidl, E. A., and Benacerraf, B. J. 1970. Carrier function in anti-hapten immune responses. I. Enhancement of responses by carrier preimmunization. *J. Exp. Med.*, **132**, 261–282.

Kaufman, S. J. 1971. Selective inhibition of cells in the immune response by actinomycin D. *J. Immunol.*, **106**, 781–785.

Kay, M. M. 1973. Cellular interactions: Scanning electron microscopy of human thymus-derived rosette-forming lymphocytes. *Clin. Immunol. Immunopathol.*, **2**, 301–309.

Kishimoto, S., Tsuyuguchi, I., and Yamamura, Y. 1969. Immune responses in aged mice. *Clin. Exp. Immunol.*, **5**, 525–530.

Kohn, R. R. 1971. *Principles of Mammalian Aging*. Englewood Cliffs, New Jersey: Prentice-Hall.

Komuro, K., and Boyse, E. A. 1973. Induction of T lymphocytes from precursor cells *in vitro* by a product of the thymus. *J. Exp. Med.*, **138**, 479–482.

Konen, T. G., Smith, G. S., and Walford, R. L. 1973. Decline in mixed lymphocyte reactivity of spleen cells from aged mice of a long-lived strain. *J. Immunol.*, **110**, 1216–1221.

Krohn, P. L. 1962. Review lectures in senescence. II. Heterochromic transplantation in the study of aging. *Proc. Roy. Soc. (London)*, *Ser. B*, **157**, 128–147.

Krohn, P. L. (ed.) 1966. *Topics in the Biology of Aging*. New York: Interscience Publishers, John Wiley.

Kysela, S., and Steinberg, A. D. 1973. Increased survival of NZB/W mice given multiple syngeneic young thymus grafts. *Clin. Immunol. Immunopathol.*, **2**, 133–136.

Lajtha, L. J., and Schofield, R. 1971. Regulation of stem cell renewal and differentiation: Possible significance in aging. *Advan. Geront. Res.*, **3**, 131–146.

Lawrence, H. S., and Landy, M. (eds.), 1969. *Mediators of Cellular Immunology*. New York: Academic Press.

Legge, J. S., and Austin, C. M. 1968. Antigen localization and the immune response as a function of age. *Australian J. Exp. Biol. Med. Sci.*, **46**, 361–365.

Levy, N. L., and Scott, D. W. 1972. Bone marrow-derived lymphoid cells (B cells): Functional depletion with cobra factor and fresh serum. *Science*, **178**, 866–867.

Linder, E., Pasternack, A., and Edgington, T. S. 1972. Pathology and immunology of age-associated disease of mice and evidence for an autologous immune complex pathogenesis of the associated renal disease. *Clin. Immunol. Immunopathol.*, **1**, 104–121.

Liu, R. K., and Walford, R. L. 1972. The effect of lowered body temperature on lifespan and immune and non-immune processes. *Gerontologia*, **18**, 363–388.

Lyngbye, J., and Kroll, J. 1971. Quantitative immunoelectrophoresis of proteins in serum from normal population: Season-, age-, and sex-related variations. *Clin. Chem.*, **17**, 495–500.

McCay, C. M., Crowell, M. F., and Maynard, L. A. 1935. The effect of retarded growth upon the length of life span and upon the ultimate body size. *J. Nutr.*, **10**, 63–79.

Mackay, I. R. 1972. Ageing and immunological function in man. *Gerontologia*, **18**, 285–304.

Makinodan, T. 1973. Cellular basis of immunosenescence. *INSERM*, **27**, 153–166.

Makinodan, T., and Adler, W. H. 1975. The effects of aging on the differentiation and proliferation potentials of cells of the immune system. *Federation Proc.*, **34**, 153–158.

Makinodan, T., and Albright, J. F. 1967. Proliferative and differentiation manifestations of cellular immune potential. *Progr. Allergy*, **10**, 1–36.

Makinodan, T., Perkins, E. H., and Chen, M. G. 1971.

Immunologic activity of the aged. *Advan. Geront. Res.*, 3, 171-198.

Makinodan, T., Perkins, E. H., Shekarchi, I. C., and Gengozian, N. 1960. Use of lethally irradiated isologous mice as *in vitro* tissue cultures of antibody-forming cells. *In*, M. Holub and L. Jaroskova (eds.), *Mechanisms of Antibody Formation*, pp. 182-189. Prague: Publ. House of the Czechoslovak Acad. Sci.

Makinodan, T., and Peterson, W. J. 1962. Relative antibody-forming capacity of spleen cells as a function of age. *Proc. Nat. Acad. Sci.*, 48, 234-238.

Makinodan, T., and Peterson, W. J. 1964. Growth and senescence of the primary antibody-forming potential of the spleen *J. Immunol.*, 93, 886-896.

Marbrook, J. 1967. Primary immune response in cultures of spleen cells. *Lancet*, 2, 1279-1281.

Mathies, M., Lipps, L., Smith, G. S., and Walford, R. L. 1973. Age-related decline in response to phytohemagglutinin and pokeweed mitogen by spleen cells from hamsters and a long-lived mouse strain. *J. Geront.*, 28, 425-430.

Medvedev, Z. A. 1964. The nucleic acids in development and aging. *Advan. Geront. Res.*, 1, 181-202.

Menon, M., Jaroslow, B. N., and Koesterer, R. 1974. The decline of cell-mediated immunity in aging mice. *J. Geront.*, 29, 499-505.

Metcalf, D., and Moulds, R. 1967. Immune responses in preleukaemic and leukaemic AKR mice. *Intern. J. Cancer*, 2, 53-58.

Metcalf, D., Moulds, R., and Pike, B. 1966. Influence of the spleen and thymus on immune responses in ageing mice. *Clin. Exp. Immunol.*, 2, 109-120.

Micklem H. S., Ford, C. E., Evans, E. P., and Gray, J. 1966. Interrelationships of myeloid and lymphoid cells: Studies with chromosome-marked cells transfused into lethally irradiated mice. *Proc. Roy. Soc. (London), Ser. B,* 165, 78-102.

Miller, J. F. A. P., Sprent, J., Basten, A., and Warner, N. L. 1972. Selective cytotoxicity of anti-kappa serum for B lymphocytes. *Nature*, 237, 18-20.

Miller, R. G., and Phillips, R. A. 1969. Separation of cells by velocity sedimentation. *J. Cellular Physiol.*, 73, 191-201.

Mishell, R. I., and Dutton, R. W. 1967. Immunization of dissociated spleen cell cultures from normal mice. *J. Exp. Med.*, 126, 423-442.

Moore, M. A. S., and Owen, J. J. T. 1967. Stem cell migration in developing myeloid and lymphoid systems. *Lancet*, 2, 658-659.

Morton, J. I., and Siegel, B. V. 1969. Response of NZB mice to foreign antigen and development of autoimmune disease. *J. Reticuloendothel. Soc.*, 6, 78-93.

Mosier, D. E. 1967. A requirement for two cell types for antibody formation *in vitro*. *Science*, 158, 1573-1575.

Nakakuki, K., Shisa, H., and Nishizuka, Y. 1967. Prevention of AKR leukemia by thymectomy of varying ages. *Acta Haematol.*, 38, 317-323.

Naor, D., and Sulitzneau, D. 1967. Binding of radio-iodinated bovine serum albumin to mouse spleen cells. *Nature*, 214, 687-688.

Nossal, G. J. V., Ada, G. L., and Austin, C. N. 1964. Antigens in immunity. IV. Cellular localization of ^{125}I- and ^{131}I-labeled flagella in lymph nodes. *Australian J. Exp. Biol. Med. Sci.*, 42, 311-330.

Oh, Y. H., and Conrad, R. A. 1972. Effect of aging on acetate incorporation in nuclei of lymphocytes stimulated with phytohemagglutinin. *Life Sci.*, 11, 677-684.

Okumura, K., and Tada, T. 1971. Regulation of hemocytotrophic antibody formation in the rat. VI. Inhibitory effect of thymocytes on the hemocytotrophic antibody response. *J. Immunol.*, 107, 1682-1689.

Orgel, L. E. 1963. The maintenance of the accuracy of protein synthesis and its relevance to ageing. *Proc. Nat. Acad. Sci.*, 49, 517-521.

Owen, J. J. T. 1972. The origin and development of lymphocyte populations. *In*, R. Porter and J. Knight (eds.), *Ciba Foundation Symposium on Acquired Immunity*, pp. 35-54. New York: Associated Scientific Publishers.

Pantelouris, E. M. 1972. Thymic involution and ageing: A hypothesis. *Exp. Geront.*, 7, 73-81.

Paul, J. R., and Bunnell, W. W. 1932. The presence of heterophile and antibodies in infectious mononucleosis. *Am. J. Med. Sci.*, 183, 90-104.

Penn, I., and Starzl, T. E. 1972. Malignant tumors arising *de novo* in immunosuppressed organ transplant recipients. *Transplantation*, 14, 407-417.

Perkins, E. H. 1971. Phagocytic activity of aged mice. *J. Reticuloendothel. Soc.*, 9, 642.

Perkins, E. H., and Makinodan, T. 1971. Nature of humoral immunologic deficiencies of the aged. *In*, *Proceedings from the First Rocky Mountain Symposium on Aging*. Fort Collins, Colorado: Colorado State University.

Perkins, E. H., Makinodan, T., and Seibert, C. 1972. Model approach to immunological rejuvenation of the aged. *Infect. Immunity*, 6, 518-524.

Perlman, P., and Holm, G. 1969. Cytotoxic effects of lymphoid cells *in vitro*. *Advan. Immunol.*, 11, 117-193.

Peter, C. P. 1973. Possible immune origin of age-related pathological changes in long-lived mice. *J. Geront.*, 28, 265-275.

Peterson, W. J., and Makinodan, T. 1972. Autoimmunity in aged mice, occurrence of autoagglutinating factors in the blood of aged mice with medium and long life-spans. *Clin. Exp. Immunol.*, 12, 273-290.

Phillips, S. M., and Wegman, T. G. 1973. Active suppression as a possible mechanism of tolerance in tetraparental mice. *J. Exp. Med.*, 137, 291-300.

Pierpaoli, W., and Sorkin, E. 1967. Relationship between thymus and hypophysis. *Nature*, 215, 834-837.

Pisciotta, A. V., Westring, D. W., Deprey, C., and Walsh, B. 1967. Mitogenic effect of phytohaemagglutinin at different ages. *Nature*, 215, 193-194.

Prehn, R. T. 1971. Evaluation of the evidence for immune surveillance. *In*, R. T. Smith and M. Landy (eds.), *Immune Surveillance*, pp. 451–462. New York: Academic Press.

Price, G. B., and Makinodan, T. 1972a. Immunologic deficiencies in senescence. I. Characterization of intrinsic deficiencies. *J. Immunol.*, 108, 403–412.

Price, G. B., and Makinodan, T. 1972b. Immunologic deficiencies in senescence. II. Characterization of extrinsic deficiencies. *J. Immunol.*, 108, 413–417.

Price, G. B., and Makinodan, T. 1973. Aging: Alteration of DNA-protein information. *Gerontologia*, 19, 58–70.

Proceedings of the 2nd International Congress of Immunology. 1974. Amsterdam: North Holland Press.

Proffit, M. R., Hirsch, M. S., and Black, P. H. 1973. Murine leukemia: A virus-induced autoimmune disease? *Science*, 182, 821–823.

Quinn, R. P., Price, G. B., Ellis, J. M., and Makinodan, T. 1973. Catabolic half-lives of immunoglobulin and albumin as a function of age in mice. *J. Geront.*, 28, 257–264.

Rabinowitz, Y. 1964. Separation of lymphocytes, polymorphonuclear leukocytes and monocytes on glass columns, including tissue culture observations. *Blood*, 23, 811–828.

Raff, M. C. 1971. Surface antigenic markers for distinguishing T and B lymphocytes in mice. *Transplant. Rev.*, 6, 52–80.

Raidt, D. J., Mishell, R. I., and Dutton, R. W. 1968. Cellular events in the immunological response. Analysis and *in vitro* response of mouse spleen cell populations separated by differential flotation in albumin gradients. *J. Exp. Med.*, 128, 681–698.

Reif, A. E., and Allen, J. M. V. 1964. The AKR thymic antigen and its distribution in leukemias and nervous tissues. *J. Exp. Med.*, 120, 413–433.

Roberts-Thomson, I. C., Whittingham, S., Young-chaiyud, U., and Mackay, I. R. 1974. Ageing immune response, and mortality. *Lancet*, 2, 368–370.

Roitt, I. V. 1971. *Essential Immunology*. Oxford, England: Blackwell Scientific Publications.

Roseman, J. 1969. X-ray resistant cell required for the induction of *in vitro* antibody formation. *Science*, 165, 1125–1127.

Ross, M. H., and Bras, G. 1971. Lasting influence of early caloric restriction on prevalence of neoplasms in the rat. *J. Nat. Cancer Inst.*, 47, 1095–1113.

Rowley, D. A., Fitch, F. W., Stuart, F. P., Köhler, H., and Cosenza, H. 1973. Specific suppression of immune responses. *Science*, 181, 1133–1141.

Rowley, M. J., Buchanan, H., and Mackay, I. R. 1968. Reciprocal change with age in antibody to extrinsic and intrinsic antigens. *Lancet*, 2, 24–26.

Rutishauser, U., Millette, C. F., and Edelman, G. M. 1972. Specific fractionation of immune cell populations. *Proc. Nat. Acad. Sci.*, 69, 1596–1600.

Rygaard, J., and Povlsen, C. O. 1974. Is immunological surveillance not a cell-mediated immune fraction? *Transplantation*, 17, 135–136.

Sabin, A. B. 1947. Antibody response of people of different ages to two doses of uncentrifuged Japanese B encephalitis vaccine. *Proc. Soc. Exp. Biol. Med.*, 65, 127–130.

Santos, G. W., and Owens, A. H., Jr. 1966. Adoptive transfer of immunologically competent cells. I. Quantitative studies of antibody formation by syngeneic spleen cells in the cyclophosphamide pretreated mice. *Bull. Johns Hopkins Hosp.* 118, 109–126.

Shortman, K., Cerottini, J. C., and Brunner, K. T. 1972. The separation of sub-populations of T and B lymphocytes. *European J. Immunol.*, 2, 313–319.

Shortman, K., and Palmer, J. 1971. The requirement for macrophages in the *in vitro* immune response. *Cell. Immunol.*, 2, 399–410.

Siminovitch, L., Till, J. E., and McCulloch, E. A. 1964. Decline in colony-forming ability of marrow cells subjected to serial transplantation into irradiated mice. *J. Cellular Physiol.*, 64, 23–31.

Smith, G. S., Walford, R. L., and Mickey, R. 1973. Lifespan and incidence of cancer and other diseases in selected long-lived inbred mice and their F_1-hybrids. *J. Nat. Cancer Inst.*, 50, 1195–1213.

Solomonova, K., and Vizev, St. 1973. Immunological reactivity of senescent and old people actively immunized with tetanus toxoid. *Z. Immunitätsforsch.*, 146, 81–90.

Stjernsward, J. 1966. Age dependent tumor-host barrier and effect of carcinogens initiated immune depression of rejection of isografted methyl cholanthrene induced sarcoma cells. *J. Nat. Cancer Inst.*, 37, 505–512.

Strehler, B. L. 1967. Cellular aging. *Ann. N. Y. Acad. Sci.*, 138, 661–679.

Stutman, O. 1974. Tumor development after 3-methylcholanthrene in immunologically deficient athymic-nude mice. *Science*, 183, 534–536.

Stutman, O., Yunis, E. J., and Good, R. A. 1968. Deficient immunologic functions of NZB mice. *Proc. Soc. Exp. Biol. Med.*, 127, 1204–1207.

Tait, N. N. 1969. The effect of temperature on the immune response in cold-blooded vertebrates. *Physiol. Zool.*, 42, 29–35.

Teague, P. O., Friou, G. J., Yunis, E. J., and Good, R. A. 1972. Spontaneous autoimmunity in aging mice. *In*, M. M. Sigel and R. A. Good (eds.), *Tolerance, Autoimmunity and Aging*, pp. 33–61. Springfield, Illinois: Charles C. Thomas.

Teague, P. O., Yunis, E. J., Rodey, G., Fish, A. J., Stutman, O., and Good, R. A. 1970. Autoimmune phenomena and renal disease in mice. Role of thymectomy, aging, and involution of immunologic capacity. *Lab. Invest.*, 22, 121–130.

Teller, M. N. 1972. Age changes and immune resistance to cancer. *Advan. Geront. Res.*, 4, 25–43.

Tengerdy, R. P., Heinzerling, R. H., and Nockels, C. F. 1972. Effect of vitamin E on the immune response of hypoxic and normal chickens. *Infect. Immunity*, 5, 987–989.

Thomsen, O., and Kettel, K. 1929. Die stärke der menschlichen isoagglutinine und entsprechenden blutkörperchenrezeptoren in verschiedenen lebensaltern. *Z. Immunitätsforsch.*, **63**, 67–93.

Till, J. E., and McCulloch, E. A. 1961. A direct measurement of the radiation sensitivity of normal mouse bone marrow cells. *Radiation Res.*, **14**, 213–222.

Trainin, N. 1974. Thymic hormones and the immune response. *Physiol. Rev.*, **54**, 272–315.

Volkman, A., and Gowans, J. L. 1965. The origin of macrophages from bone marrow in the rat. *Brit. J. Exp. Pathol.*, **46**, 62–70.

Waldorf, D. S., Willkens, R. F., and Decker, J. L. 1968. Impaired delayed hypersensitivity in an aging population. Association with antinuclear reactivity and rheumatoid factor. *J. Am. Med. Assoc.*, **203**, 831–834.

Walford, R. L. 1969. *The Immunologic Theory of Aging.* Copenhagen: Munksgaard.

Walford, R. L. 1974. The immunologic theory of aging: Current status. *Federation Proc.*, **33**, 2020–2027.

Walford, R. L., Liu, R. K., Mathies, M., Gerbase-Delima, M., and Lipps, L. 1974. Longterm dietary restriction and immune function in mice, response to sheep red blood cells and to mitogens. *Mech. Age. Dev.*, **2**, 447–454.

Walford, R. L., Smith, G. S., and Waters, H. 1971. Histocompatibility systems and disease states with particular reference to cancer. *Transplant Rev.*, **7**, 78–111.

Wekerle, H., Lonai, P., and Feldman, M. 1972. Fractionation of antigen reactive cells on a cellular immunoadsorbent: Factors determining recognition of antigens by T-lymphocytes. *Proc. Nat. Acad. Sci.*, **69**, 1620–1624.

White, A., and Goldstein, A. L. 1970. Thymosin, a thymic hormone influencing lymphoid cell immunological competence. *In*, G. E. W. Wolstenholme and J. Knight (eds.), *Hormones and the Immune Response, Ciba Foundation Study Group No. 36*, pp. 3–23. London: J. and A. Churchill.

Wigzell, H., and Stjernswärd, J. 1966. Age-dependent rise and fall of immunological reactivity in the CBA mouse. *J. Nat. Cancer Inst.*, **37**, 513–517.

Wigzell, H., Sundquist, K. G., and Yoshida, T. O. 1972. Separation of the cells according to surface antigens by the use of antibody-coated columns. Fractionation of cells carrying immunoglobulins and blood group antigens. *Scand. J. Immunol.*, **1**, 75–87.

Wioland, M., Sabolovic, D., and Burg, C. 1972. Electrophoretic mobilities of T and B cells. *Nature (New Biol.)*, **237**, 274–276.

World Health Organization. 1973. *Cell-Mediated Immunity and Resistance to Infection, Technical Report Series No. 519.* Geneva: The Organization.

Wu, A. M., Till, J. E., Siminovitch, L., and McCulloch, E. A. 1968. Cytological evidence for a relationship between normal hematopoietic colony-forming cells and cells of the lymphoid system. *J. Exp. Med.*, **127**, 455–464.

Yunis, E. J., Fernandes, G., Teague, P. O., Stutman, O., and Good, R. A. 1972. The thymus, autoimmunity and the involution of the lymphoid system. *In*, M. M. Sigel and R. A. Good (eds.), *Tolerance, Autoimmunity and Aging*, pp. 62–119. Springfield, Illinois: Charles C. Thomas.

Zacharski, L. R., Elveback, L. R., and Linman, J. W. 1971. Leukocyte counts in healthy adults. *Am. J. Clin. Pathol.*, **56**, 148–150.

16
AGING OF THE EXCRETORY SYSTEM:
Kidney and Bladder

Ralph Goldman

VA Wadsworth Hospital Center
and
University of California, Los Angeles

The aging changes of the kidney, both structural and functional, have been extensively studied. The process can be considered to begin in the embryo, where the pronephros and mesonephros of the lower vertebrates are sequentially developed, only to be replaced by the metanephros of the mammal. Oliver (1939) proposes that the regression and disappearance of the pronephros and mesonephros represent senescence of these organs prior to birth. It is generally believed that this successive organ development and replacement is due to the sequential shunting of blood from the regressing to the developing organs. If regression is due to vascular insufficiency, such insufficiency can hardly be called abnormal and pathologic. This point is particularly relevant because much of the evidence points to primary changes in the vasculature of aging kidneys. One of the fundamental problems is to determine if this vascular change is universal, and thus a manifestation of aging, or selective, and thus a manifestation of disease.

CHANGES IN RENAL ANATOMY WITH AGE

The kidney grows markedly from birth to maturation, reaches a maximum, and then, with increasing acceleration, loses mass with age. Roessle and Roulet (1932) give values of 50 grams for the two kidneys at birth, 270 grams for the third and fourth decades, and a gradually accelerating decline to 185 grams in the ninth decade. Dunnill and Halley (1973) report the combined volumes of both kidneys to be 20 ml at birth and 250 ml in healthy adults aged 20-25; in old age the volume declines, but no values are given. Examination of their data suggests that the volume is about 200 ml from the eighth decade on. Changes in the volume of the cortex are more marked with the volume declining to less than half of the maximum adult values. Tauchi, Tsuboi, and Sato (1958) present graphic material from a relatively large sample but no numerical data. The median weight appears to decline from 250 grams in the 40 to 49 year group to 200 grams in the 70+ year group.

The weight of the rat kidney has been documented by Arataki (1926). The two kidneys weigh a little more than 50 mg at birth and rapidly grow to more than 500 mg in 30 days. The maximum weight of 2.5 grams in males and 1.9 grams in females is reached at 150 days. There is a slight decline at 350 days but a more marked drop to 1.7 grams for males and

409

1.4 grams for females at 500 days. From these data the gross loss in renal weight in both men and rats is between 20 percent and 30 percent.

The Glomeruli

The total number of glomeruli per kidney in adults of several species has been established with reasonable confidence:

man	700,000 to 1,200,000
dog	400,000 to 500,000
cat	150,000 to 225,000
rabbit	90,000 to 250,000
rat	20,000 to 30,000

Early counts of glomeruli in man gave variable results ranging from a low of 0.56×10^6 (Sappey, 1889, cited by Moore, 1931) to 5.7×10^6 (Traut, 1923, also cited by Moore, 1931). The high values are obviously too high, but the low values could well have been due to factors relating to old age or disease. Moore (1931) determined the number of glomeruli per kidney in 29 individuals ranging in age from 1 to 73 years. He concluded that the human kidney from birth to 40 years contains 800,000 to 1,000,000 glomeruli, with occasional values as low as 600,000 and as high as 1,200,000, and that there is a loss with age so that by the seventh decade the number may be reduced by one-third to one-half. He also found that there was no evidence for postnatal nephro-genesis in humans, and that each kidney had approximately the same number of glomeruli. However, 5 of the 20 individuals under 40 years had between 500,000 and 700,000 glomeruli, and 3 of the 9 over 40 years had more than 700,000 glomeruli.

Dunnill and Halley (1973) counted the glomeruli in 18 individuals whose ages ranged from 1 day to 73 years. Two infants, aged 1 and 3 days, had average counts of 1,050,000 glomeruli per kidney, and the mean value for all kidneys from 13 individuals less than 38 years was $(0.98 \pm 0.11) \times 10^6$, while in the 5 individuals above this age, the mean number was $(0.72 \pm 0.07) \times 10^6$.

Arataki (1926) found that in the rat there are 10,700 glomeruli at birth, 31,000 at maturity, and 20,000 at 500 days. There is definite evidence of the formation of new glomeruli during the first 100 days of life. The number remains stable until 350 days, then declines. Glomeruli in the outer portion of the cortex are smaller than those in the juxtamedullary region and at birth measure 55 as compared to 68 microns in diameter, with a weighted average of 61 microns. At 100 days the median diameter is 100 microns, and at 150 days it is 110 microns. Glomerular enlargement then continues more slowly, and reaches 123 microns at 500 days. Throughout this period the diameter of the convoluted tubules remains constant at 40 microns. The number of glomeruli per mm^3 of cortex decreases from 1000 at birth, to 70 at 100 days, to 60 at 500 days. The number per mm^3 is somewhat greater in the female than the male. The reduction in the number of glomeruli per unit volume of cortex is due both to the increase in glomerular size and to the maturation of the renal tubules. Thus the glomeruli make up 11 percent of the cortex at birth and 3.5 percent from 30 days to 150 days, after which there is a slow increase to 5.2 percent in males and 6.4 percent in females at 500 days.

At birth the filtering surface of human glomeruli is estimated to be $0.2m^2$ (Dunnill and Halley, 1973). The mean value for all kidneys over 16 years was 1.6 ± 0.7 m^2. In two subjects aged 66 and 73 years, the area was 0.9 m^2. The same investigators found that the cell to lumen ratio in the glomeruli decreased from 48.5 percent during the first year to 41.1 percent after age 16, with no subsequent change with age. Cell types were not differentiated, but Wehner (1968) reported that the mesangium increased significantly from a mean of 6.2 percent of glomerular volume to 10.4 percent in old age. Dunnill and Halley also report that the glomeruli comprise 18 percent of the cortical volume in the newborn but only 8.6 percent in the adult; there is no evidence of change with aging. Electron microscopic and PAS studies reveal reduplication and focal thickening of both glomerular and tubular basement membranes (Farquhar, Vernier, and Good, 1957; Darmady, Offer, and Woodhouse, 1973). This is of interest because of recent reports of capillary basement membrane thickening as a possible universal aging phenomenon with obvious physiologic implications (Kilo, Vogler, and Williamson, 1972).

One difficulty in the acceptance of renal involution has been the lack of visible evidence of glomerular and nephron obsolescence (Oliver, 1939; Tauchi, Tsuboi, and Sato, 1958; Darmady, Offer, and Woodhouse, 1973). Scarred glomeruli and other signs of change seem insufficient to account for a loss of one-third of the original nephrons. Perhaps the scars are less marked because the process is scattered and very slowly continuous. Yet, as early as the seventh intrauterine month glomeruli begin to degenerate in the pelvic and peri-arcuate region, and by the seventh year degenerated juxtamedullary glomeruli can be seen. From the ninth intrauterine month, there is scattered atrophy of cortical glomeruli (Ljungqvist, 1963). When serially observed, most of these glomeruli do not form the classical hyaline scar. Yet some scars are present, and increase with age, although they never exceed 10 percent (Tauchi, Tsuboi, and Sato, 1958).

Other attempts have been made to assess the status of glomeruli. Using histologic criteria, Sworn and Fox (1972) found that there was a significant correlation between age and number of abnormal glomeruli. The regression line drops from the equivalent of 95 percent normal glomeruli up to age 40 years to 63 percent at 90 years. Yet until age 80, all individuals possessed at least 50 percent normal glomeruli. These authors state that if a kidney is to be used for transplantation, and 90 percent normal glomeruli are desired, the cut-off age should be 50 years.

The Tubules

In his pioneer review of the aging urinary system, Oliver (1939) devoted considerable attention to the results of his own micro-dissections. He found little correlation between the size of the glomerulus and the size of the tubule and that the tubule does not inevitably degenerate after loss of its glomerulus. When they do degenerate, the tubules become reduced in volume and are then replaced by connective tissue with little evidence of inflammatory or round cell infiltrate, suggesting a response to gradually increasing ischemia. Tubular hypertrophy occurs in the remaining nephrons and is limited almost entirely to the proximal convoluted tubule, which may become as much as 12 times normal in size. This change appears to result from both hypertrophy and hyperplasia of tubule cells. The glomerulus may be normal, enlarged, atrophied, or destroyed.

In contrast, Tauchi, Tsuboi, and Sato (1958) found that in the senescent kidney there was a decrease in the volume of the glomeruli, a dilatation of the tubular lumen, and a decrease in the number of cells of both, although the glomerular cells were atrophic and the tubular cells hypertrophic. It was their impression that these observations cast doubt on the primary importance of vascular insufficiency as the cause of senescent regression.

The relative decrease in the glomerular component of the cortex which occurs immediately after birth is due to the increase in the length and volume of the tubules, primarily in the proximal convoluted portion. The mean length and volume of the proximal tubule at term are 2.09 mm and 0.004 mm^3, respectively; at 4 months, 4.72 mm and 0.013 mm^3; at 1 year, 6.78 mm and 0.017 mm^3; at maturity, 19.36 mm and 0.076 mm^3; and at extreme old age (over 80 years), 12.50 mm and 0.052 mm^3 (Darmady, Offer, and Woodhouse, 1973). The ratio of the glomerular surface area to the proximal tubular volume decreases from 29.4 at term to 11.8 at 4 months, 7.78 at 1 year, and stabilizes at 3.2 throughout maturity and into old age. Analysis reveals that the decline in proximal tubular length is continuous from maturity and does not start abruptly at a specific age. It also appears that this is due to a disproportionate loss of juxtamedullary nephrons and may be of significance in the loss of concentrating ability with age. Dunnill and Halley (1973) found the cortical tubular basement membrane to increase from 0.8 m^2 at birth to a mean of 8.7 ± 2.3 m^2 over the age of 16 years and to be linearly related to renal cortical volume.

In the course of their microdissection studies, Darmady, Offer, and Woodhouse (1973) failed to find evidence for aglomerular nephrons as reported by Oliver (1939). In addition, they found no evidence of compensatory hypertrophy or hyperplasia in the single nephron. An interesting and possibly important observation was the presence of distal tubular diverticuli. These varied from side pouches to pedunculated sacs and were in the region of attachment to the macula densa. They connect to the tubular lumen and have been noted to contain detritus and bacteria; they may therefore be of clinical significance. The diverticula are rare in childhood, but after age 16 to 18 the number increased linearly with age. At age 90 they average 300 per 100 nephrons.

The tubular basement membrane, like that of the glomerulus, thickens with age (Scott, 1964; Darmady, Offer, and Woodhouse, 1973). Scott, in examining the basement membranes of rats, found them to be irregularly thickened independent of dietary variations. The thickening was accompanied by a regular aberration of the adjacent portion of the tubule cells, which protrude into the membrane. He postulates that the protrusion may represent a compensation for the effects of the thickening basement membrane.

The Renal Vasculature

Oliver (1939) proposed that the senescent changes in the kidney were all the product of ischemic atrophy, produced by vascular alterations which were part of aging, and were not pathologic in origin. There is much evidence to support vascular regression as a major component of the process. An early, and detailed, description of the course of ischemic obsolescence of glomeruli was presented by MacCallum (1939) and was summarized by McManus and Lupton (1960). Briefly, the first stage is a progressive collapse of the glomerular tuft, followed by a simplification and reduction in the vascular channels. Hyaline is deposited within both the residual glomerular tuft and in the space of Bowman's capsule. Identifiable structures disappear rapidly. The obsolete glomerulus may be reabsorbed and disappear entirely; reabsorption is suggested because of the scantiness of the cellular response. This

process can leave a single vessel in place of the glomerular capillary, thus producing a shunt between the afferent and efferent arterioles analagous to the arterioli recti of Ludwig. Indentification of this process and demonstration of arteriolar shunts does much to satisfy the objection that regression of glomeruli must leave tangible evidence of their former presence.

Ljungqvist (Ljungqvist and Lagergren, 1962, Ljungqvist 1963 and 1964) has performed extensive microangiographic studies which confirm the presence and development of the shunts and relate to the life cycle of the kidney. Pelvic and juxtamedullary glomeruli degenerate to form shunts as early as the seventh intrauterine month (Ljungqvist, 1963). Scattered cortical glomeruli begin to atrophy after the ninth fetal month, and juxtamedullary glomeruli external to the arcuate vessels, after the seventh year of life. More careful examination revealed that in the cortical area, atrophy of a glomerulus resulted in the abrupt termination of the arteriole (Figure 1). Surprisingly, these arterioles remain patent, despite their blind ends, and become more numerous with age but are still relatively uncommon. In the juxtamedullary region the afferent and efferent arterioles are of the same caliber, unlike the outer cortex where the efferent arteriole is considerably smaller. In this region there is increasing evidence of aglomerular vessels leading to the vasa rectae, but a majority of the glomeruli still remain intact. A smaller number of altered juxtamedullary glomeruli can be seen which are only partially filled. Another vascular manifestation of aging is a tortuosity and spiralling of the interloular artery as it proceeds toward the capsule (Ljungqvist and Lagergren, 1962). Recently Takazakura, Wasabu, Handa, Takada, Shinoda, and Takeuchi (1972) have confirmed all of these observations. They observed shunting in 9 percent of the juxtamedullary glomeruli at birth, with a linear increase with age which reached 100 percent during the ninth decade. This observation, alone, is strong evidence that there is a normal, age-related change in renal vascular anatomy and function independent of disease. In disease states, including hypertension, the

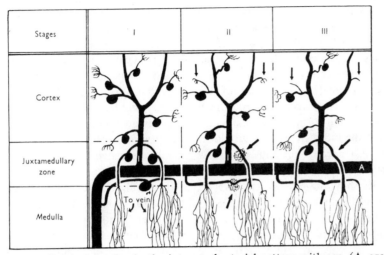

Figure 1a. Diagram showing changes in the intrarenal arterial pattern with age. (A, arcuate artery. I, interlobular artery.) Stage I. Basic adult pattern showing glomerular arterioles. Stage II. Partial degeneration of some glomeruli. Two cortical afferent arterioles ramify into remnants of glomerular tufts (small arrows). Two juxtamedullary arterioles pass through partially degenerated glomeruli (large arrows). There is slight spiraling of interlobular arteries and afferent arterioles. Stage III. Two cortical afferent arterioles now end blindly (small arrows), and two juxtamedullary arterioles are a glomerular (large arrows). The corresponding glomerular tufts have degenerated completely. The spiraling of interlobular arteries and afferent arterioles is now more pronounced. (From Ljungqvist and Lagergren, *J. Anat.*, 1962, by permission of the publisher.)

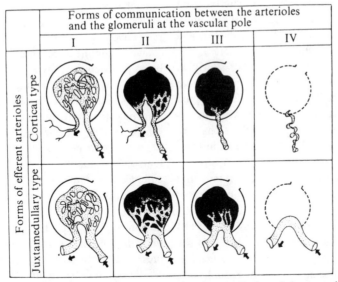

Figure 1b. Diagram of the degenerative process in the cortical and juxtamedullary nephrons. (From Takazakura, Sawabu, Handa, Takada, Shinoda, and Takeuchi. 1972. Reprinted from *Kidney Internationl,* 2, 225, by permission of the publishers.)

amount of shunting was increased independent of age. Similar observations are reported by Reynes, Coulet, and Diebold (1968).

Davidson, Talner, and Downs (1969) radio- graphed kidneys injected with radio-opaque media at postmortem examination. They found that the normal renal vessels taper from hilum to cortex and the arcuate arteries curve gently.

Before age 40 there is normally very little deviation from this pattern. Abnormalities appear between the ages of 40 and 80, although the age progression is irregular. After age 80, all kidneys show some degree of abnormality. The most frequent finding is the failure of the vessels to taper. The arcuate arteries may become angulated and tortuous, and there may be notching at the bifurcations. The interlobar arteries may also become tortuous and show luminal irregularities. The changes in the arcuate arteries show the best correlation with age. Polar areas of ischemia are often seen.

There has been little consensus regarding the histologic changes in the arteries and arterioles of the kidney with age. Muscular arteries have been reported to undergo deposition of collagen between the intima and the internal elastic lamina, fraying, splitting, reduplicating, and calcifying the elastic lamina, and replacing muscular cells with collagen. These changes are not usually associated with any decrease in luminal size. Oliver (1939) recognized these age changes in the renal vasculature as did Tauchi, Tsuboi, and Sato (1958), Williams and Harrison (1937), Yamaguchi, Omae, and Katsuki (1969), Darmady, Offer, and Woodhouse (1973), and others. These authors are also in general agreement that the changes occur rather slowly in the larger arteries but develop later and more rapidly in the smaller ones. It is also accepted that hypertension is associated with an acceleration and intensification of these changes. Tauchi, Tsuboi, and Okutomi (1971), in comparing a large number of autopsy tissues of Japanese and Caucasian males, found that sclerosis appeared earlier and was more intense in the Japanese than in the Caucasians. Recently Jackson, Puchtler, and Sweat (1968) have challenged the evidence for splitting of the elastic lamina. They produced histochemical evidence that what appears to be reduplicated elastin is actually collagen. In either case the age-related changes result in diminished elasticity.

Little change is seen in the arterioles. Moritz and Oldt (1937) found that only 16 percent of subjects over age 60 years, without evidence of hypertension, showed mild to moderate arteriolar changes, but moderate to severe changes were noted in 97 percent of hypertensives. Similar observations were made by Williams and Harrison (1937), who noted that 13 percent of elderly normotensives showed arteriolar changes as opposed to 58 percent of elderly benign hypertensives, and by Bell (1946), who found lesions in 16 percent of normotensives over the age of 50. The arteriolar changes of intimal proliferation, medial hypertrophy, and necrosis are relatively rare in the absence of hypertension. The one arteriolar lesion commonly associated with aging is mild hyalinization.

If, as Oliver states, all renal change with age is due to ischemia, it is somewhat paradoxical that there is no better anatomical evidence for such ischemia. The presence of vascular change, in the absence of luminal narrowing, does not provide such evidence. In this regard the results of Yamaguchi, Omae, and Katsuki (1969) are of interest: the ratios of lumen diameter to wall thickness in the small arteries were 3.91 in the young and 3.84 in the old and in arterioles were 2.52 in the young and 2.66 in the old. In neither case was the difference significant. Both were significantly different from the values obtained in persistent, severe hypertension of 2.26 and 1.51 for small arteries and arterioles, respectively.

Two anatomical changes in the veins have been reported by Payan and Gilbert (1967, 1972). The first is a micronodular phlebosclerosis, consisting of a fibromuscular nodule involving the wall, but not the intima, of a venule, which can be seen with low power microscopy to be protruding into the vascular lumen. The nodules are most common in the adrenal, less frequent in the renal cortex, and were not seen in other organs. They increased in number with age. The other observation was of interrupted, eccentric, longitudinal muscle fibers in the renal veins. These bundles are not present at birth, are only occasionally seen in childhood, and are found in 20–33 percent of adults and 40 percent of individuals over 60 years. The significance of these findings is not known, and they are not associated with hypertension. They were not found in the renal veins of rats at any age.

The Interstitial Tissue

There is considerable evidence that although the cortex shows very little increase in connective tissue with age, there is a significant increase in the medulla, particularly in the pyramids. Keresztury and Megyeri (1962) examined the pyramids in 89 cadavers, ranging in age from 1 to 85 years. A rich cellular population is gradually replaced by intercellular material, especially after 50 years of age, which is so extensive that they consider the term medullary sclerosis to be appropriate. The tissue is vascularized, so they postulate that the process is due to reduced blood supply rather than to vascular occlusion. In severe sclerosis, the tubules may be obstructed and dilated, but there may be no corresponding reduction in function. Histochemical staining showed the presence of finely dispersed sudanophilic fat which paralleled in amount the presence of sclerosis. Finely dispersed deposits of calcium were also noted but did not appear to be related to the sclerotic process; they were found in 32.3 percent of cases under 50 years and in 41.8 percent of those over 50 years of age. Keresztury and Megyeri credit Helpap (1933) with similar prior observations regarding pyramidal sclerosis and Prym (1909) with the observation of medullary fat deposition with age.

McGavack and Kao (1960) examined the soluble collagen, insoluble collagen, and elastin in a number of tissues of 1-, 8-, and 24-month-old rats. There were no significant differences in the renal content of these proteins at various ages. In contrast, Schaub (1963) found the soluble collagen to be 30 percent of the total at birth and to fall to 4 percent at 10 months, with stability thereafter. The total amount of collagen, measured as hydroxyproline, increased from 304 to 857 mg/100 grams defatted dry weight. Ber, Allalouf, Wasserman, and Sharon (1969) determined the concentration of acid mucopolysaccharides (AMPS), expressed as uronic acid, and of hydroxyproline in dry, defatted kidney tissue of male rats as a function of age. They found that the uronic acid increased threefold from birth to 8 months, then decreased by one-third to 18 months. On the other hand, hydroxyproline, representing collagen, increased continuously at all ages and was over two and one-half times as concentrated at 18 months as at birth. Since basement membrane contains collagen, and therefore hydroxyproline, some of the incre-

ment may have come from the basement membranes of the glomeruli, tubules, and blood vessels which are known to increase with age, but this should account for only a minor part of the increase.

Inoue, Sawada, Fukunaga, and Yoshikawa (1970) extended the study to humans by studying 20 kidneys obtained at postmortem from cadavers ranging from 1 to 84 years. They obtained tissue from the cortex and the papillary regions of the medulla. There were no age changes in the concentration of AMPS in the cortex, but there was a threefold increase from birth to age 40 in the medulla, with a modest subsequent decline, closely following the pattern found in the rat. In a later report (Inoue, Sawada, and Yoshikawa, 1973) they confirmed the rise in AMPS in the papilla to age 70 but noted a decrease in water content after age 50, so that there is an age-related change in the ratio AMPS: water. They speculate that this may correlate with the age-related decrement in urinary concentrating ability.

RENAL PHYSIOLOGY

Glomerular Filtration

Probably the first quantitative study of the effect of age upon renal function was that of Lewis and Alving (1938), who studied urea clearance, serum urea concentration, and maximal urine concentration as functions of age. They found that the regression with age could be defined by the formula: C_{urea} (ml/min.) = 136.6 − 0.912 × age (years). All clearances are standardized to 1.73 m² body surface area. The scatter around the mean remained relatively constant until the ninth decade, when more variability became apparent.

Davies and Shock (1950) reported the inulin clearances of 70 men who had been rigorously screened for evidence of disease which could affect renal function and who were equally distributed throughout the age range of 24 to 89 years. Although a straight line was not the most perfect fit, the regression with age according to the method of least squares was highly significant and the calculated formula was:

C_{inulin} (ml/min.) =

153.2 − 0.96 × age (years)

Olbrich, Ferguson, Robson, and Stewart (1950) studied 50 individuals, 36 men and 14 women, over age 60. They also divided their subjects into those with diastolic pressures below and those above 105 mm of mercury. The inulin clearance was 136.0 ml/min. for the controls (average age 30) and 92.1 and 76.5 ml/min. for the normotensive and hypertensive aged subjects, respectively (average age approximately 74). In addition, they found that the mean maximum urea clearance was 82.4 ml/min. for normal young men, 62.3 ml/min. for old men, and 53.3 ml/min. for old men and women with diastolic hypertension. Although these studies are not strictly comparable, it is clear that there is a significant, probably continuous decrement in the filtration rates with age.

There have been many subsequent confirmatory reports, some exploring the phenomenon directly, others incidental to other investigations. Examples include the work of McDonald, Solomon, and Shock (1951); Kluetsch, Heidland, and Oebek (1962); Oddie, Meade, Myhill, and Fisher (1966); Lindeman, Lee, Yiengst, and Shock (1966); Adler, Lindeman, Yiengst, Beard, and Shock (1968); and Tschebotarew and Kalinowskaja (1968). An extremely interesting presentation is made by Wesson (1969), who plotted the individual results of nearly 40 different reports which had not necessarily been made with particular reference to age, all standardized to 1.73 m² body surface (Figure 2). The data were much more complete for men than for women, but in both the filtration rate was at a maximum at age 15, declined gradually to age 45, and then more rapidly thereafter. The approximate values for men at age 15, 45, and 75 years were 138, 120, and 83 ml/min., and for women at the same ages were 123, 111, and 84 ml/min.

Olbrich, Woodford-Williams, Irvine, and Webster (1957) followed their initial report with further studies which indicated that prostatism caused a greater decrease in function than age alone and that infection resulted in an even further reduction. Half of the patients in a small series showed a statistically insignificant improvement after prostatectomy.

Dontas and his associates (Dontas Papanayiotou, Marketos, and Papanicolaou, 1968; Dontas, 1969; Marketos, Papanayiotou, and Dontas, 1969b; Dontas, Marketos, and Papanayiotou, 1972) have also shown in several studies that infection reduces renal function. Marketos, Papanayiotou, and Dontas (1969a) demonstrated that administration of an anabolic steroid will increase the inulin clearance of males as much as 23 percent, although it is without effect in women. These studies are significant in that a number of clinically inapparent conditions may affect renal function and thus amplify the observed age-related decrements.

The initial report of Lewis and Alving (1938) that the urea clearance decreases with age has also been repeatedly confirmed. As a result of this decreased clearance, the blood urea concentration rises, although this rise may be masked by a decreasing intake of protein. Lewis and Alving found that the rate of rise was approximated by the equation:

BUN (mg/100 ml) =

$$7.56 + 0.1119 \times \text{age (males)}$$

This is somewhat less than the values derived by Keating, Jones, Elveback, and Randall (1969):

Urea (mg/100 ml) =

$$28.96 + 0.131 \times \text{age (males), and}$$

Urea (mg/100 ml) =

$$21.87 + 0.170 \times \text{age (females).}$$

The numerical values presented by Milne and Williamson (1972) are more in agreement with the latter values. The serum urea is dependent not only upon the level of renal function but on the level of protein intake as well. The discrepancies noted in these data may be dietary in origin; however, the age-related slopes are similar.

Rowe, Andres, Tobin, Norris, and Shock (1976) studied the relationship of creatinine clearance to age in a large number of men followed for more than a decade. The subjects were rigorously screened to exclude possible disease. At least one clearance was obtained from each of 548 male subjects, and at least

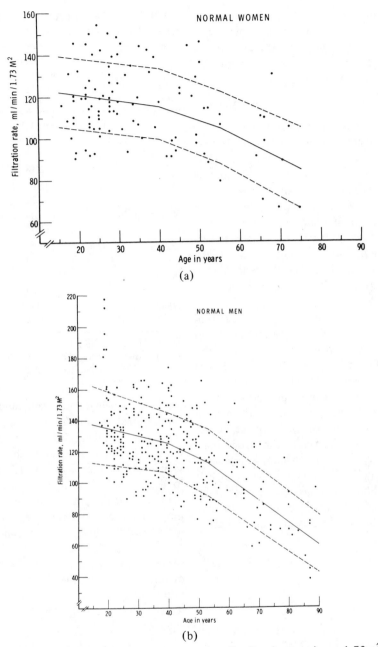

Figure 2. The relationship of age to the filtration rate (inulin clearance) per 1.73m² surface area in normal men and women. The solid line is the mean, by age, and the dashed lines represent the limits of one standard deviation. (From Wesson, *Physiology of the Human Kidney,* Grune and Stratton, New York, 1969, by permission of the publisher.)

three serial determinations, 18 to 24 months apart, were obtained from 293 of these sub-jects. A true creatinine method was used, and urine collection periods were 24 hours in order to minimize the effects of diurnal and activity variations and the inevitable, small collection errors. The study revealed a highly significant reduction in creatinine clearance with age start-ing at age 34 and accelerating after age 65. There was no significant relationship between blood pressure and creatinine clearance, and prostatism, which was present to some degree in 80 percent of subjects over 60 years, also did not appear to have any effect. The regression equation obtained was:

$$C_{cr}(\text{ml/min.}) = 165.57 - 0.80 \times \text{age (years)}$$

The consistency of the results is indicated by the small standard deviations, which for 10-year groups ranged from 3.74 to 1.35 ml/min. (Figure 3, Table 1). Since this study was part of a longitudinal evaluation of aging change, it was also possible to obtain serial determinations for up to 10 years from a large number of the subjects. It had been suspected that there may be a selective mortality which would bias the results. An analysis of the data from the serial studies failed to reveal a significant variation from the cross-sectional data.

Although the creatinine clearance fell from 140 ml/min. at 20 years to 97 ml/min. at 80 years, the serum creatinine rose only from 0.808 mg/100 ml. to 0.843 mg/100 ml. The failure of the serum creatinine to rise significantly is due to an almost proportionate decrease in creatinine production which is a reflection of the decrease in body cell mass, particularly of muscle. This has important practical clinical applications. Hansen, Kampmann, and Laursen (1970) have pointed out that half life in the body of drugs such as penicillin, amino-glucosides, tetracycline, and digoxin may be twice as long in older as in younger individ-

TABLE 1. AGE RELATED CHANGES IN CREATININE CLEARANCE.

Age interval	No. subjects	Creatinine clearance ml/min/ 1.73m²	Serum creatinine concentration mg/100 ml
17–24	10	140.2 ±3.74	0.808 ±0.026
25–34	73	140.1 ±2.48	0.808 ±0.010
35–44	122	132.6 ±1.77	0.813 ±0.009
45–54	152	126.8 ±1.35	0.829 ±0.008
55–64	94	119.9 ±1.74	0.837 ±0.012
65–74	68	109.5 ±2.04	0.825 ±0.012
75–84	29	96.9 ±2.94	0.843 ±0.019

Values indicate mean ± 1 SEM.
From Rowe, Andres, Tobin, and Shock, *J. Gerontology*, 1976, by permission of the publisher.

uals, even when the dosage is modified by the conventional use of the serum creatinine concentration. Lindberg, Nilsson, Bucht, and Kallings (1966) have also noted that while drugs such as chloramphenicol, which are metabolized, do not have rising blood levels with falling renal function, the same is not true of their metabolic products, which may have physiologic activity. Finally, it is possibly of importance to note that Rowe *et al.* (1976) demonstrated, in a smaller study of 55 male subjects of various ages, that the regression of individual ratios of creatinine clearance to inulin clearance with age was relatively slight as defined by the equation:

$$C_{cr}/C_{in} = 1.22 + 0.0012 \times \text{age (years)}$$

Almost all age-related studies of glomerular filtration have been carried out in humans. One study, performed by Gregory and Barrows (1969) on rats, is notable because it does not seem to conform with the human observations. These investigators cannulated the carotid artery and jugular vein and catheterized the bladder of rats with fine polyethylene catheters, which were then tunneled under the skin to the

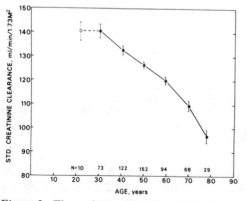

Figure 3. The relationship of standard true creatinine clearance and age. (From Rowe *et al. J. Gerontology,* 1976, by permission of the publisher.)

back of the neck. The animals were allowed to recover, and inulin clearances were performed serially on unanesthetized animals. The clearances of inulin in ml/min./100 grams were 0.83 ± 0.04 in 12-month-old animals, 0.83 ± 0.07 in 24-month-old animals, and 0.78 ± 0.04 in 30-month-old animals. Thus, no significant reduction was noted with age. Goldman (1967) found a constant ratio of kidney function to body weight in rats weighing from 150 to 450 grams, which tends to confirm this observation.

The Renal Blood Flow

The derivation of renal plasma flow (RPF) from p-aminohippurate (PAH) clearance has often been challenged because the extraction ratio is rarely determined. Miller, McDonald and Shock (1951) examined the renal extraction of PAH in 27 subjects between the ages of 23 and 75 years. The mean extraction ratio was 91.3 percent with a range of 86.5 percent to 96.8 percent and an S.D. of 2.5 percent. The mean value for those under 50 years was 91.8 percent and for those over 50 years was 91.1 percent. This difference is insignificant and is surprising in view of the progressive loss of juxtamedullary nephrons without loss of the affiliated vascular supply. The data also indicated that there was no correlation between the extraction ratio and the rate of renal blood flow.

With the establishment of the validity of the method at all ages, the reported studies can be evaluated. The early work of Davies and Shock (1950), using diodrast rather than PAH clearances, showed a progressive and consistent decrease in RPF from 649.3 ml/min./1.73 m^2 in the fourth decade to 288.8 ml/min. in the ninth decade. Earlier work by Goldring, Chasis, Ranges, and Smith (1940) had suggested a possible age-related decrease in RPF between the third and sixth decades. Age-related decrements in renal plasma flow have also been reported by Olbrich et al. (1950, 1957); McDonald, Solomon, and Shock (1951); Kluetsch, Heidland, and Oebek (1962); Lindeman et al. (1966); and Adler et al. (1968). The previously noted combined data of Wesson (1969) demonstrate a peak value of 670 ml/min. for males in the

second decade, gradually decreasing to 610 ml/min. at age 45, then more rapidly to 350 ml/min. at age 75. The comparable values for women are 650 ml/min. at age 15, 565 ml/min. at age 45, and 300 ml/min. at age 75 (Figure 4). There seems little doubt that there is a universal, moderate decrease in blood flow during early maturity which markedly accelerates after the age of 50 years. The regression equation obtained by Davies and Shock was:

$$C_D \text{ (ml/min.)} = 840 - 6.44 \times \text{age (years)}$$

This is equivalent to a decrease of 53 percent between the ages of 20 and 70 years. A subsequent study by Watkin and Shock (1955) yielded the following regressions:

$$C_{PAH} \text{ (ml/min.)} = 822 - 6.75 \times \text{age (years)}$$

These results are remarkably consistent.

The Filtration Fraction

It is generally reported that the filtration fraction rises with age, although the data are not as clear as for the corresponding decreases in the glomerular filtration rate (GFR) and RPF. The early data of Davies and Shock (1950) show a slight upward trend from about 0.19 to 0.23 between early maturity and the ninth decade, but these differences are not significant at less than three decade intervals. Some of the data used by Olbrich et al. (1950) use the standards obtained from Goldring and Chasis (1944) and may not be comparable. However, using their own young controls and their aged males, both a small series, the filtration fractions were 0.238 and 0.243, respectively. In a somewhat larger group of aged males and females, all with a diastolic pressure above 100, the filtration fraction was 0.277. In this study it would seem that the filtration fraction increases only when there is overt hypertension. The series of McDonald, Solomon, and Shock (1951) utilized 20 young men, mean age 36.6 years, 20 middle-aged men, mean age 58.8 years, and 14 old men, mean age 76.9 years. The derived filtration fractions were 0.189, 0.206, and 0.232, respectively. Although there were several individuals in the old group who had hypertension or a history of congestive failure, the me-

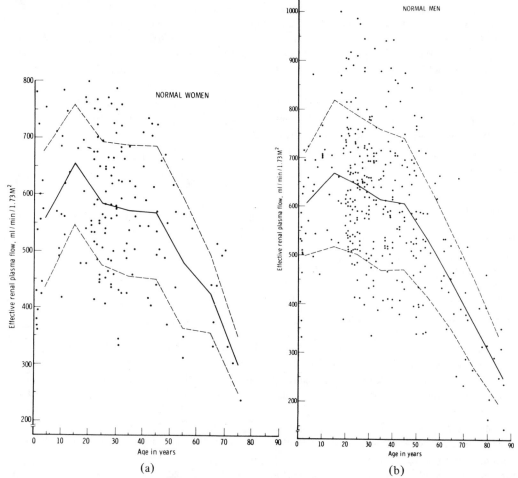

Figure 4. The relationship of age to effective renal plasma flow (PAH or diodrast clearances). (From Wesson, *Physiology of the Human Kidney*, Grune and Stratton, New York, 1969, by permission of the publisher.)

dian values for these subjects did not differ from the median for the entire group. Kluetsch, Heidland, and Oebek (1962) found a mean filtration fraction of 0.169 for 36 men aged 17 to 39 years, 0.195 for men aged 40 to 59 years, but only 0.175 for 8 men aged 60 to 69 years. Lindeman *et al.* (1966) obtained values of 0.217, 0.222, and 0.229 in small groups of young, middle-aged, and old men. The filtration fractions have been calculated from the graphic presentation of Wesson (1969) and are presented in Table 2. Since the values for GFR and RPF are derived by measurement from Figures 2 and 4, they are only approximate. These filtration fractions are relatively constant through the fifth decade in women and the sixth decade in men, then rise. This rise was

TABLE 2. AVERAGE VALUES FOR GFR, RPF, AND FILTRATION FRACTION (FF) BY AGE AND SEX.[a]

	♀			♂		
Age	GFR	RPF	FF	GFR	RPF	FF
15	123	655	0.188	138	665	0.208
25	119	585	0.203	132	650	0.203
35	117	575	0.203	128	615	0.208
45	112	570	0.196	121	610	0.198
55	105	480	0.219	110	530	0.208
65	94	425	0.221	96	445	0.216
75	84	300	0.280	80	350	0.229
85				66	250	0.264

[a]The individual GFR and RPF values are derived from Figures 2 and 4 and are approximations. The filtration fractions are computed from these data.

quite marked in the eighth decade for women and in the ninth for men, although the combined number of subjects examined is small.

It has been reported that the peripheral resistance of the vascular system increases with age (Landowne, Brandfonbrener, and Shock 1955). A rise in the filtration fraction would be of great significance, since the kidney receives so large a fraction of the cardiac output, and changes in intrarenal resistance play a disproportionate role in altering the peripheral resistance. There is a slight decrease in the fraction of the total cardiac output received by the kidney with age (Landowne and Stanley, 1960; Bender, 1965; Lee, Lindeman, Yiengst, and Shock, 1966). Both the diastolic and mean arterial pressures rise with age, although not in proportion to the rise in systolic pressure (Russek, Rath, Zohman, and Miller, 1943; Pickering, 1955; Master and Lasser, 1961).

A critical experiment was performed by McDonald, Solomon, and Shock (1951), whose work was previously cited. In three groups of male subjects, young, middle-aged, and old, they established that there was an age-related decrement in the GFR and RPF and that there was a slight, but definite, progressive increase in the filtration fraction. The subjects, after preparation with aminopyrine, were administered pyrogen intravenously (5×10^7 killed typhoid organisms, 0.05 ml TAB vaccine). Following the infusion, all three groups had a decrease in the diastolic and mean arterial pressures, and the middle-aged and old groups had a fall in the systolic pressures as well. The pulse rates increased moderately in all. The GFR remained constant, but all three groups showed an increase in the RPF which was proportionately greater with age. As a result, there was a decrease in the filtration fraction to 0.115, 0.123, and 0.122 for the young, middle-aged, and old groups, respectively. Most significant was the disappearance in the age-related differential indicating that the relatively reduced RPF with age is a physiologic, not an anatomic, phenomenon and that the anatomic decrement in the nephrons is matched by the anatomic decrement in the vascular system (Figure 5). Calculations, using Lamport's formula (1943), showed that both the afferent and efferent arterioles were involved in the pressure regulation. A further interpretation of the data was

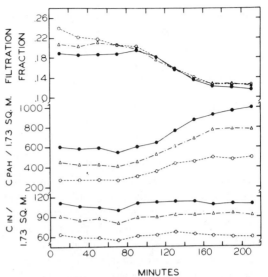

Figure 5. Changes in glomerular filtration rate (C_{IN}), effective renal plasma flow (C_{PAH}), and filtration fraction during the pyrogen reaction. ○——○, mean values for 14 subjects aged 70–85 years. △----△ mean values for 20 subjects aged 50–69 years. ●——●, mean values for 20 subjects aged 20–49 years. (From McDonald, Solomon, and Shock, *J. Clin. Invest.*, 1951, by permission of the publisher.)

made by Landowne and Shock (1951). These findings are of great importance, since they imply that there is a physiological increase in the peripheral resistance with age and that the age-related increase in the blood pressure is not due to vascular rigidity and systolic overshoot alone.

Hollenberg, Adams, Solomon, Rashid, Abrams, and Merrill (1974) have studied renal blood flow by the radioactive xenon washout technique, and, although the method does not allow direct comparison, the results are in apparent conflict with those just cited. The subjects studied were unique, since they were 207 potential kidney transplant donors who showed no apparent abnormality despite intensive examination and laboratory study. Twenty-four hour creatinine clearances were determined using total serum chromogen and were found to regress according to the equation:

$$C_{cr}(\text{ml./min.}) = 135.0 - 0.84 \times \text{age (years)}$$

The renal blood flow was determined by infusing radioactive xenon through the renal arterial catheter after performing the screening renal arteriograms, allowing an interval of 45 min. after the last contrast injection. The method provides data from which the flow per gram of kidney tissue can be calculated. The mean flow regresses according to the equation:

Mean flow (ml/gram/min.)

$$= 4.39 - 0.026 \times \text{age (years)}$$

These data show that the perfusion per gram of kidney is reduced with age in addition to the decrease caused by the reduction in renal size. Making the assumptions that the average combined kidney weights total 300 grams at age 20, 275 grams at age 40, 250 grams at age 60, and 225 grams at age 80, and an average hematocrit is 45 percent, and using the creatinine clearance values given, the filtration fractions are 0.185, 0.200, 0.217, and 0.237. In view of the assumptions, these values are of the same order as the combined data of Wesson and clearly indicate a rising filtration fraction (Table 2).

In a smaller number of subjects (19), varying amounts of acetylcholine were injected into the renal artery before pulsing with xenon. This resulted in an increased blood flow per unit volume; the magnitude of this increase was very slightly less marked in the old than in the young. Making the same assumptions, the fractions were 0.106, 0.115, 0.125, and 0.137, clearly indicating that the filtration fractions were not equalized. This may indicate that the data of McDonald et al. (1951) are in conflict or that acetylcholine is not as effective a vasodilator as pyrogen. However, a tenfold increase in the dose of acetylcholine further increased the flow but did not change the relationship. The converse experiment in 12 subjects, the injection of angiotensin amide, caused a decrease in unit blood flow, but in this instance the older individuals were more responsive. The filtration fractions were 0.251, 0.278, 0.312, and 0.358. Because the rapid, or cortical, component of flow decreased more rapidly than did the mean value for flow, it was assumed that cortical nephrons are more rapidly lost than are juxtamedullary nephrons. The authors argue that it has been shown that the juxtamedullary nephrons have a higher filtration fraction than do the cortical nephrons, and a selective loss of the latter

would lead to an increase in the mean filtration fraction. An interesting additional finding was that the sodium-induced increment in the renal blood flow is progressively decreased and is absent at age 80.

These two studies are important, since they deal with the anatomic versus the physiologic mechanisms for the reduction in blood flow. If the anatomic lesions are primary, then they must precede the loss of nephrons. If the physiologic mechanisms are primary, then measures directed at this defect might reduce the rate of nephron loss. The effects upon cardiovascular dynamics of the two methods by which reduced renal blood flow can be achieved deserve further study.

Renal Tubular Function

Tests of proximal tubular function include measurements of maximal excretion of PAH or diodrast (Tm_{PAH} or Tm_D) and of maximal reabsorption of glucose (Tm_G). Studies by Davies and Shock (1950) showed a convincing decrement in the Tm_D from 54.6 mg I/min./1.73 m^2 body surface area in the third decade to 30.8 mg I/min. in the ninth, representing 43.5 percent decrease during the period. The derived regression equation is:

$$Tm_D \text{ (mg/min.)} = 66.7 - 0.40 \times \text{age (years)}$$

Studies by Watkin and Shock (1955) showed the regression of Tm_{PAH}, which also measures tubular excretion, to be:

$$Tm_{PAH} \text{ (mg/min.)} =$$

$$120.6 - 0.865 \times \text{age (years)}$$

The changes in Tm_G were examined by Miller, McDonald, and Shock (1952), and they found a decrease from a mean of 358.7 mg/min./1.73 m^2 in the third decade to 219.2 mg/min. in the ninth decade. This represents a 47.6 percent decrease in the 70 years. The regression equation for Tm_G is:

$$Tm_G \text{ (mg/min.)} = 432.8 - 2.604 \times \text{age (years)}$$

It is significant that the studies of Shock's group in Baltimore have shown that, using the calculated function at age 20 years as 100 percent, the GFR decreased 0.722 percent/year (Davies and Shock, 1950) and 0.68 percent (Miller, McDonald, and Shock 1952). The Tm_D decreased 0.678 percent (Davies and Shock, 1950), the Tm_{PAH} decreased 0.651 percent (Watkin and Shock, 1955), and the Tm_G decreased 0.68 percent (Miller, McDonald, and Shock, 1952). The identity of the various measures of proximal tubular function and their close agreement with the GFR is strong evidence in favor of the loss of nephron units as the basis of the deterioration of function with age. This contrasts with the greater rate of loss of RPF, 0.906 percent per year.

Although the Tm_G represents a predictable value in a group of individuals, and measures the maximum amount of glucose which can be reabsorbed by a kidney, each nephron has its own Tm_G which varies from its fellows. Therefore, at a given glucose load some nephrons may be spilling glucose into the urine, while others may not yet have reached their saturation level. The effect of age upon this "splay" in renal function was examined by Butterfield, Keen, and Whichelow (1967). They surveyed a large population and found that about 4 percent had glycosuria when tested after breakfast and that about 30 percent had glycosuria after the glucose tolerance test. On closer examination, it was found that the glucose "threshold" ranged from 130 to 310 mg% and that low thresholds were less likely to occur as the age increased. Thus glycosuria can be misleading as a test for diabetes mellitus. In youth there will be an excessive number of false positives and a relatively smaller number of false negatives; with age the reverse will be true. In addition, this variability has implications for the use of glycosuria in the management of diabetics.

The concentration of the urine is primarily the function of the counter-current mechanism of the loop of Henle in the medulla, of the distal cortical tubule, and of the collecting ducts and requires the integrity of the tubule cells and the maintenace of the renal medullary concentration gradient. Lewis and Alving (1938) found the regression of the maximum urinary specific gravity with age to be:

Specific gravity =

$$1.036 - 0.00015 \times \text{age (years)}$$

At 40, the maximum specific gravity is 1.030, decreasing to 1.023 at age 90. It does not fall below 1.026 before age 65 years but then was below 1.026 in 14 of 21 subjects. Lindeman, Van Buren, and Raisz (1960) examined 14 healthy young men and 50 patients hospitalized with disease not affecting renal function or electrolyte metabolism. Urinary osmolalities were determined after 18 to 24 hr. of dehydration. The hospitalized patients showed a highly correlated decrement with age, from 1,052 mosm/L at age 20 to 765 at age 90.

$$\text{Osmolality} = 1,134 - 4.1 \times \text{age (years)}$$

The mean maximum concentrating ability of the normal young men was 1,189 mosm/L, which was somewhat higher than predicted from the hospitalized patients. Rowe, De-Fronzo, and Shock (unpublished observations) have recently obtained similar results.

Miller and Shock (1953) approached the problem of urinary concentrating ability in another way. Young, middle aged, and old men, average ages 34.6, 54.9, and 73.3 years, respectively, were studied by initiating a water diuresis, followed by the infusion of 0.5 milliunits aqueous pitressin intravenously per kilogram body weight. From preinjection values of 15.06, 11.50, and 11.85 ml urine/min., the urine flows dropped to a minimum of 1.09, 1.33, and 2.10 ml/min. respectively. More dramatically, the U/P inulin ratios increased from 8.39, 8.58, and 7.42 to maximum values of 117.68, 76.87, and 44.65.

Lindeman et al. (1966) produced a maximum water diuresis, then observed the effects of suboptimal, continuous infusions of pitressin (8.0 mu/hr.). Maximum free-water clearance was found to be closely correlated to the GFR, and the reduction in the free-water clearance in response to the standard antidiuretic stimulus was correlated to the maximal free-water clearance and thus the GFR. The regression of maximum osmolality with age was found to be in close agreement with the previously determined value:

$$\text{Osmolality} = 1,109 - 3.54 \times \text{age (years)}$$

However, the data show that the C_{H_2O}/C_{cr} ratio falls as the GFR decreases with age and that the rate of loss of diluting capacity exceeds the rate of loss of GFR. Very similar data are shown by Dontas, Marketos, and Papanayiotou (1972) who also demonstrated that the GFR/Tm_{PAH} does not change. In both studies the decrease in functions was more marked in patients with infection.

Within a narrowed range of adaptability, the kidney of the older individual appears capable of maintaining normal acid-base balance (Shock and Yiengst, 1950; Adler *et al.*, 1968). The administration of an acid load produces a comparable reduction in the serum bicarbonate and urinary pH at all ages. The maximum rate at which the acid load can be excreted is closely related to the residual glomerular filtration rate and is therefore slower in the older individual. Depression of the serum bicarbonate persists for a longer period. Analysis of ammonia and phosphate excretion indicates that the relative ammonia production is slightly decreased but that there is a slightly increased titratable acidity. The response to base loads is similarly delayed and prolonged. If the presentation of acid-base loads to the older individual does not exceed the capacity for excretion, a normal balance may be maintained, but large loads may overwhelm the regulatory mechanisms.

The general assumption has been made that the nocturia of old age is due to reduction in the ability to concentrate urine, to infection, to the increasing probability of urinary tract obstruction, particularly by prostatic hypertrophy, or to a combination of all of these factors. Rubin and Nagel (1951) noted that many patients with nocturia have normal renal function and an absence of infection. They suggested that in these patients nocturia might be due to occult congestive failure. It seems most likely that the nocturia is due to a basic disturbance in the diurnal rhythm of excretion, as documented by Lobban and Tredre (1967). This reversal of the normal cycle of urine formation, with a nocturnal increase, can then be augmented by heart failure and a number of other disorders. The basic mechanism is probably central, rather than renal, in origin.

COMPENSATORY RENAL HYPERTROPHY

Removal of one kidney results in the compensatory hypertrophy of the contralateral, normal remaining kidney. There is a rapid increase in renal size and function during the first 3 days to 1 week, followed by a slower and smaller increase for 3 weeks. The size and function probably remain stable from that point, although recent evidence suggests a moderately continuing increase for many months. MacKay, MacKay, and Addis (1926, 1932), studying rats, were probably the first to demonstrate that the degree of compensatory hypertrophy decreases with the age of the individual at the time of nephrectomy. Protein intake also governs the extent of the hypertrophy, the greater the intake the greater the enlargement. However, the age-related decrease in protein intake does not account for all of the observed change. They found that the decreased responsiveness was continuous throughout life, and that while in youth it amounted to 50 percent, in old rats it was reduced to 30 percent. Verzar (1954) and Verzar and Hugin (1955) found that in developing rats, up to the age of 6 months, there was a 40 percent increase and that from that time on the increase was 25 percent. Females showed a slightly smaller response than did males. Barrows, Roeder, and Olewine (1962) showed a 43 percent increase in weight at 8 weeks in 12-month-old rats and a 31 percent increase in 31-month-old rats. Konishi (1962) studied rats aged 140 and 665 days at the time of nephrectomy and noted the influence of basal and high protein diets as well as age. On a basal diet the increases were 16.5 percent and 10.0 percent, respectively, while on a high protein diet they were 32.8 percent and 23.9 percent.

Renal compensatory hypertrophy in humans has been of recent clinical interest because of the success with kidney transplantation. The results have been essentially the same as those noted in rats. Ogden (1967) found a significant reduction in response which progressed with age in donors who provided kidneys for transplantation. The glomerular filtration rate and effective renal plasma flow (ERPF) were determined in 28 renal homograft donors an average of 3 years after transplantation (range 21 to 48 months). There was a significant inverse correlation between age at the time of nephrectomy and function 3 years later. The correlation between GFR and donor age was $r = -0.53$, $P < 0.01$ and between ERPF and donor age was $r = -0.43$, $P < 0.05$. There were 17 donors for whom both pre- and posttransplant values were available. Although the inverse correlation between ERPF and age was of only borderline significance, the inverse relationship of age to the ratio of postoperative to preoperative ERPF was highly significant ($r = -0.65, P < 0.01$).

A more elaborate study was done by Boner, Shelp, Neton, and Rieselbach (1973). These investigators performed inulin, iothalamate, creatinine, and urea clearances before and at intervals for up to 4 years after nephrectomy. A total of 259 studies were performed on 49 kidney donors, 22 females and 27 males, 21 to 63 years of age. The data were subjected to multiple-linear regression analyses. At the time of initial posttransplant study, 1 to 3 weeks after surgery, the increase in single remaining kidney function was the same in subjects under and those over 40 years; 66.3 percent versus 66.2 percent of the total preoperative value (the initial GFRs averaged 115 and 105 ml/min., respectively). However, there was then a continuing, slower increase in hypertrophy which continued at least 4 years. The GFR of a 20-year-old increased to 74 percent and that of an 80-year-old to 65 percent, in 4 years, with a linear distribution at intermediate ages.

It has been noted that the number of glomeruli does not increase after early life in the rat or after birth in man. Therefore, the compensatory enlargement is not due to an increase in the number of nephrons (Arataki, 1926; Moore, 1929; Moore and Hellman, 1930). The compensation is produced by enlargement of the residual nephrons. The glomeruli increase in diameter, and thus in volume, and the tubules enlarge. Konishi (1962) showed by counting the number of mitotic figures that the area of greatest hyperplastic response was in the proximal tubule and that the peak was at 7 days. His data suggest that there is more hyperplasia in the old than in the young rats. Dicker and Shirley (1973) found, in contrast, that cortical RNA/DNA ratios suggest a primary cellular hyperplasia in young animals but hypertrophy of existing cells as the major mechanism for nephron enlargement in older animals. Barrows, Roeder, and Olewine (1962) found the increase in DNA to be proportional to the increase in body weight at all ages and infer that at all ages there is a comparable proportionality between the contributions of cellular hyperplasia and

hypertrophy. However, it can be argued that in this last study the use of rats of 12 and 30 months compared mature animals with a select group of longevous animals which might not reflect the response of young animals on one hand and normally aging animals on the other.

Phillips and Leong (1967) determined the rate of mitosis using tritiated thymidine and autoradiography. They used a relatively large number of weanling rats of 4 weeks and 4-month-old adults. Preliminary study showed that there were few mitotic figures or labeled cells in the medulla, and all of the counts were performed on the cortex. The maximum number of mitoses and labeled cells was found in the tubule cells at 36 hr. and occurred in both groups. The base line labeling index was 0.59 percent for the young and 0.11 percent for the 4-month rats. This increased to 3.6 percent and 1.2 percent, respectively, and remained elevated for at least 6 weeks, although at a lower level. The base line mitotic indices were 0.056 percent and 0.0062 percent, respectively, and rose to 0.30 percent and 0.088 percent at 36 hr. Weight gain began at this time. The stromal cells showed increased mitotic figures and labeling 57 hr. after nephrectomy and remained at a higher level for longer than did the tubule cells. The glomerular cells show a small and insignificant increase in the indices at 2 weeks. These results confirmed those of Reiter, McCreight, and Sulkin (1964). They both suggest a similar timing and magnitude of increase for the young and the mature rats, but since the older animals start at a much lower base, it does not seem possible that both groups can have the same level of hyperplasia. These data seem to support the concept of predominant hyperplasia in the young and hypertrophy in the older animals.

THE BLADDER

The trigone is derived from the mesodermal cloacal membrane which also gives rise to the vagina, uterus, and fallopian tubes. The detrusor muscle is derived from the hind-gut of of the primitive cloaca and consists of a network of smooth muscle fibers which arch over the trigone, and it is the expansion of this portion of the bladder which accommodates to the volume of contained urine. There is no true internal sphincter; competency is maintained by the tone of the tissue and a concentration of elastic tissue surrounding the urethra at the bladder neck. The muscle fibers of both the trigone and the detrusor are so arranged that contraction opens rather than closes the orifice. The external sphincter is striated muscle which is part of the pelvic floor and surrounds the urethra a short distance below its origin in the bladder.

The external sphincter is innervated by voluntary motor nerves; constriction prevents urinary flow and relaxation is necessary for urination. The primary innervation of the detrusor muscle appears to be parasympathetic through the second, third, and fourth sacral nerves. With normal micturition the external sphincter is voluntarily relaxed, and the trigone contracts, occluding the ureteral orifices to prevent reflux and pulling open the urethral orifice, in which function it is assisted by the arching fibers of the detrusor. The bladder becomes elongated longitudinally, and the urethral opening becomes funnel shaped. Further contraction of the detrusor then expels the urine. The highest level of control of micturition has been localized in the frontal cortex, particularly on the dominant side, but there are also centers of control in the hypothalamus, the midbrain, and the cervical cord.

A review of the anatomical and physiological changes in the bladder with age has been presented by Brocklehurst (1972) who noted increasing edema, round cell infiltration, and occasional lymphoid follicles. Trabeculae and diverticula are often present. Mucosal prolapse at the external female urethral orifice was frequent and was found in two-thirds of elderly incontinent women. Swaiman and Bradley (1967) failed to find a significant age-related variation in collagenous or total protein composition of bladder detrusor muscle or urethrovesical junction. They concluded that changes in bladder capacity with age were due to neural maturation and not to structural alteration.

Brocklehurst, Dillane, Griffiths, and Fry (1968) examined the urinary symptomatology of 182 men and 375 women above the age of 65 years. They found that 70 percent of the men and 61 percent of the women had nocturnal frequency which increased with advancing age. Precipitancy of micturition, the sudden imperative necessity to void, occurred in 28 percent of the men and 32 percent of the women. Incontinence was reported in 17 percent of men and 23 percent of women. In 3 percent of the men and 12 percent of the women this was stress incontinence only. Difficulty in passing urine was found in 13 percent of the men, usually in association with infection, and in 3 percent of the women. Precipitancy was associated with infection, but infection was not a factor in nocturia or incontinence. In a series of 70 patients on geriatric wards, Wilson (1948) found 46 with precipitancy, 46 with frequency, 25 with incontinence, and only 14 who were symptom free. He concluded that these findings were so common as to be almost normal. Brocklehurst and Dillane (1966a, 1966b) performed cystometric studies on 40 continent and 100 incontinent aged women. Their results are summarized in the following table:

	Normal adults under 65	Normal adults over 65	Incontinent adults over 65
Residual urine (ml)	0	0–100	10+
Bladder capacity (ml)	500–600	250–600	50–350
Desire to void (ml)	250–300	150–300	0–350
Uninhibited contractions	0	±	+
Leakage	0	0	+

The bladder capacity decreases with age without any apparent anatomical cause. The frequency and volume of residual urine also increases, even in women for whom prostatic enlargement cannot be a factor. The sensation of needing to void becomes more variable. In youth it most frequently appears when the bladder is little more than half full. In the aged, the sensation may not occur until the bladder is almost filled to capacity, and in many individuals there is no sensation at all. These changes can easily account for the increasing precipitancy. During filling, small bladder contraction waves of less than 3 cm water occurred with increased frequency and were noted in 80 percent. Waves of more than 4 cm water were less frequent, although they were found in almost all of the individuals with incontinence. Leakage around the catheter during the study was also associated with a significantly higher incidence of incontinence. Perhaps most significant was the fact that 83 percent of the patients with incontinence had overt cerebral disease. The absence of local factors, and the high frequency of central nervous system disease, suggest that the manifestations could be explained on a central basis.

Very similar results were obtained in a group of 61 men whose mean age was 75, all of whom were incontinent of urine (Thompson, 1964). Seventy-five percent had a bladder capacity of less than 300 ml and 42 percent less than 100 ml. Uninhibited bladder contractions were present in 55 percent at a capacity of less than 100 ml, very few had no residual urine, and one-third had more than 100 ml.

In a continuation of their studies Brocklehurst and Dillane (1967a) obtained cystograms of 47 incontinent women. In 50 percent of those in whom upright or voiding films could be obtained, there was funneling of the bladder outlet with a reduction in the length of the competent urethra. Evidence of a neurogenic bladder, the presence of trabeculation, cellules, or diverticula, were found in 62 percent. Diverticula were common in this group, 32 percent, although they usually are considered rare in women. Brocklehurst and Dillane believe that the cause, in most cases, is functional obstruction at the bladder neck due to neuromuscular incoordination rather than to an anatomic obstruction, and they note that diverticulum formation becomes more common with advancing age in other hollow viscera as well. Age changes in connective tissue may also play a role. Parvinen, Sourander, and Vuorinan (1965) performed a similar study in 59 women, and their findings were almost identical.

A variety of therapies have been attempted for the control of senile incontinence, and most have been of little benefit. The most promising have been those which block the parasympathetic innervation to the bladder and thus increase bladder capacity and reduce spontaneous, uninhibited bladder contractions. Brocklehurst and Dillane (1967b) found propantheline and orphenadrine, in combination, to be the most effective, followed by orphenadrine alone and

atropine; the unfavorable side effects of cholinergic drugs must be considered in the treatment of older individuals. Similarly, Whitehead (1967), in a double-blind study, found propantheline to have some effect in reducing urinary frequency, in women more than in men, and in the ambulant more than in the mentally deteriorated.

It is well established that urinary tract infections increase abruptly with age (Miall, Kass, Ling, and Stuart, 1962; Freedman, Phair, Seki, Hamilton and Nefzger, 1965; Sourander, Ruikkal, and Gouross, 1965; Sourander, 1966; Brocklehurst et al. 1968; Kunin and McCormack, 1968). The data seem to indicate that in women under the age of 65 years the incidence of urinary tract infections is stable and generally less than 6 percent, but that after that age the incidence suddenly jumps to over 20 percent. A similar phenomenon is seen in men, except that the early infection rate is lower and the critical age seems to be 70. It is strongly suggestive that there is some change which occurs at this time which is responsible for this increase in vulnerability. At least two mechanisms are possible as a result of specific bladder changes. The first is gross anatomical change which could lead to retention and stasis. The second is the possibility that in some way the bladder contributes to the sterilization of the urine and that this power is lost as a senescent change. Brocklehurst et al. (1968) surveyed 557 old people living in their homes. In men, there was a relationship between infection and prostatic hypertrophy and genitourinary surgery. In women there was no correlation between infection and parity, operative interference at parturition, or later gynecologic surgery. This correlates well with the result of Sourander's studies (Sourander, Ruikkal, and Gouross, 1965, Sourander, 1966), although in hospitalized patients gynecologic abnormalities clearly contributed to the frequency of infection. Infection did not seem to be related to incontinence, nocturia, or intellectual status, except for loss of recent memory in women. Although residual urine is usually associated with infection, it was not commented upon in these studies.

Freedman (1969) reports studies which suggest possible changes in the bladder defenses against infection. An inoculum of 10^3 or 10^5 *E. coli* was made into the bladders of a group of rats 2 months of age and another group 1 year old. After 4 or 5 days the cultures of both kidneys and the urine of 29 young rats were sterile, while similar cultures were positive in 7 out of 14 of the older rats. Similar, but more challenging experiments were carried out on unilaterally nephrectomized animals. Only 2 of 23 young rats, nephrectomized 1 week previously, showed positive cultures, but 6 of 9 old rats, nephrectomized 6 months previously, continued to have positive cultures. Freedman (1967) notes that there is a delicate balance between bacterial multiplication and host defense mechanisms in the bladder. The simple establishment of water diuresis in normal rats reduces the ability to clear the bladder of bacteria by many orders of magnitude. Despite the frequency of bacteriuria, both Sourander (1966) and Brocklehurst, Dillane, Griffiths, and Fry (1968) agree that it appears to be relatively benign in old age.

REFERENCES

Adler, S., Lindeman, R. D., Yiengst, M. J., Beard, E., and Shock, N. W. 1968. Effect of acute acid loading on urinary acid excretion by the aging human kidney. *J. Lab. Clin. Med.*, **72**, 278–289.

Arataki, M. 1926. On the postnatal growth of the kidney, with special reference to the number and size of the glomeruli. (Albino Rat). *Am. J. Anat.*, **36**, 399–450.

Barrows, C. H., Jr., Roeder, L. M., and Olewine, D. A. 1962. Effect of age on renal compensatory hypertrophy following unilateral nephrectomy in the rat. *J. Geront.*, **17**, 148.

Bell, E. T. 1946. *Renal Diseases.* 1st ed., p. 322. Philadelphia: Lea & Febiger.

Bender, A. D. 1965. The effect of increasing age on the distribution of peripheral blood flow in man. *J. Am. Geriat. Soc.*, **13**, 192–198.

Ber, A., Allalouf, D., Wasserman, L., and Sharon, N. 1969. Age-related changes in renal connective tissue of rats. *Gerontologia*, **15**, 252–257.

Boner, G., Shelp, W. D., Neton, M., and Rieselbach, R. E. 1973. Factors influencing the increase in glomerular filtration rate in the remaining kidney of transplant donors. *Am. J. Med.*, **55**, 169–174.

Brocklehurst, J. C. 1972. Aging of the human bladder. *Geriatrics*, p. 154 (February).

Brocklehurst, J. C., and Dillane, J. B. 1966a. Studies of the female bladder in old age I. *Gerontol. Clin.*, **8**, 285–305.

Brocklehurst, J. C., and Dillane, J. B. 1966b. Studies of the female bladder in old age II. *Gerontol. Clin.*, **8**, 306–319.

Brocklehurst, J. C., and Dillane, J. B. 1967a. Studies of the female bladder in old age III. *Gerontol. Clin.*, **9**, 47–58.

Brocklehurst, J. C., and Dillane, J. B. 1967b. Studies of the female bladder in old age IV. *Gerontol. Clin.*, **9**, 182–191.

Brocklehurst, J. C., Dillane, J. B., Griffiths, J., and Fry, J. 1968. The prevalence and symptomatology of urinary infection in an aged population. *Gerontol. Clin.*, **10**, 242–253.

Butterfield, W. J. H., Keen, H., and Whichelow, M. J. 1967. Renal glucose threshold variations with age. *Brit. Med. J.*, **4**, 505–507.

Darmady, E. M., Offer, J., and Woodhouse, M. A. 1973. The parameters of the aging kidney. *J. Pathol.*, **109**, 195–207.

Davidson, A. J., Talner, L. B., and Downs, W. M. 1969. A study of the angiographic appearance of the kidney in an aging normotensive population. *Radiology*, **92**, 975–983.

Davies, D. F., and Shock, N. W. 1950. Age changes in glomerular filtration rate, effective renal plasma flow, and tubular excretory capacity in adult males. *J. Clin. Invest.*, **29**, 496–506.

Dicker, S., and Shirley, D. G. 1973. Compensatory renal growth after unilateral nephrectomy in the new-born rat. *J. Physiol.*, **228**, 193–202.

Dontas, A. S. 1969. Renal disease in old age. *Proc. 8th Intern. Congr. Geront.*, **1**, 386–390.

Dontas, A. S., Marketos, S., and Papanayiotou, P. 1972. Mechanisms of renal tubular defects in old age. *Postgrad. Med. J.*, **48**, 295–303.

Dontas, A. S., Papanayiotou, P., Marketos, S. G., and Papanicolaou, N. T. 1968. The effect of bacteriuria on renal functional patterns in old age. *Clin. Sci.*, **34**, 73–81.

Dunnill, M. S., and Halley, W. 1973. Some observations on the quantitative anatomy of the kidney. *J. Pathol.*, **110**, 113–121.

Farquhar, M. G., Vernier, R. L., and Good, R. A. 1957. The application of electron microscopy in pathology. Study of renal biopsy tissues. *Schweiz. Med. Wochenschr.*, **87**, 501–510.

Freedman, L. R. 1967. Experimental pyelonephritis XIII. On the ability of water diuresis to increase susceptibility to *E. coli* bacteriuria in the normal rat. *Yale J. Biol. Med.*, **39**, 255–266.

Freedman, L. R. 1969. Experimental pyelonephritis XV. Increased susceptibility to *E. coli* infection in old rats. *Yale J. Biol. Med.*, **42**, 30–38.

Freedman, L. R., Phair, J. P., Seki, M., Hamilton, H. B., and Nefzger, M. D. 1965. The epidemiology of urinary tract infections in Hiroshima. *Yale J. Biol. Med.*, **37**, 262–282.

Goldman, R. 1967. Endogenous creatinine clearance by rats. *Proc. Soc. Exp. Biol. Med.*, **125**, 1021–1024.

Goldring, W., and Chasis, H. 1944. *Hypertension and Hypertensive Disease.* New York: The Commonwealth Fund.

Goldring, W., Chasis, H., Ranges, H. A., and Smith, H. W. 1940. Relations of effective renal blood flow and glomerular filtration to tubular excretory mass in normal man. *J. Clin. Invest.*, 19, 739-750.

Gregory, J. G., and Barrows, C. H. 1969. The effect of age on renal functions in female rats. *J. Geront.*, 24, 321-323.

Hansen, J. M., Kampmann, J., and Laursen, H. 1970. Renal excretion of drugs in the elderly. *Lancet*, 1, 1170.

Helpap, K. 1933. Uber anfsteigende Schrumpfniere durch Sklerose des Nierenmarks. *Virchows Arch. Pathol. Anat.*, 288, 383-392.

Hollenberg, N. K., Adams, D. F., Solomon, H. S., Rashid, A., Abrams, H. L., and Merrill, J. P. 1974. Senescence and the renal vasculature in normal man. *Circulation Res.*, 34, 309-316.

Inoue, G., Sawada, T., Fukunaga, Y., and Yoshikawa, M. 1970. Levels of acid mucopolysaccharides in aging human kidneys. *Gerontologia*, 16, 261-265.

Inoue, G., Sawada, T., and Yoshikawa, M. 1973. Change in acid mucopolysaccharides level and water content in the papillary region of human kidneys. *Gerontologia*, 19, 73-78.

Jackson, J. G., Puchtler, H., and Sweat, F. 1968. Investigation of staining, polarization and fluorescence-microscopic properties of pseudo-elastic fibers in the renal arterial system. *J. Roy. Microscop. Soc.*, 88, 473-485.

Keating, F. R., Jr., Jones, J. D., Elveback, L. R., and Randall, R. V. 1969. The relation of age and sex to distribution of values in healthy adults of serum calcium, inorganic phosphorus, magnesium, alkaline phosphatase, total proteins, albumin and blood urea. *J. Lab. Clin. Med.*, 73, 825-834.

Keresztury, S., and Megyeri, L. 1962. Histology of renal pyramids with special regard to changes due to aging. *Acta Morphol. Acad. Sci. Hung.*, 11, 205-215.

Kilo, C., Vogler, N., and Williamson, J. R. 1972. Muscle capillary basement membrane changes related to aging and diabetes mellitus. *Diabetes*, 21, 881-905.

Kluetsch, K., Heidland, A., and Oebek, A. 1962. The age factor in renal hemodynamics. *Klin. Wochschr.*, 40, 1002-1003.

Konishi, F. 1962. Renal hyperplasia in young and old rats fed a high protein diet following unilateral nephrectomy. *J. Geront.*, 17, 151-153.

Kunin, C. M., and McCormack, R. C. 1968. An epidemiologic study of bacteriuria and blood pressure among nuns and working women. *New Engl. J. Med.*, 278, 635-642.

Lamport, H. 1943. Improvements in calculation of renal resistance to blood flow. Charts for osmotic pressure and viscosity of blood. *J. Clin. Invest.*, 22, 461-470.

Landowne, M., Brandfonbrener, M., and Shock, N. W. 1955. The relation of age to certain measures of performance of the heart and circulation. *Circulation*, 12, 567-576.

Landowne, M., and Shock, N. W. 1951. An interpretation of the calculated changes in renal resistance with age. *J. Geront.*, 6, 334-339.

Landowne, M., and Stanley, J. 1960. Aging of the cardiovascular system. *In*, N. W. Shock (ed), *Aging... Some Social and Biological Aspects*, pp. 159-187. Washington, D.C.: *American Association for the Advancement of Science.*

Lee, T. D., Jr., Lindeman, R. D., Yiengst, M. J., and Shock, N. W. 1966. Influence of age on the cardiovascular and renal responses to tilting. *J. Appl. Physiol.*, 21, 55-61.

Lewis, W. H., Jr., and Alving, A. S. 1938. Changes with age in the renal function in adult men. *Am. J. Physiol.*, 123, 500-515.

Lindberg, A. A., Nilsson, L. H., Bucht, H., and Kallings, L. O. 1966. Concentration of chloramphenicol in the urine and blood in relation to renal function. *Brit. Med. J.*, 2, 724-728.

Lindeman, R. D., Lee, T. D., Jr., Yiengst, M. J., and Shock, N. W. 1966. Influence of age, renal disease, hypertension, diuretics, and calcium on the antidiuretic responses to suboptimal infusions of vasopressin. *J. Lab. Clin. Med.*, 68, 206-223.

Lindeman, R. D., Van Buren, H. C., and Raisz, L. G., 1960. Osmolar renal concentrating ability in healthy young men and hospitalized patients without renal disease. *New Engl. J. Med.*, 262, 1306-1309.

Ljungqvist, A. 1963. Fetal and postnatal development of the intrarenal arterial pattern in man. A microangiographic and histologic study. *Acta Paediat.*, 52, 443-454.

Ljungqvist, A. 1964. Structure of the arteriole-glomerular units in different zones of the kidney. *Nephron*, 1, 329-337.

Ljungqvist, A., and Lagergren, C. 1962. Normal intrarenal arterial pattern in adult and ageing human kidney. A. microangiographical and histological study. *J. Anat. Lond.*, 96, 285-298.

Lobban, M. C., and Tredre, B. E. 1967. Diurnal rhythms of renal excretion and of body temperatures in aged subjects. *J. Physiol.* (London), 188, 48P-49P.

MacCallum, D. B. 1939. The bearing of degenerating glomeruli on the problem of the vascular supply of the mammalian kidney. *Am. J. Anat.*, 65, 69-103.

McDonald, R. K., Solomon, D. H., and Shock, N. W. 1951. Aging as a factor in the renal hemodynamic changes induced by a standardized pyrogen. *J. Clin. Invest.*, 30, 457-462.

McGavack, T., and Kao, K. T. 1960. The influence of age and sex on the soluble collagen, insoluble collagen and elastin of rat tissues. *Exp. Med. Surg.*, 18, 104-123.

MacKay, L. L., MacKay, E. M., and Addis, T. 1926. Influence of age on degree of renal hypertrophy produced by high protein diets. *Proc. Soc. Exp. Biol. Med.*, **24**, 335.

MacKay, E. M., MacKay, L. L., and Addis, T. 1932. The degree of compensatory hypertrophy following unilateral nephrectomy. I. The influence of age. *J. Exp. Med.*, **56**, 255–265.

McManus, J. F. A., and Lupton, C. H., Jr. 1960. Ischemic obsolescence of renal glomeruli. *Lab. Invest.*, **9**, 413–434.

Marketos, S., Papanayiotou, P., and Dontas, A. S. 1969a. Glomerular filtration rate in elderly men and women under the influence of a new anabolic steroid. *Nephron*, **6**, 478–483.

Marketos, S., Papanayiotou, P., and Dontas, A. S. 1969b. Bacteriuria and non-obstructive renovascular disease in old age. *J. Geront.*, **24**, 33–36.

Master, A. M., and Lasser, R. P. 1961. Blood pressure elevation in the elderly. *In*, A. M. Brest and J. H. Moyer (eds.), *Hypertension. Recent advances.* Philadelphia: Lea & Febiger.

Miall, W. E., Kaas, E. H., Ling, J., and Stuart, K. L. 1962. Factors influencing arterial pressure in the general population in Jamaica. *Brit. Med. J.*, **2**, 497–506.

Miller, J. H., McDonald, R. K., and Shock, N. W. 1951. The renal extraction of p-aminohippurate in the aged individual. *J. Geront.*, **6**, 213–216.

Miller, J. H., McDonald, R. K., and Shock, N. W. 1952. Age changes in the maximal rate of renal tubular reabsorption of glucose. *J. Geront.*, **7**, 196–200.

Miller, J. H., and Shock, N. W. 1953. Age differences in the renal tubular response to antidiuretic hormone. *J. Geront.*, **8**, 446–450.

Milne, J. S., and Williamson, J. 1972. Plasma urea concentration in older people. *Gerontol. Clin.*, **14**, 32–35.

Moore, R. A. 1929. Number of glomeruli in kidney of adult white rat unilaterally nephrectomized in early life. *J. Exp. Med.*, **50**, 709–712.

Moore, R. A. 1931. Total number of glomeruli in the normal human kidney. *Anat. Rec.*, **48**, 153–168.

Moore, R. A., and Hellman, L. M. 1930. The effect of unilateral nephrectomy on the senile atrophy of the kidney in the white rat. *J. Exp. Med.*, **51**, 51–57.

Moritz, A. R., and Oldt, M. R. 1937. Arteriolar sclerosis in hypertensive and non-hypertensive individuals. *Am. J. Pathol.*, **13**, 679–728.

Oddie, T. H., Meade, J. H., Jr., Myhill, J., and Fisher, D. A. 1966. Dependence of renal clearance of radioiodide on sex, age and thyroidal status. *J. Clin. Endocrinol.*, **26**, 1292–1296.

Ogden, D. A. 1967. Donor and recipient function 2 to 4 years after renal homotransplantation. *Ann. Internal Med.*, **67**, 998–1006.

Olbrich, O., Ferguson, M. H., Robson, J. S., and Stewart, C. P. 1950. Renal function in aged patients. *Edinb. Med. J.*, **57**, 117–127.

Olbrich, O., Woodford-Williams, E., Irvine, R. E., and Webster, D. 1957. Renal function in prostatism. *Lancet*, **1**, 1322–1324.

Oliver, J. R. 1939. Urinary system. *In*, E. V. Cowdry (ed.), *Problems of Ageing: Biological and Medical Aspects*, pp. 257–277. Baltimore: Williams & Wilkins.

Parvinen, M., Sourander, L. B., and Vuorinan, P. 1965. Cystographic studies of old women. *Gerontol. Clin.*, **7**, 343.

Payan, H. M., and Gilbert, E. F. 1967. Micronodular phlebosclerosis. An aging change of the venules of the kidneys and adrenal. *Angiology*, **18**, 384–393.

Payan, H. M., and Gilbert, E. F. 1972. Interrupted eccentric longitudinal muscle fibers of the kidney and adrenal veins. *Am. Heart J.*, **84**, 76–81.

Phillips, T. L., and Leong, G. F. 1967. Kidney cell proliferation after unilateral nephrectomy as related to age. *Cancer Res.*, **2**, 286–292.

Pickering, G. W. 1955. *High Blood Pressure.* New York: Grune & Stratton.

Prym, P. 1909. Fett in Markintestitium der Neire. *Virchows Arch. Pathol. Anat.*, **196**, 322–329.

Reiter, R. J., McCreight, C. E., and Sulkin, N. M. 1964. Age differences in cellular proliferation in rat kidneys. *J. Geront.*, **19**, 485–489.

Reynes, M., Coulet, T., and Diebold, J., Jr. 1968. Microvascularization of normal and aging kidney. *Pathol.- Biol.*, **16**, 1081–1089.

Roessle, R., and Roulet, F. 1932. *Mass und Zahl in der Pathologie*. Berlin: J. Springer.

Rowe, J. W., Andres, R., Tobin, J. D., Norris, A. H., and Shock, N. W. 1976. The effect of age on creatinine clearance in man: A cross-sectional and longitudinal study. *J. Geront.*, **31**, 155–163.

Rowe, J. W., DeFronzo, R. A., and Shock, N. W. 1974. Personal communication.

Rubin, S. W., and Nagel, H. 1951. Nocturia in the aged. *J. Am. Med. Assoc.*, **147**, 840–841.

Russek, H. I., Rath, M. M., Zohman, B. L., and Miller, I. 1943. The influence of age on blood pressure. *Am. Heart J.*, **32**, 468–479.

Schaub, M. C. 1963. Qualitative and quantitative changes of collagen in parenchymatous organs of the rat during ageing. *Gerontologia*, **8**, 114–122.

Scott, E. B. 1964. Modification of the basal architecture of renal tubule cells in aged rats. *Proc. Soc. Exp. Biol. Med.*, **117**, 586–590.

Shock, N. W., and Yiengst, M. J. 1950. Age changes in the acid-base equilibrium of the blood of males. *J. Geront.*, **5**, 1–4.

Sourander, L. B. 1966. Urinary tract infection in the aged. *Ann. Med. Internae. Fenniae Suppl.*, **55**, 45.

Sourander, L. B., Ruikkal, I., and Gouross, M. 1965. Correlation between urinary tract infection, prolapse conditions and function of the bladder in aged female hospital patients. *Gerontol. Clin.*, **7**, 179–184.

Swaiman, K. F., and Bradley, W. E. 1967. Quantitation of collagen in the wall of the human bladder. *J. Appl. Physiol.*, **22**, 122–124.

Sworn, M. J., and Fox, M. 1972. Donor kidney selection for transplantation. *Brit. J. Urol.*, **44**, 377–383.

Takazakura, E., Wasabu, N., Handa, A., Takada, A., Shinoda, A., and Takeuchi, J. 1972. Intrarenal vascular changes with age and disease. *Kidney International*, 2, 224-230.

Tauchi, H., Tsuboi, K., and Okutomi, J. 1971. Age changes in the human kidney of the different races. *Gerontologia*, 17, 87-97.

Tauchi, H., Tsuboi, K., and Sato, K. 1958. Histology and experimental pathology of senile atrophy of the kidney. *Nagoya Med. J.*, 4, 71-97.

Thompson, J. 1964. Cystometry in the investigation of urinary incontinence. *In*, W. F. Anderson and B. Isaacs, *Current Achievements in Geriatrics*, pp. 103-114. London: Cassell.

Tschebotarew, D. F., and Kalinowskaja, E. G. 1968. Adaptation capacity of the aging kidney. *Z. Alternsforsch.*, 21, 35-42.

Verzár, F. 1954. Conpensatory hypertrophy of kidney and adrenal in the lifespan of rats. *In, Old Age in the Modern World. Report of the Third Congress of the International Association of Gerontology*, pp. 139-151. Edinburgh and London: Livingstone.

Verzár, F. 1969. Compensatory hypertrophy in old age. *In*, W. W. Nowinski and R. J. Goss (eds.), *Compensatory Renal Hypertrophy*, pp. 271-282. New York: Academic Press.

Verzár, F., and Hugin, F. 1955. Functional Hypertrophy in the aged. *Schweiz. Med. Wochschr.*, 85, 687-688.

Watkin, D. M., and Shock, N. W. 1955. Agewise standard value for C_{In}, C_{PAH} and Tm_{PAH} in adult males. *J. Clin. Invest.*, 34, 969.

Wehner, H. 1968. Stereologische Untersuchungen am Mesangium normaler menschlicher Nieren. *Virchows Arch. Abt. A. Pathol. Anat.*, 344, 286-294.

Wesson, L. G. 1969. *Physiology of the Human Kidney*, pp. 98-100. New York and London: Grune & Stratton.

Whitehead, J. A. 1967. Urinary incontinence in the aged. *Geriatrics*, 22(1), 154-158.

Williams, R. H., and Harrison, T. R. 1937. A study of the renal arteries in relation to age and to hypertension. *Am. Heart J.*, 14, 645-658.

Wilson, T. S. 1948. Incontinence of urine in the aged. *Lancet*, 2, 374-377.

Yamaguchi, T., Omae, T., and Katsuki, S. 1969. Quantitative determination of renal vascular changes related to age and hypertension. *Japan Heart J.*, 10, 248-258.

17
INFLUENCE OF AGING ON THE LUNG

Robert A. Klocke

State University of New York at Buffalo

Assessment of the influence of aging upon any organ system is difficult since changes associated with time are often indistinguishable from those of disease. This distinction is particularly difficult in the case of the lung since it has a remarkable ability to repair injury, often leaving only minimal residua which later appear to represent degenerative changes (Liebow, 1964). As a result, it is frequently assumed that certain disease states are exaggerations of changes which normally take place with time (Azcuy, Anderson, and Foraker, 1962), rather than arising from separate etiologic processes.

Evaluation of certain aspects of pulmonary aging in man is further complicated because samples of pulmonary tissue can only be obtained from diseased lungs at surgery or from normal lungs after death. The potential for the introduction of bias in such cases is obvious. Consequently, present knowledge of the morphologic and biochemical changes accompanying aging has many more deficiencies than information concerning functional alterations.

MORPHOLOGY

With advancing age, the costal cartilages may calcify, and kyphosis increases in frequency (Bickerman, 1952; Takahashi and Atsumi, 1955). The latter change in the shape of the thorax, predominately the result of degenera-tive changes in the intervertebral discs and increased spinal curvature, enlarges the anterior-posterior thoracic diameter and may give the appearance of a "barrel chest" (Takahashi and Atsumi, 1955; Pierce and Ebert, 1958a). Since similar changes in chest configuration are observed in obstructive pulmonary emphysema; this condition has been termed *postural* or *senile emphysema* (Bickerman, 1952). However, Pierce and Ebert (1958a) demonstrated that elderly people with this anatomic change do not have any of the functional characteristics of emphysema and, indeed, are similar in all respects except chest configuration to other individuals in the same age group. Accordingly, the term *senile emphysema* has been largely discarded since it falsely implies the presence of disease.

While the relative volume of conductive airways remains the same throughout life, Weibel (1964) has demonstrated in a small but well-studied series that alveolar duct volume increases with advancing age at the expense of alveolar volume. Microscopically, the alveolar ducts and higher order respiratory bronchioles enlarge at the expense of the surrounding alveoli which become more shallow and broad. Ryan, Vincent, Mitchell, Filley, and Dart (1965) coined the term *ductectasia* to describe this change and reported that the presence of ductectasia in 63 normal lungs was highly correlated with age. Ductectasia was absent below the age of 40, and its frequency increased to 81 percent by the ninth decade. Alveolar septae were not destroyed and these authors concluded that the dilatation of these structures was not an early manifestation of panacinar emphysema. This conclusion was similar to that of Wright (1961) who observed that the elastic fibers forming the supportive parenchymal framework were uniformly reduced in number and thickness, particularly in the area where the alveolar ducts open into alveoli. He concluded that this alternation in elastic tissue in the normal lungs of the aged is a diffuse uniform atrophy distinct from the nonuniform destructive changes seen in emphysema. Despite this diminution in elastic tissue in the alveolar ducts and alveoli, the ultrastructure of elastic fibers as examined by electron microscopy remains unchanged with age (Adamson, 1968). In addition, apparent morphologic reduction in elastic tissue has not been reflected in biochemical quantitation of elastic tissue (Pierce and Ebert, 1965).

The alveoli increase in number from 24 million at birth to approximately 300 million by the eighth year of life (Weibel, 1964). Following this maturation, alveolar number remains constant. In contrast, in a cross-sectional study of normal individuals, the internal surface area of the lung increased from 20-30 m² at birth to 70-80 m² at age 20 but thereafter declined at a rate of 0.27 m²/year (Thurlbeck, 1967). Since alveolar number is constant but internal surface area decreases with age, the average surface area of an alveolus must decline. This is consistent with the observation in aged lungs of destruction of alveolar septae, the prime criterion for the microscopic diagnosis of emphysema (Azcuy, Anderson, and Foraker, 1962; Liebow, 1964). However, most studies of the incidence of this microscopic change have not reported supporting clinical data. Auerbach, Garfinkel, and Hammond (1974) correlated rupture of alveolar septae, i.e. "emphysema", with age and smoking history. In all categories of cigarette smokers, the degree of emphysema was great (1.23 to 2.50 on a 0 to 4 scale) and increased as a function of age. However, in those individuals who had never smoked regularly, the index of emphysema was only 0.05 in

subjects under 60 and 0.11 in those over 70 on the same 0 to 4 scale. This slight difference does not appear to be statistically significant, raising the question of whether the occurence of these histologic changes is truly a function of age if other contributing factors are properly weighed. In addition, loss of alveolar septae may not be directly representative of the actual clinical state of an individual.

Liebow (1964) and Semmens (1970) have reported thickened pulmonary arterial walls in older subjects. Both authors described enlargement of the intimal layer of the wall due to deposition of a relatively acellular material. In addition, Semmens also observed thickening of the medial layer. In the latter work, the author noted that wall thickness was increased particularly in arteries 1.5 to 5.0 mm in diameter. In smaller arteries (100-500μ) wall thickness is relatively constant for a vessel of any given diameter in young individuals, but considerable variation exists in the aged (Simons and Reid, 1969). In arterioles smaller than 100μ, walls are invariably 5μ thick under the age of 40 but range from 3 to 12μ in subjects over 65. Despite the increase in wall thickness of arteries of all sizes in the aged, these changes are not as severe as those associated with pulmonary or cardiac disease.

Hernandez, Anderson, Holmes, Morrone, and Foraker (1965) have reported an increase in bronchial mucous glands in elderly people (mean age 79.9 years) as compared to a younger group of subjects (mean age 59.4 years). This correlation of thickness of the gland layer with age could not be attributed to inhalant exposure since all subjects lived in the same area and did not use tobacco. Large thin lung sections revealed minimal evidence of emphysema in these people. Hypertrophy of bronchial mucous glands is often used as an index of chronic bronchitis, but it is difficult to equate the glandular hypertrophy in these subjects with disease since clinical information is not provided. As a result, the significance of this morphologic finding is unclear, and further correlation of clinical symptomatology with anatomic findings is needed.

In a series of 100 autopsy cases equally divided between elderly patients (over 90 years of age) and middle-aged subjects (40-50 years), in addition to intimal arterial thickening, Liebow (1964) also found calcification of bronchial cartilages, loss of alveolar septae, and epithelial proliferation in the older group. Focal scarring also was more common in the elderly, as might be expected since the period of risk for pulmonary insult was greater. Liebow (1964) concluded that the lungs of older individuals do not have any pathologic changes which are not present in diseased lungs of younger people. Nevertheless, this does not necessarily indicate that disease merely accelerates processes which normally accompany aging.

BIOCHEMICAL ALTERATIONS

Little is known about biochemical changes as they relate to aging of the lungs. The demonstration of decreased elastic recoil of the lung in aged subjects (Pierce and Ebert, 1958a) prompted several teams of investigators to study the composition of pulmonary connective tissue. Surprisingly, multiple investigations indicated that total pulmonary elastin content, rather than decreasing, actually increased with age (Pierce, 1964). Collagen content was fourfold greater than elastin content in young individuals and remained constant with time. As a result of the increase in elastin, the collagen/elastin ratio decreased to approximately two by age 70.

Pierce and Ebert (1965) studied small portions of lung parenchyma following careful dissection to remove all extraneous structures except blood vessels less than 50μ in diameter. They found that elastin and collagen content of lung parenchyma was constant and independent of age. Chemical analysis of pleural tissue revealed increased elastin content in specimens from older individuals. They concluded that the increase in total pulmonary elastin content previously associated with age was a result of increasing elastin concentration in the concentration in the pleura, septae, bronchi, and vessels and that there was no significant change in the connective tissue composition of the lung parenchyma *per se*. These findings were later confirmed by John and Thomas (1972) who also demonstrated a decrease in cross-linking in

elastic connective tissue, perhaps accounting for some of the observed decrease in elastic recoil of the lungs of older individuals. In contrast, Pierce and Ebert (1965) have concluded that collagenous rather than elastic connective tissue is primarily responsible for the elastic behavior of the lungs. While collagenous tissue has relatively little longitudinal distensibility, these investigators point out that its helical distribution in the primary lobule is remarkably similar to a coiled spring. Like a spring, its elasticity may be dependent upon shearing stress rather than axial stretch of the fibers. They postulate that a disintegration of the pulmonary fibrous network with advancing age leads to the observed decrease in lung elasticity.

Despite the attention focused on the composition of pulmonary connective tissue, other factors may be important in the decline of lung elasticity which accompanies aging. The majority of the retractive force developed by the lung is not due to tissue elasticity but is the result of surface-active forces developed at the air-tissue interface (Radford, 1964). Pulmonary surfactant is responsible for maintaining the stability of this interface and influences the elastic forces generated at the interface. Unfortunately, nothing is known of the influence of age on these factors. At this date it is apparent that the exact mechanisms responsible for the decreased lung elasticity associated with age are unclear.

PULMONARY FUNCTION

Lung Volumes

Lung volumes have been the most frequently and thoroughly studied aspect of the influence of aging on pulmonary function. Although there are some quantitative differences among investigations due to variation of methods and selection of subjects, almost all reports are in excellent qualitative agreement. These data have been collected and discussed in the extensive review of Muiesan, Sorbini, and Grassi (1971) and will be summarized here.

The three factors showing the highest correlation with lung volumes are age, sex, and height.

Weight and body surface area, since the latter is directly influenced by weight, have poor predictive value in estimating lung volume.

In cross-sectional studies of the general population, total lung capacity is less in older individuals. However, when correction is made for the lesser height of older subjects, it is apparent that total lung capacity is independent of age. Because these studies were cross-sectional rather than longitudinal in nature, it is not possible to separate the effects of two factors: (1) Average height of the general population has increased in the last 50 years; and (2) there is a slight decline in an individual's height throughout his later life. Nevertheless, it is apparent from these data that measurements of total lung capacity are best predicted by height alone, and if age does influence total lung capacity, its effect is minimal. The majority of these studies included men only and, therefore, although total lung capacity appears to be constant as a function of age in women, this conclusion is less secure than in the male population.

While there is constancy of total pulmonary volume throughout life, the various subdivisions of this volume are markedly influenced by age. All reports describe decrements of vital capacity associated with age (Figure 1). The mean decrease of these reports is 26.4 ml/year for males and 21.6 ml/year for females. While men have larger vital capacities initially, the rate of decline with age is the same for both sexes ($.10 > p > .05$). There is a strong influence of height on predicted vital capacity which is not apparent in Figure 1 due to the normalization of the data to a height of 170 cm. Other less well-defined factors are also operative in the determination of the vital capacity. For example, the normal value reported by Morris, Koski, and Johnson (1971), indicated by the number 10 in Figure 1, were obtained in nonsmoking individuals who lived in a pollution-free environment. These predicted values are clearly greater than those reported in all other studies which were performed on smoking, urban populations.

Because the vital capacity decreases with age and total lung capacity remains constant, residual volume must increase with age. This has been the reported experience of all workers. The ratio of residual volume to total lung capacity (RV/TLC) increases from approximately 20 percent at age 20 to 35 percent at age 60. It appears that this increase in RV/TLC takes place predominately after age 40 (Brody, Johnson, Townley, Herrera, Snider, and Campbell, 1974).

Similarly, with the exception of the Veterans Administration-Army cooperative study (Boren, Kory, and Syner, 1966), there is agreement that the functional residual capacity increases significantly with age in both males and females. However, this increase is less than the proportional increase in residual volume with age. Boren, Kory, and Snyer (1966) studied

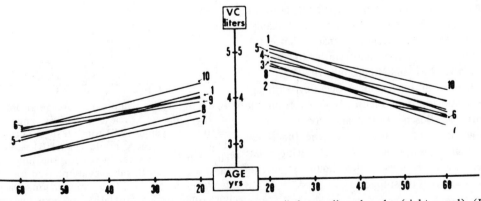

Figure 1. Changes in vital capacity with age in females (left panel) and males (right panel). (Reproduced from Muiesan, G., Sorbini, C. A., and Grassi, V. 1971. Respiratory function in the aged. *Bull. Physio-pathol. Respir*, 7, 973–1007 [Figure 1].)

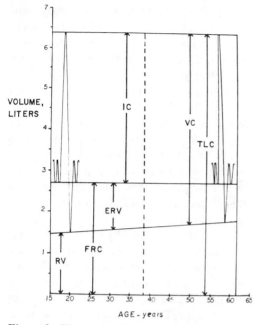

Figure 2. Diagrammatic representation of the effect of age upon the subdivisions of lung volume in males. In this study total lung capacity (TLC), inspiratory capacity (IC), and functional residual capacity (FRC) remained constant. Residual volume (RV) increased while vital capacity (VC) and expiratory reserve volume (ERV) decreased. The mean value for age is represented by the dashed line and the extremes of age represent two standard deviations from the mean. (Reproduced from Boren, H. G., Kory, R. C., and Syner, J. C. 1966. The Veterans Administration-Army cooperative study of pulmonary function: II. The lung volume and its subdivisions in normal men. *Am. J. Med.*, **41**, 96–114 [Figure 8].)

their subjects in a semirecumbent position; this may be responsible for the lack of changes in the functional residual capacity since this volume is affected significantly by posture (Leblanc, Ruff, and Milic-Emili, 1970).

Changes in lung volume occuring with age are summarized in Figure 2, taken from the work of Boren, Kory, and Syner (1966). Other than the constancy of the functional residual capacity in this study which was mentioned previously, this figure represents a consensus of most reports.

Static Mechanical Properties

The volume assumed by the total respiratory system in response to a constant distending pressure is dependent upon the interaction of the volume-pressure characteristics of its two component parts—the lung and the chest wall. The characteristics of the lung (L) and chest wall (W) are quite different, and the resulting volume-pressure relationship for the respiratory system (RS) reflects the attributes of both components (Panels A and B, Figure 3). The pressure required to maintain the system at a

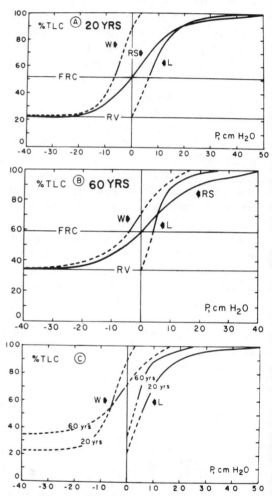

Figure 3. Static volume-pressure relationships of the lung (L), chest wall (W), and total respiratory system (RS) for "ideal" 20-year-old (Panel A) and 60-year-old (Panel B) subjects. The volume-pressure curves for the lungs and chest walls of both subjects are plotted together in Panel C to facilitate comparison. Dashed lines indicate extrapolation of existing data. (Reproduced from Turner, J. M., Mead, J., and Wohl, M. E. 1968. Elasticity of human lungs in relation to age. *J. Applied Physiol.*, **25**, 664–671 [Figure 7].)

volume is equal to the algebraic sum of the pressures required to maintain the two components at the same volume. For example, when no net pressure is applied to the system (intersection of curve RS with the ordinate), the elastic recoil of the lung exactly balances the tendency of the chest wall to expand. As a result, the entire system is at its resting volume, the functional residual capacity (FRC). Any change in system volume above or below FRC requires the application of a net positive or negative force. The volume-pressure relationships shown in Figure 3 are obtained under static conditions and do not include the pressures necessary to overcome resistance to flow as gas enters or leaves the lungs.

The influence of age on the static mechanical properties of the respiratory system has been investigated in many laboratories with conflicting results. Turner, Mead, and Wohl (1968) have pointed out that some of the divergent findings may have resulted from artifacts in measurement of esophageal pressures or from failure to provide a standard volume history prior to measurements. In addition, different workers measured compliance, the change in volume produced per unit change in pressure, under different conditions (inspiration versus expiration) and with varying methods (static versus dynamic).

Turner, Mead, and Wohl (1968) observed that the volume-pressure curve of the lung was shifted to the left, i.e., the pressure needed to distend the lung to a given volume decreased with age. This indicates that elastic recoil, the tendency of the lung to collapse, decreases with increasing age. Other investigators have reported similar findings (Frank, Mead, and Ferris, 1957; Pierce and Ebert, 1958b). While there has been confusion in the past, it now appears that static lung compliance increases with age so that the volume-pressure curve of the lung is not only shifted to the left but also has a steeper slope in the elderly (Turner, Mead, and Wohl, 1968).

Mittman, Edelman, Norris, and Shock (1965), using a positive pressure breathing method, demonstrated that chest wall compliance decreased with age, i.e., the thorax was more resistant to deformation in older individuals. The positive pressure breathing technique has

been criticized on the grounds that it provides falsely low measurements of chest wall compliance as compared to other more desirable techniques performed under general anesthesia (Van Lith, Johnson, and Sharp, 1967). Despite this drawback, measurements with this technique correlate reasonably well with more exact measurements, and, although absolute values of chest wall compliance may be in error, the method is probably valid for determining trends with age.

Combining the data on chest wall compliance of Mittman and his coworkers with their own data on lung compliance, Turner, Mead, and Wohl (1968) have synthesized a description of the volume-pressure (V-P) relationships of the total respiratory system. To illustrate the effects of aging, they have compared "ideal" 20- and 60-year-old subjects (Figure 3). The increase in lung compliance seen with age is reflected by the steeper slope of the V-P curve of the lung (L) in the 60 year old. Decreased elastic recoil shifts the curve to the left, i.e., at any given lung volume the curve of the older individual lies closer to the zero pressure line. The decreased compliance of the chest wall at the level of the functional residual capacity in the elderly is indicated by the shallow slope of the chest wall V-P curve (W). The reduction in chest wall compliance is slightly greater than the increase in lung compliance, resulting in a moderate decrease in total compliance of the respiratory system of the 60-year-old subjects (RS). As pointed out by Turner, Mead, and Wohl (1968), the work expenditure of the 60 year old to overcome elastic forces during normal breathing would be 20 percent greater than that of the 20 year old. The older subject would expend 70 percent of his total elastic work in distending the chest wall whereas the comparable figure for the younger individual would be only 40 percent. The chest wall and lung V-P curves of both individuals are compared in the bottom panel of the figure.

While most physiologic studies refer to the structures surrounding the lung as "chest wall," this is not a uniform structure and in reality is composed of two separate entities—the rib cage and the diaphragm. The alterations in physical properties of these structures differ slightly with age. Expansion of the rib cage accounts for 40 percent of the change in lung volume in young individuals; movement of the diaphragm is responsible for the remainder. The rigidity of the rib cage increases with age and the relative contribution of the rib cage to alterations in lung volume decreases to 30 percent of the total by the eighth decade (Rizzato and Marazzini, 1970). The reduction of the relative contribution of the rib cage is most pronounced at lung volumes less than the functional residual capacity.

Dynamics of Ventilation

All reports of ventilatory capacity uniformly indicate a reduction of indices of airflow with advancing age. The maximum voluntary ventilation, maximal expiratory flow rate, maximum mid-expiratory flow, and the forced expiratory volume in 1 second all decrease by approximately 20 percent to 30 percent throughout the adult years (Muiesan, Sorbini, and Grassi, 1971). Although there is generalized agreement that flow rates decrease with age, controversy exists concerning the cause of this decrease. Since the rate of flow achieved in the lungs is dependent upon (1) the applied pressure and (2) the resistance to movement of gas and tissues, alteration of either or both of these two factors could be responsible for the observed decrease in flows seen with age. Fry and Hyatt (1960) demonstrated that maximum flow rates are a function of lung volume, higher flows being achieved at larger lung volumes. Their work indicated that flow at large lung volumes was "effort-dependent," i.e., flow increased with the generation of increased intrapleural pressure by the respiratory muscles. However, as lung volume decreased, flow became independent of applied intrapleural pressure once a certain level of pressure was attained.

DuBois and Alcala (1964) concluded that the decreased force exerted by the respiratory muscles of the aged was in part responsible for observed decreases in flow. However, this factor would be operative only at "effort-dependent" lung volumes since even their subjects in the 75–90 year range were able to generate expiratory pressures sufficient to attain maximum flows at "effort-independent" volumes.

It seems unlikely that an increase in total pulmonary resistance is responsible for the decrease in indices of flow with age since measurements of total pulmonary resistance show little (Frank, Mead, and Ferris, 1957; Muiesan, Sorbini, Solinas, and Grassi, 1970) or no increase (Pierce and Ebert, 1958b; DuBois and Alcala, 1964) in older individuals. However, Mead, Turner, Macklem, and Little (1967) concluded that the relationship between lung elastic recoil and the resistance of a peripheral segment of the airways may limit flow at lower lung volumes. They theorize that the critical driving pressure for flow at "effort-independent" lung volumes is not intrapleural pressure, but the pressure supplied by the elastic recoil of the lungs. Since, as discussed in the previous section, lung elastic recoil declines with age, the available pressure to generate flow would also decrease with age. Furthermore, these authors calculated that the resistance of the "up-stream segment," the peripheral portion of the airways which they felt limited flow, increased markedly at lower lung volumes with advancing age. Since resistance of this critical segment can increase without exhibiting much effect on total pulmonary resistance, this change in resistance may not be reflected by an appreciable increase in overall pulmonary resistance. Support for this theory is provided by the demonstration of decreased dynamic compliance with increasing respiratory frequency in older individuals (Cohn and Donoso, 1963; Muiesan et al. 1970). This abnormality has been claimed by Woolcock, Vincent, and Macklem (1969) to be the most sensitive indicator of increased resistance of small peripheral airways. Despite this indirect evidence, further investigation is clearly needed to completely delineate the critical factors which result in the reduction of flow rates in older subjects.

Gas Exchange

Many investigators have documented a progressive increase in the alveolar-arterial oxygen difference, $(A - a)_{O_2}$, with age (Bates, Macklem, and Christie, 1971; Muiesan, Sorbini, and Grassi, 1971). Alveolar oxygen tension remains constant, but arterial oxygen pressure declines with age, increasing the difference between the two pressures. The decrease in arterial P_{O_2} can not be ascribed to alveolar hypoventilation since alveolar gas tensions and arterial P_{CO_2} are normal. Similarly, shunting of venous blood into the systemic circulation is unlikely since Mellemgaard (1966) demonstrated that intrapulmonary shunting is responsible for only a small fraction of the total $(A - a)_{O_2}$ and that drainage of bronchial and thebesian veins into the left heart causes less than half of the observed $(A - a)_{O_2}$. The magnitude of shunting from both sources is independent of age, and thus could not be responsible for the increasing $(A - a)_{O_2}$.

Two remaining possibilities for the decrease in arterial P_{O_2} with age are (1) diffusion impairment and (2) mismatching of alveolar ventilation and pulmonary blood flow.

According to an overwhelming consensus, the carbon monoxide diffusing capacity decreases linearly with age (Bates, Macklem, and Christie, 1971; Muiesan, Sorbini, and Grassi, 1971). Measurements of two components of the diffusing capacity, capillary blood volume, and the pulmonary membrane diffusing capacity, are both decreased. There is no data available for variation with age of the third component, the chemical reaction rate of CO with erythrocytes. However, the interpretation of these findings is difficult because many factors affect the diffusing capacity measurement even though they have no relation to diffusion (Bates, Macklem, and Christie, 1971). Because of the sensitivity of this test to artifactual and physiological variations, most authors are hesitant to attribute the reduction in arterial P_{O_2} with age to the corresponding decrement of the diffusing capacity.

A more likely explanation for the decreasing arterial oxygen tension associated with aging is uneven distribution of inspired gas and pulmonary blood flow. Using inert gas clearance during oxygen breathing, Edelman, Mittman, Norris, and Shock (1968) demonstrated age differences in the uniformity of ventilatory distribution. In order to reach a 2 percent end-tidal nitrogen concentration, subjects over 60 required 30 percent more

ventilation than men in their third and fourth decade. Interestingly, when the breathing pattern was altered so that large tidal volumes were utilized, there was no change in younger individuals, but the clearance indices of older subjects improved and became similar to the younger group. The reason for this improvement was not immediately apparent.

Although ventilation and pulmonary blood flow are distributed normally in both old and young subjects following a vital capacity maneuver, pulmonary ventilation to the lower lung zones is decreased in older individuals during normal tidal breathing (Holland, Milic-Emili, Macklem, and Bates, 1968). These authors concluded that loss of lung elastic recoil and an increased tendency to airway collapse resulted in airway closure during part or all of the breathing cycle in the dependent lung zones of the elderly. As a result, the ratio of ventilation to perfusion in these areas would fall, leading to a decrease in arterial oxygenation. Both Anthonisen, Danson, Robertson, and Ross (1969/70) and Leblanc, Ruff, and Milic-Emili (1970) demonstrated that the lung volume at which airway closure occurred, the "closing volume," increased linearly with age above 20 years. Data from the latter study indicated that at age 64, airway closure occurred in seated normals at resting lung volume (functional residual capacity) (Figure 4). In the supine position, airway closure occurred at age 44 due to the decrease in the functional residual capacity with change in posture. These findings are compatible with the improvement of ventilatory uniformity produced by large tidal volumes (Edelman et al., 1968) since deep breathing would increase lung volume above the closing volume, open closed airways, and improve distribution of inspired gas (Bates, Macklem, and Christie, 1971).

While this explanation of the inverse relationship between age and arterial oxygenation appears plausible, a disquieting note is injected by the observation that the alveolar-arterial nitrogen difference does not correlate with age (Bachofen, Hobi, and Scherrer, 1973). Since this parameter is an indicator of ventilation-perfusion inequality, it should increase if this proposed mechanism is correct. More direct

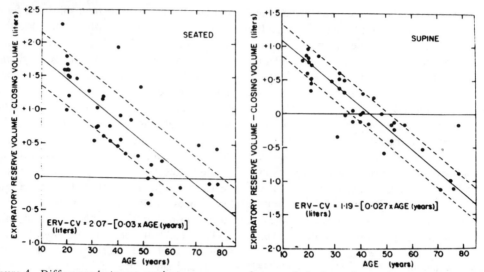

Figure 4. Difference between expiratory reserve volume and closing volume above residual volume, in liters, as a function of age in seated (left panel) and supine (right panel) subjects with regression lines (solid) ± 1.0 SD (dashed). The functional residual capacity is indicated by the horizontal line intersecting the ordinate at zero. (Reproduced from Leblanc, P., Ruff, F., and Milic-Emili, J. 1970. Effects of age and body position on "airway closure" in man. *J. Applied Physiol.*, 28, 448–451 [Figure 6].)

evidence is necessary to complete our understanding of this problem.

Exercise Capacity

Maximal oxygen uptake, the parameter most commonly used as an index of aerobic exercise capacity, peaks at age 20 and then declines with increasing age (Muiesan, Sorbini, and Grassi, 1971). If maximal uptake is expressed as a function of body weight, cross-sectional studies indicate that from age 10 throughout life there is a linear decrease of 0.40 ml/(kg-min) per year of life in males (Dehn and Bruce, 1972) (Figure 5). Thus, from age 20 to 60, average maximal oxygen uptake decreases by one-third, although there is considerable variation among individuals. On the basis of their data on subjects followed for 2 years, as well as other published data, Dehn and Bruce (1972) in longitudinal studies concluded that the decrease in maximal oxygen uptake with age was twice as great as that in cross-sectional studies. They felt that this discrepancy probably resulted from undefined truncation of the population in cross-sectional studies. The data of Åstrand, Åstrand, Hallbäck, and Kilbom

(1973) from a 21-year study indicated a lesser decrease in maximal oxygen uptake than seen in other longitudinal studies. However, their subjects probably improved their physical conditioning prior to the second observation; this is a factor known to improve maximal oxygen uptake (Dehn and Bruce, 1972; Tzankoff, Robinson, Pyke, and Brawn, 1972). Although most exercise studies have been performed on males, it appears that the proportional decrease in maximal oxygen uptake with age in females is similar if their smaller initial exercise capacity is taken into consideration (Åstrand et al., 1973).

Physical conditioning increases exercise capacity in young men (Dehn and Bruce, 1972). Similarly, in older males (44–66 years) Tzankoff et al. (1972) demonstrated an increase of 17 percent in maximal oxygen uptake following 6 months of physical training. Adams and deVries (1973) observed a 21 percent increase in oxygen uptake in females (52–79 years) after a 3-month training period. Although this was a significant improvement in comparison to pretraining studies, this improvement did not differ from the average in nontrained individuals. This most likely was the result of the small

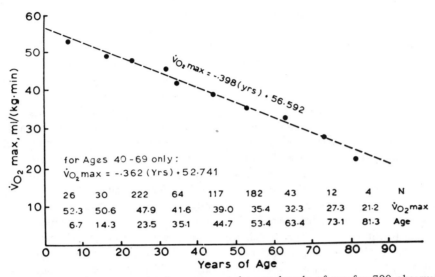

Figure 5. Regression of mean maximal oxygen uptake per decade of age for 700 observations in healthy males, recalculated from 17 studies in the literature. When corrected for body weight, maximal oxygen uptake decreases uniformly from childhood throughout life. (Reproduced from Dehn, M. M., and Bruce, R. A. 1972. Longitudinal variations in maximal oxygen intake with age and activity. *J. Applied Physiol.*, **33**, 805–807 [Figure 1].)

control population used in this study as most reports generally support the beneficial effect of conditioning on exercise capacity.

Variation among individuals, in addition to physical conditioning, is an important factor in determining exercise capability. Saltin and Grimby (1968) reported that former athletes (mean age 53 years) who had been sedentary for at least 10 years still had an average maximal oxygen uptake which was 20 percent higher than would be expected for their age. However, in comparison to athletes of comparable prowess and age who had continued physical training, maximal oxygen uptake was 25 percent lower. These data may be interpreted as showing that either athletes are a select group in the general population or that previous training has a beneficial influence on performance in later life. It is not known which alternative is correct.

PULMONARY DISEASE IN THE AGED

The incidence of pulmonary diseases is greater in older individuals than in the general population. Usually it is difficult to assess if this is due to pulmonary aging *per se*. The incidence

of serious infectious pulmonary diseases is far greater in the elderly and may be the result of associated debilitating diseases. However, there is evidence that body defenses, such as the delayed hypersensitivity response to antigens, are altered in the elderly. Waldorf, Willkens, and Decker (1968) attempted to sensitize healthy elderly people to a challenge of dinitrochlorobenzene. Only 72 percent of the group were sensitized as compared to 96 percent of a younger control group. This decrease was due to a lower rate of sensitization of subjects over 70 years; 94 percent of those under 70 responded. Interestingly, 16 subjects had positive tuberculin skin tests even though they did not respond to the dinitrochlorobenzene challenge. The authors felt that perhaps the elderly could respond to an antigen to which they had been sensitized in the past but could no longer respond to a new challenge. This and other unknown changes accompanying aging may be causal factors in the age-related incidence of pneumonia (Reimann, 1963; Sullivan, Dowdle, Marine, and Hierholzer, 1972) and tuberculosis (Stead, 1967).

While mortality from pneumonia has decreased dramatically, the incidence of the disease has remained relatively stable in recent years (Reimann, 1963). Deaths due to pneumonia in children and younger adults have decreased tenfold since 1900. The mortality rate has decreased in infants and the elderly, but the decrement has been less pronounced, and pneumonia is still a major cause of death. Age is a significant risk factor, but its direct effect is unclear since the presence of multiple associated diseases, e.g., cancer, as seen in the aged, also increases the mortality rate due to pneumonia (Sullivan *et al.,* 1972).

Although the total tuberculosis case load is decreasing in recent years, the peak incidence has shifted to an older segment of the population (Stead, 1967). This clearly results from a different pathogenesis of the disease in the older individual. Stead (1967) has marshalled impressive evidence that tuberculosis in the elderly is almost entirely of the reinfection type rather than the primary type. In the latter case, disease results from exposure to and dissemination from an individual with active tuberculosis. In reinfection tuberculosis, the source of the disease is a dormant tuberculous infection acquired years previously during a subclinical illness. Stead (1967) has hypothesized that body resistance declines and the previously dormant infection becomes activated due to aging or coexisting disease. Because the fraction of tuberculin positive individuals, i.e., the reservoir of dormant infection, is decreasing as older people die, the incidence of reinfection tuberculosis in the aged may decrease in the future.

Pulmonary embolism is a frequent cause of death in the elderly, increasing with age in linear fashion (Morrell, 1970). The exact incidence is uncertain since clinical diagnosis during life is extremely difficult and reliance is necessarily placed on autopsy series. There is no evidence that this condition is a direct result of aging; it is almost always associated with debilitating and immobilizing diseases. A major factor limiting our knowledge is the lack of a convenient laboratory technique to make a conclusive diagnosis. At present, radioisotopic lung scanning is the most helpful diagnostic aid. Although abnormal lung scans have been reported in elderly individuals without obvious disease (Friedman, Schub, Smith, and Solomon, 1970), studies in subjects selected according to more strict criteria of normalcy do not have perfusion defects (Kronenberg, L'Heureux, Ponto, Drage, and Loken, 1972).

Two other groups of diseases, lung neoplasms and chronic obstructive pulmonary disease, are related to both age and cigarette smoking. In reports on anatomic changes associated with emphysema, Auerback and his colleagues (1972, 1974) observed increasing morphologic evidence of emphysema with age in smokers. The average degree of emphysema increased slightly with age in nonsmokers but remained well below that seen in any category of cigarette smoker. If the diagnosis of emphysema is based on clinical rather than pathological criteria, the same relative importance of age and smoking history is obtained (U.S. Department of Health, Education, and Welfare, 1967).

In the case of pulmonary malignancies a similar, but more conclusive, picture emerges. Death rates from lung cancer increase fourfold throughout the adult life of a nonsmoker (U.S. Department of Health, Education, and Welfare, 1967). However, the risk of developing lung cancer in an elderly moderate smoker (10–19 cigarettes/day) is ten times as great as that of a nonsmoker. With further increase in the degree of exposure to tobacco, the risk increases almost linearly. Although the data for females are less striking, the conclusion is similar.

While age affects the incidence of obstructive lung disease and pulmonary neoplasms, the smoking factor is far more significant in the causation of disease in our elderly population.

REFERENCES

Adams, G. M., and deVries, H. A. 1973. Physiological effects of an exercise training regimen upon women aged 52 to 79. *J. Geront.,* **28,** 50–55.

Adamson, J. S. 1968. An electron microscopic comparison of the connective tissue from the lungs of young and elderly subjects. *Am. Rev. Respirat. Diseases,* **98,** 399–406.

Anthonisen, N. R., Danson, J., Robertson, P. C., and Ross, W. R. D. 1969/70. Airway closure as a function of age. *Resp. Physiol.,* **8,** 58–65.

Åstrand, I., Åstrand, P. O., Hallbäck, I., and Kilbom, A. 1973. Reduction in maximal oxygen uptake with age. *J. Appl. Physiol.*, **35**, 649–654.

Auerbach, O., Garfinkel, L., and Hammond, E. C. 1974. Relation of smoking and age to findings in lung parenchyma: A microscopic study. *Chest*, **65**, 29–35.

Auerbach, O., Hammond, E. C., Garfinkel, M. A., and Benante, C. 1972. Relation of smoking and age to emphysema. *New Engl. J. Med.*, **286**, 853–857.

Azcuy, A., Anderson, A. E., and Foraker, A. G. 1962. The morphological spectrum of aging and emphysematous lungs. *Ann. Internal Med.*, **57**, 1–17.

Bachofen, H., Hobi, H. J., and Scherrer, M. 1973. Alveolar-arterial N_2 gradients at rest and during exercise in healthy men of different ages. *J. Appl. Physiol.*, **34**, 137–142.

Bates, D. V., Macklem, P. T., and Christie, R. V. 1971. *Respiratory Function in Disease*, 2nd ed., 75–92, 96–100. Philadelphia: W. B. Saunders.

Bickerman, H. 1952. The respiratory system in the aged. *In*, A. I. Lansing (ed.), *Cowdry's Problems of Ageing*, pp. 562–613. Baltimore: Williams & Wilkins.

Boren, H. G., Kory, R. C., and Syner, J. C. 1966. The Veterans Administration-Army cooperative study of pulmonary function: II. The lung volume and its subdivisions in normal men. *Am. J. Med.*, **41**, 96–114.

Brody, A. W., Johnson, J. R., Townley, R. G., Herrera, H. R., Snider, D., and Campbell, J. C. 1974. The residual volume. Predicted values as a function of age. *Am. Rev. Respirat. Diseases*, **109**, 98–105.

Cohn, J. E., and Donoso, H. D. 1963. Mechanical properties of lung in normal men over 60 years old. *J. Clin. Invest.*, **42**, 1406–1410.

Dehn, M. M., and Bruce, R. A. 1972. Longitudinal variations in maximal oxygen intake with age and activity. *J. Appl. Physiol.*, **33**, 805–807.

DuBois, A. B., and Alcala, R. 1964. Airway resistance and mechanics of breathing in normal subjects 75 to 90 years of age. *In*, L. Cander and J. H. Moyer (eds.), *Aging of the Lung*, pp. 156–162. New York: Grune & Stratton.

Edelman, N. H., Mittman, C., Norris, A. H., and Shock, N. W. 1968. Effects of respiratory pattern on age differences in ventilation uniformity. *J. Appl. Physiol.*, **24**, 49–53.

Frank, N. R., Mead, J., and Ferris, B. G. 1957. The mechanical behavior of the lungs in healthy elderly persons. *J. Clin. Invest.*, **36**, 1680–1687.

Friedman, S. A., Schub, H. M., Smith, E. H., and Solomon, N. A. 1970. Perfusion defects in the aging lung. *Am. Heart J.*, **79**, 160–166.

Fry, D. L., and Hyatt, R. E. 1960. Pulmonary mechanics. A unified analysis of the relationship between pressure, volume and gas flow in the lungs of normal and diseased human subjects. *Am. J. Med.*, **29**, 672–689.

Hernandez, J. A., Anderson, A. E., Holmes, W. L., Morrone, N., and Foraker, A. G. 1965. The bronchial glands in aging. *J. Am. Geriat. Soc.*, **13**, 799–804.

Holland, J., Milic-Emili, J., Macklem, P. T., and Bates, D. V. 1968. Regional distribution of pulmonary ventilation and perfusion in elderly subjects. *J. Clin. Invest.*, **47**, 81–92.

John, R., And Thomas, J. 1972. Chemical compositions of elastins isolated from aortas and pulmonary tissues of humans of different ages. *Biochem. J.*, **127**, 261–269.

Kronenberg, R. S., L'Heureux, P., Ponto, R. A., Drage, C. W., and Loken, M. K. 1972. The effect of aging on lung perfusion. *Ann. Internal Med.*, **76**, 413–421.

Leblanc, P., Ruff, F., and Milic-Emili, J. 1970. Effects of age and body position on "airway closure" in man. *J. Appl. Physiol.*, **28**, 488–451.

Liebow, A. A. 1964. Biochemical and structural changes in the aging lung. Summary. *In*, L. Cander and J. H. Moyer (eds.), *Aging of the Lung*, pp. 97–104. New York: Grune & Stratton.

Mead, J., Turner, J. M., Macklem, P. T., and Little, J. B. 1967. Significance of the relationship between lung recoil and maximum expiratory flow. *J. Appl. Physiol.*, **22**, 95–108.

Mellemgaard, K. 1966. The alveolar-arterial oxygen difference: Its size and components in normal man. *Acta Physiol. Scand.*, **67**, 10–20.

Mittman, C., Edelman, N. H., Norris, A. H., and Shock, N. W. 1965. Relationship between chest wall and pulmonary compliance and age. *J. Appl. Physiol.*, **20**, 1211–1216.

Morrell, M. T. 1970. The incidence of pulmonary embolism in the elderly. *Geriatrics*, **25**, 138–153.

Morris, J. F., Koski, A., and Johnson, L. C. 1971. Spirometric standards for healthy nonsmoking adults. *Am. Rev. Respirat. Diseases*, **103**, 57–67.

Muiesan, G., Sorbini, C. A., and Grassi, V. 1971. Respiratory function in the aged. *Bull. Physio-Pathol. Respir.*, **7**, 973–1007.

Muiesan, G., Sorbini, C. A., Solinas, E., and Grassi, V. 1970. Ventilatory dynamics in aging subjects. *In*, P. Archangeli *et al.* (ed.), *Normal Values for Respiratory Function in Man*, pp. 227–237. Torino, Italy: Panminerva Medica.

Pierce, J. A. 1964. Biochemistry of aging in the lung. *In*, L. Cander and J. H. Moyer (eds.), *Aging of the Lung*, pp. 61–69. New York: Grune & Stratton.

Pierce, J. A., and Ebert, R. V. 1958a. The barrel deformity of the chest, the senile lung and obstructive pulmonary emphysema. *Am. J. Med.*, **25**, 13–22.

Pierce, J. A., and Ebert, R. V. 1958b. The elastic properties of the lungs in the aged. *J. Lab. Clin. Med.*, **51**, 63–71.

Pierce, J. A., and Ebert, R. V. 1965. Fibrous network of the lungs and its change with age. *Thorax*, **20**, 469–476.

Radford, E. P. 1964. Static mechanical properties of mammalian lungs. *In,* W. O. Fenn and H. Rahn (eds.), *Handbook of Physiology. Respiration.,* Sect. 3, Vol. I, Chap. 15, pp. 429–449. Washington, D.C.: American Physiological Society.

Reimann, H. A. 1963. Prevention and treatment of pneumonias in the older person. *Geriatrics,* 18, 432–443.

Rizzato, G., and Marazzini, L. 1970. Thoracoabdominal mechanics in elderly men. *J. Appl. Physiol.,* 28, 457–460.

Ryan, S. F., Vincent, T. N., Mitchell, R. S., Filley, G. F., and Dart, G. 1965. Ductectasia; an asymptomatic pulmonary change related to age. *Med. Thorac.,* 22, 181–187.

Saltin, B., and Grimby, G. 1968. Physiological analysis of middle-aged and old former athletes. *Circulation,* 38, 1105–1115.

Semmens, M. 1970. The pulmonary artery in the normal aged lung. *Brit. J. Diseases Chest,* 64, 65–72.

Simons, P., and Reid, L. 1969. Muscularity of pulmonary artery branches in the upper and lower lobes of the normal young and aged lung. *Brit. J. Diseases Chest,* 63, 38–44.

Stead, W. W. 1967. Pathogenesis of the sporadic case of tuberculosis. *New Engl. J. Med.,* 227, 1008–1012.

Sullivan, R. J., Dowdle, W. R., Marine, W. M., and Hierholzer, J. C. 1972. Adult pneumonia in a general hospital. *Arch. Internal Med.,* 129, 935–942.

Takahashi, E., and Atsumi, H. 1955. Age differences in thoracic forms as indicated by thoracic index. *Human Biol.,* 27, 65–74.

Thurlbeck, W. M. 1967. Internal surface area and other measurements in emphysema. *Thorax,* 22, 483–496.

Turner, J. M., Mead, J., and Wohl, M. E. 1968. Elasticity of human lungs in relation to age. *J. Appl. Physiol.,* 25, 664–671.

Tzankoff, S. P., Robinson, S., Pyke, F. S., and Brawn, C. A. 1972. Physiological adjustments to work in older men as affected by physical training. *J. Appl. Physiol.,* 33, 346–350.

U.S. Department of Health, Education, and Welfare. 1967. *The Surgeon General's Report: The health consequences of smoking.* Public Health Service Publication No. 1696.

Van Lith, P., Johnson, F. N., and Sharp, J. T. 1967. Respiratory elastances in relaxed and paralyzed states in normal and abnormal men. *J. Appl. Physiol.,* 23, 476–486.

Waldorf, D. S., Willkins, R. F., and Decker, J. L. 1968. Impaired delayed hypersensitivity in an aging population. *J. Am. Med. Assoc.,* 203, 831–834.

Weibel, E. R. 1964. Morphometrics of the lung. *In,* W. O. Fenn and H. Rahn (eds.), *Handbook of Physiology. Respiration.,* Sect. 3, Vol. I, chap. 7, pp. 285–306. Washington, D.C.: American Physiological Society.

Woolock, A. J., Vincent, N. J., and Macklem, P. T. 1969. Frequency dependence of compliance as a test for obstruction in the small airways. *J. Clin. Invest.,* 48, 1097–1106.

Wright, R. R. 1961. Elastic tissue of normal and emphysematous lungs. *Am. J. Pathol.,* 39, 355–367.

18
MUSCLE

E. Gutmann
Institute of Physiology, Czechoslovak Academy of Sciences

HISTORICAL ASPECTS, RESEARCH TRENDS, AND METHODOLOGY

Historical Aspects and Research Trends

Old age is a period when disorders of the locomotor system prevail. These disorders include muscle atrophy, slowness, and a rapid decline in the efficiency of motor functions. These motor disorders were at first explained in terms of pathological changes in bone, ligaments, and joints, rather than in muscle itself (Mc Keown, 1965). The morphological changes in muscle with old age were not expected to become noticeable until a very late stage, and secondary changes due to disease, nutritional deficiencies, and disuse were considered to be of primary importance (Rubinstein, 1960). The first physiological observations concerned the relatively early decline in muscular strength which occurred in varying degrees among different muscle groups (Ufland, 1933; Birren, 1959). The considerable variations in aging muscle had also been noted in morphological studies. These variations remained unexplained until (a) the homogeneity of different motor units (Kugelberg and Edström, 1968) constituting different muscles, and (b) the properties and reactions of different muscles were progressively clarified. Such properties as contractility, myosin, and enzymes in adult muscle (cf. Close, 1972), developmental changes (Gutmann, Melichna and Syrový, 1974) and aging differences (Gutmann

and Hanzlíková, 1972a, 1972b), were further elucidated.

From a physiological point of view, the marked decline in efficiency of motor function is a very complex phenomenon and includes changes in motivation, receptors, nervous pathways, central synaptic mechanisms, and effectors. For some time, neurophysiological studies concentrated on changes in receptors and peripheral pathways, without reporting significant alterations in peripheral effector mechanisms, i.e., the myoneural junction and skeletal muscle itself (Magladery, 1959). Progressive identification of several regulatory influences exerted by the motor neuron on skeletal muscle fibers, including impulse and long-term, nonimpulse ("neurotrophic") activities (Gutmann and Hník, 1962; Miledi, 1963; Guth, 1968; Harris, 1974) have opened the way to more detailed studies and explanations of the alterations occurring in muscles of old age. Biochemical studies also began at a descriptive level with data on muscle constituents, especially ion distribution (Lowry, Hastings, Hull, and Brown, 1942; Yiengst, Barrows, and Shock, 1959), and later concentrated on changes in the energetics of muscular contraction, e.g., creatinephosphate (CP) and ATP (Ermini and Verzár, 1968; Ermini, Szelényi, Moser, and Verzár, 1971). A large body of inconclusive data on changes in activities of enzymes involved in energy supply and utilization (cf. Finch, 1972) was accumulated mainly from experimentation with liver, and the lack of uniformity did not encourage detailed studies on muscle. However, the findings of decreases of Mg^{2+} activated in 8–10 vs. 25–31-month-old-rats (Rockstein and Brandt 1962) and Ca^{2+} activated myosin ATPase activity in 3- vs. 36-month-old rats (Syrový and Gutmann, 1970) suggested more profound metabolic disturbances of the contractile proteins. The increasing interest of gerontological research in questions of primary molecular mechanisms of aging related to the regulation of protein synthesis provided an approach to experimentation from which the question of genetically programmed aging or error accumulation could be attacked (see Hahn, 1971; Cristofalo, 1972; Orgel, 1973). For a long period this approach did not concern muscle research because of technical difficulties. The increased degradation (Hájek, Gutmann, and Syrový, 1965), decreased synthesis of proteins (Srivastava and Chaudhary, 1969), and the reduction in the concentration of polysomes (Srivastava, 1969) indicate a basic disturbance of protein synthesis in muscle with age.

Meanwhile, gerontological research, deeply influenced by studies of aging of clones of mammalian cells in tissue culture (Hayflick 1970; Cristofalo, 1972; Orgel, 1973) was concerned with a more precise formulation of several recurrent questions. What are the essential differences between young and old cells? Do these differences limit their life span because of a genetically dictated program or because of random events related to errors in molecular synthesis? Are intra or extracellular mechanisms of primary importance? How far can experiences from clonal aging be applied to aging in vivo? These questions may be explored at different levels: the organ (muscle), the tissue (muscle fibers), the isolated muscle cell, and the subcellular level. Several problems have inhibited research in aging muscle. Muscle exhibits a considerable cell heterogeneity, including mesenchymal cells, Schwann cells of neurogenic origin, muscle cells involved in synthesis of specific contractile proteins, and endothelial cells. The membranes of the muscle cells are highly organized, especially with regard to the localization of specific receptors for the transmitter (ACh) at the site of neuromuscular contact (Katz, 1966). Muscle cells are considered to be postmitotically fixed cells, as are neurons. This is however, only partly true since satellite cells are presumed to develop into myoblasts (Kelly and Zacks, 1969) and are thus "potential intermitotic cells" (Cowdry, 1952). They are numerous in early development, decline rapidly in number in adult muscle (Allbrook, Han, and Hellmuth, 1971), but still survive and exhibit new proliferative capacity in grafted or injured adult muscle. The muscle cell is still essentially "noncycling" and thus does not permit comparable studies on senescent decline of proliferative capacity as do fibroblasts, which are preferentially used in in vitro studies. Different muscle cells exhibit great variations in metabolic type, as evidenced by their histochemical heterogeneity.

The regulation of muscle is essentially a multiple process (Gutmann, 1973) and includes neuronal, hormonal, vasomotor, and other interactions. Delineation of the mechanisms of nerve-muscle cell interaction may be considered to be essential for the understanding of senescent change in the muscle cell. This interaction has been successfully explored in tissue culture work (cf. Crain and Peterson, 1974; Harris, 1974; Lentz, 1974). This type of research, including a comparison of in vivo and in vitro observations, will in time supply relevant information on the primary events in aging of the muscle cell.

Methodology

General methodological postulates for gerontological research have to be expanded by specific methodological methods relevant to muscle tissue. Highly inbred strains of insects with a short life span can be appropriately managed with respect to environmental factors. However, the size of the muscles and the complex neuroendocrine regulation (Wigglesworth, 1970) introduce difficulties in technique and interpretation. Most work on muscle concerns the rat and the mouse which remain the animals of choice. One advantage of these systems is that overall motor activity (e.g., in actographic studies) can easily be followed. While the incidence of myopathies may increase in old age (Haleem, 1972), they are, however, not specific.

Research on muscle in old age should take into account the marked diversity among muscles with different functions and the heterogeneity of muscle fibers constituting an individual muscle. The latter is due to the fact that a single muscle is largely composed of different motor units, defined by Sherrington (1929) as the population of muscle fibers innervated by a single neuron. The main groups of motor units, muscles, and muscle fibers, slow and fast with respect to speed of contraction, can clearly be distinguished. There is a marked correlation between the properties of muscle fibers innervated by the same neuron (Burke, Levine, Zajac, Tsairis, and Engel, 1971). The fact that "fast" and "slow" motoneurons differ in excitability and other parameters (Eccles, Eccles, and Lundberg, 1958) and that fast and slow muscles and muscle fibers exhibit contractile (cf. Close, 1972) and biochemical (cf. Beatty and Bocek, 1970) differences had been observed relatively early. Histochemical analysis of muscle fibers identified different enzymatic activities and distinguished two to three types of muscle fibers exhibiting an inverse relationship between oxidative and glycolytic enzyme activity (Dubowitz and Pearse 1960) and differences in ATPase activity (Engle, 1962). Thus, although motor units are homogeneous, the heterogeneity of muscles arises from the intermingling of different types of motor units in a distinct muscle (Kugelberg and Edström, 1968; Burke et al., 1971). Few muscles are homogeneous, i.e., are composed of a single type of muscle fiber, such as the soleus muscle of the guinea pig (though not of the rat). The physiological type of a muscle will depend primarily on the proportions of fast and slow motor neurons innervating the muscle. The muscle type should therefore always be stated exactly.

Loss and atrophy of cells have been repeatedly considered to be two of the most important changes (cf. Strehler, 1962). Weight changes in muscles should be stated in percent of body weight, the rate of decrease of muscle weight being significantly higher than that of body weight and differing in different muscles (Tauchi, Yoshika, and Kobayashi, 1971). Fac-

tors affecting development of muscle, such as sexual differences (Griffin and Goldspink, 1973) should be considered (cf. Goldspink, 1972). Few muscles are suitable for counting the total number of muscle fibers. Muscles with a parallel fiber course between the tendon insertion points (such as the levator ani or the diaphragm muscle) are most suitable. Total fiber counts are preferable to counts of a given area related to a transverse section of the muscle. With respect to the heterogeneity of many muscles, information on percent decrease of different muscle fiber types in a distinct muscle may be necessary (Tauchi, Yoshika, and Kobayashi, 1971). Control muscles must be taken from animals at an age when no further developmental increase of number or size of muscle fibers occurs and when physiological parameters (e.g., contraction time) are relatively constant. In morphological studies, quantitative "morphometric" methods (Sitte, 1967) with respect to volume of mitochondria and other cell organelles should be applied. In enzymatic studies, the reference points should be clearly stated. With respect to age-dependent changes in the number of muscle fibers, enzyme activities should be expressed not only on the basis of weight, but if possible also per single muscle fiber (Tuček and Gutmann, 1973). Since enzyme activities are closely related to specific physiological states, interspecies comparisons may lead to misinterpretations (Finch, 1972). This review is therefore focused on changes in rat and mouse muscle. Much of the data on rates of degradation and synthesis of proteins only have relative value, since usually there is no differentiation between changes in intra and extracellular compartments and the reports do not take into account changes in permeability or kinetics of the precursor pool in incorporation studies. The difficulties encountered with cellular systems are partly overcome by studies of RNA and protein synthesis in cell free systems (Breuer and Florini, 1965; Srivastava and Chaudhary, 1969). Molecular studies on the properties of myosin are especially important. Physiological studies should whenever possible use single muscle cell preparations, which generate more precise data on membrane characteristics and rates of transmitter release at endplates (Gutmann, Hanzlíková, and Vyskočil, 1971). Studies on muscle in old age will of course have a goal of contributing to the discovery of primary cellular events in the aging process. To achieve this aim, application of the methods of molecular biology, tissue culture with clones of distinct muscle cells, electrophysiological and biochemical studies at a cellular level, and definition of neuromuscular relations *in vitro* and *in vivo* become increasingly important.

CHANGES IN AGING MUSCLES

Morphological Changes

Gross Morphology, Number, and Sizes of Muscle Fibers. The decrease of muscle weight relative to body weight is a very characteristic sign of old age and has been documented in the rat (Rockstein and Brandt, 1961; Tauchi, Yoshika, and Kobayashi, 1971) and the mouse (Rowe, 1969). An increase of extracellular and decrease of intracellular components in muscles of old age were suggested by previous studies (Lowry, Hastings, Hull, and Brown, 1942, Yiengst, Barrows, and Shock, 1959), and the related trend of a rise in extracellular water, sodium, and chloride and a decrease in intracellular potassium content has been confirmed in rats (Frubel-Osipova, 1969) and man (Dubois, 1972). Gross histological observations show an increase of collagen and fat (Rubinstein, 1960). Elongation of Achilles tendon with loss of the reflex in man (70–90 years old) (Grischko and Litovtschenko, 1964) could often be observed and may be due to shortening of muscle. The increase in collagen might be only relative to the increase of fat tissue (Lindner, 1972). An increase in the hydroxyproline content in aging heart muscle has been described (Tomanek, Taunton, and Liskop, 1972). The increase in collagenous fibers (even if only relative) may be important in the decrease of substrate supply. Degenerative changes in muscle fibers are rare and irregular, although myopathic changes resembling dystrophy are described in old age (Berg, 1956; Berg and Simms, 1961; Jennekens, Tomlinson, and Walton, 1971; Haleem, 1972). These myopathic changes are more common in the external ocular muscles in which a higher incidence of "Ringbinden" (obliquely running myofibrils) is also observed (Rebeiz, Moore, Holden, and Adams, 1972). They are also found in other muscles and in muscle diseases. The very late onset of degenerative changes and their irregularity in onset in different muscles suggest that they are not primary changes in aging muscle but occur secondarily in connection with nutritional deficiencies, cachexia, or chronic disuse (see Rubinstein, 1960; Adams, 1969). The decrease of muscle mass is due to decrease both in number (Gutmann and Hanzlíková, 1966; Rowe, 1969; Tauchi, Yoshika, and Kobayashi, 1971) and diameter (Frubel-Osipova, 1969; Rowe, 1969; Tuček and Gutmann, 1973) of the fibers. The changes are not uniform in muscles of different function. A decrease in both number and volume in "white" (fast) and in number alone in "red" (slow) muscle fibers has been hypothesized on the basis of percentage changes of "red" fibers (with high oxidative activity) in the senescent tibialis anterior muscle (Tauchi, Yoshika, and Kobayashi, 1971). A more rapid decline in the number of muscle fibers in the slow soleus as compared with the fast extensor digitorum longus (EDL) muscle has been reported (Tuček and Gutmann, 1973). The number of muscle fibers in the soleus muscle decreased by 39 percent in muscles of old animals (Gutmann and Hanzlíková, 1966). Color (red and white) does not necessarily correlate with speed of contraction. In the slow (red) soleus muscle of the rat, a preferential atrophy of Type II muscle fibers (with high ATPase activity) is conspicuous (Gutmann and Hanzlíková, 1972a) (Figure 1), resembling the preferential atrophy of Type II fibers in denervated muscle (Engel, 1962). A small, if any, decrease in number and diameter of muscle fibers is observed in the diaphragm (Tuček and Gutmann, 1973). Different types of motor units, muscles, and muscle fibers exhibit different reactions to the aging process (Gutmann and Hanzlíková, 1976), and this is reflected by random involvement in focal grouping of atrophic fibers (Fujisawa, 1974). The increase of variation in fiber size in aging muscles (Jennekens, Tomlinson, and Walton, 1971) and the occurrence of

(a)

(b)

Figure 1. Cross sectional through the soleus muscle of a 3-month-old (a) and 30-month-old (b) rat, stained for actomyosin ATPase activity. Note two types, Type I (low) and Type II (high enzyme activity) of muscle fibers with similar size in (a) and preferential decrease of enzyme activity and antrophy of Type II muscle fibers in (b). Scale bar represents 50 μm.

hypertrophic fibers also reflect differential behavior of different muscle fibers but may be due to compensatory hypertrophy in some surviving fibers (Adams, 1969). The changes in intrafusal muscle fibers are much less conspicuous than those of extrafusal ones. There are few changes in old age with respect to number and diameter of these fibers (Gutmann and Zelená, 1962; Swash and Fox, 1972). The absolute and relative number of muscle spindles, however, differ considerably in different muscles. In spite of reduction of the diameter of spindles themselves, no decrease of number of spindles in aging muscles of man has been reported (Voss, 1971).

Ultrastructural Changes. Ultrastructural changes in aging muscle have been studied mainly in the rat (Gutmann and Hanzlíková, 1972b; Hanzlíková and Gutmann, 1975). The changes

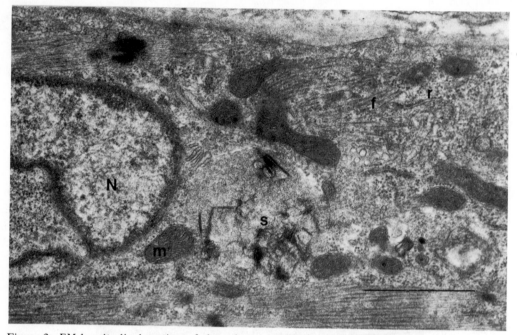

Figure 2. EM longitudinal section of the soleus muscle of a 31-month-old rat. Note formation of an autophagic vacuole near the muscle nucleus (N) with segregation of degenerating material (s), increased number of ribosomes (r), and some newly synthesized myofilaments (f), m (mitochondria). Scale bar represents 1.0 μm.

concern all structures, some of them showing a general reaction of the muscle cell to neuromuscular disturbance. The marked reduction of muscle fibers is apparently closely connected with the progressive and marked reduction of number and size of myofibrils. This process apparently proceeds very slowly at the periphery of the muscle fiber where disintegration and loss of myofibrils as well as "abortive" synthesis of new myofilaments can be observed (Figure 2). The basement membrane is maintained and thickened in many cases, and there is an increased covering of collagenous fibrils. Protrusions and fingerlike projections of the sarcolemma into the extracellular space disturb the regular assembly of single muscle fibers, and a high accumulation of ribosomes inside the newly proliferating, undifferentiated sarcolemmal processes is part of the "abortive" or "compensatory" proteosynthetic reaction. This is apparently related to the relative increase of sarcoplasmatic proteins observed in incorporation studies (Hájek, Gutmann, and Syrový, 1965). There is extensive

proliferation of the tubular T system beneath the sarcolemma, and enlarged terminal cisternae engulf the myofibrils. Diadic couplings of the sarcoplasmic reticular elements with the sarcolemma, observed until now only in developing muscle (Schiaffino and Margreth, 1969), can be seen in senescent muscle, and the overdeveloped T system joins to form pentades instead of triad complexes of the T system as in denervated muscle (Pellegrino and Franzini, 1963) (Figure 3). An increase in the number of nuclei (Frubel-Osipova, 1969) and a relative increase in DNA concentration has been observed (Drahota and Gutmann, 1961) as in cases of denervation (Gutmann and Žák, 1961) and in muscle disease but may also be due to activation of fibroblasts. While mitotic figures of the nuclei are not seen, nuclear fragmentation and occasionally a central nuclear location are observed. The nuclear chromatin is highly condensed at the periphery, and nucleoli may be attached to the nucleolemma. Satellite cells are present and might be a source of "abortive" regeneration, but no quantitative studies sug-

Figure 3. EM longitudinal section of the levator ani muscle of a 34-month-old rat. Increased number of parallel terminal cysternae. Scale bar represents 1.0 μm.

gesting their increase in senescent muscles have been reported. Disintegration of myofilaments is coupled with proliferation of sarcoplasmic reticulum and increased ribosomal activity. In some subsarcolemmal regions containing free myofilaments, triads and Z bands are probably sites of new synthesis, an "abortive regenerative" growth process in senescent muscle. Cytoplasmic degradation and autophagic processes appear to be confined to the periphery of the muscle fiber. Large autophagic vacuoles, multivesicular bodies, and increased activity of the Golgi apparatus are observed. Lipofuscin granules are regularly seen in the slow senescent muscles, especially in the perinuclear region in the proximity of the Golgi apparatus and among the accumulated mitochondria (Figure 4). The relation between degenerated mitochondrial and lipofuscin granules has also been described in senescent myocardial cells (Travis and Travis, 1972), mitochondrial degradation occurring in autophagic vacuoles. Irregularities and streaming of Z line material, rod formation, and target fibers considered to be specific for de-

Figure 4. EM longitudinal section of the soleus muscle of a 29-month-old rat. Lipofuscin granules between centrally located nuclei. Scale bar represents 1.0 μm.

nervation (Engel, 1961) are found in muscles of very (28–36 months) old rats.

Innervation

The changes in innervation of senescent muscle fibers deserve special attention in view of the close metabolic relationship of the neuron and the muscle cell (exhibited also in the "aging motor unit") and of the many morphological and metabolic changes in senescent muscle resembling those of denervated muscles (Drahota and Gutmann, 1961; Gutmann, Hanzlíková, and Jakoubek, 1968). Degeneration and loss of central neurons have repeatedly been described (see Andrew, 1938; Arendt, 1972). However, the question of definite cell loss has remained open (see Gutmann and Hanzlíková 1972a, 1972b). A decrease of proteosynthesis in spinal motor neurons (see Gutmann, Hanzlíková, and Jakoubek, 1968) and old age changes in motor nerve fibers occur, including occasional fragmentation of myelin sheaths and their degrada-

tion in Schwann cells and macrophages with appearance of intraaxonal vacuoles filled with glycogen granules and convolutions of axoplasm (Gutmann and Hanzlíková, 1972b). However, complete axonal degeneration, at least in motor nerve fibers, is a very rare occurrence. The decrease in number of muscle fibers contrasts with a lack of decrease of number of motor nerve fibers, at least in rats 24–28 months old. Consequently there is a decrease in size of the motor unit. This finding is substantiated by studies on endplate structures in senescent muscles (Gutmann, Hanzlíková, and Vyskočil, 1971). Practically no disintegration of terminal axons could be found, but the number of synaptic vesicles appear to be increased. Accumulation of vesicles and mitochondria, the occurrence of neurotubules and some neurofilaments in the terminal axons, and the finding in the axons suggested disturbance in proximodistal transport of proteins (Gutmann and Hanzlíková, 1972b). The primary synaptic clefts are enlarged, the basement membrane considerably

Figure 5. Motor endplate in levator ani muscle of a 36-month-old rat. Note terminal axon (t) with densely packed synaptic vesicles (v), enlarged primary cleft (c) of neuromuscular junction, thickened basement membrane (b), and irregular junctional infoldings (ji). Scale bar represents 1.0 μm. (From Gutmann, E., and Hanzlíková, V. 1975c. Changes in neuromuscular relationships in aging. *In*, J. M. Ordy and K. R. Brizzee (eds.), *Neurobiology of Aging*, pp. 193–207. New York: Plenum Press.)

thickened, and the postsynaptic junctional folds are widely branched (Figure 5). No withdrawal of Schwann cells from the endplates, as seen in later stages of denervation (Miledi and Slater, 1968), is found. Formation of collagen fibrils at the endplate region may be increased. Earlier observations on changes of the "subneural apparatus" illustrated by cholinesterase (ChE) activity, the "unfolding," irregularities in outline, and decrease in size of the endplate (Gutmann and Hanzlíková, 1965) demonstrate a primary decrease of enzyme activity at the endplate. This does not provide evidence for structural changes and wrongly suggested a resemblance to the postdenervation state. The irregular pattern of the endplates and the findings of collateral regeneration with thickened end bulbs suggested, however, a compensatory axonal growth after disappearance of muscle fibers. A continuous process of endplate elaboration during development and aging has also been suggested by Tuffery (1971). Very rarely, a disconnection of axonal terminals from irregular and disorganized postsynaptic structures could be observed in the soleus muscle of very old rats, indicating the final stage of random loss of neuromuscular contact (Gutmann and Hanzlíková, 1976). The characteristic and primary feature is, however, the loss of muscle fibers with relatively intact terminal axons, exhibiting a characteristic sign of old age changes in muscle.

Biochemical and Histochemical Changes

Metabolic changes in senescent muscles may be due to (a) intrinsic breakdown of cellular function, (b) changes in stability of the internal environment, and/or (c) changes in intercellular relationships. The decrease in basal metabolic rate or in oxygen uptake in old age may be due to atrophy and decrease of number of cells (Shock, 1961). Data on the decrease in oxygen consumption in senescent muscle (Frubel-Osipova, 1969) have to be reinterpreted from this point of view. Intrinsic changes in muscle cells might be expected at the level of transcription of genetic information from DNA on to intermediary messenger RNA. No evidence for such a mechanism which would suggest an "aging

program" in muscle or other cells exists to date (see Hahn, 1971).

Senescent muscle atrophy and loss of muscle cells indicate a disturbance of protein metabolism, especially a change in balance between synthesis and degradation and/or in turnover of proteins. No change in turnover of proteins in senescent muscle is suggested by incorporation studies (see Gutmann and Hanzlíková, 1972b). However, these data can be considered only preliminary with respect to the marked heterogeneity of turnover rates for various proteins (see Schimke, 1974; Goldberg, 1974). Concentration of RNA (expressed as P/mg N) in muscles of 24-month-old rats (Drahota and Gutmann, 1961) and in muscles of 320-day-old mice (μg RNA/mg protein) decreased (Srivastava, 1969), and there was also a progressive age-dependent decrease in the ratio of DNA as well as RNA to protein content in all subcellular fractions of muscle of the mouse (Srivastava and Chaudhary, 1969). An increase of concentration of RNA (mg/gram wet weight) with age has been described in muscles of the rat (Kanungo, Koul, and Reddy, 1970): however, these data have to be recalculated, considering the decrease in water content and in number of muscle fibers in senescent muscle. More relevant is the finding of a progressive decline in the concentration of polysomes with age in mouse skeletal muscle (Srivastava, 1969). There is a decrease of incorporation of labeled precursors into the proteins of senescent muscle of the rat (Gutmann and Hanzlíková, 1972b) and into RNA and proteins of the homogenate and various fractions of muscle of mice in vivo.

A decrease in proteosynthesis with age is also suggested by incorporation studies showing a decrease of the ratio of RNA/protein (Kanungo, Koul, and Reddy, 1970). However, the possible changes in precursor pool and in membrane permeability make interpretations difficult. Proteosynthetic capacity of ribosomes, isolated from rat muscle, decreases with age (Breuer and Florini, 1965). RNA polymerase isolated from nuclei (Britton, Sherman, and Florini, 1972) and in vitro incorporation of precursors into proteins by cell free systems (Srivastava and Chaudhary, 1969) decrease with age probably due to decreases in the content of polysomes in the aging muscle. Not consistent with these findings are observations of Wulff, Samis, and Falzone (1967) on an increase of RNA synthesis with age. Increased thymidine-^{3}H incorporation was interpreted as a compensatory process, a conclusion similar to that of Pelc (1965). However, more exact studies of the kinetics of incorporation with time, excluding reutilization of precursors, are necessary. The shift of percentage partition of proteins from contractile to sarcoplasmic types and the progressive increase of proteolytic activity (Hájek, Gutmann, and Syrový, 1965; Gutmann, Hanzlíková, and Jakoubek, 1968) suggest an increased degradation of proteins.

The changes in senescent muscle should be studied with respect to specific RNA species and proteins to answer the question of whether control of protein synthesis is disturbed at the level of specific mRNA.

There is apparent specificity, for example, for initiation of myosin mRNA (Heywood, 1970). Recent advances in the ability to utilize mammalian mRNAs for protein synthesis suggest that in time the basic disturbance of RNA and protein metabolism in the senescent muscle cell will be explained in specific terms. However, thus far our knowledge of RNA and protein synthesis in senescent muscle is only fragmentary.

Concerning changes in enzyme activities, questions such as (a) a decline of activity, (b) a failure of an intrinsic regulatory system, and (c) failure to react to regulatory agents have to be answered (cf. Moog, 1971). Studies on changes in enzyme activities usually involve liver, kidney, and brain tissue (see Finch, 1972) and generally conclude that enzyme activities remain essentially unchanged throughout life. Table 1 shows that with respect to enzymes involved with energy supply and utilization, there was a decrease in activity in fast muscles, more marked in the glycolytic than in the oxidative enzymes. The changes in enzyme activities (given in U/gram wet weight) are smaller than the total changes in view of the loss of total number of muscle fibers, but relatively smaller in the diaphragm (which does not show a decrease in the number of muscle fibers in old age). The changes differ in fast (EDL) and slow soleus muscles and are reflected by changes in enzyme pattern, i.e., the ratio of glycolytic to oxidative enzymes. This ratio decreases markedly in fast muscle, rendering it less able to use substrate anaerobically. The relatively increased capacity for glucose phosphorylation suggests a greater role of glucose oxidation in senescent fast muscle. The ratio of TPDH/HK decreases from about 600 to 200, and similarly changed are the ratios of other glycolytic enzymes to hexokinase (Bass, Gutmann, and Hanzlíková, 1975). The ratio of anaerobic glycolytic/aerobic oxidative enzymes does not change significantly in slow muscle, i.e., the basically aerobic oxidative type of metabolism remains little affected. The decrease in enzyme activities was least marked in the diaphragm (Bass, Gutmann, and Hanzlíková, 1974). Metabolic differences between fast and slow muscles are established during development (Gutmann and Syrový, 1967; Bass, Lusch, and Pette, 1970) and are very marked in adult muscles (Pette and Staudte, 1973). There is a definite trend to a reduction of these differences in old age (Bass, Gutmann, and Hanzlíková, 1975). A loss of differences in glycogen and potassium content between fast and slow muscles was also found in senescent rats (Drahota and Gutmann, 1963). The data are still very incomplete and should be complemented by studies of enzyme changes in different cellular constituents. There is a decrease of pyruvate dehydrogenase and oxygen uptake in mitochondria in senescent muscles (Keul, Doll, and Keppler, 1969) and also in mitochondrial turnover and half life (cf. Rechcigl, 1971).

The decrease in ATP (Ermini and Verzár, 1968; Frubel-Osipova, 1969), ATP/ADP ratio (Ermini et al., 1971), glycogen (Drahota and Gutmann, 1963), and creatinephosphate (CP) (Ermini, 1970) reflects a deficiency in energetics of muscular contraction in old age. This is especially marked in restitution after a work load, for instance, in resynthesis of proteins and glycogen (Drahota and Gutmann, 1962) and CP (Ermini, 1970). Creatinephosphokinase does not decrease, and decreased production of ATP and CP is thought to be due to decreased respiratory activity in senescent muscle (Ermini, 1974). Calcium activated myosin ATPase activity decreases in (fast or mixed) muscles (Syrový

TABLE 1. AGE-RELATED CHANGES OF ENERGY SUPPLY-ENZYME ACTIVITIES IN RAT MUSCLE.[a]

Enzyme	Type of muscle	Compared in months	% change	Change given per unit	Ref.
Triosephosphate dehydrogenase	EDL[a]	3 vs. 28–36	−48	weight	Bass, Gutmann, and Hanzlíková, 1975
	SOL		−38		
	Diaphragm		−49		
Lactate dehydrogenase	EDL	3 vs. 28–36	−41	weight	Bass, Gutmann, and Hanzlíková, 1975
	SOL		ns		Schmukler and Barrows, 1966
	Diaphragm		ns		Singh and Kanungo, 1968
	Thigh	12 vs. 24	−19		
	Gastrocnemius	7 vs. 22	−17		
LDH-isozyme composition		7 vs. 22	no change		Schmukler and Barrows, 1967
Glycerol -3-phosphate dehydrogenase	EDL	3 vs. 28–36	−43	weight	Bass, Gutmann, and Hanzlíková, 1975
	SOL		ns		
	Diaphragm		−46		
Fumarase	Diaphragm	12 vs. 24	−11	protein	Zorzoli, 1968
Hexokinase	EDL	3 vs. 28–36	ns		Bass, Gutmann, and Hanzlíková, 1975
	SOL		−30	weight	
	Diaphragm		ns		
Malate dehydrogenase	EDL	3 vs. 28–36	ns	weight	Bass, Gutmann, and Hanzlíková, 1975
	SOL		−58		
	Diaphragm		ns		
	Thigh	12 vs. 24	ns		Schmukler and Barrows, 1966
MDH -isozyme composition	Thigh	12 vs. 24	no change		Schmukler and Barrows, 1967
Citrate synthetase	EDL	3 vs 28–36	ns		Bass, Gutmann, and Hanzlíková, 1975
	SOL		−35	weight	
	Diaphragm		ns		
	"red"	5 vs. 15–30	−52	protein	Ermini et al., 1971
	"white"		−35		
Aldolase	"red"	5 vs. 15–30	ns	protein	Ermini et al., 1971
	"white"				
Creatine kinase	"red"	10 vs. 25–35	no change	mMP/g	Ermini, 1970
	"white"				

[a]EDL = extensor digitorum longus
 SOL = soleus
 ns = no significant change

and Gutmann, 1970; Gutmann and Syrový, 1974) and so does the Mg^{2+} activated myosin (Rockstein and Brandt, 1962). However, little change in myofibrillar Ca^{2+} activated ATPase activity was reported in the gastrocnemius muscle by Rockstein and Brandt (1962) and by Ermini (1970). In general, age-related disturbances in enzyme activities become much more apparent after exposure of the cells to different stimuli (Finch, 1972; Adelman, 1972). Decrease in ACh synthesis by 40 percent in EDL and soleus muscle (Tuček and Gutmann, 1973) and in the gastrocnemius muscle (Frolkis et al., 1973) in the terminal nerve endings is observed and is apparent even when relating enzyme activity to single muscle fibers (Tuček and

Gutmann, 1973). The decrease in ChE activity (Gutmann and Hanzlíková, 1965; Frolkis, et al., 1973), a postsynaptic enzyme apparently induced by ACh (see Harris, 1974), resembles the age-related decrease of induction capacity of hormones on enzyme activities in other organs (see Adelman, 1972) and cells in tissue cultures (see Cristofalo, 1972).

Histochemical studies give information about changes in different motor units and in different muscles. There is a decrease of glycolytic and oxidative enzymes in fast and slow muscles and a characteristic reduction of the differences of muscle fibers with respect to enzyme activities, resulting in a loss of the mosaic fiber pattern characteristic for almost all muscles. This "dedifferentiation" is also clearly seen with respect to ATPase activity. Fibers with high myosin ATPase activity (Type II) appear to be preferentially affected, especially in the soleus muscle where loss of enzyme activity is coupled with preferential atrophy of Type II muscle fibers (see Gutmann and Hanzlíková, 1972a). The mixed fiber pattern with respect to succinic dehydrogenase, phosphorylase, and ATPase activity is, however, maintained in the diaphragm, where the biochemical changes are also least marked. This is explained by the maintenance of functional activity of this muscle related to respiration. However, the percentage of red fibers (with high SDH activity) decreases with age even in the diaphragm (Liebermann, Maxwell, and Faulkner, 1972). A marked decrease in number and diameter of white fibers and a decrease in number alone of red fibers was found in the tibialis anterior muscle of senescent rats (Tauchi, Yoshika, and Kobayashi, 1971). A different but irregular distribution of oxidative enzyme activities in different muscles of senescent man has also been described (Jennekens, Tomlinson, and Walton, 1971). A characteristic feature of senescent muscle is the "type grouping" of muscle fibers (Bass, Gutmann, and Hanzlíková, 1975), i.e., the appearance of compact fields of muscle fibers with the same enzyme activity, apparently belonging to the same motor neuron. Such type grouping has been described in reinnervated muscle (Karpati and Engel, 1968) and is considered to be due to collateral regenera-

tion and reinnervation of muscle fibers (Kugelberg, Edström, and Abruzzese, 1970). This has been suggested also by the change in innervation pattern of senescent muscle (Gutmann and Hanzlíková, 1965; Tuffery, 1971). There is a marked increase in lysosomal enzymes, especially interstitially, and a marked decline in alkaline phosphatase of endothelial cells, suggesting a decrease in capillarization of senescent muscle (Gutmann and Hanzlíková, 1975b). It is possible to conclude that there is a decline of enzyme activities (differing, however, in different muscles) combined with a general trend toward a loss of metabolic differences of muscles and muscle fibers with different function. The marked change in activities of enzymes involved in neuromuscular control suggests the importance of extrinsic controlling agents. However, the increase of collagenous fibrils, activation of lysosomal enzymes (Gutmann and Hanzlíková, 1975b), and decrease in capillary formation all participate in the decrease of substrate supply. Moreover, it would appear that the enzymes also remain capable of responding to regulatory agents in old age, as reported in studies of other tissues (Finch, 1972; Adelman, 1972). Selective changes in senescent cell activities are apparently directed by selective changes in the pattern of gene activity as in embryogenesis (Davidson, 1971). Such genetic changes could apply both to intra and extracellular mechanisms. A differentiation of these mechanisms and a definition of the failure of intrinsic regulatory systems in senescent muscle is not yet possible.

Physiological Changes in Senescent Muscles

Membrane Characteristics. There is an increase in extracellular components, water, sodium, and chloride (Lowry et al., 1942; Yiengst, Barrows, and Shock, 1959) and a slight decrease in intracellular potassium content (Yiengst, Barrows, and Shock, 1959; Friedman, Sréter, and Friedman, 1963; Frubel-Osipova, 1969; Dubois, 1972). The relative constancy of intracellular constituents is, however, maintained (Joseph, 1966), and no decrease of resting potential in senescent muscle fibers is observed (Gutmann, Hanzlíková, and Vyskočil, 1971). No data on membrane resistance and capacitance of single senescent muscle fibers are available. A knowledge of the type of muscle fiber is important, slow soleus muscle fibers having a higher membrane resistance (Luff and Atwood, 1972).

Neuromuscular Relations

Action potentials of single senescent muscle fibers of rats elicited by stimulation of nerve do not exhibit significant alterations with respect to amplitude, width, or rise time (Gutmann, Hanzlíková, and Vyskočil, 1971). A reduction in the number of functioning motor units (MU) in men over 60 years of age on the basis of electromyographic (EMG) studies has been reported and denervation has been suggested as the underlying mechanism (Brown, 1972; Campbell, McComas, and Petito, 1973). However, the EMG definition of MU is open to criticism since distribution of muscle fibers of a single unit is scattered (see Kugelberg and Edström, 1968) and not confined to compact territories as previously assumed (Buchthal and Rosenfalck, 1973). The small size of the senescent MU makes observations difficult (Brown, 1973). The decrease in size but not in number of motor units (Gutmann and Hanzlíková, 1966) is in agreement with the finding of marked reduction but not with the finding of loss in frequency of spontaneous transmitter release (Figure 6) and of a lack of extrajunctional sensitivity to ACh in single muscle fibers (Gutmann, Hanzlíková, and Vyskočil, 1971). Degenerative changes in elderly subjects (Arnold and Harriman, 1970) and in 34-month-old rats (Steenis and Kroes, 1971) have been described, but exclusion of disease is difficult. The extremely rare degeneration of terminal axons and the reduction of the number of muscle fibers do not apparently result in a decrease in the number of MU. Some disturbances of membrane characteristics and neuromuscular transmission may be expected in single muscle fibers, as evidenced by the loss of normal differences in resistance to tetrodotoxin between junctional and extrajunctional areas (Vyskočil, 1974). However, these disturbances progress very slowly, have a random character in single muscle fibers, and are thus distinct from dener-

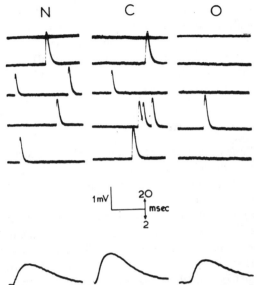

Figure 6. Oscillographic recording of miniature endplate potentials—m.e.p.p.'s—recorded from the muscle fiber at the endplate zone of a 3-month-old normal (N) animal, from a muscle, highly atrophic, of a 3-month-old castrated (C) animal, and from a muscle of a 28-month-old animal (O). Note reduction of spontaneous transmitter release in senescent muscle. Frequency of m.e.p.p.'s (sec^{-1}) was in N: 1.69 ± 0.19 (5931), in C: 1.74 ± 0.13 (6112), and 0.3 ± 0.05 (1880) in O. Numbers in brackets indicate the numbers of evaluated m.e.p.p.'s. Three rats were used in each group. (From Vyskočil, F., and Gutmann, E. 1969. Spontaneous transmitter release from motor nerve endings in muscle fibres of castrated and old animals. *Experientia,* 25, 945–946.)

vation changes. Clinical EMG studies usually involve activities from a number of MU. Duration of the action potential was found to be increased (Peterson and Kugelberg, 1949; Frubel-Osipova, 1969; Sacco, Buchthal, and Rosenfalck, 1962). The amplitudes of individual motor unit action potentials may be increased (Campbell, McComas, and Petito, 1973), and this may indicate an increase of cross-sectional area by a process of collateral regeneration. In general, a decrease of amplitude and an increase in number of polyphasic potentials (but a lack of fibrillation potentials) appear to be typical signs of the EMG in old people (Carlson, Alston, and Feldman, 1964; Frubel-Osipova, 1969). Excitability changes of whole muscle are difficult to interpret. The frequency with which muscles react to stimulation ("lability") was found to be lower in senescent muscles (Titov, 1965; Frubel-Osipova, 1969), and this has been explained by an increase of absolute and relative refractory periods.

Contractile Behavior

Prolongation of contraction time (CT), latency period, and relaxation period by about 13 percent and a decrease of maximal rate of tension development in different fast or mixed senescent muscles have been described repeatedly in the rat (Syrový and Gutmann, 1970; Gutmann, Hanzlíková, and Vyskočil, 1971) and in man (Frubel-Osipova, 1969; Campbell, McComas, and Petito, 1973) and correspond to a decrease of myosin ATPase activity (Syrový and Gutmann, 1970; Gutmann and Syrový, 1974). Fast and slow muscles exhibit a different behavior in old age. A small prolongation of CT was at first found in the slow soleus muscle of the rat (Syrový and Gutmann, 1970; Vyskočil and Gutmann, 1972). However, later studies showed a shortening of CT in most soleus muscles of very old rats corresponding to an increase in myosin-ATPase activity (Gutmann and Syrový, 1974). Peripheral factors (such as contractures) resulting in shortening of CT or even in denervated muscle may be responsible. Moreover, the slow soleus muscle of the rat exhibits a temporary postnatal shortening of CT (Close, 1972) and a process of dedifferentiation in the soleus muscle, regressing to an earlier stage of development, may occur in old age (Gutmann and Hanzlíková, 1976).

Dynamic Work Output of Senescent Muscle

A linear decrease in muscle strength in man beginning by the age of 35 (Welford, 1959) is a dominant feature (Shock, 1961). The decrease in maximal strength, differing in different muscle groups (Ufland, 1933; Norris and Shock, 1960) and in the capacity for continuous exertion, are easily described or recorded in EMG studies (Mitolo, 1968) but difficult to interpret in terms of physiological mechanisms. Complex factors evidently participate. A motivational

decrease in old people may be an important factor, and decline of maximal intensity of work that older people can perform is partly explained by the reduction of maximal capacity of the cardiovascular system to deliver oxygen to the working muscle (Skinner, 1973). Moreover, changes in joints and ligaments (McKeown, 1965) will affect measurements. Complex criteria thus have only a limited value.

The Motor Unit in Old Age

The age-dependent disturbances of motor function are apparently related to changes in the motor unit (MU). The basic characteristics of different voluntary movements will be decided by the number of units acting, the speed of their mobilization, and by the interplay of different MU. The varying functional and metabolic behavior of different (fast and slow) MU has to be considered. Isolated MU have not yet been delineated histochemically in man. The decrease in tetanic tension output of senescent muscle may be explained primarily by the decrease in size and not in number of motor units and is apparently responsible at least to some extent for the decrease in muscle strength. Slow MU appear to be more affected by the aging process, as evidenced by the more marked atrophy (with respect to body weight) of the slow soleus muscle and the more conspicuous ultrastructural findings in this muscle (Hanzlíková and Gutmann, 1975). Fast muscles may, however, be composed of fast-white and fast-red MU with regard to activities of oxidative enzymes. The fast-red muscle fibers and units of the tibialis anterior muscle appear to be less affected by a decrease of diameter of muscle fibers (Tauchi, Yoshika, and Kobayashi, 1971). However, both the single fast and slow MU (see Close, 1972) of the slow soleus muscle of the rat are composed of muscle fibers with high oxidative activity, the fast exhibiting a preferential atrophy (see Gutmann and Hanzlíková, 1972a). The differential response of different MU makes general conclusions difficult. However, a "dedifferentiation" of senescent MU with respect to loss of histochemical differences between different types of muscle fibers, i.e., a change from the mixed to a more uniform fiber type, appears to be a characteristic feature. The progressive prolongation of CT of fast and the often observed shortening of CT of slow muscles show that this trend levels out differences between muscles which differ in function as well as in contractile behavior. The differential changes probably interfere with the smooth flow of continuous motor performance. This may affect interplay of different MU and partly explain the decrease in effectiveness of coordination of activities of muscle groups described in man (Shock and Norris, 1970). A reduced coordination ability has been considered the most likely cause for the deficit of power output in older people. A decreased speed of mobilization, especially of fast MU, may be due to a decrease of velocity of impulse conduction, especially marked in the distal regions of the axon (Campbell, McComas, and Petito, 1973), and a decreased synthesis (Tuček and Gutmann 1973) and release of the transmitter (Gutmann, Hanzlíková, and Vyskočil, 1971). Further factors include a general increase of latency period (probably related to the disorganization of the sarcotubular system) and of relaxation time (probably related to the relative increase of the elastic component). Considerations of changes in the senescent MU can, however, not explain all the motor disturbances in old age. Complex mechanisms at different levels of the nervous system participate in the decline of motor performance (Magladery, 1959; Gutmann and Hanzlíková, 1972b). The increased central synaptic delay from 1.13 msec in adult to 1.86 msec in old rats (Wayner and Emmers, 1958) may be mentioned in relation to segmental levels, while the decrease in motivation for movement is more closely related to suprasegmental levels.

Denervation, Reinnervation, Regeneration, and Compensatory Hypertrophy

Few data are available on changes of senescent muscles during denervation and reinnervation. Both denervation and muscle atrophy in old age are apparently the result of protein degradation exceeding protein synthesis. Denervation atrophy is accompanied by an increased degradation of proteins (Hájek, Gutmann, and Syrový,

1964; Goldberg, 1969), a preferential shift to synthesis of sarcoplasmatic proteins, and a decrease of proteosynthetic capacity of isolated ribosomes (Klemperer, 1972). This is also the case in senescent muscle atrophy. However, there are also considerable differences between the two types of atrophy, as demonstrated by incorporation studies (see Gutmann and Hanzlíková, 1972b). The exact analysis of these differences has not yet been performed. A different reaction to denervation can be observed in muscle of young and senescent animals. In senescent denervated muscles, there is a large decrease of proteins, while the increase in DNA is less pronounced. There is an absolute decrease of RNA content in contrast to the temporary increase of RNA content in denervated muscles of young animals. In denervated muscles of both young and old animals, the increased free amino acid pool (lower in senescent muscles) assists incorporation of amino acids into proteins of denervated muscles. It was concluded that the process of degradation of newly synthesized proteins is more pronounced in denervated senescent muscles (see Gutmann and Hanzlíková, 1972b). Fast muscles of young and old animals always react to denervation with a prolongation of contraction time. However, the slow soleus muscle shows a shortening of contraction time in muscles of young but a prolongation of contraction time in muscles of old animals after denervation (Gutmann and Hanzlíková, 1976).

The process of reinnervation of senescent muscles following nerve interruption demonstrates the marked decrease of proteosynthetic capacity in senescent muscles induced by the regenerating neuron. Recovery of total RNA content and proteins is extremely delayed and deficient (Drahota and Gutmann, 1961). There is no recovery of a normal mosaic (histochemical muscle fiber pattern). Deficiencies in recovery of a normal histochemical fiber spectrum, a considerable type grouping, and a large variety of fiber sizes are all characteristic features of reinnervated senescent muscle, and this is explained by the decline of differentiating capacity of senescent MU. During reinnervation, there is a progressive shortening of CT in fast muscles, the values approaching those found in young animals. However, the senescent slow soleus muscle shows a shortening of CT after its initial prolongation, related to the denervation process. Thus, a differential response with respect to CT is observed in fast and slow muscles both during de and reinnervation. A return to ontogenetically early features, different in fast and slow muscles (Gutmann and Hanzlíková, 1975a) may be operative. This process of regeneration of senescent muscle fibers can be studied in minced and free muscle grafts in which regeneration following degeneration can be observed (Studitsky, 1959). Senescent muscle does regenerate (Gutmann and Hanzlíková, 1975a). However, the degree of recovery is very low with respect to weight and tetanic tension output. CT in regenerated fast muscles remains slow, whereas in grafted muscles of young animals, a change from a slow to a fast muscle can be observed (Carlson and Gutmann, 1972). The histochemical fiber pattern, which in grafts from young animals changes from a uniform to a mixed one, remains more uniform even 60 days after grafting, though recovery of muscle fiber size may proceed relatively successfully. The defect of differentiation capacity is thus seen both in reinnervation and regeneration studies. Intense activation of lysosomal enzymes, especially in the interstitial tissues, results in a very irregular assembly of myofilaments contrasting with the regular assembly in grafted muscles of young animals (Gutmann and Hanzlíková, 1975b). Compensatory hypertrophy in senescent muscle decreases with age (Tomanek and Woo, 1970; Macková and Hník, 1972). No such decrease in capacity of compensatory functions is observed in other organs (for ref. see Hruza, 1972). Compensatory hypertrophy of muscle, observed after extirpation of a muscle of the contralateral side in young animals, does not occur in muscles of 24-month-old animals (Drahota and Gutmann, 1962).

Specific and Nonspecific Changes in Senescent Muscles

Senescent muscle atrophy shows specific features, primarily with respect to neuronal regulation. Neuronal impulse and nonimpulse ("neurotrophic") activities may be distinguished, and

a decline of the trophic function of the neuron is assumed. This disturbance is caused by a decrease in the synthesis of neurotrophic agents and probably by a slowing of axoplasmic transport. The result of this is a slowly progressing disturbance of neuromuscular contact, resulting in a loss of muscle fibers. The random character and the slowness of the process make it difficult to identify the final stage of the event, i.e., disconnection of the neuromuscular contact. Generally there is an absence of ultrastructural evidence of endplate degeneration and of electrophysiological evidence of denervation. Maintenance of the number of motor neurons (at a time at which muscle fiber number decreases) and the marked reduction of spontaneous transmitter release reveal the specific features of senescent muscle atrophy. These features are distinct from denervation atrophy which is characterized by an absence of release of transmitter and of neurotrophic agents, nerve degeneration, and specific membrane and intracellular metabolic changes in muscle (see Gutmann and Hanzlíková 1972a, 1972b). Senescent muscle atrophy is also distinct from disuse atrophy (Figure 6), which is characterized by the lack, or a small reduction, of spontaneous transmitter release (Vyskočil and Gutmann, 1969) and transmitter synthesis (Gutmann, Tuček, and Hanzlíková, 1969) and by lack of electrophysiological evidence of denervation. Axoplasmic transport is closely related to the trophic function of the neuron; however, this trophic control is not confined to transmitter release at postsynaptic receptor sites but also includes trophic substances which may enter the postsynaptic cell (cf. Gutmann, 1964; Guth, 1968). Differentiation of the neurotrophic agents is difficult but will define more exactly the specificity of the senescent muscle change. Many changes in senescent muscle are, however, not specific. Since the speed of contraction is basically regulated by nerve-impulse activity (Gutmann, 1973), its prolongation may be due to disuse or other peripheral factors. The histochemical pattern of muscle fibers is apparently also regulated primarily by impulse activity. For instance, the percentage of red fibers increases with increased impulse activity and decreases with age (Liebermann, Maxwell, and Faulkner, 1972). Neither changes in contraction properties nor "dedifferentiation" of the histochemical fiber pattern needs be a specific senescent muscle change. Many ultrastructural features of senescent muscle can also be considered nonspecific.

FACTORS AFFECTING THE RATE OF CHANGES IN SENESCENT MUSCLES

Effect of Exercise and Disuse

The metabolic responses of the adult organism to intensive and repeated motor activity ("training") have been studied, especially with respect to the dramatic increase in oxygen uptake, cardiac output, pulmonary ventilation, and blood flow. Performance capacity declines with advancing age, and maximal capacity of the cardiovascular system to deliver oxygen to the working muscle is reduced relatively early in the aging process (see Skinner, 1973). However, oxygen supply by the circulatory system does not appear to be the main limiting factor for performance (see Kaijser, 1973), and the importance of a decrease in muscle cell activities themselves is increasingly stressed. Regularly performed endurance exercise results in a twofold increase in the capacity of skeletal muscle for aerobic metabolism (Holloszy, 1967). There is an increase in oxygen uptake of skeletal muscle mitochondria in "trained" rats and a decrease in senescent (> 36-month) rats (Keul, Doll, and Keppler, 1969). Further cellular disturbances are apparent in deficiencies of recovery after a work load, e.g., in low and delayed resynthesis of proteins (Drahota and Gutmann, 1962) and in decreased mobilization of glucose (Jakovlev, Leschkevitsch, Rogozkin, and Tschagovec, 1963), RNA (Krasnova, 1972), and phosphocreatine (Ermini and Verzár, 1968). These findings also indicate the peripheral factors involved in the more marked fatigability of senescent muscles (see Frubel-Osipova, 1969). Stimulation of sympathetic nerve fibers results in restoration of contractility of fatigued muscle. This effect is much less pronounced in senescent muscles (Frolkis, 1970). The functional capacity of

old people with endurance training is certainly higher than in "untrained" people (Karvonen, 1969; Skinner, 1973). General effects of training include the increase of enzyme activities (cf. Keul, Doll, and Kepler, 1969) and smaller fluctuations in cellular (e.g., in decrease and resynthesis of glycogen in muscle) (Gutmann, Sobolová, and Vrbová, 1953) and systemic functions related to a process of more economic functional integration. These training effects are also apparent in old age (see Muravov, 1969), but exercise tolerance declines (Brunner and Meshulam, 1970). It must be remembered that the adaptation effects of the training process are achieved only with a relatively high work load and that they are apparent not so much in resting levels of different activities but in their reactions to increased loads. "Trainability" of old people does therefore decline in old age, and little improvement can be expected if training is started late in life (see Skinner, 1973). On the other hand, disuse resulting in lack of mobilization of adaptive capacities of the organism (Verzár, 1965; Frolkis, 1970) can *a priori* be expected to lead to marked regressive changes in the neuromuscular system. This is also indicated by the less marked senescent changes in muscles continuously activated, e.g., the diaphragm and heart muscle. Disuse affects practically all functions of the organism (cf. Muravov, 1969) and results in general decrease of "fitness," the "hypokinetic disease" (Kraus and Raab, 1961). Domestication of animals is especially connected with a decrease of motor activity, and data on "slower" aging in tissues of wild animals stress the importance of such considerations (see Hruza, 1972).

Nutritional Factors

There are few controlled experiments on the effect of changes in caloric intake on muscle in old age. With respect to the increase of life span in rats with reduced caloric intake (McCay, 1952), such effects might be expected. However, a knowledge of total motor activity would be necessary in experiments concerning effects of reduction of caloric intake on muscle. Inadequate diet in old age may result in changes described as "old age dystrophy" of muscle (Verzár, 1959). These changes cannot be considered as specific for old age and may also be seen in other pathological processes (Adams, 1969). Onset of skeletal muscle degeneration, a condition which rarely appeared in rats before 800 days, was found to be delayed after dietary restriction (Berg and Simms, 1961).

Hormonal Factors

Hormone-dependent changes in muscle may be due to (a) reduced secretion, (b) decreased hormone secretion in response to motor activity, (c) decreased utilization of the hormone, and (d) altered responsiveness of the muscle cell. A number of hormones, especially the somatotropic and thyrotropic, are of great importance in the regulation of protein metabolism during developmental growth, and changes in synthesis of these hormones might be significant in the development of senescent muscle atrophy. As judged from the serum levels of pituitary hormones, which may remain high in old age (McGavack, 1967; Schmidt, 1972), decrease in secretory activity does not seem to be the decisive factor at least at rest. However, different hormones, especially the growth hormone, interact with muscular activity, which is reduced in old age. For instance, reduced secretion of growth hormone (Laron, Doron, and Amikam, 1970) in old age and decreased mobilization of glucose (Jakovlev et al., 1963) in response to exercise in fact imply a diminished output of hormones and might potentiate the decrease of adaptive functions despite increased sensitivity of some organs to hormonal influences with old age (Frolkis, 1970). If decreased secretion is observed, it appears to be derived especially from a decreased utilization of the hormone as a result of the accompanying general atrophy (Gussek, 1972). The changes in senescent muscle are therefore probably not directly related to changes in activity of pituitary hormones. The site of action of the growth hormone is still uncertain. A direct action of androgens on muscle is assumed.

The well-documented decrease of gonadal function and the androgen-dependent atrophy in target muscles deserve special consideration. Metabolic consequences of an age-related reduction in the production of gonadal hormones might be expected, related to a "castration" effect on muscle in old age. The effect of androgens could be direct, mediated through other hormones (Voss, 1973), or indirect, related to change in motor activity. The direct effect of testosterone on proteosynthesis and contractility is marked only in target muscles (e.g., the levator ani of the rat) and also *in vitro* (Burešová and Gutmann, 1971), and consequently, atrophy after castration is marked only in muscles with high receptor specificity (see Kochakian, 1966). Moreover, atrophy due to hormone deficiency exhibits features of "disuse" atrophy and differs from other types of atrophy (Gutmann, 1970). Castration and the administration of testosterone both affect total motor activity as well (Asdell, Doornenbal, and Sperling, 1962) and may result in secondary changes in the synthesis of muscle proteins. Testosterone administration after castration, even in old animals, markedly increases the synthesis of ACh in target muscles and also (though to a much lesser degree) in nontarget muscles (Koštířová, Tuček, Gutmann, and Dupalová, 1974). Therefore, any effects of "senescent castration" resulting in muscle atrophy are secondary rather than primary events in the aging process of muscle. Due to such secondary mechanisms related to change in motor activity, an earlier decline of the speed of contraction in nontarget muscles can also be observed after castration (see Gutmann and Hanzlíková, 1972b).

Type of Muscle

The rate of aging varies in different muscles, e.g., the diaphragm shows late atrophy and the slow soleus muscle early atropy. MU are endowed with specific histochemical features, and their reactivity apparently differs in old age. For instance, specific features such as the preferential atrophy of Type II (with high ATPase activity) muscle fibers in slow muscles and the relatively more marked decrease of activities of glycolytic enzymes in fibers of fast muscles are related to the muscle type. The progressive appearance of scattered and grouped muscle fiber atrophy with respect to size (Rebeiz et al., 1972) reflects changes in single MU, exhibiting common metabolic features. The appearance of lipofuscin is especially seen in the soleus and in extraocular muscles. The latter also show some specific features in a relatively early decrease of number of myofibrils, degeneration of sarcoplasm, and an increasing number of circular myofibrils (see Adams, 1969).

Neural, Myogenic, and Vascular Factors

Differentiation of neural and myogenic factors affecting senescent muscle atrophy is very difficult, as, for example, in comparing "myopathic" and neurogenic disorders. No single criterion permits such delineation (see Hudgson and Pearse, 1969). Degenerative changes are in fact superimposed on a long-lasting denervation process (see Gutmann and Zelená, 1962). The involvement of neural factors in old age is demonstrated by the decrease of mediator synthesis (Tuček and Gutmann, 1973) and release (Gutmann, Hanzlíková, and Vyskočil, 1971), processes which produce denervationlike changes and even loss of muscle fibers but are distinct from denervation and disuse atrophy. It is more difficult to prove involvement of myogenic factors. "Myopathic" or dystrophic features in senescent muscles (see Verzár, 1959) do not demonstrate such factors. It must be remembered that the synthesis and assembly of myofibrils in embryonic muscles proceed at first in the total absence of nerves or hormones (see Fishman, 1970) and that some molecular properties of myosin of embryological and adult muscle may be identical (Sreter, Holtzer, Gergely, and Holtzer, 1972). Moreover some properties of muscle (e.g., hormone sensitivity) are primarily of myogenic nature (Hanzlíková and Gutmann, 1974), and inductive neural factors (changing for instance the fiber pattern of muscle) gradually start operating at later stages of development (see Gutmann and Hanzlíková, 1975a) and are gradually lost in old age. These considerations indicate that we have to expect an interaction of myogenic

mechanisms in senescent muscle, the character of which remains unclear.

Decrease of density of capillaries in senescent muscle has been observed (Pařízková, Eiselt, Šprynarová, and Wachtlová, 1971). Increase in collagen fibrils (Lindner, 1972), changes in the ground substance of connective tissue (Sobel, 1967), including the increased thickness of the basement membrane of capillaries (Kilo, Vogler, and Williamson, 1972) and of muscle fibers at the endplates, and the decrease of noradrenalin (Frolkis et al., 1970) may also result in inadequate transfer of metabolites between capillaries and muscle cell and between neuron and muscle cell. Further research may clarify the interaction of the mechanisms which are involved in this aging process.

Comparative Aspects

Life span in animals differs considerably, but there are apparently no comparative data on "life span" of different muscle cells. Such data on senescent involution, which in fact is terminated by cell death, should be of great interest. Cell death as a programmed event has also been described as a general process in development (Glücksmann, 1951), and a marked resemblance between senescence and development has been assumed by some authors. The timing of developmental involution suggests an intrinsic "death clock" which may actually comprise a (genetically controlled) program of accelerated senescence (Saunders and Fallon, 1966). However, senescent and developmental involution of muscle present different pictures, and different mechanisms may be operative. This is best seen in the differences between developmental and senescent involution in mammalian and insect muscles. In developmental involution, e.g., in involution of the levator ani muscle in female rats or in the intersegmental muscles of the silk moth (Lockshin and Williams, 1965), rapid degeneration occurs. A severe disorganization of all sarcoplasmic elements can be observed, the contractile material loses its characteristic structure as if it were condensed into an amorphous mass, and many lysosomes are found. Especially pronounced is the lysosomal reaction in developmental involution of insect muscles. Lysosomes appear to play an important role in the breakdown process in which the mitochondria particularly are rapidly destroyed. The mechanism of lysis appears to be related to the temporally correlated appearance of lysosomes and disappearance of mitochondria and would suggest a rapid decrease of respiration over 40 hours after ecdysis (Lockshin and Beaulton, 1974). No such dramatic changes are observed in senescent involution, in which rapid loss of neurons or muscle fibers is never seen. In senescent involution of muscles, the changes may be confined to a loss of glycogen and alterations of mitochondria (Johnson and Rowley, 1972). It is of interest that in developmental involution over 4 days in insect muscles, resulting in complete destruction after ecdysis, terminal axons are still intact (Gutmann, Srihari, and Hanzlíková, 1974) even in very old (imago) animals. In senescent involution of mammalian muscle, deficiencies in neuronal protein synthesis and axoplasmic transport are apparent, but terminal axons are still maintained at a time when, due apparently to a progressive disturbance of neuromuscular contact, the muscle fibers have lost their structural integrity. Lack of neural or hormonal agents at certain developmental stages apparently initiates rapid involution and cell death. Once the motor unit is established, its life span is probably limited, and senescent involution proceeds, possibly initially as a nervous system programmed aging process and slowly resulting in disturbance and finally in disconnection of neuromuscular contact. The life spans of neuron and muscle cells thus differ. The process of developmental involution may be affected by hormonal and neuronal influences and may be reversible. For instance, maintenance of the levator ani muscle in female rats (missing in adults) can be ensured, and involution avoided, by androgens. Lysis of muscles undergoing developmental involution in the insect can also be changed by different agents affecting lysosomal activity (Lockshin and Beaulton, 1974). No such reversible changes have been demonstrated in senescent involution. Different mechanisms may therefore be postulated for developmental and senescent involution, the latter apparently dependent on a genetic program of cell death.

REFERENCES

Adams, E. D. 1969. Pathological reactions of the skeletal muscle fiber in man. *In*, J. N. Walton (ed.), *Disorders of Voluntary Muscle*. pp. 143–202. London: J. and A. Churchill.

Adelman, R. C. 1972. Age dependent control of enzyme adaptation. *In*, B. L. Strehler (ed.), *Advances in Gerontological Research*, pp. 1–23. New York: Academic Press.

Allbrook, D. B., Han, M. F., and Hellmuth, A. E. 1971. Population of muscle satellite cells in relation to age and mitotic activity. *Pathology*, **3**, 233–243.

Andrew, W. 1938. The Purkinje cell in man from birth to senility. *Z. Zellforsch.*, **28**, 292–304.

Arendt, A. 1972. Altern des Zentralnervensystems. *In*, *"Altern"*, *Handbuch der allg. Pathol.*, Vol. 6/4, pp. 490–542. Berlin: Springer Verlag.

Arnold, N., and Harriman, D. G. F. 1970. The incidence of abnormality in control human peripheral nerves studied by single axon dissection. *J. Neurol. Neurosurg. Psychiat.*, **33**, 55–61.

Asdell, S. A., Doornenbal, H., and Sperling, G. A. 1962. Sex steroid hormones and voluntary exercise in the rat. *J. Reprod. Fertility*, **3**, 26–32.

Bass, A., Gutmann, E., and Hanzlíková, V. 1975. Biochemical and histochemical changes in energy-supply-enzyme pattern of muscles of the rat during old age. *Gerontologia*, **21**, 31–45.

Bass, A., Lusch, G., and Pette, D. 1970. Postnatal differentiation of the enzyme activity pattern of energy-supplying metabolism in slow (red) and fast (white) muscles of chicken. *Eur. J. Biochem.*, **13**, 289–292.

Beatty, C. H., and Bocek, R. M. 1970. Biochemistry of the red and white muscle. *In*, R. J. Briskey, R. G. Cassens, and B. B. Marsh (eds.), *The Physiology and Biochemistry of Muscle as a Food*, pp. 155–191. Madison, Wisconsin: University of Wisconsin Press.

Berg, B. N. 1956. Muscular dystrophy in aging rats. *J. Geront.*, **11**, 134–139.

Berg, B. N., and Simms, H. S. 1961. Nutrition and longevity in the rat. III. Food restriction beyond 800 days. *J. Nutr.*, **74**, 23–32.

Birren, J. E. 1959. Principles of research on aging. *In*, J. E. Birren (ed.), *Handbook of Aging and the Individual*, pp. 1–42. Chicago: University of Chicago Press.

Breuer, C. D., and Florini, J. R. 1965. Amino acid incorporation into protein by cell-free systems from rat skeletal muscle. IV. Effects of animal age, androgens and anabolic agents on activity of muscle ribosomes. *Biochemistry N. Y.*, **4**, 1544–1549.

Britton, V. J., Sherman, F. G., and Florini, J. R. 1972. Effect of age on RNA synthesis by nuclei and soluble RNA polymerase from liver and muscle of C 57 BL/6J mice. *J. Geront.*, **27**, 188–192.

Brown, W. F., 1972. A method for estimating the number of motor units and the changes in motor unit count with aging. *J. Neurol. Neurosurg. Psychiat.*, **35**, 845–852.

Brown, W. F. 1973. Functional compensation of human motor units in health and disuse. *J. Neurol. Sci.*, **20**, 199–209.

Brunner, D., and Meshulam, N. 1970. Physical fitness of trained elderly people. *In*, D. Brunner and E. Jokl, (eds.), *Physical Activity and Aging*, Medicine and Sport, Vol. 4, pp. 80–88. Basel: S. Karger.

Buchthal, F., and Rosenfalck, P. 1973. On the structure of motor units. *In*, J. E. Desmedt (ed.), *New Developments in EMG and Clinical Neurophysiology*, Vol. 1, pp. 71–85. Basel: S. Karger.

Burešová, M., and Gutmann, E. 1971. Effect of testosterone on protein synthesis and contractility of the levator ani muscle of the rat. *J. Endocrinol.*, **50**, 643–651.

Burke, R., Levine, D. N., Zajac, F. E., Tsairis, P., and Engel, W. K. 1971. Mammalian motor units. Physiological-histological correlation in three types in cat gastrocnemius. *Science*, **174**, 709–712.

Campbell, M. J., McComas, A. J., and Petito, F. 1973. Physiological changes in aging muscles. *J. Neurol. Sci.*, **36**, 174–182.

Carlson, B. M., and Gutmann, E. 1972. Development of contractile properties of minced muscle regenerates in the rat. *Exp. Neurol.*, **36**, 239–249.

Carlson, K. E., Alston, W., and Feldman, J. 1964. Electromyographic study of aging in skeletal muscle. *Am. J. Phys. Med.*, **43**, 141–145.

Close, R. I. 1972. Dynamic properties of mammalian skeletal muscles. *Physiol. Rev.*, **52**, 129–197.

Cowdry, E. V. 1952. *Problems of Ageing*. Baltimore: Williams & Wilkins.

Crain, S. M., and Peterson, E. R. 1974. Development of neural connections in culture. *In*, D. B. Drachman (ed.), Trophic functions of the neuron. *Ann. N. Y. Acad. Sci.*, **228**, 6–34.

Cristofalo, V. J. 1972. Animal cell cultures as a model system for the study of aging. *In*, B. L. Strehler (ed.), *Advances in Gerontological Research*, Vol. 4, 45–79. New York: Academic Press.

Davidson, R. L. 1971. Regulation of differentiation in cell hybrids. *Federation Proc.*, **30**, 926–930.

Drahota, Z., and Gutmann, E. 1961. The influence of age on the course of reinnervation of muscle. *Gerontologia*, **5**, 88–109.

Drahota, Z., and Gutmann, E. 1962. The effect of age on compensatory and "postfunctional hypertrophy" in cross-striated muscle. *Gerontologia*, **6**, 81–90.

Drahota, Z., and Gutmann, E. 1963. Long term regulatory influences of the nervous system on some metabolic differences in muscles of different function. *Physiol. Bohemoslov.*, **12**, 339–348.

Dubois, H. 1972. Water and electrolyte content of human skeletal muscle. Variations with age. *Rev. Franc. Etudes Clin. Biol.*, **17**, 503–513.

Dubowitz, V., Pearse, A. G. E. 1960. A comparative biochemical study of oxidative enzymes and phosphorylase activity in skeletal muscle. *Histochemie*, **2**, 105–117.

Eccles, J. C., Eccles, R. M., and Lundberg, A. 1958. The action potentials of the alpha motoneurones supplying fast and slow muscles. *J. Physiol.*, **142**, 275–291.

Engel, W. K. 1961. Muscle target fibres: A newly recognized sign of denervation. *Nature*, **191**, 389–390.

Engel, W. K. 1962. The essentiality of histo- and cytochemical studies of skeletal muscle in the investigation of neuromuscular disease. *Neurology*, **12**, 778–784.

Ermini, M. 1970. Das Altern der Skelettmuskulatur. *Gerontologia*, **16**, 231–237.

Ermini, M. 1974. Biochemische Aspekte der Skelettmuskelalterung. *In*, D. Platte (ed.), *Experimentelle Gerontologie*. pp. 35–47. Stuttgart: G. Fischer.

Ermini, M., Szelényi, I., Moser, P., and Verzár, F. 1971. The aging of skeletal (striated) muscle by changes of recovery metabolism. *Gerontologia*, **17**, 300–311.

Ermini, M., and Verzár, F. 1968. Decreased restitution of creatin phosphate in white and red skeletal muscles during ageing. *Experientia*, **24**, 902–903.

Finch, C. E. 1972. Enzyme activities, gene function and ageing in mammals. *Exp. Geront.*, **7**, 53–67.

Fishman, D. 1970. The synthesis and assembly of myofibrils in embryonic muscle. *Curr. Top. Dev. Biol.*, **5**, 235–280.

Friedman, S. M., Sréter, F. A., and Friedman, C. L. 1963. The distribution of water, sodium and potassium in the aged rat. A pattern of adrenal preponderance. *Gerontologia*, **7**, 44–52.

Frolkis, V. V. 1970. *Regulation, Adaptation and Aging*. Leningrad: Nauka.

Frolkis, V. V., Bezrukov, V. V., Bogatskaya, L. N., Verkhratsky, N. S., Zamostian, V. P., Sevtchuk, V. G., and Shtchegolova, I. V. 1970. Catecholamines in the metabolism and functions regulation in aging. *Gerontologia*, **16**, 129–140.

Frolkis, V. V., Bezrukov, V. V., Duplenko, I. V., Shtchegolova, I. V., Sevtchuk, V. G., and Verkhratsky, N. S. 1973. Acetylcholine metabolism and cholinergic regulation of functions in aging. *Gerontologia*, **19**, 45–57.

Frubel-Osipova, S. I. 1969. The neuromuscular system (in Russian). *In*, D. F. Chebotarev, N. V. Malkovskij, and V. V. Frolkis (eds.), *The Basis of Gerontology*, pp. 128–139. Moskva: Meditsina.

Fujisawa, K. 1974. Some observations on the skeletal musculature of aged rats. Part 1. Histological aspects. *J. Neurol. Sci.*, **22**, 353–366.

Glücksmann, A. 1951. Cell death in normal vertebrate ontogeny. *Biol. Rev.*, **26**, 59–80.

Goldberg, A. L. 1969. Protein turnover in skeletal muscle. II. Effects of denervation and cortisone on protein catabolism in skeletal muscle. *J. Biol. Chem.*, **244**, 3223-3229.

Goldberg, A. L. 1974. Regulation and importance of intracellular protein degradation. *In*, F. O. Schmitt and F. G. Worden (eds.), *The Neurosciences*, III., pp. 827-834. Cambridge, Massachusetts: MIT Press.

Goldspink, G. 1972. Postembryonic growth and differentiation of striated muscle. *In*, G. H. Bourne (ed.), *The Structure and Function of Muscle*, Vol. 1, pp. 179-236. New York and London: Academic Press.

Griffin, G. E., and Goldspink, G. 1973. The increase in skeletal mass in male and female mice. *Anat. Record*, **117**, 465-469.

Grischko, F. I., and Litovtschenko. S. V. 1964. Physiological characteristics of the neuro-muscular system in people of old age (in Russian). *Fiziol. Zh. Akad. Nauk. Ukr. RSR*, **10**, 31-37.

Gussek, D. J. 1972. Endocrine mechanisms and aging. *In*, B. L. Strehler (ed.), *Advances in Gerontological Research*, Vol. 4, pp. 105-166. New York: Academic Press.

Guth, L. 1968. "Trophic" influences of nerve on muscle. *Physiol. Rev.*, **48**, 645-687.

Gutmann, E. 1964. Neurotrophic relations in the regeneration process. *In*, M. Singer and J. P. Schadé (eds.), *Mechanisms of Neural Regeneration. Progress in Brain Research*, Vol. 13, pp. 72-114. Amsterdam: Elsevier.

Gutmann, E. 1970. Nervous and hormonal mechanisms in the aging process. *Exp. Geront.*, **5**, 357-366.

Gutmann, E. 1973. The multiple regulation of muscle fiber pattern in cross striated muscle. *Nova Acta Leopoldina*, **38**, 193-218.

Gutmann, E., and Hanzlíková, V. 1965. Age changes of motor endplates in muscle fibres of the rat. *Gerontologia*, **11**, 12-24.

Gutmann, E., and Hanzlíková, V. 1966. Motor unit in old age. *Nature*, **209**, 921-922.

Gutmann, E., and Hanzlíková, V. 1972a. Basic mechanisms of aging in the neuromuscular system. *Mech. Age. Dev.*, **1**, 327-349.

Gutmann, E., and Hanzlíková, V. 1972b. *Age Changes in the Neuromuscular System*, pp. 1-195. Bristol, England: Scientechnica.

Gutmann, E., and Hanzlíková, V. 1975a. Denervation, reinnervation and regeneration of senile muscles. *In*, E. Holečková and V. J. Cristofalo (eds.), *Impairment of Cellular Functions During Aging in vivo*. pp. 431-440. New York: Plenum Press.

Gutmann, E., and Hanzlíková, V. 1975b. Lysosomal enzymes in senescent muscles. Unpublished data.

Gutmann, E., and Hanzlíková, V. 1975c. Changes in neuromuscular relationships in aging. *In*, J. M. Ordy and K. R. Brizzee (eds.), *Neurobiology of Aging*, pp. 193-207. New York: Plenum Press.

Gutmann, E., and Hanzlíková, V. 1976. Fast and slow motor units in aging. *Gerontologia*, **22**, 280-300.

Gutmann, E. Hanzlíková, V., and Jakoubek, B. 1968. Changes in the neuromuscular system during old age. *Exp. Geront.*, **3**, 141-146.

Gutmann, E., Hanzlíková, V., and Vyskočil, F. 1971. Age changes in cross striated muscle of the rat. *J. Physiol.*, **219**, 331-343.

Gutmann, E., and Hník, P. 1962. Denervation studies in research of neurotrophic relationships. *In*, E. Gutmann (ed.), *The Denervated Muscle*, pp. 13-56. Prague: Publishing House of the Czechoslovak Academy of Sciences.

Gutmann, E., Melichna, J., and Syrový, I. 1974. Developmental changes in contraction time, myosin properties and fibre pattern of fast and slow skeletal muscles. *Physiol. Bohemoslov.*, **23**, 19-27.

Gutmann, E., Sobolová, G., and Vrbová, G. 1953. Degradation and resynthesis of glycogen in denervated and tenotomized muscle after exercise. *Theorie a praxe těl. vých. a sportu* (in Czech), **1**, 213-220.

Gutmann, E., Srihari, T., and Hanzlíková, V. 1974. Persistance des axons au cours des dernier stades d' involution des muscles du vol chez Acheta domestica. *C. R. Acad. Sci.* (Paris), **279**, 517-573.

Gutmann, E., and Syrový, I. 1967. Metabolic differentiation of the anterior and posterior latissimus dorsi of the chicken during development. *Physiol. Bohemoslov.*, **16**, 232-243.

Gutmann, E., and Syrový, I. 1974. Contraction properties and myosin-ATPase activity of fast and slow senile muscles. *Gerontologia*, **20**, 239-244.

Gutmann, E., Tuček, S., and Hanzlíková, V. 1969. Changes in cholinacetyltransferase and cholinesterase activities in the levator ani muscle of rats following castration. *Physiol. Bohemoslov.*, **18**, 195-203.

Gutmann, E., and Žák, R. 1961. Nervous regulation of nucleic acid level in cross-striated muscle. *Physiol. Bohemoslov.*, **10**, 493-500.

Gutmann, E., and Zelená, J. 1962. Morphological changes in the denervated muscle. *In*, E. Gutmann (ed.), *The Denervated Muscle*, pp. 57-102. Prague: Publishing House of the Czechoslovak Academy of Sciences.

Hahn, H. P. von, 1971. Failures of regulation mechanisms as causes of cellular aging. *In*, B. L. Strehler (ed.), *Advances in Gerontological Research*, Vol. 3, pp. 1-38. New York: Academic Press.

Hájek, I., Gutmann, E., and Syrový, I. 1964. Proteolytic activity in denervated and reinnervated muscle. *Physiol. Bohemoslov.*, **13**, 32-38.

Hájek, I., Gutmann, E., and Syrový, I. 1965. Proteolytic activity in muscles of old animals. *Physiol. Bohemoslov.*, **14**, 481-487.

Haleem, M. A. 1972. Myopathies in elderly. *Gerontol. Clin.*, **14**, 361-377.

Hanzlíková, V., and Gutmann, E. 1974. Absence of androgen-sensitivity in the grafted soleus muscle innervated by the pudendal nerve. *Cell. Tiss. Res.*, **154**, 121-129.

Hanzlíková, V., and Gutmann, E. 1975. Ultrastructural changes in senile muscles. *In*, E. Holecková and V. J. Cristofalo (eds.), *Impairment of Cellular Func-*

tions During Aging in vitro and in vivo, pp. 421–440. New York: Plenum Press.

Harris, A. J. 1974. Inductive functions of the nervous system. *Ann. Rev. Physiol.*, **36**, 251–305.

Hayflick, L. 1970. Aging under glass. *Exp. Geront.*, **5**, 291.

Heywood, S. 1970. Specifity of mRNA binding factor in eukaryotes. *Proc. Nat. Acad. Sci.*, **67**, 1782–1788.

Holloszy, J. O. 1967. Biochemical adaptations in muscle. Effects of exercise on mitochondrial oxygen uptake and respiratory enzyme activity in striated muscle. *J. Biol. Chem.*, **242**, 2278–2284.

Hruza, Z. 1972. Aging of cells and molecules. *In, Handbuch der allg. Pathol.*, VI/4, pp. 83–108. Berlin: Springer Verlag.

Hudgson, P., and Pearse, G. W. 1969. Ultramicroscopic studies of diseased muscle. *In*, J. N. Walton (ed.), *Disorders of Voluntary Muscle*, pp. 277–317. London: Churchill.

Jakovlev, N. N., Leschkevitsch, L. G., Rogozkin, V. A., and Tschagovec, N. P. 1963. Adaptation to intensive muscular activity in adults and old age. *Fiziol. Zh. USSR*, **49**, 1067–1070.

Jennekens, F. G. I., Tomlinson, B. E., and Walton, J. N. 1971. Histochemical aspects of five limb muscles in old age. *J. Neurol. Sci.*, **14**, 259–276.

Johnson, B. G., and Rowley, W. A. 1972. Age related ultrastructural changes in the flight muscle of the mosquito *Culex tarsalis*. *J. Insect Physiol.*, **18**, 2375–2389.

Joseph, N. R. 1966. Intracellular hydration of ions in relation to age. *Gerontologia*, **12**, 155–173.

Kaijser, L. 1973. Oxygen supply as a limiting factor in physical performance. *In*. J. Koul (ed.), *Limiting Factors of Physical Performance*, pp. 145–156. Stuttgart: G. Thieme.

Kanungo, M. S., Koul O., and Reddy, K. R. 1970. Concomitant studies on RNA and protein synthesis in tissues of rats of various ages. *Exp. Geront.*, **5**, 261–269.

Karpati, G., and Engel, K. 1968. Type grouping in skeletal muscle after experimental reinnervation. *Neurology*, **18**, 447–455.

Karvonen, M. J. 1969. The aging endurance athlete. *Proc. 8th Intern. Congr. Geront.*, Washington, D.C., **1**, 40–42.

Katz, B. 1966. *Nerve, Muscle and Synapse*, New York: McGraw-Hill.

Kelly, A. M., and Zacks, S. T. 1969. The histogenesis of rat intercostal muscle. *J. Cell. Biol.*, **57**, 135–153.

Keul, J., Doll, E., and Keppler, D. 1969. *Muskelstoffwechsel*. München: J. A. Barth.

Kilo, C., Vogler, N., and Williamson, J. R. 1972. Muscle capillary basement membrane changes related to aging and to diabetes mellitus. *Diabetes*, **21**, 881–905.

Klemperer, H. G. 1972. Lowered proportion of polysomes and decreased amino acid incorporation by ribosomes from denervated muscle. *FEBS Letters*, **28**, 169–172.

Kochakian, C. D. 1966. Regulation of muscle growth by androgens. *In*, E. J. Briskey, R. G. Cassens, and

J. C. Trautmann (eds.), *The Physiology and Biochemistry of Muscle as a Food*, Vol. 1, pp. 81–112. Madison, Wisconsin: University of Wisconsin Press.

Kostířová, D., Tuček, S., Gutmann, E., and Dupalová, H. 1974. The effect of testosterone on the activities of choline acetyltransferase and cholinesterase in rat levator ani and soleus muscles. *Physiol. Bohemoslov.*, **24**, 63–64.

Krasnova, A. F. 1972. Age related characteristics of the dynamics of the nucleic acid and protein metabolism during and after muscular activity. *Fiziol. Zh. USSR*, **58**, 540–544.

Kraus, B., and Raab, W. 1961. *Hypokinetic Disease*. Springfield, Illinois: Charles C Thomas.

Kugelberg, E., and Edström, L. 1968. Differential histochemical effects of muscle contractions on phosphorylase and glycogen in various types of fibers: Relation to fatigue. *J. Neurol. Neurosurg. Psychiat.*, **31**, 415–423.

Kugelberg, E., Edström, L., and Abruzzese, M. 1970. Mapping of motor units in experimentally reinnervated rat muscle. *J. Neurol. Neurosurg. Psychiat.*, **33**, 319–329.

Laron, Z., Doron, M., and Amikam, B. 1970. Plasma growth hormone in men and women over 70 years of age. *In*, D. Brunner and E. Jokl (eds.), *Physical Activity and Aging*, Medicine and Sport, Vol. 4, pp. 126–131. Basel: S. Karger.

Lentz, T. L. 1974. Neurotrophic regulation at the neuromuscular junction. *In*, D. B. Drachman (ed.), Trophic functions of the neuron. *Ann. N. Y. Acad. Sci.*, **228**, 323–337.

Liebermann, D. A., Maxwell, L. C., and Faulkner, J. A. 1972. Adaptation of guinea pig diaphragm muscle to aging and endurance training. *Am. J. Physiol.*, **222**, 556–560.

Lindner, J. 1972. Altern des Bindegewebes. *In, Handbuch der allgemeinen Pathologie*, Vol. 6/4 "Altern," pp. 245–368. Berlin: Springer Verlag.

Lockshin, R. A., and Beaulton, J. 1974. Programmed cell death, cytochemical evidence for lysosomes during the normal break down of the intersegmental muscles. *J. Ultrastruct. Res.*, **46**, 43–62.

Lockshin, R. A., and Williams, C. M. 1965. Programmed cell death, III. Neural control of the break down of the intrasegmental muscles in saturnid moths. *J. Insect Physiol.*, **11**, 601–610.

Lowry, C. H., Hastings, A. B., Hull, T. Z., and Brown, A. N. 1942. Histochemical changes associated with aging. II. Skeletal and cardiac muscle in the rat. *J. Biol. Chem.*, **143**, 271–280.

Luff, A. R., and Atwood, H. L. 1972. Membrane properties and contraction of single muscle fibers in the mouse. *Am. J. Physiol.*, **222**, 1435–1440.

McCay, C. M. 1952. Chemical aspects and the effect of diet upon aging. *In*, E. V. Cowdry (ed.), *Problems of Aging*. Baltimore: Williams & Wilkins.

McGavack, T. H. 1967. Endocrine ichnography of aging. *In*, L. Gitman (ed.), *Endocrines and Aging*, pp. 36–50. Springfield, Illinois: Charles C Thomas.

McKeown, F. 1965. *Pathology of the Aged*, pp. 1–361. London: Butterworth.

Macková, E., and Hník, P. 1972. Time course of compensatory hypertrophy of slow and fast rat muscles in relation to age. *Physiol. Bohemoslov*, **21**, 9–17.

Magladery, J. W. 1959. Neurophysiology of aging. *In*, J. E. Birren (ed.), *Handbook of Aging and the Individual*, pp. 173–186. Chicago: University Chicago Press.

Miledi, R. 1963. An influence of nerve not mediated by impulses. *In*, E. Gutmann and P. Hník (eds.), *The Effect of Use and Disuse on Neuromuscular Functions*, pp. 35–40. Prague: Publishing House of the Czechoslovak Academy of Sciences.

Miledi, R., and Slater, C. R. 1968. Electrophysiology and electromicroscopy of rat neuromuscular junctions after nerve degeneration. *Proc. Roy. Soc. (London) Ser. B*, **169**, 289–305.

Mitolo, M. 1968. Electromyography on aging. *Gerontologia*, **14**, 54–61.

Moog, F. 1971. The control of enzyme activity in mammals in early development and in old age. *In*, M. Rechcigl and D. C. Washington (eds.), *Enzyme Synthesis and Degradation in Mammalian Systems*, pp. 47–76. Basel: S. Karger.

Muravov, I. V. 1969. Motor activities in old age. (in Russian). *In*, D. F. Chebotarev, I. V. Mankovski, and V. V. Frolkis (eds.), *Basis of Gerontology*, pp. 546–568. Moskva: Meditzina.

Norris, A. H., and Shock, N. W. 1960. Exercise in the adult years—with special reference to the advanced years. *In*, W. R. Johnson (ed.), *Science and Medicine of Exercise and Sports*, Chap. 24, pp. 466–490. New York: Harper.

Orgel, L. R. 1973. Aging of clones of mammalian cells. *Nature*, **243**, 441–445.

Parízková, J., Eiselt, E., Šprynarová, S., and Wachtlová, M. 1971. Body composition, aerobic capacity, and density of muscle capillaries in young and old man. *J. Appl. Physiol.*, **31**, 323–324.

Pelc, S. R. 1965. Renewal of DNA in non-dividing cells and ageing. *Exp. Geront.*, **1**, 215–222.

Pellegrino, C., and Franzini, C. 1963. An electron microscope study of denervation atrophy in red and white skeletal muscle fibres. *J. Cell Biol.*, **17**, 327–349.

Petersen, I., and Kugelberg, E. 1949. Duration and form of action potentials in the normal human muscle. *J. Neurol. Neurosurg. Psychiat.*, **12**, 124–128.

Pette, D., and Staudte, W. 1973. Differences between red and white muscles. *In*, J. Keul (ed.), *Limiting Factors of Physical Performance*, pp. 23–35. Stuttgart: G. Thieme.

Rebeiz, J. J., Moore, M. J., Holden, E. M., and Adams, R. D. 1972. Variations in muscle status with age and systemic diseases. *Acta Neuropathol.* (Berl.), **22**, 127–144.

Rechcigl, M. 1971. Intracellular protein turn over and the role of synthesis and degradation of enzyme levels. *In*, M. Rechcigl (ed.), *Enzyme Synthesis and Degradation in Mammalian Systems*, pp. 236–310. Basel: S. Karger.

Rockstein, M., and Brandt, K. 1961. Changes in phosphorus metabolism of the gastrocnemius muscle in aging white rats. *Proc. Soc. Exp. Med.*, **107**, 377–380.

Rockstein, M., and Brandt, K. 1962. Muscle enzyme activity and changes in weight in ageing white rats. *Nature*, **196**, 142–143.

Rowe, R. W. D. 1969. The effect of senility on skeletal muscles in the mouse. *Exp. Geront.*, **4**, 119–126.

Rubinstein, L. J. 1960. Aging changes in muscle. *In*, G. H. Bourne (ed.), *Structure and Function of Muscle*, Vol. 2, pp. 209–226. New York: Academic Press.

Sacco, G., Buchthal, F., and Rosenfalck, P. 1962. Motor unit potentials at different ages. *Arch. Neurol.* (Chicago), **6**, 366–373.

Saunders, J. W., and Fallon, J. F. 1966. Cell death in morphogenesis. *In*, M. Locke (ed.), *Major Problems in Developmental Biology*, pp. 289–314. New York and London: Academic Press.

Schiaffino, S., and Margreth, A. 1969. Coordinated development of the sarcoplasmic reticulum and T system during postnatal differentiation of rat skeletal muscle. *J. Cell Biol.*, **41**, 855–875.

Schimke, T. R. 1974. Principles underlying the regulation of synthesis and degradation of proteins in animal tissues. *In*, F. O. Schmitt and F. G. Worden (eds.), *The Neurosciences* III, pp. 813–825. Cambridge, Massachusetts: MIT Press.

Schmidt, R. 1972. Das Altern endokriner Drüsen. *In*, "Altern," *Handbuch der allg. Pathologie*, 6/4, pp. 582–652. Berlin: Springer Verlag.

Schmukler, M., and Barrows, C. H. 1966. Age differences in lactic and malic dehydrogenases in the rat. *J. Geront.*, **21**, 109–111.

Schmukler, M., and Barrows, C. H. 1967. Effect of age on dehydrogenase heterogeneity in the rat. *J. Geront.*, **22**, 8–13.

Sherrington, C. S. 1929. Some functional problems attaching to convergence. *Proc. Roy. Soc.* (London) *Ser. B*, **105**, 332–362.

Shock, N. W. 1961. Physiological aspects of aging in man. *Ann. Rev. Physiol.*, **23**, 97–122.

Shock, N. W., and Norris, A. H. 1970. Neuromuscular coordination as a factor in age changes in muscular exercise. *In*, D. Brunner, E. Jokl, and K. Lexington (eds.), *Medicine and Sport*, Vol. 4, pp. 92–99. Basel and New York: S. Karger.

Singh, S. N., and Kanungo, M. S., 1968. Alterations in lactate dehydrogenase of the brain, heart, skeletal muscle and liver of rats of various ages. *J. Biol. Chem.*, **243**, 4526–4529.

Sitte, H. 1967. Morphometrische Untersuchungen an Zellen. *In*, E. R. Weibel and H. Elias (eds.), *Quantitative Methods in Morphology*, pp. 167–198. Berlin: Springer Verlag.

Skinner, J. S. 1973. Age and performance. *In*, J. Keul (ed.), *Limiting factors of skeletal performance*, pp. 271–282. Stuttgart: G. Thieme.

Sobel., H. 1967. Aging of ground substance in connective tissue. *In*, B. L. Strehler (ed.), *Advances in Gerontological Research*, Vol. 2, pp. 205–277. New York and London: Academic Press.

Sreter, P., Holtzer, S., Gergely, J., and Holtzer, H. 1972. Some properties of embryonic myosin. *J. Cell Biol.*, **55**, 586–594.

Srivastava, U. 1969. Polyribosome concentration of mouse skeletal muscle as a function of age. *Arch. Biochem. Biophys.*, **130**, 129–139.

Srivastava, U., and Chaudhary, K. D. 1969. Effect of age on protein and ribonucleic acid metabolism in mouse skeletal muscle. *Can. J. Biochem.*, **47**, 231–235.

Steenis, G., and Kroes, R. 1971. Changes in the nervous system and musculature of old rats. *Vet. Pathol.*, **8**, 320–332.

Strehler, B. L. 1962. *Time, Cells and Aging*. New York and London: Academic Press.

Studitsky, A. N. 1959. *Experimental surgery of muscles* (in Russian). Moskva: Izdat. Adad. Nauk USSR.

Swash, M., and Fox, K. P. 1972. The effect of age on human skeletal muscle. Studies of the morphology and innervation of muscle spindles. *J. Neurol. Sci.*, **16**, 417–432.

Syrový, I., and Gutmann, E. 1970. Changes in speed of contraction and ATPase activity in striated muscle during old age. *Exp. Geront.*, **5**, 31–35.

Tauchi, H., Yoshika, T., and Kobayashi, H. 1971. Age changes of skeletal muscles of rats. *Gerontologia*. **17**, 219–227.

Titov, G. A. 1965. Functional state of the neuromuscular apparatus in response to heavy loads. (In Russian). *In*, D. F. Chebotarev (ed.), *Physical Culture*; *A Source of Longevity*, pp. 226–233. Moscow: Physical Culture Sport Press.

Tomanek, R. J., Taunton, C. A., and Liskop, K. S. 1972. Relationship between age, chronic exercise and connective tissue of the heart. *J. Geront.*, **27**, 33–38.

Tomanek, R. J., and Woo, J. K. 1970. Compensatory hypertrophy of the plantaris muscle in relation to age. *J. Geront.*, **25**, 23–29.

Travis, D. F., and Travis, A. 1972. Ultrastructural changes in the left myocardial cells with age. *J. Ultrastruct. Res.*, **39**, 124–130.

Tuček, S., and Gutmann, E. 1973. Choline acetyltransferase activity in muscles of old rats. *Exp. Neurol.*, **38**, 349–360.

Tuffery, A. R. 1971. Growth and degeneration of motor endplates in normal cat hind limb muscles. *J. Anat.*, **110**, 221–247.

Ufland, J. A. 1933. Einfluss des Lebensalters, des Geschlechts, der Konstitution und des Berufes auf die Kraft verschiedener Muskelgruppen. *Arbeitsphysiologie*, **6**, 653–664.

Verzár, F. 1959. Muscular dystrophy in old age. *Gerontol. Clin.*, **1**, 41.

Verzár, F. 1965. *Experimentelle Alternsforschung*. Stuttgart: Enke.

Voss, H. 1971. Tabelle der absoluten und relativen Muskelspindelzahlen der menschlichen Skelettmuskulatur. *Anat. Anz.*, **129**, 562–572.

Voss, H. E. 1973. Einflüsse der Androgene auf Organe ausserhalb der Genitalsphere und des Endocriniums. *In*, H. E. Voss and G. Oertel (eds.), *Androgene* I, pp. 528–590. Handb. exp. Pharmakol. 35/1. Berlin: Springer Verlag.

Vyskočil, F. 1974. Action potentials of the rat diaphragm and their sensitivity to tetrodotoxin during postnatal development and old age. *Pflügers Arch.*, **352**, 155–163.

Vyskočil, F., and Gutmann, E. 1969. Spontaneous transmitter release from motor nerve endings in muscle fibres of castrated and old animals. *Experientia*, **25**, 945–946.

Vyskočil, F., and Gutmann, E. 1972. Spontaneous transmitter release from nerve endings and contractile properties in the soleus and diaphragm muscles of senile rats. *Experientia*, **28**, 280–281.

Wayner, M. J., and Emmers, R. 1958. Spinal synaptic delay in young and aged rats. *Am. J. Physiol.*, **194**, 403–405.

Welford, A. T. 1959. Psychomotor performance. *In*, J. E. Birren (ed.), *Handbook of Aging and the Individual*, pp. 562–613. Chicago: University of Chicago Press.

Wigglesworth, V. B. 1970. *Insect Hormones*, pp. 1–179. Edinburgh: Oliver & Boyd.

Wulff, V. J., Samis, H. V., and Falzone, J. A. 1967. The metabolism of ribonucleic acid in young and old rodents. *In*, B. L. Strehler (ed.), *Advances in Gerontological Research*, Vol. 2, pp. 37–76. New York and London: Academic Press.

Yiengst, M: J., Barrows, C. H., and Shock, N. W., 1959. Age changes in the chemical composition of muscle and liver in the rat. *J. Geront.*, **14**, 400–404.

Zorzoli, A. 1968. Fumarase activity in mouse tissues during development and aging. *J. Geront.*, **23**, 506–508.

19
AGING OF SKELETAL-DENTAL SYSTEMS AND SUPPORTING TISSUES*

Edgar A. Tonna

New York University Dental Center

With the passage of time, the phenomenon of aging makes its impression felt upon both the skeletal and dental systems. The changes which occur in their component structures and functional variations in response to aging as presently understood is the subject of this chapter.

SKELETAL SYSTEM

General Skeletal Aging

The skeleton must furnish the elements and provide the functions necessary for the sequence of growth, development, remodeling, maintenance, and repair from birth to death of the organism. We often lose sight of the fact that aging is a natural consequence of living and that age changes occur and accumulate with time and affect the functional activity and reparative potentials. These changes are universally progressive, presently irreversible, functionally deleterious, etiologically intrinsic, and possibly multiple in origin. Since their accumulation is initially subtle, they may exert insignificant effects in young organisms. In older individuals, the factor of aging gains in impor-

tance, particularly in consideration of the response to trauma and repair, since occasionally the processes of bone formation and remodeling must be reactivated to meet with emergency demands. This raises the question of the status and magnitude of the reparative potential of bones following the significant accumulation of age changes and skeletal disease processes associated with aging.

Axial and Appendicular Skeleton. Assessment of chronologic age changes involving comparisons between various bones is a highly complex matter, since the baselines for comparisons differ, and this affects many measurements. Clinical data reveal increased incidence of osteoporosis, long bone fractures, vertebral atrophy, and compression fractures in the older segment of the human population. With increasing age, vertebral and rib bone exhibit a marked decrease in the amount of ash (slightly more so in females than males) from a maximum in the 21–30-year-old group to less than 50 percent (vertebra) and 65 percent (rib) in the 81–90-year-old group. A much larger difference exists, however, in the rates of atrophy between male and female femoral cortical thickness. It is marked in the female approaching that rate determined for tra-

*The author's research was supported by grants from NICHD (HD-03677), NIDR (DE-03014), and the U.S. Atomic Energy Commission.

becular bone. The rates of atrophy for both cortical and trabecular bone differ in axial and appendicular skeleton (Bartley and Arnold, 1967). At the iliac crest, cortical and trabecular bone mass decrease significantly with age in women, but not in men (Dequeker, Remans, Franssen, and Waes, 1971). Trotter, Broman, and Peterson (1960) find that the densities of bone decrease with age at a uniform and parallel rate within each sex and race group. In lumbar vertebrae, however, the percentage of the marrow cavity occupied by mineralized bone matrix decreases more rapidly in females than males as a function of age (Bromley, Dockum, Arnold, and Jee, 1966). Increased resorption of bone with aging is generally more obvious in trabecular than cortical areas. In vertebrae, although the number of traverse trabeculae decrease, the vertical struts remain (Atkinson, 1967). Porosity follows a spiral pattern in the femoral cortex, while at the mandible the alveolar cortex, is more porous than the basal region. Collectively, these studies show that the cortical bone of the female atrophies markedly with age while that of the male does not. This could account for the higher incidence of normal fractures in aged females. Although the rate of vertebral atrophy appears to be similar in both sexes, vertebral trabecular bone is less mineralized in females. This may explain the higher incidence of vertebral collapse or compression fracture in the aging female (Bartley and Arnold, 1967). These conclusions are supported by the findings of Bartley, Arnold, Haslam, and Jee (1966) in which a high correlation was found between the crushing strength and reduced ash content of vertebral bone with increasing age.

Resorption of bone throughout the adult skeleton normally occurs in physiologically discrete foci via internal remodeling. The average size of the focus is altered only slightly throughout life (Frost, 1963). The number of resorption foci per unit bone, however, increases significantly with increasing age (Sedlin, Villanueva, and Frost, 1963).

Bone Cell Compartment Aging

Bone tissue (Ham and Harris, 1971) consists of fibrogenic and osteogenic cell compartments, and age changes are recognized in the cells of all compartments.

Within the same organism, the timing of changes with age differs in periosteal and endosteal cells. Endosteal bone cells show consistently higher biochemical activities than periosteal cells of similar type, and age changes appear much later at the endosteum than they do at the periosteum.

Fibrogenic Cells and Matrix. Schubert and Hamerman (1968) state that, in man, "the physical properties and composition of connective tissues appear to change in a very short span of time from birth to about 5 years. From the age of 10 to 30 there is little alteration, and after 40 a further slow progressive change." In addition, age changes which are common to tissue collagen in general are expected to occur at the fibrous periosteum as elsewhere, i.e., changes in fiber diameter, degree of intrafibrillar order of crystallinity, thermal shrinkage behavior, chemically induced swelling, solubility, and metabolism (Gross, 1961). Jackson (1965) has placed a different light on collagen and aging, regarding the coincidental changes as part of the normal growth and developmental requirements necessary to achieve the optimal functional state of supporting tissues. The turnover rate of collagen is very low, except in uterus, cervix, and skin. However, significant variations in this low rate are seen in different tissues, being highest in bone as a consequence of continued skeletal remodeling (Neuberger, Perrone, and Slack, 1951).

Much less data are available on the age changes associated with elastic tissue. Fraying, fragmentation, and changes in staining properties are known for the elastic tissue of skin and blood vessels (Kohn, 1971). Cross-linking components including desmosine, isodesmosine, and lysinonorleucine increase with maturation (Franzblau, Sinex, and Faris, 1966) and possibly with aging of the animal (King, 1957). The relationship of time-associated changes in the elastic tissue of bone is yet to be explored (Murakami, and Emery, 1974). At the ultrastructural level, fragmentation is not observed, as has been reported at the histological level (Tonna, 1974a). This, however, may be due to the limitations of sample thickness of electron microscopic preparations. Microfibrils tend to permeate the entire thickness of the elastin fiber bundle with age, but further study is required. Only exiguous information exists on the synthesis and degradation of elastin. Although histological breakdown of elastin in a variety of tissues is recognized, new synthesis in damaged tissues is yet to be demonstrated (Gross, 1961).

The ground substance also reflects age concomitant changes (Sobel, 1967); however, research has been directed more to its carbohydrate moieties than to the noncollagenous proteins and lipids. The subject of aging and the intercellular matrix of connective tissues is considered in detail in Chapter 9 in this volume. Further reference to this topic will be made in particular association with bone and cartilage matrix.

The ultrastructure of fibroblasts has been reported by Movat and Fernando (1962), Porter (1964), and Ross and Benditt (1961). The cellular complement of the fibrous periosteum in young mice, as in other mammals including man, consists of functionally active fibroblasts separated by large bundles of collagen through which run elastic bundles of smaller dimension. With increasing age, maturation of collagen and elastic tissue is observed. Cells reveal significant age concomitant changes. Ultrastructural changes lead to diminished matrical precursor formation as functional fibroblasts are converted to extensively elongated fibrocytes. In 2-year-old mice, the remaining residual cells are exceedingly small in size and exhibit equally small, compact, hyperchromatic, pyknotic nuclei. Rough endoplasmic reticulum essentially disappears, while the Golgi complex becomes a simplified structure. A thin rim of cytoplasm reveals several mitochondria, often undergoing degeneration, cytoplasmic vacuoles, few free ribosomes, and a reduced number of degenerating cytoplasmic extensions. Age pigment (lipofuscin) makes its appearance at 1 year of age, and more cells reveal pigment granules thereafter (Tonna, 1974a, 1975).

Osteogenic Cells and Matrix. In the short-lived mouse and rat, cellular changes occur rapidly

with increasing age. The number of periosteal osteoblasts diminishes significantly and remains low throughout the animal's life span (Tonna and Pillsbury, 1959). As a consequence, periosteal thickness is reduced (Tonna and Cronkite, 1961c). Diminished mitochondrial numbers, volume, and average surface also occur (Tonna and Pillsbury, 1959). Reduction in activities of respiratory enzymes (Tonna, 1958, 1959) and adenosine triphosphatase (ATPase) (Tonna and Severson, 1971) accompanies mitochondrial changes. These alterations are coincidental with the physiological reduction of skeletal growth and as such represent changes concomitant with aging, but not primary age changes. Alkaline and acid phosphatase activity is marked at the osteogenic layer of the periosteum and is very low at the fibrous layer in animals of all ages. Since the reactions persist in older animals after bone formation diminishes (Tonna, 1958), the capacity for bone formation is retained should reactivation become necessary in response to trauma.

Protein synthesis by aging bone cells has been investigated autoradiographically in the mouse utilizing H^3-histidine (Tonna and Cronkite, 1962c; Tonna, Cronkite, and Pavelec, 1962), H^3-glycine (Tonna, Cronkite, and Pavelec, 1963; Tonna, 1964), and H^3-proline (Tonna, 1965a, 1966a, 1966b, 1971a, 1971b; Tonna and Pavelec, 1971) as precursors. A decrease in incorporation of these precursors into protein is observed and the peak occurs later in aging mice. The initial decrease in activity may be largely attributed to reduced physiologic demands. This is best seen in applied stress studies, such as in femoral fractures. Graphical analyses (Tonna, 1971b) also show significant age concomitant changes by 26 weeks of age, paralleling the histocytomorphological changes alluded to earlier.

The magnitude of protein synthesis by bone cells is reflected in their RNA activity (Burchard, Fontaine, and Mandel, 1959). All bone cells stain positively when using Brachet's method for RNA (Tonna, 1965b, 1966c). Staining increases as precursor cells differentiate into functional osteoblasts and diminishes when osteoblasts are transformed into osteocytes. With increasing age RNA staining decreases. Autoradiographic studies have been conducted on skeletal cells using H^3-cytidine (Young, 1963) and H^3-uridine (Owen, 1967; Singh and Tonna, 1973, 1974) as RNA markers. With increasing age, the maximum incorporation of H^3-uridine decreases.

Protein-bound sulfhydryl (PBSH) and disulfide groups (PBSS) studied in aging skeletal tissues of mice reveal gradually diminishing values (Pavelec, Tonna, and Fand, 1967). PBSH and PBSS groups are abundant in the cytoplasm of skeletal cells (osteoblasts and osteoclasts) involved in bone formation and resorption.

Little is known about the synthesis and degradation of glycosaminoglycans in aging bone matrix. There are many glycosaminoglycans, including several chondroitin sulfates (chondrotin-4-sulfate, chondroitin-6-sulfate), keratosulfate, hyaluronic acid, and neutral mucopolysaccharides which are complexed with proteins forming glycoproteins (Meyer, 1956). In bone, about one-third of the hexosamine consists of chondroitin-4-sulfate and small amounts of hyaluronic acid. The other two-thirds is derived from glycoproteins including sialoprotein (Herring, 1964). In human compact bone, Vajlens (1971) reports that the glycosaminoglycan concentration per weight of collagen is about 0.8 percent to 0.6 percent in older individuals. The chondroitin sulfates isolated from various age groups do not differ in degree of sulfation and molecular size distribution after maturity is attained. Advancing age does not result in significantly altered concentrations in compact bone. Analysis of cancellous bone from vertebral bodies reveals a decrease in total hexosamine content with advancing age (Casuccio, Bertolin, and Falzi, 1962). Data based on total hexosamine content, however, may reflect changes in glycoprotein rather than sulfated glycosaminoglycans. In rat bone epiphysis, S^{35}-sulfate uptake diminishes with increasing age, implying a decrease in sulfated glycosaminoglycan synthesis (Dziewiatkowski, 1954; Tonna and Cronkite, 1959, 1960).

Although there are numerous reports on the ultrastructure of skeletal cells, few articles are available on bone cell aging (Tonna, 1972a, 1972b, 1973a, 1974a, 1975; Tonna and Lampen, 1972). Significant ultrastructural changes occur with increasing age of mouse periosteum (Tonna, 1974a). Age pigment (lipofuscin) appears in residual osteogenic cells and postfunctional osteoblasts at about 52 weeks of age. In very old (104- to 130-week-old) mice, small residual cells exhibit highly pyknotic and hyperchromatic nuclei. The cytoplasm and remaining organelles show extensive degenerative changes with obvious accumulation of large pigment granules. Occasional periosteal cells have a characteristically functional nucleus, centrioles and cytoplasmic organelles exhibiting some level of residual integrity. These cells may account for the retainment of the propensity of the periosteum to respond to trauma despite severe age changes (Tonna, 1965b, 1966c). As such, the "old" periosteum retains its capacity to replenish the functional cell compartment in response to skeletal emergencies throughout the life span of the organism.

Osteocytes. During the active phase of bone growth and development most osteoblasts, become osteocytes, requiring ≈ 6 to 32.4 days in the mouse (Tonna, 1966a). With increasing age and curtailment or cessation of matrix production, osteoblasts remain at the bone surface and subsequently exhibit age changes. Osteocytes are seen to undergo degenerative changes similar to age changes observed in young animals (Jande and Bélanger, 1971, 1973: Tonna, 1972a). Different degrees of necrosis and death are noted in deeply positioned osetocytes in cortical bone, whereas, near-surface cells are observed in various phases of functional activity. With increasing age, aging osteocytes become more numerous. In very old animals extensive cell death occurs and even surface cells are involved in significant age changes. Tonna (1966a) reports that in a light microscopic study, the number of empty lacunae show little increase up to 1 year of age (3.7 percent), whereas a larger number of empty lacunae (31 percent) are observed in 2-year-old mice.

The observed sequential changes which occur during aging indicate that soon after formation of the osteocyte, ultrastructural changes occur signaling a reduction in RNA production, protein synthesis, and Golgi and mitochondrial activity. These alterations lead to reduced cytoplasm and functional activity of the cell. Eventually glycogen, lysosomes, autophagic bodies, and age pigment accumulate (Tonna, 1972a). Vacuolization, necrosis, and cell death occur. Consequently, once an osteoblast becomes an osteocyte, the cell is committed to a one-way path ending in death. Should the lacunae become opened due to osteoclastic activity during bone resorption, contrary to previous assumptions the osteocyte is not freed, but destroyed in the process at all ages (Tonna, 1972b).

Osteoclasts. The skeleton is endowed with specialized syncytial cells called osteoclasts which are responsible for bone (mineral and matrical) removal. These cells, essential to skeletal remodeling, are characteristically large, multinucleated cells, having large numbers of mitochondria and are rich in acid phosphatase (Schajowicz and Cabrini, 1958; Burstone, 1959) and adenosine triphosphatase (Severson, Tonna, and Pavelec, 1967; Tonna and Severson, 1971). At the ultrastructural level the cells exhibit "ruffled borders" (Scott and Pease, 1956). Osteoclasts can appear in large numbers at any age in response to fractures (Tonna, 1960b) and following parathyroid hormone treatment (Heller, McLean, and Bloom, 1950). Consequently, the capacity for osteoclastogenesis is not diminished by aging (Tonna, 1966d). Osteoclasts do not divide, and their origin resides in the fusion of cells of the osteogenic layer (Tonna, 1960a, 1960b; Tonna and Cronkite, 1961a, 1968; Young, 1964). The fate of osteoclasts is, however, uncertain. Degenerating cells are not encountered (Tonna, 1960b). On this basis, it remains possible that such cells may dissociate into precursor cells from which they arise. Studies on rodents show that the size of the osteoclastic population decreases with increasing age (Tonna, 1960a, 1960b, 1966d). Osteoclast formation does not normally occur in adult animals. The turnover of H^3-histidine is diminished with advancing age, and the osteoclasts seen in older animals appear to be "holdovers" from an earlier time period. These cells are not as active metabolically as newly generated cells in old animals following skeletal trauma. Some morphological differences between young and old osteoclasts

also exist (Tonna, 1966d). Such cells appear to be discontiguous with the bone surface unlike the younger cells.

Osteogenic Cell Kinetics and Response to Trauma. Limited information is now available as to the effects of age on skeletal repair and bone cell kinetics (Tonna, 1961, 1965a, 1965b, 1966c, 1967; Tonna and Cronkite, 1962a, 1963, 1964). The proliferative activity of the femoral periosteum of the BNL mouse (in terms of percent labeling with tritiated thymidine) is high at 1 week of age (8.5 percent) but falls significantly to a low level by 8 weeks (0.7 percent), remaining at about (0.5 percent) throughout the animal's life span unless interrupted by trauma. Kinetic values are subject to species' differences, anatomical source, and location variations.

The cellular compartments of the femoral periosteum fall into "fast" and "slow" proliferative categories. The fibrous layer is "slow" while the metaphyseal endosteum is "fast," i.e., in the fast category, cell transit times are shorter through the cell cycle. Specific proliferative levels are dictated by the physiological needs at a given anatomical location and the age of the animal. Transit times for the cell cycle of the osteogenic cells have been estimated for the BNL mouse (Tonna and Cronkite 1962a, 1963), rat (Young, 1962a, 1962b), and rabbit (Owen, 1963, 1970; Owen and MacPherson, 1963). These studies have been performed on young animals, and no report has yet appeared on the cellular kinetics of progressively older skeletal tissues. Such a study is currently in progress in the author's laboratory. Beyond 26 weeks of age, cell proliferative activity is so low that obtaining data for kinetic calculations becomes most difficult. This does not imply that if the femur of older animals is traumatized, the periosteum will be incapable of responding. Studies of femoral fracture (Tonna, 1965b, 1966c, 1967; Tonna and Cronkite, 1961b, 1961c, 1962b) show that despite a decrease in the cell proliferative potential with increasing age and significant morphological and biochemical age changes, osteogenic cells do not lose their ability to respond to trauma; aging does not alter the potential response of skeletal cells, but apparently diminishes mainly the quantitative aspects of the process. Aging does not interrupt or alter the sequence of bone reparative events, although prolongation of the various phases of repair is observed. The organism, therefore, is endowed with a suitable and adequate mechanism for response to skeletal traumatic emergencies throughout its life span. However, the responsibility of fracture repair falls upon the vital progeny of old cells which are reproduced in response to trauma (Tonna, 1967; Tonna and Cronkite, 1962b). Significant uptake of H^3-glycine, an amino acid utilized extensively in matrix production, is exhibited by the progeny of old osteogenic cells, not by the old cells themselves.

Cartilage Cell Compartment Aging

Numerous studies of cartilage obtained from animal and human surgical procedures or postmortem reveal progressive age changes (M. Silberberg and R. Silberberg, 1961). Such changes occur in both weight bearing and non–weight bearing joints, starting as early as 20 or 30 years (Jeffery, 1960).

General Gross and Histologic Changes. The typical translucent, bluish appearance of articular cartilage becomes altered by age 20 to an opaque yellowish structure. By age 30, cracking, fraying, and shredding of the surface are seen. Tears lead to fibrillation of the surface, which exhibits tangential cracks or deep vertical fissures.

Chondrocytes cluster in larger numbers within individual lacunae forming islands of cells especially at the transitional and radial zones. Progressive cell death occurs, forming masses of irregular bodies (M. Silberberg and R. Silberberg, 1961). The depth of the cartilage layers decreases to a point where removal of the calcified zone occurs. Subchondral bone then becomes eburnated as it is rubbed smooth to a highly polished, ivorylike finish. New bone (osteophytes) may be seen to form at the margins. The subchondral bone marrow becomes hyperemic and extravasation of red blood cells and fibrosis occur.

The synovial membrane also exhibits age changes including fibrosis, formation of a villous membrane, and focal accumulation of mononuclear cells. Synovial fluid is more viscous in older subjects as the levels of hyaluronate decrease beyond the fourth decade (Jebens and Monk-Jones, 1959).

At the intervertebral disk, the percentage of water decreases with age (Hansen, 1956). After 30 years in man, progressive degenerative changes occur in the nucleus pulposus affecting both cells and matrix. The number of cells decreases and a loss of metachromatic material occurs. This tissue loses its turgor becoming friable in the oldest age groups. Cartilage age changes, together with the decrease in mineral content and structural strength of bone, result in increased incidence of vertebral atrophy and compression fractures in older individuals.

The entire epiphyseal plate undergoes aging as proliferative and hypertrophic activity declines and closure of the plate occurs. The abundance of matrix formed pushes the cell columns further apart. Various zones of the plate diminish in thickness as cell numbers decrease. Islands made up of cells develop, and eventually cells undergo degenerative age changes. The residual matrix becomes more fibrillar, while the mineralized surfaces of the plate become progressively wider. Ossification encroaches upon the residual islands of cells and cell remnants.

Chondrogenic Cells and Matrix. In aging cartilage, significant morphological changes are known to occur in chondrocytes and in their by-products as reflected in the ground substance. Stidworthy, Masters, and Shetlar (1958) report that in the human the glycosaminoglycan content of costal cartilage decreases with age. While the chondroitin sulfate content decreases continuously from birth to old age, the keratosulfate content increases to a plateau, which appears to be maintained even in senescence (Kaplan and Meyer, 1959). In young costal cartilage, the keratosulfate content is negligible while in aged samples it constitutes more than 50 percent of the total glycosaminoglycans. A striking decrease in hexuronic acid occurs by the third decade and is due primarily to the loss of chondroitin-4-sulfate, since chondroitin-6-sulfate decreases only slightly. Galactosamine or uronic acid measurements show that the chondroitin sulfate at age 85 is about one-sixth of that in the newborn while the glucosamine which reflects keratosulfate increases about fourfold to age 30 and remains constant thereafter (Sobel, 1967). A high ratio of light to heavy fractions of proteoglycans (2.2) is maintained from the newborn to 16 years of age; the ratio is 1.2 at 24 years and diminishes to 0.63 by 63 years of age (Rosenberg, Johnson, and Schubert, 1965). At the articular cartilage of the knee the information is not clear, since Loewi (1953) reported that the hexosamine content was lower at age 5 than at age 40, while Anderson, Ludowieg, Harper, and Engelman (1964) claim to find no change between 10 and 80 years. In studies of rabbit epiphyseal plate, the content of chondroitin-4-sulfate was higher, chondroitin-6-sulfate lower, and karatan sulfate constant in a comparison between young and older samples (Greer, Skinner, Zarins, and Mankin, 1972).

The uptake of (S^{35}) sulfate which essentially reflects chondroitin sulfate, is decreased at the epiphyseal plate of aging rats (Dziewiatkowski, 1954) and at articular and epiphyseal cartilages of aging mice (Tonna and Cronkite, 1960). Most enzymes studied in the articular cartilages of aging guinea pigs show a decline with age (Silberberg, Stamp, Lesker, and Hasler, 1970); Silberberg, Hasler, and Lesker, 1973). Glycolytic enzyme and isocitric dehydrogenase activity change inversely with the tissue DNA content. The activity of individual chondrocytes appears to increase with respect to these enzymes as the cell numbers decline with age. An age-linked rise in myokinase and creatine phosphokinase is, however, observed. In mice, an increase in ATPase activity occurs at the articular cartilage, and a decrease in activity is seen at the epiphyseal plate of older animals (Severson, Tonna, and Pavelec, 1968; Tonna and Severson, 1971).

A series of autoradiographic studies of aging mouse cartilage has been reported in which H^3-histidine, H^3-glycine, and H^3-proline were utilized (Tonna, 1964, 1965a, 1966b, 1971a, 1971b; Tonna and Cronkite, 1962c; Tonna, Cronkite, and Pavelec, 1962, 1963). The total uptake and the rates of uptake and turnover diminish with increasing age, and the peak uptake shifts to later time periods. The shift in peak uptake time is attributed to cellular age

changes. However the absence of the shift in H^3-proline uptake time by old articular cartilage points to the importance of this amino acid in the maintenance of the integrity of the matrix and in the viability of the articular cartilage. It is a reflection of the physiological requirement for normal joint function throughout the life span of the organism despite accumulating age changes in both cells and matrix.

Protein bound sulfhydryl (PBSH) and disulfide (PBSS) groups reveal similar distribution patterns in both mouse articular and epiphyseal plate cartilage cells. PBSS groups are also detected in cartilage matrix. As the demands for growth diminish, the activity of both groups decreases. This level is further reduced with increasing age (Pavelec, Tonna, and Fand, 1967).

The uptake, turnover, and utilization of H^3-uridine have been studied in aging mouse femoral cartilage (Singh and Tonna, 1972; Tonna and Singh, 1973). With increasing age, peak values are significantly reduced and the curves flattened, indicating a decline in the magnitude and rate of uptake.

The ultrastructural details of the life cycle of articular cartilage cells have been reported in the rabbit (Barnett, Cochrane, and Palfrey, 1963) and mouse (Silberberg, Silberberg, and Fier, 1964). In the mouse, dying cells are not commonly observed in growing cartilage but are frequent after cessation of growth. Microscars are observed as replacement of disintegrated cartilage cells. While the production of ground substance by chondrocytes appears to become altered with time, the capacity for matrix precursor production is retained. However in old mice superficial chondrocytes produced a dense matrix containing atypical, short fibrils. The surface matrix exhibits increased vacuolization and blister formation, while nearby cells remain intact.

The accumulation of lipids within cells of progressively older cartilage zones is not considered evidence of degeneration; the lipid pattern is influenced by age (Collins, Ghadially, and Meachim, 1965). The localization and distribution of extracellular lipids in aging cartilage have not been reported.

Chondrogenic Cell Kinetics and Response to Trauma. Cell numbers decrease with increasing age in human articular cartilage (Stockwell, 1967) and epiphyseal plate; however in articular cartilage, growth continues at an extremely slow pace (M. Silberberg and R. Silberberg, 1961). The proliferative rates of articular cartilage are noticeably slower in older organisms, while the initial proliferative activity of the epiphyseal plate is twice as high as that of articular cartilage (Tonna and Cronkite, 1964). The turnover rates for the plate are actually much higher, since the peak labeling is 17.5 percent for articular cartilage and 58 percent for the plate. Within 14 days, the labeling diminishes to 11.13 percent for articular cartilage and to 0.33 percent for the plate, where the labeled cells are eliminated during longitudinal bone growth. In the immature rabbit, the labeling of the knee joint is 0.3 percent following an intraarticular injection of H^3-thymidine, while in the mature animal it is zero (Mankin, 1962, 1963). Of all skeletal tissues studied articular cartilage exhibits the lowest proliferative activity (Tonna, 1965b). In the human adult, mitotic figures are not seen and synthesis of DNA cannot be demonstrated (Mankin, 1964).

A labeling index study of aging mouse cartilage using H^3-thymidine shows a progressive fall in percent labeling with increasing age (Tonna, 1961). No cell cycle kinetics of aging cartilage cells has been reported. Unfortunately, too few studies have been devoted to the effects of age on the repair of cartilage and the significance of the latent growth potential. The degree of success of the limited reparative process is, however, dependent on such factors as depth of the wound, proximity to blood vessels, protection from abrasion, and the age of the animal (Sokoloff, 1969).

Aging and Skeletal Disease Processes

Senile Osteoporosis. The literature of the last three decades is full of contradictory theories as to the cause and treatment of osteoporosis. X-rays show decreasing bone density or radiolucency, especially of the axial skeleton. Frequently there are vertebral fractures and ballooning of the intervertebral disks as a result of bone loss. Increased resorption of bone is always more obvious in trabecular bone than cortical bone. An increased level of bone resorption occurs with advancing age in normal persons. In senile osteoporosis, the level of resorption is often increased above nonosteoporotic individuals of similar age, while new bone formation appears within normal limits. In most cases the level of resorption appears to be a distinguishing feature of osteoporotic bone (Jowsey, 1966). Females are more susceptible than males, accounting for the increased incidence of normal fractures in females. Vertebral atrophy appears to be similar in both sexes, but the female exhibits a lower mineral baseline than the male, possibly accounting for a higher incidence of vertebral collapse and compression fractures in the female (Bartley and Arnold, 1967). A bone loss of 40 percent in women occurs between years 40 and 80 while in men it begins between 55 and 65 years of age (Morgan and Newton-Jones, 1969). Furthermore, these authors report that the rates of bone loss do not increase but remain constant with increasing age. In persons 30–40 years of age, a linear decline at the rate of about 10 percent per decade is seen in women, and one of 5 percent per decade is seen in men. One must bear in mind that the number of histological resorption foci per unit bone increases significantly with increasing age, while the average size of the focus is altered only slightly throughout the life of the individual (Frost, 1963).

Numerous authors suggest that the etiology of senile osteoporosis is related to: lack of exercise, deficiency in lactase, diminished estrogen levels, the inability to adapt to low calcium diets, association with low calcium intake, or a small increase in parathyroid hormone secretion in response to a small decrease in the serum calcium level. Numerous parameters may well be responsible for the disorder. Atkinson (1969) goes so far as to state that "senile osteoporosis, rather than being a degenerative disease of old age, seems to be an extension of a developmental process."

Degenerative Joint Disease. Degenerative joint disease (osteoarthritis) offers a dilemma with respect to aging, since the histologic description of age changes conform to osteoarthritic changes; consequently, the relationship of aging to degenerative joint disease becomes difficult to define. It is not known whether the degenerative changes will always occur with time if the patient lives long enough or whether a particular response of the individual to the altered cartilage is required. In either case, advancing age is a significant factor in degenerative joint disease. Osteoarthritis, exhibiting the morphological characteristics of degenerative joint disease in man, has been recognized in a large variety of animals (Fox, 1939). In a study of the sternoclavicular joints of individuals ranging in age from the first to tenth decades, Silberberg, Frank, Jarrett, and Silberberg (1959) report that age alterations and osteoarthritis appear during the third decade. The incidence and severity of osteoarthritis increases to the age of 80 years, with a striking decrease after 90 years. Males exhibit lesions of greater severity than females, and Negroes appear to be more susceptible than Caucasians. Osteoarthritis occurs in different bones including weight and nonweight bearing types, but degenerative changes are described as occurring in parts of the body which bear the greatest weight and shock (Fox, 1939).

Studies of the joints in man (Sokoloff, 1969) and mouse disclose the early appearance of scattered foci of proliferation, as well as hypertrophy of chondrocytes associated with or followed by degeneration of matrix and cells (Silberberg and Silberberg, 1941). The ultrastructure of aging articular cartilage has been described in the mouse (Silberberg, Silberberg, and Fier, 1964), rabbit (Davies, Barnett, Cochrane, and Palfrey, 1962), and man (Meachim, 1967). Studies of human material from birth to 95 years of age show that a significant reduction of all glycosaminoglycan fractions occurs in osteoarthritic cartilage without change in distribution (Hjertquist and Lemperg, 1972). Matrical alterations may exert profound effects on the integrity of cellular activity and the biomechanical properties of cartilage itself. As a consequence, the dormant growth potential of cartilage cells may be released and the subsequent growth may set off a chain of events which lead to the complex structural lesion of osteoarthritis (Silberberg et al., 1959). A study of humans 4 to 90 years of age (Anderson, et al., 1964) relates osteoarthritis to mechanical stress and not to a generalized deficiency of joint surface matrix.

Osteoarthritis is more frequent in relatives of patients with multiple arthritic involvement than in a comparable unselected population (Kellgren, Lawrence, and Bier, 1963). The onset, incidence, and severity of lesions vary markedly in different strains of mice (Silberberg, 1972; Silberberg and Silberberg, 1941). Hereditary factors can scarcely be minimized. Hormonal influence on cartilage and osteoarthritis also exists (Silberberg and Silberberg, 1964). Nutritional parameters may well be involved in the pathogenesis of osteoarthritis as in the biochemical composition of chondrocyte nutrients or the integrity of the vascular supply. This subject has been inadequately investigated.

Schubert and Hamerman (1968), suggest that high levels of lysosomal enzymes may affect the mechanical properties of joints by reducing the exclusion of large molecules from the synovial fluid. If such enzymes, which could arise from chondrocytes, gain access to cartilage, the degradation of proteoglycans would lead to loss of elasticity, erosion, and degenerative changes. The present discourse emphasizes the fact that numerous factors must be considered under the subject of osteoarthritis. Further studies are necessary to unravel the intimate relationship which exists between age changes and osteoarthritis.

Nutrition. Nutritional studies of bone have largely centered on calcium intake, bone density, and osteoporosis. At all levels of calcium intake animals show some increase in bone density with increasing age. Rats receiving 0.1 percent dietary calcium, however, never achieve the high bone density of those with higher calcium intakes (Williams, Mason, and McDonald, 1964). Nordin (1962) suggests that human adults can adapt to low calcium intake by increased resorption or decreased elimination of calcium. Individuals failing to adapt eventually become osteoporotic. Evidence also exists to suggest that some forms of senile osteoporosis may be due to calcium deficiency (Malm, 1958).

The most serious effects of nutrition are on cartilage and the possible role in the pathogenesis of osteoarthritis. A lifelong consumption of a qualitatively adequate, but quantitatively restricted, diet can decrease the incidence and severity, as well as retard the onset of senile osteoporosis in mice (Silberberg and Silberberg, 1957) and rats (Saxton and Silberberg, 1947). These effects are undoubtedly related to the simultaneous retardation of age changes in cartilage. The ultrastructural response of articular cartilage chondrocytes to fasting and refeeding was studied in mice (Silberberg, Silberberg, and Hasler, 1967). Fasting for 2 to 3 days was sufficient to produce significant ultrastructural changes. Signs of cellular breakdown and degeneration were evident. Fibrillar microscars were also formed. The reverse of these changes occurred shortly after refeeding; however, residual damage to cells and matrix, such as the microscars, were retained as evidence of more permanent damage.

Hormonal Effects. With respect to skeletal aging the effects of hormones are generally those which either enhance or retard the aging process and the associated osteopathies. Somatotropic hormone (STH) exerts its influence on the proliferative cells of the epiphyseal plate and on those of the articular cartilage. Hypophysectomy results in cessation of growth, and cell columns of the epiphyseal plate become shorter than normal, taking on the appearance seen in old rats (Becks, Asling, Simpson, Li, and Evans, 1949). Subsequently, the plate is closed by bone marking the cessation of growth. STH administration results in prompt reactivation of skeletal growth, but increased incidence of degenerative joint disease also occurs (Silberberg and Silberberg, 1957). Thyroid hormone and STH act synergistically in promoting skeletal growth. In the absence of the thyroid, the integrity of articular cartilage of mice is lost (Silberberg and Hasler, 1968). Where STH is essential to stimulate osteogenesis, thyroxine is necessary for growth hormone to stimulate chondrogenesis.

Androgens are necessary for full skeletal growth, and orchiectomy in young animals leads to significant skeletal retardation. In humans there occurs a delay in epiphyseal plate closure. The resulting skeleton is, in general, delicate and sometimes osteoporotic. Aging is retarded and the incidence of degenerative joint disease is decreased in articular carti-

lage (Silberberg, Thomasson, and Silberberg, 1958). Androgen administration hastens skeletal development, causing premature closure of the epiphyses and enhances skeletal aging (Puche and Romano, 1971). Gonadotropins elicit skeletal responses resembling those of androgens, mainly from increased production of androgens.

In the growing skeleton, ovarian deficiency affects both endochondral and intramembranous ossification. Ovarian deficiency in the adult human does not exert noticeable skeletal effects. In rats and mice, osteoporosis is often observed following ovariectomy (Bernick, 1970; Silberberg and Silberberg, 1971); however, in women it is yet to be proven that ovarian deficiency is the cause of postmenopausal osteoporosis. On the other hand, extirpation of the ovaries prior to commencement of menopause may lead to postcastrational osteoporosis. Also, Frost (1961) reports a significant increase in the osteoclastic activity of ribs of postmenopausal women compared with younger women, although bone resorption is not solely dependent on osteoclastic activity. Unequivocal results have been obtained in the treatment of osteoporotic individuals with estrogens and androgens. It would appear from a comparison of the fracture rates in estrogen- and androgen-treated osteoporotic women that androgens do not exert the same beneficial effects as estrogens (Henneman and Wallach, 1975) i.e., estrogens arrest the height loss and improve Roentgenographic changes of the spinal column associated with osteoporosis. The responsible abnormality of osteoporotic bone is now recognized as being increased resorption of bone rather than decreased formation (Riggs, Jowsey, Kelly, Jones, and Maher, 1969). Estrogens decrease bone resorption without affecting formation. Ovariectomy in mice results in delayed onset, decreased incidence, and an attenuated course of osteoarthritis. This, however, may be explained on the basis of the retardation of age changes in articular cartilage (Silberberg, Goto, and Silberberg, 1958). In ovariectomized mice, progesterone administration augments the aging of articular cartilage and promotes the development of senile osteoporosis, counteracting the effects of castration which are known to retard and attenuate these events (Silberberg and Silberberg, 1965).

Adrenocorticotropic hormone (ACTH) elicits metabolic changes which are, by and large, equivalent to those induced by specific adreno-cortical steroids. Cortisone and its analogues significantly affect the rate of bone growth and resorption, with skeletal changes ranging from osteoporosis to metaphyseal sclerosis. Osteo-porosis is induced in rats following cortisone treatment when the rate of bone resorption is increased by maintaining the animals on a cal-cium deficient diet (Storey, 1960). In man, osteoporosis associated with Cushing's syn-drome differs from other types of osteoporoses of diverse etiology. A common feature, how-ever, exists in that bone resorption is increased while the rate of bone formation is variable.

The possibility that calcitonin might be useful in the treatment of osteoporosis has aroused clinical interest. However, there exists sugges-tive evidence that the bone response to calcit-onin may diminish with increasing age, which may reduce its therapeutic value in the treat-ment of skeletal problems associated with the aged (Care and Duncan, 1967). The effects of parathyroid hormone (PTH) deficiency or ad-ministration in progressively older organisms is unexplored; this is also true of calcitonin. More-over, the effect of age *per se* on PTH and cal-citonin levels is unknown at present. Presum-ably data on this key question will be available in the next few years.

For more detailed treatment of the subject the reader is referred to the reviews by Silber-berg and Silberberg (1971) and Tonna (1974b).

DENTAL SYSTEM

Aging of Dental Tissues

The oral tissues undergo remarkable age changes. Attrition of teeth may occur from in-sufficient diet, masticatory habits, or occlusion. Loss of the dentition, usually through perio-dontal disease, leads to alterations and restric-tions in the diet resulting in poor nutrition which in turn may accelerate the aging of oral tissues. Poor nutrition may cause loose dental prostheses and, in turn, traumatic ulceration. At the tissue level, significant age changes occur in the teeth and all parodontal tissues. Such

changes lead to the typical gerodontic problems which include: tissue friability, abnormal taste sensations and stomatodynia (pain in the mouth), excessive bone loss and postmeno-pausal osteoporoses, delayed wound healing, fungal infections, and causalgias. To this list must be included increased incidence of perio-dontal disease, oral cancer, and temporoman-dibular (TM) joint disease.

General Dentition. Most living tissues exhibit the capacity to repair and renew various com-ponents; the dentition of man and some mam-mals are regarded as exceptions. A renewal mechanism of limited capacity, however, does exist for dentin by virtue of secondary dentin formation. With sufficient use, the crowns of teeth undergo attrition. Other mammals, how-ever, possess continuously growing teeth. Non-mammalian vertebrates, in the majority, exhibit the continuous replacement of lost teeth, but it is not known whether the capacity of poly-phyodont species to replace their teeth dimin-ishes with increasing age. Animals in the natural state appear to depend on their dentition for their ultimate survival. Furthermore, the poten-tial length of life for most mammals depends upon the durability of their dentition. The survival of modern man depends little on his dentition. The rate of wear today is so small that his dentition could probably serve for a life span of 200 years (Miles, 1972). A Russian population study shows that the loss of teeth is twice as prevalent in the maxilla than in the mandible (Basiyan, 1966). Attrition is the most conspicuous change with increasing age, in ad-dition to the progressive loss of teeth. The re-sultant total wear in aged individuals differs significantly, since the rates of attrition depend on the consistency and nature of the diet, applied muscular force, variations in eating habits, occlusal pattern, and dental loss.

Enamel. The most striking change in enamel with increasing age is the loss of substance due to attrition. Age changes in enamel are difficult to observe at the microscopic level, and most of the information available today stems from physical and chemical analysis. There are con-flicting reports as to whether the organic matrix of enamel increases, decreases, or remains un-changed with increasing age (Frank, 1950;

Savory and Brudevold, 1959; Stack, 1955). There exists some evidence of addition or change in the organic matrix, since the surface layer of enamel accumulates a brown pigmentation with increasing age and becomes more resistant to decay as the pigment exhibits increased resistance to acids (Bhussry and Bibby, 1957).

With increasing age the permeability of enamel appears to decrease (Blake, 1958). In young dogs, the enamel is not permeable to tetanus toxin, but is permeable to the toxin dissolved in glucose or sucrose. Pulpal preparations from these animals injected into mice produce the symptoms of tetanus (Berggren and Hedström, 1951). Localized accumulation of a variety of elements is known to occur in the superficial layers of older teeth, suggesting a continuous uptake from the oral environment during aging. These include lead, iron, copper, and tin, the latter being related to the presence of amalgam.

Dentin. Dentin is a vital tissue and responds to stimuli as does bone. Reparative dentin is formed in response to stimuli which include mild or extensive attrition, caries, or operative procedures. A number of authors claim from extensive human aging studies that age rather than external irritation is the primary factor inducing formation of reparative dentin (Philippas and Applebaum, 1966, 1967, 1968). Reparative dentin formation is also observed in aging mice whose teeth reveal the absence of caries and obvious stimuli (Tonna, 1973b). Whatever the reason for its formation, odontoblastic processes are probably damaged, but may continue to form dentin or may undergo degeneration. These cells are replaced by undifferentiated pulpal cells. Zach, Topal, and Cohen (1969) were unable to find labeled odontoblasts or observe histodifferentiation of pulpal cells into odontoblasts up to 14 days following cavity preparations in rats. The kinetics of the process by which odontoblasts replace the destroyed cells requires clarification.

In an orderly fashion, there occurs with increasing age a gradual extension of the processes responsible for translucency from the root apex towards the crown, until the entire root may be effected. Miles (1972) concludes

that changes leading to translucency are associated with the ultimate disappearance of odontoblasts. Mild stimuli, such as slow attrition or chronic caries, are believed to result in the formation of translucent or sclerotic dentin. Philippas and Applebaum (1966, 1967, 1968) claim, as in the case of reparative dentin, that transparency occurs during normal aging and is unrelated to attrition, caries, or erosion. The transparency itself appears to represent deposition within the dentinal tubules of mineral salts or calcified organic matrix with the same refractive index as intertubular dentin. The resulting impermeability does not extend to all substances, including bacterial toxins. A study of 126 maxillary molars from individuals to 79 years of age (Witte and Fullmer, 1967) shows a progressive decrease with increasing age of basic dye (azure A, pH 3.31) uptake by dentin. The authors conclude that in the absence of dentin turnover (which is unlike bone), progressive linkages occur with increasing age, reducing the availability of anionic groups associated with glycosaminoglycans.

Dentin can also respond to irritations of greater severity. The odontoblastic processes degenerate and die along the entire length of the dentinal tubules, while the reparative dentin formed seals the pulpal ends. This so-called *dead tract or metamorphosed dentin* is opaque to transmitted light; the empty tubules contain air or gas. The opaque areas become more extensive with age, and this spread is independent of peripheral injuries (Lefkowitz, 1942). It was concluded that dead tract dentin occurs as a progressive age change which follows the general pattern of commencement in the crown and proceeds towards the root apex. The change is seen as secondary to senescent degeneration of odontoblasts.

The fluoride content of dentin increases progressively with age, reaching a peak at about 55 years (Jackson and Wedmann, 1959), while the water content decreases with age (Toto, Kastelic, Duyvejonck, and Rapp, 1971). These phenomena, however, appear to be physical events occurring only concomitantly with aging.

Dental Pulp. The pulpal volume decreases with increasing age with the continued deposition of dentin; however, the pattern of dentin deposition varies among different types of teeth (Seltzer, 1972). By about 71 years, the pulp canal of a number of teeth becomes almost obliterated. Aging also adversely affects the blood vessels of the pulp. As age increases, the vascularity decreases and its overall architecture is reduced. In older teeth, blood vessels become arteriosclerotic and diminish the blood supply to cells of the coronal portion of the pulp (Bernick, 1967a). In man, arteriosclerotic changes occur as early as 40 years of age. Retrogressive changes are also found in the nerves of the teeth, involving calcification and apparent decrease in the number of nerve branches in the coronal pulp with increasing age (Bernick, 1967b).

The cellular composition of the human pulp undergoes marked fluctuations from birth to about 23 years, after which time a steady decrease in cell numbers occurs until at age 70, the number of cells are reduced by 50 percent (Fröhlich, 1970). Possibly, this results as a consequence of reduced circulation. In aging rats decrease in numbers continues to 75 percent of the original values (Pinzon, Kozlov, and Burch, 1967). The kinetics of rat molar pulp cells at various ages has been reported by Pinzon, Toto, and O'Malley (1966). This study also shows a significant decrease in the number of regenerating cells with increasing age.

Fibroblasts show degeneration with increasing age, as characterized by smaller size and number of organelles including the rough endoplasmic reticulum, mitochondria, and the Golgi complex (Han, 1968). Odontoblasts also degenerate with advancing age. Ultrastructural studies reveal an increase in vacuole numbers and gradual degenerative changes leading to the absence of cells over some or all of the pulpal surfaces (Bhussry, 1968).

Matrical changes in the aging pulp lead to fibrosis and increase in argyrophilic reticular fibers and in the number and thickness of collagen fibers (Bhussry, 1968).

Pulpstones (denticles) are often found in teeth which appear to be normal and in both functional and unerupted teeth. They are seen to increase in number and size with advancing age (Orban, 1966). The formation of numerous denticles is also seen following overdoses of vitamin D (Aprile and Aprile, 1947). Diffuse calcification in those teeth which present pulpstones and painful symptoms may be secondary to injury which initially induced pulpstone formation and, eventually, has led to a degeneration and inflammation of the surviving pulp. Nevertheless, advancing age favors their development, and they are more common in older teeth. Hill (1934) reports 66 percent calcifications in the pulps of individuals 10 and 30 years of age, 80 to 82.5 percent in 30 and 50 year olds and 90 percent in individuals over 50 years of age. Bernick (1967b) reports similar findings of 90 percent calcification in the pulps of older teeth. The process first involves the neurilemma and then the nerves themselves.

Aging of Parodontal Tissues

The supporting tissues of the dentition, including cementum, gingiva, periodontal ligament, and alveolar bone, are known as the parodontal tissues.

Cementum. Unlike bone, cementum is not normally resorbed, and upon death of cementocytes during aging, cementoblasts provide a new layer of cementum. This capacity appears to be retained throughout the life span of the organism. A linear relationship between the thickness of cementum and age is reported by Zander and Hürzeler (1958). The rate of cementum formation decreases with age, but the total mass increases to a point of reducing the apical foramen often to the detriment of the pulp (Tonna, 1973b). This process keeps the attachment components intact.

Aging of acellular cementum is not readily discerned microscopically, but cellular cementum exhibits degeneration and death of cementocytes and empty lacunae eventually appear at the light microscopic level. Surface layers of cementum show normal cementocytes residing in lacunae. In the deeper layers, pyknotic, hyperchromatic nuclei can be seen in smaller cells exhibiting increased lacunar space (Gottlieb, 1942). A more recent electron microscopic study of young rat molar cementocytes (Jande and Bélanger, 1970) reveals degenerative changes similar to those observed in aging osteocytes (Tonna, 1973a). Current unpublished ultrastructural studies in the author's laboratory reveal similarities between the aging of cementocytes and osteocytes. Although the death of cementocytes is coincidental with increased age and perhaps occurs in response to the release of physiological demands (Tonna and Pavelec, 1971), reduction in the accessibility to nutritive substances (Miles, 1961) and the clearing of cell waste products may in fact be of primary concern to cell viability, if not an augmenting factor in cellular degeneration.

The deposition of cementum appears to occur in response to functional stress, although relatively thick layers of cementum occur at the roots of unerupted teeth of aged individuals (Miles, 1961). Extensive deposition of cementum (hypercementosis) also occurs. Excementoses or spurs are formed, at times leading to ankylosis with alveolar bone or becoming detached, form cementicles. This is seen in the mouse and is observed to increase with increasing age (Tonna, 1973b).

The labeling indices of the cementum are exceedingly low. A progressive decrease is encountered with increasing age with some terminal rise in very old animals, probably for the same reasons that exist for gingival labeling indices (Stahl, Tonna, and Weiss, 1969; Tonna, Weiss, and Stahl, 1972). Despite the low labeling indices and accumulated aging, proliferative activity can be reactivated following trauma in the oldest animals (Tonna and Stahl, 1974; Tonna, Stahl, and Weiss, 1969).

Gingiva. Variations in the degree of keratinization of the gingiva are generally considered part of the aging process. Unlike skin, with increasing age the gingiva shows reduced keratinization (Courtney, 1972).

Belting, Schour, Weinmann, and Shepro (1953) report on evidence that apical migration of the gingival attachment in the rat correlates with age, but not with the degree or sites of inflammation. Baer and Bernick (1957), in a contrary finding, claim recession to be directly related to the severity of local inflammatory process and not in any way related to age in the mouse. Several observations on various species including the mouse (Tonna, 1973b), in which gingival disease is not as widespread as in man, lend support to the view that gingival recession is associated with aging. This association may well be of a secondary nature. Most probably, gingival insults of one type or another augment the process. Endocrine and systemic nutritional states also affect the process in hamsters, and the rate of epithelial down growth is retarded by the addition of aureomycin to the diet (Rushton, 1955). In either case, detachment of the collagen fibers of the corium from the cementum of the root surface and absence of cementum formation in the region may be due to the penetration of bacterial toxins which invoke chemotaxis, proliferative activity, and dissolution of connective tissue, accounting for epithelial down growth.

The labeling indices of human gingival tissue apparently increase with advancing age (Meyer, Marwah, and Weinmann, 1956). Similar findings are recorded for experimental animals (Hansen, 1966; Stahl, Tonna, and Weiss, 1969; Tonna, Weiss, and Stahl, 1972). The increased proliferative activity of noncontinuously erupting teeth in man and experimental animals is believed to reflect the demands for continued repair resulting from the action of local injurious agents. Some degree of gingivitis is common to gingival tissues. In humans, periodontal disease becomes more prevalent with increasing age (Waerhaug, 1966). Subcrevicular inflammations are also known to increase significantly with age in the mouse (Tonna, 1972c). Katzberg (1952) believes that elevated indices may relate to an increased rate of cellular desquamation with age. The proliferative response of gingival tissue to trauma remains high with increasing age (Tonna and Stahl, 1974; Tonna, Stahl, and Weiss, 1969).

Another gingival change attributed to aging is the loss of the characteristic pattern of stippling (Greene, 1962). The absence or reduced stippling in the aged is significant, since it serves as a useful diagnostic criterion for periodontal disease.

Periodontal Ligament. The thickness of the periodontal ligament decreases in the aged and loses the regular arrangement of the principal fibers (Coolidge, 1937). Furthermore, the thickness of the ligament is greater in functional teeth than in unerupted teeth in the aged and teeth which have lost their occlusion. Mice also show a marked decrease in ligament thickness with increasing age, facilitating ankylosis (Tonna, 1973b). The loss of thickness is claimed to reflect a change in dietary habits due to premature loss of teeth, or decreased ability to adequately masticate coarser foods in the aged, rather than a physiologic aging process (Courtney, 1972). The findings in mice cannot be explained by these hypotheses.

Cementicles are sometimes found in the periodontal ligament, especially, in older individuals and in aging mice (Tonna, 1973b). Increased fibrosis and decreased cellularity of the periodontal connective tissue also occurs with increasing age, including arteriosclerosis (Grant and Bernick, 1972).

Both the cell numbers and labeling indices are found to decrease with aging of the periodontal ligament in H^3-thymidine studies using large populations of mice and rats (Stahl, Tonna, and Weiss, 1969; Tonna, Weiss, and Stahl, 1972). Some rise in labeling is observed in very old animals in response to increased incidence of inflammatory disease (Tonna, 1972c). However, the periodontal ligament remains capable of responding to trauma, even in old animals, by exhibiting a formidable increase in labeling indices (Tonna and Stahl, 1974). Similar results are reported in response to pulpal injuries in rats of different age (Stahl, Weiss, and Tonna, 1961; Stahl, Tonna, and Weiss, 1970c).

Alveolar Bone. With advancing age alveolar bone resorption (senile atrophy) occurs; this may be related to gingival recession (Gottlieb and Orban, 1938). A study of 123 clinically healthy subjects 11 to 70 years of age reveals statistically significant alveolar bone resorption but insignificant crest height reduction with age (Dean Boyle, Via, and McFall, 1973). The existence of the alveolar process is believed to be dependent upon the presence of teeth, since loss of the dentition is followed by a gradual resorption (Miles, 1961). Alveolar process resorption, however, may occur with-

out the former loss of teeth. The mouse reveals extensive resorption of the alveolar crest with increasing age and no tooth loss (Tonna, 1973b). It appears more probable that tooth loss, inflammatory processes, and other perturbations augment the process, as tooth loss augments mandibular osteoporosis.

Cellular proliferative activity diminishes in the rat and mouse to very low levels with increasing age (Stahl, Tonna, and Weiss, 1969; Tonna, Weiss, and Stahl, 1972). At about 52 weeks in the rat and 78 weeks in the mouse, crestal labeling indices become significantly elevated. The presence of inflammation is believed to account for the elevated response. Alveolar bone is unique in that an adjacent inflammatory process of one magnitude or another is usually present (Tonna, 1972c). Furthermore, species differences exist; the proliferative activity of rat bone is higher than that of the mouse at all ages. In response to gingival injury, reactivation of cell proliferation occurs at all ages (Tonna and Stahl, 1974; Tonna, Stahl, and Weiss, 1969).

Aging of the Maxilla, Mandible, and Temporomandibular Joint

Maxilla and Mandible. During the course of mandibular growth, the angle between the horizontal and vertical rami, which in the newborn is obtuse, becomes almost a right angle as in adults. In senescence, the angle again becomes obtuse; such mandibles are, however, edentulous. This alteration was thought to result mainly from long term absence of teeth than from aging *per se* or senile osteoporosis (Keen, 1945). A recent study denies this claim and demonstrates that the mandibular angle maintains a stable configuration from adulthood to old age regardless of the edental status (Israel, 1973). Rogers, Johnson, and Burzynski (1964) find no discernible changes in aging guinea pig maxillary and mandibular bone.

Temporomandibular Joint. A study of the temporomandibular joint of 100 subjects of both sexes, 18 to 67 years of age, shows that the remodeling increases rapidly between the ages of 18 and 25, after which age has no significant influence (Mongini, 1972). This finding is difficult to accept in view of the fact that degenerative changes comparable to osteoarthritis are known to occur at the mandibular condyle during aging (Bauer, 1941). Joint changes are correlated with increasing age, and they become more pronounced with the loss of the posterior dentition. Calcific nodules are not uncommon in the articular joint surfaces of old individuals. The mandibular condyle becomes reduced in size and the articular surfaces become flattened with advancing age (Vaughn, 1943). Occlusal abnormality, either due to tooth loss or mandibular changes with age, undoubtedly results in transmission of stress through the joint and leads to disturbances in joint function. It is entirely possible that the temporomandibular joint changes result from the cumulative effects of stress and trauma rather than from aging (Miles, 1961). On the other hand, cellular changes associated with the aging of joints are also known (M. Silberberg and R. Silberberg, 1961); it is reasonable to assume that altered joint function will be augmented by age changes, and in turn joint stress and trauma will contribute to cellular degeneration augmenting the effects of aging.

Aging of the Oral Mucosa, Tongue and Salivary Glands

Oral Mucosa and Tongue. The oral cavity is lined by a mucous membrane which includes the specialized mucosa covering the tongue. The morphologic structure of the membrane is highly variable depending upon the function at defined sites and the mechanical influences which are involved. Although the gingiva is part of the oral mucosa, it has been discussed earlier under the heading parodontal tissues. The clinical age changes of the oral mucosa include a loss of elasticity, a tendency to undergo hyperkeratosis, and delayed repair; the membrane is thin, relatively dry, and easily abraded. Microscopically, one observes atrophy of the surface epithelium and degenerative changes in the underlying connective tissue (McCarthy and Shklar, 1961). Nodular varicose enlargement of superficial veins under the

surface of the tongue called "caviar" tongue are a common finding (Kocsard, Ofner, and D'Abrera, 1970a). Numerous large Fordyce spots (sebaceous glands) are seen on the cheeks of old individuals; these tend to increase in number with age (Miles, 1963). Although the angiokeratoma of Fordyce, caviar tongue, venous lake, and senile angioma are common in persons over 70 years of age, they need not be considered a primary cause. Instead, they probably result from diminished tissue support of venous vessels and increased venous pressure (Kocsard, Ofner, and D'Abrera, 1970b). Shklar (1966) reports that polysaccharides of human oral mucosa increase with age. This change appears to represent degenerative alterations of the mucosa. Mast cell numbers increase with age, but the cause is unknown. The cause of mucosal atrophy cannot be established, but a correlation with decreased vascularity may be postulated. A decrease in steroid hormones and diminished salivary secretion in advanced age may also be contributing factors to age alterations.

Pedreira (1951) reports that in old age a decrease in keratinization occurs in various parts of the oral mucosa of males 60 to 80 years of age. Montgomery (1951), on the other hand, finds no significant differences with age.

Cellular kinetic studies of rat oral mucosa show a decrease in the rate of tissue proliferation in the initial stages of life, thereafter remaining virtually constant (Lavelle, 1968). Hermel, Schönwetter, and Samueloff (1970) find no difference in the sensitivity to salty taste, but a decreased sensitivity to sweet, sour, and bitter taste in the older age group. Arey, Tremain, and Monzingo (1935) report that children have an average of 248 taste buds per circumvallate papilla; the elderly (74 to 85 years) exhibit only an average of 88 buds. More than half of the buds of the elderly are atrophied. Furthermore, the loss of filiform papillae from the dorsum of the tongue leads in severe instances to a smooth glazed surface. This condition is known to occur in a variety of systemic disorders, iron and vitamin (especially riboflavin) deficiencies, etc. Therapeutic failures are usually seen in the elderly, and this is believed due to the inability of the papillae to regenerate after a long period of atrophy. A decrease in the number of taste nerve endings also occurs with increasing age, with some acceleration especially beyond 60 years of age (Rollin, 1973).

Salivary Glands and Salivary Secretion. The salivary glands, in addition to producing saliva, play a role in iodine metabolism, store a nerve growth stimulating factor, and secrete parotin, a hormonelike substance which lowers the serum calcium level, increases P^{32} uptake, and enhances the calcification of teeth and bones when administered to rabbits. Thus, the salivary glands not only affect the oral cavity but exert systemic effects as well. The role of salivary factors on dental caries, calculus formation, and the oral microflora contributing to periodontal disease has yet to be studied under well-controlled experimental conditions. A minimal effort has been made on the effects of age-altered glands on the oral biology of the aged. Church (1955) shows that in the salivary glands of aging rats, there occurs an increase in the number of oncocytes and marked nuclear changes. The duct cells also exhibit small, pyknotic nuclei. Lymphocytic infiltration and obstruction of gland lumina is a common feature. The parotid glands also show fatty degeneration of the parenchyma. A high proportion of the parotid gland of aged human subjects shows fatty changes and fibrosis (Bauer, 1950).

The rat submandibular gland exhibits decreased RNA but no significant change in the concentration of DNA with age (Bogart, 1967). Adelman, Stein, Roth, and Englander (1972) find a reduced magnitude of isoproterenol-induced DNA synthesis in rat salivary glands with increasing age. Burzynski (1971) reports that the glycoprotein-bound hexose: protein nitrogen ratio is significantly decreased in the submaxillary glands of aging guinea pigs. A significant decrease in salivary amylase is also seen in subjects over the age of 60 (Meyer, Spier, and Neuwelt, 1940). Brawley (1935), finds no age change in the pH of saliva. The inorganic phosphorus content, however, increases slightly with increasing age (Wainwright, 1943).

Aging and Dental Disease Processes

Osteoporosis. As in aging skeletal structures elsewhere, senile osteoporosis is also observed in association with dental bone, e.g., the mandible and the maxilla. Osteoporotic changes in the mandible increase with age, affecting some areas more than others as judged by variations in mineral density (Manson and Lucas, 1962). Shortly after maturity, the jaw begins to show signs of involution, initially appearing in regions defined by Enlow and Harris (1964) as sites of resorption during growth. Resorption which contributes to the remodeling of the jaw during growth persists, becoming more extensive with age. The osteoporotic process which is recognized with increasing age is not dependent upon the presence or absence of teeth for its inception, while such changes appear to be a major cause of tooth loss in the adult rather than the result of it (Atkinson and Woodhead, 1968). Histologically, the resorption of mouse alveolar bone does not appear to result from osteoporotic changes or to be related to senile osteoporosis (Tonna, 1972c).

Periodontal Disease. One of the most common chronic diseases of mankind is periodontal disease. In the United States alone, approximately 74 percent of the adult population 18 to 79 years of age exhibits some degree of this disease (National Center for Health Statistics, 1960-1962). However, the specific causes of the disease are still unknown. Inflammation is, however, an essential component (Stallard, Orban, and Hove, 1970). A variety of local and systemic factors are believed to influence the incidence and severity of the disease including: nutritional status, generalized infections, oral health and hygiene, host resistance, immunologic activity, ionizing radiation, hormones, bacterial endotoxins, aging, and other factors. The same observation has been made in a number of laboratory animals (Miles, 1961; Stahl, Tonna, and Weiss, 1969; Tonna, Weiss, and Stahl, 1972). Periodontal disease encountered in young persons implies that aging is not essential to the etiology of the disease; several combined factors can initiate the condition. On the other hand, one cannot disregard the significant increase in incidence and severity of the disease with increasing age (Waerhaug, 1966). Aging, an endogenous factor coupled with cofactors, e.g., reduced tissue resistance to bacterial infection, malnutrition, etc., may well explain the induction of periodontal disease. To this must be added the underlying genetic constitution of the organism which appears to set the range of susceptibility to the disease. The magnitude of this parameter and the degree of its importance to the etiology of this disease is unknown. In a recent human study, Hansen (1973) reports evidence in favor of the hypothesis that individuals showing a greater degree of biological aging, in respect to their chronologic age, would also show a greater severity of certain oral variables than those individuals appearing biologically younger.

Dental Caries. Numerous factors influence the occurrence of dental caries in humans (Scherp, 1971). The age-specific prevalence of dental caries by tooth type can be described by a family of curves rising with increasing age. This relationship is analogous to the law of radioactive decay, describing the probability of occurrence of random events (Burch and Jackson, 1966a). Whereas the proportion of people in the population with maxillary incisor caries increases with age, the mean number of affected sites or teeth per person remains constant from 17 years onwards (Jackson and Burch, 1969). In an extensive study of 36,235 permanent maxillary incisors of individuals 11 to over 60 years of age, Jackson and Burch (1970) report the existence of caries-vulnerable and caries-resistant sites which appear to be qualitative in kind. These studies strongly refute the acidogenic theory of dental caries formation. All the ingredients for acid production, i.e., saliva, bacteria, and fermentable carbohydrates, are present on the tooth surface in most if not all mouths of individuals; nevertheless, not all teeth or given tooth sites develop decay. This is not to deny the importance of acid in tooth decay, but other factors significant in the etiology of dental caries are involved. The complex process which culminates in dental caries is initiated by one or more independent random events, where the number of events (n) depends on the site and tooth type. The value n is unity for the first lesions in permanent molars, maxillary premolars, maxillary incisors, and mandibular premolars; it is 2 for canines and 3 for mandibular incisors (Burch and Jackson, 1966b). The anatomical sites of lesions on teeth are, however, highly nonrandom. Most attacks on permanent maxillary incisor teeth affect particular sites. Furthermore, when homologous pairs (right-left) teeth are examined for the prevalence of asymmetrical tooth decay versus symmetrical decay involving both members of a pair, it is found that the asymmetrical/symmetrical ratio falls from 5.6 at 11 to 12 years of age, to approximately 2 at 30 to 34 years, then remains nearly constant to at least 65 years of age (Jackson and Burch, 1970). These outstanding studies lead the authors to conclude that given the appropriate genetic predisposition, the age distributions show that caries involvement is initiated by a single random event with a constant average rate of 0.054/year; it is suggested that this event is a special form of somatic gene mutation in a central growth-control stem cell, the target cells in dental caries being the odontoblasts. The dysfunction of a particular set or sets of damaged odontoblasts leads to the precarious degeneration of specific parts of the protein matrix of the tooth (Little, 1962). Damaged odontoblasts probably fail to maintain the integrity of the protein matrix in the enamel and dentin. The denuded crystallites of the tooth are then rendered vulnerable to the action factors, e.g., acids, chelating agents, bacterial enzymes, etc.

Malnutrition. Nutrition is related to oral health through the numerous metabolic pathways responsible for the development and maintenance of the various oral structures. The susceptibility to disease is dependent to a varying extent upon these pathways. Nutrition is also related to oral health by setting the oral environment surrounding the teeth and supporting tissues in which microbial agents abound. Research involving human subjects and experimental animals demonstrates the intimate relationship between the choice and composition of the diet, dental caries, and periodontal disease. Each exhibit a complex etiology involving microbial agents and host susceptibility to the disease processes and the oral environment.

Oral tissues reflect nutritional deficiencies more readily than other tissues, probably because of the greater mechanical, chemical, and thermal stresses imposed on them. Pre-eruptive effects of diet have been demonstrated on the histologic structure, chemical composition, gross morphology, tooth size, eruption time, and caries susceptibility (Shaw, 1970). Studies involving the proliferative response of injured parodontal tissues of rats maintained on a low-protein diet show lower rates in noninjured, low protein fed rats, than in noninjured controls. This lower baseline does not appear to be significant to the repair of injury in young animals (Stahl, Tonna, and Weiss, 1970a), but some effect is observed in the older age group (Stahl, Tonna, and Weiss, 1970b). The data suggest that aging and malnutrition may reduce the compensatory response to injury after the initial peaks of repair activity are completed.

It is unfortunate that to date little attention has been directed to the effects of malnutrition on the oral biology of the aged segment of the human population and experimental animals, since the results of general or specific malnutrition involving deficiencies in vitamins, minerals, carbohydrates, or proteins directed to preeruptive teeth and young subjects differ significantly from the results anticipated in older subjects. In the latter, the processes of eruption, growth, and development are not involved. On the other hand, age changes are concomitant with increased susceptibility to oral disease, trauma, microbial infections, reduced rate of tissue reparability, and increased incidence of systemic disturbances. The special oral-dental problems of the aged are complex by virtue of these and other parameters alluded to earlier. Malnutrition is seen to be an additional and significant stressing factor added to the battery of existing stressors, resulting in further augmentation of the general degenerative condition experienced with aging.

Oral Cancer. Although many classical types of neoplasias found in the various tissues of the body may be seen in tissues of the oral cavity, few appear concomitant with aging. Ameloblastoma (adamantinoma), a locally invasive, highly destructive tumor of the lower jaws which occurs most often in the mandible in the region of the molars and ramus, exhibits an incidence which spans the ages of 6 months to 73 years of age, the average age being the fourth decade (Glickman, 1967). Oral malignancies comprise approximately 5 percent of all malignant disease, having an annual incidence of 23,000 new cases and 5,000 deaths. About 90 percent of the oral malignancies are squamous cell carcinomas. Irritation from jagged edges of carious teeth, poorly fitting prosthetic devices, and chemical and thermal stimulation from tobacco and trauma are common to the oral cavity, and much conjecture has been raised as to the significance of these parameters in the induction of oral cancer (Glickman, 1967). Renstrup, Smulow, and Glickman (1962) show that chronic irritation hastens the onset of clinically induced malignancy in a study of the hamster cheek pouch. Carcinoma of the lower lip, generally appears at the age of 50 and exhibits a significantly higher frequence in the male of approximately 90 percent. Carcinoma of the tongue is seen most frequently in males in the fifth and sixth decade. Tumors of salivary gland origin also occur, mixed tumors (pleomorphic adenomas) being the most frequent tumor encountered. The parotid gland is a common site; the submaxillary gland is occasionally involved. Mixed tumors are found less frequently elsewhere. These epithelial tumors are believed to be derived from duct cells or from embryonic cells involved in the formation of salivary glands. They occur at any age, but the incidence is higher in the second to fourth decade. Another malignancy of salivary gland origin is papillary cystadenoma lymphomatosum (Warthin's tumor). This is a benign, uncommon tumor which generally occurs in the vicinity of the parotid gland. It is seen more frequently in males in the fifth and sixth decade. Thompson and Bryant (1950) believe that the tumors arise from cellular proliferation of parotid duct epithelium accompanied by accumulations of lymphoid tissue.

SUMMARY

Due to the severe restriction in length of the manuscript, the subheadings under the subject of aging of skeletal-dental systems and associated tissues are covered only in brief detail. In an attempt to include the numerous contents without leaving out significant areas, the writing is necessarily telegraphic. In addition, many excellent references are not included. The literature on the subject matter as a whole is at best exiguous, with too many areas exhibiting little clinical experimental attention or follow-up. This is truly unfortunate, since a number of tissue changes which are recognized as "normal" to aging in reality represent widely occurring diseases whose incidence and severity increase with age, namely: senile osteoporosis, degenerative joint disease, periodontal disease, etc. Despite our sophisticated sciences and techniques, the etiology of not one of these diseases is known. In most instances covering these and other situations, our knowledge is obscure as to the primary or secondary relationship of age concomitant changes. The various types of stresses to which an individual is subject, including mechanical, bacterial, chemical, inflammatory, etc., may serve as inductors or augmentors of certain age changes and age-associated diseases. However, we exhibit little evidence at the present time of the ability to distinguish the cause and effect relationships associated with the phenomenon of aging.

REFERENCES

Adelman, R. C., Stein, G., Roth, G. S., and Englander, D. 1972. Age-dependent regulation of mammalian DNA synthesis and cell proliferation *in vivo*. *Mech. Age. Dev.*, **1**, 49–59.

Anderson, C. E., Ludowieg, J., Harper, H. A., and Engleman, E. P. 1964. The composition of the organic component of human articular cartilage. *J. Bone Joint Surg.*, **46A**, 1176–1183.

Aprile, E. C. de, and Aprile, H. 1947. Topografia de los conductos radiculares. *Rev. Odontologia*, **35**, 686–692.

Arey, L. B., Tremain, M. J., and Monzingo, F. L. 1935. The numerical and topographical relation of taste buds to human circumvallate papillae throughout the life-span. *Anat. Record*, **64**, 9–25.

Atkinson, P. J. 1967. Variation in trabecular structure of vertebrae with age. *Calc. Tiss. Res.*, **1**, 24–32.

Atkinson, P. J. 1969. Structural aspects of ageing bone. *Gerontologia*, **15**, 171–173.

Atkinson, P. J., and Woodhead, C. 1968. Changes in human mandibular structure with age. *Arch. Oral Biol.*, **13**, 1453–1463.

Baer, P. N., and Bernick, S. 1957. Age changes in the periodontium of the mouse. *Oral Surg., Oral Med., Oral Pathol.*, **10**, 430–436.

Barnett, C. H., Cochrane, W., and Palfrey, A. J. 1963. Age changes in articular cartilage of rabbits. *Ann. Rheumatic Diseases*, **22**, 389–400.

Bartley, M. H., Jr., and Arnold, J. S. 1967. Sex differences in human skeletal involution. *Nature*, **214**, 908–909.

Bartley, M. H., Arnold, J. S., Haslam, R. K., and Jee, W. S. S. 1966. The relationship of bone strength and bone quality in health, disease and aging. *J. Geront.*, **21**, 517–521.

Basiyan, G. V. 1966. Age-specific features particular to masticatory disturbances and the incidence of complete loss of teeth among urban residents. *Stomatologia*, **45**, 61–63.

Bauer, W. H. 1941. Osteo-arthritis deformans of temporomandibular joint. *Am. J. Pathol.*, **17**, 129–140.

Bauer, W. H. 1950. Old age in human parotid glands with special reference to peculiar cells in uncommon salivary gland tumors. *J. Dental Res.*, **29**, 686.

Becks, H., Asling, C. W., Simpson, M. E., Li, C. H., and Evans, H. M. 1949. The growth of hypophysectomized female rats following chronic treatment with pure pituitary growth hormone. III. Skeletal changes: Tibia, metacarpal, costochondral junction, and caudal vertebrae. *Growth*, **13**, 175–189.

Belting, C. M., Schour, I., Weinmann, J. P., and Shepro, M. J. 1953. Age changes in the periodontal tissues of the rat molar. *J. Dental Res.*, **32**, 332–353.

Berggren, H., and Hedström, H. 1951. Experimental studies *in vivo* on the permeability of enamel with particular regard to the effect of sugar solutions. *J. Dental Res.*, **30**, 161–168.

Bernick, S. 1967a. Age changes in the blood supply to human teeth. *J. Dental Res.*, **46**, 544–550.

Bernick, S. 1967b. Effect of aging on the nerve supply to human teeth. *J. Dental Res.*, **46**, 694–699.

Bernick, S. 1970. Histochemical study of bone in gonadectomized rats. *Calc. Tiss. Res.*, **5**, 170–182.

Bhussry, B. R. 1968. Modification of the dental pulp organ during development and aging. *In*, S. B. Finn (ed.), *Biology of the Dental Pulp Organ*, pp. 146–165. Birmingham: University of Alabama Press.

Bhussry, B. R., and Bibby, B. G. 1957. Surface changes in enamel. *J. Dental Res.*, **36**, 409–416.

Blake, G. C. 1958. An experimental investigation into the permeability of enamel and dentin with reference to its relation to dental caries. *Proc. Roy. Soc. Med.*, **51**, 678–682.

Bogart, B. I. 1967. The effect of aging on the histochemistry of the rat submandibular gland. *J. Geront.*, **22**, 272–275.

Brawley, R. E. 1935. Studies of the pH of normal resting saliva I. Variations with age and sex. *J. Dental Res.*, **15**, 55–77.

Bromley, R. G., Dockum, N. L., Arnold, J. S., and Jee, W. S. S. 1966. Quantitative histological study of human lumbar vertebrae. *J. Geront.*, **21**, 537–543.

Burch, P. R. J., and Jackson, D. 1966a. The greying of hair and the loss of permanent teeth considered in relation to an autoimmune theory of aging. *J. Geront.*, **21**, 522–528.

Burch, P. R. J., and Jackson, D. 1966b. Periodontal disease and dental caries some new aetiological considerations. *Brit. Dental J.*, **120**, 127–134.

Burchard, J., Fontaine, R., and Mandel, P. 1959. Métabolisme des acides ribonucléiques de l'os de lapin et de rat *in vivo. C. R. Soc. Biol. (Paris)*, **153**, 334–337.

Burstone, M. S. 1959. Histochemical demonstration of acid phosphatase activity in osteoclasts. *J. Histochem. Cytochem.*, **7**, 39–41.

Burzynski, N. J. 1971. Aging in guinea pig salivary gland. *J. Geront.*, **26**, 204–207.

Care, A. D., and Duncan, T. 1967. Age as a factor in the response to thyrocalcitonin secretion. *J. Endocrinol. (Brit.)*, **37**, 107–108.

Casuccio, C., Bertolin, N., and Falzi, M. 1962. Dell' osteoporosi senile. *La Clin. Orthop.*, **14**, 1–57.

Church, L. E. 1955. Age changes in the nucleics of salivary glands of Wistar Institute rats. *Oral Surg., Oral Med., Oral Pathol.*, **8**, 301–314.

Collins, D. H., Ghadially, F. N., and Meachim, G. 1965. Intracellular lipids of cartilage. *Ann. Rheumatic Diseases*, **24**, 123–135.

Coolidge, E. D. 1937. The thickness of the human periodontal membrane. *J. Am. Dental Assoc.*, **24**, 1260–1270.

Courtney, R. 1972. Age changes in the periodontium and oral mucous membrane. *J. Mich. Dental Assoc.*, **54**, 335–342.

Davies, D. V., Barnett, C. H., Cochrane, W., and Palfrey, A. J. 1962. Electron microscopy of articular cartilage in the young adult rabbit. *Ann. Rheumatic Diseases*, **21**, 11–22.

Dean Boyle, W., Jr., Via, W. F., Jr., and McFall, W. T., Jr. 1973. Radiographic analysis of alveolar crest height and age. *J. Periodontol.*, **44**, 236–243.

Dequeker, J., Remans, J., Franssen, R., and Waes, J. 1971. Aging patterns of trabecular and cortical bone and their relationships. *Calc. Tiss. Res.*, **7**, 23–30.

Dziewiatkowski, D. D. 1954. Effect of age on some aspects of sulfate metabolism in the rat. *J. Exp. Med.*, **99**, 283–298.

Enlow, D. H., and Harris, D. B. 1964. A study of postnatal growth of the human mandible. *Am. J. Orthodont.*, **50**, 25–50.

Fox, H. 1939. Chronic arthritis in wild mammals. *Trans. Am. Phil. Soc.*, **31**, 73–148.

Frank, R. 1950. Études sur l'infrastructure micro-scopique de l'email et sur la surface libre coronaire de la dent. *Schweiz. Monatsschr. Zahnheilk.*, **60**, 1109–1121.

Franzblau, C., Sinex, F. M., and Faris, B. 1966. Chemistry of maturation of elastin. *In*, N. W. Shock (ed.), *Perspectives in Experimental Gerontology*, pp. 98–105. Springfield, Illinois: Charles C. Thomas.

Fröhlich, E. 1970. Alterveranderungen der pulpa und des paradontiums. *Deut. Zahnäerztl. Z.*, **25**, 175–183.

Frost, H. M. 1961. Post-menopausal osteoporosis; a disturbance in osteoclasia. *J. Am. Geriat. Soc.*, **9**, 1078–1085.

Frost, H. M. 1963. *Bone Remodelling Dynamics*, pp. 5–108. Springfield, Illinois: Charles C. Thomas.

Glickman, I. 1967. The oral cavity. *In*, S. L. Robbins (ed.), *Pathology*, 3rd ed., pp. 770–817. Philadelphia: W. B. Saunders.

Gottlieb, B. 1942. Biology of the cementum. *J. Periodontol.*, **13**, 13–17.

Gottlieb, B., and Orban, B. 1938. *Dental Science and Dental Arts.* S. M. Gordon (ed.). London: H. Kimpton.

Grant, D., and Bernick, S. 1972. The periodontium of ageing humans. *J. Periodontol.*, **43**, 176–182.

Greene, A. H. 1962. A study of the characteristics of stippling and its relation to gingival health. *J. Periodontol.*, **33**, 176–182.

Greer, R. B., Skinner, S., Zarins, A., and Mankin, H. J. 1972. Distribution of acidic glycosaminoglycans in rabbit growth plate cartilage. *Calc. Tiss. Res.*, **9**, 194–199.

Gross, J. 1961. Ageing of connective tissue; the extracellular components. *In*, G. H. Bourne (ed.), *Structural Aspects of Ageing*, Chap. 11, pp. 177–195. New York: Hafner.

Ham, A. W., and Harris, R. 1971. Repair and transplantation of bone. *In*, G. H. Bourne (ed.), *The Biochemistry and Physiology of Bone*, Chap. 10, pp. 338–367. New York: Academic Press.

Han, S. S. 1968. The fine structure of cells and intercellular substances of the dental pulp. *In*, S. B. Finn (ed.), *Biology of the Dental Pulp Organ*, pp. 103–139. Birmingham: University of Alabama Press.

Hansen, E. R. 1966. Mitotic activity in the oral epithelium of the rat, variations according to age and time of day. *Odontologisk tidskrift*, **74**, 196–201.

Hansen, G. C. 1973. An epidemiologic investigation of the effect of biologic aging on the breakdown of periodontal tissue. *J. Periodontol.*, **44**, 269–277.

Hansen, H. J. 1956. Studies of the pathology of the lumbosacral disc in female cattle. *Acta Orthopaed. Scand.*, **25**, 161–182.

Heller, M., McLean, F. C., and Bloom, W. 1950. Cellular transformations in mammalian bones induced by parathyroid extract. *Am. J. Anat.*, **87**, 315–347.

Henneman, P. H., and Wallach, S. 1957. The use of androgens and estrogens and their metabolic effects. A review of the prolonged use of estrogen and androgen in post-menopausal and senile osteoporosis. *Arch. Internal Med.*, **100**, 715–723.

Hermel, J., Schönwetter, S., and Samueloff, S. 1970. Taste sensation and age in man. *J. Oral Med.*, **25**, 39–42.

Herring, G. M. 1964. Chemistry of bone matrix. *Clin. Orthop.*, **36**, 169–181.

Hill, T. J. 1934. Pathology of the dental pulp. *J. Am. Dental Assoc.*, **21**, 820–844.

Hjertquist, S.-O., and Lemperg, R. 1972. Identification and concentration of the glycosaminoglycans of human articular cartilage in relation to age and osteoarthritis. *Calc. Tiss. Res.*, **10**, 223–237.

Israel, H. 1973. The failure of aging or loss of teeth to drastically alter mandibular morphology. *J. Dental Res.*, **52**, 83–90.

Jackson, D. S. 1965. Temporal changes in collagen—aging or essential maturation. *In*, W. Montagna (ed.), *Aging, Advances In Biology of Skin*, Vol. 6, pp. 219–228. New York: Pergamon Press.

Jackson, D., and Burch, P. R. J. 1969. Dental caries as a degenerative disease. *Gerontologia*, **15**, 203–216.

Jackson, D., and Burch, P. R. J. 1970. Dental caries: Distribution, by age-group, between homologous (right-left) mesial and distal surfaces of human permanent maxillary incisors. *Arch. Oral Biol.*, **15**, 1059–1067.

Jackson, D., and Wedmann, S. M. 1959. The relationship between age and the fluorine content of human dentin and enamel: A regional survey. *Brit. J. Dent.*, **107**, 303–309.

Jande, S. S., and Bélanger, L. F. 1970. Fine structural study of rat molar cementum. *Anat. Record*, **167**, 439–463.

Jande, S. S., and Bélanger, L. F. 1971. Electron microscopy of osteocytes and the pericellular matrix in rat trabecular bone. *Calc. Tiss. Res.*, **6**, 280–289.

Jande, S. S., and Bélanger, L. F. 1973. The life cycle of the osteocyte. *Clin. Orthop.*, **94**, 281–305.

Jebens, E. H., and Monk-Jones, M. E. 1959. On the viscosity and pH of synovial fluid and the pH of blood. *J. Bone Joint Surg.*, **41B**, 388–400.

Jeffery, M. R. 1960. The waning joint. *Am. J. Med. Sci.*, **239**, 104–124.

Jowsey, J. 1966. Quantitative microradiography: A new approach in the evaluation of metabolic bone disease. *Am. J. Med.*, **40**, 485–491.

Kaplan, D., and Meyer, K. 1959. Ageing of human cartilage. *Nature*, **183**, 1267–1268.

Katzberg, A. A. 1952. The influence of age on the rate of desquamation of the human epidermis. *Anat. Record*, **112**, 418.

Keen, J. A. 1945. A study of the angle of the mandible. *J. Dental Res.*, **24**, 77–86.

Kellgren, J. H., Lawrence, J. S., and Bier, F. 1963. Genetic factors in generalized osteoarthritis. *Ann. Rheumatic Diseases*, **22**, 237–255.

King, A. L. 1957. Some studies in tissue elasticity, *In*, J. W. Remington (ed.), *Tissue Elasticity*, pp. 123–130. Baltimore: Waverly Press.

Kocsard, E., Ofner, F., and D'Abrera, V. St. E. 1970a. The histopathology of caviar tongue. *Dermatologica*, **140**, 318–322.

Kocsard, E., Ofner, F., and D'Abrera, V. St. E. 1970b. The phlibectasis of old-incidence and diagnostic importance. *J. Am. Geriat. Soc.*, **18**, 31–38.

Kohn, R. R. 1971. *Principles of Mammalian Aging*, p. 39. Found Dev. Biol. Series. Englewood Cliffs, New Jersey: Prentice-Hall.

Lavelle, C. L. B. 1968. The effect of age on the oral mucosa of the rat *(Rattus norwegicus)*. *Dent. Practit.*, **18**, 356–357.

Lefkowitz, W. 1942. The "vitality" of the calcified dental tissues. V.Protective metamorphosis of the dentin. *J. Dental Res.*, **21**, 423–428.

Little, K. 1962. The place of dental caries among the degenerative diseases. *N. Y. J. Dentistry*, **32**, 361–364.

Loewi, G. 1953. Changes in the ground substance of ageing cartilage. *J. Pathol. Bacteriol.*, **65**, 381–388.

McCarthy, P. L., and Shklar, G. 1961. Diseases of the oral mucosa. *In*, *Normal Anatomy, Histology and Histochemistry of the Oral Mucosa*, Chap. 1, pp. 1–10, New York: McGraw-Hill.

McCay, C. M., Maynard, L. A., Sperling, G., and Osgood, H. S. 1941. Nutritional requirements during the latter half of life. *J. Nutr.*, **21**, 45–60.

Malm, O. J. 1958. Calcium requirement adaptation in adult men. *Scand. J. Clin. Lab. Invest.*, **10**, *Suppl.* **36**, 1–280.

Mankin, H. J. 1962. Localization of tritiated thymidine in articular cartilage. II. Repair in immature cartilage. *J. Bone Joint Surg.*, **44A**, 688–698.

Mankin, H. J. 1963. Localization of tritiated thymidine in articular cartilage of rabbits. III. Mature articular cartilage. *J. Bone Joint Surg.*, **45A**, 529–540.

Mankin, H. J. 1964. Mitosis in articular cartilage of immature rabbits. A histologic, stathmokinetic (colchicine) and autoradiographic study. *Clin. Orthop.*, **34**, 170–183.

Manson, J. D., and Lucas, R. B. 1962. A microradiographic study of age changes in the human mandible. *Arch. Oral Biol.*, **7**, 761–769.

Meachim, G. 1967. The histology and ultrastructure of cartilage. *In*, C. A. L. Bassett (ed.), *Cartilage Degradation and Repair*, pp. 3–13. Washington, D.C.: National Academy of Science, National Research Council.

Meyer, K. 1956. The mucopolysaccharides of bone, *In*, G. E. Wolstenholme and C. M. O'Connor (eds.), *Bone Structure and Metabolism*, pp. 65–74. Boston: Little, Brown.

Meyer, J., Marwah, A. S., and Weinmann, J. P. 1956. Mitotic rate of gingival epithelium in two age groups. *J. Invest. Dermatol.*, **27**, 237–247.

Meyer, J., Spier, E., and Neuwelt, F. 1940. Basal secretion of digestive enzymes in old age. *Arch. Internal Med.*, **65**, 171–184.

Miles, A. E. W. 1961. Ageing in the teeth and oral

tissues. *In*, G. H. Bourne (ed.), *Structural Aspects of Ageing*, pp. 352–397. New York: Hafner.

Miles, A. E. W. 1963. *Dental Anthropology*. D. Brothwell (ed.), pp. 191–209. Oxford: Pergamon Press.

Miles, A. E. W. 1972. "Sans teeth": Changes in oral tissues with advancing age. *Proc. Roy. Soc. Med.*, **65**, 801–806.

Mongini, F. 1972. Remodelling of the mandibular condyle in the adult and its relationship to the condition of dental arches. *Acta Anat.*, **82**, 437–453.

Montgomery, P. W. 1951. A study of exfoliative cytology of normal human oral mucosa. *J. Dental Res.*, **30**, 12–18.

Morgan, D. B., and Newton-Jones, H. F. 1969. Bone loss and senescence. *Gerontologia*, **15**, 140–154.

Movat, H. Z., and Fernando, N. V. P. 1962. The fine structure of connective tissue 1. The Fibroblast. *Exp. Molec. Path.*, **1**, 509–534.

Murakami, H., and Emery, M. A. 1974. The role of elastic fibres in the periosteum in fracture healing in guinea pigs. I. Histological studies of the elastic fibres in the periosteum and the osteogenic cells and the cells that form elastic fibres. *Can. J. Surg.*, **10**, 359–370.

National Center for Health Statistics: Dental Findings in Adults by Age, Race, Sex, United States, 1960–1962. Pub. No. 1000, Series 11, No. 7. Washington, D.C.: Government Printing Office.

Neuberger, A., Perrone, J. C., and Slack, H. G. B. 1951. The relative metabolic inertia of tendon collagen in rat. *Biochem. J.*, **49**, 199–204.

Nordin, B. E. C. 1962. Calcium balance and calcium requirement in spinal osteoporosis. *Am. J. Clin. Nutr.*, **10**, 384–390.

Orban, B. J. 1966. Dentin. *In*, H. Sicher (ed.), *Oral Histology and Embryology*, pp. 96–126. St. Louis: C. V. Mosby.

Owen, M. E. 1963. Cell population kinetics of an osteogenic tissue. *J. Cell Biol.*, **19**, 19–32.

Owen, M. E. 1967. Uptake of [³H]-uridine into precursor pools and RNA in osteogenic cells. *J. Cell Sci.*, **2**, 39–56.

Owen, M. E. 1970. The origin of bone cells. *Intern. Rev. Cytol.*, **28**, 213–238.

Owen, M. E., and MacPherson, S. 1963. Cell population kinetics of an osteogenic tissue. *J. Cell Biol.*, **19**, 33–44.

Pavelec, M., Tonna, E. A., and Fand, I. 1967. The localization and distribution of protein-bound sulfhydryl and disulfide groups in skeletal tissues of mice during growth and aging. *J. Geront.*, **22**, 185–190.

Pedreira, R. A. 1951. A study of the keratinization of the oral mucosa of aged males. *J. Dental Res.*, **6**, 88–91.

Philippas, G. G., and Applebaum, E. 1966. Age factor in secondary dentin formation. *J. Dental Res.*, **45**, 778–789.

Philippas, G. G., and Applebaum, E. 1967. Age changes in the permanent upper lateral incisor. *J. Dental Res.*, **46**, 1002–1009.

Philippas, G. G., and Applebaum, E. 1968. Age changes in permanent upper canine teeth. *J. Dental Res.*, **47**, 411–417.

Pinzon, R. D., Kozlov, M., and Burch, W. P. 1967. Histology of rat molar pulp at different ages. *J. Dental Res.*, **46**, 202–208.

Pinzon, R. D., Toto, P. D., and O'Malley, J. J. 1966. Kinetics of rat molar pulp cells at various ages. *J. Dental Res.*, **45**, 934–938.

Porter, K. R. 1964. Cell fine structure and biosynthesis of intercellular macromolecules. *Biophys. J.*, **4**, 167–201.

Puche, R. C., and Romano, M. C. 1971. A time course study of the effects of testosterone on the femoral metaphyses of young mice. *Calc. Tiss. Res.*, **7**, 103–107.

Renstrup, G., Smulow, J. B., and Glickman, I. 1962. Effect of chronic mechanical irritation on chemically induced carcinogenesis in the hamster cheek pouch. *J. Am. Dental Assoc.*, **64**, 770–777.

Riggs, B. L., Jowsey, J., Kelly, P. J. Jones, J. D., and Maher, F. T. 1969. Effect of sex hormones on bones in primary osteoporosis. *J. Clin. Invest.*, **48**, 1065–1072.

Rogers, J. B., Johnson, W. L., and Burzynski, N. J. 1964. Growth patterns and age changes in the dentition, maxilla, and mandible of the guinea pig. *J. Geront.*, **19**, 517–519.

Rollin, H. 1973. Elektrische Geschmacksschwellen der Zunge und des weichen Gaumens, II. Einfluss von Lebensalter, Geschlecht und Rauchgewohnheiten. *Arch. Klin. exp. Ohr.-, Nas.- u. Kehlk. Hielk.*, **204**, 81–88.

Rosenberg, L., Johnson, B., and Schubert, M. 1965. Proteinpolysaccharides from human articular and costal cartilage. *J. Clin. Invest.*, **44**, 1647–1656.

Ross, R., and Benditt, E. P. 1961. Wound healing and collagen formation. I. Sequential changes in components of guinea pig skin wounds observed in the electron microscope. *J. Biophys. Biochem. Cytol.*, **11**, 677–700.

Rushton, M. A. 1955. Dental effects of dietary aureomycin. *Brit. Dental J.*, **98**, 313–317.

Savory, A., and Brudevold, F. 1959. The distribution of nitrogen in human enamel. *J. Dental Res.*, **38**, 436–442.

Saxton, J. A., Jr., and Silberberg, M. 1947. Skeletal growth and aging in rats receiving complete or restricted diets. *Am. J. Anat.*, **81**, 445–475.

Schajowicz, F., and Cabrini, R. L. 1958. Histochemical localization of acid phosphatase in bone tissue. *Science*, **127**, 1147–1148.

Scherp, H. W. 1971. Caries: Prospects and prevention. *Science*, **173**, 1199–1205.

Schubert, M., and Hamerman, D. 1968. Aging and osteoarthritis. *In*, *A Primer on Connective Tissue Biochemistry*, Chap. 8, pp. 247–268. Philadelphia: Lea & Febiger.

Scott, B. L., and Pease, D. C. 1956. Electron microscopy of the epiphyseal apparatus. *Anat. Record*, **126**, 465–495.

Sedlin, E. D., Villanueva, A. R., and Frost, H. M. 1963. Age variations in the specific surface of Howship's lacunae as an index of human bone resorption. *Anat. Record*, **146**, 201–207.

Seltzer, S. 1972. Classification of pulpal pathosis. *Oral Surg.*, *Oral Med.*, *Oral Pathol.*, **34**, 269–270.

Severson, A. R., Tonna, E. A., and Pavelec, M. 1967. Histochemical demonstration of adenosine triphosphatase in osteoclasts. *J. Histochem. Cytochem.*, **15**, 550–552.

Severson, A. R., Tonna, E. A., and Pavelec, M. 1968. Localization and distribution of adenosine triphosphatase activity in the femurs of young mice. *Anat. Record*, **161**, 57–68.

Shaw, J. H. 1970. Preeruptive effects of nutrition on teeth. *J. Dental Res.*, **49**, 1238–1260.

Shklar, G. 1966. The effects of aging upon oral mucosa. *J. Invest. Dermatol.*, **47**, 115–120.

Silberberg, M., Frank, E. L., Jarrett, S. R., and Silberberg, R. 1959. Aging and osteoarthritis of the human sternoclavicular joint. *Am. J. Pathol.*, **35**, 851–865.

Silberberg, M., and Silberberg, R. 1941. Age changes of bones and joints in various strains of mice. *Am. J. Anat.*, **68**, 69–95.

Silberberg, M., and Silberberg, R. 1961. Ageing changes in cartilage and bone. *In*, G. H. Bourne (ed.), *Structural Aspects of Ageing*, Chap. 8, pp. 85–108. New York: Hafner.

Silberberg, M., and Silberberg, R. 1971. Steroid hormones and bones. *In*, G. H. Bourne (ed.), *The Biochemistry and Physiology of Bone*, 2nd ed., Vol III, *Development and Growth*, pp. 401–484. New York: Academic Press.

Silberberg, M., Silberberg, R., and Hasler, M. 1967. Effects of fasting and refeeding on the ultrastructure of articular cartilage. *Pathol. Microbiol.*, **30**, 283–302.

Silberberg, R. 1972. Articular aging and osteoarthrosis in dwarf mice. *Pathol. Microbiol.*, **38**, 417–430.

Silberberg, R., Goto, G., and Silberberg, M. 1958. Degenerative joint disease in castrate mice I. Effects of ovariectomy of various ages. *A.M.A. Arch. Pathol.*, **65**, 438–441.

Silberberg, R., and Hasler, M. 1968. Electron microscopy of articular cartilage: The effect of acute hyperthyroidism. *Pathol. Microbiol.*, **31**, 25–40.

Silberberg, R., Hasler, M., and Lesker, P. A. 1973. Aging of the shoulder joint of guinea pigs. Electron microscopic and quantitative histochemical aspects. *J. Geront.*, **28**, 18–34.

Silberberg, R., and Silberberg, M. 1957. Changes in bones and joints of underfed mice bearing anterior hypophyseal transplants. *Endocrinology*, **60**, 67–75.

Silberberg, R., and Silberberg, M. 1961. Male sex hormones and osteoarthrosis in mice. *J. Bone Joint Surg.*, **43A**, 243–248.

Silberberg, R., and Silberberg, M. 1964. Pathogenesis of osteoarthrosis. *Pathol. Microbiol.*, **27**, 447–457.

Silberberg, R., and Silberberg, M. 1965. Aging changes and osteoarthrosis in castrate mice receiving progesterone. *J. Geront.*, **20**, 228–232.

Silberberg, R., Silberberg, M., and Fier, D. 1964. Life cycle of articular cartilage cells: An electron microscope study of the hip joint of the mouse. *Am. J. Anat.*, **114**, 17–47.

Silberberg, R., Stamp, W., Lesker, P. A., and Hasler, M. 1970. Aging changes in ultrastructure and enzymatic activity of articular cartilage of guinea pigs. *J. Geront.*, **25**, 184–198.

Silberberg, R., Thomasson, R., and Silberberg, M. 1958. Degenerative joint disease in castrate mice. II. Effects of orchiectomy at various ages. *A.M.A. Arch. Pathol.*, **65**, 442–448.

Singh, I. J., and Tonna, E. A. 1972. Autoradiographic evaluation of H³-uridine utilization by aging mouse cartilage. *Gerontologist*, **12**, 41.

Singh, I. J., and Tonna, E. A. 1973. An autoradiographic study of the utilization of tritiated uridine by osteoblasts of young mice. *Anat. Record*, **175**, 243–251.

Singh, I. J., and Tonna, E. A. 1974. An autoradiographic evaluation of the utilization of H³-uridine by osteoblasts of aging mice. *J. Geront.*, **29**, 1–10.

Sobel, H. 1967. Aging of ground substance in connective tissue. *In*, B. L. Strehler (ed.), *Advances in Gerontological Research*, Vol. 2, pp. 205–284. New York: Academic Press.

Sokoloff, L. 1969. *The Biology of Degenerative Joint Disease*, pp. 24–30, 63. Chicago: University of Chicago Press.

Stack, M. V. 1955. The chemical nature of the organic matrix of bone, dentin, and enamel. *Ann. N.Y. Acad. Sci.*, **60**, 585–595.

Stahl, S. S., Tonna, E. A., and Weiss, R. 1969. The effects of aging on the proliferative activity of rat periodontal structures. *J. Periodontol.*, **24**, 447–450.

Stahl, S. S., Tonna, E. A., and Weiss, R. 1970a. Autoradiographic evaluation of gingival response to injury: IV. Surgical trauma in low-protein-fed young adult rats. *J. Dental Res.*, **49**, 725–732.

Stahl, S. S., Tonna, E. A., and Weiss, R. 1970b. Autoradiographic evaluation of gingival response to injury: V. Surgical trauma in low-protein-fed mature rats. *J. Dental Res.*, **49**, 537–545.

Stahl, S. S., Tonna, E. A., and Weiss, R. 1970c. Autoradiographic evaluation of periapical responses to pulpal injury. *Oral Surg.*, *Oral Med.*, *Oral Pathol.*, **29**, 270–274.

Stahl, S. S., Weiss, R., and Tonna, E. A. 1961. Autoradiographic evaluation of periapical responses to pulpal injury. I. Young rats. *Oral Surg.*, *Oral Med.*, *Oral Pathol.*, **28**, 249–258.

Stallard, R. E., Orban, J. E., and Hove, K. A. 1970. Clinical significance of the inflammatory process. *J. Periodontol.*, **41**, 620–624.

Stidworthy, G., Masters, Y. F., and Shetlar, M. R.

1958. The effect of aging on mucopolysaccharide composition of human costal cartilage as measured by hexosamine and uronic acid content. *J. Geront.*, **13**, 10–13.

Stockwell, R. A. 1967. The cell density of human articular and costal cartilage. *J. Anat.*, **101**, 753–763.

Storey, E. 1960. Bone changes associated with cortisone administration in the rat. *Brit. J. Exp. Pathol.*, **41**, 207–213.

Thompson, A. S., and Bryant, H. C., Jr. 1950. Histogenesis of capillary cystadenoma lymphomatosum (Warthin's tumor) of the parotid salivary gland. *Am. J. Pathol.*, **26**, 807–849.

Tonna, E. A. 1958. Histologic and histochemical studies on the periosteum of male and female rats of different ages. *J. Geront.*, **13**, 14–19.

Tonna, E. A. 1959. Post-traumatic variations in phosphatase and respiratory enzyme activities of the periosteum of aging rats. *J. Geront.*, **14**, 159–163.

Tonna, E. A. 1960a. Periosteal osteoclasts, skeletal development and aging. *Nature*, **185**, 405–406.

Tonna, E. A. 1960b. Osteoclasts and the aging skeleton: A cytological, cytochemical and autoradiographic study. *Anat. Record*, **137**, 251–270.

Tonna, E. A. 1961. The cellular complement of the skeletal system studied autoradiographically with tritiated thymidine (H^{3}TDR) during growth and aging. *J. Biophys. Biochem. Cytol.*, **9**, 813–824.

Tonna, E. A. 1964. An autoradiographic evaluation of the aging cellular phase of mouse skeleton using tritiated glycine. *J. Geront.*, **19**, 198–206.

Tonna, E. A. 1965a. Protein synthesis and cells of the skeletal system. *In*, C. P. Leblond and K. Warren (eds.), *Use of Radioautography in Investigation of Protein Synthesis. Symposium for Cell Biology*, Vol. 4, pp. 215–245. New York: Academic Press.

Tonna, E. A. 1965b. Skeletal cell aging and its effects on the osteogenetic potential. *Clin. Orthop.*, **40**, 57–81.

Tonna, E. A. 1966a. A study of osteocyte formation and distribution in aging mice complemented with H^3-proline autoradiography. *J. Geront.*, **21**, 124–130.

Tonna, E. A. 1966b. An autoradiographic comparison of the utilization of amino acids by skeletal cells concomitant with aging. *In, Biology and Clinical Medicine, Proc. 7th Intern. Congr. Geront.*, **1**, 225–232.

Tonna, E. A. 1966c. Response of the cellular phase of the skeleton to trauma. *Periodont.*, **4**, 105–144.

Tonna, E. A. 1966d. H^3-histidine and H^3-thymidine autoradiographic studies of the possibility of osteoclast aging. *Lab. Invest.*, **15**, 435–448.

Tonna, E. A. 1967. The source of osteoblasts in healing fractures in animals of different ages. *In*, R. A. Robinson (ed.), *Healing of Osseous Tissues*, pp. 93–110, National Academy of Sciences Conference, Warrington, Virginia.

Tonna, E. A. 1971a. An autoradiographic study of H^3-proline utilization by aging mouse skeletal tissues. II. Cartilage cell compartments. *Exp. Geront.*, **6**, 405–415.

Tonna, E. A. 1971b. An autoradiographic study of H^3-proline utilization by aging mouse skeletal tissues. III. Estimation and comparison of the turnover of different cell compartments. *Gerontologia*, **17**, 273–288.

Tonna, E. A. 1972a. Electron microscopic evidence of alternating osteocytic-osteoclastic and osteoplastic activity in the perilacunar walls of aging mice. *Conn. Tiss. Res.*, **1**, 221–230.

Tonna, E. A. 1972b. An electron microscopic study of osteocyte release during osteoclasis in mice of different age. *Clin. Orthop.*, **87**, 311–317.

Tonna, E. A. 1972c. Parodontal inflammation and aging in the laboratory mouse. *J. Periodontol.*, **43**, 403–410.

Tonna, E. A. 1973a. An electron microscopic study of skeletal cell aging. II. The osteocyte. *Exp. Geront.*, **8**, 9–16.

Tonna, E. A. 1973b. Histological age changes associated with mouse parodontal tissues. *J. Geront.*, **28**, 1–12.

Tonna, E. A. 1974a. Electron microscopy of aging skeletal cells. III. The periosteum. *Lab. Invest.*, **32**, 609–632.

Tonna, E. A. 1974b. Hormonal influence on skeletal growth and regeneration. *In*, J. LoBue and A. S. Gordon (eds.), *Humoral Control of Growth and Differentiation*, Vol. I., Chap. 14, pp. 265–359. New York: Academic Press.

Tonna, E. A. 1975. Accumulation of lipofuscin (age pigment) in aging skeletal connective tissues as revealed by electron microscopy. *J. Geront.*, **30**, 3–8.

Tonna, E. A., and Cronkite, E. P. 1959. Histochemical and autoradiographic studies on the effects of aging on the mucopolysaccharides of the periosteum. *J. Biophys. Biochem. Cytol.*, **6**, 171–177.

Tonna, E. A., and Cronkite, E. P. 1960. Autoradiographic studies of changes in S^{35}-sulfate uptake by the femoral diaphyses during aging. *J. Geront.*, **15**, 377–382.

Tonna, E. A., and Cronkite, E. P. 1961a. Use of tritiated thymidine for the study of the origin of the osteoclast. *Nature*, **190**, 459–460.

Tonna, E. A., and Cronkite, E. P. 1961b. Cellular response to fracture studies with tritiated thymidine. *J. Bone Joint Surg.*, **43A**, 352–362.

Tonna, E. A., and Cronkite, E. P. 1961c. Autoradiographic studies of cell proliferation in the periosteum of intact and fractured femora of mice utilizing DNA labeling with H^3-thymidine. *Proc. Soc. Exp. Biol. Med.*, **107**, 719–721.

Tonna, E. A., and Cronkite, E. P. 1962a. An autoradiographic study of periosteal cell proliferation with tritiated thymidine. *Lab. Invest.*, **11**, 455–462.

Tonna, E. A., and Cronkite, E. P. 1962b. Changes in the skeletal cell proliferative response to trauma concomitant with aging. *J. Bone Joint Surg.*, **44A**, 1557-1568.

Tonna, E. A., and Cronkite, E. P. 1962c. Utilization of tritiated histidine (H³HIS) by skeletal cells of adult mice. *J. Geront.*, **17**, 353-358.

Tonna, E. A., and Cronkite, E. P. 1963. The periosteum: Autoradiographic studies on cellular proliferation and transformation utilizing tritiated thymidine. *Clin. Orthop.*, **30**, 218-232.

Tonna, E. A., and Cronkite, E. P. 1964. A study of the persistence of the H³-thymidine label in the femora of rats. *Lab. Invest.*, **13**, 161-171.

Tonna, E. A., and Cronkite, E. P. 1968. Skeletal cell labeling following continuous infusion with tritiated thymidine. *Lab. Invest.*, **19**, 510-515.

Tonna, E. A., Cronkite, E. P., and Pavelec, M. 1962. An autoradiographic study of the localization and distribution of tritiated histidine in bone. *J. Histochem. Cytochem.*, **10**, 601-610.

Tonna, E. A., Cronkite, E. P., and Pavelec, M. 1963. A serial autoradiographic analysis of H³-glycine utilization and distribution in the femora of growing mice. *J. Histochem. Cytochem.*, **11**, 720-733.

Tonna, E. A., and Lampen, N. 1972. Electron microscopy of aging skeletal cells. I. Centrioles and solitary cilia. *J. Geront.*, **27**, 316-324.

Tonna, E. A., and Pavelec, M. 1971. An autoradiographic study of H³-proline utilization by aging mouse skeletal tissues. I. Bone cell compartments. *J. Geront.*, **26**, 310-315.

Tonna, E. A., and Pillsbury, N. 1959. Mitochondrial changes associated with aging of periosteal osteoblasts. *Anat. Record*, **134**, 739-760.

Tonna, E. A., and Severson, A. R. 1971. Changes in the localization and distribution of adenosine triphosphatase activity in skeletal tissues of the mouse concomitant with aging. *J. Geront.*, **26**, 186-193.

Tonna, E. A., and Singh, I. J. 1973. The uptake and utilization of ³H-uridine by young mouse cartilage cells studied autoradiographically. *Lab. Invest.*, **28**, 300-304.

Tonna, E. A., and Stahl, S. S. 1974. Comparative assessment of the cell proliferative activities of injured parodontal tissues in aging mice. *J. Dental Res.*, **53**, 609-622.

Tonna, E. A., Stahl, S. S., and Weiss, R. 1969. Autoradiographic evaluation of gingival response to injury - II. Surgical trauma in young rats. *Arch. Oral Biol.*, **14**, 19-34.

Tonna, E. A., Weiss, R., and Stahl, S. S. 1972. The cell proliferative activity of parodontal tissues in aging mice. *Arch. Oral Biol.*, **17**, 969-982.

Toto, P. D., Kastelic, E. F., Duyvejonck, K. J., and Rapp, G. W. 1971. Effect of age on water content in human teeth. *J. Dental Res.*, **50**, 1284-1285.

Trotter, M., Broman, G. E., and Peterson, R. R. 1960. Densities of bones of White and Negro skeletons. *J. Bone Joint Surg.*, **42A**, 50-58.

Vajlens, L. 1971. Glycosaminoglycans of human bone tissues. I. Pattern of compact bone in relation to age. *Calc. Tiss. Res.*, **7**, 175-190.

Vaughn, H. C. 1943. A study of the temporomandibular articulation. *J. Am. Dental Assoc.*, **30**, 1501-1507.

Waerhaug, J. 1966. Epidemiology of periodontal disease—Review of the literature. *In*, S. P. Ramfjord, D. A. Kerr, and M. M. Ash (eds.), *World Workshop in Periodontics*, p. 181. Ann Arbor: University of Michigan.

Wainwright, W. W. 1943. Human saliva. XV. Inorganic phosphorus content of resting saliva of 650 healthy individuals. *J. Dental Res.*, **22**, 403-414.

Williams, D. E., Mason, R. L., and McDonald, B. B. 1964. Bone density measurements throughout the life cycle of the rat. *J. Nutr.*, **84**, 373-382.

Witte, W. E., and Fullmer, H. M. 1967. Effects of age on dentin demonstrated with azure A. *J. Dental Res.*, **46**, 218-221.

Young, R. W. 1962a. Cell proliferation and specialization during endochondrial osteogenesis in young rats. *J. Cell Biol.*, **14**, 357-370.

Young, R. W. 1962b. Regional differences in cell generation time in growing rat tibiae. *Exp. Cell Res.*, **26**, 562-567.

Young, R. W. 1963. Nucleic acids, protein synthesis and bone. *Clin. Orthop.*, **26**, 147-159.

Young, R. W. 1964. Specialization of bone cells. *In*, H. M. Frost (ed.), *Bone Biodynamics*, pp. 117-139. Boston: Little, Brown.

Zach, L., Topal, K., and Cohen, G. 1969. Pulpal repair following operative procedures. *Oral Surg., Oral Med., Oral Pathol.*, **28**, 587-597.

Zander, H. A., and Hürzeler, B. 1958. Continuous cementum apposition. *J. Dental Res.*, **37**, 1035-1044.

20
AGING OF THE SKIN AND ITS APPENDAGES

Victor J. Selmanowitz
New York Medical College — Metropolitan Hospital Center
Orentreich Foundation for the Advancement of Science
Ronald L. Rizer
Orentreich Foundation for the Advancement of Science
and
Norman Orentreich
New York University School of Medicine
Orentreich Foundation for the Advancement of Science

Skin, the most accessible organ of the human species for the scientific study of aging, is regionally heterogeneous in composition, function, and susceptibility to influences from within and outside the body. Inadequate allowance for these factors accounts for reports rife with contradictions about what constitutes aging of skin *per se.*

Some of these points will be clarified in the sections that follow. Unless otherwise specified, the skin referred to will be of the human variety.

BIOLOGIC FEATURES OF AGING SKIN

The diminishing physiological function and reserve capacity of the skin that occur with aging usually have little if any effect on human longevity. The life-sustaining potential of skin outlasts that of other decompensating vital organs. (In the wild, however, a factor such as the progressive slowing in the rate of wound healing with aging [Orentreich and Selmanowitz, 1969] would have a crucial effect on survival.) Serial transplantation of compatible skin from old to young mice (Krohn, 1965) has shown that such grafts can achieve a chronological age far in excess of the maximum recorded life span of the host.

Epidermis

Aging epidermis undergoes progressive cytoarchitectural disarray in the superficial stratum corneum, intermediate stratum malpighii, and germinative basal layer. Variations appear in the size, shape, and staining properties of the cells and their components. Major axes and surface area of stratum corneum cells tend to increase throughout life (Plewig, 1970).

Age-associated atrophy of epidermis is pronounced in areas most exposed to the environment such as the face, neck, upper ("V") portion of the chest, and dorsal surfaces of the hands and forearms. Thinning of the epidermis and flattening of the epidermal-dermal interface have also been observed in skin of the mid-back which is less exposed to sunlight and weather (Montagna, 1965). However no statistically significant change in the thickness of epidermis of unexposed skin of the buttocks was found in 28 individuals ranging in age from 25 to 76 years (Freeman, 1971).

The activities of 14 enzymes representative of major metabolic pathways were studied in epidermis from the lower part of the abdomen in 63 subjects ranging in age from 1 month to 90 years. No age-associated difference of activity in any of the enzymes was found (Yamasawa, Cerimele, and Serri, 1972).

Long-term effects of environmental actinic damage superimposed on intrinsic aging of the skin are dependent in degree on the complexion of the individual, the intensity, frequency, and duration of exposure of the area of skin under consideration, and the time elapsed for the changes to gradually evolve as in radiodermatitis (Epstein, 1962). Fair-skinned, blue- or green-eyed blondes or redheads are most susceptible to the epidermal and dermal degenerative effects of solar radiation. More darkly complexioned Caucasians are somewhat better protected. Negro skin, by virtue of its extensive melanization, and also possibly because of a larger number of cell layers in the stratum corneum for reflection and dissipation of radiant energy (Weigand, Haygood, and Gaylor, 1974; Knox, 1966), remains in the best state of preservation following exposure to environmental radiation.

In elderly individuals, the barrier efficiency of the stratum corneum in restricting transepidermal penetration of water and certain chemicals is reduced (i.e., epidermal permeability is increased compared to young adult skin) in the relatively shielded area of the mid-back. However, the rate of clearance of these chemicals following entry into the skin (percutaneous absorption) is reduced, presumably on account of reduced diffusion in the altered dermis and decreased blood flow (Christophers and Kligman, 1965).

Slowing in the rate of cell replacement in the stratum corneum of "normal" forearm skin of aged people, more pronounced in men than in women, may be taken as an indicator of reduced mitotic activity in the epidermis (Baker and Blair, 1968). Epithelization of open wounds and dermabraded facial skin takes more time with increasing age. The usual reservation holds for the imposition of long-term actinic effects. However, the rate of epithelization is also slowed in fur-covered animals (Orentreich and Selmanowitz, 1969).

Microscopic studies on the mitotic activity of epidermis have led to confusion in the interpretation and evaluation of a general trend with aging. The situation has been complicated by a lack of reconciliation with factors such as different methods of determination, rhythmic variations in mitotic cycling, peculiarities of the species and, especially in the case of man, superimposed long-term effects of actinic damage (Baker and Blair, 1968).

Studies of cell labeling by radioactive precursors of DNA have provided a scheme to clarify the dynamics of reduced mitotic activity and regenerative capacity with aging (Gelfant and Smith, 1972). Within a mitotically active population of cells (such as the basal layer of the epidermis), there are cells which exit from the mitotic cycle for extended periods in the pre-DNA synthetic phase (G_1) or the post-DNA synthetic phase (G_2). Regeneration is accomplished to a considerable degree by tapping these pools and mobilizing their G_1- and G_2-blocked cells back into mitotic cycling. Factors involved with aging, some perhaps of an immunologic or extracellular nature, would seem to hold the noncycling cells in restraint so that their proportion increases; hence overall mitotic activity is reduced and regenerative release is lessened. Such an increase in noncycling cells has been demonstrated in mouse ear epidermis. The proposition of "reserve forces" ready-and-able for mobilization in the young host but in the elderly weary for the wait and age-associated changes is indeed a tempting one for the conception of wound healing and more subtle reparative processes in the skin. The scheme has also been applied to other organs and tissues in a manner consonant with their age-associated compensatory proliferative capacities and effects on longevity.

Melanocytes

A reduction in the number of 3,4-dihydroxy-phenylalanine (dopa)-reactive epidermal melanocytes, about 20 percent of the surviving population for each increment of 10 years between ages 27 and 65, was determined for skin of the buttocks in a limited number of Caucasian males. Approximately half that rate of decline was reported for abdominal skin (Quevedo, Szabó, and Virks, 1969). The malpighian cell/melanocyte ratio in the epidermis of the thigh increases with advancing age (Fitzpatrick, Szabó, and Mitchell, 1965).

There exists in the skin a pool of melanocytes (or precursors thereof), with little or no dopa-reactivity, upon which ultraviolet irradiation draws to induce an increased number of dopa-positive cells with relatively large cell bodies and elaborate dendrites. The number of melanocytes activated in this manner decreases with aging, indicating a diminished reserve capacity. Melanocytes that remain in senescent skin tend to be larger than their young counterparts, possibly the result of functional hypertrophy (Fitzpatrick, Szabó, and Mitchell, 1965; Walsh, 1964).

Graying of hair is usually an important marker of aging but can begin in early adulthood in those genetically predisposed. The melanocytes at the base of the hair follicle are subjected to the "wear-and-tear" of its cyclic activities and become fewer and less productive of pigment.

Melanotic coloration of the skin is also under endocrine influence and should be viewed in the context of changing hormonal status with aging or pathological states.

Dermis

Significant alterations in the dermis occur throughout life. In the fetal dermis, collagen fibers are fine and fibrillar, whereas in mature dermis, coarse collagen bundles are present. Progressive thickening and aggregation of collagen fibers are most evident up to 20 years of age, after which the increments lessen. In the fetal dermis, elastic fibers are quite delicate and are mainly found in the proximity of the pilosebaceous units. During development and aging the elastic fibers become more numerous and thicker. Elastin in older subjects is more cross-linked and more calcified (Partridge, 1970), but so-called elastosis in actinically damaged skin may be largely due to a structural modification of collagen resulting in elastinlike tinctorial properties (Hall, 1961).

The rate of collagen synthesis during early growth and maturation is high, with a concomitant formation of intramolecular covalent cross-links. The most newly-synthesized collagen is extractable in salt solutions or dilute acids. As covalent cross-linking proceeds with maturation, the collagen undergoes less metabolic turnover and is less extractable in protein solvents. However, there is no marked increase in the number of covalent cross-links with advanced aging (Cannon and Davison, 1973). Rather, there is an apparent reorientation or redistribution of preexisting cross-links, so that stable intermolecular covalent cross-links predominate (Cannon and Davison, 1973; Vančiková and Deyl, 1973). This increase in the stability of dermal collagen makes the skin of older subjects more stiff and less pliable.

In the relatively unexposed skin of the trunk, the soluble collagen fraction decreases with aging, while the insoluble, highly stable collagen fraction increases. On the other hand, actinically damaged skin does not show this decrease in the soluble collagen fraction, but rather a striking decrease in the insoluble collagen fraction. In both the exposed and relatively unexposed skin, elastin or elastinlike material increases with aging, but in exposed skin the increase is far greater (Sams and Smith, 1965).

Dermal ground substance, the plasticizing component of the skin, also changes throughout life. Hyaluronic acid and dermatan sulfate are the major glycosaminoglycans in the ground substance. There are smaller amounts of chondroitin 4- and 6-sulfates. Smith, Davidson, and Taylor (1965) have shown that the total cutaneous glycosaminoglycan content decreases rapidly from birth to adolescence but shows no major decrease thereafter. However, in the more actinically damaged skin of adults, the total glycosaminoglycan content approximates that of a young child.

In a more recent study where the subjects ranged in age from 6 months *in utero* to 96 years, Fleischmajer, Perlish, and Bashey (1973) showed that in abdominal skin the soluble pool of dermal glycosaminoglycans decreased significantly in early development, remained stable from then through middle age, and declined again in old age. Hyaluronic acid decreased dramatically from birth until 5 years of age, with no change from 5 years through 50 years of age. Thereafter a significant decline occurred. However, dermatan sulfate did not show a significant decrease from birth to 5 years of age but declined markedly from 5 years to 96 years of age. Therefore, there appears to be a selective decrease in the content of the glycosaminoglycan components with development and aging.

Wrinkles of the skin, to be considered again, are closely related to age-associated changes in the dermis. Aged skin and actinically damaged skin lose their tone and elasticity, resulting in sagging and wrinkling. Wrinkling is particularly evident where the skin is frequently folded, as on the face, and the skin on flexor surfaces of joints; "wear-and-tear" of mechanical stress is thus implicated (Montagna and Parakkal, 1974).

Nerve Endings

Pacinian and Meisner's corpuscles of digital skin decrease in number throughout life. Those corpuscles remaining with advancing age are less cohesively organized and progressively show degenerative changes or an increase in dimension with lobular irregularities in form or a combination of both processes. These changes are sufficiently typical to enable approximate prediction of the bearer's age. Adjacent free nerve endings may undergo relatively little histologic change (Cauna, 1965).

Microcirculation

A decrease in the number of capillary loops and other blood vessels in the superficial dermis has been observed in regions of skin with age-associated flattening of the epidermal-dermal interface (Davis and Lawler, 1961). With common baldness of the scalp there is progressive diminution of the deep dermal blood vessels with the passage of time (Montagna and Parakkal, 1974).

Sweat Glands

Eccrine glands show changes of advanced age in the disarray and shrinkage of secretory cells, luminal dilatation and decreased output of sweat, and sometimes complete involution of the secretory coil. Histochemical changes include reductions in succinic dehydrogenase and phosphorylase activities. The connective tissue about the secretory tubules becomes excessively fibrotic, with diminution in blood vessels and acetylcholinesterase-containing nerves. The eccrine ducts tend to be preserved. Sudorific response to local adrenergic stimulation is lessened. Response to cholinergic stimulation of sweating seems to be hormonally dependent, being less in aged than in young adult males but tending in females to increase with advanced age (Silver, Montagna, and Karacan, 1965).

Reduced density of intact eccrine glands, determined morphologically or functionally, is a feature of exposed and covered skin and of glyphic skin of the digits (Juniper and Dykman, 1967). Involution with aging may be more pronounced among eccrine glands arranged in a dial motif around hair follicles than among freely distributed glands (Oberste-Lehn, 1965).

Lipofuscin granules, notable from childhood within cells of the eccrine secretory tubules, increase in number and size with the passage of years. By 60 years of age the accumulated lipofuscin may occupy about 5–10 percent of intracellular volume (the same order of accumulation as in cardiac muscle). It is uncertain if or to what extent the function of the cell is compromised by "age pigment" per se.

Apocrine glands, which are hormonally influenced, may undergo attenuation of secretory epithelium accompanied by ballooning of the tubules and a decreased output. Lipofuscin accumulates in the cells of the secretory tubules (Cawley, Hsu, Sturgill, and Harman, 1973). Many of the apocrine glands in aged subjects, when routinely processed for histological examination, appear indistinguishable from those of young adults.

Pilosebaceous Apparatus

Cyclic activity of the hair follicle and the type of hair produced by the follicle are dependent upon a complex interplay of genetic, endocrine, and aging factors. During the catagen stage of the hair cycle when hair growth ceases, a major portion of the hair bulb involutes; the remaining follicle enters into the resting or telogen stage of the cycle. After a characteristic interval of time, the telogen follicle actively undergoes a period of dramatic cytoarchitectural remodeling, going into the anagen stage, and a new hair is formed. The old hair is usually shed at this time. Whether the type of hair produced is fine, short, nonpigmented *vellus* hair, or coarse, long, pigmented *terminal* hair is dependent on the duration of anagen and the size of the hair follicle. Both characteristics change with age. From the third decade on there is a progressive transition of the vellus hairs in the ears of males into terminal hairs, usually on the tragus and antitragus (Montagna and Giacometti, 1969). The opposite transition, from terminal to vellus hair growth, occurs in age-associated common baldness of the scalp (Barman, Pecoraro, and Astore, 1969). Both transitions are examples of selective patterns of sequential gene modification. The miniaturization of hair follicles in common baldness is not associated with a decrease in their number, except in advanced age. The importance of the genetic constitution of the hair follicle and the age of the individual cannot be overemphasized. In women with virilizing syndromes there is a wide variation in the capacity of the hair follicles to respond to androgens. Maguire (1964) had repeatedly injected, subcutaneously, a long-acting testosterone ester into a single site in the beard area of five postmenopausal women. Two of the women produced vigorous growth of terminal hair at the injection site in four months; two had sparse hair growth in one year; and one showed no growth. Prior to testosterone injection, all of the women had typically short, unpigmented, thin vellus facial hair barely noticeable on visual inspection. However, the action of a potent androgenic steroid hormone effected a transformation of hair types, and thus follicle differentiation, by selective gene activation. The variable effect of this gene activation is a function of age.

Loss of axillary and pubic hair may reflect diminished endocrine function rather than aging *per se*. In the female, androgens from the adrenal cortex are primarily responsible for axillary and pubic hair maintenance. In Addison's disease, this hair does not develop. In the male, testicular androgens dominate adrenal androgens, and axillary and pubic hair growth is maintained, even in Addison's disease. Hair in these areas can be regrown in aged individuals by systemic or local administration of androgens.

The pigmentation in a hair produced by a given follicle can be interrupted intermittently before permanent graying is established. Comaish (1972) and several others have reported cases where white hair became repigmented. These observations imply that melanocytes are not completely lost in follicles as a result of the aging process, but that their function is impaired.

Sebaceous glands do not atrophy with advanced age, although some enter into a resting or inactive stage. Diminution of sebum production on the forehead in old age is thought to be related to the reduced endogenous (gonadal and adrenal) androgen production. In a study of 261 males and 173 females varying in age from 4 to 88 years, Strauss and Pochi (1968) showed that sebum production increased dramatically at the time of puberty in both sexes. In men, sebum production on the forehead remained high until about the eighth decade of life when it declined moderately. In women, however, a significant decline in sebum production over the same area was observed after the age of 50 years, roughly correlating with the time of menopause.

The increase in sebum secretion seen in patients with Parkinson's disease is not due to increased androgren circulation but is related to the decrease in dopamine in the mid-brain. Replacement therapy with L-dopa lowers sebum secretion towards normal levels (Burton, Cartlidge, and Shuster, 1973). The inhibition of sebum secretion is apparently not directly due to L-dopa, since L-dopa has no effect on normal subjects with seborrhea (Burton, Libman, Hall, and Shuster, 1971).

Shuster and Thody (1974) have presented evidence in the rat that a sebotrophic hormone is secreted by the neurointermediate lobe of the pituitary and that its release is controlled by an inhibiting factor. Sebum secretion is markedly diminished by removal of the posterior lobe, even though the anterior is left intact and is histologically normal. Replacement therapy with α-melanocyte stimulating hormone (α-MSH) completely restored sebum secretion in posterior hypophysectomized rats. MSH is controlled by the hypothalamic release of melanocyte inhibitory factor (MIF), which may be under control of the limbic system. In parkinsonism, mid-brain dopamine is decreased, and it is conjectured that MIF is not present in sufficient amounts to inhibit MSH release. An increase in circulating MSH in patients with parkinsonism supports this view (Shuster, Thody, Goolamali, Burton, Plummer, and Bates, 1973). The restoration of normal sebum secretion by the administration of L-dopa in parkinsonism suggests that the release of MIF depends on normal levels of midbrain dopamine.

Nails

Important gerontologic data and a most impressive superimposed cycle have been recorded in relation to the rate at which nails grow linearly outward. In a study of thumbnail growth among 257 individuals (Orentreich and Sharp, 1967), an average decline was found from 0.83 mm/week among subjects in their third decade to 0.52 mm/week in the ninth decade group—a 38 percent decrease. Males had a rate of nail growth more rapid than females until about the sixth decade. From then there was approximate equalization until the eighth decade, after which the rate in males fell progressively below females.

Cyclic changes are superimposed on this decline in rate of nail growth with aging. With instrumentation to determine the rate of nail growth in less than hourly intervals (based on the mechanical-optical principle described by Basler [1937] and further developed in our organization but not yet published), a circadian rhythm has been observed with slowing at nighttime. Seasonal variations in the Northeastern U.S. Temperate Zone indicate a trend for a maximal rate in November and a minimal

in July. Though cross-sectional data may suggest a steady decline in the rate of fingernail growth from maturity to senescence, analysis of longitudinal data from measurements in one man for over 30 years to date (Bean 1968, 1974) has shown remarkable 7-year plateau periods of relatively constant rate alternating with 7-year periods of marked decline (Orentreich and Selmanowitz, 1969). Other declines with aging may also be found subject to alternating multiyear periods of relative stability and rapid decay.

Additional influences on the rate of nail growth include variation among digits (e.g., the nail of the middle finger grows faster than the thumbnail); manual activities, nail-biting, and other habits involving nails; extremes of environmental temperature; racial differences; nutritional status; hormonal status (e.g., increased rate with pregnancy); infections (ungual, periungual, systemic); circulatory changes (involving blood vessels or lymphatics); and neurotrophic disorders. With proper allowances for, or regulation of the various influential factors, be they cyclic or otherwise, the determination of the rate of linear nail growth may prove an invaluable measurement of physiologic age.

For an animal model, we have studied the rate of claw growth in 16 beagles kept under controlled environmental conditions. Combined cross-sectional and longitudinal data have indicated that starting from a yearly-averaged rate of nail growth of 1.9 mm/week in the first 2 years of life, there was an approximate yearly decrease of 2.5 percent until the 15th year of life. The equivalent computation in man gives 0.5 percent average yearly decline $(0.83 - 0.52/60 \times 100)$. Interestingly, then, in a canine species with a life span about one-fifth that of the average human being, the percent-rate of decline was five times faster (Orentreich, Selmanowitz, and Stanislowski, 1972).

Lavelle (1968) reported that along the life span of certain short-lived rodent species there were no consistent age-associated changes in the rate of nail growth. The distinguishing growth pattern of epithelial tissues of such rodents was further reflected by the finding of the same investigator that there were no consistent age changes in the rate of incisor tooth eruption in rats between the ages of 32–1,029 days.

In addition to the age-related decline in the rate of linear nail growth in human beings, other changes may develop in man with respect to the appearance of the fingernails and toenails during advanced years (so-called senile nails). Such nails appear dull, opaque, and sometimes yellowish, greenish, or gray. They are ridged longitudinally and are prone to split into layers. Histologic changes in the dermis of the nail bed include thickening of the walls of the blood vessels and merging of elastic and other connective tissue. These changes are due in part to actinic damage, the nail plate tending to increase the effect of sunlight on the tissues beneath (Rook, Wilkinson, and Ebling, 1972). Toenail dystrophies in the aged are often related to circulatory impairment.

GERIATRIC DERMATOSES

Though dermatologic problems are common in the elderly, a specific relationship to an intrinsic aging process of the integument is often questionable. Most irregularities of so-called aging skin are actually either long-term effects of environmental exposure, especially actinic damage to susceptible skin; or reflective of underlying circulatory, neurotrophic, hormonal, and metabolic disturbances; or continuations of processes already evident from early adulthood or middle age. Representative examples will be presented.

Wrinkles and Furrows

Actinic insult ultimately contributes in large measure to wrinkling of the skin, usually most marked on face, neck (cutis rhomboidalis nuchae), and dorsa of hands. Owing to atrophy of the epidermis and degenerative changes in dermal connective tissue, the exposed skin becomes dry, yellowish, and leathery with loss of resiliency as occurs in the wizened ("senile") countenance of the elderly. In addition, alterations in subcutaneous fat and musculoskeletal structure in the remodeling

of later years also emphasize the deeper wrinkles and furrows and contribute to the pendulous draping of the skin (dermatochalasis). Absorption of alveolar bone of the maxilla and mandible and as a consequence a reduced vertical facial dimension contribute to furrowed pockets at the corners of the mouth where saliva may pool and moniliasis develop in perlèche (angular chelilitis) of the elderly. Gross and microscopic comparisons of skin from the cheeks of the face compared to those of the buttocks illustrate many of these points.

Benign Proliferations

Epidermal. Seborrheic keratoses are common, circumscribed, variably pigmented outgrowths, microscopically of verrucoid or interconnecting strand configuration. They may appear almost anywhere on the skin and may be found in young adults. The passage of years allows new keratoses to appear and preexisting ones to enlarge; hence the association with aging.

Keratoacanthoma is a keratotic crateriform papule or nodule which, when solitary, occurs most frequently after the fifth decade with a predilection for exposed surfaces. Rapid growth and atypicality of malpighian cells belie the benign course of spontaneous regression in most cases. In addition to the major factor of actinic damage to fair skin, some cases are related to prolonged topical contact with petroleum products.

Melanocytic and Nevocytic. "Senile" lentigines are the pigmented macules seen frequently in whites of middle age and beyond on the dorsa of the hands and forearms and on the face (exposed areas). Melanocytes are increased in number in epidermal ridges that are elongated and club shaped.

Nevi undergo regression and disapperance with advanced aging via reduction in the number of nevocytes and separation of the nevocytes from the epidermis and from each other by connective tissue.

Dermal Connective Tissue. Pseudoscars of circumscribed subepidermal fibrosis almost devoid of elastic tissue, clinically stellate or linear in configuration, appear on the dorsa of the fore-arms and hands of Caucasians especially after 60 years of age. Senile purpura are commonly found nearby (Colomb, 1972). Solar damage and mechanical trauma may be factors in both conditions.

Cutaneous nodules of fibrotic tissue and of histiocytic and vascular components (derma-tofibromas, histiocytomas), fairly common on limbs, may be seen in young adults but, since these persist while new ones develop, more are found with increasing age (Selmanowitz, Lerer, and Orentreich, 1970).

Vascular. "Senile" angiomas (de Morgan's spots) are cherry- or ruby-red vascular papules which may be seen in early adulthood. They increase in number and size with aging and occur on both exposed and covered surfaces. Angiokeratomas develop on the scrotum during middle and old age.

Facial telangiectases of middle and later years are of tortuous linear course and are usually related to previous actinic exposure and rosa-cea. Venous lakes are seen on the lips and ears of the elderly.

Adnexal. "Senile" sebaceous hyperplasia, though more common and pronounced after mid-life, is occasionally seen in young adults. This sebaceous gland proliferation, which often appears clinically as small yellowish papules surrounding a central umbilication, is certainly not specific for senescence of the skin and may represent a nevoid predisposition of variably delayed appearance.

Premalignant and Malignant Lesions

It would be especially inaccurate to subdivide the most common of these lesions into cate-gories of specific cutaneous structures since there are chemically inductive and structural interactions of epidermal, dermal, and adnexal elements. Microscopic hallmarks of these con-ditions include atypical cellular appearance and disorganization.

The most common premalignant cutaneous lesion, the actinic or solar keratosis (synony-mous terms preferable to "senile" keratosis), usually appears as a rough-surfaced patch less than a centimeter in diameter. Sites of predi-lection, where multiple keratoses may develop, are the face and dorsa of the hands and fore-arms. On occasion there is progression to dermally invasive carcinoma. Fair-skinned persons exposed a great deal to the environ-ment, especially in geographic locations where solar electromagnetic energy is intense, are liable to develop actinic keratoses during early adulthood (Selmanowitz and Silverberg, 1968). A darker complexion and/or lesser exposure delay their appearance, sometimes until old age, or avoid the problem altogether. Premalignant keratoses are less frequently related to occupa-tional or medicinal exposure to arsenicals and petroleum products.

Leukoplakia refers to potentially precan-cerous keratotic dysplasia of mucous and semi-mucous epithelium. Various external and in-ternal factors may be involved, and old age is not a prerequisite.

Bowen's disease, a type of intraepidermal (*in situ*) squamous cell carcinoma, usually appears as a reddish plaque on covered skin. Associations with arsenical exposure (the effects of which may take many years to become evident) and internal malignancies would relate to the onset in later years.

Epidermal carcinomas of basal and squamous cell varieties (the former being the most com-mon carcinoma in whites) are in their cutane-ous distribution and ages of onset in good part governed by the same factors described under actinic keratosis. However the far greater frequency of basal cell carcinoma on certain areas of the face compared to the dorsa of the hands and forearms also indicates intrinsic regional variation in susceptibility thought to be related to pilosebaceous differences.

Lentigo maligna is a variably melanotic lesion of atypical melanocytes which spreads consid-erably in the course of years. Though most common from the fifth decade on and usually located on exposed surfaces, exceptions are notable for earlier onset and involvement of generally shielded areas. Dark melanomatous nodules which eventually develop in the lesion have less malignant propensity than other melanomas.

Malignant melanoma is of increased incidence in the latter half of life. The time-mediated allowance for development (though melanoma may be found even from the outset of life) involves numerous predisposing factors: genetic, hormonal, immunologic, traumatic; also fair complexion and exposure.

Sarcomas of dermal origin are rare and not at all confined to the elderly. Kaposi's multiple hemorrhagic sarcoma, perhaps not actually a sarcoma by strict meaning of the term, is not too rare and becomes progressively more frequent with advancing years in Caucasians of European derivation. Multifocal vascular plaques and nodules of proliferative capillary vessels and connective tissue autochthonously arise in skin and internal organs. The course of the disease tends to be protracted.

Other cutaneous malignancies that may develop in the elderly though not restricted to later years include lymphomas, reticuloses, varieties of leukemia, and metastases from internal neoplasms. These can present as scaly patches, plaques, papules, nodules, or diffuse infiltrates of the skin.

Poikiloderma atrophicans vasculare bespeaks a dyschromic, atrophying, and telangiectatic dermatosis. The course is protracted and slowly progressive. The condition may portend a lymphoma or reticulosis (e.g., mycosis fungoides), or an "autoimmune" disease (e.g., dermatomyositis), or without such demonstrable association may be a prodromal process evolving at a rate slower than the life span of the host (Wolf and Selmanowitz, 1970). Clinical and microscopic features of the condition are also shared by radiodermatitis and various genodermatoses (e.g., Werner's syndrome, xeroderma pigmentosum, dyskeratosis congenita), indicating a common pathway of cutaneous reactivity in a variety of disorders and probably, to some degree, in aging of the skin.

Other Dermatoses

Certain conditions involving the skin tend to be less severe or more slowly progressive in the elderly when compared to young adults (e.g., psoriasis, certain "autoimmune diseases") (Spencer and Kierland, 1970). Others have more dire implications. For example, *Herpes zoster* eruption ("shingles") in the aged is more frequently followed by persistent neuralgia and is more often indicative of underlying malignancy. Still others are almost confined to the geriatric group, e.g., bullous pemphigoid.

Decreased performance of cutaneous glands affects surface lubrication and resident microflora (Sommerville, 1969). Pruritus may result from scaly dryness or "chapping" of the skin (asteatosis, xerosis, winter itch). *Candida albicans* can be isolated with higher incidence from skin of geriatric subjects as compared to younger adults, and inflammatory, pruritic lesions of intertriginous moniliasis can be troublesome in the elderly. The age-associated tendency towards higher blood glucose level may contribute to the development of moniliasis.

Other cutaneous conditions relating to so-called senile pruritus include contact dermatitis (recall the factors of increased epidermal permeability and decreased percutaneous absorption), drug reactions, seborrheic dermatitis, psoriasis, seborrheic keratoses with associated skin tags, nummular eczema, lichen chronicus, and atopic dermatitis. Pruritus may indicate internal disease be it hormonal (e.g., diabetes mellitus, thyrotoxicosis), parenchymatously degradative (e.g. hepatic or renal failure), circulatory (e.g., stasis dermatitis), neurologic-neuropsychiatric (e.g., "little strokes," delusions of parasitosis), or malignant. Some residual cases of pruritus are relegated to an "essential" (cause undetermined) category.

Only two further examples of conditions involving the skin which are of particular importance in later years can be included in the scope of this review. Scaly and variably inflammatory patches of seborrheic dermatitis, in such locations as the scalp, forehead, eyebrows, nasolabial folds, and chest, may first appear or become exacerbated in relation to stressful situations (e.g., "heart attack") or neurovascular problems (e.g., arteriosclerotic parkinsonism). Problems with lower extremity skin, including pruritus, burning sensation, atrophy, indolent ulceration, and onychodystrophy, are related to underlying circulatory deficiencies (venous, arterial, and lymphatic) and neurotrophic influence. It will generally be found that additional dermatoses of the elderly described in references at the end of this chapter (Spencer and Kierland, 1970; Domonkos, 1968) are related to underlying disorders rather than to primary aging of skin viewed as an entity unto itself.

PROGEROID SYNDROMES

As a word, *progeria* (from the Greek, meaning prematurely old) has general uses for the concept of premature aging. Although certain features of syndromes to be discussed are apparently akin to those associated with natural aging, others not of the character of senescence are as much in evidence. Also, certain features associated with aging are entirely lacking. Here we shall emphasize the patients' general appearance and cutaneous manifestations; further details in these areas and those concerning internal manifestations are found in appropriate references (e.g., Leider and Selmanowitz, 1976). Tissue culture findings will be consolidated at the end of the chapter.

Hutchinson-Gilford Syndrome (Progeria)

Sometimes evident within the first days of life are a cyanotic tinge of the circumoral and nasolabial regions, cutaneous thickenings of the lower portions of the trunk and proximal portions of the limbs, and wrinkling and/or brownish pigmentation of the skin. Loss of hair and lightening of what remains to a blondish-red color are additional hints of what is to follow. Pronounced retardation of bodily growth becomes conspicuous after the first year or two.

Cutaneous alterations further develop during infancy and childhood. Nails become hypoplastic and dystrophic. The expanse of skin becomes diffusely atrophic (except for the sclerotic plaques), xerotic, and mottled in a brownish-orange hue.

The fully developed clinical appearance is stereotypic. Affected individuals look like very little, very old, wizened creatures. The facies is characteristic for the prominent balding scalp relative to hypoplasia of the face (especially micrognathia), the beaked nose with visible contour of the cartilages, the thin lips, and the crowded dentition. The thorax is pyriform and the abdomen protrudes. Tautness of skin and lack of subcutaneous fat emphasize the knobbiness of the joints and also emphasize muscles, ligaments, tendons, and blood vessels. The characteristic erect posture of such a person resembles that of a bow-legged equestrian but withal suggests joint stiffness and instability. Death follows cardiovascular or cerebral complications sometime between the ages of 7 and 27 years.

Changes found in connective tissue include excessively cross-linked structure in collagen, decreased rate of collagenolysis, less acid-soluble collagen and more insoluble residue compared to age-matched controls. The cutaneous, musculoskeletal, and vascular changes display generalized mesenchymal dysplasia in terms of aberrant growth and synthesis, turnover and remodeling of tissues and organs.

Werner's Syndrome (Progeria of the Adult)

Graying of hair may begin in childhood but more often appears in the teens and early 20's. Generalized hypotrichosis soon supervenes. Early cessation of physical growth results in short stature and thin limbs. Remaining symptoms and signs of this recessively inherited disorder emerge during the second and third decades, but exceptions with respect to earlier and later onset are notable.

Cutaneous changes are progressively more severe toward the acral points of the face, forearms, and hands, and especially legs and feet. Atrophy, dyschromia, and scaliness are constant features; telangiectases sometimes develop and the skin appears poikilodermatous. The degenerate and also sclerotic skin, being uncushioned for lack of subcutaneous fat and also tautly stretched, is restrictive of motion of joints, deforming of digits, and revealing of anatomic features of the musculoskeletal and venous systems below.   Nails become dystrophic.

Thick keratoses develop on points of pressure and friction like the digits, soles, ankles, knees, elbows and, less often, on the ears or over the ischial tuberosities. Separation of these callosities is followed by painful and persistent ulcers. Peripheral vascular disease adds the factor of ischemia on the ulcerations and may further predispose to gangrene, osteomyelitis, and soft tissue calcification.

The face develops a tightly-drawn, pinched expression, and the cadaverlike retraction of tissues is all the more emphasized by pseudo-exophthalmos, beaked nose, circumoral radial furrows, taut lips, protuberant teeth, and recessive chin. Other cardinal features of Werner's syndrome are cataracts (posterior cortical and subcapsular), hypogonadism, diabetes mellitus, generalized arteriosclerosis, cardiopathy, and propensity to neoplasia. The conglomerate of changes produces an individual who looks 20–30 years older than his years and one whose life span will be correspondingly shortened.

Other Syndromes

Werner's syndrome and the Hutchinson-Gilford syndrome have been nosologically linked to the term *progeria* and, in a sense, have been adopted by gerontologists as *the* models in which to study unleashed progressions to premature aging or facsimiles thereof. Yet there are other rare syndromes which, at least in some of their aspects, could qualify in the same vein. Some of these will be briefly highlighted.

The dominantly inherited syndrome of *myotonic muscular dystrophy (Steinert's disease)* has numerous features overlapping those of Werner's syndrome. Clinical disturbances, many of which may become apparent during the second and third decades with slow progression thereafter, include male frontal alopecia, testicular atrophy and other endocrinopathy, cataracts, myotonia and atrophy of selective muscles, and cutaneous pilomatricomas.

In *Rothmund's and Thomson's syndromes* (considered together), poikilodermatous changes in selective locations commence in infancy and ultimately resemble chronic radiodermatitis. Photosensitivity is common but

shielded surfaces are also degeneratively affected. Keratoses grow out on hands, feet, and over joints elsewhere. Epidermal carcinomas may develop within the keratoses or in atrophic sites. Other features include dental dysplasia (a marker for the heterozygous "carrier"), cataracts, generalized hypotrichosis, hypogonadism and other endocrinopathy, skeletal anomalies, characteristic facies, and retardation of growth. Life span is not necessarily curtailed.

Cutaneous manifestations of *xeroderma pigmentosum* include variable degrees of photosensitivity, dryness and heavy "freckling" (hence "xeroderma pigmentosum"), progressive poikilodermatous degeneration (especially of exposed surfaces), angiomas, fibromas, keratoacanthomas, premalignant keratoses, and ultimately a host of malignancies which, together with generalized infection, spell out an early demise. Ocular involvement includes photophobia (an early symptom), pigmentations, deformations of the eyelids and related inflammatory lesions of the ocular surface, and neoplastic lesions of the lids, conjunctiva, cornea, and iris. Associated findings include somatic and sexual retardation and many neurologic abnormalities. Clinical variations are notable concerning the integumental and ocular manifestations for different ages of onset (infancy and early childhood being most common) and different rates of progression, and, concerning the associated findings alluded to, for their presence or degrees of involvement. Deficiencies in DNA repair following damages by ultraviolet irradiation or chemicals have been demonstrated in most but not in all patients tested and are thought, by natural progress of the disease, to be related to the cutaneous and ocular changes and to accelerated neuronal loss in the central nervous system (Robbins, Kraemer, and Lutzner, 1974).

Ectodermal findings in *dyskeratosis congenita* include cutaneous atrophy, telangiectasia, and dyschromia; precocious alopecia; ungual, exocrine, and dental dysplasias; and mucosal leukoplakia with neoplastic consequences. Other features include retardation of growth and sexual development and overall frailty. Clinical features of this rare genetic disorder are noted in childhood and lethal consequences of general debilitation, bone marrow hypoplasia, susceptibility to infection, and carcinomatosis supervene between the second and fifth decade (Steier, Van Voolen, and Selmanowitz, 1972).

Certain facial characteristics in the *Hallerman-Streiff syndrome,* namely a bulging forehead, beaked nose, atrophic skin and consequent visibility of subcutaneous veins, along with early lightening and diminution of scalp hair, hypotrichosis of the eyebrows and elsewhere, dental dysplasia, and general retardation of physical development, have led to the erroneous diagnosis of Hutchinson-Gilford "progeria" by several authors. Among the distinguishing features of Hallerman-Streiff syndrome, alopecia of the scalp follows dehiscent cranial sutures, cutaneous atrophy is not generalized, ocular manifestations (including congenital cataracts and microphthalmia) are prominent, and life span is longer.

As a final example, we shall briefly mention that *Cockayne's syndrome* has some progeric semblance outwardly, that photosensitivity plays a role, and that neurologic and retinal abnormalities are related to neuronal atrophy and deficient metabolism of phytanic acid. The reader is now referred to the literature for distinguishing features of this syndrome (Lasser, 1972) and for features of other disorders that might serve as gerontologic models.

DERMAL TISSUE CULTURE

Martin, Sprague, and Epstein (1970) measured the replicative life span of cutaneous fibroblast-type cells in tissue culture in relationship to the decade of normally aging donors. From fetal skin an average growth potential of approximately 44 cell doublings was achieved in serial subculture (excluding the number of cell generations used by the primary explants in attaining the first confluent monolayer). From the first through the ninth decades there was a regression coefficient of -0.20 cell doublings per year. Fibroblasts from three patients with Werner's syndrome (37, 48, and 49 years old) had fewer than 12 doublings, far below the mean of decade-matched controls.

Among patients with either Werner's syndrome or the Hutchinson-Gilford syndrome, differing results obtained from tissue culture studies of cutaneous fibroblasts can be accounted for by variable expressivity in the subjects, inconstant sites for sampling coupled to different degrees of cutaneous involvement, and diverse laboratory procedures (Leider and Selmanowitz, 1976).

Abnormalities reported in Werner's syndrome include: (a) cells difficult to establish in culture (although decreased cloning efficiency is also a feature in the diabetic diathesis apart from that which occurs in Werner's syndrome); (b) markedly prolonged lag phase prior to initiation of growth; (c) reduced replicative life span of cultivated cells, the finding most emphasized but with reported exception; (d) gross changes in the morphologic evolution of the culture; (e) rapid onset of degenerative changes in the form of granular, PAS-positive cytoplasmic inclusions; and (f) decreased incorporation of tritiated thymidine. Though these changes in the main occur in fibroblasts ordinarily derived from elderly donors, they are more pronounced in patients with Werner's syndrome who are half their years. Whether the inordinately restricted replicative life span *in vitro* and other tissue culture abnormalities in Werner's syndrome reflect an unleashed aging phenomenon or some other phenomenon of diseased fibroblasts is a moot question at the current state of knowledge.

In the Hutchinson-Gilford syndrome, there have been reports of failure to establish cultures of cutaneous fibroblasts or attainment of only a few subcultures, but other investigators have not found any major restriction in the replicative life span. Cloning efficiency, mitotic activity, and DNA synthesis have been found to be markedly reduced in the fibroblasts of fully affected individuals, while parents' fibroblasts have lesser degrees of these deficiencies as would be expected from obligatory heterozygotes.

In xeroderma pigmentosum, difficiencies in the DNA repair mechanism have been demonstrated in cutaneous fibroblasts, epidermis, conjunctival epithelium, and peripheral blood lymphocytes. Studies combining cellular fusion and ultraviolet irradiation of cutaneous fibroblasts derived from separate patients have revealed multiple defects in the nuclear DNA repair mechanism (by complementary corrections of these defects among dual origin nuclei contained in the fused cell) and genetic heterogeneity for the condition in point.

ACKNOWLEDGMENT

The authors acknowledge the assistance of Mrs. Desna Donovan in editing and preparing this chapter.

REFERENCES

Baker, H., and Blair, C. P. 1968. Cell replacement in the human stratum corneum in old age. *Brit J. Dermatol.*, **80**, 367-372.

Barman, J. M., Pecoraro, V., and Astore, I. 1969. Biological basis of the inception and evolution of baldness. *J. Geront.*, **24**, 163-168.

Basler, A. 1937. Wachstumsvorgänge am vollentwickelten Organismus. *Med. Klin.*, **33**, 1664-1666.

Bean, W. B. 1968. Nail growth: Twenty-five years' observation. *Arch. Internal Med.*, **122**, 359-361.

Bean, W. B. 1974. Nail growth: 30 years of observation. *Arch. Internal Med.*, **134**, 497-502.

Burton, J. L., Cartlidge, M., and Shuster, S. 1973. Effect of L-dopa on the seborrhea of parkinsonism. *Brit. J. Dermatol.*, **88**, 475-479.

Burton, J. L., Libman, L. J., Hall, R., and Shuster, S. 1971. Laevo-dopa in acne vulgaris. *Lancet*, **2**, 370.

Cannon, D. J., and Davison, P. F. 1973. Cross-linking and aging in rat tendon collagen. *Exp. Geront.*, **8**, 51-62.

Cauna, N. 1965. The effects of aging on the receptor organs of the human dermis. *In*, W. Montagna (ed.), *Advances in Biology of Skin*, Vol. VI, *Aging*, pp. 63-96. Oxford: Pergamon Press.

Cawley, E. P., Hsu, Y. T., Sturgill, B. C., and Harman, L. E. 1973. Lipofuscin ("wear and tear" pigment) in human sweat glands. *J. Invest Dermatol*, **61**, 105-108.

Christophers, E., and Kligman, A. M. 1965. Percutaneous absorption in aged skin. *In*, W. Montagna (ed.), *Advances in Biology of Skin*, Vol. VI, *Aging*, pp. 163-175. Oxford: Pergamon Press.

Colomb, D. 1972. Stellated spontaneous pseudoscars. *Arch. Dermatol.*, **105**, 551-554.

Comaish, S. 1972. White scalp hairs turning black—an unusual reversal of the aging process. *Brit J. Dermatol.*, **86**, 513-514.

Davis, M. J., and Lawler, J. C. 1961. Capillary microscopy in normal and diseased human skin. *In*, W. Montagna and R. A. Ellis (eds.), *Advances in Biology of Skin*, Vol. 2, pp. 79-97. Oxford: Pergamon Press.

Domonkos, A. N. 1968. The aging skin. *Cutis*, **4**, 539-549.

Epstein, E. 1962. *Radiodermatitis*. Springfield, Illinois: Charles C. Thomas.

Fitzpatrick, T. B., Szabó, G., and Mitchell, R. E. 1965. Age changes in the human melanocyte system. *In*, W. Montagna (ed.), *Advances in Biology of Skin*, Vol. VI, *Aging*, pp. 35-50. Oxford: Pergamon Press.

Fleischmajer, R., Perlish, J. S., and Bashey, R. I. 1973. Aging of human dermis. *In*, C. L. Robert (ed.), *Frontiers of Matrix Biology*, Vol. 1, pp. 90-106. Basel: S. Karger.

Freeman, R. G. 1971. Effects of aging on the skin. *In*, E. B. Helwig and F. K. Mostofi (eds.), *The Skin*, pp. 244-260. Baltimore: Williams &Wilkins.

Gelfant, S., and Smith, J. G. 1972. Aging: Non cycling cells an explanation. *Science*, **178**, 357-361.

Hall, D. A. 1961. *The Chemistry of Connective Tissue*, pp. 51-55. Springfield, Illinois: Charles C. Thomas.

Juniper, K., and Dykman, R. A. 1967. Skin resistance, sweat-gland counts, salivary flow, and gastric secretion: Age, race, and sex differences, and intercorrelations. *Psychophysiology*, **4**, 216-222.

Knox, J. M. 1966. The aging skin. *J. Am. Med. Women's Assoc.*, **21**, 659-661.

Krohn, P. L. 1965. Transplantation and aging. *In*, P. L. Krohn (ed.), *Topics in the Biology of Aging*, pp. 125-148. New York: Interscience Publishers; John Wiley.

Lasser, A. E. 1972. Cockayne's syndrome. *Cutis*, **10**, 143-148.

Lavelle, C. 1968. The effect of age on the rate of nail growth. *J. Geront.*, **23**, 557-559.

Leider, M., and Selmanowitz, V. J. 1976 Revision. Unit 4-30: Werner's syndrome (progeria of the adult); Unit 4-31: The Rothmund-Thomson syndrome(s); Unit 4-33: Hutchinson-Gilford syndrome (progeria); Unit 4-39: Poikiloderma atrophicans vasculare. *In*, D. J. Demis, R. L. Dobson, and J. McGuire (eds.), *Clinical Dermatology*, Vol. 1. New York: Harper & Row.

Maguire, H. C. 1964. Facial hair growth over site of testosterone injection in women. *Lancet*, **1**, 864.

Martin, G. M., Sprague, C. A., and Epstein, C. J. 1970. Replicative life-span of cultivated human cells: Effects of donor's age, tissue and genotype. *Lab. Invest.*, **23**, 86-92.

Montagna, W. 1965. Morphology of the aging skin: The cutaneous appendages. *In*, W. Montagna (ed.), *Advances in Biology of Skin*, Vol. VI, *Aging*, pp. 1-16. Oxford: Pergamon Press.

Montagna, W., and Giacometti, L. 1969. Histology and cytochemistry of human skin. XXXII. The external ear. *Arch. Dermatol.*, **99**, 757-767.

Montagna, W., and Parakkal, P. F. 1974. *The Structure and Function of Skin*. 3rd ed. New York: Academic Press.

Oberste-Lehn, H. 1965. Effects of aging on the papillary body of the hair follicles and on the eccrine sweat glands. *In*, W. Montagna (ed.), *Advances in*

Biology of Skin, Vol. VI, *Aging,* pp. 17–34. Oxford: Pergamon Press.

Orentreich, N., and Selmanowitz, V. J. 1969. Levels of biological functions with aging. *Trans. N.Y. Acad. Sci.,* Series II, Vol **31**, No. 8, pp. 992–1012.

Orentreich, N., Selmanowitz, V. J., and Stanislowski, E. 1972. Nailgrowth decline with aging. Abstract #109. *In,* Vol 3, *Ninth International Congress of Gerontology,* Kiev, Russia.

Orentreich, N., and Sharp, N. J. 1967. Keratin replacement as an aging parameter. *J. Soc. Cosmetic Chemists,* **18,** 537–547.

Partridge, S. M. 1970. Biological role of cutaneous elastin. *In,* W. Montagna, J. P. Bentley, and R. L. Dobson (eds.), *Advances in Biology of Skin,* Vol. 10, pp. 69–87. New York: Meredith Corporation.

Plewig, G. 1970. Regional differences of cell sizes in the human stratum corneum. Part II. Effects of sex and age. *J. Invest. Dermatol.,* **54,** 19–23.

Quevedo, W. C., Szabo, G., and Virks, J. 1969. Influences of age and UV on the populations of dopa-positive melanocytes in human skin. *J. Invest. Dermatol.,* **52,** 287–290.

Robbins, J. H. Kraemer, K. H., Lutzner, M. A., et al. 1974. Xeroderma pigmentosum. *Ann. Internal Med.,* **80,** 221–248.

Rook, A., Wilkinson, D. S., and Ebling. F. J. G. 1972. *Textbook of Dermatology,* 2nd ed., p. 1668. Oxford: Blackwell Scientific Publications.

Sams, W. M., Jr., and Smith, J. G., Jr. 1965. Alterations in human dermal fibrous connective tissue with age and chronic sun damage. *In,* W. Montagna (ed.), *Advances in Biology of Skin,* Vol. VI, *Aging,* pp. 199–210. Oxford: Pergamon Press.

Selmanowitz, V. J., Lerer, W., and Orentreich, N. 1970. Multiple noduli cutanei and urinary tract abnormalities. A possible significant association. *Cancer,* **26,** 1256–1260.

Selmanowitz, V. J., and Silverberg, S. G. 1968. How young can a senile keratosis be? *Cutis,* **4,** 279–282.

Shuster, S., and Thody, A. J. 1974. The control and measurement of sebum secretion. *J. Invest. Dermatol.,* **62,** 172–190.

Shuster, S., Thody A. J., Goolamali, S. K., Burton,

J. L., Plummer, N. A., and Bates, D. 1973. Melanocyte-stimulating hormone and parkinsonism. *Lancet,* **1,** 463–465.

Silver, A. F., Montagna, W., and Karacan, I. 1965. The effect of age on human eccrine sweating. *In,* W. Montagna (ed.), *Advances in Biology of Skin,* Vol. VI, *Aging,* pp. 129–150. Oxford: Pergamon Press.

Smith J. G., Jr., Davidson, E. A., and Taylor, R. W. 1965. Human cutaneous acid mucopolysaccharides: The effects of age and chronic sun damage. *In,* W. Montagna (ed.), *Advances in Biology of Skin,* Vol. VI, *Aging,* pp. 211–218. Oxford: Pergamon Press.

Sommerville, D. A. 1969. The effect of age on the normal bacterial flora of the skin. *Brit. J. Dermatol.,* **81,** 14–22.

Spencer, S. K., and Kierland, R. R. 1970. The aging skin: Problems and their causes. *Geriatrics,* **24,** 81–89.

Steier, W., Van Voolen, G. A., and Selmanowitz, V. J. 1972. Dykeratosis congenita: Relationship to Fanconi's anemia. *Blood,* **XXXIX,** 510–521.

Strauss, J. S., and Pochi, P. E. 1968. The changes in human sebaceous gland activity with age. *In,* A. Baccaredda-Boy, G. Moretti, and J. R. Frey (eds.), *Biopathology of Pattern Alopecia,* pp. 166–170. Basel: S. Karger.

Vančiková, O., and Deyl, Z. 1973. Aging of connective tissue. Solubilization of collagen from animals varying in age and species by reagents capable of splitting aldimine bonds. *Exp. Geront.,* **8,** 297–306.

Walsh, R. J. 1964. Variation in the melanin content of New Guinea natives at different ages. *J. Invest. Dermatol.,* **42,** 261–265.

Weigand, D. A., Haygood, C., and Gaylor, J. R. 1974. Cell layers and density of Negro and Caucasian stratum corneum. *J. Invest. Dermatol.,* **62,** 563–568.

Wolf, D. J., and Selmanowitz, V. J. 1970. Poikiloderma vasculare atrophicans. *Cancer,* **25,** 682–686.

Yamasawa, S., Cerimele, D., and Serri, F. 1972. The activity of metabolic enzymes of human epidermis in relation to age. *Brit. J. Dermatol.,* **86,** 134–140.

5 WHOLE ANIMAL LEVEL

21
PATHOBIOLOGY

Arthur C. Upton
State University of New York at Stony Brook

INTRODUCTION

In contrast to preceding chapters which are concerned with age-dependent changes primarily at the level of the individual cell, tissue, organ, or organ system, this chapter considers such changes at the level of the organism as a whole. Because different parts of the body are functionally interdependent, minor modifications in some cells or organs may lead to profound changes in others. Thus, age-dependent changes in the organism must be viewed as the end result of a complex sequence of alterations at various levels of organization, evolving out of the biological amplification of molecular modifications, through biochemical and pathophysiological pathways. The study of the pathobiology of aging at the level of the whole animal is therefore the study of the genesis and evolution of all such changes in the aggregate and of the extent to which their development depends on the interaction of various genetic, constitutional, and environmental influences.

INFLUENCE OF AGE ON LIFE EXPECTANCY, HOMEOSTASIS, VIGOR, AND INCIDENCE OF DISEASE

Life Expectancy

In most organisms, the probability of dying fluctuates up to a certain age, after which it rises progressively with time, owing to deteriorative changes that lower vitality, increase vulnerability to disease, and thereby limit the life span to a maximum characteristic for that species (Lansing, 1959; Comfort, 1964; Timiras, 1972; Sacher, 1976). Although the process of deterioration, or senescence, differs in detail from one organism to another, in humans it manifests itself after childhood in a logarithmic increase in the probability of dying with advancing age. In man, the likelihood of death doubles about once every 8 years after age 30, depending on the specific population (Figure 1). This relationship was first described mathematically by Gompertz (1825) and has since been known as Gompertz's function or Gompertz's Law. A comparable logarithmic increase of the age-specific death rate is observed in aging mammals of other species, provided that they are protected against intercurrent death from malnutrition, predation, or infection. For example, the mortality curves for selected populations of mice may be so similar in shape to those of humans as to be largely superimposable when adjusted for the species difference in overall life span (Figure 2).

From inspection of Figures 1 and 2, it is evident that there is a high and declining rate of mortality during infancy and childhood, which is presumably unrelated to senescence. It is also evident that the rate of mortality in young adults varies appreciably, depending on the geographical population (Figure 1) and on the

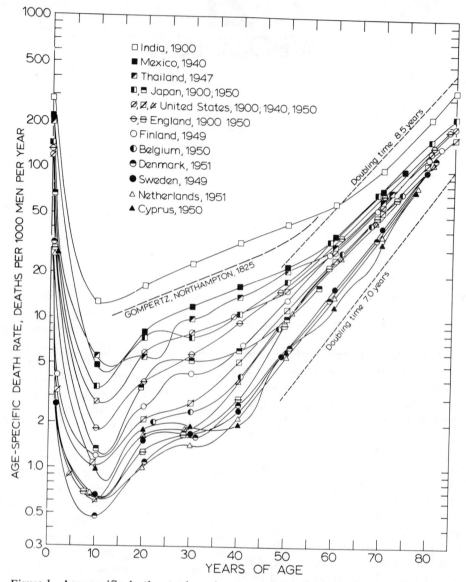

Figure 1. Age-specific death rates in various countries and years. (From Jones, 1955.)

cause of death (Figure 2). Interpretation of the gerontological significance of mortality data thus depends on the ability to distinguish between deaths that are attributable to the effects of aging and those that are attributable to other causes. Although this distinction often remains tentative in our present state of knowledge, it is noteworthy that differences similar to those in Figure 1 exist between populations of Swedish women living many years ago and those living more recently. Mortality curves for the successive populations diverge most markedly during childhood and early adult life (Figure 3). The most obvious explanation for such differences in life expectancy lies in the dramatic reduction in mortality from infectious diseases that has occurred in advanced countries within the past century as a result of improvements in nutrition, sanitation, public health, and medical care (Figure 4). Further evidence of this reduction comes from comparative studies on the mortality of

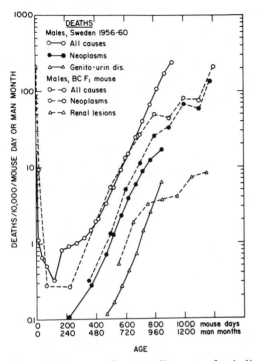

Figure 2. Age-specific mortality rates for indicated causes in Swedish males and BCF$_1$ male mice. (From Grahn, 1970.)

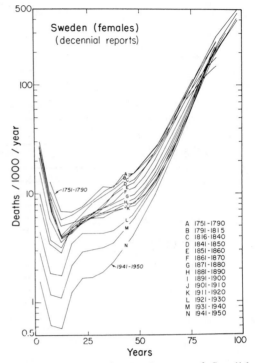

Figure 3. Age-specific death rates of Swedish females in various periods from 1751 to 1950. (From Jones, 1959.)

successive generations (Figures 5-7). Those born and reared in recent times enjoy lower death rates at essentially all ages than their predecessors, with the differences again being most dramatic early in life, causing the survival curve for recent cohorts to become progressively more rectangular in shape (Figure 7).

The tendency for the risk of death to attain roughly the same rate of increase in all elderly populations, irrespective of variations in mortality earlier in life, is paralleled by similar age-dependent increases in the rates of such diseases as arteriosclerosis, including its various complications, and cancer (Figure 8). These causes of death do not account for the slope of the curve, however, since even if they could be prevented, the resulting curve (i.e., the ALL-AS-NEOPL curve in Figure 8) would lie roughly parallel to the original (i.e., ALL CAUSES) curve, but displaced slightly to the right (Kohn, 1976). The population would then merely die from other diseases—notably influenza and pneumonia—and accidents, the risks of which rise faster during old age than the overall risk of death

from all causes (Kohn, 1963, 1976). The similar increase with age in the rates of different diseases, in animals (Simms, 1967) as well as in humans, implies that the progression of deteriorative changes in various tissues of the body is influenced by a "common factor" (Figure 9). Although yet to be identified, such a factor may be subject to the influences of other variables, such as: species, age, sex, diet, metabolism, and other constitutional and environmental determinants.

The gains in life expectancy associated with improvements in the environment have not been confined to the early years of life, since even in middle age, the mortality curves of recently born cohort populations (Figure 6) fail to converge with those of populations born earlier (Figures 3,6). This persistent displacement has been interpreted as evidence that improved health early in life leads to a lasting reduction in "physiological age" (Jones, 1959).

The final slope of the mortality curve in later decades of life, as contrasted with its intercept,

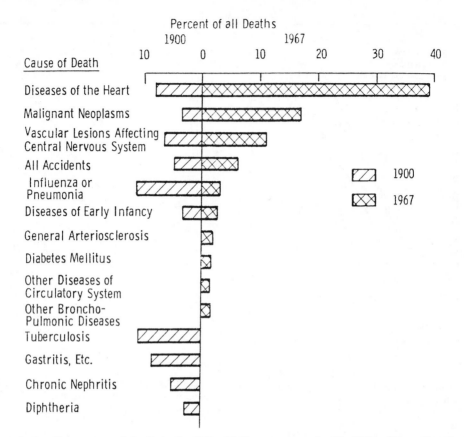

Figure 4. Leading causes of death in the U.S., 1967, as compared with 1900. (From Donabedian, Axelrod, Swearingen, and Jameson, 1972.)

seems to be affected relatively little by ordinary variations in the environment (Figures 1, 3, 6). Because the increase in risk of death from all causes is paralleled by a similar increase in the risk of death from most major diseases, the constancy of the curve implies the existence of some relatively invariant process of age-dependent deterioration, or "physiologic aging," associated with growing vulnerability to stress, injury, and disease, in general.

Homeostasis

Adaptation to stress, involving readjustment of biological conditions to equilibrium, is slower in the elderly than in the young (Shock, 1960; Comfort, 1968; Bertolini and de Sabata, 1969; Kohn, 1971; Timiras, 1972). The gradual decline in ability to maintain regulatory equilibrium is viewed in several theories as central to the process of aging, death being conceived

as a chance (stochastic) event (Figure 10), resulting from disruptive effects of strains that would be tolerated at younger ages (Selye and Prioreschi, 1960; Strehler and Mildvan, 1960; Sacher and Trucco, 1962; Comfort, 1964; Sacher, 1968). The stochastic theories of death also tentatively explain how a gradual decrement in physiological performance (Figure 11) can give rise to an exponentially rising probability of death (Sacher, 1968). With progressive deterioration in physiological (Figure 11), hormonal (Gusseck, 1972, Timiras, 1972; Finch, 1976a; Andres and Tobin, 1976), and neural (Timiras, 1972; Finch, 1976a) regulation, there is an age-dependent decline in resistance to radiation (Storer, 1965; Kohn, 1971), cold stress (Finch, Foster, and Mirsky, 1969), and other physiological (Kohn, 1971; Timiras, 1972) and emotional stresses (Kimmel, 1974). It should be noted in passing, however, that not all functions change so dramatically as is

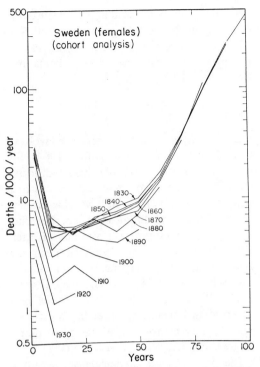

Figure 5. Age-specific death rates of Swedish females, analyzed by cohorts, 1830-1930. (From Jones, 1959.)

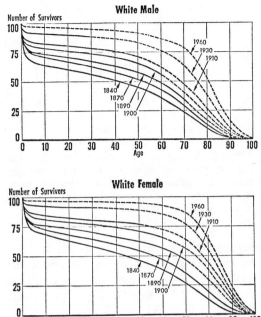

Figure 7. Survivorship from birth to successive ages in U.S. white males and females analyzed by year of birth 1840-1960, with projections as indicated by dashed portions of curves. (From Jacobson, 1964.)

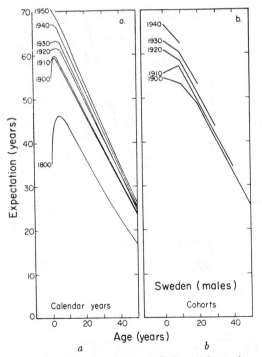

Figure 6. Life-expectancy of Swedish males, analyzed by (a) calendar year, 1800-1950, and (b) cohort, 1900-1940. (From Jones, 1959.)

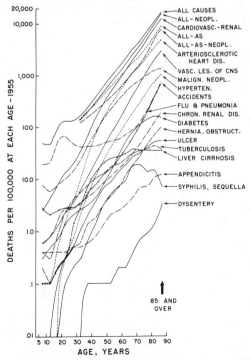

Figure 8. Age-specific death rates for major causes, in the U.S., 1955. (From Kohn, 1963.)

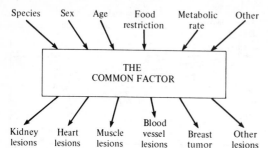

Figure 9. Schematic representation of the "common factor" postulated to influence the rate of progression of age-dependent lesions in various tissues, and some of the agents affecting it. (From Simms, 1967.)

suggested by the curves in Figure 11. The decrements indicated therein may themselves be misleading to the extent that they include cross-sectional data reflecting contributions from subpopulations with certain diseases. The overriding importance of hormonal factors in some senescent changes (Finch, Foster, and Mirsky, 1969; Selye, 1970; Finch, 1976b; Andres and Tobin, 1976) is exemplified in the

dramatic alterations leading to death after spawning in Pacific salmon, which result from adrenal cortiscosteroid toxicosis and can be prevented by castration during immaturity (Robertson, 1961).

Vigor

It is generally agreed that senescence involves a general decline in vigor (Comfort, 1964), but this process is yet to be fully characterized and quantified. Diminution with age in muscular strength (Figure 12), physical working capacity (Daly, Barry, and Birkhead, 1968; Henschel, 1970), psychomotor performance (Birren, 1964; Davies and Tune, 1969; Gutmann and Hanzlikova, 1972; Harkins, Nowlin, Ramm, and Schroeder, 1974), and creativity (Dennis, 1966; Botwinick, 1967, 1973) have been observed in humans. In mice, the capacity to sustain physical exercise, expressed in output of gram-calories, declines with age (Figure 13).

The above changes are detectable too early in life to result from debilitating effects of age-

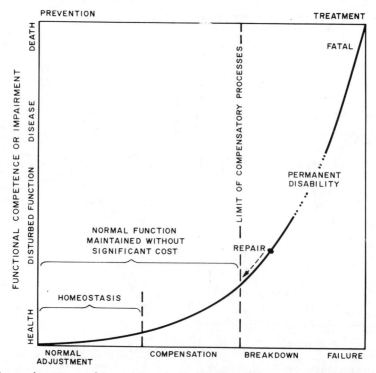

Figure 10. Successive stages of homeostasis, from normal adjustment to breakdown, failure, and death. (From Timiras, 1972.)

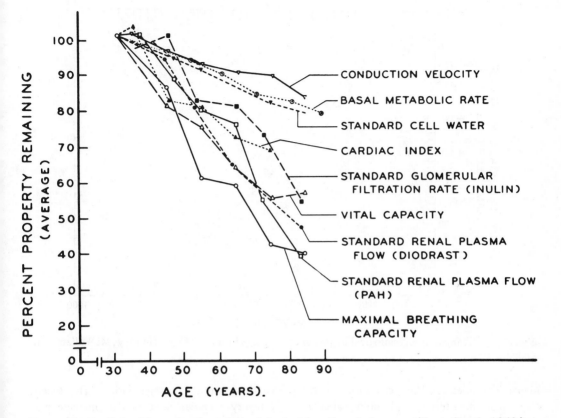

Figure 11. Decline with age in selected physiological functions in humans. (From Shock, 1960.)

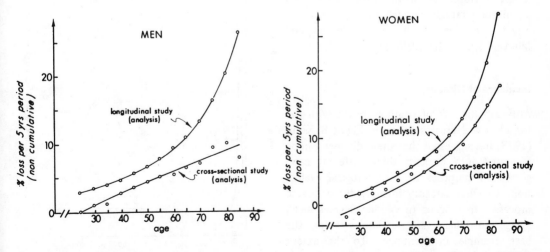

Figure 12. Relative loss of muscular strength with age in men and women. (From Clement, 1974.)

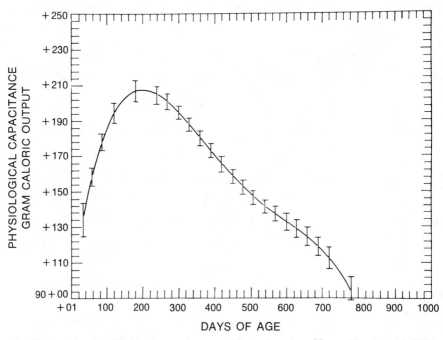

Figure 13. Changes in physiological capacitance with age in mice. (From Hensley, McWilliams, and Oakley, 1964.)

dependent diseases. They can more plausibly be explained in terms of physiological changes in the central nervous system (see Chapters 10-11), muscular system, and other vital organ systems (see Chapters 16-18). The loss of vigor, viewed in the context of the entropic or informational theories of aging (see Chapter 2), extends to the hypothesis that age-dependent mortality occurs when the organism can no longer perform the work needed to restore equilibrium rapidly enough to cope with the effects of a given challenge (Strehler and Mildvan, 1960; Atlan, 1968).

Incidence of Disease

Although the risk of death increases with age for all of the diseases shown in Figure 8, Kohn (1973) has suggested that these diseases can be separated into at least three different categories for purposes of gerontological evaluation. The first category includes those disease processes that occur to varying degrees in all aging individuals, arteriosclerosis being the best example in mammals. To the extent that arteriosclerotic changes are universal, progressive, and irreversible, they would inevitably prove fatal if some other cause of

death did not intervene earlier. The second category includes diseases that increase with age but are not universal in the population; one such example is neoplasia. Some forms of neo-

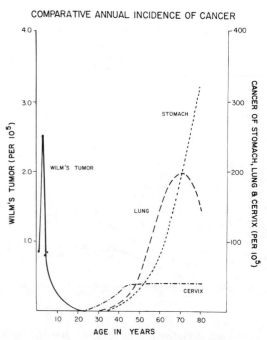

Figure 14. Age-specific incidence of several types of cancer in humans. (From Doll, 1970.)

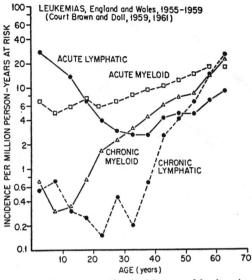

Figure 15. Age-specific incidence of leukemias in humans. (From Upton, 1964.)

plasia may attain peak incidence levels at earlier ages than others (Figures 14, 15), reflecting age variations in susceptibility, age differences in time of exposure to cancer-inducing stimuli, differences in the time required for induction and evolution of the cancer process, and/or dying off of susceptible subpopulations. The third category comprises diseases that are not causally related to aging but have more serious consequences in older individuals, e.g., pneumonia, influenza, other infectious, inflammatory, or toxic reactions, and accidents.

DISEASES ASSOCIATED WITH AGING

Spontaneous Diseases

Although some age-dependent diseases have been shown to result from the influence of environmental agents, most of the degenerative diseases of aging have yet to be linked to such agents, except possibly in the role of modifiers or cofactors. Such diseases are generally assumed to arise primarily through intrinsic causes and thus to occur "spontaneously" with advancing age.

Since the diseases of aging have already been discussed in previous chapters on relevant organ systems, they will not be reviewed here except to comment (for purposes of overall perspective) on their place in the aging of the

organism as a whole. Most prominent among the spontaneous diseases accounting for death in aging humans are arteriosclerosis, cancer, diabetes, hypertension, and renal disease (Figure 8). Of these, the leading cause of death is arteriosclerosis and its various complications. Similarly, in other species of mammals, cardiovascular changes, renal diseases, and neoplasms are among the most prominent lesions associated with aging (Figure 16).

As emphasized above, arteriosclerotic changes are universal, progressive, and incompletely reversible, affecting to varying degrees all mammals. Hence, although the form and severity of the arteriosclerotic process may be influenced by genetic and environmental factors, its occurrence in some form is a more or less constant accompaniment of aging. Depending on the anatomical distribution and severity of arteriosclerotic changes, they may lead to functional impairment and degeneration in virtually any organ of the body, thereby complicating any other senescent processes that may also be present. As discussed elsewhere, the manifestations of arteriosclerosis and its complications may vary markedly, depending on genetic and environmental influences (Kohn, 1976). Atherosclerotic changes, which are prevalent and severe in some human populations, may be relatively inconspicuous in others and may be even more variable among nonhuman species (Roberts and Straus, 1965). Conversely, the deposition of amyloid, which is seldom severe in humans, may be the most consistent and prominent vascular lesion in aging mice of certain strains (Cohen, 1965). Proliferative forms of arteriopathy may, likewise, characteristically accompany aging in some animals (Upton, Conklin, Cosgrove, Gude, and Darden, 1967; Beach, Bair, Pirani, Cox, and Dixon, 1974), although such changes are relatively rare in humans.

Constant among the changes affecting blood vessel walls in arteriosclerosis are degenerative changes of elastin and collagen (Kohn, 1976). These changes steadily progress throughout life, largely unopposed by mechanisms of biological repair (Balazs, 1976; Kohn, 1976). The extent to which the resulting deterioration of the extracellular microenvironment contributes to the overall decline in physiological function that occurs with advancing age (Figure

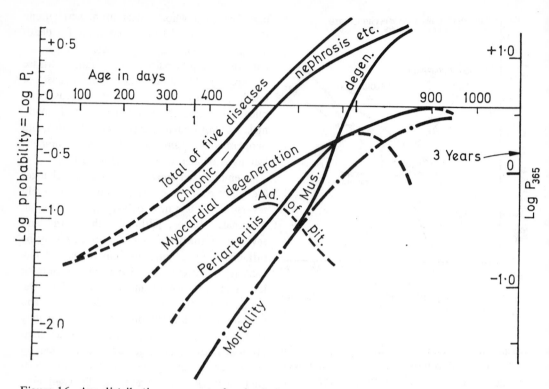

Figure 16. Age distribution on onset of major lesions, as compared with mortality from all causes, in aging rats. (From Simms, 1967.)

11) is yet to be fully determined but may be presumed to be appreciable.

Neoplasms, benign and malignant, comprise another major category of disease and death in old age (Figures 8, 14, 15). As emphasized elsewhere (Doll, 1970; Ponten, 1976) not all forms of cancer show the same relationship between incidence and age. Four different patterns characterize the majority of common neoplasms (Figures 14, 15). The first pattern, typified by Wilm's tumor of the kidney (Figure 14), shows a peak incidence early in life, followed by a decline; some other neoplasms in this category, e.g., acute lymphatic leukemia (Figure 15), show an uninterrupted increase in incidence throughout adult life, with virtually no cases in childhood. The third pattern, exemplified by cancer of the lung, shows a gradual increase up to a certain age, after which the incidence declines (Figure 14). The fourth, typified by carcinoma of the breast and carcinoma of the cervix (Figure 14), shows a rise in incidence until middle age, after which the

rate of increase slows or ceases. Many forms of cancer increase in proportion to a power function of the age; the power of the age that provides the best fit for cancer of the gastrointestinal tract is approximately five or six, for cancer of the skin (other than melanoma), four, and for cancer of the prostate, approximately eleven (Doll, 1970). To explain the power relationship between cancer incidence and age, various theories have been generated, including the hypotheses that cancer occurs when a critical number of neighboring cells becomes altered, or that the disease is the end-result of a succession of mutational changes, some or all of which may be inherited (Doll, 1970; Knudson, 1973). In fact the age relationship is compatible with many models, all of which must take into account the multistage nature of the cancer process and the evidence that its initiation and progression may be influenced by many interacting variables (Doll, 1970, Farber, 1973; Knudson, 1973).

Epidemiologic studies imply that susceptibility to radiation-induced leukemia increases with age at irradiation in adult human populations, such that the excess attributable to a given dose of radiation approximates a constant multiple of the natural age-specific incidence (Figure 17), as opposed to a constant number of additional cases, irrespective of age. This relationship suggests that the effects of radiation are similar to those of aging. There is no evidence that susceptibility to the induction of other neoplasms bears the same relationship to age (Doll, 1970; National Academy of Science, 1972).

The incidence of bronchial carcinoma in cigarette smokers increases with the duration of exposure, at a rate almost exactly paralleling the rise with age in nonsmokers, implying that the "natural" occurrence of the tumors in nonsmokers might result from cumulative exposure to a carcinogenic agent present in

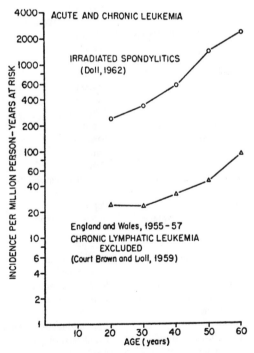

Figure 17. Age-specific incidence of leukemia (all types excluding chronic lymphatic) in patients treated with spinal irradiation for ankylosing spondylitis, in relation to age at onset of treatment, as compared with age-specific incidence of leukemia (all types excluding chronic lymphatic) in population of England and Wales. (From Upton, 1964.)

the atmosphere and inhaled from birth (Doll, 1970). The increase in incidence with age that is characteristic of many other neoplasms might, similarly, be attributed to prolonged exposure to carcinogenic stimuli (Doll, 1970). The possible contribution of other influences such as the age-dependent decline in immunological competence (Teller, 1972; Cheney and Walford, 1973; Makinodan, 1976), activation of latent oncogenic viruses (Rauscher and O'Connor, 1973; Rowe, 1973), disturbances in hormonal regulation (Andres and Tobin, 1976), and other age-dependent changes (Farber, 1973; Ponten, 1976) must also be considered in any critical assessment of age-incidence relationships.

A comprehensive review of the relation between neoplasia and aging is beyond the scope of this chapter. Cogent discussions and references are available elsewhere (Garner and Brown, 1967; Kohn, 1971; Andrew, 1969; Doll, 1970; Hollander, 1973; Smith, Walford, and Mickey, 1973; Ponten, 1976).

Infectious Diseases

Even in the *germfree* state, animals develop many of the neoplasms and nonneoplastic lesions that are characteristic of senescence in their conventional counterparts, although not necessarily in the same relative frequencies and severities (Walburg and Cosgrove, 1967; Gordon, 1968; Saloman, 1968; Pollard and Kajima, 1970; Walburg, 1973). It is evident, therefore, that microbial contaminants of the environment do not generally play a decisive role in the pathogenesis of the diseases of aging. Such agents may contribute, however, to the development of lesions in tissues that are normally in direct contact with mircoorganisms or concerned indirectly with antimicrobial defenses (Pleasants, 1968). Infection may also supervene in aging individuals as a complication of underlying circulatory disturbances, urinary retention, altered immunological responsiveness, or other degenerative changes (Höring, 1969).

Activation of latent oncogenic viruses (Ponten, 1976) appears to constitute an important mechanism of neoplasia in aging individuals. The lengthening list of such growths now includes viral tumors of virtually every type, with examples in nearly all of the commonly studied species of vertebrates (Table 1). Viewed historically, moreover, viral oncology is still in an early stage of evolution (Rowe, 1973).

The first phase of viral oncology (roughly from 1910 to 1935) was dominated by studies of avian tumor viruses, in which

TABLE 1. VIRUSES THAT INDUCE NEOPLASMS IN ANIMALS.

Common name of virus	No. of major isolates	Host of origin	Produces neoplasia in:	Tumor type in animals
Mouse leukemia (MLV)	16	Mouse	Mouse, rats, hamsters	Leukemia, lymphoma
Mouse sarcoma (MSV)	6	Mouse	Mouse, rats, hamsters, cats, tissue culture	Sarcomas
Polyoma (Py)	2	Mouse	Mouse, hamsters, tissue culture	All types except leukemia
Mammary tumor (MTV)	2	Mouse	Mouse	Carcinoma
Chicken leukemia (ALV)	4	Chicken	Chicken, tissue culture	Leukemia
Twiehaus	1	Chicken	Chicken, quail, hamster	Reticuloendotheliosis
Chicken sarcoma	9	Chicken	Chicken, quail, turkey, duck, hamster, monkey, snake, tissue culture	Sarcoma
Marek's (MHV)	1	Chicken	Chicken	Lymphoma
CELO	1	Chicken	Hamster	Sarcoma
Cat leukemia (FLV)	4	Cat	Cat	Leukemia, lymphoma
Cat sarcoma (FSV)	3	Cat	Cat, rat, dog, monkey, tissue culture	Sarcoma
G. pig leukemia	1	G. pig	G. pig	Leukemia
G. pig herpes	1	G. pig	G. pig	Sarcoma
Deer fibroma	1	Deer	Deer	Fibroma
Squirrel fibroma	1	Squirrel	Squirrel	Fibroma
Shope fibroma	1	Rabbit	Rabbit	Fibroma
Shope papilloma	1	Rabbit	Rabbit	Papilloma
Dog sarcoma	1	Dog	Dog, tissue culture	Sarcoma
Dog mast cell	1	Dog	Dog	Carcinoma
Lucké	1	Frog	Frog	Carcinoma
Human adeno	31[a]	Man	Hamster, mouse, tissue culture	Sarcoma, lymphoma
Wart	1	Man	Man	Papilloma
Hybrids[b]	7	Monkey, man, cat mouse	Hamster, cat, tissue culture	Sarcoma, lymphoma
Yaba	1	Monkey	Monkey, man	Histiocytoma
H. saimiri	1	Monkey	Monkey	Lymphoma
Simian adeno	6	Monkey	Hamster, tissue culture	Sarcoma, lymphoma
SV40[c]	1	Monkey	Hamster, mouse, tissue culture	Lymphosarcoma
Graffi hamster	2	Hamster	Hamster	Lymphoma, papilloma
Bovine papilloma	1	Cow	Cow, horse, mouse, hamster	Papilloma, fibroma, sarcoma
Bullhead papilloma	1	Fish	Fish (bullhead catfish)	Papilloma
	110			

[a] As of May 1970 approximately 12 of 31 human adenoviruses induce malignancies in hamsters. These 12 and the remaining 19 induce discrete foci of transformed (apparently cancerous) cells in tissue cultures.
[b] Hybrid = Genotypic recombinants of 2 different viruses, e.g., SV40 + adeno; cat leukemia + mouse sarcoma.
[c] Simian virus 40.

From Rauscher and O'Connor, 1973.

efforts to establish etiologic relationships in terms of Koch's postulates were frustrated repeatedly by expectations that are now known not to be strictly applicable to oncogenic viruses; namely, that the virus causes rapid onset of disease and remains readily detectable thereafter. Failure to fulfill Koch's postulates consistently, especially in mammalian tumors, prevented the viral hypothesis from gaining general credence at that time (Rowe, 1973). The second period (from about 1935 to 1960) saw the discovery of a growing number of mammalian tumor viruses, the realization that such viruses usually require specific genetic, physiologic, or environmental cofactors, and the recognition that the resulting neoplasms might develop only after a long latency, appear in but few of the infected animals, and be noninfectious themselves (Rowe, 1973). During the third era (in the early 1960's), it became evident that tumorigenesis by DNA viruses was characteristically accompanied by integration of viral genes into the genome of the host cell, after which the viral genes could be expressed without any required production of infectious virus. These observations served to reconcile the lack of correlation between patterns of cancer incidence and epidemiological evidence for an infectious causative agent. The observations also suggested that any DNA virus might conceivably exert carcinogenic effects under appropriate circumstances, thus stimulating a search for oncogenic activity among common viruses. This has since led to the demonstration of tumorigenesis by adenoviruses and the implication of *Herpes simplex* in certain types of cancer (Rowe, 1973). The fourth and most recent phase of viral oncology has seen the emergence of the revolutionary concept that RNA tumor viruses, like their DNA counterparts, contribute genetic information which becomes part of the genome of the host cell. With this latest development in viral oncology, tumor viruses have come to be considered more properly as endogenous, rather than exogenous, to the host (Rowe, 1973).

The viral information that is integrated into the genome of the host cell is viewed in each of the two currently prevailing hypotheses—the "oncogene" hypothesis (Huebner and Todaro, 1969; Huebner et al., 1970) and the "protovirus" hypothesis (Temin and Baltimore, 1972)—as constituting part of the normal inheritance of the cell. The "oncogene" hypothesis postulates that the genome of C-type RNA viruses consists of (1) "virogenes," which code for replication of the virus, and (2) "oncogenes," which code for neoplastic transformation of the host cell. Such viral genomes are held to be widespread in vertebrates, to be transmitted vertically in the germ line, and to play a role in normal cellular growth and differentiation by coding for alloantigens, or differentiation antigens, on the cell surface. According to this theory, cancer is envisioned to result from derepression of viral oncogenes through the action of external carcinogens or through spontaneously occurring, stochastic, somatic mutational events, without necessarily any derepression of virogenes or virus production. The "protovirus" hypothesis, on the other hand, postulates that genetic information is transmitted within or among somatic cells from the DNA in "protovirus" regions of the genome by RNA intermediates and thence, via reverse transcriptase, back into DNA sequences which are reinserted into the genome. It is proposed that through this mechanism existing genes can be amplified, and new DNA sequences evolved in differentiation, without affecting the stability of the germ line. It is the "misevolution" of protoviruses, either by mutation of their base sequences or by misinsertion into the wrong sites in the genome, that is postulated to result in neoplastic transformation of the affected cell.

Although knowledge of the genetic composition of oncogenic viruses and of the mechanisms regulating their expression is still meager, it is clear that viral mutants are constantly being formed which differ in their transformation and replication abilities, host cell range, specification of virus-associated cell surface antigens, and other properties. Depending on the nature of a given mutation, the mutant may be said to be "defective" for the property in question. The occurrence of genetic interactions between defective and nondefective mutants, and between defective mutants and host cell genomes, has been indicated by "marker rescue" phenomena. However genetic mapping of the oncogenic viruses and characterization of their genetic interactions are still at a rudimentary stage (Tooze, 1973).

The genetic heterogeneity among tumor viruses is paralleled by heterogeneity among host cells in susceptibility to transformation by a given virus, reflecting the complexity of interactions between viral and host cell genomes. In avian cells, as well as mouse cells (Table 2), several genetic loci have been found to influence the control of spontaneous and induced virus activation, expression of viral antigen, susceptibility to dissemination of viral infection, and the host's ability to respond immunologically to virus-induced antigens in the transformed cells.

Although with the exception of the wart virus, viral agents have yet to be implicated conclusively in the pathogenesis of neoplastic lesions in humans, the susceptibility of human cells to virus-induced "neoplastic" transformation *in vitro* is amply documented (Rauscher and O'Connor, 1973). There is growing indirect evidence implicating viruses in human neoplasia: e.g., (1) the frequent occurrence of characteristic virus particles in the cells of certain malignancies; (2) the association of group-specific, possibly viral or virus-mediated, antigens with the cells of some neoplasms; (3) the presence of reverse transcriptase of viral type in certain cancer cells; and (4) the presence in certain cancer cell nuclei of DNA base sequences complementary with the base sequences of known or suspect tumor viruses

TABLE 2. GENES AFFECTING THE EXPRESSION OF ENDOGENOUS MURINE LEUKEMIA VIRUS.

Linkage group	Location	Designation	Allele	Expression	Phenotype	Mouse strain
I	viral?	V_1	V_1	dominant	N-tropic MLV release	AKR
			V_1	recessive	no MLV release	
unknown not I, VIII, IX	viral?	V_2	V_2	dominant	N-tropic MLV release	AKR
			V_2	recessive	no MLV release	
unknown not VIII	viral?	Ind	Ind^+	dominant	N-tropic MLV release	Balb/c
			Ind^-	recessive	no MLV release	NIH-Swiss
unknown	?	none	+	dominant	gs antigen	AKR
			−	recessive	no gs antigen	C57BL
unknown	?	none	+	dominant	MLV release if gs^+ gene is present	AKR
			−	recessive	no MLV release	
unknown	?	Mlv-1	$Mlv-1^a$	recessive	gs antigen	B10, D2
			$Mlv-1^b$	dominant	no gs antigen	
VIII	host	Fv-1	$Fv-1^n$	recessive	susceptibility to N-tropic MLV	AKR, C58
			$Fv-1^b$	recessive	susceptibility to B-tropic MLV	C57BL/6 Balb/c
IX	host	H-2	$H-2^k$	semidominant	early leukemia	AKR
			$H-2^b$	semidominant	late leukemia	$AKR/H-2^b$
IX	viral?	Tla	Tla^+	dominant	epistatic for TL antigen expression	A, C58
			Tla^-	recessive	no TL antigen	AKR, C57BL/6
IX	viral?	G_{ix}	G_{ix}^+	semidominant	G_{ix} antigen	129
			G_{ix}^-	semidominant	no G_{ix} antigen	
unknown not IX	viral?	none	+	dominant	G_{ix} antigen	129
			−	recessive	no G_{ix} antigen	

From Tooze, 1973.

(Rauscher and O'Connor, 1973; Tooze, 1973).

The mechanisms by which latent viruses become activated in aging animals remain to be fully elucidated; however, leukemogenesis by whole-body irradiation in C57BL mice appears to involve radiation-induced depression of immunity to an endogenous leukemia virus (Haran-Ghera and Peled, 1968). The virus is immunogenic to nonirradiated animals, hence rarely emerging in such animals except during senescence (Haran-Ghera, 1973). Radiation-induced immunosuppression has, likewise, been implicated as a factor in leukemogenesis in RF mice, based on the reciprocal correlation between the incidence of lymphoid neoplasms and the severity of chronic glomerular lesions containing antiviral antibody in such animals (Clapp and Yuhas, 1973). The occurrence of a similar chronic immunological response against endogenous C-type viruses has been demonstrated in nonirradiated nonleukemic AKR (Oldstone, Aoki, and Dixon, 1972), RF (Hanna, Snodgrass, Tennant, Yuhas, and Batzing, 1973), and B6C3Fl (Batzing, Yurcomic, and Hanna, 1974) mice, indicating that classical tolerance to endogenous viral antigens is incomplete in these animals. Based on such evidence, and the observation that viral antigens are detectable in mouse tissues most consistently either prior to immunological maturity or during immunological senescence, it has been suggested that susceptibility to leukemogenesis is inversely correlated with antiviral immunity in mouse strains of low-leukemia incidence (Hanna et al., 1973; Yuhas, Tennant, Hanna, and Clapp, 1973).

The induction of virus release by radiation, chemical carcinogens, and chemical mutagens is also yet to be fully explained. In this process, however, iododeoxyuridine (IUdR) and bromodeoxyuridine (BUdR) have been found to be vastly more effective than x-rays, the former inducing the release of murine virus in about 1 percent of cells, as compared with 0.001–0.01 percent of cells in the case of x-rays. The evidence suggests that the induction of virus involves excision of the integrated viral DNA, in this respect resembling induction of lambda phage and other integrated viral genomes. The release of endogenous virus is also more readily induced in the cells of established lines and lines that have become transformed than in newly cultured or nontransformed cells (Tooze, 1973). In this regard, it is noteworthy that cells from patients with chromosomal aberrations possess enhanced susceptibility to viral transformation *in vitro* (Miller and Todaro, 1969) which may be of gerontologic significance in view of the rising frequency of chromosomal abnormalities with advancing age (Jacobs, Brunton, and Court Brown, 1963; Jarvik, Yen, and Moralishvili, 1974). The possibility that viruses may be involved in the pathogenesis of nonneoplastic chronic and degenerative lesions of aging is suggested by the *slow (progressive) virus infections* (Abinanti, 1971; Gajdusek, 1972) and so-called autoimmune diseases (Lewis, 1974), since the characteristics of these diseases (Table 3) include: (1) long incubation period (months to years), (2) insidious onset of illness, (3) protracted clinical course, (4) fatal outcome, and (5) pathologic changes unlike those typical of acute viral diseases (Abinanti, 1971). The organs and tissues affected include the brain, kidney, lung, reticuloendothelial system, liver, and vascular system (Abinanti, 1971; Gajdusek, 1972;

TABLE 3. EXAMPLES OF SLOW VIRAL INFECTIONS.

Virus	Host	Organ primarily affected
Kuru	Man	Brain
Subacute sclerosing panencephalitis	Man	Brain
Creutzfeldt-Jakob disease	Man	Brain
Progressive multifocal leukoencephalopathy	Man	Brain
Scrapie	Sheep	Brain
Visna	Sheep	Brain
Maedi	Sheep	Lung
Progressive pneumonia	Sheep	Lung
Lymphocytic choriomeningitis	Mouse	Kidney, brain, liver
Aleutian mink disease	Mink	Reticuloendothelial system
Mink encephalopathy	Mink	Brain

From Davies, Dulbecco, Eisen, Ginsberg, Wood, and McCarty, 1973.

Lewis, 1974). The pathologic changes have features in common with those lesions characteristic of senescence. Hence the possibility must be considered that the latter may in some instances result from activation of latent viruses, without necessarily any infectious virus being readily detectable at the time of death. In this connection, it is noteworthy that oncogenic viruses have, in certain instances, been reported to cause deleterious effects apart from their oncogenic effects *per se*. In mice, the presence of the mammary tumor agent has been interpreted to decrease longevity (Storer, 1966a) and to impair immunological responsiveness (Griswold, Heppner, and Calabresi, 1973) in the absence of mammary tumor formation. Impairment of the immune response has also been reported to follow infection with leukemia viruses in the mouse (Hanna, *et al.*,

1973; Shearer, Mozes, Haran-Ghera, and Bentwich, 1973).

INFLUENCE OF ENVIRONMENTAL FACTORS

Additional evidence relating age-dependent morbidity and mortality to environmental factors is the suggested correlation between day-to-day health practices (i.e., regularity of meals, hours of sleep, smoking habits, and alcohol consumption) and the rates of age-specific morbidity (Belloc and Breslow, 1972) and mortality (Figure 18). The above observations, along with the additional evidence reviewed elsewhere (Barrows and Roeder, 1976; Sacher, 1976), indicate that environmental factors influence age-dependent disease and death rates through a complex series of mechanisms. The

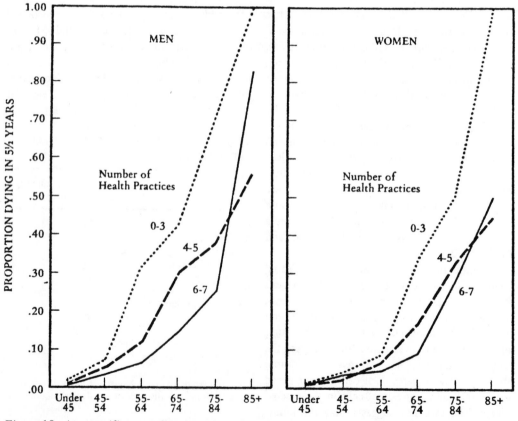

Figure 18. Age-specific mortality rates in a study population of men and women, in relation to number of health practices. (From Belloc, 1973). Note that men and women with 6–7 favorable health practices show consistently lower death rates than do those with only 0–3 such health practices.

variations attributable to environmental factors are relatively small in comparison with the large differences among the various species (Rockstein, Chesky, and Sussman, 1976). Hence it may be concluded that the longevity normally attainable by a given species is determined primarily by its genetic constitution.

INFLUENCE OF GENETIC FACTORS

Familial Concordance

Correlation between longevity and ancestry is well documented in laboratory animals and human beings (Lansing, 1959; Kallman and Jarvik, 1959; Glass, 1960; Comfort, 1964; Abbott, Murphy, Bolling, and Abbey, 1974). In inbred laboratory mice, animals of long-lived strains have a mean life span more than twice as long as do those of short-lived strains (Storer, 1966b). Likewise, human offspring of long-lived parents tend to outlive those of shorter-lived parents (Table 4). Monozygotic twins show a closer correlation in longevity than do dizygotic twins of the same sex (Table 5).

Although the role of specific genes in longevity is yet to be defined, survival represents the summation of various physiologic processes changing throughout life and in response to environmental factors. Hence, gradations in survival must be attributed to interactions of many

TABLE 4. LONGEVITY OF HUMAN OFFSPRING IN RELATION TO THE LONGEVITY OF THEIR PARENTS.[a]

| Father's Age at Death (years) | MOTHER'S AGE AT DEATH (YEARS) | | |
| | Under 60 | 60–80 | Over 80 |
	Offspring's mean age at death (years)		
Under 60	32.8 (128)[b]	33.4 (120)	36.3 (74)
60–80	35.8 (251)	38.0 (328)	45.0 (172)
Over 80	42.3 (131)	45.5 (206)	52.7 (184)

[a]From Pearl (1922), after Bell (in Kallman and Jarvik, 1959).
[b]Figures in parentheses indicate numbers of offspring on which mean is based.

genes, any one of which generally produces only minor variations in the life span.

Specific Diseases

Exceptions to the above generalization, that single genes ordinarily exert only minor effects, include the rare syndromes of progeria—infantile progeria (Hutchinson-Gilford syndrome) and adult progeria (Werner's syndrome). These syndromes present many of the characteristics of premature senescence, and some forms appear to be transmitted as autosomal

TABLE 5. LIFE SPAN DIFFERENCES IN SAME-SEX MONOZYGOTIC, AS COMPARED WITH DIZYGOTIC, TWINS OVER 60.

| Type of twins | Year of analysis | No. of pairs | INTRAPAIR LIFE SPAN DIFFERENCES (Expressed in Months) | | |
			Male	Female	Total
One-egg (monozygotic) pairs	1950	11	48.0	18.2	34.4
	1954	24	50.6	22.9[a]	37.9[b]
	1958	41	60.0	36.9[b]	48.7
Two-egg (dizygotic) pairs	1950	17	73.8	41.3	68.1
	1954	37	68.9	65.6[a]	67.0[b]
	1958	45	64.5	68.2[b]	66.5

[a]Difference between one-egg and two-egg pairs significant at 1 percent level of confidence.
[b]Difference between one-egg and two-egg pairs significant at 5 percent level of confidence.
From Kallman and Jarvik, 1959.

recessive traits (Epstein, Martin, and Schultz, 1966). A progerialike familial syndrome has also been reported in rabbits (Pearce and Brown, 1960). Aside from the aforementioned inherited syndromes, the genetic constitutions known to affect the life span have been found to do so through modification of susceptibility to some specific life-shortening disease, such as diabetes mellitus, cancer, or renal disease. The regulation of susceptibility to such diseases may be polygenic and complex as indicated by the multiplicity and diversity of genetic factors influencing susceptibility to leukemia in the mouse (Table 2), which act through widely differing pathways on the pathogenesis of the neoplasm.

Hybrid Vigor

Cross-breeding between animals of two moderately long-lived strains characteristically produces offspring of longer life span, the effect being maximal in the first generation (Chai, 1959; Comfort, 1964). If, however, one of the parental strains is abnormally susceptible to an early fatal disease, such as leukemia, the incidence of the disease, and hence the mean survival time, may be intermediate in its F_1 hybrid offspring (Law, 1954).

The greater longevity of hybrids is typically associated with increased size, fertility, and hardiness. Although postconceptional influences may be responsible to varying degrees in certain instances, the effect is preponderantly attributable to the generally favorable influence of heterozygosity, homozygosity tending to shorten life by increasing predisposition to specific diseases (Glass, 1960; Comfort, 1964).

Sex Differences

In virtually all animals, the female outlives the male. The observed differences range from about 6 years in humans to about 171 days in the spider, 150 days in the rat, 51 days in the beetle, and 2 days in the fruit fly (Kallman and Jarvik, 1959). The consistency of the sex difference throughout the animal kingdom, despite wide differences in social behavior and physiology, implies a common basic mechanism, that is unrelated to the paucity and lack of redundancy of genes on the small Y-chromosome (Comfort, 1964). Sex-linked genes do not generally appear to play a major role in the determination of longevity (Medvedev, 1966).

SELECTION OF ANIMAL MODELS

Objectives and Relevance

Although limitation of life span appears to be universal among animals, the duration of survival and the immediate causes of death vary from one species to another (Lansing, 1959; Comfort, 1964; Rockstein, Chesky, and Sussman, 1976). Because of the complexity, diversity, and particular chronology of age-dependent pathophysiologic alterations in human beings, no other species provides a faithful replica of all aspects of human aging. Nevertheless, specific aspects of the process appear to be duplicated to varying degrees in many other species. The selection of a suitable model system depends, therefore, on the particular aspect to be investigated and the condition under which it is to be studied.

Control of Variables

To the extent that senescence reflects a summation of physiologic processes changing with time under the influence of interactions between genetic and environmental variables, the experimental study of aging should seek to define and control such variables insofar as possible. Without rigorous control, experiments may not be consistently reproducible, and efforts to elucidate the respective roles of the involved variables may be compromised. Ideally, model studies of aging should utilize animal test systems that are defined genetically and maintained under environmental conditions that are also specified and controlled with respect to microbial flora, nutrition, ambient temperature, relative humidity, atmospheric pressure, light, sound, population density, mode of care, feeding regimen, and other variables.

Genetic Considerations

The mouse is the only other vertebrate approaching man in the degree to which its genetic constitution has been characterized. At present, more than 240 different inbred strains of mice are known, each having one or more properties distinguishing it from the others (Staats, 1972). From among these strains and their intercross hybrids, an enormous variety of phenotypes may be obtained, any one of which can be particularly advantageous for the study of a given age-dependent process.

Major investigative advantages to be derived from the use of inbred animals include (1) the opportunity for systematic manipulation of allelic differences as a means for analyzing the cause of phenotypic variations and, ultimately, their biological and molecular mechanisms; (2) the relatively high degree of homogeneity among members of an inbred line, which enables greater uniformity and reproducibility of experimental results; (3) the predictability of responses in animals of the same genotype, which facilitates accumulation of an expanding body of knowledge on processes influencing the phenomena in question; (4) transplantation of cells and tissues without histoincompatibility reactions, which permits the relative importance of age-dependent changes to be investigated at different levels of biological organization through the use of donors and recipients differing in their respective ages (Russell and Meier, 1966; Russell, 1969, 1972; Festing, 1971).

Microbial Considerations

In the presence of certain microbial contaminants that are widely distributed in most conventional animal colonies, many laboratory rodents succumb to intercurrent infection before reaching old age. A notable example is the assortment of chronic respiratory diseases that are prevalent in mice, rats, rabbits, and guinea pigs infected with microorganisms of the pleuropneumonia group (Innes, 1965; Nelson, 1967). To the extent that such intercurrent mortality must be avoided if animals are to provide valid models for the study of aging, measures to prevent infection are required. These range from relatively modest improvements in sanitation, isolation, and husbandry techniques to more elaborate steps involving Caesarean derivation under aseptic conditions and the maintenance of germfree or specific-pathogen-free (SPF) colonies. Experience with germfree animals in gerontologic research is still sufficiently limited that the advantages and disadvantages of such animals are not yet fully apparent (Gordon, 1968; Pleasants, 1968; Pollard and Kajima, 1970; Walburg, 1973). Experience with SPF animals is similarly limited at present (Serrano, 1971; Walburg, 1972). To the extent that both types of animals can harbor vertically transmitted and poorly defined microorganisms, such as viruses of the leukemia-sarcoma complex and other oncogenic agents, such animals are not strictly "germfree" or gnotobiotic in the classical sense. This limitation notwithstanding, they represent the closest approximation available thus far to the ideal of the microbially defined animal, in which microflora-dependent processes are defined and standardized.

Data to be Collected

The records of a life span experiment should define the materials, methods, and conditions of the study and should describe the life history of the population under investigation, including its complete life table, actuarial statistics, and detailed information on the age-distribution, clinical course, and pathology of the major lesions associated with death in the population. Without such information, the gerontologic significance of the survival curve or of any particular lesion related to it may defy analysis.

Animal Models for Specific Purposes

The diversity of animal models used for studying age-dependent changes in various cells, tissues, and organs is too comprehensive to be summarized here. References to numerous examples will be found in previous chapters of this volume on specific organ systems. In addition, useful reviews of various aspects of the subject are available elsewhere (Ribelin and McCoy, 1965; Hollander, 1973; Getty and Ellenport, 1974). As indicated above, the selection of a given model must be based on careful consideration of the purpose for which it is intended.

REFERENCES

Abbott, M. H., Murphy, E. A., Bolling, D. R., and Abbey, H. 1974. The familial component in longevity. A study of offspring of nonagenarians. II. Preliminary analysis of the completed study. *Johns Hopkins Med., J.,* **134,** 1–16.

Abinanti, F. R. 1971. Chronic and degenerative diseases of man: The value of natural and experimentally induced diseases of animals. *In,* Animal Models for Biomedical Research, **IV,** pp. 31–46. Washington, D.C.: National Academy of Sciences.

Andres, R., and Tobin, J. 1976. Endocrine systems. *In,* J. E. Birren (ed.), *Handbook of the Biology of Aging,* Chap. 14. New York: Van Nostrand Reinhold.

Andrew, W. 1969. Tumors and aging. National Cancer Institute Monograph No. 31, pp. 129–140.

Atlan, H. 1968. Strehler's theory of mortality and the second law of thermodynamics. *J. Geront.* **23,** 196–200.

Balazs, E. 1976. Intercellular matrix of connective tissue. *In,* J. E. Birren, (ed.), *Handbook of the Biology of Aging,* Chap. 9. New York: Van Nostrand Reinhold.

Barrows, C. H., and Roeder, L. 1976. Nutrition. *In,* J. E. Birren (ed.), *Handbook of the Biology of Aging,* Chap. 23. New York: Van Nostrand Reinhold.

Batzing, B. L., Yurcomic, M., and Hanna, M. G. 1974. Autogenous immunity to endogenous RNA tumor virus: Chronic humoral immune response to virus envelope antigens in B_6 C3F1 mice., *J. Nat. Cancer Inst.,* **52,** 117–132.

Beach, J. E., Bair, A. M. J. N., Pirani, C. L., Cox, G. E., and Dixon, F. J. 1974. An unusual form of proliferative arteriopathy in macaque monkeys (Macacea sps). *Exp. Molec. Path.,* **21,** 322–338.

Belloc, N. B. 1973. Relationship of health practices and mortality. *Preventive Medicine,* **2,** 67–81.

Belloc, N. B., and Breslow, L. 1972. Relationship of physical health status and health practices. *Preventive Medicine,* **1,** 409–421.

Bertolini, A. M., and Sabata, V. de 1969. *Gerontologic Metabolism,* pp. 663–681. Springfield, Illinois: Charles C. Thomas.

Birren, J. E. 1964. *The Psychology of Aging.* Englewood Cliffs, New Jersey: Prentice-Hall.

Botwinick, J. 1967. *Cognitive Processes in Maturity and Old Age.* New York: Springer.

Botwinick, J. 1973. *Aging and Behavior.* New York: Springer.

Chai, C. K. 1959. Life span in inbred and hybrid mice. *J. Heredity,* **50,** 203–208.

Cheney, K. E., and Walford, R. L. 1973. Immune function and dysfunction in relation to age. *Life Sci.* I. **14,** 2075–2084.

Clapp, N. K., and Yuhas, J. M. 1973. Suggested correlation between radiation-induced immunosuppression and radiogenic leukemia in mice. *J. Nat. Cancer Inst.,* **51,** 1211–1215.

Clement, F. J. 1974. Longitudinal and cross-sectional assessments of age changes in physical strength as related to sex, social class, and mental ability. *J. Geront.,* **29,** 423–429.

Cohen, A. S. 1965. The constitution and genesis of amyloid. *Intern. Rev. Exp. Pathol.,* **4,** 159–243.

Comfort, A. 1964. *Aging. The Biology of Senescence.* New York: Holt, Rinehart and Winston.

Comfort, A. 1968. Physiology, homeostasis, and aging. *Gerontologia,* **14,** 224–234.

Daly, J. W., Barry, A. J., and Birkhead, N. C. 1968. The physical working capacity of older individuals. *J. Geront.,* **23,** 134–139.

Davies, B. D., Dulbecco, R., Eisen, H. N., Ginsberg, H. S., Wood, W. B. Jr., and McCarty, M. 1973. *Microbiology.* 2nd ed., p. 1219. Hagerstown: Harper and Row.

Davies, D. R., and Tune, G. S. 1969. *Human Vigilance Performance,* New York: American Elsevier.

Dennis, W. 1966. Creative productivity between the ages of 20 and 80 years. *J. Geront.,* **21,** 1–8.

Doll, R. 1970. Cancer and aging: The epidemiological evidence. *In, Tenth International Cancer Congress,* pp. 133–160. Chicago: Year Book Medical Publishers.

Donabedian, A., Axelrod, S. J., Swearingen, C., and Jameson, J. 1972. *Medical Care Chart Book.* 5th Edition. Ann Arbor, Michigan: Bureau of Public Health Economics, University of Michigan School of Public Health.

Epstein, C. J., Martin, G. M., and Schultz, A. L. 1966. Werner's syndrome: A review of its symptomatology, natural history, pathologic features, genetics, and relationship to the natural aging process. *Medicine* (Baltimore), **45,** 177–221.

Farber, E. 1973. Carcinogenesis-cellular evolution as a unifying thread: Presidential address. *Cancer Res.,* **33,** 2537–2550.

Festing, M. F. W., 1971. The use of inbred strains, F_1 hybrids, and noninbred strains in research. *In, Defining the Laboratory Animal,* pp. 156–168. Washington, D. C.: National Academy of Sciences.

Finch, C. E. 1976a. Neuroendocrine and autonomic aspects of aging. *In,* J. E. Birren (ed.), *Handbook of the Biology of Aging,* Chap. 11. New York: Van Nostrand Reinhold.

Finch, 1976b. The regulation of physiological changes during mammalian aging. *Quart. Rev. Biol.,* in press.

Finch, C. E., Foster, J. R., and Mirsky, A. E. 1969. Aging and the regulation of cell activities during exposure to cold. *J. Gen. Physiol.,* **54,** 690–712.

Gajdusek, D. C. 1972. Slow virus infection and activation of latent virus infections in aging. *Advan. Geront. Res.,* **4,** 201–218.

Garner, F. M., and Brown, R. J. 1967. Bibliography of comparative oncology. Washington, D.C.: Armed Forces Institute of Pathology.

Getty, R., and Ellenport, C. R. 1974. Laboratory animals in aging studies. *In,* W. I. Gay (ed.), *Methods of Animal Experimentation,* Vol. V, pp. 41–181. New York: Academic Press.

Glass, H. B. 1960. Genetics of aging. *In*, N. W. Shock (ed.), *Aging: Some Social and Biological Aspects.* American Association for the Advancement of Science, Washington, D.C.; Publ. No. 65, pp. 67–99.

Gompertz, B. 1825. On the nature of the function expressive of the law of human mortality and on a new mode of determining life contingencies. *Phil. Trans. Roy Soc.. London*, pp. 513–585.

Gordon, H. A. 1968. Is the germ-free animal normal? A review of its anomalies in young and old age. *In*, M. E. Coates (ed.), *The Germ-Free Animal in Research*, pp. 127–150. New York: Academic Press;

Grahn, D. 1970. Biological effects of protracted low dose radiation exposure of man and animals. *In*, R. M. Fry, D. Grahn, M. L. Griem, and J. H. Rust, (eds.), *Late Effects of Radiation*, pp. 101–136. London: Taylor and Francis.

Griswold, D. E., Heppner, G. H., and Calabresi, P. 1973. Alteration of immunocompetence by mammary tumor virus. *J. Nat. Cancer Inst.*, **50**, 1035–1038.

Gusseck, D. J. 1972. Endocrine mechanisms and aging. *Advan. Geront. Res.*, **4**, 105–166.

Gutmann, E., and Hanzlikova, V. 1972. *Age Changes in the Neuro-muscular System*, pp. 106–113. Bristol, England: Scientechnica Publ.

Hanna, M. G., Jr., Snodgrass, M. J., Tennant, R. W., Yuhas, J. M., and Batzing, B. L. 1973. The interaction of RNA tumor viruses and the immune system: Immune capacity and pathogenesis. *In*, W. S. Ceglowski and H. Friedman (eds.), *Virus Tumorigenesis and Immunogenesis*, pp. 59–89, New York: Academic Press.

Haran-Ghera, N. 1973. The role of immunity in radiation leukemogenesis. *In*, R. M. Dutcher and L. Chieco-Bianchi (eds.), *Unifying Concepts of Leukemia, Bibl. heamat, No. 39*, pp. 671–676. Basel: S. Karger.

Haran-Ghera, N., and Peled, A. 1968. The mechanism of radiation action in leukemogenesis. IV. Immune impairment as a coleukemogenic factor. *Israel J. Med. Sci.*, **4**, 1181–1187.

Harkins, S. W., Nowlin, J. B., Ramm, D., and Schroeder, S. 1974. Effects of age, sex, and time-on-watch on a brief continuous performance task. *In*, E. Palmore (ed.), *Normal Aging II*, pp. 140–150. Durham, North Carolina: Duke University Press.

Henschel, A. 1970. Effects of age on work capacity. *Am. Ind. Hyg. Assoc. J.*, **31**, 430–436.

Hensley, J. C., McWilliams, P. C., and Oakley, G. E. 1964. Physiological capacitance. A study in physiological age determination. *J. Geront.*, **19**, 317–321.

Hollander, C. F. 1973. Guest editorial. Animal models for aging and cancer research. *J. Nat. Cancer Inst.*, **51**, 3–5.

Höring, F. O. 1969. Infektionen in Alter. *Z. Geront.*, **2**, 67–68.

Huebner, R. J., Kelloff, G. J., Sarma, P. S., Lane, W. T., Turner, H. C., Gilden, R. V., Orszlan, S.,

Meier, H., Myers, D. D., and Peters, R. L. 1970. Group-specific (gs) antigen expression of the C-type RNA tumor virus genome during embryogenesis: Implications for ontogenesis and oncogenesis. *Proc. Nat. Acad. Sci.*, **67**, 366–376.

Huebner, R. J., and Todaro, G. J. 1969. Oncogenes of RNA tumor viruses as determinants of cancer. *Proc. Nat. Acad. Sci.*, **64**, 1087–1094.

Innes, J. R. M. 1965. Lesions of the respiratory tract of small laboratory animals. *In*, W. E. Ribelin and J. R. McCoy (ed.), *The Pathology of Laboratory Animals*, pp. 49–59. Springfield, Illinois: Charles C. Thomas.

Jacobs, P. A., Brunton, M., and Court Brown, W. M. 1963. Change of human chromosome count distributions with age: Evidence for a sex difference. *Nature*, **197**, 1080–1081.

Jacobson, P. H. 1964. Cohort survival for generations since 1840. *Milbank Mem. Fund Quart.*, **42**, 36–53.

Jarvik, L. F., Yen, Fu-Sun, and Moralishvili, E. 1974. Chromosome examinations in aging institutionalized women. *J. Geront.*, **29**, 269–276.

Jones, H. B. 1955. A special consideration of the aging process, disease, and life expectancy. University of California Radiation Laboratory, Berkeley.

Jones, H. B. 1959. The relation of human health to age, place, and time. *In*, J. E. Birren (ed.), *Handbook of Aging and the Individual*, pp. 336–363. Chicago: University of Chicago Press.

Kallman, E. J., and Jarvik, L. F. 1959. Individual differences in constitution and genetic background. *In*, J. E. Birren (ed.), *Handbook of Aging and the Individual*, pp. 216–263. Chicago: University of Chicago Press.

Kimmel, D. C. 1974. *Adulthood and Aging, an Interdisciplinary, Developmental View*, pp. 343–390. New York: John Wiley.

Knudson, A. G., Jr. 1973. Mutation and human cancer. *In*, G. Klein and S. Weinhouse (eds.), *Advan. in Cancer Res.*, **17**, 317–352. New York: Academic Press.

Kohn, R. R. 1963. Human aging and disease. *J. Chronic Diseases*, **16**, 5–21.

Kohn, R. R. 1971. *Principles of Mammalian Aging.* Englewood Cliffs, New Jersey: Prentice-Hall.

Kohn, R. R. 1973. *Aging.* Kalamazoo, Michigan: Upjohn.

Kohn, R. R. 1976. Heart and cardiovascular system. *In*, J. E. Birren (ed.), *Handbook of the Biology of Aging*, Chap. 12. New York: Van Nostrand Reinhold.

Lansing, A. I. 1959. General biology of senescence. *In*, J. E. Birren (ed.), *Handbook of Aging and the Individual*, pp. 119–135. Chicago: University of Chicago Press.

Law, L. W. 1954. Recent advances in experimental leukemia research. *Cancer Res.*, **14**, 659–709.

Lewis, R. M. 1974. Spontaneous autoimmune diseases of domestic animals. *Intern. Rev. Exp. Path.*, **13**, 55–82.

Makinodan, T. 1976. Immunity and aging. *In*, J. E.

Birren (ed.), *Handbook of the Biology of Aging*, Chap. 15. New York: Van Nostrand Reinhold.

Medvedev, Zh A. 1966. *Protein Biosynthesis and Problems of Heredity, Development and Aging*, pp. 469–530. New York: Plenum Press.

Miller, R. W., and Todaro, G. 1969. Viral transformation of cells from persons at high risk of cancer. *Lancet*, 1, 81–82.

National Academy of Sciences, Committee on the Biological Effects of Ionizing Radiation. 1972. The effects on populations of exposure to low levels of ionizing radiation, pp. 186–187. Washington, D. C.: National Academy of Sciences, National Research Council.

Nelson, J. B. 1967. Respiratory infections of rats and mice, with emphasis on indigenous mycoplasms. *In*, E. Cotchin and F. J. C. Roe (ed.), *Pathology of Laboratory Rats and Mice*, pp. 259–294. Philadelphia: F. A. Davis.

Oldstone, M. B., Aoki, T., and Dixon F. J. 1972. The antibody response of mice to murine leukemia virus infection: Absence of classical immunological tolerance. *Proc. Nat. Acad. Sci*, 69, 134–138.

Palmore, E. 1974. Health practices and illness. *In*, *Normal Aging II*, pp. 49–55. Durham, North Carolina: Duke University Press.

Pearce, L., and Brown, W. H. 1960. Hereditary premature senescence in the rabbit. *J. Exp. Med.*, 111, 485–516.

Pearl, R. 1922. *The Biology of Death*. Philadelphia: J. P. Lippincott.

Pleasants, J. R. 1968. Characteristics of the germ-free animal. *In*, M. E. Coates (ed.), *The Germ-free Animal in Research*, pp. 115–126, New York: Academic Press.

Pollard, M., and Kajima, M. 1970. Lesions in aged germfree rats. *Am. J. Pathol.* 61, 24–36.

Ponten, J. 1975. Abnormal cell growth, *In*, J. E. Birren (ed.), *Handbook of the Biology of Aging*, Chap. 22. New York: Van Nostrand Reinhold.

Rauscher, F. J., Jr., and O'Connor, T. E. 1973. Virology. *In*, J. F. Holland and E. Frei III (eds.), *Cancer Medicine*, pp. 15–44. Philadelphia: Lea & Febiger.

Ribelin, W. E., and McCoy, J. R. 1965. *The Pathology of Laboratory Animals*. Springfield, Illinois: Charles C. Thomas.

Roberts, J. C., Jr., and Straus, R. (eds.). 1965. *Comparative Atherosclerosis*. New York: Harper (Hoeber).

Robertson, O. H. 1961. Prolongation of the life span of kokanee salmon (*Oncorhynclus nerka kemerlyi*) by castration before beginning of gonad development. *Proc. Nat. Acad. Sci.*, 47, 609–621.

Rockstein, M., Chesky, J., and Sussman, M. 1976. Comparative biology and evolution of aging. *In*, J. E. Birren (ed.), *Handbook of the Biology of Aging*, Chap. 1. New York: Van Nostrand Reinhold.

Rowe, W. P. 1973. Genetic factors in the natural history of murine leukemia virus infection: G. H. A.

Clowes Memorial Lecture. *Cancer Res.*, 33, 3061–3068.

Russell, E. S. 1969. The importance of animal genetics in biomedical research. *In, Genetics in Laboratory Animal Medicine*, pp. 1–8 Washington, D.C. National Academy of Sciences.

Russell, E. S. 1972. Genetic considerations in the selection of rodent species and strains for research in aging. *In*, D. C. Gibson (ed.), *Development of the Rodent as a Model System of Aging*, pp. 33–53, Bethesda: Government Printing Office.

Russell, E. S., and Meier, H. 1966. Constitutional diseases. *In*, E. L. Green (ed.), *Biology of the Laboratory Mouse*, 2nd ed., pp. 571–587. New York: McGraw-Hill.

Sacher, G. A. 1968. Molecular versus systemic theories on the genesis of aging. *Exp. Geront.*, 3, 265–271.

Sacher, G. A. 1976. Life table modification and prolongation. *In*, J. E. Birren (ed.), *Handbook of the Biology of Aging*, Chap. 24. New York: Van Nostrand Reinhold.

Sacher, G. A., and Trucco, E. 1962. The stochastic theory of mortality. *Ann. N.Y. Acad. Sci.*, 96 (4), 985–1007.

Saloman, J. C. 1968. Carcinogenesis in axenic animals *In*, M. E. Coates (ed.), *The Germ-free Animal in Research*, pp. 227–236. London: Academic Press.

Selye, H. 1970. Stress and aging. *J. Am. Geriat. Soc.*, 18, 669–680.

Selye, H., and Prioreschi, P. 1960. Stress theory of aging. *In*, N. W. Shock (ed.), *Aging . . . . Some Social and Biological Aspects*, pp. 261–272. Washington, D.C.: American Association for the Advancement of Science.

Serrano, L. J. 1971. Defined mice in a radiobiological experiment. *In, Defining the Laboratory Animal*, pp. 13–43. Washington, D.C.: National Academy of Sciences.

Shearer, G. M., Mozes, E., Haran-Ghera, N., and Bentwich, Z. 1973. Cellular analysis of immunosuppression to synthetic polypeptide immunogens induced by a murine leukemia virus, *J. Immunol.*, 110, 736–741.

Shock, N. W. 1960. Discussion on mortality and measurement, *In*, B. L. Strehler, J. D. Ebert, H. B. Glass, and N. W. Shock (eds.), *The Biology of Aging: A Symposium*, pp. 22–23. Washington, D.C.: American Institute of Biological Sciences.

Simms, H. S. 1967. Longevity studies in rats. I. Relation between life span and age of onset of specific lesions. *In*, E. Cotchin and F. J. C. Roe (eds.), *Pathology of Laboratory Rats and Mice*, pp. 733–746. Philadelphia: F. A. Davis.

Smith, G. S., Walford, R. L., and Mickey, M. R. 1973. Life span and incidence of cancer and other diseases in selected long-lived inbred mice and their F_1 hybrids. *J. Nat. Cancer Inst.*, 50, 1195–1213.

Staats, J. 1972. Standardized nomenclature for inbred strains of mice: Fifth listing. *Cancer Res.*, 32, 1609–1646.

Storer, J. B. 1965. Radiation resistance with age in normal and irradiated populations of mice. *Radiation Res., 25,* 435–459.

Storer, J. B. 1966a. Nonspecific life shortening in male mice exposed to the mammary tumor agent. *J. Nat. Cancer Inst., 37,* 211–215.

Storer, J. B. 1966b. Longevity and gross pathology at death in 22 inbred mouse strains. *J. Geront., 21,* 404–409.

Strehler, B. L., and Mildvan, A. S. 1960. A general theory of mortality and aging. *Science, 132,* 14–21.

Teller, M. N. 1972. Age changes and immune resistance to cancer. *Advan. Geront. Res., 4,* 25–44.

Temin, H. M., and Baltimore D. 1972. RNA-directed DNA synthesis in RNA tumor viruses. *Advan. Virus Res., 17,* 129–186.

Timiras, P. S. 1972. *Developmental Physiology and Aging.* New York: Macmillan.

Tooze, J. (ed.) 1973. *The Molecular Biology of Tumor Viruses.* Cold Spring Harbor, New York: Cold Spring Harbor Laboratory.

Upton, A. C. 1964. Comparative aspects of carcinogenesis by ionizing radiation, *In,* C. C. Congdon and P. Mori-Chavez (eds.), International symposium on the control of cell division and the induction of cancer, National Cancer Institute Monograph 14, pp. 221–239. Washington, D.C.: Government Printing Office.

Upton, A. C., Conklin, J. W., Cosgrove, G. E., Gude, W. D., and Darden, E. B. 1967. Necrotizing polyarteritis in aging RF mice. *Lab. Invest., 16,* 483–487.

Walburg, H. E. Jr. 1972. Microbiological definition and relevant microbiological considerations in rearing, maintenance, and care of the laboratory rodent for research in aging. *In,* D. C. Gibson (ed.), *Development of the Rodent as a Model System of Aging,* pp. 23–29. Washington, D.C.: Government Printing Office.

Walburg, H. E., Jr. 1973. Carcinogenesis in gnotobiotic rodents. *In,* J. B. Heneghan (ed.), *Germfree Research,* pp. 115–122. New York: Academic Press.

Walburg, H. E., Jr., and Cosgrove, G. E. 1967. Aging in irradiated and unirradiated germfree ICR mice. *Exp. Geront., 2,* 143–158.

Yuhas, J. M., Tennant, R. W., Hanna, M. G., Jr., and Clapp, N. K. 1973. Radiation-induced immunosuppression. Its role in radiation leukemogenesis in the intact RF mouse. *In,* C. L. Sanders, R. H. Busch, J. E. Ballou, and D. D. Mahlum (eds.), *Radionuclide Carcinogenesis,* CONF. 720505, pp. 312–321. Springfield, Virginia: Office of Info Services, U.S. Dept. of Commerce.

22
ABNORMAL CELL GROWTH (NEOPLASIA) AND AGING

Jan Pontén

University of Uppsala (Sweden)

INTRODUCTION

Prokaryotic existence is a highly successful mode of adaptation. Bacterial reproduction is fast and limited only by the availability of suitable external metabolites and sources of energy. To become competitive, a multi-cellular organism has to evolve efficient mechanisms for growth control and cellular specialization. These two requirements cannot be met unless the primitive method of species propagation by simple division of autonomous single cells is replaced by a more sophisticated scheme. This has been achieved in all higher organisms by the development of a special germ cell line in which the genetic information for any single species is embodied in specific nuclear DNA sequences which are faithfully reproduced in generation after generation. Variability is insured by exchanges of genes between the gametes, and aging does not affect the germ cell line. Extinction of a species has never been ascribed to "species senescence" but only to adverse environmental circumstances.

Although presumably equipped with the same DNA sequences as the germ cells, an assembly of somatic cells seems predetermined to die. All available evidence indicates that somatic death and its premonitory senescent stage are not primarily environmental except for certain lower organisms with so-called indeterminate growth, and perennial plants (cf. Sheldrake, 1974). Senescence appears to be essentially dependent on intrinsic cellular or organismic factors. One question which this review tries to answer is whether these same factors also cause or facilitate the development of neoplasia.

Death of somatic cells can be permanently prevented by their malignant transformation. This can be shown by serial syngeneic transplantation of normal and neoplastic tissue *in vivo*. Whereas the former always enters irreversible degeneration (Daniel and Young, 1971; Davis, Upton, Satterfield, 1971; Williamson and Askonas, 1972), the later can be transferred apparently indefinitely without any impaired vitality (Hayflick, 1966). A malignant tumor lineage thus in some ways resembles a germ cell line.

Age is linked to neoplasia in yet another way in that a correlation exists between the age of individual animals and development of cancer. The life span of different species varies greatly; however, its chronologic length seems unrelated to the risk of developing neoplasia. A 2-year-old mouse approaching its death is thus comparable to a 70-year-old human being from the point of view of percentage cancer incidence.

Any discussion about the relationship between abnormal cell growth and aging needs a working definition of both concepts. I will restrict the term abnormal growth to describe only the aberrant multiplication generally termed neoplasia. This can operationally be defined (from the point of view of the whole organism) as useless cell reduplication which goes on without any physiologic stimuli. The defining feature—loss of physiologic growth control—is an intrinsic property of a permanently altered neoplastic cell. The process by which a normal cell acquires this property is called a neoplastic transformation.

Neoplasias are customarily divided into benign and malignant forms. I will use the term malignant to mean neoplastic cell populations with an apparently indefinite capacity for replication. A benign tumor is, on the other hand, composed of neoplastic cells with a finite growth potential. Such a population will—at least in the human where the most thorough observations have been made—behave in any of the following ways: grow to a certain size and then remain stationary with no further cell proliferation, e.g., fibromas, lipomas, and pigment nevi; grow to a certain size until a balance is reached between proliferation and cell loss (e.g., basal cell papillomas); grow to a certain size and then regress (e.g., virus induced squamous cell papillomas); grow progressively to a stage where it may become dangerous to life (e.g., meningeomas, pituitary adenomas).

Any benign neoplastic cell can undergo malignant transformation, although it is difficult to ascertain if this risk is greater than for the corresponding normal cells. Usually this does not seem to be the case. Carcinoma in pleomorphic salivary gland adenoma is, for instance, only a rare complication (Eneroth, Blanck, and Jakobsson, 1968; Moberger and Eneroth, 1968).

Aging is harder to define than neoplasia. In a multicellular organism, it is primarily appreciated at the level of the whole animal. Intuitively one may think of it as an irreversible physiologic degenerative process which eventually causes somatic death by a breakdown of the integrated function of the whole individual and/or decreased resistance to many diseases.

Senescence is probably just the final part of a total genetic program which sequentially determines embryogenesis, postnatal development, puberty, menopause, etc. (Curtis, 1966). Aging may therefore in one sense start immediately after fertilization; here, however, the term is used in a more conventional sense, i.e., as a synonym to senescence. Senescent degenerative changes have been well established in birds, mammals, reptiles, and amphibia where they seem to conform to a general pattern (the aging syndrome).

The basic question we are asking is whether neoplasia in general or any specific tumors are part of the aging syndrome or if the increased risk of cancer in old age is a coincidence which does not depend on age *per se*. If the former hypothesis is true, we cannot expect to avoid cancer by any environmental measures, and cancer incidence will never be substantially reduced unless we understand the basic mechanisms of aging.

The relationship between aging and neoplasia can be looked at from different points of view. At an *evolutionary level*, one may ask if there is a relationship between aging and neoplasia in different species. Do all species which show a defined aging syndrome also develop tumors? At the level of the *individual organism*, one may ask if senescence as such predisposes to neoplasia, or if the apparent increase in tumor incidence with increasing age is fortuitous. At the *tissue level*, one may ask if the well-established patterns of organ senescence are involved in tumorigenesis. Do organs or tissues which are affected early or extensively by aging show a high tumor incidence? At the level of the *individual somatic cell*, I will discuss if senescence, defined as a progressive decline in proliferative potential in a multiplying population of cultivated cells, is related to neoplastic transformation.

The probability of occurrence of a neoplastic transformation varies enormously for different cells. Unfortunately, no species has been adequately studied to answer precisely how this probability relates to the age of the organism. The distribution of tumors in different organs is a species characteristic reflected in widely varying incidence figures for specific tumors in different species (Dawe, 1973). This multitude of tumor types and their peculiar, partly species-dependent organ distribution severely confounds the issue of relationship between age and cancer. It is necessary to extend the questioning to many specific types of tumors and not to limit it to neoplasia in general.

EVOLUTIONARY ASPECTS OF THE RELATION BETWEEN CANCER AND AGING

If cancer were part of an aging syndrome, one would expect it to occur predictably in all species which display such a syndrome. Unfortunately, because there are no absolute constitutive definitions of either aging or neoplasia covering their occurrence in all the diverse forms of the living world, a precise analysis cannot be performed. An extensive and thoughtful review on comparative neoplasia was published recently (Dawe, 1973).

In *mammals* and *birds*, where the aging syndromes seem very similar, there is no doubt that malignant neoplasias (benign tumors have only been defined and investigated to any extent in humans) occur in all species. It is also clear that most cancers are diseases of middle age or old life. One exception is contagious viral leukemias in cats (Hardy, Old, Hess, Essex, and Colter, 1973; Jarrett *et al.*, 1974) and fowl (Burmester, 1957) which affect relatively young animals. Another is so-called embryonal carcinomas and such tumors as neuroblastoma, acute lymphatic leukemia, and osteogenic sarcoma which occur more frequently in children or adolescents.

A relevant finding is that the tumor spectrum varies widely among different species. Mammary cancer is very rare in the cow but common in mice and humans. Sertoli cell tumors and mastocytomas are frequent in dogs but rare in most other species. Leukemias and lymphomas are common in many species, but the proportion of the different varieties is not the same (cf. Engelbreth-Holm, 1938).

The obvious implication from these differences in the tumor spectrum is that if cancer is part of an aging syndrome in mammals and birds, the type of cancer seen with age appears to be somewhat specific for different animals, although cancer as a general descriptive term does increase with age in most species.

Reptiles, not "the most attractive animals for cancer research in the laboratory" (Dawe, 1973), have not been investigated to any degree. Aging seems, however, to proceed according to a pattern similar to that of mammals. In general, fairly few tumors have been found in reptiles (cf. Schlumberger and Lucké, 1948), perhaps because these often long-lived animals have only rarely been followed to the end of their physiologic life span.

Amphibians also seem to become senescent according to a defined aging pattern. Malignant tumors, notably renal adenocarcinomas, in the frog (Lucké, 1934) are well established. Their relation, if any, to aging in the frog has not been determined. The same holds true for other less thoroughly investigated neoplasms.

Fishes are bearers of a variety of tumors. This has been definitely established in many species of *bony fish* (cf. Wellings, 1969. Mawdesley-Thomas, 1971; Nigrelli and Ruggieri, 1974). In contrast, the daddy sculpin even at the age of 3 to 4 years was found to be devoid of tumors (Falkmer and Boquist, 1976).

Cartilaginous fish (Chondrichthyes) are particularly interesting from a phylogenetic point of view, because they represent the most primitive of all the Gnathostomian vertebrates (cf. Jarvik, 1964). Here, tumors seem to be rare. The majority of the few published examples have been melanomas (Wellings, 1969). The paucity of neoplasia in Chondrichthyes may be due to a lack of studies. However, Dawe (1973) has made the interesting speculation that there may be a more fundamental reason. Chrondrichthyes have shown less evolutionary advancement than the osteichthyes, which have developed a large variety of widely diversified species, capable of life in fresh water and even in air. Dawe (1973) suggests that genomic instability and mutability may facilitate neoplasia, as well as promoting evolutionary diversification.

Phylogenetically, the *Agnatha* (The Cyclostomes or "jawless fish") form an even more interesting group. They are considered a sister group to all the Gnathostomian vertebrates, forming a separate evolution line, known for more than 500 million years (cf. Jarvik, 1964). The main two extant phyla of the Cyclostomes are the hagfish (*Myxinoidei*) and the lampreys (*Petromyzonitia*). Both lampreys and hagfish were believed to be practically devoid of tumors (cf. Dawe, 1973). However, when a large number of these animals were dissected, the picture changed dramatically (Falkmer, Östberg, and Emdin, 1973; Östberg, Boquist, and Falkmer, 1973; Falkmer, 1974). Thus, the hagfish population in the Gullmar Fiord on the Swedish West-Coast had an unusually high incidence of hepatic tumors. The relation between hepatoma and age in the hagfish is unknown, particularly since various populations of this animal show large variations in tumor incidence. In the lamprey, practically no tumors were recorded.

When turning to the *invertebrates*, it should be stressed that the term *invertebrates* simply means "all other animals" (when the vertebrates have been exempted). Consequently, the number of species and their heterogeneity are both almost inconceivably great—some 95 to 97 percent of all extant animal species on earth are invertebrates. Some kind of subdivision is obtained by using Karl Grobben's two evolutionary lines, viz., the protostomian and the deuterostomian. The latter includes the vertebrates and such invertebrate species as the Echinoderms and Tunicates which during the larval stage have some traits in common with the vertebrates. The large majority of the invertebrate species are found along the protostomian evolution line, such as the mollusks, arthropods, annelids, etc.

It is generally maintained that both deuterostomian and protostomian invertebrates only rarely develop neoplasia. There are no obvious reasons for such a lack of tumors (cf. Dawe, 1973), and it is reasonable to assume that it is rather a lack of comprehensive studies, as in the case of the hagfish. Some support for such an assumption stems from the fact that *Drosophila* and oysters are those invertebrate species where tumors have been most thoroughly described and studied. Here, scientists with primary interests in genetics but with insight into tumor biology and pathology have had ample opportunities to study a large number of the same species over a long period of time. This is a prerequisite for an adequate study of the tumor pathology of a species.

One reason why some invertebrates would lack tumors is the occurrence of autotomy, i.e., the capacity to autoamputate part of the body and then replace it by complete regeneration (Dawe, 1968). By this mechanism tumors could be removed. Another possibility is that invertebrates have highly efficient DNA repair mechanisms and therefore resist potentially carcinogenic mutations (Dawe, 1969). Since body growth and physiologic cell divisions seem comparatively rare in adult invertebrates, it is also possible that the relative lack of dividing cells serves as a protective shield against neoplastic transformations which only rarely manifest themselves in stationary or nearly stationary cell systems. Good and Finstad (1969) have proposed that the T-cell lymphoid system found in vertebrates has evolved as a necessary mechanism to counteract the increased risk of neoplasia. This increased risk is postulated to depend on an increased deployment of DNA for cellular diversification. Since this has occurred without any appreciable increase in the amount of DNA per cell, the number of redundant genes is presumed to have decreased, thus increasing the likelihood that any mutations which might occur will have a phenotypic effect (Dawe, 1973).

Tumors in *Drosophila* have a peculiar biology. So-called melanomas have been much studied (Harshberger and Taylor, 1968). These are, however, very different from the neoplastic processes described by the same term in vertebrates (Dawe, 1973). The *melanomas* of *Drosophila* are pigmented aggregates of lamellocytes. They are routinely found in larvae and do not grow after pupation. They could be defense reactions to foreign bodies or parasites and have no adverse effect on the viability of the flies.

Another proliferative disorder also under genetic influence is characterized by uncontrolled proliferation of the cystocytes which, however, remain confined to the egg chamber (King, 1969). Probably this is a benign neoplasm.

The only likely malignant neoplasm in *Drosophila* is the so-called neuroblastoma (Granoff, Gravell, and Darlington, 1969; Hadorn, 1969; Gateff and Schneiderman, 1969). These populations composed of undifferentiated cells form indefinitely transplantable lines. A transplant will appreciably shorten the life span of its bearer. Neuroblastoma has no relation to aging. It originates from imaginal disc blastema and should, if anything, be comparable to "embryonal carcinomas" in mammals.

Drosophila is also the only invertebrate species where aging has been systematically studied. *Drosophila* flies are known to die according to predictable statistics. If death is preceded by anything like the aging syndrome in vertebrates it is unknown.

The overall impression of the relation between aging and cancer in different species is first of all that few species have been well studied besides mammals. In insects, exemplified by *Drosophila*, there are no reports of neoplasia toward the end of their life span. This is not due to total absence of neoplasia, because at least the existence of neuroblastomas from imaginal disc blastema seems well documented (Granoff, Gravell, and Darlington, 1969). In birds and mammals, in spite of widely different tumor spectra in different species, malignant neoplasms occur in a high frequency in middle-aged and old individuals. On the evolutionary level, aging behaves as a constant companion of somatic life, at least in Gnathostomian vertebrates. The same regularity has not been shown for any specific type of tumor or the generality of cancer. Most likely, neoplasia is therefore not an obligate part of an evolutionary pattern, and in this respect it bears no fundamental relation to aging. This, of course, does not exclude the possibility that aging may enhance the risk of neoplasia by a mechanism common to all living matter.

AGING AND NEOPLASIA IN INDIVIDUAL ORGANISMS

The Concept of an Aging Syndrome

Aging should be considered a syndrome of alterations which gradually and with time become manifest in all individuals of a population. Many of these alterations facilitate the development of deadly diseases and are therefore indirect causes of death.

One of the well-studied examples of an indisputable age change is the increased resistance to deformation shown by the human lens (presbyopia).

Figure 1 shows loss of accommodation measured in dioptries plotted against age. A linear decrease is found from 10–50 years when the lens has lost practically all mobility. All individuals are affected at approximately the same rate and interindividual variations are comparatively small. A diminished power of accommodation is not subjectively noted until reading becomes difficult. If one would put this "clinical horizon" at the arbitrary level of two dioptries and plot incidence of "difficult reading" against age, one would obtain a steep sigmoid curve of the type also shown in Figure 1. This may be regarded as a typical plot for an alteration belonging to the aging syndrome. It illustrates that precursor changes can start long before senile

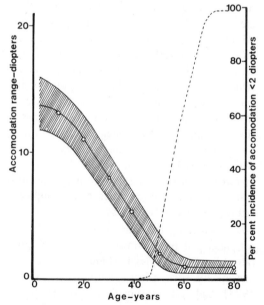

Figure 1. Loss of accommodation as a function of age in a healthy human population. The shaded area indicates the limits within which 95% of the measurements fall. Modified from Friedenwald (1952) together with a theoretical plot of incidence of "difficult reading," defined as a maximal power of accommodation ⩽ 2 dioptries, against age in a human population.

deteriorations become noted and that the changes eventually manifest themselves in 100 percent of the individuals.

Statistical Analysis of Cancer and Aging

The question if neoplasia is a part of an aging syndrome can be approached by statistical analysis of tumor incidence in relation to age in very much the same fashion as with lack of accommodative power.

The perfect study of the relation between neoplasia and biological age still remains to be done. It would require a large population raised under conditions which minimized all non-age-dependent causes of disease and death and exposure to external carcinogens. Careful autopsies, including thorough microscopic investigation of all organs, have to be performed at regular intervals. Reliable criteria of neoplasia have to be applied. The species under investigation should not have any unnoticed regressing or "dormant" tumors or be the victim of epidemics caused by tumor viruses.

Animal Studies. These have mainly been performed in mice and will only be used to exemplify important principles.

Storer (1966) compared 22 inbred mouse strains with respect to longevity and frequency of tumors. The mean life span differed widely. For example, male AKR/J mice only survived for 326 ± 16 days compared to 748 ± 19 days for LP/J. Hereditary life shortening factors acted by facilitating the development of a variety of diseases. Leukemia played a large role in causing premature deaths in many of the short-lived strains. Ninety percent of the AKR/J mice were thus found to have lymphoma at death. In contrast, only 55 percent of the LP/J mice had any tumors. These were of varied type and started late in life.

The important message from these and many other similar studies is that Medelian genes govern the development of many malignant murine tumors (Table 1). Whenever a gene has shortened the life span, it has apparently done so by facilitating a specific disease. The conclusion is that neoplasias in mice may arise independently of the aging process as such.

The association between neoplasia and aging established in the genetic studies of the mouse may be a very special case. It has been shown that lymphoma (Gross, 1951) and mammary carcinoma (Bittner, 1936), two of the foremost examples of apparent hereditary malignancies, owe their development to the action of RNA tumor viruses. The infection, spread, and oncogenicity of these agents seem to depend essentially on cellular genes (cf. Tooze, 1973). Development of these cancers therefore requires not only the appropriate susceptibility genes but also the ubiquitous presence of oncogenic RNA viruses. The relevant question may be whether non-virus-associated neoplasias which also tend to occur in the very old mice are hereditary, and if so, whether the responsible genes are associated with the aging syndrome.

There are few studies on large populations of noninbred mice with respect to the age incidence of various neoplasias. Andervont and Dunn (1962) observed a diversified tumor spectrum dominated by pulmonary tumors, granulosa cell tumors, reticulum cell sarcoma, hepatomas, hemangioendotheliomas and mammary tumors. The incidence rose with age, and 64 percent of the tumor-bearing mice were over 25 months old.

For other laboratory or wild populations of animals, there seem to be no sufficiently extensive statistical studies of the exact prevalence of tumors in different ages. All studies agree, however, that biologically old animals are much more prone to develop tumors than are young ones. It would be valuable to know if the apparent relative decline in tumor incidence noted in the very old humans (see below) has any correspondence in the rest of the animal kingdom and if there is any species which has a natural tumor incidence of 100 percent in the senile period of life.

Studies in Man.

Malignant Tumor. Our knowledge of tumor frequency and its relation to age in man is still imperfect. Various national cancer registries have calculated incidence figures based on clinical data including histologic diagnoses of cancer. There figures are, however, underestimates of an unknown magnitude since tumors

TABLE 1. ONCOLOGIC CHARACTERISTICS OF INBRED MOUSE STRAINS.

Neoplasm	Strains	Incidence of neoplasm
Mammary gland tumors	C3H	Almost 100% in ♀♀
	A	High in breeding ♀♀; low in virgin
	DBA	High in breeding ♀♀
	RIII	High in breeding ♀♀
	BALB/c	Incidence low, but high following introduction of mammary tumor agent
	C57BR	Do not develop spontaneous mammary tumors: 55% after
	C57W	introduction of mammary-tumor agent
Pulmonary tumors	A	90% in mice living to 18 months
	SWR	80% in mice living to 18 months
	BALB/c	26% in ♀♀; 29% in ♂♂
	BL	26% in mice of all ages
Hepatomas	C3H	85% in males 14 months old
	C3Hf	72% in males 14 months old
	C3He	78% in males 14 months old
		91% in breeding ♂♂; 59% in virgin ♀♀; 30% in breeding ♀♀; and 38% in force-bred ♀♀
Leukemia and other reticular cell neoplasms	C58	High leukemia
	AKR	High leukemia
	C57BL	Hodgkin's-like lesion, reticular cell neoplasm Type B in liver and spleen, approximately 25% at 18 months
Papilloma and carcinoma	HR	Papillomas occurred in all mice, both haired and hairless, painted with methylcholanthrene, and the carcinomatous transformation occurred in most of the animals
	I	Most susceptible of 5 strains tested with methylcholanthrene
Subcutaneous sarcomas	C3H	Occurred spontaneously in 57 of 1,774 C3H and C3Hf ♀♀
		Most susceptible of 8 strains tested with carcinogenic hydrocarbons
	CBA	High occurrence after subcutaneous injection of methylcholanthrene
Stomach lesion	I	Occurs in practically all mice of this strain
	BRS	Occurs following injection with methylcholanthrene and
	BRSUNT	spontaneously
Adrenal cortical tumors	CE	High occurrence following castration
	NH	High occurrence of spontaneous adenoma
		High occurrence of carcinoma following castration
Teratomas, testicular	129	1% congenital
Interstitial cell tumors of testis	A	Readily induced with estrogens
	BALB/c	High incidence following treatment with stilbestrol
Pituitary adenoma	C57BL	Occurred in almost all mice treated with estrogens
Hemangioendotheliomas	HR	19 to 33% in untreated mice
		54 to 76% in mice injected with 4-o-tolylazo-o-toluidine
	BALB/c	High occurrence particularly in interscapular fat pad and lung in mice treated with o-aminoazotoluene
Ovarian tumors	C3He	47% in virgin ♀♀; 37% in breeding ♀♀; 29% in force-bred ♀♀
Myoepitheliomas	A and BALB/c	Occur in region of salivary gland and clitoral gland
Harderian gland tumors	C3H	Occur in C3H and hybrids resulting from out-crossing C3H

Modified from Dawe, 1973.

which have given no symptoms or which have not been diagnosed properly are not systematically included.

There are only a few studies which go beyond the crude cancer incidence data of the conventional registries. I will rely on a series of such studies carried out in Malmö, Sweden, under the direction of Folke Linell.

Malmö, with a population of about 250,000, has only one department of pathology and one general hospital serving the entire area. Since 1958 all autopsies have been carried out under a strict, thorough, and uniform regimen aimed at detection of all significant diseases. The autopsy rate has been raised from 50 percent to about 70 percent presently. Statistical probes have indicated that this sample is representative for all clinically diagnosed malignancies for the entire Malmö population (Berge, 1967).

The Swedish system of individual identification of all citizens by their birth numbers made it possible to check the medical record of each autopsied person. Not only the presence of tumors at the time of death but also tumors diagnosed previously could thus be recorded.

The Malmö series gives an individual-based longitudinal, although retrospective, estimate of tumor incidence based on histologically diagnosed neoplasias and is probably one of the most reliable cancer incidence studies. Age incidences for adenocarcinoma of the prostate and colon have been singled out for further discussion here.

Prostatic Carcinoma. The open circles of Figure 2 give the incidence of carcinoma detected clinically and pathologically in autopsies in the Malmö area. A linear increase is seen including even ages above 90 where the incidence is over 30 percent. This curve includes all clinically detected cancers and those which were routinely noted in a postmortem examination. The continuous increase with age is compatible with prostatic carcinoma being part of the aging syndrome. The failure to approach the expected 100 percent incidence in the 90 to 100-year-old men (cf. Figure 1) could be explained by a failure to detect all carcinomas. The upper curve of Figure 2 illustrates the incidence in an autopsy series (Lundberg and Berge, 1970)

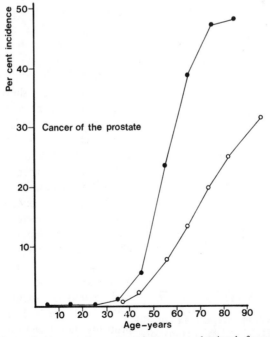

Figure 2. Incidence of prostatic carcinoma against age obtained from thorough microscopic analysis of glands removed at autopsies in the Malmö material (filled circles) (Lundberg and Berge, 1970) and incidence of prostatic carcinoma detected clinically and/or pathologically in the Malmö material (open circles) (see text).

where all prostatic glands were scrutinized for cancer. Its shape coincides with that of other similar studies (Liavåg, 1968; Franks, 1972). It shows that the true incidence of carcinoma detectable by current morphologic techniques is (a) higher than that normally observed clinically and/or pathologically, and (b) does not increase after the age of 80 where it seems to approach asymptotically a level of about 50 percent. Therefore prostatic carcinoma has not on available statistical grounds been shown to be an authentic part of an aging syndrome; instead, it behaves as a disease which strikes in old age in a large segment but not in the whole male human population. To make this conclusion certain one would, however, like to have access to an even larger "over-80 material" than currently published series.

Cancer of Colon and Rectum. The incidence of carcinoma of the colon (including the rectum) is given in Figure 3.

The curve which includes both sexes is different from the incidence curve of pros-

tatic carcinoma in one important respect. The incidence figures are lower by a factor of approximately 200 and are consequently far below 100 percent, even at very old age.

The curve resembles that of occult prostatic carcinoma by being sigmoid with a steep rise between 55 and 75. After 80, the incidence remained stationary at about 0.25 percent. This figure is too low to regard cancer of the bowel as part of an aging syndrome. The shape of the curve of Figure 3 is typical for a large number of malignancies in humans (cf. Higginson and Muir, 1973). The principal difference between those malignancies is only the absolute incidence levels.

Cancers in General. It is possible to claim that the overall incidence of cancer follows an age distribution compatible with malignant transformation being part of an aging syndrome. All those malignancies with no further increase in incidence above 80 (e.g., colon carcinoma) could be special cases. Other less easily diagnosed tumors could occur in large numbers in the very old, so that the composite curves would indeed approach 100 percent at the end of the physiologic human life span.

It is deplorable that even the best materials do not include all types of malignant tumors. Squamous and basal cell carcinomas of the skin have never been systematically diagnosed clinically or in autopsies of symptomless individuals. It is, therefore, theoretically possible that these two diseases show an unsuspected rapid and progressive increase with age even after 80. Available data on clinically diagnosed squamous cell carcinomas of the skin speak, however, against this possibility.

Total cancer incidence has been computed for the Malmö material. Figure 4 excludes basal cell carcinoma of the skin. Some other skin cancers may have been undetected in the autopsies.

Figure 4 demonstrates, with the reservations above, that the overall cancer incidence shows an approximately linear increase between 45-80 years of age. The incidence doubles for each period of about 9 years. But after 80 further increase is slight, and the curve would probably not reach any higher than an incidence of about 45 percent (or 60-70 percent if microscopic prostatic carcinomas and basal cell

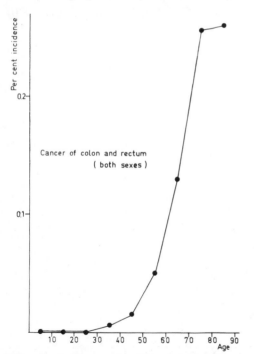

Figure 3. Incidence of colon carcinoma against age. Figures extracted from a special study of the Malmö material (From Berge, Ekelund, Mellner, Phil, and Wenckert, 1973.)

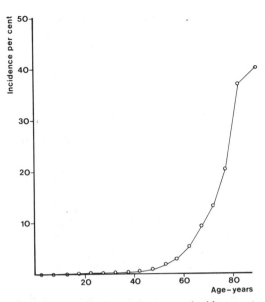

Figure 4. Total observed cancer incidence at different ages in the Malmö material. It excludes all basal cell skin carcinomas. About half the number of prostatic carcinomas can also be assumed to have been "missed," because the careful analysis of this gland illustrated in Figure 2 was not part of the procedure. The age figures are based on age at death for the tumors first detected at the autopsy. For tumors diagnosed during life, age is based on the time at which the malignant tumor was first unequivocally verified.

carcinoma were included) even at the age of 100. The absence of an increase in the very old is supported by a recent autopsy study of 3,535 patients over 65 years old (Suen, Lau, and Yermakov, 1974) in which the cancer incidence for males 76–85 years old was 42.9 percent, whereas it was 33.7 percent for people over 84. Saxton, Handler, and Bauer (1950) had previously noted a similar trend for several common neoplasms in a large autopsy series.

Benign Tumors. Benign tumors have only been studies in humans. As a group they are more common than malignant ones. Pigmented nevi, for instance, are invariably present after puberty (Lever, 1967).

One common tumor—basal cell papilloma—deserves serious consideration as a possible part of an aging syndrome. These distinctive lesions ("senile warts") are not found before puberty (except in certain rare hereditary conditions) and are unusual before 40, when they begin to increase rapidly in incidence. Although this has never been quantified, old people seem to always have senile warts, often in rather large number (cf. Lever, 1967).

From a general biological point of view, senile warts may well fulfill criteria of being part of an aging syndrome. No other etiology has been found. Basal cell papillomas do not seem to carry any virus. They occur on any parts of the body and do not seem to depend on the sunlight or any other exterior carcinogens. No method of preventing senile warts from occurring has been found (cf. Lever, 1967).

There may be other benign neoplasms which are part of an aging syndrome, but this is far from clear. Of special interest in this connection is so-called benign gammopathy (Waldenström, 1961), i.e., the occurrence of monoclonal protein in serum (M-component) of the same principal type as in myeloma. The disorder is rare before 50 and increases progressively with age to give an incidence figure of 3 percent in persons over 70 years (Hällén, 1966). Minor degrees of neoplastic production of immunoglobulin are not detected by this method, and benign gammopathy detected by serum electrophoresis is most probably only the top of the iceberg. Clonal benign neoplastic proliferation of Ig secreting (and nonsecreting?) lymphoid cells may well turn out to be part of an aging syndrome.

Critical Analysis of Statistical Evidence for Tumors as Part of an Age Syndrome. In this review neoplasia has been treated not as one disease but as many. There is no good reason for regarding malignant tumors as part of an aging syndrome. Each tumor seems to have its own characteristic age spectrum and for none (except possibly prostatic carcinoma) is there any proof of a continuing linear increase beyond the age of 80. Many are strongly influenced by the biological age of the bearer with a rapidly increasing incidence between 50 and 80 years of age in the human species. Others show a flat age incidence curve, and some childhood tumors are virtually nonexistent after adolescence. Animal data are consistent with the conclusion (Loeb, 1945;

Saxton, 1952; Kohn, 1963) that cancer is not part of the aging syndrome.

Another strong argument at least against individual types of malignancies as part of an aging syndrome is the large variation of the tumor spectrum shown in different parts of the world (cf. Higginson and Muir, 1973) in spite of a largely identical pattern of aging.

THE FACILITATING EFFECT OF AGE ON THE DEVELOPMENT OF TUMORS

In the two previous sections, compelling evidence has been reviewed that neoplasia is not part of an aging syndrome but a group of diseases many of which strike in middle age or old life. This naturally raises the question of the nature of the facilitating effect which biological age seems to have on carcinogenesis.

Theoretically there are a number of ways by which age can promote the development of neoplasia. All these are deeply involved in general theories on the etiology of cancers. I will discuss the following: (a) accumulation of somatic mutations, (b) increased sensitivity to oncogenic viruses, (c) increased sensitivity to external carcinogens, (d) decreased immuno-

logic resistance against neoplastic cells, (e) increased tendency to hormone imbalance, and (f) intrinsic age-related cell alterations which could influence cellular susceptibility to neoplastic transformation.

Accumulation of Somatic Mutations

The validity of this theory requires (a) that somatic mutations are an important cause of tumors and (b) that the number of such mutations increases with biological age.

The most extensive experiments on somatic mutations in aged individuals have been performed on mouse lines (Crowley and Curtis, 1963; Curtis and Crowley, 1963).

Figure 5 displays the findings in two inbred strains of mice (Crowley and Curtis, 1963). Both strains showed an increase in percent chromosome aberration with age. In the long-lived C57BL/6J strain, the increase was slow and moderate in contrast to the short-lived A/HEJ strain. Studies in the dog have given similar results with the important difference that the rate of accumulation of aberrations with age was much slower in the long-lived dog compared to the short-lived mouse (Curtis, Leith, and Tilley, 1966).

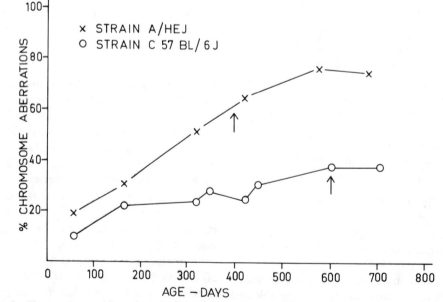

Figure 5. Chromosome abberations in liver cells of two different inbred strains of mice, plotted as a function of age. The median life span of each strain is indicated by the arrows. (Data from Crowley and Curtis, 1963.)

The liver is the only organ whose age incidence of spontaneous mutations has been systematically studied. Brain and other stationary cells cannot be studied because mitosis cannot be induced. In constantly regenerating systems such as bone marrow, mutated cells are believed to be eliminated rapidly, and this is thought to be the reason for the absence of any increased number of chromosome aberrations with age in such cells (Curtis, 1966).

If we accept that somatic mutations increase with age, it remains to examine if such mutations facilitate neoplasia, i.e., if the somatic mutation hypothesis for cancer is true.

Irradiation is a well-known mutagen and also a prominent carcinogen. The literature contains no direct attempts to correlate induction of chromosome alterations and tumors in the same experiment, and few studies include data on histologic types and organ distribution of the arising neoplasms. From a vast amount of data on irradiation caused tumors, it seems, however, very likely that there is some correlation between the capacity of ionizing radiation to produce chromosome damage and to induce malignant tumors under various experimental conditions (Upton, 1973).

Irradiation is known to shorten the life span of animals. According to many observers, the whole aging syndrome starts earlier and becomes severe more rapidly in irradiated than nonirradiated animals (Lindop and Rotblat, 1961). The tumor spectrum is usually somewhat different after x-ray treatment (Kohn and Guttman, 1963) with tumors tending to start earlier in life; but this is difficult to interpret since irradiation will have an effect on the immunologic defense apart from its mutagenic activity. (See chapter 24 in this volume for a different analysis of radiation and life shortening.)

Indirect *in vivo* evidence for a positive statistical correlation between induced or spontaneous mutations and cancers of the type cited can probably never prove a cause/effect relation. *In vitro* systems seem worth exploring. That mass cultures of human fibroblasts with chromosome aberrations (Moorhead and Saksela, 1965) may be extra sensitive to transformation is suggested by the finding that phase III (aging) cells (Jensen, Koprowski, and Pontén, 1963) and cells from Down's syndrome (Todaro and Martin, 1967) show an increased susceptibility to transformation by Simian virus 40.

Mutations are generally detrimental to cell viability. There is no *a priori* reason why damaged rather than healthy cells should be more susceptible to transformation. In spite of a high proportion of chromosome breaks in phase III human fibroblasts, spontaneous neoplastic transformation never occurs (Pontén, 1971). Susceptibility of damaged cells may totally depend on the transforming agent. If it, in very simple terms, carries a transformation gene capable of switching off normal growth control, there is no reason why an already mutated cell would become more efficiently neoplastic than its normal counterpart. If, on the other hand, it acts nonspecifically by increasing the number of mutations and a certain constellation of such events if necessary for transformation, then already altered cells may be more easily transformed than normal ones.

To sum up, there is evidence favoring accumulation of somatic mutations with increasing biological age. In the few systems studied, the rate of this accumulation seems to relate directly to the longevity of a species or of different inbred strains within one species. The theory that somatic mutations are the very cause of aging is, however, not proven and even difficult to reconcile with certain facts. Some indirect evidence is compatible with mutated cells showing an increased susceptibility to subsequent malignant transformation. It is possible that the somatic mutation theory eventually will turn out to explain aging and some of its facilitating effect on many types of cancer, although it seems at present much more likely that mutations and/or chromosomes alterations are secondary epiphenomena at least in relation to aging.

Increased Sensitivity to Oncogenic Viruses

A simple explanation of tumors in old age would be that the senescent organism is unduly sensitive to oncogenic virus. This theory, of

TABLE 2. TYPES OF ONCOGENIC VIRUSES.

Classification of virion	Popular group designation	Site of maturation	Prototype virus	Type of lesion	Proliferative lesion transmitted under natural conditions
DNA					
Large					
Membrane-bound	Pox	Cytoplasmic inclusion	Shope rabbit fibroma	Solid benign neoplasia	Yes
Medium					
Membrane-bound	"Herpes-type"	Nucleus	Lucké frog kidney carcinoma[a]	Solid malignant neoplasia	Yes
Naked	Adeno	Nucleus	Adenovirus 12	Solid malignant neoplasia	No
Small					
Naked	Papova	Nucleus	1. Human wart	Solid benign neoplasia	Yes
			2. Shope rabbit papilloma	Solid benign neoplasia	Yes
			3. S–E polyoma	Solid malignant neoplasia	No
RNA					
Medium					
Membrane-bound	"Myxo-like"[b]	Cytoplasm	1. Rous sarcoma	Solid malignant neoplasia	_[c]
			2. Bittner mouse mammary cancer[d]	Solid malignant neoplasia	Yes
			3. Avian leukosis	Leukemia and solid lymphoma	Yes
			4. Gross mouse leukemia	Aleukemic leukemia	Yes

[a]Frog kidney carcinoma virus of Lucké. Tentative classification on a basis of: (a) reproduction and maturation in the nucleus; and (b) morphological similarity to "herpes-like" viruses, known to be of DNA type.

[b]So-called because of budding from cell membranes, as is characteristic for the myxoviruses. Hemagglutination, which is characteristic of the myxoviruses, does not occur with the RNA tumor viruses.

[c]Laboratory strain isolated from a particular spontaneous tumor. Other similar tumors occur spontaneously in chickens with low frequency, but the relationship among etiologic agents is unknown.

[d]Mammary gland carcinoma virus of Bittner. Tentative classification on a basis of budding from cytoplasmic membranes, as is characteristic for the RNA myxoviruses and "myxo-like" tumor viruses.

Modified from Rauscher and O'Connor, 1973.

course, requires that oncogenic viral genomes are indeed an important cause of cancer.

The vast field of tumor virology has been reviewed repeatedly (Gross, 1961; Pontén, 1971; Tooze, 1973). Table 2 lists the most common and best studied oncogenic viruses.

The only types of infectious oncogenic agents for which biological universality has been claimed are the RNA B and C-type viruses (Huebner and Todaro, 1969). Obviously the mechanism by which the virus is spread becomes of utmost importance if a general role for cancer is claimed.

Horizontal Infection. Horizontal infection has without exception been most effective in the newborn animal with a rapid increase in host resistance sometimes within a few days after birth.

The pronounced susceptibility of the newborn has been shown for oncogenic C-type viruses (Gross, 1951; Burmester, 1957), mammary carcinoma virus of mice (Bittner, 1936), Simian virus 40 (Eddy, 1964), polyoma virus (Stewart and Eddy, 1959) and adenovirus (Trentin, Yabe, and Taylor, 1962). There is strong evidence that the major reason for this age-related susceptibility is the immaturity of the immunologic apparatus at birth.

Increased sensitivity to horizontal infection by oncogenic virus in old age is a most unlikely explanation for the age distribution of cancer, since all experimental evidence indicates that young individuals are most sensitive to infection.

Vertical Infection. Vertical infection is defined as the transmission from parents to embryos of viral genes. This can occur via a chronically infected virus-shedding ovary (Burmester, 1957), but the form which interests us here is one in which the viral genes are so closely associated with the cellular genome that they are carried along with it in the germ line as well as in the somatic cells. How these viral genes have become associated with the cellular genomes is a matter of considerable dispute. Some may become integrated into the cellular genome after regular horizontal infections between animals even belonging to zoologically distant species (Benveniste and Todaro, 1974) or between cells within an animal (Rowe and Pincus, 1972). Others may be ancient, permanent parts of the cellular genomes with a capacity to "break lose" as viral genes under appropriate conditions.

Viral genes of the described nature have only been established for the RNA viruses under natural conditions. In all likelihood, they exist as provirus DNA copies of the respective viral RNAs (Temin, 1964; Hill and Hillova, 1972). Usually these genes are silent, "repressed," but under certain circumstances they may be activated. In this context it is important if their activation is related to the age of the host.

Huebner and a large group of collaborators (see below) have made extensive analyses of inbred and noninbred mouse strains using gs-antisera, electron microscopy, and infectiosity tests as their principal tools for detection of C-virus genomes in animals of different ages. Genomic expression has been correlated with development of lymphomas. "Provirus" DNA is considered present in all murine cellular genomes regardless of age or strain (Huebner and Todaro, 1969). It is probably also to some extent transcribed into RNA. In young embryos, translation into gs-antigen and assembly

of noninfectious C-particles budding from the cell membrane can almost always be established (Huebner, Kelloff, Sarma, Lane, and Turner, 1970; Huebner, 1970; Gardner, Officer, Rongey, Estes, Turner, and Huebner, 1971; Vernon, Lane, and Huebner, 1973). In older embryos and newborn animals of certain strains, there was a tendency to lesser signs of viral activity, since the amount of gs-antigen and number of C-particles decreased (Huebner et al., 1970). The postnatal development varied widely between strains and individual mice. The high lymphoma incidence strain AKR showed infectious virus in newborns and adult animals. Development of lymphoma started early, and hardly any animal survived to old age. In the low incidence noninbred NIH Swiss strain, virions were found, which, however, were noninfectious (Vernon, Lane, and Huebner, 1973).

A minor proportion of wild mice showed increased numbers of C-particles and increased percentage of gs-antigen-positive tissues by age. The few animals which developed "spontaneous" lymphomas after their capture, with occasional exceptions, belonged to the category where gs-antigen and C-particles appeared.

The findings above are difficult to interpret. Gs-antigen and C-particles are strongly associated with hematopoietic cells. Their appearance and disappearance from a certain organ is therefore correlated to its participation in blood formation. Age-related patterns of viral expression can therefore in certain situations be artifacts due to redistribution of cells rather than genomic derepression. As soon as infectious particles are produced, and even a moderate synthesis cannot be detected with current methods, there is ample opportunity for spread within the animal (Rowe and Pincus, 1972) and for recombination with preexisting endogenous genomes (Weiss, Mason and Vogt, Virology 1973)—a situation which could easily become unanalyzable.

Infection by a C-particle is not, when this is shown, necessarily synonomous with oncogenic properties. Many isolates of RNA C-type particles have never been shown to induce leukemia or any other disease.

In spite of the above and other difficulties, it seems possible to discern a pattern where biological age (or cell differentiation?) influences the expression of C-type genomes in mice. There is first a stage in early embryonic life where gs-antigen and particles are produced in abundance. The second period when C-type genomes again tend to become active is in adult life of the short-lived AKR mice when there is a rather strong association with overt occurrence of leukemia (Rowe and Pincus, 1972).

The findings briefly summarized above and similar observations in fowl (Payne and Chubb, 1968) led Huebner and Todaro (1969) to formulate their well-known oncogene theory. In extended form, it postulates that each somatic cell in mammals, birds, and probably other animals harbors oncogenes. These are negative DNA copies of the genetic material of the RNA tumor viruses of B and C-type. Activation of the oncogene will lead to more or less complete production of the corresponding RNA viruses and sometimes to a neoplastic transformation of the cells in question. The oncogenes are postulated to be spontaneously activated by aging but also by a host of carcinogens (Igel et al., 1969; Kaplan, 1950). Oncogenes are the ultimate mediators of a neoplastic transformation; their presence and activation explain the development of the "generality of cancer" (Todaro and Huebner, 1969).

The theory can be criticized on several points. Its only experimental basis is studies on lymphoma and mammary cancer in mice and lymphoma in chickens. The tumor spectrums of wild mice and many low leukemia strains are characterized by a variety of tumors which are not transmissible by C or B-viruses (although they may carry such agents as passengers). There are no experiments to show that these, which may be more representative for "the generality of cancer" than the lymphomas, are related to oncogenic RNA virus. Appearance of infective C-virus under relatively crude in vivo conditions may be caused by trivial infection from the outside or more subtly by horizontal spread within the organism rather than by switching on of repressed oncovirogenes. Many C-virus isolates although infective do not cause a neoplastic transformation. Furthermore, in spite of very extensive efforts, no human C-virus has been detected.

To sum up, the theory that RNA tumor virus associated oncogenes are responsible for cancer has not received sufficient experimental support to make it an acceptable explanation for the occurrence of any tumors other than certain lymphomas in chickens, mice, and cats and mammary caricnomas in mice. It cannot presently explain how the majority of natural malignancies arise. Since these are the ones strongly associated with age, the oncogene theory has so far failed to give any explanation for the mechanism by which tumor incidence is increased in old age. The DNA "proviruses" of cellular genomes may turn out to be important for other functions rather than growth control (Temin, 1971).

Chemical Carcinogens, Aging, and Cancer

From epidemiological data it has been guessed that a major portion of all malignant tumors in man are caused by external chemicals (Higginson and Muir, 1973). These cancers show the type of age incidence curves illustrated in Figure 3.

Chemical carcinogenesis under natural conditions is apparently a very complex process. Only in certain situations is it possible to ascribe a given tumor to a specific carcinogen with a high degree of probability, e.g., bronchial cancer in a heavy smoker. In many cases the picture is mixed with possible exposure to a number of carcinogens. For example, what exactly caused carcinoma of the renal pelvis in a smoking worker in the dye industry (aromatic amines) who had habitually consumed phenacetin to alleviate his headache and who lived in an area with heavy air pollution and a high background of ionizing irradiation? It is in all probability an interaction between largely unknown endogenous host factors and a variety of synergistic or antagonistic chemicals of different carcinogenic potential for different organs (together with promotors?) which determines if a particular individual will contract cancer (cf. Wogan, 1974; Stenbäck, Garcia, and Shubik, 1974). In animal experiments, the situation is simplified by the administration of large doses of one single carcinogen, but still all possible endogenous and exogenous cocarcinogens cannot be controlled.

Two circumstances would, either alone or in combination, explain why chemically induced cancers would occur in old individuals: (1) Chemical carcinogens could be more effective in old than young tissues. (2) An old individual could have more time to accumulate a chemical carcinogen and/or manifest the resulting malignant tumor. The latter alternative is, of course, not a true facilitation but a more passive and in a sense trivial effect of the passage of time.

Surprisingly few attempts have been made to resolve whether old tissues are more susceptible than young ones to chemical carcinogenesis. Cowdry and Suntzeff (1944) exposed the skin of young and old mice of two strains of different sensitivity to methylcholanthrene. In the highly susceptible strain, essentially all mice contracted tumors regardless of age at exposure. But particularly in the interval between 3-7 months after exposure to the carcinogen, the proportion of tumors was consistently higher in the "young" than in the "old" group. A similar experiment in a less susceptible strain failed to show the same difference. Engelbreth-Holm and Jensen (1953) found 20-day-old mice to be most susceptible to chemical carcinogenesis. Resistance was larger both in younger and older mice. Della Porta, Capitano, Parmi, and Colnaghi (1967) found urethane to be a much more efficient carcinogen in baby than in older mice. The subject was reviewed by Della Porta and Terracini (1969) and Homburger (1974).

Only recently has a critical experiment been performed where all factors but tissue age were kept constant. Ebbesen (1973, 1974) transplanted old and young skin to young syngeneic mice. After exposure to DMBA there was a more than threefold increase in the incidence of carcinoma in the old versus the young transplants. This elegant experiment indicates very strongly that senescent tissues *per se* have an increased sensitivity to a chemical carcinogen. Chemically caused cancers in old individuals may therefore be explained on other grounds than a decreased general immune resistance or hormone imbalance.

It has often been discussed whether cancers in man differ in malignancy depending on the age of the host. The most common statement is that a cancer is clinically more malignant the younger the patient is (Lees and Park, 1949). Superficial analyses are bound to be misleading since many morphologically distinct childhood cancers (acute leukemia, osteogenic sarcoma, neuroblastoma, nephroblastoma, and so on) are unusually malignant and cannot be compared with cancers in general. The only reliable study would be one in which a specific well-defined tumor was singled out and analyzed with respect to growth rate, spread, and prognosis in patients of different ages. Although feasible, such a study has not, to my knowledge, been performed. We are thus not certain if less-differentiated tumors tend to occur at a younger age than well-differentiated, if comparable tumors tend to metastasize differently, or if growth rate varies depending on host age.

To sum up, chemically induced tumors tend to occur comparatively late in life. Nothing definitely disproves that this is simply due to a longer exposure to the carcinogens combined with a long latent time; however, some recent experiments suggest that at least old mouse skin may be intrinsically more susceptible to chemical carcinogens than young skin.

Decreased Immunologic Resistance Against Neoplastic Cells

From a vast immunologic literature, two facts can reasonably safely be extracted. The first is that malignant cells in experimental animals and man often but not always become antigenic to their host, who then may mount a specific immunologic response. This is usually biologically ineffective in the primary host, but aspects of it can be detected and amplified *in vitro* and *in vivo* with suitable experimental procedures. The second is that certain autoimmune diseases and related disorders increase with age and that some physiologic immune reactions tend to weaken in life (Walford, 1969).

The problem is whether the pathological responses of the immune mechanism which increase with age could also facilitate development of cancer and thus explain its age distribution.

Paramount to the theme of immunology, cancer, and aging is the concept of immunosurveillance (Burnet, 1957, 1964, 1970, 1971). This theory states that aberrant cells, many of which are potentially malignant, arise in large numbers in all tissues of the body. As part of their abnormality, these cells will have membrane changes sufficiently distinctive to elicit an autoimmune reaction, which is cytotoxic and thus eliminates cancers in their nascent state. Immunosurveillance would then become the most important means by which the body cleanses itself of malignant cells. Failure of immune surveillance is the essential cause of cancer because it permits unchecked growth of aberrant cells (Burnet, 1967; Good and Finstad, 1969). Obviously a failing immunosurveillance as part of an aging syndrome would explain the prevalence of cancer of senescence.

The immune surveillance theory demands that all tumors be capable of stimulating immunity when very small. This is contradicted by certain data (Old, Boyse, Clarke, and Carswell, 1962; Potter, Hoskins, and Oxford, 1969) in which very small tumor inocula were capable of "sneaking through" an immunologic defense which was effective against higher tumor cell doses. It has also been found that the tumors in mice which show the highest degrees of antigenicity are either those which are induced by virulent strains of oncogenic virus or those which come up after a short latent time because a large amount of a potent chemical carcinogen was given (Prehn, 1957). These are not the situations encountered outside of the laboratory. Most spontaneous murine tumors have little or no capacity to immunize the host although a degree of antigenicity can almost always be demonstrated in lymphocytotoxic tests *in vitro* (Baldwin, 1974). It is difficult to invoke a failing immune surveillance as the primary cause for the emergence of weakly antigenic tumors.

Although theoretically attractive, the immunosurveillance theory of cancer has thus not received sufficient experimental support to become generally accepted. Prehn (1970) has discussed the pros and cons for the theory in detail.

Already established tumors multiplying beyond the reaches of immunosurveillance generally grow progressively in their primary host, regardless of whether one can experimentally demonstrate an immune reaction. Many explanations have been advanced such as presence of blocking antibodies (Hellström and Hellström, 1970), antigen-antibody complexes, or soluble tumor-specific antigens (Hellström, Hellström, and Sjögren, 1970). Also a "central" immunologic depression has not been ruled out. Apparently, malignant tumors influence their hosts in a very complex, still largely not understood fashion with temporal and spatial differences in the degree, quality, and direction of the antitumoral response. The net result of this immunologic host-tumor cell interplay is usually insignificant as far as tumor growth is concerned. In certain situations which may be amplified experimentally, the result may either be enhancement or inhibition of tumor growth.

The current state of tumor immunology should make it clear that any age-related changes in the immunologic system cannot be expected to be easily analyzed and that a uniform and predictable effect on tumor incidence and growth would be surprising to find (cf. Kripke and Borsos, 1974).

Because of the uncertainty about the importance of immunological repsonses in spontaneous neoplasia, in general it seems premature to speculate about their possible effect on the age incidence of cancer (Walford, 1969). Nothing contradicts that the similarity in age incidence curves between certain immunologic disorders (types of acquired hemolytic anemia, chronic rheumatoid arthritis) and many types of cancer is purely coincidental.

To sum up, there is only weak suggestive evidence favoring the idea that an age-related breakdown of the immunologic system is a major factor in explaining the increased tumor incidence in aging populations of animals or humans.

Hormone Imbalance

The hormone changes which occur with age can be broadly divided into those which are part of a physiologic program and those which are pathologic. The physiologic program of endocrine changes with biological age is exceedingly complex and varies from species to species. It has sometimes been assumed that these alterations are the very cause of aging, but this is contradicted by the failure to prolong life by endocrine measures. If anything, the integrity of the endocrine system seems better preserved than most other organ systems in old age—a fact which also speaks against hormones as the driving force for senescence (cf. Curtis, 1966).

Even if hormonal changes are not the etiology of aging, they could be important in causing cancer to develop. Mammary tumors in mice can be quoted as an outstanding example of the influence of the endocrine environment. Castration and hypophysectomy strongly reduce cancer incidence, whereas multiple pregnancies have the opposite effect (Wynder, 1959; Macmahon and Cole, 1969).

Human breast cancer is also influenced by hormones. Chronic anterior pituitary secretory insufficiency and castration since youth are known to reduce the risk of subsequent mammary carcinoma (Wynder, 1959; Macmahon and Cole, 1969). These are, however, extreme examples. A more important piece of information would be the outcome of a long-term prospective study of hormone levels in healthy women. Would the group which contracted breast cancer be different than those females which remained free of the disease? Sampling of urine from 5,000 women prior to development of breast cancer has suggested a subnormal excretion of androgen metabolites as a predisposing factor (Bulbrook, Hayward, and Spicer, 1971). These interesting findings need to be extended and confirmed before their value can be determined.

The same considerations apply to prostatic carcinoma—a disease which may be exclusively human, at least in its spontaneous form (Prout, 1973). Although there has been much speculation about hormone imbalance as the cause of prostatic carcinoma, there is no solid study excluding or confirming an endocrine dysfunction preceding the development of cancer. Since the incidence of this disease is so high (Figure 2), and its pathology, bio-chemistry, hormone responsiveness, and clinical course are rather well understood, it would seem most relevant to assemble the required data on hormone levels in blood and urine. An age-related endocrine pathology might very well prove to be the factor which facilitates the development of this disease.

Endometrial carcinoma in humans is clearly under hormonal influence. The profile of high-risk subjects includes menstrual dysfunction, a late menopause (probably with many anovulatory cycles) and estrogen producing ovarian tumors; ovariectomy of young subjects reduces the risk (cf. Novak and Woodruff, 1974).

Additional examples can be quoted to show that endogenous endocrine activity plays a role in the development of cancer from hormone influenced tissues both in animals and man.

The factor of age is difficult to assess in all these cases. There is, however, no proof that physiologic age-dependent changes in hormone secretion are the etiology of any malignancies. If this were ever demonstrated to be true, it would be a strong reason to regard these cancers as part of an aging syndrome.

It is important to make a distinction between hormones as causative or growth modulating agents. The latter case, that already manifest malignant tumors can be positively or negatively influenced by hormones, has been made abundantly clear in the clinic and in experiments. The much more difficult question, whether hormones can achieve a malignant cell transformation, has never been satisfactorily answered (Heidelberger, 1973).

Endocrine changes, particularly those concerning gonadal hormones, are part of the aging syndrome taken in a broad sense. No proof exists that these physiologic alterations can primarily cause cancer. Already manifest malignancies exemplified by human prostatic carcinoma seem, however, to profit from the normal relative excess of androgens in old males, as shown by the effectiveness of anti-androgen therapy. This mainly concerns histologically well-differentiated adenocarcinomas and is thus not a general phenomenon, even for prostatic carcinoma. In an indirect manner, the hormone environment of the aged may therefore facilitate the proliferation of existing malignancies exemplified by a proportion of the carcinomas of the prostate and the breast in animals and man. It is possible that a similar situation will eventually also be found for other cancers, including those which are not controlled by conventional hormones, in which still undetected circulating growth factors could play a role.

Cellular Senescence *in vitro* and Malignant Transformation

From a large literature on the establishment of permanent cell lines *in vitro* (Hayflick, 1965 and 1966; Hay, 1967; Cristofalo, 1970; Pontén, 1971; Macieira-Coelho, 1973), the following facts seem well established.

Only a few nonneoplastic cell types are serially propagable. These are fibroblasts, lymphoblastoid cells, and astrocytes. "Fibroblasts" is then used as a descriptive term for spindle-shaped cells which tend to grow in parallel in tight bundles. Details of their behavior such as number of possible doublings, terminal cell density, etc., vary depending on their source (lung, skin, synovia, etc.). Populations of lymphoblastoid cells (Nilsson and Pontén, 1975) and astrocytes (Westermark, 1973) appear, on the other hand, to be homogenous.

Fibroblasts of human (Swim and Parker, 1957; Hayflick and Moorhead, 1961) and avian (Pontén, 1970) origin have a finite life span *in vitro*. No spontaneous transformations to infinite growth have been observed in these species. Fibroblast populations of murine origin, on the other hand, invariably undergo spontaneous transformation and become capable of indefinite proliferation (Sanford *et al.*, 1950; Rothfels, Kupelwieser, and Parker, 1963; Todaro and Green, 1963; Sanford *et al.*, 1970) (Figure 6). Fibroblasts from other (less exhaustively) studied species take an intermediate position, i.e., rare spontaneous transformations have been recorded (cf. Pontén, 1971).

Astrocytes of human origin invariably die out in culture after an average of 20 divisions not counting the unknown number of cell doublings which precede the formation of the first monolayer (Pontén and Macintyre, 1968). Astrocytes of rat origin have been observed to

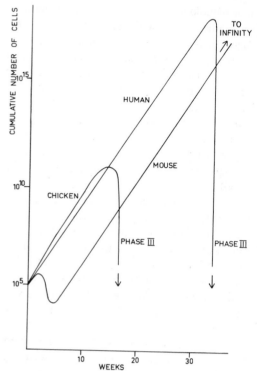

Figure 6. Total population size obtainable from embryonic human, chicken, and mouse fibroblasts. The starting material is assumed to be one primary culture containing 5×10^6 cells. The arrows pointing downwards indicate points of termination of a finite population life. Only mouse fibroblasts have been shown capable of undergoing "infinite growth transformation."

transform spontaneously, although this cell type has not been systematically investigated.

Lymphoid cells of normal mouse, calf, cat, and rabbit origin do not produce established lines but deteriorate rapidly after explantation *in vitro*. Human lymphoid organs, on the other hand, readily give rise to infinitely propagable lymphoblastoid cell lines (Moore and Minowada, 1969; Nilsson, 1971).

Solid malignant tumors and lymphomas in mice and other rodents readily give rise to established lines *in vitro* composed of the neoplastic cells. Solid malignant tumors of human origin only rarely survive *in vitro* to give established lines (Moore and Koike, 1964; Pontén and Saksela, 1967; Pontén and Macintyre, 1968); the same holds true for lymphomas and leukemias with the notable exception of

Burkitt's lymphoma (cf. Nilsson and Pontén, 1975).

One conclusion from the observations above is that the species origin has a strong influence on the behavior *in vitro* of otherwise comparable cells. Fibroblasts and astrocytes of two "stable" species, man and chicken, have no tendency toward spontaneous infinite growth transformation, in contrast to rodents (particularly mice?) where the same tendency is pronounced. Lymphoblastoid cells seem to contradict this conclusion; however, their infinite growth, when of human origin, is only possible after infection by Epstein-Barr virus (EBV) and may therefore be a special case (Pope, Horne, and Scott, 1968).

It follows from these considerations that "aging *in vitro*," i.e., the eventual irreversible degeneration of serially propagable healthy cells (Hayflick and Moorhead, 1961), can only be studied in a few model systems in which both the cell and species origin have to be "right." In practice, the available models have been restricted to human and avian fibroblasts or human astrocytes. Any conclusions about the relations between aging and neoplasia *in vitro* are therefore of limited scope.

The three described models seem to age according to the same gross pattern *in vitro*. The most prominent feature is a stage of luxuriant growth (phase II) followed by a rapid decline (phase III) which terminates in total loss of the cultures. Cell biological and metabolic parameters of this process have been summarized by Macieira-Coelho (1973).

A most straightforward experiment is to compare phase II ("young") to phase III ("old") cells with respect to their sensitivity to neoplastic transformation. It has been shown that old human lung fibroblasts are more sensitive to transformation by SV40 than young fibroblasts (Jensen, Koprowski, and Pontén, 1963; Todaro, Wolman, and Green, 1963). This manifests itself as a shorter latent time before the characteristic altered growth pattern is detected and as a higher percentage of cells which score as infected by the presence of the virus-specific intranuclear T-antigen (Carp and Gilden, 1966). The transformed cells from phase III cultures seem, on the other hand, less viable than those of phase II cell origin (Jensen, Koprowski, and Pontén, 1963).

Phase II chicken cells were induced to grow faster after transformation by Rous sarcoma virus (RSV), but their total number of possible doublings were nevertheless decreased in comparison with control cells (Pontén, 1970). Bovine phase II fibroblasts transformed by RSV also failed to undergo infinite growth transformation (Stenkvist, 1966).

The interpretation of these results in terms of aging and cancer is very difficult. The only experiment which suggests that senescent cells are more susceptible to transformation are those in which SV40 was added to human fibroblasts (Jensen, Koprowski, and Pontén, 1963; Todaro, Wolman, and Green, 1963). Mass cultures towards the end of their life span are, however, heterogenous with respect to their content of phase II and phase III cells (cf. Macieira-Coelho, 1973). Therefore it cannot be excluded that the few cells in the aging cultures which transformed were descendants of remaining phase II cells rather than cells at the very end of their life span *in vitro*. It should also be recalled that the transformation predominantly concerned morphology and the capacity to divide in spite of a high local cell density and not a potential for infinite growth.

It seems as if there is no solid experimental support to regard phase III ("aged") cells as generally more susceptible to neoplastic transformation *in vitro* than their corresponding young predecessors. But the crucial experiments remain to be done in which individual phase III cells with an estimable potential of future cell cycles are transformed by defined carcinogens and compared with phase II cells. Such experiments could prove very illuminating in distinguishing between current theories about senescence of diploid cells *in vitro*.

Aging and Cancer as Part of the Same Ontogenetic Program

The idea of a "biological clock" for cellular aging assumes that the finite life span of normal cells *in vitro* is a reflection of a general program for somatic cell growth and differentiation, according to which all groups and categories of cells are programmed to undergo series of proliferative and differentiative events during the lifetime of an individual. Certain cells, for instance phylogenetic vestiges or so-called fetal organs, are already eliminated in embryonic life; others are eliminated later during adolescence (e.g., the human thymus), and still others deteriorate in old age. Most of the latter will not reach this stage *in vivo,* but if survival is prolonged by cultivation outside of the body, their mortality is exposed. The biological clock hypothesis is vague. Since the molecular background of such a biologic clock is entirely conjectural, it is impossible to test its validity by experiment.

There is some indirect *in vivo* support for a relation between a "biological clock" and carcinogenesis. The most important argument is, of course, that this theory is compatible with the relation of cancer to *biological* rather than *chronological* age. Protein synthetic errors (Orgel, 1963; Fulder and Holliday, 1975) or somatic mutations would, for instance, not be expected to accumulate with such vastly different speeds which the differences in the longevity of animals seem to require unless they were coupled to "biological" rather than chronologic time. A programmed biological clock could be intrinsically set to fit all kinds of life spans, organ developments, and living forms.

Some evidence for a biological clock for aging can be inferred from the age relations of certain human cancers. Osteogenic sarcoma, a malignant transformation of osteoblasts, has its peak incidence between 15-20 years (Glücksmann, 1951; Saunders, 1966). This coincides approximately with the approaching quiescence of the metaphyseal growth zones of the limbs rather than with the phase of the most rapid osteoblastic multiplication which is in embryos and infants. Similarily, neuroblastomas and medulloblastomas, two malignant tumors of early childhood, make their appearance not during embryonic life but rather at a point when the "clock" for neuroblasts and medulloblasts begins to run out. Very speculatively, an analogous argument could be construed to explain,

for instance, why mammary carcinomas peak in the climacteric breast when the epithelium begins to quiet down and perhaps atrophy and why prostatic carcinoma peaks later when the "male climacterium" starts to bring the specific cells susceptible to transformation to quiescence.

Solid facts about the causes and conditions responsible for cellular senescence *in vitro* and *in vivo* are still too meager to permit more than vague speculations about how they could facilitate neoplasia. The theory about a preprogrammed biological clock is not incompatible with an enhanced susceptibility for neoplastic transformation but is so vague and in such desperate lack of molecular support that it does not provide much help for any deeper understanding of the relation between aging and cancer.

ACKNOWLEDGMENTS

I have profited greatly from interesting discussions with my Swedish colleagues Thorbjörn Berge (Skövde) and Sture Falkmer (Umeå). Their kind cooperation is gratefully acknowledged. Frank Bittkowski drew the figures and Kerstin Lindberg gave excellent secretarial help. Experiments from our group at the Wallenberg Laboratory in Uppsala, Sweden were supported by the Swedish Cancer Fund.

REFERENCES

Andervont, H. B., and Dunn, T. B. 1962. Occurence of tumors in wild house mice. *J. Nat. Cancer Inst.*, **28**, 1153–1163.

Baldwin, R. W. 1974. Tumour-specific antigens. *In*, F. Homburger (ed.), *The Physiopathology of Cancer.* Vol. 1, P. Shubik (ed.), *Biology and Biochemistry*, pp. 314–392. Basel-München-Paris-London-New York-Sydney: S. Karger.

Benveniste, R. E., and Todaro, G. J. 1974. Evolution of C-type viral genes: Inheritance of exogenously acquired viral genes. *Nature,* **252,** 456–459.

Berge, T. T. 1967. The metastasis of carcinoma with special references to the spleen. *Acta Pathol. Microbiol. Scand. Suppl.*, **188**.

Berge, T., Ekelund, G., Mellner, C., Phil, B., and Wenckert, A. 1973. Carcinoma of the colon and rectum in a defined population. *Acta Chir. Scand. Suppl.*, **438**.

Bittner, J. J. 1936. Some possible effects of nursing on the mammary gland tumour incidence in mice. *Science*, **84**, 162 (only).

Bulbrook, R. D., Hayward, J. L., and Spicer, C. C. 1971. Relation between urinary androgen and corticoid excretion and subsequent breast cancer. *Lancet*, **ii**, 395–402.

Burmester, B. R. 1957. Transmission of tumor inducing avian viruses under natural conditions. *Tex. Symp. Cancer Res.*, **15**, 92–110.

Burnet, F. M. 1957. Cancer–A biological approach. IV. Practical applications. *Brit. Med. J.*, **1**, 844–847.

Burnet, F. M. 1964. Immunological factors in the process of carcinogenesis. *Brit. Med. Bull.*, **20**, 154–158.

Burnet, F. M. 1967. Immunological aspects of malignant disease. *Lancet*, **i**, 1171–1174.

Burnet, F. M. 1970. *Immunological Surveillance.* Sydney: Pergamon Press.

Burnet, F. M. 1971. Immunological surveillance in neoplasia. *Transplant. Rev.*, **7**, 3–25.

Carp, R. I., and Gilden, R. V. 1966. A comparison of the replication cycles of simian virus 40 in human diploid and African green monkey kidney cells. *Virology*, **28**, 150–162.

Cowdry, E. V., and Suntzeff, V. 1944. Influence of age on epidermal carcinogenesis induced by methylcholanthrene in mice. *Yale J. Biol. Med.*, **17**, 47–58.

Cristofalo, V. J. 1970. Metabolic aspects of aging in diploid human cells. *In*, E. Holeckova and V. J. Christofalo, *Aging in Cell and Tissue Culture*, pp. 83–119. New York: Plenum Press.

Crowley, C., and Curtis, H. 1963. The development of somatic mutations in mice with age. *Proc. Nat. Acad. Sci.*, **49**, 626–628.

Curtis, H. J. 1966. Biological mechanisms of aging. *In*, I. N. Kugelmass (ed.), *The Bannerstone Division of American Lectures in Living Chemistry*, pp. 1–133. Springfield, Illinois: Charles C. Thomas.

Curtis, H., and Crowley, C. 1963. Chromosome aberrations in liver cells in relation to the somatic mutation theory of aging. *Radiation Res.*, **19**, 337–344.

Curtis, H. J., Leith, J., and Tilley, J. 1966. Chromosome aberrations in liver cells of dogs of different ages. *J. Geront.*, **21**, 268–270.

Daniel, C. W., and Young, L. J., 1971. Influence of cell division on an aging process. Life span of mouse mammary epithelium during serial propagation *in vivo*. *Exp. Cell Res.*, **65**, 27–32.

Davis, M. L., Upton, A. C., and Satterfield, L. C. 1971. Growth and senescence of the bone marrow stem cell pool in RFU/Un mice. *Proc. Soc. Exp. Biol. Med.*, **137**, 1452–1456.

Dawe, C. J. 1968. Invertebrate animals in cancer research. *Gann Monogr.*, **5**, 45–55.

Dawe, C. J. 1969. Phylogeny and oncogeny. *Nat. Cancer Inst. Monograph*, **31**, 1–39.

Dawe, C. J. 1973. Comparative neoplasia. *In*, J. F. Holland and E. Frei (eds.), *Cancer Medicine*, pp. 193–240. Philadelphia: Lea & Febiger.

Della Porta, G., Capitano, J., Parmi, L., and Colnaghi,

M. I. 1967. Cancerogenesi da uretano in topi neomati, lattanti e adulti dei ceppi C57BL, C3H, BC3F$_1$, C3Hf e SWR. *Tumori*, **53**, 81–102.

Della Porta, G., and Terracini, B. 1969. Chemical carcinogenesis in infant animals. *Prog. Exp. Tum. Res.*, **11**, 334–363.

Ebbesen, P. 1973. Papilloma induction in different aged skin grafts to young recipients. *Nature*, **241**, 280–281.

Ebbesen, P. 1974. Aging increases susceptibility of mouse skin to DMBA carcinogenesis independent of general immune status. *Science*, **183**, 217–218.

Eddy, B. E. 1964. Simian virus 40 (SV40): An oncogenic virus. *Progr. Exp. Tum. Res.*, **4**, 1–26.

Eneroth, C.-M., Blanck, C., and Jakobsson, P. Å. 1968. Carcinoma in pleomorphic adenoma of the parotid gland. *Acta Otolaryng.*, **66**, 477–492.

Englebreth-Holm, J. 1938. Tumor-producing viruses in fowls. *Acta Pathol. Microbiol. Scand.*, *Suppl*, **38**, 26–36.

Engelbreth-Holm, J., and Jensen, Em. 1953. On the mechanism of experimental carcinogenesis. X. The influence of age and of growth hormone on skin carcinogenesis in mice. *Acta Pathol. Microbiol. Scand.*, **XXXII**, 257–262.

Falkmer, S. 1974. Primary liver carcinoma and other tumors in a large population of a primitive vertebrate the Atlantic hagfish, *Myxine glutinosa.* Paper read at *The XIth Internat. Cancer Congr.*, *Florence*, October 20–26, 1974.

Falkmer, S., and Boquist, L. 1976. Onto- and phylogenetical aspects on insulin-producing islet-cell tumores. *Horm. Metab. Res. In* "Hypoglycemia" (eds. R. Leoine and E. S. Pfeiffer) Horm. Metab. Res. The Hypoglycemia Proceedings of the European Symposium, Rome, 1974, Vol. 6, pp. 55–62. Georg Thieme Publ. Stuttgart.

Falkmer, S., Östberg, Y., and Emdin, S. 1973. Tumors of the liver of the hagfish, *Myxine glutinosa. Acta Reg. Soc. Scient. Litt. Gothoburg.*, *Ser. Zool.* **8**, 70–72.

Franks, L. M. 1972. The incidence of carcinoma of prostate: An epidemiological survey. *In*, E. Grundmann and H. Tulinius (eds.), *Current Problems in the Epidemiology of Cancer and Lymphomas*, pp. 149–155. Berlin-Heidelberg-New York: Springer Verlag.

Friedenwald, J. S. 1952. The eye. *In* Cowdry's Problems of Ageing, Biological and Medical Aspects, A. Lansing (ed.), pp. 239–259. Williams and Wilkins Company, Baltimore, USA.

Fulder, S. J. and Holliday, R. 1975. A rapid rise in cell variants during the senescence of populations of human fibroblasts.

Gardner, M. B., Officer, E. J., Rongey, R. W., Estes, J. D., Turner, H. C., and Huebner, R. J. 1971. C-type RNA tumour virus genome expression in wild house mice. *Nature*, **232**, 617–620.

Gateff, E., and Schneiderman, H. A. 1969. Neoplasms

in mutant and cultured wild-type tissues of *Drosophila*. *Nat. Cancer Inst. Monograph*, **31**, 365-397.

Glücksmann, A. 1951. Cell deaths in normal vertebrate ontogeny. *Biol. Rev. Cambridge Phil. Soc.*, **26**, 59-86.

Good, R. A., and Finstad, J. 1969. Essential relationship between the lymphoid system immunity, and malignancy. *Nat. Cancer Inst. Monograph*, **31**, 41-58.

Granoff, A., Gravell, M., and Darlington, R. W. 1969. Studies on the viral etiology of the renal adenocarcinoma of Rana pipiens (Lucké tumor). *In*, M. Mizell (ed.), *Biology of Amphibian Tumors*, pp. 279-295. New York: Springer-Verlag.

Gross, L. 1951. "Spontaneous" leukemia developing in C3H mice following inoculation in infancy with AK leukemic extracts, or AK embryos. *Proc. Soc. Exp. Biol.*, **76**, 27-32.

Gross, L. 1961. *Oncogenic Viruses*, pp. 153-281. New York: Pergamon Press.

Hadorn, E. 1969. Proliferation and dynamics of cell heredity in blastema cultures of drosophila. *Nat. Cancer Inst. Monograph*, **31**, 351-364.

Hällén, H. 1966. Discrete gamma globulin (M)-components in serum. Clinical study of 150 subjects without myelomatosis. *Acta Med. Scand. Suppl.*, **462**.

Hardy, W. D., Old, L. J., Hess, P. W., Essex, M., and Cotter, S. 1973. Horizontal transmission of feline leukemia virus. *Nature*, **244**, 266-269.

Harshberger, J. C., and Taylor, R. E. 1968. Neoplasms of insects. *Ann. Rev. Entomol.*, **13**, 159-190.

Hay, R. J. 1967. Cell and tissue culture in aging research. *Advan. Geront. Res.*, **37**, 614-636.

Hayflick, L. 1965. The limited *in vitro* lifetime of human diploid cell strains. *Exp. Cell Res.*, **37**, 614-636.

Hayflick, L. 1966. Senescence and cultured cells. *Perspectives Exptl. Gerontol.*, **14**, 195-211.

Hayflick, L., and Moorhead, P. 1961. The serial cultivation of human diploid cell strains. *Exp. Cell Res.*, **25**, 585-621.

Heidelberger, C. 1973. Chemical oncogenesis in culture. *Advan. Cancer Res.*, **18**, 317-366.

Hellström, K. E., and Hellström, I. 1970. Immunological enhancement as studied by cell culture techniques. *Ann. Rev. Microbiol.*, **24**, 373-398.

Hellström, I., Hellström, K. E., and Sjögren, H. O. 1970. Serum mediated inhibition of cellular immunity to methylcholanthrene-induced murine sarcomas. *Cell Immunol.*, **1**, 18-30.

Higginson, J., and Muir, C. S. 1973. Epidemiology. *In*, J. F. Holland and E. Frei (eds.), *Cancer Medicine*, pp. 241-306. Philadelphia: Lea & Febiger.

Hill, M., and Hillova, J. 1972. Recovery of the temperature-sensitive mutant of Rous sarcoma virus from chicken cells exposed to DNA extracted from hamster cells transformed by the mutant. *Virology*, **49**, 309-313.

Homburger, F. 1974. Modifiers of carcinogenesis. *In*, F. Homburger (ed.), *The Physiopathology of Cancer*.

Vol. 1, P. Shubik (ed.), *Biology and Biochemistry*, pp. 110-154. Basel-München-Paris-London-New York-Sydney: S. Karger.

Huebner, R. J. 1970. Identification of leukemogenic viruses: Specifications for vertically transmitted, mostly "Switched off" RNA tumor viruses as determinants of the generality of cancer. *Comp. Leuk. Res. Bibl. Haemat.*, **35**, 22-44.

Huebner, R. J., Kelloff, G. J., Sarma, P. S., Lane, W. T., and Turner, H. C. 1970. Group-specific antigen expression during embryogenesis of the genome of the C-type RNA tumor virus. Implications for ontogenesis and oncogenesis. *Proc. Nat. Acad. Sci.*, **67**, 366-376.

Huebner, R. J., and Todaro, G. 1969. Oncogenes of RNA tumor viruses as determinants of cancer. *Proc. Nat. Acad. Sci.*, **64**, 1087-1094.

Igel, H. J., Huebner, R. J., Turner, H. C., Kotin, P., and Falk, H. L. 1969. Mouse leukemia virus activation by chemical carcinogens. *Science*, **166**, 1624-1626.

Jarrett, W., Jarrett, O., Mackey, L., Laird, H., Hardy, W. J., and Essex, M. 1974. Horizontal transmission of leukemia virus and leukemia in the cat. *J. Nat. Cancer Inst.*, **51**, 833-841.

Jarvik, E. 1964. Specializations in early vertebrates. *Ann. Soc. Roy. Zool. Belique*, **94**, 11-95.

Jensen, F., Koprowski, H., and Pontén, J. 1963. Rapid transformation of human fibroblast cultures by simian virus 40. *Proc. Nat. Acad. Sci.*, **50**, 343-348.

Kaplan, H. S. 1950. Influence of thymectomy, splenectomy and gonadectomy on incidence of radiation-induced lymphoid tumors in strain C57 black mice. *J. Nat. Cancer Inst.*, **11**, 83-90.

King, R. C. 1969. Hereditary ovarian tumors of *Drosophila melanogaster*. *Nat. Cancer Inst. Monograph*, **31**, 323-345.

Kohn, R. 1963. Human aging and disease. *J. Chronic Diseases*, **16**, 5-21.

Kohn, H. I., and Guttman, P. H. 1963. Age at exposure and the late effects of X-rays, survival and tumor incidence in CAF$_1$ mice irradiated at 1 to 2 years of age. *Radiation Res.*, **18**, 348-373.

Kripke, M. L., and Borsos, T. 1974. Immune surveillance revisited. *J. Nat. Cancer Inst.*, **52**, 1393-1395.

Lees, J. C., and Park, W. W. 1949. The malignancy of cancer at different ages: A histological study. *Brit. J. Cancer*, **III**, 186-197.

Lever, W. 1967. *Histopathology of the Skin*. 4th ed. Philadelphia and Toronto: J. B. Lippincott.

Liavåg, I. 1968. The localization of prostatic carcinoma. *Scand. J. Urol. Nephrol.*, **2**, 65-71.

Lindop, P. J., and Rotblat, J. 1961. Long-term effects of a single whole-body exposure of mice to ionizing radiations. I. Life-shortening. *Proc. Roy. Soc. (London)*, **154**, 332-368.

Loeb, L. 1945. Cancer and the process of ageing. *Biol. Symposia*, **11**, 197-216.

Lucké, B. 1934. A neoplastic disease of the kidney of the frog, *Rana pipiens*. *Am. J. Cancer*, **20**, 352-379.

Lundberg, S., and Berge, T. 1970. Prostatic carcinoma. *Scand. J. Urol. Nephrol.*, 4, 93–97.

Macieira-Coelho, A. 1973. Aging and cell division. *Front. Matrix Biol.*, 1, 46–77.

Macmahon, B., and Cole, P. 1969. Endocrinology and epidemiology of breast cancer. *Cancer*, 24, 1146–1150.

Mawdesley-Thomas, L. E. 1971. Neoplasia in fish: A review. *In*, T. C. Cheng (ed.), *Current Topics in Comparative Pathology*, pp. 87–170. New York and London: Academic Press.

Moberger, G., and Eneroth, C.-M. 1968. Malignant mixed tumors of the major salivary glands with special reference to the histological structures in metastases. *Cancer*, 21, 1198–1211.

Moore, G. E., and Koike, K. 1964. Growth of human tumor cells *in vitro* and *in vivo*. *Cancer*, 17, 11–20.

Moore, G. E., and Minowada, J. 1969. Human hematopoietic cell lines: A progress report. *In*, P. Farnes (ed.), *Hemic Cells in Vitro*, pp. 100–114. Baltimore: Williams & Wilkins.

Moorhead, P. S., and Saksela, E. 1965. The sequence of chromosome aberrations during SV40 transformation of a human diploid cell strain. *Hereditas*, 52, 271–284.

Nigrelli, R. F., and Ruggieri, G. D. 1974. Hyperplasia and neoplasia of the thyroid in marine fishes. *Mount Sinai J. Med.*, 51, 283–293.

Nilsson, K. 1971. Human hematopoietic cells in continuous culture. *Acta Universitatis Upsaliensis. Abstracts of Uppsala Dissertations from the Faculty of Medicine, 107.* Stockholm, Sweden: Almqvist & Wiksell.

Nilsson, K., and Pontén, J. 1975. Classification and biological nature of established human hematopoietic cell lines. *Intern. J. Cancer*, 15, 321–341.

Novak, E. R., and Woodruff, J. D. 1974. *Novak's Gynecologic and Obstetric Pathology: With Clinical and Endocrine Relations.* Philadelphia: W. B. Saunders.

Old, L. J., Boyse, E. A., Clarke, D. A., and Carswell, E. A. 1962. Antigenic properties of chemically induced tumors. *Ann. N. Y. Acad. Sci.*, 101, 80–106.

Orgel, L. E. 1963. The maintenance of the accuracy of protein synthesis and its relevance to ageing. *Proc. Nat. Acad. Sci.*, 49, 517–521.

Östberg, Y., Boquist, L., and Falkmer, S. 1973. Tumors or hamartomas in endocrine pancreas of the hagfish, *Myxine glutinosa*. *Acta Reg. Soc. Scient. Litt. Gothoburg, Ser. Zool.*, 8, 73–75.

Payne, L. N., and Chubb, R. 1968. Studies on the nature and genetic control of an antigen in normal chick embryos which reacts in the COFAL test. *J. Gen. Virol.*, 3, 379–391.

Pontén, J. 1970. The growth capacity of normal and Rous virus transformed chicken fibroblasts *in vitro*. *Intern. J. Cancer*, 6, 323–332.

Pontén, J. 1971. Spontaneous and virus induced transformation in cell culture. *In*, S. Gard, C. Hallauer, and K. F. Meyer (eds.), *Virology Monographs, Handbook of Virus Research*, pp. 1–253. Wien and New York: Springer-Verlag.

Pontén, J., and Macintyre, E. 1968. Long-term culture of normal and neoplastic human glia. *Acta Pathol. Microbiol. Scand.*, 74, 465–486.

Pontén, J., and Saksela, E. 1967. Two established *in vitro* cell lines from human mesenchymal tumors. *Intern. J. Cancer*, 2, 434–447.

Pope, J. H., Horne, M. K., and Scott, W. 1968. Transformation of foetal human leukocytes *in vitro* by filtrates of human leukaemic cell line containing herpes-like virus. *Intern. J. Cancer*, 3, 857–866.

Potter, C. W., Hoskins, J. M., and Oxford, J. S. 1969. Immunological relationships of some oncogenic DNA viruses. *Arch. Ges. Virusforsch.*, 27, 73–86.

Prehn, R. T. 1957. Immunity to methylcholanthrene-induced sarcomas. *J. Nat. Cancer Inst.*, 18, 769–778.

Prehn, R. T. 1970. Immunosurveillance, regeneration and ocogenesis. *Progr. Exp. Tum. Res.*, 14, 1–24.

Prout, G. R. 1973. Prostate gland. *In*, J. F. Holland and E. Frei (eds.), *Cancer Medicine*, pp. 1680–1694. Philadelphia: Lea & Febiger.

Rauscher, F. J., and O'Connor, T. E. 1973. Virology. *In*, J. F. Holland and E. Frei (eds.), *Cancer Medicine*, pp. 15–44. Philadelphia: Lea & Febiger.

Rothfels, K. H., Kupelwieser, E. B., and Parker, R. C. 1963. Effects of X-irradiated feeder layers on mitotic activity and development of aneuploidy in mouse-embryo cells *in vitro*. *Can. Cancer Conf.*, 5, 191–223.

Rowe, W. P., and Pincus, Th. 1972. Quantitative studies of naturally occurring murine leukemia virus infection of AKR mice. *J. Exp. Med.*, 135, 429–436.

Sanford, K., Barker, B. E., Parshad, R., Westfall, B. B., Woods, M. W., Jackson, J. L., King, D. R., and Peppers, E. V. 1970. *J. Nat. Cancer Inst.*, 45, 1071–1096.

Sanford, K. K., Earle, W. R., Shelton, E., Schilling, E. L., Duchesne, E. M., Likely, G. D., and Becker, M. N. 1950. Production of malignancy *in vitro*. XII. Further transformations of mouse fibroblasts to sarcomatous cells. *J. Nat. Cancer Inst.*, 11, 351–375.

Saunders, J. W. 1966. Death in embryonic systems. *Science*, 154, 604–612.

Saxton, J. A., Jr. 1952. Cancer and ageing. *In*, A. I. Lansing (ed.), *Cowdry's Problems of Ageing*, pp. 950–961. Baltimore: Williams & Wilkins.

Saxton, J. A., Handler, F. P., and Bauer, J. 1950. Cancer and aging. *Arch. Pathol.*, 50, 813–827.

Schlumberger, H. G., and Lucké, B. 1948. Tumors of fishes, amphibians and reptiles. *Cancer Res.*, 8, 657–754.

Sheldrake, A. R. 1974. The ageing, growth and death of cells. *Nature*, 250, 381–385.

Stenbäck, F., Garcia, H., and Shubik, P. 1974. Present status of the concept of promoting action and cocarcinogenesis in skin. *In*, F. Homburger (ed.), *The Physiopathology of Cancer*. Vol 1., P. Shubik (ed.), *Biology and Biochemistry*, pp. 155–225. Basel-München-Paris-London-New York-Sydney: S. Karger.

Stenkvist, B. 1966. Long-term cultivation of human and bovine fibroblastic cells morphologically transformed *in vitro* by Rous sarcoma virus. *Acta Pathol. Microbiol. Scand.*, **67**, 67–82.

Stewart, S. E., and Eddy, B. E. 1959. Properties of a tumor-inducing virus recovered from mouse neoplasms. *In, Perspectives in Virology*, pp. 245–255. New York: John Wiley; London: Chapman & Hall.

Storer, J. B. 1966. Longevity and gross pathology at death in 22 inbred mouse strains. *J. Geront.*, **21**, 404–409.

Suen, K. C., Lau, L. L., and Yermakov, V. 1974. Cancer and old age. An autopsy study of 3,535 patients over 65 years old. *Cancer*, **33**, 1164–1168.

Swim, H. E., and Parker, R. F. 1957. Culture characteristics of human fibroblasts propagated serially. *Am. J. Hyg.*, **66**, 235–243.

Temin, H. 1964. Nature of the provirus of Rous sarcoma. *Nat. Cancer Inst. Monograph*, **17**, 557–570.

Temin, H. 1971. The protovirus hypothesis: Speculations on the significance of RNA-directed DNA synthesis for normal development and for carcinogenesis. *J. Nat. Cancer Inst.*, **46**, III (Guest Editorial).

Todaro, G. J., and Green, H. 1963. Quantitative studies of the growth of mouse embryo cells in culture and their development into established lines. *J. Cell Biol.*, **17**, 299–313.

Todaro, G. J., and Huebner, R. J. 1969. Oncogenes of RNA tumor viruses as determinants of cancer. *Proc. Nat. Acad. Sci.*, **64**, 1087–1094.

Todaro, G. J., and Martin, G. M. 1967. Increased susceptibility of Down's syndrome fibroblasts to transformation by SV40. *Proc. Soc. Exp. Biol. Med.*, **124**, 1232–1236.

Todaro, G. J., Wolman, S. R., and Green, H. 1963. Rapid transformation of human fibroblasts with low growth potential into established cell lines by SV40. *J. Cellular Comp. Physiol.*, **62**, 257–265.

Tooze, J. (ed.) 1973. *The Molecular Biology of Tumour Viruses*. Cold Spring Harbor, New York: Cold Spring Harbor Laboratory.

Trentin, J. J., Yabe, Y., and Taylor, G. 1962. The quest for human cancer viruses. *Science*, **137**, 835–841.

Upton, A. C. 1973. Radiation. *In*, J. F. Holland and E. Frei (eds.), *Cancer Medicine*, pp. 90–101. Philadelphia: Lea & Febiger.

Vernon, M. L., Lane, W. T., and Huebner, R. J. 1973. Prevalence of type-C particles in visceral tissues of embryonic and newborn mice. *J. Nat. Cancer Inst.*, **51**, 1171–1174.

Waldenström, J. 1961. Studies on conditions associated with disturbed gamma globulin formation (gammopathies). *Harvey Lectures*, **56**, 211–231.

Walford, R. L. 1969. *The Immunologic Theory of Aging*. A/S Copenhagen: Munksgaard, J. Jørgensen.

Weiss, R. A., Mason, W. S. and Vogt, P. K. 1973. Genetic recombinants and heterozygotes derived from endogenous and exogenous avian RNA tumor viruses. *Virology* **52**, 535–552.

Wellings, S. R. 1969. Neoplasia and primitive vertebrate phylogeny: Echinoderms, prevertebrates and fishes. *Nat. Cancer Inst. Monograph*, **31**, 59–128.

Westermark, B. 1973. Growth control of normal and neoplastic human glia-like cells in culture. *Acta Universitatis Upsaliensis. Abstracts of Uppsala Dissertation n Medicine*, *164*. Uppsala, Sweden: Kå-We Composer & Fotosats.

Williamson, A. R., and Askonas, B. A. 1972. Senescence of an antibody-forming cell clone. *Nature*, **238**, 337–339.

Wogan, G. N. 1974. Naturally occurring carcinogens. *In*, F. Homburger (ed.), *The Physiopathology of Cancer*. Vol. 1, P. Shubik (ed.), *Biology and Biochemistry*, pp. 64–109. Basel-München-Paris-London-New York-Sydney: S. Karger.

Wynder, E. L. 1959. Identification of women at high risk for breast cancer. *Cancer*, **24**, 1235–1240.

23
NUTRITION

Charles H. Barrows, Jr.
Gerontology Research Center,
National Institute on Aging
National Institutes of Health and
the Baltimore City Hospitals

and

Lois M. Roeder
University of Maryland School of Medicine

INTRODUCTION

The survival of an organism is dependent upon its nutritional state. Recently, emphasis has been placed on the effects of perinatal nutrition, whereas in the past, nutritional studies examined the growth period to establish the requirements for optimal growth and survival. Unfortunately, little effort has been made to identify changes which may occur in nutritional requirements during adulthood and senescence. It is generally accepted that intakes moderately above the recommended allowances are optimal for the well-being of the organism. However, a number of studies carried out on animals have demonstrated that longevity was increased when the intakes of certain nutrients were lower than the recommended allowances. Similarly, very high intakes of some nutrients have been reported to shorten life span (Silberberg and Silberberg, 1955). Little information is available regarding the influence of the nutritional status of an organism at one period in life on the remaining periods. Therefore, an attempt will be made to review the pertinent literature on (1) the effect of age after the ces-

sation of growth on nutritional requirements, and (2) the effect of nutrition on life span. This information may provide useful knowledge for the optimal nutrition of the aged and for an understanding of the basic mechanisms of biological aging.

EFFECT OF AGE ON NUTRITIONAL STATUS

There are many variables that make the assessment of nutritional requirements in human subjects difficult. This is especially so in the United States due to the marked differences in genetic background, social environment, and economic status of the population. These variables have a marked impact on the nutrition of the individual. Furthermore, the great selection of foods available complicates the problem. Other difficulties arise because of the various ways of assessing nutritional status. These include records of dietary intake, plasma, blood, or tissue contents of the nutrient, urinary or fecal excretion under various intakes, and the measurement of a biochemical system in which the nutrient plays a role. At present, nutritionists do not agree on the adequacy of any one method for the assessment of nutritional status. Although there seem to be many reports on the subject of nutrition and aging, many are difficult to interpret due either to a small population, lack of adequate age distribution, and/or questionable techniques. There are data which can be drawn upon to gain some knowledge of nutritional problems of the aged.

There are two general types of studies on assessment of dietary intake and nutritional status. The first includes national or regional surveys of large segments of the population. The second includes studies on a smaller, limited number of subjects as part of specific laboratory investigations. It is important to describe the characteristics of each of these populations in terms of socioeconomic and other factors since these have a marked impact on nutritional status.

National Surveys

In order to assess the nutritional status of the general population in the United States, the Department of Agriculture has obtained information at various times since 1936 on nutrient intakes of large numbers of individuals. The most recent study was in 1965 (U.S. Department of Agriculture, 1968) on 14,500 persons from 6,174 households. The survey did not include those living in institutions and rooming houses and thus omitted many of the aged who were ill or disabled. The results showed that, except for calcium, the average nutrient intakes per day for men aged 55 and over were adequate, whereas the intakes of thiamine, riboflavin and calcium of women in this age group were 87, 84, and 64 percent respectively, of the recommended dietary allowances (RDAs) (National Academy of Sciences-National Research Council, 1968). Calcium intakes declined with age in men and averaged 84 percent of the RDAs for this group. When individuals with low incomes were evaluated separately, it was found that dietary adequacy (based on RDAs) declined with income. Of those with incomes after taxes of less than $3,000, 63 percent had inadequate diets.

The Ten-State Nutrition Survey, conducted by the U.S. Department of Health, Education, and Welfare (Center for Disease Control, 1972), was designed to assess the nutritional status of groups considered to be a risk for undernutrition, such as poverty groups, migrant workers, Spanish-speaking people in the southwest United States, inner-city residents, and individuals in industrial states who had migrated from the South in the previous 10-20 years. These groups were selected from districts with average incomes in the lowest quartile according to the 1960 Census. However, the income characteristics of some of these districts had changed between 1960 and the time of the survey.

The assessment involved a series of clinical and biochemical measurements and a dietary evaluation. In this survey, the standards of intake were developed by an *ad hoc* committee using as guidelines the RDAs of the National Research Council (1968) and the FAO/WHO reports (World Health Organization (WHO) Technical Report Series, 1962, 1965, 1967, 1970; Food and Agriculture Organization (FAO) Nutrition Studies, 1957) on requirements for various nutrients. The standards selected for protein and iron were similar, but others were about 50 percent of those in the RDAs. It was concluded that persons 60 years of age and older consumed far less food than needed to meet the nutritional standards for their age, sex, and weight. No subgroup met the caloric standard, and other limiting nutrients were protein, iron, and vitamin A. Although the differences were minor, the Ten-State Survey tended to report lower intakes than the USDA study.

The clinical assessments used in the Ten-State Survey included skeletal weight, obesity, and dental evaluations. After age 50, skeletal weight generally decreased with age, reflecting the loss and thinning of bone. Low income groups had lower skeletal weights than high income groups, but the rate of bone loss was independent of economic status. Obesity was more prevalent in higher than lower income groups. The percentages in females in the 45 to 55-year-old age group were 50 percent for blacks and 40 percent for whites. These percentages declined markedly with age to about 20-25 percent in both races by age 75-85. Men of both races had lower incidences of obesity and there were no age-associated patterns. The major dental problem in adults was periodontal disease, which increased with age to over 90 percent in nearly every subgroup of the survey population by age 65-75 years. However, there were no correlations between dental disorders and several selected biochemical measures (serum albumin, plasma vitamin A, and serum vitamin C). Taken as a whole, the clinical assessments did not indicate a high incidence of severe malnutrition in the older subjects examined.

Similarly, the biochemical tests for nutritional status did not suggest marked age-associated nutritional deficiencies. For example, the mean hemoglobin values in this population, although consistently lower than generally accepted normal values, were not age-dependent. There was a low incidence of deficient or low values for serum protein, albumin, vitamin A or C. Finally, the excretions of riboflavin, thiamine, or iodine in urine showed no marked age changes among adult groups.

The preliminary findings of the first Health and Nutrition Examination Survey (HANES) for the United States population in 1971-1972 (National Center for Health Statistics, 1974) represent civilian, noninstitutionalized persons from 1 to 74 years of age. The complete study will include the total population, as well as those groups considered to be high risk for malnutrition—the poor, preschool children, women of childbearing age, and the elderly. The preliminary results include data on 10,126 persons, who represented a 72.8 percent response of the individuals selected for sampling. Since it was assumed that the main evidence of malnutrition in this population would be early subclinical symptoms, the measures of nutritional status emphasized early risk signals and included (1) 24-hour food consumption, (2) biochemical tests (hematocrit, hemoglobin, serum iron, percent transferrin saturation, total serum protein, albumin, and vitamin A), (3) clinical signs of malnutrition, and (4) anthropometric measurements. The final, still unpublished report will include data on serum folate, vitamin C, magnesium, cholesterol and total iron-binding capacity and urinary creatinine, thiamine, riboflavin, and iodine.

The guidelines for classifying and interpreting biochemical data were essentially those used by the Ten-State Nutrition Survey (Center for Disease Control, 1972). The standards for evaluating the dietary intake data were developed by an *ad hoc* advisory group upon consideration of a variety of standards (National Center for Health Statistics, 1974). For persons 60 years and older, these daily standards were as follows:

Sex	Calories (per kg)	Protein (g per kg)	Ca (mg)	Iron (mg)	Vitamin A (I.U.)	Vitamin C (mg)
M	34	1.0	400	10	3,500	60
F	29	1.0	600	10	3,500	55

The data on dietary intakes were grouped according to age, race, and income status. The results indicated that, among persons over 60 years of age with incomes above the poverty level (Orshansky, 1968), 16 percent of the white and 18 percent of the Negro population consumed less than 1,000 calories per day. In those with incomes lower than the poverty level, these percentages rose to 27 and 36 percent, respectively. The intake of protein as well as of calories in this age group was also related to income in both races. Protein intakes per 1,000 calories showed no variation with race or income, indicating that it was closely related to caloric consumption. Calcium intakes were less than the standards for 37 percent of all persons over 60. The intakes of vitamin A were below standards in 52 to 62 percent and consumption of vitamin C was low in 39 to 59 percent in all adults in this age group.

The only biochemical indications of nutritional problems among the elderly in this study were the high percentages of Negro adults aged 60 years and over with low values for hemoglobin (29.6 percent) and hematocrit (41.7 percent). However, iron deficiency was not considered the cause, since most of this group did not have low levels of serum iron or percentage of transferrin saturation. The biochemical tests have not been completed, nor are the clinical assessments available from this study.

Taken as a whole, these surveys do not indicate consistent evidence of poor nutritional status or of marked deficiences in nutrient intake among older members of most populations in the United States. However, significant percentages of many of the groups studied consumed less than the recommended amounts of certain nutrients, especially of protein, calcium, ascorbic acid, and vitamin A. One of the most consistent findings was that low intakes were more likely to occur if income was low. The same conclusion about the relationship between poverty and diets containing less than the RDAs was reached by Watkin (1968), who indicated that nutrient intake or nutritional status of the elderly was more related to health and poverty than to age *per se*.

Some estimates of the frequency of nutritional deficiencies among the aged are found in studies reported by Brewer, Furnivall, Wagoner, Lee, Alsop, and Ohlson (1956) and by Chinn (1956). In the latter study, the nutritional status of approximately 500 elderly patients admitted to a hospital for long-term illnesses over a period of 3 years was assessed. The data showed that only 35 percent had significant primary nutritional problems. Of these, 15 were undernourished, whereas the remaining 20 had a problem of obesity. Similar data were obtained by Brewer on 107 subjects who were admitted to county institutions for the aged in Michigan. Nutritional assessment was made on the basis of the concentration of hemoglobin and plasma levels of ascorbic acid, vitamin A, and carotene. Only 5 to 10 percent of the residents could be considered in a poor nutritional state with respect to vitamin A and ascorbic acid. Brin, Dibble, Peel, McMullen, Bourquin, and Chen (1965) examined 234 elderly subjects whose average age was 71.0 ± 8.9 years (Mean ± S.D.). They measured hematocrits and evaluated nutritional status with respect to ascorbic acid, vitamin A and carotene, riboflavin, and thiamine. The latter was estimated on the basis of urinary excretion as well as three parameters of erythrocyte transketolase activity. They concluded that 5 percent of the men and 13 percent of the women had hematocrits in the deficient range according to Inter-departmental Committee on Nutrition for National Defense (ICNND) (1963) criteria. Plasma ascorbic acid levels were low in only 8 percent of the whole population. Plasma vitamin A and carotene levels were in the acceptable to high range, and urinary riboflavin excretion values showed no deficiencies. Thiamine deficiency was indicated for 18 percent of the population if the stan-

dards of ICNND (1963) were used and for 21 percent on the basis of Pearson's criteria (1962). However, a biochemical defect, on the basis of the erythrocyte transketolase data, was evident in only 6 percent of the group. The authors concluded that this ambulant, well, aged, surveyed population was fairly well nourished. Therefore, on the basis of these low frequencies of nutritional deficiencies and the complete lack of information on the effect of continued long-term vitamin therapy in older people, it seems unwise to propose mass vitamin and other nutrient supplements to the aged at this time: therapy should be administered on the merits of individual cases.

In addition to these surveys, there are a few studies in which the subjects are carefully selected in order to focus on age as an isolated variable and which include a variety of measurements in addition to dietary intake. Davis, Gershoff, and Gamble (1969) recently reviewed the studies of vitamin and mineral nutrition in the United States reported during the interval 1950-1968. The data were subdivided into groups according to sex and age, but neither the summaries of results nor discussion was focused on differences associated with age. However, examination of the findings does not suggest severely deficient consumption in the over-50 age groups.

Similarly Kelsay (1969) compiled the results of approximately 60 individual dietary intake studies published between 1957 and 1967 on over 30,000 subjects. Only 10 of these studies were directed toward evaluating nutrient intakes of the elderly. The dietary intake data from these 10 studies were somewhat variable. Although none of the studies showed a high percentage of the groups with markedly inadequate intake, there was evidence of less than recommended levels of consumption of certain nutrients. Those likely to be low included protein, riboflavin, niacin, thiamine, iron, and particularly calcium, vitamin A, and vitamin C.

Laboratory Investigations

Vitamins. There are a small number of carefully conducted studies which deserve consideration in more detail. Kirk has presented data for both men and women on the plasma and blood levels of total carotenes, alpha and beta carotenes, vitamin A (Kirk and Chieffi, 1948), thiamine (Kirk and Chieffi, 1949), DPN (Kirk, 1954), total ascorbic acid (Kirk and Chieffi, 1953a), and alpha tocopherol (Chieffi and Kirk, 1951). The results were calculated as linear regressions, but the only statistically significant age-associated difference was a decrease in the blood ascorbic acid level in men. Morgan and associates conducted studies on 250 men and 280 women between the ages of 50 and 80 years and failed to demonstrate any effect of age on the serum content of vitamin A, carotene (Gillum, Morgan, and Sailer, 1955), or ascorbic acid (Morgan, Gillum, and Williams, 1955). Similar results were obtained in another study by Brewer, et al. (1956) on a small number of subjects. Horwitt (1953) measured thiamine and riboflavin levels in serum in young and old subjects under conditions of depletion and repletion. There were no age differences in either initial serum levels, rates of depletion or repletion, or levels attained following the periods of depletion or repletion.

On the other hand, there is evidence that there are age-wise differences in certain other vitamin levels. For example, Ranke, Tauber, Horonick, Ranke, Goodhart, and Chow (1960) estimated the pyridoxalphosphate (PLP) levels by the activity of serum glutamin-oxalacetic acid transaminase (SGOT), an enzyme system that requires PLP for its activity. The data demonstrated marked age decrements (21 percent for men and 30 percent for women) in the activities of the enzyme and, therefore, suggested age-dependent decreases in serum PLP levels. Rose, Gyorgy, Spiegel, Brin, Butler, and Shock (1974), in a study carried out on 617 community-dwelling subjects, found that the average PLP of men not taking a vitamin supplement ($N = 414$) was 12.3 ± 6.4 ng/ml and that 41 percent had values below the suggested lower acceptable limit of 10. They reported a negative correlation of plasma PLP with age ($r = -0.22$). For those subjects taking supplements, PLP levels were related to dosage. Similarly, age-dependent decrements in vitamin B_{12} levels have been reported by Gaffney, Horonick, Okuda, Meier, Chow, and Shock

(1957). In one experiment, 144 subjects were studied. Of these, 89 were ambulant, apparently healthy males slected from the Infirmary Division at Baltimore City Hospitals. The remaining 55 subjects were physicians and other male staff members of the participating research insititutions. In a second study, all 97 subjects were apparently healthy inmates who had been in a state penal institution for at least 5 years prior to the test. The same range was represented in both studies. The results were essentially the same, i.e., approximately a 35 percent decrement in vitamin B_{12} levels over the age span of 25 to 70 years, although the variance seemed to be reduced in the second study. These data indicate that deficiency states among the elderly are found only for selected vitamins. There is no evidence for a general increase in vitamin requirements with age.

Proteins and Amino Acids. Most data on the effects of age on protein requirements were obtained by the nitrogen balance technique. The results of these studies are not in complete agreement, as shown by the data (Table 1) of Kountz, Hofstatter, and Ackermann (1947, 1951), Ohlson, Brewer, Cederquist, Jackson, Brown, and Roberts (1948), and Schulze (1955). A similar lack of agreement on the effect of age is found when the requirements for the amino acids are considered. For example, Tuttle, Swenseid, Mulcare, Griffith, and Bassett (1957) fed 5 men aged 52 to 68 a diet that contained amino acids in amounts that exceeded Rose's minimal recommended allowance for 25-year-old male subjects (Table 2). When fed either this diet or one that contained twice the amount of tryptophan, all subjects were in negative nitrogen balance. These data indicate an increased requirement for one or more of the essential amino acids with age. On the other hand, in a study carried out by Watts, Mann, Bradley, and Thompson (1964), 6 Negro men 65 to 85 years of age were fed semipurified diets containing essential amino acids in ratios corresponding to the FAO references protein and the pattern of milk protein (Table 2). Although the amounts of the essential amino acids fed these subjects were actually lower

TABLE 1. THE EFFECT OF AGE ON PROTEIN REQUIREMENTS.

Investigator	Subjects (N)	Age	Sex	Estimated requirements (g/kg/day)
Kountz, Hofstatter, and Ackermann (1947)	27	41–86	M	>1.0
Kountz, Hofstatter, and Ackermann (1951)	4	69–76	M	0.7
Schulze (1955)	4	61–79	M	0.5
Ohlson et al. (1948)	8	50–75	F	0.9 (0.7 – 1.3)

than those fed the subjects of Tuttle, both diets were adequate for maintaining nitrogen equilibrium in all subjects. A comparison of the other variables in these two studies failed to explain the apparent age-associated differences in requirements in the study by Tuttle et al. (1957). For example, the caloric intakes of Tuttle's subjects (30 to 41 kcal per kilogram) were similar to those of Watts' (28 to 44 kcal per kilogram). However, the dietary periods used by Tuttle were 4 to 6 days, while those of Watts were 7 to 12 days. The greatest difference may be found in the total nitrogen intake, which, in the study of Tuttle, was 7 g, while that of Watts was 10 g. At present little can be stated regarding the effects of age on protein and amino acid requirements.

Interpretation of these studies is made diffi-cult by the quality of protein used, caloric intake, lack of simultaneous study of young subjects, and the observation that subjects can be maintained at nitrogen equilibrium at various levels of nitrogen intake. This latter point has been expressed by Hegsted (1952), who also pointed out that an individual on self-selected diets would show a nitrogen balance varying from positive balance through equilibrium to negative balance, depending upon changing factors of stress and/or food intake. Horwitt (1953) reported that 31 individuals who were in positive nitrogen balance when fed a diet containing 11 g of nitrogen per day immediately went into negative balance when the intake was reduced to 6.5 g per day. However, when this same low intake was continued over a 3-month period, these individuals returned to a

TABLE 2. COMPARISON OF DAILY INTAKES OF AMINO ACIDS IN VARIOUS STUDIES WITH THE MINIMAL REQUIREMENTS OF ROSE.

Essential amino acid	Rose's minimum diet for 25-year male (g)	Tuttle's AA I (g)	FAO PATTERN 360 mg TRYPT		MILK PATTERN 580 mg S-AA[c]	
			Amount fed (g)	% of Rose's minimum	Amount fed (g)	% of Rose's minimum
Isoleucine	0.70	1.28	1.08	154	1.01	144
Leucine	1.10	1.72	1.22	111	1.54	140
Lysine	0.80	1.39	1.08	135	1.25	156
Methionine	1.10	1.12[a]	1.20	109	0.58	53
Phenylalanine	1.10	1.56[b]	1.44	131	1.58	144
Threonine	0.50	0.77	0.72	144	0.72	144
Tryptophan	0.25	0.38	0.36	144	0.24	96
Valine	0.80	1.29	1.08	135	1.10	138
Histidine	–	0.43	–	–	–	–
Amino acid N	0.74	1.11	0.96	–	0.95	–

[a]Calculated from published data: 0.56 g methionine + 0.45 g cystine.
[b]Calculated from published data: 0.96 g phenylalanine + 0.60 g tyrosine.
[c]Amino acid mixture patterned after milk proteins fed at level of 580 mg methionine per day.

With permission of Journal of Gerontology, Watts et al., 1964.

positive nitrogen balance. No differences between the young and old subjects were found in these studies.

Calcium. Many of the factors that make interpretation of the data on the effect of age on protein and amino acid requirements difficult also apply to data on the requirements for calcium. This is shown in the summary of the data of Bogdonoff, Shock, and Nichols (1953), Ackermann and Toro (1953a,b), Ohlson, *et al.* (1952), and Roberts, Kerr, and Ohlson (1948) shown in Table 3. Therefore, the only estimates available suggest the calcium intakes necessary to establish equilibrium (840 to 1,020 mg per day) exceeded the RDA of 800 mg per day. However, care should be taken in interpreting these data due to the large variation among subjects and the possibility of establishing calcium equilibrium at various levels of intake. This latter point is evident from the data of the following studies. Malm (1958) reported that, regardless of age, prisoners who were in calcium equilibrium on intakes of 937 mg per day could maintain calcium balance on intakes estimated to be as low as 440 mg per day. In addition, Hegsted, Moscoso, and Collazos (1952) determined that Peruvian prisoners could maintain calcium equilibrium on mean intakes of only 216 mg per day.

TABLE 3. THE EFFECT OF AGE ON CALCIUM REQUIREMENTS.

Investigator	Subjects (N)	Age	Sex	Estimated requirements (mg/day)
Bogdonoff, Shock, and Nickols (1953)	7	66–83	M	850
Ackermann and Toro (1953b)	8	70–88	M	1,020
Ohlson et al. (1952)	135	30–89	F	840
Roberts, Kerr, and Ohlson (1948)	9	52–74	F	929
Ackermann and Toro (1953a)	8	48–83	F	920

NUTRITIONAL DEFICIENCIES AND PHYSIOLOGICAL IMPAIRMENTS

There is little evidence to correlate age-associated nutritional deficiency states with clinical findings, physiological functions, or biochemical changes. Chieffi and Kirk (1949), in a study of 106 subjects aged 16 to 99 years, found no significant correlation between vitamin A levels in serum and (1) dark-adaption time, (2) the number of epithelial cells excreted daily in the urine, or (3) the percentage of keratinized cells in the urinary sediment. However, the frequency of dryness of the skin, conjunctivitis, and the percent of keratinized cells in conjunctival smears were higher in subjects with low vitamin A plasma levels (1 to 15 μg percent) than in those with high levels (25 to 60 μg percent). The differences between the groups were not marked and could not be considered clinically useful. Gillum, Morgan, and Sailer (1955) attempted to relate the frequency of gingivitis in subjects over 50 years to serum levels of ascorbic acid. However, they found that the incidence of the disease was essentially the same over the range of serum ascorbic acid levels from 0 to 1.1 + mg percent. In addition, although thickening of the bulbar conjunctiva was noted in 94 percent of the subjects, this condition was not marked in individuals whose serum vitamin A levels were low. In a more recent study, Davis, et al. (1966) attempted to find biochemical and hematological changes attributable to low serum levels of vitamin B_{12}. In this study of 275 subjects aged 49 to 89 years, there were no significant correlations between the serum vitamin B_{12} level and (1) serum lactic acid concentration, (2) serum lactic dehydrogenase activity, or (3) hematocrit. Taken as a whole, these data indicate that vitamin deficiency states, if they exist in some old subjects, are generally not severe enough to be manifested by clinical or biochemical changes.

Two bone diseases which occur with increasing incidence as age progresses and which may be of nutritional origin are osteomalacia and osteoporosis. The first is an undermineralization of the bone during its formation. Since it is correctable by vitamin D therapy (Sandstead and Pearson, 1973), it appears to be a result of a deficiency of this nutrient. Active adults do not need a dietary source of vitamin D due to adequate conversion of its precursor in skin by ultraviolet irradiation by the sun. Elderly persons, on the other hand, frequently have very limited or no exposure to sunlight, and may be at risk for vitamin D insufficiency. The second disease, osteoporosis, is an excessive resorption of bone resulting in a reduced ratio of bone mass to bone volume and is of more complex etiology. In a recent review, Nordin (1971) cited several reports which showed that about 50 percent of trabecular bone and 5 percent of cortical bone is lost between youth and old age. The proportions of these two types of bone in the total skeleton are such that overall bone loss with age is 15 percent. The rate of loss is highest among postmenopausal women. The high frequency of the disease among the elderly was also shown by Gitman and Kamholtz (1965), who performed routine x-ray examinations of the dorsal lumbar spine on all admissions to a large geriatric facility. They found that in a group of 933 females, the incidence of osteoporosis increased linearly from approximately 50 percent between the ages of 65 to 70 to 90 percent in women over 90 years. In men, however, the frequency was much lower and ranged from approximately 15 percent in the 65 to 70-year-old group to 30 percent in the individual over 90.

Unfortunately, the reports of attempts to relate calcium intake to the incidence of osteoporosis are not in complete agreement. Lutwak (1963) and Nordin (1961) reported that the average intakes of calcium of subjects with osteoporosis are statistically lower than those of normal subjects. On the other hand, Garn, Rohmann and Wagner (1967) found no correlation between the intake of calcium and the cortical thickness of the second metacarpal in 382 subjects ranging in age from 25–85 years. Likewise, Smith and Frame (1965), in a radiographic survey of 2,000 women 45 years of age or older, found no significant differences in the calcium intake of the subjects with high or low vertebral densities or vertebral compressions. The difficulty in correlating calcium intake with the incidence or severity of osteoporosis has been recently discussed by Garn (1970), who pointed out at least four variables of dietary origin (re-duced calcium intake, altered calcium to phosphorus ratio, decreased protein intake, or a change in acid-base balance) that could contribute to bone loss in the adult. It has also been proposed that postmenopausal osteoporosis is excessive bone resorption due to loss of the protective action of estrogens against parathyroid hormone (Nordin, 1971). The type of osteoporosis associated with extreme old age in men as well as women may be due to impaired calcium absorption as a result of vitamin D deficiency. Thus, although both of these types of osteoporosis are associated with impaired calcium balance, it is possible that neither is due to dietary calcium insufficiency. The role of fluoride in the disease process remains unclear. Although it has been used therapeutically to increase bone density, very high (perhaps toxic) doses are required. Furthermore, there were no differences in bone characteristics determined at autopsy or in the incidence of the diseased between populations in high, as compared to low fluoride areas (Yasumura, 1972). The specific relationship between the nutritional status calcium, vitamin B, and fluoride, and this physiological impairment cannot be defined.

REVERSAL OF DEFICIENCIES BY SUPPLEMENTATION

There are a number of examples that indicate that nutritional deficiency states associated with age can be corrected simply by supplementation with the specific nutrient. Kirk and Chieffi (1953b) administered 100 mg of ascorbic acid daily to 19 elderly subjects whose serum ascorbic acid levels were low (approximately 0.25 mg percent). In 16 of the 19 subjects, the blood levels of the vitamin rose immediately to values approximately 1.2 mg percent and were maintained at these high levels during the 12-week supplementation period. Following the withdrawal of the supplement, the levels dropped very rapidly to those originally observed. Similar results were obtained by Davis, Lawton, Prouty, and Chow (1965) when 20 μg of vitamin B_{12} per day was administered orally to 40 elderly men whose initial serum vitamin B_{12} levels were low (150 μg per ml).

When the supplement was withdrawn, the serum levels of the vitamin returned to the original low values. Similarly, Chernish, Helmer, Fauts, and Hohlstaedt (1957) demonstrated that values comparable to those of young individuals may be attained by old subjects following the oral administration of vitamin B_{12}. Yiengst and Shock (1949) administered 100,000 units of vitamin A orally to subjects between 40 and 89 years of age and observed marked elevations in the plasma levels of the vitamin in all age groups. No age differences were found. Finally, Ranke *et al.* (1960) showed that the activities of serum glutamic-oxalacetic transaminase in old subjects could be raised to those of young individuals by the oral administration of vitamin B_6. Rose *et al.* (1974) found that plasma levels of this vitamin (measured as pyridoxal phosphate) were related to the dosage of supplement taken. They reported that if the supplement was high (above 2 mg), only 5 percent of the subjects had plasma vitamin levels below the acceptable range.

These data show conclusively that when low plasma levels of vitamins occur in older individuals, they can be reversed by the administration of the specific nutrient. In addition, these studies provide evidence that there is no impairment in absorption of vitamins in elderly subjects. These findings are in agreement with other studies on the absorption of nitrogen in older individuals. For example, Chinn, Lavik, and Cameron (1956) reported no decrements in the rate of digestion of ^{131}I-labeled albumin in 12 subjects 72 to 88 years of age. Similarly, Watkin *et al.* (1955) and Bogdonoff, Shock, and Nichols (1953), using the nitrogen-balance technique, found no decrease in nitrogen absorption with age.

In view of the uncertainty regarding the relationship between calcium intake and osteoporosis, it is not surprising that a lack of agreement exists in the literature regarding the therapeutic effects of increased calcium intake. Bogdonoff, Shock, and Nichols (1953), Lutwak and Whedon (1963), Nordin (1962), and Harrison, Fraser, and Mullan (1961) have shown that an increase in dietary calcium resulted in positive calcium balance in older individuals. However, in the report by Harrison, Fraser, and Mullan

(1961), the senile osteoporotics in the study group maintained positive calcium balance on high intakes of calcium (i.e., 40 mg per kilogram body weight per day), but showed no increase in bone density estimated radiographically. In contrast, Schmid (1962) and Nordin and Smith (1964) found increases in radiographic density in osteoporotics given dietary calcium supplements. There is still controversy regarding the beneficial effects of increased calcium intake in older individuals.

Since older individuals apparently can correct nutritional deficiencies by increasing their dietary intake, a logical explanation for the existence of age-related deficiencies in various nutrients is a decreased intake among the older people, particularly those of low income levels. In order to evaluate the influence of age on dietary intake in the absence of the economic factor a study was carried out by McGandy, Barrows, Spanias, Meredith, Stone and Norris (1966) on a group of apparently healthy, highly educated, successful men engaged in or retired from professional and managerial occupations. Seven-day dietary histories were obtained on a group of 250 individuals between the ages of 23 and 99 years who resided in the Baltimore-Washington area. The results showed a marked decline with age in total daily caloric intake, as well as progressive decreases with age in the intakes of iron, thiamine, riboflavin, niacin, calcium, and vitamin A. However, except for calcium, the National Research Council's suggested allowances were met by the majority of subjects. The data on the effect of age on daily caloric intakes were analyzed as shown in Figure 1. Figure 1A shows the age decrement in total dietary Calories (a decline of 12.4 Calories per day per year), while Figure 1B shows the basal metabolism of the same subjects which fell by 5.23 Calories per day per year. The difference, which amounts to 7.6 Calories per day per year, (Figure 1C) must be related to the reduction in Calories required for other purposes, including physical activity. Interviews were conducted with 167 of the subjects to obtain an estimate of their physical activities. Table 4 gives the mean values and standard deviations of the calculated daily energy expenditures for the subjects in this sample which were lower in

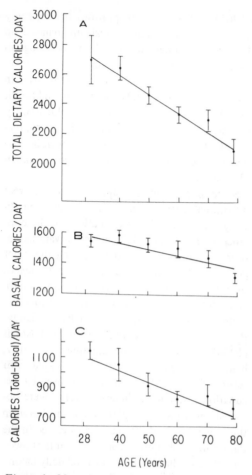

Figure 1. Mean total caloric intakes (A); basal metabolic rates (B); and energy expenditures (C). (With permission of *Journal of Gerontology*, McGandy *et al.*, 1966.)

TABLE 4. ENERGY EXPENDITURE REQUIRED FOR REPORTED ACTIVITIES IN MEN OF DIFFERENT AGES.

Age group	N	ENERGY EXPENDITURE (cal/day)	
		Mean	S. D.
20–34 years	13	1,175	307
35–44 years	32	1,166	333
45–54 years	41	982	280
55–64 years	34	950	269
65–74 years	36	928	239
75–99 years	13	640	245

With permission of *Journal of Gerontology*, McGandy *et al.*, 1966.

old than young individuals. The age decrement in total caloric intake can be accounted for by the age-associated decrease in basal metabolism plus the decline in physical activity.

FOOD ADDITIVES

Harman (1956) proposed that aging may be due in part to the deleterious side effects of free radicals produced in the normal course of metabolism. He proposed that raising the concentrations of compounds such as cysteine and other chemicals capable of reacting rapidly with free radicals would tend to slow the aging process and thus lead to an extension of the normal life span. In the first study to test this proposal (Harman, 1957), weanling AKR male mice and C_3H female mice, which develop spontaneous lymphatic leukemia and mammary carcinoma respectively, were used. The experimental animals were offered *ad libitum* a powdered diet to which was added one of the following compounds: cysteine hydrocholoride (1.0 percent), 2-mercaptoethylamine hydrochloride (MEA) (1.0 percent) 2,2'-diaminodiethyl disulfide dihydrochloride (0.5 percent), ascorbic acid (2.0 percent), and 2-mercaptoethanol (0.5 percent). None of these five compounds statistically influenced the life span of C_3H or AKR mice. In the second study (Harman, 1961), these same strains as well as Swiss male mice were employed. The mice were fed *al libitum* a pellet mouse diet which contained MEA (1 percent), 2,2'diaminodiethyl disulfide (1 percent), hydroxylamine hydrochloride (1 and 2 percent), or cysteine hydrochloride (1 percent). Again, none of the differences in life span was statistically significant. In the third study of this series (Harman, 1968), weanling LAF male mice were used. The control animals were offered *ad libitum* either a powdered commercial diet (Rockland, Teklad Inc.) or a synthetic diet (20 percent casein, 68 percent sucrose, 5 percent corn oil, and adequate amounts of vitamins and minerals). The experimental mice were also fed *ad libitum* and received one of these diets to which the compounds to be tested were added. The addition of MEA (0.5,

1 percent) to the commercial diet or the addition of cysteine hydrochloride, propyl gallate, 2,6-di-*tert*-butyl hydroquinone, or hydroxylamine hydrochloride to the synthetic diet failed to increase the mean life span. However, when MEA was added to the synthetic diet, life span increased by 12%. The inclusion of 2,6-di-*tert*-butyl 4-methylphenol (BHT) at the level of 0.25 percent and 0.50 percent increased longevity by 17.6 and 44.6 percent, respectively. One major difficulty in interpreting the results of this study is that the mean life span of the control mice fed the commercial diet was 20.0 months, whereas that of the control animals fed the synthetic diet was 14.5 months. The author pointed out that this finding may be due to the higher frequency of amyloidosis in the animals fed the synthetic control diet (60 percent) as compared to that of those offered the commercial diet (20 percent). Furthermore, the life spans of the treated synthetic diet groups were less than that of the mice fed the commercial diet.

Kohn (1971) carried out a series of three experiments to test the effect of antioxidants (MEA and BHT) on the life span of C57BL/6J female mice. The compounds were added to Wayne Mouse Breeder Blox, which served as the control diet. The MEA was maintained at a level of 1 percent of the diet in both the first and second studies. The other antioxidant (BHT) caused early weight losses and death when offered at the 1 percent level. Therefore, it was varied between 0.2 and 0.5 percent throughout the life span of the animals in the second and third studies. The results of these experiments indicated that when the control animals had a 50 percent survival time of 121 weeks and a maximum life span of 148 weeks, the antioxidants were without effect. When the survival of the controls was suboptimal, the agents increased the life span but not beyond optimal control values. It was concluded by Kohn (1971) that antioxidants do not inhibit aging but increase life span by beneficially affecting some harmful environmental or nutritional factors.

Tappel, Fletcher, and Deamer (1973) carried out studies on the effects of three diets on various criteria related to aging in 9-month-old retired breeder CDI male mice. One diet served as a control and contained normal amounts of antioxidants, such as vitamin E. Two test diets contained supplements of antioxidants and related nutrients, including vitamin E, BHT, selenium, ascorbic acid, and methionine. The results showed no significant differences in mortality among the various groups. Animals fed the diet supplemented with high levels of antioxidants had significantly lower amounts of fluorescent products in the testes than the other mice. No other age-related index was affected by diet.

Oeriu and Vochitu (1965) proposed that aging is associated with increases in the concentrations of cysteine and oxidized glutathione, as well as decreases in the activities of thiolic enzymes. Furthermore, compounds which contain sulfhydryl groups such as cysteine and N-formylcysteine have been shown to exert a favorable action on various age-related enzymatic changes. Therefore, the effect of treatment with compounds which contain sulfhydryl groups initiated at 13 months on the subsequent life span of male mice, female rats, and female guinea pigs was investigated. The animals were fed natural product diets *ad libitum*. They were given 21 subcutaneous injections on alternate days of either cysteine (30 mg/per kilogram), a combination of thiazolidincarboxylic acid (30 mg/per kilogram) and folic acid (0.75 mg/per kilogram), or saline. Although the treated animals lived somewhat longer than the controls, no statistical analysis of the data was presented. Furthermore, the strains of the various species were not given so that the survival curves cannot be compared with other published data. However, the life spans of the animals in this study seemed short, even among the treated animals. Taken as a whole, these studies do not offer convincing statistical evidence that the addition of various antioxidants increases the life span of mammals.

DIETARY RESTRICTION

McCay, Crowell, and Maynard (1935); McCay, Maynard, Sperling, and Barnes (1939), and McCay, Sperling, and Barnes (1943) carried out a series of three studies which supported earlier observations (Osborne and Mendel, 1915) that nutritional deprivation delays maturation and increases life span. Essentially, McCay and his associates fed an adequate diet *ad libitum* to control animals and only enough food to maintain the body weight of the animals in the retarded groups. However, the authors indicated that when any of the retarded group appeared to be failing from the deficiency of calories, the entire group was supplemented until they gained 10 g. At the end of the periods of 300, 500, 700, and 1,100 days, the various groups of retarded animals were fed *ad libitum*. The results indicated that animals subjected to dietary restriction lived longer than those fed *ad libitum*. Since these early studies, the increased life span associated with underfeeding has been reported in rats by Berg and Simms (1960), Ross (1959), and Riesen, Herbst, Walliker, and Elvehjem (1947), in mice by Visscher, Ball, Barnes, and Sivertsen (1942), in fish by Comfort (1963), in *Daphnia* by Ingel, Wood, and Banta (1937), in *Drosophila* by Loeb and Northrop (1917), and in rotifers by Fanestil and Barrows (1965). It is apparent that underfeeding influences some basic biological phenomenon which results in an increased life span. The biological mechanisms responsible for these effects are unknown.

Physiological and Biochemical Variables

In a recent study by Leto, Kokkonen, and Barrows (1975), attempts were made to determine the degree to which increases in life span of mice brought about by protein restriction may be associated with changes in a number of selected physiological and biochemical variables. Female C57BL/6J mice obtained from the Jackson Laboratories at the age of 30 days were randomly distributed into two groups and individually housed. One group was fed a diet which contained 26 percent casein, 4 percent fat, 15 percent cornstarch, 49 percent sucrose, a balanced salt mixture, and adequate amounts of all the known vitamins. The second group was offered a similar diet except that it contained 4 percent casein. The difference in the protein content was made up with sucrose to keep the diets isocaloric. Both groups of mice were offered water and their respective diet *ad libitum*

throughout the study. Ten mice from each group were sacrificed at 1, 3, 7, and 13.5 months and when the remaining animals reached 50 percent mortality. This was 23.5 and 28 months in the control ($N = 61$) and restricted ($N = 83$) groups respectively.

Although the body weights were lower in the restricted animals as compared to the controls, the ratios of the various organ weights to body weight were not markedly affected by the diets. The involution of the thymus occurred at the same time in both groups of mice.

Rectal temperatures were measured with calibrated, rapid response thermistors using a telethermometer. Although no age-associated differences were seen, significantly lower body temperatures were observed at all ages in the protein-restricted animals than in the controls throughout each 36-hour test period (Table 5). The largest differences between the groups and the lowest temperatures were obtained during the early afternoon hours when the animals were resting and maintained at a normal room temperature (24°C). Lowering the ambient temperature from 24 to 18.5°C had little effect on the rectal temperature of the mice except for an increase of 1.2°C in the lowest values recorded in the protein-restricted animals (Fig. 2). These data indicate that the restricted mice are capable of increasing body temperature under certain stimuli. Little information is available on the effect of body temperature on the life span of homeothermic animals. In poikilothermic animals, the life span increases with decreased environmental temperature (Alpatov and Pearl, 1929; Strehler, 1961). With the use of the Arrehnius equation, and assuming that the activation energy (18,400 calories) found for poikilotherms (Strehler, 1961) is applicable to mice, it is possible to estimate the expected increase in life span due to the lower body temperature associated with dietary restriction. The mean maximal difference in body temperature at various ages was -0.9°C (Table 5). However, the mean lowering of body temperature over a 24-hour period was 0.65°C. The calculated increase in life span due to the lowered body temperature (0.65°C) of restricted mice amounts to 1.5 mo.

The oxygen consumptions of these mice

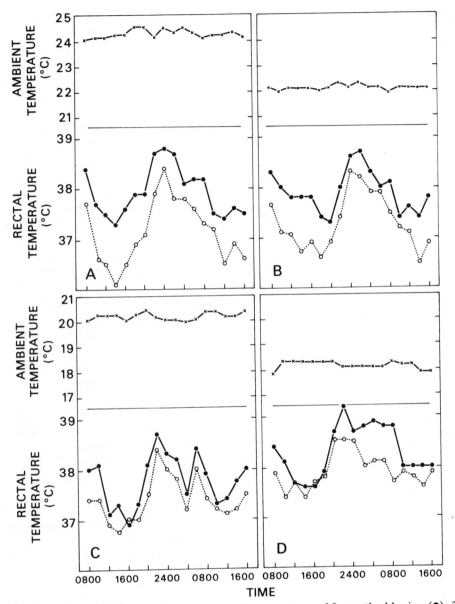

Figure 2. Effect of ambient temperatures on rectal temperatures of 8-month-old mice; (●): 26 percent casein diet; (○): 4 percent casein diet. (With permission of *Journal of Gerontology*, Leto *et al.*, 1976.)

were measured at essentially bimonthly periods from 1 to 27 months of age. Oxygen comsump-tion per unit body weight of control animals in-creased significantly from 1 month to 4 months and then remained stable until 15 months of age (Table 6). Following this age, the consump-tion decreased to 24 months and then increased in later life. This age-associated pattern was also observed in the restricted animals. However, the

oxygen consumption was 21 percent higher in these animals than in the controls. Calculation of the oxygen consumption on the basis of lean body mass failed to alter the observations regarding the effect of age or diet on this variable.

Interpretation of these results is difficult since there is not complete agreement among data available on the effects of oxygen con-

TABLE 5. THE EFFECT OF LOW PROTEIN FEEDING AND AGE ON RECTAL TEMPERATURE AT THE POINT OF MAXIMAL DIFFERENCES IN FEMALE C57BL/6J MICE.

Age (months)	RECTAL TEMPERATURE[a]		
	Control	Low Protein	P Difference
1	37.6 ± 0.2^b		
2	38.1 ± 0.1	37.7 ± 0.3	0.01
4	38.3 ± 0.1	37.8 ± 0.2	0.05
8	37.6 ± 0.1	36.4 ± 0.3	0.001
12	37.7 ± 0.1	36.5 ± 0.2	0.001
14	38.2 ± 0.1	37.4 ± 0.2	0.01
16	37.8 ± 0.2	37.2 ± 0.1	0.01
19	37.5 ± 0.2	36.4 ± 0.3	0.01
22	38.1 ± 0.1	36.6 ± 0.2	0.001
24	38.1 ± 0.2	36.9 ± 0.3	0.001
27	37.7 ± 0.2	36.9 ± 0.2	0.01
Mean	37.9	37.0	

[a]Degrees in centigrade, ambient temperature 24°C.
[b]Mean ± SEM.

With permission of *Journal of Gerontology*, Leto *et al.*, 1976.

sumption on the life span of animals. For many years (Rubner, 1908), a rough inverse correlation has been described among various species, i.e., the higher the oxygen uptake per unit body

TABLE 6. THE EFFECT OF LOW PROTEIN FEEDING ON OXYGEN CONSUMPTION OF C57BL/6J FEMALES.

Age (months)	OXYGEN CONSUMPTION		
	Control	Low Protein	P Difference
1	2.05 ± 0.05^a	—	
2	2.13 ± 0.07	2.54 ± 0.10	0.001
4	2.52 ± 0.12	2.97 ± 0.09	0.01
6	2.43 ± 0.19	3.12 ± 0.08	0.001
12	2.50 ± 0.09	2.85 ± 0.11	0.01
15	2.61 ± 0.10	3.20 ± 0.10	<.001
20	2.32 ± 0.11	2.86 ± 0.08	<.001
24	2.27 ± 0.14	2.71 ± 0.16	0.05
27	2.54 ± 0.08	3.17 ± 0.14	<.001
Mean	2.41	2.92	

[a]$ml0_2/g/hr$, Mean ± SEM.

With permission of *Journal of Gerontology*, Leto *et al.*, 1976.

weight, the shorter the life span. However Storer (1967) reported a direct relationship between oxygen consumption and life span among 18 strains of mice. If there is a direct relationship between these variables, the degree to which longevity is increased due to the increased basal metabolic rate associated with dietary restriction may be estimated from a regression equation calculated from the data of Storer (1967). The results indicate that the life span of the restricted rats in this study would be increased by 1.9 months. Therefore, even employing assumptions which would maximize the effect of these variables on longevity, changes in body temperature and basal oxygen consumption will not account for the 4.5-month increase in life span observed in mice fed a low protein diet.

Biochemical measurements reported in various studies did not indicate that mice subjected to dietary restriction were necessarily like younger animals. For example, Leto, Kokkonen, and Barrows (1976) found an increase (32 percent) in the collagen content of skin during the first 3 months, after which no age-associated changes were observed. However, a marked decrease with age in the amount of skin collagen which was extractable with acetic acid occurred over the total life span (Figure 3). Diet did not markedly affect either of these age-dependent variables.

Earlier studies carried out in rats (Ross, 1959) and in rotifers (Fanestil and Barrows, 1965) indicated that age changes in enzymatic activities occurred later in the life of animals whose longevity was increased by dietary restriction. Ross (1959) showed that rats fed a diet containing 8 percent casein lived 840 days whereas those fed a commercial diet containing 25 percent protein lived 729 days. The same maximal activity of ATPase of liver was observed in both groups of animals but occurred at 200 days in the controls and at 600 days in the longer lived experimental group. Similarly Fanestil and Barrows (1965) showed that the life span of the rotifer could be increased from 34 days when offered fresh pond water and algae daily to 45 days when algae was offered only every other day. Although the same maximal activity of lactic dehydrogenase (LDH) was

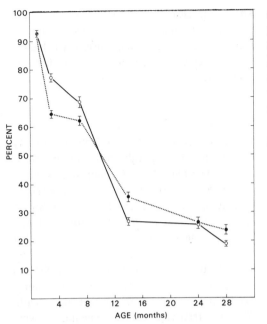

Figure 3. Effect of age and diet on the extractable collagen of skin; (●): 26 percent casein diet; (○): 4 percent casein diet. (With permission of *Journal of Gerontology*, Leto et al., 1976.)

observed in both groups of animals, it occurred at 15 days and 36 days in the control and restricted animals, respectively. Estimates of the activities of malic dehydrogenase (MDH) provided essentially the same results. The enzymatic activities were expressed as the total amount of enzyme per rotifer. In order to minimize the influence of differences in body mass on changes in the enzymatic activities, a ratio of MDH/LDH was calculated in individual animals. In control rotifers, the ratio decreased markedly at the age of 13 days. In restricted animals, this age-associated change did not occur until the 30th day of life.

The enzymatic activities studied by Leto, Kokkonen, and Barrows (1976) on C57BL/6J mice did not follow these alterations in age-associated patterns of changes. The concentrations of DNA were not markedly affected by age in either control or experimental animals but were higher in the kidneys and livers of the restricted mice than in the control mice throughout their life span. Age had little effect on the activities of cholinesterase, alkaline phosphatase, lactic and malic dehydrogenase, and succinoxidase when expressed per unit of DNA. However, catheptic activity increased approximately five-fold and almost linearly throughout life. Feeding the low protein diet resulted in marked decreases in the activities of four (cholinesterase, lactic and malic dehydrogenase, and succinoxidase) of the six enzymes studied. Similar results were obtained when the activities of the enzymes were estimated in kidney, viz., an age-associated increase in cathepsin and reduced activities in the other enzymes attributable to low dietary protein. In heart, the activities of lactic and malic dehydrogenase and alkaline phosphatase increased during early life. This was followed by a slight decrease with age in the activities of the former enzymes, but alkaline phosphatase decreased markedly. There was essentially no effect due to feeding the low dietary protein.

Although a consistent age pattern of changes is not apparent between control and restricted animals, there may be a common factor among these various studies as well as a more recent study by Ross (1969), who varied the protein and/or caloric intake of rats throughout their life span. In general, the enzymatic activities were consistently low in restricted animals. Thus far, in the rat, of 41 enzymes in liver and 31 in kidney, only about 20 percent have been found to change with age (Finch, 1972). This fact suggests that selected parts of the genome are more subject to age-associated changes than others. Although proteins which exhibit the same enzymatic activity may vary structurally among species, the chemical characteristics of the active site are likely to be the same. Therefore, the effect of age on enzymatic activities and other biochemical systems common to various species could be similar (Barrows, 1972). If aging does indeed result from continued use of certain genes with a loss of or imperfections in transcription of information, then the reduced rate of use of informational sites would result in the delay of senescent changes found in certain enzyme systems. Assuming that low enzymatic activities indicate reduced rates of transcription, the results of these studies would support this proposal.

Diseases

The relationship between aging and many diseases remains unknown. If diseases occur as part of the aging process and may be genetically controlled, then dietary restriction should delay the onset of specific diseases as well as increase life span. Berg and Simms (1962) demonstrated that in rats a reduction of 46 percent in dietary intake was accompanied by a 25 percent increase in life span and a delay in the age at which 40 percent of the animals had chronic glomerulonephritis from 500 to 1,000 days. Other observations by these investigators indicated that the incidence of muscular dystrophy in control male rats was 74 percent at 900 days, whereas only 31 percent of the restricted animals had muscular lesions at 1,100 days. In females at age 1,100 days, the incidence of this disease was 80 percent and 41 percent respectively, for control and restricted animals. Carcinogenesis was also delayed by food restriction. For example, at 800 days of age, the total incidence of tumors was reduced in males from 58 percent to 26 percent and in females from 43 percent to 12 percent by reduction in dietary intakes.

Similar findings have been reported by Bras and Ross (1964). Approximately 1,000 male rats were distributed into five groups; four of these groups were allotted restricted amounts of semisynthetic diets so designed that the intakes of only protein (casein), or carbohydrate (sucrose), or calories differed. The fifth group was fed a commercial diet *ad libitum*. The histopathologic changes which occurred with age suggested the presence of a disease described as a progressive glomerulonephrosis (PGN). Restriction in the intakes of protein, carbohydrate, or calories markedly reduced the incidence of PGN. The most beneficial effects were obtained in those animals whose carbohydrate intake and concomitant caloric intake were reduced. The greatest incidence, as well as the earliest appearance of PGN, were found in those rats fed a commerical diet *ad libitum*. Tumor incidence was also evaluated (Ross and Bras, 1965) and, in general, it was found that low intakes of protein, carbohydrate, and/or calories reduced the incidence or the number of tumors per rat or delayed the age of appearance of the tumors.

These data clearly indicate that life span, and onset, and incidence of various diseases can be markedly altered by dietary means. The biological mechanisms which bring about these results remain unknown.

Age

Nolen (1972) reported the effects of a variety of restricted feeding regimens on the life spans of rats. The animals were obtained at weaning and fed a semipurified diet which contained 23 percent protein and 18.5 percent fat. Controls received this diet *ad libitum* throughout life. Six experimental groups were offered either 80 or 60 percent of the amount consumed by controls for one of three time intervals: (1) throughout life, (2) for 12 weeks after weaning, (3) from 12 weeks after weaning until death. When not restricted, the experimental rats were fed *ad libitum*. The results indicated that restriction of dietary intake either throughout life or from 12 weeks after weaning until death, prolonged life span, whereas early restriction followed by *ad libitum* feeding did not. Reduction of intake to 60 percent was more effective than 80 percent restriction.

Ross (1967) maintained rats on a commerical diet offered *ad libitum* from weaning (21 days) until 300 days of age. He then divided them into groups and placed them on different dietary regimens for the remainder of the life span. The protein contents of 5 diets varied from 8 to 50.9 percent. The level of allotment of each diet was also varied and ranged from 40 to 100 percent of the amount consumed by animals fed *ad libitum*. A mortality index was calculated for each group from their respective age-specific mortality rates after 300 days. Beneficial effects on this index were observed for three groups of animals, i.e., those offered either 60 or 70 percent of *ad libitum* intakes of the commercial diet (23 percent protein) or 52 percent of the *ad libitum* intake of a formulated diet which contained 21.6 percent vitamin-free casein.

Miller and Payne (1968) also varied the dietary regimen of rats. A stock diet which contained 12 percent of Net Dietary Protein calories (NDp Cals %) was offered *ad libitum* throughout life to one group. Two other groups received this diet diluted with starch to yield 6 and 4 NDp Cals % respectively for life. An additional group was fed the stock diet until 120 days of age, followed by the 4 NDp Cals % diet. A fifth group received a protein-free diet. A significant extension of the life span beyond that of the stock-fed animals was seen in those given the diluted stock (4 NDp Cals %) from 120 days of age until death. If they received this experimental diet throughout life, the longevity was significantly decreased.

Barrows and Roeder (1965) subjected animals at more advanced ages, 13 and 19 months, to a 50 percent reduction in intake of a commercial (25 percent protein) diet. The reductions were calculated for individual animals from their *ad libitum* intakes measured for 3 weeks prior to initiation of restriction. This dietary regimen failed to increase the life span of these animals. In fact, the mean age at death for all restricted rats combined was slightly (1.8 months) but significantly lower than that of *ad libitum* fed controls.

Roeder (1973) investigated the effect of very early (perinatal) undernourishment on biochemical changes associated with senescence in the rat. Undernutrition was effected during the gestation and lactation periods by subjecting the mother to a 50 percent reduction in intake of a commerical (24 percent protein) diet. At weaning, the pups were offered this diet *ad libitum*. Certain biochemical variables known to change with age were measured in these animals and in the offspring of unrestricted mothers. The expected age-dependent increase in catheptic activity of liver and kidney (Barrows and Roeder, 1965) occurred prematurely in the experimental animals. In addition, the rate of development of albuminuria in the second year of life was significantly greater in the perinatally undernourished than control group. These findings were interpreted as evidence of accelerated aging. The role of nutrition is difficult to evaluate, but during the postweaning period of *ad libitum* intakes, the experimental animals were relatively overfed since they consumed greater amounts of feed per unit of body size than controls. However, the mean life span of the progeny of 7 control and 6 experimental animals were 104 and 107 weeks respectively and were not significantly different.

In addition, Kahn (1968) reported a similar effect on biochemical changes associated with aging in the offspring of mice who were intermittently starved during gestation. The animals experienced a premature decline in hemoglobin levels during adulthood when compared to the progeny of *ad libitum* fed controls.

Since the numbers of animals used in most of these studies were small (10 or less per group) and the ages at which diets were changed were quite variable, it is difficult to draw general conclusions about critical intervals of life with respect to the effect of nutrition on age-associated biochemical changes and longevity. Nevertheless, the results indicate that it may be possible to impose specific types of dietary restrictions, even after the cessation of growth, to beneficially affect life span. On the other hand, the data also suggest that perinatal undernutrition may have a deterimental effect in that it seems to accelerate the biochemical changes which occur during aging. It is apparent that our previous thinking that the growth period was the only one during which dietary manipulations could influence age-associated physiological and biochemical changes as well as life span must be reevaluated.

SUMMARY

As man ages, a reduction in caloric intake and most nutrients occurs. This appears to be due to a decrease in basal metabolic rate and a marked reduction in physical activity. The frequency of not meeting the recommended dietary allowances is low in high economic groups, although some marginal deficiencies may be seen. Rarely are these deficiencies manifested in clinical or physiological changes. However, as income decreases, especially to or below poverty levels, nutritional deficiencies become more frequent and severe. The dietary intakes of protein, niacin, thiamine, and iron, particularly of calcium, vitamin A and vitamin C are most likely to be low. Therefore, it would seem that poverty and health influence nutritional status in man to a greater extent than age *per se*.

Different forms of underfeeding have been

shown to increase the life span of a large number of species of animals. The biological mechanisms responsible for this are unknown. The increase in life span of restricted animals is accompanied by a reduced incidence and severity, and a delay in the age at onset, of various diseases. At present, it is not known whether the increased longevity is due solely to changes in age-related diseases. However, data indicate that the increased life span is not associated with changes in body temperature or oxygen consumption in restricted animals. In biochemical studies, increased longevity is frequently associated with an increase in the age of occurrence of changes in certain enzymatic activities. However, this finding is not uniform among all studies. Although it was formerly believed that the growth period was the critical interval in which nutritional manipulations could affect life span, more recent data suggest that beneficial effects may be produced by dietary changes in adulthood. However, dietary restrictions during the perinatal period may be detrimental with respect to the rate of development of age-associated changes in the organism. It is apparent that greater research efforts must be made in order to gain an understanding of the mechanisms by which dietary manipulations alter life span.

REFERENCES

Ackermann, P. G., and Toro, G. 1953a. Calcium and phosphorus balance in elderly men. *J. Geront.*, **8**, 289–300.

Ackermann, P. G., and Toro, G. 1953b. Effect of added vitamin D on the calcium balance in elderly males. *J. Geront.*, **8**, 451–457.

Alphatov, W., and Pearl, R. 1929. Experimental studies on the duration of life. XII. Influences of temperature during the larval period and adult life of the imago of *Drosophila melanogaster*. *Am. Naturalist*, **63**, 37–67.

Barrows, C. H. 1972. Nutrition, aging and genetic program. *Amer. J. Clin. Nutr.*, **25**, 829–833.

Barrows, C. H., and Roeder, L. M. 1965. The effect of reduced dietary intake on enzymatic activities and life span of rats. *J. Geront.*, **20**, 69–71.

Berg, B. N., and Simms, H. S. 1960. Nutrition and longevity in the rat. II. Longevity and onset of disease with different levels of food intake. *J. Nutr.*, **71**, 255–263.

Berg, B. N., and Simms, H. S. 1962. Relation of nutrition to longevity and onset of disease in rats. *In*, N. W. Shock (ed.), *Biological Aspects of Aging*, pp. 35–37. New York: Columbia University Press.

Bogdonoff, M. D., Shock, N. W., and Nichols, M. P. 1953. Calcium, phosphorus, nitrogen, and potassium balance studies in the aged male. *J. Geront.*, **8**, 272–288.

Bras, G., and Ross, M. H. 1964. Kidney disease and nutrition in the rat. *Toxicol. Appl. Pharmacol.* **6**, 247–262.

Brewer, W. D., Furnivall, M. E., Wagoner, A., Lee, J., Alsop, B., and Ohlson, M. A. 1956. Nutritional status of the aged in Michigan. *J. Am. Dietet. Assoc.*, **32**, 810–815.

Brin, M., Dibble, M. V., Peel, A., McMullen, E., Bourquin, A., and Chen, N. 1965. Some preliminary findings on the nutritional status of the aged in Onondaga County, New York. *Amer. J. Clin. Nutr.*, **17**, 240–258.

Center for Disease Control. 1972. *Ten-State Nutrition Survey, 1968–1970*. DHEW Publ. No. (HSM) 72-8134. Health Services and Mental Health Administration. Washington, D.C.: Government Printing Office.

Chernish, S. M., Helmer, O. M., Fauts, P. J., and Hohlstaedt, K. G. 1957. The effect of intrinsic factor on the absorption of vitamin B_{12} in older people. *Amer. J. Clin. Nutr.*, **5**, 651–658.

Chieffi, M., and Kirk, J. E. 1949. Vitamin studies in middle-aged and old individuals. II. Correlation between vitamin A plasma content and certain clinical and laboratory findings. *J. Nutr.*, **37**, 67–79.

Chieffi, M., and Kirk, J. E. 1951. Vitamin studies in middle-aged and old individuals. VI. Tocopheral plasma concentration. *J. Geront.*, **6**, 17–19.

Chinn, A. B. 1956. Some problems of nutrition in the aged. *J. Am. Med. Assoc.*, **162**, 1511–1513.

Chinn, A. B., Lavik, P. S., and Cameron, D. B. 1956. Measurement of protein digestion and absorption in aged persons by a test meal of I^{131}-labeled protein. *J. Geront.*, **11**, 151–153.

Comfort, A. 1963. Effect of delayed and resumed growth on the longevity of a fish (*lebistes recticulatus, Peters*) in captivity. *Gerontologia*, **8**, 150–155.

Davis, R. L., Lawton, A. H., Barrows, C. H., Jr., and Hargen, S. M. 1966. Serum lactate and lactic dehydrogenase levels of aging males. *J. Geront.*, **21**, 571–574.

Davis, R. L., Lawton, A. H., Prouty, R., and Chow, B. F. 1965. The absorption of oral vitamin B_{12} in an aged population. *J. Geront.*, **20**, 169–172.

Davis, T. R. A., Gershoff, S. N., and Gamble, D. F. 1969. Review of studies of vitamin and mineral nutrition in the United States (1950–1968). *J. Nutrit. Ed.*, **1** (Suppl. 1), 40–57.

Fanestil, D. D., and Barrows, C. H., Jr. 1965. Aging in the rotifer. *J. Geront.*, **20**, 462–469.

Finch, C. E. 1972. Enzyme activities, gene function and ageing in mammals (Review). *Exp. Geront.*, **7**, 53–67.

Food and Agriculture Organization. 1957. *Caloric requirements, Rome,* Nutrition Studies No. 15.

Gaffney, G. W., Horonick, A., Okuda, K., Meier, P., Chow, B. F., and Shock, N. W. 1957. Vitamin B_{12} serum concentrations in 528 apparently healthy human subjects of ages 12–94. *J. Geront.,* **12,** 32–38.

Garn, S. M. 1970. *The Earlier Gain and the Later Loss of Cortical Bone in Nutritional Perspective.* Springfield, Illinois: Charles C. Thomas.

Garn, S. M., Rohmann, C. G., and Wagner, B. 1967. Bone loss as a general phenomenon in men. *Federation Proc.,* **26,** 1729–1736.

Gillum, H. L., Morgan, A. F., and Sailer, F. 1955. Nutritional status of the ageing. V. Vitamin A and carotene. *J. Nutr.,* **55,** 655–670.

Gitman, L., and Kamholtz, T. 1965. Incidence of radiographic osteoporosis in a large series of aged individuals. *J. Geront.,* **20,** 32–33.

Harman, D. 1956. Aging: A theory based on free radical and radiation chemistry. *J. Geront.,* **11,** 298–300.

Harman, D. 1957. Prolongation of the normal life span by radiation protection chemicals. *J. Geront.,* **12,** 257–263.

Harman, D. 1961. Prolongation of the normal life span and inhibition of spontaneous cancer by antioxidants. *J. Geront.,* **16,** 247–254.

Harman, D. 1968. Free radical theory of aging: Effect of free radical reaction inhibitors on the mortality rate of male LAF, mice. *J. Geront.,* **23,** 476–482.

Harrison, M., Fraser, R., and Mullan, B. 1961. Calcium metabolism in osteoporosis. Acute and long-term responses to increased calcium intake. *Lancet,* **1,** 1015–1019.

Hayflick, L. 1965. The limited *in vitro* life-time of human diploid cell strains. *Exp. Cell Res.,* **37,** 614–636.

Hegsted, D. M. 1952. False estimates of adult requirements. *Nutrit. Rev.,* **10,** 257–259.

Hegsted, D. M., Moscoso, I., and Collazos, C. 1952. A study of the minimum calcium requirements of adult men. *J. Nutr.,* **46,** 181–201.

Horwitt, M. 1953. Dietary requirements of the aged. *J. Am. Dietet. Assoc.,* **29,** 443–448.

Ingle, L., Wood, T. R., and Banta, A. M. 1937. A study of longevity, growth, reproduction and heart rate in *Daphnia langispina* as influenced by limitations in quantity of food. *J. Exp. Zool.,* **76,** 325–352.

Inter-departmental Committee on Nutrition for National Defense. 1963. *Manual for Nutrition Surveys,* 2nd ed. Bethesda, Maryland: National Institutes of Health.

Kahn, A. J. 1968. Embryogenic effect on post-natal changes in hemoglobin concentration with time. *Growth,* **32,** 13–17.

Kelsay, J. L. 1969. A compendium of nutritional status studies and dietary evaluation studies conducted in the United States 1957–1967. *J. Nutr.,* **99** (Suppl. 1), 119–166.

Kirk, J. E. 1954. Blood and urine vitamin levels in the aged. *In, Symposium on Problems of Gerontology,* pp. 73–94. New York: Nat. Vitamin Found.

Kirk, J. E., and Chieffi, M. 1948. Vitamin studies in middle-aged and old individuals. I. The vitamin A, total carotene and $\alpha + \beta$ carotene concentrations in plasma. *J. Nutr.,* **36,** 315–322.

Kirk, J. E., and Chieffi, M. 1949. Vitamin studies in middle-aged and old individuals. III. Thiamine and pyruvic acid blood concentrations. *J. Nutr.,* **38,** 353–360.

Kirk, J. E., and Chieffi, M. 1953a. Vitamin studies in middle-aged and old individuals. XI. The concentration of total ascorbic acid in whole blood. *J. Geront.,* **8,** 301–304.

Kirk, J. E., and Chieffi, M. 1953b. Vitamin studies in middle-aged and old individuals. XII. Hypovitaminemia C. Effect of ascorbic acid administration on the blood ascorbic acid concentration. *J. Geront.,* **8,** 305–311.

Kohn, R. R. 1971. Effect of antioxidants on life-span of C57BL mice. *J. Geront.,* **26,** 378–380.

Kountz, W. B., Hofstatter, L., and Ackermann, P. 1947. Nitrogen balance studies in elderly people. *Geriatrics,* **2,** 173–182.

Kountz, W. B., Hofstatter, L., and Ackermann, P. G. 1951. Nitrogen balance studies in four elderly men. *J. Geront.,* **6,** 20–33.

Leto, S., Kokkonen, G., and Barrows, C. H. 1976. Dietary proteins, life span and physiological and biochemical variables in female mice. *J. Geront.,* **31**(2), 144–148.

Loeb, J., and Northrop, J. H. 1917. On the influence of food and temperature upon the duration of life. *J. Biol. Chem.,* **32,** 103–121.

Lutwak, L. 1963. Osteoporosis. A disorder of nutrition. *N.Y. State J. Med.,* **63,** 590–593.

Lutwak, L., and Whedon, C. D. 1963. Osteoporosis. *In, Disease-a-Month* (April), pp. 1–39. Chicago, Illinois: Year Book Medical Publishers.

McCay, C. M., Crowell, M. F., and Maynard, L. A. 1935. The effect of retarded growth upon the length of life span and upon the ultimate body size. *J. Nutr.,* **10,** 63–79.

McCay, C. M., Maynard, L. A., Sperling, G., and Barnes, L. L. 1939. Retarded growth, life span ultimate body size and age changes in the albino rat after feeding diets restricted in calories. *J. Nutr.,* **18,** 1–13.

McCay, C. M., Sperling, G., and Barnes, L. L. 1943. Growth, ageing, chronic diseases, and life span in rats. *Arch. Biochem.,* **2,** 469–479.

McGandy, R. B., Barrows, C. H., Jr., Spanias, A., Meredith, A., Stone, J. L., and Norris, A. H. 1966. Nutrient intakes and energy expenditure in men of different ages. *J. Geront.,* **21,** 581–587.

Malm, O. J. 1958. *Calcium Requirements and Adaptation in Adult Men.* Oslo: Oslo University Press.

Miller, D. S., and Payne, P. R. 1968. Longevity and protein intake. *Exp. Geront.,* **3,** 231–234.

Morgan, A. F., Gillum, H. L., and Williams, R. I.

1955. Nutritional status of the aging. III. Serum ascorbic acid and intake. *J. Nutr.*, **55**, 431–448.

National Academy of Sciences–National Research Council. 1968. *Recommended Dietary Allowances*, 7th Ed. National Research Council Publ. 1964. Washington, D.C.: National Research Council.

National Center for Health Statistics. 1974. *First Health and Nutrition Examination Survey, United States*, 1971–1972, DHEW Publ. No. (HRA) 74-1219-1 Health Services Administration. Washington, D.C.: Government Printing Office.

Nolen, G. A. 1972. Effect of various restricted dietary regimens on the growth, health and longevity of albino rats. *J. Nutr.*, **102**, 1477–1494.

Nordin, B. E. C. 1961. The pathogenesis of osteoporosis. *Lancet*, **1**, 1011–1014.

Nordin, B. E. C. 1962. Calcium balance and calcium requirements in spinal osteoporosis. *Am. J. Clin. Nutr.*, **10**, 384–390.

Nordin, B. E. C. 1971. Clinical significance and pathogenesis of osteoporosis. *Brit. Med. J.*, **1**, 571–576.

Nordin, B. E. C., and Smith, D. A. 1964. The treatment of osteoporosis. *Triangle*, **6**, 273–277.

Oeriu, S., and Vochitu, E. 1965. The effect of the administration of compounds which contain sulfhydryl groups on the survival rates of mice, rats, and guinea pigs. *J. Geront.*, **20**, 417–419.

Ohlson, M. A., Brewer, W. D., Cederquist, D. C., Jackson, L., Brown, E. G., and Roberts, P. H. 1948. Studies of protein requirements of women. *J. Am. Dietet. Assoc.*, **24**, 744–749.

Ohlson, M. A., Brewer, W. D., Jackson, L., Swanson, P. P., Roberts, P. H., Mangel, M., Leverton, R. M., Chaloupka, M., Gram, M. R., Reynolds, M. S., and Lutz, R. 1952. Intakes and retention of nitrogen, calcium and phosphorus by 136 women between 30 and 85 years of age. *Federation Proc.*, **11**, 775–783.

Orshansky, M. 1968. The shape of poverty in 1966. *Soc. Sec. Bull.*, **31**, 3–32.

Osborne, T. B., and Mendel, L. B. 1915. The resumption of growth after long continued failure to grow. *J. Biol. Chem.*, **23**, 439–454.

Pearson, W. N. 1962. Biochemical appraisal of nutritional status in man. *Am. J. Clin. Nutr.*, **11**, 462–467.

Ranke, E., Tauber, S. A., Horonick, A., Ranke, B., Goodhart, R. S., and Chow, B. F. 1960. Vitamin B$_6$ deficiency in the aged. *J. Geront.*, **15**, 41–44.

Reisen, W. H., Herbst, E. J., Walliker, C., and Elvehjem, C. A. 1947. The effect of restricted caloric intake on the longevity of rats. *Am. J. Physiol.*, **148**, 614–617.

Roberts, P. H., Kerr, C. H., and Ohlson, M. A. 1948. Nutritional status of older women. Nitrogen, calcium, phosphorus retentions of nine women. *J. Am. Dietet. Assoc.*, **24**, 292–299.

Roeder, L. M. 1973. Effect of the level of nutrition on rates of cell proliferation and of RNA and protein synthesis in the rat. *Nutrit. Rep. Intern.*, **7**, 271–288.

Rose, C. S., Gyorgy, P., Spiegel, H., Brin, M., Butler, M., and Shock, N. W. 1974. Vitamin B$_6$ status of American adult males. *Federation Proc.*, **33**, 697.

Ross, M. H. 1959. Protein, calories and life expectancy. *Federation Proc.*, **18**, 1190–1207.

Ross, M. H. 1967. Life expectancy modification by change in dietary regimen of the mature rat. *In, Proceedings of the Seventh International Congress of Nutrition*, Vol. 5, pp. 35–38.

Ross, M. 1969. Aging, nutrition and hepatic enzyme activity patterns in the rat. *J. Nutr.*, **97**, 562–602.

Ross, M., and Bras, G. 1965. Tumor incidence patterns and nutrition in the rat. *J. Nutr.*, **87**, 245–260.

Rubner, M. 1908. *Das Problem der Lebensdauer und seine Beziehungen zu Wachstum und Ernährung.* Muchen: R. Oldenbourg.

Sandstead, H. H., and Pearson, W. N. 1973. Clinical evaluation of nutrition status. *In*, R. S. Goodhart and M. E. Shils (eds.), *Modern Nutrition in Health and Disease*, 5th ed., pp. 562–586. Philadelphia: Lea & Febiger.

Schmid, O. 1962. *Die Ernährung des Menschen über 50 Jahre.* Stuttgart: Paracelsus-Verlag.

Schulze, W. 1955. Protein metabolism and requirement in old age. *In, Old Age in the Modern World*, pp. 122–127. London: E. & S. Livingstone.

Silberberg, M., and Silberberg, R. 1955. Diet and life span. *Physiol. Rev.*, **35**, 347–362.

Smith, R. W., Jr., and Frame, B. 1965. Concurrent axial and appendicular osteoporosis. Its relation to calcium retention. *New Eng. J. Med.*, **273**, 73–78.

Storer, J. B. 1967. Relation of lifespan to brain weight, body weight and metabolic rates among inbred mouse strains. *Exp. Geront.*, **2**, 173–182.

Strehler, B. L. 1961. Studies on the comparative physiology of aging. II. On the mechanism of temperature of life-shortening in *Drosphilia Melanogaster. J. Geront.*, **16**, 2–12.

Tappel, A., Fletcher, G., and Deamer, D. 1973. Effect of antioxidants and nutrients on lipid peroxidation fluorescent products and aging parameters in the mouse. *J. Geront.*, **28**, 415–424.

Tuttle, S. G., Swenseid, M. E., Mulcare, D., Griffith, W. H., and Bassett, S. H. 1957. Study of the essential amino acid requirements of men over fifty. *Metab., Clin. Exp.*, **6**, 564–573.

U.S. Department of Agriculture, Agriculture Research Service (by Consumer and Food Economics Division). 1968. *Comsumption of Households in the United States, Spring 1965.* Household Food Consumption Survey 1965–66, Rept. No. 1. Washington, D.C.: Government Printing Office.

Visscher, M. B., Ball, Z. B., Barnes, R. H., and Sivertsen, I. 1942. The influence of caloric restriction upon the incidence of spontaneous mammary carcinoma in mice. *Surgery*, **11**, 48–55.

Watkin, D. M. 1968. Nutritional problems today in the elderly in the United States. *In*, A. N. Exton-Smith and D. L. Scott (eds.), *Vitamins in the Elderly*, pp. 66–77. Bristol, England: John Wright and Sons.

Watts, J. H., Mann, A. N., Bradley, L., and Thompson, D. J. 1964. Nitrogen balance of men over 65 fed the FAO and milk patterns of essential amino acids. *J. Geront.*, **19**, 370–374.

World Health Organization. 1962; 1965; 1967; 1970. *Calcium requirements, Rome*, Tech. Rept. No. 230; *Protein requirements, Rome*, Tech, Rept. No. 301; *Requirements of vitamin A, thiamine, riboflavin and niacin, Rome*, Tech. Rept. No. 362; *Requirements of ascorbic acid, vitamin D, vitamin B_{12}, folate and iron, Geneva*, Tech. Rept. No. 452. Geneva: World Health Organization.

Yasumura, S. 1972. Physiological changes in metabolic disorders of bone and an evaluation of agents used in their treatment. *Semin. Drug Treat.*, **2**, 1–13.

Yiengst, M. J., and Shock, N. W. 1949. Effect of oral administration of vitamin A on plasma levels of vitamin A and carotene in aged males. *J. Geront.*, **4**, 205–211.

24
LIFE TABLE MODIFICATION
AND LIFE PROLONGATION

George A. Sacher*

Argonne National Laboratory

INTRODUCTION

Synopsis

This chapter offers a survey and critique of experimental efforts to extend the lifespan. The problem is many-sided, not only in regard to the multiplicity of biological hypotheses, but also in regard to many basic methodological and theoretical questions that have not yet been thoroughly examined. Although some aspects of biochemical mechanisms and of mathematical models for mortality and aging are touched on, the primary concern is to refine the phenomenological analysis of life table modification so that it can become an effective instrument for testing hypotheses about theory and mechanism. The statistical estimation of parameters is not discussed, despite its importance.

A sound disciplinary basis for research on life table modification cannot be developed if the inquiry is limited to the prolongation of life, because life-lengthening and life-shortening are inseparably intertwined. Thus, experimentation into the life-shortening effects of ionizing radiation becomes very relevant in life table modification.

We examine the problem of paradoxical life prolongation by toxic substances, which is an aspect of the larger topic of paradoxical stimulation (hormetic effects) in general. The evidence for such phenomena is examined in relation to the methodological problem of drawing valid inferences from life prolongation experiments.

The analysis of the effects of environmental agents on life tables leads to the demonstration that there are two basic kinds of parameters governing longevity: rate of aging and vulnerability. Although some treatments may affect both, it is likely that most treatments affect predominantly one or the other. For this reason, every treatment is, insofar as is possible, considered in terms of the evidence for its effect on each parameter.

The question of the effects of therapies on these two specific actuarial parameters is important in human applications, as changes in these parameters have very different consequences for subsequent survival. It is also important in relation to the mechanism of life-prolongation, especially since no pharmacological anti-aging therapy has yet brought about an unequivocal reduction in the rate-of-aging parameter.

*Work supported by the U.S. Energy Research and Development Administration.

THE RELATION OF MORTALITY TO THE PHYSIOLOGICAL STATE OF THE ORGANISM

The Life Table and the Survival Characteristics

The *life table* was developed to meet the needs of the insurance industry. Life table analysis is a highly developed numerical procedure for transforming raw mortality data to an accurate tabular form (Dublin, Lotka, and Spiegelman, 1949). Except for some weak requirements for "smoothness" in the sequences of numerical values, the actuarial life table has no theoretical content.

This empirical approach to mortality processes is not a satisfactory conceptual basis for the examination of life table modification undertaken here because, although it gives abundant numerical detail, it provides no information concerning meaningful life table modifications, i.e., those that can be expected as consequences of various classes of chemical or physical treatments applied to animal or human populations.

The approach here is to represent the mortality process in adults by a comparatively simple mathematical model that satisfies two conditions: (1) the small number of parameters in the model (two, or at most three for our present purposes) adequately describe the mortality process for the unperturbed population, and also for the perturbations produced by various procedures; and (2) the mortality parameters are related to those of the molecular degradations that underlie the aging process by a mathematical theory of mortality. A mathematical function that satisfies the first of these conditions and is chosen as a model of the mortality process for a taxonomic group is called a *survival characteristic*.

A survey of the plant and animal kingdoms would produce a great diversity of survival characteristics, but it would not be correct to assume that they are all generated by a single kind of aging process. Mammals (the primary concern of this chapter) are a monophyletic group that is homogeneous both in physiology and in reproductive factors that shape the population

biology and the somatic aging processes of its members. All mammals, like most other vertebrates, are *iteroparous* (i.e., have multiple litters) and have reproductive spans that are long relative to their development times. *Semelparous* forms with a single reproductive cycle, such as annual plants, have profoundly different population structures and aging processes (Cole, 1954). The length of the reproductive span required for an adequate rate of increase per generation, and the length of the maturation period, are major factors determining the characteristic species longevity (Table 1A). Most mammals have determinate growth, but some (e.g., Norway rats) retain a limited potential for somatic growth into middle age. Physical aging in mammals is essentially a continuous process proceeding at an almost uniform rate throughout adult life (Shock, Ch. 25). There is no evidence for the presence of genetically controlled humoral triggering of a discrete aging phase, such as that which occurs in annual plants (Woolhouse, 1974) and in some insects and fishes (Rockstein, Chesky and Sussman, Ch. 1). The apparent absence of triggered aging in mammals is noteworthy. However, it is consistent with their population biology as iteroparous animals, because interoparity places a premium on life maintenance rather than life termination.

Although the molecular aging of mammals is a uniform process, the mammalian survival curve in a favorable environment is sigmoid in shape, which implies that the risk of death increases as a function of age. The mathematical nature of that increase has been investigated for a diverse set of mammalian species, and the conclusion is that the age-specific death rate increases exponentially with age (Figure 1B) (Sacher and Staffeldt, 1972). This relation of death rate to age is the *Gompertz equation* (Gompertz, 1825):

$$q_x = q_o e^{\alpha x} \qquad (1)$$

where

$q_x = d_x/hL_x$ is the death rate at age x,

d_x is the number of deaths between age x and age $x + h$

L_x is the number alive at age x

TABLE 1A. MAXIMUM LIFESPANS, IN YEARS, OF SOME MAMMALIAN SPECIES.

Species		Maximum lifespan in years
Rodents		
Norway rat	*Rattus norvegicus*	4
Pocket mouse*	*Perognathus longimembris*	8
Gray squirrel	*Sciurus carolinensis*	15
Monotremes and marsupials		
Echidna*	*Tachyglossus aculeatus*	50
Virginia opossum	*Didelphis virginianus*	5
Kangaroo	*Macropus robustus*	20
Bats		
Indian fruit bat	*Pteropus giganteus*	17
Little brown bat*	*Myotis lucifugus*	24
Primates		
Orang-utan	*Pongo pygmaeus*	50
Capuchin monkey	*Cebus capucinus*	40
Brown lemur	*Lemur fulvus*	31
Carnivores		
Coyote	*Canis latrans*	16
Brown bear[†]	*Ursus arctos*	37
Bobcat	*Felis rufus*	25
Ungulates		
Asiatic elephant	*Elephas maximus*	70
Syrian wild ass	*Equus hemionus*	36
Hippopotamus	*Hippopotamus amphibius*	51
Whales		
Finback	*Balaenoptera physalus*	80
Pilot whale	*Globicephala melaena*	50

*Hibernating species.
[†]Winter sleep is not hibernation.
Data from Sacher (1972).

For further discussion of life table functions, see Rockstein, Chesky and Sussman (Ch. 1).

The Gompertz equation can also be written

$$G_x = \ln q_x = G_o + \alpha x, \qquad (2)$$

which is a special form of the *Gompertz function*,

$$G_x = G_o + \phi(x) \qquad (3)$$

where $\phi(x)$ can be a curvilinear function of x (Brues and Sacher, 1952). The Gompertz function is important in that there is a theoretical basis and experimental support for the postulate that the function $\phi(x)$, obtained by plotting logarithm of death rate versus age, is approximately a linear measure of the time course of aging injury in the population (Sacher, 1956; Sacher and Trucco, 1962b). The linear form, equation (2), is adequate for most of this discussion, because the mortality rate of homogeneous populations of adult experimental mammals that are maintained free of disease and given adequate diets is described by the linear equation remarkably well (Sacher and Staffeldt, 1972; Figure 1B).

Because the rate of increase in mortality with

Figure 1. Plots of survivorship (A) and of logarithm of rate of mortality or Gompertz function (B), versus age, for wild-type populations of five rodent species bred and reared in captivity (Sacher and Staffeldt, 1972). The straight lines were fitted to the Gompertz function points by weighted least squares. Slopes and intercepts are from Table 1B. (From Sacher and Staffeldt, unpublished.)

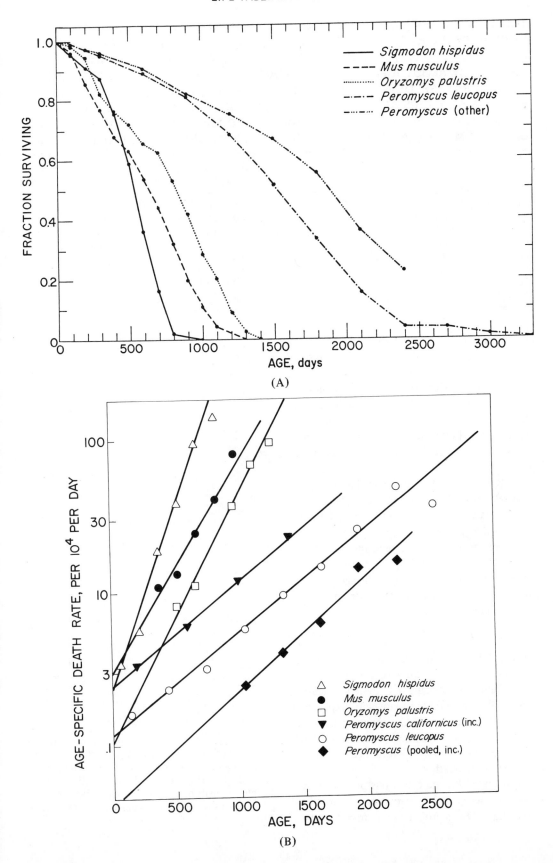

(A)

(B)

TABLE 1B. LIFE EXPECTANCY, E_o, INITIAL DEATH RATE, q_o, DOUBLING TIME OF MORTALITY RATE, T_d, RESTING METABOLIC RATE, M, AND LIFETIME ENERGY DISSIPATION LED ($= E_o M$), FOR 8 SPECIES OF MAMMALS. THE LED ESTIMATES ARE LOW BY ABOUT A FACTOR OF 2 BECAUSE THEY ARE COMPUTED FROM THE RESTING RATHER THAN THE AVERAGE DAILY METABOLIC RATES. DATA FOR RODENTS AND DOGS ARE UNPUBLISHED WORK DONE AT ARGONNE NATIONAL LABORATORY; LIFE TABLE FOR THOROUGHBRED FROM COMFORT (1958); OTHER DATA FROM ALTMAN AND DITTMER, HANDBOOK OF BIOLOGICAL DATA.

	E_o days	q_o (day)$^{-1}$	T_d days	M cal/g day	LED kcal/g
Mus musculus (house mouse)	602	3.0×10^{-4}	220	248	149
Sigmodon hispidus (cotton rat)	514	2.2×10^{-4}	125	159	82
Oryzomys palustris (rice rat)	789	1.1×10^{-4}	197	338	267
Peromyscus leucopus (white-footed mouse)	1,475	1.2×10^{-4}	447	309	456
Peromyscus californicus (California mouse)	1,100	2.4×10^{-4}	441	355	391
Canis familiaris (beagle dog)	3,617	2.7×10^{-5}	812	39	141
Equus caballus (tho'bred mare)	6,329	6.0×10^{-6}	1332	17.7	112
Homo sapiens (U.S. white female 1969)	27,700	1.5×10^{-7}	3100	24	665

age, α in equation (2) (in dimensions of reciprocal time), is an awkward unit, the rate of mortality will also be represented by the *doubling time*, $T_d = 0.693/\alpha$, i.e., the time required for the death rate to increase by a factor of two. This time is constant, independent of age and death rate, for a population that obeys the Gompertz equation. The other parameter, G_o, is called the *vulnerability* parameter, for it measures the initial vulnerability to disease, before the onset of aging. It is, therefore, related to the genetically determined vigor of the genotype.

The expectation of life depends on both parameters and, for a Gompertz population, the relation of life expectancy from age zero, E_o, to α and q_o is, to a satisfactory approximation (Sacher, 1960)

$$E_o = -\alpha^{-1} \ln(1.76 q_o \alpha^{-1}) \qquad (4)$$

The wide range of life expectancies among mammals (Table 1B) is due to both the vulnerability and rate-of-aging parameters. Figure 2 shows that the 30-fold increase in life expectancy from mouse to man is accompanied by a 15-fold increase in doubling time of mortality rate, and an almost 500-fold decrease in q_o (Sacher in preparation).

If increased life expectancy is produced by a decrease of q_o and α in *constant* ratio, then, from Eq. 4, E_o is proportionate to α^{-1}, and the

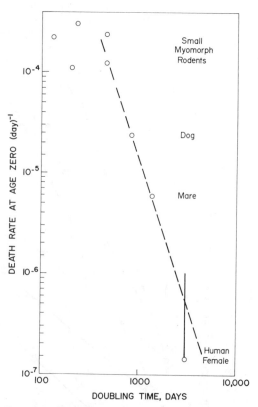

Figure 2. Relation of the slope, α, to the intercept, q_o, of the Gompertz equation for several rodent species, dog, horse, and man. Data from Table 1. The slope of the linear relationship in double logarithmic coordinates indicates that q_o varies as a highly accelerated function of α (Original results of G. A. Sacher.)

life tables are similar in form, i.e., one can be transformed into another by a change of time scale. However, it can be seen in Figure 2 that q_o decreases *more rapidly* than α so $q_o\alpha^{-1}$ decreases, and hence, E_o increases more rapidly than α^{-1}. The increased life expectation leads to a "rectangularization" or an increase in the width of the shoulder of the survivorship curve. The tendency toward rectangularization of the survivorship curve is a result of two other trends in the evolution of large body and brain size: reduction in litter size, and lengthened period of dependence.

The Sacher-Trucco theory is, in a strict sense, a phenomenological theory of mortality which seeks to establish a quantitative functional relationship between the vital physiological state of the organism in a given time interval and its probability of dying in that and subsequent intervals. It does not introduce any assumption as to aging, but rather, allows one to infer that if the physical aging process has a particular time course, then, because of the nature of the conditional stability of living organisms, the mortality curve must have a certain shape. Conversely, if the shape of the mortality curve is known, then the time course of the aging injury curve can be inferred.

Theories of aging have as their goal the demonstration of a particular mechanism as being responsible both for the aging process and for the shape of the mortality curve. Such theories would be of no use for our present purpose, because in considering aging and mortality as a single process, it becomes impossible to discuss life table modification without unwarranted assumptions about the nature of aging. Some theories are also disqualified because they postulate various kinds of unobservable events as the cause of aging.

Effect of Cellular Injury on the Parameters of the Survival Characteristic: Radiation Life Shortening

More is known about the effects of ionizing radiations on the survival characteristics of experimental animals than about any other physicochemical agent. The present section is concerned with the analysis of life shortening induced in experimental populations and in

man by comparatively high radiation doses and dose rates. Another kind of effect on survival, which is observed only at low doses, is discussed separately.

When experimental animal populations are given single doses of ionizing radiation, an acute injury process is initiated that runs its course within 30 days in most species (Casarett, 1968). A typical mouse strain exposed to ^{60}Co gamma rays has a sigmoid dosage-survival curve with a LD50/30 (the dose for 50 percent killed in 30 days) of 600 to 1000 Roentgens (R). The survivors of sublethal or fractionally lethal dosages show age-dependent mortality earlier than unirradiated controls, and the displacement of mortality toward earlier ages increases with dose.

The survivorship curves from a typical study of life shortening produced by single doses of gamma rays in young mice are given in Figure 3 (Furth, Upton, Christenberry, Benedict, and Moshman, 1954). They show a displacement of the mortality process to earlier ages, almost as if each radiation dose had subtracted a certain number of days from the after-survival of each member of the irradiated population. This

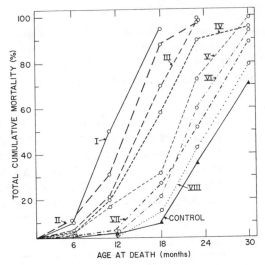

Figure 3. Cumulative mortality for samples of female LAF_1 mice exposed to the radiations from a nuclear detonation (operation Greenhouse). (From Furth, J., Upton, A. C., Christenberry, K. W., Benedict, W. H., and Moshman, J. 1954. Some late effects in mice of ionizing radiation from an experimental nuclear detonation. *Radiology*, **63**, 562–570.)

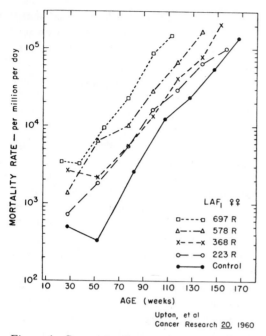

LAF₁ ♀♀

□----□	697 R
△-·-△	578 R
×- - -×	368 R
○—○	223 R
●—●	Control

Upton, et al
Cancer Research 20, 1960

Figure 4. Gompertz diagram for mice exposed to the radiations from a nuclear detonation (operation Greenhouse). Adjacent dose levels pooled for the analysis. (From Upton, A. C., Kimball, A. W., Furth, J., Christenberry, K. W., and Benedict, W. H. 1960. Some delayed effects of atom-bomb radiations in mice. *Cancer Research,* **20** (8, part II), 1–60.)

hypothesis is suggested more forcibly in Figure 4, in which the age-specific death rate curves for the several doses are plotted on a log scale versus age, i.e., as a Gompertz plot (Sacher, 1956; Upton, Kastenbaum, and Conklin, 1963). By the chi-square test they appear to form a family of straight lines, parallel to each other and to the control line (Sacher, 1956; 1976a).

The relation between irreparable injury and dose for single radiation doses can be calculated as the mean upward displacement of the Gompertz function intercept per unit dose. Estimates for mouse, rat, guinea pig, and dog in Table 2 (Sacher, 1966) show that these species experience equal upward displacement of the Gompertz intercept per Roentgen of dose. The apparent invariance of effect among species is evidence for the theory that the Gompertz function is an approximately linear measure of the tissue injury underlying the actuarial aging process. This demonstration is important because, unless we know that a given change in the physicochemical state of the tissues has a predictable relationship to a change in the rate of mortality, we have no basis for a rational analysis of the effects of anti-aging drugs on the life table.

When the effects of ionizing radiation on Gompertz functions are represented by a family of straight lines, as in Figure 4, they can, with equal consistency, be interpreted as arising from either, (a) adding an increment of age to the chronological age of each treated population, i.e., displacing the curves to the left, or (b) adding an increment of permanent injury to the accumulating aging injury represented by the control line, i.e., displacing the Gompertz line

TABLE 2. DISPLACEMENT OF THE INTERCEPT, G_0, OF THE GOMPERTZ FUNCTION BY SINGLE DOSES OF IONIZING RADIATIONS, FOR MOUSE, RAT, GUINEA PIG, AND DOG. EXPRESSED AS THE DISPLACEMENT PER UNIT DOSE, $\Delta G/D$. NOTE THAT $\Delta G/D$ IS NEARLY CONSTANT DESPITE AN EIGHTFOLD VARIATION IN GOMPERTZ SLOPE (COLUMN 5) AND COMPARABLE VARIATION OF LIFE EXPECTANCY. FROM SACHER (1966).

Species, reference	Sex	Radiation quality	$\Delta G/D$ R^{-1}	Gompertz slope $(day)^{-1}$
Mouse (1)	Female	x and γ rays	0.00299	0.00675
Mouse (1)	Male	x and γ rays	0.00172	0.00675
Rat (2)	Male & female	x ray	0.00324	0.00606
Guinea Pig (3)	Male & female	x ray	0.00357	0.00162
Dog (4)	Female	x ray	0.00380	0.00085

(1) Sacher 1956; (2) Boche 1954; (3) Kimeldorf, Phillips and Jones 1966; Rust, *et al.* 1966; (4) Andersen and Rosenblatt 1969, and unpublished data from Argonne National Laboratory.

upward. The first model assumes implicitly that the irradiation does not initiate new cases of disease, but instead promotes the development of pre-existing diseases, and thereby decreases the time to death. This hypothesis has particular bearing on the induction of cancer by carcinogens.

The second model implies that the radiation exposure leaves a residue of virtually permanent molecular and cellular injury, which, by depressing cell and tissue functions to a level equivalent to that which would occur at a later age in the course of natural aging, increases the vulnerability to disease to that level characteristic of the later age.

It is not easy to decide between these two independent modes of disease induction because of the difficulty of establishing the nature of the proximate radiation lesion, and the nature of the initiation and promotion processes in carcinogenesis and systemic disease. The "added injury" model (model *b*) is the more plausible explanation for the increased mortality from infectious diseases and systemic degenerative diseases, because the existence of residual physiological and biochemical injury in irradiated animals and man is readily demonstrable.

If exposure to ionizing radiations occurs daily for the duration of life starting at young adult age, the survival curves get progressively steeper, in contrast to the pattern for single doses. The Gompertz plots form a divergent fan of lines (Figure 5) (Grahn, 1960) instead of a family of parallel lines. These changes are consistent with the theoretical view developed above, for if each separate dose produces a parallel displacement of the Gompertz function, then the summation of the effects of the daily doses should be a line with a slope related to the size of the daily dose (Sacher, 1956).

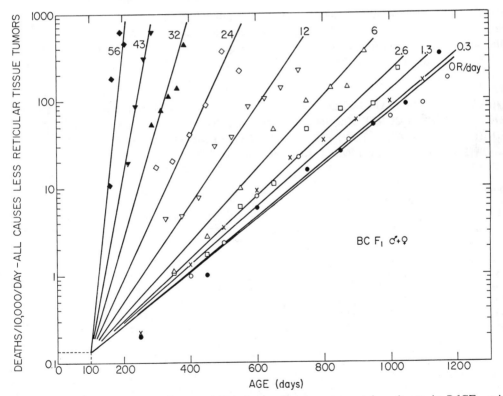

Figure 5. Gompertz diagrams for mortality from all causes except lymphoma in B6CF$_1$ mice exposed to ^{60}Co gamma rays for the duration of life, beginning at age 100 days. The straight lines are fitted by least squares, subject to the constraint that all lines have a common origin. (From Grahn, D. 1970. Biological effects of protracted low dose radiation exposure to man and animals. *In*, R. J. M. Fry, D. Grahn, M. L. Griem, and J. H. Rust (eds.), *Late Effects of Radiation*, pp. 101–136. London: Taylor & Francis.)

An unexplained feature of radiation life shortening is that the amount of shortening produced per Roentgen decreases as the age at exposure increases (Jones and Kimeldorf, 1964; Yuhas, 1971; Sacher, unpublished observations), and mouse populations irradiated at advanced ages sometimes have lower mortality rates, and longer life expectancies, than their controls. The implications of this finding in the theory of the aging process and mortality are not clear, but suppression of cancer development may be a factor. Rebound of proliferative tissues in the late phase of recovery from radiation injury, which is a prominent feature of the radiation syndrome, may have more functional significance for old animals than for young ones.

Mortality and Morbidity from Specific Diseases

Many independent studies of late effects of single doses of radiation show that almost all diseases occur earlier in irradiated populations, and in about the same degree (Table 3) (Upton,

Kastenbaum, and Conklin, 1963; Lindop and Rotblat, 1961). The leukemias are elicited to a greater degree by radiations than are other diseases. Under some conditions, 70 to 80 percent of irradiated populations of some mouse strains die from lymphoid leukemia (Upton, 1960). Radiation-induced leukemia in mouse (Brues and Sacher, 1952) and man (Jablon, Ishida, and Yamasaki, 1965), is distinguished by a wave of incidence that occurs earlier than any other major neoplastic or degenerative disease, and subsides well before the end of the lifespan, whereas other radiation-induced diseases continue to appear. In the mouse, this wave begins within 2 months after exposure and ends after about 1 year, while in man, another type of leukemia, myeloid leukemia, increases 1 or 2 years after exposure and subsides in about 15 years.

Mortality rate data by themselves are insufficient to completely characterize the life table modification produced by a specific treatment. Data are also needed regarding the course of the disease in the living population, and the effect of life-prolongation therapy on the mean time

TABLE 3. PERCENTAGE INCIDENCE OF VARIOUS DISEASES IN IRRADIATED SAS-4 MICE AND THEIR CONTROLS, IN RELATION TO SIZE OF x-RAY DOSE GIVEN AT FOUR WEEKS OF AGE. INCIDENCE CORRECTED FOR MORTALITY FROM COMPETING CAUSES. FROM LINDOP AND ROTBLAT (1961).

Dose (R)	NEOPLASTIC DISEASES					NON-NEOPLASTIC DISEASES				
	Leukemia	Pulmonary tumors	Liver tumors	Ovarian tumors	Other tumors	Pulmonary	Renal	Liver	Intestinal	n.a.d.*
Males										
0	6.5	16.0	10.2		8.3	10.7	17.6	10.2	5.0	15.5
50	11.7	17.3	14.4		7.6	11.8	10.1	4.6	7.2	15.3
98	12.0	16.2	9.7		8.6	12.3	13.0	6.5	7.6	14.1
198	11.1	17.8	12.4		7.8	8.6	14.0	8.7	5.9	13.7
350	13.8	17.9	11.9		12.5	8.0	11.9	6.6	5.0	12.4
457	12.8	13.5	14.4		8.2	11.6	10.2	5.3	5.9	18.1
Females										
0	16.4	13.6	1.8	12.4	9.7	10.1	7.6	7.4	4.6	16.4
50	17.9	14.7	1.2	15.0	5.1	6.9	8.8	12.1	3.7	14.6
98	14.4	14.8	2.4	20.4	8.3	6.8	7.0	7.1	3.8	15.0
198	17.5	11.6	2.3	19.9	8.6	5.3	5.9	10.1	3.2	15.6
350	17.8	13.4	6.2	12.4	10.7	9.9	2.8	9.7	2.9	14.2
457	19.2	11.2	5.3	13.9	8.2	10.1	4.9	5.3	3.1	18.8

*n.a.d. = no diagnosis.

required for progress from the earliest recognizable stage of the disease to its terminal form. Such information is obtained by *morbidity studies*, in which defined living populations are sampled to obtain information about the prevalence of specified diseases and their rates of development. This is accomplished in human populations by epidemiological studies, and in animal populations by protocols, in which adequate samples of animals are sacrificed at a series of equal age intervals, and thoroughly examined for diseases. At least two studies of disease morbidity in mouse populations are under way, in conjunction with research programs on late radiation effects.

The *prevalence* of a disease is the probability that the disease will be observed in living members of a defined age class. If certain restrictions are satisfied (i.e., prevalence and death rate not too high, low probability of death from competing diseases) then T_x, the mean duration of the disease at age x, given a prevalence probability P_x and age-specific mortality rate from the disease, q_x, is

$$T_x = P_x/q_x \qquad (5)$$

The prevalence of tumors of the reticular tissue of mice was estimated for a number of ages throughout adult life (Fry, Sacher, Tyler, Ainsworth, Allen, and Staffeldt, 1975) and increased with age in parallel with the mortality rate (Figure 6, Fry, *et al.*, 1975). This implies a relatively constant *residence time* of the disease throughout life. The mean residence time for murine reticular tissue tumors was estimated to be less than 200 days. This may be the typical pattern for steadily progressing fatal diseases, but it is not an adequate model for chronic diseases with low fatality. When disease residence times can be determined for treated populations and their controls, it will be possible to distinguish between the effects of treatment on the initiation of diseases and on their duration.

Decreased Longevity in Fruit Flies with Reduced Environmental Radiation Exposure

Planel and his associates at the University of Toulouse have evaluated the results of maintaining fruit flies in environments in which the

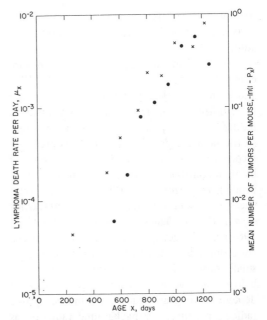

Figure 6. The age-specific mortality rate (circles) and prevalence (crosses) for reticular tissue tumors (thymic lymphomas) of B6CF$_1$ mice, both on a logarithmic scale *versus* age. The parallelism of the two curves indicates a constant residence time, which is on the order of 200 days. (From Fry *et al.*, 1975.)

levels of ionizing radiations are lower than those that prevail in the natural terrestrial environment. Two populations of *D. melanogaster* were compared. The control group experienced the normal ambient radiation exposure, while the experimental group, from egg to death, experienced 10 percent of the natural gamma ray background irradiation. The outcome (five trials for each sex, involving a total of 10,000 flies) was a decrease of average survival time from 9.73 weeks for controls to 9.01 weeks in the shielded group, a difference of 7.4 percent (Planel and Giess, 1973). The decreased survival time was observed only in populations that were kept radiation-deficient throughout adult life; the radiation level during development was irrelevant. Their curves for the radiation-deficient populations seem to be parallel to the control curves, but it is not known whether the hypothesis of a 7 percent increase in steepness of the curves for the radiation-deficient groups can be rejected. If the appearance of parallelism were to be borne out by experimentation, it would mean that the deprivation of a part of natural radiation exposure throughout adult life adds a constant risk factor in the mortality at adult ages.

About half the natural background exposure comes from the body burden of ^{14}C, ^{3}H, ^{40}K, and from the alpha and beta emitters of the radium decay sequence. No effort was made to reduce these components of the radiation dose, so the radiation-deficient populations probably received about half the radiation dose received by their controls. Possibly, the depression of reproductive performance (Planel, Soleilhavoup, Giess, and Tixador, 1967a), development (Planel, et al., 1967b; Planel, Soleilhavoup and Geiss 1969) and longevity in the radiation-deprived condition are related to the hormetic effects of small doses of ionizing radiation discussed below. On the other hand, organisms might depend on the statistically uniform level of free radicals produced by background radiation as primers for certain metabolic reactions. This hypothesis is not highly plausible, because metabolizing tissues produce hydrogen peroxide (Aebi, 1963) and superoxide (Fridovich, 1972). In rat organs, the rate of metabolic production of hydrogen peroxide is 1 to 10 μM/g of tissue per hour, greater by a factor of 10^{10} than the rate of peroxide production by background radiation.

Relation Between the Molecular Lesions of Ionizing Radiation and Aging

When the effects of ionizing radiations on the life table first became known, it was often concluded that radiations "accelerate" the aging process; hence, radiation was seriously considered as a tool for research into the mechanisms of aging. That opinion is no longer widely held because several lines of evidence indicate that the primary lesions of aging and radiation are not identical.

Radiation damage that shortens life characteristically causes permanently increased mortality rates, and hence is presumably inaccessible to repair. The amount of this irreparable damage produced per Roentgen depends on the dose and the time-pattern of administration, usually decreasing as the exposure time increases (Sacher, 1956, 1976a). This indicates that the irreparable injury is not fixed immediately at the time that the radiation is absorbed, but arises subsequently from a transient precursor. It can be estimated that this precursor state has a mean lifetime of a few days in mice, and that the production of irreparable injury in the cell depends on an interaction with a second independent injury event produced within that time interval. The inference that two events are involved is based on the fact that the yield of irreparable injury increases as a quadratic function of dose (Sacher, 1956, 1973). This implies that the life-shortening action of ionizing radiations is due primarily to the production of chromosome breaks leading to deleterious rearrangements (Sacher 1956, 1976a). This hypothesis is *prima facie* plausible because the dose dependence for the production of chromosome breaks by ionizing radiations, and for the cell sterilization or death caused by asymmetric chromosomal rearrangements (e.g., dicentrics, acentrics, and rings) are quantitatively consistent with the hypothesis. Other hypotheses are also espoused, however, and there is at this time no consensus about the nature of the molecular lesion leading to late systemic radiation damage.

The yield per Roentgen of visible specific-locus gene mutations in somatic cells decreases as exposure time increases (Russell, 1968). This suggests that gene mutation by ionizing radiation, previously thought to be an irreversible one-step event, is a more complex phenomenon involving a transitory precursor phase, and raises the possibility that the spontaneous gene mutations of the natural aging process are also multistage processes.

Curtis (Curtis, 1963; Crowley and Curtis, 1963; Curtis and Crowley, 1963) proposed a somatic mutation theory of aging that identified mutations in somatic cells as the basic aging lesion. The term "mutation" is extremely broad, for it can include any kind of change of the genetic material that leads to heritable genetic change. It is not entirely clear what Curtis meant the term to include; in testing the hypothesis he used abnormal mitotic figures as a measure of mutation frequency, which indicates that he considered chromosome abberations to be a primary lesion of aging as well as radiation life shortening. This specific form of the somatic mutation hypothesis is not well substantiated, for Curtis' data on chromosome abberations induced by x rays and fast neutrons show that radiation doses that produce large increases in frequency of aberrations in liver cells do not commensurately shorten life span (Curtis, Tilley, and Crowley, 1964; Stevenson and Curtis, 1961).

Clark and Rubin (1961) used haploid and diploid males and females of the wasp *Habrobracon* to test the somatic mutation hypothesis. Haploid and diploid males had essentially the same lifespan as diploid females. Diploid males and diploid females given 10,000 to 50,000 R showed almost equal life shortening; but haploid males had a considerably shorter life span than diploid males. The degree of differential sensitivity between haploids and diploids depended on the developmental stage at which radiation exposure was given. Clark and Rubin concluded that their results disprove the hypothesis that somatic mutations are the cause of aging. However, their conclusion is not justified in view of recent evidence that species longevity is correlated with the level of an endonuclease for DNA repair (Hart and Setlow, 1974). Hence, it is possible that haploid longevity is assured by higher levels of repair enzymes. However, the results on wasps definitely disprove the hypothesis that the radiation lesion is the same as the aging lesion. If radiation life shortening in wasps is caused primarily by chromosome abberations, then natural aging is not.

To recapitulate, exposure to ionizing radiations produces a kind of primary injury that remains permanently imbedded in the molecular constitution of the organism. This fact made it possible to find the mathematical transformation that makes radiation injury additive with itself and with the injury of natural aging, and this led, in turn, to the development of the theory of the probabilistic relationship between the level of cellular-molecular injury in a population and its expected death rate. These conclusions are quite general and can be carried over to the analysis of life prolongation by anti-aging therapies. However, present evidence indicates that aging is not due to the same molecular lesion as radiation life shortening. Thus, the efficacy of a drug as a protective agent against radiation life shortening is not necessarily related to its efficacy in life prolongation.

The Role of Compensatory and Adaptive Systemic Responses: Paradoxical Stimulation and the Concept of Hormesis

A life-prolongation treatment can be considered to be potentially efficacious if it prolongs life, but such a demonstration is not by itself sufficient evidence. It is still necessary to show that the life-prolongation is achieved by what we can call a *proper action*; that is, a reduction of the accumulation of an aging lesion by a specific chemical mechanism or a direct protection against age-dependent disease or deterioration.

The importance of requiring evidence that life prolongation results from a proper action arises from the fact that paradoxical stimulation effects are evoked by a variety of organic and inorganic substances (Luckey, 1963, 1968, 1974; Townsend and Luckey, 1960). Characteristically, stimulatory effects are produced by an agent in low doses, and are qualitatively different from the effect produced over a wide range of higher dosages. The hypothesis that these are instances of a general pharmacological law was first formulated by Arndt and Schulz (Schulz, 1888). More recently, Luckey introduced the term *hormoligosis* to describe the class of phenomena in which "small" quantities of a depressive or toxic agent are stimulatory. This occurrence of a stimulatory effect is called *hormesis* or hormetic action.

The problem in aging is to distinguish between a life-prolongation effect that arises from the proper action of a drug and one that arises from a hormetic action. It can be argued that the life prolongation is the important consideration, regardless of whether it is achieved by a proper or a hormetic action. This argument fails on several counts, of which the most important is that hormetic response is primarily a function of the *state* of the organism, rather than of the stimulus. Also, although hormetic stimulation may enable the animal to approach its potential longevity, so far as is known it does not increase that potential. Hence, hormetic effects are unlikely to occur in the healthy active individual, and are more likely to be significant in the ill or depressed individual. Although these characteristics of individual organisms determine the response, the hormetic effect is operationally defined only by the statistical differences between populations. This is a source of serious difficulty in studying hormetic phenomena.

A hormetic effect that has been extensively studied is stimulation of growth in domestic animals by antibiotics. Luckey (1956, 1958) found that low doses of terramycin and penicillin increase growth in conventionally reared turkey poults, and also in poults reared germ-free. He reviews evidence that penicillin stimulates growth in germ-free chicks, and that inactivated penicillin retains its growth-stimulation potency. These findings support the hypothesis of a hormetic action of these antibiotics, distinct from their proper antibiotic actions.

The insecticides are another heterogeneous group of toxic compounds that are alike in having hormetic effects on growth. Luckey (1968) examined the effects of small doses of 14 pesticides on the growth of house crickets, *Acheta domesticus*. Twelve of these preparations showed growth stimulation over a range of concentrations centered at about 1 percent of the lethal dose for each. Laws (1971) reports an inhibition of tumor incidence by DDT, and Ottoboni (1972) observed an increase of reproductive lifespan in female rats that were fed low doses of DDT.

The stimulatory effects of minor environmental perturbations on the neuroendocrine maturation of infant rats have been extensively investigated (Levine, Alpert, and Lewis, 1958). These effects may have features in common with the stimulatory effects of environment "enrichment" during development on the growth of the cerebral cortex of laboratory rats (Diamond, Rosenzweig, Bennett, Lindner, and Lyon, 1972). Environmental enrichment, even late in adult life, has a beneficial effect on learning rates of rats (Doty, 1966). These latter effects are especially interesting because they are the consequences of environmental changes that increase the sensory information inputs to the subjects, but are not stressful.

Hormetic Effects on the Longevity of Rodents and Insects

Hormetic effects on mortality rates and longevity are not as well known, except in response to low levels of ionizing radiations. The paucity of scientific information concerning the adaptive value of external stimulation has fostered the view that "stress" is generally deleterious to health and survival. Gerobiology has a vital stake in the development of a less distorted perspective on this matter.

Improved survival has been observed in mice and rats subjected to comparatively severe (but not injurious) physiological and sensory stresses. In one experiment, inbred mice were subjected to daily electric shock, intermittent exposure to a cool (60°F) environment, or a combination of these treatments throughout adult life. The stressed groups, all treatments and both sexes combined, lived 39 days longer than the controls, a non-significant increase (Ordy, Samorajski, Zeman, and Curtis, 1967). In this same experiment, brains were irradiated with 500 rads of deuterons. In the comparison of stressed and unstressed mice without brain irradiation, mortality rates of stressed groups were slightly lower than for unstressed, and in two of six contrasts (three stress conditions for each sex) the decrease was significant. In the brain-irradiated groups, mortality rates of stressed irradiated were lower than the like-sex control in five of six contrasts, and three of these were significant. The pattern of mortality rates in these groups was in perfect rank order agreement with the pattern of life expectations in the independent survival time experiments.

Reincke, Stutz, and Hunstein (1970) examined the effect of three acute non-lethal stresses—starvation for 9 days, water deprivation for six days, or forced swimming for 11–13 minutes—on the longevity and tumor incidence of groups of rats that were also given acute exposure to 280 R of x-rays. These groups were compared with groups that received 280 R only, and to untreated controls. Both sexes of the stressed, irradiated groups showed the same increase of incidence of malignant tumors as the unstressed irradiated group. Survival curves and age-specific mortality rate curves showed that all three groups of stressed irradiated males lived longer than the unstressed irradiated males. In females, two of the three irradiated stress conditions had increased survival over the unstressed irradiated group by almost the same amount as the males, but they did not equal the control female survival, which was about three months longer than the male control survival.

The results of Ordy, *et al.* and Reincke, Stutz, and Hunstein are consistent on comparable points and indicate that moderate physiological stress can lead to decreased mortality rate and increased survival time in intact mice, and, to an equal or greater degree, in mice or rats exposed to ionizing radiations. Since the physiologically stressed, irradiated rats had the same increase of radiation-induced malignant neoplasms as the unstressed irradiated, the improved survival of the stressed must be due primarily to physiological factors such as increased vigor and decreased vulnerability to non-neoplastic disease.

The life-shortening and carcinogenic effects of comparatively large doses of ionizing radiations can be accounted for in terms of the cellular and molecular mechanisms of radiation injury. However, when the doses are in a range such that the life shortening expected (by extrapolation from higher doses) is a small fraction of the normal survival time, the observed life shortening sometimes is significantly less than the expectation, and occasionally, there is a paradoxical increase of life expectation above the control value.

Lorenz, *et al.* (1954) exposed groups of LAF_1 mice to radium gamma rays for 8 hr per day, beginning at young adult age and continuing until all were dead. The levels of daily dose given were 8.8, 4.4, 2.2, 1.1, and 0.11 R/day.

The control group had a different pattern of mortaility than any of the irradiated groups, characterized by relatively higher mortality at early ages and a shallower survival curve. In the Gompertz plot of the age-specific mortality rates for the six groups (Figure 7), the heterogeneity between the mortality of the control and the 5 irradiated groups has the form of a displacement of the Gompertz function intercepts of all irradiated groups to a common point below the control intercept, as if irradiation had effected a net decrease of vulnerability. Superimposed on this is the accumulated radiation life shortening effect, expressed in a linear increase of Gompertz function slope with daily dose. These findings were confirmed in a later study (Lorenz, Hollcroft, Miller, Congdon, and Schweisthal, 1955).

Carlson gave gamma irradiation to rats for 12

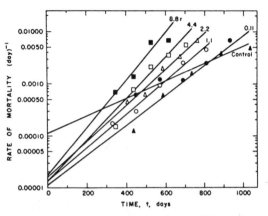

Figure 7. Gompertz plots for LAF_1 mice given low-level exposure to radium gamma rays for the duration of life. Straight lines fitted to the data by weighted least squares. Note that the q_o values for exposed groups lie below the value. (From Sacher, G. A. 1956. On the statistical nature of mortality with especial reference to chronic radiation mortality. *Radiology, 67,* 250-257.)

months at daily doses ranging from 0.3 to 4.0 R/day. Increase of median and maximum survival time above control values was observed in the exposed groups over this entire dose range, with a significant peak increase of 30 percent at 2.5 R/day (Carlson, Scheyer, and Jackson, 1957; Carlson and Jackson, 1959). However, the median survival time of 650 days at 2.5 R/day is no greater than what is expected for a control rat population in a current laboratory environment. Hence, the exposed group did not experience real life prolongation, but rather a nullification of some of the life-shortening effects of a deleterious environment. This is characteristic of the paradoxical life prolongation produced by ionizing radiations. Tryon (1971) found increased survival of irradiated chipmunks in the wild.

When chronic irradiation experiments are done with high standards of animal maintenance, hormetic effects diminish in magnitude but do not disappear entirely. Grahn (1970) observed both sexes of three inbred mouse strains and one F_1 hybrid during daily gamma irradiation at doses ranging from 0.3 to 56 R/day. Figure 8 shows that there are no paradoxical reversals in the relation of survival time to daily dose in any of the 8 groups, but except for the F_1 hybrid, which had the longest control survival, there is a tendency for a

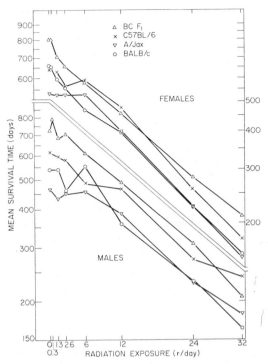

Figure 8. Relation of mean after survival time (MAS) of four mouse genotypes to daily dose. MAS on a logarithmic scale. Note existence of a plateau at low daily doses for the animals with shorter control survival, and its absence for the BCF_1 mice. (From Grahn, D. 1970. Biological effects of protracted low dose radiation exposure of man and animals. *In*, R. J. M. Fry, D. Grahn, M. L. Griem, and J. H. Rust (eds.), *Late Effects of Radiation*, pp. 101–136. London: Taylor & Francis.)

shoulder to appear at dose levels of 6 R/day and below. This shoulder region is broader and flatter for males and for the genotypes with the shorter control survival times.

In another experiment, Sacher and Grahn (1964) gave LAF_1 mice 0 or 6 R/day under the same conditions as above, and again found less decrease of survival time at 6 R/day than expected. There is a significantly lower variability of survival times in the 6 R/day group than in controls, which is due to a decreased incidence of early deaths in the 6 R/day group as compared to the controls. This characteristic is also observable in the experiments of Lorenz, *et al.* (1954) and Grahn (1970). The shoulder on the dose-effect curve, and the decreased variance of survival time, are not explained by

the proper actions of ionizing radiations and must be considered hormetic effects.

In the mouse experiments that yielded either paradoxical oversurvival or less than the expected life shortening, the tumor incidence in all irradiated groups decreased with dose in the expected manner, so there is no hormetic effect on tumor induction. The Gompertz function slopes for mortality from all causes also show the expected dependence on dose down to the lowest level (Figure 5; Sacher, 1973). These characteristics, together with those discussed above, lead to the conclusion that hormetic longevity effects generally have the form of a non-cumulative decrease of vulnerability that does not modify the aging process or the accumulation of irreparable radiation injury.

Paradoxically increased survival time has been observed for a number of insect species of several orders after single exposures to x or gamma rays (review by Ducoff, 1972). Ducoff (1975) describes life prolongation in the flour beetle, *Tribolium*, and discusses some possible mechanisms. *Drosophila* given x-ray treatment periodically for the duration of life (Sacher, 1963) showed the same pattern of improved mean survival time accompanied by decreased standard deviation and decreased variation between replicate samples as described above for irradiated mice.

The Nature and Biological Role of Hormesis

It is not possible in this survey to discuss the theory of hormesis in depth, but at least the outline of a phenomenological theory must be indicated.

There is an inclination to explain these phenomena by postulating stress response or enzyme induction. These are not satisfactory explanations, since many adaptations or learned responses of the organism ultimately involve either increase or *de novo* initiation of enzyme synthesis. Similarly, if all environmental changes are defined as stresses, and all adaptations to the environment are called stress responses, the terms lose all value as scientific explanations. At present, a desired scientific explanation of hormesis is one that will help us to understand it as a property of the operating characteristic of organisms, and to establish its relation to other categories of adaptive behavior.

A deleterious environmental agent is related to the organism in two fundamentally different ways. First, it causes specific molecular changes in the organism, such as denaturation or inhibition of enzymes, alteration of the structure of DNA, destabilization of membranes, etc. These changes bring about the injury or pharmacological action that is the proper action of the agent. Second, the organism detects the effects of the agent systemically by monitoring vital physiological parameters. The critical feature of physiological signaling is that the signals decrease in magnitude as the displacement of the system from its normal state diminishes. In textbook discussions of homeostatic mechanisms from the standpoint of control theory (Yamamoto and Brobeck, 1965), the analysis is carried out deterministically, as if all the signals and responses of the organism are exact and free from error. This assumption is adequate for analysis of large disturbances, but it is not so for the analysis of regulation in the normal range or for small departures from it. In that domain, signal levels are so low that the uncertainty in the organism's information about its actual state may be relatively high, and hence the precision of the adaptive response is correspondingly low. However, if the organism is perturbed by a major environmental disturbance, signal levels and signal:noise ratios rise and the precision of response is increased.

A theory of the increased survival produced by ionizing radiations and other noxious agents (Sacher and Trucco, 1962a) was based on the limiting informational effect on precision of physiological performance, as discussed above, and on a statistical theory of mortality (Sacher and Trucco, 1962b). The latter demonstrates that the rate of failure of physiological performance, including death, rises exponentially with the magnitude of the fluctuations of performance. They inferred that a decrease in the magnitude of fluctuations brought about by the signals from a physiological disturbance can result in a decrease of mortality rates over a range of low injury levels that more than compensates for the increased mortality expected from the direct toxic action of the agent.

The occurrence of hormetic action should be considered in all cases of experimental life prolongation, even where there is prior justification for the hypothesis that the agent has efficacy for life prolongation. In particular, the question of mode of action should be kept open if prolongation is only demonstrable relative to a control group with survival considerably shorter than the best recorded for the strain or species. Kohn (1971) made this point about the results of his experimental test of an antioxidant treatment. In a series of replicate trials, he obtained prolongation only in those trials in which the controls were short-lived. His data support the Sacher-Trucco theory, for an alternative description of Kohn's data is that the variance of responses among the replicate groups is smaller than the among-group variance of the controls, i.e., the same phenomenon that is observed in replicate groups of chronically irradiated mice.

Hormesis is in one sense an obstacle in the path of gerobiological research, and efforts to understand and annul it would be well justified. A first step is to breed vigorous animal genotypes and a second step is to develop living environments that are optimal for their behavioral, physiological, and immunological health. This may require the restoration of some of the periodic and aperiodic stimulations that have been systematically excluded from our "controlled laboratory environment". An important objective criterion of success is the production of rectangular survival curves that can be replicated with little variation.

In another sense, hormesis may be an important key to the understanding of the conditional stability of organisms, and of the ways in which that stability is contingent upon certain properties of the environment and on a dynamic organism-environment relationship.

ENVIRONMENTAL AND GENETIC DETERMINATION OF THE SURVIVAL CHARACTERISTIC

Life Tables in the Wild and in Captivity

The rodent species that were found by Sacher and Staffeldt (1972) to have Gompertzian survival characteristics (Table 1B) are only a few generations removed from the wild. In their native environments, these species have survival characteristics approaching the exponential form and life expectancies of a few hundred days at most (Snyder, 1956).

The environmental factors of parasitism, predation, and privation that cause high mortality in the wild do not appear to act cumulatively or to modify the aging process, for animals removed from the wild to good captive environments live about as long as animals born in captivity.

The argument that "aging does not occur in the wild" is controverted by the results of many population studies on the survival of species ranging from fishes to elephants (Beverton and Holt, 1959; Laws and Parker, 1968; Deevey, 1947; Bourlière, 1957, 1959; Spinage, 1972). Within the limits of the data, the aging rates in the wild are about as expected from experience with captive populations.

The transition from the survival characteristic of the wild to that of captivity is shown in Figure 9A and B. This is scaled approximately for a mouse-like rodent, and Figure 9B shows how the survival curve shifts from exponential to rectangular form as the environmentally imposed age-independent mortality (Figure 9A) progressively decreases, until the full extent of the underlying Gompertzian survival characteristic is revealed. The more general survival characteristic needed to represent the transitional curves is the Gompertz-Makeham equation,

$$q_x = q_o e^{\alpha x} + \beta \qquad (6)$$

The L_x and q_x curves in Figure 9 were computed using fixed values of q_o and α and a range of values of the Makeham term, β. The Gompertz-Makeham equation is useful for fitting data from populations of zoo animals, domestic animals, or household pets, where the accidental mortality, though high, is low enough to allow the terminal senescent mortality to appear (Comfort, 1957, 1960).

Although the accidental mortality in the wild is different in kind from the mortality due to senescence, they are related, for the life expectancies of mammals in the wild and in captivity are in ratios ranging from less than 1:2 for some large species to about 1:4 for some small rodents. These ratios are consistent with the basic iteroparous reproductive pattern of mammals (Cole, 1954), and with the systematic decrease

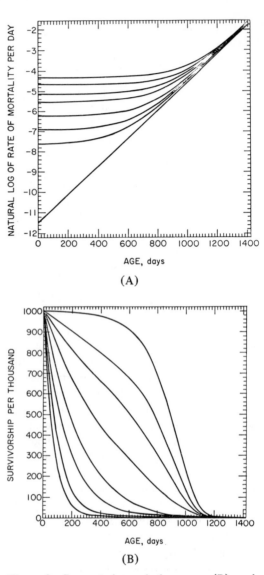

(A)

(B)

Figure 9. Computed survival curves (B) and rate of mortality curves (A) to illustrate how a change in the age-independent mortality—the Makeham term, Eq. 6—affects the shape of the mortality functions. The exponential shape is seen in wild populations, the intermediate diagonal forms in life curves from zoo and domestic animal populations, and the rectangular forms in good laboratory conditions. (Unpublished work by G. A. Sacher.)

of reproductive rate as body and brain size increase (Sacher and Staffeldt, 1974). In short, the Gompertzian parameters of each species are aspects of the reproductive fitness of the species, and as such are the genetically determined consequences of natural selection.

Genetic Determination of the Survival Characteristic

The present section will examine whether inherited differences in longevity are due to variation in the vulnerability parameter, the rate-of-aging parameter, or both. Very few investigations have examined this question explicitly, and the available evidence is not definitive.

The first quantitative estimate of the heritability of longevity among inbred strains of laboratory mice was made by Storer (1966), based on samples of males and females of 22 inbred strains maintained at Jackson Laboratory. Festing and Blackmore (1971) did a similar study. Both studies agree that the heritability, i.e., the fraction of the total longevity variance that is genetically determined, ranges from 20 to 30 percent and is somewhat higher for females than for males.

These calculations assume implicitly that every mouse of a given genotype has the same genetically determined lifespan, so that all would live equally long in a hypothetical constant environment. Hence, all variation of survival time around the genotype mean is considered to be due to the "environmental variance". This assumption may be appropriate for the great majority of genetically determined morphological traits, but it is not applicable to longevity. What all members of an isogenic strain inherit in common is a characteristic physiological *stability* that is expressed in the age-dependent mortality curve for the population; no physically realizable degree of control of the environment can reduce the dispersion of ages at death for these genotypes much below the dispersions now obtained in the best laboratory environments (Sacher, 1956; Sacher and Trucco, 1962b).

There is an instructive analogy between this conception of genetically determined stability and radioactive decay. Radioisotopes have characteristic nuclear stabilities (the same for every atom) and decay exponentially. It is physically meaningless to say that all atoms would have the same lifetime except for environmental fluctuations; and, despite the complexity of biological systems, it is equally absurd to make an equivalent assertion about the longevity of organisms. Theories of aging

based on this postulate, such as the theory of Szilard (1959) for example, are contradicted by the results of life table studies on isogenic populations.

The basic postulate of this paper is that the genetic determination of the adult survival characteristic is exercised by biological stability parameters, one governing the initial vulnerability to disease and death, and the other governing the rate at which the vulnerability increases with age.

In the first life table analysis of the inheritance of longevity in *Drosophila*, Pearl (1922) observed that the F_1 hybrids of two inbred strains lived longer than either parent. It appears that longevity differences between inbreds and their F_1 hybrids are primarily due to differences in the vulnerability parameter, but statistical analysis is needed for a decision.

More recently, crosses of two inbred strains of *Drosophila subobscura* yielded progeny of the two reciprocal crosses which lived almost twice as long as the parents (Figure 10A) (Clarke and Smith, 1955; Smith, Clarke, and Hollingsworth, 1955). Despite the great increase of mean lifetime, the slopes of the parent and F_1 Gompertz curves are very nearly the same (Figure 10B), indicating that the improved longevity is due to a decreased vulnerability parameter rather than to a decreased rate of aging (Sacher, unpublished).

Chai (1959) and Grahn (1972) determined life tables for several inbred strains of mice and some F_1 and F_2 hybrids. In terms of the Gompertz parameters, the longer-lived mice had lower vulnerability in the common environment, but had no perceptible decrease in aging rate. Storer (1966), Festing and Blackmore (1971), and Smith, Walford, and Mickey (1973) give biometric data for several dozen inbred mouse strains and hybrids. Their data are equivocal. Nash and Kidwell (1973) conducted a diallele analysis of longevity, fecundity, and body weight of 3 strains. Except for significant sex and sex x inbred terms (which probably arose because the female progeny were bred throughout their lives) no significant genetic components for longevity were found. However, significant positive heterosis was found for the four reproductive and body weight variables.

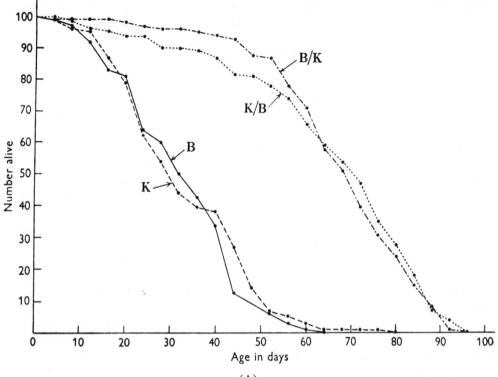

(A)

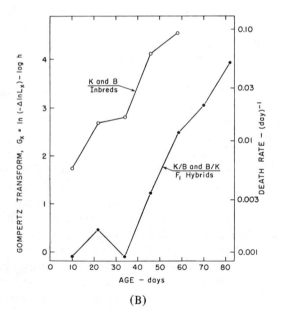

(B)

Figure 10. Survivorship and Gompertz diagrams for inbred and hybrid fruit flies, *Drosophila subobscura,* showing the effect of hybridization. Strains *K* and *B* crossed reciprocally to make the *K/B* and *B/K* hybrids. (Figure 10A from Clarke, J. M. and Smith, J. M., 1955; Figure 10B from unpublished work by G. A. Sacher.)

The literature on the inheritance of longevity in man is extensive and controversial. Cohen (1964) reviewed this material and found methodological flaws in all the studies. Although the studies overestimate the heritable longevity variance, its existence seems real.

A recent study by Hammond, Garfinkel, and Seidman (1971) may give evidence about the inheritance of the specific Gompertz parameters. A large population of U.S. men and women was followed for 6 years and was placed in seven classes on the basis of the summed longevity of the parents and grandparents. Age-specific mortality rates were computed in five-year intervals by sex in each heredity class for various categories of cardiovascular disease and for all remaining causes of death. For all disease categories, the mortality increased from the class with greatest ancestral longevity (class 1), to that with least ancestral longevity (class 7). The increase of age-specific mortality rate was a nearly constant factor in all age intervals from 40–44 to 65–69. The factor of increase for males from class 1 to class 7 was about 2 for coronary heart disease and various other categories of heart disease, and less than 1.5 for other diseases. These results indicate that the difference between the individuals with short-lived and those with long-lived families is an age-independent difference in their vulnerabilities to cardiovascular and other diseases, and not a difference in the rate of increase of risk with age. Hammond, Garfinkel, and Seidman point out that the probands "inherited" socio-economic and behavioral characteristics as well as genetic factors. Although there is no way to separate the contributions of the two, the absence of divergence in mortality ratios among these longevity classes is interesting. Cohen's (1964) discussion of the methodology of research on familial inheritance of longevity is a valuable introduction to the design of future studies in this field.

Effects of Secular Socio-Economic Change on the Human Survival Characteristic

The best conspectus of the human life table is still the treatise of Dublin, Lotka, and Spiegelman (1949). The most accessible resource for world-wide demographic information is the United Nations Demographic Yearbook (United Nations, 1975).

An examination of socio-economic influences on life tables from a biological point of view was carried out by Jones (1955), based on premises very similar to those employed in this chapter. He shows that economic progress is accompanied by decreased mortality from infectious disease, with the result that the life tables shift progressively in the direction of a smaller Makeham term (Equation 6) in the survival characteristic. At advanced ages the Makeham term is unimportant, and Jones is therefore able to show that the doubling time, T_d, for mortality at late ages has been almost constant over the past century, so that the effect of improved nutrition and health on degenerative disease and cancer in old age has been to decrease the vulnerability term, G_o, without evident alteration of T_d.

Human societies have been undergoing accelerated change for the past two centuries, so that a *current life table*, based on the current population structure and the age-distribution of the deaths recorded in a period of one or a few years, gives a distorted representation of the aging process in the population. This is because each age-class in a current life table is a member of a distinct cohort with a distinct life history of nutrition, health care, and living and working conditions. In countries with uniform death statistics and registration going back a century or more, it is possible to follow a specified cohort from birth to complete dying out, or to the current age, and thus to construct a series of cohort life tables (Case, 1956a, b). However, cohort life tables suffer from other disadvantages, because the mortality rate at a given age is a function also of the quality of health care in the year in which it occurred.

Sacher (1957, 1960) proposed a model for analyzing a set of current life tables, preferably covering a time span of 50 years or more, into three additive components of the Gompertz function: (1) a mortality process as a function of age that estimates the course of mortality as it would be for the same population in a stationary environment; (2) a secular function arising from nutritional and other conditions that prevailed during the period of infancy and childhood in each cohort; and (3) a second secular function associated with the effectiveness of medical practices, and with the accuracy of reporting causes of death in a given calendar year. Kermack, McKendrick, and McKinley (1934) took a different approach.

The three components are assumed to contribute additively to the Gompertzian mortality rate for a specified age class and calendar year.

$$G_{ij} = \alpha_i + \beta_j + \gamma_k \qquad (7)$$

where $G_{ij} = \ln q_{ij}$, the logarithm of the age-specific death rate at age i in year j

$i = 1, \ldots, n$ are the age classes

$j = 1, \ldots, m$ are the calendar years for which the current life tables were constructed

$k \equiv j - i + n = 1, \ldots, n + m - 1$ are the years of birth of the $n + m - 1$ cohorts.

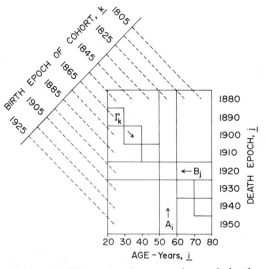

Figure 11. Illustrating how an observed death rate in a specific age interval, occurring in a specific calendar year, can be represented as a product of three factors: an intrinsic age factor and two secular factors expressive of two kinds of environmental influences. The death rate q_{ij} at age i (centered at age 55 years) in year j (1920) is the product of an intrinsic aging function A_i, a factor for the epoch of death B_j (year 1920) that is constant for all ages, and a factor for the epoch of birth k (1865 in the diagram) that is constant on the diagonal for all members of the cohort. The additive form of this model is stated in terms of the Gompertz function, $G_{ij} = \alpha_i + \beta_j + \gamma_k$.

The contributions of these functions are shown in Figure 11. The age function, α_i, is constant by columns; the function for the current effectiveness of health care and reporting, β_j, is constant by rows; and γ_k, the function for the influences operating on each cohort, is constant on diagonals from upper left to lower right. If all cells in the $n \times m$ mortality table are filled, there are $n \times m$ observations with which to estimate the $2n + 2m - 1$ terms of the three functions. This is done by solving the $2n + 2m - 1$ equations (Equation 7) simultaneously by least squares, where n, m must satisfy the inequality $n \times m - 2n - 2m + 1 > 0$. The solution contains three arbitrary constants. Two are eliminated by setting $\Sigma \beta_j = 0$ and $\Sigma \gamma_k = 0$. Evaluation of the third constant is done either by the use of additional information, such as prior knowledge about the shape of some part of one of the three functions, or by estimating the time-trend of one of the secular functions. For example, if m is more than 50 years, then the cohort function, γ_k, can be estimated back to the early 19th century, and it is usually safe to assume that γ_k is independent of time for the first few years.

This procedure for secular analysis was used by Sacher in analyzing the mortality from tuberculosis in Connecticut from 1880 to 1940. The current life tables and the cohort life tables for tuberculosis mortality (Merrill, 1947) are in Figure 12A and B. The results of Sacher's analysis are given in Figure 13. The cohort effect (the epoch-of-birth factor, parameter α in Equation 7) is stationary for 60 years, from 1815 to 1975, then begins an accelerating decline. The factor for current health care (the epoch-of-death factor, parameter β in Equation 7) declines fairly steadily from 1880 to 1940, and is somewhat less important than the cohort factor in reducing tuberculosis mortality in that period.

The mortality rate function corrected for secular trends in Figure 13 shows a constant rate after age 25, whereas the cohort mortality curves presented by Merrill (1947) (Figure 12) shows a decline. However, the cohort curves are not corrected for the β-term for changing current health conditions, and so are biased toward decreasing mortality rates as age in-

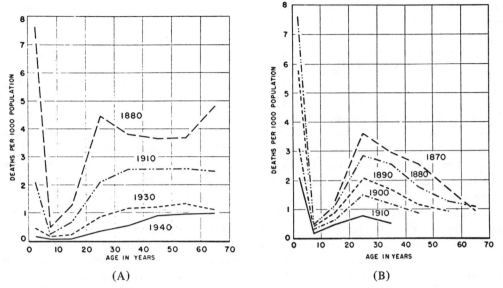

Figure 12. Current life tables (A) and cohort life tables (B) for mortality from tuberculosis in Connecticut in the years 1880 to 1940. (From Merrill, 1947.)

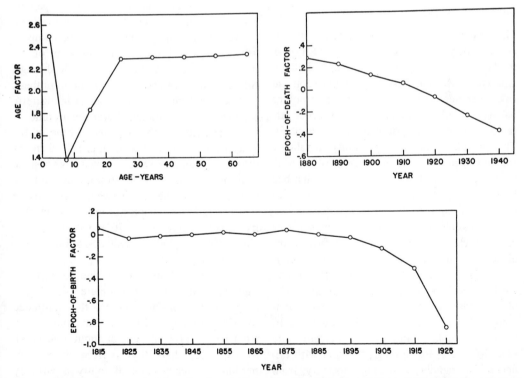

Figure 13. The two secular functions and the actuarial aging function computed for the tuberculosis mortality in Connecticut, based on the data in Figure 12. (From Sacher, 1957, 1960. Reproduced with permission of the National Academy of Sciences.)

creases. The aging function in Figure 13 resembles the current life table for 1880, as is proper, for prior to 1880 the cohort term and the term for current health care are constant.

Thus, the cohort life table can give a representation of the intrinsic aging process that is as distorted as that given by the current life table. The procedures of simultaneous analysis are therefore essential for a true perspective. Epidemiologists and statisticians have developed estimation procedures for various circumstances (Portman, Lucas, Elston, and Greenberg, 1963; Barrett, 1973).

It is imperative that we begin now to apply secular trend analysis to analysis of mortality in the United States and other countries where large-scale clinical trials of anti-aging drugs may be conducted because, without the refined predictions of mortality that these procedures can provide, there will be little possibility of evaluating life table modification effects over a long term.

Effects of a Sustained Low-Level Insult: Cigarette Smoking

The epidemiology of cigarette smoking and its consequences in human morbidity and mortality has been investigated in the United States and Great Britain. The large populations at risk, together with the stability of smoking behavior, make it possible to construct life tables for defined populations of smokers. This provides a unique opportunity to validate for human populations the analysis of environmental effects on life table parameters that had been developed on the basis of experience with animal populations.

The possible relationship between smoking and bronchiogenic carcinoma was first recognized early in the century by chest surgeons (citations in Wynder and Graham, 1950), and led to their study which showed that in a series of 605 cases of verified bronchiogenic carcinoma, 96.5 percent had histories of heavy to moderate smoking and only 2 percent were nonsmokers. These findings, together with evidence for rapidly increasing mortality from lung cancer in the general population (Kennaway and Kennaway, 1937, 1947), led to the initiation of three major studies of smoking and mortality in the United States (Kahn, 1966; Hammond and Horn, 1954, 1958; Hammond, 1966, 1969) and the United Kingdom (Doll and Hill, 1956, 1966).

The Dorn Study was based on 247,992 white, male U.S. veterans who were policyholders of U.S. Government life insurance (Kahn, 1966). Individuals were classified by their smoking habits; the categories were 1-9, 10-20, 21-39, and 40 or more cigarettes per day, plus a group of nonsmokers. Age-specific death rates were determined by 10-year intervals from 35 through 84 years, for all causes of death and for a number of specific causes.

The Gompertz functions for the mortality rates of the 5 exposure levels were fitted with straight lines by Forbes and Gentleman (1973), using a weighted least squares procedure. The outcome is a family of Gompertz lines that are displaced upward in a regular series from the nonsmoker to the 40+ group, with slopes that are virtually parallel, and independent of level of consumption. This contrasts sharply with the effect of continuous exposure to gamma rays, in which a range of daily doses produces a divergent fan of lines (Figure 5). Since divergent Gompertz lines are an indication of the indefinite accumulation of irreparable damage, the lack of divergence suggests the hypothesis that lesions leading to lung cancer in cigarette smokers are not cumulative over the lifetime.

The question of the persistence time of the precancerous lesion can be approached in another way, because there is now a large population of individuals who stopped smoking at various times in the past. Three studies estimate that the time for the excess lung cancer mortality rate to decrease by 50 per cent, $T_{1/2}$, is about 5 years (Doll and Hill, 1956; Hammond, 1966; Kahn, 1966).

A model for lung cancer due to cigarette smoking is constructed in Figure 14A. Injury is produced continuously by the continued smoking insult (line b), but each injury increment has a finite half time of about 5 years (a), so that in less than 20 years from the onset of smoking a steady state of injury is virtually established (c). This injury *summates* with the injury due to natural aging (which does accu-

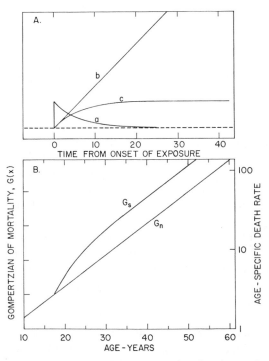

Figure 14. A model to account for the observed mortality from lung cancer in cigarette smokers. (Original work by G. A. Sacher.)

mulate indefinitely, Figure 14B, G_n), and the constant increment of cellular injury leads to an increase of mortality rates from lung cancer by a constant multiplicative factor at all ages (G_s), owing to the exponential relation of increased mortality risk to increased physical tissue damage (Sacher and Trucco, 1962b). The nonstationary phase is over by age 40 years, so there is little possibility of observing it in the lung cancer mortality rate statistics.

It is remarkable that a cellular lesion predisposing to cancer is subject to repair. Possibly, the precancerous lesion consists of a population of transformed epithelial cells (Saccomanno, Saunders, Archer, Auerbach, and Brennan, 1970), and the "repair" that occurs is due to the loss of transformed cells as a result of their decreased proliferative capacity or increased death rate. The second stage of the induction process, leading to active tumor growth, must occur within the lifespan of the transformed cell or clone. The linear dose-dependence of lung tumor induction suggests that this second transformation does not re-

quire exposure to the carcinogen in tobacco smoke, but a carcinogen present in levels not influenced by smoking is not excluded.

The success in analyzing the smoking hazard is due to the lack of gross health effects. The most serious chronic diseases directly associated with smoking are emphysema and bronchitis, which disable only a few smokers. The difficulties of investigating the actuarial effects of consumption of the more addictive drugs, such as alcohol and psychotropic chemicals, are much greater, because alcoholism and drug addiction become progressive diseases for a considerable fraction of users. They are, therefore, more physiologically and socially disruptive in their effects, and patterns of consumption are less stable, so that the definition of risk groups becomes more difficult.

Trace Elements

The problem of trace elements in the diet is assuming increasing importance in nutrition, medicine, and public health. The magnitude and difficulty of the problem is illustrated by the case of selenium (Scott, 1973). Selenium is an essential element for the laboratory rat, several domestic animals, and probably is essential for man also. Selenium deficiency in the rat diet results in degenerative processes, including pancreatic fibrosis. These results can be overcome by as little as 0.02 ppm selenium in the diet. The role of selenium is complex, but it is known to participate in the metabolism of vitamin E and peroxidase. Selenium deficiency in the diets of livestock and poultry has led to widespread losses from cardiac myopathy, muscular dystrophy and poor growth, and to increased mortality from various diseases. However, the regulations of the U.S. Food and Drug Administration until recently prohibited the addition of selenium to animal feeds because selenium at high levels is carcinogenic and this required the F.D.A. to apply the Delaney Amendment, which prohibits the addition to foods and feeds of anything that has been shown to be a carcinogen. After extensive review and hearings, a revised regulation was issued in 1974 permitting selenium to be added to the rations of poultry and swine to give optimal levels for growth, provided that amounts above normal do not appear in edible portions of the carcass.

The case of selenium epitomizes the difficult decision processes involved in establishing the best environment for man and his domestic animals. These problems will recur, for there are other trace elements that have beneficial or essential roles at low levels, and yet are carcinogenic at high dose levels.

Studies on the effects of lifetime feeding of trace elements have been carried out for a number of elements. The work of Schroeder and his colleagues is important because they investigated the effects of a number of elements and valence states on the longevity and disease incidence of rats and mice. A nutritionally adequate base diet low in trace elements was established, then trace elements were added, usually at concentrations of a few micrograms per gram to produce levels that are higher by large factors than the levels in the environment. Growth curves were obtained, survival was followed to complete dying out, and pathology and tissue analyses were performed (Schroeder, Vinton, and Balassa, 1963a, b; Schroeder, Balassa, and Vinton, 1964, 1965; Schroeder, Mitchener, Balassa, Kanisawa, and Nason, 1968; Schroeder, Kanisawa, Frost, and Mitchener, 1968; Schroeder, Mitchener, and Nason, 1970; Schroeder and Mitchener, 1971a and b, 1972; Schroeder, Mitchener, and Nason, 1974; Schroeder and Kraemer, 1974; Kanisawa and Schroeder, 1967, 1969). About half of the elements tested had no effects on growth, survival time, or tumor incidence. Increased growth was observed in rats fed chromium in two different valence states, tetravalent titanium, and niobium. Several of the elements assayed produced significant life shortening in rats, but none of them belonged to the growth-stimulating group. All metals tested inhibited growth in mice, but only germanium shortened life significantly. Tumor incidence in rats was increased significantly only by selenium fed as the selenate. There was no significant survival difference between the selenate and control groups, but one rat that was fed selenate lived for 5 years, which is at least 1 year longer than any other rat in all their published experience (Schroeder and Mitchener, 1971a). This animal

was not included in the average survival of the selenate-fed group. The incidence of benign and malignant tumors in the selenate-fed group (62.5 percent and 41.7 percent, respectively) was more than double the incidence in controls (30.8 percent and 16.9 percent). This is paradoxical because the selenate-fed rats, with the high tumor incidence, lived as long as the controls. Unfortunately, the age-distribution of the tumors was not reported. These complex findings suggest that there were two opposed actions of selenate in this experiment, a carcinogenic action and a beneficial action of unknown nature, which may be related to the role of selenium in vitamin E metabolism. Significant prolongation of life in mice was achieved with trivalent chromium (Schroeder, Vinton, and Balassa, 1963a), yttrium, and palladium (Schroeder and Mitchener, 1971b). There was a borderline significant increase of malignant tumors in the mice fed palladium.

Two experimental modifications would make an extended series of tests of chemical agents of this kind more productive. One is to introduce a comparative-genetic dimension by using several mouse strains and their hybrids, and also by using two species more physiologically different than the mouse and rat. These changes would give cumulative value to the data as the number of elements tested increased, because the genetic correlations of the responses of different genotypes to the different elements would yield, at virtually no additional cost, much additional knowledge about the genetic factors operating in the modification of longevity or tumor incidence. A serial killing protocol to gain information about the prevalence of tumors and other diseases at different ages would also be valuable. Information about the prevalence of tumors in the selenate group and its control, for example, would help to clarify the finding of increased tumor incidence in treated populations with no decrease in survival time (Schroeder and Mitchener, 1971a).

Trace Metals in Drinking Water and Cardiovascular Disease

The role of trace metals in mortality from cardiovascular disease has come under intensive study, following the demonstration by Kobayashi (1957) that the death rates in Japan from cerebral hemorrhage and heart disease by prefecture have a high positive correlation with the acidity of the local river water. In the United States, the only measure of drinking water initially available nationwide is the hardness index, which measures the mineral content, primarily calcium and magnesium. There is a significant *negative* correlation of total death rate, and of death rate from cardiovascular disease, but not from other diseases, with the hardness of water (Enterline, Rikli, Sauer, and Hyman, 1960), in agreement with Kobayashi (1957). This finding has been confirmed in Great Britain, Sweden, The Netherlands, Canada, and South America (reviewed by Schroeder and Kraemer, 1974). It was subsequently shown that the concentrations of 11 constituents of drinking water and 7 trace elements also had negative correlations with hypertensive heart disease and cerebral vascular lesions in men by state, and with arteriosclerotic heart disease by city (Schroeder, 1960; 1966).

These consistent findings led to the postulation of a protective "water factor," whose nature remains elusive. The possibility that some trace metal constituent has a protective action is discounted due to lack of consistent correlation. Alternatively, Schroeder (1969, Schroeder and Kraemer 1974) suggested that soft waters are more corrosive, and thus able to dissolve cardiotoxic metals, such as cadmium or antimony, from galvanized domestic water pipes.

The hypothesis that corrosiveness is the water factor has interesting implications since cadmium, a likely corrosion product, is present at increasing levels in water, air, and food (Perry et al., 1961), and may be a cause of the mild-to-moderate hypertension present in modern man, with its added risk of ventricular fibrillation or cerebral vascular accident (Anderson, le Riche, and MacKay, 1969; Perry, 1972; Schroeder and Kraemer 1974).

The experimental and human epidemiological data on trace metals make it clear that finding a balance that maximizes human health and longevity will be difficult. The possible interaction of beneficial, life-prolonging effects with mutagenic or carcinogenic activity, which is adumbrated by the studies on trace metals, may become a matter of concern for gerontology, because it may give rise to medicolegal problems when attempts are made to initiate trials of life-prolonging drugs on human populations for it is possible that some effective life-prolonging drugs may act at higher dose levels as tumor initiating or promoting agents.

RELATION OF THE SURVIVAL CHARACTERISTIC TO TEMPERATURE AND THE RATE AND QUANTITY OF METABOLISM: POIKILOTHERMIC ORGANISMS

Effect of Ambient Temperature on the Metabolism, Development, and Longevity of *Drosophila*

This section will examine the effects of temperature on the survival characteristics of insects, and also on their energy metabolism, rate of development, failure rate in development, and egg production. Loeb and Northrop (1917) established for fruit flies that the mean lifespan varies inversely with the ambient temperature. This rule holds for all temperatures above the optimum ambient temperature for the species, and for a range below optimum down to temperatures at which torpor becomes incompatible with survival. Sacher (1967) has reviewed and analyzed much of this data, which also applies to many other cold-blooded species.

The most informative representation of the relation of longevity to temperature is the plot of mean survival time on a logarithmic scale *versus* temperature on a reciprocal scale, the well-known Arrhenius diagram. Figure 15 shows that in this coordinate system the dependence of survival on temperature for *Drosophila subobscura* has two distinct branches. At temperatures below 25°C there is a branch of low slope on which the activation energy is 22.4 kcal, and above this temperature there is a transition to a branch with a much steeper slope, with activation energy of 182 kcal (Hollingsworth, 1969a). The transition begins at about 25°C but the steeper branch is not fully attained until temperatures reach 30°C. This high value of the activation energy may indicate heat death

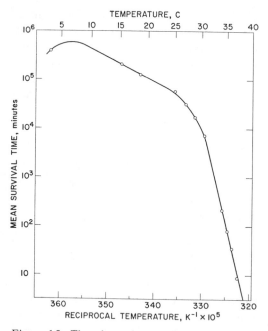

Figure 15. The dependence of mean survival time of adult *Drosophila subobscura* on ambient temperature. The mean survival time is plotted on a logarithmic scale against reciprocal temperature. (Reproduced from Hollingsworth, M. J. 1969. Temperature and length of life in Drosophila. *Experimental Gerontology*, **4**, 49–55. By permission of Pergamon Press.)

due to protein denaturation. Hence, the viable range of this species lies well within the upper and lower temperature limits of the low-slope branch.

Although all poikilothermic species have this kind of two-branched relation of survival time to temperature, the slope of the low-slope branch and the temperature at which the transition to the steeper branch occurs varies considerably among species. *Drosophila melanogaster*, which tolerates a wider range of temperature than *D. subobscura*, does not depart appreciably from the low-slope branch until the temperature exceeds 30°C, at least 5°C higher than *D. subobscura* (Strehler, 1961). The low-slope branch for *D. melanogaster* has an activation energy of 18 kcal, considerably lower than the value for *D. subobscura*.

Most of the enzymatically catalyzed reactions have activation energies in the range from 10 to 30 kcal (Laidler, 1958), and the overall

metabolic rates of many insects fall in the same range (Sacher, 1967). If the activation energies for metabolic rate and for reciprocal survival time are equal, then the product (metabolic rate) × (Survival time), is a constant independent of temperature, equal to the number of calories expended per lifetime. Constancy of the number of calories dissipated per lifetime at different temperatures is an implication of the rate-of-living hypothesis, which states that the duration of life is determined by the exhaustion of a vital substance that is consumed at a rate proportional to the metabolic rate (Pearl, 1928). Attempts to test this hypothesis by temperature-step experiments (Shaw and Bercaw, 1962; Clarke and Smith, 1961a, b; Lamb, 1968; Hollingsworth, 1969b; 1970; Strehler, 1961; Smith 1958a) have not yielded a clear conclusion.

Most of the publications cited on temperature and longevity in insects report the results in terms of the mean survival time and standard deviation, and the consistent finding is that the standard deviation is very nearly proportional to the mean, i.e., the coefficient of variation is nearly constant. This result can be translated into the statement that the rate of actuarial aging increases with the temperature. It is not possible to determine how the vulnerability parameter varies with temperature, but in view of the direct variation of the standard deviation, the prolongation of life at low temperatures is primarily due to a reduced rate of aging.

Temperature Dependence of Aging Viewed as an Aspect of Reproductive Fitness

We will now examine the alternative view that theories of the kind discussed in the previous section cannot be operable because they fail to take into account the fact that the life table of a species is an essential aspect of its reproductive fitness, and, like every other fitness variable, is therefore optimized with respect to the species habitat. In regard to ambient temperature, the minimum set of environmental parameters is the mean and the standard deviation of temperature fluctuations. A more complete characterization would include the temporal characteristics of cyclical and random fluctuations. In this section we show that insect development and reproduction is optimized to the thermal parameters of their habitats and, that longevity is probably also optimized. These considerations are important for the debate on hypothermia as a means of prolonging human life.

To establish the thesis that a species longevity is governed by the requirements of reproduction, dispersal, etc., in the thermal environment to which it is genetically adapted, it must be shown that the appropriate longevity parameter is indeed optimized for the range of environmental parameters encountered (Sacher, 1967). Little information about the relation of energy metabolism to temperature for adult insects was available in 1967, hence adaptation to the thermal environment was studied by an analysis of development and temperature. A curve for the relation of development rate (reciprocal of development time) to temperature for *Drosophila* eggs is given in Figure 16. The major characteristics of this curve are reproduced in the development of the eggs, larvae, and pupae of all insect species examined (Sacher, 1967 for review). The metabolic rate as a function of temperature has also been measured for some of these species and in every such case, the metabolic rate function has less curvature than the growth rate function (Richards, 1964). Because of the relations in Figure 16, the caloric cost of development, (metabolic rate) X (development time), per gram of insect tissue synthesized, is always a concave curve such as that in Figure 16 (Sacher, 1967). The minimum metabolic cost, i.e., the maximum efficiency of growth, occurs at an intermediate temperature that is always well below 30°C, despite the fact that the maximum rate of growth of these same species is near or beyond 30°C.

The rate of developmental error, estimated from either the mortality rate or the frequency of developmental anomaly, for all developmental stages of all insects studied, has a minimum at an intermediate temperature not very different from the temperature for maximum energetic efficiency of development (Menusan, 1934; Sacher, 1967).

During the egg and pupal stages, insects are

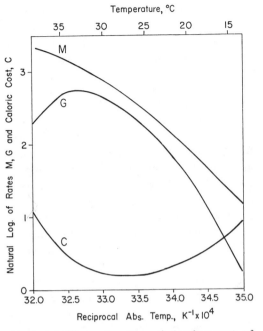

Figure 16. The energetics of development of *Drosophila* eggs. Curve G gives an Arrhenius plot for rate of development (reciprocal of development time) against reciprocal temperature, curve M gives the metabolic rate, in calories per gram, against reciprocal temperature, and curve C gives the developmental cost in calories, which is the metabolic rate multiplied by the development time. (From Sacher, G. A. 1967. The complementarity of entropy terms for the temperature-dependence of development and aging. *Ann. N.Y. Acad. Sci.,* **138**, 680–712.)

immobile, and therefore exposed to the full range of environmental temperature fluctuation. However, larvae are mobile and hence can select a more optimal environmental temperature. Corresponding to this characteristic, the energetic efficiency of development decreases more steeply on each side of the temperature optimum for the larval stage than for the egg or pupal stages of all species studied. Also, the rate of developmental error increases more rapidly with displacement from the temperature optimum for larvae than for eggs or pupae. This illustrates how closely insects are adapted to their thermal environments (Sacher, 1967; David and Clavel, 1969).

Similar adaptation to the temperature of the habitat is indicated for insect longevity and aging. The lifetime caloric expenditure of *Drosophila melanogaster* is a convex function of temperature, with a shallow maximum at about 20°C (Sacher, 1967). Ross and Sacher (1975) measured the survival of female houseflies, *Musca domestica*, at 9 temperatures from 17°C to 36°C, and the metabolic rates at early, middle, and late life of the flies at 9 temperatures. The lifetime caloric expenditure was found to be a convex curve with a maximum at about 26°C, consistent with the temperature optimum for egg production. These findings, while not conclusive, support the hypothesis that the rate of aging per calorie dissipated is a minimum at the temperature to which the insects are best adapted. These phenomena are also observed in the development of vertebrates. There is evidence that errors in the development of chicken eggs increase sharply if incubation temperature is displaced more than 1°C on *either* side of its optimum (Barott, 1937).

The adjustment of development to the temperature of the habitat extends to the diel temperature cycle. In regimes of daily temperature variation that approximate those of their habitat, the rate of insect development is greater than at a constant temperature equal to the mean of the temperature cycle (Parker, 1930; Huffaker, 1944). Moreover, the energetic efficiency of growth in an optimal diel thermal cycle is greater than at any constant temperature (Parker, 1930).

Pittendrigh (1960) compared the effects of (a) constant ambient temperature and (b) sinusoidal temperature variation with a 16°C amplitude and 24-hour period, both conditions with 12:12 LD, on the viability of an allele that is semilethal as a homozygote in *Drosophila melanogaster*. The proportion of females homozygous for the semilethal allele that reached maturity was significantly greater in the thermoperiodic regime than at constant temperature.

Under conditions of one-step or periodic temperature fluctuation (Clarke and Smith, 1961a, b; Hollingsworth, 1966; Lamb, 1968) survival was longer than expected on the rate-of-living hypothesis; the threshold hypothesis was equally unsuccessful in accounting for

the data. An alternative explanation for the effects of stepped and cycled temperature on longevity may be considered (Sacher, 1967) viz. the hypothesis that the maintenance of the adult insect has its maximum energetic efficiency, and is attended by the lowest rate of accumulation of aging error, in periodically varying temperature regimes that have some features of the variations in the natural environment. This hypothesis accounts for the fact that fluctuating temperature regimes yield better survival and developmental efficiency than the expectation from the rate-of-living hypothesis. It also provides a basis for the interpretation of experiments on the effect of photoperiod on longevity.

This hypothesis is supported by the work of Halbach (1973). The rotifer, *Brachionus calyciflorus* was reared and maintained at a constant temperature of 20°C or at temperatures varying sinusoidally from 15°C to 25°C, with a mean of 20°C. The average life durations were significantly different: 10.6 ± 0.3 days for constant and 12.0 ± 0.4 days for varying temperature. In the varying temperature regime the maturation time was significantly shorter (35.2 *versus* 51.9 hrs), the reproductive performance was improved, and the intrinsic rate of natural increase, r, (Cole, 1954) was increased about 25 percent.

Effect of Environment During Development on the Longevity of *Drosophila*

Alpatov and Pearl (1929) found that fruit flies maintained at a temperature of 28°C during development and at 25°C during adult life have shorter life spans than flies reared at 18°C and maintained as adults at 25°C. Smith (1958b) compared developmental temperatures of 25°C and 15°C and found the same advantage of lower developmental temperature. Burcombe and Hollingsworth (1970) observed that the temperature of development in *D. subobscura* has no influence on adult longevity in either sex of two reciprocal F_1 hybrids when the adults are maintained at 15°C, but that flies reared at 15°C have survival times one-fourth to one-half longer when kept at 30°C than flies reared at 30°C. On the other hand, *D. melano-*

gaster, which has a higher optimum temperature than *D. subobscura*, has reduced survival times at 25°C after being reared at 13°C (David and Cohet, 1971), and also reduced fecundity (Cohet, 1973).

Increased temperature during development decreases the development time and also decreases the body size at emergence. Variation of larval density per culture vial at constant temperature has the opposite effect on development: increased larval density produces increased development time and decreased body size at emergence. Lints and Lints (1969a and b, 1971a and b) confirmed earlier work on the relation of adult longevity to developmental temperature, and also showed that increase of larval density leads to increased adult survival. Hence, the concordant biological factor for longevity is the rate of development: a lower rate is accomplished by lower developmental temperature or higher density in the larval stage, both of which prolong adult survival. This result is clearest for the shorter development times, from 8 to 14 days, although from 14 to 26 days life span no longer increases with development time, and may decrease (Lints and Lints, 1971a, b; David and Cohet, 1971). This suggests that there are nonlinear interactions of development rate, density, and temperature which influence adult longevity. These considerations underline the need to examine the hypothesis that sufficiently large departures, in either direction, from the optimum development temperature or development time will reduce the subsequent longevity potential. In order to determine these nonlinear terms, developmental environments must be employed in which a range of larval densities is incubated at each of several temperatures. The importance of the result amply justifies the cost of this definitive experiment. If development time is increased by reducing the nutritive content of the medium with number of larvae held constant, the adult flies are smaller, just as for increased density, but the mean lifetime of the adults of both sexes is reduced (David, Cohet, and Fouillet 1971). The reason for the different effects of these two treatments is not known.

In the experiments reported above, the investigators interpret the differences in longevity as arising from effects on the aging process. However, insofar as the data permit any conclusions, they indicate that the differences in adult survival at constant temperatures are due to variation of the *vulnerability parameter rather than the rate-of-aging parameter*. The longer adult mean survival times arising from lower development rates have constant, or even decreased standard deviations, in sharp contrast to the increasing standard deviation with increased mean survival time of adult flies kept at different temperatures. Recall also that the improved survival of F_1 hybrids of inbred *Drosophila* strains is associated with decreased vulnerability rather than decreased aging rate (Smith, Clarke, and Hollingsworth 1955).

The conclusion that manipulation of the developmental schedule affects the vulnerability rather than the rate of aging is consistent with the higher error rates generated by a suboptimal developmental history. This is known to lead to increased variability and mortality during development (David and Clavel, 1969) and would also leave permanent damage in the surviving adults. Such constitutional damage would tend to cause increased vulnerability to disease, as exemplified by the effects of exposure to ionizing radiations early in life. It is less easy to understand how it can bring about more rapid accumulation of aging injury during subsequent life.

Effect of Photoperiod and Diel Period on Longevity of *Drosophila*

Several studies indicate that the survival of *Drosophila melanogaster* is affected by the light: dark (LD) cycle. Fruit flies maintained in continuous light (LL) throughout adult life have shorter life expectations than controls on a 12:12 LD cycle (Erk and Samis, 1970; Pittendrigh and Minis, 1972). Conversely, flies kept in continuous dark (DD) at 25°C during imaginal life outlive controls on a 12:12 LD cycle by a wide margin (Allemand, Cohet, and David 1973). The difference is a very nonlinear function of LD ratio, for survival in 95 percent darkness is similar to survival in 50 percent darkness. Curiously, females experience 43 percent greater extension of life than do males. Allemand, Cohet, and David have evidence that rejects the hypothesis that the longer survival in continuous darkness is due either to decreased activity (flies do not fly in darkness) or to decreased egg production. Deprivation of light is almost as great for the flies in 95 percent darkness as in continuous darkness, yet they experience no extension of life. Hence, it is possible that even a brief flash of light is a *Zeitgeber* (timing signal) that initiates the daytime metabolic activity pattern, and that these metabolic activities then go on to completion without the need for further light.

Because the free-running circadian period is rarely an exact 24-hour day in length (Buenning, 1964), it is important to determine whether a small change in day length will have deleterious effects on aging and longevity. Pittendrigh and Minis (1972) found that such a deleterious effect exists for fruit flies kept on a 50:50 LD regime with periods of 21, 24 or 27 hours, or in continuous light. The flies on the 24-hour day length had the longest median survival times and longest maximum spans in the three experiments that went to complete dying out. Pittendrigh and Minis interpreted their findings as arising from the discrepancy between T, the period of the diel cycle, and τ, the free-running circadian period of the organism. However, their hypothesis about the role of the photoperiod is brought into question by the finding of Allemand, Cohet, and David (1973) that fruit flies in complete darkness live considerably longer than they do in a wide range of 24-hour LD cycles.

Effect of Ambient Temperature on the Longevity of Poikilothermic Vertebrates

Some reptiles and fish are adapted to habitats that vary considerably in mean temperature; and several of these species which live in cooler environments live longer (Bourlière, 1957). An experimental disadvantage of poikilothermic vertebrates is that even very small species may have long lifespans. The guppy (*Poecilia reticulata*) and medaka (*Oryzias latipes*) (Egami and Etoh, 1969) can live for at least 6 years (Comfort, 1963). Fortunately, there are cypronidont fishes with an annual reproductive cycle which

are temperature-tolerant, hardy, and yet have short life spans (Liu and Walford, 1969, 1970). Liu and Walford (1966) maintained *Cynolebias bellottii* at constant temperatures of 16°C or 22°C. The group at 22°C had a median survival time of 10.5 months, and maximum survival for the males of 17 months, while the group at 16°C had an extrapolated median survival time of 21 months. The slope of the survivorship curve at 16°C was decreased in about the same ratio as the increase of median survival time. Therefore, the longer survival at the lower temperature was mainly due to a decreased rate of aging, similar to insects at low temperatures. The same temperature characteristic is observed in other *Cynolebias* species (Liu and Walford, 1970).

The actuarial evidence for a decreased aging rate at lower body temperature is supported by data showing a decreased rate of increase of insoluble collagen (Walford, Liu, Troup, and Hsiu, 1969).

Liu and Walford (1972) studied *Cynolebias bellottii* during temperature steps from either 15°C or 20°C. Although there was excess mortality at a critical time, fish transferred from 20°C to 15°C at 8 months of age (which is about half the life expectation at 20°C for these fish) appeared to survive at least as long as the fish kept at 15°C. The effects of these temperature regimes on the Gompertz parameter cannot be evaluated. The convenient *Cynolebias* model developed by Liu and Walford deserves to be extensively exploited because more can be learned from it that may be applicable to mammals.

RELATION OF THE SURVIVAL CHARACTERISTIC TO TEMPERATURE AND THE RATE AND QUANTITY OF METABOLISM AND FUNCTION: HOMEOTHERMIC VERTEBRATES

Energy Metabolism and Constitutional Factors in the Longevity of Mammals

Rubner (1908) first noted that various domestic animals with a wide range of body weights and life spans have almost constant lifetime energy dissipation (LED) in calories per gram of body tissue. This near-constancy arises because the metabolic rate per gram varies as the $-1/4$ power of body weight, and life span varies about as the $+1/4$ power, so their product is almost independent of body weight (Sacher, 1959). The mammalian LED is estimated to be about 200 Kcal/g (Rubner, 1908). Friedenthal (1910) pointed out that LED varies between species, being about four times greater for man, than a group of domestic animals and that the species differences in LED fit an allometric relation to brain weight. Sacher (1959, 1976), employing a more diverse sample of species and more accurate longevity records, confirmed both of these generalizations, but found a systematic trend toward increase of LED with metabolic rate. The relation of LED to the constitutional variables body weight, S, brain weight, E, and resting metabolic rate, in cal/g/day, M_r, can be represented in terms of a multiple regression of LED on M_r and on the *index of cephalization*, I,

$$I = ES^{-2/3}$$

This change in variable is advantageous because I is orthogonal to M_r, whereas E and S are highly correlated with M_r. The relation of life span, L, to I and M_r is (Sacher, 1959),

$$L = 18I^{.636}M^{-.744}$$

where L is in years. The relation of LED to I and M_r is then

$$LED = 365LM_r = 6600 \cdot I^{.636}M_r^{.256}$$

Hence, if M_r is constant, LED increases with index of cephalization, while if I is constant, LED increases with resting metabolic rate. Thus, small, active mammals, e.g., weasels, voles, and some mice, have high LED's, and primates and other highly cephalized mammals do also. The LED's for mammals range from about 100 to 1000 kcal/g (Table 1B). Although these formulae were based on data from mammals, the same relations seemed to hold for all vertebrates. In particular, the tortoises and other large reptiles with long life spans fall into subordinate positions when their longevity is expressed in caloric units. Man is unequalled in the amount of metabolic use he can make of his body.

Torpor and Hibernation as Factors in the Longevity of Mammals

Two different kinds of thermoregulation are utilized by mammals in adjusting to low environmental temperatures (Whittow, 1973). The homeothermic thermoregulator responds by decreasing heat loss to the environmental and increasing heat production in order to minimize the decrease of its core temperature. If these mechanisms fail, rapid fall of body temperature is followed by coma.

The other thermoregulatory strategy is heterothermy, in which the individual is a bistable system that can exist in either of two states: the active state, with characteristic mammalian homeothermy and metabolic rate, or the torpid state, with body temperature only slightly above ambient and metabolic rate depressed to a small fraction of the rate in the active state. There are two physiologically distinct kinds of torpor, diel torpor, which lasts, at most, a fraction of a day, and hibernation, which may last for weeks or months. Some heterothermic species, such as insectivorous bats, use both forms, but ground hogs and others use hibernation exclusively (Kayser, 1961).

The long life spans of some insectivorous bats of temperate latitudes are documented. Survival longer than 15 years is recorded for several species (Cockrum, 1956) and there are records of more than 20 years. The small insectivorous bats of temperate latitudes have low metabolic rates and body temperatures in comparison to other small mammals, and readily enter torpor (McNab, 1969). If we consider that they have an active metabolic rate about two-thirds that of a small terrestrial mammal, and spend 75 percent of each day in torpor and 4 to 6 months of the year in hibernation, the annual energy budget is probably not more than 20 percent of that for a small mouse. Therefore, the bat's LED over a 20-year life span is no greater than that of a mouse in 4 years.

Larger hibernating mammals, such as marmots, do not gain longevity over otherwise similar non-hibernators for several reasons. The depression of body temperature and metabolic rate is smaller in magnitude as body size increases, their hibernation period is shorter, and they are precluded, again by their large body size, from going into diurnal torpor.

Some small desert rodents, such as the little pocket mouse *Perognathus longimembris*, with body weight less than 10g and a life span approaching 8 years (Egoscue, Bittmenn, and Petrovich, 1970), are longer-lived than other small rodents, in part because of a lower metabolic rate in the waking state and in part because of highly developed diel torpor. The duration of torpor can be controlled in these animals by food restriction (Bartholomew and Cade, 1957), so they offer an attractive model system for the analysis of the relation of aging to metabolism and body temperature.

Relation of Rat Longevity to Ambient Temperature

The effect of ambient temperatures on the longevity and diseases of the laboratory rat will now be considered.

Heroux and Campbell (1960) maintained rats for their adult life spans at 6°C or 30°C on conventional diets fed *ad libitum*: average survival of the cold-acclimated rats (n = 13) was 560 days; that of the warm-acclimated rats (n = 10) was 708 days. Room temperature controls were not run. The cold-acclimated group had an increase incidence of testicular hypoplasia, glomerulonephritis, myocardial fibrosis, and periarteritis nodosa, although pulmonary diseases and neoplasms were less.

Kibler and Johnson (1961), Johnson, Kintner, and Kibler (1963) and Kibler, Silsby, and Johnson (1963) examined the effects of 9°C, 28°C and 34°C environments on the growth, food consumption, resting oxygen consumption, and body temperature of rats. The mean age at death at 9°C was 445 ± 14.5 days, and at 28°C was 646 ± 22.0 days (Kibler, Silsby, and Johnson, 1963). The 9°C group had lower body weights but higher food, water, and oxygen consumption. Oxygen consumption per gram was 75 percent higher than in 28°C controls. Rectal temperatures were similar and declined with age in both groups, while oxygen consumption per gram remained relatively constant with age for each group. Survival curves for this experiment were not reported, so it is

not possible to draw a definitive conclusion about the effects of increased metabolic rate on the Gompertz parameters. However, we can estimate that the standard deviation of survival times was 112 days at 9°C and 170 days at 28°C. This indicates that the mean doubling time of mortality rate, T_d, was about 66 percent as long at 9°C as at 28°C, and this is almost the same as the 69:100 ratio of survival times. Hence, it can be tentatively inferred that the rate of aging is about 50 percent greater in the population that has a 75 percent higher specific metabolic rate, and that the decreased survival is due primarily to the increased aging rate. The LED is about 21 percent greater (1.75 × 0.69) in the 9°C rats.

Carlson, Scheyer, and Jackson (1957) maintained rats for lifetimes at 5°C and 26°C, as part of an experiment in which rats at these two temperatures were given chronic low-level exposures to gamma rays. The group at 26°C had median survival of 460 days from the beginning of the experiment at 120 days of age, and the 5°C group survived 240 days, or 52 percent as long. Body weight of the 5°C group was about 370g, 16 percent less than the 26°C control. Food intake per kg body weight per 24 hours was 104g, increased by a factor of 2.3 over the 26°C group. Hence, the LED is 20 percent greater in the 5°C rats (2.3 × 0.52), in agreement with Kibler, Silsby, and Johnson (1963). The authors give a plot of probit of survival against logarithm of age, and the 5°C and 26°C survival curves are parallel on this grid. This implies that the mean doubling time of the mortality rate of the 5°C group is decreased in the same ratio as the mean survival time, so that the shortened survival is attributable to an increased rate of actuarial aging, as in the experiment of Kibler, Silsby, and Johnson (1963).

Kibler and Johnson (1966) also compared a high temperature, 34°C, to a temperature of 28°C. In addition to groups fed *ad libitum* at these temperatures, a group was kept at 28°C with a food intake matching that of the *ad libitum* group at 34°C. Body weight at 34°C was lower than in the 28°C *ad libitum* group, and food and oxygen consumption were lower per animal, but higher on a per gram basis. Interestingly, the rats with matched food intake at 28°C lived 80 days longer than the rats that consumed the same amount of food at 34°C. The authors divided the rats in each environmental temperature condition into two subgroups with rectal temperatures above or below the group median. The group held at 34°C as a whole had an average body temperature of about 39°C, somewhat more than 1°C higher than the controls. The subgroup with higher rectal temperature in the 34°C group averaged 39.3°C, 0.7°C higher than the subgroup with lower rectal temperatures, and had survival times 101 days shorter. It follows (although not noted by the authors) that almost the entire difference in survival between the 34°C group and the 28°C group with matched intake was due to the 34°C subgroup with rectal temperatures above 39°C. Within the 28°C group, the subgroups with low and high rectal temperatures, averaging 37.7°C and 38.2°C respectively, did not differ in survival. In sum, these results suggest that the capacity of the rat to maintain its health deteriorates rapidly when its mean body temperature exceeds 39°C, only 1°C above the normal, but there is no indication that survival is correlated with body temperatures for temperatures below 39°C.

Effect of Caloric Intake on the Survival Characteristic and Diseases of Rats and Mice

Osborne, Mendel, and Ferry (1917) and McCay and Crowell (1934) opened the field of caloric restriction studies by observing that rats kept in a state of retarded growth by diets limited in calories have prolonged lifespans. Subsequent experiments (McCay, Crowell, and Maynard, 1935; McCay, Maynard, Sperling, and Barnes, 1939; McCay, Maynard, Sperling, and Osgood, 1941) established the main features of the caloric restriction phenomenon (McCay, 1942).

Respiratory disease, a major cause of death in fully-fed rats, was reduced in incidence, as was tumors. The restricted rats remained lively and young-looking, but were prone to cataracts in late life. Life expectations are not increased in the same degree as life spans because mortality at early ages, from causes related to the inability to adapt fully to severe growth retardation, is in excess of control mortality. When restricted rats were allowed access to unlimited food at any age up to 1000 days, they gained weight rapidly and their body weights approached those of rats fully fed since birth. They also began to age in the ways characteristic for fully-fed rats. Resumption of growth in adult restricted rats on resumption of unrestricted feeding was reported earlier by Osborne and Mendel (1915).

Berg and Simms (1960a, b, 1961) studied the diseases and longevity of male and female rats on three dietary regimens: (1) unrestricted diet: (2) 33 percent less than the unrestricted; and (3) 46 percent less than the unrestricted. The 33 percent restricted group was followed to age 800 days, and the 46 percent restricted to age 1200 days. Food intake and body weight are given in Table 4.

TABLE 4. FOOD INTAKE AND BODY WEIGHT FOR RATS IN THE EXPERIMENT OF BERG AND SIMMS (1960A AND B, 1961). SEE TEXT FOR SURVIVAL DATA.

		Unrestricted	33% restricted	46% restricted
		male		
sample size	n	31	42	38
daily food intake	g	19.5	13.0	10.5
body weight	g	448	342	275
		female		
samples	n	58	22	17
daily food intake	g	13.0	8.7	7.0
body weight	g	280	207	161

The 46 percent dietary restricted group showed a 40 percent reduction of body weight, with little retardation of skeletal growth or sexual maturity. The onset of cardiac, vascular, and renal lesions was delayed and the cumulative lifetime incidence of these lesions was lower. Although appearance of tumors was delayed, the lifetime tumor incidence was as great in restricted as in unrestricted rats. The median survival of 46 percent restricted male rats was 1005 days, 230 day longer than the control median. Control females lived 930 days and the expectation of 46 percent restricted females was probably close to 1300 days, for 73 percent of the females survived when the experiment was terminated to 1200 days. The age-specific death rates for the unrestricted and 46 percent restricted rats of Berg and Simms are plotted on Figure 17 as solid and open circles, respectively.

The analysis of the effects of restricted food intake was carried further by the work of Ross and his colleagues. In the first experiment (Ross, 1959), four calorically restricted diets gave all combinations of high and low protein intake (HP and LP) and high and low carbohydrate intake (HC and LC). The restricted diets began at 21 days of age. The controls had unrestricted intake of Purina Lab Chow. More than 1600 male Charles River COBS rats were used. Adult body weights were an increasing linear function of cumulative caloric intake over the weight range from 170g (LP-LC) to 450g (HP-HC) (Table 5). The effects of these regimes on survival were presented graphically as curves of

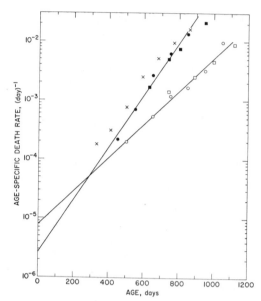

Figure 17. Gompertz diagram for rats maintained on restricted caloric intakes and their controls. (Data of Berg and Simms, 1960b; and Ross, 1959.) A control population of Jones and Kimeldorf (1963) is also shown. Open symbols are restricted populations, closed symbols and crosses are controls. Squares are Berg and Simms data, circles are Ross data, and crosses are Jones and Kimeldorf data.

percent survival from 90 to 1400 days (Ross, 1959). The unrestricted group averaged 729 days survival from birth with a maximum of 1072 days (Table 5). The survival curve for this group showed an earlier and steeper descent than any of the restricted groups, which had average survivals ranging from 925 to 950 days. The groups with high protein intake were

TABLE 5. COMPUTED LIFETIME CALORIC INTAKE PER ANIMAL AND PER GRAM OF BODY WEIGHT, SHOWING THAT LIFETIME CALORIC INTAKE PER GRAM IS NEARLY CONSTANT FOR THE FIVE CONDITIONS OF RESTRICTED AND UNRESTRICTED CALORIC INTAKE. BASED ON DATA OF ROSS (1969). LP, HP ARE LOW AND HIGH PROTEIN, LC, HC ARE LOW AND HIGH CALORIES, "AD LIB" IS UNRESTRICTED RAT CHOW DIET.

	Units	LP-LC	HP-LC	LP-HC	HP-HC	Ad lib
Average daily caloric intake	kcal/day	18	30	47	47	75
Average survival time	days	990	990	890	945	780
Calories/animal lifetime	kcal	17820	28700	41830	44415	58500
Average body weight	g	170	280	400	450	600
Calories/gram lifetime	kcal/g	105	106	105	98.7	97.5

markedly superior in the first half of the dying-out process, and the HP-LC group had the longest average survival. However, the LP-LC group, which had high early mortality from caecal impaction, showed the best late-life survival. The LP-HC group shared the early mortality of the LP-LC group and also had the steep late mortality seen in the HP-HC group.

Ross (1969) showed that the caloric intakes of the five dietary groups are linearly related to their life spans, with a slope of about – 3.9 days/Kcal/day. This result can be examined in another way. Table 5 gives the average daily caloric intake, life expectancy from birth, and adult body weights of the five diet groups. From these, the lifetime energy intake per gram of tissue can be calculated, and the bottom line shows that this value varies by only 7.5 percent over the five groups. The variation that does occur is systematic, being positively correlated with life expectation and negatively with body weight and caloric intake. The small magnitude of variation suggests that there is a fundamental aspect of the longevity potential of the cells of the rat that remains invariant in the face of major changes in constitution and life span. The extensive biochemical and histological measurements of the livers of these diet groups (Ross, 1969) should be examined to determine whether any aspects of the cellular makeup and enzymatic activity of the liver share this invariance property. Unfortunately, this analysis cannot be applied to the data of Berg and Simms because it is not possible to estimate mean survival times for their treatment groups.

The increase in longevity under caloric restriction is largely due to decreased tumor incidence and retarded appearance of tumors. The incidence of neoplasms is a linearly increasing function of caloric intake level or body weight (Ross, Bras, and Ragbeer, 1970; Ross and Bras, 1965, 1973). The relation of tumor incidence to the number of cells at risk in the tissue of rats at different levels of growth retardation has not been examined, but deserves to be, in the light of the invariance demonstrated above.

Some diseases are less strongly linked to caloric intake. Kidney disease, specifically progressive glomerulonephrosis (PGN), depends on level of protein intake under conditions of lifetime intake of a fixed diet. Cumulatively, more than 60 percent of rats with high protein intake had PGN, while rats on low protein intake had only a 15 percent incidence (Bras and Ross, 1964, 1966).

The effects of caloric restriction on the Gompertzian parameters can be evaluated from the excellent survival studies by Berg and Simms (1960b) and Ross (1959). Figure 17 gives the age-specific mortality rates for the 40 percent restriction group of Berg and Simms and the HP-LC group of Ross. The two experiments agree in all important features. Both show the same pattern of control mortality. The consistency of life tables for rats in modern laboratory environments is underlined by the data on a population of 747 conventionally fed and maintained Sprague Dawley male rats reported by Jones and Kimeldorf (1963). These three control life tables yield a pooled estimate of 66 days for the doubling time of the mortality rate T_d. The high degree of consistency in this estimate is welcome, because 66 days is a remarkably low value in comparison to 100 days for laboratory mice, and longer doubling times for all other rodent species (Sacher and Staffeldt, 1972). The restricted groups in the two experiments agree in having longer doubling times. The T_d is about 105 days for the Berg and Simms restricted group and 130 days for the Ross group. This is almost double the control value, and is the best estimate available of the efficacy of caloric restriction for retarding aging.

The extrapolated death rate at birth, q_o, for the control Gompertz line is 2.7×10^{-6}/day, remarkably low in comparison to the values found for other rodent species. However, this necessarily goes with the short doubling time, for the rat has about the same life expectancy as the mouse, which is only possible if a low q_o compensates for a low T_d. The q_o for the restricted groups is 8×10^{-6}/day, threefold higher than the control q_o. This is an indication of the magnitude of the deleterious actuarial effects of caloric restriction, which have been described by all investigators. The increase of q_o is greater for more extreme degrees of restriction, such as Ross' HP-HC group. If we could determine how T_d and q_o separately depend on the degree of restriction, it would be possible to arrive at an optimum level of restriction.

Other ways of optimizing the life prolongation effect include maintaining different degrees of restriction at different ages. Ross (1966, 1972) examined several "step" patterns, in which intake was either increased from a low value, or decreased from a high value, and reported that rats fed *ad libitum* to age 300 days followed by restriction to 10 g/day had an increase of after-expectation of 430 days from age 400 days as compared to controls fed *ad libitum*. This increase was almost equal to that observed for rats fed *ad libitum* from weaning to 70 days followed by 6 g/day, but not as great as the increase of expectation for rats fed 6 g/day throughout life beginning at weaning.

Caloric restriction limited to early life has a lasting influence on the lifetime tumor incidence (Ross and Bras, 1971). The reduction of tumor incidence is not so great as that accomplished by lifetime restriction. Moreover, it appears that a limited period of restriction delays the onset of tumor incidence, but the incidence, when it begins, accumulates at the same rate as in controls. The incidence under lifetime restriction accumulates at a slower rate, comparable to the twofold increase of doubling time for mortality rates for all causes, as discussed above. Tannenbaum (1947) and Tannenbaum and Silverstone (1949, 1953) maintained mice on restricted food intake and also found a decrease incidence of tumors and increased survival.

Many of the effects of caloric restriction in rodents can be reproduced in fishes. Comfort (1963) showed that caloric restriction increases the lifespan of the guppy (*Poecilia reticulata*), and that the capacity for resumption of growth after resumption of unrestricted feeding is unimpaired after 1500 days. The rate of regeneration of the tail web in the guppy has no decrement with age, and is greater in the retarded fish than in controls at all ages tested (Comfort and Doljanski, 1958). The retarded fish has median survival of 1400 days, as against 1000 for controls, but the maximum survival of 1800 days was only 100 days greater

than control. The retarded fish showed delayed onset of mortality, but died out thereafter in parallel with controls. There was, therefore, a reduction of vulnerability without reduction in the rate of actuarial aging. This is in contrast to the rat (Figure 17).

Influence of Self-Selection of Diet and Temporal Pattern of Food Intake on Longevity and Diseases of Rats

Rats are able to make a self-selection of dietary components that yield optimum growth, compensate for specific dietary deficiencies, and ameliorate systemic disease conditions such as diabetes or hormone deficiencies (Lát, 1967). Rats given unrestricted access to an adequate, fixed diet show rapid growth and large adult body size, just as rats on self-selected diets do, but there is still a question as to whether lifetime self-selection of diet components has different effects on longevity than a fixed diet.

Ross and Bras (1974, 1975) set up a lifetime experiment to examine the effects of dietary self-selection (S-S) on the longevity and disease incidence of rats, in comparison to three groups fed on each of three diets separately that were presented to the S-S group for its free choice. The three diets varied in the relative amounts of protein, carbohydrates and total calories, and all groups had unrestricted access to food. The S-S group as a whole showed the best growth and highest mature body weights. However, there were large individual differences in the dietary patterns of individual S-S rats. The amount of calories consumed during the first 200 days of life was inversely correlated with the life expectancy. This correlation diminished with age, and food consumption after 400 days had no predictive value for longevity. Independent partial correlations of survival time with protein intake and carbohydrate intake were also observed (Ross and Bras, 1975). Although life expectation did not differ between the S-S and fixed groups these groups differed importantly in the cumulative incidence of late-appearing degenerative and neoplastic diseases. There were more tumors and more diseases of the kidney, heart, and prostate gland in the S-S group than in any of the groups fed the same three diets singly. The proportion of tumors was two and one-half times greater in the S-S group, and the types of tumors were also different.

In view of the extensive evidence that rats have the ability to improve their well-being by self-selection of diet components when a demonstrable dietary lack is present, one must ask whether some as yet unknown aspect of the well-being of the animals is also served by self-selection in the absence of deficiency, and why this is associated with increased disease in late life. Also, since the increased cancer incidence did not shorten life, there is reason to infer that there was either a compensatory decrease in mortality from other diseases, or a deferred onset of cancer incidence, perhaps related to decreased vulnerability or increased vigor.

Ross averaged individual consumption in 100-day blocks, so the detailed patterns of cyclical or random variation in preferences could not be examined. The subject of 24-hour and other periodicities in the synthesis and activity of liver enzymes is currently under investigation by Potter and his colleagues, with special reference to the relation of this cyclical behavior, or its disturbance, to tumor incidence and aging (Yager, Lichtenstein, Bonney, Hopkins, Walker, Dorn, and Potter, 1974). These investigations may throw light on Ross' findings concerning the influence of self-selection on tumor incidence and may also provide an explanation for the finding that food deprivation every fourth, third, or second day leads to prolonged survival (Carlson and Hoelzel, 1946, 1947). This may have general significance for all caloric restriction experiments, for the food intake of restricted animals occurs during a short period of each day, so a severely restricted animal is also an animal on a strict cyclical program of food intake and enzyme induction. It will be necessary eventually to do experiments that distinguish the cyclic and caloric aspects of dietary restriction.

Effect of Restricted and Accelerated Growth on the Longevity and Diseases of Rats and Mice

A classical hypothesis of aging is Bidder's (1932) claim that growth and aging are antagonistic processes, so that organisms with indefinite growth do not undergo senescence. However, the guppy, *Poecilia reticulata*, which grows at a diminishing rate throughout its life span, and experiences very little age-decrement in its ability to regenerate lost tail tissue, nevertheless undergoes physical and actuarial senescence (Comfort, 1963). Comfort considered the persistence of regeneration to be proof against Bidder's hypothesis.

The experiments on restricted food intake emphasized the somewhat different point that animals that are prevented by underfeeding from exhausting their capacity for growth have a delayed senescence. This is equally true for the guppies and rats.

Widdowson and Kennedy (1962) investigated the effect of retarded early growth on longevity and disease incidence in the rat. Growth was retarded by forming large and small litters. The rats suckled in large litters grew more slowly before and after weaning and had lower adult body weights, due to both a smaller lean body mass and a much smaller fat depot. The growth-retarded group had a slightly different distribution of ages at death than the controls, but the life expectancy and maximum life span were not increased. The retarded group had a higher cumulative incidence of respiratory diseases, but a lower incidence of tumors and kidney diseases. Widdowson and Kennedy concluded that nutritionally retarded growth does not promote longevity.

Silberberg, Jarrett, and Silberberg (1961, 1962) investigated the effects of underfeeding or feeding a high-fat diet during the growth period on subsequent survival of C57BL/6, DBA/2, and A mice. The underfed groups received 60 percent of the *ad libitum* intake, and the high-fat diet consisted of the stock diet enriched with 25 percent lard. The diets were fed for 1 or 3 months, followed by *ad libitum* feeding of the stock diet for the remainder of life. The high-fat diet had slight effects on body weight and juvenile mortality, but subsequent survival did not differ from the controls. The underfed groups of both sexes had erratic weight behavior, with some groups fully regaining the weight deficit and others only partially. There was a marked excess of juvenile mortality in the underfed groups, but the subsequent mortality experience of the survivors did not differ significantly from the controls. The conclusion is that moderately retarded or increased rates of growth have no influence on the subsequent lifespan of mammals.

Effects of Physical and Sexual Activity on Survival of Rats and Mice

The effects of exercise and physical work on health and longevity are of great theoretical and practical importance, but little data is available.

McCay *et al.* (1941) maintained rats on a regime of restricted food intake with or without controlled, involuntary exercise in a motor-driven drum and found that the group on a regime of dietary restriction with exercise survived longer than the restricted, non-exercised groups.

A study of the effect of a brief daily period of controlled exercise on the survival of rats with unrestricted dietary intake was conducted by Retzlaff, Fontaine, and Furuta (1966). There were 25 males and 31 females in the exercise groups, with an equal number of littermate controls. The exercised rats, which were required to run 840 meters in 10 min. every 24 hr., had a 25 percent increase in resting metabolism, 13 percent increase in daily food intake, and a decreased rate of weight gain. In both sexes, the exercise group had a later onset of mortality and a displacement of the survival curve about 200 days to the right, so that the effect of exercise was to decrease disease vulnerability without decreasing the rate of aging.

Edington, Cosmas, and McCafferty (1972) forced rats to run at a rate of 10 m/min. for 20 minutes, 5 days a week. Exercise was started at four ages ranging from 120 to 600 days. The exercised groups were fed 20 g of laboratory chow per day and the controls were fed 15 g per day in order to maintain equality of body weight with the exercised groups. The groups which were started at 120 and 300 days of age had significantly lower mortality than their matched controls, while the groups that began exercise at 450 to 600 days had significantly increased mortality. It was concluded that there is a "threshold age," beyond which it is not advantageous to commence an exercise program. This conclusion should not be ac-

cepted uncritically, since only a single level of forced exercise without any conditioning period was employed. It is more appropriate to view these findings as an indication that the optimum amount and intensity of exercise decreases at advanced ages.

Goodrick (1974) allowed mice voluntary activity in exercise wheels beginning at age 23 months. Male mice experienced a significant increase in longevity (after-survival of 7.4 months as compared to 4.5 months for controls) but females did not. However, the control females and the exercised females lived as long as the exercised males. Both sexes showed increased open field exploration behavior and decreased emotionality in the exercised groups.

The effects of mating on the longevity of male rats have been investigated repeatedly, but the results are inconclusive. Asdell, Doornenbal, Joshi, and Sperling (1967) found no significant differences among the mean lifespans of groups of male rats that were: (1) unbred, (2) bred, (3) castrated at 45 days of age, or (4) castrated and implanted with androgens. Drori and Folman (1969) found a significantly longer mean survival time in a group of 28 mated rats as compared to an equal number of paired litter-mate controls, but the experimental conditions were such that the differences cannot be unequivocally attributed to the physiological effects of mating *per se*.

Mated female mice and rats have shorter lives than virgins (Mühlbock, 1959), but this is probably due to the metabolic burdens of multiple pregnancies. In at least one colony of Sprague Dawley rats, virgin animals of both sexes have a lower incidence of atherosclerosis (Wexler, 1964) and differ strikingly from breeders in their response to ischaemia (Wexler & Saroff, 1970).

When houseflies are kept in large populations of mixed or single sex, the males have life spans about half as long as females (Rockstein and Lieberman, 1959), associated with earlier abrasion and loss of wings in the male. Restriction of physical activity and mating by confining flies individually in small vials led to a slight increase in mean survival time of females, but male survival increased to about 50 days, more than double the survival of males caged in large groups, and slightly superior to the survival of isolated females (Raglan and Sohal, 1973). These investigators attribute the increased survival of the confined males to decreased physical activity and reduction of mating activity. However, surgically dewinged males caged in groups had even shorter survival times than intact males, so other factors must be operative in addition to the quantitative reduction of physical activity. Metabolic rates were not measured. Survival curves were presented by Ragland and Sohal (1973), but life table analysis was not done. The survival data shown suggest that changes in the caging conditions brought about both a decreased vulnerability and a decreased actuarial aging rate. If confirmed by quantitative analysis, this would support their suggestion that "it may be more fruitful to study metabolic changes due to physical activity, rather than temperature-induced metabolic changes, in relation to longevity and aging."

Polednak (1972a, b, and c) investigated the longevity and mortality from cardiovascular and renal disease among former Harvard College athletes and their classmates. The after-expectancy of life of athletes born in the period 1860–1889 was not significantly affected by the type of sport, but there was a small decrease of expectancy with increased extent of participation. This pattern was also observed for coronary heart disease and other cardiovascular diseases. Body build was more mesomorphic in the athletes with three or more varsity letters, but apparently physique was not responsible for the correlation of heart disease with level of participation. In comparisons among varsity lettermen, athletes in intramural sports, and nonathletes, in regard to mean age at death from natural causes (Polednak, 1972c), the varsity athletes had the shortest lives, but the differences were small and not statistically significant. Longevity of men who participated in intramural athletics was as great as, or slightly (but insignificantly) greater than, that of nonathletes, despite the larger body size of the former.

The Free Radical Hypothesis and Antioxidant Therapy

Harman (1956) developed the free radical hypothesis of aging (Harman, 1973; Pryor, 1971),

and investigated the life table modifications produced by a variety of chemical antioxidants administered to mice throughout their adult lives. It was uniformly intermixed into the solid food ration, which was a standard mouse diet formula or a semi-synthetic diet. Free radical inhibitors were fed to AKR mice and to C3H mice (Harman, 1957) and he tested the same agents on these strains and on Swiss mice (Harman, 1961, 1962) (Table 4). Tumor incidence and survival time was scored and average body weights were reported. None of the agents tested was consistently life-prolonging over the three strains and two experiments. The greatest extension observed was 3.8 months in C3H female mice given 2-mercaptoethylamine HCl (MEA) in the second study. This 26 percent increase was statistically significant, and was accompanied by a delayed onset of mortality from mammary tumors, but without any decrease in lifetime tumor incidence. The C3H female mouse has a high incidence of a virus-induced mammary tumor. Hydroxylamine hydrochloride greatly decreased mammary tumor incidence ($1/24$, as compared to $11/36$ in controls) but did not prolong life. There was no evidence for life prolongation in AKR mice, but the AKR is a short-lived strain that has virtually a 100 percent incidence of fatal leukemia by 10 months. There was no significant effect on the longevity of Swiss mice, which had fairly normal control survival and relatively low tumor incidence. Body weights were not much depressed in any of the treated groups, so that food intake was presumably comparable in all groups. Since food intake was not reported, the actual intake of the antioxidants cannot be estimated.

Subsequently 6 free radical inhibitors were tested on LAF$_1$ mice fed a semi-synthetic diet, and one agent, MEA, was also tested on a commercial diet (Harman, 1968a and b). Of the agents tested, MEA had apparent efficacy on the commercial diet and on the semi-synthetic diet, and butylated hydroxytoluene (BHT) was effective with the semi-synthetic diet. All other agents were ineffective or slightly toxic. Body weight differences were small but sufficient in the case of MEA and BHT so that the possibility of a life prolongation effect arising from caloric restriction (Tannenbaum and Silverstone, 1953; Silberberg and Silberberg, 1954; Silberberg, Jarrett, and Silberberg, 1962) cannot be excluded.

Buu-Hoi and Ratsimamanga (1959) tested the efficacy of an antioxidant, nordihydroguaiaretic acid, that is employed commercially as a food preservative. They fed 12 mated pairs the antioxidant for 796 days at a level of 20 mg per kg of alimentation and, "afin de se rapprocher des conditions de vie normale," the basic balanced diet was supplemented for 1 day every 15 days with a free choice of foods including liver, pork bones, lard, vegetables, and sweetened tea containing 10 percent alcohol. After 796 days, 2 of 24 controls survived, both females, whereas among those fed the free radical inhibitor, 8 survived, 2 males and 6 females. The females in the treated group also bore twice as many litters.

Comfort, Youhotsky-Gore and Pathmanathan (1971) evaluated the effects of another free radical inhibitor, ethoxyquin, administered in a standard pelleted diet, on the longevity of C3H mice. The mice fed ethoxyquin lived 100 days longer than controls and there was no sex difference. The treated group weighed as much as the controls for the first 125 days, but fell below controls at later ages by amounts ranging from 10 to 20 percent.

An implication of the free radical theory is that the rate of aging increases as the amount of unsaturated fat in the body tissues increases, because the unsaturated bonds are the sites of lipid peroxidation. Harman (1971) tested this by feeding mice and rats semi-synthetic diets containing 5, 10 or 20 percent by weight of lard, olive oil, safflower oil, or menhaden oil. Vitamin E (DL-α-tocopherol acetate), 20 mg/kg of diet, was added. This was estimated to be more than adequate to avert vitamin E deficiency in the animals receiving 20 percent menhaden oil, the most readily peroxidized diet. No evidence of overt vitamin E deficiency was observed in any diet group. The diets were approximately isocaloric in composition, for the lipids, in excess of the 5 percent base level, replaced the same number of calories of glucose in the semi-synthetic diet. Food consumption was restricted by giving the same number of calories of diet to all 15 diet groups. Despite this precaution, the body weights

tended to increase with the level of dietary fat. Since the mice were caged in groups of 10 and the rats in groups of four, the food intakes of individual animals were not known. The data on mammary carcinoma in C3H female mice indicated that mammary tumor incidence increased with the fat content of the diet and, at a fixed fat content, with the degree of unsaturation of the lipids. The results with menhaden oil were markedly lower than expected, but possibly some highly unsaturated fatty acids in menhaden oil are not readily hydrolyzed by the rat's digestive enzymes, so that the lipid actually absorbed may have been more saturated than that ingested. Increasing the fat content or degree of unsaturation of the diet reduced the longevity of C3H female mice significantly, perhaps because of the large increase of mammary carcinoma, but produced only a small decrease of longevity in Swiss male mice or Charles River male rats. Increased "peroxidizability" of lipids alone had little effect on longevity. This may be evidence that an excess of vitamin E gives adequate protection against lipid peroxidation. However, no evidence was given on the relationship between the degree of unsaturation of dietary fat and the unsaturation of lipids in the body tissues.

Despite the number of experiments, it is not possible to reach a conclusive actuarial evaluation of the effects of antioxidant treatment of the survival characteristic. The control mice in the experiments of Harman and of Comfort, Youhotsky-Gore, and Pathmanathan had typical survival for those times and the experimental conditions. The doubling times of the mortality rates, T_d, ranged from 100 to 130 days, consistent with the general experience with laboratory mice that are not tumor-prone and are free of epidemic disease. The short life expectations, 450 to 550 days, in these experiments are therefore due to a comparatively high value of the vulnerability parameter, q_o. The prolongations that were observed in treated groups can only be interpreted as arising from a decrease in the vulnerability parameter: there is no evidence, in any experiment, for a decrease in the rate of aging, or for an increase of maximum life span to or beyond the potential span for the mouse strains used.

This conclusion is underlined by the results of

Kohn (1971), who fed two antioxidants, MEA and BHT, to retired breeder C57BL mice. In three replicate experiments, when the control mice had good mean survival time the agents were without effect, but in those trials with suboptimal control survival, the antioxidant groups had longer life spans than their controls, but not beyond optimal control values.

Harman (1972) recognized that free radical inhibitors fail to increase the maximal life span, and conjectured that this arises from the fact that they do not protect certain organelles, particularly the mitochondria. However, evidence that free radicals have a direct reaction path to the primary aging lesion is slight. Most of the lipids in membranes turn over rapidly, so that most, if not all, of the damage produced by peroxidation is repaired and would not be cumulative. The site and nature of the irreparable damage are unknown, as are the kinetics. The failure to effect a decreased aging rate with antioxidants should also be viewed with the perspective that *no* other chemical agent has yet been shown to reduce the rate of actuarial aging, even when life expectancy is increased.

Marechal, Lion, and Duchesne (1973) measured the ESR signals from the fresh-frozen brain tissue of 11 species of birds and 11 species of mammals, and examined the relation of signal intensity to maximum life span. Signal intensity decreased as species life span increased for both birds and mammals, and in almost the same degree, but the birds as a group had signal levels about 40 percent higher than mammals of comparable longevity. The decrease of signal from mouse to man amounted to about 35 percent. They conclude that this trend is due to a decrease of organic free radicals in the brains of the longer-lived species.

Rahman (1976) carried out similar measurements on the brain tissues of young animals from four species of small myomorph rodents, two of which (*Mus musculus* and *Praomys natalensis*) have life expectancies of about 600 days, and two (*Peromyscus leucopus* and *P. californicus insignis*) have expectancies of about 1500 days (Table 1). Despite great care in preparation and measurement, the within-species variation was too great (4.3 to 9.3 for the long-lived, *versus* 3.7 to 7.1 for the short-

lived) to allow a significant difference to be observed. The magnitude of variation of the ESR signal from mouse to man (35 percent) is small in comparison to the 30-fold ratio of life spans, and may be more closely related to other factors, such as the rate of metabolism of brain tissue, rather than to longevity *per se.*

Molecular oxygen plays a central role in the reactions leading to the formation of peroxides and superoxides, and this led Gerschman (Gerschman, Gilbert, Nye, Dwyer, and Fenn 1954; Gerschman, Gilbert, and Caccamise, 1958; Gerschman, 1959) to propose that oxygen poisoning and ionizing radiation injury have many features in common. Sobel (1970) exposed 41 mice to 1.08 atmospheres of oxygen for a total of 72 days over a period of 168 days, with 250 to 390 days of follow-up. No effects on mortality, growth, or nitrogen metabolism were observed, nor were there any differences in hyaluronic acid and collagen content, or in the fluorescence of collagen.

Further studies of the role of oxygen are desirable, preferably beginning with an invertebrate model that allows more flexible and direct control of tissue oxygen levels, temperature, and other physico-chemical variables.

Membrane Stabilization

There are two general approaches to the prolongation of life by retardation of age changes in membranes. The nonspecific approach is to inhibit the peroxidation of membrane lipids by means of free radical scavengers. The more specific method, reviewed here, is to use a heterogeneous group of drugs that increase the stability of cell and organelle membranes (Weissmann, 1969; Hochschild, 1971a). The lysosomes play an especially important role in the life and death of cells because of the powerful hydrolytic enzymes they contain: this has led to the theory that the lysosomes are a major factor in the aging process (DeDuve and Wattiaux, 1966 DeDuve, 1968). Hence the lysosomal membrane stabilizers are of particular interest, including such diverse molecules as salicylates, antihistamines, and certain corticosteroids.

Hochschild has investigated the life-prolonging action of a number of alleged membrane stabilizers on fruit flies and mice. Two experiments were performed with fruit flies, the first with an F_1 hybrid of two inbred strains of *D. melanogaster*, and the second with one of the parent inbred strains (Hochschild, 1971b). The control samples of the two genotypes had life expectancies of 80 and 73 days for males and 80 and 68 days for females, good longevities at the maintenance temperature of 22°C. Of several corticosteroids tested, hydrocortisone acetate consistently increased mean survival time, ranging from 20 to 40 percent in two sexes in two experiments. Triamcinoline had comparable effectiveness in the second experiment. Prednisolone and its derivatives were not effective. The protection by hydrocortisone was independent of dose down to the lowest dose tested, 10 mg/ml of medium. Among the salicylates, aspirin and salicylamide were effective. Other analgesics and antipyretics tested were ineffective, as were some antihistamines, phenothiazines, chloroquine derivatives, colchicine, and procaine HCl. On the whole, the effectiveness of these drugs for life prolongation in *Drosophila* was not correlated with their effectiveness for stabilizing mammalian cell membranes *in vitro* (Weissmann, 1969).

Hochschild presented survival curves for all those treatment groups that showed significant increase of survival time. With no exceptions, the protected groups experienced either a constant displacement of the survival curve to the right of controls at all levels of survival, i.e., a parallel curve, or a decrease in the amount of displacement as dying-out proceeded, i.e., a steeper curve. The maximum survival time was increased in several trials, but the percent increase was never as great as the increase of median survival time. In terms of the two Gompertz function parameters, the modification of the survival characteristic for *Drosophila* produced by the membrane stabilizers that were effective in prolonging life was due to a decreased vulnerability to disease, and not to a decrease of the aging rate.

Consideration of the possible mechanism of action of the membrane stabilizers suggests that this is the kind of actuarial effect to be expected. The dose-independent life prolongation conferred by both cortisone acetate and aspirin indicates that all available receptor sites were saturated by the lowest doses, so the lysosomes were maintained in a non-progressive stabilized state, independent of age. This could account for a decrease of death rates by a constant factor, but not for a decrease by a progressively increasing factor. Although these results do not support the hypothesis that decreased stability of the lysosome membrane is a primary cause of aging, they are nevertheless important, for deferral of mortality without slowing down the aging process is a desirable goal in its own right.

Hochschild (1973) found no significant effect of membrane stabilizers on mean survival time in mice. However, 8 of 10 of his treated groups had smaller standard deviations of survival time than his control group, and this difference appears to be significant for most groups. This suggests that lifetime maintenance of the lysosomes at a higher than normal level of stability may have a cumulative deleterious effect on mice which is actuarially equivalent to an increase in the rate of aging. The same may be true for fruit flies, since most treatments yielded slightly steeper survival curves. The difference is that there was a net increase of survival time for the flies because of a more than compensatory decrease in vulnerability, while in mice there is only slight initial indication of a decrease in vulnerability, and it is overtaken by the subsequent acceleration of the mortality process.

Bellamy (1968) administered prednisolone phosphate continuously, in drinking water, to a short-lived population of inbred mice, beginning at weaning. There was a large increase in survival time in both sexes of treated mice compared to controls but the treated mice had normal mouse survival curves (50 percent dead at about 700 days, while the control mice of both sexes were almost all dead at 440 days). The prednisolone-treated groups showed retardation of growth and of deposition of collagen as compared to the controls. There was no postmortem pathology examination of the mice, so the reason for the early death of controls and its prevention by prednisolone is unknown. Until that point is clarified, prednisolone should not be considered to be an effective life prolongation drug. Forbes (1975) administered prednisolone to 50 female DBA/2J mice beginning at 232 days of age. It was administered in the drinking water at a level of 3.0–3.2 μg/ml. There was no difference in survival from the controls, which lived 775 days.

Hormones and Metabolic Factors

The medical and popular press of the 1920's and 30's contained many accounts of the rejuvenating power of "gland" therapy, but virtually none of that work has been validated. One exception is the work of Korenchevsky, who began in the 1930's a series of investigations on the relation of various hormones and vitamins, especially the sex hormones, to the aging process in male and female rats (e.g., Korenchevsky, 1942, 1948, 1950; Korenchevsky and Jones, 1947; Korenchevsky and Paris, 1950; Korenchevsky, Paris, and, Benjamin, 1950). Although his work was primarily histological, it merits attention because it exemplifies the optimization approach to life prolongation research. Thus, he gives evidence (Korenchevsky and Jones, 1948: Korenchevsky, Paris, and Benjamin, 1950) that the balanced administration of two or more hormones can reduce some damaging effects due to hyperhormonization produced by a single hormone. The tendency of endocrinological stimulation of aging tissues to be accompanied by widespread meta-hyperplasias and adenomatous growths is documented (Korenchevsky and Paris, 1950).

Friedman and Friedman (1963) took note of the fact that both man and rat show a disturbance of salt and water metabolism in advanced age. They carried out two experiments in which male rats were given saline suspension of whole posterior pituitary powder three times weekly beginning at 24 months of age. In the second experiment the posterior pituitary powder was supplemented with pitressin (vasopressin). Mortality was reduced in the treated group in the following 6 to 7 months, after which the experiment was terminated. The reduction of mortality is significant, but the data do not permit any conclusion about the specific actuarial parameters affected. The Friedmans describe the effect as a temporary reduction of the death rate, and that may be correct, for in the seventh month of treatment the mortality

in the treated group increased considerably and the difference from controls dwindled. However, the crude dried posterior pituitary, presumably from cattle or pigs, may have elicited an immune reaction in the treated animals.

Subsequently, a small decrease in mortality of rats treated with desiccated posterior pituitary powder was reported by Friedman and Friedman (1964) and, physiological measurements were also made which showed superior sodium excretion and a more powerful isometric tension response in the stimulated gastrocnemius muscle of the pituitary-treated rats. The treated group also failed to show the hypertrophy of kidney, heart, adrenal, and pituitary shown by the controls.

Robertson and Brailsford (1928) administered desiccated thyroid to rats at levels that caused a moderate increase of metabolic rate and found that life expectancy was decreased.

There is evidence that the androgens have a life-shortening effect and that reduction of androgen levels prolongs life. Hamilton and Mestler (1969) compared populations of eunuchs and intact males and females in an institution for the mentally retarded. The eunuchs lived to a median age of 69.3 years, as compared to 55.7 years for intact males. Hamilton (1965) and Hamilton, Hamilton, and Mestler (1969) also found that castrated male cats lived longer than intact males, and about as long as intact or spayed females. However, Mühlbock (1959) found no significant effect of gonadectomy on either sex of DBA_f mice. Asdell, et al. (1967) found that administration of testosterone to gonadectomized male and female rats reduced their life expectancies by a non-significant amount.

This action of androgens has been linked to their labilizing effect on lysosomal membranes (Hochschild, 1971b), on the basis of evidence that testosterone and progesterone increase the permeability of lysosomal membranes.

Comparison of the life tables of eunuchs and intact males reported by Hamilton and Mestler (1969) indicates that the increased longevity of eunuchs is probably due to reduction of vulnerability factors rather than to a reduction of the rate of aging. Castration led to a more rectangular life table, with decreased mortality at early ages, especially for the subgroup castrated before puberty. However, the subsequent mortality accelerated somewhat more rapidly than did the non-castrate mortality, and the survival curves converged at advanced ages.

Levo dopa (L-dopa, L-3,4-dihydroxyphenylalanine) has a life-prolonging effect on males of a short-lived population of albino mice (Cotzias, et al. 1974). The use of L-dopa, (a precursor of brain dopamine) for the treatment of Parkinson's disease (Cotzias, Van Woert, and Schiffer, 1967; Cotzias, Papavasilou, and Gellene, 1969) is accompanied by side effects in both humans and mice. Fixed doses of L-dopa given to mice are highly toxic, producing motor hyperactivity, autonomic disturbances and convulsions. Male mice that consumed 40 mg of L-dopa per day in their food, the highest sublethal dose, had an initial period of toxicity accompanied by loss of weight and thinning of hair, but subsequently adapted fully and regained the lost weight. Thereafter, they maintained good health and appearance, and experienced greatly reduced mortality up to the end of the 18-month study as compared to their controls (Cotzias, Miller, Nicholson, Maston, and Tang, 1974).

Segall (1975; personal communication, June 1975), finds that rats fed diets deficient in tryptophan had considerably extended reproductive spans. The rats were sterile during the period of tryptophan deficiency, but regained fertility at 26 months of age, 9 months beyond the maximum fertile age in control rats. There are also indications that longevity is comparably increased. Tryptophan is an essential amino acid that is a precursor of the neurotransmitter serotonin (5-hydroxytryptamine), which has a depressant influence on CNS activity that is, on the whole, antagonistic to the stimulatory action of L-dopa. Hence, the findings of Segall (1975) and those of Cotzias, et al. (1974) are consistent in pointing to the importance of the level of CNS activity for the maintenance of vigorous function and low vulnerability to disease. (Discussion of the neurotransmitters and aging is given by Finch in Chapter 11).

The Cross-Linkage Theory of Aging and Lathyrogen Therapy

The theory that aging is due to the cross-linkage of protein and DNA molecules has been exten-sively examined at the biochemical and biophysical level (Bjorksten, 1963), but there is little data on the modification of life tables by retardation of cross-linkage. Caloric restriction, which prolongs life in rats, also delays the increase of collagen cross-linkage (Everitt, 1971), but the causal sequence is not known. Prednisolone, which has an equivocal life-prolongation effect, also retards collagen aging (Bellamy, 1968).

One direct approach to testing this theory is the long-term administration of lathyrogens, chemicals that inhibit the formation of collagen cross-linkages. Kohn and Leash (1967; see also LaBella, 1968) performed such an experiment, administering β-aminopropionitrile (BAPN) to rats for their lifetimes, beginning at weaning. There was retardation of growth and a reduction of benign tumors by almost a factor of three, but no significant change of survival at dosage levels that did not inhibit growth too severely. Kohn does not consider this result to be conclusive, because the reduction of cross-linkage by BAPN may be operating at the wrong collagen bonds. He suggests that penicillamine is a more rational anti-cross-linkage agent because it affects only the cross-linkage in mature, insoluble collagen, and is, therefore, less likely to interfere with collagen synthesis.

Procaine

The beneficial effects of procaine (novocaine) on the psychic function, health, and survival of old people (Aslan, 1956) has been the focus of much research. An extensive investigation of the effects of procaine on the survival and on some behavioral, morphological, and physiological characteristics of white rats was carried out by Aslan, Vrabiescu, Domilescu, Campeanu, Costiniu, and Stanescu, (1965). Rats of the French Wistar strain received 4 mg procaine per kg body weight on a schedule of three parenteral injections per week for 4 weeks, followed by an intermission period of 1 month, repeated for the entire life span, beginning at either 2 months or 6 months of age. Controls received saline injections. There were 1840 rats of both sexes in the experiment, equally divided between experimentals and controls. Survival and pathology were determined for all but 60 rats that were killed at 24 months of age for histology. Samples of the treated groups were drawn at random for the psychological and physiological measurements at ages 16 and 24 months. Survival time was significantly increased in the males but not in females. The age at beginning of the therapy made no difference. The Gompertz plots for the male rats are given in Figure 18. It is clear that the effect of procaine on the survival of males is due entirely to a decrease of the vulnerability parameter. Causes of death differed little between treated groups and controls, and body weights were not consistently related to treatment. The old, treated animals showed better psychomotor performance than controls in the maze learning task. In both rate of learning and running speed, the females were comparable at age 24 months to controls at age 18 months. This indicates that in both sexes, but especially in females, procaine treatment had more benefit for central nervous system functions than it did for the retardation of disease processes.

The search for the mechanism of procaine action should take account of the fact that it does not have a cumulative anti-aging action, but rather produces a non-cumulative displacement of the steady state of the organism. This is expressed in improved psychophysiological performance and a reduction of disease incidence and mortality rates by a constant factor as long as administration is continued. These characteristics are consistent with recent evidence that procaine acts as an inhibitor of monoamine oxidase, for an action of this kind could understandably modify the psychophysiological steady state, but it is not easy to understand how it could have a cumulative action. The mean decay time of the improved psychophysiological state must, therefore, be on the order of days or weeks. This parameter could be evaluated by initiating and terminating treatment at several ages. The findings of Aslan, *et al.* may be related to the life prolongation found by Cotzias, *et al.* (1974) with L-dopa, and the preservation of reproductive capacity described by Segall (1975) with restriction of a serotonin precursor.

Parabiosis

Heterochronic parabiosis (the surgical joining of the circulations of two animals of different ages) is, like heterochronic transplantation, a

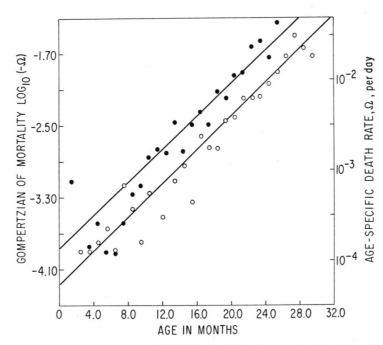

Figure 18. Gompertz diagrams for control (solid circles) and procaine-treated rats (open treated circles) to show parallelism of the mortality rate trends. This implies that the life prolongation effected by procaine is due to reduction of vulnerability, not to decrease of aging rate. (Data of Aslan *et al.*, 1965.) Lines fitted by weighted least squares.

useful tool for the study of aging processes; various physiological and immunological questions have been answered by its use. An experiment on the effects of parabiosis on longevity was carried out by Ludwig and Elashoff (1972), who maintained 275 homochronic (same age) and heterochronic (different age) pairs of rats in parabiosis for their joint life spans and obtained survival curves. The age difference between pairs of unequal age was 280 days, and the surgery was done when the young members, and both members of like-age pairs, were 60–85 days old.

Parabiosis of males was disadvantageous to the survival of homochronic parabionts and to the young member of the heterochronic pairs, while the survival of the older members was about equal to the single control survival. In females, parabiosis decreased the longevity of the young heterochronic parabiont, while the homochronic pairs lived as long as single controls and the older heterochronic parabiont lived significantly longer. An alternative way of expressing their results is to say that the survival time at a given fractional survival of the heterochronic parabionts at death (average of ages of young and old pair members) is quite close to the survival time of the homochronic pairs at the same fraction surviving, as if the aging injury is averaged over the two members of the heterochronic pairs. Tauchi (1972) describes the pathology observed in parabionts, with special reference to the causes of the early deaths.

CONCLUSION

This survey shows that a number of diverse chemical and physical treatments have been found to possess life-prolonging efficacy in animal experiments. It is seen also that increases in life expectation may be due either to decrease of a parameter governing the rate of aging, or to decrease of another parameter governing the age-independent vulnerability to disease and death. In terms of these actuarial criteria, the surprising conclusion emerges that all efficacious pharmacological therapies tested achieve their effects by reduction of disease vulnerability, and not by decrease of the aging rate.

It was found, however, that two non-pharma-cological treatments, caloric restriction in rats and reduction of body temperature for poikilotherms, prolong life by decreasing the rate of actuarial aging. In both cases, the decrease of aging rate is explicable as a consequence of a decrease of the rate of energy metabolism, a mode of action that is fundamentally different from the actions proposed for the various chemical agents.

These observations indicate that life prolongation must hereafter be viewed as a two-dimensional concept, and that every life-prolonging drug must be categorized in terms of the extent to which it affects each of the two major life table parameters.

The problem of distinguishing between proper and hormetic actions must be faced, and the fact that effective pharmacological agents are so frequently found to reduce the vulnerability parameter makes this examination more crucial, for the same kind of actuarial effect is produced by hormetic actions.

Although this review has been deliberately critical, it is heartening to observe that there is a body of accomplishment that survives critical examination. If future theory and experiment takes account of the concepts and methods developed here, there is good reason to expect that progress will be more rapid in the future.

Acknowledgment. The author is indebted to S. A. Tyler and Carol Fox for statistical and computational assistance, and to R. J. M. Fry, W. P. Norris, Y.-E. Rahman, E. Staffeldt, and P. H. Duffy for the use of unpublished data.

REFERENCES

Aebi, H. 1963. Detection and fixation of radiation-produced peroxide by enzymes. *Radiation Res.*, suppl. **3**, 130–149.

Allemand, R., Cohet, Y. and David, J. 1973. Increase in the longevity of adult *Drosophila melanogaster*. *Exp. Geront.*, **8**, 279–283.

Alpatov, W. W., and Pearl, R. 1929. Experimental studies on the duration of life. XII. Influence of temperature during the larval period and adult life on the duration of the life of the imago of *Drosophila melanogaster*. *Am. Naturalist.*, **63**, 37–67.

Andersen, A. C., and Rosenblatt, L. S. 1969. The effect whole-body X-irradiation on the median lifespan of female dogs (beagles). *Radiation Res.*, **39**, 177–200.

Anderson, T. W., le Riche, W. H., and MacKay, J. S. 1969. Sudden death and ischemic heart disease. Correlation with hardness of local water supply. *New Engl. J. Med.*, **280**, 805–807.

Asdell, S. A., Doornenbal, H., Joshi, S. R., and Sperling, G. A. 1967. The effect of sex steroid hormones on the longevity of rats. *J. Reprod. Fertility*, **14**, 113–120.

Aslan, A. 1956. Novocain als eutrophischer Faktor und die Möglichkeit einer Verlängerung der Lebensdauer. *Ther. Umschau. Bern*, **9**, 165–173.

Aslan, A., Vrabiescu, A., Domilescu, C., Campeanu, L., Costiniu, M., and Stanescu, S. 1965. Long-term treatment with procaine (Gerovital H₃) in albino rats. *J. Geront.*, **20**, 1–8.

Barott, H. G. 1937. Effect of temperature, humidity and other factors on hatch of hens' eggs and on energy metabolism of chick embryos. *U. S. Dept. Agriculture Technical Bulletin, No.* 553.

Bartholomew, G. A. and T. J. Cade. 1957. Temperature regulation, hibernation, and estivation in the little pocket mouse, *Perognathus longimembris*. *J. Mammal.* **38**: 60–72.

Barrett, J. C. 1973. Age, time and cohort factors in mortality from cancer of the cervix. *J. Hyg., Camb.*, **71**, 253–259.

Bellamy, D. 1968. Long-term action of prednisolone phosphate on a strain of short-lived mice. *Exp. Geront.*, **3**, 327–333.

Berg, B., and Simms, H. S. 1960a. Nutrition and longevity in the rat. I. Food intake in relation to size, health and fertility. *J. Nutr.*, **71**, 242–255.

Berg, B. N., and Simms, H. S. 1960b. Nutrition and longevity in the rat. II. Longevity and onset of disease with different levels of food intake. *J. Nutr.*, **71**, 255–263.

Berg, B. N., and Simms, H. S. 1961. Nutrition and longevity in the rat. III. Food restriction beyond 800 days. *J. Nutr.*, **74**, 23–32.

Beverton, R. J. H., and Holt, S. J. 1959. A review of the lifespans and mortality rates of fish in nature and their relation to growth and other physiological characteristics. *In*, G. E. W. Wolstenholme and M. O'Connor (eds.), *Ciba Foundation Colloquia on Ageing. Vol. 5. The Lifespan of Animals*, pp. 142–177. Boston: Little, Brown.

Bidder, G. P. 1932. Senescence. *Brit. Med. J., ii*, 5831.

Bjorksten, J. 1963. Aging, primary mechanism. *Gerontologia*, **8**, 179–192.

Boche, R. D. 1954. Effects of chronic exposure to X-radiation on growth and survival. *In*, H. A. Blair (ed.), *Biological Effects of External Radiation*, pp. 220–252. New York: McGraw-Hill.

Bodansky, M., and Engel, S. L. 1966. Oxytocin and the lifespan of male rats. *Nature*, **210**, 751.

Bourlière, F. 1957. The comparative biology of aging: A physiological approach. *In*, G. E. W. Wolstenholme and M. O'Connor (eds.), *Ciba Foundation Colloquia on Ageing. Vol. 3.* Methodology of the study of ageing, pp. 20–30. Boston: Little, Brown.

Bourlière, F. 1959. Lifespans of mammalian and bird populations in nature. *In*, G. E. W. Wolstenholme and M. O'Connor (eds.), *Ciba Foundation Colloquia on Ageing. Vol. 5. The Lifespan of Animals*, pp. 99–103. Boston: Little, Brown.

Bras, G., and Ross, M. H. 1964. Kidney disease and nutrition in the rat. *Toxicol. Appl. Pharmacol.*, **6**, 247–262.

Bras, G., and Ross, M. H. 1966. Protein intake and the incidence of kidney disease in the rat. *In*, *Proceedings of the Seventh International Congress of Nutrition, Hamburg, Vol.*, **5**, 226–229.

Brues, A. M., and Sacher, G. A. 1952. Analysis of mammalian radiation injury and lethality. *In*, J. J. Nickson (ed.), *Symposium on Radiobiology*, pp. 441–465. New York: John Wiley and Sons.

Buenning, E. 1964. *The Physiological Clock*. New York: Academic Press.

Burcombe, J. V., and Hollingsworth, M. J. 1970. The relationship between developmental temperature and longevity in *Drosophila*. *Gerontologia*, **16**, 172–181.

Buu-Hoi, N. P., and Ratsimamanga, A. R. 1959. Action retardante de l'acide nordihydroguaiarétique sur le vieillisément chez le rat. *C. R. Soc. Biol.*, **153**, 1180–1182.

Carlson, A. J., and Hoelzel, F. 1946. Apparent prolongation of the lifespan of rats by intermittent fasting. *J. Nutr.*, **31**, 363–373.

Carlson, A. J., and Hoelzel, F. 1947. Growth and longevity of rats fed omnivorous and vegetarian diets. *J. Nutr.*, **34**, 81–96.

Carlson, L. D., and Jackson, B. H. 1959. The combined effects of ionizing radiation and high temperature on the longevity of the Sprague-Dawley rat. *Radiation Res.*, **11**, 509–519.

Carlson, L. D., Scheyer, W. J., and Jackson, B. H. 1957. The combined effects of ionizing radiation and low temperature on the metabolism, longevity, and soft tissues of the white rat. I. Metabolism and longevity. *Radiation Res.*, **7**, 190–197.

Casarett, A. P. 1968. *Radiation Biology*. Englewood Cliffs, N.J.: Prentice-Hall.

Case, R. A. M. 1956a. Cohort analysis of mortality rates as an historical or narrative technique. *Brit. J. Prevent. & Social Med.*, **10**, 159–171.

Case, R. A. M. 1956b. Cohort analysis of cancer mortality in England and Wales, 1911–1954 by site and sex. *Brit. J. Prevent. Social Med.*, **10**, 172–199.

Chai, C. K. 1959. Life span in inbred and hybrid mice. *J. Heredity*, **50**, 203–208.

Clark, A. M., and Rubin, M. A. 1961. The modification by X-irradiation of the life span of haploids and diploids of the wasp, *Habrobracon* sp. *Radiation Res.*, **15**, 244–253.

Clarke, J. M., and Smith, J. M. 1955. The genetics and cytology of *Drosophila subobscura*. XI. Hybrid vigour and longevity. *J. Genet.*, **53**, 172–180.

Clarke, J. M., and Smith, J. M. 1961a. Independence of temperature of the rate of ageing in *Drosophila subobscura*. *Nature*, **190**, 1027–1028.

Clarke, J. M., and Smith, J. M. 1961b. Two phases of ageing in *Drosophila subobscura*. *J. Exp. Biol.*, **38**, 679–684.

Cockrum, E. L. 1956. Homing, movements, and longevity in bats. *J. Mammalogy*, **37**, 48–57.

Cohen, B. H. 1964. Family patterns of mortality and life span. *Quart. Rev. Biol.*, **39**, 130–181.

Cohet, Y. 1973. Reduction de la fécondité et du potentiel reproducteur de la *Drosophila* adulte consecutive au développement larvaire à basse température. *C. R. Acad. Sci. (Paris)*, **277**, 2227–2230.

Cole, L. C. 1954. The population consequences of life history phenomena. *Quart. Rev. Biol.*, **29**, 103–137.

Comfort, A. 1957. Survival curves of mammals in captivity. *Proc. Zool. Soc. Lond.*, **128**, 349–364.

Comfort, A. 1958. Coat colour and longevity in Thoroughbred mares. *Nature*, **182**, 1531–1532.

Comfort, A. 1960. Longevity and mortality in dogs of four breeds. *J. Geront.*, **15**, 126–129.

Comfort, A. 1963. Effect of delayed and resumed growth on the longevity of a fish (*Lebistes reticulatus*, Peters) in captivity. *Gerontologia*, **8**, 150–155.

Comfort, A., and Doljanski, F. 1958. The relation of size and age to rate of tail regeneration in *Lebistes reticulatus*. *Gerontologia*, **2**, 266–283.

Comfort, A., Youhotsky-Gore, I., and Pathmanathan, K. 1971. Effect of ethoxyquin on the longevity of C3H mice. *Nature*, **229**, 254–255.

Cotzias, G. C., Miller, S. T., Nicholson, A. R., Jr., Maston, W. H., and Tang, L. C. 1974. Prolongation of the life-span in mice adapted to large amounts of L-Dopa. *Proc. Nat. Acad. Sci.*, **71**, 2466–2469.

Cotzias, G. C., Papavasilou, P. S., and Gellene, R. 1969. Modification of parkinsonism—chronic treatment with L-Dopa. *New Engl. J. Med.*, **280**, 337–345.

Cotzias, G. C., Van Woert, M. H., and Schiffer, L. M. 1967. Aromatic amino acids and modification of parkinsonism. *New Engl. J. Med.*, **276**, 374–379.

Crowley, C., and Curtis, H. J. 1963. The development of somatic mutations in mice with age. *Proc. Nat. Acad. Sci.*, **49**, 626–628.

Curtis, H. J. 1963. Biological mechanisms underlying the aging process. *Science*, **141**, 686–694.

Curtis, H. J., and Crowley, C. 1963. Chromosome aberrations in liver cells in relation to the somatic mutation theory of aging. *Radiation Res.*, **19**, 337–344.

Curtis, H. J., Tilley, J., and Crowley, C. 1964. The cellular differences between acute and chronic neutron and gamma ray irradiated mice. *In, Biological Effects of Neutron and Proton Irradiations, Vol. III*, pp. 143–155. Vienna: International Atomic Energy Agency.

Dalderup, L. M., and Visser, W. 1971. Influence of extra sucrose, fats, protein and of cyclamate in the daily food on the lifespan of rats. *Experientia*, **27**, 519–521.

David, J., and Clavel, M. F. 1969. Influence de la témperature sur le nombre, le pourcentage d'éclosion et la taille des oeufs pondus per *Drosophila melanogaster*. *Ann. Soc. ent. Fr. (N.S.)*, **5**, 161–177.

David, J., and Cohet, Y. 1971. Réduction de la longévité de drosophiles adultes par élevage à basse température. *C. R. Acad. Sci. (Paris)*, **273**, 1028–1031.

David, J., Cohet, Y., and Fouillet, P. 1971. Ralentissement de la croissance et longévité des drosophiles adultes: influence d'une sous-alimentation larvaire. *C. R. Soc. Biol.* **165**, 2100.

De Duve, C. 1968. Lysosomes as targets for drugs. *In*, P. N. Campbell (ed.), *The Interaction of Drugs and Subcellular Components in Animal Cells*, pp. 155–169. London: J. & A. Churchill.

DeDuve, C., and Wattiaux, R. 1966. Functions of lysosomes. *Ann. Rev. Physiol.*, **28**, 435–492.

Deevey, E. S., Jr. 1947. Life tables for natural populations of animals. *Quart. Rev. Biol.*, **22**, 283–314.

Diamond, M. C., Rosenzweig, M. R., Bennett, E. L., Lindner, B., and Lyon, L. 1972. Effects of environmental enrichment and impoverishment on rat cerebral cortex. *J. Neurobiol.*, **3**, 47–64.

Doll, R., and Hill, A. B. 1956. Lung cancer and other causes of death in relation to smoking. *Brit. Med. J.*, part 2, 1071–1081.

Doll, R., and Hill, A. B. 1966. Mortality of British doctors in relation to smoking: Observations on coronary thrombosis. *In*, W. Haenszel (ed.), *Epidemiological Study of Cancer and Other Chronic Diseases*, pp. 205–268. U. S. Department of Health, Education and Welfare.

Doty, B. 1966. Age and avoidance conditioning in rats. *J. Geront.*, **21**, 287–290.

Drori, D., and Folman, Y. 1969. The effect of mating on the longevity of male rats. *Exp. Geront.*, **4**, 263–266.

Dublin, L. I., Lotka, A. J., and Spiegelman, M. 1949. *Length of Life*, revised edition. New York: Ronald Press.

Ducoff, H. S. 1972. Causes of death in irradiated adult insects. *Biol. Rev.*, **47**, 211–240.

Ducoff, H. S. 1975. Form of the increased longevity of *Tribolium* after X-irradiation. *Exp. Geront.* (in press).

Edington, D. W., Cosmas, A. C., and McCafferty, W. B. 1972. Exercise and longevity: Evidence for a threshold age. *J. Geront.*, **27**, 341–343.

Egami, N., and Etoh, H. 1969. Life span for the small fish, *Oryzias latipes*. *Exp. Geront.*, **4**, 127–129.

Egoscue, H. F., Bittmenn, J. G., and Petrovich, J. A. 1970. Some fecundity and longevity records for captive small animals. *J. Mammalogy*, **51**, 622–623.

Enterline, P. E., Rikli, A. E., Sauer, H. I., and Hyman, M. 1960. Death rates for coronary heart disease in metropolitan and other areas. *Public Health Reports*, **75**, 759–766.

Erk, F. C., and Samis, H. V., Jr. 1970. Light regimes and longevity. *Drosophila Information Serv.*, **45**, 148.

Everitt, A. V. 1971. Food intake, growth and the ageing of collagen in rat tail tendon. *Gerontologia*, **17**, 98–104.

Festing, M. F. W., and Blackmore, D. K. 1971. Life span of specified-pathogen-free (MRC category 4) mice and rats. *Lab. Anim.* **5**, 179–192.

Forbes, W. F. 1975. The effect of prednisolone

phosphate on the life-span of DBA/2J mice. *Exp. Geront.* **10:** 27–29.

Forbes, W. F., and Gentleman, J. F. 1973. A possible similar pathway between smoking-induced life shortening and natural aging. *J. Geront.*, **28,** 302–311.

Fridovich, I. 1972. Superoxide radical and superoxide dismutase. *Accounts of Chem. Res.*, **5,** 321–326.

Friedenthal, H. 1910. Ueber die Giltigkeit des Massenwirkung für den Energieumsatz der lebendigen Substanz. *Zbl. Physiol.*, **24,** 321–327.

Friedman, S. M., and Friedman, C. L. 1963. Effect of posterior pituitary extracts on the life-span of old rats. *Nature*, **200,** 237–238.

Friedman, S. M., and Friedman, C. L. 1964. Prolonged treatment with pituitary powder in aged rats. *Exp. Geront.*, **1,** 37–48.

Fry, R. J. M., Sacher, G. A. Tyler, S. A., Ainsworth, E. J., Allen, K. H., and Staffeldt, E. F. 1975. A comparison of the incidence of tumors obtained by two methods of sampling. *In*, *Argonne National Laboratory, Division of Biological and Medical Research Annual Report for 1974*, No. ANL-75-30, pp. 95–98.

Furth, J., Upton, A. C., Christenberry, K. W., Benedict, W. H., and Moshman, J. 1954. Some late effects in mice of ionizing radiation from an experimental nuclear detonation. *Radiology*, **63,** 562–570.

Gerschman, R. 1959. Oxygen effects in biological systems. *In, Proc. XXI Internat. Congr. Cienc. Physiol., Buenos Aires*, p. 1.

Gerschman, R., Gilbert, D. L., and Caccamise, D. 1958. Effect of various substances on survival time of mice exposed to different high oxygen tensions. *Amer. J. Physiol.*, **192,** 563–571.

Gerschman, R., Gilbert, D. L., Nye, S. W., Dwyer, P., and Fenn, W. O. 1954. Oxygen poisoning and X-irradiation: A mechanism in common. *Science*, **119,** 623.

Giess, M. C., and Planel, M. H. 1973. Influence de la radio-protection effectuée a différents stades sur la longévité de *Drosophila melanogaster*. *C. R. Acad. Sci. (Paris)*, **276,** 1029–1032.

Giess, M. C., Planel, H., and Blanquet, Y. 1971. Recherches sur l'influence des radiations ionisantes naturelles sur la genèse d'une mutation spontanée chez *Drosophila melanogaster*. *C. R. Soc. Biol.* **165,** 706–709.

Gompertz, B. 1825. On the nature of the function expressive of the law of human mortality and on a new mode of determining life contingencies. *Phil. Trans. Roy. Soc. London*, 513–585.

Goodrick, C. L. 1974. The effects of exercise on longevity and behavior of hybrid mice which differ in coat color. *J. Geront.*, **29,** 129–133.

Grahn, D. 1960. Genetic control of physiological processes: The genetics of radiation toxicity in animals. *In*, R. S. Caldecott and L. A. Snyder (eds.), *Symposium on Radioisotopes in the Biosphere*, pp. 181–200. Minneapolis: The Center for Continuation Study, University of Minnesota.

Grahn, D. 1970. Biological effects of protracted low dose radiation exposure of man and animals. *In*, R. J. M. Fry, D. Grahn, M. L. Griem, and J. H. Rust (eds.), *Late Effects of Radiation*, pp. 101–136. London: Taylor and Francis.

Grahn, D. 1972. Data collection and genetic analysis in the selection and study of rodent model systems in aging. *In*, D. C. Gibson (ed.), *Development of the Rodent as a Model System of Aging*, pp. 55–56. Bethesda, Md.: National Inst. of Child Health and Human Development.

Grahn, D., Fry, R. J. M., and Lea, R. A. 1972. Analysis of survival and cause of death statistics for mice under single and duration-of-life gamma irradiation. *In, Life Sciences and Space Research, Vol.* **10,** pp. 175–186. Berlin: Akademie-Verlag.

Halbach, U. 1973. Life table data and population dynamics of the rotifer *Brachionus calyciflorus* Pallas as influenced by periodically oscillating temperature. *In*, W. Wieser (ed.), *Effects of Temperature on Ectothermic Organisms*, pp. 217–228. New York: Springer-Verlag.

Hamilton, J. B. 1965. Relationship of castration, spaying and sex to survival and duration of life in domestic cats. *J. Geront.* **20:** 96–104.

Hamilton, J. B., Hamilton, R. S., and Mestler, G. E. 1969. Duration of life and causes of death in domestic cats: Influence of sex, gonadectomy, and inbreeding. *J. Geront.*, **24,** 427–437.

Hamilton, J. B., and Mestler, G. E. 1969. Mortality and survival: Comparison of eunuchs with intact men and women in a mentally retarded population. *J. Geront.*, **24,** 395–411.

Hammond, E. C. 1966. Smoking in relation to the death rates of one million men and women. *In*, W. Haenszel (ed.), *Epidemiological Study of Cancer and Other Chronic Diseases*, pp. 126–204. U. S. Department of Health, Education and Welfare.

Hammond, E. C. 1969. Life expectancy of American men in relation to their smoking habits. *J. Nat. Cancer Inst.*, **43,** 951–962.

Hammond, E. C., Garfinkel, L., and Seidman, H. 1971. Longevity of parents and grandparents in relation to coronary heart disease associated variables. *Circulation*, **43,** 31–44.

Hammond, E. C., and Horn, D. 1954. The relationship between human smoking habits and death rates: A follow-up study of 187,766 men. *J. Am. Med. Assoc.*, **155,** 1316–1328.

Hammond, E. C., and Horn, D. 1958. Smoking and death rates–Report on forty-four months of follow-up of 187,783 men. *J. Am. Med. Assoc.*, **166,** 1159–1171.

Harman, D. 1956. Aging: A theory based on free radical and radiation chemistry. *J. Geront.*, **11,** 298–300.

Harman, D. 1957. Prolongation of the normal life span by radiation protection chemicals. *J. Geront.*, **12,** 257–263.

Harman, D. 1961. Prolongation of the normal lifespan

and inhibition of spontaneous cancer by antioxidants. *J. Geront.*, **16**, 247–254.

Harman, D. 1962. Role of free radicals in mutation, cancer, aging and the maintenance of life. *Radiation Res.*, **16**, 753–773.

Harman, D. 1968a. Free radical theory of aging: Effect of free radical reaction inhibitors on the mortality rate of male LAF$_1$ mice. *J. Geront.*, **23**, 476–482.

Harman, D. 1968b. Free radical theory of aging: Effect of free radical inhibitors on the life span of male LAF$_1$ mice—second experiment. *Gerontologist*, **8**, (3, part II), 13.

Harman, D. 1971. Free radical theory of aging: Effect of the amount and degree of unsaturation of dietary fat on mortality rate. *J. Geront.*, **26**, 451–457.

Harman, D. 1972. The biologic clock: The mitochondria? *J. Am. Geriat. Soc.*, **20**, 145–147.

Harman, D. 1973. Free radical theory of aging. *Triangle*, **12**, 153–158.

Hart, R. W., and Setlow, R. B. 1974. Correlation between deoxyribonucleic acid excision-repair and life-span in a number of mammalian species. *Proc. Nat. Acad. Sci.*, **71**, 2169–2173.

Heroux, O., and Campbell, J. S. 1960, A study of the pathology and life span of 6°C- and 30°C-acclimated rats. *Lab. Invest.*, **1**, 205–315.

Herz, Z., Folman, Y., and Drori, D. 1969. The testosterone content of the testes of mated and unmated rats. *J. Endocrinol.*, **44**, 127–128.

Hochschild, R. 1971a. Effect of membrane stabilizing drugs on mortality in *Drosophila melanogaster*. *Exp. Geront.*, **6**, 133–151.

Hochschild, R. 1971b. Lysosomes, membranes and aging. *Exp. Geront.*, **6**, 153–166.

Hochschild, R. 1973a. Effects of dimethylaminoethyl *p*-chlorophenoxyacetate on the life span of male Swiss Webster albino mice. *Exp. Geront.*, **8**, 177–183.

Hochschild, R. 1973b. Effect of dimethylaminoethanol on the life span of senile male A/J mice. *Exp. Geront.*, **8**, 185–191.

Hochschild, R. 1973c. Effects of various additives on *in vitro* survival time of mouse macrophages. *J. Geront.*, **28**, 447–449.

Hochschild, R. 1973d. Effects of various additives on *in vitro* survival time of human fibroblasts. *J. Geront.*, **28**, 450–451.

Hochschild, R. 1973e. Effects of various drugs on longevity in female C57BL/6J mice. *Gerontologia*, **19**, 271–280.

Hollcroft, J., Lorenz, E., Miller, E., Congdon, C. C., Schweisthal, R., and Uphoff, D. 1957. Delayed effects in mice following acute total-body X-irradiation: Modification by experimental treatment. *J. Nat. Cancer Inst.*, **18**, 615–640.

Hollingsworth, M. J. 1966. Temperature and the rate of aging in *Drosophila subobscura*. *Exp. Geront.*, **1**, 259–267.

Hollingsworth, M. J. 1968. Environmental temperature and life span in poikilotherms. *Nature*, **218**, 869–870.

Hollingsworth, M. J. 1969a. Temperature and length of life in *Drosophila*. *Exp. Geront.*, **4**, 49–55.

Hollingsworth, M. J. 1969b. The effect of fluctuating environmental temperatures on the length of life of adult *Drosophila*. *Exp. Geront.*, **4**, 159–167.

Hollingsworth, M. J. 1970. The threshold theory of aging. *Gerontologia*, **16**, 252–258.

Hollingsworth, M. J., and Burcombe, J. V. 1970. The nutritional requirements for longevity in *Drosophila*. *J. Insect Physiol.*, **16**, 1017–1025.

Huffaker, C. B. 1944. The temperature relations of immature stages of the malarial mosquito, *Anopheles quadrimaculatus* Say, with a comparison of the developmental power of constant and variable temperatures in insect metabolism. *Ann. Entomol., Soc. Amer.*, **37**, 1–27.

Irving, L., Krog, H., and Monson, M. 1955. The metabolism of some Alaskan animals in winter and summer. *Physiol. Zool.*, **28**, 173–185.

Jablon, S., Ishida, M., and Yamasaki, M. 1965. Studies on the mortality of A-bomb survivors. Description of the samples and mortality, 1950–1960. *Radiation Res.*, **25**, 25–52.

Johnson, H. D., Kintner, L. D., and Kibler, H. H. 1963. Effects of 48°F (8.9°C) and 83°F (28.4°C) on longevity and pathology of male rats. *J. Geront.*, **18**, 29–36.

Jones, D. C., and Kimeldorf, D. J. 1963. Lifespan measurements in the male rat. *J. Geront.*, **18**, 316–321.

Jones, D. C. L., and Kimeldorf, D. J. 1964. Effect of age at irradiation on life span in the male rat. *Radiation Res.*, **22**, 106–115.

Jones, H. B. 1955. A special consideration of the aging process, disease, and life expectancy. *University of California Radiation Laboratory, Berkeley, California.* UCRL-3105, pp. 1–68. U. S. Atomic Energy Commission.

Kahn, H. A. 1966. The Dorn study of smoking and mortality among U.S. veterans: Report on eight and one-half years of observance. *In*, W. Haenszel (ed.), *Epidemiological Study of Cancer and Other Chronic Diseases*, pp. 1–125. U.S. Department of Health, Education and Welfare.

Kanisawa, M., and Schroeder, H. A. 1967. Life term studies on the effect of arsenic, germanium, tin, and vanadium on spontaneous tumors in mice. *Cancer Res.*, **27**, 1192–1195.

Kanisawa, M., and Schroeder, H. A. 1969. Life term studies on the effect of trace elements on spontaneous tumors in mice and rats. *Cancer Res.*, **29**, 892–895.

Kayser, C. H. 1961. *The Physiology of Natural Hibernation*. Oxford: Pergamon Press.

Kennaway, N. M., and Kennaway, E. L. 1937. A study of the incidence of cancer of the lung and larynx. *J. Hyg. Camb.*, **36**, 236–267.

Kennaway, E. L., and Kennaway, N. M. 1947. A further study of the incidence of cancer of the lung and throat. *Cancer*, **1**, 260–298.

Kermack, W. O., McKendrick, A. G., and McKinley, P. L. 1934. Death rates in Great Britain and Sweden. *Lancet*, **226**, 698–703.

Kibler, H. H., and Johnson, H. D. 1961. Metabolic rate

and aging in rats during exposure to cold. *J. Geront.*, **16**, 13–16.

Kibler, H. H., and Johnson, H. D. 1966. Temperature and longevity in male rats. *J. Geront.*, **21**, 52–56.

Kibler, H. H., Silsby, H. D., and Johnson, H. D. 1963. Metabolic trends and life spans of rats living at 9 C and 28 C. *J. Geront.*, **18**, 235–239.

Kimeldorf, D. J., Phillips, R. D., and Jones, D. C. 1966. Longevity in neutron-exposed guinea pigs. *J. Geront.*, **21**, 265–267.

Kobayashi, K. 1957. Geographical relationship between the chemical nature of river water and death-rate from apoplexy. *Ber. Ohara Inst. landwirtschl. Biol.*, **11**, 12–21.

Kohn, R. R. 1971. Effect of antioxidants on life span of C57BL mice. *J. Geront.*, **26**, 378–380.

Kohn, R. R., and Leash, A. M. 1967. Long-term lathyrogen administration to rats, with special reference to aging. *Exp. Molec. Pathol.*, **7**, 354–361.

Korenchevsky, V. 1942. Natural relative hypoplasia and the problem of ageing. *J. Pathol. Bacteriol.*, **54**, 13–24.

Korenchevsky, V. 1948. Effects of sex and thyroid hormones on the processes of ageing in female rats. *Brit. Med. J.*, **i**, 728.

Korenchevsky, V. 1950. The effect of vitamins on the heart lesions produced by thyroid hormone in the rat. *J. Pathol. Bacteriol.*, **62**, 53–60.

Korenchevsky, V., and Jones, V. E. 1947. The effects of androsterone, oestradiol, and thyroid hormone on the artififical premature "climacteric" of pure gonadal origin produced by ovariectomy in rats. III. Effects on histological structure of vagina, uterus, adrenals, and thyroid. *J. Geront.*, **2**, 116–136.

Korenchevsky, V., and Jones, V. E. 1948. The effects of progesterone, oestradiol, thyroid hormone, and androsterone on the artificial premature "climacteric" of pure gonadal origin produced by ovariectomy in rats. *J. Geront.*, **3**, 21–39.

Korenchevsky, V., and Paris, S. K. 1950. Co-operative effects of endocrinological factors and process of aging in producing adenoma-like structures in rats. *Cancer*, **3**, 903–922.

Korenchevsky, V., Paris, S. K., and Benjamin, B. 1950. Treatment of senescence in female rats with sex and thyroid hormones. *J. Geront.*, **5**, 120–157.

LaBella, F. S. 1968. The effect of chronic dietary lathyrogen on rat survival. *Gerontologist*, **8**, 13.

Laidler, K. J. 1958. *The Chemical Kinetics of Enzyme Action.* Oxford: The Clarendon Press.

Lamb, M. J. 1968. Temperature and lifespan in *Drosophila. Nature*, **220**, 808–809.

Lát, J. 1967. Self-selection of dietary components. *Handbook of Physiology, Section 6, Alimentary Canal*, **1**, pp. 367–386. Washington, D.C.: American Physiological Society.

Laws, E. R. 1971. Evidence of antitumorigenic effects of DDT. *Proc. Environ. Health*, **23**, 181–184.

Laws, R. M., and Parker, I. S. C. 1968. Recent studies on elephant populations in East Africa. *Symp. Zool. Soc. Lond.*, **21**, 319–359.

Levine, S., Alpert, M., and Lewis, G. W. 1958. Differential maturation of an adrenal response to cold stress in rats manipulated in infancy. *J. Comp. Physiol. Psychol.*, **51**, 774–777.

Lindop, P. J., and Rotblat, J. 1961. Long-term effects of a single whole-body exposure of mice to ionizing radiations. II. Causes of death. *Proc. Roy. Soc. Lond.*, **B154**, 350–368.

Lints, F. A. 1971. Life span in *Drosophila. Gerontologist*, **17**, 33–51.

Lints, F. A., and Lints, C. V. 1968. Respiration in *Drosophila.* II. Respiration in relation to age by wild, inbred and hybrid *Drosophila melanogaster* imagos. *Exp. Geront.*, **3**, 341–349.

Lints, F. A., and Lints., C. V. 1969a. Respiration in *Drosophila.* III. Influence of preimaginal environment on respiration and ageing in *Drosophila melanogaster* hybrids. *Exp. Geront.*, **4**, 81–94.

Lints., F. A., and Lints., C. V. 1969b. Influence of preimaginal environment on fecundity and ageing in *Drosophila melanogaster* hybrids. I. Preimaginal population density. *Exp. Geront.*, **4**, 231–244.

Lints, F. A., and Lints, C. V. 1971a. Influence of preimaginal environment on fecundity and ageing in *Drosophila melanogaster* hybrids. *Exp. Geront.*, **6**, 417–427.

Lints, F. A., and Lints, C. V. 1971b. Influence of preimaginal environment on fecundity and ageing in *Drosophila melanogaster* hybrids. III. Developmental speed and life-span. *Exp. Geront.*, **6**, 427–445.

Liu, R. K., and Walford, R. L. 1966. Increased growth and lifespan with lowered ambient temperature in the annual fish, *Cynolebias adloffi. Nature*, **212**, 1277–1278.

Liu, R. K., and Walford, R. L. 1969. Laboratory studies on lifespan, growth, aging and pathology of the annual fish, *Cynolebias bellottii* Steindachner. *Zoologica, N.Y.* **54**, 1–16.

Liu, R. K., and Walford, R. L. 1970. Observations on the lifespans of several species of annual fishes and of the world's smallest fishes. *Exp. Geront.*, **5**, 241–246.

Liu, R. K., and Walford, R. L. 1972. The effect of lowered body temperature on lifespan and immune and non-immune processes. *Gerontologia*, **18**, 363–388.

Loeb, J., and Northrop, J. H. 1917. On the influence of food and temperature upon the duration of life. *J. Biol. Chem.*, **32**, 103–126.

Lorenz, E., Hollcroft, J. W., Miller, E., Congdon, C. C., and Schweisthal, R. 1955. Long-term effects of acute and chronic irradiation in mice. I. Survival and tumor incidence following chronic irradiation of 0.11 R per day. *J. Nat. Cancer Inst.*, **15**, 1049–1058.

Lorenz, E., Jacobson, L. O., Heston, W. E., Shimkin, M., Eschenbrenner, A. B., Deringer, M. K., Doniger, J., and Schweisthal, R. 1954. Effects of long-continued total-body gamma irradiation on mice, guinea pigs, and rabbits. III. Effects on life span, weight, blood picture, and carcinogenesis and the role of the intensity of radiation. *In*, R. E. Zirkle (ed.), *Biological Effects of External X and Gamma Radiation,* National Nuclear Energy Series, Div. IV, *Vol.* **22B**, pp. 24-148. New York: McGraw-Hill.

Luckey, T. D. 1956. Mode of action of antibiotics: Evidence from germfree birds. *In, First International Conference on Uses of Antibiotics in Agriculture, Washington, D. C.,* pp. 135-145. National Academy of Science and National Research Council.

Luckey, T. D. 1958. Modes of action of antibiotics in growth stimulation. *Recent Progress in Microbiology, Symposia held at VII International Congress for Microbiology,* pp. 340-349.

Luckey, T. D. 1963. Antibiotic action in adaptation. *Nature,* **198,** 263-265.

Luckey, T. D. 1968. Insecticide hormoligosis. *J. Econ. Entomol.,* **62,** 7-12.

Luckey, T. D. 1974. Hormology with inorganic compounds. *Environ. Qual. Safety, Suppl.* **1,** 81-103.

Ludwig, F. C., and Elashoff, R. M. 1972. Mortality in syngeneic rat parabionts of different chronological age. *Trans. N.Y. Acad. Sci.,* **134,** 582-587.

McCay, C. M. 1941. Diet and Aging. *J. Am. Dietet. Assoc.,* **17,** 540-545.

McCay, C. M. 1942. Chemical aspects and the effect of diet upon aging. *In,* E. V . Cowdry (eds.), *Problems of Ageing,* second edition, pp. 680-727. Baltimore: Williams and Wilkins.

McCay, C. M., and Crowell, M. F. 1934. Prolonging the life span. *Sci. Monthly,* **39,** 405-414.

McCay, C. M., Crowell, M. F., and Maynard, L. A. 1935. The effect of retarded growth upon the length of life span and upon the ultimate body size. *J. Nutr.,* **10,** 63-79.

McCay, C. M., Ellis, G. H., Barnes, L. L., Smith, C. A. H., and Sperling, G. 1931. Chemical and pathological changes in aging and after retarded growth. *J. Nutr.,* **18,** 15-25.

McCay, C. M., Maynard, L. A., Sperling, G., and Barnes, L. L. 1939. Retarded growth, life span, ultimate body size and age changes in the albino rat after feeding diets restricted in calories. *J. Nutr.,* **18,** 1-13.

McCay, C. M., Maynard, L. A., Sperling, G., and Osgood, H. S. 1941. Nutritional requirements during the latter half of life. *J. Nutr.,* **21,** 45-60.

McNab, B. 1969. The economics of temperature regulation in neotropical bats. *Comp. Biochem. Physiol.,* **31,** 227-268.

Marechal, R., Lion, Y., and Duchesne, J. 1973. Radicaux libres organiques et longévité maximale chez les mamifères et les oiseaux. *C. R. Acad. Sci. (Paris),* **277,** 1085-1087.

Menusan, H., Jr. 1934. Effects of temperature and humidity on the life processes of the bean weevil, *Bruchus obtectus* Say. *Ann. Entomol. Soc. Amer.,* **27,** 515-526.

Merrill, M. 1947. Time-specific life tables contrasted with observed survivorship. *Biometrics,* **3,** 129-136.

Molnar, K. 1973. Subbiological aspects of ageing and the concept of biological cathode protection. *Mech. Age. Dev.,* **1,** 319-326.

Mühlbock, O. 1959. Factors influencing the life-span of inbred mice. *Gerontologia,* **3,** 177-183.

Nash, D. J., and Kidwell, J. F. 1973. A genetic analysis of lifespan, fecundity, and weight in the mouse. *J. Heredity,* **64,** 87-90.

Nolen, G. A. 1972. Effect of various restricted dietary regimes on the growth, health and longevity of albino rats. *J. Nutr.,* **102,** 1477-1494.

Ordy, J. M., Samorajski, T., Zeman, W., and Curtis, H. J. 1967. Interaction effects of environmental stress and deuteron irradiation of the brain on mortality and longevity in C57BL/10 mice. *Proc. Soc. Exp. Biol. Med.,* **126,** 184-190.

Osborne, T. B., and Mendel, L. B. 1915. The resumption of growth after long continued failure to grow. *J. Biol. Chem.,* **23,** 439-454.

Osborne, T. B., Mendel, L. B., and Ferry E. L. 1917. The effect of retardation of growth upon the breeding period of duration of life in rats. *Science,* **45,** 294-295.

Ottoboni, A. 1972. Effect of DDT on reproductive lifespan in the female rat. *Toxicol. Appl. Pharmacol.,* **22,** 497-502.

Parker, J. R. 1930. Some effects of temperature and moisture upon *Melanoplus mexicanus mexicanus* Saussure and *Camnula pellucida* Scudder (Orthoptera). *Univ. Montana Agric. Exp. Sta. Bull. No. 223,* pp. 1-132.

Pearl, R. 1922. *The Biology of Death.* Philadelphia: J. B. Lippincott.

Pearl, R. 1928. *The Rate of Living.* New York: Alfred Knopf.

Perry, H. M., Jr. 1972. Hypertension and the geochemical environment. *Bull. N.Y. Acad. Sci.,* **199,** 202-215.

Perry, H. M., Jr., Tipton, I. H., Schroeder, H. A., Steiner, R. L., and Cook, M. J. 1961. Variation in the concentration of cadmium in human kidney as a function of age and geographic origin. *J. Chronic Diseases,* **14,** 259-271.

Pittendrigh, C. S. 1960. Circadian rhythms and the circadian organization of living systems. *Symp. on Quant. Biol.,* **25,** 159-182.

Pittendrigh, C. S., and Minis, D. H. 1972. Circadian systems: Longevity as a function of circadian resonance in *Drosophila melanogaster. Proc. Nat. Acad. Sci.,* **69,** 1537-1539.

Planel, M. H., and Giess, M. C. 1973. Diminution de la longévité de *Drosophila melanogaster* sous l'effect de la protection vis-a-vis des radiations ionisantes naturelles. *C. R. Acad. Sci. (Paris)* **276,** 809-812.

Planel, H., Soleilhavoup, J. P., and Giess, M. C. 1969. Influence de milieu et de la souche sur le rôle de l'irradiation naturelle chez *Drosophila melanogaster. C. R. Acad. Sci. (Paris),* **268,** 584-587.

Planel, H., Soleilhavoup, J. P., Giess, M. C., and

Tixador, M. R. 1967a. Action des radiations ionis-antes naturelles sur la reproduction des métazoaires: Recherches chez "*Drosophila melanogaster.*" *C. R. Acad. Sci.* (*Paris*), **264**, 755–758.

Planel, H., Soleihavoup, J. P., Giess, M. C., and Tixador, M. R. 1967b. Mise en évidence d'un retard de développement de *Drosophila melanogaster* par diminution de la radioactivité naturelle ambiante. *C. R. Acad. Sci.* (*Paris*), **264**, 865–868.

Polednak, A. P. 1972a. Mortality from renal diseases among former college athletes. *Ann. Internal. Med.*, **77**, 919–922.

Polednak, A. P. 1972b. Longevity and cardiovascular mortality among former college athletes. *Circulation*, **46**, 649–654.

Polednak, A. P. 1972c. Longevity and cause of death among Harvard College athletes and their classmates. *Geriatrics*, **27**, 53–64.

Portman, R. M., Lucas, H. L., Elston, R. C., and Greenberg, B. G. 1963. Estimation of time, age, and cohort effects. Raleigh, North Carolina, North Carolina State College, *Institute of Statistics Mimeographed Series No. 372.*

Prausnitz, S., and Süsskind, C. 1962. Effects of chronic microwave irradiation on mice. *I.R.E. Trans. Biomed. Electronics*, PGME-4, pp. 104–108.

Preskorn, S., Edwards, H., Justesen, D. R., Nielson, A., and Werder, A. 1976. Tumor growth and longevity in mice after fetal irradiation by 2450-MHz microwaves. *J. Surg. Oncol.* (in press).

Pryor, W. A. 1971. Free radical pathology. *Chem. Eng. News*, **34**, 34–51.

Ragland, S. S., and Sohal, R. S. 1973. Mating behavior, physical activity and aging in the housefly *Musca domestica. Exp. Geront.*, **8**, 135–145.

Rahman, Y. E. 1976. Unpublished results.

Reincke, U., Stutz, E., and Hunstein, W. 1970. Life span and tumor incidence in rats subjected to severe stress before whole body X-irradiation. *In, Proceedings of the First European Symposium on Late Effects of Radiation, Casaccia Nuclear Center*, pp. 151–172.

Retzlaff, E., Fontaine, J., and Furuta, W. 1966. Effect of daily exercise on life-span of albino rats. *Geriatrics*, **21**, 171–177.

Richards, A. G. 1964. The generality of temperature effects on developmental rate and oxygen consumption in insect eggs. *Physiol. Zool.*, **37**, 199–211.

Robertson, T. B., and Brailsford, T. 1928. The influence of thyroid alone and of thyroid administered together with nucleic acids upon the growth and longevity of the white mouse. *Australian J. Exp. Biol. Med. Sci.*, **5**, 69–88.

Rockstein, M., and Lieberman, H. M. 1959. A life table for the common house fly, *Musca domestica. Gerontologia*, **3**, 23–36.

Ross, M. H. 1959. Protein, calories and life expectancy. *Fed. Proc.*, **18**, 1190–1207.

Ross, M. H. 1961. Length of life and nutrition in the rat. *J. Nutr.*, **75**, 197–210.

Ross, M. H. 1964. Nutrition, disease and length of life. *In*, G. E. W. Wolstenholme and M. O'Connor (eds.), *Diet and Bodily Constitution*, pp. 91–103. Boston: Little, Brown.

Ross, M. H. 1966. Life expectancy modification by change in dietary regimen of the mature rat. *Proc. Seventh Internat. Congr. Nutr.*, **5**, 35–38.

Ross, M. H. 1969. Aging, nutrition and hepatic enzyme activity patterns in the rat. *J. Nutr.*, **97**, Suppl. 1, part II, 563–602.

Ross, M. H. 1972. Length of life and caloric intake. *Amer. J. Clin. Nutr.*, **25**, 834–838.

Ross, M. H., and Batt, W. G. 1956. Alkaline phosphatase activity and diet. *J. Nutr.*, **60**, 137–144.

Ross, M. H., and Batt, W. G. 1957. Diet-age pattern for hepatic enzyme activity. *J. Nutr.*, **61**, 39–49.

Ross, M. H., and Bras, G. 1965. Tumor incidence patterns and nutrition in the rat. *J. Nutr.*, **87**, 245–260.

Ross, M. H., and Bras, G. 1971. Lasting influence of early caloric restriction on prevalence of neoplasms in the rat. *J. Nat. Cancer Inst.*, **47**, 1095–1113.

Ross, M. H., and Bras, G. 1973. The influence of protein under and overnutrition on spontaneous tumor prevalence in the rat. *J. Nutr.*, **103**, 944–963.

Ross, M. H., and Bras, G. 1974. Dietary preference and diseases of age. *Nature*, **250**, 263–265.

Ross, M. H., and Bras, G. 1975. Food preference and length of life. *Science* (in press).

Ross, M. H., Bras, G., and Ragbeer, M. S. 1970. Influence of protein and caloric intake upon spontaneous tumor incidence of the anterior pituitary gland of the rat. *J. Nutr.*, **100**, 177–189.

Ross, R., and Sacher, G. A. 1976. Unpublished results.

Rubner, M. 1908. *Das Problem der Lebensdauer und seine Beziehungen zum Wachstum und Ernährung.* Munich: Oldenbourg.

Russell, W. L. 1968. Recent studies on the genetic effects of radiation in mice. *Pediatrics*, **41**, 223–230.

Rust, J. H., Robertson, R. J., Staffeldt, E. F., Sacher, G. A., and Fry, R. J. M. 1966. Effects of lifetime periodic gamma-ray exposure on the survival and pathology of guinea pigs. *In*, P. J. Lindop and G. A. Sacher (eds.), *Radiation and Ageing*, pp. 217–244. London: Taylor and Francis.

Saccomanno, G., Saunders, R. P., Archer, V. E., Auerbach, O., and Brennan, L. 1970. Metaplasia to neoplasia. *In*, P. Nettesheim, M. G. Hanna, Jr., and J. W. Deatherage, Jr. (eds.), *Morphology of Experimental Respiratory Carcinogenesis*, pp. 63–80. AEC Symposium Series, *Vol.* **21**, Oak Ridge, USAEC Division of Technical Information.

Sacher, G. A. 1956. On the statistical nature of mortality with especial reference to chronic radiation mortality, *Radiology*, **67**, 250–257.

Sacher, G. A. 1957. Discussion. *In, Mammalian Aspects of Basic Mechanisms of Radiobiology*. NAS-

NRC Publ. *No.* **513,** Report No. 21, pp. 121–125, 137–142.

Sacher, G. A. 1958. Entropic contributions to mortality and aging. *In*, H. Yockey, H. Quastler and R. Platzman (eds.), *Symposium on Information Theory in Biology*, pp. 317–330. New York: Pergamon Press.

Sacher, G. A. 1959. Relation of lifespan to brain weight and body weight in mammals. *In*, G. E. W. Wolstenholme and M. O'Connor (eds.), *CIBA Foundation Colloquia on Ageing, Vol.* **5,** *The Lifespan of Animals*, pp. 115–133. London: Churchill.

Sacher, G. A. 1960. Analysis of life tables with secular terms. *In*, B. L. Strehler (ed.), *The Biology of Aging*, pp. 253–257. Baltimore: Waverly Press.

Sacher, G. A. 1963. Effects of X-rays on the survival of *Drosophila melanogaster. Physiol. Zool.,* **36,** 295–311.

Sacher, G. A. 1966. The Gompertz transformation in the study of the injury-mortality relationship. Application to late radiation effects and ageing. *In*, P. J. Lindop and G. A. Sacher (eds.), *Radiation and Ageing, Proceedings of a Colloquium held in Semmering, Austria, June, 1966*, pp. 411–441. London: Taylor and Francis.

Sacher, G. A. 1967. The complementarity of entropy terms for the temperature-dependence of development and aging. *Ann. N.Y. Acad. Sci.,* **138,** (Art. 2), 680–712.

Sacher, G. A. 1972. Table of Lifespans of Mammals F.A.S.E.B. *Handbook of Biological Data*.

Sacher, G. A. 1973. Dose dependence for life shortening by X-rays, gamma rays and fast neutrons. *In*, J. P. Duplan and A. Chapiro (eds.), *Advances in Radiation Research, Biology and Medicine, Vol.* **3,** pp. 1425–1432. New York: Gordon and Breach.

Sacher, G. A. 1976a. Dose, dose rate, radiation quality and host factors for radiation-induced life shortening. *In*, K. S. Smith (ed.), *Aging, carcinogenesis, and radiation biology*, pp. 419–517. New York, Plenum.

Sacher, G. A. 1976b. Evaluation of entropy and information terms governing mammalian longevity. *In*, R. Cutler (ed.), *Interdiscipl. Topics Geront.,* **9,** 69–82. Basel, Karger.

Sacher, G. A., and Grahn, D. 1964. Survival of mice under duration-of-life exposure to gamma rays. I. The dosage-survival relation and the lethality function. *J. Nat. Cancer Inst.,* **32,** 277–321.

Sacher, G. A., and Staffeldt, E. 1972. Life tables of seven species of laboratory-reared rodents. *Gerontologist,* **12** (3, part II), 39 (abstract).

Sacher, G. A., and Staffeldt, E. 1974. Relation of gestation time to brain weight for placental mammals: Implications for the theory of vertebrate growth. *Am. Naturalist,* **108,** 593–615.

Sacher, G. A., and Trucco, E. 1962a. A theory of the improved performance and survival produced by small doses of radiations and other poisons. *In*, N. W. Shock (ed.), *Biological Aspects of Aging, Proceedings Fifth International Association of Geron-*

tology, San Francisco, August, 1960, pp. 244–251. New York: Columbia University Press.

Sacher, G. A., and Trucco, E. 1962b. The stochastic theory of mortality. *Ann. N.Y. Acad. Sci.,* **96,** 985–1007.

Scholander P. F., Hock, R., Walters, V., and Irving, L. 1950. Adaptation to cold in arctic and tropical mammals and birds in relation to body temperature, insulation and basal metabolic rate. *Biol. Bull.,* **99,** 259–271.

Schroeder, H. A. 1960. Relation between mortality from cardiovascular disease and treated water supplies. *J. Am. Med. Assoc.,* **172,** 1902–1908.

Schroeder, H. A. 1966. Municipal drinking water and cardiovascular death rates. *J. Am. Med. Assoc.,* **195,** 125–129.

Schroeder, H. A. 1969. The water factor. *New Engl. J. Med.,* **280,** 836–838.

Schroeder, H. A., Balassa, J. J., and Vinton, W. H., Jr. 1964. Chromium, lead, cadmium, nickel and titanium in mice: Effect on mortality, tumors and tissue levels. *J. Nutr.,* **83,** 239–250.

Schroeder, H. A., Balassa, J. J., and Vinton, W. H., Jr. 1965. Chromium, cadmium and lead in rats: Effects on life span, tumors and tissue levels. *J. Nutr.,* **86,** 51–66.

Schroeder, H. A., Kanisawa, M., Frost, D. V., and Mitchener, M. 1968. Germanium, tin and arsenic in rats: Effects on growth, survival, pathological lesions and life span. *J. Nutr.* **96,** 37–45.

Schroeder, H. A., and Kraemer, L. A. 1974. Cardiovascular mortality, municipal water, and corrosion. *Arch. Environ. Health* **28,** 303–311.

Schroeder, H. A. and Mitchener, M. 1971a. Selenium and tellurium in rats: Effect on growth, survival and tumors. *J. Nutr.* **101,** 1531–1540.

Schroeder, H. A. and Mitchener, M. 1971b. Scandium, chromium (VI), gallium, yttrium, rhodium, palladium, indium in mice: Effects on growth and life span. *J. Nutr.* **101,** 1431–1438.

Schroeder, H. A. and Mitchener, M. 1972. Selenium and tellurium in mice. *Arch. Environ. Health* **24,** 66–71.

Schroeder, H. A., Mitchener, M., Balassa, J. J., Kanisawa, M., and Nason, A. P. 1968. Zirconium, niobium, antimony and fluorine in mice: Effects on growth, survival and tissue levels. *J. Nutr.* **95,** 95–101.

Schroeder, H. A., Mitchener, M., and Nason, A. P. 1970. Zirconium, niobium, antimony, vanadium and lead in rats: Life term studies. *J. Nutr.* **100,** 59–68.

Schroeder, H. A., Mitchener, M., and Nason, A. P. 1974. Life-term effects of nickel in rats: Survival, tumors, interactions with trace elements and tissue levels. *J. Nutr.* **104,** 239–243.

Schroeder, H. A., Vinton, W. H., Jr., and Balassa, J. J. 1963a. Effect of chromium, cadmium and other trace metals on the growth and survival of mice. *J. Nutr.,* **80,** 39–47.

Schroeder, H. A., Vinton, W. H., Jr., and Balassa, J. J. 1963b. Effects of chromium, cadmium and lead on the growth and survival of rats. *J. Nutr.*, **80**, 48–54.

Schulz. H. 1888. Veber Hefegifte. *Arch Ges. Physiol.* **42**, 517–541.

Scott, M. L. 1973. The selenium dilemma. *J. Nutr.* **103**, 803–810.

Segall, P. 1975 (abstract). Aging and CNS monoamines. *Proc. Xth Int. Congr. Gerontology*, Jerusalem, Israel.

Shaw, R. F. and Bercaw, B. L. 1962. Temperature and life-span in poikilothermous animals. *Nature*, **196**, 454–457.

Silberberg, R., Jarrett, S. R., and Silberberg, M. 1961. Life span of mice fed enriched or restricted diets during growth. *Am. J. Physiol.* **200**, 332–334.

Silberberg, R., Jarrett, S. R., and Silberberg, M. 1962. Longevity of female mice kept on various dietary regimens during growth. *J. Geront.* **17**, 239–244.

Silberberg, M. and Silberberg, R. 1954. Factors modifying the lifespan of mice. *Am. J. Physiol.* **177**, 23–26.

Smith, G. S., Walford, R. L., and Mickey, M. R. 1973. Lifespan and incidence of cancer and other diseases in selected long-lived inbred mice and their F_1 hybrids. *J. Natl. Cancer Inst.* **50**, 1195–1213.

Smith, J. M. 1958a. Prolongation of the life of *Drosophila subobscura* by a brief exposure of adults to a high temperature. *Nature* **181**, 496–497.

Smith, J. M. 1958b. The effects of temperature and of egg-laying on the longevity of *Drosophila subobscura*. *J. Exp. Biol.* **35**, 832–842.

Smith, J. M., Clarke, J. M., and Hollingsworth, M. J. 1955. The expression of hybrid vigour in *Drosophila subobscura*. *Proc. Roy. Soc. Lond. B.*, **144**, 159–171.

Smith, L. C. and Dugal, L. P. 1966. Influence of testosterone on the spontaneous running activity of white rats. *Canad. J. Physiol. Pharmacol.* **44**, 682–686.

Snyder, D. P. 1956. Survival rates, longevity and population fluctuations in the white-footed mouse, *Peromyscus leucopus* in southeastern Michigan. *Misc. Publ. Mus. Zool. Univ. Mich.* **95**, 1–33.

Sobel, H. 1970. Follow-up on mice exposed to 1.08 atm. oxygen in nitrogen for a substantial portion of lifespan. *Aerospace Med.* **41**, 524–525.

Spinage, C. A. 1972. African ungulate life tables. *Ecology* **53**, 645–652.

Stevenson, K. G. and Curtis, H. J. 1961. Chromosomal aberrations in irradiated and nitrogen mustard treated mice. *Radiation Res.* **15**, 774–784.

Storer, J. B. 1966. Longevity and gross pathology at death in 22 inbred mouse strains. *J. Geront.* **21**, 404–409.

Strehler, B. L. 1961. Studies on the comparative physiology of aging. II. On the mechanism of temperature life-shortening in *Drosophila melanogaster*. *J. Gerontol.* **16**, 2–12.

Szilard, L. 1959. On the nature of the aging process. *Proc. Natl. Acad. Sci.* **45**, 30–42.

Tannenbaum, A. 1947. Effects of varying caloric intake upon tumor incidence and tumor growth. *Ann. N.Y. Acad. Sci.* **49**, 6–17.

Tannenbaum, A. and Silverstone, H. 1949. The influence of the degree of caloric restriction on the formation of skin tumors and hepatomas in mice. *Cancer Res.* **9**, 724–727.

Tannenbaum, A. and Silverstone, H 1953. Nutrition in relation to cancer. *Advan. Cancer Res.* **1**, 452–501.

Tauchi, N. 1972. Parabiosis between young and old rats. *Proc. IXth Int. Congr. Geront. Kiev, U.S.S.R.*, Vol. **3**, p. 56 (Abstract).

Thung, P. J., Boot, L. M., and Mühlbock. O. 1956. Senile changes in the oestrous cycle and in ovarian structure in some inbred strains of mice. *Acta Endocrinol.* **23**, 8–32.

Townsend, J. F. and Luckey, T. D. 1960. Hormologosis in pharmacology. *J. Am. Med. Assoc.* **173**, 44–48.

Tryon, C. A. 1971. The effect of exposure to 200 and 400 R of ionizing radiation on the survivorship curves of the eastern chipmunk (*Tamias striatus*) under natural conditions. In *Radionuclides in Ecosystems, Third National Symposium on Radioecology*, May 10–12, Oak Ridge, Tenn. pp. 1037–1041.

Ulland, B. M., Weisburg, H. H., Yamamoto, R. S., and Weisburg, E. K. 1972. Antioxidants and carcinogenesis. *Toxicol. Appl. Pharmacol.* **22**, 281 (abstract).

United Nations. 1949 to present. Demographic yearbook. New York, United Nations.

Upton, A. C. 1957. Ionizing radiation and the aging process. A review. *J. Geront.* **12**, 306–313.

Upton, A. C. 1960. Ionizing radiation and aging. *Gerontologia* **4**, 162–176.

Upton, A. C. 1961. The dose-response relation in radiation-induced cancer. *Cancer Res.*, **21**, 717–729.

Upton, A. C., Kastenbaum, M. A., and Conklin, J. W. 1963. Age-specific death rates of mice exposed to ionizing radiation and radiomimetic agents. *Symp. on Cellular Basis and Aetiology of Late Somatic Effects of Ionizing Radiations*, pp. 285–294. Proc. ed. by R. J. C. Harris, New York: Academic Press.

Upton, A. C., Kimball, A. W., Furth, J., Christenberry, K. W., and Benedict, W. H. 1960. Some delayed effects of atom-bomb radiations in mice. *Cancer Research*, **20** (8, part II), 1–60.

U.S. Surgeon General's Office. 1964. Smoking and Health. Report of the Advisory Committee to the Surgeon General of the Public Health Service. Public Health Service publication no. 1103, 387 p. Washington, D.C., Supt. of Documents, U. S. Gov't. Printing Office.

U.S. Surgeon General's Office. 1967. The health consequences of smoking: A Public Health Service

Review: 1967. Public Health Service publication no. 1969, revised, 227 p. Washington, D.C., Supt. of Documents, U.S. Govt. Printing Office.

Walford, R. L., Liu, R. K., Troup, G. M., and Hsiu, J. 1969. Alterations in soluble/insoluble collagen ratios in the annual fish, *Cynolebias bellottii*, in relation to age and environmental temperature. *Exp. Geront.* **4**, 103–109.

Walker, A. D., Stevenson, D. E., Robinson, J., Thorpe, E., and Roberts, M. 1969. Toxicology and pharmacology of dieldrin. *Toxicol. Appl. Pharmacol.* **15**, 345–370.

Weissmann, G. 1969. The effects of steroids and drugs on lysosomes. *In*, J. J. Dingle and H. B. Fell (eds.), *Lysosomes in Biology and Pathology*, *Vol.* **1**. pp. 276–295. Amsterdam: North-Holland.

Went, F. 1957. *The Experimental Control of Plant Growth*. Waltham, Mass., Chronica Botanica.

Wexler, B. C. 1964. Spontaneous coronary arteriosclerosis in repeatedly bred male and female rats. *Circulation Res.* **14**, 32–43.

Wexler, B. C. and Saroff, J. 1970. Metabolic changes in response to acute cerebral ischemia following unilateral carotid artery ligation in arteriosclerotic versus non-arteriosclerotic rats. *Stroke*, **1**, 38–57.

Whittow, G. C. (ed.), 1973. *Comparative Physiology of Thermoregulation*. New York: Academic Press.

Widdowson, E. M. and Kennedy, G. C. 1962. Rate of growth, mature weight and life-span. *Proc. Roy. Soc. London, Series B, Biological Sciences*, **156**, 96–108.

Woolhouse, H. W. 1974. Longevity and senescence in plants. *Sci. Prog.*, Oxf. **61**, 123–147.

Wynder, E. L. and Graham, E. A. 1950. Tobacco smoking as a possible etiologic factor in bronchiogenic carcinoma. *J. Am. Med. Assoc.* **143**, 329–336.

Yager, J. D., Jr., Lichtenstein, M. J., Bonney, R. J., Hopkins, H. A., Walker, P. R., Dorn, C. G., and Potter, V. R. 1974. Effects of various feeding and exercise regimens on rat growth and survival. *J. Nutr.* **104**, 273–286.

Yamamoto, W. S. and Brobeck, J. R. 1965. *Physiological Controls and Regulations*. W. B. Saunders: Philadelphia.

Yuhas, J. M. 1971. Age and susceptibility to reduction in life expectancy: an analysis of proposed mechanisms. *Exp. Geront.* **6**, 335–343.

25
SYSTEMS INTEGRATION

Nathan W. Shock, Ph.D.
National Institute on Aging,
National Institutes of Health, and
the Baltimore City Hospitals

INTRODUCTION

Previous chapters of this book have placed primary emphasis on describing the changes that take place in cells, tissues, and organs with aging. However, most performances of the total animal require the coordinated activities of a number of organ systems. This chapter will examine the effects of aging on some of the integrative processes and mechanisms involved. These mechanisms range from the ways in which cells respond to increased metabolic demands to the ways in which the activities of different organ systems work together to achieve adaptation of the animal to variations in environmental demands. Since questions of interactions between cells, between organ systems, and the idea of control mechanisms have only recently been approached by physiologists, relatively little experimental data on the effects of age on these mechanisms is as yet available. However, a few specific examples will be explored as an indication of the approach, rather than as a complete story. Actually, aging, as we see it in the total animal, may be more a function of the breakdown in integrative mechanisms than of changes in individual cells, tissues, or organs.

HOMEOSTASIS

It has long been known that, in the mammal, all cells require for effective functioning a high degree of uniformity of temperature, acidity, oxygen content, electrolyte composition, and osmotic pressure in their environment. Uniformity of this internal environment is achieved by specific activities of all the organ systems of the body, and control of their activity is primarily through neural or endocrine mechanisms. It was Claude Bernard (1859) who first enunciated the general physiological principle that the maintenance of the constancy of the internal cellular environment of the body is essential to maintenance of life in the animal. Cannon (1929, 1939, 1942) expanded the concept and was the first to introduce the term "homeostasis" to designate the maintenance of this steady state of the cellular environment.

The common denominator of the extracellular fluids of the body is the blood plasma. Studies have shown that age has little effect on the acidity of the blood, or its electrolyte content, glucose content, and osmotic pressure. However, aging has a significant effect on the rate at which these variables are returned to resting levels after they have been displaced either experimentally or by responses to environmental factors. The rate at which readjustment occurs is substantially slower in the old than in the young. It is apparent, therefore, that age has an impact on the ability of the animal to adjust to stresses.

CONTROL MECHANISMS

Evaluation of the effectiveness of a control mechanism can be made only if a standard displacing stimulus can be applied and the rate of readjustment to normal values can be measured. Thus, the experimental design can quantify differences in the overall effectiveness of a mechanism, but cannot distinguish between changes in the sensitivity of the sensing mechanism which identifies the displacement and the effectiveness of the mechanisms involved in readjusting the displacement. In order to make this distinction, experiments must be designed to isolate and quantify each step involved in the total response. In many instances, such analytical experiments can be carried out only in an animal model.

An indication of the role of integrative mechanisms in age decrements in performance can be seen in Figure 1 (Shock, 1972). In this figure the average performance of 30-year-old subjects is taken as 100 percent and the average decrement, as percent of this 30-year-old figure, is projected linearly to age 80. From the variables selected it may be seen that variables associated with the maintenance of the internal environment under resting conditions show no age trend (curve A for fasting blood glucose or pH of the blood). Nerve condition velocity, which involves measurements in a single organ system, shows an average decrement of about 15 percent between the ages of 30 and 80 years (curve B). Resting cardiac index (curve C) falls by about 30 percent, whereas vital capacity and renal blood flow (curve D) are, in the 80 year olds, only about one-half the average values for 30 year olds. Maximum breathing capacity (curve E) and maximum oxygen uptake (curve F) fall by 60 percent and 70 percent, respectively. These performances require the integrated activity of the cardiovascular, nervous, muscular, and respiratory systems, and show the greatest decrements with age.

It must be emphasized that these idealized curves are based on cross-sectional data which identify age differences rather than age changes. There is no assurance that age changes in any individual or in all subpopulations follow this path. This question can be answered only from repeated measurements made in the same individual as he ages. Such longitudinal data are not yet available for these physiological characteristics.

Neuromuscular Coordination

The role of neuromuscular coordination in age decrements in the performance of rhythmic exercise is illustrated by the fact that the maxi-

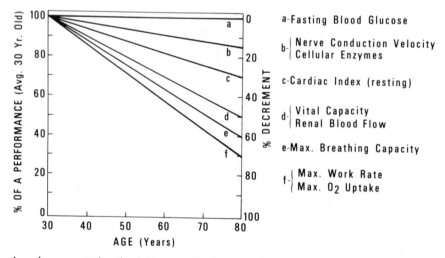

Fig. 1. Age decrements in physiological functions in males. Mean values for 20- to 35-year-old subjects are taken as 100%. Decrements shown are schematic linear projections: (a) fasting blood glucose; (b) nerve conduction velocity and cellular enzymes; (c) resting cardiac index; (d) vital capacity and renal blood flow; (e) maximum breathing capacity, and (f) maximum work rate and maximum oxygen uptake. (From: Shock 1972).

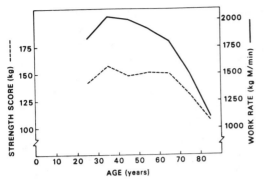

Fig. 2. Age trends in muscle strength compared with trends in coordinated cranking performance utilizing the same muscles. ———, Work rate (arm operated crank) vs. age; - - - -, strength score for arm and shoulder muscles. (Adapted from: Shock and Norris 1970).

mum rate of cranking a bicycle ergometer begins to show a decrement as early as age 40, whereas the static strength of the muscles involved in performing this work does not begin to diminish appreciably until age 65 or 70 (Figure 2) (Shock, 1974; Shock and Norris, 1970). It is therefore clear that, from a gross standpoint, impairment in some performances with age is a reflection of impairment in control mechanisms.

Assessment of Integrative and Control Mechanisms

The effectiveness of organ system integration and control mechanisms can be determined by estimating how well the organism adapts to increased demands made upon it by changes in the environment and by the rate at which displacements in physiological characteristics can be returned to normal or resting values. Measurements of this type are focused on determining the immediate response to a stress or a displacing stimulus. In addition to the immediate response, animals tend to adapt when a given stress or change in conditions is experienced periodically or continuously. Thus, animals exposed to chronic hypoxia, as when moved to higher altitudes, adapt to this change in the lowered oxygen content of the air by increasing the number of red cells in circulating blood. Such adaptations in response to a chronic stimulus may require days or weeks to achieve.

We will therefore examine some of the age differences in the effectiveness of the animal to readjust to both immediate and long term stresses, many of which are a part of daily living. In the context of this discussion, stress is used to imply any change in environment or activity which requires readjustments on the part of the individual. Thus, the stress may or may not be deleterious.

TEMPERATURE REGULATION AND CONTROL

Mechanisms of Temperature Regulation

In mammals the internal or core temperature of the body is closely regulated between 36 and 38°C. This core temperature is most reliably estimated by rectal temperature, the temperature of the urine immediately after its passage, or by ear temperature (determined by a thermocouple or thermistor inserted into the ear). The temperature of the mouth is not reliable as a measurement of central temperature, particularly in elderly people, unless special methods are used, partly because of the difficulty of assuring adequate mouth closure. Temperatures recorded from the armpit are also highly unreliable as an estimate of body core temperature. Skin temperatures are also highly variable, and depend on the area where the temperature is recorded as well as on the environmental temperature.

In order to maintain a uniform core temperature, a close balance must be maintained between the heat production and the heat loss (DuBois, 1948). Heat production is represented by the basal heat production or basal metabolism plus the extra metabolism and heat, which is generated, primarily, by muscular activity (there is some contribution from the activity of other tissues of the body). Heat is lost primarily by radiation, convection, and evaporation of moisture from the skin. Regulation of the amount of heat loss is effected, primarily, by changes in the amount of blood flowing to the skin, which in turn depends upon the integrated activity of the nervous system. Receptors sensitive to slight changes in central blood temperature are located in the hypothalamus of the brain. In addition, there are pathways from skin receptors for temperature to the brain, which also monitor temperatures at the periphery. The different pathways from the brain send impulses through the sympathetic nerve trunks of the lateral columns of the spinal cord to sympathetic ganglia. Post-ganglionic fibers innervate cutaneous blood vessels as well as sweat glands (Cooper, 1966). With a rise in core body temperature vasodilitation occurs in the skin so that more blood is brought to the surface and hence more heat can be dissipated. With a fall in temperature the opposite effect occurs, namely, vasoconstriction of the vessels in the skin so that less blood is exposed to the outside environment and less heat is lost.

As a second line of defense against a rise in temperature, the sweat glands are activated so that heat loss is further augmented by evaporation of sweat from the skin. Under conditions of lowered temperature, shivering, which augments heat production from muscular contraction, will occur.

Basal Heat Production or Basal Metabolism

As shown in Figure 3, a number of studies indicate that basal heat production falls progressively with age in adults over the age of 30

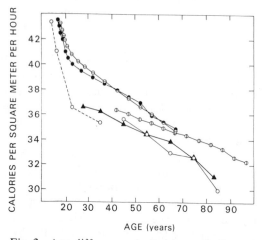

Fig. 3. Age differences in basal metabolism of males aged 15 to 95 years. ○---○, data from Shock, 1955; ●——●, data from Boothby, Berkson and Dunn 1936; ⊖—⊖, data from Dubois 1936; ○——○, data from Shock and Yiengst 1955; ▲——▲, data from GRC Longitudinal Study–Shock, Andres and Norris, unpublished.

(Boothby, Berkson, and Dunn, 1936; DuBois, 1936; Shock, 1942, 1955; Shock and Yiengst, 1955). Although average values differ somewhat among different studies, the slopes of the regression of basal metabolism on age after age 30 (1.66 calories/m^2/hour/decade) are markedly uniform except for two studies, Lewis (1938) and the Baltimore Longitudinal Study (Shock, Andres, and Norris, 1975), in which the regression slope was only 0.8 calories/m^2/hour/decade. The Lewis study was conducted on normal subjects aged 40 to 95 years, who lived in New York City and came to the hospital for tests each morning on an outpatient basis. Results from the Baltimore Longitudinal Study, which are based on normal community-residing subjects (Stone and Norris, 1966), showed a regression on age of 0.93 calories/m^2/hour/decade. In contrast to the Lewis study, the Baltimore subjects were tested under morning basal conditions, after having spent the night in the hospital. The original report of Shock and Yiengst (1955) was based on determinations made on an institutional population (Old Peoples' Home).

Although the regression of basal metabolism on age is statistically significant, it must be pointed out that individual variations, around the regression line, are quite large. In fact, some subjects in their 80's may have metabolic rates as high as the average for the 40-year-old subjects. On the average, basal metabolism falls from about 38 calories/m^2/hour at age 30 to about 30 calories/m^2/hour at age 80, resulting in an average decrement of about 15 percent over this age span. A detailed statistical analysis of records of basal metabolism for over 8,600 subjects selected from the literature by Quenouille, Boyne, Fisher, and Leitch (1951) led them to conclude that, "when all other variables have been taken into account, the mass data for adults of both sexes and all racial groups analyzed conformed to the rule that basal metabolism declines at the rate of 3 percent per decade from age 3 to over 80." This value would be approximately 1.08 calories/m^2/hour/decade, which is significantly less than a regression constant of 1.37 ± 0.017, calculated on data from more homogeneous populations (see Shock and Yiengst, 1955).

Basal Metabolism and Tissue Loss

The fall in metabolic rate with age has led to the assumption that aging is associated with a "slowing of metabolism," presumably at the cellular level. Since thyroid hormone is the primary regulator of the rate of cellular metabolism, studies have been directed toward determining age changes in the ability of the thyroid gland to produce or release thyroxin. None of these studies were able to produce definitive evidence that the function of the thyroid gland was adversely influenced by aging (Gregerman, 1967). Consequently, other explanations of the fall in total heat production with age must be explored.

Since heat loss from any body is determined by its surface area, heat production has traditionally been related to surface area in order to reduce the effects of body size on measurements. Since surface area of the human body is calculated from height and weight (DuBois and DuBois, 1916), it can be greatly influenced by the amount of bone, fat, and other low oxygen uptake tissues which contribute to body weight. Fat individuals, because of their increased body weight, will have a high surface area and a low heat production per unit of surface area, compared with other individuals with the same amount of functioning tissue but free from excess weight due to fat. Since the water content of cells is very stable and does not change significantly with age (Lowry and Hastings, 1952), it is reasonable to utilize the water content of the body as a more appropriate index of the amount of metabolizing tissue in the individual than surface area. Consequently, measurements of total body weight were made in subjects by the antipyrine dilution technique (Shock, Watkin, Yiengst, Norris, Gaffney, Gregerman, and Falzone, 1963). Figure 4 shows that basal oxygen consumption per liter of body water is not influenced by age. Hence, the fall in basal metabolism, calculated as calories/m²/hour with age, is simply a reflection of the loss of metabolizing tissue (or increase in body fat) with advancing age. The tissues in the elderly produce heat at the same rate as the young.

The Role of Activity in Total Heat Production

In addition to the basal heat production, heat generated as a result of activities must also be eliminated. Two-hundred-fifty-two community-

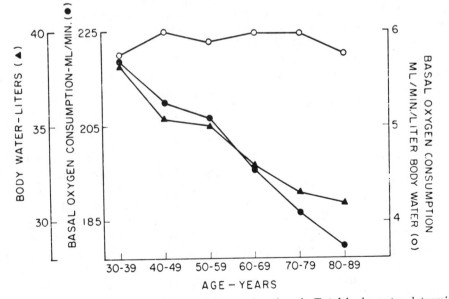

Fig. 4. Effect of age on basal metabolism in normal males. ▲, Total body water determined as antipyrine space; ●, basal O_2 consumption, ml/min; ○, basal O_2 consumption, ml/min/l body water. (From: Gregerman 1967).

residing men, aged 20 to 79, served as subjects in a study designed to determine age differences in daily activities and to relate total heat production to dietary intake (McGandy, Barrows, Spanias, Meredith, Stone, and Norris, 1966). Each subject received detailed instructions from trained nutritionists in order to collect a 7-day record of all foods eaten. After verification with the nutritionists, the data from each record were coded for computer analyses of mean daily nutrient intakes.

Physical activity was estimated from a detailed interview covering specific activities at home, at work and recreation (including active or passive participation in sports), and variations in activity patterns, such as trips and seasonal sports. The amount of time spent in each activity was expressed as a daily average for each subject. The time spent in seasonal and infrequent activities were expressed as an annual total and then divided by 365. Total daily energy expenditures were calculated for each subject by using values for each activity as reported in the literature. The total caloric intake of these subjects fell from 2,688 calories per day in 20- to 34-year-olds to 2,093 calories per day in 75- to 99-year-olds (Figure 5). The middle line of Figure 5 shows the average basal metabolism expressed as calories per day for these subjects and the bottom line the total calories per day assignable to daily activities. These curves show that, as a result of reduced physical activity among the elderly, the activity calories fall somewhat more than basal metabolism. As a result, the total heat elimination required in elderly subjects is substantially less than that in the young.

Basal Body Temperature

Under resting or basal conditions, body temperature of elderly persons is maintained within the same limits as that in the young, that is, between 35 and 37°C (Shock, 1952). Howell (1950) recorded both mouth and axillary temperatures in 326 males aged 65 to 91. The average values were compared with similar measurements made in 50 male and female nurses aged 20 to 30 years. The average values were slightly lower (0.02°F for mouth and 0.64°F

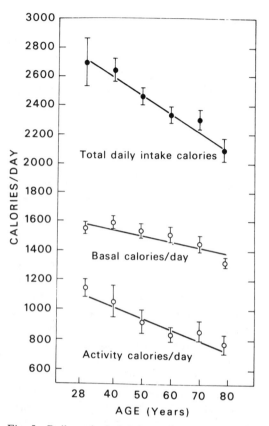

Fig. 5. Daily caloric intake and expenditure in normal males. ●——●, total daily caloric intake; O——O (upper curve), basal caloric expenditure per day; O---O (lower curve), daily caloric expenditure for activity. Vertical lines represent ±1 standard curve of the mean. (From: Shock 1972).

for the axilla) in the aged group than in the nurses. Since the latter group also included females, who show significantly lower temperatures than males, it cannot be concluded that an age difference exists.

In a more recent study, Howell (1972) has reported axillary temperatures taken with an electric thermometer in 105 female convalescent patients aged 60 to 100 years. Temperatures were recorded for both the right and left axilla. Mean values for each decade, beginning at age 60, were 36.1, 35.9, 35.8, 35.8, and 36.0°C (a single centenarian was tested). Although the mean values for right and left axilla did not differ significantly, individual subjects showed a variation from 0.2°C to as much as 1.4°C between the two arms. These observations failed to demonstrate any significant age trend in body temperature between the ages of 60 and 100 years.

Hypothermia

In Great Britain, estimates of the incidence of death due to hypothermia vary from 100 or so returns on the Registrar General's death certificates to over 20,000 deaths yearly as estimated by Taylor (1964). The incidence of hypothermia is believed to be substantially greater among the elderly than among other age groups (Wollner and Spalding, 1973). In order to test this hypothesis, Fox, Woodward, Exton-Smith, Green, Donnison, and Wicks (1973) conducted a survey which included 1,020 subjects (391 males and 629 females) selected at random from 100 constituency sampling points in Great Britain by a systematic probability sampling method. Measurements of mouth and urine specimen temperatures were recorded for each subject during the morning hours (8:00-10:00 A.M.) and again in the late afternoon (4:00-6:00 P.M.). All temperatures were recorded by specially trained nurses, who visited the subject in his or her own home. Environmental temperatures were also recorded. Body temperature, as measured by the urine technique, was not related to either the room or external temperature, whereas it was significantly correlated with other body temperatures (hand and mouth temperatures). Figure 6 summarizes the results of this study and compares them with observations made in comparable surveys conducted in other populations (Fox, MacGibbon, Davies, and Woodward, 1973; Fox, Woodward, Fry, Collins, and MacDonald, 1971; Ivy, 1944; and Salvosa, Payne, and Wheeler, 1971). There is a remarkably close agreement between morning temperatures observed in different populations of subjects living in their own homes. In all of the studies, average values for mouth temperatures were approximately 36.0 to 36.2°C, with a standard deviation of about 0.8°. If the usual clinical definition of hypothermia (temperatures below 35°C) is used, the incidence of hypothermia in the elderly at home was relatively low.

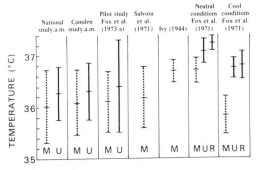

Fig. 6. Body temperature in subjects aged 65 years and over as well as young subjects. The elderly subjects were living in their own homes. Mean and standard deviation of the distributions are shown. M = mouth; U = freshly voided urine; R = rectal temperature. (Redrawn from Fox, *et al.* 1973).

MacMillan, Corbett, Johnson, Crampton Smith, Spalding, and Wollner (1967) have shown that survivors of accidental hypothermia in the elderly show an impairment of their temperature regulating mechanisms which may persist for as long as three years following hypothermia. Ear temperatures were recorded while subjects were exposed to a cooling environment, induced by blowing air (at a nonspecified temperature) over the subject as he lay almost naked under a radiant heat cradle. Cooling continued until trunk skin temperature fell to 21°C, core body temperature fell by at least 1°C, or the subject complained of discomfort. On moderate cooling, chilling was absent, metabolic rate did not rise, and there was defective vasoconstriction in the elderly subjects. In contrast to control subjects aged 70 to 94, who showed no drop in core body temperature on exposure to cold for a period of 70 minutes, survivors of accidental hypothermia aged 66 to 99 showed a fall in core body temperature, over the 70-minute cooling period, of 1 to 2.5°C. In these patients, although the body temperature was low, the subjects did not report feeling cold. Present evidence indicates that, although, in general, elderly people are able to maintain their resting body temperatures, there is a group of subjects who seem to have a higher risk of developing hypothermia. Although it seems likely that the defect of temperature regulation precedes the hypothermic state, definitive evidence for this is not available.

Skin Temperature

Skin temperatures are, on the average, lower than the core body temperature. However, skin temperatures are greatly influenced by the degree of vasodilitation or constriction in the part observed and are primarily dependent upon the adjustments being made at any given point in time to regulate the body core temperature. In general, the temperature of the fingers and toes is slightly lower in the old than in the young, largely because of the diminished circulation of the skin of the aged (Köng, 1939). In a group of 40 elderly women, aged 69 to 93, and living in their own homes, skin temperature over the sternum and over the neck averaged $33.3 \pm 1.65°C$ and $33.4 \pm 1.26°C$, respectively, as compared with a mouth temperature of $35.8 \pm 0.56°C$ (Salvosa et al., 1971).

Response to Cold

Although, under resting conditions, the older individual is able to maintain body temperature within normal limits, there is evidence that the response to high or low environmental temperatures is less effective in the old than in the young. When mammals are exposed to a cold environment, the initial response is vasoconstriction of the blood vessels in the skin to reduce heat loss. The next line of defense is an increase in heat production, which is effected by a rise in metabolic rate and by increased muscular activity (evidenced by shivering).

Munk (1910-11) reported occurrence of shivering in elderly subjects immersed in water at reduced temperatures that did not produce shivering in young subjects. The response to exposure to cold has been studied in more detail by Krag and Kountz (1950). Thirteen subjects aged 57 to 91 and six aged 22 to 36 were exposed in a closed cabinet to ambient temperatures of 5 to 15°C for 45 to 120 minutes. Iron-constantine thermocouples recorded rectal temperatures and surface temperatures of the abdomen, back, and the midpoints of

the lower arm and leg. Serial determinations of oxygen consumption by the closed circuit method were also made. During the exposure to the cold the young subjects showed little change in rectal temperature, whereas the aged subjects showed a fall of 0.5 to 1.0°C during exposure. Shivering was much more marked among the young subjects than in the elderly. Actually, one elderly subject, whose body temperature dropped by 2.5 degrees, experienced no bodily distress and only mild shivering. Among the young subjects, the change in body temperature during exposure to the cold was less than 0.5°C. In contrast, 10 of the 13 elderly subjects had a fall in rectal temperature of 0.5° or more, and of these five had a fall of 1° or more. However, within the total group, the mean increase in oxygen consumption following cold exposure was significantly higher in the old than in the young individuals. Therefore, it seems that, although the elderly subject can increase heat production as well as the young, the mechanisms involved in conserving heat are not as effective. As a result, body temperature in the elderly diminishes in the cold.

Thermal Comfort for the Elderly

It is commonly believed that, for thermal comfort, elderly people require a higher environmental temperature than do young. In fact, the Handbook of the Society of Heating, Refrigerating, and Air Conditioning Engineers states that, "all men and women over 40 years of age prefer a temperature for comfort 1.0° effective temperature higher than that desired by persons below this age" (1967). This is based on ratings of comfort, as for example the statements, "cold, cool, slightly cool, comfortable, slightly warm, warm, or hot," made by subjects exposed to different temperatures.

There are, however, a number of studies which fail to substantiate the conclusion that older people prefer warmer temperatures. For example, Rohles (1969) recorded the responses of 64 subjects with a mean age 75 years to two questionnaires in which they were asked to classify temperatures from 32°F to 110°F as "cooler than comfortable, comfortable, and warmer than comfortable." The distribution of comfortable temperatures agreed with experimentally derived findings on college age and middle-aged adults, and offered no support to the conclusion that older subjects preferred a temperature higher than that desired by the young and middle-aged.

Watts (1971) conducted interviews on 18 females subjects aged 74 to 86 in their own homes. Continuous 24- or 48-hour recordings of dry bulb temperatures were made in each dwelling using a thermohygrograph. Dry bulb temperatures in the living and sleeping quarters of the subjects varied between 8 and 18°C. On each visit the subject was asked to rate her thermal feelings and to report any change in thermal feelings she would prefer. No evidence was found that any of the subjects were unable to experience cold or cold discomfort. All of the subjects responded to the experience of cold discomfort with some appropriate voluntary thermal regulatory behavior, such as adding more clothing. However, an analysis of the thermal preference data suggests that some of the old people experienced cold and warmth at lower environmental temperatures than that reported by the middle-aged population. The important finding is that while the room temperatures were often cool by Institute of Heating and Ventilation Engineers standards (1965), many of the subjects did not experience them as cool. The range of air temperatures over which these subjects voted "slightly warm" (11.8 to 19.5°C) was much lower than the equivalent range for young active females (15.3 to 28°C).

These findings are in accord with the laboratory investigations of Krag and Kountz (1950) and of Horvath, Radcliffe, Hutt, and Spurr (1955). Horvath noted that, "in contrast to the marked complaints of discomfort made by the younger subjects, . . . older subjects generally did not complain of the cold and reported little or no discomfort during the entire exposure." Horvath also noted that, although the older subjects apparently did not experience discomfort sensations, they were less able than the young subjects to maintain their body temperature during cold exposure. Although the data are scanty, it is possible that older subjects

are less sensitive to the sensation of coldness and are therefore less likely to take appropriate action to conserve heat when exposed to lower temperatures.

Adaptation to Cold Environments

Adjustment and adaptation to cold environments is also less effective in old mice than in young. Finch, Foster, and Mirsky (1969) measured rectal temperatures in 10- and 30-month-old mice during exposure to temperatures of 9 to 10°C over a period of three hours. Figure 7 shows that, over the 3-hour period, rectal temperatures in the young mice fell to approximately 35°, whereas in the old mice the temperature dropped to approximately 27°C.

Grad and Kral (1957) found a significantly higher mortality rate on exposure to cold in old female C57BL mice than in the young. When the animals were adapted to the cold environment by a gradual reduction in environmental temperature, 95 percent of the young mice survived a temperature of 1.5 to 3.5°C for seven days, whereas only 20 percent of the old

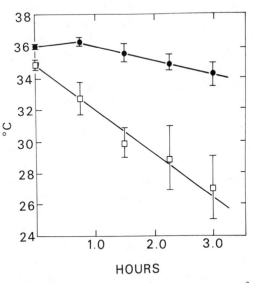

Fig. 7. Effect of age on colon temperature of mice during 3-hour exposure to cold (9–10°C). Mean temperature, ±1 SE$_{mn}$ for 7 mice per age group. ●, young adult mice (10 mo old); □, senescent mice (30 mo old). (From: Finch, *et al.* 1969).

animals survived this stress. Continued exposure to temperatures of 9 to 11°C induced significantly greater increases in oxygen consumption, food intake, and blood sugar in the young than in the old animals. Body weight decreased less in the young than in the old. It is therefore apparent that, although the old animals were able to adapt to the stress, their effectiveness is much less than that of the young.

Response to Heat

With a rise in environmental temperature associated with an increase in body temperature, the first compensatory change which occurs is a vasodilitation of the blood vessels in the skin, followed by an increase in sweating and an augmentation of the heart rate and respiration. All of these adjustments tend to increase heat loss from the body. Although counter productive to eliminating heat, there is also an increase in basal metabolism.

Krag and Kountz (1952) subjected 26 individuals (14 aged 57 to 95 years and 12 aged 21 to 32 years) to ambient temperatures of 38 to 45°C for 60 to 90 minutes. Measurements of rectal, oral, and skin temperatures, as well as pulse rate, respiration rate, and oxygen consumption were made. Rectal temperatures were increased by 1 to 2° in both old and young subjects. Following termination of heat exposure there was a delay of 10 to 30 minutes before the rectal temperature began to fall. This delay amounted, on the average, to 12.9 minutes in the young, and was much greater in the aged (mean of 21.2 minutes). Pulse rate increased with heat exposure in both the old and the young. The young increased their heart rate by 22 beats per minute per 1° rise in rectal temperature, whereas the increase in the old was only 18.5 beats per minute per degree C. Oxygen consumption during heat exposure increased significantly more in the young than in the old. There was also greater variation with respect to the increase in oxygen consumption in the aged than in the young. As a whole, these results indicate that adaptive responses to a rise in environmental temperature were less effective in the old than in the young.

Hellon, Lind, and Weiner (1956) studied the physiological reactions of 18 young (19 to 31 years, mean 26) and 18 older (39 to 45 years, mean 43) coal miners to four hours of physical work in a hot environment (temperature 37.8° C dry bulb, 29.4°C wet bulb). The work consisted of stepping on and off a 12-inch high stool at the rate of 12 steps per minute. Twenty to thirty minute work periods alternated with 20 to 30 minute rest periods for the four hour exposure. Rectal and skin temperatures were recorded, as well as sweat production, blood pressure, pulse rate, and blood flow through the right arm. There were no age differences in the rectal temperatures recorded during the first work period. However, by the end of the second, third, and fourth work periods, the increments in rectal temperature above the pre-heat values were significantly greater in the old group. No age differences in skin temperature were observed. Thus there was a small but significantly greater heat gain in the older subjects. There was no significant age difference in total amount of sweat produced, although the younger men evaporated more sweat than the older men during the work periods and less in the rest periods. These results suggest a slower reaction of sweat glands to the additional heat load of work on the part of the older men and has been substantiated in other studies (Hellon and Lind, 1956).

The increase in heart rate as a result of the heat exposure was slightly higher in the old than in the young. The most striking age difference in response to the hot environment was a significantly greater increase in forearm blood flow observed in the older men (Figure 8). These results indicate that, although the older subjects increased forearm blood flow largely due to vasodilitation of the blood vessels in the skin, the increased flow was still inadequate to provide sufficient heat loss to prevent the rise in body temperature.

Pickering (1936) found that under standard conditions the maximum heat output in calories per minute per unit volume of the hand was approximately 33% lower at age 70 than at age 25. The rate of water loss from the surface of the finger and the toe tips was significantly lower in the aged than in the young

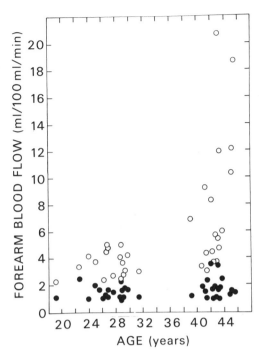

Fig. 8. Forearm blood flows before entry into the hot chamber (●) and after 3 hours in the heat (○) for subjects aged 20–46. (Redrawn from Hellon, *et al*. 1956).

subjects (Burch, Cohn, and Neumann, 1942), thus reducing the potential heat loss from evaporation.

Adaptation to Hot Environments

Robinson, Belding, Consolazio, Horvath, and Turrell (1965) studied the acclimatization to work in the heat in four men, aged 44 to 60, who had been tested under the same circumstances 21 years earlier. The work, heat stress, and duration of exposure were those orginally found to cause marked hyperpyrexia and circulatory strain in unacclimatized men (mean age 31 years) on the first day in the heat. In this highly selected group of four men, tolerance on the first day of exposure to work in the heat was no less than when they were younger. During exposure to exercise in a hot environment, body temperatures and heart rates of the older men were lowered on successive days of exposure, and the work was judged progressively easier. Final values of body temperature reached after 5 to 7 days

of exposure were about the same as observed originally after the same number of exposures. Thus these older men exhibited about the same degree of strain during work in the heat as they did 20 years earlier, and acclimatized about as well.

Henschel, Cole, and Lyczkowskyj (1968) measured the capacity of 32 females (average age 69 years) and 68 males, averaging 72 years (age range 60 to 93 years), to tolerate an extended heat work load under controlled laboratory conditions. Subjects were recruited from members of the American Association of Retired Persons living in the St. Petersburg area and were above average with respect to health and activity. Standard tests involved four 5-minute work periods on a bicycle ergometer. The work was conducted in a constant temperature room set at 92°F dry bulb and 82°F wet bulb temperature. Pulse rate, ventilation rate, oxygen consumption, and oral temperature were measured during the last minute of each work period. Each subject completed the test on two occasions, once in the spring and again in the fall after a summer exposure to a natural hot, humid environment. Response to the work load did not vary significantly from similar tests carried out on young and middle-aged subjects. Nor were there significant differences between tests conducted in the spring and in the fall. Thus, there was no evidence of impairment in performance in these highly selected subjects when subjected to a moderate work load.

Heat Stroke and the Effect of Environmental Temperature on Mortality

The death rate from heat stroke rises sharply after age 60. For instance, Shattuck and Hilferty (1932) have tabulated the incidence of heat stroke in Massachusetts between 1900 and 1930. These observations show an increase from 8 per 100,000 deaths between the ages of 70 to 79, to 80 per 100,000 deaths for ages 90 to 100. Friedfield (1949) has also shown that mortality rates in institutions for the aged increased during periods of prolonged high temperatures. Driscoll (1971a) has correlated weather characteristics and daily mortality in ten major metropolitan areas in the United States. In this analysis, July days were isolated on which both the daily maximum temperature and dew point were greater than one standard deviation above their means. On these days, excess deaths per day ranged from 43.7 in New York to 2.2 in Seattle. Oechsli and Buechley (1970) analyzed mortality data from three hot spells (temperatures 100 to 107°F) in Los Angeles. The daily numbers of deaths increased with increasing temperature and with advancing age. The time lag between temperature maximum and mortality maximum was about one day, which is similar to Kutschenreuter's findings for data from New York (1950).

MacPherson, Ofner, and Welch (1967) analyzed daily mortalities in a large institution for the elderly in relationship to environmental temperature. From the age of 70 years onward there was a progressive decrease in the ability of patients to adjust to changes in environmental temperature, as indicated by their increased mortality rate. In all age groups (50 to 99 years), death rates on the coldest days (50 to 59°F) were greater than the mean annual death rate by an amount varying from 7 to 69 percent. In the 60 to 69 year age group, there was no systematic effect of temperature on daily mortality. In the 70 to 79 year age group, both extremes of temperatures were unfavorable. Temperature intervals of 60 to 69°F and 70 to 79° appeared almost equally favorable. In the 80 to 89 year group, a comparatively warm temperature of 70 to 79° was associated with a marked reduction in mortality. In the 90 to 99 year age group, the decrease in mortality rate was even more marked in the interval of 70 to 79°F, and any departure from this temperature range sharply increased the mortality rate. The effect of successive hot days seemed to be accumulative. Schuman, Anderson, and Oliver (1964) have reported similar findings based on analysis of mortality during successive heat waves in Michigan.

REGULATION OF THE ACID BASE BALANCE OF THE BLOOD

In most mammals the acidity or pH of the cellular environment must be maintained within fairly narrow limits (pH 7.35 to 7.45) if cells are to function properly. The acidity of the blood, or its pH, is primarily determined by the ratio of the concentration of bicarbonate to that of carbonic acid. Under normal circumstances this ratio is approximately 20 to 1, resulting in a pH of 7.40. Under conditions of increased metabolic activity, as for example during muscular exercise, the liberation of acid metabolites which reduces the bicarbonate content of the blood tends to disturb this ratio.

Regulation of the acid base balance of the blood is effected primarily by two mechanisms. The first mechanism is regulated by changes in respiration rate and volume, which alter the elimination or retention of carbon dioxide from the blood. These processes represent effective devices for rapid adjustments in the pH of the blood by alterations of its carbonic acid content. When fixed acids are released into the blood, carbonic acid is displaced from a large pool of bicarbonate present, and consequently tends to lower the bicarbonate concentration. The increased carbonic acid is readily eliminated under normal circumstances through the lungs, restoring the system to equilibrium (pH of 7.40). On the other hand, conditions leading to the accumulation of bicarbonate may be compensated temporarily by reduced ventilation and a consequent increase in the amount of carbonic acid in the blood. Thus the ratio of bicarbonate to carbonic acid concentration is maintained with a normal pH.

The second mechanism of importance in regulating acid base equilibrium is the kidneys. It is through the kidneys that increased quantities of fixed acids are eliminated (Berliner, 1966). Adjustment by this mechanism requires considerably more time than adjustment of the carbonic acid mechanism. Both processes are, of course, dependent upon the adequacy of the blood supply to the kidneys and the lungs.

Role of the Lungs in Acid Base Regulation

Fine adjustments of the acidity (pH) of the blood are made by increasing or decreasing the amount of carbon dioxide eliminated through the lungs. These adjustments in respiration rate and volume are regulated by cells in the respiratory center of the brain, which are extremely sensitive to slight changes in the CO_2 tension of the blood. It is extremely difficult to design experiments to test the sensitivity of the respiratory center to changes in CO_2 tension since these cells can respond to very slight changes (of the order of 0.1 mm Hg of CO_2 tension). Analytical techniques now available can at best detect variations of only 1 mm Hg of CO_2 tension in the circulating blood. Although there are significant age changes in pulmonary characteristics, such as vital capacity, residual volume, and maximum breathing capacity (see Chapter 18), these characteristics have only minimal effects on elimination of CO_2 from the blood by way of the lungs. The primary characteristic of the lungs, which will play a significant role in CO_2 elimination, is the permeability of cells of the lung which separate the blood flowing in the capillaries from the air spaces of the lung. This characteristic is estimated by measuring the diffusion capacity of the lung for carbon dioxide. Because of technical problems, diffusion capacity of the lung is estimated by measurements of the rate of diffusion of carbon monoxide from the blood. It must be recognized that the overall measurements of maximum diffusing capacity are the end result of the interplay between a number of factors, as for example, (a) the difference in partial pressure of the alveolar gas and the mixed venous blood entering the pulmonary capillaries, (b) the duration of the contact between blood traversing the capillary and the alveolar gas, (c) the cardiac output, (d) transit time of a red blood cell through the alveolar capillary network of the lung, (e) the number of capillaries perfused, as well as (f) the dimensions and spatial configurations of the pulmonary capillary bed. In addition, the diffusion characteristics of the cellular membranes themselves play a role. Molecular weight and solubility coefficients of a gas also affect its rate of diffusion. Figure 9 summarizes results from a number of studies of the diffusion capacity of the lung (Burrows, Kasik, Niden, and Barclay, 1961; Cohn, 1964; Cohn, Carroll, Armstrong, Shepard, and Riley, 1954; Donevan, Palmer, Varvis, and Bates,

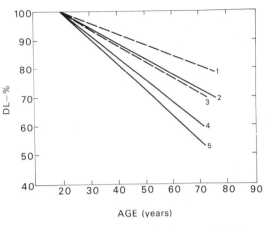

Fig. 9. Age decrements in maximum diffusing capacity of the lung. Mean values for 20-year-old subjects are taken as 100%. Decrements shown are schematic linear projections of data for diffusing capacity for carbon monoxide determined by the single breath method: (1) ---females, Gaensler, unpublished data; (2) —males, Gaensler, unpublished data; (3) ---females, Burrows, *et al.* 1961; (4) — males, Burrows, *et al.* 1961; (5) —males, McGrath and Thomson 1959. (From: Cohn 1964).

1959, and McGrath and Thomson, 1959). These studies are in agreement in showing a significant age decrement averaging approximately 8 percent per decade in diffusion capacity. There is some evidence that the decline is somewhat less in women than in men. It must be recognized that this is an overall effect and cannot be interpreted in terms of age changes in capillary bed or of the characteristics of the alveolar-blood membrane.

The Role of the Kidney in Acid Base Regulation

Under resting or basal conditions, the pH of the blood is maintained within normal limits of 7.35 to 7.45 even into advanced old age (Shock and Yiengst, 1950). However, the rate at which the pH is restored to normal values following an experimental displacement is significantly slower in the old than in the young. Oral ingestion of ammonium chloride shifts the pH of the blood toward the acid side. Compensation for this displacement is made by increasing ex-

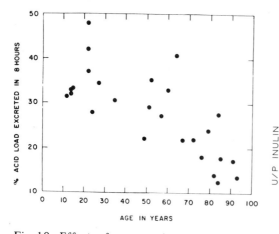

Fig. 10. Effect of age on the percent of the ingested acid excreted in the urine over an 8-hour period. (From: Adler, *et al.* 1968).

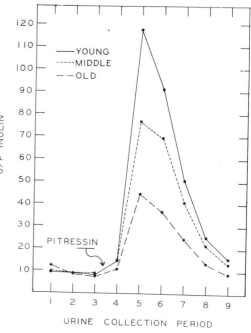

Fig. 11. Mean values of U/P inulin ratio for each of three age groups before and after the intravenous administration of pitressin. Urine collection periods 1 to 9 represent 9 consecutive 12-minute periods. Pitressin was administered immediately after the conclusion of period 3. (From: Miller and Shock, 1953).

cretion of acids through the kidney. Adler, Lindeman, Yiengst, Beard, and Shock (1968) found that young subjects were able to correct the reduction in pH of the blood, following oral administration of 10 grams of ammonium chloride, in a period of 6 to 8 hours, whereas elderly subjects required 18 to 24 hours. The deficit in the elderly is due primarily to the age-related decrement in glomerular filtration rate. Figure 10 shows that, with increasing age, the percent of the acid load excreted in 8 hours is significantly reduced. It is important to note that even the older subjects were ultimately able to readjust their acid base equilibrium after a displacing stimulus had been applied. The older subject simply requires more time to achieve the same result.

Kidney Response to Antidiuretic Hormone

Other experiments have shown that response of the kidney to a normal physiological stimulus is less effective in old than in young subjects. For example, Miller and Shock (1953) have shown that the renal response to antidiuretic hormone is progressively less when young, middle-aged, and old subjects are compared (Figure 11). In these experiments a maximum urine flow was first induced in all subjects by water ingestion accompanied by the intravenous infusion of inulin. Under these conditions the renal tubular cells excrete a maximum amount of

water, so that the ratio of the concentration of inulin in the blood plasma to the concentration of inulin in the urine is very low. With exposure to antidiuretic hormone (pitressin), the cells of the renal tubules reduce the amount of water excreted, so that the ratio of urine to plasma concentration of inulin rises markedly. Figure 11 shows that the response of the young subjects was substantially greater than that of the old. The U/P ratio was used in order to eliminate the effect of loss of glomeruli in the kidneys of the elderly subjects. Urine flows were lower in the old than in the young subjects because fewer glomeruli are available to contribute to the formation of urine.

REGULATION OF BLOOD SUGAR LEVELS

The effects of age on carbohydrate metabolism and glucose tolerance, which characterizes the rate of return of blood sugar levels to resting levels following an increase induced by administration of glucose, have been described in detail in Chapter 15. However, a discussion of control mechanisms and aging would be incomplete without mention of the primary findings. A broad spectrum of endocrine and metabolic functions play a role in regulating blood sugar levels. The important finding is that, even in advanced old age, these mechanisms are capable of maintaining the fasting blood sugar level within fairly close limits. However, when blood sugar levels are increased, the rate of return to the fasting levels diminishes progressively with age (Silverstone, Brandfonbrener, Shock, and Yiengst, 1957). Since the release of insulin from the β cells of the pancreas plays a primary role in effecting this adjustment, detailed studies have been carried out which show that, while there is no age impairment in the ability of the β cells to release insulin, they become less sensitive to increases in blood sugar levels with advancing age. In old subjects, a greater increase in blood sugar level is required to stimulate the β cells of the pancreas to release insulin into the blood stream than is the case in young subjects. Thus, for this particular regulatory system, it can be shown that the age defect lies in the sensing mechanism.

OTHER ENDOCRINE REGULATION

All of the endocrine glands play an important role in regulating many physiological activities, ranging from cellular metabolism to the cyclic events associated with the menstrual cycle. Since the details of regulatory functions of specific endocrine glands have been presented in Chapter 15, they will not be repeated here.

PHYSIOLOGICAL STRESS OF EXERCISE

The performance of physical work involves the integrated activity and coordination of many different organ systems. The primary requirements involve the delivery of an increased supply of oxygen to muscle tissues and the removal of waste products. Each of these functions requires the integrated activities of the cardiovascular system, the pulmonary system, the muscular system, the nervous system, and,

to some extent, the endocrine system. Delivery of oxygen to functioning tissues is aided by dilation of the capillary bed, followed by an increase in pulse rate, blood pressure, cardiac output, and circulation rate. Simultaneously, the excess carbon dioxide produced at the tissue level must be eliminated through the lungs and excess acid neutralized by the buffer system of the blood and ultimately eliminated through the kidneys. The increase in heat production resulting from muscular activity is dissipated by vasodilitation of the vessels in the skin and by augmented sweating. Endocrine factors also play a part in the adjustment to exercise. Release of epinephrine from the adrenal medulla increases the glucose available to the contracting muscle by its release from the glycogen stores in the liver and by increasing the utilization of free fatty acids. There may also be a contraction of the spleen, with a release of additional red cells into the blood stream to augment the capacity for transport of oxygen from lungs to tissues. Thus, the maximum work that can be achieved or maintained is a result of the interplay of many factors which must be adequately coordinated.

Maximum Oxygen Uptake

Measurement of the maximum oxygen uptake that can be achieved during performance of strenuous exercise represents an overall estimate of the effectiveness of all organ systems involved. Numerous studies have shown that, with increasing age, both maximum oxygen uptake and maximum ventilation volume reach a maximum at age 25 or 30, and diminish progressively up to the age of 75 or 80 (Åstrand, I. 1958, 1960, 1967; Åstrand, P. O. 1952, 1956; Benestad, Halvorsrud, and Anderson, 1968; Binkhorst, Pool, van Leeuwen, and Bouhuys, 1966; Fischer, Pařizková, and Roth, 1965; Hollmann, Venrath, and Valentin, 1959; Robinson, 1938; and Valentin, Venrath, von Mallinckrodt, and Gürakar, 1955). Figure 12 summarizes the data from a number of these studies (Norris and Shock, 1974). Since different types of exercise (treadmill, bicycle ergometer) served as the tasks in these studies,

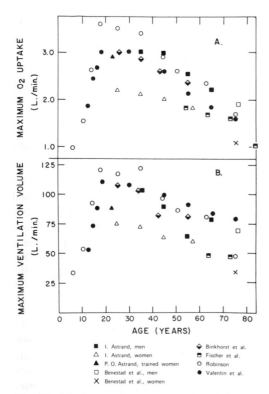

Fig. 12. Maximum oxygen uptake (A) and maximum ventilation volume (B) values (l/min) are plotted against age (years) for the experimental conditions of I. Åstrand's (1958) men and (1960) women, P. O. Åstrand's (1952) trained women, Benestad, *et al.* (1968) men and women, Binkhorst, *et al.* (1966), Fischer, *et al.* (1965), Robinson (1938), and Valentin, *et al.* (1955). (From: Norris and Shock 1974).

the absolute values show considerable variation. However, the general conclusion that maximal oxygen uptake significantly diminishes with age can be drawn. The maximum oxygen uptake achieved by 25 to 30-year-old subjects is approximately 10 times the basal oxygen uptake of 0.3 l/minute. By the age range of 70 to 75, the maximum oxygen uptake falls to about five times the basal levels.

It must be recognized that many factors other than age influence the maximum oxygen uptake. Primary among them is physical fitness. In fact, trained athletes at any age have maximum oxygen intakes that are much greater than untrained individuals. Values for sedentary workers are significantly lower than those for individuals of the same age who engage in systematic exercise. Furthermore, programs of systematic exercise can improve the maximum oxygen uptake in sedentary, middle-aged males (see p. 656, *Physical training and age*).

Dill has reported the results of a longitudinal study of maximal oxygen uptake measurements made on himself between the ages of 37 and 71 years (Dill, 1942; Dill, Horvath, and Craig, 1958; Dill, Robertson, Balke, and Newton, 1964). At age 40, Dill was able to attain a maximal oxygen uptake of 3.3 l/minute. At age 50 this value dropped to 2.9 l/minute, and at age 66 to 2.8 l/minute. At 71 years he achieved a maximum oxygen uptake of 2.1 l/minute. A similar decrement in maximum work rate was reported by Dawson and Hellebrandt (1945) based on measurements made on Dawson over the age span of 40 to 71 years. Thus the age decrement observed in cross-sectional studies also occurs in longitudinal observations made on at least two subjects.

Maximum Heart Rate

Under conditions of exercise, the increase in blood flow required for the delivery of oxygen to the tissues is achieved primarily by an increase in heart rate, with very little change in the amount of blood ejected from the heart with each beat. Consequently, one of the major factors limiting maximum oxygen uptake in the elderly is the progressive decrement, with age, of the maximum heart rates that can be attained (Robinson, 1938). In middle-aged subjects, heart rate may increase from its resting level of about 60 beats per minute to as much as 200 beats per minute. In contrast, Fischer, Pařizková, and Roth (1965) have reported maximum pulse rates, during strenuous exercise, of 125 beats per minute in normal males 70 to 90 years of age.

The physiological basis for this inability of the elderly to accelerate the heart rate is not known. However, studies on animals indicate that a broad spectrum of factors may be involved. For example, Rothbaum, Shaw, Angell, and Shock (1974) found that in unanesthetized rats the reduction in heart rate induced by an increase in blood pressure is significantly less in senescent animals than in young adults.

Further evidence of impaired control of heart rate may be found in the results of studies on changes in heart rate following postural changes in young and old subjects. Norris, Shock, and Yiengst (1953) as well as Graybiel and McFarland (1941) have shown that, when subjects are passively tilted from supine to the upright position, the normal response of an increment in pulse rate is less in old subjects than in young. These results have been attributed to diminished sensitivity of the carotid sinus mechanism to changes in the blood pressure. These experiments show that the mechanisms involved in the control of heart rate are less effective in the old than in the young.

Other experiments conducted on isolated heart muscle from old and young rats have shown that the time required for contraction and relaxation is longer in the old than in the young (Weisfeldt, Loeven, and Shock, 1971). After each heart beat there is a refractory period during which the heart does not respond to a stimulus. Thus, the senescent heart, which requires more time for both contraction and relaxation, cannot initiate the next beat as quickly as can the young heart. As a result, the maximum rate that can be achieved is lower in the old than in the young.

Age and Submaximal Work Rates

The capacity to perform light to moderate physical work is not grossly age dependent, at least up to 65 years of age. Henschel (1970) conducted a survey of some 4,000 coal miners and their wives. Work was performed on a bicycle ergometer with a resistance to pedaling set to produce work energy expenditures of 2, 3, 4, and 5 times resting levels. Pulse rates, pulmonary ventilation, and oxygen consumption were measured at rest and at the end of each work period of 4-6 minutes. At none of the four levels of work was there an age effect on the increment in pulse rate or oxygen consumption. Pulmonary ventilation during each work level became slightly higher with increasing age.

Norris and Shock (1957) also found that, with increasing age, the increment in respiratory volume necessary to provide a given increment in oxygen uptake was greater in the old than in the young. In other words, the older subjects required a higher ventilation volume for a given level of oxygen uptake than did the young. This age difference is probably related to age changes in the alveolar ventilation and capillary blood flow through the lung, since it is known that, in the aged, areas of exchange between the blood and the alveolar spaces of the lung are often impaired.

Although there is no evidence of impairment in the ability to perform work at low or moderate levels with age, physiological responses at a given low level work load are greater in the old than in the young, and the rate of recovery of oxygen consumption, heart rate, and blood pressure are somewhat smaller in the old than in the young (Norris and Shock, 1957).

Berg (1947) has shown the existence of age differences in the rate of recovery of oxygen uptake and CO_2 elimination following moderate levels of exercise. He found that the recovery time constants for CO_2 elimination increased from 35 seconds for subjects 20 years of age to 60 seconds for subjects 60 years old, while the recovery time constants for oxygen uptake were increased from 28 seconds at 20 years to 35 seconds at 60 years. Although the exact mechanisms for these age differences are not known, it is clear that, in terms of overall adaptation to exercise, older subjects are less effective than young ones.

Mechanical Efficiency

The mechanical efficiency of individuals in performing work can be calculated as the amount of work done (kilogram meters) per liter of oxygen consumed. Although the oxygen consumption can be measured with some degree of precision, it is difficult to accurately estimate the amount of work done. Hence, many unknown factors, such as the viscosity of the muscle and the work needed to move the body, arms, or legs, etc. against gravity, require energy (oxygen consumption), but the work done cannot be measured. It is only the external work done, as measured by the ergometer or treadmill, that can enter into the calculation of efficiency. The total work performed is always somewhat indeterminate so that values for mechanical efficiency reported by various investigators show a wide range of variation, although most of them fall within the limits of 15 to 18 percent, while values as high as 25 percent have been reported (Burger and Hause, 1943; Rhyming, 1953). Although I. Åstrand (1960) found significantly lower mechanical efficiencies in old subjects than young ones at moderate levels of work, most other studies have failed to demonstrate any age difference in efficiency. However, Norris, Shock, and Yiengst (1955) found a decrease in mechanical efficiency in subjects over 70 years of age, especially at very low work rates. It is extremely doubtful whether or not the impaired performance in strenuous exercise in older people can be attributed to reduced efficiency, that is, a requirement of more oxygen in order to perform a given amount of work.

Physical Training and Age

It has long been known that, with continued repetition of an exercise regime, young adults will show significant improvements in performance. With training, the maximum oxygen uptake that can be achieved with maximal effort increases, heart rate drops, and the rise in blood pressure associated with the exercise is less. The exact mechanisms of this improvement in response are not well established, but the effects are well known among athletes. In order to obtain the maximum effects of training, the exercise bouts must be severe enough to produce maximum physiological displacements. In view of this requirement, the question has been raised concerning whether training can be achieved when the work load imposed is less than maximum, and whether or not middle-aged and older people can benefit from training.

Numerous studies have shown that middle-aged and older men who engage in regular physical activities are able to develop higher maximum oxygen uptakes during exercise than are sedentary men or women (Åstrand, P. O. 1956; Fischer, Pařizková, and Roth, 1965; Ribisl,

1969). Robinson, Dill, Ross, Robinson, Wagner, and Tzankoff (1973) studied the physiological adjustments of 10 men, aged 18 to 22 years, to work during a 6-month strenuous athletic training program. The same men were restudied twice, first when they were 41 to 44 years old and again when they were 50 to 54. The changes during training at all ages were (a) a marked improvement in maximal work capacity, (b) decreases in heart rate at rest and during work, and (c) a 3 percent increase in body weight. The data showed that the physical fitness and work capacity of the men at age 41 to 54 years depended on their habits of exercise, diet, and smoking through the years, and not on training or work capacity in their youth. In fact, it is claimed by some investigators that the age decrement in exercise performance and maximum oxygen uptake may be compensated for, at least in part, by regular participation in exercises which require endurance (Sucec, 1969).

A number of investigators have tested the effects of periodic exercise continued over periods from six weeks to seven months. Determinations were made of the maximum oxygen uptake before, during, and after the training periods. Some investigators, such as Schuster and Stanley (1970), have failed to find any significant physiological changes after six months of training. However, most studies have reported some improvement in work performance following periods of physical training. Improvement in maximum oxygen uptake, heart rate response, or blood pressure response to exercise has been reported in some studies but not in others.

Tzankoff, Robinson, Pyke, and Brawn (1972) tested the effects of training in 15 sedentary men, aged 44 to 66 years. Training, which extended over a 6–month period, was fairly vigorous, and included activities such as tennis, handball, paddle ball, swimming, jogging, and walking. The younger men, aged 44 to 53 years, had higher maximal oxygen uptakes and blood lactate levels than the older men, aged 54 to 66 years, during exhausting work on a treadmill. After training, maximal oxygen uptake increased in all subjects, although heart rate and blood pressure responses to the exercise did not change. The older men showed as much improvement after training as did the young.

Regimens of strenuous physical exercise may be hazardous, especially for older subjects. Kilbom, Hartley, Saltin, Bjure, Grimby, and Åstrand (1969) carried out an 8 to 10 week training program with 50 sedentary male employees (aged 20 to 50 years) of a Stockholm insurance company. The training program included running, muscle strength exercises, and ball playing two to three times per week. Of the 50 subjects, eight failed to complete the training regime. Among the 50 subjects who started the training, 48 percent had troublesome complications during at least one week of the training period, usually within two to three weeks after the training started. Among these were six cases of achilles peritendinitis, eight cases of sprained ankle, 11 cases with symptoms from the calf and knee, one case of tuberculum major fracture, and four cases of headache. No significant differences in vital capacity, maximum ventilation volume, heart volume, or blood pressure resulted from the training.

Mann, Garrett, Farhi, Murray, and Billings (1969) have also reported a high (49 percent) incidence of complications of the locomotor apparatus (joints and muscles) following physical sessions. In view of these potential complications, it is clear that adequate precautions must be taken when sedentary individuals are exposed to intensive physical training.

A number of studies have indicated that training with relatively light loads of exercise may, at least, result in feelings of well-being, even if objective evidence of improved physical condition, such as an increase in maximum oxygen uptake, cannot be demonstrated. Wallin and Schendel (1969) found that heart rate, during a standard exercise test, was slightly lower in subjects after a 10 week jogging regime than before. The subjects were 21 sedentary males, aged 31 to 60 years, who jogged at least three days a week for 10 weeks. The training had no effect on blood pressure.

De Vries (1970) tested the effect of physical training in 112 males, aged 51 to 87, who were recruited from a retirement community in Los Angeles. The training regimen consisted of 15 to 20 minutes of calisthenics, 15 to 20 minutes of running and walking, 15 to 20 minutes static stretching or swimming (30 minutes, one day per week) three times each week, for periods of 6, 18, and 42 weeks. Although no significant changes were found in any of the hemodynamic measures (cardiac output, stroke volume, total peripheral resistance), oxygen transport capacity (measured by oxygen pulse and respiratory volume at a heart rate of 145 beats per minute), work capacity, and vital capacity improved significantly with training. It was concluded that older men can respond to physical training, and that the response does not depend on their having trained vigorously in youth. This conclusion contrasts with that of Hollmann (1964) and Nöcker (1965), who concluded that training is of little value in persons over 60 years of age unless they have undergone vigorous training earlier in life.

Although it is more difficult to motivate women than men to participate in physical training programs, a number of studies have shown that women who do participate also show improvement in work performance and in physiological response to exercise (Adams and de Vries, 1973; Profant, Early, Nilson, Kusumi, Hofer, and Bruce, 1972; Wessel and van Huss, 1969).

The effectiveness of training programs is greatly influenced by the level of motivation of the subjects. However, even light exercise (walking on a treadmill at low work loads) carried out five days a week for 12 weeks resulted in a significant lowering of heart rate during maximum exercise in elderly men living in a state institution (Stamford, 1972). In these subjects, who were less than enthusiastic about the program, no effect was found after six weeks of training. It is apparent that sedentary, middle-aged, and perhaps even older people can improve their capability of performing physical work if they are willing to carry out an exercise regime.

Life Span of Athletes

Since many early studies show that individuals who had participated in active sports during their college or high school years lived, on the average, slightly longer than the general population (Montoye, 1967), many have assumed that participation in sports and athletic activities will increase life span. All of these studies, although they showed an advantage in length of life for former athletes, suffer from a number of serious limitations. First, age at death of the former athletes was compared with insurance tables or statistics based on the general population. Many of the university graduates in these early investigations entered the clergy or other professions which have a more favorable life expectancy than the general population (Dublin, Lotka, and Spiegelman, 1949). Secondly, mortality data was incomplete in all the studies, that is, the studies were terminated before all of the subjects in a given cohort had died. Dublin corrected the first limitation of these studies by comparing the life expectancies of 4,976 former athletes of eight eastern universities with 38,269 graduates of these same universities (classes of 1870 to 1905). In this study no difference was found between life expectancy of the former athletes and their classmates. Polednak and Damon (1970) have reviewed follow-up studies of longevity of former athletes. In three cohort studies, recognized athletes, that is, lettermen or sportsmen, were compared with a group of their less athletic peers. In no case did the athlete group have significantly different longevity from a random group of college men. However, honor men or intellectuals had a two-year longevity advantage over athletes and the general group of nonathletes. Thus, there is no evidence that those who participate in competitive sports in early life live any longer than those who do not.

Exercise and Heart Disease

Numerous epidemiological studies have indicated a lower incidence of coronary artery disease in populations engaged in physical activity as part of their work regime when compared to populations of sedentary workers. However, all of these studies suffer from a number of limitations. Such groups often differ with respect to other variables, such as diet, living conditions, etc., which may also play a role. For example,

Morris, Heady, Raffle, Roberts, and Parks (1953) showed that the incidence of coronary artery disease was higher among London bus drivers than among conductors. The difference was ascribed to the fact that conductors were engaged in physical activity, that is, climbing stairs to the upper level of the London buses to collect fares whereas the bus drivers remained seated throughout their work day. However, in a follow-up study it was found that the same difference in incidence of coronary artery disease occurred in applicants for positions as drivers or conductors prior to their employment. Thus the difference in the incidence of coronary artery disease could be explained on the basis of preselection factors. Furthermore, stress associated with driving a bus through heavy traffic versus ticket collection may have been equally important in contributing to differences in disease incidence.

Taylor, Klepetar, Keys, Parlin, Blackburn, and Puchner (1962) also compared the incidence of coronary artery disease in railway office workers with yard switchmen. Here again, the incidence of heart disease was somewhat less among the physically active switchmen than the sedentary office workers.

Taylor, Buskirk, and Remington (1973) tested the effects of an exercise regime extending over a period of 18 months in 209 male volunteers selected at three universities (Minnesota, Penn State, and Wisconsin). The exercise regime included calisthenics, jogging, walking, and volleyball for sessions of one hour, three times per week. The dropout rate among subjects was high, that is, 50% were lost to the study by the end of four months in the program at Penn State and Wisconsin and approximately seven months in the Minnesota program. The cardiovascular condition, measured by treadmill grade at which pulse rate increased to 140 beats per minute, was increased in the treatment group over that of the control group at both Minnesota and Penn State. However, the duration of the experiment was too short and the number of subjects too small to permit analysis of differences in the incidence of coronary artery disease in the exercise and control groups. It is, however, of interest that Karvonen, Orma, Punsar, Kallio, Arstila, Luomanmaki, and Takkunen (1970) found a high incidence of coronary artery disease among a population in East and West Finland who performed heavy work. These men worked in logging operations during the winter and on their own farms for the rest of the year. It is thus very clear that high rates for coronary artery disease do exist in the presence of heavy occupational work.

In view of the lack of clear evidence of the effect of exercise on the incidence of coronary artery disease, the Task Force on Arteriosclerosis of the National Heart and Lung Institute (1972) concluded that there was not enough evidence to warrant a trial of exercise in the primary prevention of coronary heart disease. The report of the Intersociety Commission for Heart Disease Resources (1970) reached a similar conclusion.

OTHER ENVIRONMENTAL STRESSES

Changes in the environment also impose changes in conditions to which the animal must adapt. These changes relate primarily to temperature, air pollution, and lowered oxygen tension associated with life at high altitudes. The reduced ability of older people to adapt to changes in environmental temperature have already been discussed in the section on Temperature Regulation.

Air Pollution

Numerous studies have shown the association between air pollution and death rate (Driscoll, 1971b; Greenburg, Jacobs, Drolette, Field, and Braverman, 1962; Hechter and Goldsmith, 1961; Lave and Seskin, 1972; McCarroll, 1967; Martin and Bradley, 1960). McCarroll (1967), in a study of deaths in New York City, found that periods of high air pollution were associated with an increase in deaths which was more pronounced in subjects over 65 years of age than among younger groups, although the difference between the age groups was not subjected to a test of statistical significance. Other studies have shown that, although air pollution increases death rates in general, the effect is greater among people over age 65 than among middle-aged adults.

Altitude and Hypoxia

The primary adaptation to lowered oxygen tension of the air at high altitudes is a marked increase in respiratory volume, followed by an increase in the hemoglobin concentration of whole blood. Within a few days, young subjects increase the hemoglobin content of their blood from about 8.5 gm per 100 ml to as much as 10-11 gm per 100 ml of blood. This response requires more time with increasing age. The final increase in hemoglobin content of the blood is also lower. Dill, Terman, and Hall (1963) compared responses of six subjects, aged 58 to 71 years, with respect to adaptation to the 5,000-10,000 feet altitude at the White Mountain Research Station in 1962. With some of the subjects, results could be compared with their responses acquired when they participated in high altitude expeditions in 1929 and 1935. In the 1935 expeditions, all of the subjects (who were then 29 to 38 years old) responded with the usual increase in hemoglobin concentration for the first 6 to 8 days. On the other hand, five of the six subjects in the 1962 party exhibited a decrease in hemoglobin during the first few days. The greatest decrease was observed in the oldest subject. Thus, an adaptive response was markedly impaired as the age of the subjects increased.

Weihe (1966) has exposed rats raised at 540 meters altitude to an altitude of 3,450 meters for three periods of up to 16 days, at intervals of 8 to 10 days between the altitude exposures. Acclimatization to the increased altitude was assessed in terms of the reduction in food intake and body weight. The ability to acclimatize decreased with age and repetition of exposures.

Verzár and Flückinger (1955) found that the drop in body temperature associated with exposure to low oxygen tensions (high altitudes) was restored to normal values in one to two days in young rats, whereas the body temperature remained depressed in the old rats.

AGING AS THE BREAKDOWN OF REGULATORY MECHANISMS

A number of investigators have advanced a general hypothesis that aging is primarily a reflection of the breakdown of integrative mechanisms. This point of view has been presented by Cannon (1942). Shock (1952), and Verzár (1957). Timiras (1972, 1975) has recently summarized some of the data on age changes in neural and endocrine control mechanisms.

Dilman (1971) has suggested that the key process in aging is a gradual elevation of the threshold of sensitivity of the hypothalamus to feedback suppression. Since the hypothalamus and the pituitary gland play a key role in regulating the activities of many other endocrine glands, an impairment in its sensitivity could have far-reaching effects in many other organ systems. However, the evidence for a reduction in the sensitivity of the hypothalamus with increasing age is far from convincing. For example, he claims that the fall in growth hormone in the plasma which follows an increase in blood sugar level in the young is reversed in old subjects, i.e., growth hormone levels increase. Examination of his data show, however, that the old subjects in his studies were also suffering from diseases such as endometrial carcinoma, breast carcinoma, or coronary heart disease. Thus his data confound the effects of disease and age. Furthermore, his arguments in support of his theory are often based on observations which are in error, as shown by more recent studies (for example, his presumptions that blood insulin levels increase with age and that "muscular tissue becomes progressively less sensitive to the hormone").

In the light of recent studies, neither of these assertions are true (Chapter 15). This theory proposes that changes within a single organ have far-reaching effects, thus explaining a number of the phenomena of aging. However, like many other theories that have preceded it, it is still based on very uncertain circumstantial evidence. Until direct experimental evidence, in which a specific, quantitatively measured stimulus can be applied to the hypothalamus and an appropriate response (that can also be measured quantitatively) is available, this theory of aging is of little value.

Frolkis (1966, 1968) has advanced the hypothesis that the essence of aging is the sum total of unequal changes in regulatory processes at the molecular, cellular, and systemic levels of the organism. Unfortunately, most of the experimental data upon which this hypothesis is based has been published in the Russian literature, and only summaries are available in English. The essence of Frolkis' theory is that, during aging, the sensitivity of a series of effectors (heart, blood vessels, skeletal muscles, etc.) to the action of humoral factors increases, whereas their sensitivity to neural influences decreases. (Sensitivity is defined as the excitation threshold or the minimal stimulation which will cause a functional response. Reaction ability is defined as the maximum effect obtained with intensified stimulation.) Experimentally, Frolkis attempts to distinguish between sensitivity and maximum effect by comparing effects obtained at low levels of stimulation with those observed with increasing intensity of stimulation. He reports many observations to show that, with increasing age, the minimum stimulus of a hormone (or drug) decreases, i.e., the sensitivity to the chemical stimulus increases, whereas in the aged animal, the maximum response diminishes. In contrast, the electrical excitation threshold of nerve trunks was greater in the old than in the young animals.

Although Frolkis attempts to rationalize the presumed increase in sensitivity to humoral factors and the decrease in sensitivity to neural influences, the case is not very convincing. Part of this is due to the fact that many of the critical observations and experiments are presented as a statement of fact, without details of the experimental conditions and design. A number of these statements are not in accord with observations reported by other investigators. For example, Tuttle (1966) has shown that the sensitivity of aortic strips to norepinephrine was much greater in strips taken from 1-year-old than from 2-year-old rats. No increase in tension developed by the strips was observed at norepinephrine concentrations less than 1×10^{-7} M/l in 2-year-old strips, whereas the 1-year-old strips showed a response at a concentration of 1×10^{-8} M/l. At all concentrations of norepinephrine, the response (tension developed) was significantly greater in the 1-year-old than the 2-year-old strips.

The initial step in the action of most hormones consists of specific binding to target cell receptors. Thus the response of a cell to a hormone is in part dependent on the ability of the cell to bind the hormone. Roth (1974, 1975) has shown that, with increasing age of rats, there is a reduction in the number of binding sites in a number of tissues for glucocorticoid hormones. Furthermore, Roy, Milin, and McMinn (1974) have shown a loss of a liver androgen receptor which is correlated with decreased production of an androgen-dependent globulin by the liver in rats over 750 days of age. This loss of binding sites in tissue from senescent animals may be the basis for the reduction in responsiveness to various stimuli as reviewed by Gusseck (1972) and Adelman (1972).

In view of the mounting evidence that aging is associated with a reduction in sensitivity and responsiveness of tissues to hormones and other substances, Frolkis' hypothesis that presumes an increase in sensitivity to humoral agents as contrasted with a reduction in sensitivity to neural influences with advancing age cannot be accepted.

SUMMARY

This chapter has presented currently available evidence to support the premise that aging in the total animal may be more than the summation of changes that take place at the cellular, tissue, or organ level. Life of the total animal requires the integrated activity of all of the organ systems of the body to meet the stresses of living.

The effects of age on regulatory mechanisms has been illustrated with respect to the adaptation of body temperature to environmental changes and the ability to perform muscular work. These examples show that, with advancing age, regulatory mechanisms are less effective. Much work remains to be done to identify the mechanisms which are critical in explaining the reduced effectiveness of adaptation, which is associated with aging in the total animal.

REFERENCES

Adams, G. M., and de Vries, H. A. 1973. Physiological effects of an exercise training regimen upon women aged 52 to 79. *J. Geront.*, **28**, 50–55.

Adelman, R. C. 1972. Age dependent control of enzyme adaptation. *In*, B. L. Strehler (ed.), *Advances in Gerontological Research*, Vol. 4, pp. 1–23. New York: Academic Press.

Adler, S., Lindeman, R. D., Yiengst, M. J., Beard, E., and Shock, N. W. 1968. Effect of acute loading on urinary acid excretion by the aging human kidney. *J. Lab. Clin. Med.*, **72**, 278–289.

American Society of Heating, Refrigeration, and Air Conditioning Engineers. 1967. *ASHRAE handbook of fundamentals*. New York: The Society.

Åstrand, I. 1958. The physical work capacity of workers 50–64 years old. *Acta Physiol. Scand.*, **42**, 73–86.

Åstrand, I. 1960. Aerobic work capacity in men and women with special reference to age. *Acta Physiol. Scand.*, **49**, 45–60.

Åstrand, I. 1967. Aerobic work capacity. Its relation to age, sex and other factors. *Circulation Res.*, **20**, Suppl. I, I-211–I-217.

Åstrand, P. O. 1952. *Experimental studies of physical working capacity in relation to sex and age.* Copenhagen: Munksgaard.

Åstrand, P. O. 1956. Human physical fitness with special reference to sex and age. *Physiol. Rev.*, **36**, 307–335.

Benestad, A. M., Halvorsrud, J., and Anderson, K. L. 1968. The physical fitness of old Norwegian men and women. *Acta Med. Scand.*, **183**, 73–78.

Berg, W. E. 1947. Individual differences in respiratory gas exchange during recovery from moderate exercise. *Am. J. Physiol.*, **149**, 597–610.

Berliner, R. W. 1966. Urine formation. *In*, C. H. Best and N. B. Taylor (eds.), *The Physiological Basis of Medical Practice*, pp. 1665–1702. Baltimore: Williams & Wilkins, 8th ed.

Bernard, C. 1859. *Leçons sur les propriétés physiologiques et les alterations pathologiques des liquides de l'organisme*. Paris: Baillière.

Binkhorst, R. A., Pool, J., van Leeuwen, P., and Bouhuys, A. 1966. Maximum oxygen uptake in healthy non-athletic males. *Inter. Z. Angew. Physiol.*, **22**, 10–18.

Boothby, W. M., Berkson, J., and Dunn, H. L. 1936. Studies of the energy metabolism of normal individuals. A standard for basal metabolism with a nomogram for clinical application. *Am. J. Physiol.*, **116**, 468–484.

Burch, G. E., Cohn, A. E., and Neumann, C. 1942. A study of the rate of water loss from the surfaces of the finger tips and toe tips of normal and senile subjects and patients with arterial hypertension. *Am. Heart J.*, **23**, 185–196.

Burger, M., and Hause, W. H. 1943. Über die Okonomie korplicher Arbeit in den verschnedenen Altersstufen. *Z. Alternsforsch.*, **4**, 229–236.

Burrows, B., Kasik, J. E., Niden, A. H., and Barclay, W. R. 1961. Clinical usefulness of the single-breath pulmonary diffusing capacity test. *Am. Rev. Respirat. Diseases*, **84**, 789–806.

Cannon, W. B. 1929. The sympathetic division of the autonomic system in relation to homeostatis. *Arch. Neurol. Psychiat., Chicago*, **22**, 282–294.

Cannon, W. B. 1939. The William Henry Welch Lectures. II. Homeostasis in senescence. *J. Mt. Sinai Hosp., N.Y.*, 5, 598–606.

Cannon, W. B. 1942. Aging of homeostatic mechanisms. *In*, E. V. Cowdry (ed.), *Problems of Ageing*, pp. 567–582. Baltimore: Williams & Wilkins, 2nd ed.

Cohn, J. E. 1964. Age and the pulmonary diffusing capacity. *In*, L. Cander and J. H. Moyer (eds.), *Aging of the Lung*, pp. 163–172. New York: Grune & Stratton.

Cohn, J. E., Carroll, D. G., Armstrong, B. W., Shepard, R. H., and Riley, R. L. 1954. Maximal diffusing capacity of the lung in normal subjects of different ages. *J. Appl. Physiol.*, 6, 588–597.

Cooper, K. E. 1966. Temperature regulation and the hypothalamus. *Brit. Med. Bull.*, 22, 238–242.

Dawson, P. M., and Hellebrandt, F. A. 1945. The influence of aging in man upon his capacity for physical work and upon his cardiovascular response to exercise. *Am. J. Physiol.*, 143, 420–427.

de Vries, H. A. 1970. Physiological effects of an exercise training regimen upon men aged 52 to 88. *J. Geront.*, 25, 325–336.

Dill, D. B. 1942. Effects of physical strain and high altitudes on the heart and circulation. *Am. Heart J.*, 23, 441–454.

Dill, D. B., Horvath, S. M., and Craig, F. N. 1958. Responses to exercise as related to age. *J. Appl. Physiol.*, 12, 195–196.

Dill, D. B., Robinson, S., Balke, B., and Newton, J. L. 1964. Work tolerance: Age and altitude. *J. Appl. Physiol.*, 19, 483–488.

Dill, D. B., Terman, J. W., and Hall, F. G. 1963. Hemoglobin at high altitude as related to age. *Clin. Chem.*, 9, 710–716.

Dilman, V. M. 1971. Age-associated elevation of hypothalamic threshold to feedback control and its role in development, ageing and disease. *Lancet*, 1, 1211–1219.

Donevan, R. E., Palmer, W. H., Varvis, C. J., and Bates, D. V. 1959. Influence of age on pulmonary diffusing capacity. *J. Appl. Physiol.*, 14, 483–492.

Driscoll, D. M. 1971a. The relationship between weather and mortality in ten major metropolitan areas in the United States, 1962-1965. *Int. J. Biometeor.*, 15, 23–39.

Driscoll, D. M. 1971b. Base lines for measuring adverse effects of air pollution: Some evidence for weather effects on mortality. *Environ. Res.*, 4, 233–242.

Dublin, L. I., Lotka, A. J., and Spiegelman, M. 1949. *Length of life: A study of the life table.* New York: Ronald Press.

DuBois, D., and DuBois, E. F. 1916. A formula to estimate the approximate surface area if height and weight be known. *Arch. Internal Med.*, 17, 863–871.

DuBois, E. F. 1936. *Basal metabolism in health and disease.* Philadelphia: Lea & Febiger, 3rd ed.

DuBois, E. F. 1948. *Fever and the regulation of body temperature.* Springfield, Ill.: C. C Thomas.

Finch, C. E., Foster, J. R., and Mirsky, A. E. 1969. Ageing and the regulation of cell activities during exposure to cold. *J. Gen. Physiol.*, 54, 690–712.

Fischer, A., Pařizková, J., and Roth, Z. 1965. The effect of systematic physical activity on maximal performance and functional capacity in senescent men. *Inter. Z. Angew. Physiol.*, 21, 269–304.

Fox, R. H., MacGibbon, R., Davies, L., and Woodward, P. M. 1973. Problem of the old and the cold. *Brit. Med. J.*, 1, 21–24.

Fox, R. H., Woodward, P. M., Exton-Smith, A. N., Green, M. F., Donnison, D. V., and Wicks, M. H. 1973. Body temperatures in the elderly; a national study of physiological, social and environmental conditions. *Brit. Med. J.*, 1, 200–206.

Fox, R. H., Woodward, P. M., Fry, A. J., Collins, J. C., and MacDonald, I. C. 1971. Diagnosis of accidental hypothermia of the elderly. *Lancet*, 1, 424–427.

Friedfield, L. 1949. Heat reaction states in the aged. *Geriatrics*, 4, 211–216.

Frolkis, V. V. 1966. Neurohumoral regulations in the aging organism. *J. Geront.*, 21, 161–167.

Frolkis, V. V. 1968. Regulatory process in the mechanism of aging. *Exp. Geront.*, 3, 113–123.

Grad, B., and Kral, V. A. 1957. The effect of senescence on resistance to stress. I. Response of young and old mice to cold. *J. Geront.*, 12, 172–181.

Graybiel, A., and McFarland, R. A. 1941. The use of the tilt table test in aviation medicine. *J. Aviation Med.*, 12, 1–20.

Greenburg, L., Jacobs, M. B., Drolette, B. M., Field, F., and Braverman, M. M. 1962. Report of an air pollution incident in New York City, November 1953. *Public Health Reports*, 77, 7–16.

Gregerman, R. I. 1967. The age-related alteration of thyroid function and thyroid hormone metabolism in man. *In*, L. Gitman (ed.), *Endocrines and Aging*, pp. 161–173. Springfield, Ill.: C. C Thomas.

Gusseck, D. J. 1972. Endocrine mechanisms and aging. *In*, B. L. Strehler (ed.), *Advances in Gerontological Research, Vol. 4*, pp. 105–166. New York: Academic Press.

Hechter, H. H., and Goldsmith, J. R. 1961. Air pollution and daily mortality. *Am. J. Med. Sci.*, 241, 581–588.

Hellon, R. F., and Lind, A. R. 1956. Observations on the activity of sweat glands with special reference to the influence of ageing. *J. Physiol.*, 133, 132–144.

Hellon, R. F., Lind, A. R., and Weiner, J. S. 1956. The physiological reactions of men of two age groups to a hot environment. *J. Physiol.*, 133, 118–131.

Henschel, A. 1970. Effects of age on work capacity. *Am. Ind. Hyg. Assoc. J.*, 31, 430–436.

Henschel, A., Cole, M. B., and Lyczkowskyj, O. 1968. Heat tolerance of elderly persons living in a subtropical climate. *J. Geront.*, 23, 17–22.

Hollmann, W. 1964. Changes in the capacity for maximal and continuous effort in relation to age. *In*, E. Jokl and E. Simon (eds.), *International Research in*

Sport and Physical Education, pp. 369–371. Springfield, Ill.: C. C Thomas.

Hollmann, W., Venrath, H., and Valentin, H. 1959. Über das Verhalten von Ventilation und Stoffwechsel gesunder männlicher Personen verschiedenen Alters bei leichter und mittelschwerer Arbeit. *Z. Alternsforsch.*, **13**, 60–67.

Horvath, S. M., Radcliffe, C. E., Hutt, B. K., and Spurr, G. B. 1955. Metabolic responses of old people to a cold environment. *J. Appl. Physiol.*, **8**, 145–148.

Howell, T. H. 1950. *Old Age: Some Practical Points in Geriatrics and Gerontology.* London: H. K. Lewis Co., 2nd ed.

Howell, T. H. 1972. Axillary temperatures in aged women. *Age and Ageing*, **1**, 250–253.

Institute of Heating and Ventilation Engineers. 1965. *Guide, Sect. 4, Comfort.* London: The Institute.

Intersociety Commission for Heart Disease Resources. 1970. Report on primary prevention of the atherosclerotic diseases. *Circulation*, **42**, A–55.

Ivy, A. C. 1944. What is normal or normality? *Quart. Bull. Northwestern Univ. Med. School*, **18**, 22–32.

Karvonen, M. J., Orma, E., Punsar, S., Kallio, V., Arstila, M., Luomanmaki, K., and Takkunen, J. 1970. Coronary heart disease in seven countries. VI. Five-year experience in Finland. *Circulation*, **41–42**, Suppl. I, I–52–I–62.

Kilbom, A., Hartley, L. H., Saltin, B., Bjure, J., Grimby, G., and Åstrand, I. 1969. Physical training in sedentary middle-aged and older men. I. Medical evaluation. *Scand. J. Clin. Lab. Invest.*, **24**, 315–322.

Köng, F. 1939. Hauttemperaturmessungen an Männern von über 6 Jahren. *Z. Ges. Exp. Med.*, **107**, 98–105.

Krag, C. L., and Kountz, W. B. 1950. Stability of body function in the aged. I. Effect of exposure of the body to cold. *J. Geront.*, **5**, 227–235.

Krag, C. L., and Kountz, W. B. 1952. Stability of body function in the aged. II. Effects of exposure of the body to heat. *J. Geront.*, **7**, 61–70.

Kutschenreuter, P. H. 1950. Weather does affect mortality. *ASHRAE* (Am. Soc. Heating, Refrig., Aircond. Engrs), **2**, 39–43.

Lave, L. B., and Seskin, E. P. 1972. Air pollution, climate and home heating: Their effects on U.S. mortality rates. *Am. J. Public Health*, **62**, 909–916.

Lewis, W. H., Jr. 1938. Changes with age in basal metabolic rate in adult men. *Am. J. Physiol.*, **121**, 502–516.

Lowry, O. A., and Hastings, A. B. 1952. Quantitative histochemical changes in aging. *In*, A. I. Lansing (ed.), *Cowdry's Problems of Ageing*, pp. 105–138. Baltimore: Williams & Wilkins, 3rd ed.

McCarroll, J. 1967. Measurements of morbidity and mortality related to air pollution. *J. Air Pollution Control Assoc.*, **17**, 203–209.

McGandy, R. B., Barrows, C. H., Jr., Spanias, A., Meredith, A., Stone, J. L., and Norris, A. H. 1966. Nutrient intakes and energy expenditure in men of different ages. *J. Geront.*, **21**, 581–587.

McGrath, M. W., and Thomson, M. L. 1959. The effect of age, body size and lung volume change on alveolar-capillary permeability and diffusing capacity in man. *J. Physiol.*, **146**, 572–582.

MacMillan, A. L., Corbett, J. L., Johnson, R. H., Crampton Smith, A., Spalding, J. M. K., and Wollner, L. 1967. Temperature regulation in survivors of accidental hypothermia of the elderly. *Lancet*, **2**, 165–169.

MacPherson, R. K., Ofner, F., and Welch, J. A. 1967. Effect of prevailing air temperature on mortality. *Brit. J. Prevent. Social Med.*, **21**, 17–21.

Mann, G. V., Garrett, H. L., Farhi, A., Murray, H., and Billings, F. T. 1969. Exercise to prevent coronary heart disease. *Am. J. Med.*, **46**, 12–27.

Martin, A. E., and Bradley, W. H. 1960. Mortality, fog and atmospheric pollution; an investigation during the winter of 1958–59. *Monthly Bull. Min. Health Public Health Lab. Serv., Lond.*, **19**, 56–72.

Miller, J. H., and Shock, N. W. 1953. Age differences in the renal tubular response to antidiuretic hormone. *J. Geront.*, **8**, 446–450.

Montoye, H. J. 1967. Participation in athletics. *Can. Med. Assoc. J.*, **96**, 813–820.

Morris, J. N., Heady, J. A., Raffle, P. A. B., Roberts, C. G., and Parks, J. W. 1953. Coronary heart disease and physical activity of work. *Lancet*, **2**, 1053–1057; *Lancet*, **1**, 1111–1120.

Munk, F. 1910–1911. Wirking von Temperatur und anderen Hautreizen auf das Gefässystem. *Z. Exp. Path. Therap.*, **8**, 337–345.

National Heart and Lung Institute. 1972. *Arteriosclerosis: Report by the National Heart and Lung Institute Task Force on Arteriosclerosis.* Vol. 1, 41 pp. Vol. 2, 365 pp. Washington, D.C.: U.S. Gov't. Printing Off.

Nöcker, J. 1965. Die Bedeutung des Sportes für den alten menschen. *In*, W. Doberauer, A. Hittmair, R. Nissen, and F. H. Schulz (eds.), *Handbuch der prakitschen Geriatrie, Bd. 1*, pp. 176–199. Stuttgart: F. Enke.

Norris, A. H., and Shock, N. W. 1957. Age changes in ventilatory and metabolic responses to submaximal exercise. *In, 4th Congress of the International Association of Gerontology, Merano, Italy, July 14–19, 1957*, pp. 512–522. Fidenza: Tito Mattioli.

Norris, A. H., and Shock, N. W. 1974. Exercise in the adult years. *In*, W. R. Johnson and E. R. Buskirk (eds.), *Science and Medicine of Exercise and Sport*, pp. 346–365. New York: Harper & Row.

Norris, A. H., Shock, N. W., and Yiengst, M. J. 1953. Age changes in heart rate and blood pressure responses to tilting and standardized exercise. *Circulation*, **8**, 521–526.

Norris, A. H., Shock, N. W., and Yiengst, M. J. 1955. Age differences in ventilatory and gas exchange responses to graded exercise in males. *J. Geront.*, **10**, 145–155.

Oechsli, F. W., and Buechley, R. W. 1970. Excess mortality associated with three Los Angeles September hot spells. *Environ. Res.*, **3**, 277–284.

Pickering, G. W. 1936. The peripheral resistance in persistent hypertension. *Clin. Sci.*, **2**, 209–235.

Polednak, A. P., and Damon, A. 1970. College athletics, longevity and cause of death. *Human Biol.*, **42**, 28–46.

Profant, G. R., Early, R. G., Nilson, Karen L., Kusumi, F., Hofer, Verona, and Bruce, R. A. 1972. Responses to maximal exercise in healthy middle-aged women. *J. Appl. Physiol.*, **33**, 595–599.

Quenouille, M. H., Boyne, A. W., Fisher, W. B., and Leitch, I. 1951. *Statistical studies of recorded energy expenditure in man. Part I. Basal metabolism related to sex, stature, age, climate and race.* Farnham Royal, England: Commonwealth Bur. Animal Nutrit., Tech. Comm. No. 17.

Rhyming, I. 1953. A modified Harvard step test for the evaluation of physical fitness. *Arbeitsphysiologie*, **15**, 235–250.

Ribisl, P. M. 1969. Effects of training upon the maximal oxygen uptake of middle aged men. *Inter. Z. Angew. Physiol.*, **27**, 154–160.

Robinson, S. 1938. Experimental studies of physical fitness with relation to age. *Arbeitsphysiologie*, **10**, 251–323.

Robinson, S., Belding, H. S., Consolazio, F. C., Horvath, S. M., and Turrell, E. S. 1965. Acclimatization of older men to work in heat. *J. Appl. Physiol.*, **20**, 583–586.

Robinson, S., Dill, D. B., Ross, J. C., Robinson, R. D., Wagner, J. A., and Tzankoff, S. P. 1973. Training and physiological aging in man. *Federation Proc.*, **32**, 1628–1634.

Rohles, F. H. 1969. Preference for the thermal environment by the elderly. *Human Factors*, **11**, 37–41.

Roth, G. S., 1974. Age-related changes in specific glucocorticoid binding by steroid-responsive tissues of rats. *Endocrinology*, **94**, 82–90.

Roth, G. S. 1975. Age-related changes in glucocorticoid binding by rat splenic leukocytes: possible cause of altered adaptive responsiveness. *Federation Proc.*, **34**, 183–185.

Rothbaum, D. A., Shaw, D. J., Angell, C. S., and Shock, N. W. 1974. Age differences in the baroreceptor response of rats. *J. Geront.*, **29**, 488–492.

Roy, A. K., Milin, B. S., and McMinn, D. M. 1974. Androgen receptor in rat liver: hormonal and developmental regulation of the cytoplasmic receptor and its correlation with the androgen-dependent synthesis of α_{2u}-globulin. *Biochim. Biophys. Acta*, **354**, 213–232.

Salvosa, C. B., Payne, P. R., and Wheeler, E. F. 1971. Environmental conditions and body temperatures of elderly women living alone or in local authority home. *Brit. Med. J.*, **4**, 656–659.

Schuman, S. H., Anderson, C. P., and Oliver, J. T. 1964. Epidemiology of successive heat waves in Michigan in 1962 and 1963. *J. Am. Med. Assoc.*, **189**, 733–738.

Schuster, B., and Stanley, E. 1970. Experiences with physical conditioning programs in middle-aged men. *Indust. Med. & Surg.*, **39**, 472–476.

Shattuck, G. C., and Hilferty, M. M. 1932. Sunstroke and allied conditions in the United States. *Am. J. Trop. Med.*, **12**, 223–245.

Shock, N. W. 1942. Standard values for basal oxygen consumption in adolescents. *Am. J. Diseases Children*, **64**, 19–32.

Shock, N. W., 1952. Ageing of homeostatic mechanisms. *In*, A. I. Lansing (ed.), *Cowdry's Problems of Ageing*, pp. 415–446. Baltimore: Williams & Wilkins, 3rd. ed.

Shock, N. W. 1955. Metabolism and age (review). *J. Chronic Diseases*, **2**, 687–703.

Shock, N. W. 1972. Energy metabolism, caloric intake and physical activity of the aging. *In*, L. A. Carlson (ed.), *Nutrition in Old Age (X Symposium of the Swedish Nutrition Fdn.)*, pp. 12–23. Uppsala: Almqvist & Wiksell.

Shock, N. W. 1974. Physiological aspects of aging. *In*, *Troisième Age et Vieillissement*, pp. 89–111. Paris: J. B. Baillière.

Shock, N. W., Andres, R., and Norris, A. H. 1975. Unpublished data.

Shock, N. W., and Norris, A. H. 1970. Neuromuscular coordination as a factor in age changes in muscular exercise. *In*, D. Brunner and E. Jokl (eds.), *Medicine and Sports. Vol. 4. Physical Activity and Aging*, pp. 92–99. Basel: S. Karger.

Shock, N. W., Watkin, D. M., Yiengst, M. J., Norris, A. H., Gaffney, G. W., Gregerman, R. I., and Falzone, J. A. 1963. Age differences in the water content of the body as related to basal oxygen consumption in males. *J. Geront.*, **18**, 1–8.

Shock, N. W., and Yiengst, M. J. 1950. Age changes in the acid base equilibrium of the blood of males. *J. Geront.*, **5**, 1–4.

Shock, N. W., and Yiengst, M. J. 1955. Age changes in basal respiratory measurements and metabolism in males. *J. Geront.*, **10**, 31–40.

Silverstone, F. A., Brandfonbrener, M., Shock, N. W., and Yiengst, M. J. 1957. Age differences in the intravenous glucose tolerance test and the response to insulin. *J. Clin. Invest.*, **36**, 504–514.

Stamford, B. A. 1972. Physiological effects of training upon institutionalized geriatric men. *J. Geront.*, **27**, 451–455.

Stone, J. L., and Norris, A. H. 1966. Activities and attitudes of participants in the Baltimore Longitudinal Study. *J. Geront.*, **21**, 575–580.

Succec, A. 1969. Oxygen uptake and heart rate in middle-aged males participating in an adult fitness program. *Am. Correct. Therap. J.*, **23**, 98–103.

Taylor, G. 1964. The problem of hypothermia in the elderly. *Practitioner*, **193**, 761–767.

Taylor, H. L., Buskirk, E. R., and Remington, R. D. 1973. Exercise in controlled trials of the prevention of coronary heart disease. *Federation Proc.*, **32**, 1623–1627.

Taylor, H. L., Klepetar, E., Keys, A., Parlin, W., Blackburn, H., and Puchner, T. C. 1962. Death rates among physically active and sedentary employees of the railroad industry. *Am. J. Public Health*, **52**, 1697–1707.

Timiras, P. S. 1972. Decline in homeostatic regulation. *In*, P. S. Timiras, *Developmental Physiology and Aging*, pp. 542–563. New York: McMillan Co.

Timiras, P. S. 1975. Aging of homeostatic control systems. Introductory remarks. *Federation Proc.*, **34**, 81–82.

Tuttle, R. S. 1966. Age related changes in the sensitivity of rat aortic strips to norepinephrine and associated chemical and structural alterations. *J. Geront.*, **21**, 510–516.

Tzankoff, S. P., Robinson, S., Pyke, F. S., and Brawn, C. A. 1972. Physiological adjustments to work in older men as affected by physical training. *J. Appl. Physiol.*, **33**, 346–350.

Valentin, H., Venrath, H., von Mallinckrodt, H., and Gürakar, M. 1955. Die maximale Sauerstoffaufnahme in den verschiedenen Altersklassen Eine praktisch wichtige Herz-Kreislauf-Funktionsprüfung im Vitamaxima-Bereich. *Z. Alternsforsch.*, **9**, 291–309.

Verzár, F. 1957. Studies on adaptation as a method of gerontological research. *Ciba Collq. on Aging*, **3**, 60–72.

Verzár, F., and Flückinger, E. 1955. Lack of adaptation to low oxygen pressure in aged animals. *In*, *Old Age and the Modern World* (3rd International Congress of Gerontology), pp. 524–532. London: E. & S. Livingstone Ltd.

Wallin, C. C., and Schendel, J. S. 1969. Physiological changes in middle-aged men following a ten-week jogging program. *Res. Quart.*, **40**, 600–606.

Watts, A. J. 1971. Hypothermia in the aged: A study of the role of cold sensitivity. *Environ. Res.*, **5**, 119–126.

Weihe, W. H. 1966. Influence of age, physical activity and ambient temperature on acclimatization of rats to high altitudes. *Federation Proc.*, **25**, 1342–1346.

Weisfeldt, M. L., Loeven, W. A., and Shock, N. W. 1971. Resting and active mechanical properties of trabeculae carneae from aged male rats. *Am. J. Physiol.*, **220**, 1921–1927.

Wessel, J. A., and van Huss, W. D. 1969. The influence of physical activity and age on exercise adaptation of women, 20–69 years. *J. Sports Med.*, **9**, 173–180.

Wollner, L., and Spalding, J. M. K. 1973. The autonomic nervous system. *In*, J. C. Brockelhurst (ed.), *Textbook of Geriatric Medicine and Gerontology*, pp. 235–254. Edinburgh & London: Churchill Livingstone.

26
SELECTED
TABULAR MATERIAL
ON AGING

N. O. Calloway
Madison General Hospital
and
Paula L. Dollevoet
University of Nebraska Medical School

TABLE 1. AVERAGE VALUES OF GLYCOGEN CONTENTS, mg PER 100 g, OF TISSUE OF THE VARIOUS PARTS OF THE CENTRAL NERVOUS SYSTEM AT THREE DIFFERENT AGES.

	Cortex	Caudate nucleus	Thalamus	Colliculi	Cerebellum	Medulla	Cord
New born cat	23 [12–32] (16)	–	48 [30–89] (5)	45 [33–68] (3)	107 [47–158] (7)	101 [72–164] (6)	137 [126–151] (3)
5 to 8 week old cat	45 [25–66] (15)	36 [32–43] (4)	30 [28–32] (3)	38 [37–38] (3)	97 [62–139] (7)	35 [22–48] (6)	47 [34–56] (6)
Adult cat	68 [42–120] (10)	46 [26–96] (9)	27 [19–39] (9)	28 [21–30] (6)	32 [10–53] (9)	31 [23–47] (8)	25 [10–53] (6)
Newborn dog	18 [14–23] (12)	34 [28–47] (6)	44 [20–88] (15)	60 [33–93] (12)	65 [44–98] (16)	122 [90–157] (12)	127 [75–200] (13)
5 to 8 week old dog	31 [24–45] (10)	39 [31–62] (10)	53 [35–74] (9)	56 [31–75] (9)	69 [50–91] (10)	58 [33–85] (9)	45 [26–63] (11)
Adult dog	73 [45–108] (7)	58 [44–71] (7)	62 [41–68] (6)	50 [37–60] (7)	35 [23–46] (6)	39 [21–47] (6)	29 [15–31] (6)

The numbers in brackets are the extreme upper and lower values. These values show the same general trend as the averages and similarly indicate which differences are significant.

Values in parentheses are the number of animals used.

Annette Chesler and Harold E. Himwich, *Arch. Biochem.*, 1943, **2**, (2), June.

TABLE 2. LIFE HISTORY DATA FOR BODY WEIGHT (g), OXYGEN CONSUMPTION RATE (ml O_2/g/min.) AND TOTAL OXYGEN UPTAKE (ml O_2 · min.) BY SEX FOR C57BL/6 MICE. OXYGEN UTILIZATION MEASUREMENTS WERE AT 30°C. FOR 17 MALES AND 17 FEMALES.

Age (Days)	BODY WEIGHT (g)		OXYGEN CONSUMPTION (ml O_2/g/min.)				OXYGEN UPTAKE (ml O_2/min.)	
	Male	Female	Male	±S.D.[a]	Female	±S.D.[a]	Male	Female
0	1.44	1.44	0.056	0.016	0.060	0.012	0.081	0.086
1	1.62	1.70	0.057	0.011	0.058	0.012	0.092	0.099
2	1.91	2.04	0.057	0.001	0.062	0.010	0.103	0.126
3	2.40	2.58	0.068	0.008	0.066	0.010	0.163	0.170
4	2.97	3.12	0.070	0.010	0.073	0.011	0.208	0.228
5	3.52	3.71	0.068	0.008	0.069	0.012	0.239	0.256
6	4.11	4.25	0.076	0.010	0.078	0.007	0.312	0.332
7	4.62	4.82	0.084	0.008	0.085	0.011	0.388	0.410
8	5.21	5.18	0.088	0.004	0.088	0.009	0.458	0.456
9	5.75	5.90	0.087	0.005	0.088	0.008	0.500	0.513
10	6.29	6.41	0.091	0.005	0.093	0.006	0.572	0.596
11	6.82	6.94	0.094	0.009	0.091	0.015	0.641	0.632
12	7.26	7.35	0.089	0.007	0.092	0.012	0.646	0.676
13	7.72	7.79	0.090	0.011	0.096	0.011	0.695	0.748
14	8.05	8.10	0.089	0.010	0.090	0.009	0.716	0.729
15	8.28	8.34	0.080	0.014	0.087	0.011	0.662	0.726
16	8.57	8.51	0.086	0.016	0.089	0.012	0.737	0.757
17	8.98	8.94	0.085	0.017	0.088	0.017	0.763	0.787
18	9.46	9.45	0.074	0.010	0.079	0.011	0.700	0.747
19	10.22	10.10	0.078	0.011	0.078	0.010	0.797	0.788
20	10.94	10.86	0.072	0.014	0.069	0.015	0.788	0.749
22	12.43	12.25	0.076	0.011	0.078	0.010	0.945	0.956
24	14.53	13.68	0.065	0.009	0.067	0.008	0.941	0.917
26	16.67	15.34	0.070	0.006	0.072	0.008	1.167	1.104
28	18.46	16.71	0.077	0.009	0.074	0.011	1.421	1.237
30	20.41	17.62	0.067	0.007	0.069	0.008	1.367	1.216
35	22.30	18.04	0.060	0.008	0.061	0.006	1.338	1.100
40	23.85	18.34	0.067	0.008	0.066	0.006	1.598	1.210
45	28.59	19.00	0.064	0.005	0.060	0.008	1.830	1.140
50	26.50	19.33	0.061	0.009	0.059	0.005	1.617	1.140
52	26.92	19.84	0.066	0.008	0.059	0.005	1.777	1.151
54	27.27	19.93	0.066	0.007	0.063	0.013	1.833	1.256
56	27.73	20.18	0.067	0.009	0.056	0.007	1.858	1.130
58	28.10	20.30	0.060	0.007	0.054	0.005	1.686	1.096
60	28.35	20.47	.0.056	0.008	0.055	0.005	1.588	1.126
65	28.95	20.90	0.059	0.005	0.056	0.007	1.708	1.170
70	29.46	21.12	0.064	0.008	0.059	0.007	1.885	1.246
75	29.68	21.45	0.067	0.008	0.064	0.008	1.989	1.373
80	28.22	21.62	0.069	0.006	0.062	0.007	1.947	1.340
85	30.11	21.57	0.074	0.006	0.068	0.008	2.228	1.467
90	32.82	21.65	0.073	0.006	0.072	0.011	2.396	1.559
95	30.69	21.90	0.063	0.009	0.057	0.006	1.933	1.248
100	31.07	22.19	0.067	0.010	0.062	0.006	2.079	1.376
110	31.74	22.86	0.066	0.008	0.057	0.007	2.095	1.303
120	32.34	23.14	0.069	0.008	0.059	0.004	2.225	1.365
130	32.36	23.49	0.071	0.005	0.059	0.005	2.298	1.386
140	32.94	23.89	0.058	0.006	0.051	1.910	1.190	1.218
150	33.82	23.99	0.068	0.008	0.066	0.008	2.300	1.583
160	33.58	24.16	0.072	0.010	0.067	0.008	2.418	1.619

TABLE 2. *(Continued)*

Age (Days)	BODY WEIGHT (g)		OXYGEN CONSUMPTION (ml O$_2$/g/min.)				OXYGEN UPTAKE (ml O$_2$/min.)	
	Male	Female	Male	±S.D.[a]	Female	±S.D.[a]	Male	Female
170	33.54	24.81	0.066	0.012	0.059	0.007	2.214	1.464
180	34.76	25.11	0.069	0.008	0.062	0.008	2.398	1.557
190	34.29	25.01	0.073	0.008	0.077	0.012	2.503	1.926
200	33.09	24.59	0.073	0.006	0.072	0.008	2.416	1.770
220	31.89	23.87	0.076	0.011	0.067	0.006	2.424	1.600
240	31.91	23.50	0.089	0.009	0.070	0.008	2.840	1.645
260	33.01	24.23	0.073	0.011	0.072	0.008	2.410	1.745
280	31.84	24.46	0.081	0.007	0.074	0.010	2.579	1.810
300	33.35	24.46	0.080	0.009	0.081	0.011	2.668	1.981
320	33.67	24.78	0.079	0.004	0.067	0.008	2.660	1.660
340	33.71	24.61	0.079	0.006	0.070	0.012	2.663	1.723
360	33.70	25.07	0.079	0.008	0.076	0.017	2.662	1.905
420	33.81	24.81	0.074	0.008	0.067	0.010	2.520	1.662
480	33.30	24.90	0.071	0.008	0.070	0.008	2.364	1.743
540	33.45	24.93	0.062	0.009	0.069	0.007	2.074	1.720
600	33.59	25.12	0.054	0.011	0.047	0.005	1.814	1.181
660	33.60	25.17	0.058	0.006	0.055	0.006	1.949	1.384
720	33.68	25.34	0.049	0.004	0.049	0.007	1.650	1.242
780	34.04	25.09	0.028	0.005	0.027	0.009	0.953	0.677

[a]±S.D. = standard deviation of the mean.

Raleigh K. Pettegrew and Keith L. Ewing, *J. Gerontol.*, 1971, **26**, (3), 381–385.

TABLE 3. AGE CHANGES IN ENZYME ACTIVITY[a] OF ARTICULAR CARTILAGE OF THE UPPER EXTREMITY OF MALE GUINEA PIGS.

	2 Weeks	12 Weeks	1 Year	2½ Years
Hexokinase (mM)	35 ± 1	23 ± 1	158 ± 21	353 ± 10
Phosphoglucomutase (M)	0.64 ± 0.03	0.47 ± 0.04	4.80 ± 0.63	1.18 ± 0.16
Phosphorylase (total) (mM)	11.9 ± 0.8	8.2 ± 0.8	55.8 ± 2.1	75.3 ± 4.2
Glucose-6-P dehydrogenase (mM)	100 ± 11	85 ± 5	442 ± 59	637 ± 32
Phosphofructokinase (mM)	23.3 ± 0.7	7.8 ± 0.5	55.5 ± 2.4	160.0 ± 6.0
Aldolase (mM)	21 ± 1	25 ± 1	155 ± 20	326 ± 11
α-glycerol-P dehydrogenase (mM)	5.3 ± 0.9	7.6 ± 0.9	61.9 ± 2.5	76.2 ± 4.3
Pyruvic Kinase (M)	0.52 ± 0.02	0.39 ± 0.01	5.09 ± 0.71	7.66 ± 0.52
Lactic dehydrogenase (M)	2.17 ± 0.77	1.08 ± 0.81	4.37 ± 0.88	10.90 ± 1.00
Sulfatase (μM)	0.28 ± 0.02	0.45 ± 0.09	1.17 ± 0.12	0.89 ± 0.15
β-galactosidase (mM)	0.75 ± 0.11	0.84 ± 0.08	1.87 ± 0.16	1.42 ± 0.17
Cathpsin D (g)	0.83 ± 0.06	1.12 ± 0.10	2.58 ± 0.50	1.78 ± 0.16
β-glucuronidase (mM)	1.12 ± 0.08	0.96 ± 0.10	2.95 ± 0.32	1.68 ± 0.12

[a]Calculated as moles (M), millimoles (nM), micromoles (μM), or gram (g/g DNA/hour).

Note—± Indicates standard error.

TABLE 4. AGE CHANGES IN ENZYME ACTIVITY[a] OF ARTICULAR CARTILAGE OF THE UPPER EXTREMITY OF FEMALE GUINEA PIGS.

	2 Weeks	12 Weeks	1 Year	2½ Years
Hexokinase (mM)	243 ± 22	152 ± 40	144 ± 7	87 ± 1
Phosphoglucomutase (M)	3.11 ± 0.37	1.74 ± 0.33	2.60 ± 0.12	0.33 ± 0.02
Phosphorylase (total) (mM)	62.4 ± 4.4	58.2 ± 6.8	23.6 ± 1.5	21.3 ± 1.8
Glucose-6-P dehydrogenase (mM)	775 ± 71	396 ± 34	447 ± 46	108 ± 5
Phophofructokinase (mM)	159.0 ± 11.0	64.4 ± 3.2	42.8 ± 1.6	35.1 ± 2.2
Aldolase (mM)	186 ± 13	214 ± 9	92 ± 4	132 ± 9
α-glycerol-P dehydrogenase (mM)	77.6 ± 3.6	66.7 ± 2.8	31.0 ± 7.8	19.4 ± 2.9
Pyruvic Kinase (M)	4.01 ± 0.50	1.87 ± 0.50	3.81 ± 0.08	2.08 ± 0.08
Lactic dehydrogenase (M)	12.80 ± 1.40	5.81 ± 0.51	6.54 ± 0.44	2.55 ± 0.04
Sulfatase (μm)	1.69 ± 0.19	1.95 ± 0.30	0.78 ± 0.12	1.45 ± 0.17
β-galactosidase (mM)	3.17 ± 0.24	2.48 ± 0.30	1.56 ± 0.36	1.30 ± 0.20
Cathepsin D (Hb) (g)	1.89 ± 0.39	4.47 ± 0.48	2.47 ± 0.66	3.67 ± 0.39
β-glucuronidase (mM)	6.38 ± 0.50	3.30 ± 0.45	3.13 ± 0.49	2.73 ± 0.45

[a]Calculated as moles (M), millimoles (mM), micromoles (μM), or gram (g)/kilogram dry weight/hour.

Note – ± Indicates standard error.

TABLE 5. AGE CHANGES IN ENZYME ACTIVITY[a] OF ARTICULAR CARTILAGE OF THE UPPER EXTREMITY OF FEMALE GUINEA PIGS.

	2 Weeks	12 Weeks	1 Year	2½ Years
Hexokinase (mM)	58 ± 1	21 ± 1	326 ± 11	118 ± 6
Phosphoglucomutase (M)	0.74 ± 0.04	0.31 ± 0.01	7.00 ± 0.85	0.48 ± 0.03
Phosphorylase (total) (mM)	14.9 ± 0.9	8.2 ± 0.8	63.3 ± 1.6	28.9 ± 0.9
Glucose-6-P dehydrogenase (mM)	185 ± 7	560 ± 8	1070 ± 82	164 ± 9
Phosphofructokinase (mM)	37.9 ± 1.2	9.0 ± 0.5	96.3 ± 1.3	47.7 ± 1.1
Aldolase (mM)	44 ± 8	21 ± 1	207 ± 12	180 ± 5
α-glycerol-P dehydrogenase (mM)	18.5 ± 0.7	9.5 ± 0.7	70.1 ± 3.6	26.4 ± 1.2
Pyruvic Kinase (M)	0.96 ± 0.05	0.26 ± 0.01	9.92 ± 0.57	2.83 ± 0.72
Lactic dehydrogenase (M)	3.05 ± 0.20	8.16 ± 0.72	9.19 ± 0.20	3.47 ± 0.14
Sulfatase (μM)	0.70 ± 0.02	0.47 ± 0.03	1.10 ± 0.16	1.11 ± 0.11
β-galactosidase (mM)	1.21 ± 0.04	0.81 ± 0.06	1.37 ± 0.13	0.93 ± 0.10
Cathepsin D (g)	1.60 ± 0.08	1.07 ± 0.11	3.68 ± 0.80	2.84 ± 0.20
β-glucuronidase (mM)	2.30 ± 0.12	0.85 ± 0.10	3.01 ± 0.31	2.00 ± 0.23

[a]Calculated as moles (M), millimoles (mM), micromoles (μM), or gram (g)/g DNA/hour.

Note – ± Indicates standard error.

R. Silberberg, M. Hasler, and P. Lesker, *J. Gerontol.*, 1973, 28, (1), 18–34, p. 24.

TABLE 6. AGE-RELATED CALCIUM CONCENTRATIONS[a] IN CARDIAC AND SKELETAL MUSCLES, SKIN, AND AORTA OF FISCHER AND A $\times$ C RATS.

Rat strain	AGE (months)									
	1	2	4	8	12	16	19	21	22	28
Cardiac Muscle										
Fischer	11.59 ±.30 (12)	13.49 ±1.43 (6)	12.96 ±1.60 (5)	8.35 ±.63 (6)	9.90 ±.35 (12)	8.52 ±.38 (13)	9.59 ±.40 (13)	8.76 ±.32 (3)		
A $\times$ C	12.39 ±.76 (6)	12.43 ±.98 (11)				10.66 ±1.20 (6)			8.31 ±.53 (5)	9.65 ±.18 (2)
Skeletal Muscle										
Fischer	15.70 ±.54 (12)	15.75 ±1.33 (6)	12.98 ±.69 (6)	11.17 ±.23 (6)	12.85 ±.88 (12)	10.94 ±.30 (13)	11.46 ±.28 (13)	11.14 ±.10 (4)		
A $\times$ C	17.27 ±.41 (6)	13.84 ±.45 (12)				11.91 ±.44 (6)			11.65 ±.29 (5)	13.35 ±1.12 (3)
Skin										
Fischer	18.19 ±.50 (12)	15.81 ±1.37 (6)	15.66 ±1.22 (6)	12.70 ±1.60 (6)	14.57 ±.61 (12)	11.46 ±.49 (13)	12.47 ±.58 (13)	10.88 ±.64 (4)		
A $\times$ C	22.06 ±1.71 (6)	17.83 ±.82 (12)				12.32 ±1.11 (6)			10.25 ±.53 (5)	12.21 ±1.32 (3)
Aorta										
Fischer	108.07 ±6.52 (10)	102.78 ±12.76 (5)	95.03 ±7.98 (5)	88.17 ±10.72 (6)	76.34 ±3.34 (12)	64.89 ±3.98 (13)	75.56 ±5.24 (13)	74.51 ±3.90 (3)		
A $\times$ C	105.25 ±9.52 (6)	117.58 ±12.32 (11)				66.69 ±3.73 (5)			63.75 ±4.67 (4)	69.57 ±3.68 (2)

[a]Calcium concentrations are mean values ±S.E. expressed as mEq/kg dry tissue. Numbers in parentheses are numbers of animals.

M. J. McBroom and A. K. Weiss, *J. Gerontol.*, 1973, 28, (2), 143–151, p. 145.

TABLE 7. AGE-RELATED CALCIUM CONCENTRATIONS[a] IN KIDNEY, LUNG, AND CEREBRAL CORTEX OF FISCHER AND A × C RATS.

Rat strain	AGE (months)									
	1	2	4	8	12	16	19	21	22	28
Kidney										
Fischer	13.86 ±.29 (12)	17.07 ±.81 (5)	16.22 ±1.06 (5)	13.33 ±1.07 (6)	15.13 ±.43 (12)	14.97 ±.43 (13)	15.03 ±.44 (13)	14.80 ±.44 (4)		
A × C	12.92 ±.37 (6)	13.39 ±.60 (12)				15.35 ±.64 (6)			14.03 ±1.22 (5)	18.49 ±.32 (3)
Lung										
Fischer	24.33 ±.67 (12)	23.37 ±1.75 (6)	23.01 ±.38 (5)	22.64 ±.90 (6)	26.81 ±.52 (11)	25.07 ±1.00 (12)	28.60 ±1.35 (13)	21.52 ±.71 (4)		
A × C	25.32 ±.04 (6)	22.67 ±.68 (12)				24.05 ±1.56 (6)			19.92 ±3.06 (5)	28.16 ±2.41 (3)
Cerebral Cortex										
Fischer	13.52 ±.49 (12)	11.79 ±.40 (6)	11.89 ±1.01 (5)	13.03 ±1.51 (4)	13.36 ±.87 (12)	16.38 ±1.74 (12)	20.37 ±2.17 (11)	19.42 ±1.64 (4)		
A × C	11.30 ±.30 (6)	12.26 ±.25 (10)				13.62 ±.71 (6)			15.33 ±2.14 (4)	15.15 ±.79 (3)

[a]Calcium concentrations are mean values ±S.E. expressed as mEq/kg dry tissue. Numbers in parentheses are numbers of animals.

M. J. McBroom and A. K. Weiss, *J. Gerontol.*, 1973, 28, (2), 143–151, p. 144.

TABLE 8. EFFECT OF AGE ON TOTAL HYALURONIC HEXOSAMINE (HAH), CHONDROITIN SULFATE HEXOSAMINE (CSH), AND HYDROXYPROLINE (HOPr-S) IN SKIN; ON NITROGEN (N) AND HYDROXYPROLINE (HOPr-C) IN CARCASS OF MALE SWISS MICE.

Age (days)	100–250	250–350	350–500	500–650	650–750
Weight (g)	41.6 ± 0.5 (72)	45.0 ± 0.6 (62)	45.4 ± 0.7 (85)	46.2 ± 0.8 (83)	47.7 ± 1.2 (51)
Femur Length (cm)	1.69 ± .01 (72)	1.72 ± .01 (62)	1.71 ± .01 (85)	1.70 ± .01 (83)	1.71 ± .01 (51)
HAH (µg)	450 ± 20 (41)	430 ± 17 (38)	399 ± 16 (44)	377 ± 16 (41)	328[a] ± 20 (18)
		[403 ± 32 (15)	383 ± 24 (18)	369 ± 26 (20)	267 ± 31 (4)]
CSH (µg)	242 ± 10 (41)	234 ± 10 (38)	210 ± 9 (42)	209 ± 8 (40)	185[a] ± 8 (16)
		[228 ± 15 (15)	184 ± 13 (16)	186 ± 10 (20)	168 ± 30 (4)]
HOPr-S (mg)	89.2 ± 2.1 (72)	89.8 ± 2.2 (62)	85.4 ± 2.3 (85)	81.4 ± 2.0 (83)	71.2[a] ± 2.2 (51)
HOPr-C (mg)	213.8 ± 3.6 (29)	299.6 ± 5.5 (20)	247.7 ± 5.8 (30)	255.2 ± 4.9 (30)	261.1[a] ± 7.6 (9)
N (mg)	607.6 ± 8.8 (49)	642.5 ± 10.4 (32)	678.3 ± 8.4 (45)	643.8 ± 8.6 (51)	625.5[a] ± 15.8 (24)
		[681.8 ± 19.4 (11)	647.3 ± 16.8 (15)	643.3 ± 17.0 (19)	577.8 ± 28.3 (7)]

Note–Figures in parenthesis are numbers of mice in each group. Figures in brackets show one experimental group which demonstrated decreases similar to data for C57BL/6aa males.

[a]Statistically significant decrease compared with peak value.

H. Sobel, M. J. Hewlett, and H. E. Hrubant, J. Gerontol., 1970, 25, (2), 102–104, p. 103.

TABLE 9.[a]   UREA CLEARANCE AND URINE CONCENTRATION TESTS AT DIFFERENT AGES.

| Age (years) | UREA CLEARANCE TEST | | ADDIS-SHERVKY CONCENTRATION TEST | |
	Number of persons in group	as % of the clearance in young normal men	Number of persons in group	Specific gravity of urine
40–49	20	95 (72–124)	8	1.0293 (1.0258–1.0362)
50–59	20	86 (54–127)	4	1.0287 (1.0258–1.0316)
60–69	20	82 (44–113)	8	1.0277 (1.0230–1.0308)
70–79	20	65 (37–119)	7	1.0253 (1.0179–1.0327)
80–89	20	61 (19–111)	11	1.0238 (1.0210–1.0281)

Lewis and Alving, *Am. J. Physiol.*, 1938, **123**. Recalculated and abbreviated (V.K.) from original data.

TABLE 10.[a]   AGE CHANGES OF GLOMERULAR FILTRATION AND EFFECTIVE BLOOD PLASMA FLOW IN HUMAN KIDNEYS.

Age groups (years)	Number of men in group	Inulin clearance and glomerular filtration rate cc/min./1.73 sq m	Diodrast clearance and renal plasma flow cc/min./1.73 sq m
20–29	9	122.8 (93.7–145.8)	613.5 (480.8–724.0)
30–39	9	115.0 (95.6–125.3)	649.3 (502.0–804.0)
40–49	10	121.2 (77.2–162.3)	573.8 (396.0–734.8)
50–59	11	99.3 (74.3–118.9)	500.4 (340.7–616.8)
60–69	10	96.0 (57.7–150.8)	442.1 (253.4–534.0)
70–79	9	89.0 (60.8–123.5)	354.0 (234.4–519.4)
80–89	12	65.3 (31.4–96.4)	288.8 (147.2–462.4)

Davies and Shock, *J. Clin. Invest.*, 1950, **29**, 500–501. In brackets—range of variations. Abbreviated (V.K.) from original data.

[a]*Physiological & Pathological Ageing*, p. 438.

TABLE 11. THE MAXIMUM RATE OF RENAL TUBULAR REABSORPTION OF GLUCOSE.

Age (years)	Number of subjects	Reabsorption rate of glucose (mg/min.)
20–29	3	358.7 (324–395)
30–39	9	333.6 (236–395)
40–49	12	315.1 (240–380)
50–59	14	308.2 (236–452)
60–69	14	260.2 (170–394)
70–79	15	239.3 (128–306)
80–86	9	219.2 (143–282)

Miller, McDonald, and Shock, *J. Gerontol.*, 1952, 7, 197–198. In brackets–range of variations. Abbreviated (V.K.) from original data.

Physiological & Pathological Ageing, p. 439.

TABLE 12.[a] PERCENTAGE DISTRIBUTION OF CASES ACCORDING TO MATERNAL AGE.

Data and source	Births in maternity hospital (Malpas)	Mongolism (Penrose)	Deformities of nervous system (Malpas)	Deformities of nervous system (Penrose)	Central placenta praevia (Penrose)
Number of cases	13,964	224	140	144	35
Maternal age group					
16–20	7.6	1.8	2.1	2.1	0.0
21–25	30.0	5.3	24.3	24.2	8.6
26–30	29.0	7.2	25.7	19.5	17.1
31–35	19.0	16.9	19.3	24.9	34.3
36–40	11.0	30.8	19.3	19.5	22.9
41–45	3.0	31.3	7.1	9.0	14.2
46–50	0.34	15.9	2.1	0.7	2.9

[a]L. S. Penrose, M.D., *J. Mental Sci.*, 1939, 85, p. 1143.

TABLE 13.[a] INCIDENCE COMPARED WITH STANDARD MATERNAL AGE GROUPINGS.

Data	Births in maternity hospital	Mongolism	Deformities of nervous system (a)	Deformities of nervous system (b)	Central placenta praevia
Maternal age group					
16–20	1.0	0.3	0.3	0.3	0.0
21–25	1.0	0.2	0.8	0.8	0.3
26–30	1.0	0.4	0.9	0.7	0.6
31–35	1.0	0.9	1.0	1.3	1.8
36–40	1.0	2.8	1.8	1.8	2.1
41–45	1.0	10.4	2.4	3.0	4.7
46–50	1.0	43.9	6.2	2.1	8.5

[a]L. S. Penrose, M.D., *J. Mental Sci.*, 1939, 85, p. 1143.

TABLE 14.[a] FREQUENCIES OF 144 CONGENITAL ABNORMALITIES OF THE NERVOUS SYSTEM IN RELATION TO AGE OF MOTHERS.

(The frequencies are expressed relative to the frequency for the youngest age group which is arbitrarily designated as unity.) (Penrose, 1939).

Maternal age group	Abnormalities
16–20	1
21–25	2.7
26–30	2.3
31–35	4.3
36–40	6.0
41–45	10.0
46–50	7.0

Curt Stein, *Principles of Human Genetics*, p. 336.
The distribution of defective children, and of their normally developed siblings, by maternal age at the time that the children were born. Note in column 6 that the ratio of defective children to their normally developed siblings increased directly with maternal age.

[a]D. P. Murphy, *Ann. N.Y. Acad. Sci.*, "Maternal Age and Malformation," 1954, 57, p. 505.

TABLE 15.[a] CHILD DEVELOPMENT BY MATERNAL AGE.

Ages of mothers (years) (1)	DEFECTIVE		NORMAL		Col. 3 divided by col. 5 (6)
	Number (2)	% (3)	Number (4)	% (5)	
10 to 14	0	–	1	–	–
15 to 19	43	7.1	130	8.2	0.866
20 to 24	163	26.8	505	31.9	0.840
25 to 29	176	29.0	516	32.6	0.890
30 to 34	111	18.3	277	17.5	1.045
35 to 39	86	14.2	123	7.8	1.820
40 to 44	24	4.0	28	1.8	2.241
45 to 49	4	0.6	4	0.2	3.000
Total	607	100.0	1584	100.0	–

The distribution of defective children, and of their normally developed siblings, by maternal age at the time that the children were born. Note in column 6 that the ratio of defective children to their normally developed siblings increased directly with maternal age.

[a]D. P. Murphy, *Ann. N.Y. Acad. Sci.*, 1954, 57, "Maternal Age and Malformation," p. 505.

TABLE 16. DISAPPEARANCE OF ^{3}H-EPINEPHRINE FROM THE BLOOD OF YOUNG AND OLD RATS.

Group	Number of animals	% remaining radioactivity after $2 \cdot 5$ min ± S.E.	% change	Significance
Young (2 months)	12	$23 \cdot 1 \pm 1 \cdot 8$	+56%	$P < 0 \cdot 0025$
Old (15 months)	7	$36 \quad \pm 4 \cdot 1$		
Young (2 months)	11	$24 \cdot 1 \pm 2 \cdot 0$	+57%	$P < 0 \cdot 0025$
Old (15 months)	11	$42 \cdot 2 \pm 5 \cdot 3$		
Young (2 months)	6	$21 \quad \pm 3 \cdot 4$	+183%	$P < 0 \cdot 001$
Old (18 months)	6	$59 \cdot 9 \pm 7 \cdot 5$		

TABLE 17.[a] MEAN RECOGNITION, RECALL, AND RECOGNITION MINUS RECALL SCORES BY AGE.

Age range	Number	Recognition	Recall	Recognition minus recall
20–29	36	20.01	13.78	6.42
30–39	23	19.48	12.30	7.17
40–49	32	19.53	10.01	9.47
50–59	21	19.90	9.57	10.24
60+	22	20.09	7.50	12.59

[a]David Schonfield, *Nature*, 1965, 208, (918), "Memory changes with age," p. 169, Nov.

TABLE 18.[a]

Calander year	Mean age at menarche ± S.D.
1932	13.53
1934	13.5 ± 1.1
1937	13.01 ± 1.1
1940	13.1
1948	12.9 ± 1.4
1953	12.8 ± 1.1
1962	12.8 ± 1.1
1966	12.60 ± 2.0

[a]Leona Zacharias, Ph.D., and Richard J. Wurtman, M.D., *New Engl. J. Med.*, 1969, 280, (873).

TABLE 19.[a] MEAN MENARCHEAL AGES IN THE UNITED STATES AS REPORTED IN PROSPECTIVE STUDIES, 1934–1966.

Year	Age at menarche (Yr) Mean ± SD
1934	13.53
1937	13.1 ± 1.1
1940	13.1
1948	12.9 ± 1.4
1953	12.8 ± 1.1
1962	12.8 ± 1.1
1966	12.60 ± 2.0

[a]Leona Zacharias, Ph.D., and Richard J. Wurtman, M.D., *New Engl. J. Med.*, 1969, 280, (873).

TABLE 20. MEAN MENARCHEAL AGES IN THE UNITED STATES AS REPORTED IN RETROSPECTIVE STUDIES,[a] 1932-1964.

Year	AGE AT MENARCHE (yr) Mean ± SD	Standard Error	Number of subjects	Population studied
1944[b]	14.3 ± –	–	–	Residents of Colored Orphan Asylum, Riverdale, N.Y.
1932	13.5 ± 1.1	–	185	Residents of Hebrew Orphan Asylum in New York
	13.1 ± 1.2	–	352	Students of Horace Mann School (private) in New York, N.Y.
1944[c]	13.07 ± 1.1	–	113	Residents of Colored Orphan Asylum, Riverdale, N.Y.
1943	12.6 ± 1.1	–	200	Participants in Brush Foundation Regular Series, Cleveland, O.
1962[d]	13.17	±0.03	–	Students at Wellesley College, Wellesley, Mass.
1964	12.46 ± 0.85	–	236	Nursing students in Greater Boston, Mass.
1968	12.65 ± 1.2	–	6217	American student nurses in all parts of U.S.

[a]Those in which women are questioned about their age at menarche after the event.
[b]Data obtained in 1910-1914.
[c]Data obtained in 1935-1940.
[d]Data obtained in 1958.
Leona Zacharias, Ph.D., and Richard J. Wurtman, M.D., *New Engl. J. Med.*, p. 873, 1969, 280.

TABLE 21.[b] VITAMIN B_{12} CONTENT OF HUMAN VASCULAR TISSUE IN VARIOUS AGE GROUPS.

Age group (years)	N	Mn. Nanograms of Vitamin B_{12}/g wet tissue	S.E.	Mn. Nanograms of Vitamin B_{12}/g tissue nitrogen	S.E.
		Normal aortic tissue[a]			
0-1	5	2.30	0.52	61.0	15.5
1-9	4	4.10		99.8	
10-19	5	4.22	0.39	91.0	11.6
20-29	11	6.55	1.01	157.1	22.0
30-39	14	6.18	0.93	153.9	21.9
40-49	8	5.84	1.37	160.8	38.6
50-59	16	5.85	0.63	151.7	16.0
60-69	16	7.00	0.84	192.2	21.5
70-82	4	7.42		207.0	

[a]Thoracic descending aorta
[b]S. Hosoda & J. E. Kirk, *J. Gerontol.*, 1969, 24, (3), 298-301.

TABLE 22.[a] RELATION OF CELL NUMBER IN CORTICAL SECTIONS WITH AGE.

Specimen–Age	A	B	C	E	F	H	K
HC 3–Newborn	3829	2501	2711	2510	2818	3376	2546
HC 1–18 years	1019	1078	1394	1628	1749	1725	1684
HC 10–45 years	1186	1034	936	1110	1250	1214	1202
HC 5–95 years	947	864	892	1342	1377	1111	1382

[a]Harold Brody, *J. Comp. Neurol.*, 1955, 102, "Organization of the Cerebral Cortex III: A Study of Aging in the Human Cerebral Cortex," p. 511-556.

TABLE 23.[a] SIMPLE REACTION TIMES. (In Seconds)

Author	Type of reaction[b]	Teens	20s	30s	40s	50s	60s	70s	80s	Notes
Galton (1899); see also Koga and Morant (1923)	Press key in response to light	0.187	0.182	0.181	0.190	0.186	0.206	0.205	—	Subjects were visitors to an international health exhibition. The figures have been calculated approximately from those given by Koga & Morant.
	Press key in response to sound	.158	.154	.158	.159	.157	.167	.174		
Miles (1931a)	Press key in response to sound	—	.23	.24	.22	.20	.28	.30	.28	100 subjects: fewer in the twenties and eighties than other ranges. The twenties ranged from 25 to 29 only. Data from a much larger sample are given in Fig. 1.
	Release key in response to sound	—	.21	.22	.22	.22	.23	.26	.28	
	Lift foot response to sound	—	.22	.22	.24	.24	.26	.27	.30	
Bellis (1933)	Press key in response to light									20 subjects in each age range except the highest which had 10. Equal numbers of men and women in each range. Scores are means of best five readings by each subject.
	Men	.24	.22	.26	.27	.38	—	—	—	
	Women	.32	.26	.34	.36	.44	—	—	—	
	Press key in response to sound in headphones									
	Men	.23	.19	.24	.25	.37	—	—	—	
	Women	.31	.20	.30	.30	.42	—	—	—	
De Silva (1936)	"Brake reaction time" in a test designed to simulate car driving (subject raised foot from accelerator pedal and transferred it to brake on seeing red flash of a traffic light)	.418	.418	.428	.422	.455	.465	—	—	2000 subjects. The age range of the teens is 16–19 and of the sixties, 61–65. The figures are approximate only, having been taken from a graph included in De Silva's paper.
Fieandt et al. (1956)	Pressing button in response to light	0.228	.201	.201	.217	.212	.217	0.245	0.353	The age ranges were 11–14, 21–24, 29–36, 39–47, 49–56, 59–67, 69–79, and 80–88. Each of the 120 subjects gave five readings. The two extremes of these were excluded and the scores were the means of the remaining three.
Cesa-Bianchi (1955)	Response to light	—	.215	.186	.202	.207	.214	—	—	268 subjects mostly between 30 and 59. The oldest age range was 60–66. Very full scores given for individual subjects.
	Response to sound	—	0.157	0.161	0.179	0.167	0.187	—	—	

[a] *Handbook of Aging and the Individual*, A. T. Welford, p. 568.
[b] All are made with the hand unless otherwise stated.

TABLE 24. NUMBER AND PROPORTION OF ALL PERSONS AND FEMALES WHO ARE 60-69, 70-79, 80 AND OVER AND 100 AND OVER IN THE UNITED STATES (1960) AND THE SOVIET UNION (1959).

| | 60–69 | | 70–79 | | 80 and Over | | 100 and Over | |
| | | | Number in thousands | | | | | |
	Number	Proportion	Number	Proportion	Number	Proportion	Number	Proportion
All persons								
U.S.A.	13,400	7.4	7,792	4.3	2,509	1.3	10.3	.00006
U.S.S.R.	11,736	5.6	6,168	2.9	1,803	.8	21.7	.00010
Females								
U.S.A.	7,060	7.7	4,248	4.6	1,481	1.6	6.5	.00007
U.S.S.R	7,637	6.6	4,148	3.6	1,283	1.4	16.3	.00014

Source: Demographic Yearbook 1963, United Nations, 1964, New York.

Walter C. McKain, Ph.D., *The Gerontologist*, 1967, 7, (72).

TABLE 25. INCIDENCE OF LOCALIZED SEMINAL VESICLE AMYLOID.[a]

Age range	Patients studied	Seminal vesicle amyloid	Percentage
40–60	52	4	7.7
61–75	70	15	22.5
76–90	38	13	34.2

[a]Summarized from Bursell (27).

John R. Wright, M.D., Evan Calkins, M.D., William J. Breen, M.D., Gisela Stolte, M.D., and Russell T. Schultz, M.D., *Medicine*, 1969, **48**, (46).

TABLE 26. SKELETAL MEASUREMENTS OF GUINEA PIGS BY AGE GROUPS.

Group[a]	Humerus	Ulna	Radius	Femur	Tibia	Fibula	Angle to angle	Ant.–Post.
Stillbirth	19.5	22.8	18.3	20.6	23.3	21.4	16.8	26.2
3 months	32.8	36.4	29.4	39.8	43.2	38.9	26.6	42.8
6 months	34.9	38.7	30.7	41.7	44.8	41.9	27.8	44.3
9 months	35.5	39.1	31.1	41.9	44.8	43.0	29.9	45.5
1 year	37.3	41.3	32.1	43.9	47.9	42.2	30.5	47.2
2 years	36.7	40.6	32.2	43.5	46.5	44.6	32.4	47.4
3 years	36.5	40.2	31.8	42.4	45.9	44.3	32.2	46.1
4 years	37.0	41.3	32.5	43.6	47.1	45.6	33.0	46.3

[a]Thirty animals in each group.

Aging Around the World: Proceed V Congress of the Internal Assoc. of Gerontology, Medical and Clinical Aspects of Aging, 1962, ed. H. T. Blumenthal, Columbia Univ. Press, New York.

TABLE 27. WEIGHT OF AMERICAN BOYS.[a]

Age	MEAN Lb.	MEAN Kg	STANDARD DEVIATION Lb.	STANDARD DEVIATION Kg
3 months	14.3	6.5	1.5	0.7
6 months	18.7	8.5	1.8	0.8
9 months	21.7	9.8	2.2	1.0
1 year	23.8	10.8	2.5	1.1
1½ years	29.9	12.2	2.7	1.2
2 years	29.2	13.2	3.0	1.4
2½ years	31.5	14.3	3.3	1.5
3 years	33.5	15.2	3.6	1.6
3½ years	35.9	16.3	4.0	1.8
4 years	38.1	17.3	4.3	2.0
4½ years	40.5	18.4	4.6	2.1
5 years	42.8	19.4	5.0	2.3
6 years	48.2	21.9	5.8	2.6
7 years	54.2	24.6	7.0	3.2
8 years	61.0	27.7	8.8	4.0
9 years	68.4	31.0	10.9	4.9
10 years	76.8	34.8	12.9	5.9
11 years	85.6	38.8	16.2	7.3
12 years	95.2	43.2	19.0	8.6
13 years	105.7	47.9	21.0	9.5
14 years	119.1	54.0	22.2	10.1
15 years	132.3	60.0	21.4	8.7
16 years	141.9	64.4	20.3	9.2
17 years	147.6	66.9	19.6	8.9

[a]Modified from Simmons.[16]

E. H. Watson and G. H. Lowrey, *Growth and Development of Children*, 5th ed., 1967, Year Book Medical Publ., Chicago.

TABLE 28. WEIGHT OF AMERICAN GIRLS.[a]

Age	MEAN Lb.	MEAN Kg	STANDARD DEVIATION Lb.	STANDARD DEVIATION Kg
3 months	13.0	5.9	1.5	0.7
6 months	17.0	7.7	1.8	0.8
9 months	19.7	8.9	2.1	1.0
1 year	21.9	9.9	2.5	1.1
1½ year	25.0	11.3	3.0	1.4
2 years	27.6	12.5	3.0	1.4
2½ years	30.1	13.6	3.6	1.6
3 years	32.5	14.7	3.9	1.8
3½ years	35.0	15.9	4.2	1.9
4 years	37.2	16.9	4.6	2.1
4½ years	40.0	18.1	5.2	2.4
5 years	42.3	19.2	5.8	2.6
6 years	48.3	21.9	7.6	3.4
7 years	54.5	24.7	8.9	4.0
8 years	61.9	28.1	10.5	4.8
9 years	69.6	31.6	12.9	5.8
10 years	78.1	35.4	14.7	6.7
11 years	88.4	40.1	17.0	7.7
12 years	100.4	45.5	18.8	8.5
13 years	110.5	50.1	18.7	8.5
14 years	120.1	54.5	18.6	8.4
15 years	126.6	57.4	18.4	8.3
16 years	130.5	59.2	18.2	8.2
17 years	133.5	60.5	18.1	8.2

[a]Modified from Simmons.[16]

E. H. Watson and G. H. Lowrey, *Growth and Development of Children*, 5th ed., 1967, Year Book Medical Publ., Chicago.

TABLE 29. MORTALITY IN THE U.S. WHITE POPULATION FROM VARIOUS CAUSES. DEATH RATE PER 100,000.

Cause of death	Year of study	MALES					FEMALES				
		35–74	35–44	45–54	55–64	65–74	35–74	35–44	45–54	55–64	65–74
1. Malignant Neoplasms	1968	329.39	50.89	172.93	484.60	975.91	245.05	65.09	178.67	330.96	543.06
2. Heart Disease	1968	725.79	100.28	385.72	1024.28	2031.00	305.43	25.85	97.00	335.64	1085.22
3. Tuberculosis	1966		2.2	6.0	14.7	24.8		1.3	2.1	3.0	4.9
4. Parkinson's Disease	1967			0.4	2.5	13.6			0.2	1.7	8.7
5. Influenza and Pneumonia	1974	43	8	21	52	143	22	5	12	24	65
6. Chronic Respiratory Diseases	1973	50	3	14	70	189	11	2	6	16	26
7. Cerebrovascular Diseases	1968	111	12	38	123	443	87	12	32	82	314
8. Diabetes	1968	26	5	12	35	84	27	4	9	32	94
9. Suicide	1973	30	23	29	36	35	11	12	14	12	8

Statistical Bulletin of the Metropolitin Life Insurance Company: 1. **54**:2 Feb. 1973; 2. **53**:2, 4 Nov. 1972; 3. **51**:8 Jan. 1970; 4. **51**:6 March 1970; 5. **55**:6 Feb. 1974; 6. **54**:7 July 1973; 7. **54**:6 April 1973; 8. **54**:6 Dec. 1973; 9. **54**:2 Aug. 1973.

TABLE 30. AGE CHANGES IN Mg-ATPase ACTIVITY AND WEIGHT OF GASTROCNEMIUS MUSCLE OF THE MALE WHITE RAT.

	1	2	3	4
Strain	Median age – months	ATPase activ.	Muscle wt. – grams	Muscle wt./ body wt. × 10⁻³
Sprague	9.5 (7–12)	.69 (±.13)	4.58	11.93
Dawley	16.5 (13–20)	.51 (±.18)	4.63	9.47
	26.0 (23–28)	.24 (±.07)	2.45	6.69
CFN	8.0 (5–12)	.79 (±.15)	4.10	8.92
	17.5 (14–18)	.58 (±.10)	4.89	9.34
	26.0 (24–33)	.37 (±.05)	4.55	7.91

Values in parentheses, column 1, show actual ranges of ages for the various median age groups. Data in columns 2 and 3 represent median enzyme activity and gastrocnemius muscle mass values for 10 animals of each median age group. ATPase activity is expressed in μg of P released in 15 minutes, per gram of fresh muscle mass. Values in parentheses in column 2 are probable deviation. (From Rockstein and Brandt, 1961).

Aging Life Processes, 1969. ed. Seymour Bakerman, pub. Charles C. Thomas, Springfield, Ill.

TABLE 31. TOTAL FREE FATTY ACIDS OF HUMAN BRAIN AT DIFFERENT AGES.

Age	Wt. % total lipid (± standard deviation)	% Dry wt.	mM/100 g. fresh wt.	Total lipid % fresh wt.
25-week fetus	1.58 ± 0.04	0.40	0.136	2.48
1 day	1.15 ± 0.09	0.32	0.123	3.13
3 weeks	1.97 ± 0.07	0.59	0.260	3.81
6 mo.	2.22 ± 0.10	0.78	0.447	5.77
8 mo.	1.97 ± 0.05	0.73	0.430	6.50
22 mo.	1.76 ± 0.04	0.71	0.453	7.61
6 years	1.70 ± 0.04	0.75	0.494	8.82
8.5 years	1.70 ± 0.05	0.82	0.595	10.00
10 years	1.45 ± 0.04	0.67	0.527	10.52
18 years	1.25 ± 0.04	0.67	0.487	11.31
33 years	2.07 ± 0.07	1.05	0.819	11.54
55 years	1.16 ± 0.04	0.55	0.417	10.58
98 years	1.13 ± 0.03	0.49	0.356	9.28

A. Yamamoto and G. Rouser, *J. Gerontol.* 1973, **28**, (2), 140–142.

TABLE 32. ANALYTICAL VALUES FOR TWO DIFFERENT PREPARATIONS OF ELASTIN FROM THE AORTAS OF CATTLE OF DIFFERENT AGES.

	PURIFIED WITH WATER[a]				PURIFIED WITH SODIUM HYDROZIDE[b]			
	Calcium (%)	Sialic acid (%)	Desmo-sines[c]	R[d]	Calcium (%)	Sialic acid (%)	Desmo-sines[c]	R[d]
Foetal	0.125	0.34	9	0.33	0.80	0.08	3	1.02
2 yr	0.550	0.67	12	1.80	0.50	0.13	5	1.00
4 yr	0.650	0.38	14	1.80	0.55	0.26	7	1.13
7 yr	0.700	0.20	15	1.00	0.71	0.04	11	1.80

[a] Autoclaved at 15 lb/in.^{2} pressure, then washed with water 80–90°.
[b] Treated with 0.1 N NaOH at 98° for three 15-min. periods.
[c] ¼ residues/1000 residues.
[d] Ratio of susceptibility of elastin to attack by insoluble and soluble forms of elastase (Hall, 1968a).

D. A. Hall, *Exp. Geront.* 1968. **3**, p. 81.

TABLE 33. FAT, FAT-FREE MASS, CELL MASS OF WOMEN.

Age (years)	Number	FAT		FAT-FREE MASS		CELL MASS	
		Mean	SD	Mean	SD	Mean	SD
Absolute amounts (kg)							
18–25	89	18.8	4.94	37.5	4.02	21.3	2.28
25–35	33	19.8	10.36	38.6	5.17	21.9	2.94
35–45	44	22.5	7.94	39.0	5.16	22.1	2.93
45–55	72	29.3	9.16	37.8	4.23	21.4	2.42
55–65	54	27.9	7.93	35.3	4.21	20.0	2.39
65–85	13	28.5	6.57	34.5	2.94	19.6	1.67
Relative amounts (%)							
18–25	89	33.04	5.26	66.96	5.26	37.98	2.98
25–35	33	32.22	8.72	67.78	8.72	38.45	4.94
35–45	44	35.91	7.56	64.09	7.56	36.36	4.29
45–55	72	42.71	7.84	57.29	7.84	32.50	4.45
55–65	54	43.52	7.21	56.48	7.21	32.04	4.09
65–85	13	44.76	6.20	55.24	6.20	31.34	3.52

L. P. Novak, *J. Gerontol.*, 1972, **27**, (4), 438–443.

TABLE 34. TOTAL AND LABILE HYDROXYPROLIN IN THE OVARY OF RATS.

	Age (months)	Number	Dry matter %	Total hydroxyprolin g % dry matter	Labile hydroxyprolin %	P
I	2–4	7	25.3 ± 2.36	1.84 ± 0.22	12.01 ± 1.12	–
II	7–8	8	26.2 ± 2.91	2.61 ± 0.22	5.10 ± 1.03	I/II P < 0.01
III	12–14	6	27.3 ± 2.84	2.73 ± 0.22	4.16 ± 0.89	I/III P < 0.001
IV	20–24	7	27.5 ± 2.36	2.51 ± 0.22	3.81 ± 0.63	I/IV P < 0.01
V	30–34	6	28.1 ± 2.41	2.32 ± 0.23	1.87 ± 0.18	IV/V P < 0.05 III/V P < 0.01

I. Takáes, *Gerontologia*, 1968 **14**, (3), 176 (177).

TABLE 35. TOTAL BODY POTASSIUM OF MEN AND WOMEN.

Age (years)	Number	mEq		mEq/kg		GRAMS		GRAMS/kg	
		Mean	SD	Mean	SD	Mean	SD	Mean	SD
				Men					
18–25	27	4,051	455.3	56.1	5.54	158.5	17.79	2.18	0.204
25–35	58	4,126	401.8	53.5	4.59	161.4	15.71	2.09	0.188
35–45	33	4,110	566.7	52.7	3.40	160.7	22.17	2.06	0.133
45–55	37	3,775	525.2	49.5	4.17	147.6	16.63	1.94	0.169
55–65	42	3,607	433.2	47.8	3.89	141.0	16.93	1.87	0.158
65–85	18	3,168	234.3	43.4	3.71	123.9	9.15	1.69	0.157
				Women					
18–25	89	2,555	273.4	45.6	3.57	99.9	10.69	1.79	0.144
25–35	33	2,626	352.3	46.2	5.93	102.7	13.77	1.81	0.236
35–45	44	2,655	351.3	43.7	5.11	103.6	13.84	1.71	0.199
45–55	72	2,575	290.9	39.1	5.39	100.7	11.38	1.53	0.215
55–65	54	2,403	286.6	38.2	4.53	93.2	10.19	1.49	0.179
65–85	13	2,351	200.0	37.6	4.33	91.9	7.81	1.47	0.184

TABLE 36. FAT, FAT-FREE MASS, CELL MASS OF MEN.

Age (years)	Number	FAT		FAT-FREE MASS		CELL MASS	
		Mean	SD	Mean	SD	Mean	SD
Absolute amounts (kg)							
18–25	27	13.4	7.37	59.5	6.69	33.7	3.79
25–35	58	17.2	6.72	60.6	5.90	34.4	3.35
35–45	33	17.9	4.85	60.4	8.32	34.2	4.72
45–55	37	21.1	5.75	55.4	6.24	31.4	3.54
55–65	42	23.1	6.68	53.0	6.36	30.0	3.61
65–85	18	26.9	6.01	46.5	3.44	26.4	1.95
Relative amounts (%)							
18–25	27	17.79	8.14	82.22	8.14	46.64	4.62
25–35	58	21.71	6.76	78.29	6.76	44.41	3.84
35–45	33	22.76	5.02	77.24	5.02	43.82	2.84
45–55	37	27.39	6.09	72.61	6.09	41.19	3.46
55–65	42	29.94	5.80	70.06	5.80	39.74	3.29
65–85	18	36.24	5.43	63.76	5.43	36.17	3.08

TABLE 37. HEIGHT AND WEIGHT: MAN, NORTH AMERICAN.

Specifications	HEIGHT (M)		HEIGHT (F)		WEIGHT (M)		WEIGHT (F)	
	cm	in.	cm	in.	kg	lb	kg	lb
BIRTH:								
Negro	49.6	19.5	48.7	19.1	3.2	7.1	3.1	6.8
White	50.8	20.0	50.2	19.7	3.5	7.8	3.4	7.6
Period 1860–1900	50.4	19.8						
Period 1930–1950	50.7	19.9						
2 yr:								
Japanese	83.8	33.0	82.4	32.4				
White	89.6	35.2	85.4	33.6	13.4	29.6	12.5	27.5
Period 1860–1900	81.6	32.1						
Period 1930–1950	86.9	34.2						
7 yr:								
Dutch	123.3	48.5			22.9	50.4		
Finnish	121.2	47.7			23.5	51.7		
Indian, American	120.8	47.6	117.0	46.0	21.6	47.5	20.3	44.7
Italian	119.3	47.0			22.7	49.9		
Japanese			114.1	44.9			20.7	45.6
Japanese, reared in Japan	113.9	44.8	112.7	44.4	20.4	44.9	19.7	43.3
Mexican			117.0	46.0			21.0	46.2
Negro	120.9	47.5	120.4	47.3			22.1	48.6
White	122.5	48.2	121.6	47.9	24.0	52.8	23.4	51.6
Lower economic groups	M,F 119.3 cm;	47.0 in.			M,F 22.1 kg;	48.6 lb.		
Upper economic groups	M,F 120.8 cm;	47.6 in.			M,F 22.9 kg;	50.4 lb.		
Unskilled, semiskilled	121.4	48.7			23.3	51.3		
Managerial, professional	123.6	48.7			24.5	53.9		
Poorest residential dist.			118.9	46.8			21.4	47.1
Best residential dist.			122.0	48.0			22.8	50.2
Period 1860–1900	114.3	45.0						
Period 1930–1950	112.4	48.2						
Northeastern USA	119.6	47.1	118.4	46.6	22.9	50.4	22.5	49.5
Northcentral USA	120.0	47.2	118.9	46.8	22.7	49.9	22.2	48.8
Southcentral USA	118.9	46.8	118.1	46.5	22.2	48.8	21.4	47.1
Western USA	118.6	46.7	118.9	46.8	21.9	48.2	21.4	47.1

TABLE 37. (Continued)

Specifications	HEIGHT (M) cm	HEIGHT (M) in.	HEIGHT (F) cm	HEIGHT (F) in.	WEIGHT (M) kg	WEIGHT (M) lb	WEIGHT (F) kg	WEIGHT (F) lb
10 yr:								
Indian, American			131.7	51.8			27.3	60.1
Japanese			129.6	51.0			27.8	61.2
Japanese, reared in Japan	127.6	50.2	127.3	50.1	26.4	58.1	26.1	57.4
Mexican			132.2	52.0			28.2	62.0
Negro	135.3	53.2	135.2	53.1			30.7	67.5
White	137.9	54.3	137.7	54.2	32.0	70.7	31.8	70.3
Lower economic groups	M,F 135.0 cm;	53.1 in.			M,F 29.7 kg;	65.3 lb.		
Upper economic groups	M,F 136.6 cm;	53.8 in.			M,F 31.1 kg;	68.4 lb.		
Unskilled, semiskilled	137.8	54.3			32.3	71.1		
Managerial, professional	140.7	55.4			34.3	75.5		
Poorest residential dist.			134.3	52.9			29.0	63.8
Best residential dist.			138.7	54.6			31.8	70.0
Period 1860–1900	129.6	51.0						
Period 1930–1950	139.2	54.8						
Northeastern USA	135.1	53.2	135.1	53.2	30.5	67.1	30.3	66.7
Northcentral USA	135.4	53.3	134.4	52.9	30.5	67.1	30.1	66.2
Southcentral USA	134.9	53.1	134.1	52.8	30.2	66.4	29.3	64.5
Western USA	134.9	53.1	134.6	53.0	29.6	65.1	28.6	62.9
11 yr:								
Dutch	144.3	56.8			33.8	74.4		
Finnish	141.6	55.7			33.4	73.5		
Indian, American	138.9	54.7			30.3	66.7		
Italian	139.1	54.8			32.1	70.6		
Japanese, reared in Japan	132.1	52.0	132.5	52.2	28.8	63.4	29.2	64.2
Mexican	138.2	54.8						
Negro	140.9	55.4	141.2	55.5				
White	142.7	56.2	143.5	56.5	35.2	77.6	35.8	79.0
14 yr:								
Indian, American			150.8	59.4			42.8	94.2
Japanese			150.6	59.3			43.3	95.3
Japanese, reared in Japan	148.4	58.4	146.7	57.8	40.5	89.1	41.2	90.6
Mexican			152.0	59.8			44.5	97.9
Negro	156.5	61.5	154.7	60.8	48.0	105.8	47.7	105.2
White	160.0	63.0	158.2	62.3	48.9	107.9	49.1	108.5
Period 1860–1900	151.8	59.8						
Period 1930–1950	163.7	64.4						
Northeastern USA	155.4	61.2	155.7	61.3	45.2	99.4	48.1	105.8
Northcentral USA	155.7	61.3	155.2	61.1	45.8	100.8	46.5	102.3
Southcentral USA	155.7	61.3	155.4	61.2	44.6	98.1	45.2	99.4
Western USA	153.2	60.3	153.9	60.6	41.2?	90.6?	45.7	100.5
15 yr:								
Dutch	168.6	66.4			50.5	111.1		
Finnish	164.4	64.7			52.1	114.6		
Indian, American	160.5	63.2			45.2	99.4		
Italian	161.4	63.5			50.9	112.0		
16 yr:								
Japanese, reared in Japan	157.7	62.1	150.3	59.2	49.1	108.0	47.2	103.8
Negro	161.0	63.3	158.1	62.1	53.0	116.9	53.0	116.9
White	166.6	65.6	160.5	63.2	55.1	121.7	52.1	115.0
19 yr:								
Japanese, reared in Japan	161.1	63.4	150.7	59.2				
Negro	172.9	67.9	159.9	62.8	68.1	150.2		
White	173.8	68.3	164.6	64.7	68.5	151.2	58.2	128.6
Period 1860–1900	172.1	67.8						
Period 1930–1950	175.6	69.1						

TABLE 37. (Continued)

Specifications	HEIGHT (M)		HEIGHT (F)		WEIGHT (M)		WEIGHT (F)	
	cm	in.	cm	in.	kg	lb	kg	lb
25 yr:								
Japanese, reared in Japan	161.8	63.7	150.4	59.2				
Period 1860–1900	171.8	67.6						
Period 1930–1950	173.5	68.3						

North Americans of different racial backgrounds, socio-economic conditions, geographical areas, and different periods in American history. Data for the Negro were collected about 1925; White, Cleveland, Ohio. 1920–35; Japanese, 1920–40; Japanese, reared in Japan, 1951; Dutch, Finnish, Italian, 1930–40; American Indian, Mexican, 1920–40. Lower economic groups; children of unskilled and semiskilled workers, 16 states in USA, 1937–39; upper economic groups; all occupational groups other than unskilled and semiskilled workers, 16 states in USA, 1937–39. Unskilled, semiskilled and managerial, professional: Oregon boys of northwest European ancestry, studied in 1950. Roughly 25% in unskilled and semiskilled category, 49% in the excluded (middle) category, and 25% in the managerial and professional category. Poorest and best residential districts; white girls of Minneapolis, Minn., and Ottawa Canada, 1930–45. Period 1860–1900 and period 1930–1950: investigations at each age were selected to approximate similar ethnic and socio-economic sampling in the 2 periods. Geographical sections of USA: about 1935. Values at age 7 are averages of means of ages 6 and 8.

W. Spector, *Handbook of Biological Data*, P. 177.

TABLE 38. PART II: RELATED TO AGE AT MAXIMUM GROWTH INCREASE.

Age Yr.	Number of subjects	Weight kg	Height cm	Number of subjects	Weight kg	Height cm	Number of subjects	Weight kg	Height cm
	MGI at 12.5–13.5 yr			MGI at 14.0–15.5 yr			MGI at 16.0–17.0 yr		
Males									
7	77	24.0	120.7	317	22.9	118.9	98	21.6	117.4
8	97	27.1	126.6	387	25.5	124.6	127	23.9	122.7
9	109	30.1	132.1	429	28.2	130.0	135	26.3	127.9
10	112	33.3	137.3	452	31.0	135.1	139	28.0	132.8
11	112	37.1	142.6	453	34.1	139.9	141	31.3	137.3
12	112	42.5	149.4	454	37.6	144.8	141	34.0	141.7
13	112	50.4	159.8	454	41.6	150.1	141	36.8	146.0
14	112	57.2	166.8	454	48.3	158.3	141	39.9	150.3
15	111	61.8	170.0	449	55.8	166.4	141	45.0	156.4
16	102	64.4	171.2	426	60.7	170.5	141	52.5	165.0
17	76	66.1	171.9	336	63.5	172.3	114	58.3	170.5
18	32	67.3	172.3	144	65.5	173.0	44	62.1	173.0
	MGI at 10.5–11.5 yr			MGI at 12.0–13.0 yr			MGI at 13.5–14.5 yr		
Females									
7	109	23.1	119.0	259	21.7	116.9	112	20.8	115.8
8	140	25.9	124.8	339	24.2	122.6	145	23.1	121.1
9	153	29.0	130.6	383	26.9	127.9	170	25.4	126.2
10	155	33.3	137.3	407	29.7	133.1	175	27.8	131.0
11	155	39.4	146.0	413	33.2	138.5	177	30.6	135.8
12	155	45.9	152.4	413	38.3	145.7	177	33.8	140.7
13	155	50.2	155.6	413	44.3	153.0	177	38.8	147.5
14	153	52.9	157.0	411	49.1	156.8	177	44.7	154.2
15	145	54.4	157.7	400	52.0	158.5	173	49.2	157.4
16	128	55.0	158.0	374	53.5	159.2	157	51.5	158.9
17	90	55.3	158.2	294	54.4	159.6	109	53.1	159.5
18	26	55.1	158.4	130	54.6	159.9	49	53.9	159.8

Values are for subjects, dressed in indoor clothing but without shoes, from three towns near Boston, Mass. Ancestry: 63% N. European, 24% Iranian, 7% Jewish, 4% South European, 1% Negro and mixed. MGI = maximum growth increase.

TABLE 39. GROWTH: VERTEBRATES OTHER THAN MAMMALS—PART III: BODY LENGTH AND WEIGHT: FISHES.

Age: Ages are completed years; Max. = age at maximum length and/or weight. Length measurements give total length—from tip of head (jaws closed) to tip of tail—unless otherwise indicated.

Species (Common Name)	Age	Length (cm)	Weight (kg)	Species (Common Name)	Age	Length (cm)	Weight (kg)
PISCES				*Lepisosteus osseus*	1 yr	16	
Acipenser fulvescens	1 yr	24	0.068		2 yr	32	
(Lake Sturgeon)[a]	2 yr	30	0.136		10 yr	102	
	4 yr	45	0.390		Maximum	160	18.00
	6 yr	54	0.720	*Lepomis macrochirus*	1 yr	5	0.005
	8 yr	60	1.000	(Bluegill)	2 yr	9	0.026
	10 yr	71	1.400		4 yr	16	0.070
	Maximum	168	50.000		6 yr	20	0.170
Carassius auratus	1 yr	9	—		8 yr	23	0.340
(Goldfish)	2 yr	14	—		10 yr	23	0.340
Clupea pallasi	1 yr	6			Maximum	29	1.955
(Pacific Herring)[a]	2 yr	14		*Melanogrammus aeglefinus*	1 yr	20	—
	4 yr	21		(Haddock)[a]	2 yr	30	0.29
	6 yr	24			4 yr	45	0.90
	8 yr	26			6 yr	55	1.53
	10 yr	28			8 yr	61	—
	Maximum	40	0.310		Maximum	90	—
Coregonus clupeaformis	1 yr	15	0.030	*Micropterus salmoides*	1 yr	11	0.023
(North American Lake	2 yr	23	0.085	(Largemouth Black Bass)	2 yr	20	0.12
Whitefish)	4 yr	42	0.700		4 yr	34	0.57
	6 yr	53	1.360		6 yr	41	1.02
	8 yr	58	2.270		8 yr	46	1.36
	10 yr	64	2.780		10 yr	51	1.81
	Maximum	71[a]	4.880		Maximum	95	10.48
Cyprinus carpio	1 yr	18	0.09	*Osmerus mordax*	1 yr	14	0.023
(Carp)	2 yr	31	0.45	(American Smelt)	2 yr	18	0.036
	4 yr	48	1.80		4 yr	25	0.110
	6 yr	53	2.50		Maximum	36	0.141
	8 yr	58	3.20	*Perca flavescens*	1 yr	7.0	0.003
	10 yr	66	5.10	(Yellow Perch)	2 yr	12.0	0.03
	Maximum	127	37.88		4 yr	20.0	0.11
Esox lucius	1 yr	20	0.09		6 yr	25.0	0.23
(Northern Pike)	2 yr	38	0.27		8 yr	27.0	0.285
	4 yr	61	1.10		10 yr	30.0	0.37
	6 yr	79	2.10		Maximum	41.9	1.913
	8 yr	97	2.95	*Polyodon spathula*	1 yr	25	0.077
	10 yr	107	4.50		2 yr	64	1.35
	Maximum	120	28.00		4 yr	84	2.27
Gadus morbua	1 yr	16			6 yr	97	3.40
(Atlantic Cod)	2 yr	41			8 yr	102	5.00
	4 yr	64			10 yr	112	6.80
	6 yr	81			Maximum	188[a]	74.00
	Maximum	142	25.00	*Pomoxis annularis*	1 yr	7	0.006
Ictalurus punctatus	1 yr	8	0.045	(White Crappie)	2 yr	15	0.03
(Channel Catfish)	2 yr	15	0.135		4 yr	25	0.21
	4 yr	30	0.230		6 yr	32	0.45
	6 yr	41	0.680		8 yr	38	0.71
	8 yr	53	1.630		Maximum	40	0.865
	10 yr	69	4.300				
	Maximum	127	24.050				

TABLE 39. (*Continued*)

Species (Common Name)	Age	Length (cm)	Weight (kg)	Species (Common Name)	Age	Length (cm)	Weight (kg)
Salmo salar	1 yr	4	0.011		6 yr	53	1.59
(Atlantic Salmon)[a]	2 yr	10	0.033		8 yr	56	–
	4 yr	76	4.54		Maximum	80	6.58
	6 yr	107	16.00	*Thunaris thynnus*	1 yr	64	–
	Maximum	120	47.00	(Bluefin Tuna)[a]	2 yr	82	–
Salmo trutta	1 yr	10	0.025		4 yr	118	–
(Brown Trout)	2 yr	20	0.095		6 yr	153	–
	4 yr	36	0.88		Maximum	311	726
	6 yr	56	1.80				
	8 yr	64	4.26	**AGNATHA**			
	Maximum	120	18.50	*Petromyzon marinus*	1 yr	3.8	–
Salvelinus fontinalis	1 yr	10	0.025	(Sea Lamprey)	2 yr	7.9	–
(Eastern Brook Trout)	2 yr	16	0.06		4 yr	43.0	–
	4 yr	35	0.65		Maximum	84.0	1.14

[a] Fork length, measured from tip of snout to end of rays in center of caudal fin.
[b] Standard length, measured from tip of snout (upper jaw) to end of vertebral column.
[c] Total length.

P. L. Altman and D. S. Dittmer, *Biology Data Book*, 1964, p. 104.

TABLE 40. BODY WEIGHT AND HEIGHT: MAN, NORTH AMERICAN PART I: RELATED TO RATE OF MATURING.

	MALES						FEMALES					
Age yr.	Accelerated weight kg	(38 Subj) Height cm	Average weight kg	(105 Subj) Height cm	Retarded weight kg	(31 Subj) Height cm	Accelerated weight kg	(27 Subj) Height cm	Average weight kg	(108 Subj) Height cm	Retarded weight kg	(25 Subj) Height cm
1	10.8	78.5	10.4	78.0	10.6	74.4	10.9	77.7	9.8	73.9	9.6	71.9
2	14.1	89.4	13.3	87.9	12.4	83.3	13.7	87.4	12.7	87.4	11.7	84.6
3	16.1	98.0	15.7	96.5	13.9	91.7	15.7	96.0	14.7	95.2	13.9	93.2
4	18.8	105.4	17.7	103.6	16.2	100.6	19.1	104.9	17.0	103.1	15.3	100.1
5	20.8	113.0	19.4	111.0	18.3	107.4	21.8	112.8	18.7	109.5	17.2	105.9
6	23.5	119.9	21.6	116.3	20.0	114.0	24.1	119.1	21.2	116.6	19.5	113.0
7	25.8	127.0	24.0	123.7	22.0	119.4	26.0	125.0	24.0	122.2	21.6	119.9
8	29.5	133.4	26.4	129.3	24.8	125.5	30.3	132.1	27.2	128.0	23.2	125.0
9	33.8	139.4	30.3	134.9	27.3	131.6	35.6	140.0	30.1	133.9	27.1	130.8
10	39.0	145.5	33.6	141.5	30.0	137.4	41.8	145.5	34.5	140.0	29.4	135.4
11	44.1	151.4	37.3	146.0	33.3	141.7	49.4	153.4	39.3	146.0	31.7	141.0
12	49.8	157.0	41.4	150.1	36.6	146.4	56.6	160.3	45.0	154.2	35.4	146.6
13	56.7	166.6	46.0	156.0	40.9	150.0	59.5	163.3	51.0	160.0	39.4	151.9
14	61.0	174.0	52.6	164.1	45.4	156.7	61.2	164.6	54.9	163.1	44.9	158.5
15	67.1	179.6	60.7	173.0	50.9	163.1	62.9	165.1	58.4	164.6	49.2	162.1
16	69.9	182.1	64.7	178.1	59.4	172.0	63.2	165.6	59.7	165.6	52.0	163.8
17	70.7	182.1	67.9	179.1	64.9	176.5	62.4	165.6	60.0	165.9	54.1	164.6
18	–	–	69.9	180.1	68.4	179.1	61.0	165.6	59.8	165.9	54.0	164.8

Values for individuals and for specific groups of individuals vary widely from average weight–height values. Variations are particularly great for boys ages 12–17 years and for girls 10–15 years. For additional information consult Hathaway, Milicent L., 1957, Heights and Weights of Children and Youth in the United States, Home Economics Research Report No. 2, U.S. Dept. of Agriculture, Wash. D.C.

Values are for subjects living in Calif. Weights and Heights were interpolated from a large graph based on mean values established at 2% intervals of mature height.

P. L. Altman and D. S. Dittmer, *Growth*, p. 337.

TABLE 41. BODY WEIGHT AND HEIGHT: MAN, NORTH AMERICAN
PART III: RELATED TO AGE AT PUBESCENCE.

Age yr	MALES								
	Number of subjects	Weight kg	Height cm	Number of subjects	Weight kg	Height cm	Number of subjects	Weight kg	Height cm
	Pubescence before 14 yrs			Pubescence at 14–15 yrs			Pubescence at 15 yr or later		
6	35	22.4	119.9	9	20.4	115.3	8	19.7	115.8
7	46	24.9	125.5	15	23.1	121.9	12	21.9	120.3
8	60	27.4	130.8	18	25.4	127.3	18	23.8	125.7
9	65	30.5	136.1	19	28.6	133.6	25	25.7	130.6
10	81	34.1	141.7	22	32.1	138.7	24	28.4	135.1
11	89	37.6	147.1	29	34.3	143.5	25	30.8	140.0
12	96	42.1	152.9	40	36.7	147.1	29	33.8	144.3
13	105	47.4	159.8	54	41.1	152.4	35	37.0	148.6
14	112	53.3	167.1	87	46.7	159.5	50	40.8	153.2
15	90	58.9	173.5	86	53.1	167.1	70	46.7	160.5
16	79	63.0	176.3	73	58.4	173.0	79	52.4	167.1
17	42	65.8	176.5	53	61.9	176.3	55	57.3	171.7
18	9	66.5	176.5	20	63.9	177.8	20	61.0	179.1

Age yr	FEMALES								
	Menarche before 13 yr			Menarche at 13–14 yr			Menarche at 14 yr or later		
6	19	22.5	119.4	7	20.0	112.8	5	19.6	113.0
7	33	24.6	123.4	12	23.7	122.4	13	21.4	117.9
8	44	27.4	129.4	15	25.6	126.5	13	24.0	124.2
9	58	31.2	135.4	19	29.2	131.3	18	25.8	128.0
10	62	35.9	141.7	21	32.1	137.4	19	28.3	133.8
11	75	40.7	148.3	27	36.6	143.0	25	31.4	137.9
12	85	46.3	155.4	37	41.5	151.1	36	35.1	144.3
13	93	51.8	160.0	53	47.1	156.7	48	39.4	151.6
14	115	54.8	162.1	91	50.8	160.8	70	44.6	157.2
15	108	56.4	162.8	105	53.5	162.6	84	49.4	161.8
16	98	57.4	163.6	96	54.4	163.3	74	52.1	163.3
17	61	47.7	163.3	74	54.5	162.6	58	52.9	163.3

Values are for subjects, weighed in the nude, from well-to-do professional classes, living in or near Chicago, Illinois.

P. L. Altman and D. S. Dittmer, *Growth*, 1962, p. 338–39.

TABLE 42. BODY WEIGHT AND HEIGHT FOR TWO SOCIO-ECONOMIC GROUPS: MAN, NORTH AMERICAN.

Age Yr	PROFESSIONAL OR SKILLED			SEMISKILLED OR UNSKILLED		
	Number of subjects	Weight kg	Height cm	Number of subjects	Weight kg	Height cm
			MALE			
4.5	306	18.0 (13.2–22.8)	106.2 (95.6–116.8)	492	17.3 (13.3–21.3)	104.3 (93.7–114.9)
7.5	2466	24.4 (17.8–31.0)	123.9 (112.9–124.9)	2544	23.5 (17.3–29.7)	122.6 (111.2–134.0)
10.5	3230	32.9 (22.1–43.7)	139.5 (126.7–152.3)	3258	31.2 (21.4–41.0)	137.6 (125.0–150.2)
13.5	3430	44.3 (27.9–60.7)	155.1 (138.3–171.9)	2684	42.0 (26.4–57.6)	152.9 (136.7–169.1)
16.5	2534	61.3 (43.7–78.9)	172.3 (159.3–185.3)	1372	59.3 (42.3–76.3)	170.9 (156.7–185.1)
			FEMALE			
4.5	388	17.5 (12.9–22.1)	105.5 (95.9–115.1)	587	16.8 (12.6–21.0)	103.6 (93.0–114.2)
7.5	2464	24.0 (16.4–31.6)	122.9 (111.5–134.3)	2838	23.0 (16.0–30.0)	121.5 (110.3–132.7)
10.5	2967	32.6 (20.4–44.8)	138.9 (125.7–152.1)	3179	31.3 (20.1–42.5)	137.6 (124.2–151.0)
13.5	2696	45.8 (30.2–61.4)	155.6 (143.4–168.8)	2361	44.0 (28.6–59.4)	154.3 (140.7–167.9)
16.5	2135	53.2 (40.0–66.4)	161.2 (149.6–172.4)	1106	52.7 (38.9–66.5)	160.9 (149.5–172.3)

Socio-economic classification was determined by the occupation of the principal wage earner supporting the child's family. Values are for white subjects wearing light underclothing. Values in parentheses are ranges, estimate "b" (cf. Introduction).

P. L. Altman and D. S. Dittmer, *Growth*, 1962, p. 339.

TABLE 43. ORGAN SIZE AND AGE.

Age	20's Avg	20's %BW	30's Avg	30's %BW	40's Avg	40's %BW	50's Avg	50's %BW	60's Avg	60's %BW	70's Avg	70's %BW	80's Avg	80's %BW	90's Avg	90's %BW	GMS
	25.4		35.2		45.2		56.0		64.5		73.3		83.8		92.0		
Adrenal R & L	24.8	.03	15.3	.02	15.4	.02	25.1	.04	16.7	.02	19.6	.03	14.6	.02			mm
Aorta, Abd	30.5		33.5		38.3		42.2		42.4		52.0		48.8		48.0		mm
Aorta, Thor	37.0		46.5		51.0		52.1		53.8		61.3		65.8		55.0		g
Brain	1325	1.8	1399	1.8	1233	1.8	1350	2.1	1300	1.9	1270	2.0	1198	1.8			g
Heart	345	.46	466	.59	429	.62	425	.65	444	.64	463	.72	369	.56	390	.64	g
Kidney, L	177	.24	200	.26	186	.27	180	.28	177	.26	149	.23	145	.22	110	.18	g
Kidney, R	163	.22	181	.23	174	.25	166	.25	173	.25	146	.23	138	.21	105	.17	g
Liver	1855	2.5	1929	2.5	1662	2.4	1625	2.5	1569	2.3	1398	2.2	1273	1.9	1000	1.6	g
Lung, L	513	.68	601	.77	572	.83	605	.93	575	.83	539	.83	612	.93	690	1.1	g
Lung, R	525	.7	780	.99	634	.92	692	1.1	706	1.0	640	.99	722	1.1	690	1.1	g
Pancreas	96.8	.13	113	.14	108	.16	116	.18	112	.16	105	.16	103	.16	110	.18	g
Pituitary[a]	0.6	.8	0.5	.64	.77	1.1	.734	1.1	.72	1.0	.69	1.1	.7	1.1			g
Prostate	22.3	.03	46.3	.06	28.0	.04	26.2	.04	40.6	.06	52.9	.08	50.4	.08			g
Spleen	199	.27	214	.27	157	.23	164	.25	184	.27	138	.21	120	.18	95	.16	g
Testes (L & R)			35.7	.05	32.3	.05	40.8	.06	42.1	.06	45.3	.07	32.9	.05			g
Thyroid			25.5	.03	23.2	.03	53	.08	32.6	.05	26.2	.04	29.5	.05			g
Ventricle, L	16		16.9		17		18.2		18.5		17.9		18.8		17		mm
Ventricle, R	3.6		3.7		3.7		4.6		4.9		4.6		3.8		3		mm
Height	69.1		70.1		67.9		67.5		67.3		66.1		66.2		64.5		In.
Weight	165		173		152		144		153		143		145		135		Lbs.

[a]On percentage of body weight—10^{-3}.

Calloway, Foley, and Lagerbloom: J. Am. Geriat. Soc., 1964, 13, (20).

TABLE 44. AVERAGE WEIGHTS OF ADULTS.
Average Weights in Pounds and Kilograms (In Indoor Clothing).

MAN

Height (in shoes)			15–16 yrs		17–19 yrs		20–24 yrs		25–29 yrs		30–39 yrs		40–49 yrs		50–59 yrs		60–69 yrs	
ft.	in.	cm	lb	kg	lb	kg	lb	kg	lb	kg	lb	kg	lb	kg	lb	kg	lb	kg
5	0	152.4	98	44.5	113	51.3	122	55.3	128	58.1	131	59.4	134	60.8	136	61.7	133	60.3
5	0½	153.7	100	45.4	114.5	51.9	123.5	56	129.5	58.7	132.5	60.1	135.5	61.5	137.5	62.4	134.5	61
5	1	154.9	102	46.3	116	52.6	125	56.7	131	59.4	134	60.8	137	62.1	139	63	136	61.7
5	1½	156.2	104.5	47.4	117.5	53.3	126.5	57.4	132.5	60.1	135.5	61.5	138.5	62.8	140.5	63.7	137.5	62.4
5	2	157.5	107	48.5	119	54	128	58.1	134	60.8	137	62.1	140	63.5	142	64.4	139	63
5	2½	158.8	109.5	49.7	121	54.9	130	59	136	61.7	139	63	142	64.4	143.5	65.1	140.5	63.7
5	3	160	112	50.8	123	55.8	132	59.9	138	62.6	141	64	144	65.3	145	65.8	142	64.4
5	3½	161.3	114.5	51.9	125	56.7	134	60.8	139.5	63.3	143	64.9	146	66.2	147	66.7	144	65.3
5	4	162.6	117	53.1	127	57.6	136	61.7	141	64	145	65.8	148	67.1	149	67.6	146	66.2
5	4½	163.8	119.5	54.2	129	58.5	137.5	62.4	142.5	64.6	147	66.7	150	68	151	68.5	148	67.1
5	5	165.1	122	55.3	131	59.4	139	63	144	65.3	149	67.6	152	68.9	153	69.4	150	68
5	5½	166.4	124.5	56.5	133	60.3	140.5	63.7	146	66.2	151	68.5	154	69.9	155	70.3	152	68.9
5	6	167.6	127	57.6	135	61.2	142	64.4	148	67.1	153	69.4	156	70.8	157	71.2	154	69.9
5	6½	168.9	129.5	58.7	137	62.1	143.5	65.1	149.5	67.8	155	70.3	158.5	71.9	159.5	72.3	156.5	71
5	7	170.2	132	59.9	139	63	145	65.8	151	68.5	157	71.2	161	73	162	73.5	159	72.1
5	7½	171.5	134.5	61	141	64	147	66.7	153	69.4	159	72.1	163	73.9	164	74.4	161	73
5	8	172.7	137	62.1	143	64.9	149	67.6	155	70.3	161	73	165	74.8	166	75.3	163	73.9
5	8½	174	139.5	63.3	145	65.8	151	68.5	157	71.2	163	73.9	167	75.8	168	76.2	165.5	75.1
5	9	175.3	142	64.4	147	66.7	153	69.4	159	72.1	165	74.8	169	76.7	170	77.1	168	76.2
5	9½	176.5	144	65.3	149	67.6	155	70.3	161	73	167.5	76	171.5	77.8	171.5	78.2	170.5	77.3
5	10	177.8	146	66.2	151	68.5	157	71.2	163	73.9	170	77.1	174	78.9	175	79.4	173	78.5
5	10½	179.1	148	67.1	153	69.4	159	72.1	165	74.8	172	78	176	79.8	177.5	80.5	175.5	79.6
5	11	180.3	150	68	155	70.3	161	73	167	75.8	174	78.9	178	80.8	180	81.6	178	80.8
5	11½	181.6	152	68.9	157.5	71.4	163.5	74.2	169.5	76.9	176.5	80.1	180.5	81.9	182.5	82.8	180.5	81.9
6	0	182.9	154	69.9	160	72.6	166	75.3	172	78	179	81.2	183	83	185	83.9	183	83
6	0½	184.2	156.5	71	162	73.5	168	76.2	174.5	79.2	181	82.1	185	83.9	187	84.8	185.5	84.1
6	1	185.4	159	72.1	164	74.4	170	77.1	177	80.3	183	83	187	84.8	189	85.7	188	85.3
6	1½	186.7	161.5	73.3	166	75.3	172	78	179.5	81.4	185.5	84.1	189.5	86	191.5	86.9	190.5	86.4
6	2	188	164	74.4	168	76.2	174	78.9	182	82.6	188	85.3	192	87.1	194	88	193	87.5
6	2½	189.2	166.5	75.5	170	77.1	176	79.8	184	83.5	190.5	86.4	194.5	88.2	196.5	89.1	195.5	88.7

WOMAN

Height (in shoes)			15–16 yrs		17–19 yrs		20–24 yrs		25–29 yrs		30–39 yrs		40–49 yrs		50–59 yrs		60–69 yrs	
ft.	in.	cm	lb	kg	lb	kg	lb	kg	lb	kg	lb	kg	lb	kg	lb	kg	lb	kg
4	10	147.3	97	44	99	44.9	102	46.3	107	48.5	115	52.2	122	55.3	125	56.7	127	57.6
4	10½	148.6	98.5	44.7	100	45.6	103.5	46.9	108.5	49.2	116	52.6	123	55.8	126	57.2	128	58.1
4	11	149.9	100	45.4	102	46.3	105	47.6	110	49.9	117	53.1	124	56.2	127	57.6	129	58.5
4	11½	151.1	101.5	46	103.5	46.9	106.5	48.3	111.5	50.6	118.5	53.8	125.5	56.9	128.5	58.3	130	59
5	0	152.4	103	46.7	105	47.6	108	49	113	51.3	120	54.4	127	57.6	130	59	131	59.4
5	0½	153.7	105	47.6	107	48.5	110	49.9	114.5	51.9	121.5	55.1	128.5	58.3	131.5	59.6	132.5	60.1
5	1	154.9	107	48.5	109	49.4	112	50.8	116	52.6	123	55.8	130	59	133	60.3	134	60.8
5	1½	156.2	109	49.4	111	50.3	113.5	51.5	117.5	53.3	124.5	56.5	131.5	59.6	134.5	61	135.5	61.5
5	2	157.5	111	50.3	113	51.3	115	52.2	119	54	126	57.2	133	60.3	136	61.7	137	62.1
5	2½	158.8	112.5	51	114.5	51.9	116.5	52.8	120.5	54.7	127.5	57.8	134.5	61	138	62.6	139	63
5	3	160	114	51.7	116	52.6	118	53.5	122	55.3	129	58.5	136	61.7	140	63.5	141	64
5	3½	161.3	115.5	52.4	118	53.5	119.5	54.2	123.5	56	130.5	59.2	138	62.6	142	64.4	143	64.9
5	4	162.6	117	53.1	120	54.4	121	54.9	125	56.7	132	59.9	140	63.5	144	65.3	145	65.8
5	4½	163.8	119	54	122	55.3	123	55.8	127	57.6	133.5	60.6	141.5	64.2	146	66.2	147	66.7
5	5	165.1	121	54.9	124	56.2	125	56.7	129	58.5	135	61.2	143	64.9	148	67.1	149	67.6
5	5½	166.4	123	55.8	125.5	56.9	127	57.6	131	59.4	137	62.1	145	65.8	150	68	151	68.5
5	6	167.6	125	56.7	127	57.6	129	58.5	133	60.3	139	63	147	66.7	152	68.9	153	69.4
5	6½	168.9	126.5	57.4	128.5	58.3	130.5	59.2	134.5	61	140.5	63.7	149	67.6	154	69.9	155	70.3
5	7	170.2	128	58.1	130	59	132	59.9	136	61.7	142	64.4	151	68.5	156	70.8	157	71.2
5	7½	171.5	130	59	132	59.9	134	60.8	138	62.6	144	65.3	153	69.4	158	71.7	159	72.1
5	8	172.7	132	59.9	134	60.8	136	61.7	140	63.5	146	66.2	155	70.3	160	72.6	161	73
5	8½	174	134	60.8	136	61.7	138	62.6	142	64.4	148	67.1	157	71.2	162	73.5	163	73.9
5	9	175.3	136	61.7	138	62.6	140	63.5	144	65.3	150	68	159	72.1	164	74.4	165	74.8
5	9½	176.5	—	—	140	63.5	142	64.4	146	66.2	152	68.9	161.5	73.3	166.5	75.5	—	—
5	10	177.8	—	—	142	64.4	144	65.3	148	67.1	154	69.9	164	74.4	169	76.7	—	—
5	10½	179.1	—	—	144.5	65.5	146.5	66.5	150.5	68.3	156.5	71	166.5	75.5	171.5	77.8	—	—
5	11	180.3	—	—	147	66.7	149	67.6	153	69.4	159	72.1	169	76.7	174	78.9	—	—
5	11½	181.6	—	—	149.5	67.8	151.5	68.7	155.5	70.5	161.5	73.3	171.5	77.8	177	80.3	—	—
6	0	182.9	—	—	152	68.9	154	69.9	158	71.7	164	74.4	174	78.9	180	81.6	—	—
6	3	190.5	169	—	172	78	178	80.8	186	84.4	193	87.5	197	89.4	199	90.3	198	89.8
6	3½	191.8	—	—	174	78.9	179.5	81.4	188	85.3	196	88.9	200	90.7	202	91.6	201	91.2
6	4	193	—	—	176	79.8	181	82.1	190	86.2	199	90.3	203	92.1	205	93	204	92.5

Diem and Konrad, "Scientific Tables," *Documenta Geigy*, 1962, p. 623.

TABLE 45.[a] DIAMETER AND SURFACE SIZES OF MYOFIBRES IN THE HUMAN HEART AT DIFFERENT AGES.

	RANGE OF VARIATIONS IN MEASURED MYOFIBRES	
	Diameter (μ)	Surface size (sq. μ)
Newborn	5–8	20–50
3	10–15	78–176
9	11–15	93–176
17	16–25	203–440
21	16–27	203–572
32	16–25	203–490
43	18–30	254–706
50–53	16–30	226–706
55–56	16–28	203–615
62–68	12–27	113–572
70–73	15–25	176–490
75–78	12–25	113–490

Dogliotti, *Z. Anat. Entw.*, 1931, **76**, (716) (abbreviated table).

[a]*Physiological and Pathological Ageing*, p. 396.

TABLE 46.[a] PERCENTAGE OF CASES IN EACH AGE DECADE WITH VARIOUS DEGREES OF DEVELOPMENT OF ELASTIC TISSUE IN THE HEART; AND THE AMOUNT OF COLLAGENOUS TISSUE.

Age (years)	DEVELOPMENT OF ELASTIC TISSUE (% OF CASES)				Collagenous tissue (sq. μ) per 1000 sq. μ of myocardial tissue
	Absent	Scarce	Moderate	Abundant	
0–10	92	8	–	–	17.6–27
10–20	52	40	8	–	14.2–28
20–30	12	68	16	5	18
30–40	8	48	32	12	37.6
40–50	–	48	32	20	28.2–30.8
50–60	–	36	44	20	27
60–70	–	16	52	32	18
70–90	–	12	68	20	12–43.6

Dogliotti, *Z. Anat. Entw.*, 1931, **96**, (703).

[a]*Physiological and Pathological Ageing*, p. 396.

TABLE 47.[a] AVERAGE MEASUREMENTS OF A POPULATION BY AGE AND SEX.
(N = 27,515 Males and 33,562 Females).

	HEIGHT[b] (INCHES)		WEIGHT[c]		WEIGHT ADJUSTED FOR HEIGHT	
	Males	Females	Males	Females	66-inch males	62-inch females
14	61.10	60.77	94.3	99.6	113.9	103.8
14.5	62.43	61.35	101.1	105.2	115.4	107.4
15.5	64.51	62.03	111.7	110.0	117.7	109.9
16.5	65.92	62.14	120.0	112.8	120.3	112.3
17.5	66.31	62.16	124.5	114.4	123.3	113.9
18.5	66.74	62.30	127.8	116.0	124.8	115.0
19.5	66.94	62.26	131.2	115.7	127.4	114.8
20.5	66.92	62.42	131.6	118.0	127.9	116.6
21.5	67.34	62.41	136.0	117.3	130.6	115.9
22.5	67.04	62.35	135.0	117.7	130.8	116.5
23.5	66.83	62.26	135.3	117.0	132.0	116.1
24.5–29.5	66.76	62.12	134.3	117.3	133.6	116.9
29.5–34.5	66.73	61.99	138.4	119.6	135.8	119.6
34.5–39.5	66.64	61.87	139.0	122.3	136.7	122.7
39.5–44.5	66.09	61.60	137.2	125.8	136.9	127.0
44.5–49.5	65.89	61.48	137.2	128.3	137.6	129.9
49.5–54.5	65.69	61.24	137.2	130.2	138.3	132.5
54.5–59.5	65.55	60.96	137.5	129.8	139.1	132.9
59.5–64.5	65.07	60.66	136.8	127.1	140.2	131.1
64.5–69.5[d]	64.67	60.38	136.4	123.1	141.2	128.0
69.5–74.5[e]	64.64	59.96	136.0	118.9	140.9	125.0
74.5 and over[e]	63.83	60.00	125.4	117.8	133.2	123.8
All ages	66.02	61.92	132.3	119.5	132.2	119.7

[a]Source: Kemsley, 1950, Table 1, p. 163. Kemsley editor, Social Survey, London.
[b]Estimated height without shoes.
[c]Estimated nude weight.
[d]Fewer than 100 females in this interval.
[e]Fewer than 50 males and 50 females in this age interval.

TABLE 48.[a] EXPECTATION OF LIFE FOR WHITE MALES AND FEMALES BY GEOGRAPHIC DIVISION.

| | EXPECTATION OF LIFE (IN YEARS) | | | |
| | WHITE | MALES | WHITE | FEMALES |
Geographic Division	Age 0	Age 45	Age 0	Age 45
United States	66.3	26.9	72.0	31.1
New England	66.9	26.6	72.1	30.8
Middle Atlantic	66.2	26.0	71.2	29.9
East North Central	66.5	26.8	71.9	30.8
West North Central	67.8	28.2	73.3	32.1
South Atlantic	66.0	26.9	72.5	31.7
East South Central	66.0	27.6	71.8	31.6
West South Central	66.1	27.7	72.6	32.6
Mountain States	65.4	27.4	71.9	32.0
Pacific States	66.1	26.6	72.9	31.8

[a] SOURCE: *United States Vital Statistics*, 1949–51.

TABLE 49. AGE AND TOTAL NITROGEN OF HUMAN BRAIN.

Age (Years)	Dry substance (%)	Nitrogen (%)	Nitrogen in fresh tissue[a] (%)
21–30	23.2	7.27	1.69
31–40	23.2	7.30	1.69
41–50	22.9	7.40	1.69
51–60	22.8	7.55	1.72
61–70	22.5	7.53	1.69
71–74	21.7	7.28	1.58
75–80	21.7	7.12	1.55
81–84	22.0	6.85	1.51
85–90	22.0	6.80	1.50

[a] Calculated from Bürger's (1957) data on percentages of dry substances and of total nitrogen in dry substance.

TABLE 50. EFFECT OF PARENTAL AGE ON MEAN LIFE-SPANS OF 1429 SENESCENT TWIN INDEX PAIRS AND THEIR SIBLINGS.

	MOTHER DIED			FATHER DIED			EITHER PARENT DIED			BOTH PARENTS DIED		
	Under 55	55–69	70 and Over	Under 55	55–69	70 and Over	Under 55	55–69	70 and Over	Under 55	55–69	70 and Over
Twins and sibs:												
Sons	55.8	58.8	59.6	56.3	57.2	60.2	55.9	57.4	59.6	51.8	59.6	61.4
Daughters	64.8	60.0	66.4	63.0	64.3	65.3	64.1	62.0	65.7	62.1	59.3	66.8
Total	58.5	57.8	62.1	58.5	60.0	61.5	58.5	59.0	61.8	55.9	59.4	62.9
Sibs only:												
Sons	48.6	51.6	52.9	48.5	50.4	53.4	48.5	50.9	53.1	45.8	55.1	55.2
Daughters	55.7	50.8	60.0	51.6	57.5	58.3	53.7	54.3	59.1	54.3	55.8	60.7
Total	51.7	51.2	56.4	49.9	54.0	55.8	50.9	52.7	56.1	49.5	55.4	57.9

Franz J. Kallmann and Lissy F. Jarvik, *Handbook of Aging and the Individual*, p. 246.

TABLE 51. PERCENTAGE WATER AND NITROGEN CONTENT OF RABBIT BRAIN PARTS.

	AGE									
	77 Days (5)[a]		4 Years (2)		5 Years (4)		6 Years (2)		10 Years (1)	
	H_2O	Nitrogen	H_2O	Nitrogen	H_2O	Nitrogen	H_2O	Nitrogen	H_2O	Nitrogen
Cortex	82.5	1.97	80.9		79.8	2.05	81.3	1.85	73.3	2.41
Caudate	80.4	2.14	79.5		80.1	2.02	79.5	1.96	80.4	2.29
Thalamus	80.4	1.92			77.5	1.74	77.6	1.87	81.7	2.11
Colliculi	78.9	1.90	76.0		75.0	1.97	76.4	1.92	76.2	1.99
Cerebellum:										
Lateral lobes	80.0	1.97	78.8		77.7	2.02	78.9	1.98	67.7	2.00
Paraflocculi	80.6	2.02	78.8		77.5	2.11	78.9	1.97	77.3	2.07
Vermis	80.9	2.13	78.3		78.2	2.20	79.9	1.93	78.9	2.36
Medulla	74.6	1.85	70.8		70.1	1.94	71.1	1.86	70.5	1.98
Cervical spinal cord	73.0	1.81			66.7	1.88	69.2	1.65	67.6	1.94

[a]Number of animals in parentheses.

Williamina A. and Harold E. Himwich, *Handbook of Aging and the Individual*, p. 206.

700 WHOLE ANIMAL LEVEL

TABLE 52.[a] ASCORBIC ACID CONCENTRATION IN HUMAN PITUITARY, CEREBRAL CORTEX, MYOCARDIUM, AND PECTORAL MUSCLE.

Age group	PITUITARY		CEREBRAL CORTEX				MYOCARDIUM				PECTORAL MUSCLE			
	Number[b]	mg/g wet weight	Number[b]	mg/g wet weight	Number[b]	mg/g tissue nitrogen	Number[b]	mg/g wet weight	Number	mg/g tissue nitrogen	Number[b]	mg/g wet weight	Number[b]	mg/g tissue nitrogen
30–39	6	0.988	6	0.180	6	14.1	5	0.055	5	1.8	4	0.043	4	1.6
40–49	4	.447	5	.122	5	10.4	5	.038	5	1.5	5	.028	5	1.1
50–59	15	.521	16	.140	14	11.1	13	.030	12	1.3	14	.030	13	1.2
60–69	17	.511	16	.153	16	11.4	14	.040	14	1.6	13	.033	13	1.0
70–79	4	.497	11	.149	11	11.9	11	.039	10	1.6	10	.031	10	1.2
80–89	1	0.455	1	0.103	1	8.0	4	0.049	2	2.1	3	0.019	1	0.4

[a] Adapted from Schaus, *J. Clin. Nutr.*, 1957, 5: 39–41.
[b] Number of specimens.

TABLE 53. MAXIMUM STRENGTH AT DIFFERENT AGES AS A PERCENTAGE OF STRENGTH AT AGES 20-29.

		AGE RANGE					
Author and Muscle Group	20–29		30–39	40–49	50–59	60–69	70–79
1. Uffland (1935):							
Grip, right hand	100	(41.6)[a]	96.4	90.9	78.0	64.9	
Biceps, right flexor	100	(31.8)	93.4	83.6	66.0	54.1	
Wrist, right flexor	100	(29.3)	96.9	93.1	85.9	75.4	
Thumb, right flexor	100	(12.4)	96.8	96.8	85.3	79.8	
Wrist, right extensor	100	(24.3)	99.2	94.2	88.9	79.3	
Back strength	100	(134.6)	95.4	89.8	79.2	64.3	
2. Galton; see Ruger and Stoessiger (1927):							
Grip, right hand	100	(37.4)	99.8	97.8	93.2	85.9	74.9
Pull (across chest)	100	(33.7)	99.4	95.1	87.9	78.0	65.5
3. Cathcart et al. (1935):							
a) Employed men:							
Grip, right hand	100	(52.7)	99.4	96.3	91.3	82.2	
Back strength	100	(171.6)	100	97.0	93.1	85.3	
b) Unemployed men:							
Grip, right hand	100	(46.1)	97.1	94.1	87.2	80.9	
Back strength	100	(150.2)	99.3	93.7	87.7	84.9	
4. Burke et al. (1953):							
Maximum grip strength	100	(56.3)	95.0	91.5	86.9	78.8	64.4

		AGE RANGE						
	23–27		28–32	33–37	38–42	43–47	48–52	53–68
5. Fisher and Birren (1947):								
Grip, right hand	100	(56.0)	96.8	95.2	93.5	89.9	86.2	83.6

[a]Numbers in parentheses are kilograms.

A. T. Welford, *Handbook of Aging and the Individual*, p. 565.
James E. Birren, ed., Univ. of Chicago Press 1959.

TABLE 54. EFFECT OF AGE AND PUPIL SIZE ON CRITICAL FLICKER FUSION.

	CRITICAL FLICKER FUSION	
Age	Pupils not dilated	Pupils dilated
20–30	40.2	42.8
31–40	39.2	42.6
41–50	34.4	42.6
51–60	31.8	40.8
61–70	31.6	38.4

*Source: Weekers and Roussel, *Ophthalmologia*, 1946, **112**, 305–19.

TABLE 55. SIMPLE AUDITORY REACTION TIMES OF FINGER, JAW AND FOOT.
(In Milliseconds)

	AGE GROUPS (32 SUBJECTS IN EACH)		Difference Between Age Groups
	19–36	61–91	
Finger	182	232	50
Jaw	194	254	60
Foot	202	260	58

*From Birren and Botwinick, *J. Gerontol.*, 1955a, **10**, 429–32.

TABLE 56. REACTION TIMES AND MOVEMENT TIMES IN AN AIMING TASK.
(In Seconds)

	AGE GROUP			
	Twenties	Thirties	Forties	Fifties
Time from appearance of signal to beginning of responding movement	0.86	0.99	1.29	1.37
Duration of responding movement	1.18	1.20	1.14	1.22

*From Szafran, *Quart. J. Exper. Psychol.*, 1951, **3**, 111–18.

TABLE 57.[a] MEAN NUMBER OF NERVOUS SYMPTOMS FOR EACH AGE GROUP FOR THREE GROUPS OF ENLISTED NAVAL PERSONNEL VARYING IN DEGREE OF STRESS.

Experience group	AGE GROUP					
	18–20	21–23	24–26	27–29	30–32	33–45
United States only	3.2	3.9	4.5	5.0	5.3	5.3
Overseas non-combat	4.8	5.0	5.8	6.1	6.9	8.2
Overseas combat	6.0	6.2	6.6	7.2	8.2	8.7

[a]Source: After Kuhlen, 1951. (unpublished)

TABLE 58.[a] PERCENTAGE OF POSITIVE REACTIONS OF PUPILS TO LIGHT AND ACCOMMODATION.

Age	Number of subjects	LIGHT		ACCOMMODATION		NEITHER	
		One	Both	One	Both	One	Both
65–69	16	6	69	0	69	6	12
70–74	57	9	60	0	60	9	25
75–79	72	12	54	7	36	10	24
80–84	32	3	50	0	19	3	44
85–91	9	0	33	0	0	0	67
Mean	–	9	54	3	41	8	28

[a]Source: Howell, *Brit. Med. J.*, 1949, **1**, (4592), 56–58.

TABLE 59. AGE AND DESOXYRIBONUCLEIC ACID IN HUMAN BRAIN.

Age (Years)	Brain weight[a] (g)	DRY WEIGHT[a] %	DRY WEIGHT[a] Grams	DNA[a] (%)	DNA (g)
16–20	1384	22.2	307.2	0.75	23.04
21–30	1394	23.2	323.4	0.77	24.90
31–40	1375	23.2	319.0	0.54	17.23
41–50	1358	22.9	311.0	0.68	21.15
51–60	1345	22.8	306.7	1.05	32.20
61–70	1310	22.5	294.8	1.23	30.65
71–80	1263	21.7	274.1	1.23	33.71
81–84	1166[b]	22.0[b]	256.5	1.17	30.01
85–90	1166[b]	22.0[b]	256.5	1.38	35.40
90–93	1166[b]	22.0[b]	256.5	1.44	36.94

[a] Adapted from Bürger (1957).
[b] Average given by Bürger (1957) for 81–93 years.

TABLE 60.[a] AGE AND WATER CONTENT OF RAT BRAIN.

Age (Days)	Water (%)	Age (Days)	Water (%)
8	88.2	182	78.2
9	88.1	204	78.0
15	84.6	248	77.9
25	81.2	289	77.3
45	79.3	328	77.3
61	79.3	363	77.5
82	78.7	409	77.5
97	78.5	452	77.3
119	78.4	489	77.2
144	78.4	529	76.7
169	78.5		

[a] Adapted from Donaldson & Hatai (1931).

A. Williamina and H. E. Himwich, *Neurochemistry of Aging*, p. 200 and 209.

TABLE 61.[a] CHANGES IN THE VARIABILITY OF SIMPLE AUDITORY REACTION TIMES.
(In Milliseconds)

	AGE GROUP 18–39	AGE GROUP 65–75	AGE GROUP 76–86
Variation between subjects (standard deviation of median readings)	10.6	16.4	22.2
Variation between readings (mean of the semi-interquartile ranges for the individual subjects)	9.3	11.0	14.0
Mean reaction time (mean of the medians for the individual subjects)	122	131	145

[a] Obrist, *J. Psychol*., 1953, **35**, 259–66.

TABLE 62.[a] PREVALENCE AND ANNUAL INCIDENCE RATES FOR IMPAIRED HEARING (ANY STAGE) ACCORDING TO AGE AND SEX, BASED ON NATIONAL HEALTH SURVEY EXPERIENCE OF 1935 AND 1936.

Age Period	PREVALENCE DEAFNESS CASES [ANY STAGE][b] PER 1000 POPULATION		INCIDENCE AVERAGE ANNUAL RATE[c] OF NEW CASES PER 100,000 POPULATION	
	Male	Female	Male	Female
Under 5	0.49	0.43	–	–
5–14	2.95	2.26	33	24
15–24	3.51	2.93	6	7
25–34	4.76	4.99	13	21
35–44	9.70	9.28	49	43
45–54	14.93	15.45	52	62
55–64	29.27	26.43	143	110
65–74	73.64	54.68	444	283
75 and over	175.08	135.95	1014	813

[a]Source: Beasley (1940). W. C. Laryngoscope **50**, 856–905.
[b]Equivalent to an average hearing loss of 47 db. or more for 1024 and 2048 cps.
[c]New cases per year at each single-year age throughout specified age period.

TABLE 63.[a] DEMOGRAPHIC AND SEX-SPECIFIC VARIATIONS IN LIFE-EXPECTANCY.

	DIFFERENTIAL LIFE-EXPECTANCY									
	At birth		Age 40		Age 60		Age 70		Age 85	
	Male	Female	Male	Female	Male	Female	Male	Female	Male	Female
Brazil (1949–51)	49.80	55.96	25.45	31.21	12.80	16.60	8.34	10.68	3.57	4.49
Canada (1950–52)	66.33	70.83	32.45	35.63	16.49	18.64	10.41	11.62	4.27	4.57
England and Wales (1954)	67.58	73.05	31.49	36.21	15.13	18.83	9.33	11.64	3.97	4.72
France (1950–51)	63.6	69.3	30.4	35.0	15.1	18.1	9.1	11.1	3.4	4.2
India (1941–50)	32.45	31.66	20.53	21.06	10.13	11.33	6.51	7.53	3.06	3.69
Japan (1955)	63.88	68.41	31.15	35.11	15.33	18.59	9.56	12.05	–	–
Norway (1946–50)	69.25	72.65	35.16	36.96	18.39	19.45	11.43	12.03	4.55	4.64
Sweden (1946–50)	69.04	71.58	33.84	35.29	17.05	18.03	10.40	10.89	3.89	4.11
United States (1955)										
White	67.4	73.6	31.8	36.7	16.2	19.4	10.5	12.4	5.1	5.4
Others	61.0	65.8	28.7	31.9	15.7	18.3	11.9	14.0	8.1	8.9
West Germany (1952–53)	64.56	68.48	32.32	34.67	16.20	17.46	9.84	10.42	3.72	4.02

[a]Source: *United Nations Yearbook*, 1956.

TABLE 64. DISTRIBUTION BY AGE GROUP OF GREEK SKULLS (FOUND ON THE MAINLAND) FROM DIFFERENT PERIODS.

	Neolithic -Early Bronze (3500- 2000 B.C.)	Middle Bronze (2000- 1400 B.C.)	Late Helladic III (1400- 1150 B.C.)	Cephallenia, Submycenean[a] (1200- 1050 B.C.)	Early Iron Central Greece (1150- 650 B.C.)	Classical Period (650- 150 B.C.)	Roman Period (150 B.C.- 450 A.D.)	Byzantine Period (450- 1300 A.D.)	Total Series
				MALES					
Subadult (19)	7.4%	0 %	0 %	0 %	3.7%	1.9%	0 %	3.2%	8%
Young adult (28)	55.6	43.5	43.9	33.3	37.0	26.9	27.8	51.6	39.4
Middle-aged adult (46)	33.3	52.2	48.8	63.4	59.3	61.6	66.6	42.0	54.6
Old adult (66)	3.7	4.3	7.3	3.3	0	9.6	5.6	3.2	5.2
Number of skulls	27	23	41	30	27	52	18	31	249
				FEMALES					
Subadult (19)	17.6	23.1	18.5	9.1	18.7	11.1	0	11.1	14.1
Young adult (28)	64.7	53.8	70.4	63.6	50.0	55.6	80.0	66.7	63.0
Middle-aged adult (46)	17.7	23.1	11.1	27.3	31.3	29.6	20.0	22.2	22.2
Old adult (66)	0	0	0	0	0	3.7	0	0	.7
Number of skulls	17	13	27	11	16	27	15	9	135

[a]The Cephallenia skulls are geographically rather than chronologically separated from the first subperiod of the Early Iron Age of Central or Circum-Isthmian Greece.

J. Lawrence Angel, *J. of Gerontol.*, 1947, 2, (1), p. 19, January.

TABLE 65. AGE CHANGES IN KIDNEYS OF WISTAR INSTITUTE RATS.

Average size of glomeruli (glomerular tufts) in different age groups of Wistar Institute rats, as obtained by measurement of short and long diameters of 50 glomeruli in each animal. The probable error is given for each diameter. Kidney weights for each group are included in this table.

Size characteristics of glomeruli and combined weight of two kidneys	Group I 75–100 days (9 animals)	Group II 300 days (11 animals)	Group IIIab 868–1170 days (30 animals)
Average size of glomeruli			
Short diameter in μ	73.43 ± 1.093	74.40 ± 1.449	96.45 ± 0.689
Long diameter, in μ	89.28 ± 0.999	91.30 ± 1.884	117.76 ± 0.809
Range in size within group			
Short diameter, μ	66.02 – 79.50	54.82 – 82.80	83.92 – 110.24
Long diameter, μ	83.90 – 97.16	67.76 – 106.84	103.58 – 133.06
Combined weight of two kidneys, g	1.989 ± 0.095	2.149 ± 0.127	2.687 ± 0.035

Andrew Warren and Dennis Pruett, *Am. J. Anat.*, 1957, **100**, (1), p. 55, January.

TABLE 66. ALBUMIN AND GLOBULIN FRACTIONS IN HUMAN BLOOD SERUM AT DIFFERENT AGES.

Age (years)	PERCENT OF TOTAL PROTEINS		Alb./Glob.
	Albumin	Globulin	
10–20	63.35	36 65	1.73
21–30	61.65	38.35	1.61
31–40	57.88	42.12	1.37
41–50	56.80	43.20	1.32
51–60	54.14	45.86	1.28
61–70	52.85	47.15	1.12
Over 70	51.87	48.13	1.08

Nocker and Bemm. Quot. by Burger, *Alternund Krankheit,* p. 270, G. Thieme, Leipzig, 1957.

TABLE 67. FIBRIN CONTENT IN HUMAN PLASMA.

Age (years)	FIBRIN CONTENT, g PERCENT	
	in men	in women
10–20	0.321	0.364
20–30	0.366	0.372
30–40	0.374	0.394
40–50	0.435	0.440
50–60	0.457	0.471
60–70	0.461	0.481

Z. Schultz, *Altersf.*, 1951, 5: 196.

TABLE 68. CIRCULATING GONADOTROPIN AND TESTOSTERONE LEVELS, URINARY STEROID EXCRETION, BONE MATURATION AND WHOLE BODY ^{40}K CONTENT IN 253 MALES IN RELATION TO AGE AND SEXUAL DEVELOPMENT.

Age (yr)	Number	Puberty stage[a]	CLINICAL DATA					24-HR URINE CONTENT							SERUM		PLASMA
			Testis diameter cm	Penis length cm	Bone maturation score [47]	^{40}K cpm	^{40}K cpm/kg	Creatinine g	Total 17-KS[b] mg	Androsterone mg	Etiocholanolone mg	DHA[c] mg	Estrogens µg	17-OCHS[d] mg	FSH[e] µg LER-907/100 ml	LH[f] µg LER-907/100 ml	Testosterone ng/100 ml
0.2-2.0	11	P_1	1.4 ± 0.4[g]	2.7 ± 0.5	8 ± 7										7.0 ± 2.4	1.2 ± 0.4	13 ± 10
2.1-4.0	7	P_1	1.2 ± 0.4	3.3 ± 0.4	53 ± 16										7.5 ± 1.4	1.3 ± 0.6	11 ± 4
4.1-6.0	13	P_1	1.5 ± 0.6	3.9 ± 0.9	127 ± 31										7.8 ± 2.5	1.5 ± 0.5	20 ± 9
6.1-8.0	21	P_1	1.8 ± 0.3	4.2 ± 0.8	199 ± 55	59.9 ± 6.3	2.7 ± 0.1	0.49 ± 0.08	0.9 ± 0.4	0.07 ± 0.05	0.07 ± 0.05	0.02 ± 0.01	2.2 ± 0.5	2.8 ± 1.2	10.0 ± 1.5	1.7 ± 0.5	14 ± 7
8.1-10.0	25	P_1	2.0 ± 0.5	4.9 ± 1.0	321 ± 69	74.1 ± 6.9	2.5 ± 0.3	0.50 ± 0.10	1.2 ± 0.6	0.09 ± 0.08	0.09 ± 0.08	0.02 ± 0.01	2.5 ± 0.8	3.3 ± 1.1	10.3 ± 2.8	1.9 ± 0.4	21 ± 12
10.1-12.0	53	P_2	2.7 ± 0.7	5.2 ± 1.3	494 ± 137	92.7 ± 11.7	2.3 ± 0.4	0.85 ± 0.19	2.5 ± 1.1	0.35 ± 0.22	0.35 ± 0.22	0.07 ± 0.05	5.2 ± 1.7	4.7 ± 1.6	12.6 ± 3.6	2.0 ± 0.5	41 ± 46
12.1-14.0	51	P_2	3.4 ± 0.8	6.2 ± 2.0	628 ± 150	110.0 ± 20.2	2.6 ± 0.4	1.01 ± 0.16	3.3 ± 1.3	0.54 ± 0.32	0.54 ± 0.32	0.20 ± 0.20	5.9 ± 3.4	4.8 ± 1.3	13.6 ± 3.1	2.5 ± 0.8	131 ± 172
14.1-16.0	26	P_3	4.1 ± 1.0	8.6 ± 2.4	811 ± 155	155.8 ± 27.7	2.7 ± 0.5	1.31 ± 0.34	5.2 ± 2.0	1.80 ± 0.31	1.80 ± 0.31	1.03 ± 0.30	16.2 ± 2.7	5.1 ± 2.7	15.8 ± 4.1	3.1 ± 0.7	328 ± 211
16.1-18.0	10	P_4	5.0 ± 0.5	9.9 ± 1.7	967 ± 28	189.2 ± 19.1	2.9 ± 0.4								15.7 ± 3.5	4.1 ± 1.1	532 ± 191
18.1-20.0	6	P_5	5.0 ± 0.3	11.0 ± 1.1	992	189.6 ± 19.4	2.8 ± 0.3								20.2 ± 6.1	3.6 ± 0.6	564 ± 157
20.1-25.0	30	P_5	5.2 ± 0.6	12.4 ± 1.6	1000	190.1 ± 20.0	2.8 ± 0.3								17.0 ± 3.9	4.2 ± 1.0	605 ± 194

[a] This represents the stage of puberty most prevalent in each age group.
[b] 17-KS: 17-ketosteroids.
[c] DHA: dehydroepiandrosterone.
[d] 17-OHCS: 17-hydroxycorticosteroids.
[e] FSH: follicle-stimulating hormone.
[f] LH: luteinizing hormone.
[g] Mean ± standard deviation.

Jeremy S. D. Winter & Charles Faiman, *Pediat. Res.*, 6, 1972, 126-135, "Pituitary-Gonadal Relations in Male Children and Adolescents."

TABLE 69. AGING OF PIG SKIN.

Composition and calculations	Fetus 46 days	Fetus 90 days	Newborn	3 weeks	4-6 weeks	Adult
Water[a]	937	902	836	782	778	685
Na^a	135.5	106.4	131.6	115.3	111.5	119.1
K^a	30.2	43.8	47.2	56.9	53.8	38.2
Cl^a	100.0	89.8	95.7	95.5	99.6	110.9
Ca^a	10.9	12.5	10.9	13.8	10.8	13.4
Mg^a	4.6	8.0	7.9	10.0	10.0	6.4
$\Sigma (c_i)''$ [b]	273.4	250.2	283.9	279.6	275.3	278.1
$\Sigma (c_i)'' z_i{}^a$	812,	80.9	101.9	100.5	86.5	66.2
Equivalent weight	830	1,350	1,950	2,750	3,300	7,000
$\Delta \mu_{Na}{}^{o}$ [c]	0.20	0.29	0.14	0.16	0.16	0.17
D'' [c]	70	67	74	73	73	72
$\Delta \mu_{Na}{}^{c}$	0.17	0.12	0.08	0.02	0.01	0.05
E (mV.)[c]	-7.5	-5.3	-3.5	-0.9	-0.4	-2.2
Collagen N (g)	0.43	4.0	11.5	22.8	39.7	70.8

[a]Water in g per kg. ion concentrations in meq. per kg water. $\Sigma (c_i)'' z_i$ expressed as meq. per kg water. Analytical data of Widdowson and Dickerson [2].
[b]$\Sigma (c_i)''$ expressed as mmoles per kg water.
[c]Calculated by means of equations (5), (11), (12), (13) and (14). Values of $\Delta \mu_{Na}{}^{o}$ and $\Delta \mu_{Na}$ in kcal per equivalent.

N. R. Joseph, H. R. Catchpole, and M. B. Engel, *Gerontologia*, 1969, **15**.

27
AGING AND GASTROINTESTINAL FUNCTION

Kowit Bhanthumnavin
and
Marvin M. Schuster

INTRODUCTION

Nowhere in the body is cellular turnover more rapid than in the gastrointestinal tract. The intestines have a greater surface area than any other part of the body. Vast quantities of materials are secreted and absorbed daily by gastrointestinal organs, and motility is active and vigorous in the tubular components of the alimentary tract. Therefore, it would appear that this organ system should be a fertile area for the study of the effects of aging on function and structure. The following discussion attempts to compile and evaluate information currently available in this area.

ESOPHAGUS

Motility

The upper esophageal sphincter at resting stage is closed, and its resting pressure is higher than the adjacent areas. Upon swallowing, the upper esophageal sphincter relaxes, allowing a bolus to pass through, then closes forcing the bolus into the upper esophagus. Transport of the bolus is accomplished normally by a peristaltic contraction. There are two types of esophageal peristalsis, primary and secondary types. Primary peristaltic wave occurs following deglutition, while the secondary peristaltic wave occurs when the upper portion of the esophagus is distended locally either by an experimental balloon or reflux of stomach contents. Secondary peristalsis is indistinguishable from the primary type.

In certain circumstances, in the distal one-to two-thirds of the esophagus, a localized series of ring-like, simultaneous, nonperistaltic contractions occurs spontaneously or after swallowing, giving an appearance, in a barium study, of a "cork screw" pattern. These are termed "tertiary" contractions and they appear to increase with age.

The lower esophageal sphincter, a physiological zone, has a resting pressure which is higher than the adjacent esophageal and stomach areas. Mechanical and chemical factors, as well as drugs, have been shown to influence its resting pressure and strength of contractions (Table 1).

Recent work suggests that endogenous gastrin may play a role in maintaining lower esophageal sphincter contraction (Lipshutz and Cohen 1972). Upon swallowing, the lower sphincter

TABLE 1. FACTORS AFFECTING TONAL QUALITY OF THE LOWER ESOPHAGEAL SPHINCTER

Factors that increase tone	Factors that decrease tone
Hormones: gastrin	Hormones: secretin, estrogens, progesterones
Alkalies: antacids orally	Acids: antral gastric acid, ingested acids
Drugs: methacholine, bethanechol, metoclopramide	Smoking
	Vagotomy
	Drugs: alcohol, anticholinergics, essence of peppermint
	Rapid drinking of iced beverages
	Fatty food

immediately relaxes and remains so until the peristaltic wave passes through it.

Patterns of esophageal motility have been studied, by both manometric and cineradiographic technics, in a group of nonagenarians without known esophageal disease (Soergel, Zboralske and Amberg, 1964; Zboralske, Amberg, Soergel, 1964). In this age group, peristaltic waves occur in only 50 percent of swallows as compared with 90–95 percent in a normal young age group. Furthermore, 45 percent of the swallows were followed by nonperistaltic or tertiary waves, while only 10 percent occurred in the young. The lower esophageal sphincter failed to relax in over half of the swallows, and there was a significant delay of esophageal emptying in the elderly. This pattern was called "presbyesophagus."

It would be of interest to study esophageal motility patterns of individuals on a longitudinal basis. This type of study could answer questions as to whether changes observed in presbyesophagus were age-related or the consequence of other underlying diseases, such as diabetes mellitus (Mandelstam and Lieber, 1969).

Other esophageal disorders, which may occur more often in the elderly, include diffuse spasm, achalasia, and scleroderma of the esophagus (Wolf, Brahms and Khilnani, 1959).

Hiatal Hernia

Hiatal hernia is common in the elderly. In persons under the age of 30 years its incidence is less than 10 percent, but increases to 60 percent or more in persons over the age of 60 years (Wolf, Brahms, and Khilnani, 1959; Pridie, 1966; Stilson, Sanders and Gardiner,

1969). However, only a small number of hiatal hernia patients have reflux symptoms. This may be explained by the observation that the lower esophageal sphincter pressure was neither influenced by its location above or below the diaphragm, nor by any change in surrounding pressure (Fyke, Code and Schlegel, 1956). The resting lower esophageal sphincter pressure is decreased in patients with symptomatic gastroesophageal reflux, whether hernia is present or not (Winans and Harris, 1967). This has raised the possibility that gastrin deficiency may be present and may be an important factor responsible in decreased sphincter pressure (Rosenberg and Harris, 1971; Cohen and Harris, 1972; Lipshutz, Gaskins, Lukash, and Sode, 1974).

Studies (Farrell, Castell, and McGuigan, 1974) of the responsiveness of the lower esophageal sphincter, in patients with gastroesophageal reflux and under normal controls, to protein meals, acid, alkaline perfusion, and pentagastrin infusion suggests that reduced gastrin release may contribute to the development of lower esophageal incompetence. However, diminished lower esophageal sphincter responsiveness to pentagastrin, and the absence of significant differences in basal serum gastrin levels suggests that additional factors are involved in the production of lower esophageal sphincter incompetence.

The resting lower esophageal pressure in pernicious anemia is lower than normal, and pressure responds poorly to exogenous as well as endogenous gastrin stimulations. There is no correlation between the high serum gastrin levels and lower esophageal sphincter pressure in these patients (Farrell, Nebel, McGuire, and Castell, 1973).

Achalasia of the esophagus is characterized by a failure of the lower esophageal sphincter to relax upon swallowing, together with non-peristaltic contraction in the body. The precise mechanism is not known. The lower esophageal sphincter in this disease is supersensitive to gastrin (Cohen, Lipshutz, and Hughes, 1971).

In conclusion, the normal esophagus in the aged responds differently than in the young. There is decreased peristaltic response, increased nonperistaltic response, delayed transit time, and frequent failure of the lower esophageal sphincter to relax upon swallowing. Also, motility disturbances may occur as a result of other underlying patho-physiological states that commonly occur in the aged. Recent work (Hollis and Castell 1974) suggests that esophageal motor changes in the elderly are more likely caused by disease than by aging, per se. The only change in motility in healthy aged subjects was reduced amplitude of contraction, assumed to be due to weakened esophageal smooth muscle. It would be pertinent to observe esophageal motility change in a longitudinal follow up.

STOMACH

Motility

The rate of gastric emptying, [as a function of aging], has not been studied. However, the emptying rate is delayed in atrophic gastritis (which is age-related) and in gastric cancer (Davies, Kirkpatrick and Owen, Shields R. 1971).

Secretion

Basal and maximal histamine-stimulated acid output decreases more in men, with age, than in women (Baron, 1963). In both men and women aged 50 and over, the basal and histalog-stimulated secretion is less than in the age group 20-49 (Grossman, Kirsner and Gillespie, 1963). There is a further decrease in acid secretion in men aged 60 and over. Females secrete acid amounting to 55 percent of male basal secretion and 65 percent of male histalog-stimulated secretion. Unfortunately, there were no histological studies of these

patients with which to correlate the reduction in gastric acid secretion in the aged group, and the dose of histalog used was only 0.5 mg/kg of body weight. Andrews, Haneman, Arnold, Booth, and Taylor (1967) found that all but one of their 24 asymptomatic subjects over 60 years of age showed atrophic gastritis, and that acid secretion was decreased following maximal histamine stimulation test.

Recently, Bernier, Vidon, and Mignon (1973) found no difference in acid output at any age, if the results are expressed against the exchangeable potassium pool and not body weight.

Atrophic Gastritis

The subject of gastritis has recently been reviewed (Jeffries, 1973; Phillips, 1972). The common form of gastritis in the elderly is chronic atrophic gastritis. Siurala, Isokoski, Varis, and Kekki, M., (1968) and Isokoski, Krohn, Varis, (1969) studied a random sample of the adult population of a Finnish commune by gastric biopsy and with tests for parietal cell antibody (PCA). They showed that (a) 40 (28 percent) of 142 subjects biopsied had atrophic gastritis; (b) females exceeded males by a factor of two; (c) there was a rise in the prevalence of atrophic gastritis with advancing age; and (d) 8 percent of the sample had a positive test for PCA.

Atrophic gastritis is histologically characterized by thinning of the gastric mucosa and muscular wall. The mucosa is diffusely infiltrated with lymphocytes, eosinophils and plasma cells. The gastric glands are destroyed or lost. This process may be manifested as patchy lesions over the gastric mucosal surface, or it may be confined to a specific region such as the antral or fundic area. The severity of the lesion is graded according to the degree of loss of gastric glands. Gastric atrophy is characterized by an apparent loss of normal fundic glands. In pyloric metaplasia, residual gastric glands may be replaced by pyloric type glands.

With increasing severity, the gastric mucosa may be transformed into cells resembling intestinal epithelial cells (consisting of mucus-secreting goblet cells, simple columnar cells with brush border) and also Paneth and

Kultschitzky cells at the base of the crypts of Lieberkuhn. There is no villus formation. This change may be recognized by an endoscopic examination (Korn, 1974). Chronic gastritis is frequently found in association with gastric ulcer, pernicious anemia, recurrent gastritis, and gastric carcinoma. There is pathological evidence that metaplasia of the gastric mucosa to an intestinal type of epithelium is a precancerous condition (Morson, 1962).

In a review of the nature and significance of chronic atrophic gastritis (Strickland and Mackay, 1973), two types of lesions (Types A and B) were described on the basis of gastric morphology, function, and pathogenesis. Type A atrophic gastritis shows sparing of the antral mucosa, a positive PCA reaction, [diffuse character] changes in the corpus mucosa, and severe impairment of gastric secretion. Type B atrophic gastritis shows antral involvement, a negative PCA reaction, change in the corpus mucosa of focal character, and moderate impairment of gastric secretion. Patients with Type B gastritis tend to have various gastrointestinal symptoms and a higher incidence of cancer, while Type A gastritis is probably genetically determined and associated with pernicious anemia and other autoimmune diseases. Prednisone has been shown to stimulate regeneration of gastric parietal cells in patients with atrophic gastritis and pernicious anemia, particularly those who had the highest titer of circulating parietal cell antibodies (Jeffries, Todd and Sleisenger, 1966).

Although the parietal cell antibodies are found in atrophic gastritis, a causal relationship is not clear. There are other factors that cause gastric mucosa injury which, if prolonged or repeated, may lead to chronic atrophic gastritis (there has been no definite documentation for this). Potentially injurious factors include aspirin (Palmer, 1972; Cooke, 1973), alcohol (Lawson, 1964), bile salts and acids, and hypogammaglobulinemia (Twomey, Jordan, Jarrold, et al., 1969).

Significant numbers of gastric ulcer patients are middle-aged and elderly, with a slight male predominance occurring: 14 percent over the age of 60 (Cutler, 1958; Fenger, Amdrup,

Christiansen, 1973), 13 percent over the age of 65 (Levrat, Pasquier, Lambet, and Tissot, 1966). Relatively few ulcers developed for the first time after the age of 60, but those that do appear are often accompanied by severe hemorrhage or perforation (Cutler, 1958). Hitchock, MacLean and Sullivan, (1957) reported that advanced age, with reduced cardiac, renal and especially pulmonary reserve, and gastric ulcer are the major causes of high mortality in patients with bleeding peptic ulcer.

In conclusion, changes in the gastric physiology in the aged are the hyposecretion of acid, intrinsic factors, and pepsin, and the increased incidence of atrophic gastritis leading to the development of intestinal metaplasia. The latter change is thought to be a precancerous condition. Atrophic gastritis increases the risk of carcinoma of the stomach twenty-fold over age-matched controls (Hitchock, MacLean and Sullivan, 1957). Diminished absorption of iron and vitamin B_{12} occurs as a consequence of the physiological changes. Significant numbers of elderly patients have gastric ulcer and frequently, its complications. Bleeding gastric ulcer in elderly persons, especially with diminished pulmonary reserve, carries a high mortality risk.

There is little information on age-related changes in gastric motility and emptying and control factors. Changes in these functions may account for some of the nonspecific, upper gastrointestinal symptoms in the elderly.

SMALL INTESTINE

The data concerning age-related morphological changes in the small intestine are meager. This is partly due to difficulty in obtaining specimens before significant autolysis occurs. In humans, Peyer's patches are decreased in number and there is reduction in number of lymphatic follicles in individual patches (Cornes, 1965). However, Chin (1973) found, by electron microscopy in the mouse, that most of the age-related changes were seen in the stroma and the reticular cells rather than in the lymphoid components of the patch.

Cell renewal or transit time in the crypts of the descending colon is prolonged in aged mice

(Cameron, 1972). In 19-month-old mice, the transit time is 54 hours, while it is only 40 hours in the 3-month-old mice. The transit time of mouse small intestine mucosal epithelium is also prolonged in the aged (Lesher, Fry, and Kohn, 1961). Gorbach, Nahas, Lerner, and Weinstein (1967) studied the microflora of the feces of 70 normal individuals, aged 20 to 100 years. They found that elderly subjects, 70-100 years old, harbored fewer anaerobic lactobacilli and larger numbers of fungus and coliforms than younger persons.

Information on intestinal enzymes in the aged is scarce. Using glucose-1-phosphate and glucose-6-phosphate as substrates to study the kinetics of intestinal phosphomonoesterases in female mice aged 11 months and 34 months, Sayeed (1967) found diminished value of V_{max} but no differences in K_m value in the older animals. This finding suggests that there is a decrease in enzymatic concentration in the aged, but that the enzyme structure remains the same.

Although dietary history in the elderly is often unreliable and direct measurement of diet intake is tedious, evidence strongly suggests that reduced nutritional intake is the important factor in folic acid and ascorbic acid deficiencies. Poor income, physical and mental deterioration, loneliness, and intercurrent diseases are, to a large part, responsible for the poor intake of food in the elderly. Despite increased evidence of low serum vitamin levels, clinical manifestations of the appropriate vitamin deficiency are not common (Girdwood, Thomson and Williamson, 1967). Data on serum vitamin levels in longitudinal studies is lacking. There have been several reports on the small intestine absorptive functions in the aged. However, the information available is fragmentary and often speculative. Frequently, the results are not related to aging but to the effects of growth. Some of these studies will be reviewed.

D-xylose Absorption Test

D-xylose is a pentose sugar which is absorbed predominantly from the jejunum by an active process (Csaky and Lassen, 1964). The pathway is similar to that of the hexose sugars; e.g., glucose and galactose (Alvarado, 1966). Absorption of D-xylose does not require the presence of pancreatic enzymes or bile salts; hence, impairment of the absorption usually indicates small intestine mucosal disease. Normal adults excrete at least 25 percent of the ingested xylose in the urine over 5-hour periods (Finlay, Hogarth, and Wightman, 1964). Usually a dose of 5 or 25 g of xylose is given to the fasted patients, although the larger dose tends to cause diarrhea. Blood samples are collected at 2-hour intervals, and urine is collected for 5 hours after ingestion.

Factors affecting D-xylose absorption in the presence of normal jejunal mucosa are renal insufficiency, achlorhydria, rapid or delayed gastrointestinal transit, vomiting, dehydration, intestinal bacterial overgrowth, malnutrition, and endocrine disorders—particularly thyroid and pituitary disorders. Age is also a factor (Texter, Cooper, Vidinli, and Finlay, 1964; Fowler and Cooke, 1960). Guth (1968) performed 25 g D-xylose tolerance tests on 29 patients ranging in age from 36 to 95 years. He found no difference in urinary excretion in subjects between the ages of 30 and 69. Xylose excretion decreased in subjects in the 70 to 79-year age group, and decreased even more among subjects over the age of 80. In the later group, hourly blood values were lower, reached peak levels later, and the blood disappearance rate was slower.

Hence, in subjects over 80 years, there was decreased ability of the small bowel to absorb, and of the kidney to excrete D-xylose. Kendall (1970), using 5 g D-xylose for oral absorption as well as an intravenous infusion dose, found that the 5-hour urinary excretion of D-xylose diminished after the age of 60. However, in all age groups, the percentage of xylose excreted after an oral dose was the same as that excreted after an intravenous dose. He attributed this finding to aging kidney function and not to a failing intestinal absorption. Unfortunately, his studies did not include people over 80 years. Guth's findings (1968) of diminished intestinal absorption as well as poor renal excretion of D-xylose in an 80 and over group still remain unchallenged.

Disturbances in cellular proliferation, reduced transit time of jejunal mucosal cells, impaired absorption of monosaccharides, essential and non-essential amino acids, as well as vitamin B_{12} have been observed in undernutrition and protein caloric malnutrition states (Deo and Ramalingswami, 1964; Wiseman, 1971; Adibi and Raworth, 1970). However, the effects on small intestine function in the aged have not been investigated.

Pénzes, Simon and, Winter (1968) studied radiomethionine absorption, in vivo, in female rats aged 6, 14, and 26 months. They found that intestinal absorption of this amino acid increases as the animal becomes older. At dosage 9.49×10^2 mg per 100 g of body weight, the 6, 14, and 26 month rats absorb methionine, expressed as percent of the total dose, as follows: 39.05 ± 5.57, 42.73 ± 7.59, and 48 ± 8.74, respectively. When the dose of methionine is increased to 3.25×10^3 mg/100g body weight, the results are as follows: 40.97 ± 4.06, 41.09 ± 6.66, and 44.75 ± 4.26, respectively. They also found that the values of specific activity of liver proteins increase with age. Pénzes (1968), using 2.5, 8, and 27.5-month-old female rats to study in vivo ^{14}C lysine absorption, found that the old rat absorbed nearly as much as the young but more than the adult rat. He attributed the finding to increased requirement for lysine in the young and aged animal.

Reports on age-related diminished absorption of various nutrients, such as L-valine (Ning, Reiser, and Christiansen, 1968), iron, strontium and lead (Forbes and Reina, 1972) and calcium (Harrison and Harrison, 1951), mainly derive from studies on different rates of absorption from animals of all ages. Bullamore, Gallagher, Wilkinson, Nordin, and Marshall (1970) measured calcium absorption, by plasma radioactivity after intake of oral calcium isotopes in 75 men and 150 women aged 20-95 years. Absorption of calcium fell with age after about 60 years, and everyone over 80 had significant malabsorption. Bullamore, et. al., suggested that the mechanism was due to vitamin D deficiency. Radioactive calcium was given to patients over 40 years old; yet the age group of the study ranged from 20 to 95 years old. Hence, these results require confirmation.

Ziemlanski, Wartanowicz, and Palaszewska (1971) studied intestinal absorption of tritiated pteroyl monoglutamic acid, ^3H-PGA, in rat everted gut sac. They reported that the ^3H-PGA absorption was highest in rats aged 3 to 6 weeks and that the rate of absorption diminished and became stable after the age of 15 to 30 weeks. Their studies reflected the effect of growth, not aging, on folic acid absorption. Bhanthumnavin, Wright, and Halsted (1974) found no difference in the rate of absorption of ^3H-PGA in everted gut sacs from rats aged 1.5, 6, 12, and 24 months. Hurdle, Picton, and Williams (1965) also found no difference between folic acid absorption in a group of aged humans with low serum folate levels, and those of the same age group or younger, whose serum folate was normal.

In conclusion, there has been no concrete evidence to show [apart from Guth's work (1968), in persons aged 80 and over] that diminished absorption of nutrients occurs in normal elderly persons. This may be explained on the basis of the enormous reserve absorptive capacity of the small intestine mucosa, as shown by Dowling and Booth (1966). Evidence strongly points to reduced intake and poor preparation of food as the main causes for low serum vitamins and minerals in elderly persons; other possibilities include increased body-loss and increased body utilization. There is a paucity of information in these two areas. Maldigestion and malabsorption in the elderly, as consequences of various pathological states, have been reviewed by Balacki and Dobbin (1974).

COLON

The function of the colon is to receive ileal contents—absorb water, sodium, and chloride and secrete potassium, bicarbonate, and mucus—into the lumen, process these modified contents, and store them until evacuation of feces is socially convenient. Studies of colonic motility have been mainly confined to the distal colon and rectum due to their ready accessibility. These have been reviewed recently (Sklar, 1972; Portis and King, 1952; Manier, 1974; Jordan, Kepes, Hayes, and Hammond, 1954).

Common Colonic Disturbances in Aging

As a person ages he tends to become consti-
pated, prone to laxative abuse, and is likely
to have diverticulosis. Functional bowel symptoms also become more prominent (Sklar,
1972). (Constipation may be defined as the
infrequent and difficult passage of excessively
dry stool). Portis and King (1952) found that
32 percent of 66 female and 67 male ambu-
latory patients, aged 60 to 83 without
gastrointestinal organic abnormality, had
persistent constipation. There are several
contributing factors leading to this disorder,
and they may be divided into those affecting
filling and those affecting emptying of the
rectosigmoid (Manier, 1974). They are due
to not enough bulk in the diet to stimulate
colonic motility, the abuse of laxatives (Jordan,
et al., 1954), decreased fluid intake, decreased
muscle tone and motor function of the colon,
blunting or loss of defecation reflex, organic
lesion (e.g., poor dentition leading to decreased
intake) anorectal lesions, and medication, (e.g.,
sedatives, tranquilizers, antihypertensive agents,
and narcotics (Hootnick, 1956). Constipation
may occur as a result of neurological disorder,
such as Hirschsprungs' disease or spinal cord
lesions, or an endocrine disorder, such as
hypothyroidism. Other causes of constipation
in the elderly are depression, functional bowel
syndrome, and irritable colon syndrome.
Colonic motility in constipation has been
discussed earlier. Chronic constipation may lead
to megacolon and overflow fecal incontinence
("senile megacolon") (Todd, 1971). Recently,
Engel, Nikoomanesh, and Schuster (1974)
described a biofeedback technique for
managing fecal incontinence in patients with
neurological lesions.

Diarrhea is an imbalance in the mechanisms
controlling secretion and absorption of water
resulting in an excessive loss of water and
electrolytes in the feces. Usually it occurs as
a consequence of multiple factors involving
osmotic, secretory, permeability, transport,
and motility components (Low-Beer and Read
1971). The major cause of diarrhea in the
elderly is laxative abuse (Cummings, 1974).
Over 90 percent of the patients suffering
from this condition are women. They may
display other symptoms, such as marked weight
loss, lethargy, anorexia, weakness, electrolyte
disturbances, and melanosis coli. Motility disturbances of diarrhea have been discussed
earlier.

Diverticulosis

The incidence of diverticular disease of the
colon increases with age (Hughes, 1969;
Manousos, Truelove, and Lumsden, 1967;
Parks, 1969; Slack, 1962). Radiological surveys
on healthy subjects demonstrate diverticula in
about 8 percent of adults under age 60 and in
40 percent of individuals over age 70
(Manousos; et al., 1967). They are more
common in females, and are rarely found
in individuals who are less than age 30. A
colonic diverticulum is an abnormal herniation
of the mucosa through the circular muscle
layer between the bands of taenia coli and in
close association with the point of penetration
of blood vessels into the wall. In addition to the
anatomic weakening of the wall, high intraluminal pressures within the colon generated
by sustained muscular contraction play a
significant pathogenetic role (Edwards, 1936).
Early in the course, herniation may be reversible (Marcus and Watt, 1964). Morson,
et al. (1963a, 1963b) found that the taenia
coli and circular muscle layers, in surgically
respected specimens with diverticulosis, were
thickened and firm. The mucosal surface was
trabeculated with sacculation of the mucous
membrane, between the circular muscles,
creating redundant folds and shortening
the colon, thus adding to the functional narrowing. The thickened muscle layers show no
evidence of hyperplasia or hypertrophy.
Inflammation was entirely absent from
one-third of these specimens. Muscle abnormality, in diverticular disease, is probably the
result of increased tone in both taenia and
circular fibers.

Colonic motility studies on this condition
result in conflicting reports. Painter and
Truelove (1964) found no major differences in
the basal, intraluminal pressure in normal
controls and patients with diverticulosis.
However, Arfwidsson (1964), and Parks and
Connell (1969) found higher intraluminal

pressure in diverticulosis patients at basal conditions. Under stimulation by eating, or by morphine or neostigmine administration, the intraluminal pressure in the diverticulosis patient increased 3-to-5-fold above normal. Parks (1970) studied colonic motility in the normal remaining colon, following resection of the diverticulosis portion. He found that the normal segment had an abnormal response to stimuli similar to regions of established disease, and he suggested that there was a primary muscular abnormality which existed before the appearance of the diverticula.

Change of diet from bulky, high residue to low residue food, (e.g., refined sugar and flour) is thought to cause narrowing of the colonic lumen, increased intraluminal pressure, and increase in incidence of diverticulosis. This concept is supported by animal studies and anthropological surveys. Carlson and Hoelzel (1949) found that the colonic lumen was reduced in size, and that diverticulosis could be produced in rat colon with a low residue diet; whereas the condition could be prevented by feeding a high roughage diet. Diverticulosis seems to be a disease of Western civilization and may be related to dietary differences, particularly the refinement of flour and sugar (Painter, 1970; Painter and Burkitt, 1971). Diverticulosis is rare in the rural parts of Africa, Asia, and South America where diet consists of large quantities of high residue diet. However, the incidence increases as the socioeconomic status of these areas improves and as the refined diet is achieved. Painter and Burkitt (1971) treated 70 patients with painful spastic diverticular disease, for an average of 21.5 months, with high residue diet containing unprocessed bran, and found this program to be 85 percent effective in eliminating the diverticular symptoms. Certain features of the experimental design have raised questions concerning the results, however.

In conclusion, colonic dysfunction in the aged commonly occurs in the form of constipation and diverticulosis. The roles of dietary change, and environmental influences need further study. Study along longitudinal lines should contribute further knowledge concerning colonic function in the aged.

LIVER

Morphology

Reports on gross and morphologic changes that take place in the liver with normal aging are conflicting. There is progressively diminished liver weight, taking into account reduced body weight after the age of 50 or 60 years (Boyd, 1933; Calloway, Foley, and Lagerbloom, 1965; Thompson and Williams, 1965). However, Morgan and Feldman (1957) found at autopsy that 86 percent of the livers of 75 persons aged 75 and over were of normal weight. Histological study of aged livers of mice and humans (Andrew, Brown and Johnson, 1943; Carr, Smith and Keil, 1960) revealed changes in parenchymal cells and their nuclei. There were variations in parenchymal cell size; giant, hyperchromatic, irregularly shaped nuclei in the parenchymal cells; multiple nuclei (5 to 15) within giant nuclei; large, round or oval, poorly stained, intranuclear inclusions; binucleate cells and clear perinuclear zones. There was no increase in connective tissue stroma. Periportal cellular infiltration is observed only in mice.

Schaffner and Popper (1959) reported that histological examination of the liver, in aged and infirm people, demonstrates a pattern of "nonspecific reactive hepatitis," characterized by ductular proliferation, portal and periportal inflammatory infiltration, focal necrosis, Kupffer cell mobilization, and evidence of regeneration. Sklar, Kirsner, and Palmer (1956) found no changes in liver function or histology when they studied 300 patients over the age of 65. Electron microscopic changes of intranuclear inclusion in the aged liver cell have been noted (Kleinfield, Grieder, and Fajela, 1956). Their significance is not known. In vivo experiments show that regeneration of lever parenchyma is depressed in older animals (Bucher and Glinos, 1950).

Hepatic Enzymes

Knowledge of hepatic enzymes in the aged is scanty. Ross (1969) studied hepatic ATPase, alkaline phosphatase, histidase, and catalase in 1,000 male rats of seven age groups ranging from 21-1,000 days. For each of the enzymes studied, the activity levels were found to vary with the age and the diet of the rat. Wilson's (1972) studies of hepatic enzymes in young (3-10 days), adult (6 months), middle-aged (18 months), and old (30 months) male and female, C_{57} and C_3H mouse livers and lungs, revealed complex patterns of change. Alkaline phosphatase, acid phosphatase, β-glucuronidase, G-6 PDH, LDH, SDH, cytochrome oxidase, glucose-6-phosphatase, 5'-nucleotidase, glycogen phosphorylase, phosphoglucomutase, ATPase, and NAD diaphorase, were measured. In livers of males, glycogen phosphorylase was unchanged; acid phosphatase and phosphoglucomutase increased and glucose-6-phosphatase decreased with age. In livers of females, similar patterns of change were found except that 5'-nucleotidase was constant, whereas ATPase increased with age. Light and electron microscopic studies showed no changes in enzyme localization with age. The most common quantitative changes were found in the mitochondrial enzymes SDH, which showed peak activity at 18 months, and LDH, which showed peak activity at 6 months. No correlation between enzymatic changes and liver function was made.

Age has been known as a factor in drug metabolism that occurs actively in the liver (Williams 1972). The majority of the reactions of drug metabolism are carried out by enzymes which are located mainly in the smooth endoplasmic reticulum of hepatic microsomes. The drug metabolizing system in the microsomes contains two catalysts, namely, an NADPH-oxidizing flavoprotein, NADPH-cytochrome C reductase, and a carbon monoxide-binding hemoprotein called cytochrome P-450. These enzymes may be induced by many drugs and chemicals. Kato and Takanaka (1968a and b) reported that the activities of microsomal NADPH-linked electron transport systems and oxidation and reduction of drugs in liver microsomes were markedly decreased with aging. Phenobarbital induces these enzymes in younger rats, while it has no effect on rats over 600-days old.

Kanungo and Gandhi (1972) studied the effect of adrenalectomy and cortisone administration on the activity of cytoplasmic and mitochondrial malate dehydrogenase of livers of young (9-10 weeks) and old (60-70 weeks) rats. They found that the decrease after adrenalectomy and the increase after administration of cortisone to adrenalectomized rats on the cytoplasmic isoenzymes were lower in old rats. Adrenalectomy decreased and cortisone increased the activity of the mitochondrial isoenzymes of young rats, but not of old rats. Cortisone, however, induced both mitochondrial and cytoplasmic isoenzymes of the regenerating liver at both ages. Kanungo and Gandhi concluded that the change in activities of the enzymes seen in old age might be due to changes in template activity concerned with enzyme synthesis from the corresponding genes, which apparently did not change with age. Other age-dependent impairments of enzyme induction have been reported on tyrosine aminotransferase by Finch, Foster, and Mirsky (1969), and on glucokinase by Adelman (1970). Evidence of change of hepatic enzymes in aged humans is lacking.

Liver Function

Morphological and histological changes do occur in the liver with age; and some reduction in hepatic enzyme concentrations and enzyme response to external stimuli also occur. However, it is known that the liver has a large reserve capacity, and 80 percent may be resected without evidence of hypofunction (Magath, 1922). Cohen, Giltman, and Lipschutz (1960) studied liver function in 59 patients, 49 women and 10 men, 65 years of age and over, who were free from any disease known to alter liver function tests. The tests included total bilirubin, direct reacting bilirubin, serum glutamic oxaloacetic transaminase, serum glutamic pyruvic transaminase, alkaline phosphatase, thymol turbidity, and cephalin flocculation. Bromsulphalein retention determination was performed in several patients who had evidence of an abnormal test. There was no distinct increase in abnormalities associated with aging and multiple abnormalities in a single patient were the exception. Calloway and Merrill (1965) studied BSP retention and

TABLE 2. SERUM PROTEIN PATTERNS IN AGED NORMAL HUMANS*

	Albumin	Alpha 1	Alpha 2	Beta	Gamma	A/G Ratio
Per cent of Total Serum Protein	46.07	6.30	12.69	17.33	16.17	0.88
Grams of Protein per 100 ml Serum	2.8	0.38	0.77	1.05	1.07	6.08

*Adapted from Karel, et al. (1956).

bilirubin clearance in 73 adult male patients without liver disease, aged 20-90 years, and found no differences in either test. However, other reports on the effect of age on liver function, with particular reference to BSP retention (Hollander, deLeeuw-Israel and Arp-Neefjess, 1968; Grodsk, Kolb, Franska, and Nemechek, 1970) mainly concern the changes due to growth. They compare the results of fetal to 1-month-old rats and 3-month-old, to 6-month-old rats. Rats become senescent at 2 years, which is equivalent to a human span 70 years.

The results of studies of BSP retention tests in aged humans (Thompson and Williams, 1965; Koff, Garvey, Burney, and Bill, 1973) emphasize the importance of longitudinal study. Thompson and Williams (1965) studied 32 male subjects whose age ranged from 20 to 93 years. There was no abnormality below the age of 50. Above that age BSP retention was abnormal, although other liver functions remained within normal limits. They found that the BSP retention was due to a reduction in the storage capacity of the liver for the dye. Experimental design may have been inadequate. In contrast, Koff, et al. (1973) measured BSP retention in 904 healthy veterans participating in a longitudinal study of aging. They found no relationship between mean BSP retention and aging. The frequency of abonrmal values did not change with increasing age in the cohort studied.

Hepatic blood flow is known to decrease with age. Landowne, and Stanley (1960) calculated a fall in hepatic blood flow of 0.3 percent per year, based on normal flow values and the average weight change of the liver with age. Sherlock, Bearn, Billing, and Paterson (1950), using the bromsulphalein technique, demon-

strated a definite reduction in blood flow to the liver averaging 1.5 percent per year. Thus, in a person aged 65, the hepatic blood flow will decrease by 40-45 percent, as compared to those aged 25.

Electrophoretic serum protein patterns in the aged show a relative and absolute decrease in albumin and all the globulin fractions, particularly of the beta and gamma globulin components (Rafsky, Brill, Stern, Carey, 1952; Karel, Wilder and Beber, 1956). The mechanism of hypoalbuminemia is thought to be due to a diminished rate of albumin synthesis, secondary to a progressive decrease in efficiency of liver function associated with senescence (Karel, et al., 1956). However, it may be related to deficiency of dietary protein. Beauchene, Roeder, and Barrows (1970) found age-associated increases in the incorporation of ^{14}C from acetate-2-^{14}C, of ^{3}H from UL-^{3}H-L-isoleucine into liver protein and serum albumin, following administration of the isotopes to rats. This mechanism was due to increased urinary albumin and protein excretion in the old, as compared to younger animals.

It may be concluded that, in the aged, the liver gets smaller in relation to body weight after the age of 50-60 years. Some characteristic changes are observed by light microscopy, while others are found by electron microscopic study. There are changes in hepatic enzymes particularly the inducible microsomal enzymes concerned with oxidation and reduction mechanisms. This is important in drug metabolism and detoxification processes. In summary, there does not seem to be an age-dependent liver function change, including BSP retention. Reduction in serum albumin and increase in serum globulins (particularly the beta and gamma fractions) occur in the aged. The precise mechanism of these phenomena has not been defined.

PANCREAS

Rosenberg, Friedland, and Janowitz (1966) studied peak volume and bicarbonate responses after intravenous administration of secretin to 103 persons, 59 of whom were over the age of 50. There was little difference in the results when related to sex or age.

Information on age-related pancreatic histological changes is scanty, partly due to rapid post-mortem changes of the organ. Andrew (1944) described comparable cellular changes in the pancreas of senescent rats and humans. Squamous metaplasia in both the interlobular and intralobular ducts, as well as proliferation of the cells of these ducts, were observed. General loss of basophilic staining quality in acinar cells, nuclear atrophy, and increase in nucleolar substance occurs.

In conclusion, information on pancreatic histology in the aged is scanty. There is no significant difference in pancreatic exocrine function in the elderly.

GALL BLADDER

Gall Bladder in the Aged

Cholelithiasis is common in the elderly, occurring in 38 percent of autopsied patients, 70 to 80 years of age (Newman and Northrop, 1959). In the United States, [it is estimated] that 10 percent of men and 20 percent of women between the ages of 55 and 65 years have gallstones (Friedman, Kannel and Dawber, 1959).

Surgical management has been the traditional treatment for cholelithiasis in the elderly with symptoms or complications (Glenn, 1969; Shirazi, 1972; Grodsinsky, Brush and Ponka, 1972). However, knowing that bile in cholesterol gallstone patients is supersaturated with cholesterol (lithogenic bile), Thistle and Hofmann (1973) treated patients with chenodeoxycholic acid (CDC) for 4 months, causing fasting duodenal bile to become unsaturated with cholesterol. With continued

treatment up to 2 years, radiolucent gallstones decreased in size or disappeared in 6 out of 7 patients (Danzinger, Hofmann, Thistle, et al., 1972). This finding has subsequently been confirmed (Bell, Whitney, and Dowling, 1972).

CDC may provide a model for future medical treatment for asymptomatic radiolucent gallstones in functioning gall bladders (Thistle and Hofmann, 1973). The mechanism of action of CDC may be via the dual actions of increasing the bile acid pool (Danzinger, et al., 1973) and decreasing cholesterol synthesis (Schoenfield, Bonorris and Ganz, 1973) and biliary secretion (Adler, Duane, Bennion, and Grundy, 1973).

Long term administration of CDC is required to dissolve the stones, and recurrence of gallstones occurs following cessation of therapy. Serum transaminase elevations of less than three-fold were observed in 9 out of 32 patients receiving CDC (Thistle and Hofmann, 1973). With continued therapy, however, this elevation was transient in 8 and persistent in 1 patient, at less than twice the normal value. Bell, Mok, Thwe, Murphy, Henry, Dowling (1974), using 0.5-1.5 g CDC per day in 25 patients with gallstones, found no significant change in liver function or histology. Infusion of cholic acid, via a T-tube in the common bile duct, was effective in dissolving gallstones distal to the tube (Mok, Perry, and Hermon Dowling, 1974). Phenobarbital and synthetic detergent quaternary amines also influence saturation of cholesterol in the bile.

Hence, when a surgical approach, in management of cholelithiasis in the elderly, may not be possible due to other concurrent diseases, gallstones may be dissolved by oral administration of drugs. The long-term effect of this therapy is not yet fully known.

CONCLUSION

Despite many inviting and promising features which the gastrointestinal system presents for the study of aging, little substantial information is available concerning the effects of aging on this organ system. This stems only in part from the lack of a basic understanding of the aging process in general. The alimentary system has such an immense reserve that considerable curtailment of normal function can occur without appreciably affecting measurable physiological processes. Perhaps future refinements in experimental techniques will overcome this handicap. In addition, studies must be designed so that they clearly differentiate between the effects of aging and the effects of diseases that increase in frequency with longevity. Longitudinal studies in healthy animals or volunteer subjects appear to provide the best opportunity for gathering useful information.

Acknowledgment is made to the Gerontology Research Center, National Institute of Child Health and Human Development, for use of its facilities under its Guest Scientist Program and to the Postgraduate Medical Foundation, University of Sidney, Sidney, Australia for a research fellowship grant for Dr. Bhanthumnavin.

REFERENCES

Adibi, S. A., and Raworth, A. E. 1970. Impaired jejunal absorption rates of essential amino acids induced by either dietary caloric or protein deprivation in man. *Gastroenterology*, 59, 404–413.

Adelman, R. C. 1970. Reappraisal of Biological Ageing. *Nature* 228, 1095–1096.

Adler, R., Duane, W., and Bennion L., and Grundy S. 1973. Effect of bile acid feeding on biliary cholesterol secretion (abstr). *Gastroenterology* 64, 689.

Alvarado, F. 1966. D-xylose active transport in the hamster small intestine. *Biochim. Biophys. Acta.* (Amst), 112, 292–306.

Andrew, W. 1944. Senile changes in the pancreas of Wistar Institute rats and of man with special regard to the similarity of locule and cavity formation. *Am. J. Anat. 74,* 97.

Andrew, W., Brown, H. M., and Johnson, J. B. 1943. Senile changes in the liver of mouse and man, with special reference to the similarity of the nuclear alterations. *Am. J. Anat. 72,* 199.

Andrews, G. R., Haneman, B., Arnold, B. J., Booth, J. C., and Taylor, K. 1967. Atrophic gastritis in the aged. *Aust. Ann. Med.* 16, 230.

Arfwidsson, S. 1964. Pathogenesis of multiple diverticula of the sigmoid colon in diverticular disease. *Acta. Chir. Scand. Suppl., 342.*

Balacki, J. A. and Dobbin, W. O. III. 1974. Maldigestion and Malabsorption: making up for lost nutrients. *Geriatrics*, 157–166, May.

Baron, J. H. 1963. Studies of basal peak acid output for an augmented histamine test. *Gut,* 4, 136.

Beauchene, R. E., Roeder, L., and Barrows, C. H., Jr. 1970. The interrelationships of age, tissue protein synthesis and proteinuria. *Gerontology*, 25, 359–363.

Bell, G. D., Mok, H. Y. I., and Thwe, M., et al. 1974. Liver structure and function in cholelithiasis: effect of chenodeoxycholic acid. *Gut*, 15, 165–172.

Bell, G. D., Whitney, B., and Dowling, R. H. 1972. Gallstone dissolution in man using chenodeoxycholic acid. *Lancet*, 2, 1213–1216.

Bernier, J. J., Vidon, N., and Mignon, M. 1973. The value of a cooperative multicenter study for establishing a table of normal values for gastric acid secretion and as a function of sex, age and weight. *Biol. Gastroenterol.* (Paris), 6, 287–296.

Bhanthumnavin, K., Wright, J. R., and Halsted, C. H. 1974. Intestinal transport of tritiated folic acid (^{3}H-PGA) in the everted gut sac of the rat at different ages. *Johns Hopkins Med J.,* 135, 152–160.

Boyd, E. 1933. Normal variability in weight of adult human liver and spleen. *Arch. Pathol.,* 16, 350.

Bucher, N. L. R., and Glinos, A. D., 1950. The effect of age on regeneration of rat liver. *Cancer Res.,* 10, 324.

Bullamore, J. R., Gallagher, J. C., Wilkinson, R., Nordin, B. E. C., and Marshall, D. H. 1970. Effect of age on calcium absorption. *Lancet*, 535–537, (Sept. 2).

Cameron, I. L. 1972. Cell proliferation and renewal in aging mice. *J. Gerontology,* 27, 162–172.

Calloway, N. O., Foley, C. F., and Lagerbloom, P. 1965. Uncertainties in geriatric data. 11 Organ size. *J. Am. Geriat. Soc.,* 13, 20.

Calloway, N. O. and Merrill, R. S. 1965. The aging adult liver I. Bromsulphalein and bilirubin clearances. *J. Am. Geriat. Soc.,* 13, 594–598.

Carlson, A. J. and Hoelzel, F. 1949. Relations of diet to diverticulosis in colon in rats. *Gastroenterology,* 12, 108–115.

Carr, R. D., Smith, M. J., and Keil, P. G. 1960. The liver in the aging process. *Arch. Pathol.,* 70, 15–18.

Chin, K. N. 1973. Ultrastructure of Peyer's patches in the aged mouse. *Acta. Anat.,* 84, 523–533.

Cohen, T., Giltman, L., and Lipshutz, E. 1960. Liver function studies in the aged. *Geriatrics* 15, 824–836.

Cohen, S. and Harris, L. D. 1972. The lower esophageal sphincter. *Gastroenterology,* 63, 1066–1073.

Cohen, S., Lipshutz, W. H. and Hughes, W. 1971. Role of gastrin super sensitivity in the pathogenesis of lower esophageal sphincter hypertension in achalasia. *J. Clin. Invest.,* 50, 1241–1246.

Cooke, A. R. 1973. Progress report. The role of acid in the pathogenesis of aspirin-induced gastrointestinal erosions and hemorrhage. *Digest. Dis.* 18, 225–237.

Cornes, J. S. 1965. Number, size and distribution of Peyer's patches in the human small intestine. II. The effect of age on Peyer's patches. *Gut* 6, 230.

Csaky, T. Z. and Lassen, U. V. 1964. Active intestinal transport of D-xylose. *Biochim. Biophys. Acta* (Amst.), 82, 215–217.

Cummings, J. H. 1974. Progress report. Laxative Abuse. *Gut.* **15**, 758–766.

Cutler, C. W. 1958. Clinical patterns of peptic ulcer after sixty. *Surg. Gynecol. Obstet.,* **107**, 23–30.

Danzinger, R. G., Hofmann, F., Thistle, J. L. et al. 1972. Dissolution of cholesterol gallstones by chenodeoxycholic acid. *New. Engl. J. Med.,* **286**, 1–7.

Danzinger, R. G., Hofmann, A. F., and Thistle, J. L. et al. 1973. Effect of oral chenodeoxycholic acid on bile acid kinetics and biliary lipid composition in women with cholelithiasis. *J. Clin. Invest.,* **52**, 2809–2821.

Davies, W. T., Kirkpatrick, J. R., and Owen, G. M. 1971. Gastric emptying in atrophic gastritis and carcinoma of the stomach. *Scand. J. Gastro.,* **6**, 297.

Deo, M. G. and Ramalingswami, V. 1964. Absorption of Co^{58} labelled cyanocobalamine in protein deficiency. *Gastroenterology* **46**, 167–174.

Deo, M. G. and Ramalingswami, V. 1965. Reaction of the small intestine to induced protein malnutrition in Rhesus monkeys—a study of cell population kinetics in the jejunum. G. E. **49**, 150–157.

Dowling, R. H. and Booth, C. C. 1966. Functional compensation after bowel resection in man: *Lancet* **2**, 146.

Edwards, H. C. 1936. Diverticula of the intestine. *Ann. Surg.* **103**, 230–254.

Engel, T. N., Nikoomanesh, P., and Schuster, M. M., 1974. Operant conditioning in the treatment of faecal incontinence. *New. Engl. J. Med.* **290**, 646–649.

Farrell, R. L., Castell, D. O., and McGuigan, J. E. 1974. Measurements and comparisons of lower esophageal sphincter pressures and serum gastrin levels in patients with gastroesophageal reflux. *Gastroenterology* **67**, 415–422.

Farrell, R. L., Nebel, O. T., McGuire, A. T., and Castell, D. O. 1973. The abnormal lower esophageal sphincter in pernicious anemia. *Gut* **14**, 767–772.

Fenger, C., Amdrup, E., and Christiansen, P. 1973. Gastric Ulcer I. Analysis of 701 patients. *Acta. Chir. Scand.* **139**, 455–459.

Finch, C. E., Foster, J. R., and Mirsky, A. E. 1969. Aging and the regulation of cell activities during exposure to cold. *J. Gen. Physiol.,* **54**, 690–712.

Finlay, J. M., Hogarth, J., and Wightman, K. J. R. 1964. Clinical evaluation of the D-xylose tolerance test. *Ann. Internal Med.,* **61**, 411.

Forbes, G. B. and Reina, J. C. 1972. Effect of age on gastrointestinal absorption (Fe, Sr, Pb) in the rat. *J. Nutr.,* **102**, 647–652.

Fowler, D. and Cooke, W. T. 1960. Diagnostic significance of D-xylose tolerance test. *Gut* **1**, 67.

Friedman, D. K., Kannel, W. B., Dawber, T. R. 1959. The autopsy incidence of gallstones. *Int. Surg.,* **109**, 1.

Fyke, F. E., Jr., Code, C. F., Schlegel, J. F. 1956. The gastroesophageal sphincter in healthy human beings. *Gastroenterologia,* **86**, 135–150.

Girdwood, R. H., Thomson, A. D., Williamson, J. 1967. Folate status in the elderly. *Brit. Med. J.,* **2**, 670.

Glenn, F. 1969. Indications for operation in biliary tract disease among the elderly. *Geriatrics,* 98–103 (August).

Gorbach, S. I., Nahas, L., Lerner, P. I., and Weinstein, L. 1967. Studies of intestinal microflora I. Effects of diet, age and periodic sampling on numbers of fecal microorganisms in man. *Gastroenterology,* **53**, 845–855.

Grodsk, G. M., Kolb, H. J., Franska, R. E., Nemechek, C. 1970. Effect of age on development of hepatic carriers for bilirubin. A possible explanation for physiologic jaundice and hyperbilirubinemia in the new born. *Metabolism,* **19**, 246–252.

Grossman, M. I., Kirsner, J. B., Gillespie, I. E. 1963. Basal and histalog stimulated gastric secretion in control subjects and in patients with peptic ulcer or gastric cancer. *Gastroenterology,* **45**, 14–26.

Guth, P. H. 1968. Physiologic alteration in small bowel function with age. The absorption of D-xylose. *Am. J. Digest Diseases,* **13**, 565–571.

Harrison, H. E. and Harrison, H. C. 1951. Studies with radiocalcium: the intestinal absorption of calcium. *J. Biol. Chem.,* **188**, 83–90.

Hitchock, C. R., MacLean, L. D., and Sullivan, W. A. 1957. The secretory and clinical aspects of achlorhydria and clinical aspects of achlorhydria and gastric atrophy as precursors of gastric cancer. *J. Nat. Cancer Inst.,* **18**, 795.

Hollander, C. F., de Leeuw-Israel, R. F., and Arp-Neefjess, J. 1968. M. Bromsulphalein (BSP) clearance in aging rats. Exp. Geront., **3**, 147–153.

Hollis, J. B. and Castell, D. O. 1974. Esophageal function in old men: a new look at "presbyesophagus." Ann. Internal Med., **80**, 371–374.

Hootnick, H. L. 1956. Constipation in elderly patients due to drug therapy. *J. Am. Geriat. Soc.,* **4**, 1021–1930.

Hughes, L. E. 1969. Postmortem survey of diverticular disease of the colon. I. Diverticulosis and diverticulitis. II. The muscular abnormality in the sigmoid colon. *Gut* **10**, 336, 344.

Hurdle, A. D. F., T. C. Picton, Williams, T. C. 1966. Folic acid deficiency in elderly patients admitted to hospital. *Brit. Med. J.,* **2**, 202–205.

Isokoski, M., Krohn, K., and Varis, K., and Siuralla, M. 1969. Parietal cell and intrinsic factor antibodies in a Finnish rural population sample. *Scand. J. Gasteroenterol.,* **4**, 521.

Jeffries, G. H. Gastritis. Dis. a Month, 1973. July pp. 1–32.

Jeffries, G. H., Todd, J. E., and Sleisenger, M. H. 1966. The effect of prednisolone on gastric mucosal histology, gastric secretion and vitamin B_{12} absorption in patients with pernicious anemia. *J. Clin. Invest.,* **45**, 803.

Jordan, M., Kepes, M., Hayes, R. B., and Hammond,

W. 1954. Dietary habits of persons living alone. *Geriatrics*, 9, 230-232.

Kanungo, M. S., and Gandhi, B. S. 1972. *Proc. Nat. Acad. Sci. U.S.A.,* Induction of Malate Dehydrogenase Iso-enzymes in liver of young and old rats. 69, 2035-2038.

Karel, J. L., Wilder, V. M. and Beber, M. 1956. Electrophoretic serum protein patterns in the aged. *J. Am. Geriat. Soc.,* 4, 667-682.

Kato, R. and Takanaka, A. 1968a. Metabolism of drugs in old rats (II) Metabolism in vivo and effect of drugs in old rats. *Jap. J. Pharmacol.,* 18, 389-396.

Kato, R. and Takanaka, A. 1968b. Effect of phenobarbital on electron transport system, oxidation and reduction of drugs in liver microsomes of rats of different ages. *J. Biochem.,* 63, 406-408.

Kendall, M. J. 1970. The influence of age on the xylose absorption test. *Gut,* 11, 488-501.

Kleinfield, G. F., Grieder, M. G. and Fajela, W. J. 1956. Electron microscopy of intra-nuclear inclusions found in human rat liver parenchyma cells. *J. Biophys Biochem. Cytol.,* (Suppl.) 2, 435.

Koff, R. S., Garvey, A. J., Burney, S. W., and Bell, B. 1973. Absence of an age effect on sulfobromophalein retention in healthy men. *Gastroenterology,* 65, 300-302.

Korn, E. R. 1974. Intestinal metaplasia of the gastric mucosa. *Am. J. Gastroenterol.,* 61, 270-275.

Landowne, M. and Stanley, J. 1960. Aging of the cardiovascular system in aging, some social and biological aspects. *In* N. W. Shock (ed.), Washington, D.C. American Association for the Advancement of Science, 159.

Lawson, H. H. 1964. Effect of duodenal contents on the gastric mucosa under experimental conditions. *Lancet,* 1, 469.

Lesher, S., Fry, R. J. M., and Kohn, H. I. 1961. Influence of age on transit time of cells of mouse intestinal epithelium. I. Duodenum. *Lab. Invest.,* 10, 291.

Levrat, M., Pasquier, J., Lambet, R., and Tissot, A. 1966. Peptic ulcer in patients over 60. Experience in 287 cases. *Amer. J. Digest Diseases,* 11, 279-285.

Lipshutz, W. H. and Cohen, S. 1972. The genesis of lower esophageal sphincter pressure: its identification through the use of gastrin antiserum. *J. Clin. Invest.,* 51, 522-529.

Lipshutz, W. H., Gaskins, R. D., and Lukash, W. M., Sode, J. 1974. Hypogastrinemia in patients with lower esophageal sphincter incompetence. *Gastroenterology,* 67, 423-427.

Low-Beer, T. S. and Read, A. E. 1971. Progress Report on diarrhea; mechanisms and treatment. *Gut,* 12, 1021-1036.

Magath, T. B. 1922. Production of chronic liver insufficiency. *Am. J. Physiol.,* 59, 485.

Mandelstam, P. and Lieber, A. 1969. Esophageal dysfunction in diabetes. *Brit. Med. J.,* 466, May.

Manier, J. W. 1974. Diarrhea and constipation: mechanism and treatment. *Semin. Drug Treat.,* 3, 321-329, (Spring).

Manousos, O. N., Truelove, S. C., and Lumsden, K. 1967. Prevalence of colonic diverticulosis in general population of Oxford area. *Brit. Med. J.,* 3, 762-763.

Marcus, R. and Watt, J. 1964. The pre-diverticular state. *Brit. J. Surg.,* 5, 676-682.

Mok, H. Y. I., Perry, P. M., Hermon Dowling, R. 1974. The control of bile acid pool size: effect of jejunal resection and phenobarbitone on bile acid metabolism in the rat. *Gut,* 15, 247-253.

Morgan, Z. R. and Feldman, M. 1957. Liver, biliary tract and pancreas in aged: an anatomic and laboratory evaluation. *J. Am. Geriat. Soc.,* 5, 59.

Morson, B. C. 1962. Pre-cancerous lesions of upper gastrointestinal tract. *J. Am. Med. Assoc.,* 179, 311-315.

Morson, B. C. 1963a. The muscle abnormality in diverticular disease of the sigmoid colon. *Brit. J. Radiol.,* 36, 385-392.

Morson, B. C., 1963b. The muscle abnormality in the divercula disease of the colon. *Proc. Roy. Soc. Med.,* 9, 798-800.

Newman, H. F. and Northrup, J. D. 1959. The autopsy incidence of gallstones, *Int. Surg.,* 109, 1.

Ning, M., Reiser, S., and Christiansen, P. A. 1968. Variation in intestinal transport of L-valine in relation to age. *Proc. Soc. Exp. Biol. Med.,* 799-803.

Painter, N. S. 1970. Diverticular disease of the colon: a disease of Western civilization. DM.

Painter, N. S. 1971. A Etiology of Diverticular Dis. *Brit. Med. J.,* 2, 156.

Painter, N. S. and Burkitt, D. P. 1971. Diverticular disease of the colon: a deficiency disease of Western civilization. *Brit. Med. J.,* 11, 450-454.

Painter, N. S. and Truelove, S. C. 1964. The intraluminal pressure patterns in diverticulosis of the colon. Part I. Resting patterns of pressure. *Gut,* 5, 201-207.

Palmer, E. D. 1972. Gastritis: a reevaluation. *Medicine,* 33, 199-290.

Parks, T. G. 1969. Natural history of diverticular disease of the colon. A review of 521 cases. *Brit. Med. J.* 4, 639.

Parks, T. G. 1970. Rectal and colonic studies after resection of the sigmoid for diverticula disease. *Gut.,* 11, 121.

Parks, T. G. and Connell, A. M. 1969. Motility studies in diverticular disease of the colon. I. Basal activity and response to food assessed by open-ended tube and miniature balloon techniques. *Gut.,* 10, 534.

Pénzes, L., Simon, G., Winter, M. 1968. Effect of concentration on the intestinal absorption and utilization of radiomethionine in old age. *Exp. Geront.,* 3, 257-263.

Persdie, R. B. 1966. Incidence and coincidence of hiatus hernia. *Gut.,* 7, 188.

Phillips, S. F. 1972. Pathophysiology of gastritis: recent concepts and clinical significance. *Southern Med. J.,* 65, 1187-1191.

Portis, S. A. and King, J. C. 1952. The gastrointestinal tract in the aged. *J. Am. Med. Assoc.,* 148, 1073-1079.

Rafsky, H. A., Brill, A. A., Stern, K. G., Carey, H. Electrophoretic studies in the serum of normal aged individuals. *Am. J. Med. Sci.,* **224,** 522-528.

Rosenberg, I. R., Friedland, N., Janowitz, H. D., Dreiling, D. A. 1966. The effect of age and sex upon human pancreatic secretion of fluid and bicarbonate. *Gastroenterology,* **50,** 191.

Rosenberg, S. and Harris, L. D. 1971. Heartburn and hormones. The mechanism of lower esophageal sphincter incompetence. (Abstract) *Gastroenterology,* **60,** 711.

Ross, M. H. 1969. Aging, nutrition and hepatic enzyme activity patterns in the rat. *J. Nutr.,* **97,** 565.

Sayeed, M. 1967. Age related changes in intestinal phosphomonoesterases. *Fed. Proc.,* **26,** 259.

Schaffner, F. and Popper, H. 1959. Non-specific reactive hepatitis in aged and infirm people. *Amer. J. Digest Diseases,* **4,** 389.

Schoenfield, L. J., Bonorris, G. G., Ganz, P. 1973. Induced alterations in the rate-limiting enzymes of hepatic cholesterol and bile acid synthesis in the hamster. *J. Lab. Clin. Med.,* **82,** 858-868.

Sherlock, S., Bearn, A. G., Billing, B. H., Paterson, J. 1950. C.S. Splanchnic blood flow in man by the bromsulphalein method. The relation of peripheral plasma bromsulphalein level to the calculated flow. *J. Lab. Clin. Med.,* **35,** 923.

Shirazi, S. and Printen, K. 1972. Gallstone Illeus: Review of forty cases. *J. Am. Geriat. Soc.,* **20,** 335-339.

Siurala, M., Isokoski, M., Varis, K. et al. 1968. Prevalence of gastritis in a rural population: bioptic study of subjects selected at random. *Scand. J. Gastroenterol.,* **3,** 311.

Sklar, M. Functional bowel distress and constipation in the aged. *Geriatrics,* Sept. 1972, 79-85.

Sklar, M., Kirsner, J. B., Palmer, W. L. 1956. Symposium on medical problems of aged: gastrointestinal disease in the aged. *Med. Clin. N. Am.,* **40,** 223.

Slack, W. W. 1962. The anatomy, pathology and some clinical features of diverticulitis of the colon. *Brit. J. Surg.,* **50,** 185.

Soergel, K. H., Zboralske, F. F., and Amberg, J. R. 1964. Presbyesophagus: esophageal motility in nonagenarians. *J. Clin. Invest.,* **43,** 1472-1479.

Stilson, W. C., Sanders, I., Gardiner, G. A. 1969. Hiatel hernia and gastroesophageal reflux. *Radiology,* **93,** 1323-1327.

Strickland, R. G. and Mackay, I. R. 1973. Progress report: a reappraisal of the nature and significance of chronic gastritis. *Digest Dis.,* **18,** 426-440.

Texter, E. C., Cooper, J. A. D., Vidinli, M., Finlay, J. M. 1964. Laboratory procedures in the diagnosis of malabsorption. *Med. N. Am.,* **48,** 117.

Thistle, J. L. and Hofmann, A. F. 1973. Efficiency and safety of CDC for dissolving gallstones. *New Engl. J. Med.,* **289,** 655-659.

Thistle, J. L. and Schoenfield, L. J. 1971. Induced alterations in composition of bile of persons having cholelithiasis. *Gastroenterology,* **61,** 488-496.

Thompson, E. N. and Williams, R. 1965. Effect of age on liver function with particular reference to bromsulphalein excretion. *Gut.* **6,** 266-269.

Todd, I. P. 1971. Some aspects of adult megacolon. *Proc. Roy. Soc. Med.* **64,** 561-565.

Twomey, J. J., Jordan, P. H., and Jarrold, T. Trubowitz, S, Ritz, N. D. and Conn H. O. 1969. The syndrome of immunoglobulin deficiency and pernicious anemia. *Amer. J. Med.,* **47,** 340-350.

Williams, R. T. 1972. Progress Report. Hepatic metabolism of drugs. *Gut.* **13,** 579-585.

Wilson, P. D. 1972. Enzyme patterns in young and old mouse livers and lungs. *Gerontologia,* **18,** 36-54.

Winans, C. S. and Harris, L. D. 1967. Quantitation of lower esophageal sphincter competenee. *Gastroenterology,* **52,** 773-778.

Wiseman, G. 1970, 1971. Effect of undernutrition in intestinal active transport of sugars and amino acids. Nutricia Symposium. Metabolic Processes in the fetus and new born infants, 22-24, Oct. 1970, 1971.

Wolf, B. S., Brahms, S. A., and Khilnani, M. R. 1959. The incidence of hiatal hernia in routine barium meal examinations. *Mt. Sinai J. Med., N.Y.,* **26,** 598.

Zboralske, F. F., Amberg, J. R., and Soergel, K. H. 1964. Presbyesophagus: Cine-radiographic manifestations. *Radiology,* **82,** 463.

Ziemlanski, S., Wartanowicz, and Palaszewska, M. 1971. Effect of age and various diets on folic acid absorption in the alimentary tract. *Acta Phsiol. Polon.* **22,** 219-224.

AUTHOR INDEX

SUBJECT INDEX

Propranolol, 282, 284

Prostaglandins, 349, 350

Prostate: atrophy of, 346–348; benign hypertrophy, 216, 318–346-349, 416, 426, 427–ethnic studies of, 346; testosterone levels, 347–; carcinoma of, 347, 522; and dihydrotestosterone, 349; morphological changes, 346, 347; and renal function, 416, 424; testosterone stimulation, 110, 349; vascular changes, 347; weight *vs* age, 693

Protein synthesis: age decreases, 26, 169–171, 180, 264; in cell cycle, 108; elementary protein error theory, 64; end product analysis, 57, 58; evaluation methods, 57, 58; missynthesis, 64, 65, 78; post-translational changes, 64–66, 78; regulation with age, 63, 169–171, 180

See also Transcription and Translation

Proteoglycans: and collagen, 224; in matrix, 222, 237, 238

Proteolysis, 65, 66

Protozoans: studies on, 8, 14, 123, 177, 178, 572, 574, 575, 610

Puberty: menarche, 319, 325; reproductive system and, 318; and sebum production, 500; stages of, 707

Pulmonary disease: in animal models, 531; bronchitis, 433; cancer, 442, 520, 522, 523; deaths from *vs* age, 681; embolism, 442; emphysema, 432, 433; immunity and, 441; incidence in aged, 441, 515; pneumonia–age related incidence, 441, 515; deaths from, 295, 296, 441, 442, 515–517–; and smoking, 433, 442, 523; tuberculosis–age related incidence, 441, 442; deaths from, 516, 517

Pulmonary function: diffusion capacity, 651; tests for, 650, 651

Pulmonary system

See Lung

Purkinje cells, 245, 263, 264

Puromycin, 107, 108

Pyridoxalphosphate, 565, 569

Quail: studies on, 23, 524

Rabbits: studies on, 10, 13, 65, 247, 273, 290, 297, 320, 328–330, 332, 334, 343, 344, 364, 474, 476, 486, 524, 530, 531

Radiation: acute, 45, 47, 48, 587; and age at exposure, 590; *vs* aging injury, 45–51, 587, 592–596; and chromosome aberrations, 45, 46, 48, 592, 593; chronic, 45, 595, 596, 614; and disease incidence, 589, 590; dose of, 590; and Gompertz, 588, 589, 595, 596; injury repair, 48, 49, 113, 592; ionizing, 45; and life span, 45, 587, 588, 592–597; protection against, 44, 45; and somatic mutation aging theory, 592, 593

Radioautography

See Autoradiography

Radioimmunoassay: estrogens, 331; glucagon, 365; insulin, 358, 365

Rat: adipose tissue, 80, 81; age changes–calcium levels, 670, 671; cardiac, 25, 26, 273, 282, 284, 285, 287, 301, 303, 305–308; in cell cycle, 174; in mitochondria, 247, 303; in muscle, 17, 214; in nerve cells, 18, 247; vascular, 290, 294, 301, 306, 311–; age pigments, 249–254, 331; antioxidant studies, 44, 571; body temperature, 24, 274, 614, 615; brain studies, 264; catecholamine metabolism, 266, 267; cellular respiration, 83, 84, 88, 89; chro-

matin of, 110; collagen in, 307, 308, 332, 684; dentition studies, 482–484, 487, 488, 502; dietary self-selection, 618, 619; diet effects, 7, 247, 303, 306, 399, 400, 461, 478, 479, 571, 572, 576, 606, 614–620; DNA of, 47, 70; endocrine system–ACTH, 371; corticosterone, 272, 369, 370; hypothalamus, 325, 326, 341; insulin, 362, 363; LH, 272; pituitary, 321, 322, 341, 365, 366; thyroid, 372, 373–; environmental studies, 614, 615; enzyme studies, 26, 67, 68, 77, 89, 267–270, 303, 306, 574, 684, 714, 716, 717; excretory studies, 409, 410, 414, 415, 418, 419, 424, 425, 427, 428, 706; eye studies, 12; hematocrit, 19; immunological studies, 384, 399, 400; intercellular matrix of, 224, 225, 235, 236; lifespan–male *vs* female, 530; modification of, 7, 8, 17, 399–402, 461, 571, 572, 576, 614–621, 627, 628–; lipid studies, 78–80, 303, 306; lipofuscin in, 249–254; liver regeneration, 49, 67, 68, 109, 110, 112, 114, 128; metabolic studies, 24, 25, 78–80, 82–84, 88, 89, 303, 613, 614, 625, 714; monoamines of, 272; muscle studies, 446–449, 464, 480; neoplasia, 266, 340, 341, 524, 576; neurotransmitters, 266, 267, 272, 325, 326; oxygen consumption, 24, 25, 132, 164; parabiosis, 627, 628; prostate, 349; radiation effects, 588; reproductive studies, 22, 320, 324, 325, 344–corpora lutea, 329; decline of, 320, 326; follicles, 329; oocyte numbers, 326; vaginal smears, 336–; salivary glands of, 109, 110, 112, 115–117, 372, 374, 486; skeletal studies, 472, 476, 478, 479; stress responses, 25, 26, 132, 247, 248, 252; ultrastructural changes, 321; water content in, 703

See also Rat, species and strains

Rat, species and strains: A×C, 670, 671; albino, 264, 267; BHE, 363; Birmingham, 341; BN, 79; CFN, 17, 684; Charles River, 363, 622; Donryu, 17; Fischer, 19, 21, 24, 270, 670, 671; Lewis, 79; Long Evans, 268; Norway, 583, 584; McCollum, 17; *Oryzomys palustria*, 585, 586; Osborne-Mendel, 19; *Sigmodon hispidus*, 585, 586; Sprague-Dawley–cardiac studies, 25; DNA, 70; enzymes of, 67, 270, 684; eye lens, 12; insulin level, 363; life span, 17, 620; lipid analysis, 78, 79; neoplasia in, 266, 341–; Walter Reed, 26; Wistar–blood studies, 19; cardiac, 25; insulin level, 363; lifespan, 7, 17; neuroendocrine, 264, 267–270; skeletal muscle, 17; stress response, 26–; Zivic-Miller, 24, 25

Reaction time: *vs* age (table), 678, 701–703

Recall, 676

Receptors: for ACh, 446; cytoplasmic *vs* membrane, 374; hormonal, 349, 350, 357, 373, 374–age changes, 374; cAMP, 349, 350, 374; prostaglandins, 349, 350–; immunoglobulin, 395; muscle membrane, 446; skin, 255; steroid, 272

Renal aging

See Kidney

Reproduction: age and offspring number, 22, 320, 321; aneuploidy and age, 328; and DDT, 594;. failure of and genetics, 350; female–age effect on cycles, 325; and deliveries, 319, 320; general changes, 321–342; hormone effects, 322–342; initiation, 318; stages of, 319; termination of, 319–; gamete "microaging," 328, 344, 350; hormone dependency, 318–350 (passim); implantation failure, 328, 334, 335; and life span, 9, 27, 28, 178, 318, 583; litter size, 22, 320, 321, 583; male–decline, 342; hormone effects, 342–349–; of rodents, 318–